Get started with your **Connected Casebook**

Redeem your code below to access the **e-book** with search, highlighting, and note-taking capabilities; **case briefing** and **outlining** tools to support efficient learning; and more.

1. Go to www.casebookconnect.com
2. Enter your access code in the box and click **Register**
3. Follow the steps to complete your registration and verify your email address

If you have already registered at CasebookConnect.com, simply log into your account and redeem additional access codes from your Dashboard.

ACCESS CODE:
Scratch off with care.

STXT97908586571

Is this a used casebook? Access code already redeemed? Purchase a digital version at **CasebookConnect.com/catalog**.

If you purchased a digital bundle with additional components, your additional access codes will appear below.

"I liked being able to search quickly while in class."

"Being able to highlight and easily create case briefs was a fantastic resource and time saver for me!"

"I loved it! I was able to study on the go and create a more effective outline."

For technical support, please visit http://support.wklegaledu.com.

FOREIGN RELATIONS
LAW

ASPEN CASEBOOK SERIES

FOREIGN RELATIONS LAW

Cases and Materials

Seventh Edition

Curtis A. Bradley

William Van Alstyne Professor of Law
Duke University School of Law

Ashley S. Deeks

E. James Kelly, Jr.—Class of 1965 Research Professor of Law
University of Virginia School of Law

Jack L. Goldsmith

Henry L. Shattuck Professor of Law
Harvard Law School

Published by Wolters Kluwer in New York.

Wolters Kluwer Legal & Regulatory U.S. serves customers worldwide with CCH, Aspen Publishers, and Kluwer Law International products. (www.WKLegaledu.com)

To contact Customer Service, e-mail customer.service@wolterskluwer.com, call 1-800-234-1660, fax 1-800-901-9075, or mail correspondence to:

> Wolters Kluwer
> Attn: Order Department
> PO Box 990
> Frederick, MD 21705

Printed in the United States of America.

1 2 3 4 5 6 7 8 9 0

ISBN 978-1-5438-1365-4

Library of Congress Cataloging-in-Publication Data

Names: Bradley, Curtis A., author. | Deeks, Ashley S., author. | Goldsmith, Jack L., author.
Title: Foreign relations law : cases and materials / Curtis A. Bradley, William van Alstyne Professor of Law, Duke University School of Law; Ashley Deeks, E. James Kelly, Jr. - Class of 1965, Research Professor of Law, University of Virginia School of Law; Jack L. Goldsmith, Henry L. Stattuck Professor of Law, Harvard Law School.
Description: Seventh edition. | New York : Wolters Kluwer, [2020] | Series: Aspen casebook series | Includes bibliographical references and index. | Summary: "Casebook for law school courses on Foreign Relations Law, offering a mix of cases, statutes, and executive branch materials, as well as extensive notes and questions and discussion of relevant historical background"—Provided by publisher.
Identifiers: LCCN 2019055402 (print) | LCCN 2019055403 (ebook) | ISBN 9781543813654 (hardcover) | ISBN 9781543817515 (ebook)
Subjects: LCSH: United States—Foreign relations—Law and legislation. | LCGFT: Casebooks (Law)
Classification: LCC KF4651 .B73 2020 (print) | LCC KF4651 (ebook) | DDC 342.73/0412—dc23
LC record available at https://lccn.loc.gov/2019055402
LC ebook record available at https://lccn.loc.gov/2019055403

About Wolters Kluwer Legal & Regulatory U.S.

Wolters Kluwer Legal & Regulatory U.S. delivers expert content and solutions in the areas of law, corporate compliance, health compliance, reimbursement, and legal education. Its practical solutions help customers successfully navigate the demands of a changing environment to drive their daily activities, enhance decision quality, and inspire confident outcomes.

Serving customers worldwide, its legal and regulatory portfolio includes products under the Aspen Publishers, CCH Incorporated, Kluwer Law International, ftwilliam.com, and MediRegs names. They are regarded as exceptional and trusted resources for general legal and practice-specific knowledge, compliance and risk management, dynamic workflow solutions, and expert commentary.

To Kathy, David, and Liana

—Curtis A. Bradley

To Michael and Tate

—Ashley S. Deeks

To Leslie, Jack, and Will

—Jack L. Goldsmith

Summary of Contents

Contents

Preface

This casebook examines the constitutional and statutory law that regulates the conduct of U.S. foreign relations. The topics covered include the distribution of foreign relations authority between the three federal branches, the relationship between the federal government and the states in regulating foreign relations, and the status of international law in U.S. courts. In addition to including excerpts of the major Supreme Court decisions in this area (and some lower court decisions that we thought would be helpful for teaching purposes), we have included a variety of non-case materials, including historical documents; excerpts of statutes, treaties, and Executive Branch pronouncements and memoranda; and detailed Notes and Questions.

One of our goals in the book is to give students a sense of the rich history associated with foreign relations law. History is especially important in this field because much of the content of U.S. foreign relations law has developed in response to, and thus can best be understood in light of, discrete historical events. Historical research also has played a significant role in foreign relations scholarship. As a result, much of the first chapter is devoted to history, and we sketch the historical origins of all of the major foreign relations doctrines as they are presented.

Despite these historical materials, the focus of the book is on contemporary controversies, such as debates over the validity of executive agreements, the nature and limits of the war power, the scope of the treaty power, the legitimacy of international human rights litigation, and the propriety of judicial deference to the Executive Branch. In addition to describing the positions taken on these issues by institutional actors, we have attempted to give students some exposure to the extensive academic debates on these topics. We have avoided, however, including long excerpts of law review articles, which, in our experience, are not the best vehicle for teaching. Instead, we have attempted to weave the relevant academic arguments into the Notes and Questions that follow each set of cases and materials.

Without advocating any particular approach to constitutional interpretation, we have also attempted to get students to focus closely on the text of the Constitution—a practice that we believe will be useful to them as lawyers. In addition, we emphasize issues of constitutional structure, especially federalism and separation of powers. Regardless of one's views about the legal relevance of these structural principles to foreign relations (a matter of some debate), we believe it is important to understand these principles, at least for their political significance. A related theme of the book concerns "legal process" questions about the relative competence of various institutional actors to conduct U.S. foreign relations, questions that overlap with work that has been done in the political science area.

The casebook also emphasizes continuities and discontinuities between foreign relations law and "mainstream" constitutional law, statutory law, and federal jurisdiction issues. Indeed, we believe that many important constitutional law and federal courts doctrines—such as the political question doctrine, federal common law, and dormant preemption—have some of their most interesting applications in the foreign relations context. As a result, it is our hope that the book will appeal not only to students interested in international studies, but also to students interested in domestic constitutional and jurisdictional issues. We also hope that domestic law scholars will be tempted by this book to teach a course in foreign relations law.

Foreign relations law is a fast-changing field, and this seventh edition takes account of numerous developments since the last edition. Among other things, it contains an excerpt of the Supreme Court's 2018 decision in *Trump v. Hawaii* upholding the Trump administration's "travel ban"; a discussion of recent developments in the litigation over state and local "sanctuary jurisdictions"; an account of the Trump administration's withdrawal from various international agreements; an excerpt of the Supreme Court's 2018 decision in *Jesner v. Arab Bank*, concerning corporate liability under the Alien Tort Statute; and a discussion of the air strikes against Syria in 2017 and 2018. This edition also takes account of the *Restatement (Fourth) of the Foreign Relations Law of the United States*, which was published in 2018. The Notes and Questions in the book have also been updated throughout to take account of recent scholarship, important lower court decisions, and legislative developments.

This edition generally retains the organizational structure of the last edition, in which the book is divided into four thematic Parts: Introduction; Government Institutions; International Law in the U.S. Legal System; and International Crime, War, and Terrorism. In Chapter 2, we have moved up the section on deference to the Executive Branch so that it appears earlier in the chapter, and we have made *Trump v. Hawaii* the main case in that section. In Chapter 4, we have deleted what was Section C, concerning a jurisdictional federal common law of foreign relations, because the cases have become dated and the issue is currently of less interest than it once was. In Chapter 5, we have separated out and expanded the materials on treaty interpretation and presented them earlier in the chapter. Finally, we have added a new appendix (Appendix A), containing the Articles of Confederation.

A significant change in this edition is the addition of a new co-author: Ashley Deeks, from the University of Virginia School of Law. Professor Deeks brings particular expertise in the area of national security law. She has contributed throughout this edition, and particularly to Chapters 8, 9, and 10.

Although (and indeed because) we have participated as scholars in many of the debates implicated by the cases and materials in this book, we have tried hard to present the issues and questions in a balanced manner. We welcome feedback on this and any other aspect of the casebook.

Curtis A. Bradley
Ashley S. Deeks
Jack L. Goldsmith
November 2019

Acknowledgments

In preparing this seventh edition, we are thankful for the support that we have received from our respective deans at Duke, Harvard, and Virginia. The law library staff at our schools have also provided invaluable assistance. In preparing all of the editions of this casebook, we have learned a tremendous amount from interactions with our students. For comments on the sixth edition, which we have considered in making revisions, we thank Mark Feldman and Eric Posner. For research, we thank Elena Chachko.

The three of us have all worked in the Executive Branch. Professor Goldsmith served as Special Counsel to the General Counsel at the Department of Defense (2002-2003) and as Assistant Attorney General in the Justice Department's Office of Legal Counsel (2003-2004); Professor Deeks served as the Assistant Legal Adviser for political-military affairs in the State Department's Office of the Legal Adviser (2008-2010); and Professor Bradley served as the Counselor on International Law in the State Department's Office of the Legal Adviser (2004). We have benefited greatly from these experiences and, to the extent that the information is not confidential, we have attempted to incorporate what we have learned into this casebook.

The authors would like to thank the following copyright holders for permission to excerpt their materials:

Bradley, Curtis A., & Flaherty, Martin S. (2004). Executive Power Essentialism and Foreign Affairs. Michigan Law Review, 102(4), 545. doi: 10.2307/4141924.

Hongju Koh, Harold "Remarks: Twenty-First-Century International Lawmaking" (2013). Faculty Scholarship Series. 4698. As published in Georgetown Law Journal, 101. https://digitalcommons.law.yale.edu/fss_papers/4698.

Neuman, Gerald L. (2004). The Uses of International Law in Constitutional Interpretation. The American Journal of International Law, 98(1), 82. doi: 10.2307/3139258.

Editorial Notice

In editing the cases and other materials in this book, we have used ellipses to indicate deletions and brackets to indicate additions. We have not generally signified the deletion of citations or footnotes, and we have not used ellipses at the end of the excerpted material. We have retained citations within the excerpted material only when we thought the citations served a pedagogical purpose, or when the citations were needed to identify the source of a quotation.

Overview of International Law and Institutions

Because U.S. foreign relations law often intersects with international law, students may find it useful to acquaint themselves at the outset of this course with the basic sources of international law and some of the most important international institutions. The following is a brief overview.*

1. Sources of International Law

International law can be divided into two categories: public international law and private international law. Traditionally, public international law regulated the interactions between nations, such as the laws of war and the treatment of diplomats. Since the mid-twentieth century, it also has regulated to some extent the way that nations treat their own citizens. Private international law, by contrast, encompasses issues relating to transactions and disputes between private parties, such as international commercial standards, international choice of law rules, and the standards for enforcing foreign judgments. References in this course to international law are primarily references to public international law.

There are two principal sources of public international law: treaties and customary international law. Treaties are, quite simply, binding agreements among nations. All such agreements are referred to as "treaties" under international law, regardless of what they are called under each nation's domestic law. By contrast, under U.S. domestic law, "treaties" refers only to the international agreements concluded by the President with the advice and consent of two-thirds of the Senate and does not include "executive agreements" made by the President alone or with a majority approval of Congress.

There are both "bilateral" treaties (between two nations) and "multilateral" treaties (among multiple nations). Typical bilateral treaties include extradition agreements, Friendship, Commerce, and Navigation treaties, and Bilateral Investment Treaties. Multilateral treaties—some of which resemble international legislation in their scope and detail—cover a wide range of subjects, including international trade, the environment, and human rights.

Customary international law results from the general practices and beliefs of nations. By most accounts, customary international law forms only after nations have consistently followed a particular practice out of a sense of legal obligation. It is also commonly accepted that nations that persistently object to an emerging customary international law rule are not bound by it, as long as they do so before the rule becomes settled. Nations that remain silent, however, may become bound by the rule, even if they did not expressly support it. Silence, in other words, is considered a form of implicit acceptance.

---

* For more extensive discussions, see, for example, Restatement (Third) of the Foreign Relations Law of the United States §§101-103 (1987); David J. Bederman, International Law Frameworks (2001); Mark W. Janis, International Law (6th ed. 2012); and Sean D. Murphy, Principles of International Law (2d ed. 2012). For an overview of the status of international law in the United States, see Curtis A. Bradley, International Law in the U.S. Legal System (2d ed. 2015).

Treaties and customary international law have essentially equal weight under international law. As a result, if there is a conflict between these two sources of international law, the later of the two will be controlling. International and domestic adjudicators will likely attempt to reconcile these two sources, however, if that is reasonably possible. Although it is not uncommon for treaties to supersede customary international law, there are relatively few examples in which customary international law has superseded a treaty.

Before the twentieth century, customary international law was the principal source of international law. Subjects regulated by customary international law included maritime law, the privileges and immunities of diplomats, and the standards for neutrality during wartime. Although customary international law continues to play an important role today, its importance has been eclipsed to some extent by the rise of multilateral treaties, which now regulate many areas previously regulated by customary international law.

Some customary international law rules are said to constitute *jus cogens*, or "peremptory" norms. A *jus cogens* norm is, according to one widely accepted definition, "a norm accepted and recognized by the international community of States as a whole as a norm from which no derogation is permitted and which can be modified only by a subsequent norm of general international law having the same character."* These norms transcend requirements of national consent, such that nations are not allowed to opt out of them, even by treaty. Norms frequently described as *jus cogens* norms are the prohibitions (now contained in treaties) on genocide, slavery, and torture.

2. International Institutions

The United Nations was established at the end of World War II, pursuant to the United Nations Charter, a multilateral treaty. Today, 193 nations—essentially all the nations in the world—are parties to the Charter and thus members of the United Nations. The purposes of the United Nations, according to the Charter, are to maintain international peace and security; develop friendly relations among nations; achieve international cooperation in solving economic, social, cultural, and humanitarian problems, and in promoting respect for human rights and fundamental freedoms; and to be a center for harmonizing the actions of nations in attaining these ends.

The central deliberative organ of the United Nations is the General Assembly, which is made up of representatives of all the member nations. The General Assembly is an important forum for discussion and negotiation, but it does not have the power to make binding international law. Instead, it conducts studies and issues non-binding resolutions and recommendations reflecting the views of its members.

The principal enforcement arm of the United Nations is the Security Council. The Council is made up of representatives from fifteen nations. Five nations (China, France, Russia, the United Kingdom, and the United States) have permanent seats on the Council, as well as a veto power over the Council's decisions. The other ten seats on the Council are filled by representatives of other nations elected by the General Assembly. Under the United Nations Charter, the Council is given "primary responsibility for the maintenance of international peace and security." To address any threat to the peace, breach of the peace, or act of aggression, "the Council may

---

* Vienna Convention on the Law of Treaties, art. 53, May 23, 1969, 1155 U.N.T.S. 331.

call upon the members of the United Nations to apply" measures not involving the use of armed force, such as economic sanctions. If the Council determines that such non-military measures are inadequate, it may authorize "such action by air, sea, or land forces as may be necessary to maintain or restore international peace and security." The Charter obligates each member to "accept and carry out the decisions of the Security Council." .

Another component of the United Nations system is the International Court of Justice (also sometimes referred to as the "World Court"), which is based in The Hague, in the Netherlands. There are fifteen judges on the Court, and they are elected to staggered nine-year terms. The Court has jurisdiction over two types of cases: contentious cases and cases seeking an advisory opinion. In contentious cases, only nations may appear as parties. In cases seeking advisory opinions, certain international organizations may also be parties. To be a party to a contentious case before the International Court of Justice, a nation must ordinarily be a party to the Statute of the International Court of Justice (a multilateral treaty) and have consented to the Court's jurisdiction. Consent to jurisdiction can be given in several ways: a special agreement between the parties to submit their dispute to the Court; a jurisdictional clause in a treaty to which both nations are parties; or a general declaration accepting the compulsory jurisdiction of the Court.

In addition to the United Nations system, there are a variety of international institutions established to administer particular treaty regimes. A prominent example is the World Trade Organization (WTO), which was established in 1995 to administer the General Agreement on Tariffs and Trade and related agreements. The WTO has its own dispute settlement body, which adjudicates trade disputes between member nations. To enforce its decisions, the dispute settlement body can authorize the prevailing party to impose trade sanctions on the losing party. Another example is the International Criminal Court, based in The Hague, which has jurisdiction to try and punish certain international offenses, such as genocide.

Finally, there are regional international institutions, the most prominent of which is the European Union (EU). The EU currently is made up of 28 member countries.* The EU has a number of constitutive organs, including a European Parliament, which is elected by individuals in the member countries; a Council of the European Union, which has representatives from the member governments; and a European Commission (an executive body). It also has a European Court of Justice, based in Luxembourg, which interprets and applies the treaty commitments of the Union. Although not part of the EU system, there is also a European Court of Human Rights, based in Strasbourg, France, which interprets and applies the European Convention for the Protection of Human Rights and Fundamental Freedoms (which has been ratified by over 40 countries). The decisions of both the Court of Justice and the Court of Human Rights are binding on the member countries.

---

* In June 2016, the United Kingdom voted in a referendum to leave the Union.

FOREIGN RELATIONS LAW

PART I

INTRODUCTION

1

Historical and Conceptual Foundations

This chapter introduces some of the recurring themes of this casebook. Section A does so in the context of describing the historical origins of the Constitution's foreign relations provisions. Section B then analyzes the constitutional issues implicated by the United States' first foreign relations crisis after ratification of the Constitution—the 1793 Neutrality Controversy. Section C examines some of the conceptual issues that arise in identifying the sources of the federal government's foreign relations powers. The chapter concludes with a note on approaches to constitutional interpretation.

A. CONSTITUTIONAL BACKGROUND

An understanding of history is often useful for understanding legal doctrine. It is particularly useful when studying foreign relations law. The Constitution was written against the background of, and was designed in part to redress, concrete foreign relations problems that arose in the pre-constitutional period. In addition, constitutional text does not specifically address many practical issues concerning the allocation and proper exercise of foreign relations powers. Judges, officials, and scholars therefore commonly consult historical materials from the Founding period to help clarify or flesh out the meaning of the text. As we shall see, however, these materials are often unclear or contested, and frequently do not yield definitive answers.

Post-Founding history is also relevant to foreign relations law. Because of the relative lack of textual guidance, the details of constitutional foreign relations law have been developed through the practices of government in discrete historical contexts. When judges decide foreign relations law cases, they often consider this history. Moreover, because of various limitations on judicial review in the foreign relations context, courts have played a relatively modest role in developing and regulating foreign relations law. As a result, much of the law in this area has emerged through political branch practice and interpretation outside the purview of courts; to understand the law, therefore, one must understand the historical practices out of which it emerges. Furthermore, the world has changed a great deal since the Founding. The United States has gone from a new and relatively weak nation to a military and economic superpower, and the international threats and challenges it faces today are substantially different from those it faced in the late 1700s. As we shall see, the constitutional law of foreign relations has developed to meet the evolving challenges of international relations.

1. Declaration of Independence

In September 1774, representatives of the British colonies in America met in the First Continental Congress for the purpose of responding to British sanctions (known as the "Intolerable Acts") that were themselves responses to earlier acts of colonial defiance. In October 1774, Congress petitioned the king to redress grievances, agreed on sanctions, and resolved to meet the following year. The Second Continental Congress convened in May 1775, approximately three weeks after fighting had broken out between the British and the Americans at Lexington and Concord. It was not until June of 1776, however, that a consensus formed in favor of independence. At this point, it was clear to all involved that the financial, political, and military support of continental European countries would be crucial in achieving victory over the British. And this, in turn, raised questions about the proper conduct of foreign relations and the requirements of international law. Richard Henry Lee, the delegate from Virginia who introduced the resolution of independence, maintained that "[n]o state in Europe will either [enter into treaties] or Trade with us so long as we consider ourselves Subjects of [Great Britain]." He later added: "It is not choice then but necessity which calls for Independence, as the only means by which foreign allies can be obtained." *See* Bradford Perkins, *The Creation of a Republican Empire*, 1776-1865, 1 Cambridge History of American Foreign Relations 19 (1993). On June 11, 1776, the Continental Congress chose committees to draft a declaration of independence, prepare a plan of confederation, and draft a model commercial treaty. Independence, union, and foreign relations were thus viewed as inextricably related.

But where did the power to conduct foreign relations for the United States rest—with the Continental Congress or the States? No written governmental compact bound the States together or defined the Continental Congress's powers. And the Declaration of Independence itself was unclear as to whether the United States was a nation or a confederate union of 13 States. On the one hand, its famous first sentence begins: "When in the Course of human events, it becomes necessary for *one people* to dissolve the political bands which have connected them with another. . . ." (Emphasis added.) On the other hand, the document is entitled "The unanimous Declaration of *the thirteen united States* of America."* (Emphasis added.) And its closing paragraph provides:

> We, therefore, the Representatives of the united States of America, in General Congress, Assembled, appealing to the Supreme Judge of the world for the rectitude of our intentions, do, in the Name, and by Authority of the good People of these Colonies, solemnly publish and declare, That these United Colonies are, and of Right ought to be Free and Independent States; that they are Absolved from all Allegiance to the British Crown, and that all political connection between them and the State of Great Britain, is and ought to be totally dissolved; and that as Free and Independent States, they have

---

* Thomas Jefferson's original draft, later changed by Congress, read: "A Declaration of the Representatives of the United States of America, in General Congress assembled." *See* 1 The Papers of Thomas Jefferson 423 (Julian P. Boyd ed., 1950).

full Power to levy War, conclude Peace, contract Alliances, establish Commerce, and to do all other Acts and Things which Independent States may of right do.

1 The Papers of Thomas Jefferson 432 (Julian P. Boyd ed., 1950).

Moreover, some state constitutions during this period contemplated state foreign relations powers. Article 18 of New York's April 20, 1777, constitution provided that "the governor shall . . . by virtue of his office, be general and commander-in-chief of all the militia, and admiral of the navy of this State. . . ." Similarly, Article 26 of the South Carolina Constitution of 1776 stated that "the president and commander-in-chief [of South Carolina]" would have the power "to make war or peace, or enter into any final treaty" only with the "consent of the general assembly and legislative council." In addition, several states negotiated directly with European nations for loans, arms, clothing, and the like—in direct competition with, and to the great annoyance and disadvantage of, the Continental Congress's official representative and treaty negotiator, Benjamin Franklin.

Despite these suggestions of residual foreign relations powers in the individual former colonies, the Continental Congress conducted foreign relations for the United States. The Continental Congress agreed on a model commercial treaty (the so-called Plan of 1776) in the fall of 1776 and sent a delegation, led by Franklin, to France. The French Foreign Minister, Vergennes, received this delegation, and after much hesitation (having to do with uncertainty about the outcome of the Revolutionary War), the United States and France signed two treaties—of alliance and of commerce—in Paris on February 6, 1778.

The Treaty of Alliance bound together France and the United States for the duration of the Revolutionary War, and it also created obligations that would potentially apply in future conflicts in which they were involved. The treaty provided that "[i]f War should break out between France and Great Britain, during the continuance between the United States and England," France and the United States "shall make it a common cause, and aid each other mutually." More generally, the treaty committed both parties to preserving the United States' "liberty, Sovereignty, and independence," divided up North American possessions, and required that the allies consult one another before concluding a peace treaty with Britain. The countries also agreed to defend one another's North American possessions after the war ended. The Treaty of Amity and Commerce aimed to facilitate good relations by recognizing "a firm, inviolable, and universal Peace, and a true and sincere Friendship between" France and the United States. The two countries guaranteed one another most-favored-nation trading status, agreed to protect nationals living within one another's jurisdiction, and promised not to seize one another's merchant ships. And in a provision that would become a major source of contention, the treaty allowed the ships and privateers of each nation to enter the other's ports and sell their prizes, and denied those privileges to "foreign Privateers . . . in enmity with either Nation."

These treaties constituted the first official recognition of the United States as an independent nation. The Continental Congress ratified these treaties on May 4, 1778. The Continental Congress also authorized several other treaty delegations prior to the ratification of the Articles of Confederation, but no additional treaties were concluded during this period.

Some years later, when the United States was operating under the Constitution, the Chief Justice of the Supreme Court, Samuel Chase, reflected on the source of the national government's foreign relations authority during the Revolutionary War period. In Ware v. Hylton, 3 U.S. (3 Dall.) 199 (1796), the Court held that, by virtue of the Supremacy Clause in Article VI of the Constitution, the obligations of the 1783 peace treaty between the United States and Great Britain overrode contrary provisions in a 1777 Virginia statute. In the course of analyzing the Continental Congress's foreign relations authorities from its first meeting in 1774 until the ratification of the Articles of Confederation in 1781, Chief Justice Chase observed:

> It appears to me that the powers of Congress during that whole period were derived from the people they represented, expressly given, through the medium of their state conventions or state legislatures, or that after they were exercised, they were impliedly ratified by the acquiescence and obedience of the people. . . . The powers of Congress originated from necessity, and arose out of, and were only limited by, events, or in other words they were revolutionary in their very nature. Their extent depended on the exigencies and necessities of public affairs. It was absolutely and indispensably necessary that Congress should possess the power of conducting the war against Great Britain, and therefore if not expressly given by all (as it was by some of the states), I do not hesitate to say that Congress did rightfully possess such power. The authority to make war of necessity implies the power to make peace, or the war must be perpetual. I entertain this general idea—that the several states retained all internal sovereignty, and that Congress properly possessed the great rights of external sovereignty—Among others, the right to make treaties of commerce and alliance, as with France on 6 February 1778. In deciding on the powers of Congress and of the several states before the confederation, I see but one safe rule—namely, that all the powers actually exercised by Congress before that period were rightfully exercised, on the presumption not to be controverted, that they were so authorized by the people they represented by an express, or implied grant, and that all the powers exercised by the state conventions or state legislatures were also rightfully exercised on the same presumption of authority from the people.

For similar sentiments about the source of the national government's foreign relations authority during the revolutionary period, see Penhallow v. Doane, 3 U.S. 54, 80-81 (1795) (Paterson, J.), and Chisholm v. Georgia, 2 U.S. 419, 470 (1793) (Jay, C.J.).

2. Articles of Confederation

The Continental Congress adopted the Articles of Confederation in November 1777 and submitted them to the States, which approved them in March 1781. The Articles ostensibly gave broad foreign relations power to "the united states in congress assembled," where each state had a vote and a nine-vote majority was required to approve any law. Among other things, the Continental Congress was given the "sole and exclusive power of determining on peace and war," "of sending and receiving ambassadors," and of "entering into treaties and alliances." In addition, the individual states were expressly prohibited from engaging in certain foreign relations activities without Congress's consent, such as sending and receiving ambassadors, entering into treaties, engaging in war, and keeping troops or vessels of war in times of peace. The Articles created no independent executive branch and established no federal court system (although Congress did establish an appellate admiralty court).

Within just a few years, there was widespread agreement that the structure and powers of the national government under the Articles of Confederation were inadequate to manage U.S. foreign relations. Congress created a Department of Foreign Affairs, but it was understaffed and lacked the independent authority to make decisions or act. The Articles also failed to give Congress the legal authority to raise revenue or regulate foreign commerce. Without substantial sources of revenue, Congress could not fund an adequate military to secure U.S. borders and otherwise protect the country's interests. When Spain closed New Orleans and the lower Mississippi River to American navigation in 1784, for example, the U.S. government lacked the military means to change the situation. The absence of a general commerce power led American exports to suffer. Individual states controlled tariffs, which meant that Congress could not encourage other countries to lower duties on American goods because it could not guarantee reciprocal treatment in the United States. Moreover, because Congress could not impose a uniform trade policy, it could not credibly threaten to retaliate against trade restrictions imposed by other nations. Thus, for example, Great Britain closed its Caribbean possessions to American trade but was able to continue flooding the States with inexpensive imports.

Congress also had difficulty fulfilling the United States' international legal obligations. The Treaty of Paris, which ended the Revolutionary War between the United States and United Kingdom, was made during the period of the Articles of Confederation. It recognized American independence and acknowledged a "firm and perpetual peace between" the two countries. The treaty also required the United States to compensate British creditors for pre–Revolutionary War debts and confiscated property. But since the federal government lacked revenues to pay compensation, and since there were no federal courts to enforce this treaty provision, creditors sought relief in state courts, which refused to honor the debts. In retaliation for this noncompliance with the treaty, Great Britain refused to honor its treaty commitment to vacate forts along the western frontier. And more generally, other nations saw that the United States could not ensure compliance with its treaties, and refused to enter into new ones with it.

These structural problems were hard to rectify under the Articles, which could only be amended by a unanimous vote of all 13 States. When representatives from the States ultimately decided to draft a Constitution, foreign relations were a significant consideration. "Nothing contributed more directly to the calling of the 1787 Constitutional Convention than did the spreading belief that under the Articles of Confederation, Congress could not effectively and safely conduct foreign policy." Walter LaFeber, *The Constitution and United States Foreign Policy*, 74 J. Am. Hist. 697 (1987). For more on the foreign relations deficiencies of the Articles period, see Bradford Perkins, *The Creation of a Republican Empire, 1776-1865, in* 1 Cambridge History of American Foreign Relations 54-59 (1993); Jack N. Rakove, *Making Foreign Policy — The View from 1787, in* Foreign Policy and the Constitution 1-3 (Robert A. Goldwin & Robert A. Licht eds., 1990).

3. United States Constitution

It is against this background that the foreign relations provisions of the United States Constitution were drafted. You should now read the entire Constitution in Appendix A. Pay particular attention to the following provisions: Article I, §1, cl. 1; Article I, §8, cls. 1, 3, 4, 10-16, 18; Article I, §9, cls. 5-6; Article I, §10, cls. 1-3; Article II, §1, cl. 1; Article II, §2, cls. 1-2; Article III, §§1-2; Article VI, §2; and Amendment X.

What follows are excerpts from *The Federalist Papers* concerning the weaknesses of the national government under the Articles of Confederation and the virtues of the foreign relations provisions of the new Constitution. *The Federalist Papers* consist of 85 newspaper essays written by Alexander Hamilton, John Jay, and James Madison during the 1787-1788 deliberations over the proposed U.S. Constitution. These essays reflect the opinions of three prominent proponents of the Constitution attempting to persuade others to support ratification. They are not definitive accounts of the original understanding of the Constitution's foreign relations provisions, but they have been influential in subsequent debates about these provisions. We include them here to provide a sense of the foreign relations concerns of the Founders and some of their justifications for the Constitution's foreign relations provisions. As we study specific constitutional issues throughout this casebook, we will examine the historical background of the pertinent constitutional provisions in more detail.

Federalist No. 3 (Jay)

It is of high importance to the peace of America that she observe the laws of nations towards all [powers with whom she has treaties and other relations], and to me it appears evident that this will be more perfectly and punctually done by one national government than it could be either by thirteen separate States or by three or four distinct confederacies. . . .

Because, under the national government, treaties and articles of treaties, as well as the laws of nations, will always be expounded in one sense and executed in the same manner—whereas adjudications on the same points and questions, in thirteen States, or in three or four confederacies, will not always accord or be consistent; and that, as well from the variety of independent courts and judges appointed by different and independent governments, as from the different local laws and interests which may affect and influence them. The wisdom of the convention, in committing such questions to the jurisdiction and judgment of courts appointed by and responsible only to one national government, cannot be too much commended.

Federalist No. 4 (Jay)

Leave America divided into thirteen or, if you please, into three or four independent governments—what armies could they raise and pay—what fleets could they ever hope to have? If one was attacked, would the others fly to its succor, and spend their blood and money in its defense? Would there be no danger of their being flattered into neutrality by its specious promises, or seduced by a too great fondness for peace to decline hazarding their tranquillity and present safety for the sake of neighbors, of whom perhaps they have been jealous, and whose importance they are content to see diminished? Although such conduct would not be wise, it would, nevertheless, be natural.

But whatever may be our situation, whether firmly united under one national government, or split into a number of confederacies, certain it is, that foreign nations will know and view it exactly as it is; and they will act toward us accordingly. If they see that our national government is efficient and well administered, our trade prudently regulated, our militia properly organized and disciplined, our resources and finances discreetly managed, our credit re-established, our people free, contented, and united, they will be much more disposed to cultivate our friendship than provoke our resentment. If, on the other hand, they find us either destitute of an effectual government (each State doing right or wrong, as to its rulers may seem convenient), or split into three or four independent and probably discordant republics or confederacies, one inclining to Britain, another to France, and a third to Spain, and perhaps played off against each other by the three, what a poor, pitiful figure will America make in their eyes!

Federalist No. 11 (Hamilton)

The importance of the Union, in a commercial light, is one of those points about which there is least room to entertain a difference of opinion. . . . This applies as well to our intercourse with foreign countries as with each other. . . .

If we continue united, we may counteract a policy so unfriendly to our prosperity in a variety of ways. By prohibitory regulations, extending, at the same time, throughout the States, we may oblige foreign countries to bid against each other, for the privileges of our markets. This assertion will not appear chimerical to those who are able to appreciate the importance of the markets of three millions of people — increasing in rapid progression, for the most part exclusively addicted to agriculture, and likely from local circumstances to remain so — to any manufacturing nation; and the immense difference there would be to the trade and navigation of such a nation, between a direct communication in its own ships, and an indirect conveyance of its products and returns, to and from America, in the ships of another country. Suppose, for instance, we had a government in America, capable of excluding Great Britain (with whom we have at present no treaty of commerce) from all our ports; what would be the probable operation of this step upon her politics? Would it not enable us to negotiate, with the fairest prospect of success, for commercial privileges of the most valuable and extensive kind, in the dominions of that kingdom?

Federalist No. 15 (Hamilton)

We may indeed with propriety be said to have reached almost the last stage of national humiliation. There is scarcely any thing that can wound the pride or degrade the character of an independent nation which we do not experience. Are there engagements to the performance of which we are held by every tie respectable among men? These are the subjects of constant and unblushing violation. Do we owe debts to foreigners and to our own citizens contracted in a time of imminent peril for the preservation of our political existence? These remain without any proper or satisfactory provision for their discharge. Have we valuable territories and important posts in the possession of a foreign power which, by express stipulations, ought long since to have been surrendered? These are still retained, to the prejudice of our interests, not less than of our rights. Are we in a condition to resent or to repel the aggression? We have neither troops, nor treasury, nor government. Are we even in a condition to remonstrate with dignity? The just imputations on our own faith, in respect to the same treaty, ought first to be removed. Are we entitled by nature and compact to a free participation in the navigation of the Mississippi? Spain excludes us from it. Is public credit an indispensable resource in time of public danger? We seem to have abandoned its cause as desperate and irretrievable. Is commerce of importance to national wealth? Ours is at the lowest point of declension. Is respectability in the eyes of foreign powers a safeguard against foreign encroachments? The imbecility of our government even forbids them to treat with us. Our ambassadors abroad are the mere pageants of mimic sovereignty.

Federalist No. 42 (Madison)

The *second* class of powers, lodged in the general government, consist of those which regulate the intercourse with foreign nations, to wit: to make treaties; to send and receive ambassadors, other public ministers, and consuls; to define and punish piracies and felonies committed on the high seas, and offenses against the law of nations; to regulate foreign commerce. . . .

This class of powers forms an obvious and essential branch of the federal administration. If we are to be one nation in any respect, it clearly ought to be in respect to other nations.

The powers to make treaties and to send and receive ambassadors, speak their own propriety. . . .

The power to define and punish piracies and felonies committed on the high seas, and offenses against the law of nations, belongs with equal propriety to the general government, and is a still greater improvement on the articles of Confederation. These articles contain no provision for the case of offenses against the law of nations; and consequently leave it in the power of any indiscreet member to embroil the Confederacy with foreign nations.

Federalist No. 75 (Hamilton)

However proper or safe it may be in governments where the executive magistrate is an hereditary monarch, to commit to him the entire power of making treaties, it would be utterly unsafe and improper to intrust that power to an elective magistrate of four years' duration. . . . An avaricious man might be tempted to betray the interests of the state to the acquisition of wealth. An ambitious man might make his own aggrandizement, by the aid of a foreign power, the price of his treachery to his constituents. . . .

To have intrusted the power of making treaties to the Senate alone, would have been to relinquish the benefits of the constitutional agency of the President in the conduct of foreign negotiations. It is true that the Senate would, in that case, have the option of employing him in this capacity, but they would also have the option of letting it alone, and pique or cabal might induce the latter rather than the former. Besides this, the ministerial servant of the Senate could not be expected to enjoy the confidence and respect of foreign powers in the same degree with the constitutional representatives of the nation, and, of course, would not be able to act with an equal degree of weight or efficacy. While the Union would, from this cause, lose a considerable advantage in the management of its external concerns, the people would lose the additional security which would result from the co-operation of the executive. . . .

The fluctuating and, taking its future increase into the account, the multitudinous composition of [the House of Representatives], forbid us to expect in it those qualities which are essential to the proper execution of such a trust. Accurate and comprehensive knowledge of foreign politics; a steady and systematic adherence to the same views; a nice and uniform sensibility to national character; decision, *secrecy*, and dispatch, are incompatible with the genius of a body so variable and so numerous. The very complication of the business, by introducing a necessity of the concurrence of so many different bodies, would of itself afford a solid objection.

Federalist No. 80 (Hamilton)

It seems scarcely to admit of controversy, that the judiciary authority of the Union ought to extend to these several descriptions of cases: . . . 4th, to all those which involve the PEACE of the CONFEDERACY, whether they relate to the intercourse between the United States and foreign nations, or to that between the States themselves; . . . .

The fourth point rests on this plain proposition, that the peace of the WHOLE ought not to be left at the disposal of a PART. The Union will undoubtedly be answerable to foreign powers for the conduct of its members. And the responsibility for an injury ought ever to be accompanied with the faculty of preventing it. As the denial or perversion of justice by the sentences of courts, as well as in any other manner, is with reason classed among the just causes of war, it will follow that the federal judiciary ought to have cognizance of all causes in which the citizens of other countries are concerned.

Notes and Questions

1. What was the purpose of the Declaration of Independence? To whom was it addressed? In its first paragraph, it states that "a decent respect for the opinions of mankind" requires that the colonies "declare the causes which impel them to the separation." Why is the Declaration concerned with the "opinions of mankind"? Why did its closing paragraph refer to the foreign relations powers of the colonies?

2. What were the structural weaknesses of the Articles of Confederation with respect to the conduct of foreign relations? How were these problems addressed in the Constitution?

3. What foreign relations powers does the Constitution's text assign to Congress? To the President? To the federal courts? What role, if any, does constitutional text permit states to play in foreign relations? What does it prohibit them from doing?

4. In what ways does the Constitution help ensure U.S. compliance with international law? What status do treaties have in the U.S. legal system? What status does the "law of nations" have? For an extensive historical argument that "the founders designed the Constitution to facilitate American integration into the wider community of civilized states and ensure that the nation would comply with its international obligations," see David M. Golove & Daniel J. Hulsebosch, *A Civilized Nation: The Early American Constitution, the Law of Nations, and the Pursuit of International Recognition*, 85 N.Y.U. L. Rev. 932 (2010). For an argument that the Founders did not seek to require federal government compliance with international law but merely sought to empower the government to achieve compliance, see David H. Moore, *Constitutional Commitment to International Law Compliance?*, 102 Va. L. Rev. 367 (2016).

5. Edward Corwin famously observed that the Constitution "is an invitation to struggle for the privilege of directing American foreign policy." Edward S. Corwin, The President: Office and Powers 1787-1984, at 201 (Randall Bland et al. eds., 5th rev. ed. 1984). In what ways does the Constitution regulate this struggle? In what ways does it invite the struggle? Is it desirable that the foreign relations powers of the three federal branches, and the states, be clearly defined, or are there virtues to uncertainty with respect to such powers?

6. Do foreign relations powers inhere in sovereignty? If so, which foreign relations powers? Where was the locus of this sovereignty in 1776? During the Articles of Confederation period? If the U.S. Constitution had not allocated foreign relations powers to the national government, would the national government nevertheless possess them? Which ones? What does Chief Justice Chase's opinion in Ware v. Hylton (see subsection A.1 above) suggest about the answers to these questions?

7. For additional discussion of the United States' conduct of foreign relations during the revolutionary period, see Samuel Flagg Bemis, The Diplomacy of the American Revolution (1935); Keith L. Dougherty, Collective Action Under the Articles of Confederation (2001); Perkins, 1 Cambridge History of American Foreign Relations, *supra*; Julius W. Pratt, A History of United States Foreign Policy 39-53 (1955). For additional discussion of the foreign relations difficulties under the Articles of Confederation, see Richard B. Morris, The Forging of the Federal Union, 1781-1789 (1987); Jack N. Rakove, The Beginnings of National Politics: An Interpretive History of the Continental Congress (1979); Frederick W. Marks III, Independence on Trial: Foreign Affairs and the Making of the Constitution (1973).

B. NEUTRALITY CONTROVERSY OF 1793

In 1789, the same year the United States began operating under its new Constitution, a violent revolution occurred in France. The spillover from this revolution led to the first great crisis in the U.S. constitutional law of foreign relations. Central to the controversy were the treaties that the United States had entered into with France in 1778, described above.

When revolutionary France declared war on Great Britain, Spain, and Holland (France was already at war with Austria and Prussia) following the execution of Louis XVI in early 1793, the French-U.S. treaties raised the prospect that the United States might be drawn into the war on the side of the French. President Washington, however, was determined to avoid entanglement in the European war. As Washington explained to Gouverneur Morris, the U.S. Minister to France, it would be "unwise . . . in the extreme to involve ourselves in the contests of European Nations, where our weight could be but small; tho' the loss to ourselves would be certain." Letter from George Washington to Gouverneur Morris (Mar. 25, 1793), *in* 32 The Writings of George Washington 402 (John C. Fitzpatrick ed., 1939). The French treaties, moreover, were not the only treaties at issue, since the United States by this point also had treaties with a number of France's enemies, including (as discussed above) a peace treaty with Great Britain.

Washington's Cabinet debated what the President should do—consistent with international law and the U.S. Constitution—to stay out of the European conflict. The Cabinet first considered whether to call Congress into special session, and it decided not to do so. It then considered whether the President should issue a proclamation to prevent U.S. citizens from participating in the war, and whether such a proclamation should contain a declaration of U.S. neutrality. Secretary of State Thomas Jefferson initially argued that the President had no authority to issue a formal declaration of neutrality, because (as he later recounted to Madison) that would amount to "a declaration there should be no war, to which the Executive was not competent." The Cabinet, including Jefferson, ultimately agreed to issue a proclamation of neutrality, but, perhaps in response to Jefferson's concerns, the proclamation did not use the word "neutrality." The following is an excerpt of the proclamation:

Proclamation, April 22, 1793

32 The Writings of George Washington 430-31 (John C. Fitzpatrick ed., 1939)

Whereas it appears that a state of war exists between Austria, Prussia, Sardinia, Great Britain, and the United Netherlands, on the one part, and France on the other; and the duty and interest of the United States require, that they should with sincerity and good faith adopt and pursue a conduct friendly and impartial toward the belligerent powers:

I have therefore thought fit by these presents, to declare the disposition of the United States to observe the conduct aforesaid towards those powers respectively; and to exhort and warn the citizens of the United States carefully to avoid all acts and proceedings whatsoever, which may in any manner tend to contravene such disposition.

And I do hereby also make known, that whosoever of the citizens of the United States shall render himself liable to punishment or forfeiture under the law of nations, by committing, aiding or abetting hostilities against any of the said powers, or by carrying to any of them, those articles which are deemed contraband by the modern usage of nations, will not receive the protection of the United States against such punishment or forfeiture; and further that I have given instructions to those officers to whom it belongs, to cause prosecutions to be instituted against all persons, who shall, within the cognizance of the Courts of the United States, violate the law of nations, with respect to the powers at war, or any of them.

The Neutrality Proclamation was controversial for two reasons: it was not authorized by Congress, and it was construed by some as a repudiation of U.S. treaty obligations to France. As James Madison wrote to Jefferson on June 19, 1793:

> The proclamation was in truth a most unfortunate error. It wounds the National honor, by seeming to disregard to stipulated duties to France. . . . And it seems to violate the forms & spirit of the Constitution, by making the executive Magistrate the organ of the disposition, the duty & interest of the Nation in relation to war & peace, subjects appropriated to other departments of the Government.

Letter from James Madison to Thomas Jefferson (June 19, 1793), *in* 15 The Papers of James Madison 33 (Thomas A. Mason et al. eds., 1985).

When criticisms of this sort began to be made in public, Hamilton moved to defend the Neutrality Proclamation in seven newspaper articles under the pseudonym "Pacificus." Hamilton's defense, and in particular his conception of presidential power, alarmed Jefferson, who urged his friend Madison to respond: "Nobody answers him, & his doctrine will therefore be taken for confessed. For god's sake, my dear Sir, take up your pen, select the most striking heresies, and cut him to pieces in the face of the public." Letter from Thomas Jefferson to James Madison (July 7, 1793), *in* 26 The Papers of Thomas Jefferson, *supra*, at 444. After initial reluctance, Madison answered Hamilton in five newspaper articles under the pseudonym

"Helvidius." The Pacificus-Helvidius debate is among the most celebrated arguments in U.S. constitutional history. The themes in this debate—the nature and scope of presidential power, the separation of federal powers in foreign relations, and the proper methods of constitutional interpretation—recur throughout this casebook.

"Pacificus" No. 1

15 The Papers of Alexander Hamilton 33-43
(Harold C. Syrett & Jacob E. Cooke eds., 1969)

It will not be disputed that the management of the affairs of this country with foreign nations is confided to the Government of the [United States]. . . .

The inquiry then is—what department of the government of the [United States] is the proper one to make a declaration of Neutrality, in the cases in which the engagements of the Nation permit and its interests require such a declaration.

A correct and well-informed mind will discern at once that it can belong neither to the Legislative nor Judicial Department and of course must belong to the Executive.

The Legislative Department is not the organ of intercourse between the [United States] and foreign Nations. It is charged neither with making nor interpreting Treaties. It is therefore not naturally that Organ of the Government which is to pronounce the existing condition of the Nation, with regard to foreign Powers, or to admonish the Citizens of their obligations and duties as founded upon that condition of things. Still less is it charged with enforcing the execution and observance of these obligations and those duties.

It is equally obvious that the act in question is foreign to the Judiciary Department of the Government. The province of that Department is to decide litigations in particular cases. It is indeed charged with the interpretation of treaties; but it exercises this function only in the litigated cases; that is where contending parties bring before it a specific controversy. It has no concern with pronouncing upon the external political relations of Treaties between Government and Government. This position is too plain to need being insisted upon.

It must then of necessity belong to the Executive Department to exercise the function in Question, when a proper case for the exercise of it occurs.

It appears to be connected with that department in various capacities, as the organ of intercourse between the Nation and foreign Nations—as the interpreter of the National Treaties in those cases in which the Judiciary is not competent, that is in the cases between Government and Government—as that Power, which is charged with the Execution of the Laws, of which Treaties form a part—as that Power which is charged with the command and application of the Public Force. . . .

The second Article of the Constitution of the [United States], section 1st, establishes this general Proposition, That "The EXECUTIVE POWER shall be vested in a President of the United States of America."

The same article in a succeeding Section proceeds to designate particular cases of Executive Power. It declares among other things that the President shall be Commander in Chief of the army and navy of the [United States] and of the Militia of the several states when called into the actual service of the [United States] that he shall have power by and with the advice of the senate to make treaties; that it shall be his duty to receive ambassadors and other public Ministers and to take care that the laws be faithfully executed.

It would not consist with the rules of sound construction to consider this enumeration of particular authorities as derogating from the more comprehensive grant contained in the general clause, further than as it may be coupled with express restrictions or qualifications; as in regard to the co-operation of the Senate in the appointment of Officers and the making of treaties; which are qualifications of the general executive powers of appointing officers and making treaties: Because the difficulty of a complete and perfect specification of all the cases of Executive authority would naturally dictate the use of general terms — and would render it improbable that a specification of certain particulars was designed as a substitute for those terms, when antecedently used. The different mode of expression employed in the constitution in regard to the two powers the Legislative and the Executive serves to confirm this inference. In the article which grants the legislative powers of the [Government] the expressions are — "All Legislative powers herein granted shall be vested in a Congress of the [United States]," in that which grants the Executive Power the expressions are, as already quoted "The EXECUTIVE POWER shall be vested in a President of the [United States] of America."

The enumeration ought rather therefore to be considered as intended by way of greater caution, to specify and regulate the principal articles implied in the definition of Executive Power; leaving the rest to flow from the general grant of that power, interpreted in conformity to other parts of the Constitution, and to the principles of free government.

The general doctrine then of our constitution is, that the EXECUTIVE POWER of the Nation is vested in the President; subject only to the exceptions and qualifications which are expressed in the instrument.

Two of these have been already noticed — the participation of the Senate in the appointment of Officers and the making of Treaties. A third remains to be mentioned; the right of the Legislature "to declare war and grant letters of marque and reprisal."

With these exceptions the EXECUTIVE POWER of the Union is completely lodged in the President. . . .

And since upon general principles for reasons already given, the issuing of a proclamation of neutrality is merely an Executive Act; since also the general Executive Power of the Union is vested in the President, the conclusion is that the step, which has been taken by him, is liable to no just exception on the score of authority.

It may be observed that this Inference would be just if the power of declaring war had not been vested in the Legislature, but that this power naturally includes the right of judging whether the Nation is under obligations to make war or not.

The answer to this is, that however true it may be, that the right of the Legislature to declare war includes the right of judging whether the Nation be under obligations to make War or not — it will not follow that the Executive is in any case excluded from a similar right of Judgment, in the execution of its own functions.

If the Legislature have a right to make war on the one hand — it is on the other the duty of the Executive to preserve Peace till war is declared; and in fulfilling that duty, it must necessarily possess a right of judging what is the nature of the obligations which the treaties of the Country impose on the Government; and when in pursuance of this right it has concluded that there is nothing in them inconsistent with a state of neutrality, it becomes both its province and its duty to enforce the laws incident to that state of the Nation. The Executive is charged with the execution of all laws, the laws of Nations as well as the Municipal law, which recognizes and adopts those laws. It is consequently bound, by faithfully executing the laws of neutrality, when that is the state of the Nation, to avoid giving a cause of war to foreign Powers. . . .

It deserves to be remarked, that as the participation of the senate in the making of Treaties and the power of the Legislature to declare war are exceptions out of the general "Executive Power" vested in the President, they are to be construed strictly—and ought to be extended no further than is essential to their execution.

While therefore the legislature can alone declare war, can alone actually transfer the nation from a state of Peace to a state of War—it belongs to the "Executive Power," to do whatever else the laws of Nations, cooperating with the Treaties of the Country enjoin, in the intercourse of the [United States] with foreign Powers.

"Helvidius" Nos. 1, 2

15 The Papers of James Madison 70-72, 81-84 (Thomas A. Mason et al. eds., 1985)

Let us examine [the doctrine being propounded by Pacificus].

In the general distribution of powers, we find that of declaring war expressly vested in the Congress, where every other legislative power is declared to be vested, and without any other qualifications than what is common to every other legislative act. The constitutional idea of this power would seem then clearly to be, that it is of a legislative and not an executive nature.

This conclusion becomes irresistible, when it is recollected, that the constitution cannot be supposed to have placed either any power legislative in its nature, entirely among executive powers, or any power executive in its nature, entirely among legislative powers, without charging the constitution, with that kind of intermixture and consolidation of different powers, which would violate a fundamental principle in the organization of free governments. If it were not unnecessary to enlarge on this topic here, it could be shown, that the constitution was originally vindicated, and has been constantly expounded, with a disavowal of any such intermixture.

The power of treaties is vested jointly in the President and in the Senate, which is a branch of the legislature. From this arrangement merely, there can be no inference that would necessarily exclude the power from the executive class: since the senate is joined with the President in another power, that of appointing to offices, which as far as relate to executive offices at least, is considered as of an executive nature. Yet on the other hand, there are sufficient indications that the power of treaties is regarded by the constitution as materially different from mere executive power, and as having more affinity to the legislative than to the executive character. . . .

But the conclusive circumstance is, that treaties when formed according to the constitutional mode, are confessedly to have the force and operation of laws, and are to be a rule for the courts in controversies between man and man, as much as any other laws. They are even emphatically declared by the constitution to be "the supreme law of the land."

So far the argument from the constitution is precisely in opposition to the doctrine. As little will be gained in its favour from a comparison of the two powers, with those particularly vested in the President alone.

As there are but few, it will be most satisfactory to review them one by one.

> The President shall be commander in chief of the army and navy of the United States, and of the militia when called into the actual service of the United States.

There can be no relation worth examining between this power and the general power of making treaties. And instead of being analogous to the power of declaring war, it affords a striking illustration of the incompatibility of the two powers in the same hands. Those who are to conduct a war cannot in the nature of things, be proper or safe judges, whether a war ought to be commenced, continued, or concluded. They are barred from the latter functions by a great principle in free government, analogous to that which separates the sword from the purse, or the power of executing from the power of enacting laws. . . .

Thus it appears that by whatever standard we try this doctrine, it must be condemned as no less vicious in theory than it would be dangerous in practice. It is countenanced neither by the writers on law; nor by the nature of the powers themselves; nor by any general arrangements or particular expressions, or plausible analogies, to be found in the constitution.

Whence then can the writer have borrowed it?

There is but one answer to this question.

The power of making treaties and the power of declaring war, are royal prerogatives in the British government, and are accordingly treated as Executive prerogatives by British commentators. . . .

Leaving however to the leisure of the reader deductions which the author having omitted might not choose to own, I proceed to the examination of one, with which that liberty cannot be taken[:]

> However true it may be, (says he) that the right of the legislature to declare war includes the right of judging whether the legislature be under obligations to make war or not, it will not follow that the executive is in any case excluded from a similar right of judging in the execution of its own functions.

. . . A concurrent authority in two independent departments, to perform the same function with respect to the same thing, would be as awkward in practice, as it is unnatural in theory.

If the legislature and executive have both a right to judge of the obligations to make war or not, it must sometimes happen, though not at present, that they will judge differently. The executive may proceed to consider the question today, may determine that the United States are not bound to take part in a war, and in the execution of its functions proclaim that declaration to all the world. Tomorrow the legislature may follow in the consideration of the same subject, may determine that the obligations impose war on the United States, and in the execution of its functions, enter into a constitutional declaration, expressly contradicting the constitutional proclamation.

In what light does this present the constitution to the people who established it? In what light would it present to the world, a nation, thus speaking, through two different organs, equally constitutional and authentic, two opposite languages, on the same subject and under the same existing circumstances?

But it is not with the legislative rights alone that this doctrine interferes. The rights of the judiciary may be equally invaded. For it is clear that if a right declared by the constitution to be legislative, and actually vested by it in the legislature, leaves, notwithstanding, a similar right in the executive whenever a case for exercising it occurs, in the course of its functions: a right declared to be judiciary and vested in that department may, on the same principle, be assumed and exercised by the executive in the course of its functions: and it is evident that occasions and pretexts for the latter interference may be as frequent as for the former. So again the judiciary department may find equal occasions in the execution of its functions, for usurping the authorities of the executive: and the legislature for stepping into the jurisdiction of both. And thus all the powers of government, of which a partition is so carefully made among the several branches, would be thrown into absolute hotchpot, and exposed to a general scramble.

———————

Another important issue that arose as a result of the French Revolution was whether and how to recognize the ambassador from the revolutionary French government, Edmond Charles Genet. Washington's Cabinet worried about the possibility of rival ambassadors if a successor to Louis XVI sent his own representative. The Cabinet also was concerned that an unqualified reception of Genet would constitute acceptance of the validity of the French-American treaties. Secretary of the Treasury Alexander Hamilton and Secretary of War Henry Knox thought the ambassador should be received with qualifications so that the United States would have the option of suspending or terminating the treaties, whereas Secretary of State Thomas Jefferson and Attorney General Edmund Randolph thought he should be received without qualifications. At the President's request, the cabinet members prepared memoranda focused on whether international law allowed for suspension or termination of the treaties in light of the changes in the French government. Ultimately, Washington decided to receive Genet without qualification as the representative of France—an exercise of discretion that everyone agreed fell within the President's Article II power to "receive Ambassadors and other public Ministers."

Genet proved to be a major thorn in Washington's side, and a significant challenge to America's neutrality policy. When Genet arrived in the United States, he began to commission and arm privateers, manned by American sailors, to capture prizes on behalf of France.* He also began establishing French prize courts on U.S. soil to oversee the condemnation and sale of captured prize vessels. Genet claimed that his actions were consistent with the French-American treaties. But the British protested, arguing that these activities violated American neutrality and the law of nations.

This controversy presented Washington's Cabinet with a number of technical questions under international law. Could the French, consistent with U.S. neutrality, invoke the treaties to justify using American ports for war preparation? Could the French set up prize courts in U.S. territory? Could the warring parties recruit seamen in the United States? Could Americans sell ships to the belligerents? How far at sea could the United States prevent hostilities between the belligerent powers?

* A "privateer" is a private ship authorized by a government during wartime to attack and capture enemy vessels. A "prize" is an enemy ship and its cargo captured at sea during time of war. In effect, Genet was recruiting Americans on American soil for the purpose of attacking British shipping under French authorization.

Were U.S. ships that carried the property of one belligerent immune from capture by the other belligerent?

Washington's Cabinet eventually decided that these and related questions could best be addressed by the Justices of the Supreme Court. On July 12, 1793, the Cabinet agreed to send "letters . . . to the Judges of the Supreme court of the US requesting their attendance . . . to give their advice on certain matters of public concern which will be referred to them by the President." Cabinet Opinion on Consulting the Supreme Court, *in* 26 The Papers of Thomas Jefferson 485 (John Catanzariti ed., 1995). The Cabinet further agreed to inform the ambassadors from Great Britain and France that "the Executive of the US desirous of having done what shall be strictly conformable to the treaties of the US and the laws respecting the said cases has determined to refer the questions arising therein to persons learned in the laws." *Id.* at 484. On July 18, 1793, Jefferson sent the following letter to the Supreme Court, along with a list of 29 questions:

> The war which has taken place among the powers of Europe produces frequent transactions within our ports and limits, on which questions arise of considerable difficulty, and of greater importance to the peace of the US. These questions depend for their solution on the construction of our treaties, on the laws of nature and nations, and on the laws of the land; and are often presented under circumstances which do not give a cognisance of them to the tribunals of the country. Yet their decision is so little analogous to the ordinary functions of the Executive as to occasion much embarrassment and difficulty to them. The President therefore would be much relieved if he found himself free to refer questions of this description to the opinions of the Judges of the Supreme Court of the US whose knowledge of the subject would secure us against errors dangerous to the peace of the US and their authority insure the respect of all parties. He has therefore asked the attendance of such of the judges as could be collected in time for the occasion, to know, in the first place, their opinion, Whether the public may, with propriety, be availed of their advice on these questions? and if they may, to present, for their advice, the abstract questions which have already occurred, or may soon occur, from which they will themselves strike out such as any circumstances might, in their opinion, forbid them to pronounce on.

Letter to the Justices of the Supreme Court (July 18, 1793), *in* 26 The Papers of Thomas Jefferson, *supra,* at 520. The questions concerned the implications of both the U.S.-French treaties, as well as the customary law of nations.

On August 8, 1793, Chief Justice Jay and the Associate Justices responded to the President as follows:

> We have considered the previous question stated in a letter written by your direction to us by the Secretary of State on the 18th of last month, [regarding] the lines of separation drawn by the Constitution between the three departments of the government. These being in certain respects checks upon each other, and our being judges of a court in the last resort, are considerations which afford strong arguments against the propriety of our extra-judicially deciding the questions alluded to, especially as the power given by the Constitution to the President, of calling on the heads of departments for opinions, seems to have been purposely as well as expressly united to the executive departments.
>
> We exceedingly regret every event that may cause embarrassment to your administration, but we derive consolation from the reflection that your judgment will discern what is right, and that your usual prudence, decision, and firmness will surmount every obstacle to the preservation of the rights, peace, and dignity of the United States.

Chief Justice Jay and Associate Justices to President Washington (Aug. 8, 1793), *in* 3 The Correspondence and Public Papers of John Jay 488-89 (Henry P. Johnston ed., 1891).

In response to the Justices' letter, Washington's Cabinet prepared its own set of "regulations" reflecting its answers to the international law questions it had addressed to the Justices. These guidelines were needed in part to guide the Executive Branch in its prosecution of Americans who had engaged in privateering on behalf of the French in violation of the Neutrality Proclamation. One of the first such prosecutions was against Gideon Henfield, a U.S. citizen and the prize master of the French-commissioned ship *Citoyen Genet*. Henfield was arrested when *Citoyen Genet* brought a captured British prize into port at Philadelphia.

The prosecution of Henfield exacerbated the controversy sparked by the Neutrality Proclamation itself. Article I, §8 of the Constitution empowered Congress rather than the President to "define and punish . . . Offenses against the Law of Nations." Congress had not exercised this power with respect to neutrality. It thus seemed to many that the President was exercising a power that the Constitution gave to Congress. As John Marshall explained in his biography of George Washington:

> [The Republican newspapers] universally asked, "What law had been offended, and under what statute was the indictment supported? Were the American people already prepared to give to a proclamation the force of a legislative act, and to subject themselves to the will of the executive? But if they were already sunk to such a state of degradation, were they to be punished for violating a proclamation which had not been published when the offence was committed?"

5 John Marshall, The Life of George Washington 359 (1807).

At about the same time as Henfield's arrest, Chief Justice John Jay delivered a famous grand jury charge for the circuit court in Virginia. The charge was not delivered to the actual grand jury considering Henfield's case, but it was designed to state the law with respect to all offenders of the Neutrality Proclamation.

Grand Jury Charge of John Jay

Circuit Court for the District of Virginia, May 22, 1793
Reprinted in United States v. Henfield, 11 F. Cas. 1099, 1100-05 (C.C.D. Pa. 1793)

Gentlemen of the Grand Jury. . . .

That you may perceive more clearly the extent and objects of your inquiries, it may be proper to observe, that the laws of the United States admit of being classed under three heads of descriptions. 1st. All treaties made under the authority of the United States. 2d. The laws of nations. 3dly. The constitution, and statutes of the United States.

Treaties between independent nations, are contracts or bargains which derive all their force and obligation from mutual consent and agreement; and consequently, when once fairly made and properly concluded, cannot be altered or annulled by one of the parties, without the consent and concurrence of the other. Wide is the difference between treaties and statutes—we may negotiate and make contracts with other nations, but we can neither legislate for them, nor they for us; we may repeal or alter our statutes, but no nation can have authority to vacate or modify treaties at discretion. Treaties, therefore, necessarily become the supreme law of the land, and so they are very properly declared to be by the sixth article of the constitution. Whenever doubts and questions arise relative to the validity, operation or construction of treaties, or of any articles in them, those doubts and questions must be settled according to the maxims and principles of the laws of nations applicable to the case. The peace, prosperity, and reputation of the United States, will always greatly depend on their fidelity to their engagements; and every virtuous citizen (for every citizen is a party to them) will concur in observing and executing them with honour and good faith; . . . .

As to the laws of nations—they are those laws by which nations are bound to regulate their conduct towards each other, both in peace and war. Providence has been pleased to place the United States among the nations of the earth, and therefore, all those duties, as well as rights, which spring from the relation of nation to nation, have devolved upon us. . . . On this occasion, it is proper to observe to you, gentlemen, that various circumstances and considerations now unite in urging the people of the United States to be particularly exact and circumspect in observing the obligation of treaties, and the laws of nations, which, as has been already remarked, form a very important part of the laws of our nation. I allude to the facts and injunctions specified in the President's late proclamation; [Jay then repeats the words of the Neutrality Proclamation].

By this proclamation, authentic and official information is given to the citizens of the United States:—That war actually exists between the nations mentioned in it: That they are to observe a conduct friendly and impartial towards the belligerent powers: That offenders will not be protected, but on the contrary, prosecuted and punished. . . . The proclamation is exactly consistent with and declaratory of the conduct enjoined by the law of nations. It is worthy of remark that we are at peace with all these belligerent powers not only negatively in having war with none of them, but also in a more positive and particular sense by treaties with four of them. . . .

From the observations which have been made, this conclusion appears to result, viz.: That the United States are in a state of neutrality relative to all the powers at war, and that it is their duty, their interest, and their disposition to maintain it: that, therefore, they who commit, aid, or abet hostilities against these powers, or either of them, offend against the laws of the United States, and ought to be punished; and consequently, that it is your duty, gentlemen, to inquire into and present all such of these offences, as you shall find to have been committed within this district. What acts amount to committing or aiding, or abetting hostilities, must be determined by the laws and approved practice of nations, and by the treaties and other laws of the United States relative to such cases. . . .

On the third branch of the laws of the United States, viz: their constitution and statutes, I shall be concise. Here, also, one great unerring principle, viz: the will of the people, will take the lead. The people of the United States . . . have ordained and established [a national government] which is specified in their great and general compact or constitution—a compact deliberately formed, maturely considered, and solemnly adopted and ratified by them. . . . The statutes of the United States, constitutionally made, derive their obligation from the same source, and must bind accordingly. . . . Most essentially, therefore, is it the duty and interest of us all, that the laws be observed, and irresistibly executed.

Justice Wilson gave a similar, though more verbose, charge to Henfield's grand jury. *See Henfield*, 11 F. Cas. at 1105-15.

Henfield and several other defendants were ultimately acquitted in trials for alleged violations of the Neutrality Proclamation. There are a number of possible reasons for the acquittals, including a concern that the defendants had not received sufficient notice that their conduct was criminal, a pro-French bias among the jurors, and a belief that federal criminal law should come from Congress rather than the Executive. Whatever the reasons, Washington asked Congress at its next session to provide a statutory basis for prosecuting violations of the law of nations concerning neutrality. The following is an excerpt of the statute Congress enacted:

Neutrality Act of 1794

Ch. 50, 1 Stat. 381 (1794)

An Act in addition to the act for the punishment of certain crimes against the United States.

Sec. 1. *Be it enacted and declared by the Senate and House of Representatives of the United States of America in Congress assembled,* That if any citizen of the United States shall, within the territory or jurisdiction of the same, accept and exercise a commission to serve a foreign prince or state in war by land or sea, the person so offending shall be deemed guilty of a high misdemeanor, and shall be fined not more than two thousand dollars, and shall be imprisoned not exceeding three years. . . .

Sec. 8. *And be it further enacted and declared,* That it shall be lawful for the President of the United States, or such other person as he shall have empowered for that purpose, to employ such part of the land or naval forces of the United States or of the militia thereof, as shall be necessary to compel any foreign ship or vessel to depart the United States, in all cases in which, by the laws of nations or the treaties of the United States, they ought not to remain within the United States.

Ambassador Genet continued to defy U.S. authorities concerning American neutrality throughout the summer of 1793. He also engaged in other mischief, including making a request to Attorney General Randolph to prosecute Chief Justice Jay and Senator Rufus King for libel and organizing various plots to spark revolution in Louisiana, Florida, and Canada. Washington, on the unanimous recommendation of his Cabinet, sought and received Genet's recall. Instead of returning to France (where he likely would have been executed), Genet chose to settle down as a farmer in New York, where he subsequently married the governor's daughter.

Notes and Questions

1. What was the constitutional basis for Washington's Neutrality Proclamation? Who has the better of the debate on this issue, Pacificus or Helvidius? Whose argument is more faithful to constitutional text? When constitutional text is silent about the locus of a foreign relations power (such as the power to proclaim neutrality), what interpretive principles should one use? Original understanding? Constitutional structure? Policy?

2. Hamilton (Pacificus) articulates several justifications for the President's power to proclaim neutrality: (a) that the President has the power to proclaim neutrality by virtue of the "Vesting Clause" in Article II, which states that "[t]he executive Power shall be vested in a President of the United States of America"; (b) that the President's power to proclaim neutrality flows from his duty in Article II to "take Care that the Laws be faithfully executed"; and (c) that the text and structure of the Constitution make the President the "organ of intercourse between the United States and foreign nations." All three of these arguments recur throughout this casebook in connection with assertions of presidential power in foreign relations.

3. Is Hamilton's theory of the Vesting Clause of Article II persuasive? What explains the difference in wording between the Vesting Clause in Article I and the Vesting Clause in Article II? For a modern defense and elaboration of Hamilton's theory, see Saikrishna B. Prakash & Michael D. Ramsey, *The Executive Power over Foreign Affairs*, 111 Yale L.J. 231 (2001). For a critique of the theory, see Curtis A. Bradley & Martin S. Flaherty, *Executive Power Essentialism and Foreign Affairs*, 102 Mich. L. Rev. 545 (2004). For an originalist argument that the Neutrality Proclamation and related actions taken by the Washington Administration "were based on the principle that the Executive has the duty and the resulting power to comply with the obligations of the law of nations," see Robert J. Reinstein, *Executive Power and the Law of Nations in the Washington Administration*, 46 U. Rich. L. Rev. 373, 377 (2012).

4. Does the President's duty to "take Care that the Laws be faithfully executed" provide an independent basis for the Neutrality Proclamation, as Hamilton argues? Does this duty include a power to *interpret* the laws? What laws? Do "the Laws" include the law of nations? Isn't Congress, rather than the President, given the constitutional power to define and punish offenses against the law of nations?

5. Is it true that the President is the "organ of intercourse" between the United States and foreign nations? If so, what is the precise constitutional basis for this role? What is entailed by this role? How does this role relate to Congress's many foreign relations powers?

6. Pacificus and Helvidius disagree about whether a "concurrent authority" between the President and Congress in certain foreign relations contexts is constitutionally justified and practically necessary. This, too, is an issue that will recur throughout this casebook. Who has the better of this argument?

7. What is the status of the law of nations (referred to today as "customary international law") in the U.S. constitutional system? Unlike treaties, the law of nations is not mentioned in the Supremacy Clause or in Article III. The only mention of the term is in Article I, which gives Congress the power to define and punish offenses against the law of nations. And yet many of the documents reproduced in this chapter suggest that the law of nations is part of U.S. law. For example, John Jay states in *Federalist No. 3* that under the Constitution, the law of nations, like treaties, will "always be expounded in one sense and executed in the same manner." Hamilton states as Pacificus that the law of nations is part of the "law of the land," and argues that the President has a duty to "take care" that the law of nations is faithfully executed. And Jay's grand jury charge states that the law of nations "form[s] a very important part of the laws of our nation." Do these statements mean that the law of nations, or customary international law, is part of U.S. *federal* law? Could the law of nations have been part of "the laws of our nation" or the "law of the land" without being federal law? Why is the domestic legal status of the law of nations important?

Why do you think the Constitution only mentions the law of nations in Article I? We explore these issues in detail in Chapter 7.

8. In debating whether to retain the option of suspending or terminating the U.S.-French treaties in light of the French revolution, Washington's Cabinet addressed only the international law standards for suspension and termination. As Jefferson argued then, and is still the case today, a nation's treaties generally continue in force under international law even after significant changes in the nation's government. International law nevertheless recognizes circumstances that will allow suspension or termination of a treaty—such as when the other party to a bilateral treaty has materially breached it. Moreover, although this was not true during the Founding period, many treaties today contain clauses allowing for unilateral withdrawal, often conditioned on a required period of notice. What international law does not address, however, is how each nation is to exercise its right of suspending or terminating a treaty—for example, whether the executive arm of the government can exercise this right unilaterally without legislative participation. Instead, that issue is determined by each nation's domestic law. Section G of Chapter 5 considers the U.S. constitutional law governing the suspension and termination of treaties.

9. Why do you think Jefferson, who was a lawyer, wanted the Justices of the Supreme Court to answer the questions about international law? Why did he not simply ask the Attorney General? Why did the Justices not answer Jefferson's questions? Why would it have been "extra-judicial[]" for them to do so? Because the questions were "political"? Or because, in the words of Pacificus, a federal court may decide legal questions only "where contending parties bring before it a specific controversy"? In answering these questions, consider two facts. First, Washington and Hamilton frequently consulted Chief Justice Jay in private about legal matters relating to the Neutrality Controversy, and Jay offered his legal opinion to them in private (including writing a draft of the Neutrality Proclamation itself). Second, the Supreme Court addressed and resolved questions about the meaning of the French-American treaties and related law of nations issues in live cases and controversies presented to it. *See, e.g.,* Glass v. The Sloop Betsey, 3 U.S. (3 Dall.) 6 (1794) (ordering French prize restored to its owners after concluding that France had no right to erect prize courts in the United States). *See also* Kevin Arlyck, *The Courts and Foreign Affairs at the Founding,* 2017 B.Y.U. L. Rev. 1 (documenting how, throughout the Neutrality Crisis, "the Washington administration actively sought to enlist the help of the federal judiciary in managing a diplomatic emergency").

Whatever its true motivation, the Justices' letter to Jefferson is often cited as a precedent for a variety of judicial "nonjusticiability" doctrines, including the "case or controversy" requirement, the related prohibition on advisory opinions, the standing doctrine, and the ripeness and mootness doctrines. We discuss these doctrines in Chapter 2. On the historical background and significance of the letter from the Justices, see Stewart Jay, Most Humble Servants: The Advisory Role of Early Judges (1997).

10. The controversy sparked by *Henfield's Case*—whether a U.S. citizen could be prosecuted for a non-statutory, common law crime—was later resolved in United States v. Hudson & Goodwin, 11 U.S. 32 (1812), in which the Supreme Court declared that it had "long been settled in public opinion" that there is no federal common law of crimes. *See also* United States v. Coolidge, 14 U.S. 415 (1816) (declining to overturn *Hudson & Goodwin*). We return to this issue, as it relates to the domestic legal status of customary international law, in Chapter 7.

11. What was the constitutional basis for Congress's neutrality statute? Is it more or less clear than the President's power to declare neutrality? Which branch of government is most competent to determine U.S. neutrality policy—Congress or the President? Which branch is more responsive to the wishes of the electorate? Was it constitutional for Congress, in Section 8 of the neutrality statute, to delegate military authority to the President? Did the President already have the authority that Congress was purporting to delegate? We consider the respective powers of Congress and the President concerning the use of military force in Chapter 9.

12. The current version of the Neutrality Act is codified at 18 U.S.C. §960. The Act provides as follows:

> Whoever, within the United States, knowingly begins or sets on foot or provides or prepares a means for or furnishes the money for, or takes part in, any military or naval expedition or enterprise to be carried on from thence against the territory or dominion of any foreign prince or state, or of any colony, district, or people with whom the United States is at peace, shall be fined under this title or imprisoned not more than three years, or both.

For decisions upholding convictions under this statute, see, for example, United States v. Khan, 461 F.3d 477 (4th Cir. 2006) (conspiracy to carry out attacks against India), and United States v. Ramirez, 765 F.2d 438 (5th Cir. 1985) (conspiracy to overthrow government of Haiti). Private plaintiffs have occasionally sought to sue Executive Branch officials under the Neutrality Act, or to force the Attorney General to prosecute Executive officials under the Act, usually without success. *See, e.g.,* Ronald v. Dellums, 797 F.2d 817 (9th Cir. 1986); Sanchez-Espinoza v. Reagan, 770 F.2d 202 (D.C. Cir. 1985). For additional discussion of the Act, see Jules Lobel, *The Rise and Decline of the Neutrality Act: Sovereignty and Congressional War Powers in United States Foreign Policy,* 24 Harv. Int'l L.J. 1 (1983).

13. For more detailed accounts of the Neutrality Controversy and the constitutional debates it generated, see William R. Casto, Foreign Affairs and the Constitution in the Age of Fighting Sail (2006); David P. Currie, The Constitution in Congress: The Federalist Period, 1789-1801, at 174-82 (1997); Stanley Elkins & Eric McKitrick, The Age of Federalism: The Early American Republic, 1788-1800, at 330-54 (1993); Martin Flaherty, *The Story of the Neutrality Controversy: Struggling over Presidential Power Outside the Courts, in* Presidential Power Stories (Christopher H. Schroeder & Curtis A. Bradley eds., 2009); Jay, Most Humble Servants, *supra,* at 117-48. For additional discussion of the neutrality prosecutions, see Stewart Jay, *Origins of Federal Common Law: Part One,* 133 U. Pa. L. Rev. 1003, 1048-53 (1985); Robert C. Palmer, *The Federal Common Law of Crime,* 4 Law and Hist. Rev. 267, 286-99 (1986).

C. NATURE OF U.S. FOREIGN RELATIONS AUTHORITY

The text of the Constitution expressly assigns certain foreign relations powers to the national government, such as the power to enter into treaties (assigned to the President and Senate) and the power to declare war (assigned to Congress). As the

Neutrality Controversy demonstrates, however, some foreign relations powers do not have a clear basis in constitutional text. This raises a number of important questions:

> Where . . . is the power to recognize other states or governments; to maintain or rupture diplomatic relations; to open consulates in other countries and permit foreign governments to establish consulates in the United States; to acquire or cede territory; to grant or withhold foreign aid; to proclaim a Monroe Doctrine, an Open-Door Policy, or a Reagan Doctrine; indeed to determine all the attitudes and carry out all the details in the myriads of relationships with other nations that are 'the foreign policy' and 'the foreign relations' of the United States? The power to make treaties is granted, but where is the power to break, denounce, or terminate them? The power to declare war is there, but where is the power to make peace, to proclaim neutrality in the wars of others, or to recognize or deny rights to belligerents or insurgents, or to address the consequences of the United Nations Charter and other international agreements regulating war? Congress can enact laws to define and punish violations of international law, but where is the power to assert U.S. rights or carry out its obligations under international law, to help make new international law, or to disregard or violate law that has been made? Congress can regulate commerce with foreign nations, but where is the power to make other laws relating to U.S. foreign relations—to regulate immigration or the status and rights of aliens, or activities of citizens abroad? These "missing" powers, and a host of others, were clearly intended for, and have always been exercised by, the federal government, but where does the Constitution say that it shall be so?

Louis Henkin, Foreign Affairs and the United States Constitution 14-15 (2d ed. 1996).

Keep these questions in mind as you read the following decisions.

Ex parte Merryman

(Circuit Court, D. Md. 1861) 17 F. Cas. 144 (No. 9,487)

[On April 19, 1861, pro-secession mobs in Baltimore attempted to prevent Union troops from passing through the city on their way to guard Washington, D.C., and 4 soldiers and 12 civilians were killed in the resulting conflict. On April 27, President Lincoln authorized the commanding general of the U.S. army to suspend the writ of habeas corpus if there was resistance "at any point or in the vicinity of any military line which is now or which shall be used between the city of Philadelphia and the city of Washington." On May 25, a military commander at Fort McHenry arrested John Merryman, a Maryland resident suspected of aiding the Confederacy following the Baltimore riot. Merryman petitioned Chief Justice Taney, riding circuit in Baltimore, for a writ of habeas corpus. Taney issued the writ, but the military ignored it because of Lincoln's April 27 order. Taney then wrote the following opinion.]

TANEY, CIRCUIT JUSTICE. . . .

As the case comes before me, therefore, I understand that the President not only claims the right to suspend the writ of habeas corpus himself, at his discretion, but to delegate that discretionary power to a military officer, and to leave it to him to determine whether he will or will not obey judicial process that may be served upon him. . . .

The clause of the constitution, which authorizes the suspension of the privilege of the writ of habeas corpus, is in the 9th section of the first article. This article is devoted to the legislative department of the United States, and has not the slightest reference to the executive department. . . .

It is the second article of the constitution that provides for the organization of the executive department, enumerates the powers conferred on it, and prescribes its duties. And if the high power over the liberty of the citizen now claimed, was intended to be conferred on the President, it would undoubtedly be found in plain words in this article; but there is not a word in it that can furnish the slightest ground to justify the exercise of the power. . . .

The only power . . . the President possesses, where the "life, liberty or property" of a private citizen is concerned, is the power and duty prescribed in the third section of the second article, which requires "that he shall take care that the laws shall be faithfully executed." He is not authorized to execute them himself, or through agents or officers, civil or military, appointed by himself, but he is to take care that they be faithfully carried into execution, as they are expounded and adjudged by the co-ordinate branch of the government to which that duty is assigned by the constitution. . . .

With such provisions in the constitution, expressed in language too clear to be misunderstood by any one, I can see no ground whatever for supposing that the President, in any emergency, or in any state of things, can authorize the suspension of the privileges of the writ of habeas corpus, or the arrest of a citizen, except in aid of the judicial power. He certainly does not faithfully execute the laws, if he takes upon himself legislative power, by suspending the writ of habeas corpus, and the judicial power also, by arresting and imprisoning a person without due process of law.

Nor can any argument be drawn from the nature of sovereignty, or the necessity of government, for self-defence in times of tumult and danger. The government of the United States is one of delegated and limited powers; it derives its existence and authority altogether from the constitution, and neither of its branches, executive, legislative or judicial, can exercise any of the powers of government beyond those specified and granted; for the tenth article of the amendments to the constitution, in express terms, provides that "the powers not delegated to the United States by the constitution, nor prohibited by it to the states, are reserved to the states, respectively, or to the people."

[Merryman was subsequently released on bail and was never tried on the charges for which he was indicted.]

Chinese Exclusion Case (Chae Chan Ping v. United States)

130 U.S. 581 (1889)

[An 1888 federal statute prohibited Chinese laborers from reentering the United States under certain circumstances. This case presented two issues: First, did the statute violate treaties between the United States and China? Second, did Congress have the authority to enact the statute? We examine the first question in Chapter 5 in the materials on the last-in-time rule. The portion of the opinion excerpted below addresses the second question.]

JUSTICE FIELD delivered the opinion of the court. . . .

There being nothing in the treaties between China and the United States to impair the validity of the act of Congress of October 1, 1888, was it on any other ground beyond the competency of Congress to pass it? If so, it must be because it was not within the power of Congress to prohibit Chinese laborers who had at the time departed from the United States, or should subsequently depart, from returning to the United States. Those laborers are not citizens of the United States; they are aliens. That the government of the United States, through the action of the legislative department, can exclude aliens from its territory is a proposition which we do not think open to controversy. Jurisdiction over its own territory to that extent is an incident of every independent nation. It is a part of its independence. If it could not exclude aliens it would be to that extent subject to the control of another power. As said by this court in the case of The Exchange, 7 Cranch, 116, 136, speaking by Chief Justice Marshall: "The jurisdiction of the nation within its own territory is necessarily exclusive and absolute. It is susceptible of no limitation not imposed by itself. Any restriction upon it, deriving validity from an external source, would imply a diminution of its sovereignty to the extent of the restriction, and an investment of that sovereignty to the same extent in that power which could impose such restriction. All exceptions, therefore, to the full and complete power of a nation within its own territories, must be traced up to the consent of the nation itself. They can flow from no other legitimate source."

While under our Constitution and form of government the great mass of local matters is controlled by local authorities, the United States, in their relation to foreign countries and their subjects or citizens are one nation, invested with powers which belong to independent nations, the exercise of which can be invoked for the maintenance of its absolute independence and security throughout its entire territory. The powers to declare war, make treaties, suppress insurrection, repel invasion, regulate foreign commerce, secure republican governments to the States, and admit subjects of other nations to citizenship, are all sovereign powers, restricted in their exercise only by the Constitution itself and considerations of public policy and justice which control, more or less, the conduct of all civilized nations. . . .

The control of local matters being left to local authorities, and national matters being entrusted to the government of the Union, the problem of free institutions existing over a widely extended country, having different climates and varied interests, has been happily solved. For local interests the several States of the Union exist, but for national purposes, embracing our relations with foreign nations, we are but one people, one nation, one power.

To preserve its independence, and give security against foreign aggression and encroachment, is the highest duty of every nation, and to attain these ends nearly all other considerations are to be subordinated. It matters not in what form such aggression and encroachment come, whether from the foreign nation acting in its national character or from vast hordes of its people crowding in upon us. The government, possessing the powers which are to be exercised for protection and security, is clothed with authority to determine the occasion on which the powers shall be called forth; and its determination, so far as the subjects affected are concerned, are necessarily conclusive upon all its departments and officers. If, therefore, the government of the United States, through its legislative department, considers the presence of foreigners of a different race in this country, who will not assimilate with us, to be dangerous to its peace and security, their exclusion is not to be stayed because at the time there are no actual hostilities with the nation of which the foreigners are subjects. The existence of war would render the necessity of the proceeding only more obvious and pressing. The same necessity, in a less pressing degree, may arise when war does not exist, and the same authority which adjudges the necessity in one case must also determine it in the other. In both cases its determination is conclusive upon the judiciary. If the government of the country of which the foreigners excluded are subjects is dissatisfied with this action it can make complaint to the executive head of our government, or resort to any other measure which, in its judgment, its interests or dignity may demand; and there lies its only remedy. . . .

The power of exclusion of foreigners being an incident of sovereignty belonging to the government of the United States, as a part of those sovereign powers delegated by the Constitution, the right to its exercise at any time when, in the judgment of the government, the interests of the country require it, cannot be granted away or restrained on behalf of any one.

Carter v. Carter Coal Co.

298 U.S. 238 (1936)

[This case involved a challenge to a 1935 federal statute that provided for the establishment of minimum prices and collective bargaining in the coal industry. In addition to holding that the statute exceeded Congress's authority under the Commerce Clause, the Court rejected the claim that the statute could be upheld on the basis of a "general federal power, thought to exist, apart from the specific grants of the Constitution."]

MR. JUSTICE SUTHERLAND delivered the opinion of the court. . . .

The ruling and firmly established principle is that the powers which the general government may exercise are only those specifically enumerated in the Constitution, and such implied powers as are necessary and proper to carry into effect the enumerated powers. . . .

The proposition, often advanced and as often discredited, that the power of the federal government inherently extends to purposes affecting the nation as a whole with which the states severally cannot deal or cannot adequately deal, and the related notion that Congress, entirely apart from those powers delegated by the Constitution, may enact laws to promote the general welfare, have never been accepted but always definitely rejected by this court. Mr. Justice Story, as early as 1816, laid down the cardinal rule, which has ever since been followed — that the general government "can claim no powers which are not granted to it by the Constitution, and the powers actually granted, must be such as are expressly given, or given by necessary implication." Martin v. Hunter's Lessee, 1 Wheat. 304, 326. . . .

The general rule with regard to the respective powers of the national and the state governments under the Constitution, is not in doubt. The states were before the Constitution; and, consequently, their legislative powers antedated the Constitution. Those who framed and those who adopted that instrument meant to carve from the general mass of legislative powers, then possessed by the states, only such portions as it was thought wise to confer upon the federal government; and in order that there should be no uncertainty in respect of what was taken and what was left, the national powers of legislation were not aggregated but enumerated — with the result that what was not embraced by the enumeration remained vested in the states without change or impairment. . . .

[S]ince every addition to the national legislative power to some extent detracts from or invades the power of the states, it is of vital moment that, in order to preserve the fixed balance intended by the Constitution, the powers of the general government be not so extended as to embrace any not within the express terms of the several grants or the implications necessarily to be drawn there from. It is no longer open to question that the general government, unlike the states, possesses no *inherent* power in respect of the internal affairs of the states; and emphatically not with regard to legislation. The question in respect of the inherent power of that government as to the external affairs of the nation and in the field of international law is a wholly different matter which it is not necessary now to consider.

United States v. Curtiss-Wright Export Corp.

299 U.S. 304 (1936)

[On May 28, 1934, Congress enacted a joint resolution that provided that, if the President found that a prohibition on arms sales to the countries fighting in the Chaco war between Bolivia and Paraguay would promote regional peace, and the President made a proclamation to that effect, such arms sales would be illegal. The President made such a proclamation. Subsequently, four officers of the Curtiss-Wright Export Corporation, along with the corporation and two affiliates, were indicted for conspiring to sell aircraft machine guns to Bolivia, in violation of the joint resolution and proclamation. The defendants challenged their indictment on the ground that the joint resolution had unconstitutionally delegated legislative power to the President.]

MR. JUSTICE SUTHERLAND delivered the opinion of the court. . . .

Whether, if the Joint Resolution had related solely to internal affairs it would be open to the challenge that it constituted an unlawful delegation of legislative power to the Executive, we find it unnecessary to determine. The whole aim of the resolution is to affect a situation entirely external to the United States, and falling within the category of foreign affairs. The determination which we are called to make, therefore, is whether the Joint Resolution, as applied to that situation, is vulnerable to attack under the rule that forbids a delegation of the law-making power. In other words, assuming (but not deciding) that the challenged delegation, if it were confined to internal affairs, would be invalid, may it nevertheless be sustained on the ground that its exclusive aim is to afford a remedy for a hurtful condition within foreign territory?

It will contribute to the elucidation of the question if we first consider the differences between the powers of the federal government in respect of foreign or external affairs and those in respect of domestic or internal affairs. That there are differences between them, and that these differences are fundamental, may not be doubted.

The two classes of powers are different, both in respect of their origin and their nature. The broad statement that the federal government can exercise no powers except those specifically enumerated in the Constitution, and such implied powers as are necessary and proper to carry into effect the enumerated powers, is categorically true only in respect of our internal affairs. In that field, the primary purpose of the Constitution was to carve from the general mass of legislative powers *then possessed by the states* such portions as it was thought desirable to vest in the federal government, *leaving those not* included in the enumeration still in the states. Carter v. Carter Coal Co., 298 U.S. 238, 294. That this doctrine applies only to powers which the states had, is self evident. And since the states severally never possessed international powers, such powers could not have been carved from the mass of state powers but obviously were transmitted to the United States from some other source. During the colonial period, those powers were possessed exclusively by and were entirely under the control of the Crown. By the Declaration of Independence, "the Representatives of the United States of America" declared the United [not the several] Colonies to be free and independent states, and as such to have "full Power to levy War, conclude Peace, contract Alliances, establish Commerce and to do all other Acts and Things which Independent States may of right do."

As a result of the separation from Great Britain by the colonies acting as a unit, the powers of external sovereignty passed from the Crown not to the colonies severally, but to the colonies in their collective and corporate capacity as the United States of America. Even before the Declaration, the colonies were a unit in foreign affairs, acting through a common agency—namely the Continental Congress, composed of delegates from the thirteen colonies. That agency exercised the powers of war and peace, raised an army, created a navy, and finally adopted the Declaration of Independence. Rulers come and go; governments end and forms of government change; but sovereignty survives. A political society cannot endure without a supreme will somewhere. Sovereignty is never held in suspense. When, therefore, the external sovereignty of Great Britain in respect of the colonies ceased, it immediately passed to the Union. *See* Penhallow v. Doane, 3 Dall. 54, 80-81. That fact was given practical application almost at once. The treaty of peace, made on September 23, 1783, was concluded between his Brittanic Majesty and the "United States of America." . . .

The Union existed before the Constitution, which was ordained and established among other things to form "a more perfect Union." Prior to that event, it is clear that the Union, declared by the Articles of Confederation to be "perpetual," was the sole possessor of external sovereignty and in the Union it remained without change save in so far as the Constitution in express terms qualified its exercise. The Framers' Convention was called and exerted its powers upon the irrefutable postulate that though the states were several their people in respect of foreign affairs were one. Compare The Chinese Exclusion Case, 130 U.S. 581, 604, 606. In that convention, the entire absence of state power to deal with those affairs was thus forcefully stated by Rufus King:

> The states were not "sovereigns" in the sense contended for by some. They did not possess the peculiar features of sovereignty,—they could not make war, nor peace, nor alliances, nor treaties. Considering them as political beings, they were dumb, for they could not speak to any foreign sovereign whatever. They were deaf, for they could not hear any propositions from such sovereign. They had not even the organs or faculties of defence or offence, for they could not of themselves raise troops, or equip vessels, for war.

5 Elliott's Debates 212.

It results that the investment of the federal government with the powers of external sovereignty did not depend upon the affirmative grants of the Constitution. The powers to declare and wage war, to conclude peace, to make treaties, to maintain diplomatic relations with other sovereignties, if they had never been mentioned in the Constitution, would have vested in the federal government as necessary concomitants of nationality. Neither the Constitution nor the laws passed in pursuance of it have any force in foreign territory unless in respect of our own citizens; and operations of the nation in such territory must be governed by treaties, international understandings and compacts, and the principles of international law. As a member of the family of nations, the right and power of the United States in that field are equal to the right and power of the other members of the international family. Otherwise, the United States is not completely sovereign. The power to acquire territory by discovery and occupation (Jones v. United States, 137 U.S. 202, 212), the power to expel undesirable aliens (Fong Yue Ting v. United States, 149 U.S. 698, 705 et seq.), the power to make such international agreements as do not constitute treaties in the constitutional sense (Altman & Co. v. United States, 224 U.S. 583, 600-601), none of which is expressly affirmed by the Constitution, nevertheless exist as inherently inseparable from the conception of nationality. This the court recognized, and in each of the cases cited found the warrant for its conclusions not in the provisions of the Constitution, but in the law of nations.

In Burnet v. Brooks, 288 U.S. 378, 396, we said, "As a nation with all the attributes of sovereignty, the United States is vested with all the powers of government necessary to maintain an effective control of international relations." *Cf.* Carter v. Carter Coal Co., *supra.*

Not only, as we have shown, is the federal power over external affairs in origin and essential character different from that over internal affairs, but participation in the exercise of the power is significantly limited. In this vast external realm, with its important, complicated, delicate and manifold problems, the President alone has the power to speak or listen as a representative of the nation. He *makes* treaties with the advice and consent of the Senate; but he alone negotiates. Into the field of negotiation the Senate cannot intrude; and Congress itself is powerless to invade it. As Marshall said in his great argument of March 7, 1800, in the House of Representatives, "The President is the sole organ of the nation in its external relations, and its sole representative with foreign nations." Annals, 6th Cong., col. 613. . . .

It is important to bear in mind that we are here dealing not alone with an authority vested in the President by an exertion of legislative power, but with such an authority plus the very delicate, plenary and exclusive power of the President as the sole organ of the federal government in the field of international relations—a power which does not require as a basis for its exercise an act of Congress, but which, of course, like every other governmental power, must be exercised in subordination to the applicable provisions of the Constitution. It is quite apparent that if, in the maintenance of our international relations, embarrassment—perhaps serious embarrassment—is to be avoided and success for our aims achieved, congressional legislation which is to be made effective through negotiation and inquiry within the international field must often accord to the President a degree of discretion and freedom from statutory restriction which would not be admissible were domestic affairs alone involved. Moreover, he, not Congress, has the better opportunity of knowing the conditions which prevail in foreign countries, and especially is this true in time of war. He has his confidential sources of information. He has his agents in the form of diplomatic, consular and other officials. Secrecy in respect of information gathered by them may be highly necessary, and the premature disclosure of it productive of harmful results. . . .

When the President is to be authorized by legislation to act in respect of a matter intended to affect a situation in foreign territory, the legislator properly bears in mind the important consideration that the form of the President's action—or, indeed, whether he shall act at all—may well depend, among other things, upon the nature of the confidential information which he has or may thereafter receive, or upon the effect which his action may have upon our foreign relations. This consideration, in connection with what we have already said on the subject, discloses the unwisdom of requiring Congress in this field of governmental power to lay down narrowly definite standards by which the President is to be governed. . . .

In the light of the foregoing observations, it is evident that this court should not be in haste to apply a general rule which will have the effect of condemning legislation like that under review as constituting an unlawful delegation of legislative power. The principles which justify such legislation find overwhelming support in the unbroken legislative practice which has prevailed almost from the inception of the national government to the present day. . . .

Practically every volume of the United States Statutes contains one or more acts or joint resolutions of Congress authorizing action by the President in respect of subjects affecting foreign relations, which either leave the exercise of the power to his unrestricted judgment, or provide a standard far more general than that which has always been considered requisite with regard to domestic affairs. . . .

The result of holding that the joint resolution here under attack is void and unenforceable as constituting an unlawful delegation of legislative power would be to stamp this multitude of comparable acts and resolutions as likewise invalid. And while this court may not, and should not, hesitate to declare acts of Congress, however many times repeated, to be unconstitutional if beyond all rational doubt it finds them to be so, an impressive array of legislation such as we have just set forth, enacted by nearly every Congress from the beginning of our national existence to the present day, must be given unusual weight in the process of reaching a correct determination of the problem. A legislative practice such as we have here, evidenced not by only occasional instances, but marked by the movement of a steady stream for a century and a half of time, goes a long way in the direction of proving the presence of unassailable ground for the constitutionality of the practice, to be found in the origin and history of the power involved, or in its nature, or in both combined. . . .

The uniform, long-continued, and undisputed legislative practice just disclosed rests upon an admissible view of the Constitution which, even if the practice found far less support in principle than we think it does, we should not feel at liberty at this late day to disturb.

We deem it unnecessary to consider, *seriatim*, the several clauses which are said to evidence the unconstitutionality of the Joint Resolution as involving an unlawful delegation of legislative power. It is enough to summarize by saying that, both upon principle and in accordance with precedent, we conclude there is sufficient warrant for the broad discretion vested in the President to determine whether the enforcement of the statute will have a beneficial effect upon the reestablishment of peace in the affected countries; whether he shall make proclamation to bring the resolution into operation; whether and when the resolution shall cease to operate and to make proclamation accordingly; and to prescribe limitations and exceptions to which the enforcement of the resolution shall be subject.

Notes and Questions

1. There are at least three theories concerning the source of the federal government's foreign relations powers. The first theory is that the federal government has only the foreign relations powers delegated to it in the Constitution. This delegated powers theory is expressed by Justice Taney in *Merryman*. As made clear in

Carter Coal Co., this is also the theory of governmental power that has long been applied to the national government's exercise of *domestic* power. Under this theory, the federal government would not necessarily be limited to the foreign affairs powers specifically mentioned in the Constitution. It might also possess powers that could be *implied* from the specific grants and from other constitutional provisions (such as the Necessary and Proper Clause, the Executive Power Clause, and the Take Care Clause). *Cf.* The Legal Tender Cases, 79 U.S. 457, 534 (1870) ("[I]t is not indispensable to the existence of any power claimed for the Federal government that it can be found specified in the words of the Constitution, or clearly and directly traceable to some one of the specified powers. Its existence may be deduced fairly from more than one of the substantive powers expressly defined, or from them all combined.").

The second theory—embraced in *The Chinese Exclusion Case*—is that foreign relations powers inhere in the "sovereignty" that is implicitly vested by the Constitution in the national government. *See also* Fong Yue Ting v. United States, 149 U.S. 698, 711 (1893) ("The United States are a sovereign and independent nation, and are vested *by the Constitution* with the entire control of international relations, and with all the powers of government necessary to maintain that control and to make it effective.") (emphasis added). The third theory—articulated in *Curtiss-Wright*—also postulates that foreign relations powers inhere in U.S. national sovereignty, but this theory relies on an extraconstitutional source for these sovereignty-based powers, such as the British Crown or international law. What practical differences are there, if any, between these theories?

2. Justice Sutherland wrote both *Carter Coal* and *Curtiss-Wright* within a span of six months. Taken together, the decisions stand for the proposition that federal power with respect to domestic affairs derives from the Constitution and is subject to constitutional limitation, while federal power with respect to foreign affairs has an extraconstitutional source and is subject to significantly weaker constitutional constraints. Justice Sutherland had articulated a version of this theory of federal sovereignty in 1910 while a Republican senator from Utah. *See* George Sutherland, *The Internal and External Powers of the National Government*, 191 N. Am. Rev. 373 (1910). Nine years later, he published a revised version of the theory. *See* George Sutherland, Constitutional Power and World Affairs (1919). In *Curtiss-Wright*, Justice Sutherland was, as one commentator puts it, "in the happy position of being able to give [his] writings and speeches the status of law." David M. Levitan, *The Foreign Relations Power: An Analysis of Mr. Justice Sutherland's Theory*, 55 Yale L.J. 467, 476 (1946). For a discussion of why Sutherland, one of the conservative "Four Horsemen" known for "strict construction" of the Constitution and abhorrence of broad federal power in the context of New Deal legislation, would indulge such a broad view of federal power in the foreign relations context, see G. Edward White, *The Transformation of the Constitutional Regime of Foreign Relations*, 85 Va. L. Rev. 1 (1999).

3. Does Sutherland's distinction between constitutional powers in the domestic and external realms make sense? How can courts tell whether a case raises an issue of domestic or external power? Couldn't *Curtiss-Wright* itself be characterized as a domestic case because it involved attempted sales by an American company and its U.S. citizen officers? Couldn't *Merryman* be characterized as a foreign relations case because it involved the exercise of military control over insurgents in the context of the Civil War? In an era of globalization, is the domestic/foreign distinction a workable basis for such important differences in constitutional doctrine?

4. How tenable is the Court's claim in *Curtiss-Wright* that the foreign relations powers of the federal government are derived from a source other than the U.S. Constitution? Is this claim consistent with the historical materials we considered above in Section A? With the idea of a limited national government regulated by a written Constitution? With the actual allocation of foreign relations powers in the Constitution itself? With the Court's assertion that presidential power in foreign affairs, "like every other governmental power, must be exercised in subordination to the applicable provisions of the Constitution"? If the national government does have extraconstitutional foreign relations powers, what are they? In any event, why is the source of the national government's foreign relations powers relevant to the issue specifically before the Court in *Curtiss-Wright*—that is, whether Congress could delegate to the President the authority to prohibit arms sales to foreign countries?

For criticism of the Court's assertion of extraconstitutional foreign relations powers, see, for example, Michael D. Ramsey, *The Myth of Extraconstitutional Foreign Affairs Power,* 42 Wm. & Mary L. Rev. 379 (2000) (arguing that the Founders did not understand that the national government would have extraconstitutional powers), and Sarah H. Cleveland, *Powers Inherent in Sovereignty: Indians, Aliens, Territories, and the Nineteenth Century Origins of Plenary Power over Foreign Affairs,* 81 Tex. L. Rev. 1, 14 (2002) (making similar originalist arguments and adding that "[t]he doctrine's origins instead lie in a peculiarly unattractive, late-nineteenth-century nationalist and racist view of American society and federal power"). *But see* Richard B. Morris, *The Forging of the Union Reconsidered: A Historical Refutation of State Sovereignty over Seabeds,* 74 Colum. L. Rev. 1056, 1060-68 (1974) (defending the *Curtiss-Wright* theory on historical grounds). For additional discussion of *Curtiss-Wright* and its historical context, see H. Jefferson Powell, *The Story of Curtiss-Wright Export Corporation,* in Presidential Power Stories (Christopher H. Schroeder & Curtis A. Bradley eds., 2009).

5. Despite academic criticism of the reasoning in *Curtiss-Wright,* the Supreme Court has sometimes cited and quoted from the decision approvingly. In a 2004 Indian law decision, the Supreme Court referred favorably to the theory of foreign affairs powers espoused in *Curtiss-Wright,* stating:

> Moreover, "at least during the first century of America's national existence . . . Indian affairs were more an aspect of military and foreign policy than a subject of domestic or municipal law." Insofar as that is so, Congress' legislative authority would rest in part, not upon "affirmative grants of the Constitution," but upon the Constitution's adoption of preconstitutional powers necessarily inherent in any Federal Government, namely powers that this Court has described as "necessary concomitants of nationality." United States v. Curtiss-Wright Export Corp., 299 U.S. 304, 315-22 (1936). . . .

United States v. Lara, 541 U.S. 193, 201 (2004). And, in a 2005 decision concerning a federal criminal prosecution relating to the evasion of Canadian liquor taxes, the Court quoted from *Curtiss-Wright* for the proposition that "the Executive is 'the sole organ of the federal government in the field of international relations.'" Pasquantino v. United States, 544 U.S. 349, 369 (2005). In Zivotofsky v. Kerry, 135 S. Ct. 2076, 2090 (2015), however, the Court emphasized that *Curtiss-Wright* "dealt with congressionally authorized action, not a unilateral Presidential determination" and that the decision "did not hold that the President is free from Congress' lawmaking power in the field of international relations." (*Zivotofsky,* including its relationship to *Curtiss-Wright,* is discussed in detail in subsection C.2 of Chapter 3.)

In describing the President as the "sole organ" in foreign affairs, Justice Sutherland in *Curtiss-Wright* was quoting from a speech that John Marshall made in Congress in 1800, when he was a member of the House of Representatives. For discussion of the political context of Marshall's speech, see Michael Van Alstine, *Taking Care of John Marshall's Political Ghost*, 53 St. Louis L.J. 93 (2008). *See also* Martin S. Flaherty, *Organs Misused and Used: A Comment on the Sole Organ Problem*, 53 St. Louis L.J. 137 (2008). The meaning and implications of the "sole organ" idea are explored in Chapter 3.

6. What are the implications of the Court's suggestion in *Curtiss-Wright* that international law notions of sovereignty are the source of the U.S. foreign relations power? International law might dictate that nationhood requires, for example, the ability to engage in international relations and make treaties. But does it also specify the particular allocation of foreign relations power *within* a sovereign—for example, between political branches, or between national and sub-national governments? If international law notions of sovereignty provide the source for the national government's foreign relations power, do they also provide limitations? For example, if nations are prohibited from engaging in certain acts, such as waging aggressive war, does this mean that the U.S. government lacks the constitutional power to do so? In other words, does the Constitution require that the national government act as a *lawful sovereign*?

7. The issue in *The Chinese Exclusion Case* concerned Congress's power to exclude aliens. Nevertheless, the Court perceived the need to assert that, "For local interests the several States of the Union exist, but for national purposes, embracing our relations with foreign nations, we are but one people, one nation, one power." Similarly, the issue in *Curtiss-Wright* was whether Congress's statutory delegation of certain arms embargo powers to the President was constitutional. And yet the Court talks a great deal about the power of states in foreign affairs. Why are these federalism issues relevant to the scope of federal foreign relations powers?

8. President Lincoln implicitly responded to *Merryman* in his famous July 4, 1861 message to a special session of Congress:

> [T]he legality and propriety of [suspending the writ of habeas corpus] are questioned; and the attention of the country has been called to the proposition that one who is sworn to "take care that the laws be faithfully executed," should not himself violate them. . . . The whole of the laws which were required to be faithfully executed, were being resisted, and failing of execution, in nearly one-third of the States. Must they be allowed to finally fail of execution, even had it been perfectly clear, that by the use of the means necessary to their execution, some single law, made in such extreme tenderness of the citizen's liberty, that practically, it relieves more of the guilty, than of the innocent, should, to a very limited extent, be violated? To state the question more directly, are all the laws, but one, to go unexecuted, and the government itself go to pieces, lest that one be violated? Even in such a case, would not the official oath be broken, if the government should be overthrown, when it was believed that disregarding the single law, would tend to preserve it?

Message to Congress in Special Session of July 4, 1861, *in* 4 The Collected Works of Abraham Lincoln 421, 429-30 (Roy P. Basler ed., 1953). Can constitutional limitations—relating either to constitutional structure or to individual rights—be suspended in a national emergency? Which ones? For how long? And who decides—the President, the Congress, or the courts? These issues, which have renewed contemporary relevance in light of the September 11, 2001 terrorist attacks on the United

States, are explored in detail in other parts of this casebook, especially Chapters 9 and 10. Note that Lincoln went on in his message to argue that, in any event, the suspension of the writ of habeas corpus was constitutional:

> The provision of the Constitution that "The privilege of the writ of habeas corpus, shall not be suspended unless when, in cases of rebellion or invasion, the public safety may require it," is equivalent to a provision—is a provision—that such privilege may be suspended when, in cases of rebellion, or invasion, the public safety does require it. It was decided that we have a case of rebellion, and that the public safety does require the qualified suspension of the privilege of the writ which was authorized to be made. Now it is insisted that Congress, and not the Executive, is vested with this power. But the Constitution itself, is silent as to which, or who, is to exercise the power; and as the provision was plainly made for a dangerous emergency, it cannot be believed the framers of the instrument intended, that in every case, the danger should run its course, until Congress could be called together; the very assembling of which might be prevented, as was intended in this case, by the rebellion.

Id. at 430-31. We shall return to this issue of who has the power to suspend the writ of habeas corpus as well. For now, note that all of the Justices in Hamdi v. Rumsfeld, 542 U.S. 507 (2004), which concerned the detention of a U.S. citizen "enemy combatant" in the war on terrorism, appeared to assume that only Congress could suspend the writ of habeas corpus.

9. The significance of *Curtiss-Wright* was debated in the course of the Iran-Contra affair in the 1980s. That affair, in a nutshell, involved National Security Council (NSC) officials in the Reagan Administration skirting congressional prohibitions (known as the Boland Amendments) on the expenditure of U.S. funds in support of rebel forces in Nicaragua (known as the "Contras"). These NSC activities caused a national scandal when it became known that profits from secret arms sales to Iran were being used to help finance the Contras. In his testimony before Congress, Colonel Oliver North invoked *Curtiss-Wright* as a justification for ignoring the Boland Amendments. The final congressional report contained a majority report and a minority report, and these reports articulated differing views of the implications of *Curtiss-Wright*. The majority report stated:

> [One] does not have to be a proponent of an imperial Congress to see that [*Curtiss-Wright*] has little application to the situation here. We are not confronted with a situation where the President is claiming inherent constitutional authority in the absence of an Act of Congress. Instead, to succeed on this argument the Administration must claim it retains authority to proceed in derogation of an Act of Congress—and not just any act, at that. Here, Congress relied on its traditional authority over appropriations, the "power of the purse," to specify that no funds were to be expended by certain entities in a certain fashion. . . . While each branch of our Government undoubtedly has primacy in certain spheres, none can function in secret disregard of the others in any sphere.

Report of the Congressional Committees Investigating the Iran-Contra Affair, S. Rep. No. 100-216, H. Rep. No. 100-433 (1987), at 406 (majority report). The minority report stated:

> [The] Constitution gives the President some power to act on his own in foreign affairs. What kinds of activities are set aside for him? The most obvious—other than the Commander-in-Chief power and others explicitly listed in Article II—is the one named in *Curtiss-Wright:* The President is the "sole organ" of the government in foreign affairs. . . . [Congress] may not use its control over appropriations, including salaries,

to prevent the executive or judiciary from fulfilling Constitutionally mandated obligations. The implications of the Boland amendments is obvious. If any part of the amendments would have used Congress's control over salaries to prohibit executive actions
that Congress may not prohibit directly, the amendments would be just as unconstitutional as if they had dealt with the subject directly.

Id. at 473, 476 (minority report). How do the views in these reports compare with
the Pacificus-Helvidius debate? Which view is more persuasive? We consider additional implications of *Curtiss-Wright* for presidential power in foreign affairs, and for
presidential-congressional relations, in Chapter 3.

10. Scholars disagree about the original source of the federal government's
foreign relations powers. For the view that the states retained powers of "external
sovereignty" in the postrevolutionary period, and that the United States acquired
these powers through the Articles of Confederation and the Constitution rather
than from Great Britain, see Levitan, The Foreign Relations Power, *supra*, at 478-
90; Claude H. Van Tyne, *Sovereignty in the American Revolution: An Historical Study,*
12 Am. Hist. Rev. 529 (1907). *See also* Charles A. Lofgren, *United States v. Curtiss-
Wright Export Corporation: An Historical Reassessment,* 83 Yale L.J. 1, 29-30 (1973)
("Far from supporting the contention that external sovereignty devolved on the
federal government ultimately from Great Britain and hence has an extraconstitutional base, Sutherland's historical evidence and judicial precedents suggest
the opposite: Federal power in foreign affairs rests on explicit and implicit constitutional grants and derives from the ordinary constitutive authority."). For
the view that the states never possessed foreign relations powers, see Morris,
The Forging of the Federal Union, *supra*; Curtis Putnam Nettels, *The Origins
of the Union and of the States,* 72 Proceedings Mass. Hist. Soc'y 68 (1957-1960).
For an account that emphasizes the uncertainties associated with this issue, see
Jack P. Greene, Peripheries and Center: Constitutional Development in the
Extended Politics of the British Empire and the United States, 1607-1788, at
153-80 (1986).

11. The American Law Institute (ALI) is a private organization established
in 1923 with the goal of helping to clarify and simplify the law. Its members consist of experienced lawyers, legal academics, and judges. ALI publishes extensive
"Restatements" of areas of law that contain a mix of black-letter propositions, comments, and Reporters' notes. These Restatements typically reflect years of drafting
by appointed Reporters and the incorporation by the Reporters of feedback from
expert advisors, outside groups, ALI's Council, and the general membership of ALI.
Although not binding, Restatements are often influential and courts frequently rely
on their accounts of the law.

In 1965, ALI published a Restatement (Second) of the Foreign Relations Law of
the United States. (It was referred to as a "Restatement (Second)" because it was part
of the second series of Restatement projects.) In 1987, ALI published a Restatement
(Third) of the Foreign Relations Law of the United States, which both expanded on
the coverage of the Restatement (Second) and departed from the positions of that
Restatement on some topics. In 2012, a group of eight appointed Reporters (including one of the authors of this casebook) began work on a Restatement (Fourth)
of Foreign Relations Law, addressing three topics: treaties, jurisdiction, and sovereign immunity. In 2017, they completed their work on these topics and obtained
approval of their drafts from ALI's membership, and the Restatement (Fourth)
was published in late 2018. There are select references to it, and to the earlier
Restatements, throughout this casebook.

Note on Approaches to Constitutional Interpretation

As you might have studied in a constitutional law course, there are a variety of approaches to constitutional interpretation. The approaches most relevant to foreign relations law, greatly simplified, include the following.

A. *Originalism.* This approach focuses on the text of the Constitution as it was understood around the time of the framing. There are two distinct but overlapping strands of originalist thought. Those who focus on original *intent or understanding* emphasize the expectations and views of the drafters and ratifiers of the Constitution. Those who focus on original *meaning* look primarily to the public meaning of the Constitution's often technical language when it was adopted. Both approaches demand study, in different ways and for different purposes, of historical materials, such as the records of the state ratifying conventions, the *Federalist Papers,* and the notes from the federal Constitutional Convention of 1787, as well as evidence of how a term was understood or used prior to the Constitution or in the initial years after it began operating. Originalism is often invoked, among other contexts, in debates about the Constitution's distribution of war authority between Congress and the President. Similarly, there has been significant debate about the Founders' understanding of the domestic status of the "law of nations."

Can a study of Founding history provide concrete answers to contemporary foreign relations law disputes? Even if Founding history does provide concrete answers, why should it be binding hundreds of years later, when the nation, and the foreign relations issues it faces, are dramatically different? Or are modern foreign relations issues not dramatically different from the ones faced by the United States early in its history? For a discussion of the potential relevance of originalist history to foreign relations law, see Ingrid Wuerth, *An Originalism for Foreign Affairs?,* 53 St. Louis L.J. 5 (2008). For responses to this article, see Eugene Kontorovich, *Originalism and the Difficulties of History in Foreign Affairs,* 53 St. Louis L.J. 39 (2008), and Stephen I. Vladeck, *Foreign Affairs Originalism in* Youngstown*'s Shadow,* 53 St. Louis L.J. 29 (2008). For a comprehensive originalist analysis of constitutional foreign relations issues, see Michael D. Ramsey, The Constitution's Text in Foreign Affairs (2007).

B. *Burkeanism/Historical Gloss.* Sometimes associated with the views of the eighteenth-century British theorist Edmund Burke, the main idea here is that long-standing historical practice and tradition can inform constitutional meaning. As we will see in Chapter 3, Justice Frankfurter suggested something like this in his concurrence in the famous steel seizure decision from the early 1950s, in referring to "the gloss which life has written upon" the constitutional text. This Burkean or "historical gloss" approach differs from originalism because it considers historical materials from long after the constitutional provision was ratified. For example, one of the major arguments in favor of the constitutionality of "executive agreements"—that is, binding international agreements concluded by the President without concurrence of two-thirds of the Senate—is that the political branches have for a long time made and acquiesced in such agreements. Similarly, one argument in favor of a presidential authority to initiate limited military conflicts without congressional authorization is based on the fact that presidents have often done so, especially since World War II. Should the mere fact that a practice has been carried out for a long time make it constitutional? For discussions of this and related approaches to constitutional interpretation, see David A. Strauss, *Common Law Constitutional Interpretation,* 63 U. Chi. L. Rev. 877 (1996), and Cass R. Sunstein, *Burkean Minimalism,* 105 Mich. L. Rev. 353 (2006). For an extensive discussion of the ways in which historical practice can inform the powers of the President and Congress, see Curtis A. Bradley & Trevor W. Morrison, *Historical Gloss and the Separation of Powers*, 126 Harv. L. Rev. 421 (2012). *See also* Michael J. Glennon, *The Use of Custom in Resolving Separation of Powers Disputes*, 64 B.U. L. Rev. 109 (1984). For an account of the potential justifications for crediting historical gloss and an explanation of why these justifications have differing methodological implications, see Curtis A. Bradley, *Doing Gloss*, 84 U. Chi. L. Rev. 59 (2017).

The Supreme Court strongly endorsed this approach to constitutional interpretation in NLRB v. Noel Canning, 134 S. Ct. 2550 (2014). In that case, the Court construed the Recess Appointments Clause — "The President shall have Power to fill up all Vacancies that may happen during the Recess of the Senate, by granting Commissions which shall expire at the End of their next Session." — to allow the President to make appointments during "intra-session" as well as "inter-session" Senate recesses, and even for vacancies that pre-date the recess. (The Court nevertheless held that the recess appointments at issue in the case were invalid because they occurred during a break in Senate business that was too short to constitute a recess.) In the course of its analysis, the Court confirmed the importance of looking to historic governmental practices when resolving questions relating to the separation of powers. The Court observed that, for questions concerning "the allocation of power between two elected branches of Government," "significant weight" should be given to the practices of government and that this is true "even when the nature or longevity of that practice is subject to dispute, and even when that practice began after the founding era." For additional discussion of the decision, see Curtis A. Bradley & Neil S. Siegel, *After Recess: Historical Practice, Textual Ambiguity, and Constitutional Adverse Possession*, 2014 Sup. Ct. Rev. 1.

C. *Structuralism.* Under this approach, constitutional gaps and ambiguities can be filled in based on inferences from the way in which the Constitution allocates and limits governmental authority. Structural arguments include ones based on the Constitution's general separation of powers between the three federal branches of government, as well as the federal nature of the U.S. system of government. They also include more specific arguments based on implications from particular constitutional provisions. For example, some scholars have argued that the Constitution's requirement of senatorial advice and consent for the making of treaties implies that the President does not have the unilateral authority to terminate treaties. Other scholars have argued that the Constitution's specification of some presidential powers in Article II suggests that the first sentence of that Article should not be read (contrary to what some textualists have argued) to convey substantive authority. Yet another structural argument is that customary international law should not automatically be applied as U.S. federal law because such application would be inconsistent with the procedures for federal lawmaking specified in the Constitution. For general discussions in support of structural approaches to constitutional interpretation, see, for example, Charles Lund Black, Structure and Relationship in Constitutional Law (1968), and J. Harvie Wilkinson III, *Our Structural Constitution*, 104 Colum. L. Rev. 1687 (2004). For a skeptical view, and an argument in particular that the Constitution embodies no freestanding principle of separation of powers, see John F. Manning, *Separation of Powers as Ordinary Interpretation*, 124 Harv. L. Rev. 1939 (2011).

D. *Prudentialism/Consequentialism.* A prudential or consequentialist approach to constitutional interpretation takes account of pragmatic consequences. Prudential arguments often appear in connection with judicial tests that balance several different considerations. Even when they are not explicitly referenced, these arguments often lurk in the background of judicial decisions. In the war-on-terror materials in Chapter 10, for example, courts interpret the Executive Branch's authority in a manner that takes account of the functional needs of the government in fighting terrorism and attempts to balance those functional needs against individual liberty considerations. Similarly, in deciding whether to preempt state laws relating to foreign affairs, courts have attempted to assess the extent to which the laws are likely to create harmful consequences for U.S. foreign policy. Do such prudential considerations give the courts too much of a policy-making role? What, if anything, constrains courts' prudential assessments? For a discussion of prudential argumentation in constitutional law, see Philip Bobbitt, Constitutional Fate: Theory of the Constitution, at ch. 5 (1982).

E. *Stare Decisis*. Although not specifically an approach to constitutional interpretation, another common form of constitutional argumentation is an appeal to prior judicial decisions. The Supreme Court generally adheres to its prior decisions under a doctrine of *stare decisis*, although this doctrine is said to have somewhat less weight in the constitutional area than in the statutory area (because it is much more difficult to amend the Constitution in response to a judicial decision than to amend a statute). As a result of *stare decisis*, judicial opinions and scholarship often debate whether prior decisions control contemporary controversies or whether they are distinguishable because of differences in context. One challenge to the use of *stare decisis* in foreign relations law is that foreign relations controversies are sometimes intermittent, making reliance on precedent from a different era uncertain. For example, there has been much debate about whether World War II–era decisions concerning military detention and trial in a traditional war are controlling after September 11, 2001, with respect to the detention and trial issues in an indefinite war against non-state actor terrorists. Similarly, there has been significant debate regarding the viability in modern times of a 1920 decision by the Supreme Court, *Missouri v. Holland* (excerpted in Chapter 5), which held that the government can create domestic law pursuant to a treaty that it cannot create through legislation in the absence of a treaty. Because foreign relations law tends to have fewer precedents than other areas of constitutional law, debates over precedent sometimes concern the implications of very old decisions. As we will see, for example, scholars still debate today the implications of the Supreme Court's 1829 decision in *Foster v. Neilson*, which considered the circumstances under which a treaty is judicially enforceable.

We will explore each of these approaches to constitutional interpretation and argument in much more detail throughout this book. Note that these approaches are generally not exclusive—that is, it is possible (and in fact quite common) for a judge or scholar to rely on more than one in making a constitutional argument. *See generally* Richard H. Fallon, Jr., *A Constructivist Coherence Theory of Constitutional Interpretation*, 100 Harv. L. Rev. 1189 (1987).

PART II

GOVERNMENT INSTITUTIONS

2

Courts and Foreign Relations

This chapter considers the role of U.S. courts, especially the federal courts, in resolving foreign relations law disputes. As you will learn in this and subsequent chapters, many important questions of foreign relations law are resolved, if at all, by the political branches outside of the courts. Courts nevertheless play an important role in interpreting foreign relations law, both in deciding foreign relations law cases and, just as importantly, in setting background rules of potential judicial intervention or nonintervention that shape how the political branches address foreign relations law issues outside of court. Some of the key materials that you will read in subsequent chapters concerning the powers of the President and Congress, and the role of the states, are judicial decisions. It is therefore useful to understand early in the course what role courts can and cannot play in the area of foreign relations law.

This chapter begins by briefly describing the subject matter jurisdiction of the federal courts and some of the "justiciability" limitations on the exercise of this jurisdiction. It then considers in more detail the political question doctrine, a justiciability limitation that has had particular relevance in the area of foreign relations law. The chapter next considers the various forms of deference that courts give to the Executive Branch in foreign relations law cases. It subsequently examines the act of state doctrine, which limits the circumstances under which U.S. courts will examine the validity of foreign government acts. Finally, the chapter discusses the presumption against extraterritoriality that U.S. courts sometimes apply when construing federal statutes, as well as more general considerations of international comity that can affect judicial decisionmaking.

A. JURISDICTION OVER FOREIGN RELATIONS CASES

As discussed in Chapter 1, the constitutional Founders viewed the lack of a meaningful national judiciary as one of the central defects of the Articles of Confederation. The establishment of such a judiciary was important, they explained, for U.S. foreign relations. In *Federalist No. 80*, for example, Alexander Hamilton argued that a national judiciary was needed in order to ensure adequate enforcement of treaty obligations, as well as uniformity in treaty interpretations. He also expressed concern that state courts might be biased against foreign citizens. Noting that "the denial or perversion of justice by the sentence of courts, as well as in any other manner, is with reason classed among the just causes of war," he argued that "it will follow that the federal judiciary ought to have cognizance of all causes in which the citizens of other countries are concerned." Hamilton further argued in *Federalist No. 81* that there should be federal court jurisdiction—indeed, Supreme Court jurisdiction—over cases involving ambassadors and other representatives of foreign nations, both in order to reduce international friction and "out of respect to the sovereignties [these individuals] represent."

Article III of the Constitution addresses these and other foreign affairs concerns in a variety of ways. It provides that the "judicial Power of the United States, shall be vested in one supreme Court, and in such inferior Courts as the Congress may from time to time ordain and establish." It further provides that this judicial power shall extend to various enumerated "Cases" and "Controversies." Some of these cases and controversies have an obvious relationship to foreign affairs. Among other things, the federal courts are allowed under Article III to hear cases arising under treaties, cases affecting ambassadors, admiralty cases, and suits between U.S. citizens and foreign citizens.

By its terms, Article III does not require the creation of any federal courts other than the Supreme Court. In addition, Article III has not been construed as requiring that Congress give the federal courts all the judicial power authorized by Article III. Congress did, of course, establish lower federal courts, and it granted them jurisdiction to hear various cases and controversies. Congress has never given the federal courts the power, however, to hear all the cases and controversies covered by Article III. And it is well settled that, except for the Supreme Court's exercise of its original jurisdiction (which is narrow in scope), the federal courts may not exercise jurisdiction over a case or controversy unless that jurisdiction is authorized both by Article III and by a congressional grant of jurisdiction. (Select jurisdictional statutes are printed at the end of this casebook, in Appendix B.)

The two most important categories of Article III jurisdiction are *federal question jurisdiction* (cases "arising under this Constitution, the Laws of the United States, and Treaties") and *diversity jurisdiction* (controversies between parties of diverse citizenship). Congress has granted the federal courts jurisdiction in both of these categories, but its statutory grants have been construed to be substantially narrower than the bounds of Article III. For example, Article III federal question jurisdiction may extend to any case in which there is a federal law "ingredient." *See* Osborn v. Bank of the United States, 22 U.S. (9 Wheat.) 738, 823 (1824). The federal question jurisdiction statute (28 U.S.C. §1331), by contrast, is subject to a well-pleaded complaint rule: The federal law issue must appear on the face of the plaintiff's well-pleaded complaint and cannot arise merely by way of defense. *See* Louisville & Nashville Railroad v. Mottley, 211 U.S. 149, 152 (1908).

With respect to the diversity jurisdiction statute (28 U.S.C. §1332), the most important limitation is the requirement of complete diversity: Ordinarily, no plaintiff can share citizenship with any defendant, even if the other parties are diverse. *See* Strawbridge v. Curtiss, 7 U.S. (3 Cranch) 267, 267-68 (1806). The diversity statute also requires that the amount in controversy exceed a certain amount, currently $75,000. Defendants are allowed to remove to federal court suits brought against them in state court if the suit could have originally been filed in federal court, except that a case may not be removed on the basis of diversity jurisdiction if one or more of the defendants is a citizen of the state in which the suit is brought. *See* 28 U.S.C. §1441(b). (Other jurisdictional statutes relating to foreign affairs, such as the Alien Tort Statute (ATS) and the Foreign Sovereign Immunities Act (FSIA), are discussed elsewhere in this casebook.)

As the text of Article III suggests, and as the Supreme Court confirmed early in U.S. history, a suit between two foreign citizens does not satisfy even the minimal diversity requirements of Article III. *See* Mossman v. Higginson, 4 U.S. (4 Dall.) 12, 14 (1800); Hodgson v. Bowerbank, 9 U.S. (5 Cranch) 303, 304 (1809). As a result, to be heard in the federal courts, such suits must fall within some other category of Article III jurisdiction—for example, "Cases . . . arising under . . . the Laws of the United States." There are uncertainties, however, regarding the scope of this "arising under" jurisdiction as it relates to foreign affairs. For example, do the "Laws of the United States" include customary international law? If so, is customary international law also part of "the Laws of the United States which shall be made in Pursuance [of the Constitution]" referred to in Article VI of the Constitution? Do cases that do not involve international law but nevertheless implicate foreign affairs involve "federal common law," such that these cases arise under the laws of the United States? These and other jurisdictional questions are addressed in subsequent materials.

B. JUSTICIABILITY: STANDING, RIPENESS, MOOTNESS

As noted above, Article III allows for the exercise of federal judicial power over "Cases" and "Controversies." The Supreme Court has construed these terms as imposing certain "justiciability" limitations on the exercise of federal court jurisdiction. This section considers some of these limitations. It begins with a decision that addresses the standing of members of Congress to bring a lawsuit challenging presidential action, something that the Supreme Court sharply limited in a case that did not involve foreign affairs, Raines v. Byrd, 521 U.S. 811 (1997). *Raines* is described in the excerpt of the decision below.

Campbell v. Clinton

203 F.3d 19 (D.C. Cir. 2000)

SILBERMAN, CIRCUIT JUDGE . . . .
On March 24, 1999, President [William] Clinton announced the commencement of NATO air and cruise missile attacks on Yugoslav targets. Two days later he submitted to Congress a report, "consistent with the War Powers Resolution," detailing the circumstances necessitating the use of armed forces, the deployment's scope and expected duration, and asserting that he had "taken these actions pursuant to [his] authority . . . as Commander in Chief and Chief Executive." On April 28, Congress voted on four resolutions related to the Yugoslav conflict: It voted down a declaration of war 427 to 2 and an "authorization" of the air strikes 213 to 213, but it also voted against requiring the President to immediately end U.S. participation in the NATO operation and voted to fund that involvement. The conflict between NATO and Yugoslavia continued for 79 days, ending on June 10 with Yugoslavia's agreement to withdraw its forces from Kosovo and allow deployment of a NATO-led peacekeeping force. Throughout this period Pentagon, State Department, and NATO spokesmen informed the public on a frequent basis of developments in the fighting.

Appellants, 31 congressmen opposed to U.S. involvement in the Kosovo intervention, filed suit prior to termination of that conflict seeking a declaratory judgment that the President's use of American forces against Yugoslavia was unlawful under both the War Powers Clause of the Constitution and the War Powers Resolution ("the WPR"). *See* 50 U.S.C. §1541 *et seq.* The WPR requires the President to submit a report within 48 hours "in any case in which United States Armed Forces are introduced . . . into hostilities or into situations where imminent involvement in hostilities is clearly indicated by the circumstances," and to "terminate any use of United States Armed Forces with respect to which a report was submitted (or required to be submitted), unless the Congress . . . has declared war or has enacted a specific authorization for such use of United States Armed Forces" within 60 days. Appellants claim that the President did submit a report sufficient to trigger the WPR on March 26, or in any event was required to submit a report by that date, but nonetheless failed to end U.S. involvement in the hostilities after 60 days. The district court granted the President's motion to dismiss, and this appeal followed. . . .

The question whether congressmen have standing in federal court to challenge the lawfulness of actions of the executive was answered, at least in large part, in the Supreme Court's recent decision in Raines v. Byrd, 521 U.S. 811 (1997). *Raines* involved a constitutional challenge to the President's authority under the short-lived Line Item Veto Act. Individual congressmen claimed that under that Act, a President could veto (unconstitutionally) only part of a law and thereby diminish the institutional power of Congress. Observing it had never held that congressmen have standing to assert an institutional injury as against the executive, the Court held that petitioners in the case lacked "legislative standing" to challenge the Act. The Court observed that petitioners already possessed an adequate political remedy, since they could vote to have the Line Item Veto Act repealed, or to provide individual spending bills with a statutory exemption. . . .

There remains, however, a soft spot in the legal barrier against congressional legal challenges to executive action, and it is a soft spot that appellants sought to penetrate. In 1939 the Supreme Court in *Coleman v. Miller* voted 5-4 to recognize the standing of Kansas State legislators in the Supreme Court to challenge the actions of the Kansas Secretary of State and the Secretary of the State Senate. *See* 307 U.S. 433 (1939). That case arose out of a State Senate vote on the ratification of a constitutional amendment, the Child Labor Amendment, proposed by Congress in 1924. The State Senate split 20 to 20, and the Lieutenant Governor, the presiding officer of the Senate, then cast a deciding vote in favor. The State House subsequently also passed a ratification resolution. Thereupon the twenty State Senators who voted against ratification plus one more (who presumably had voted for the resolution) brought a mandamus action in the State Supreme Court challenging the Lieutenant Governor's right to vote. They sought an order compelling the Secretary of the Senate to erase the endorsement on the resolution and restraining the Secretary of State from authenticating the resolution and passing it on to the Governor. The Supreme Court of Kansas entertained the action but ruled against the plaintiffs on the merits. Granting certiorari, the United States Supreme Court determined that "at least the twenty senators whose votes, if their contention were sustained, would have been sufficient to defeat the resolution . . . have an interest . . . sufficient to give the Court jurisdiction," *id.* at 446, because they have a legal interest "in maintaining the effectiveness of their votes." *Id.* at 438.

In *Raines* the plaintiff congressmen had relied on *Coleman* to argue that they had standing because the presidential veto had undermined the "effectiveness of their votes." The Supreme Court noted that *Coleman* might be distinguished on grounds that the federal constitutional separation of powers concerns that underlay its decision in *Raines* . . . were not present, or that if the Court in *Coleman* had not taken the case a question of federal law—the ratification *vel non* by the Kansas Legislature—would remain as decided by the Kansas Court. But the Court thought it unnecessary to cabin *Coleman* on those grounds. Instead, the Court emphasized that the congressmen were not asserting that their votes had been "completely nullified":

> They have not alleged that they voted for a specific bill, that there were sufficient votes to pass the bill, and that the bill was nonetheless deemed defeated. . . .
>
> Nor can they allege that the Act will nullify their votes in the future in the same way that the votes of the *Coleman* legislators had been nullified . . .
>
> In addition, a majority of Senators and Congressmen can vote to repeal the Act, or to exempt a given appropriations bill. . . .

Id. at 824.

Here the plaintiff congressmen, by specifically defeating the War Powers Resolution authorization by a tie vote and by defeating a declaration of war, sought to fit within the *Coleman* exception to the *Raines* rule. This parliamentary tactic led to an extensive argument before us as to exactly what the Supreme Court meant by a claim that a legislator's vote was completely "nullified."

It is, to be sure, not readily apparent what the Supreme Court meant by that word. It would seem the Court used nullify to mean treating a vote that did not pass as if it had, or vice versa. The "nullification" alleged in this case therefore differs from *Coleman* in a significant respect. In that case, state officials endorsed a defeated ratification, treating it as approved, while the President here did not claim to be acting pursuant to the defeated declaration of war or a statutory authorization, but instead "pursuant to [his] constitutional authority to conduct U.S. foreign relations and as Commander-in-Chief and Chief Executive." *See* Letter to Congressional Leaders Reporting on Airstrikes Against Serbian Targets in the Federal Republic of Yugoslavia (Serbia and Montenegro), 35 Weekly Comp. Pres. Doc. 528 (March 26, 1999). The Court did not suggest in *Raines* that the President "nullifies" a congressional vote and thus legislators have standing whenever the government does something Congress voted against, still less that congressmen would have standing anytime a President allegedly acts in excess of statutory authority. As the government correctly observes, appellants' statutory argument, although cast in terms of the nullification of a recent vote, essentially is that the President violated the quarter-century old War Powers Resolution. Similarly, their constitutional argument is that the President has acted illegally—in excess of his authority—because he waged war in the constitutional sense without a congressional delegation. Neither claim is analogous to a *Coleman* nullification.

We think the key to understanding the Court's treatment of *Coleman* and its use of the word nullification is its implicit recognition that a ratification vote on a constitutional amendment is an unusual situation. It is not at all clear whether once the amendment was "deemed ratified," *see Raines*, 521 U.S. at 822, the Kansas Senate could have done anything to reverse that position. We think that must be what the Supreme Court implied when it said the *Raines* plaintiffs could not allege that the "[Line Item Veto Act] would nullify their votes *in the future*," and that, after all, a majority of senators and congressmen could always repeal the Line Item Veto Act. *Id.* at 824 (emphasis added). The *Coleman* senators, by contrast, may well have been powerless to rescind a ratification of a constitutional amendment that they claimed had been defeated. In other words, they had no legislative remedy. Under that reading—which we think explains the very narrow possible *Coleman* exception to *Raines*—appellants fail because they continued, after the votes, to enjoy ample legislative power to have stopped prosecution of the "war."

In this case, Congress certainly could have passed a law forbidding the use of U.S. forces in the Yugoslav campaign; indeed, there was a measure—albeit only a concurrent resolution—introduced to require the President to withdraw U.S. troops. Unfortunately, however, for those congressmen who, like appellants, desired an end to U.S. involvement in Yugoslavia, this measure was *defeated* by a 139 to 290 vote. Of course, Congress always retains appropriations authority and could have cut off funds for the American role in the conflict. Again there was an effort to do so but it failed; appropriations were authorized. And there always remains the possibility of impeachment should a President act in disregard of Congress' authority on these matters.

Appellants' constitutional claim stands on no firmer footing. Appellants argue that the War Powers Clause of the Constitution proscribes a President from using military force except as is necessary to repel a sudden attack. But they also argue that the WPR "implements" or channels congressional authority under the Constitution. It may well be then that since we have determined that appellants lack standing to enforce the WPR, there is nothing left of their constitutional claim. Assuming, however, that appellants' constitutional claim should be considered separately, the same logic dictates they do not have standing to bring such a challenge. That is to say, Congress has a broad range of legislative authority it can use to stop a President's war making, and therefore under *Raines* congressmen may not challenge the President's war-making powers in federal court.

Judge Randolph asserts that appellants lack standing because they do not claim that the President violated various statutes that depend on the existence of a war or the *imminence* of war. But that position sidesteps appellants' basic claim that the President unconstitutionally conducted a war without authority, and the logic of Judge Randolph's reasoning ("There is no suggestion that despite the vote, President Clinton *invaded* Yugoslavia by land or took some other action authorized only during a declared war.") is that if there had been a "war" appellants would have had standing. He therefore presents as an alternate reason for denying standing that the President did not "nullify" the vote against the declaration of war because he did not take any actions that constitute "war" in the constitutional sense. That analysis, however, conflates standing with the merits. At the standing stage, we must take as correct appellants' claim that the President violated the Constitution simply by ordering U.S. forces to attack Yugoslavia.

In our view Judge Randolph's criticism of our analysis does not give sufficient attention to *Raines*' focus on the political self-help available to congressmen. Even though the congressmen in *Raines* sought review before the Court of what was soon after determined in Clinton v. City of New York, 524 U.S. 417 (1998), to be an unconstitutional statute, the Court denied them standing as congressmen because they possessed political tools with which to remedy their purported injury. Our colleague notes a distinction drawn by *Raines* between "the right to vote in the future [and] the nullification of a vote in the past," and asserts that the former does not remedy the latter. But *Raines* rejected this argument, which is why the congressmen in *Raines* lacked standing whereas petitioners in *New York* were allowed to contest the President's "nullification" of particular appropriations line items. Indeed, *Raines* explicitly rejected Judge Randolph's argument that legislators should not be required to turn to politics instead of the courts for their remedy. Although the plaintiff legislators in *Raines* had already failed to stop passage of the Line Item Veto Act, the Court's response was the equivalent of "if at first you don't succeed, try and try again"—either work for repeal of the Act, or seek to have individual spending bills made exempt. *See Raines*, 521 U.S. at 824-25, 825 n.9, 830. Judge Randolph overlooks this key portion of *Raines* when he disagrees with our conclusion that plaintiffs lack standing because they may "fight again tomorrow."

RANDOLPH, CIRCUIT JUDGE, concurring in the judgment. . . .

The heart of the *Raines* decision is this: "legislators whose votes would have been sufficient to defeat (or enact) a specific legislative act have standing to sue if that legislative action goes into effect (or does not go into effect), on the ground that their votes have been completely nullified." 521 U.S. at 823.

Here, plaintiffs had the votes "sufficient to defeat" "a specific legislative action"—they defeated a declaration of war (their constitutional claim) and they blocked a resolution approving the President's continuation of the war (their statutory claim). To follow precisely the formulation in *Raines*, they would have standing only if the legislative actions they defeated went "into effect." Obviously, this did not happen: war was not declared, and the President never maintained that he was prosecuting the war with the House's approval.

Plaintiffs' reply is that the President's military action against Yugoslavia without congressional authorization had the effect of completely nullifying their votes, of making their votes worthless. With respect to their vote against declaring war, that clearly is not true. A congressional declaration of war carries with it profound consequences.[6] The United States Code is thick with laws expanding executive power "in time of war." Under these laws, the President's authority over industries, the use of land, and the terms and conditions of military employment is greatly enhanced. A declaration of war may also have the effect of decreasing commercial choices and curtailing civil liberties. . . .

The vote of the House on April 28, 1999, deprived President Clinton of these powers. The vote against declaring war followed immediately upon the vote not to require immediate withdrawal. Those who voted against a declaration of war did so to deprive the President of the authority to expand hostilities beyond the bombing campaign and, specifically, to deprive him of the authority to introduce ground troops into the conflict. There is no suggestion that despite the vote, President Clinton invaded Yugoslavia by land or took some other action authorized only during a declared war. It follows that plaintiffs' votes against declaring war were not for naught. For that reason, plaintiffs do not have standing to sue on their constitutional claim.

As to their claim under the War Powers Resolution, the beauty of this measure, or one of its defects, is in its automatic operation: unless a majority of both Houses declares war, or approves continuation of hostilities beyond 60 days, or Congress is "physically unable to meet as a result of an armed attack upon the United States," the Resolution requires the President to withdraw the troops. 50 U.S.C. §1544(b).

---

6. Although the United States has committed its armed forces into combat more than a hundred times, Congress has declared war only five times: the War of 1812, the Mexican-American War of 1848, the Spanish-American War of 1898, World War I, and World War II.

The President has nothing to veto. Congress may allow the time to run without taking any vote, or it may—as the House did here—take a vote and fail to muster a majority in favor of continuing the hostilities.

To put the matter in terms of *Raines* once again, plaintiffs had the votes "sufficient to defeat" "a specific legislative action"—they blocked a resolution authorizing the President's continuation of the war with Yugoslavia—but it is not true, in the language of *Raines*, that this "legislative action" nevertheless went "into effect." Congressional authorization simply did not occur. The President may have acted as if he had Congress's approval, or he may have acted as if he did not need it. Either way, plaintiffs' real complaint is not that the President ignored their votes; it is that he ignored the War Powers Resolution, and hence the votes of an earlier Congress, which enacted the law over President Nixon's veto. It is hard for me to see that this amounts to anything more than saying: "We, the members of Congress, have standing because the President violated one of our laws." To hold that Members of Congress may litigate on such a basis strikes me as highly problematic, not only because the principle is unconfined but also because it raises very serious separation-of-powers concerns. . . .

The majority opinion analyzes standing rather differently than I do. It says plaintiffs lack standing to pursue their statutory claim because "they continued, after the votes, to enjoy ample legislative power to have stopped prosecution of the 'war.'" For specifics, the opinion points out that Congress defeated House Concurrent Resolution 82, a resolution requiring immediate disengagement from the conflict in Yugoslavia; that "Congress always retains appropriations authority and could have cut off funds for the American role in the conflict"; and that "there always remains the possibility of impeachment." The same reason—the possibility of future legislative action—is used to defeat plaintiffs' standing with respect to their constitutional claim.

The majority has, I believe, confused the right to vote in the future with the nullification of a vote in the past, a distinction *Raines* clearly made. *See* 521 U.S. at 824. To say that your vote was not nullified because you can vote for other legislation in the future is like saying you did not lose yesterday's battle because you can fight again tomorrow. The Supreme Court did not engage in such illogic. When the Court in *Raines* mentioned the possibility of future legislation, it was addressing the argument that "the [Line Item Veto] Act will nullify the [Congressmen's] votes in the future. . . ." *Id.* This part of the Court's opinion, which the majority adopts here, is quite beside the point to our case. No one is claiming that their votes on future legislation will be impaired or nullified or rendered ineffective.

Besides, as long as Congress and the Constitution exist, Members will always be able to vote for legislation. And so the majority's decision is tantamount to a decision abolishing legislative standing. I have two problems with this. First, if we are going to get rid of legislative standing altogether, we ought to do so openly and not under the cover of an interpretation, or rather misinterpretation, of a phrase in *Raines*. If the Supreme Court had meant to do away with legislative standing, it would have said so and it would have given reasons for taking that step.

Notes and Questions

1. The Supreme Court has held that Article III of the Constitution imposes three requirements for standing: the plaintiff must have suffered (or be likely to suffer) a concrete and particularized injury; the injury must be fairly traceable to the conduct of the defendant; and it must be likely that the injury will be redressed by a favorable decision. *See, e.g.,* DaimlerChrysler Corp. v. Cuno, 547 U.S. 332, 342-44 (2006); Lujan v. Defenders of Wildlife, 504 U.S. 555, 560-61 (1992). In the foreign relations law area, private individuals often lack the concrete and particularized injury that is required in order to have standing to challenge the legality of government action.

2. The Supreme Court has made clear that a mere interest in government law compliance is not enough of a stake in a case for Article III standing. *See, e.g., Lujan,* 504 U.S. at 573-74. In addition, it is generally not sufficient for standing for someone to assert that her tax dollars are being spent for what she contends is an improper government activity. *See, e.g.,* Arizona Christian School Tuition Org. v. Winn, 563 U.S. 125 (2011). When Congress has conferred an entitlement on a class of people and authorized them to sue, however, members of the class will generally have Article III standing to challenge denials of the entitlement, as long as the denial involves some sort of injury that extends beyond a mere displeasure with a violation of the law. *See, e.g.,* Federal Election Commission v. Akins, 524 U.S. 11, 25 (1998) (allowing suit to compel disclosure of statutorily required information relevant to voting because the injury was "sufficiently concrete and specific such that the fact that it is widely shared does not deprive Congress of constitutional power to authorize its vindication in the federal courts").

3. As discussed in *Campbell,* the Supreme Court addressed the standing of members of Congress in Raines v. Byrd, 521 U.S. 811 (1997). *Raines* involved a lawsuit brought by four senators and two members of the House of Representatives who had voted against the Line Item Veto Act of 1996, which provided that the President could "cancel" items in appropriations bills after signing them into law. The legislators argued that the Act was unconstitutional because it allowed the President to make changes to federal statutes without going through the process for making new legislation set forth in Article I of the Constitution. In holding that the legislators lacked standing to sue, the Court observed that "our standing inquiry has been especially rigorous when reaching the merits of the dispute would force us to decide whether an action taken by one of the other two branches of the Federal Government was unconstitutional." The Court then proceeded to explain that the legislators here were not complaining of an injury personal to them but were instead claiming that the Line Item Veto Act "causes a type of institutional injury (the diminution of legislative power), which necessarily damages all Members of Congress and both Houses of Congress equally." In concluding that this institutional injury was not sufficient for standing, the Court distinguished Coleman v. Miller, 307 U.S. 433 (1939), in which members of the Kansas Senate were held to have standing to challenge that state's ratification of a constitutional amendment. The Kansas Senate had deadlocked on the amendment by a vote of 20-20, and a tie-breaking vote had been cast in favor of it by Kansas's Lieutenant Governor. The plaintiffs in *Coleman,* the Court explained, alleged that their votes against the constitutional amendment should have been sufficient as a constitutional matter to prevent the state from ratifying the amendment. The Court described the holding of *Coleman* as follows: "our holding in *Coleman* stands (at most) for the proposition that legislators whose votes would have been sufficient to defeat (or enact) a specific legislative Act have standing to sue if that legislative action goes into effect (or does not go into effect), on the ground that their votes have been completely nullified." That holding did not apply to the challenge to the Line Item Veto Act, reasoned the Court:

> [The legislators here] have not alleged that they voted for a specific bill, that there were sufficient votes to pass the bill, and that the bill was nonetheless deemed defeated. In the vote on the [Line Item Veto] Act, their votes were given full effect. They simply lost that vote. Nor can they allege that the Act will nullify their votes in the future in the same way that the votes of the *Coleman* legislators had been nullified. In the future, a majority of Senators and Congressmen can pass or reject appropriations bills; the Act has no effect on this process. In addition, a majority of Senators and Congressmen can vote to repeal the Act, or to exempt a given appropriations bill (or a given provision in an appropriations bill) from the Act; again, the Act has no effect on this process.

The Court concluded by noting:

> We attach some importance to the fact that appellees have not been authorized to represent their respective Houses of Congress in this action, and indeed both Houses actively oppose their suit. We also note that our conclusion neither deprives Members of Congress of an adequate remedy (since they may repeal the Act or exempt appropriations bills from its reach), nor forecloses the Act from constitutional challenge (by someone who suffers judicially cognizable injury as a result of the Act). Whether the case would be different if any of these circumstances were different we need not now decide.

A year after *Raines*, the Supreme Court held the Line Item Veto Act unconstitutional, in Clinton v. City of New York, 524 U.S. 417 (1998). The lawsuit in *Clinton* was brought by the City of New York and related parties who alleged an injury resulting from President Clinton's cancellation, pursuant to the Line Item Veto Act, of a federal statutory waiver of the federal government's right to recoup certain Medicaid-related taxes. The Court held that the plaintiffs had standing because they "alleged a 'personal stake' in having an actual injury redressed, rather than an 'institutional injury' that is 'abstract and widely dispersed.'" 524 U.S. at 430 (quoting *Raines*, 521 U.S. at 830).

Raines is an important decision for foreign relations law because many of the issues in this area involve disputes between the federal political branches. In limiting "legislative standing," *Raines* makes it more difficult for courts to adjudicate such disputes.

4. Did the court in *Campbell* correctly apply *Raines*? The plaintiffs in *Campbell* maintained that President Clinton was required by both the War Powers Resolution and the Constitution to obtain congressional authorization in order to continue his military campaign against Yugoslavia. Why wasn't President Clinton's continuation of the campaign a "nullification" of the votes that these members of Congress had successfully made in opposition to a bill that would have authorized the campaign? Is it enough of an answer to say, as the court does, that there were additional actions that Congress could have taken in opposition to the President? Or is this like saying, as Judge Randolph contends, "you did not lose yesterday's battle because you can fight again tomorrow"? On the other hand, is Judge Randolph's reason for upholding dismissal of the case—that the congressional vote against the authorization bill was not nullified because President Clinton did not claim congressional authorization—responsive to the plaintiffs' claim that President Clinton needed authorization in order to continue the military campaign lawfully?

5. In Arizona State Legislature v. Arizona Independent Redistricting Commission, 135 S. Ct. 2562 (2014), the Supreme Court held that the Arizona legislature had standing to challenge the constitutionality of a referendum adopted by Arizona voters that had removed redistricting authority from the Arizona Legislature and vested it in an independent commission. The Court distinguished *Raines v. Byrd*, noting that in that case the individual legislators had not been authorized to represent their respective houses of Congress, whereas in this case the Arizona legislature was "an institutional plaintiff asserting an institutional injury, and it commenced this action after authorizing votes in both of its chambers." The Court also reasoned that the referendum at issue would "completely nullify" any vote by the legislature to adopt a redistricting plan. In a footnote, however, the Court observed that "[t]he case before us does not touch or concern the question whether Congress has standing to bring a suit against the President" and that "a suit between Congress and the President would raise separation-of-powers concerns absent here."

6. What is the relationship between the standing requirement and the prohibition on advisory opinions invoked in the letter from the Justices discussed in Chapter 1? Recall that the Justices reasoned that "the lines of separation drawn by the Constitution between the three departments of the government" precluded them from "extra-judicially deciding the questions" presented to them. Is this the same logic underlying standing? *See* Valley Forge Christian College v. Americans United for Separation, 454 U.S. 464, 472 (1982) (standing doctrine "tends to assure that the legal questions presented to the court will be resolved, not in the rarified atmosphere of a debating society, but in a concrete factual context conducive to a realistic appreciation of the consequences of judicial action"); Lujan v. Defenders of Wildlife, 504 U.S. 555, 598 n.4 (1992) (Blackmun, J., dissenting) ("The purpose of the standing doctrine is to ensure that courts do not render advisory opinions rather than resolve genuine controversies between adverse parties."); Ronald J. Krotoszynski, Jr., *Constitutional Flares: On Judges, Legislatures, and Dialogue*, 83 Minn. L. Rev. 1, 32 (1998) ("If a federal court renders a judgment in a case in which the plaintiff lacks standing, then it has authored an advisory opinion. Indeed, such an opinion would fall squarely within the prohibition of The Correspondence of the Justices.").

7. Another standing issue concerns the ability of *foreign nations* to sue in U.S. courts. It is settled that foreign nations have standing to sue in U.S. courts when they (a) are suing private parties, and (b) are seeking to protect their own interests. *See, e.g.*, Principality of Monaco v. Mississippi, 292 U.S. 313, 324 n.2 (1934). Although foreign nations may also have standing to sue state or federal government defendants, such suits may be barred on other grounds, such as sovereign immunity, lack of a private right of action, or the political question doctrine. *See, e.g.*, Breard v. Greene, 523 U.S. 371, 377 (1998) (holding that suit by Paraguay against Virginia state officials was barred because of the lack of a private right of action in the relevant treaty, and suggesting that the suit was also barred by Virginia's sovereign immunity). A related standing issue concerns the ability of foreign governments to sue in U.S. courts on behalf of their citizens. *See, e.g.*, Estados Unidos Mexicanos v. DeCoster, 229 F.3d 332 (1st Cir. 2000) (holding that Mexico lacked *parens patriae* standing to bring discrimination claims on behalf of its nationals).

8. The Foreign Intelligence Surveillance Act of 1978 (FISA) regulates the government's use of electronic surveillance of persons suspected of being involved in espionage on behalf of a foreign power or international terrorism against the United States. As discussed more fully in Chapter 10, Congress, in 2008, amended FISA to make it easier for the government to conduct electronic surveillance of communications with non–U.S. persons located outside the United States. Under 50 U.S.C. §1881a, the government was no longer required to submit an individualized application to the Foreign Intelligence Surveillance Court (a special court created by the 1978 Act) identifying the particular targets or facilities to be monitored and instead was allowed to seek approval from the court for mass surveillance. A group of individual attorneys and various human rights, labor, legal, and media organizations—whose work requires international communications with individuals they believe the government will likely monitor under the amendment—sued the government, alleging that §1881a violated the First and Fourth Amendments, Article III of the Constitution, and the principle of separation of powers.

In Clapper v. Amnesty International USA, 568 U.S. 398 (2013), the Supreme Court held, in a 5-4 decision, that the plaintiffs lacked standing to sue. In an opinion by Justice Alito, the Court explained (quoting from *Raines v. Byrd*) that " '[o]ur standing inquiry has been especially rigorous when reaching the merits of the dispute would force us to decide whether an action taken by one of the other two branches of the Federal Government was unconstitutional.'" In this case, said the Court, the plaintiffs' fear that their communications would be intercepted was too speculative, given that the plaintiffs "have no actual knowledge of the government's . . . targeting practices," do not know whether the government would pursue surveillance of their communications under §1881a as opposed to some other provision, and do not know whether the FISA court would approve a surveillance program that covered them. Nor do the plaintiffs have standing by virtue of the costs they have incurred to avoid surveillance: "respondents cannot manufacture standing," said the Court, "merely by inflicting harm on themselves based on their fears of hypothetical future harm that is not particularly impending."

The dissenters, led by Justice Breyer, argued that the alleged harm here was not speculative. In light of the nature of the communications in question, and the capacity and motives of the government in its surveillance program, there is a "high probability," argued the dissenters, "that the Government will intercept at least some electronic communication to which at least some of the plaintiffs are parties."

Was it appropriate for the Court to disallow standing because of the plaintiffs' inability to prove something that the government had information about but refused to disclose? Or is that outcome simply the natural consequence of the secrecy required for national security operations? The *Clapper* decision was decided before Edward Snowden (who had formerly worked for the CIA and as a government contractor) made extensive disclosures to the media, beginning in May 2013, about secret U.S. government surveillance programs. These programs included mass collection and computer analysis of phone call records made by persons in the United States, as well as large-scale incidental collection of other communications by U.S. citizens. Do the disclosures undermine the Court's analysis? Regardless of their ultimate merits, the constitutional concerns raised by the plaintiffs about §1881a were far from frivolous. Does the Court's decision mean that these concerns are effectively unreviewable by the judiciary? With respect to this last question, the Court said the following:

> [O]ur holding today by no means insulates §1881a from judicial review. As described above, Congress created a comprehensive scheme in which the Foreign Intelligence Surveillance Court evaluates the Government's certifications, targeting procedures, and minimization procedures—including assessing whether the targeting and minimization procedures comport with the Fourth Amendment. Any dissatisfaction that respondents may have about the Foreign Intelligence Surveillance Court's rulings—or the congressional delineation of that court's role—is irrelevant to our standing analysis.
>
> Additionally, if the Government intends to use or disclose information obtained or derived from a §1881a acquisition in judicial or administrative proceedings, it must

[under the relevant statutory provisions] provide advance notice of its intent, and the affected person may challenge the lawfulness of the acquisition. . . .

Finally, any electronic communications service provider that the Government directs to assist in §1881a surveillance may challenge the lawfulness of that directive before the [Foreign Intelligence Surveillance Court]. . . .

Is this persuasive?

9. Standing concerns the proper *party* to bring a lawsuit. Two related justiciability doctrines—ripeness and mootness—concern the proper *timing* of federal court adjudication. The ripeness doctrine ensures that courts do not review an issue prematurely at a point when the alleged injury is still speculative. To be ripe, the alleged harm must ordinarily be "immediate" or "imminent" rather than merely "distant" or "speculative." *See, e.g.,* Poe v. Ullman, 367 U.S. 497 (1961) (plurality). As this test shows, the ripeness inquiry is related to standing, and the two inquiries often overlap. The mootness doctrine is also about timing, and is also related to standing. A case that is ripe when filed will ordinarily be dismissed as moot if it is no longer ripe at the time of the decision. *See* DeFunis v. Odegaard, 416 U.S. 312, 316 (1974). The Supreme Court has held, however, that a case that would otherwise be moot can be heard if the issue raised is capable of repetition between the same parties, yet evades judicial review. *See, e.g.,* First National Bank of Boston v. Bellotti, 435 U.S. 765, 774 (1978) (election restrictions); Roe v. Wade, 410 U.S. 113, 125 (1973) (abortion restrictions). Also, a defendant's voluntary cessation of challenged activity ordinarily will not moot a case, because the defendant simply could resume the activity after the case was dismissed. *See* United States v. W.T. Grant Co., 345 U.S. 629, 632 (1953).

C. POLITICAL QUESTION DOCTRINE

The Supreme Court's opinion in Marbury v. Madison, 5 U.S. (1 Cranch) 137 (1803), is famous for announcing the doctrine of constitutional judicial review. In that opinion, Chief Justice Marshall states that it is "emphatically the province and duty of the judicial department to say what the law is," and he suggests that for every violation of a vested legal right, there should be a legal remedy. He also suggests, however, that not all disputes are susceptible to judicial resolution. In particular, Marshall states that some government actions are "mere political act[s]" that are not "examinable in a court of justice." The materials below address the relevance of this "political question doctrine" to cases implicating foreign affairs.

Baker v. Carr

369 U.S. 186 (1962)

[This case involved an equal protection challenge to the method by which the state of Tennessee apportioned the election of members of its legislature among the state's counties. In rejecting the argument that the case presented a nonjusticiable political question, the Court surveyed its prior political question decisions, including in the foreign relations law area. It also listed six factors relevant to determining whether a case presents a nonjusticiable political question.]

MR. JUSTICE BRENNAN delivered the opinion of the Court. . . .

Foreign relations: there are sweeping statements to the effect that all questions touching foreign relations are political questions. Not only does resolution of such issues frequently turn on standards that defy judicial application, or involve the exercise of a discretion demonstrably committed to the executive or legislature, but many such questions uniquely demand single-voiced statement of the Government's views. Yet it is error to suppose that every case or controversy which touches foreign relations lies beyond judicial cognizance. Our cases in this field seem invariably to show a discriminating analysis of the particular question posed, in terms of the history of its management by the political branches, of its susceptibility to judicial handling in the light of its nature and posture in the specific case, and of the possible consequences of judicial action. . . .

It is apparent that several formulations which vary slightly according to the settings in which the questions arise may describe a political question, although each has one or more elements which identify it as essentially a function of the separation of powers. Prominent on the surface of any case held to involve a political question is found a textually demonstrable constitutional commitment of the issue to a coordinate political department; or a lack of judicially discoverable and manageable standards for resolving it; or the impossibility of deciding without an initial policy determination of a kind clearly for non judicial discretion; or the impossibility of a court's undertaking independent resolution without expressing lack of the respect due coordinate branches of government; or an unusual need for unquestioning adherence to a political decision already made; or the potentiality of embarrassment from multifarious pronouncements by various departments on one question. Unless one of these formulations is inextricable from the case at bar, there should be no dismissal for nonjusticiability on the ground of a political question's presence.

Goldwater v. Carter

444 U.S. 996 (1979)

[During the 1970s, the United States began to pursue closer relations with the People's Republic of China (PRC). The PRC made clear that a precondition to normalization of relations between the two countries was for the United States to terminate its 1954 mutual defense treaty with Taiwan. In September 1978, Congress passed (and the President signed) the International Security Assistance Act, §26 of which provided that "[i]t is the sense of the Congress that there should be prior consultation between the Congress and the executive branch on any proposed policy changes affecting the continuation in force of the Mutual Defense Treaty of 1954." In December 1978, President Jimmy Carter announced that the United States would recognize the PRC as the sole government of China and that he planned to terminate the U.S. mutual defense treaty with Taiwan, pursuant to a provision in the treaty that allowed either party to withdraw from the treaty after giving a year's notice. In response, 8 senators and 16 members of the House of Representatives sued for declaratory and injunctive relief to prevent Carter from terminating the treaty. The federal district court held that Carter's notice of termination was ineffective absent either a manifestation of the consent of the Senate to such termination by a two-thirds vote, or an approving majority vote by both houses of Congress. The court of appeals reversed, ruling on the merits that the President had the power to terminate the treaty. Without issuing a majority opinion, the Supreme Court granted *certiorari*, vacated the lower court judgment, and remanded the case with directions to dismiss the complaint.]

MR. JUSTICE POWELL, concurring.

Although I agree with the result reached by the Court, I would dismiss the complaint as not ripe for judicial review.

I

This Court has recognized that an issue should not be decided if it is not ripe for judicial review. Prudential considerations persuade me that a dispute between Congress and the President is not ready for judicial review unless and until each branch has taken action asserting its constitutional authority. Differences between the President and the Congress are commonplace under our system. The differences should, and almost invariably do, turn on political rather than legal considerations. The Judicial Branch should not decide issues affecting the allocation of power between the President and Congress until the political branches reach a constitutional impasse. Otherwise, we would encourage small groups or even individual Members of Congress to seek judicial resolution of issues before the normal political process has the opportunity to resolve the conflict.

In this case, a few Members of Congress claim that the President's action in terminating the treaty with Taiwan has deprived them of their constitutional role with respect to a change in the supreme law of the land. Congress has taken no official action. In the present posture of this case, we do not know whether there ever will be an actual confrontation between the Legislative and Executive Branches. Although the Senate has considered a resolution declaring that Senate approval is necessary for the termination of any mutual defense treaty, no final vote has been taken on the resolution. Moreover, it is unclear whether the resolution would have retroactive effect. It cannot be said that either the Senate or the House has rejected the President's claim. If the Congress chooses not to confront the President, it is not our task to do so. I therefore concur in the dismissal of this case.

II

Mr. Justice Rehnquist suggests, however, that the issue presented by this case is a nonjusticiable political question which can never be considered by this Court. I cannot agree. In my view, reliance upon the political question doctrine is inconsistent with our precedents. As set forth in the seminal case of Baker v. Carr, 369 U.S. 186, 217 (1962), the doctrine incorporates three inquiries: (i) Does the issue involve resolution of questions committed by the text of the Constitution to a coordinate branch of Government? (ii) Would resolution of the question demand that a court move beyond areas of judicial expertise? (iii) Do prudential considerations counsel against judicial intervention? In my opinion the answer to each of these inquiries would require us to decide this case if it were ready for review.

First, the existence of "a textually demonstrable constitutional commitment of the issue to a coordinate political department," *ibid.*, turns on an examination of the constitutional provisions governing the exercise of the power in question. Powell v. McCormack, 395 U.S. 486, 519 (1969). No constitutional provision explicitly confers upon the President the power to terminate treaties. Further, Art. II, §2, of the Constitution authorizes the President to make treaties with the advice and consent of the Senate. Article VI provides that treaties shall be a part of the supreme law of the land. These provisions add support to the view that the text of the Constitution does not unquestionably commit the power to terminate treaties to the President alone.

Second, there is no "lack of judicially discoverable and manageable standards for resolving" this case; nor is a decision impossible "without an initial policy determination of a kind clearly for nonjudicial discretion." Baker v. Carr, *supra*, at 217. We are asked to decide whether the President may terminate a treaty under the Constitution without congressional approval. Resolution of the question may not be easy, but it only requires us to apply normal principles of interpretation to the constitutional provisions at issue. *See* Powell v. McCormack, *supra*, at 548-49. The present case involves neither review of the President's activities as Commander in Chief nor impermissible interference in the field of foreign affairs. Such a case would arise if we were asked to decide, for example, whether a treaty required the President to order troops into a foreign country. But "it is error to suppose that every case or controversy which touches foreign relations lies beyond judicial cognizance." Baker v. Carr, *supra*, at 211. This case "touches" foreign relations, but the question presented to us concerns only the constitutional division of power between Congress and the President.

A simple hypothetical demonstrates the confusion that I find inherent in Mr. Justice Rehnquist's opinion concurring in the judgment. Assume that the President signed a mutual defense treaty with a foreign country and announced that it would go into effect despite its rejection by the Senate. Under Mr. Justice Rehnquist's analysis that situation would present a political question even though Art. II, §2, clearly would resolve the dispute. Although the answer to the hypothetical case seems self-evident because it demands textual rather than interstitial analysis, the nature of the legal issue presented is no different from the issue presented in the case before us. In both cases, the Court would interpret the Constitution to decide whether congressional approval is necessary to give a Presidential decision on the validity of a treaty the force of law. Such an inquiry demands no special competence or information beyond the reach of the Judiciary. *Cf.* Chicago & Southern Air Lines v. Waterman S.S. Corp., 333 U.S. 103, 111 (1948).[1]

Finally, the political question doctrine rests in part on prudential concerns calling for mutual respect among the three branches of Government. Thus, the Judicial Branch should avoid "the potentiality of embarrassment [that would result] from multifarious pronouncements by various departments on one question." Similarly, the doctrine restrains judicial action where there is an "unusual need for unquestioning adherence to a political decision already made." Baker v. Carr, *supra*, at 217.

If this case were ripe for judicial review, none of these prudential considerations would be present. Interpretation of the Constitution does not imply lack of respect for a coordinate branch. Powell v. McCormack, *supra*, at 548. If the President and the Congress had reached irreconcilable positions, final disposition of the question presented by this case would eliminate, rather than create, multiple constitutional

---

1. The Court has recognized that, in the area of foreign policy, Congress may leave the President with wide discretion that otherwise might run afoul of the nondelegation doctrine. United States v. Curtiss-Wright Export Corp., 299 U.S. 304 (1936). As stated in that case, "the President alone has the power to speak or listen as a representative of the Nation. He *makes* treaties with the advice and consent of the Senate; but he alone negotiates." *Id.* at 319 (emphasis in original). Resolution of this case would interfere with neither the President's ability to negotiate treaties nor his duty to execute their provisions. We are merely being asked to decide whether a treaty, which cannot be ratified without Senate approval, continues in effect until the Senate or perhaps the Congress takes further action.

interpretations. The specter of the Federal Government brought to a halt because of the mutual intransigence of the President and the Congress would require this Court to provide a resolution pursuant to our duty " 'to say what the law is.'" United States v. Nixon, 418 U.S. 683, 703 (1974), quoting Marbury v. Madison, 1 Cranch 137, 177 (1803). . . .

MR. JUSTICE REHNQUIST, with whom THE CHIEF JUSTICE, MR. JUSTICE STEWART, and MR. JUSTICE STEVENS join, concurring in the judgment.

I am of the view that the basic question presented by the petitioners in this case is "political" and therefore nonjusticiable because it involves the authority of the President in the conduct of our country's foreign relations and the extent to which the Senate or the Congress is authorized to negate the action of the President. In Coleman v. Miller, 307 U.S. 433 (1939), a case in which members of the Kansas Legislature brought an action attacking a vote of the State Senate in favor of the ratification of the Child Labor Amendment, Mr. Chief Justice Hughes wrote in what is referred to as the "Opinion of the Court":

> We think that . . . the question of the efficacy of ratifications by state legislatures, in the light of previous rejection or attempted withdrawal, should be regarded as a political question pertaining to the political departments, with the ultimate authority in the Congress in the exercise of its control over the promulgation of the adoption of the Amendment.
>
> The precise question as now raised is whether, when the legislature of the State, as we have found, has actually ratified the proposed amendment, the Court should restrain the state officers from certifying the ratification to the Secretary of State, because of an earlier rejection, and thus prevent the question from coming before the political departments. We find no basis in either Constitution or statute for such judicial action. Article V, speaking solely of ratification, contains no provision as to rejection. . . .

Id. at 450.

Thus, Mr. Chief Justice Hughes' opinion concluded that "Congress in controlling the promulgation of the adoption of a constitutional amendment has the final determination of the question whether by lapse of time its proposal of the amendment had lost its vitality prior to the required ratifications."

I believe it follows *a fortiori* from *Coleman* that the controversy in the instant case is a nonjusticiable political dispute that should be left for resolution by the Executive and Legislative Branches of the Government. Here, while the Constitution is express as to the manner in which the Senate shall participate in the ratification of a treaty, it is silent as to that body's participation in the abrogation of a treaty. In this respect the case is directly analogous to *Coleman, supra.* . . . In light of the absence of any constitutional provision governing the termination of a treaty, and the fact that different termination procedures may be appropriate for different treaties, the instant case in my view also "must surely be controlled by political standards."

I think that the justifications for concluding that the question here is political in nature are even more compelling than in *Coleman* because it involves foreign relations—specifically a treaty commitment to use military force in the defense of a foreign government if attacked. In United States v. Curtiss-Wright Corp., 299 U.S. 304 (1936), this Court said:

> Whether, if the Joint Resolution had related solely to internal affairs it would be open to the challenge that it constituted an unlawful delegation of legislative power to the

Executive, we find it unnecessary to determine. The whole aim of the resolution is to affect a situation entirely external to the United States, and falling within the category of foreign affairs. . . .

Id. at 315.

The present case differs in several important respects from Youngstown Sheet & Tube Co. v. Sawyer, 343 U.S. 579 (1952), cited by petitioners as authority both for reaching the merits of this dispute and for reversing the Court of Appeals. In *Youngstown,* private litigants brought a suit contesting the President's authority under his war powers to seize the Nation's steel industry, an action of profound and demonstrable domestic impact. Here, by contrast, we are asked to settle a dispute between coequal branches of our Government, each of which has resources available to protect and assert its interests, resources not available to private litigants outside the judicial forum. Moreover, as in *Curtiss-Wright,* the effect of this action, as far as we can tell, is "entirely external to the United States, and [falls] within the category of foreign affairs." Finally, as already noted, the situation presented here is closely akin to that presented in *Coleman,* where the Constitution spoke only to the procedure for ratification of an amendment, not to its rejection. . . .

MR. JUSTICE BRENNAN, dissenting.

I respectfully dissent from the order directing the District Court to dismiss this case, and would affirm the judgment of the Court of Appeals insofar as it rests upon the President's well-established authority to recognize, and withdraw recognition from, foreign governments.

In stating that this case presents a nonjusticiable "political question," Mr. Justice Rehnquist, in my view, profoundly misapprehends the political-question principle as it applies to matters of foreign relations. Properly understood, the political-question doctrine restrains courts from reviewing an exercise of foreign policy judgment by the coordinate political branch to which authority to make that judgment has been "constitutional[ly] commit[ted]." Baker v. Carr, 369 U.S. 186, 211-13, 217 (1962). But the doctrine does not pertain when a court is faced with the *antecedent* question whether a particular branch has been constitutionally designated as the repository of political decisionmaking power. *Cf.* Powell v. McCormack, 395 U.S. 486, 519-21 (1969). The issue of decisionmaking authority must be resolved as a matter of constitutional law, not political discretion; accordingly, it falls within the competence of the courts.

The constitutional question raised here is prudently answered in narrow terms. Abrogation of the defense treaty with Taiwan was a necessary incident to Executive recognition of the Peking Government, because the defense treaty was predicated upon the now-abandoned view that the Taiwan Government was the only legitimate political authority in China. Our cases firmly establish that the Constitution commits to the President alone the power to recognize, and withdraw recognition from, foreign regimes. *See* Banco Nacional de Cuba v. Sabbatino, 376 U.S. 398, 410 (1964); Baker v. Carr, *supra,* at 212; United States v. Pink, 315 U.S. 203, 228-30 (1942). That mandate being clear, our judicial inquiry into the treaty rupture can go no further.

Zivotofsky v. Clinton

132 S. Ct. 1421 (2012)

CHIEF JUSTICE ROBERTS delivered the opinion of the Court. . . .

I

The State Department's Foreign Affairs Manual states that "[w]here the birthplace of the applicant is located in territory disputed by another country, the city or area of birth may be written in the passport." The manual specifically directs that passport officials should enter "JERUSALEM" and should "not write Israel or Jordan" when recording the birthplace of a person born in Jerusalem on a passport.

Section 214(d) [of the Foreign Relations Authorization Act for Fiscal Year 2003] sought to override this instruction by allowing citizens born in Jerusalem to have "Israel" recorded on their passports if they wish. . . .

Petitioner Menachem Binyamin Zivotofsky was born in Jerusalem on October 17, 2002, shortly after §214(d) was enacted. Zivotofsky's parents were American citizens and he accordingly was as well, by virtue of congressional enactment. Zivotofsky's mother filed an application for a consular report of birth abroad and a United States passport. She requested that his place of birth be listed as "Jerusalem, Israel" on both documents. U.S. officials informed Zivotofsky's mother that State Department policy prohibits recording "Israel" as Zivotofsky's place of birth. Pursuant to that policy, Zivotofsky was issued a passport and consular report of birth abroad listing only "Jerusalem."

Zivotofsky's parents filed a complaint on his behalf against the Secretary of State. Zivotofsky sought a declaratory judgment and a permanent injunction ordering the Secretary to identify his place of birth as "Jerusalem, Israel" in the official documents. . . .

II

The lower courts concluded that Zivotofsky's claim presents a political question and therefore cannot be adjudicated. We disagree.

In general, the Judiciary has a responsibility to decide cases properly before it, even those it "would gladly avoid." Cohens v. Virginia, 19 U.S. (6 Wheat.) 264, 404 (1821). Our precedents have identified a narrow exception to that rule, known as the "political question" doctrine. We have explained that a controversy "involves a political question . . . where there is 'a textually demonstrable constitutional commitment of the issue to a coordinate political department; or a lack of judicially discoverable and manageable standards for resolving it.'" Nixon v. United States, 506 U.S. 224, 228 (1993) (quoting Baker v. Carr, 369 U.S. 186, 217 (1962)). In such a case, we have held that a court lacks the authority to decide the dispute before it. . . .

[The D.C. Circuit] concluded that "[o]nly the Executive—not Congress and not the courts—has the power to define U.S. policy regarding Israel's sovereignty over Jerusalem," and also to "decide how best to implement that policy." Because the Department's passport rule was adopted to implement the President's "exclusive and unreviewable constitutional power to keep the United States out of the debate over the status of Jerusalem," the validity of that rule was itself a "nonjusticiable political question" that "the Constitution leaves to the Executive alone." [T]he D.C. Circuit's opinion does not even mention §214(d) until the fifth of its six paragraphs of analysis, and then only to dismiss it as irrelevant: "That Congress took a position on the status of Jerusalem and gave Zivotofsky a statutory cause of action . . . is of no moment to whether the judiciary has [the] authority to resolve this dispute. . . ."

The existence of a statutory right, however, is certainly relevant to the Judiciary's power to decide Zivotofsky's claim. The federal courts are not being asked to supplant a foreign policy decision of the political branches with the courts' own unmoored determination of what United States policy toward Jerusalem should be. Instead, Zivotofsky requests that the courts enforce a specific statutory right. To resolve his claim, the Judiciary must decide if Zivotofsky's interpretation of the statute is correct, and whether the statute is constitutional. This is a familiar judicial exercise.

Moreover, because the parties do not dispute the interpretation of §214(d), the only real question for the courts is whether the statute is constitutional. At least since Marbury v. Madison, 1 Cranch 137 (1803), we have recognized that when an Act of Congress is alleged to conflict with the Constitution, "[i]t is emphatically the province and duty of the judicial department to say what the law is." That duty will sometimes involve the "[r]esolution of litigation challenging the constitutional authority of one of the three branches," but courts cannot avoid their responsibility merely "because the issues have political implications." INS v. Chadha, 462 U.S. 919, 943 (1983).

In this case, determining the constitutionality of §214(d) involves deciding whether the statute impermissibly intrudes upon Presidential powers under the Constitution. If so, the law must be invalidated and Zivotofsky's case should be dismissed for failure to state a claim. If, on the other hand, the statute does not trench on the President's powers, then the Secretary must be ordered to issue Zivotofsky a passport that complies with §214(d). Either way, the political question doctrine is not implicated. "No policy underlying the political question doctrine suggests that Congress or the Executive . . . can decide the constitutionality of a statute; that is a decision for the courts." *Chadha*, 462 U.S. at 941-42.

The Secretary contends that "there is 'a textually demonstrable constitutional commitment'" to the President of the sole power to recognize foreign sovereigns and, as a corollary, to determine whether an American born in Jerusalem may choose to have Israel listed as his place of birth on his passport. Perhaps. But there is, of course, no exclusive commitment to the Executive of the power to determine the constitutionality of a statute. The Judicial Branch appropriately exercises that authority, including in a case such as this, where the question is whether Congress or the Executive is "aggrandizing its power at the expense of another branch."

Our precedents have also found the political question doctrine implicated when there is " 'a lack of judicially discoverable and manageable standards for resolving'" the question before the court. Framing the issue as the lower courts did, in terms of whether the Judiciary may decide the political status of Jerusalem, certainly raises those concerns. They dissipate, however, when the issue is recognized to be the more focused one of the constitutionality of §214(d). Indeed, both sides offer detailed legal arguments regarding whether §214(d) is constitutional in light of powers committed to the Executive, and whether Congress's own powers with respect to passports must be weighed in analyzing this question. . . .

[The Court reviews the government's and the petitioner's arguments on the merits of the constitutionality of Section 214(d).]

Recitation of these arguments—which sound in familiar principles of constitutional interpretation—is enough to establish that this case does not "turn on standards that defy judicial application." Resolution of Zivotofksy's claim demands careful examination of the textual, structural, and historical evidence put forward by the parties regarding the nature of the statute and of the passport and recognition powers. This is what courts do. The political question doctrine poses no bar to judicial review of this case. . . .

Having determined that this case is justiciable, we leave it to the lower courts to consider the merits in the first instance.

[Justice Sotomayor, joined in part by Justice Breyer, concurred in part and concurred in the judgment in *Zivotofsky*. In her view, the factors from Baker v. Carr "reflect three distinct justifications for withholding judgment on the merits of a dispute." She explained:

> When a case would require a court to decide an issue whose resolution is textually committed to a coordinate political department, as envisioned by *Baker*'s first factor, abstention is warranted because the court lacks authority to resolve that issue. . . .
>
> The second and third *Baker* factors reflect circumstances in which a dispute calls for decisionmaking beyond courts' competence. . . .
>
> The final three *Baker* factors address circumstances in which prudence may counsel against a court's resolution of an issue presented.

While acknowledging that "it will be the rare case in which *Baker*'s final factors alone render a case nonjusticiable," Justice Sotomayor argued that "our long historical tradition recognizes that such exceptional cases arise, and due regard for the separation of powers and the judicial role envisioned by Article III confirms that abstention may be an appropriate response." But she agreed with the Court that this particular case did not present a political question.]

[Justice Alito concurred in the judgment. He reasoned: "Under our case law, determining the constitutionality of an Act of Congress may present a political question, but I do not think that the narrow question presented here falls within that category. Delineating the precise dividing line between the powers of Congress and the President with respect to the contents of a passport is not an easy matter, but I agree with the Court that it does not constitute a political question that the Judiciary is unable to decide."]

[Justice Breyer dissented. Like Justice Sotomayor, he emphasized all six of the *Baker* factors, and he agreed with her that prudential considerations can sometimes trigger application of the political question doctrine. Four sets of prudential considerations led him to conclude that this case presented a nonjusticiable political question:

> First, the issue before us arises in the field of foreign affairs. . . . Decisionmaking in this area typically is highly political. . . . Second, if the courts must answer the constitutional question before us, they may well have to evaluate the foreign policy implications of foreign policy decisions. . . . Third, the countervailing interests in obtaining judicial resolution of the constitutional determination are not particularly strong ones [because they do not involve] an interest in property or bodily integrity, which courts have traditionally sought to protect, [and because *Zivotofsky* does not] assert an interest in vindicating a basic right of the kind that the Constitution grants to individuals and that courts traditionally have protected from invasion by the other branches of Government. . . . Fourth, insofar as the controversy reflects different foreign policy views among the political branches of Government, those branches have nonjudicial methods of working out their differences.]

Notes and Questions

1. How much guidance do the six factors listed in *Baker v. Carr* give to the lower courts? Are some factors more important than others? How do courts know when issues demand a "single-voiced statement of the Government's views," or when "multifarious pronouncements" will cause "embarrassment"? What information and expertise would courts need to answer these questions? In applying these factors, are courts able to avoid making judgments about the merits of the case?

2. Prior to *Baker*, there was not a singular political question "doctrine." Rather, there were simply various issues that the Supreme Court thought were properly resolved by the political branches rather than the judiciary. In the foreign affairs area, this meant deferring in the course of adjudication to certain determinations made by Congress or the Executive Branch.

A good example is Jones v. United States, 137 U.S. 202 (1890). The defendant in *Jones* was prosecuted for committing murder on a Caribbean island that the President had proclaimed, pursuant to an Act of Congress, to be within the jurisdiction of the United States. The defendant argued that the Act of Congress authorizing this presidential assertion of jurisdiction was unconstitutional because it was an attempt by Congress to regulate land outside of U.S. control. The Supreme Court concluded that the question of sovereignty over the island was by its nature a "political question":

> Who is the sovereign, *de jure or de facto*, of a territory is not a judicial, but a political question, the determination of which by the legislative and executive departments of any government conclusively binds the judges, as well as all other officers, citizens and subjects of that government. This principle has always been upheld by this court, and has been affirmed under a great variety of circumstances....
>
> All courts of justice are bound to take judicial notice of the territorial extent of the jurisdiction exercised by the government whose laws they administer, or of its recognition or denial of the sovereignty of a foreign power, as appearing from the public acts of the legislature and executive, although those acts are not formally put in evidence, nor in accord with the pleadings.

For other examples, see Doe v. Braden, 57 U.S. (16 How.) 635, 657 (1853) (treaty ratification power of foreign government is a political question); Williams v. Suffolk Ins. Co., 38 U.S. 415, 420 (1839) (sovereignty of foreign nation is a political question); Foster v. Neilson, 27 U.S. (2 Pet.) 253, 308-13 (1829) (territorial boundary determination is a political question); and United States v. Palmer, 16 U.S. (3 Wheat.) 610, 633-34 (1818) (recognition of new government is a political question). *See generally* Edwin D. Dickinson, *International Political Questions in the National Courts,* 19 Am. J. Int'l L. 157 (1925).

3. Why, according to Justice Rehnquist's plurality opinion in *Goldwater,* is the issue of treaty termination political? What is Justice Powell's response?

Justice Powell supported dismissal in *Goldwater* on the ground that the case was not "ripe for judicial review." What does Justice Powell mean by ripeness in this context? What difference is there between Justice Powell's ripeness basis for dismissal and the plurality's political question basis? What difference is there between the ripeness requirement and the limitations on legislative standing discussed above in Section B?

Both Justice Rehnquist's and Justice Powell's opinions in *Goldwater* assume that, at least generally, the political branches have adequate tools with which to resolve constitutional foreign affairs issues outside the courts. Is this assumption valid? How do we know whether the Senate, for example, has sufficient leverage to protect its constitutional interests?

4. What is the overall significance of *Goldwater* regarding the termination of U.S. treaty commitments? Do the separate opinions yield a holding on this issue? Does *Goldwater* effectively mean that the President can terminate U.S. treaties with impunity?

A more recent treaty termination case is Kucinich v. Bush, 236 F. Supp. 2d 1 (D.D.C. 2002). In that case, 32 members of the House of Representatives brought suit in federal district court against President Bush and other Executive Branch officials, challenging the Bush Administration's decision to withdraw from the Anti-Ballistic Missile (ABM) Treaty. The ABM Treaty, which was ratified by the United States and the Soviet Union in 1972, strictly limited the number and location of anti-ballistic missile systems that could be deployed by each country. The House members argued that because the Constitution classifies treaties, like federal statutes, as the "supreme law of the land," the President does not have the authority to terminate a treaty without congressional consent, just as he cannot terminate a statute without congressional consent. In dismissing the suit, the court concluded that the House members lacked standing under *Raines v. Byrd.* The court also held that the case raised a nonjusticiable political question, for reasons similar to those articulated by Justice Rehnquist in *Goldwater.* The power of treaty termination is discussed more fully in Chapter 5.

5. Even after *Baker*, when courts have labeled issues "political questions," they often have meant that a political branch—often the Executive Branch—has the constitutional authority to resolve the issue in a way that is dispositive for the courts. In these cases, courts treat a political branch's resolution of the issue as valid. The first factor referred to by the Court in *Baker*—"a textually demonstrable constitutional commitment of the issue to a coordinate political department"—appears to concern this type of dispositive political branch authority. Nevertheless, some foreign affairs actions are treated as nonjusticiable in the sense that courts will not express a view about their validity, and some of the other *Baker* factors seem relevant to that issue of nonjusticiability. To take an example that is discussed in Chapter 9, a number of courts held that the lawfulness of the Vietnam War (under the U.S. Constitution and international law) was a nonjusticiable political question, without holding that the war was lawful. Similarly, in *Goldwater*, the Rehnquist plurality was not arguing that President Carter's treaty termination was constitutionally valid; rather, it was arguing that the Court should not decide the validity of the termination. Do you see the difference between saying that a political branch has the authority to dispositively resolve an issue and saying that the issue is not justiciable? On the other hand, if courts refuse to overturn a political branch action because its validity raises a nonjusticiable political question, how is that different from treating the action as constitutionally valid?

6. Although it did not concern foreign affairs, another notable political question decision by the Supreme Court is Nixon v. United States, 506 U.S. 224 (1993). In that case, Congress had voted to impeach a federal judge (Walter Nixon) for having given false testimony to a grand jury that was investigating allegations that he had accepted a bribe. In trying the impeachment, the Senate used a committee to receive evidence and hear testimony, and then the full Senate voted based on its review of the record. Nixon subsequently brought suit challenging the impeachment procedure, arguing that it violated Article I, §3, cl. 6 of the Constitution, which gives the Senate the "sole Power to try all impeachments." The responsibility to "try" impeachments, Nixon maintained, precluded the Senate from delegating to a committee the task of receiving evidence and hearing witnesses. The Supreme Court held that this challenge presented a nonjusticiable political question because the word "try" "lacks sufficient precision to afford any judicially manageable standard of review of the Senate's actions," and also because, in giving the Senate the "sole" power to try impeachments, the text of the Constitution suggested that the courts should not scrutinize the Senate's decision. In addition, the Court expressed concern about both the lack of finality that would result if impeachments could be challenged in court and the difficulty of fashioning relief.

7. Why did the Court in *Zivotofsky* refer to and apply only the first two of the six *Baker* factors? Does this decision mean that the other four factors are no longer relevant in determining whether a case presents a political question? Or that they are relevant only if one of the first two factors also is applicable? The Court cites *Marbury* for the proposition that it is the duty of the courts to decide constitutional questions, quoting from *Chadha* to the effect that Congress and the President cannot decide the constitutionality of a federal statute. Do these references mean that the political question doctrine can never apply when the constitutionality of a federal statute is at issue? *Cf.* Rucho v. Common Cause, 139 S. Ct. 2484, 2507 (2019) (holding that constitutional challenges to partisan gerrymandering of electoral districts present political questions because "[f]ederal judges have no license to reallocate political power between the two major political parties, with no plausible grant of authority in the Constitution, and no legal standards to limit and direct their decisions").

As discussed in Chapter 3, after a remand to the D.C. Circuit, the *Zivotofsky* case returned to the Supreme Court, and the Court held that Congress had invaded the President's exclusive recognition power. *See* Zivotofsky v. Kerry, 135 S. Ct. 2076 (2015).

8. Before *Zivotofsky*, lower courts frequently applied the political question doctrine in cases involving foreign affairs, and they often took into account prudential considerations in doing so. *See, e.g.,* Schneider v. Kissinger, 412 F.3d 190 (D.C. Cir. 2005) (barring a suit against the U.S. government and Henry Kissinger for their alleged role in a military coup in Chile in 1970 and the resulting death of the plaintiffs' family member, a Chilean general). Many commentators claimed that *Zivotofsky* would diminish or end this practice, and some lower courts do appear to be applying the political question doctrine more cautiously. *See, e.g.,* Hourani v. Mirtchev, 796 F.3d 1 (D.C. Cir. 2015) (declining to apply political question doctrine in case against the daughter of Kazakhstan's president, despite possible embarrassment to that nation, because under *Zivotofsky*, courts have a responsibility to decide cases before them and "cannot avoid their responsibility merely because the issues have political implications").

Nevertheless, a number of lower court decisions since *Zivotofsky* have applied the political question doctrine in a robust way and have relied on prudential considerations. In Li-Shou v. United States, 777 F.3d 175 (4th Cir. 2015), for example, the Fourth Circuit considered claims by a Taiwanese citizen against the United States for sinking her husband's ship and accidentally killing him during a counter-piracy mission. Examining all six *Baker* factors, the court characterized the case as "a textbook example of a situation in which courts should not interfere." Allowing the suit to continue, the court reasoned, risked embroiling the court in factual questions concerning "what kind of warnings were given, the type of ordinance used, the type of weapons deployed, the range of fire selected, and the pattern, timing, and escalation of the firing." The court considered itself ill placed "to second-guess such small bore tactical decisions," or even "more strategic considerations," which it concluded lacked "discernible rules and standards." To take another example, in Saldana v. Occidental Petroleum Corp., 774 F.3d 544 (9th Cir. 2014), the Ninth Circuit relied on the political question doctrine to dismiss claims against a company that provided funds to a Colombian army brigade that committed human rights abuses. The U.S. government also provided funds to that brigade. The court refused to reach the merits of the claims after concluding that they were "inextricably bound to an inherently political question" about the propriety of "the political branches' decision to provide extensive military aid to Colombia." Ruling on the merits of such a case, the court concluded, would run afoul of the fourth, fifth, and sixth *Baker* factors.

One survey of post-*Zivotofsky* decisions in the lower appellate courts concludes that "[m]any appellate judges still use the prudential *Baker* factors to dispose of cases under the political question doctrine, notwithstanding *Zivotofsky*." *See* Alex Loomis, *Why Are the Lower Courts (Mostly) Ignoring Zivotofsky I's Political Question Analysis?*, Lawfare (May 19, 2016). Why might lower court judges be more inclined than the Supreme Court to consider prudential factors when applying the political question doctrine? Might it have something to do with the fact that the Supreme Court can choose which cases it hears, whereas the lower courts cannot?

For another post-*Zivotofsky* application of the political question doctrine by a lower court, see Jaber v. United States, 861 F.3d 241 (D.C. Cir. 2017). In that case, the family members of individuals allegedly killed by a U.S. drone strike in Yemen sought a declaration that the strike was unlawful under both domestic and international law. The court concluded that the suit was barred by the political question doctrine because "the precise grounds [that the plaintiffs] raise in their Complaint call for a court to pass judgment on the wisdom of Executive's decision to commence military action—mistaken or not—against a foreign target," and "courts lack the competence necessary to determine whether the use of force was justified." The court distinguished *Zivotofsky* on the ground that the Supreme Court in that case "was not called upon to impose its own foreign policy judgment on the political branches, only to say whether the congressional statute encroached on the Executive's constitutional authority."

9. In Japan Whaling Ass'n. v. American Cetacean Society, 478 U.S. 221 (1986), the Supreme Court considered a challenge by wildlife groups to the Secretary of Commerce's decision not to certify Japan for statutory sanctions designed to protect whales, despite Japan's violation of an international whaling quota. A majority of the Court concluded that the Executive had not acted contrary to the relevant statutes. The Court rejected the argument, however, that the case posed a nonjusticiable political question. The Court explained: "As *Baker* plainly held . . . the courts have the authority to construe treaties and executive agreements, and it goes without saying that interpreting congressional legislation is a recurring and accepted task for the federal courts. It is also evident that the challenge to the Secretary's decision not to certify Japan for harvesting whales in excess of [the international] quotas presents a purely legal question of statutory interpretation."

Does this decision stand for the proposition that courts cannot invoke the political question doctrine to avoid the interpretation of foreign relations statutes? That the political question doctrine is inapplicable to non-constitutional claims? For better or worse, although the political question doctrine is most likely to be applied in foreign affairs cases that involve constitutional challenges, it is sometimes applied in cases involving statutory, international, or other non-constitutional claims, especially if the cases concern war or military affairs. *See, e.g.,* United States v. Martinez, 904 F.2d 601 (11th Cir. 1990) (challenge to government's placement of an item on list subject to the Arms Export Control Act); Smith v. Reagan, 844 F.2d 195 (4th Cir. 1988) (suit to have U.S. prisoners of the Vietnam War declared to be in captivity and subject to the terms of the Hostage Act); Iwanowa v. Ford Motor Co., 67 F. Supp. 2d 424 (D.N.J. 1999) (Alien Tort Statute and other claims against private companies for use of forced labor during World War II). Nevertheless, consistent with *Japan Whaling,* courts often decline to apply the political question doctrine in non-constitutional cases. They do, however, frequently give deference to the views of the Executive Branch concerning the meaning of foreign affairs statutes and the content of international law, as discussed below in Section D. (Indeed, the Court in *Japan Whaling* gave deference to the Executive's interpretation of the sanctions statutes at issue there.)

10. In *Goldwater,* the plaintiffs were seeking injunctive and declaratory relief. Should the requested remedy affect whether an issue is held to be a political question? For example, should courts be more willing to adjudicate foreign affairs cases involving claims for damages than those involving claims for equitable relief? *Compare* Ramirez de Arellano v. Weinberger, 745 F.2d 1500 (D.C. Cir. 1984) (en banc) (applying political question doctrine to injunctive claim based on Takings Clause), *with* Langenegger v. United States, 756 F.2d 1565 (Fed. Cir. 1985) (declining to apply political question doctrine to monetary compensation claim based on Takings Clause). *See also* Koohi v. United States, 976 F.2d 1328, 1332 (9th Cir. 1992) ("A key element in our conclusion that the plaintiffs' action is justiciable is the fact that the plaintiffs seek only damages for their injuries."). For discussion of this issue, see John M. Hillebrecht, *Foreign Affairs Cases and Political Question Analysis:* Chaser Shipping v. United States, 23 Stan. J. Int'l L. 665 (1987).

11. For additional discussion of the role of the political question doctrine in foreign affairs cases, see Thomas M. Franck, Political Questions/Judicial Answers (1992); Michael J. Glennon, *Foreign Affairs and the Political Question Doctrine,* 83 Am. J. Int'l L. 814 (1989); Jack L. Goldsmith, *The New Formalism in United States Foreign Relations Law,* 70 U. Colo. L. Rev. 1395 (1999); Louis Henkin, *Is There a "Political Question" Doctrine?,* 85 Yale L.J. 597 (1976); Jide Nzelibe, *The Uniqueness of Foreign Affairs,* 89 Iowa L. Rev. 941 (2004); Michael E. Tigar, *Judicial Review, the "Political Question Doctrine," and Foreign Relations,* 17 UCLA L. Rev. 1135 (1970). For more general discussions of the political question doctrine, see Rachel E. Barkow, *More Supreme than Court? The Fall of the Political Question Doctrine and the Rise of Judicial Supremacy,* 102 Colum. L. Rev. 237 (2002); Louis Michael Seidman, *The Secret Life of the Political Question Doctrine,* 37 John Marshall L. Rev. 441 (2004); Mark Tushnet, *Law and Prudence in the Law of Justiciability: The Transformation and Disappearance of the Political Question Doctrine,* 80 N.C. L. Rev. 1203 (2002). *See also* Alexander M. Bickel, *The Supreme Court, 1960 Term—Foreword: The Passive Virtues,* 75 Harv. L. Rev. 40 (1961).

D. DEFERENCE TO THE EXECUTIVE BRANCH

Trump v. Hawaii

138 S. Ct. 2392 (2018)

[In January 2017, shortly after taking office, President Trump signed Executive Order No. 13769 (EO-1). EO-1 directed the Department of Homeland Security (DHS) to conduct a worldwide review of the adequacy of certain information from foreign governments related to immigration of their citizens and, pending that review, halted entry of various classes of non-citizens from seven majority-Muslim countries into the United States. The order appeared not to have been extensively vetted within the Executive Branch, and there was substantial confusion about its scope and application, such as whether it applied to lawful permanent residents. After lower courts enjoined that order, the President revoked EO-1 and replaced it with Executive Order No. 13780 (EO-2), which again directed a worldwide review and temporarily restricted the entry of foreign nationals (with waivers) from six of the countries covered by EO-1. The restrictions in this order were enjoined by lower courts, although the injunctions were partially stayed by the Supreme Court. The restrictions then expired, rendering the lower court decisions moot.

In September 2017, the President issued Proclamation No. 9645, the order under review in this case. Based on the worldwide review that began under the previous orders, the Proclamation placed entry restrictions on the nationals of eight nations—Chad, Iran, Iraq, Libya, North Korea, Syria, Venezuela, and Yemen—whose systems for managing and sharing information about their nationals the President deemed inadequate. (Of these eight countries, all but North Korea and Venezuela are majority-Muslim countries.) As authority for imposing these restrictions, the President relied primarily on a provision in the Immigration and Nationality Act (INA), 8 U.S.C. §1182(f), which authorizes the President to "suspend the entry of all aliens or any class of aliens as immigrants or nonimmigrants, or impose on the entry of aliens any restrictions he may deem to be appropriate" whenever he "finds that the entry of any aliens or of any class of aliens into the United States would be detrimental to the interests of the United States." Based on §1182(f) and related authorities, the Proclamation imposed entry restrictions that varied based on the "distinct circumstances" in each of the eight countries, exempted lawful permanent residents, provided case-by-case waivers under certain circumstances, and directed DHS to continue to assess the basis for the restrictions, which resulted in the President lifting the ones on nationals from Chad after DHS determined that Chad had sufficiently improved its practices.

In this case, the State of Hawaii, three individuals with foreign relatives affected by the entry suspension, and the Muslim Association of Hawaii argued that the Proclamation violated several immigration statutes and the Establishment Clause of the U.S. Constitution. The Ninth Circuit upheld the district court's nationwide preliminary injunction barring enforcement of the restrictions.]

CHIEF JUSTICE ROBERTS delivered the opinion of the Court. . . .

III

. . . Plaintiffs argue that the Proclamation is not a valid exercise of the President's authority under the INA. In their view, §1182(f) confers only a residual power to temporarily halt the entry of a discrete group of aliens engaged in harmful conduct. . . .

By its terms, §1182(f) exudes deference to the President in every clause. It entrusts to the President the decisions whether and when to suspend entry ("[w]henever [he] finds that the entry" of aliens "would be detrimental" to the national interest); whose entry to suspend ("all aliens or any class of aliens"); for how long ("for such period as he shall deem necessary"); and on what conditions ("any restrictions he may deem to be appropriate"). . . .

The Proclamation falls well within this comprehensive delegation. The sole prerequisite set forth in §1182(f) is that the President "find[]" that the entry of the covered aliens "would be detrimental to the interests of the United States." The President has undoubtedly fulfilled that requirement here. He first ordered DHS and other agencies to conduct a comprehensive evaluation of every single country's compliance with the information and risk assessment baseline. The President then issued a Proclamation setting forth extensive findings describing how deficiencies in the practices of select foreign governments—several of which are state sponsors of terrorism—deprive the Government of "sufficient information to assess the risks [those countries' nationals] pose to the United States." Based on that review, the President found that it was in the national interest to restrict entry of aliens who could not be vetted with adequate information—both to protect national security and public safety, and to induce improvement by their home countries. The Proclamation therefore "craft[ed] . . . country-specific restrictions that would be most likely to encourage cooperation given each country's distinct circumstances," while securing the Nation "until such time as improvements occur."

Plaintiffs believe that these findings are insufficient. They argue, as an initial matter, that the Proclamation fails to provide a persuasive rationale for why nationality alone renders the covered foreign nationals a security risk. And they further discount the President's stated concern about deficient vetting because the Proclamation allows many aliens from the designated countries to enter on nonimmigrant visas.

Such arguments are grounded on the premise that §1182(f) not only requires the President to *make* a finding that entry "would be detrimental to the interests of the United States," but also to explain that finding with sufficient detail to enable judicial review. That premise is questionable. . . . But even assuming that some form of review is appropriate, plaintiffs' attacks on the sufficiency of the President's findings cannot be sustained. The 12-page Proclamation—which thoroughly describes the process, agency evaluations, and recommendations underlying the President's chosen restrictions—is more detailed than any prior order a President has issued under §1182(f). . . .

Moreover, plaintiffs' request for a searching inquiry into the persuasiveness of the President's justifications is inconsistent with the broad statutory text and the deference traditionally accorded the President in this sphere. "Whether the President's chosen method" of addressing perceived risks is justified from a policy perspective is "irrelevant to the scope of his [§1182(f)] authority." Sale v. Haitian Centers Council, 509 U.S. 155, 187-88 (1993). And when the President adopts "a preventive measure . . . in the context of international affairs and national security," he is "not required to conclusively link all of the pieces in the puzzle before [courts] grant weight to

[his] empirical conclusions." Holder v. Humanitarian Law Project, 561 U.S. 1, 35 (2010). . . .

IV

A

We now turn to plaintiffs' claim that the Proclamation was issued for the unconstitutional purpose of excluding Muslims. [The Court first ruled that the individual plaintiffs had standing to sue, because their allegation that the Proclamation kept them separated from relatives who seek to enter the country "is sufficiently concrete and particularized to form the basis of an Article III injury in fact."]

B

The First Amendment provides, in part, that "Congress shall make no law respecting an establishment of religion, or prohibiting the free exercise thereof." Our cases recognize that "[t]he clearest command of the Establishment Clause is that one religious denomination cannot be officially preferred over another." Larson v. Valente, 456 U.S. 228, 244 (1982). . . . Relying on Establishment Clause precedents concerning laws and policies applied domestically, plaintiffs allege that the primary purpose of the Proclamation was religious animus and that the President's stated concerns about vetting protocols and national security were but pretexts for discriminating against Muslims.

At the heart of plaintiffs' case is a series of statements by the President and his advisers casting doubt on the official objective of the Proclamation. [The Court reiterated numerous such statements, including candidate Trump's "Statement on Preventing Muslim Immigration" that called for a "total and complete shutdown of Muslims entering the United States until our country's representatives can figure out what is going on" and his claim "Islam hates us" and that the United States was "having problems with Muslims coming into the country"; President Trump's advisor's claim that after issuance of EO-1, the president referred to it as a "Muslim ban" and asked the advisor to "[p]ut a commission together" and "[s]how me the right way to do it legally"; the President's regret upon issuance of EO-2 that EO-1 had been "watered down" and expression of a desire for a "much tougher version" of his "Travel Ban"; and the President's retweets of links to three anti-Muslim propaganda videos.]

The President of the United States possesses an extraordinary power to speak to his fellow citizens and on their behalf. Our Presidents have frequently used that power to espouse the principles of religious freedom and tolerance on which this Nation was founded. . . . Yet it cannot be denied that the Federal Government and the Presidents who have carried its laws into effect have—from the Nation's earliest days—performed unevenly in living up to those inspiring words.

Plaintiffs argue that this President's words strike at fundamental standards of respect and tolerance, in violation of our constitutional tradition. But the issue before us is not whether to denounce the statements. It is instead the significance of those statements in reviewing a Presidential directive, neutral on its face, addressing a matter within the core of executive responsibility. In doing so, we must consider not only the statements of a particular President, but also the authority of the Presidency itself. . . .

C

For more than a century, this Court has recognized that the admission and exclusion of foreign nationals is a "fundamental sovereign attribute exercised by the Government's political departments largely immune from judicial control." Fiallo v. Bell, 430 U.S. 787, 792 (1977). Because decisions in these matters may implicate "relations with foreign powers," or involve "classifications defined in the light of changing political and economic circumstances," such judgments "are frequently of a character more appropriate to either the Legislature or the Executive." Mathews v. Diaz, 426 U.S. 67, 81 (1976).

Nonetheless, although foreign nationals seeking admission have no constitutional right to entry, this Court has engaged in a circumscribed judicial inquiry when the denial of a visa allegedly burdens the constitutional rights of a U.S. citizen. In Kleindienst v. Mandel, 408 U.S. 753, 756-57 (1972), the Attorney General denied admission to a Belgian journalist and self-described "revolutionary Marxist," Ernest Mandel, who had been invited to speak at a conference at Stanford University. The professors who wished to hear Mandel speak challenged that decision under the First Amendment, and we acknowledged that their constitutional "right to receive information" was implicated. But we limited our review to whether the Executive gave a "facially legitimate and bona fide" reason for its action. Given the authority of the political branches over admission, we held that "when the Executive exercises this [delegated] power negatively on the basis of a facially legitimate and bona fide reason, the courts will neither look behind the exercise of that discretion, nor test it by balancing its justification" against the asserted constitutional interests of U.S. citizens. . . .

A conventional application of *Mandel*, asking only whether the policy is facially legitimate and bona fide, would put an end to our review. But the Government has suggested that it may be appropriate here for the inquiry to extend beyond the facial neutrality of the order. For our purposes today, we assume that we may look behind the face of the Proclamation to the extent of applying rational basis review. That standard of review considers whether the entry policy is plausibly related to the Government's stated objective to protect the country and improve vetting processes. As a result, we may consider plaintiffs' extrinsic evidence, but will uphold the policy so long as it can reasonably be understood to result from a justification independent of unconstitutional grounds.

D

Given the standard of review, it should come as no surprise that the Court hardly ever strikes down a policy as illegitimate under rational basis scrutiny. On the few occasions where we have done so, a common thread has been that the laws at issue lack any purpose other than a "bare . . . desire to harm a politically unpopular group." Department of Agriculture v. Moreno, 413 U.S. 528, 534 (1973). . . .

The Proclamation does not fit this pattern. It cannot be said that it is impossible to "discern a relationship to legitimate state interests" or that the policy is "inexplicable by anything but animus." . . .

The Proclamation is expressly premised on legitimate purposes: preventing entry of nationals who cannot be adequately vetted and inducing other nations to improve their practices. The text says nothing about religion. Plaintiffs and the dissent nonetheless emphasize that five of the seven nations currently included in the Proclamation have Muslim-majority populations. Yet that fact alone does not support an inference of religious hostility, given that the policy covers just 8% of the world's Muslim population and is limited to countries that were previously designated by Congress or prior administrations as posing national security risks. . . .

The Proclamation, moreover, reflects the results of a worldwide review process undertaken by multiple Cabinet officials and their agencies. Plaintiffs seek to discredit the findings of the review, pointing to deviations from the review's baseline criteria resulting in the inclusion of Somalia and omission of Iraq. But as the Proclamation explains, in each case the determinations were justified by the distinct conditions in each country. Although Somalia generally satisfies the information-sharing component of the baseline criteria, it "stands apart . . . in the degree to which [it] lacks command and control of its territory." As for Iraq, the Secretary of Homeland Security determined that entry restrictions were not warranted in light of the close cooperative relationship between the U.S. and Iraqi Governments and the country's key role in combating terrorism in the region. It is, in any event, difficult to see how exempting one of the largest predominantly Muslim countries in the region from coverage under the Proclamation can be cited as evidence of animus toward Muslims. . . .

More fundamentally, plaintiffs and the dissent challenge the entry suspension based on their perception of its effectiveness and wisdom. They suggest that the policy is overbroad and does little to serve national security interests. But we cannot substitute our own assessment for the Executive's predictive judgments on such matters, all of which "are delicate, complex, and involve large elements of prophecy." Chicago & Southern Air Lines, Inc. v. Waterman S.S. Corp., 333 U.S. 103, 111 (1948). While we of course "do not defer to the Government's reading of the First Amendment," the Executive's evaluation of the underlying facts is entitled to appropriate weight, particularly in the context of litigation involving "sensitive and weighty interests of national security and foreign affairs." Holder v. Humanitarian Law Project, 561 U.S. 1, 33-34 (2010). . . .

V

Because plaintiffs have not shown that they are likely to succeed on the merits of their claims, we reverse the grant of the preliminary injunction as an abuse of discretion. . . .

JUSTICE KENNEDY, concurring.

I join the Court's opinion in full.

. . . Whether judicial proceedings may properly continue in this case, in light of the substantial deference that is and must be accorded to the Executive in the conduct of foreign affairs, and in light of today's decision, is a matter to be addressed in the first instance on remand. And even if further proceedings are permitted, it would be necessary to determine that any discovery and other preliminary matters would not themselves intrude on the foreign affairs power of the Executive.

In all events, it is appropriate to make this further observation. There are numerous instances in which the statements and actions of Government officials are not subject to judicial scrutiny or intervention. That does not mean those officials are free to disregard the Constitution and the rights it proclaims and protects. The oath that all officials take to adhere to the Constitution is not confined to those spheres in which the Judiciary can correct or even comment upon what those officials say or do. Indeed, the very fact that an official may have broad discretion, discretion free from judicial scrutiny, makes it all the more imperative for him or her to adhere to the Constitution and to its meaning and its promise.

The First Amendment prohibits the establishment of religion and promises the free exercise of religion. From these safeguards, and from the guarantee of freedom of speech, it follows there is freedom of belief and expression. It is an urgent necessity that officials adhere to these constitutional guarantees and mandates in all their actions, even in the sphere of foreign affairs. An anxious world must know that our Government remains committed always to the liberties the Constitution seeks to preserve and protect, so that freedom extends outward, and lasts.

JUSTICE BREYER, with whom JUSTICE KAGAN joins, dissenting.

The question before us is whether Proclamation No. 9645 is lawful. If its promulgation or content was significantly affected by religious animus against Muslims, it would violate the relevant statute or the First Amendment itself. . . . If, however, its sole *ratio decidendi* was one of national security, then it would be unlikely to violate either the statute or the Constitution. Which is it? Members of the Court principally disagree about the answer to this question, i.e., about whether or the extent to which religious animus played a significant role in the Proclamation's promulgation or content.

In my view, the Proclamation's elaborate system of exemptions and waivers can and should help us answer this question. That system provides for case-by-case consideration of persons who may qualify for visas despite the Proclamation's general ban. Those persons include lawful permanent residents, asylum seekers, refugees, students, children, and numerous others. There are likely many such persons, perhaps in the thousands. And I believe it appropriate to take account of their Proclamation-granted status when considering the Proclamation's lawfulness. The Solicitor General asked us to consider the Proclamation "as" it is "written" and "as" it is "applied," waivers and exemptions included. He warned us against considering the Proclamation's lawfulness "on the hypothetical situation that [the Proclamation] is what it isn't," while telling us that its waiver and exemption provisions mean what they say: The Proclamation does not exclude individuals from the United States "if they meet the criteria" for a waiver or exemption.

On the one hand, if the Government is applying the exemption and waiver provisions as written, then its argument for the Proclamation's lawfulness is strengthened. . . .

On the other hand, if the Government is *not* applying the system of exemptions and waivers that the Proclamation contains, then its argument for the Proclamation's lawfulness becomes significantly weaker. . . .

Unfortunately there is evidence that supports the second possibility, i.e., that the Government is not applying the Proclamation as written. [Justice Breyer drew evidence for this conclusion from *amicus* briefs. That evidence included the government's failure to issue guidance contemplated by the Proclamation for consular officers to follow when deciding whether to grant a waiver; its granting of waivers to only a "miniscule percentage" of those eligible; its issuance of very few nonimmigrant visas to citizens of covered countries; an affidavit in a lower court case by a consular official asserting that he and other officials do not, in fact, have discretion to grant waivers; and instructions allegedly issued to the U.S. Embassy in Djibouti, which processes visa applications for citizens of Yemen, to grant waivers "only in rare cases of imminent danger."]

Declarations, anecdotal evidence, facts, and numbers taken from *amicus* briefs are not judicial factfindings. The Government has not had an opportunity to respond, and a court has not had an opportunity to decide. But, given the importance of the decision in this case, the need for assurance that the Proclamation does not rest upon a "Muslim ban," and the assistance in deciding the issue that answers to the "exemption and waiver" questions may provide, I would send this case back to the District Court for further proceedings. And, I would leave the injunction in effect while the matter is litigated. Regardless, the Court's decision today leaves the District Court free to explore these issues on remand.

If this Court must decide the question without this further litigation, I would, on balance, find the evidence of antireligious bias, including statements on a website taken down only after the President issued the two executive orders preceding the Proclamation, along with the other statements also set forth in Justice Sotomayor's opinion, a sufficient basis to set the Proclamation aside. And for these reasons, I respectfully dissent.

JUSTICE SOTOMAYOR, with whom JUSTICE GINSBURG joins, dissenting. . . .

Although the majority briefly recounts a few of the statements and background events that form the basis of plaintiffs' constitutional challenge, that highly abridged account does not tell even half of the story. The full record paints a far more harrowing picture, from which a reasonable observer would readily conclude that the Proclamation was motivated by hostility and animus toward the Muslim faith. [Justice Sotomayor quotes from numerous additional statements by President Trump and associates, dating from December 7, 2015 to November 29, 2017, that she says support the plaintiffs' claim that the Proclamation was motivated by anti-Muslim hostility.]

. . . Taking all the relevant evidence together, a reasonable observer would conclude that the Proclamation was driven primarily by anti-Muslim animus, rather than by the Government's asserted national-security justifications. . . .

Moreover, despite several opportunities to do so, President Trump has never disavowed any of his prior statements about Islam. Instead, he has continued to make remarks that a reasonable observer would view as an unrelenting attack on the Muslim religion and its followers. Given President Trump's failure to correct the reasonable perception of his apparent hostility toward the Islamic faith, it is unsurprising that the President's lawyers have, at every step in the lower courts, failed in their attempts to launder the Proclamation of its discriminatory taint. . . .

Ultimately, what began as a policy explicitly "calling for a total and complete shutdown of Muslims entering the United States" has since morphed into a "Proclamation" putatively based on national-security concerns. But this new window dressing cannot conceal an unassailable fact: the words of the President and his advisers create the strong perception that the Proclamation is contaminated by impermissible discriminatory animus against Islam and its followers.

Rather than defend the President's problematic statements, the Government urges this Court to set them aside and defer to the President on issues related to immigration and national security. The majority accepts that invitation and incorrectly applies a watered-down legal standard in an effort to short circuit plaintiffs' Establishment Clause claim. . . .

. . . [T]he Court, without explanation or precedential support, limits its review of the Proclamation to rational-basis scrutiny. That approach is perplexing, given that in other Establishment Clause cases, including those involving claims of religious animus or discrimination, this Court has applied a more stringent standard of review. . . .

But even under rational-basis review, the Proclamation must fall. . . .

The majority insists that the Proclamation furthers two interrelated national-security interests: "preventing entry of nationals who cannot be adequately vetted and inducing other nations to improve their practices." But the Court offers insufficient support for its view "that the entry suspension has a legitimate grounding in [those] national security concerns, quite apart from any religious hostility." Indeed, even a cursory review of the Government's asserted national-security rationale reveals that the Proclamation is nothing more than a " 'religious gerrymander.' "

The majority first emphasizes that the Proclamation "says nothing about religion." Even so, the Proclamation, just like its predecessors, overwhelmingly targets Muslim-majority nations. Given the record here, including all the President's statements linking the Proclamation to his apparent hostility toward Muslims, it is of no moment that the Proclamation also includes minor restrictions on two non-Muslim majority countries, North Korea and Venezuela, or that the Government has removed a few Muslim-majority countries from the list of covered countries since EO-1 was issued. Consideration of the entire record supports the conclusion that the inclusion of North Korea and Venezuela, and the removal of other countries, simply reflect subtle efforts to start "talking territory instead of Muslim," precisely so the Executive Branch could evade criticism or legal consequences for the Proclamation's otherwise clear targeting of Muslims. The Proclamation's effect on North Korea and Venezuela, for example, is insubstantial, if not entirely symbolic. . . .

The majority next contends that the Proclamation "reflects the results of a worldwide review process undertaken by multiple Cabinet officials." . . . [The] worldwide review does little to break the clear connection between the Proclamation and the President's anti-Muslim statements. . . . The President campaigned on a promise to implement a "total and complete shutdown of Muslims" entering the country, translated that campaign promise into a concrete policy, and made several statements linking that policy (in its various forms) to anti-Muslim animus. . . .

Beyond that, Congress has already addressed the national-security concerns supposedly undergirding the Proclamation through an "extensive and complex" framework governing "immigration and alien status." Arizona v. United States, 567 U.S. 387, 395 (2012). The Immigration and Nationality Act sets forth, in painstaking detail, a reticulated scheme regulating the admission of individuals to the United States. . . . Generally, admission to the United States requires a valid visa or other travel document. To obtain a visa, an applicant must produce "certified cop[ies]" of documents proving her identity, background, and criminal history. An applicant also must undergo an in-person interview with a State Department consular officer. . . .

In addition to vetting rigorously any individuals seeking admission to the United States, the Government also rigorously vets the information-sharing and identity-management systems of other countries, as evidenced by the Visa Waiver Program, which permits certain nationals from a select group of countries to skip the ordinary visa-application process. To determine which countries are eligible for the Visa Waiver Program, the Government considers whether they can satisfy numerous criteria—e.g., using electronic, fraud-resistant passports, 24-hour reporting of lost or stolen passports, and not providing a safe haven for terrorists. The Secretary of Homeland Security, in consultation with the Secretary of State, also must determine that a country's inclusion in the program will not compromise "the law enforcement and security interests of the United States." Eligibility for the program is reassessed on an annual basis. As a result of a recent review, for example, the Executive decided in 2016 to remove from the program dual nationals of Iraq, Syria, Iran, and Sudan.

Put simply, Congress has already erected a statutory scheme that fulfills the putative national-security interests the Government now puts forth to justify the Proclamation. Tellingly, the Government remains wholly unable to articulate any credible national-security interest that would go unaddressed by the current statutory scheme absent the Proclamation. . . .

Moreover, the Proclamation purports to mitigate national-security risks by excluding nationals of countries that provide insufficient information to vet their nationals. Yet, as plaintiffs explain, the Proclamation broadly denies immigrant visas to all nationals of those countries, including those whose admission would likely not implicate these information deficiencies (e.g., infants, or nationals of countries included in the Proclamation who are long-term residents of and traveling from a country not covered by the Proclamation). In addition, the Proclamation permits certain nationals from the countries named in the Proclamation to obtain nonimmigrant visas, which undermines the Government's assertion that it does not already have the capacity and sufficient information to vet these individuals adequately.

Equally unavailing is the majority's reliance on the Proclamation's waiver program. As several *amici* thoroughly explain, there is reason to suspect that the Proclamation's waiver program is nothing more than a sham. The remote possibility of obtaining a waiver pursuant to an ad hoc, discretionary, and seemingly arbitrary process scarcely demonstrates that the Proclamation is rooted in a genuine concern for national security.

In sum, none of the features of the Proclamation highlighted by the majority supports the Government's claim that the Proclamation is genuinely and primarily rooted in a legitimate national-security interest. What the unrebutted evidence actually shows is that a reasonable observer would conclude, quite easily, that the primary purpose and function of the Proclamation is to disfavor Islam by banning Muslims from entering our country. . . .

Our Constitution demands, and our country deserves, a Judiciary willing to hold the coordinate branches to account when they defy our most sacred legal commitments. Because the Court's decision today has failed in that respect, with profound regret, I dissent.

Notes and Questions

1. It is common for courts to give deference to the views of the Executive Branch in cases perceived as implicating foreign affairs. *See, e.g.,* Jama v. Immigration & Customs Enforcement, 543 U.S. 335, 348 (2005) (referring to the Court's "customary policy of deference to the President in matters of foreign affairs"). Why is this so? Under what circumstances should courts *not* give deference? Should courts be more deferential to the Executive Branch's factual determinations than to its legal determinations? What should the courts do if the Executive's views conflict with those of Congress?

2. "Deference" can take many forms, ranging from respectful consideration to conclusive weight. On issues viewed as falling within the President's exclusive foreign affairs authority, such as the recognition of foreign governments, courts give absolute deference. This deference can be seen as an application of the political question doctrine: The issue is treated as non-justiciable once decided by the Executive. *See, e.g.,* Guaranty Trust Co. v. United States, 304 U.S. 126, 137-38 (1938) ("What government is to be regarded here as representative of a foreign sovereign state is a political rather than a judicial question, and is to be determined by the political department of the government."). As discussed further in Chapter 7, for several decades prior to Congress's enactment of the Foreign Sovereign Immunities Act (FSIA) in 1976, courts gave absolute deference to the Executive Branch about whether to accord foreign governments immunity from suit. *See, e.g.,* Republic of Mexico v. Hoffman, 324 U.S. 30, 35 (1935) ("It is therefore not for the courts to deny an immunity which our government has seen fit to allow, or to allow an immunity on new grounds which the government has not seen fit to recognize."). Chapter 7 also discusses how, even today, courts generally give absolute deference to the views of the Executive Branch about whether to grant immunity to foreign heads of state, an issue not addressed by the FSIA. *See, e.g.,* Ye v. Zemin, 383 F.3d 620, 627 (7th Cir. 2004) ("A court is ill-prepared to assess these implications and resolve the competing concerns the Executive Branch is faced with in determining whether to immunize a head of state.").

3. When Congress delegates discretionary authority to the Executive Branch concerning foreign affairs, courts typically give substantial deference to the Executive Branch concerning how to exercise that authority. This deference was evident in Part III of the majority's opinion in Trump v. Hawaii. What is the rationale for this deference? How, if at all, does it relate to the observation in *Curtiss-Wright* that legislative delegations of authority to the president in the foreign affairs field often coincide with independent presidential powers? When Congress trusts the President to make certain determinations, should courts also do so?

4. Although courts will not defer to the Executive Branch concerning the meaning of the Constitution, some constitutional standards themselves reflect a degree of deference to governmental decisionmaking. The "rational basis" review that the Court applied in Trump v. Hawaii is an example: In applying this standard, the Court required only that the government's action be plausibly related to a constitutional purpose, and it said that it could not "substitute our own assessment for the Executive's predictive judgments on such matters."

Was the Court in Trump v. Hawaii too deferential to the President, in light of the process that he had followed in issuing the first executive order and the statements that he and his associates had made? When, if ever, should a court look behind a national security rationale offered by a President in support of authorized action related to immigration? The Court relied on many factors related to the third executive order—the inclusion of non-Muslim majority countries, the extensive country specific findings, and the like—that were not present with respect to the first two orders. Would the first two orders have survived scrutiny under the Court's rationale? What do you think of Justice Sotomayor's point that despite the "new window dressing" in support of the third order, it appears to be "contaminated by impermissible discriminatory animus against Islam and its followers"? Would Justice Sotomayor's position mean that President Trump would forever be disabled from issuing immigration orders related to persons from Muslim countries?

5. Despite holding in favor of the President, the Court's opinion in Trump v. Hawaii is noteworthy for its effort to distance itself from President Trump's statements—for example, when it observes that other presidents have "espouse[d] the principles of religious freedom and tolerance on which this Nation was founded," even while acknowledging that unnamed presidents have "performed unevenly in living up to those inspiring words." Justice Kennedy's concurrence similarly seems to convey an implied critique of the President, including in the observation that "[i]t is an urgent necessity that officials adhere to these constitutional guarantees and mandates in all their actions, even in the sphere of foreign affairs." Nevertheless, the decision is very deferential to presidential authority. What is the significance in this regard of the Court's observation that "we must consider not only the statements of a particular President, but also the authority of the presidency itself"?

6. The Supreme Court has stated that, although not conclusive, the views of the Executive Branch concerning the meaning of a treaty are entitled to "great weight." *See, e.g.,* Medellin v. Texas, 552 U.S. 491, 513 (2008); Sumitomo Shoji America, Inc. v. Avagliano, 457 U.S. 176, 184-85 (1982); Kolovrat v. Oregon, 366 U.S. 187, 194 (1961). At times, the Court has used somewhat different terms to describe this deference, but it is not clear that the Court has intended these terms to reflect a different standard. *See, e.g.,* El Al Israel Airlines v. Tsui Yuan Tseng, 525 U.S. 155, 168 (1999) ("[r]espect"); Factor v. Laubenheimer, 290 U.S. 276, 295 (1933) ("of weight"). Deference to the Executive may have a significant effect on the outcome of judicial decisions involving treaties. After studying numerous treaty cases, Professor Bederman observed that judicial deference to the Executive Branch may be "the single best predictor of interpretive outcomes in American treaty cases." David J. Bederman, *Revivalist Canons and Treaty Interpretation,* 41 UCLA L. Rev. 953 (1994). On occasion, however, the Court has seemed not to accord the Executive Branch this deference. *See, e.g.,* Hamdan v. Rumsfeld, 548 U.S. 557, 630-31 (2006) (not accepting the Executive Branch's interpretation of a provision in the Geneva Conventions).

What are the justifications for treaty interpretation deference? One court explained the justifications as follows:

> Because the Executive Branch is involved directly in negotiating treaties, it is well situated to assist the court in determining what the parties intended when they agreed on a particular provision. Moreover, treaties normally carry significant foreign policy implications, matters peculiarly within the purview of the political branches of our government. A court should minimize intrusion in the conduct of foreign affairs by adopting the interpretation suggested by the Executive Branch whenever it can fairly do so. Finally, the Executive Branch generally has administrative authority over the implementation of international agreements. As in the case of domestic legislation, a court should generally give great weight to the interpretations of agencies charged with implementation of treaties because such agencies may possess significant expertise in the relevant subject matter.

Coplin v. United States, 6 Cl. Ct. 115 (1984) (Kozinski, C.J.), *rev'd on other grounds,* 761 F.2d 688 (Fed. Cir. 1985). Is this account persuasive? Do these justifications also apply to Executive Branch interpretations of customary international law? *See* Restatement (Third) of the Foreign Relations Law of the United States, §112, cmt. c (1987) ("Courts give particular weight to the position taken by the United States Government on questions of international law because it is deemed desirable that so far as possible the United States speak with one voice on such matters. The views of the United States Government, moreover, are also state practice, creating or modifying international law.").

7. The Supreme Court returned to the issue of deference to Executive Branch treaty interpretations in Abbott v. Abbott, 560 U.S. 1 (2010). The main treaty issue in the case was whether a Chilean father's "*ne exeat*" right to consent before his child's mother could take the child out of Chile to the United States constituted a "right of custody" under the Hague Convention on the Civil Aspects of International Child Abduction that triggered the treaty's remedial provisions. In ruling that it was, the majority opinion stated:

> This Court's conclusion that Mr. Abbott possesses a right of custody under the Convention is supported and informed by the State Department's view on the issue. The United States has endorsed the view that *ne exeat* rights are rights of custody. In its brief before this Court the United States advises that "the Department of State, whose Office of Children's Issues serves as the Central Authority for the United States under the Convention, has long understood the Convention as including *ne exeat* rights among the protected 'rights of custody.'" It is well settled that the Executive Branch's interpretation of a treaty "is entitled to great weight." There is no reason to doubt that this well-established canon of deference is appropriate here. The Executive is well informed concerning the diplomatic consequences resulting from this Court's interpretation of "rights of custody," including the likely reaction of other contracting states and the impact on the State Department's ability to reclaim children abducted from this country.

In dissent, Justice Stevens (joined by Justices Thomas and Breyer) stated:

> Without discussing precisely why, we have afforded "great weight" to "the meaning given [treaties] by the departments of government particularly charged with their negotiation and enforcement." We have awarded "great weight" to the views of a particular government department even when the views expressed by the department are newly memorialized, and even when the views appear contrary to those expressed by the department at the time of the treaty's signing and negotiation. In this case, it appears that both are true: The Department of State's position, which supports the Court's conclusion, is newly memorialized, and is possibly inconsistent with the Department's earlier position.
>
> Putting aside any concerns arising from the fact that the Department's views are newly memorialized and changing, I would not in this case abdicate our responsibility to interpret the Convention's language. This does not seem to be a matter in which deference to the Executive on matters of foreign policy would avoid international conflict; the State Department has made no such argument. Nor is this a case in which the Executive's understanding of the treaty's drafting history is particularly rich or illuminating. Finally, and significantly, the State Department, as the Central Authority for administering the Convention in the United States, has failed to disclose to the Court whether it has facilitated the return of children to America when the shoe is on the other foot. Thus, we have no informed basis to assess the Executive's post-ratification conduct, or the conduct of other signatories, to aid us in understanding the accepted meaning of potentially ambiguous terms.
>
> Instead, the Department offers us little more than its own reading of the treaty's text. Its view is informed by no unique vantage it has, whether as the entity responsible for enforcing the Convention in this country or as a participating drafter. The Court's perfunctory, one-paragraph treatment of the Department's judgment of this matter only underscores this point. I see no reason, therefore, to replace our understanding of the Convention's text with that of the Executive Branch.

Should courts be more discriminating in the deference they give to Executive Branch treaty interpretations, as Justice Stevens suggests? (Chapter 5 of this casebook contains additional discussion of issues relating to treaty interpretation.)

8. Deference to the Executive Branch on questions of foreign relations law can be analogized to the deference that courts sometimes give to administrative agencies concerning the meaning of the federal statutes they administer. This administrative agency deference is often referred to as "*Chevron* deference," after the Supreme Court's decision in Chevron, U.S.A., Inc. v. Natural Resources Defense Council, Inc., 467 U.S. 837 (1984). Under *Chevron* deference, courts first examine whether Congress has clearly spoken to the issue. If so, courts will simply apply the statute and not defer to the agency's interpretation. If the statute is ambiguous or does not address the issue, however, courts will defer to the agency's interpretation, unless it is unreasonable. This deference is based on the theory that, in charging the administrative agency with administering the statute, Congress may have delegated authority to the agency to fill in gaps and resolve ambiguities in the statute. The Supreme Court has held that this deference applies even to an agency's interpretation of the scope of its own jurisdiction to regulate. *See* City of Arlington v. FCC, 569 U.S. 290 (2013). For a discussion of the similarities and differences between foreign affairs deference and *Chevron* deference, see Curtis A. Bradley, Chevron *Deference and Foreign Affairs,* 86 Va. L. Rev. 649 (2000). *See also* Kevin M. Stack, *The Statutory President,* 90 Iowa L. Rev. 539 (2005); Oren Eisner, Note, *Extending* Chevron *Deference to Presidential Interpretations of Ambiguities in Foreign Affairs and National Security Statutes Delegating Lawmaking Power to the President,* 86 Cornell L. Rev. 411 (2001).

There is a lesser form of deference in administrative law known as "*Skidmore* deference" after a pre-*Chevron* decision, Skidmore v. Swift & Co., 323 U.S. 134 (1944). Under *Skidmore* deference, "[t]he weight [accorded to an administrative] judgment in a particular case will depend upon the thoroughness evident in its consideration, the validity of its reasoning, its consistency with earlier and later pronouncements, and all those factors which give it power to persuade, if lacking power to control." *Id.* at 140. For an argument that, for treaty interpretation, *Skidmore* deference is preferable to *Chevron* deference, see Evan Criddle, Scholarship Comment, Chevron *Deference and Treaty Interpretation,* 112 Yale L.J. 1927 (2003).

9. Sometimes, *Chevron* deference will be directly applicable in the foreign affairs area: When an Executive Branch agency is interpreting a foreign affairs-related statute that it is charged with administering, it may be entitled to *Chevron* deference. Should the foreign affairs nature of the statute be considered in the deference analysis in these situations? One possibility is that deference is heightened or triggered more easily in this context, because the Executive Branch will be able to claim both *Chevron* deference and general foreign affairs deference. Perhaps this is what the Supreme Court had in mind when it stated, in connection with an Executive Branch interpretation of an immigration statute, that "judicial deference to the Executive Branch [under *Chevron*] is especially appropriate in the immigration context where officials 'exercise especially sensitive political functions that implicate questions of foreign relations.'" INS v. Aguirre-Aguirre, 526 U.S. 415, 425 (1999). *See also* Abourezk v. Reagan, 785 F.2d 1043, 1063 (D.C. Cir. 1986) (Bork, J., dissenting) ("This principle of [*Chevron*] deference applies with special force where the subject of that analysis is a delegation to the Executive of authority to make and implement decisions relating to the conduct of foreign affairs.").

10. To receive deference, what form must the Executive Branch's position take? Must the position be formulated prior to the litigation? Is an *amicus curiae* brief sufficient? What if the Executive Branch's position is inconsistent with an earlier Executive Branch position? Under *Chevron,* Executive Branch litigating positions are not entitled to deference if they are "wholly unsupported by regulations, rulings, or administrative practice." Bowen v. Georgetown Univ. Hosp., 488 U.S. 204, 212 (1988); *accord* Smiley v. Citibank, 517 U.S. 735, 741 (1996). Should a similar limitation apply to foreign affairs deference? Note that, even under *Chevron*, the Executive Branch may receive deference notwithstanding a change in position on an issue. *See Smiley*, 417 U.S. at 742. For a decision declining to defer to the Executive Branch's construction of certain provisions in the Geneva Conventions because the construction was inconsistent with historical practices of the Executive Branch, see American Civil Liberties Union v. Department of Defense, 543 F.3d 59, 78-91 (2d Cir. 2008).

11. For academic discussions of foreign affairs deference, see, for example, Robert M. Chesney, *Disaggregating Deference:* Hamdan, *the Judicial Power, and Executive Treaty Interpretations*, 92 Iowa L. Rev. 1723 (2007); Robert M. Chesney, *National Security Fact Deference*, 95 Va. L. Rev. 1361 (2009); Robert Knowles, *American Hegemony and the Foreign Affairs Constitution*, 41 Ariz. St. L.J. 87 (2009); Julian Ku & John C. Yoo, Hamdan v. Rumsfeld: *The Functional Case for Foreign Affairs Deference to the Executive Branch*, 23 Const. Comm. 179 (2006); and Eric A. Posner & Cass R. Sunstein, *Chevronizing Foreign Relations Law*, 116 Yale L.J. 1170 (2007).

For academic commentary arguing that courts should play a more active and independent role in foreign relations cases, see, for example, Thomas M. Franck, Political Questions/Judicial Answers: Does the Rule of Law Apply to Foreign Affairs? (1992); K. Lee Boyd, *Universal Jurisdiction and Structural Reasonableness*, 40 Tex. Int'l L.J. 1 (2004); and Jonathan I. Charney, *Judicial Deference in Foreign Relations*, 83 Am. J. Int'l L. 805 (1989). For commentary that is more skeptical about judicial involvement in foreign relations cases, see, for example, John Yoo, *Federal Courts as Weapons of Foreign Policy: The Case of the Helms-Burton Act*, 20 Hastings Int'l & Comp. L. Rev. 747 (1997). *Cf.* Louis Henkin, *The Foreign Affairs Power of the Federal Courts:* Sabbatino, 64 Colum. L. Rev. 805, 826 (1964) ("Inevitably, the courts tend to establish rules of more-or-less general applicability, which can only relate to the needs of foreign policy grossly, and on the basis of assumptions and generalizations hardly consonant with flexibility, currentness, and consistency.").

For an empirical assessment that finds that overall Supreme Court deference to the Executive Branch (not just in the foreign affairs area) has gone down in recent decades, see Lee Epstein & Eric A. Posner, *The Decline of Supreme Court Deference to the President*, 166 U. Pa. L. Rev. 829 (2018). The authors identify two likely explanations for this shift: "The first is that the Court has become more aggressive over the last three decades. As its institutional self-confidence grew, it became increasingly willing to defy the Executive as well as Congress. The second is that a specialized Supreme Court bar has emerged, nullifying the advantage to the President formerly conferred by the [Solicitor General]."

E. ACT OF STATE DOCTRINE

We now turn to the act of state doctrine, a common law (that is, judicially developed) doctrine that limits the circumstances under which U.S. courts will examine the validity of foreign government acts. The act of state doctrine has its roots in early decisions granting foreign governments and their leaders immunity from suit. *See, e.g.*, The Schooner Exchange v. McFaddon, 11 U.S. (7 Cranch) 116 (1812); Hatch v. Baez, 7 Hun. 596 (N.Y. Sup. Ct. 1876). The first U.S. Supreme Court decision that clearly relied on the act of state doctrine was Underhill v. Hernandez, 168 U.S. 250 (1897). In that case, Underhill, an American citizen, had been living in Bolivar, Venezuela, where he had constructed a waterworks system for the city and was carrying on a machinery repair business. A revolutionary army seized control of the city and, for a time, the commander of the army refused to let Underhill leave, in an effort to coerce Underhill to operate the waterworks system and continue his repair business. Underhill eventually was allowed to leave, and he subsequently sued the commander in a U.S. federal court, seeking damages for the detention. In the meantime, the U.S. government recognized the revolutionary government as the legitimate government of Venezuela. In affirming a dismissal of Underhill's suit, the Supreme Court stated:

> Every sovereign State is bound to respect the independence of every other sovereign State, and the courts of one country will not sit in judgment on the acts of the government of another done within its own territory. Redress of grievances by reason of such acts must be obtained through the means open to be availed of by sovereign powers as between themselves.

The Supreme Court reaffirmed this doctrine in a number of decisions in the early 1900s. *See, e.g.*, American Banana Co. v. United Fruit Co., 213 U.S. 347, 357-58 (1909) (holding that actions of Costa Rican government in allegedly evicting company from property in Costa Rica could not be challenged because "a seizure by a state is not a thing that can be complained of elsewhere in the courts"); Oetjen v. Central Leather Co., 246 U.S. 297, 303-04 (1918) (explaining that the act of state doctrine "rests at last upon the highest considerations of international comity and expediency," and holding that an expropriation by the Mexican government "is not subject to reexamination and modification by the courts of this country"); Ricaud v. American Metal Co., 246 U.S. 304, 309-10 (1918) (stating that Mexico's expropriation of U.S. citizen's property could not be questioned in a U.S. court because "the act within its own boundaries of one sovereign State cannot become the subject of reexamination and modification in the courts of another").

The Supreme Court's most important decision concerning the act of state doctrine is Banco Nacional de Cuba v. Sabbatino, excerpted below. In reading *Sabbatino*, it is important to keep in mind the historical context. The decision was issued in 1964, during the height of the Cold War. The relations between the United States and Cuba were strained. Fidel Castro's Communist government had assumed power in Cuba in 1959, and, shortly thereafter, proceeded to expropriate U.S. property. The United States supported the attempted invasion of Cuba at the Bay of Pigs in 1961, and it imposed a trade embargo against Cuba in 1962. The Cuban missile crisis also occurred in 1962, during which the United States Navy blocked Soviet ships from reaching Cuba in order to compel the Soviet Union to remove nuclear missiles that it had placed there. This was also a time during which the customary international law rules of state responsibility, especially rules relating to the expropriation of foreign citizen property, were being challenged by Communist and newly independent developing countries.

Banco Nacional de Cuba v. Sabbatino

376 U.S. 398 (1964)

[Farr Whitlock, a U.S. commodities broker, contracted to purchase sugar from a subsidiary of a Cuban company, C.A.V. The sugar was to be shipped to Farr Whitlock's customer in Morocco, and Farr was to pay for it in New York upon presentation of the shipping documents and a sight draft (an instrument that it could present for payment by its customer's bank upon tendering the bill of lading to the customer).

The stock in C.A.V. was owned principally by U.S. residents. In response to a reduction in the United States' sugar quota for Cuba (by President Eisenhower, exercising power delegated to him from Congress), the Cuban government adopted a law allowing it to expropriate property in which U.S. nationals had an interest. The government subsequently expropriated C.A.V.'s property.

To obtain the release of the shipment of C.A.V.'s seized sugar (and have it shipped to its customer in Morocco), Farr Whitlock entered into a payment agreement with a Cuban government bank (Banco Exterior). However, after having the sugar shipped to its customer, receiving the shipping documents from the Cuban entity, and tendering them to the customer and receiving payment from the customer, Farr Whitlock received a claim from C.A.V. for the proceeds of the sale of the sugar. It also received a promise from C.A.V. to indemnify it for any losses as long as it did not turn the money over to Cuba.

A New York court then appointed Sabbatino as a Temporary Receiver of C.A.V.'s New York assets, and enjoined Farr Whitlock from disposing of the proceeds from its sale of the sugar. Following this, pursuant to court order, Farr Whitlock turned the proceeds over to Sabbatino. An assignee of Banco Exterior — Banco Nacional de Cuba — then brought suit against Sabbatino in the federal district court for the Southern District of New York, seeking to recover on the contract/bills of lading. Banco Nacional alleged that Farr Whitlock had unlawfully converted its property. As a defense, Farr Whitlock claimed that the expropriation violated international law and that title to the sugar therefore had not validly passed to Cuba. Both the district court and court of appeals agreed with this argument, declining to apply the act of state doctrine.]

MR. JUSTICE HARLAN delivered the opinion of the Court. . . .

IV

. . . [The Court discusses *Underhill* and the subsequent act of state decisions, including *Oetjen* and *Ricaud*, and notes that "[n]one of this Court's subsequent cases in which the act of state doctrine was directly or peripherally involved manifest any retreat from *Underhill*."]

In deciding the present case the Court of Appeals relied in part upon an exception to the unqualified teachings of *Underhill, Oetjen,* and *Ricaud* which that court had earlier indicated. In Bernstein v. Van Heyghen Freres Societe Anonyme, 163 F.2d 246, suit was brought to recover from an assignee property allegedly taken, in effect, by the Nazi Government because plaintiff was Jewish. Recognizing the odious nature of this act of state, the court, through Judge Learned Hand, nonetheless refused to consider it invalid on that ground. Rather, it looked to see if the Executive had acted in any manner that would indicate that United States Courts should refuse to give effect to such a foreign decree. Finding no such evidence, the court sustained dismissal of the complaint. In a later case involving similar facts the same court again assumed examination of the German acts improper, Bernstein v. N. V. Nederlandsche-Amerikaansche Stoomvaart-Maatschappij, 173 F.2d 71, but, quite evidently following the implications of Judge Hand's opinion in the earlier case, amended its mandate to permit evidence of alleged invalidity, 210 F.2d 375, subsequent to receipt by plaintiff's attorney of a letter from the Acting Legal Adviser to the State Department written for the purpose of relieving the court from any constraint upon the exercise of its jurisdiction to pass on that question.

This Court has never had occasion to pass upon the so-called *Bernstein* exception, nor need it do so now. For whatever ambiguity may be thought to exist in the two letters from State Department officials on which the Court of Appeals relied,[19] is now removed by the position which the Executive has taken in this Court on the act of state claim; respondents do not indeed contest the view that these letters were intended to reflect no more than the Department's then wish not to make any statement bearing on this litigation.

The outcome of this case, therefore, turns upon whether any of the contentions urged by respondents against the application of the act of state doctrine in the premises is acceptable: (1) that the doctrine does not apply to acts of state which violate international law, as is claimed to be the case here; (2) that the doctrine is inapplicable unless the Executive specifically interposes it in a particular case; and (3) that, in any event, the doctrine may not be invoked by a foreign government plaintiff in our courts.

V

Preliminarily, we discuss the foundations on which we deem the act of state doctrine to rest, and more particularly the question of whether state or federal law governs its application in a federal diversity case.[20]

We do not believe that this doctrine is compelled either by the inherent nature of sovereign authority, as some of the earlier decisions seem to imply, or by some principle of international law. If a transaction takes place in one jurisdiction and the forum is in another, the forum does not by dismissing an action or by applying its own law purport to divest the first jurisdiction of its territorial sovereignty; it merely declines to adjudicate or makes applicable its own law to parties or property

---

19. Abram Chayes, the Legal Adviser to the State Department, wrote on October 18, 1961, in answer to an inquiry regarding the position of the Department by Mr. John Laylin, attorney for *amici*:

> The Department of State has not, in the *Bahia de Nipe* case or elsewhere, done anything inconsistent with the position taken on the Cuban nationalizations by Secretary Herter. Whether or not these nationalizations will in the future be given effect in the United States is, of course, for the courts to determine. Since the *Sabbatino* case and other similar cases are at present before the courts, any comments on this question by the Department of State would be out of place at this time. As you yourself point out, statements by the executive branch are highly susceptible of misconstruction.

A letter dated November 14, 1961, from George Ball, Under Secretary for Economic Affairs, responded to a similar inquiry by the same attorney:

> I have carefully considered your letter and have discussed it with the Legal Adviser. Our conclusion, in which the Secretary concurs, is that the Department should not comment on matters pending before the courts.

20. Although the complaint in this case alleged both diversity and federal question jurisdiction, the Court of Appeals reached jurisdiction only on the former ground. We need not decide, for reasons appearing hereafter, whether federal question jurisdiction also existed.

before it. The refusal of one country to enforce the penal laws of another is a typical example of an instance when a court will not entertain a cause of action arising in another jurisdiction. While historic notions of sovereign authority do bear upon the wisdom of employing the act of state doctrine, they do not dictate its existence.

That international law does not require application of the doctrine is evidenced by the practice of nations. Most of the countries rendering decisions on the subject fail to follow the rule rigidly. No international arbitral or judicial decision discovered suggests that international law prescribes recognition of sovereign acts of foreign governments, and apparently no claim has ever been raised before an international tribunal that failure to apply the act of state doctrine constitutes a breach of international obligation. If international law does not prescribe use of the doctrine, neither does it forbid application of the rule even if it is claimed that the act of state in question violated international law. The traditional view of international law is that it establishes substantive principles for determining whether one country has wronged another. Because of its peculiar nation-to-nation character the usual method for an individual to seek relief is to exhaust local remedies and then repair to the executive authorities of his own state to persuade them to champion his claim in diplomacy or before an international tribunal. Although it is, of course, true that United States courts apply international law as a part of our own in appropriate circumstances, Ware v. Hylton, 3 Dall. 199, 281; The Nereide, 9 Cranch 388, 423; The Paquete Habana, 175 U.S. 677, 700, the public law of nations can hardly dictate to a country which is in theory wronged how to treat that wrong within its domestic borders.

Despite the broad statement in *Oetjen* that "The conduct of the foreign relations of our Government is committed by the Constitution to the Executive and Legislative . . . Departments," it cannot of course be thought that "every case or controversy which touches foreign relations lies beyond judicial cognizance." Baker v. Carr, 369 U.S. 186, 211. The text of the Constitution does not require the act of state doctrine; it does not irrevocably remove from the judiciary the capacity to review the validity of foreign acts of state.

The act of state doctrine does, however, have "constitutional" underpinnings. It arises out of the basic relationships between branches of government in a system of separation of powers. It concerns the competency of dissimilar institutions to make and implement particular kinds of decisions in the area of international relations. The doctrine as formulated in past decisions expresses the strong sense of the Judicial Branch that its engagement in the task of passing on the validity of foreign acts of state may hinder rather than further this country's pursuit of goals both for itself and for the community of nations as a whole in the international sphere. Many commentators disagree with this view; they have striven by means of distinguishing and limiting past decisions and by advancing various considerations of policy to stimulate a narrowing of the apparent scope of the rule. Whatever considerations are thought to predominate, it is plain that the problems involved are uniquely federal in nature. If federal authority, in this instance this Court, orders the field of judicial competence in this area for the federal courts, and the state courts are left free to formulate their own rules, the purposes behind the doctrine could be as effectively undermined as if there had been no federal pronouncement on the subject.

We could perhaps in this diversity action avoid the question of deciding whether federal or state law is applicable to this aspect of the litigation. New York has enunciated the act of state doctrine in terms that echo those of federal decisions decided during the reign of Swift v. Tyson, 16 Pet. 1. . . . Thus our conclusions might well be the same whether we dealt with this problem as one of state law, see Erie R. Co. v. Tompkins, 304 U.S. 64; Klaxon Co. v. Stentor Elec. Mfg. Co., 313 U.S. 487; . . . or federal law.

However, we are constrained to make it clear that an issue concerned with a basic choice regarding the competence and function of the Judiciary and the National Executive in ordering our relationships with other members of the international community must be treated exclusively as an aspect of federal law.[23] It seems fair to assume that the Court did not have rules like the act of state doctrine in mind when it decided Erie R. Co. v. Tompkins. Soon thereafter, Professor Philip C. Jessup, now a judge of the International Court of Justice, recognized the potential dangers were *Erie* extended to legal problems affecting international relations.[24] He cautioned that rules of international law should not be left to divergent and perhaps parochial state interpretations. His basic rationale is equally applicable to the act of state doctrine.

The Court in the pre-*Erie* act of state cases, although not burdened by the problem of the source of applicable law, used language sufficiently strong and broad-sweeping to suggest that state courts were not left free to develop their own doctrines (as they would have been had this Court merely been interpreting common law under Swift v. Tyson, *supra*). The Court of Appeals in the first *Bernstein* case, *supra,* a diversity suit, plainly considered the decisions of this Court, despite the intervention of *Erie,* to be controlling in regard to the act of state question, at the same time indicating that New York law governed other aspects of the case. We are not without other precedent for a determination that federal law governs; there are enclaves of federal judge-made law which bind the States. A national body of federal-court-built law has been held to have been contemplated by §301 of the Labor Management Relations Act, Textile Workers v. Lincoln Mills, 353 U.S. 448. Principles formulated by federal judicial law have been thought by this Court to be necessary to protect uniquely federal interests, D'Oench, Duhme & Co. v. Federal Deposit Ins. Corp., 315 U.S. 447; Clearfield Trust Co. v. United States, 318 U.S. 363. Of course the federal interest guarded in all these cases is one the ultimate statement of which is derived from a federal statute. Perhaps more directly in point are the bodies of law applied between States over boundaries and in regard to the apportionment of interstate waters.

. . . We conclude that the scope of the act of state doctrine must be determined according to federal law.[25]

VI

If the act of state doctrine is a principle of decision binding on federal and state courts alike but compelled by neither international law nor the Constitution, its continuing vitality depends on its capacity to reflect the proper distribution of functions between the judicial and political branches of the Government on matters bearing upon foreign affairs. It should be apparent that the greater the degree of codification or consensus concerning a particular area of international law, the

---

23. At least this is true when the Court limits the scope of judicial inquiry. We need not now consider whether a state court might, in certain circumstances, adhere to a more restrictive view concerning the scope of examination of foreign acts than that required by this Court.

24. The Doctrine of Erie Railroad v. Tompkins Applied to International Law, 33 Am. J. Int'l L. 740 (1939).

25. Various constitutional and statutory provisions indirectly support this determination, see U.S. Const., Art. I, §8, cls. 3, 10; Art. II, §§2, 3; Art. III, §2; 28 U.S.C. §§1251 (a)(2), (b)(1), (b)(3), 1332 (a)(2), 1333, 1350-51, by reflecting a concern for uniformity in this country's dealings with foreign nations and indicating a desire to give matters of international significance to the jurisdiction of federal institutions.

more appropriate it is for the judiciary to render decisions regarding it, since the courts can then focus on the application of an agreed principle to circumstances of fact rather than on the sensitive task of establishing a principle not inconsistent with the national interest or with international justice. It is also evident that some aspects of international law touch much more sharply on national nerves than do others; the less important the implications of an issue are for our foreign relations, the weaker the justification for exclusivity in the political branches. The balance of relevant considerations may also be shifted if the government which perpetrated the challenged act of state is no longer in existence, as in the *Bernstein* case, for the political interest of this country may, as a result, be measurably altered. Therefore, rather than laying down or reaffirming an inflexible and all-encompassing rule in this case, we decide only that the Judicial Branch will not examine the validity of a taking of property within its own territory by a foreign sovereign government, extant and recognized by this country at the time of suit, in the absence of a treaty or other unambiguous agreement regarding controlling legal principles, even if the complaint alleges that the taking violates customary international law.

There are few if any issues in international law today on which opinion seems to be so divided as the limitations on a state's power to expropriate the property of aliens. There is, of course, authority, in international judicial and arbitral decisions, in the expressions of national governments, and among commentators for the view that a taking is improper under international law if it is not for a public purpose, is discriminatory, or is without provision for prompt, adequate, and effective compensation. However, Communist countries, although they have in fact provided a degree of compensation after diplomatic efforts, commonly recognize no obligation on the part of the taking country. Certain representatives of the newly independent and underdeveloped countries have questioned whether rules of state responsibility toward aliens can bind nations that have not consented to them and it is argued that the traditionally articulated standards governing expropriation of property reflect "imperialist" interests and are inappropriate to the circumstances of emergent states.

The disagreement as to relevant international law standards reflects an even more basic divergence between the national interests of capital importing and capital exporting nations and between the social ideologies of those countries that favor state control of a considerable portion of the means of production and those that adhere to a free enterprise system. It is difficult to imagine the courts of this country embarking on adjudication in an area which touches more sensitively the practical and ideological goals of the various members of the community of nations.[34]

The possible adverse consequences of a conclusion to the contrary . . . is highlighted by contrasting the practices of the political branch with the limitations of the judicial process in matters of this kind. Following an expropriation of any significance, the Executive engages in diplomacy aimed to assure that United States citizens who are harmed are compensated fairly. Representing all claimants of this country, it will often be able, either by bilateral or multilateral talks, by submission to the United Nations, or by the employment of economic and political sanctions, to achieve some degree of general redress. Judicial determinations of invalidity of title can, on the other hand, have only an occasional impact, since they depend on the fortuitous circumstance of the property in question being brought into this

---

34. There are, of course, areas of international law in which consensus as to standards is greater and which do not represent a battleground for conflicting ideologies. This decision in no way intimates that the courts of this country are broadly foreclosed from considering questions of international law.

country. Such decisions would, if the acts involved were declared invalid, often be likely to give offense to the expropriating country; since the concept of territorial sovereignty is so deep seated, any state may resent the refusal of the courts of another sovereign to accord validity to acts within its territorial borders. Piecemeal dispositions of this sort involving the probability of affront to another state could seriously interfere with negotiations being carried on by the Executive Branch and might prevent or render less favorable the terms of an agreement that could otherwise be reached. Relations with third countries which have engaged in similar expropriations would not be immune from effect.

The dangers of such adjudication are present regardless of whether the State Department has, as it did in this case, asserted that the relevant act violated international law. If the Executive Branch has undertaken negotiations with an expropriating country, but has refrained from claims of violation of the law of nations, a determination to that effect by a court might be regarded as a serious insult, while a finding of compliance with international law would greatly strengthen the bargaining hand of the other state with consequent detriment to American interests.

Even if the State Department has proclaimed the impropriety of the expropriation, the stamp of approval of its view by a judicial tribunal, however impartial, might increase any affront and the judicial decision might occur at a time, almost always well after the taking, when such an impact would be contrary to our national interest. Considerably more serious and far-reaching consequences would flow from a judicial finding that international law standards had been met if that determination flew in the face of a State Department proclamation to the contrary. When articulating principles of international law in its relations with other states, the Executive Branch speaks not only as an interpreter of generally accepted and traditional rules, as would the courts, but also as an advocate of standards it believes desirable for the community of nations and protective of national concerns. In short, whatever way the matter is cut, the possibility of conflict between the Judicial and Executive Branches could hardly be avoided. . . .

Against the force of such considerations, we find respondents' countervailing arguments quite unpersuasive. Their basic contention is that United States courts could make a significant contribution to the growth of international law, a contribution whose importance, it is said, would be magnified by the relative paucity of decisional law by international bodies. But given the fluidity of present world conditions, the effectiveness of such a patchwork approach toward the formulation of an acceptable body of law concerning state responsibility for expropriations is, to say the least, highly conjectural. Moreover, it rests upon the sanguine presupposition that the decisions of the courts of the world's major capital exporting country and principal exponent of the free enterprise system would be accepted as disinterested expressions of sound legal principle by those adhering to widely different ideologies. . . .

It is suggested that if the act of state doctrine is applicable to violations of international law, it should only be so when the Executive Branch expressly stipulates that it does not wish the courts to pass on the question of validity. We should be slow to reject the representations of the Government that such a reversal of the *Bernstein* principle would work serious inroads on the maximum effectiveness of United States diplomacy. Often the State Department will wish to refrain from taking an official position, particularly at a moment that would be dictated by the development of private litigation but might be inopportune diplomatically. Adverse domestic consequences might flow from an official stand which could be assuaged, if at all, only by revealing matters best kept secret. Of course, a relevant consideration for the State Department would be the position contemplated in the court to hear the case. It is highly questionable whether the examination of validity by the judiciary should depend on an educated guess by the Executive as to probable result and, at any rate, should a prediction be wrong, the Executive might be embarrassed in its dealings with other countries. We do not now pass on the *Bernstein* exception, but even if it were deemed valid, its suggested extension is unwarranted.

However offensive to the public policy of this country and its constituent States an expropriation of this kind may be, we conclude that both the national interest and progress toward the goal of establishing the rule of law among nations are best served by maintaining intact the act of state doctrine in this realm of its application. . . .

MR. JUSTICE WHITE, dissenting.

I am dismayed that the Court has, with one broad stroke, declared the ascertainment and application of international law beyond the competence of the courts of the United States in a large and important category of cases. I am also disappointed in the Court's declaration that the acts of a sovereign state with regard to the property of aliens within its borders are beyond the reach of international law in the courts of this country. However clearly established that law may be, a sovereign may violate it with impunity, except insofar as the political branches of the government may provide a remedy. This backward-looking doctrine, never before declared in this Court, is carried a disconcerting step further: not only are the courts powerless to question acts of state proscribed by international law but they are likewise powerless to refuse to adjudicate the claim founded upon a foreign law; they must render judgment and thereby validate the lawless act. Since the Court expressly extends its ruling to all acts of state expropriating property, however clearly inconsistent with the international community, all discriminatory expropriations of the property of aliens, as for example the taking of properties of persons belonging to certain races, religions or nationalities, are entitled to automatic validation in the courts of the United States. No other civilized country has found such a rigid rule necessary for the survival of the executive branch of its government; the executive of no other government seems to require such insulation from international law adjudications in its courts; and no other judiciary is apparently so incompetent to ascertain and apply international law. . . .

I start with what I thought to be unassailable propositions: that our courts are obliged to determine controversies on their merits, in accordance with the applicable law; and that part of the law American courts are bound to administer is international law.

. . . The doctrine that the law of nations is a part of the law of the land, originally formulated in England and brought to America as part of our legal heritage, is reflected in the debates during the Constitutional Convention and in the Constitution itself. This Court has time and again effectuated the clear understanding of the Framers, as embodied in the Constitution, by applying the law of nations to resolve cases and controversies. As stated in The Paquete Habana, 175 U.S. 677, 700, "international law is part of our law, and must be ascertained and administered by the courts of justice of appropriate jurisdiction, as often as questions of right depending upon it are duly presented for their determination." Principles of international law have been applied in our courts to resolve controversies not merely because they provide a convenient rule for decision but because they represent a consensus among civilized nations on the proper ordering of relations between nations and the citizens thereof. . . .

The reasons for nonreview, based as they are on traditional concepts of territorial sovereignty, lose much of their force when the foreign act of state is shown to be a violation of international law. All legitimate exercises of sovereign power, whether territorial or otherwise, should be exercised consistently with rules of international law, including those rules which mark the bounds of lawful state action against aliens or their property located within the territorial confines of the foreign state. . . . [T]o refuse inquiry into the question of whether norms of the international community have been contravened by the act of state under review would seem to deny the existence or purport of such norms, a view that seems inconsistent with the role of international law in ordering the relations between nations. Finally, the impartial application of international law would not only be an affirmation of the existence and binding effect of international rules of order, but also a refutation of the notion that this body of law consists of no more than the divergent and parochial views of the capital importing and exporting nations, the socialist and free-enterprise nations. . . .

There remains for consideration the relationship between the act of state doctrine and the power of the executive over matters touching upon the foreign affairs of the Nation. . . .

Without doubt political matters in the realm of foreign affairs are within the exclusive domain of the Executive Branch, as, for example, issues for which there are no available standards or which are textually committed by the Constitution to the executive.[20] But this is far from saying that the Constitution vests in the executive exclusive absolute control of foreign affairs or that the validity of a foreign act of state is necessarily a political question. International law, as well as a treaty or executive agreement, see United States v. Pink, 315 U.S. 203, provides an ascertainable standard for adjudicating the validity of some foreign acts, and courts are competent to apply this body of law, notwithstanding that there may be some cases where comity dictates giving effect to the foreign act because it is not clearly condemned under generally accepted principles of international law. And it cannot be contended that the Constitution allocates this area to the exclusive jurisdiction of the executive, for the judicial power is expressly extended by that document to controversies between aliens and citizens or States, aliens and aliens, and foreign states and American citizens or States.

Notes and Questions

1. Prior to *Sabbatino*, the Supreme Court had indicated that the act of state doctrine was derived from principles of international law and international comity. Is that the way the Court conceives of the doctrine in *Sabbatino*? If not, what, according to the Court, is the source of the doctrine? Why does the Court in *Sabbatino* conceive of the doctrine in this way? For a thoughtful consideration of these and other questions relating to the decision, see Louis Henkin, *The Foreign Affairs Power of the Federal Courts:* Sabbatino, 64 Colum. L. Rev. 805 (1964).

---

20. These issues include whether a foreign state exists or is recognized by the United States, Gelston v. Hoyt, 3 Wheat. 246; The Sapphire, 11 Wall. 164, 168; the status that a foreign state or its representatives shall have in this country (sovereign immunity), Ex parte Muir, 254 U.S. 522; Ex parte Peru, 318 U.S. 578; the territorial boundaries of a foreign state, Jones v. United States, 137 U.S. 202; and the authorization of its representatives for state-to-state negotiation, Ex parte Hitz, 111 U.S. 766; In re Baiz, 135 U.S. 403.

2. One could describe the holding of *Sabbatino* in choice-of-law terms. Normally, in determining title to property, choice-of-law principles would call for applying the law of the place where the property was located. In *Sabbatino,* this presumably would mean applying the Cuban law that existed at the time of the sale of the sugar, including the Cuban expropriation decree. Courts often decline to apply foreign law, however, if it offends some fundamental public policy of the forum. *See* Restatement (Second) of Conflict of Laws §90 (1971). In *Sabbatino,* the respondents argued that Cuba had violated customary international law in expropriating the sugar, and that it would therefore violate public policy to give legal effect to the expropriation. Why does the Court reject such a public policy limitation? *See also* Anne-Marie Burley, *Law Among Liberal States: Liberal Internationalism and the Act of State Doctrine,* 92 Colum. L. Rev. 1907, 1931-36 (1992) (describing the support by academic commentators and corporate lawyers before *Sabbatino* for a public policy limitation on the act of state doctrine and how, "[a]ccording to conventional wisdom, the act of state doctrine was . . . transformed [by *Sabbatino*] from a conflicts rule, directing a court to apply a foreign law under specified conditions, to a doctrine of judicial restraint or abstention, requiring a court confronting a foreign act of state to refrain from adjudicating the validity of the act").

3. United States courts also commonly decline to enforce the penal and revenue laws of other nations. *See, e.g.,* Attorney General of Canada v. R.J. Reynolds Tobacco Holdings, Inc., 268 F.3d 103 (2d Cir. 2001); United States v. Boots, 80 F.3d 580 (1st Cir. 1996); Her Majesty the Queen, 597 F.2d 1161 (9th Cir. 1979); *see also* The Antelope, 23 U.S. (1 Wheat.) 66, 123 (1825) ("The Courts of no country execute the penal laws of another . . ."). Learned Hand described the justifications for this limitation as follows:

> Even in the case of ordinary municipal liabilities, a court will not recognize those arising in a foreign state, if they run counter to the "settled public policy" of its own. Thus a scrutiny of the liability is necessarily always in reserve, and the possibility that it will be found not to accord with the policy of the domestic state. This is not a troublesome or delicate inquiry when the question arises between private persons, but it takes on quite another face when it concerns the relations between the foreign state and its own citizens or even those who may be temporarily within its borders. To pass upon the provisions for the public order of another state is, or at any rate should be, beyond the powers of a court; it involves the relations between the states themselves, with which courts are incompetent to deal, and which are entrusted to other authorities. It may commit the domestic state to a position which would seriously embarrass its neighbor. Revenue laws fall within the same reasoning; they affect a state in matters as vital to its existence as its criminal laws. No court ought to undertake an inquiry which it cannot prosecute without determining whether those laws are consonant with its own notions of what is proper.

Moore v. Mitchell, 30 F.3d 600, 604 (2d Cir. 1929) (Hand, J., concurring); *see also* Banco Nacional de Cuba v. Sabbatino, 376 U.S. 398, 437 (1964) (noting the "desire to avoid embarrassing another state by scrutinizing its penal and revenue laws"). Courts also have reasoned that this limitation is consistent with separation of powers principles, because, if the judiciary enforced foreign penal and revenue laws, it would "risk[] being drawn into issues and disputes of foreign relations policy that are better assigned to—and better handled by—the political branches of the government." *Attorney General of Canada,* 268 F.3d at 114. This analysis resembles the analysis underlying the act of state doctrine. But if courts can properly decline to apply a foreign nation's penal and revenue laws, why can't they also decline to apply a foreign nation's expropriation laws? To put it differently, why do sovereignty and separation of powers considerations require abstention in the first situation and preclude abstention in the second? On the other hand, are the justifications for not applying foreign penal and revenue laws persuasive? For an argument that the bar on applying the penal, revenue, and other public laws of foreign nations should be reconsidered "because cooperation in the enforcement of public law would be mutually beneficial," see William S. Dodge, *Breaking the Public Law Taboo*, 43 Harv. Int'l L.J. 161, 163 (2002). *See also* European Community v. Japan Tobacco, Inc., 355 F.3d 123 (2d Cir. 2003) (concluding that the 2001 Patriot Act, which among other things amended the Racketeer Influenced Corrupt Organizations Act (RICO) to include terrorism-related offenses as predicate acts, did not show a clear intent by Congress to abrogate the revenue rule); Republic of Honduras v. Philip Morris Cos., 341 F.3d 1253 (11th Cir. 2003) (same).

4. The Supreme Court famously stated in Erie Railroad Co. v. Tompkins, 304 U.S. 64 (1938), that "[e]xcept in matters governed by the Federal Constitution or by Acts of Congress, the law to be applied in any case is the law of the State." In some cases, however, the Court has approved the development of "federal common law" — that is, law fashioned by the federal courts that displaces the relevant state law. In Clearfield Trust Co. v. United States, 318 U.S. 363 (1943), for example, the Court held that "[t]he rights and duties of the United States on commercial paper which it issues are governed by federal, rather than local, law" and that in the "absence of an applicable Act of Congress, it is for the federal courts to fashion the governing rule of law according to their own standards."

The Cuban bank's claim in *Sabbatino* (for conversion of bills of lading) was not governed by the Constitution or an act of Congress. As a result, under the *Erie* doctrine, such a case would normally be decided by looking to the law of the state in which the federal court sits, including any relevant choice-of-law rules of that state. *See* Klaxon v. Stentor Elec. Manuf. Co., 313 U.S. 487 (1941). In *Sabbatino*, however, the Court holds that the act of state doctrine is a rule of federal common law that displaces state rule. What justifications does the Court give for this holding? What are the implications of this holding? Does *Sabbatino* authorize the creation of federal common law rules to govern other foreign affairs issues?

5. The court of appeals in *Sabbatino*, in declining to apply the act of state doctrine, relied heavily on the letters quoted in footnote 19 of the Supreme Court's opinion, stating that, although the letters "are somewhat ambiguous, perhaps intentionally so[,] . . . they express a belief on the part of those responsible for the conduct of our foreign affairs that the courts here should decide the status here of Cuban decrees." 307 F.2d 845, 858 (2d Cir. 1962). Did the court of appeals misconstrue these letters? Note that the Justice and State Departments submitted an *amicus curiae* brief to the Supreme Court in *Sabbatino* urging the Court to apply the act of state doctrine. Among other things, the brief argued that "executive diplomatic action may be seriously impeded or embarrassed by American judicial decisions which undertake, in domestic lawsuits, to pass upon the validity of foreign acts." The brief also disputed the court of appeals' finding that the Executive Branch had supported judicial resolution of the expropriation issue. The letters referred to by the court of appeals, the brief argued, were mere refusals to comment, not an endorsement of the litigation. Finally, the brief argued that Executive Branch approval of the litigation should not be inferred from mere Executive Branch silence. (The issue of whether courts should defer to the Executive Branch in applying the act of state doctrine is explored in more detail in the materials below.) Why do you think that, at least in the Supreme Court, the Executive Branch opposed U.S. court adjudication of the validity of Cuba's expropriation?

6. For a general critique of the Court's reasoning in *Sabbatino,* consider the following comments by Professor Henkin:

> As a principle of the Law of American Foreign Relations, rooted in enlightened United States foreign policy, there is much to be said for Act of State, perhaps also for its application in *Sabbatino.* As constitutional law, as a reflection of the role of the federal judiciary in the application of a national policy, the Court's opinion seems torn by conflicting compulsions which it did not clearly resolve. It favored the classic Act of State doctrine but could not accept the original rationale that it was required by international law or comity. Compelled to seek a basis for the doctrine in domestic law it could not accept a rationale which would release the states from the doctrine and leave an issue important to American foreign affairs to the vagaries and idiosyncrasies of the many states. Seeking a federal basis for the doctrine in supreme federal law, it could not readily find authorization for it from Congress. And the Court was reluctant to make the doctrine depend on authorization or approval of the Executive, lest the courts be, or seem, subject to political dictation from the Department of State. And so, without fully exploring the constitutional difficulties, the Court asserted an independent judicial power to establish Act of State as supreme federal common law—apparently solely because it relates to American foreign affairs, which are "intrinsically federal," and the needs of which courts are competent to determine. The Court also rested the classic doctrine on this new foundation without explaining why its traditional scope and traditional limitations conform to the needs of American foreign policy today, or why new limitations might not now be consonant with United States policy or the needs of international order.

Louis Henkin, *The Foreign Affairs Power of the Federal Courts:* Sabbatino, 64 Colum. L. Rev. 805, 830-31 (1964). Does Henkin accurately describe the "conflicting compulsions" in the Court's opinion? What are the "constitutional difficulties" that Henkin adverts to?

7. As Justice White notes in dissent in *Sabbatino,* the Court had stated in prior decisions that international law is part of U.S. law. *See, e.g.,* The Paquete Habana, 175 U.S. 677, 700 (1900). Does the Court in *Sabbatino* reject that proposition? If not, how does it justify its refusal to apply customary international law principles governing the expropriation of foreign citizen property? Note that courts have held that a government's confiscation, within its territory, of the property of *its own citizens* does not violate customary international law. *See, e.g.,* Fogade v. ENB Revocable Trust, 263 F.3d 1274 (11th Cir. 2001); Bank Tejarat v. Varsho-Saz, 723 F. Supp. 516, 520 (C.D. Cal. 1989); F. Palicio y Compania v. Brush, 256 F. Supp. 481, 487 (S.D.N.Y. 1966).

The act of state doctrine has been criticized by a number of scholars because, among other things, it reduces the opportunities for U.S. courts to apply customary international law. *See, e.g.,* Michael J. Bazyler, *Abolishing the Act of State Doctrine,* 134 U. Pa. L. Rev. 325 (1986); Harold Hongju Koh, *Transnational Public Law Litigation,* 100 Yale L.J. 2347, 2362-64 (1991). As discussed in Chapter 7, however, the *Sabbatino* decision is sometimes invoked to support the argument that customary international law has the status in U.S. courts of supreme federal law. Can you see how the decision might be used in this way?

8. In *Sabbatino,* the Court stated that the act of state doctrine should be applied "in the absence of a treaty or other unambiguous agreement regarding controlling legal principles." The Court also stated that "the greater the degree of codification or consensus concerning a particular area of international law, the more appropriate it is for the judiciary to render decisions regarding it." Consistent with these state-ments, courts generally have not applied the act of state doctrine to bar treaty claims. *See, e.g.,* Kalamazoo Spice Extraction Co. v. Provisional Military Government of Socialist Ethiopia, 729 F.2d 422 (6th Cir. 1984); American Int'l Group, Inc. v. Islamic Republic of Iran, 493 F. Supp. 522 (D.D.C. 1980), *vacated on other grounds,* 657 F.2d 430 (D.C. Cir. 1981); *see also* Ramirez de Arellano v. Weinberger, 745 F.2d 1500, 1540 (D.C. Cir. 1984) ("[T]he doctrine was never intended to apply when an applicable bilateral treaty governs the legal merits of the controversy."), *vacated and remanded,* 471 U.S. 1113 (1985). *But cf.* Callejo v. Bancomer, S.A., 764 F.2d 1101 (5th Cir. 1985) (suggesting that act of state doctrine might bar some treaty claims). Should some *customary international law* claims be exempt from the act of state doctrine? What if there is a high degree of international consensus regarding the customary international law rule? What if the rule is considered a *jus cogens* norm?

9. In a portion of its opinion not excerpted above, the Court in *Sabbatino* rejected the respondents' argument that, because the United States had broken off diplomatic relations with Cuba, Cuba should be denied access to U.S. courts. As the Court noted, the general rule is that foreign governments and their officials may bring civil suits in U.S. courts. *See, e.g.,* The Sapphire, 78 U.S. 164, 167 (1870). Foreign governments are not allowed to sue in U.S. courts, however, if they are not "recognized" by the United States. As discussed above in the political question materials, "recognition" is determined by the Executive Branch. However, a deci-sion by the Executive Branch to cut off diplomatic relations with a government does not, by itself, constitute a decision not to recognize the government. *See, e.g.,* National Petrochemical Co. of Iran v. The M/T Stolt Sheaf, 860 F.2d 551 (2d Cir. 1988) (termination of diplomatic relations with Iran did not deprive the Iranian government of access to U.S. courts). For a general discussion of the rights of for-eign governments in the United States, see Lori Fisler Damrosch, *Foreign States and the Constitution,* 73 Va. L. Rev. 483 (1987).

10. In response to *Sabbatino,* Congress enacted the Hickenlooper Amendment to the Foreign Assistance Act of 1961 (also called the "Second Hickenlooper Amendment"), which provides as follows:

> Notwithstanding any other provision of law, no court in the United States shall decline
> on the ground of the federal act of state doctrine to make a determination on the
> merits giving effect to the principles of international law in a case in which a claim of
> title or other right to property is asserted by any party including a foreign state (or a
> party claiming through such state) based upon (or traced through) a confiscation or
> other taking after January 1, 1959, by an act of that state in violation of the principles
> of international law, including the principles of compensation and the other standards
> set out in this subsection: Provided, That this subparagraph shall not be applicable
> (1) in any case in which an act of a foreign state is not contrary to international law or
> with respect to a claim of title or other right to property acquired pursuant to an irre-
> vocable letter of credit of not more than 180 days duration issued in good faith prior
> to the time of the confiscation or other taking, or (2) in any case with respect to which
> the President determines that application of the act of state doctrine is required in that
> particular case by the foreign policy interests of the United States and a suggestion to
> this effect is filed on his behalf in that case with the court.

22 U.S.C. §2370(e)(2).

This statute was applied retroactively to the *Sabbatino* case and, as a result, Cuba's claim was ultimately dismissed. *See* 383 F.2d 166 (2d Cir. 1967). Since then, some courts have interpreted the statute narrowly, such that it applies only when

(a) there are claims of *title to property* (rather than mere breach of contract claims), and (b) the property or its proceeds is presently *located in the United States. See, e.g.,* Compania de Gas de Nuevo Laredo, S.A. v. Entex, Inc., 686 F.2d 322 (5th Cir. 1982); Banco Nacional de Cuba v. First National City Bank of New York, 431 F.2d 394 (2d Cir. 1970), *rev'd on other grounds,* 406 U.S. 759 (1972); Banco Nacional de Cuba v. Farr, 383 F.2d 166 (2d Cir. 1967). *But cf.* West v. Bancomer, S.N.C, 807 F.2d 820, 829-30 (9th Cir. 1987) (holding that the Second Hickenlooper Amendment applies to expropriation of certificates of deposit regardless of their "intangible" or "contractual" nature); Ramirez de Arellano v. Weinberger, 745 F.2d 1500, 1541 n.180 (D.C. Cir. 1984) ("It may be that a primary purpose of the statute was to prevent invocation of the act of state doctrine when property expropriated in a foreign country subsequently makes its way into the United States, but this was not the *sole* situation in which the amendment was to be activated."), *vacated and remanded,* 471 U.S. 1113 (1985).

Are these limitations supported by the language of the statute? Why do you think courts have interpreted the statute narrowly? With or without these limitations, is the statute constitutional? For an affirmative answer, see Banco Nacional de Cuba v. Farr, 383 F.2d 166 (2d Cir. 1967). *See also* Restatement (Fourth) of the Foreign Relations Law of the United States §441(1) (2018) (stating that the act of state doctrine "is subject to modification by act of Congress").

11. The Second Hickenlooper Amendment is not the only statutory restriction imposed by Congress on the act of state doctrine. In 1996, Congress enacted the Cuban Liberty and Democratic Solidarity (Libertad) Act, also known as the Helms-Burton Act. Title III of the Act authorizes U.S. nationals with claims to property confiscated by the Cuban government to sue individuals and companies around the world who are trafficking in that property. The Act further provides that "[n]o court of the United States shall decline, based upon the act of state doctrine, to make a determination on the merits in an action brought under [Title III]." Nevertheless, the Act allows presidents to suspend the allowance of this litigation for repeated six-month periods if they determine that the suspension "is necessary to the national interests of the United States and will expedite a transition to democracy in Cuba." Until 2019, every President had repeatedly invoked this suspension provision, thereby preventing litigation from proceeding under Title III of the Act. In April 2019, however, President Trump announced that he would end that suspension and allow suits to begin. The announcement drew sharp protests from the European Union, in part because many European companies have made investments in Cuba.

12. The Court in *Sabbatino* reserved judgment on the existence of a *"Bernstein"* exception to the act of state doctrine, whereby courts would decline to apply the act of state doctrine when informed by the Executive Branch that it had no objection to the litigation. (The Second Circuit had endorsed such an exception prior to *Sabbatino* in Bernstein v. N.V. Nederlandsche-Amerikaansche, 210 F.2d 375 (2d Cir. 1954), a case involving an expropriation of property by the Nazis.) In First National City Bank v. Banco Nacional de Cuba, 406 U.S. 759 (1972), three Justices (Rehnquist, Burger, and White) argued for a *Bernstein* exception. They reasoned that:

> The act of state doctrine, as reflected in the cases culminating in *Sabbatino,* is a judicially accepted limitation on the normal adjudicative processes of the courts, springing from the thoroughly sound principle that on occasion individual litigants may have to forgo decision on the merits of their claims because the involvement of the courts in such a decision might frustrate the conduct of the Nation's foreign policy. It would be

wholly illogical to insist that such a rule, fashioned because of fear that adjudication would interfere with the conduct of foreign relations, be applied in the face of an assurance from that branch of the Federal Government that conducts foreign relations that such a result would not obtain.

In splintered opinions, however, the other six Justices in *City Bank* rejected a *Bernstein* exception. Justice Powell, for example, stated in a concurrence that "the reasoning of *Sabbatino* implicitly rejects that exception" and that he "would be uncomfortable with a doctrine which would require the judiciary to receive the Executive's permission before invoking its jurisdiction." More colorfully, Justice Douglas stated in a concurrence that courts should not become "a mere errand boy for the Executive Branch which may choose to pick some people's chestnuts from the fire, but not others." And Justice Brennan argued in a four-Justice dissent that avoidance of embarrassment of the Executive Branch in foreign relations is only one of the policies underlying the act of state doctrine and that the other policies are still served when the State Department indicates that it does not oppose the litigation. Justice Brennan further observed, "As six members of this Court recognize today, the reasoning of that case is clear that the representations of the Department of State are entitled to weight for the light they shed on the permutation and combination of factors underlying the act of state doctrine. But they cannot be determinative." Although the lower federal courts have not applied a *Bernstein* exception since *City Bank*, they do continue to give some weight (but not conclusive weight) to the views of the Executive Branch in deciding whether to apply the act of state doctrine. *See, e.g.,* Environmental Tectonics v. W.S. Kirkpatrick, Inc., 847 F.2d 1052, 1062 (3d Cir. 1988), *aff'd on other grounds*, 493 U.S. 400 (1990); Kalamazoo Spice Extraction Co. v. Provisional Military Government of Socialist Ethiopia, 729 F.2d 422, 427-28 (6th Cir. 1984). Is such deference warranted? For a discussion of this issue, see Curtis A. Bradley, Chevron *Deference and Foreign Affairs*, 86 Va. L. Rev. 649, 716-21 (2000).

13. The Supreme Court has indicated that only official, public acts qualify as "acts of state" for purposes of the act of state doctrine. Thus, in Alfred Dunhill of London, Inc. v. Republic of Cuba, 425 U.S. 682 (1976), the Court refused to give effect to a repudiation of a quasi-contract obligation, noting that "[n]o statute, decree, order, or resolution of the Cuban Government itself was offered in evidence indicating that Cuba had repudiated its obligations in general or any class thereof or that it had as a sovereign matter determined to confiscate the amounts due." How formal must the government act be in order to qualify as an act of state? If government officials engage in *illegal* activities, can those activities constitute acts of state? *Compare* Republic of the Philippines v. Marcos, 818 F.2d 1473, 1483 (9th Cir. 1987) ("Since the act of state doctrine prohibits inquiry into the legality of official governmental acts, such acts surely cannot be official only if they are legal."), *opinion withdrawn*, 832 F.2d 1110 (9th Cir. 1987), *with* Sharon v. Time, Inc., 599 F. Supp. 538, 544 (S.D.N.Y. 1984) ("The actions of an official acting outside the scope of his authority as an agent of the state are simply not acts of state. In no sense are such acts designed to give effect to a State's public interests."). *See generally* Lynn E. Parseghian, Note, *Defining the "Public Act" Requirement in the Act of State Doctrine*, 58 U. Chi. L. Rev. 1151 (1991).

14. Another limitation on the act of state doctrine is that it covers only acts by a foreign government taken within its own territory. What is the basis for this limitation? Does this territorial restriction still make sense today in this era of globalization? Note that this limitation can pose some difficult "situs" questions, especially in cases involving intangible property, such as intellectual property and debt obligations. For debt cases, courts often find that the situs is the agreed-upon place of payment. *See, e.g.,* Braka v. Bancomer, S.N.C., 762 F.2d 222 (2d Cir. 1985); Allied Bank Int'l v. Banco Credito Agricola de Cartago, 757 F.2d 516 (2d Cir. 1985); Garcia v. Chase Manhattan Bank, N.A., 735 F.2d 645 (2d Cir. 1984); Perez v. Chase Manhattan Bank, N.A., 463 N.E.2d 5 (N.Y. 1984). *See generally* Margaret E. Tahyar, Note, *The Act of State Doctrine: Resolving Debt Situs Confusion,* 86 Colum. L. Rev. 594 (1986). Because of the situs limitation, courts have held that the act of state doctrine does not apply to efforts by a foreign state to expropriate property located in the United States, even if the property is owned the foreign state's own nationals. *See, e.g.,* Villoldo v. Ruz, 821 F.3d 196 (1st Cir. 2016).

15. As discussed in Chapter 7, foreign governments have long been accorded immunity from suit in U.S. courts. This immunity was essentially absolute during the nineteenth and early twentieth centuries, but is now more qualified. Since 1976, foreign governmental immunity has been regulated by a comprehensive statute, the Foreign Sovereign Immunities Act (FSIA). One of the most important exceptions to immunity under the FSIA is the exception for commercial activity. The basic idea is that when a foreign state acts like a private actor in the marketplace, it should be subject to suit like a private actor. . . .

Should a similar exception apply to the act of state doctrine? In the *Dunhill* case, cited above in Note 12, four Justices argued for a commercial activity exception to the act of state doctrine, reasoning that courts could adjudicate the validity of "purely commercial obligations" of a foreign government. To date, courts have not adopted such an exception. . . . Sometimes these [cases] consider the commercial character of a foreign government's action, and sometimes whether the policies of the act of state doctrine are implicated in a particular case. *See, e.g.,* [. . .] v. Government of Honduras, 129 F.3d . . . . In determining whether to apply a commercial exception to the act of state doctrine . . . from the FSIA. The factors to be considered, . . . may sometimes [overlap with] the commercial exception, but a commercial exception alone is not . . . For discussion of whether there should be a commercial activity exception to the act of state doctrine, see Michael D. Ramsey, *Acts of State and Foreign Sovereign Obligations,* 39 Harv. Int'l L.J. 1 (1998); Jonathan M. Wight, *An Evaluation of the Commercial Activities Exception to the Act of State Doctrine,* 19 Dayton L. Rev. 1265 (1994); Russ Schlossbach, Note, *Arguably Commercial, Ergo Adjudicable?: The Validity of a Commercial Activities Exception to the Act of State Doctrine,* 18 B.U. Int'l L.J. 139 (2000).

16. There is also an exception in the FSIA for counterclaims. Even before the FSIA was enacted, the Supreme Court had recognized a counterclaim exception to foreign sovereign immunity. *See* National City Bank of New York v. Republic of China, 348 U.S. 356, 363 (1955). The Court in *Sabbatino,* however, in a portion of the opinion not excerpted above, rejected a counterclaim exception to the act of state doctrine. The Court reasoned that (a) foreign governments could attempt to get around this exception by assigning their claims; (b) if the exception applied to assignees it could undermine the security of titles; (c) the exception would encourage claimants to engage in self-help remedies in an effort to cause the foreign government to become the plaintiff; and (d) the act of state doctrine rests on different policies than foreign sovereign immunity. Are these points persuasive? In First National City Bank v. Banco Nacional de Cuba, 406 U.S. 759 (1972), the State Department supported a counterclaim exception to the doctrine, but only Justice Douglas clearly accepted such an exception (although Justices Rehnquist, Burger, and White also appeared sympathetic to it).

17. In W.S. Kirkpatrick & Co. v. Environmental Tectonics Corp., 493 U.S. 400 (1990), the Supreme Court made clear that the act of state doctrine applies only when "the relief sought or the defense interposed would [require] a court in the United States to declare invalid the official act of a foreign sovereign performed within its own territory." In that case, one private company was suing another private company under various statutes for having obtained a construction contract from the government of Nigeria through the use of a bribe, conduct that had previously been found to violate the criminal provisions of the Foreign Corrupt Practices Act. Because bribery was also ostensibly illegal in Nigeria, if the plaintiff prevailed, it would have established that an act of the Nigerian government—the award of the contract—was unlawful. Nevertheless, the Court, in a unanimous opinion by Justice Scalia, concluded that this did not suffice to trigger the act of state doctrine. The doctrine "is not some vague doctrine of abstention," explained the Court. Rather, "[a]ct of state issues only arise when a court *must decide*—that is, when the outcome of the case turns upon—the effect of official action by a foreign sovereign." That was not the case here, since the only thing that the plaintiff needed to establish in order to prevail was that the defendant had violated U.S. law: "[R]egardless of what the court's factual findings may suggest as to the legality of the Nigerian contract, its legality is simply not a question to be decided in the present suit, and there is thus no occasion to apply the rule of decision that the act of state doctrine requires." While the suit might end up embarrassing the government of Nigeria, the Court explained that "[t]he act of state doctrine does not establish an exception for cases and controversies that may embarrass foreign governments, but merely requires that, in the process of deciding, the acts of foreign sovereigns taken within their own jurisdictions shall be deemed valid."

The Justice and State Departments filed an *amicus curiae* brief in *Kirkpatrick* arguing that the act of state doctrine should not be applied in that case. The brief contended that, in deciding whether to apply the act of state doctrine, courts should consider a variety of "comity" factors, avoid any absolute distinction between validity and motivation, and give substantial deference to the Executive Branch's views regarding "whether foreign policy concerns, together with considerations made relevant by other components of the act of state doctrine, require that the court give effect to the act of a foreign state." Although the Court agreed that the doctrine should not be applied in this case, it rejected the government's proposed approach to the issue. The Court explained:

> These urgings are deceptively similar to what we said in *Sabbatino,* where we observed that sometimes, even though the validity of the act of a foreign sovereign within its own territory is called into question, the policies underlying the act of state doctrine may not justify its application. We suggested that a sort of balancing approach could be applied—the balance shifting against application of the doctrine, for example, if the government that committed the "challenged act of state" is no longer in existence. But what is appropriate in order to avoid unquestioning judicial acceptance of the acts of foreign sovereigns is not similarly appropriate for the quite opposite purpose of expanding judicial incapacities where such acts are not directly (or even indirectly) involved. It is one thing to suggest, as we have, that the policies underlying the act of state doctrine should be considered in deciding whether, despite the doctrine's technical availability, it should nonetheless not be invoked; it is something quite different to suggest that those underlying policies are a doctrine unto themselves, justifying expansion of the act of state doctrine (or, as the United States puts it, unspecified "related principles of abstention") into new and uncharted fields.

Picking up on the Court's distinction between declining to apply the doctrine and expanding the doctrine, a number of courts since *Kirkpatrick* have concluded that, even when the requirements for the act of state doctrine are technically satisfied, the doctrine need not be applied if the foreign relations and other concerns underlying the doctrine are not implicated. *See, e.g.,* Bigio v. Coca-Cola Co., 239 F.3d 440 (2d Cir. 2000); Grupo Protexa, S.A. v. All American Marine Slip, 20 F.3d 1224 (3d Cir. 1994). For more recent applications of the act of state doctrine, see, for example, Sea Breeze Salt, Inc. v. Mitsubishi Corp., 899 F.3d 1064 (9th Cir. 2018) (holding that an antitrust challenge to the actions of a Mexican government-owned corporation concerning the exploitation of natural resources in Mexico was barred by the act of state doctrine), and Von Saher v. Norton Simon Museum of Art, 897 F.3d 1191 (9th Cir. 2018) (holding that the Dutch government's conveyance of paintings confiscated by the Nazis was an official act protected by the act of state doctrine).

18. For additional discussion of the act of state doctrine, see, for example, Anne-Marie Burley, *Law Among Liberal States: Liberal Internationalism and the Act of State Doctrine,* 92 Colum. L. Rev. 1907 (1992); Daniel C. K. Chow, *Rethinking the Act of State Doctrine: An Analysis in Terms of Jurisdiction to Prescribe,* 62 Wash. L. Rev. 397 (1987); Joseph W. Dellapenna, *Deciphering the Act of State Doctrine,* 35 Vill. L. Rev. 1 (1990); Malvina Halberstam, Sabbatino *Resurrected: The Act of State Doctrine in the Revised Restatement of U.S. Foreign Relations Law,* 79 Am. J. Int'l L. 68 (1985); Louis Henkin, *Act of State Today: Recollections in Tranquility,* 6 Colum. J. Transnat'l L. 175 (1967); Michael D. Ramsey, *Acts of State and Foreign Sovereign Obligations,* 39 Harv. Int'l L.J. 1 (1998); Note, *Rehabilitation and Exoneration of the Act of State Doctrine,* 12 N.Y.U. J. Int'l L. & Pol. 599 (1980); and Comment, *The Act of State Doctrine: A History of Judicial Limitations and Exceptions,* 18 Harv. Int'l L.J. 677 (1977). For a more general consideration of when U.S. courts do, and should, sit in judgment on foreign states, see Zachary D. Clopton, *Judging Foreign States,* 94 Wash. U. L. Rev. 1 (2016).

F. PRESUMPTION AGAINST EXTRATERRITORIALITY

Morrison v. National Australia Bank Ltd.

561 U.S. 247 (2010)

[In 1998, an Australian bank, National Australia Bank Ltd., bought HomeSide Lending, a mortgage servicing company based in Florida. For several years, National touted the success of HomeSide's business. In 2001, however, National substantially wrote down the value of HomeSide's assets, which caused National's stock price to fall. National's stock was listed on the Australian stock exchange and certain other foreign exchanges, but not on any U.S. exchange. Several Australian purchasers of National stock, seeking to represent a class of foreign stock purchasers, sued National and officers of both National and HomeSide in federal district court in New York, alleging securities fraud in violation of §10(b) of the Securities and Exchange Act of 1934 and SEC Rule 10-b, which was promulgated pursuant to §10(b). The district court dismissed the case due to insufficient contacts with the United States, and the Second Circuit affirmed.]

JUSTICE SCALIA delivered the opinion of the Court.

We decide whether §10(b) of the Securities Exchange Act of 1934 provides a cause of action to foreign plaintiffs suing foreign and American defendants for misconduct in connection with securities traded on foreign exchanges. . . .

III

A

It is a "longstanding principle of American law 'that legislation of Congress, unless a contrary intent appears, is meant to apply only within the territorial jurisdiction of the United States.'" EEOC v. Arabian American Oil Co., 499 U.S. 244, 248 (1991) (*Aramco*) (quoting Foley Bros., Inc. v. Filardo, 336 U.S. 281, 285 (1949)). This principle represents a canon of construction, or a presumption about a statute's meaning, rather than a limit upon Congress's power to legislate, see Blackmer v. United States, 284 U.S. 421, 437 (1932). It rests on the perception that Congress ordinarily legislates with respect to domestic, not foreign matters. Smith v. United States, 507 U.S. 197, 204, n.5 (1993). Thus, "unless there is the affirmative intention of the Congress clearly expressed" to give a statute extraterritorial effect, "we must presume it is primarily concerned with domestic conditions." *Aramco, supra*, at 248 (internal quotation marks omitted). The canon or presumption applies regardless of whether there is a risk of conflict between the American statute and a foreign law, see Sale v. Haitian Centers Council, Inc., 509 U.S. 155, 173-74 (1993). When a statute gives no clear indication of an extraterritorial application, it has none.

Despite this principle of interpretation, long and often recited in our opinions, the Second Circuit believed that, because the Exchange Act is silent as to the extraterritorial application of §10(b), it was left to the court to "discern" whether Congress would have wanted the statute to apply. This disregard of the presumption against extraterritoriality did not originate with the Court of Appeals panel in this case. It has been repeated over many decades by various courts of appeals in determining the application of the Exchange Act, and §10(b) in particular, to fraudulent schemes that involve conduct and effects abroad. That has produced a collection of tests for divining what Congress would have wanted, complex in formulation and unpredictable in application. . . .

[In decisions in the late 1960s and early 1970s, the Second Circuit] excised the presumption against extraterritoriality from the jurisprudence of §10(b) and replaced it with the inquiry whether it would be reasonable (and hence what Congress would have wanted) to apply the statute to a given situation. As long as there was prescriptive jurisdiction to regulate, the Second Circuit explained, whether to apply §10(b) even to "predominantly foreign" transactions became a matter of whether a court thought Congress "wished the precious resources of United States courts and law enforcement agencies to be devoted to them rather than leave the problem to foreign countries." Bersch v. Drexel Firestone, Inc., 519 F.2d 974, 985 (1975).

The Second Circuit had thus established that application of §10(b) could be premised upon either some effect on American securities markets or investors or significant conduct in the United States. It later formalized these two applications into (1) an "effects test," "whether the wrongful conduct had a substantial effect in the United States or upon United States citizens," and (2) a "conduct test," "whether the wrongful conduct occurred in the United States." SEC v. Berger, 322 F.3d 187, 192-93 (2d Cir. 2003). These became the north star of the Second Circuit's §10(b) jurisprudence, pointing the way to what Congress would have wished. Indeed, the Second Circuit declined to keep its two tests distinct on the ground that "an admixture or combination of the two often gives a better picture of whether there is sufficient United States involvement to justify the exercise of jurisdiction by an American court." Itoba Ltd. v. Lep Group PLC, 54 F.3d 118, 122 (2d Cir. 1995). The Second

Circuit never put forward a textual or even extratextual basis for these tests. As early as *Bersch*, it confessed that "if we were asked to point to language in the statutes, or even in the legislative history, that compelled these conclusions, we would be unable to respond," 519 F.2d at 993.

As they developed, these tests were not easy to administer. The conduct test was held to apply differently depending on whether the harmed investors were Americans or foreigners: When the alleged damages consisted of losses to American investors abroad, it was enough that acts "of material importance" performed in the United States "significantly contributed" to that result; whereas those acts must have "directly caused" the result when losses to foreigners abroad were at issue. And "merely preparatory activities in the United States" did not suffice "to trigger application of the securities laws for injury to foreigners located abroad." *Id.* at 992. This required the court to distinguish between mere preparation and using the United States as a "base" for fraudulent activities in other countries. But merely satisfying the conduct test was sometimes insufficient without " 'some additional factor tipping the scales'" in favor of the application of American law. District courts have noted the difficulty of applying such vague formulations. There is no more damning indictment of the "conduct" and "effects" tests than the Second Circuit's own declaration that "the presence or absence of any single factor which was considered significant in other cases . . . is not necessarily dispositive in future cases." IIT v. Cornfeld, 619 F.2d 909, 918 (1980).

Other Circuits embraced the Second Circuit's approach, though not its precise application. Like the Second Circuit, they described their decisions regarding the extraterritorial application of §10(b) as essentially resolving matters of policy. . . . While applying the same fundamental methodology of balancing interests and arriving at what seemed the best policy, they produced a proliferation of vaguely related variations on the "conduct" and "effects" tests. . . .

Commentators have criticized the unpredictable and inconsistent application of §10(b) to transnational cases. . . . Some have challenged the premise underlying the Courts of Appeals' approach, namely that Congress did not consider the extraterritorial application of §10(b) (thereby leaving it open to the courts, supposedly, to determine what Congress would have wanted). . . . Others, more fundamentally, have noted that using congressional silence as a justification for judge-made rules violates the traditional principle that silence means no extraterritorial application. . . .

The criticisms seem to us justified. The results of judicial-speculation-made-law—divining what Congress would have wanted if it had thought of the situation before the court—demonstrate the wisdom of the presumption against extraterritoriality. Rather than guess anew in each case, we apply the presumption in all cases, preserving a stable background against which Congress can legislate with predictable effects.

B

Rule 10b-5, the regulation under which petitioners have brought suit, was promulgated under §10(b), and "does not extend beyond conduct encompassed by §10(b)'s prohibition." United States v. O'Hagan, 521 U.S. 642, 651 (1997). Therefore, if §10(b) is not extraterritorial, neither is Rule 10b-5.

On its face, §10(b) contains nothing to suggest it applies abroad:

It shall be unlawful for any person, directly or indirectly, by the use of any means or instrumentality of interstate commerce or of the mails, or of any facility of any national securities exchange . . . [t]o use or employ, in connection with the purchase or sale of any security registered on a national securities exchange or any security not so registered, . . . any manipulative or deceptive device or contrivance in contravention of such rules and regulations as the [Securities and Exchange] Commission may prescribe. . . .

Petitioners and the Solicitor General contend, however, that three things indicate that §10(b) or the Exchange Act in general has at least some extraterritorial application.

First, they point to the definition of "interstate commerce," a term used in §10(b), which includes "trade, commerce, transportation, or communication . . . between any foreign country and any State." 15 U.S.C. §78c(a)(17). But "we have repeatedly held that even statutes that contain broad language in their definitions of 'commerce' that expressly refer to '*foreign* commerce' do not apply abroad." *Aramco*, 499 U.S. at 251. The general reference to foreign commerce in the definition of "interstate commerce" does not defeat the presumption against extraterritoriality.

Petitioners and the Solicitor General next point out that Congress, in describing the purposes of the Exchange Act, observed that the "prices established and offered in such transactions are generally disseminated and quoted throughout the United States and foreign countries." 15 U.S.C. §78b(2). The antecedent of "such transactions," however, is found in the first sentence of the section, which declares that "transactions in securities as commonly conducted upon securities exchanges and over-the-counter markets are affected with a national public interest." §78b. Nothing suggests that this *national* public interest pertains to transactions conducted upon *foreign* exchanges and markets. The fleeting reference to the dissemination and quotation abroad of the prices of securities traded in domestic exchanges and markets cannot overcome the presumption against extraterritoriality.

Finally, there is §30(b) of the Exchange Act, 15 U.S.C. §78dd(b), which *does* mention the Act's extraterritorial application: "The provisions of [the Exchange Act] or of any rule or regulation thereunder shall not apply to any person insofar as he transacts a business in securities without the jurisdiction of the United States," unless he does so in violation of regulations promulgated by the Securities and Exchange Commission "to prevent . . . evasion of [the Act]." (The parties have pointed us to no regulation promulgated pursuant to §30(b).) The Solicitor General argues that "[this] exemption would have no function if the Act did not apply in the first instance to securities transactions that occur abroad." Brief for United States as *Amicus Curiae* 14.

We are not convinced. In the first place, it would be odd for Congress to indicate the extraterritorial application of the whole Exchange Act by means of a provision imposing a condition precedent to its application abroad. And if the whole Act applied abroad, why would the Commission's enabling regulations be limited to those preventing "evasion" of the Act, rather than all those preventing "violation"? The provision seems to us directed at actions abroad that might conceal a domestic violation, or might cause what would otherwise be a domestic violation to escape on a technicality. At most, the Solicitor General's proposed inference is possible; but possible interpretations of statutory language do not override the presumption against extraterritoriality. *See Aramco, supra*, at 253. . . .

The concurrence claims we have impermissibly narrowed the inquiry in evaluating whether a statute applies abroad, citing for that point the dissent in *Aramco*. But we do not say, as the concurrence seems to think, that the presumption against extraterritoriality is a "clear statement rule," if by that is meant a requirement that a statute say "this law applies abroad." Assuredly context can be consulted as well. But whatever sources of statutory meaning one consults to give "the most faithful reading" of the text, there is no clear indication of extraterritoriality here. The concurrence does not even try to refute that conclusion, but merely puts forward the same (at best) uncertain indications relied upon by petitioners and the Solicitor General. As the opinion *for the Court* in *Aramco* (which we prefer to the dissent) shows, those uncertain indications do not suffice.[8]

In short, there is no affirmative indication in the Exchange Act that §10(b) applies extraterritorially, and we therefore conclude that it does not.

IV

A

Petitioners argue that the conclusion that §10(b) does not apply extraterritorially does not resolve this case. They contend that they seek no more than domestic application anyway, since Florida is where HomeSide and its senior executives engaged in the deceptive conduct of manipulating HomeSide's financial models. . . . This is less an answer to the presumption against extraterritorial application than it is an assertion—a quite valid assertion—that that presumption here (as often) is not self-evidently dispositive, but its application requires further analysis. For it is a rare case of prohibited extraterritorial application that lacks *all* contact with the territory of the United States. But the presumption against extraterritorial application would be a craven watchdog indeed if it retreated to its kennel whenever *some* domestic activity is involved in the case. The concurrence seems to imagine just such a timid sentinel, but our cases are to the contrary. In *Aramco*, for example, the Title VII plaintiff had been hired in Houston, and was an American citizen. The Court concluded, however, that neither that territorial event nor that relationship was the "focus" of congressional concern, but rather domestic employment.

Applying the same mode of analysis here, we think that the focus of the Exchange Act is not upon the place where the deception originated, but upon purchases and sales of securities in the United States. Section 10(b) does not punish deceptive conduct, but only deceptive conduct "in connection with the purchase or sale of any security registered on a national securities exchange or any security not so registered." 15 U.S.C. §78j(b). Those purchase-and-sale transactions are the objects of the statute's solicitude. . . . And it is in our view only transactions in securities listed on domestic exchanges, and domestic transactions in other securities, to which §10(b) applies.[9]

---

8. The concurrence notes that, post-*Aramco*, Congress provided explicitly for extraterritorial application of Title VII, the statute at issue in *Aramco*. All this shows is that Congress knows how to give a statute explicit extraterritorial effect — and how to limit that effect to particular applications, which is what the cited amendment did.

9. The concurrence seems to think this test has little to do with our conclusion in Part III that §10(b) does not apply extraterritorially. That is not so. If §10(b) did apply abroad, we would not need to determine which transnational frauds it applied to; it would apply to all of them (barring some other limitation). Thus, although it is true, as we have said, that our threshold conclusion that §10(b) has no extraterritorial effect does not resolve this case, it is a necessary first step in the analysis.

The concurrence also makes the curious criticism that our evaluation of where a putative violation occurs is based on the text of §10(b) rather than the doctrine in the Courts of Appeals. Although it concedes that our test is textually plausible, it does not (and cannot) make the same claim for the Court-of-Appeals doctrine it endorses. That is enough to make our test the better one.

The primacy of the domestic exchange is suggested by the very prologue of the Exchange Act, which sets forth as its object "[t]o provide for the regulation of securities exchanges . . . operating in interstate and foreign commerce and through the mails, to prevent inequitable and unfair practices on such exchanges. . . ." 48 Stat. 881. We know of no one who thought that the Act was intended to "regulat[e]" *foreign* securities exchanges—or indeed who even believed that under established principles of international law Congress had the power to do so. The Act's registration requirements apply only to securities listed on national securities exchanges. 15 U.S.C. §78*l*(a). . . .

Finally, we reject the notion that the Exchange Act reaches conduct in this country affecting exchanges or transactions abroad for the same reason that *Aramco* rejected overseas application of Title VII to all domestically concluded employment contracts or all employment contracts with American employers: The probability of incompatibility with the applicable laws of other countries is so obvious that if Congress intended such foreign application "it would have addressed the subject of conflicts with foreign laws and procedures." 499 U.S. at 256. Like the United States, foreign countries regulate their domestic securities exchanges and securities transactions occurring within their territorial jurisdiction. And the regulation of other countries often differs from ours as to what constitutes fraud, what disclosures must be made, what damages are recoverable, what discovery is available in litigation, what individual actions may be joined in a single suit, what attorney's fees are recoverable, and many other matters. The Commonwealth of Australia, the United Kingdom of Great Britain and Northern Ireland, and the Republic of France have filed *amicus* briefs in this case. So have (separately or jointly) such international and foreign organizations as the International Chamber of Commerce, the Swiss Bankers Association, the Federation of German Industries, the French Business Confederation, the Institute of International Bankers, the European Banking Federation, the Australian Bankers' Association, and the Association Francaise des Entreprises Privees. They all complain of the interference with foreign securities regulation that application of §10(b) abroad would produce, and urge the adoption of a clear test that will avoid that consequence. The transactional test we have adopted—whether the purchase or sale is made in the United States, or involves a security listed on a domestic exchange—meets that requirement.

B

The Solicitor General suggests a different test, which petitioners also endorse: "[A] transnational securities fraud violates [§]10(b) when the fraud involves significant conduct in the United States that is material to the fraud's success." Brief for United States as *Amicus Curiae* 16. Neither the Solicitor General nor petitioners provide any textual support for this test. The Solicitor General sets forth a number of purposes such a test would serve: achieving a high standard of business ethics in the securities industry, ensuring honest securities markets and thereby promoting investor confidence, and preventing the United States from becoming a "Barbary Coast" for malefactors perpetrating frauds in foreign markets. But it provides no textual support for the last of these purposes, or for the first two as applied to the foreign securities industry and securities markets abroad. It is our function to give the statute the effect its language suggests, however modest that may be; not to extend it to admirable purposes it might be used to achieve.

If, moreover, one is to be attracted by the desirable consequences of the "significant and material conduct" test, one should also be repulsed by its adverse consequences. While there is no reason to believe that the United States has become the Barbary Coast for those perpetrating frauds on foreign securities markets, some fear that it has become the Shangri-La of class-action litigation for lawyers representing those allegedly cheated in foreign securities markets. . . .

The Solicitor General points out that the "significant and material conduct" test is in accord with prevailing notions of international comity. If so, that proves that *if* the United States asserted prescriptive jurisdiction pursuant to the "significant and material conduct" test it would not violate customary international law; but it in no way tends to prove that that is what Congress has done. . . .

JUSTICE STEVENS, with whom JUSTICE GINSBURG joins, concurring in the judgment.

While I agree that petitioners have failed to state a claim on which relief can be granted, my reasoning differs from the Court's. I would adhere to the general approach that has been the law in the Second Circuit, and most of the rest of the country, for nearly four decades.

I

Today the Court announces a new "transactional test," for defining the reach of §10(b) of the Securities Exchange Act and SEC Rule 10b-5: Henceforth, those provisions will extend only to "transactions in securities listed on domestic exchanges . . . and domestic transactions in other securities." If one confines one's gaze to the statutory text, the Court's conclusion is a plausible one. But the federal courts have been construing §10(b) in a different manner for a long time, and the Court's textual analysis is not nearly so compelling, in my view, as to warrant the abandonment of their doctrine.

The text and history of §10(b) are famously opaque on the question of when, exactly, transnational securities frauds fall within the statute's compass. As those types of frauds became more common in the latter half of the 20th century, the federal courts were increasingly called upon to wrestle with that question. The Court of Appeals for the Second Circuit, located in the Nation's financial center, led the effort. . . .

The Second Circuit's test became the "north star" of §10(b) jurisprudence, not just regionally but nationally as well. With minor variations, other courts converged on the same basic approach. . . .

In light of this history, the Court's critique of the decision below for applying "judge-made rules" is quite misplaced. This entire area of law is replete with judge-made rules, which give concrete meaning to Congress' general commands. . . .

The development of §10(b) law was hardly an instance of judicial usurpation. Congress invited an expansive role for judicial elaboration when it crafted such an open-ended statute in 1934. And both Congress and the Commission subsequently affirmed that role when they left intact the relevant statutory and regulatory language, respectively, throughout all the years that followed. Unlike certain other domains of securities law, this is "a case in which Congress has enacted a regulatory statute and then has accepted, over a long period of time, broad judicial authority to define substantive standards of conduct and liability," and much else besides. Stoneridge Investment Partners, LLC v. Scientific-Atlanta, Inc., 552 U.S. 148, 163 (2008). . . .

Thus, while the Court devotes a considerable amount of attention to the development of the case law, it draws the wrong conclusions. The Second Circuit refined its test over several decades and dozens of cases, with the tacit approval of Congress and the Commission and with the general assent of its sister Circuits. That history is a reason we should give additional weight to the Second Circuit's "judge-made" doctrine, not a reason to denigrate it. . . .

II

The Court's other main critique of the Second Circuit's approach—apart from what the Court views as its excessive reliance on functional considerations and reconstructed congressional intent—is that the Second Circuit has "disregard[ed]" the presumption against extraterritoriality. It is the Court, however, that misapplies the presumption, in two main respects.

First, the Court seeks to transform the presumption from a flexible rule of thumb into something more like a clear statement rule. We have been here before. In the case on which the Court primarily relies, EEOC v. Arabian American Oil Co., 499 U.S. 244 (1991) (*Aramco*), Chief Justice Rehnquist's majority opinion included a sentence that appeared to make the same move. Justice Marshall, in dissent, vigorously objected.

Yet even *Aramco*—surely the most extreme application of the presumption against extraterritoriality in my time on the Court[6]—contained numerous passages suggesting that the presumption may be overcome without a clear directive. And our cases both before and after *Aramco* make perfectly clear that the Court continues to give effect to "*all available evidence* about the meaning" of a provision when considering its extraterritorial application, lest we defy Congress' will. Sale v. Haitian Centers Council, Inc., 509 U.S. 155, 177 (1993) (emphasis added). Contrary to Justice Scalia's personal view of statutory interpretation, that evidence legitimately encompasses more than the enacted text. Hence, while the Court's dictum that "[w]hen a statute gives no clear indication of an extraterritorial application, it has none," makes for a nice catchphrase, the point is overstated. The presumption against extraterritoriality can be useful as a theory of congressional purpose, a tool for managing international conflict, a background norm, a tiebreaker. It does not relieve courts of their duty to give statutes the most faithful reading possible.

Second, and more fundamentally, the Court errs in suggesting that the presumption against extraterritoriality is fatal to the Second Circuit's test. For even if the presumption really were a clear statement (or "clear indication") rule, it would have only marginal relevance to this case.

It is true, of course, that "this Court ordinarily construes ambiguous statutes to avoid unreasonable interference with the sovereign authority of other nations," F. Hoffmann-La Roche Ltd v. Empagran S.A., 542 U.S. 155, 164 (2004), and that, absent contrary evidence, we presume "Congress is primarily concerned with domestic conditions," Foley Bros., Inc. v. Filardo, 336 U.S. 281, 285 (1949). Accordingly, the presumption against extraterritoriality "provides a sound basis for concluding that Section 10(b) does not apply when a securities fraud with no effects in the United States is hatched and executed entirely outside this country." Brief for United States as *Amicus Curiae* 22. But that is just about all it provides a sound basis

---

6. And also one of the most short lived. *See* Civil Rights Act of 1991, §109, 105 Stat. 1071 (repudiating *Aramco*).

for concluding. And the conclusion is not very illuminating, because no party to the litigation disputes it. No one contends that §10(b) applies to wholly foreign frauds.

Rather, the real question in this case is how much, and what kinds of, *domestic* contacts are sufficient to trigger application of §10(b). In developing its conduct-and-effects test, the Second Circuit endeavored to derive a solution from the Exchange Act's text, structure, history, and purpose. . . .

The question just stated does not admit of an easy answer. The text of the Exchange Act indicates that §10(b) extends to at least some activities with an international component, but, again, it is not pellucid as to which ones. The Second Circuit draws the line as follows: §10(b) extends to transnational frauds "only when substantial acts in furtherance of the fraud were committed within the United States," or when the fraud was "'intended to produce'" and did produce "'detrimental effects within'" the United States.

This approach is consistent with the understanding shared by most scholars that Congress, in passing the Exchange Act, "expected U.S. securities laws to apply to certain international transactions or conduct." Buxbaum, *Multinational Class Actions Under Federal Securities Law: Managing Jurisdictional Conflict*, 46 Colum. J. Transnat'l L. 14, 19 (2007). It is also consistent with the traditional understanding, regnant in the 1930's as it is now, that the presumption against extraterritoriality does not apply "when the conduct [at issue] occurs within the United States," and has lesser force when "the failure to extend the scope of the statute to a foreign setting will result in adverse effects within the United States." Environmental Defense Fund, Inc. v. Massey, 986 F.2d 528, 531 (D.C. Cir. 1993). And it strikes a reasonable balance between the goals of "preventing the export of fraud from America," protecting shareholders, enhancing investor confidence, and deterring corporate misconduct, on the one hand, and conserving United States resources and limiting conflict with foreign law, on the other.[11]

Thus, while §10(b) may not give any "clear indication" on its face as to how it should apply to transnational securities frauds, it does give strong clues that it should cover at least some of them. And in my view, the Second Circuit has done the best job of discerning what sorts of transnational frauds Congress meant in 1934—and still means today—to regulate. I do not take issue with the Court for beginning its inquiry with the statutory text, rather than the doctrine in the Courts of Appeals. I take issue with the Court for beginning *and ending* its inquiry with the statutory text, when the text does not speak with geographic precision, and for dismissing the long pedigree of, and the persuasive account of congressional intent embodied in, the Second Circuit's rule.

Repudiating the Second Circuit's approach in its entirety, the Court establishes a novel rule that will foreclose private parties from bringing §10(b) actions whenever the relevant securities were purchased or sold abroad and are not listed on a domestic exchange. The real motor of the Court's opinion, it seems, is not the

11. Given its focus on "domestic conditions," Foley Bros., Inc. v. Filardo, 336 U.S. 281, 285 (1949), I expect that virtually all " 'foreign-cubed'" actions — actions in which "(1) *foreign* plaintiffs [are] suing (2) a *foreign* issuer in an American court for violations of American securities laws based on securities transactions in (3) *foreign* countries" — would fail the Second Circuit's test. As they generally should. Under these circumstances, the odds of the fraud having a substantial connection to the United States are low. In recognition of the Exchange Act's focus on American investors and the novelty of foreign-cubed lawsuits, and in the interest of promoting clarity, it might have been appropriate to incorporate one bright line into the Second Circuit's test, by categorically excluding such lawsuits from §10(b)'s ambit.

presumption against extraterritoriality but rather the Court's belief that transactions on domestic exchanges are "the focus of the Exchange Act" and "the objects of [its] solicitude." In reality, however, it is the "public interest" and "the interests of investors" that are the objects of the statute's solicitude. . . . And while the clarity and simplicity of the Court's test may have some salutary consequences, like all bright-line rules it also has drawbacks.

Imagine, for example, an American investor who buys shares in a company listed only on an overseas exchange. That company has a major American subsidiary with executives based in New York City; and it was in New York City that the executives masterminded and implemented a massive deception that artificially inflated the stock price—and which will, upon its disclosure, cause the price to plummet. Or, imagine that those same executives go knocking on doors in Manhattan and convince an unsophisticated retiree, on the basis of material misrepresentations, to invest her life savings in the company's doomed securities. Both of these investors would, under the Court's new test, be barred from seeking relief under §10(b).

The oddity of that result should give pause. For in walling off such individuals from §10(b), the Court narrows the provision's reach to a degree that would surprise and alarm generations of American investors—and, I am convinced, the Congress that passed the Exchange Act. Indeed, the Court's rule turns §10(b) jurisprudence (and the presumption against extraterritoriality) on its head, by withdrawing the statute's application from cases in which there is *both* substantial wrongful conduct that occurred in the United States *and* a substantial injurious effect on United States markets and citizens.

Notes and Questions

1. The Supreme Court has applied a presumption against extraterritoriality since early in the nation's history. For example, in United States v. Palmer, 16 U.S. 610 (1818), the Court held that a federal piracy statute did not extend to a robbery committed on the high seas by foreign citizens on board a foreign ship. Although the Court acknowledged that the words of the statute, which purported to cover "any person or persons," were "broad enough to comprehend every human being," the Court reasoned that mere "general words" should not be construed to cover the conduct of foreign citizens outside U.S. territory. In *Palmer,* the presumption was formulated as one against the application of federal laws to *foreigners* outside the United States, but over time it came to apply to U.S. citizens abroad as well. The Supreme Court continued to apply the presumption during the twentieth century, especially with respect to labor-related statutes. *See, e.g.,* McCulloch v. Sociedad Nacional de Marineros de Honduras, 372 U.S. 10, 19-22 (1963) (National Labor Relations Act); Benz v. Compania Naviera Hidalgo, S.A., 353 U.S. 138, 143-46 (1957) (Labor Management Relations Act); Foley Bros., Inc. v. Filardo, 336 U.S. 281, 285 (1949) (Eight Hour Law). As discussed in the Notes below, however, the Court has not applied the presumption to all federal statutes.

2. In EEOC v. Arabian American Oil Co., 499 U.S. 244 (1991) (*Aramco*), which is referred to extensively in *Morrison,* the Court applied the presumption against extraterritoriality to Title VII of the Civil Rights Act, which prohibits employers from discriminating on various grounds. In that case, Boureslan, a naturalized

U.S. citizen of Lebanese descent, was hired by a subsidiary of Arabian American Oil Co. (Aramco), a Delaware company that had its principal place of business in Saudi Arabia, to work as a cost engineer in Houston. A year later, he was transferred, at his request, to Saudi Arabia. After being fired in 1984, he brought suit against Aramco under Title VII, claiming that he had been discriminated against on the basis of race, religion, and national origin.

The Court explained that, because of the presumption against extraterritoriality, "[i]t is our task to determine whether Congress intended the protections of Title VII to apply to United States citizens employed by American employers outside of the United States." The Court did not find sufficient evidence of such intent in the language of Title VII. Although the statute applies to employers "engaged in an industry affecting commerce" and defines "commerce" to include "trade, traffic, commerce, transportation, transmission, or communication . . . between a State and any place outside thereof," the Court concluded that this reference was at best ambiguous about extraterritorial application. The Court also said that a finding of extraterritorial intent should not be based on "inference from boilerplate language which can be found in any number of congressional Acts, none of which have ever been held to apply overseas."

The Court further rejected the argument that Title VII's "alien exemption" provision, which provides that the statute "shall not apply to an employer with respect to the employment of aliens outside any State," showed sufficient extraterritorial intent to overcome the presumption. The Court expressed concern that if this provision were interpreted to mean that the statute applies to the employment of U.S. citizens by employers overseas, "we see no way of distinguishing in its application between United States employers and foreign employers." If the statute applied to foreign employers overseas, however, the Court noted that it would raise serious questions under international law about the authority of the United States to regulate conduct occurring in other countries. "Without clearer evidence of congressional intent to do so than is contained in the alien-exemption clause," said the Court, "we are unwilling to ascribe to that body a policy which would raise difficult issues of international law by imposing this country's employment-discrimination regime upon foreign corporations operating in foreign commerce." The Court also noted that Congress had not specified any mechanisms for enforcement of the statute overseas and had not attempted to address potential conflicts with foreign laws and procedures, further suggesting that Congress was intending only domestic application of the statute.

Justice Marshall dissented and was joined by Justices Blackmun and Stevens. Marshall argued that the majority had improperly turned the presumption against extraterritoriality into a strict clear statement rule, and he contended that "[t]he inference arising from the alien-exemption provision is more than sufficient to rebut the presumption against extraterritoriality." As for the majority's concern about having the statute apply to foreign employers overseas, Marshall argued that, because "our cases recognize that application of United States law to United States nationals abroad ordinarily raises considerably less serious questions of international comity than does the application of United States law to foreign nationals abroad," it would be entirely appropriate for the Court to construe the statute "to apply extraterritorially to United States nationals but not to foreign nationals."

3. What are the justifications for the judge-made presumption against extraterritoriality? To comply with congressional wishes? To avoid foreign relations controversy? To defer to the Executive? To comply with international law? To keep courts out of foreign affairs? Some combination? Something else?

As for international law, it is generally accepted that customary international law imposes limits on the extent to which nations may apply their laws to conduct occurring outside their territory. During the nineteenth century, these limits on "prescriptive jurisdiction" were highly territorial, which meant that nations generally were not permitted to regulate conduct abroad, except for conduct by their own nationals. These customary international law limits became less territorial in the twentieth century. Most notably, it became accepted that nations could regulate some conduct abroad when the conduct produced or was likely to produce substantial effects within their territory. Importantly, the modern presumption against extraterritoriality applies even when the application of a federal statute would not violate customary international law limits on prescriptive jurisdiction. (Customary international law limits on prescriptive jurisdiction are discussed further in Section B of Chapter 8 of this casebook, which addresses the extraterritorial application of federal criminal statutes.)

As discussed elsewhere in the casebook, U.S. courts have long attempted to construe federal statutes to avoid violations of international law, when they reasonably can do so. *See, e.g.,* Murray v. Schooner Charming Betsy, 6 U.S. (2 Cranch) 64, 118 (1804) ("[A]n act of Congress ought never to be construed to violate the law of nations if any other possible construction remains."). What is the relationship between this "*Charming Betsy*" canon of construction and the presumption against extraterritoriality?

4. Should the presumption against extraterritoriality be applied in a case, such as *Aramco*, where the defendant is a U.S. citizen or corporation? To a case, such as *Morrison*, where deceptive practices allegedly occurred within the United States? Should the Court abandon the presumption and simply attempt to discern legislative intent? Why not apply a presumption *in favor* of extraterritoriality? Or a presumption that statutes extend to the limits of Congress's powers, or to the limits of what is permitted under international law?

5. What evidence of intent must Congress provide in order to overcome the presumption? What materials is a court allowed to look at in making this determination? Can it, for example, look at the legislative history of the statute? What does *Morrison* suggest?

6. Congress quickly overturned the specific holding of *Aramco* concerning the scope of Title VII. In the Civil Rights Act of 1991, Congress amended the definition of "employee" in Title VII to provide that, "[w]ith respect to employment in a foreign country, [the term employee] includes an individual who is a citizen of the United States." Congress also added the following provisions:

> (b) It shall not be unlawful under [this statute] . . . for an employer (or a corporation controlled by an employer), labor organization, employment agency, or joint labor-management committee controlling apprenticeship or other training or retraining (including on-the-job training programs) to take any action otherwise prohibited by such section, with respect to an employee in a workplace in a foreign country if compliance with such section would cause such employer (or such corporation), such organization, such agency, or such committee to violate the law of the foreign country in which such workplace is located.
>
> (c) (1) If an employer controls a corporation whose place of incorporation is a foreign country, any practice prohibited by [this statute] engaged in by such corporation shall be presumed to be engaged in by such employer.
>
> (2) [This statute] shall not apply with respect to the foreign operations of an employer that is a foreign person not controlled by an American employer.

Does this statute show that the Court in *Aramco* erred in its original interpretation of Title VII? Or does it show the system of separation of powers working well? Consider this assessment:

> [A]ny extraterritorial interpretation would have raised tricky issues that the Court feared might create "unintended clashes between our laws and those of other nations which could result in international discord." . . .
>
> Any interpretation the *Aramco* Court could make might thus fail to capture the nuances of just what Congress would want. However, the Court could obtain more explicit legislative guidance by provoking a legislative reaction with a preference-eliciting default rule [i.e., a default rule designed to prompt Congress to provide more guidance about its preferences], such as the extraterritorial-conduct canon. This is precisely what happened. . . .
>
> [T]he preference-eliciting default rule provoked Congress into providing just the sort of nuanced specificity and limitations that the Court would have had difficulty divining.

Einer Elhauge, Statutory Default Rules: How to Interpret Unclear Legislation 205-06 (2008). Do you agree?

7. The Court applied the presumption against extraterritoriality to §10b of the Securities Exchange Act in *Morrison* despite decades of lower court precedent to the contrary. Why didn't the Court defer to the longstanding lower court interpretation? Did Congress's failure to overturn that interpretation suggest that Congress had acquiesced in it, as suggested by Justice Stevens?

Under the Court's approach, will §10b sometimes apply to foreign conduct? If so, when? What does the Court mean when it says that the presumption against extraterritoriality "here (as often) is not self-evidently dispositive"? In applying the presumption, the Court attempts to discern the "focus" of the Securities Exchange Act. How should courts determine the focus of a statute?

Congress responded quickly to *Morrison*. Within about a month of the decision, Congress enacted §929P(b) of the Dodd-Frank Wall Street Reform and Consumer Protection Act, which provides that the federal courts have jurisdiction to hear actions brought by the Justice Department and the Securities and Exchange Commission (SEC) under the Securities Exchange Act based on either:

> (1) conduct within the United States that constitutes significant steps in furtherance of the violation, even if the securities transaction occurs outside the United States and involves only foreign investors; or (2) conduct occurring outside the United States that has foreseeable substantial effect within the United States.

The statute does not, however, authorize private suits for these situations. Rather, in a separate provision, Congress directed the SEC to solicit public comment and "conduct a study to determine the extent to which private rights of action" under the Exchange Act should apply extraterritorially. Does Congress's rapid enactment of these provisions show that the Court got it wrong? Or does it show the value of the presumption against extraterritoriality?

8. The extraterritorial application of U.S. antitrust law has a long and varied history. The Sherman Antitrust Act provides that "[e]very contract, combination in the form of trust or otherwise, or conspiracy, in restraint of trade or commerce among the several States, or with foreign nations, is declared to be illegal." The Supreme Court originally construed the Act to be strictly territorial. *See* American Banana Co. v. United Fruit Co., 213 U.S. 347 (1909). In 1927, the Court said that the

Sherman Act applied to "deliberate acts, here and elsewhere, [that] brought about forbidden results within the United States." United States v. Sisal Sales Corp., 274 U.S. 268, 276 (1927). Eighteen years later, the Second Circuit, in a case referred to it because the Supreme Court did not have a quorum of disinterested Justices, held that U.S. antitrust law applies to agreements made abroad "if they were intended to affect imports and did affect them." United States v. Aluminum Co. of Am., 148 F.2d 416, 444 (2d Cir. 1945) (en banc). The Supreme Court appeared to endorse this "effects test" in later cases. *See* Matsushita Elec. Indus. Co. v. Zenith Radio Corp., 475 U.S. 574, 582 n.6 (1985); Continental Ore Co. v. Union Carbide & Carbon Corp., 370 U.S. 690, 704 (1962).

In the 1970s and 1980s, lower courts applied the effects test aggressively to regulate extraterritorial conduct, spawning controversy with some of the United States' closest trading partners. Some lower courts modified the extraterritorial scope of the Sherman Act by engaging in comity analysis that balanced the interests of foreign nations and sometimes resulted in nonapplication of the Sherman Act even when the effects test was satisfied. *See, e.g.,* Mannington Mills v. Congoleum, 595 F.2d 1287 (3d Cir. 1979); Timberlane Lumber Co. v. Bank of America, 549 F.2d 597 (9th Cir. 1976). *But see* Laker Airways v. Sabena, 731 F.2d 909 (D.C. Cir. 1984) (granting virtually no deference to other states' interests).

In 1982, Congress enacted the Foreign Trade Antitrust Improvements Act (FTAIA) in order to clarify the application of U.S. antitrust laws to foreign conduct. The FTAIA provides that the Sherman Act "shall not apply to conduct involving trade or commerce . . . with foreign nations (other than import trade or import commerce)" unless the conduct has "a direct, substantial and reasonably foreseeable effect" on domestic commerce, U.S. imports, or U.S. exports, and "such effect gives rise to a claim" under the Sherman Act.

In Hartford Fire Insurance Co. v. California, 509 U.S. 764 (1993), the Supreme Court made clear that the presumption against extraterritoriality did not apply to the Sherman Act. Instead, the Court described the Act as applying "to foreign conduct that was meant to produce and did in fact produce some substantial effect in the United States." In that case, the Court concluded that the Act could be applied to an alleged conspiracy among foreign insurance companies to affect the U.S. insurance market. The Court in *Hartford Fire* also cast doubt on the extent to which courts should consider international comity as a basis for declining jurisdiction under the Sherman Act. Although its discussion of this point was ambiguous, some commentators construed the decision as limiting comity analysis to situations involving a "true conflict" — that is, the rare situations in which compliance with U.S. law would violate foreign law. *Compare, for example,* Roger P. Alford, *The Extraterritorial Application of Antitrust Laws: A Postscript on Hartford Fire Insurance Co. v. California,* 34 Va. J. Int'l L. 213, 220 (1993) (reading the decision that way), and Robert C. Reuland, Hartford Fire Insurance Co., *Comity, and the Extraterritorial Reach of United States Antitrust Laws,* 29 Tex. Int'l L.J. 159, 161 (1994) (same), *with* Curtis A. Bradley, *Territorial Intellectual Property Rights in an Age of Globalism,* 37 Va. J. Int'l L. 505, 557-60 (1997) (contesting that interpretation).

Justice Scalia dissented in *Hartford Fire* (along with three other Justices), arguing that the Court had overlooked the *Charming Betsy* canon of construction, pursuant to which (as noted above) federal statutes will be construed, where possible, not to violate customary international law. Scalia argued that this canon provided a basis for taking into account a range of comity considerations in deciding whether to apply the Sherman Act to foreign conduct. He relied in particular on §403 of the

Restatement (Third) of the Foreign Relations Law of the United States, which contends that customary international law disallows the extraterritorial application of law if such application would be "unreasonable," and it lists various considerations that are relevant in determining reasonableness.

The Court appeared to shift toward Justice Scalia's position in Hoffman-La Roche Ltd. v. Empagran S.A., 542 U.S. 155 (2004). In that case, purchasers of vitamins filed a class action suit alleging that various vitamin manufacturers and distributors had engaged in a conspiracy to raise vitamin prices in the United States and foreign countries, in violation of U.S. antitrust law. The issue before the Supreme Court was whether foreign purchasers of the vitamins could maintain an action under the Sherman Act for their foreign harm. In concluding that the Sherman Act does not apply to the foreign effects of foreign anticompetitive conduct, where the foreign effects are independent of any domestic effects, the Court (in an opinion by Justice Breyer) reasoned:

> [T]his Court ordinarily construes ambiguous statutes to avoid unreasonable interference with the sovereign authority of other nations. . . . This rule of construction reflects principles of customary international law—law that (we must assume) Congress ordinarily seeks to follow. *See* Restatement (Third) of Foreign Relations Law of the United States §§403(1), 403(2) (1986) (hereinafter Restatement) (limiting the unreasonable exercise of prescriptive jurisdiction with respect to a person or activity having connections with another State); Murray v. Schooner Charming Betsy, 6 U.S. 64 (1804) ("[A]n act of Congress ought never to be construed to violate the law of nations if any other possible construction remains."); Hartford Fire Insurance Co. v. California, 509 U.S. 764 (1993) (Scalia, J., dissenting) (identifying rule of construction as derived from the principle of "prescriptive comity").

The Court also found that "the FTAIA's language and history suggest that Congress designed the FTAIA to clarify, perhaps to limit, but not to expand in any significant way, the Sherman Act's scope as applied to foreign commerce."

The Restatement (Fourth) of the Foreign Relations Law of the United States, published in 2018, backs away from the claim that the reasonableness considerations are required by international law. Instead, it contends that "[c]ustomary international law permits exercises of prescriptive jurisdiction if there is a genuine connection between the subject of the regulation and the state seeking to regulate," §407, and it observes that, "[i]n exercising jurisdiction to prescribe, the United States takes account of the legitimate interests of other nations *as a matter of prescriptive comity*," §402(2) (emphasis added). In explaining its departure from §403 of the Third Restatement, it notes: "[§403] is not supported by state practice. Instead, this Restatement gives effect to the principle of reasonableness by requiring a genuine connection between the subject of the regulation and the state seeking to regulate, while noting that states often seek to reduce conflicts of prescriptive jurisdiction through various rules of domestic law that are often motivated by international comity but are not required by international law."

For various perspectives on the relationship between *Hartford Fire* and *Empagran*, see John K. Setear, *A Forest with No Trees: The Supreme Court and International Law in the 2003 Term*, 91 Va. L. Rev. 579, 610-11 (2005); Christopher Sprigman, *Fix Prices Globally, Get Sued Locally? U.S. Jurisdiction over International Cartels*, 72 U. Chi. L. Rev. 265, 280-81 (2005); Jaafar A. Riazi, *Finding Subject Matter Jurisdiction over Antitrust Claims of Extraterritorial Origin*, 54 DePaul L. Rev. 1277, 1279 (2005). For a decision finding a "true conflict" that warranted dismissal of an antitrust case on comity grounds, see In re Vitamin C Antitrust Litigation, 837 F.3d 175 (2d Cir. 2016) (finding that Chinese law required the defendants to act in a way that violated U.S. antitrust law).

9. Courts apply the presumption somewhat differently with respect to criminal statutes. In particular, they decline to apply the presumption to criminal laws that are "by their nature" concerned with extraterritorial conduct. The genesis of this limitation on the presumption (which is framed somewhat differently by different circuits) is the Supreme Court's decision in United States v. Bowman, 260 U.S. 94 (1922), in which the Court stated that the presumption against extraterritoriality "should not be applied to criminal statutes which are, as a class, not logically dependent on their locality for the Government's jurisdiction, but are enacted because of the right of the Government to defend itself against obstruction, or fraud wherever perpetrated, especially if committed by its own citizens, officers or agents." Should courts be more or less reluctant to apply U.S. criminal laws extraterritorially than they are to apply U.S. civil laws extraterritorially? (The extraterritorial application of criminal law is explored in more detail in Chapter 8.)

10. Maritime law is another context in which the Court does not apply the presumption. A good example is Lauritzen v. Larsen, 345 U.S. 571 (1953), which held that a Danish seaman on a Danish ship in Havana harbor could not recover under the Jones Act. The Court did not reach this conclusion through application of the presumption against extraterritoriality, but rather by balancing seven factors that might affect the extraterritorial application of the Jones Act, namely: the place of the wrongful act, the law of the flag, allegiance or domicile of the injured, allegiance of the defendant ship owner, place of contract, inaccessibility of the foreign forum, and the law of the forum. It is unclear why *Lauritzen* used this balancing approach rather than a flat presumption against extraterritoriality, but the decision has been followed in subsequent maritime cases. *See* Hellenic Line Ltd. v. Rhoditis, 398 U.S. 306 (1970); Romero v. International Terminal Operating Co., 358 U.S. 354 (1959). Is there something about maritime law that requires a different test for extraterritoriality?

11. First enacted in 1789, the Alien Tort Statute (ATS) provides that, "The district courts shall have original jurisdiction of any civil action by an alien for a tort only, committed in violation of the law of nations or a treaty of the United States." This statute is considered extensively in Chapter 7. As discussed there, most lower courts had assumed in recent years that suits could be brought under the ATS for torts committed in other countries. In Kiobel v. Royal Dutch Petroleum Co., 133 S. Ct. 1659 (2013), however, the Supreme Court held that the presumption against extraterritoriality applies to the ATS and that nothing in the statute rebuts the presumption. The Court reached this conclusion even though the ATS refers to international law, which by definition applies outside as well as inside the United States. The Court explained that the judicial development by the federal courts of remedies for violations of international law entails the application of a form of domestic law, and that the existence of this domestic law in ATS cases makes it appropriate to apply the presumption against extraterritoriality. If anything, said the Court, "the danger of unwarranted judicial interference in the conduct of foreign policy is magnified in the context of the ATS, because the question is not what Congress has done but instead what courts may do."

12. In RJR Nabisco, Inc. v. European Community, 136 S. Ct. 2090 (2016), the Supreme Court considered the effect of the presumption against extraterritoriality on the application of the Racketeer Influenced and Corrupt Organizations Act (RICO), 18 U.S.C. §§1961-1968. RICO addresses various ways in which an "enterprise" might be controlled, operated, or funded by a "pattern of racketeering activity." "Racketeering activity" is defined to encompass the violation of numerous specifically identified federal criminal statutes, as well as a number of generically described state criminal prohibitions. Section 1962 of RICO prohibits four types of connections between a pattern of racketeering activity and an enterprise: investing income derived from a pattern of racketeering activity in an enterprise; acquiring or maintaining an interest in an enterprise through a pattern of racketeering activity; conducting the enterprise's affairs through a pattern of racketeering activity; and conspiring to violate any of the other three prohibitions. RICO provides that violations of §1962 are subject to criminal penalties, as well as civil enforcement proceedings brought by the Attorney General. RICO also creates, in §1964(c), a private civil cause of action that allows "[a]ny person injured in his business or property by reason of a violation of section 1962" to sue in federal district court and recover treble damages, costs, and attorney's fees.

In this case, the European Community and 26 of its member states sued RJR Nabisco and its related companies under RICO, alleging that the defendants were involved in a global money-laundering scheme in association with various organized crime groups. In particular, it was alleged that the defendants had helped drug traffickers from Colombia and Russia launder money through the sale of cigarettes in Europe. The plaintiffs contended that the defendants' involvement in this scheme violated each of the prohibitions in §1962, and that these violations harmed the plaintiffs in various ways, thereby giving them a cause of action under §1964(c). In response, the defendants invoked the presumption against extraterritoriality.

In an opinion by Justice Alito, the Supreme Court began its analysis by noting that this case involved two questions of extraterritoriality: "First, do RICO's substantive prohibitions, contained in §1962, apply to conduct that occurs in foreign countries? Second, does RICO's private right of action, contained in §1964(c), apply to injuries that are suffered in foreign countries?" The Court then proceeded to explain that *Morrison* and *Kiobel* established a "two-step framework for analyzing extraterritoriality issues":

> At the first step, we ask whether the presumption against extraterritoriality has been rebutted—that is, whether the statute gives a clear, affirmative indication that it applies extraterritorially. We must ask this question regardless of whether the statute in question regulates conduct, affords relief, or merely confers jurisdiction. If the statute is not extraterritorial, then at the second step we determine whether the case involves a domestic application of the statute, and we do this by looking to the statute's "focus." If the conduct relevant to the statute's focus occurred in the United States, then the case involves a permissible domestic application even if other conduct occurred abroad; but if the conduct relevant to the focus occurred in a foreign country, then the case involves an impermissible extraterritorial application regardless of any other conduct that occurred in U.S. territory.

Applying this framework, the Court first concluded that the presumption against extraterritoriality had been rebutted for some applications of §1962. The Court noted that some of the predicate offenses identified by Congress in RICO apply by their terms to foreign conduct. As a result, said the Court, "Congress's incorporation of these (and other) extraterritorial predicates into RICO gives a clear, affirmative indication that §1962 applies to foreign racketeering activity," although the Court emphasized that this was true "only to the extent that the predicates alleged in a particular case themselves apply extraterritorially." The presumption against extraterritoriality is rebutted in cases involving such predicates, reasoned the Court, even though RICO does not specifically state that it applies abroad. "While the presumption can be overcome only by a clear indication of extraterritorial effect," said the Court, "an express statement of extraterritoriality is not essential." The statutory context can also be consulted, said the Court, and here, the context of congressional incorporation of extraterritorial predicate offenses was sufficient evidence of extraterritorial intent.

In answer to the defendants' argument that the "focus" of RICO is on the enterprise being corrupted, not the pattern of racketeering, and that RICO's enterprise provision does not contain a clear indication of extraterritorial intent, the Court explained that this argument "misunderstands *Morrison*." A consideration of "focus," the Court explained, is relevant only when there is no clear indication of extraterritoriality. In this case, however, there was such a clear indication. As a result, as long as the predicate offense is determined to apply extraterritorially, "the location of the affected enterprise does not impose an independent constraint."

Up to this point, the Court was unanimous.* A 4-3 majority of the Court then proceeded to hold that the presumption against extraterritoriality was not rebutted with respect to the private cause of action established in §1964(c) of RICO. As a result, the Court concluded that §1964(c)'s reference to a "person injured in his business or property" encompasses only injury sustained in the United States. Invoking *Kiobel* and *Morrison*, the Court explained that "we separately apply the presumption against extraterritoriality to RICO's cause of action despite our conclusion that the presumption has been overcome with respect to RICO's substantive prohibitions" because "providing a private civil remedy for foreign conduct creates a potential for international friction beyond that presented by merely applying U.S. substantive law to that foreign conduct." Indeed, the Court pointed out that in prior cases, some of the plaintiffs in this case had filed *amicus curiae* briefs expressing concern about the potential for friction associated with extraterritorial private causes of action under U.S. law.

The Court acknowledged that there might not be foreign relations friction in every case, but it noted that it is the "potential for international controversy that militates against recognizing foreign injury claims without clear direction from Congress." The Court also reasoned that, while the governmental nature of the plaintiffs in this case might reduce friction in this particular case, its interpretation of §1964(c) would necessarily apply as well to cases brought by non-governmental plaintiffs. Finally, the Court found nothing in §1964(c) providing "a clear indication that Congress intended to create a private right of action for injuries suffered outside of the United States." Because the only damage claims left in the case at this point concerned foreign injury, the Court directed that the claims be dismissed.

Justice Ginsburg dissented from this part of the Court's holding, and she was joined by Justices Breyer and Kagan. She argued that the Court should not have distinguished between the extraterritorial scope of RICO's private cause of action and that of the underlying prohibited conduct, contending that the two were linked together in the statute. She also argued that this case illustrates why it is unduly restrictive to imply a domestic injury requirement in §1964(c): "All defendants are U.S. corporations, headquartered in the United States, charged with a pattern

---

* Only seven Justices participated in the case. The Court had only eight members at this point because of Justice Scalia's death, and Justice Sotomayor did not participate.

of racketeering activity directed and managed from the United States, involving conduct occurring in the United States." As a result, she said, "this case has the United States written all over it." In addition, Justice Ginsburg expressed doubt that a blanket rule against private suits for injuries abroad would reduce international friction. "Making such litigation available to domestic but not foreign plaintiffs," she contended, "is hardly solicitous of international comity or respectful of foreign interests." Finally, Justice Ginsburg argued that, to the extent that extraterritorial application of RICO would sometimes raise comity concerns, those concerns can be addressed through other doctrines such as *forum non conveniens* and limits on standing.

Does it make sense to consider the extraterritoriality of a statute's private cause of action separately from the extraterritoriality of its substantive prohibitions? Do *Morrison* and *Kiobel* support such a bifurcation? When applying the presumption to a cause of action provision, is it appropriate for the Court to shift to considering whether there is sufficient evidence of an intent to address foreign *injury* (as opposed to foreign conduct)? In any event, the Court's decision means that the federal government can bring RICO actions based on foreign injury, but private parties cannot. Is that outcome consistent with the justifications for the presumption against extraterritoriality? For additional discussion of *RJR Nabisco*, see the August 2016 essays in the AJIL Unbound "Agora" by Pamela Bookman, Hannah Buxbaum, Anthony Colangelo, William Dodge, Stephanie Francq, Paul Stephan, and Carlos Vazquez, at https://www.asil.org/blogs/introduction-agora-reflections-rjr-nabisco-v-european-community.

13. Although the Patent Act generally applies only to infringing conduct within the United States, §271(f)(2) of the Act imposes liability for exporting components of a patented invention for assembly abroad. Patent owners who prove a violation of this provision are entitled, under §284 of the Act, to "damages adequate to compensate for the infringement, but in no event less than a reasonable royalty for the use made of the invention by the infringer." In WesternGeco LLC v. ION Geophysical Group, 138 S. Ct. 2129 (2018), the Supreme Court held that damages under §284 for a violation of §271(f)(2) can include lost foreign profits, notwithstanding the presumption against extraterritoriality. In that case, WesternGeco LLC owned patents relating to a system that it used to survey the ocean floor. Another company, ION Geophysical Corporation, manufactured components for a similar system and shipped them to companies abroad, which the companies used to create their own competing surveying system. WesternGeco sued ION for patent infringement under §271(f)(2) and was awarded damages for the survey contracts that it had lost abroad as a result of ION's actions. In an opinion by Justice Thomas, the Court held that the damage award was proper.

The Court considered the "focus" of §284. The focus of a statute, the Court explained (quoting from *Morrison*) "is 'the objec[t] of [its] solicitude,' which can include the conduct it 'seeks to regulate' as well as the parties and interests it 'seeks to protec[t]' or vindicate." The Court also noted that "[i]f the statutory provision at issue works in tandem with other provisions, it must be assessed in concert with those other provisions." Applying those principles to this case, the Court concluded that the focus of §284 is "infringement," and that when that focus is applied to claims under §271(f)(2), it covers "the act of exporting components from the United States." As a result, explained the Court, "[t]he conduct in this case that is relevant to that focus clearly occurred in the United States, as it was ION's domestic act of supplying the components that infringed WesternGeco's patents." The Court also emphasized, quoting from another decision, that §284 was designed to give patent owners "complete compensation" for infringements. Justice Gorsuch dissented and was joined by Justice Breyer. Gorsuch argued that, even if the award of lost profits here did not offend the presumption against extraterritoriality, the award was not authorized by the Patent Act, because the lost profits related to the use of the invention abroad and such use is not an "infringement" under the Act.

14. A number of academic commentators have criticized the presumption against extraterritoriality, arguing that it is inconsistent with modern international law, which allows for some extraterritorial regulation; with contemporary state choice-of-law rules, which generally employ a multifactored balancing analysis, rather than a strict territorial presumption; and with the modern legislative focus of Congress, which they contend is often international in scope. *See, e.g.,* Gary B. Born, *A Reappraisal of the Extraterritorial Reach of U.S. Law,* 24 Law & Pol'y Int'l Bus. 1 (1992); Larry Kramer, *Vestiges of* Beale: *Extraterritorial Application of American Law,* 1991 Sup. Ct. Rev. 179; Jonathan Turley, *"When in Rome": Multinational Misconduct and the Presumption Against Extraterritoriality,* 84 Nw. U. L. Rev. 598 (1990). For a defense of the presumption grounded in separation of powers principles, see Curtis A. Bradley, *Territorial Intellectual Property Rights in an Age of Globalism,* 37 Va. J. Int'l L. 505, 550-61 (1997). For a defense of the presumption grounded in principles of formalism, see Jack L. Goldsmith, *The New Formalism in United States Foreign Relations Law,* 70 U. Colo. L. Rev. 1395 (1999). For an argument that the presumption should be applied only to situations in which the extraterritorial conduct does not have effects within the United States, see William S. Dodge, *Understanding the Presumption Against Extraterritoriality,* 16 Berkeley J. Int'l L. 85 (1998). For an argument that the strength of the presumption should vary depending on the extent to which extraterritorial application raises concerns under international law, see John H. Knox, *A Presumption Against Extrajurisdictionality,* 104 Am. J. Int'l L. 351 (2010). For additional discussion of the presumption, see Lea Brilmayer, *The New Extraterritoriality:* Morrison v. National Australia Bank, *Legislative Supremacy, and the Presumption Against Extraterritorial Application of American Law,* 40 Sw. L. Rev. 655 (2011); Anthony J. Colangelo, *A Unified Approach to Extraterritoriality,* 97 Va. L. Rev. 1019 (2011); William S. Dodge, Morrison*'s Effects Test,* 40 Sw. L. Rev. 687 (2011); Jeffrey A. Meyer, *Dual Illegality and Geoambiguous Law: A New Rule for Extraterritorial Application of U.S. Law,* 95 Minn. L. Rev. 110 (2010). For a consideration of why the modern Supreme Court has not used a choice-of-law model for determining the extraterritorial application of federal statutes and an argument that this development stems in part from the pressures created by the *Erie* doctrine (which typically requires that federal courts apply state law for issues not governed by federal constitutional or statutory law), see Caleb Nelson, *State and Federal Models of the Interaction Between Statutes and Unwritten Law,* 80 U. Chi. L. Rev. 657 (2013). For a symposium on extraterritoriality, see Volume 99, Issue 6 of the Cornell Law Review (2014), with articles by John Coffee, Anthony Colangelo, Eugene Kontorovich, Jenny Martinez, Juliet Moringiello and William Reynolds, Gerald Neuman, and Louise Weinberg. For a systematic examination of claims filed by foreign governments in U.S. courts, and an argument that characterizing extraterritorial application of law as "judicial imperialism" "fails to capture the ways in which the extraterritorial application of U.S. law may fit comfortably with global governance strategies," see Hannah L. Buxbaum, *Foreign Governments as Plaintiffs in U.S. Courts and the Case Against "Judicial Imperialism,"* 73 Wash. & Lee L. Rev. 753 (2016).

15. States of the United States sometimes apply their laws extraterritorially in ways that implicate U.S. foreign relations. For example, California in 1999 enacted the Holocaust Victim Insurance Relief Act, which required any insurer doing business in California that sold insurance policies to persons in Europe that were in effect between 1920 and 1945 to file certain information about those policies with the California Insurance Commissioner. A Florida Holocaust insurance act had similar reporting requirements. Both statutes imposed disclosure obligations that in some sense regulated corporate activity outside the United States. Both statutes were challenged on dormant foreign affairs preemption and related grounds, and as discussed in Chapter 4, the Supreme Court in American Insurance Ass'n v. Garamendi held that the California statute was preempted because it was inconsistent with Executive Branch policy as embodied in certain sole executive agreements. But in the courts of appeals, both statutes were also challenged on different grounds relevant to this chapter—namely, that they violated the Fourteenth Amendment Due Process Clause.

In the interstate context, when one state applies its laws in a way that regulates activity in another state, the Due Process Clause and the Full Faith and Credit Clause, taken together, have been interpreted to provide modest restrictions on the application of state and local law to activities in another state. In general, the state need only have "a significant contact or significant aggregation of contacts, creating state interests, such that choice of its law is neither arbitrary nor fundamentally unfair." Allstate Insurance Co. v. Hague, 449 U.S. 302, 312-13 (1981) (plurality opinion). The Court in *Hague* applied this standard to conclude that Minnesota could apply its insurance law of "stacking" to an accident in Wisconsin, involving a Wisconsin domiciliary who took out insurance in Wisconsin, primarily because the decedent worked in Minnesota and his wife (who was seeking recovery in the case) moved there after the litigation began. In Phillips Petroleum v. Shutts, 472 U.S. 797 (1985), by contrast, the Court applied the same standard to conclude that Kansas could not apply its law for determining interest on royalties for land leased entirely outside of Kansas and that had no other connection to Kansas.

The application of the "significant aggregation of contacts" test to state laws that apply outside the United States (as opposed to applying in another state) is somewhat uncertain because the test purports to flow from both the Due Process and Full Faith and Credit Clauses, but the latter Clause concerns only sister-state relations and does not govern the application of state law abroad. However, the Supreme Court in an older case, which was reaffirmed in *Hague* and *Shutts,* held that the Due Process Clause considered alone does regulate the extraterritorial application of state law abroad, and it emphasized the fairness of applying the law to the defendant (as opposed to concerns about offending the foreign sovereign). *See* Home Insurance Co. v. Dick, 281 U.S. 397 (1930).

What implications do these precedents have for the state Holocaust insurance statutes? In Gerling Global Reinsurance Corp. of Am. v. Gallagher, 267 F.3d 1228 (11th Cir. 2001), the Eleventh Circuit concluded that the Florida statute ran afoul of the *Hague* test to the extent that it required production of information regarding Holocaust-era policies issued outside Florida by German entities having only some corporate affiliation with insurance companies in Florida and no other contacts with the state. By contrast, in Gerling Global Reinsurance Corp. of Am. v. Low, 296 F.3d 832 (9th Cir. 2002), *reversed on other grounds*, American Insurance Ass'n v. Garamendi, 539 U.S. 396 (2003), the Ninth Circuit concluded that *Hague, Shutts,* and *Dick* were inapposite because the California laws did not affect the substance of the contractual relationship between the policyholders and the insurance companies, but rather merely required information disclosure.

How does the *Hague/Shutts* analysis differ from the presumption against extraterritoriality and the comity analysis that apply to federal statutes? Why are the analyses different? Which analysis is more restrictive?

G. INTERNATIONAL COMITY AND ABSTENTION

Ungaro-Benages v. Dresdner Bank AG

379 F.3d 1227 (11th Cir. 2004)

[The plaintiff, Ursula Ungaro-Benages, sued Dresdner Bank and Deutsche Bank, alleging that during the Nazi regime in Germany the two banks stole her family's interest in a manufacturing company. The district court dismissed the case on multiple grounds, including the political question doctrine and international comity, while also rejecting the defendants' act of state doctrine defense.]

KRAVITCH, CIRCUIT JUDGE. . . .

In the 1990s, class-action lawsuits against the German government and private German companies [arising from Nazi-era expropriations and related issues] increased dramatically in American courts, which caused considerable concern in Germany. In an effort to stem American litigation, the German government sought to enter into an international agreement with the United States to remove this litigation to an alternative forum based in Germany.

In 2000, President Clinton entered into an agreement with the German government ("the Foundation Agreement") aimed at achieving a "legal peace."[4] See Agreement concerning the Foundation "Remembrance, Responsibility and the Future," July 17, 2000, U.S.-F.R.G., 39 I.L.M. 1298. In the agreement, the German government agreed to establish a private foundation, the Foundation "Remembrance, Responsibility, and the Future" ("the Foundation"), to hear claims brought by victims of the Nazi regime. The Foundation is funded by voluntary contributions from the German government and German companies. Both the United States government and the German government argue that this fund offers compensation to victims of the Nazi regime that would not be available through traditional litigation.

In return, the United States agreed to encourage its courts and state governments to respect the Foundation as the exclusive forum for claims from the National Socialist era. The agreement, however, did not suspend or transfer lawsuits in American courts to Germany. Instead, the United States promised to file a Statement of Interest in any lawsuit dealing with WWII restitution or reparations.[6] The statement would inform United States courts that it is in the foreign policy interests of the United States for the case to be dismissed on any valid legal ground but would not suggest that the agreement itself provides an independent legal basis for dismissal. . . .

---

4. The agreement was concluded by the President without ratification by either 2/3 of the Senate or a majority vote of Congress.

6. The United States filed such a statement in this case, both before the district court and before this court.

The plaintiff argues that the [Foundation Agreement] does not cover her suit because the relevant transactions took place before World War II, but the treaty's scope includes any actions committed during the National Socialist era. Article 1 states:

> The parties agree that the Foundation "Remembrance, Responsibility and the Future" covers, and that it would be in their interests for the Foundation to be the exclusive remedy and forum for the resolution of, *all claims that have been or may be asserted against German companies arising from the National Socialist era* and World War II.

Foundation Agreement, art. I, para. 1. Furthermore, the agreement explicitly covers property claims. In Annex B, the United States government agreed to submit a statement of interest to federal courts announcing that the Foundation is the preferred forum for "the resolution of all asserted claims against German companies arising from their involvement in the National Socialist era and World War II, including without limitation those relating to . . . damage to or *loss of property, including banking assets* and insurance policies." Foundation Agreement, Annex B, para. 1 (emphasis added).

The Foundation Agreement, however, does not provide the substantive law to resolve the case before us because it neither settles the outstanding claim nor directs that all claims be transferred to the Foundation's settlement procedures. Rather, the United States simply promises to announce that such a transfer is in the United States' national interests. In Annex B, the United States government is obliged to inform domestic courts that its policy interests "favor dismissal on any valid legal ground," but "does not suggest that its policy interests concerning the Foundation in themselves provide an independent legal basis for dismissal." Foundation Agreement, Annex B, para. 7. Thus, by its own terms, the agreement does not provide a basis to dismiss or suspend litigation against German companies stemming from their actions during the National Socialist era.

Because the Foundation Agreement firmly establishes that issues related to litigation against German corporations from the National Socialist era are governed by federal law, but does not provide any substantive principles by which to adjudicate this case, we must examine federal law not based in treaty to resolve the issues presented here. . . .

[The court declined to uphold dismissal of the case under the political question doctrine, reasoning that "[a]djudication of the present claim would not interfere with the executive's handling of foreign relations or show a lack of respect to the executive's power in foreign affairs." It then turned to consider the doctrine of international comity.]

International comity reflects "the extent to which the law of one nation, as put in force within its territory, whether by executive order, by legislative act, or by judicial decree, shall be allowed to operate within the dominion of another nation." Hilton v. Guyot, 159 U.S. 113, 163 (1895). It is an abstention doctrine: A federal court has jurisdiction but defers to the judgment of an alternative forum. Turner Entm't Co. v. Degeto Film, 25 F.3d 1512, 1518 (11th Cir. 1994).[13] International comity serves as a guide to federal courts where "the issues to be resolved are entangled in international relations." In re Maxwell Communication Corp., 93 F.3d 1036, 1047 (2d Cir. 1996). The district court dismissed this case on

---

13. Abstention doctrines are prudential doctrines and this court is not obligated under American statutory law to defer to foreign courts. *Turner Entm't,* 25 F.3d at 1518 ("Federal courts have a 'virtually unflagging obligation' to exercise the jurisdiction conferred upon them. Nevertheless, in some private international disputes the prudent and just action for a federal court is to abstain from the exercise of jurisdiction.") (internal citations omitted).

international comity grounds in favor of resolution at the Foundation because the Foundation is a specialized system, supported by the United States government and the international community, for addressing Nazi era claims. The district court further considered that all of the relevant transactions leading to this suit took place in Germany and, thus, Germany was the most appropriate forum state for the resolution of these claims.

The doctrine of international comity can be applied retrospectively or prospectively. When applied retrospectively, domestic courts consider whether to respect the judgment of a foreign tribunal or to defer to parallel foreign proceedings. *See, e.g.*, Finanz AG Zurich v. Banco Economico S.A., 192 F.3d 240 (2d Cir. 1999) (affording comity in deference to concurrent foreign bankruptcy proceedings); *Turner Entm't*, 25 F.3d at 1514 (staying domestic legal proceedings to defer to concurrent German proceedings on the merits of the dispute); *see also* Canadian Southern Ry. v. Gebhard, 109 U.S. 527 (1883) (dismissing the claims of American railroad bond holders in favor of Canadian legislation and legal proceedings aimed at reorganizing the railroad's corporate structure).

When applied prospectively, domestic courts consider whether to dismiss or stay a domestic action based on the interests of our government, the foreign government and the international community in resolving the dispute in a foreign forum. *See* Bi v. Union Carbide Chems. & Plastics Co., 984 F.2d 582 (2d Cir. 1993) (dismissing the claims of Indian nationals injured by a chemical plant explosion in Bhopal based on Indian legislation granting the Indian government exclusive standing to represent all victims); *see also* Jota v. Texaco, 157 F.3d 153 (2d Cir. 1998) (considering whether to dismiss proceedings related to environmental damage in Ecuador based on Ecuador's interest in foreign or domestic resolution and holding dismissal on grounds of *forum non conveniens* and comity erroneous); Pravin Banker Assocs. v. Banco Popular Del Peru, 109 F.3d 850 (2d Cir. 1997) (considering whether to stay proceedings brought by an American holder of Peruvian debt while Peru attempted to renegotiate its commercial debt under the Brady Plan).

The analysis for both forms of international comity embody similar concerns with foreign governments' interests, fair procedures, and American public policy, but they emphasize different issues. When applied retrospectively, federal courts evaluate three factors: (1) whether the foreign court was competent and used "proceedings consistent with civilized jurisprudence," (2) whether the judgment was rendered by fraud, and (3) whether the foreign judgment was prejudicial because it violated American public policy notions of what is decent and just. Courts also consider whether the central issue in dispute is a matter of foreign law and whether there is a prospect of conflicting judgments.

Applied prospectively, federal courts evaluate several factors, including the strength of the United States' interest in using a foreign forum, the strength of the foreign governments' interests, and the adequacy of the alternative forum. Our determination of the adequacy of the alternative forum is informed by *forum non conveniens* analysis. . . .

Here, we decide to abstain based on the strength of our government's interests in using the Foundation, the strength of the German government's interests, and the adequacy of the Foundation as an alternative forum. The United States government has consistently supported the Foundation as the exclusive forum for the resolution of litigation against German corporations related to their acts during the National Socialist era. The President entered into negotiations with the German government and determined that the interests of American citizens, on the whole, would be best served by establishing the Foundation Agreement.[14] The agreement offers monetary compensation to nationals who were used as slave labor and were victims of insurance fraud as well as those deprived of their property. The fund to provide this compensation was established with the expectation that all such American litigation against German corporations would be resolved at the Foundation. In creating a comprehensive compensatory scheme for all remaining victims of the Nazi era, the Foundation Agreement may end up favoring the monetary interests of some American victims more than others. International agreements, however, often favor some domestic interests over others, and the President has the constitutional authority to settle the international claims of American citizens, even if the claimants would prefer litigation in American courts. Likewise, the German government has a significant interest in having the Foundation be the exclusive forum for these claims in its efforts to achieve lasting legal peace with the international community.

Furthermore, the Foundation is an adequate alternative forum. The tribunal has a speciality in the relevant post-war law and has relaxed standards of proof to ease the burden for the potential plaintiffs to obtain compensation. The Foundation offers victims of the Nazi era an adequate remedy, even if the Foundation cannot provide as substantial an award as American courts. *See* Piper Aircraft Co. v. Reyno, 454 U.S. 235, 254 (1981) (noting that a forum can be adequate even where there is the potential for a smaller damage award).

The plaintiff maintains that the forum does not provide her with a remedy because her claims are barred under the Foundation Agreement. Our reading of the Foundation Agreement, however, does not lead us to the conclusion that her claims necessarily would be barred. Annex A of the agreement specifically addresses claims of deprivation of property by German companies based on discrimination. That provision provides that the plaintiff's claims would be barred if her family could have received compensation under the German restitution laws. The plaintiff is free to argue to the Foundation, just as she has argued to this court, that her claims should not be barred because the defendant banks prevented her family from pursuing their property claims after the war. The Foundation is in just as good a position as this court to consider the allegedly fraudulent acts by the defendant banks and is likely to be far more familiar than this court with German law on the relevant issues. . . .

We recognize that the plaintiff would prefer to pursue her claim in federal court. She is an American citizen, and even though her claim is derivative of her grandmother, we give particular attention to her choice of forum. On balance, however, we find that the strength of the interests held by the American government and the German government outweigh the plaintiff's preference. In doing so, we note that American and German governments have entered into extensive negotiations over this subject and those negotiations affect thousands of other victims of the Nazi regime. While we do not use the Foundation Agreement as an independent legal basis to dismiss this case, we must take the governments' ongoing interests in settling claims from the National Socialist era and World War II into account in our international comity analysis. We further note that all of the relevant events implicated in this litigation took place in Germany and will involve issues of German

---

14. Even if the governments had not engaged in negotiations on this issue, the executive's statements of national interest in issues affecting our foreign relations are entitled to deference.

law. Finally, the plaintiff has an alternative forum, established in part by the United States government, where she can seek redress.

Notes and Questions

1. International comity is a multifaceted doctrine. At the most abstract level, international comity refers to the respect that U.S. courts give to the laws, acts, and decisions of foreign countries. As the Supreme Court famously stated (in a case involving an attempt to enforce a foreign judgment in a U.S. court):

> "Comity," in the legal sense, is neither a matter of absolute obligation, on the one hand, nor of mere courtesy and good will, upon the other. But it is the recognition which one nation allows within its territory to the legislative, executive, or judicial acts of another nation, having due regard both to international duty and convenience, and to the rights of its own citizens or of other persons who are under the protection of its laws.

Hilton v. Guyot, 159 U.S. 113, 163-64 (1895). *See also* Societe Nationale Industrielle Aerospatiale v. United States District Court, 482 U.S. 522, 543 n.27 (1987) ("Comity refers to the spirit of cooperation in which a domestic tribunal approaches the resolution of cases touching the laws and interests of other sovereign states."); Hartford Fire Ins. Co. v. California, 509 U.S. 764 (1993) (Scalia, J., dissenting) (defining "the comity of courts" as a decision by a court in one country to decline jurisdiction "over matters more appropriately adjudged elsewhere"). International comity arises in a variety of contexts, including the recognition and enforcement of foreign judgments, the stay or dismissal of U.S. litigation because of similar litigation already pending in a foreign country, international anti-suit injunctions, and the stay or dismissal of U.S. litigation because of a determination that the case is best brought in a foreign or international or related forum, regardless of whether proceedings have actually begun there. Below we consider each of these situations.

2. Although the Constitution's Full Faith and Credit Clause requires each U.S. state to recognize and enforce the judgments of other states, see U.S. Const. art. IV, §1, U.S. courts are not under any constitutional, federal statutory, or treaty obligation to recognize or enforce foreign judgments. As early as 1895, however, the Supreme Court held that foreign judgments are generally enforceable as a matter of common law "comity," subject to a "reciprocity" requirement whereby the foreign government would have to enforce similar U.S. judgments. *See* Hilton v. Guyot, 159 U.S. 113 (1895). Today, enforcement of foreign judgments is generally viewed as governed by state law (either under state common law or state codifications of the Uniform Foreign Money Judgments Recognition Act, 13 U.L.A. 261 (1986 & Supp.)). Under most of these state laws, courts will presumptively recognize and enforce foreign judgments, even in the absence of reciprocity, as long as the foreign court had jurisdiction, the foreign proceedings were procedurally fair, and enforcement does not offend a fundamental public policy. As a result, foreign judgments are often recognized and enforced in the United States, although these judgments receive somewhat less respect in U.S. courts than the judgments of sister states. For cases in which U.S. courts have declined to enforce foreign judgments because of public policy concerns, see, for example, Matusevitch v. Telnikoff, 877 F. Supp. 1 (D.D.C. 1995) (declining to enforce libel judgment from England because doing so would, in light of the lower speech protections in England, violate public policy); Bachchan v. India Abroad Publications, Inc., 585 N.Y.S.2d 661 (N.Y. Sup. Ct. 1992) (similar). Is it appropriate for U.S. courts to scrutinize foreign judgments in this way? Might such scrutiny undermine U.S. foreign relations?

3. In 2010, Congress enacted the "Securing the Protection of our Enduring and Established Constitutional Heritage Act," also known as the "SPEECH Act." The Act provides that:

> Notwithstanding any other provision of Federal or State law, a domestic court shall not recognize or enforce a foreign judgment for defamation unless the domestic court determines that —
>
> (A) the defamation law applied in the foreign court's adjudication provided at least as much protection for freedom of speech and press in that case as would be provided by the first amendment to the Constitution of the United States and by the constitution and law of the State in which the domestic court is located; or
>
> (B) even if the defamation law applied in the foreign court's adjudication did not provide as much protection for freedom of speech and press as the first amendment to the Constitution of the United States and the constitution and law of the State, the party opposing recognition or enforcement of that foreign judgment would have been found liable for defamation by a domestic court applying the first amendment to the Constitution of the United States and the constitution and law of the State in which the domestic court is located.

28 U.S.C. §4102(a).

The Act further provides (among other things) that:

> Notwithstanding any other provision of Federal or State law, a domestic court shall not recognize or enforce a foreign judgment for defamation unless the domestic court determines that the exercise of personal jurisdiction by the foreign court comported with the due process requirements that are imposed on domestic courts by the Constitution of the United States.

Id. at §4102(b)(1).

The legislative history of the Act expresses concern about the potential chilling effect of "libel tourism," pursuant to which plaintiffs might seek to obtain defamation judgments in jurisdictions with lower speech protections than in the United States and then attempt to enforce the judgments in the United States. For a decision applying the Act to bar enforcement of a defamation judgment rendered in Canada, see Trout Point Lodge, Ltd. v. Handshoe, 729 F.3d 481 (5th Cir. 2013).

4. In Chevron v. Naranjo, 667 F.3d 232 (2d Cir. 2012), the Second Circuit held that the Uniform Foreign Money Judgments Recognition Act does not give potential judgment-debtors a cause of action to challenge foreign judgments before enforcement of those judgments is sought. Rather, "[j]udgment-debtors can challenge a foreign judgment's validity under the Recognition Act only defensively, in response to an attempted enforcement." The court based its decision in part on considerations of international comity:

> A decision by a court in one jurisdiction, pursuant to a legislative enactment in that jurisdiction, to decline to enforce a judgment rendered in a foreign jurisdiction necessarily touches on international comity concerns. It is a particularly weighty matter for a court in one country to declare that another country's legal system is so corrupt or unfair that its judgments are entitled to no respect from the courts of other nations.

That inquiry may be necessary, however, when a party seeks to invoke the authority of our courts to enforce a foreign judgment.

But when a court in one country attempts to preclude the courts of every other nation from ever considering the effect of that foreign judgment, the comity concerns become far graver. In such an instance, the court risks disrespecting the legal system not only of the country in which the judgment was issued, but also those of other countries, who are inherently assumed insufficiently trustworthy to recognize what is asserted to be the extreme incapacity of the legal system from which the judgment emanates. The court presuming to issue such an injunction sets itself up as the definitive international arbiter of the fairness and integrity of the world's legal systems.

But cf. Chevron Corp. v. Donziger, 833 F.3d 74 (2d Cir. 2016) (upholding injunctive relief under RICO and New York common law, directed against the lead attorney for the plaintiffs and others over whom the district court had personal jurisdiction, based on evidence of fraud, bribery, coercion, and other misconduct in the foreign proceedings).

5. Sometimes courts defer out of comity not to foreign judgments, but rather to foreign judicial proceedings. In such cases, U.S. courts may decide to stay or dismiss litigation in the United States when similar or related litigation is pending in a foreign country. *See, e.g.,* Zurich v. Banco Economico, S.A., 192 F.3d 240 (2d Cir. 1999); Turner Entertainment Co. v. Degeto Film GmbH, 25 F.3d 1512 (11th Cir. 1994); *cf.* Seguros del Estado, S.A. v. Scientific Games, Inc., 262 F.3d 1164 (11th Cir. 2001) (declining to stay U.S. suit out of deference to foreign proceeding because the foreign suit involved materially different issues, documents, and parties). Courts disagree about the precise standards for this sort of "international abstention," with some courts holding that it is appropriate only in exceptional circumstances and other courts holding that there is broad discretion to avoid such duplicative litigation. *See Turner,* 25 F.3d at 1518 (describing differing approaches).

Occasionally, U.S. courts will do essentially the opposite of international abstention: they will issue a so-called anti-suit injunction to prevent persons or entities subject to their personal jurisdiction from pursuing litigation in foreign tribunals. *See, e.g.,* Laker Airways Ltd. v. Sabena, Belgian World Airlines, 731 F.2d 909 (D.C. Cir. 1984). As with stays in the face of foreign proceedings, courts disagree about the precise standards for issuing anti-suit injunctions, with some courts holding that they are appropriate whenever there is a duplication of parties and issues and the prosecution of simultaneous proceedings would frustrate the speedy and efficient determination of the case, and other courts focusing more narrowly on whether the foreign action imperils the jurisdiction of the forum court or threatens some strong national policy. *See* Quaak v. Klynveld Peat Marwick Goerdeler Bedrijfsrevisoren, 361 F.3d 11, 17-19 (1st Cir. 2004) (describing differing approaches). Considerations of comity are viewed as favoring a stay of U.S. litigation in the face of foreign parallel proceedings, and as weighing against the issuance of an anti-suit injunction that would stop a foreign proceeding.

In both situations, international comity is viewed as favoring foreign over U.S. litigation. Does this make sense? Isn't comity a two-way street? Should U.S. court reliance on comity depend on whether the foreign nation in question gives comity to U.S. proceedings?

6. International comity can involve respect not only for foreign judicial proceedings, but also for foreign laws. Consider, for example, Bi v. Union Carbide Chemical and Plastics Co., 984 F. 2d 582 (2d Cir. 1993). The issue in *Bi* was whether

U.S. courts should defer to an Indian statute that gave the Indian government exclusive standing to represent the victims of the Bhopal toxic tort disaster in India in a suit against a U.S. company and its Indian subsidiary. Pursuant to this statute, the Indian government had earlier brought suit in Indian courts to resolve the Bhopal matter, and had reached a comprehensive settlement approved by the Indian Supreme Court. The suit in *Bi* was an attempt by plaintiffs unhappy with the Indian settlement to litigate their claims in the United States. The *Bi* court, characterizing the issue as one "involving comity among nations," rejected the suit. Relying in part on the fact that India was a democratic nation, and in part on the logic of the act of state doctrine, the court reasoned:

> To grant the victims of the Bhopal disaster, most of whom are citizens of India, access to our courts when India has set up what it believes to be the most effective method of dealing with a difficult problem would frustrate India's efforts. . . . [W]ere we to pass on the validity of India's response to a disaster that occurred within its borders, it would disrupt our relations with the country and frustrate the efforts of the international community to develop methods to deal with problems of this magnitude in the future.

Why should an Indian statute rather than U.S. law determine the scope of jurisdiction in U.S. federal courts in cases involving the behavior of U.S. corporations? Why does it matter to the court that India is a democracy? Is the act of state doctrine relevant here?

7. Considerations of comity can also arise when courts are asked to abstain not in the face of a foreign judicial proceeding or law, but rather in the face of some alternate foreign or international effort to resolve issues related to the litigation. For example, in Pravin Banker Assocs. v. Banco Popular Del Peru, 109 F.3d 850 (2d Cir. 1997), a Peruvian bank that had defaulted on loans from American financial institutions sought to stay enforcement proceedings in the United States while it attempted to restructure its commercial debt under a plan worked out by U.S. Treasury Secretary Nicholas Brady. The court stated that "[u]nder the principles of international comity, United States courts ordinarily refuse to review acts of foreign governments and defer to proceedings taking place in foreign countries, allowing those acts and proceedings to have extraterritorial effect in the United States," but emphasized that international comity "remains a rule of 'practice, convenience, and expediency' rather than of law." It noted that there were two competing U.S. government policy interests in the case: foreign debt resolution under the Brady plan, and ensuring the enforceability of valid debts. Because the district court had previously granted a six-month stay (thus serving to some degree the first interest), the court of appeals concluded (in agreement with the district court) that a further stay would unduly prejudice the second interest. The court did not expressly consider Peru's interest, or the adequacy of the alternative forum. But it did note that granting a stay would have "converted what the United States intended to be voluntary and open-ended negotiations between Peru and its creditors into the equivalent of a judicially-enforced bankruptcy proceeding, for it would, in effect, have prohibited the exercise of legal rights outside of the negotiations." For somewhat similar reasoning, see Bodner v. Banque Paribas, 114 F. Supp. 2d 117, 129-30 (E.D.N.Y. 2000) (declining to defer under international comity to independent commissions formed by the French government to study and propose solutions to Holocaust-era atrocities, reasoning that the suit would not impede the commissions' work, and that in any event the commissions were too informal and did not provide "a conflicting judicial, legislative, or executive act to which this Court could reasonably defer").

8. In what ways does *Ungaro-Benages* extend the international comity doctrine beyond the decisions described in the above Notes? Why is it appropriate for a U.S. court to dismiss a case brought by a U.S. citizen, over which the court has jurisdiction, in favor of a private, non-U.S., nonjudicial claims settlement mechanism that might not provide the plaintiff with relief? Why is the Foundation an adequate alternative forum? Is it true, as the court maintains, that the private German Foundation "is in just as good a position as this court to consider the allegedly fraudulent acts by the defendant banks"? Why does it matter that "all of the relevant events implicated in this litigation took place in Germany and will involve issues of German law"?

9. In *Ungaro-Benages,* the governmental interest analysis was relatively straightforward, since both countries evinced a clear preference for the Foundation in the agreement setting it up. What would happen, however, if there were no such evidence of the governments' relative interests? How would the court decide? Does a court have competence to make such decisions in the absence of express guidance from the governments themselves?

10. More generally, what role did the Foundation Agreement play in the court's decision to abstain in *Ungaro-Benages*? Did the Foundation Agreement impose any *legal* obligations to dismiss the suit? Does it matter that the President entered into this international agreement with Germany on his own authority, without the consent of either the Senate or Congress? As we will learn in Chapter 6, the Supreme Court has recognized presidential authority to enter into so-called executive agreements of this sort, and courts have traditionally deferred to such agreements when they require dismissal of suits in U.S. courts in favor of foreign forums. The Foundation Agreement, however, does not compel dismissal in favor of a foreign forum; rather, it simply compels the Executive Branch to urge courts to so dismiss. The Executive Branch did file a "Statement of Interest" in the *Ungaro-Benages* case that stated that the "President of the United States concluded that it would be in the foreign policy interests of the United States for the Foundation to be the exclusive forum and remedy for the resolution of all asserted claims against German companies arising from their involvement in the Nazi era and World War II." Should courts defer to such presidential suggestions in this context? Would the result in the case have been different if the Executive Branch had not suggested dismissal? Would it have been different if Germany had, without U.S. cooperation or pressure, unilaterally established the Foundation to resolve Nazi expropriation claims?

11. The court's application of comity in *Ungaro-Benages* is similar to the *forum non conveniens* doctrine. Under the *forum non conveniens* doctrine as applied by federal courts, district courts have discretion to dismiss a case if they determine that there is an adequate alternate forum and various private and public interest factors weigh in favor of adjudicating the case in that forum. *See* Piper Aircraft Co. v. Reyno, 454 U.S. 235 (1981). In determining whether an alternate forum is "adequate," courts look primarily at whether the forum would have jurisdiction to hear the dispute and the ability to provide a remedy. Ordinarily, an alternate forum will not be considered inadequate merely because its laws or procedures are less favorable to the plaintiff than those of the United States. The private interest factors to be considered in the *forum non conveniens* analysis include "the 'relative ease of access to sources of proof; availability of compulsory process for attendance of unwilling, and the cost of obtaining attendance of willing, witnesses; possibility of view of premises, if view would be appropriate to the action; and all other practical problems that make trial of a case easy, expeditious and inexpensive.'" The public interest factors include "the administrative difficulties flowing from court congestion; the 'local interest in having localized controversies decided at home'; the interest in having the trial of a diversity case in a forum that is at home with the law that must govern the action; the avoidance of unnecessary problems in conflict of laws, or in the application of foreign law; and the unfairness of burdening citizens in an unrelated forum with jury duty." In considering these factors, courts apply a presumption in favor of the plaintiff's choice of forum, although less of a presumption is given when the plaintiff is a foreign citizen. The court in *Ungaro-Benages* states that its determination of the adequacy of the alternative forum is "informed by *forum non conveniens* analysis," but otherwise it treats the prospective application of comity as a separate doctrine from *forum non conveniens*. Why didn't the court simply apply the *forum non conveniens* doctrine? How does the court's application of comity differ from the *forum non conveniens* doctrine? Does it makes sense to have both a comity doctrine like the one applied by the court and a *forum non conveniens* doctrine? For a critique of the *forum non conveniens* doctrine and an argument that courts should move away from it, see Maggie Gardner, *Retiring* Forum Non Conveniens, 92 N.Y.U. L. Rev. 390 (2017).

12. The U.S. Court of Appeals for the Ninth Circuit adopted a broad interpretation of the comity doctrine in Mujica v. AirScan Inc., 771 F.3d 580 (9th Cir. 2014). That case concerned the bombing of a Colombian village by the Colombian air force in 1998, as part of a conflict with insurgents. Civilian victims of the bombing sought damages against various Colombian government defendants in the Colombian courts, and a criminal action was also brought in Colombia against three Colombian air force officers who were allegedly responsible for the bombing. While their damages action was pending in Colombia, the victims brought suit in a federal court in California against two U.S. corporations, alleging that the corporations had been involved in helping to plan and facilitate the bombing. In support of their claims, the plaintiffs relied on the Torture Victim Protection Act (TVPA), the Alien Tort Statute (ATS), and California state law. (Both the TVPA and the ATS are discussed extensively in Chapter 7 of the casebook.)

The court relied on international comity in directing a dismissal of the state law claims. International comity, the court reasoned, is a federal common law doctrine that can preempt state law, even when other bases for federal preemption are inapplicable. The court also concluded that for "adjudicatory comity"—that is, the deference that a U.S. court will show to foreign legal proceedings—no "true conflict" is required between U.S. law and foreign law in order for the U.S. court to abstain from exercising jurisdiction.

Applying the comity analysis from the Eleventh Circuit's decision in *Ungaro-Benages*, the court considered "the strength of the United States' interest in using a foreign forum, the strength of the foreign governments' interests, and the adequacy of the alternative forum." The factors relevant to the strength of the U.S. interest, the court further explained, include "(1) the location of the conduct in question, (2) the nationality of the parties, (3) the character of the conduct in question, (4) the foreign policy interests of the United States, and (5) any public policy interests." Those factors favored dismissal of the state law claims in this case, the court reasoned, because (among other things) the conduct occurred outside the United States and the U.S. government had specifically indicated that it was concerned that the litigation would undermine U.S.-Colombian relations. While acknowledging that California might have some interest in allowing the plaintiffs' claims, the court said that this interest "should not be overstated, given that Plaintiffs are not California citizens, that their claims concern events that occurred abroad, and that one Defendant (AirScan) is not a California resident corporation."

As for the strength of Colombia's interest, the court noted that Colombia had expressed concerns about the case, and that its courts had already addressed the incident in civil and criminal litigation. Finally, with respect to the adequacy of the Colombian courts, the court pointed out that the plaintiffs had managed to obtain an appreciable sum of money in their suit against the government defendants. While Colombian law now precluded the plaintiffs from seeking a secondary recovery of damages from the corporate defendants, the court reasoned that this did not make the Colombian courts inadequate because such limitations on recovery are common, and the plaintiffs could have sued the corporations originally in their action in Colombia and had not done so. One of the judges in the case dissented, complaining that the majority had "needlessly announce[d] novel standards that will thwart the ability of not only these plaintiffs, but also of every other alien who seeks to hold a U.S. corporation accountable for atrocities committed abroad."

To what extent does this decision extend the comity doctrine beyond the holding in *Ungaro-Benages*? For criticism of the decision, see William Dodge, *International Comity Runs Amok*, Just Security (Feb. 3, 2015).

13. In some cases involving conduct outside the United States, U.S. courts may require, as a precondition to suit, that the plaintiff first exhaust remedies that are potentially available in another country. As discussed in Chapter 7, such an exhaustion requirement has been mandated by Congress for suits brought under a 1992 human rights statute, the TVPA. As also discussed in that chapter, the Supreme Court has suggested that it might be appropriate for courts to impose such a requirement in cases brought under a more general statute that has been used for human rights litigation, the ATS. In Sarei v. Rio Tinto, PLC, 550 F.3d 822 (9th Cir. 2008) (en banc), the Ninth Circuit held that, while exhaustion is not required in ATS cases, it might be appropriate in select cases as a prudential matter, especially when a case has only a weak nexus to the United States. The Seventh Circuit has held that an exhaustion requirement is appropriate for cases brought under the takings of property exception to immunity in the Foreign Sovereign Immunities Act (28 U.S.C. §1605(a)(3)). *See* Abelesz v. Magyar Nemzeti Bank, 692 F.3d 661 (7th Cir. 2012); Fischer v. Magyar Allamvasutak Zrt, 777 F.3d 847 (7th Cir. 2015). (The Act is considered in Chapter 7.) Any exhaustion requirement is likely to have exceptions for situations in which pursuing relief in the foreign country would be futile, dangerous, or clearly inadequate to address the alleged harm. *Cf.* Agudas Chasidei Chabad of U.S. v. Russian Federation, 528 F.3d 924, 949 (D.C. Cir. 2008) ("Assuming that an exhaustion requirement exists . . . the only remedy Russia has identified is on its face inadequate.").

14. The court in *Ungaro-Benages* describes international comity as an "abstention" doctrine. That is, under the court's approach to comity, U.S. courts are to abstain from exercising their jurisdiction over certain international cases out of deference to, among other things, foreign government interests and proceedings (or potential proceedings). There are a number of *domestic* abstention doctrines, pursuant to which federal courts will abstain from adjudicating an issue or a case in favor of pending or future litigation in state court. Although domestic abstention doctrines are extraordinarily complex, the following three factors are usually involved:

> First, the plaintiff claims that a provision of state law is invalid by reason of federal law, whether by constitutional invalidity, or federal preemption, or the like. Second, the state legal provision is ambiguous in terms of the allegedly superseding federal provision; that is, the state provision is susceptible of being construed or applied in a way that would not run afoul of federal law. Third, the legal issue thus posed already has arisen in a pending state proceeding or would so arise in a state proceeding if the legal controversy went forward in the normal course of events.

Fleming James, Jr., Geoffrey C. Hazard, Jr., & John Leubsdorf, Civil Procedure §2.29 at 149-50 (5th ed. 2001). How, if at all, do the justifications for domestic abstention—having to do with federal courts trying to avoid resolving sensitive federal questions out of respect to the state court system—translate into the international arena? For a critique of the lower courts' reliance on a general doctrine of "international comity abstention" and an argument that the courts should specify narrower grounds for abstention in transnational cases, see Maggie Gardner, *Abstention at the Border*, 105 Va. L. Rev. 63 (2019).

15. Professors Eric Posner and Cass Sunstein link the issue of comity with the issue of deference to the Executive discussed above in Section D. They contend that, when applying comity doctrines, "courts seem to be making a presumptive judgment that to the United States, deferring to the interests of foreign sovereigns can produce benefits for Americans that outweigh the costs." They further argue that "there are strong reasons, rooted in constitutional understanding and in institutional competence, to allow the executive branch to resolve issues of international comity, at least where the underlying statute is unclear." As a result, they advocate strong deference to the Executive Branch in foreign relations law cases, along the lines of the *Chevron* doctrine in administrative law. "It follows," they contend, "that if the executive wants to interpret ambiguous statutes so as to apply extraterritorially, or so as to conflict with international law, it should be permitted to do so." *See* Eric A. Posner & Cass R. Sunstein, *Chevronizing Foreign Relations Law*, 116 Yale L.J. 1170 (2007). Derek Jinks and Neil Katyal respond that this approach to deference would "radically expand the authority of the executive to interpret and, in effect, to break foreign relations law." They contend that deference is inappropriate with respect to Executive interpretations of, or decisions to breach, international law that operates in what they call the "Executive constraining zone"—that is, in situations where international law has the status of supreme federal law, it is made at least in part outside the Executive, and it conditions the exercise of Executive power. Courts should not allow the Executive to violate such law, they contend, absent explicit congressional authorization. *See* Derek Jinks & Neal Katyal, *Disregarding Foreign Relations Law*, 116 Yale L.J. 1230 (2007).

To what extent, if at all, would the Posner and Sunstein approach entail a departure from current law? To what extent, if at all, would the Jinks and Katyal approach entail such a departure?

16. In Animal Science Products, Inc. v. Hebei Welcome Pharmaceutical Co. Ltd., 138 S. Ct. 1865 (2018), the Supreme Court unanimously held that U.S. courts are not required to accept the representations of foreign governments about the content of their law. That case involved a class action suit brought against Chinese corporations for allegedly having conspired to fix prices and limit supply for Vitamin C sold into the U.S. market, in violation of U.S. antitrust law. During the litigation, the Ministry of Commerce of the People's Republic of China filed *amicus curiae* briefs explaining that Chinese law required the defendants to engage in the actions in question, a proposition that, if accepted, would potentially lead to dismissal of the case under various doctrines. The U.S. Court of Appeals for the Second Circuit held that the Chinese government's representation should be treated as binding, reasoning that "when a foreign government, acting through counsel or otherwise, directly participates in U.S. court proceedings by providing a sworn evidentiary proffer regarding the construction and effect of its laws and regulations, which is reasonable under the circumstances presented, a U.S. court is bound to defer to those statements."

In reversing the Second Circuit, the Supreme Court noted that Rule 44.1 of the Federal Rules of Civil Procedure, which has been in place since 1966, directs that a determination of the content of foreign law "must be treated as a ruling on a question of law" and that in making such a ruling a court may consider "any relevant material or source." This rule, the Court observed, "does not address the weight a federal court determining foreign law should give to the views presented by the foreign government." The Court accepted that, as a matter of "international comity," courts "should carefully consider a foreign state's views about the meaning of its own laws," but it said that "the appropriate weight in each case will depend upon the circumstances; a federal court is neither bound to adopt the foreign government's characterization nor required to ignore other relevant materials." "Relevant considerations," continued the Court, "include the statement's clarity, thoroughness, and support; its context and purpose; the transparency of the foreign legal system; the role and authority of the entity or official offering the statement; and the statement's consistency with the foreign government's past positions." Finally, the Court explained that stronger deference was not warranted in order to obtain reciprocity by foreign courts for representations by the U.S. government about the content of its own law, since "historically, [the U.S. government] has not argued that foreign courts are bound to accept its characterizations or precluded from considering other relevant sources."*

For an analysis of the Supreme Court's citation to and discussion of foreign sovereign *amicus* briefs, and an argument that some of the same reasons underlying judicial deference to the Executive Branch apply to foreign sovereigns, see Kristen E. Eichensehr, *Foreign Sovereigns as Friends of the Court*, 102 Va. L. Rev. 289 (2016).

17. Scholars disagree about the usefulness of having a general doctrine of international comity. For example, Professor Joel Paul has argued that comity is too vague a standard and is inconsistent with the duty of courts to interpret and apply their own sovereign's will rather than the interests of foreign sovereigns. *See* Joel R. Paul, *Comity in International Law*, 32 Harv. Int'l L.J. 1 (1991). Similarly, Professor Michael Ramsey has argued that the comity concept is overly vague, and he contends that the doctrine is a substitution for, rather than an aid to, analysis. *See* Michael

---

* The Court also distinguished United States v. Pink, 315 U.S. 203 (1942), in which the Court had treated as "conclusive" a declaration from the Soviet Union about the extraterritorial effect of a nationalization decree, noting that: *Pink* was decided prior to the adoption of Rule 44.1; the declaration there was obtained by the U.S. government through diplomatic channels; there was no indication that the declaration was inconsistent with the Soviet government's past statements; and the declaration was consistent with expert evidence on point.

D. Ramsey, *Escaping "International Comity,"* 83 Iowa L. Rev. 893 (1998). By contrast, while acknowledging that comity is an amorphous concept, Anne-Marie Slaughter maintains that interactions between courts of different nations are necessary, and increasingly common, in our globalized world, and that considerations of comity are useful in addressing these relations. *See* Anne-Marie Slaughter, *Court to Court*, 92 Am. J. Int'l L. 708 (1998); *see also* Molly Warner Lien, *The Cooperative and Integrative Models of International Judicial Comity: Two Illustrations Using Transnational Discovery and Breard Scenarios*, 50 Cath. U. L. Rev. 591 (2001) (building on Slaughter's approach).

For a comprehensive account of how U.S. courts apply international comity, which the author defines as "deference to foreign government actors that is not required by international law but is incorporated in domestic law," see William S. Dodge, *International Comity in American Law*, 115 Colum. L. Rev. 2071 (2015). This article explains that "[i]n some areas of foreign relations law, like sovereign immunity and prescriptive jurisdiction, doctrines of international comity are layered on top of rules of international law," whereas "[i]n other areas, international comity does all of the work." The article also challenges what the author describes as "two enduring myths about comity: (1) that comity must be governed by standards rather than rules; and (2) that comity determinations are best left to the executive branch." For a defense of comity-based abstention and a proposal for a federal common law framework for international comity drawn from historical practice, see Thomas H. Lee & Samuel Estreicher, *In Defense of International Comity*, 92 S. Cal. L. Rev. (forthcoming). For an overview, by a sitting Supreme Court Justice, of the Court's increased focus on cases involving foreign persons and activities, and some of the challenges presented by these cases, see Stephen Breyer, The Court and the World: American Law and the New Global Realities (2015).

3

Congress and the President in Foreign Relations

This chapter considers the basic foreign relations powers of Congress and the President. Sections A and B provide an overview of the specific foreign relations powers conferred in Articles I and II of the Constitution. Section C then discusses the relationship between Congress and the President in the exercise of their constitutional foreign relations powers. Aspects of this relationship relating to the exercise of war powers will be addressed separately in Chapter 9.

The text of the Constitution does not explicitly address many important issues concerning the foreign relations authority of the federal political branches. As Professor Harold Koh has noted:

> One cannot read the Constitution without being struck by its astonishing brevity regarding the allocation of foreign affairs authority among the branches. Nowhere does the Constitution use the words "foreign affairs" or "national security." Instead, it creates a Congress, president, and federal judiciary and vests in them powers, some of which principally affect foreign affairs. Only occasionally does it explicitly condition one branch's exercise of a foreign affairs power upon another's, as in its grants to the President of the powers, with the Senate's advice and consent, to make treaties and appoint ambassadors. More frequently, the document grants clearly related powers to separate institutions, without ever specifying the relationship between those powers, as for example, with Congress's power to declare war and the President's power as commander-in-chief. Most often, the text simply says nothing about who controls certain domains as, for example, the exercise of international emergency powers or the conduct of covert action.

Harold Hongju Koh, The National Security Constitution: Sharing Power After the Iran-Contra Affair 67 (1990). Professor Edward Corwin famously noted that "the Constitution, considered only for its affirmative grants of power capable of affecting the issue, is an invitation to struggle for the privilege of directing American foreign policy." Edward S. Corwin, The President: Office and Powers 1787-1984, at 201 (Randall Bland et al. eds., 5th ed. 1984).

Notwithstanding these quotations from Koh and Corwin, do the text and structure of the Constitution offer some guidance about the scope of Congress's and the President's foreign relations powers? When the text and structure do not provide sufficient guidance, how should the Constitution's allocation of foreign affairs authority be determined? To what extent should Founding history be consulted? What weight should be given to the historic practices of the political branches? What weight should be given to functional considerations relating to the effective conduct of U.S. foreign relations? And what role, if any, should courts play in making this determination? Keep these questions in mind as you read the materials that follow.

A. SOURCES OF CONGRESSIONAL POWER

Article I of the Constitution confers on Congress numerous powers relating to the conduct of foreign relations. In addition, the Supreme Court has recognized other congressional foreign relations powers not specifically enumerated in the constitutional text. The decisions and notes below discuss some of Congress's most frequently exercised foreign relations powers—the power to make appropriations, the power to regulate foreign commerce, the power to define and punish offenses against the law of nations, the power to make laws that are necessary and proper to carry into execution other governmental powers, the implied power to regulate immigration, and, more controversially, the "inherent" sovereign power to regulate foreign affairs. Before reading these materials, read carefully Article I, Section 8 of the U.S. Constitution, in Appendix B.

Fong Yue Ting v. United States

149 U.S. 698 (1893)

[In the *Chinese Exclusion Case*, excerpted in Chapter 1, the Supreme Court upheld the constitutionality of an 1888 act of Congress that excluded certain Chinese laborers from reentering the United States. In 1892, Congress enacted a statute titled "An act to prohibit the coming of Chinese persons into the United States." Section 6 of this statute required *deportation* of Chinese laborers in the United States unless they obtained a certificate from the Collector of the Internal Revenue demonstrating that they had entered the United States before enactment of the statute. To avoid deportation, a Chinese laborer without a certificate was required to show good cause and to present "at least one credible white witness" who would verify his residency prior to 1892. Section 7 of the statute directed the Secretary of the Treasury to issue rules and regulations implementing the statute.

This case involved three writs of habeas corpus filed by Chinese laborers arrested and held by the marshal of the district for not having certificates of residence under the 1892 Act. The plaintiffs argued that Congress lacked the power to deport them, and that the deportation in any event violated the Due Process Clause of the Fifth Amendment. The circuit court dismissed the writs of habeas corpus.]

MR. JUSTICE GRAY . . . delivered the opinion of the Court. . . .

"It is an accepted maxim of international law that every sovereign nation has the power, as inherent in sovereignty, and essential to self-preservation, to forbid the entrance of foreigners within its dominions, or to admit them only in such cases and upon such conditions as it may see fit to prescribe. In the United States this power is vested in the national government, to which the constitution has committed the entire control of international relations, in peace as well as in war. It belongs to the political department of the government, and may be exercised either through treaties made by the president and senate or through statutes enacted by congress." [Nishimura Ekiu v. United States, 142 U.S. 651, 659 (1892).]

The right of a nation to expel or deport foreigners who have not been naturalized, or taken any steps towards becoming citizens of the country, rests upon the same grounds, and is as absolute and unqualified, as the right to prohibit and prevent their entrance into the country. . . .

The right to exclude or to expel all aliens, or any class of aliens, absolutely or upon certain conditions, in war or in peace, being an inherent and inalienable right of every sovereign and independent nation, essential to its safety, its independence, and its welfare, the question now before the court is whether the manner in which Congress has exercised this right in sections 6 and 7 of the act of 1892 is consistent with the Constitution.

The United States are a sovereign and independent nation, and are vested by the Constitution with the entire control of international relations, and with all the powers of government necessary to maintain that control, and to make it effective. The only government of this country which other nations recognize or treat with is the government of the Union, and the only American flag known throughout the world is the flag of the United States. . . .

In exercising the great power which the people of the United States, by establishing a written Constitution as the supreme and paramount law, have vested in this court, of determining, whenever the question is properly brought before it, whether the acts of the legislature or of the executive are consistent with the Constitution, it behooves the court to be careful that it does not undertake to pass upon political questions, the final decision of which has been committed by the Constitution to the other departments of the government. . . .

The power to exclude or to expel aliens, being a power affecting international relations, is vested in the political departments of the government, and is to be regulated by treaty or by act of Congress, and to be executed by the executive authority according to the regulations so established, except so far [as] the judicial department has been authorized by treaty or by statute, or is required by the paramount law of the Constitution, to intervene. . . .

Congress, having the right, as it may see fit, to expel aliens of a particular class, or to permit them to remain, has undoubtedly the right to provide a system of registration and identification of the members of that class within the country, and to take all proper means to carry out the system which it provides. . . .

Chinese laborers . . . like all other aliens residing in the United States for a shorter or longer time, are entitled, so long as they are permitted by the government of the United States to remain in the country, to the safeguards of the Constitution, and to the protection of the laws, in regard to their rights of person and of property, and to their civil and criminal responsibility. But they continue to be aliens, having taken no steps towards becoming citizens, and incapable of becoming such under the naturalization laws; and therefore remain subject to the power of Congress to expel them, or to order them to be removed and deported from the country, whenever, in its judgment, their removal is necessary or expedient for the public interest. . . .

The question whether, and upon what conditions, these aliens shall be permitted to remain within the United States being one to be determined by the political departments of the government, the judicial department cannot properly express an opinion upon the wisdom, the policy, or the justice of the measures enacted by

Congress in the exercise of the powers confided to it by the Constitution over this subject. . . .

Upon careful consideration of the subject, the only conclusion which appears to us to be consistent with the principles of international law, with the Constitution and laws of the United States, and with the previous decisions of this court, is that in each of [the three cases] the judgment of the circuit court dismissing the writ of habeas corpus is right, and must be affirmed.

MR. JUSTICE BREWER, dissenting. . . .

[W]hatever rights a resident alien might have in any other nation, here he is within the express protection of the Constitution, especially in respect to those guaranties which are declared in the original amendments. It has been repeated so often as to become axiomatic that this government is one of enumerated and delegated powers; and, as declared in article 10 of the amendments, "the powers not delegated to the United States by the constitution, nor prohibited by it to the states, are reserved to the states, respectively, or to the people."

It is said that the power here asserted is inherent in sovereignty. This doctrine of powers inherent in sovereignty is one both indefinite and dangerous. Where are the limits to such powers to be found, and by whom are they to be pronounced? Is it within legislative capacity to declare the limits? If so, then the mere assertion of an inherent power creates it, and despotism exists. May the courts establish the boundaries? Whence do they obtain the authority for this? Shall they look to the practices of other nations to ascertain the limits? The governments of other nations have elastic powers. Ours are fixed and bounded by a written constitution. The expulsion of a race may be within the inherent powers of a despotism. History, before the adoption of this Constitution, was not destitute of examples of the exercise of such a power; and its framers were familiar with history, and wisely, and it seems to me, they gave to this government no general power to banish. Banishment may be resorted to as punishment for crime; but among the powers reserved to the people, and not delegated to the government, is that of determining whether whole classes in our midst shall, for no crime but that of their race and birthplace, be driven from our territory.

Whatever may be true as to exclusion,—and as to that see *Chinese Exclusion* . . .—I deny that there is any arbitrary and unrestrained power to banish residents, even resident aliens. What, it may be asked, is the reason for any difference? The answer is obvious. The Constitution has no extraterritorial effect, and those who have not come lawfully within our territory cannot claim any protection from its provisions; and it may be that the national government, having full control of all matters relating to other nations, has the power to build, as it were, a Chinese wall around our borders, and absolutely forbid aliens to enter. But the Constitution has potency everywhere within the limits of our territory, and the powers which the national government may exercise within such limits are those, and only those, given to it by that instrument. Now, the power to remove resident aliens is, confessedly, not expressed. Even if it be among the powers implied, yet still it can be exercised only in subordination to the limitations and restrictions imposed by the Constitution.

MR. JUSTICE FIELD, dissenting. . . .

I had the honor to be the organ of the court in announcing [the opinion in the *Chinese Exclusion Case*]. I still adhere to the views there expressed, in all particulars; but between legislation for the exclusion of Chinese persons,—that is, to prevent them from entering the country, — and legislation for the deportation of those who have acquired a residence in the country under a treaty with China, there is a wide and essential difference. The power of the government to exclude foreigners from this country, — that is, to prevent them from entering it, — whenever the public interests, in its judgment, require such exclusion, has been repeatedly asserted by the legislative and executive departments of our government, and never denied; but its power to deport from the country persons lawfully domiciled therein by its consent, and engaged in the ordinary pursuits of life, has never been asserted by the legislative or executive departments, except for crime, or as an act of war, in view of existing or anticipated hostilities, unless the alien act of 1798 can be considered as recognizing that doctrine. . . .

. . . Aliens from countries at peace with us, domiciled within our country by its consent, are entitled to all the guaranties for the protection of their persons and property which are secured to native-born citizens. The moment any human being from a country at peace with us comes within the jurisdiction of the United States, with their consent, — and such consent will always be implied when not expressly withheld, and, in the case of the Chinese laborers before us, was, in terms, given by the treaty referred to, — he becomes subject to all their laws, is amenable to their punishment, and entitled to their protection. Arbitrary and despotic power can no more be exercised over them, with reference to their persons and property, than over the persons and property of native-born citizens. They differ only from citizens in that they cannot vote, or hold any public office. As men having our common humanity, they are protected by all the guaranties of the Constitution. To hold that they are subject to any different law, or are less protected in any particular, than other persons, is, in my judgment, to ignore the teachings of our history, the practice of our government, and the language of our Constitution. . . .

The government of the United States is one of limited and delegated powers. It takes nothing from the usages or the former action of European governments, nor does it take any power by any supposed inherent sovereignty. There is a great deal of confusion in the use of the word "sovereignty" by law writers. Sovereignty or supreme power is in this country vested in the people, and only in the people. By them certain sovereign powers have been delegated to the government of the United States, and other sovereign powers reserved to the states or to themselves. This is not a matter of inference and argument, but is the express declaration of the Tenth Amendment to the constitution, passed to avoid any misinterpretation of the powers of the general government. That amendment declares that "The powers not delegated to the United States by the Constitution, nor prohibited by it to the States, are reserved to the States, respectively, or to the people." When, therefore, power is exercised by Congress, authority for it must be found in express terms in the Constitution, or in the means necessary or proper for the execution of the power expressed. If it cannot be thus found, it does not exist. . . .

United States v. Clark

435 F.3d 1100 (9th Cir. 2006)

[Defendant Michael Lewis Clark, a U.S. citizen, resided in Cambodia, where he paid young boys to engage in sex acts. Cambodia extradited Clark to the United States, where he was charged with (among other things) violating 18 U.S.C. §2423(c), which provides: "Any United States citizen or alien admitted for permanent residence who travels in foreign commerce, and engages in any illicit sexual conduct with another person shall be fined under this title or imprisoned not more than 30 years, or both." (The relevant statute also defines "illicit sexual conduct" to include "any commercial sex act . . . with a person under 18 years of age." 18 U.S.C. §2423(f)(2).) Clark pled guilty to violating Section 2423(c) but preserved the right to appeal on the question of Congress's power to enact this statute under its authority to regulate commerce with foreign nations.]

McKeown, Circuit Judge. . . .

Under the Commerce Clause, Congress has power "to regulate Commerce with foreign Nations, and among the several States, and with the Indian Tribes." . . .

We start with the component that has dominated judicial consideration of the Commerce Clause: "among the several States." After decades of expansive reading by the courts, the mid-1990s saw a retrenchment in Commerce Clause jurisprudence beginning with the watershed case of *Lopez.* In *Lopez,* the Court held that a statute which criminalized possession of a firearm in a school zone was beyond Congress's Commerce Clause authority. United States v. Lopez, 514 U.S. 549 (1995). In so holding, the Court stressed its concern that an overly expansive view of the Interstate Commerce Clause "would effectually obliterate the distinction between what is national and what is local and create a completely centralized government." *Id.* at 557. The Court reiterated these concerns five years later in *Morrison* in striking down a provision under the Violence Against Women Act: "[T]he concern . . . that Congress might use the Commerce Clause to completely obliterate the Constitution's distinction between national and local authority seems well founded." United States v. Morrison, 529 U.S. 598, 615 (2000).

In addition to announcing a shift to a more constrained view of Congress's power over interstate commerce, *Lopez* and *Morrison* ossified the three-category framework that the Court had long applied to interstate commerce cases. . . . [T]hese three familiar categories are (1) the use of the channels of interstate commerce; (2) the instrumentalities of interstate commerce, or persons or things in interstate commerce; and (3) activities that substantially affect interstate commerce. . . .

This past term the Court introduced a new wrinkle in interstate commerce's jurisprudential fabric when it held that the Controlled Substances Act was a valid exercise of Congress's powers under the Commerce Clause. *See* Gonzales v. Raich, 545 U.S. 1 (2005). *Raich* did not alter the fundamental three-prong rubric, but the Court took a more generous view of Congress's power over interstate commerce than seen in *Lopez* and *Morrison.* . . .

[T]he Foreign Commerce Clause has followed its own distinct evolutionary path. Born largely from a desire for uniform rules governing commercial relations with foreign countries, the Supreme Court has read the Foreign Commerce Clause as granting Congress sweeping powers. . . .

The Court has been unwavering in reading Congress's power over foreign commerce broadly. There is no counterpart to *Lopez* or *Morrison* in the foreign commerce realm that would signal a retreat from the Court's expansive reading of the Foreign Commerce Clause. In fact, the Supreme Court has never struck down an act of Congress as exceeding its powers to regulate foreign commerce. . . .

Clark's case illustrates the predominance of national interests and the absence of state sovereignty concerns in Foreign Commerce Clause jurisprudence. No state has voiced an interest in the proceedings nor is there an indication of any state interest at stake in determining the constitutionality of §2423(c). Because this case is divorced from the common federal/state interplay seen in the Interstate Commerce Clause cases, we find ourselves in sparsely charted waters. We thus look to the text of §2423(c) to discern whether it has a constitutionally tenable nexus with foreign commerce. . . .

Although it is important to view the statute as a whole, parsing its elements illustrates why the statute fairly relates to foreign commerce. The elements that the government must prove under §2423(c)'s commercial sex acts prong are straightforward. First, the defendant must "travel[ ] in foreign commerce." 18 U.S.C. §2423(c). Second, the defendant must "engage[ ] in any illicit sexual conduct with another person," *id.*, which in this case contemplates "any commercial sex act, . . . with a person under 18 years of age." 18 U.S.C. §2423(f)(2). We hold that §2423(c)'s combination of requiring travel in foreign commerce, coupled with engagement in a commercial transaction while abroad, implicates foreign commerce to a constitutionally adequate degree.

Beginning with the first element, the phrase "travels in foreign commerce" unequivocally establishes that Congress specifically invoked the Foreign Commerce Clause. The defendant must therefore have moved in foreign commerce at some point to trigger the statute. In Clark's case, he traveled from the United States to Cambodia. . . .

Once in Cambodia, the second element of §2423(c) was also met, namely, "engage[ment] in any illicit sexual conduct with another person," 18 U.S.C. §2423(c), which in this case was commercial sex under §2423(f)(2). As the Supreme Court recognized centuries ago, the Commerce Clause "comprehend[s] every species of commercial intercourse between the United States and foreign nations." Gibbons v. Ogden, 22 U.S. (9 Wheat.) 1, 193 (1824). Section 2423(c) regulates a pernicious "species of commercial intercourse": commercial sex acts with minors.

The statute expressly includes an economic component by defining "illicit sexual conduct," in pertinent part, as "any commercial sex act . . . with a person under 18 years of age." 18 U.S.C. §2423(f)(2). "Commercial sex act 'is defined as' any sex act, on account of which anything of value is given to or received by any person." 18 U.S.C. §1591(c)(1). Thus, in the most sterile terms, the statute covers the situation where a U.S. citizen engages in a commercial transaction through which money is exchanged for sex acts.

The essential economic character of the commercial sex acts regulated by §2423(c) stands in contrast to the non-economic activities regulated by the statutes at issue in *Lopez* and *Morrison*. *See Morrison*, 529 U.S. at 613 ("Gender motivated crimes of violence are not, in any sense of the phrase, economic activity."); *Lopez*, 514 U.S. at 561 (explaining that firearm possession statute was purely a criminal statute). In both *Lopez* and *Morrison*, the Supreme Court voiced strong concerns over Congress's use of the Commerce Clause to enact "a criminal statute that by its terms has nothing to do with 'commerce' or any sort of economic enterprise, however broadly one might define those terms." Like the statute regulating illicit drugs at issue in *Raich*, the activity regulated by the commercial sex prong of §2423(c) is "quintessentially economic," and thus falls within foreign trade and commerce.

As in *Raich*, the fact that §2423(c) has a criminal as well as an economic component does not put it beyond Congress's reach under the Foreign Commerce Clause. Indeed, §2423(c) is far from unique in using the Foreign Commerce Clause to regulate crimes with an economic facet. . . .

The combination of Clark's travel in foreign commerce and his conduct of an illicit commercial sex act in Cambodia shortly thereafter puts the statute squarely within Congress's Foreign Commerce Clause authority. . . .

FERGUSON, CIRCUIT JUDGE, dissenting. . . .

. . . [W]hile the majority correctly notes that "[f]ederalism and state sovereignty concerns do not restrict Congress's power over foreign commerce," it fails properly to consider the restrictions on the scope of Congress's Foreign Commerce power that emanate from the constitutional text itself, which the tri-category framework also helps elucidate.

Under the tri-category framework, and contrary to the District Court's conclusion, §2423(c) is not a regulation of the channels of foreign commerce. Section 2423(c) lacks any of the tangible links to the channels of commerce that would justify upholding it under Congress's Foreign Commerce power. . . .

. . . [Section] 2423(c) neither punishes the act of traveling in foreign commerce, or the wrongful use or impediment of use of the channels of foreign commerce. Rather, it punishes future conduct in a foreign country entirely divorced from the act of traveling except for the fact that the travel occurs at some point prior to the regulated conduct. The statute does not require any wrongful intent at the time the channel is being used, nor does it require a temporal link between the "travel[ ] in foreign commerce," 18 U.S.C. §2423(c), and the underlying regulated activity. . . .

The mere act of boarding an international flight, without more, is insufficient to bring all of Clark's downstream activities that involve an exchange of value within the ambit of Congress's Foreign Commerce power. On some level, every act by a U.S. citizen abroad takes place subsequent to an international flight or some form of "travel[ ] in foreign commerce." 18 U.S.C. §2423(c). This cannot mean that every act with a bare economic component that occurs downstream from that travel is subject to regulation by the United States under its Foreign Commerce power, or the Commerce Clause will have been converted into a general grant of police power. . . .

Rather than engaging in a losing "channels of commerce" analysis, the majority applies a general "rational nexus" standard in this case, and strains to find more foreign commerce in §2423(c) than the act of boarding an international flight. Specifically, the majority characterizes the crime regulated by §2423(c), illicit sexual conduct, as sufficiently related to "Commerce with foreign Nations," art. I, §8, cl. 3, to bring it under Congress's Foreign Commerce authority.

First, the underlying regulated activity is not "quintessentially economic," simply because it has a bare economic aspect. Just as "[g]ender-motivated crimes of violence are not, in any sense of the phrase, economic activity," *Morrison*, 529 U.S. at 613, neither is "illicit sexual conduct." The plain purpose of §2423(c) is to regulate criminal conduct, not commerce. As the Supreme Court cautioned in *Lopez*, "depending on the level of generality, any activity can be looked upon as commercial." 514 U.S. at 565.

Further, the underlying act, even if considered economic or commercial, is certainly not a presence of commerce with foreign nations. In the most sterile terms, an act of paid sex with a minor that takes place overseas is not an act of commerce with other nations. Under the interpretation of the majority, the purchase of a lunch in France by an American citizen who traveled there by airplane would constitute a constitutional act of engaging in foreign commerce. Under such an interpretation, Congress could have the power to regulate the overseas activities of U.S. citizens many months or years after they had concluded their travel in foreign commerce, as long as the activities involved some sort of exchange of value—even if the partner in exchange was a U.S. entity that funneled the value back into the American economy. . . .

United States v. Bellaizac-Hurtado

700 F.3d 1245 (11th Cir. 2012)

[The Panamanian Navy, after being tipped off by the U.S. Coast Guard, captured a ship in Panamanian waters that contained 760 kilograms of cocaine, and later arrested the operators of the ship. After an exchange of diplomatic notes, Panama's Foreign Ministry consented to the prosecution of the captured individuals in the United States. The defendants were convicted under the Maritime Drug Law Enforcement Act (MDLEA), 46 U.S.C. §§70503(a), 70506, of possession and conspiracy to possess, with intent to distribute, five kilograms or more of cocaine on board a vessel subject to the jurisdiction of the United States. They appealed their convictions on the ground that the MDLEA, as applied to drug-trafficking activities in the territorial waters of Panama, exceeded the power of Congress "[t]o define and punish . . . Offences against the Law of Nations," U.S. Const., art. I., §8, cl. 10, also known as the Offenses Clause.]

PRYOR, CIRCUIT JUDGE . . . .

. . . The question whether Congress has the power under the Offences Clause to proscribe drug trafficking in the territorial waters of another nation is an issue of first impression in our Court. . . .

The power to "define" offenses against the law of nations does not grant Congress the authority to punish conduct that is not a violation of the law of nations. . . .

We and our sister circuits agree that the eighteenth-century phrase, the "law of nations," in contemporary terms, means customary international law. . . . The more difficult question involves how to determine whether a crime violates customary international law.

Our Court has referred to customary international law several times, but we have never defined it. Five of our sister circuits have adopted the definition in the Restatement (Third) of Foreign Relations, which provides that customary international law is the "general and consistent practice of states followed by them from a sense of legal obligation," Restatement (Third) of Foreign Relations §102(2) (1987). We agree with our sister circuits that customary international law is determined by examining state practice and *opinio juris*:

> Customary international law . . . consists of two components. First, there must be a general and consistent practice of states. This does not mean that the practice must be universally followed; rather it should reflect wide acceptance among the states particularly involved in the relevant activity. Second, there must be a sense of legal obligation, or *opinio juris sive necessitatis*. In other words, a practice that is generally followed but which states feel legally free to disregard does not contribute to customary law; rather, there must be a sense of legal obligation. States must follow the practice because they believe it is required by international law, not merely because that they think it is a good idea, or politically useful, or otherwise desirable.

Buell v. Mitchell, 274 F.3d 337, 372 (6th Cir. 2001). . . .

Private criminal activity will rarely be considered a violation of customary international law because private conduct is unlikely to be a matter of mutual legal concern. . . .

Courts must exercise restraint in defining violations of customary international law because customary international law is, by its nature, difficult to determine. . . .

The text of the Offences Clause does not resolve the question whether it limits the power of Congress to define and punish only those violations of customary international law that were established at the Founding or whether the power granted under the Clause expands and contracts with changes in customary international law. The Supreme Court has not resolved the issue. . . .

We need not decide whether the power granted to Congress under the Offences Clause changes with the evolution of customary international law because, under either approach, the result is the same. Drug trafficking was not a violation of customary international law at the time of the Founding, and drug trafficking is not a violation of customary international law today.

When the Constitution was ratified, the range of conduct that could be viewed as a violation of customary international law was even more limited than it is today. In his *Commentaries on the Laws of England,* William Blackstone explained that, because offenses against the law of nations are "principally incident to whole states or nations," they "can rarely be the object of the criminal law of any particular state." 4 William Blackstone, Commentaries at *68. As a result, "[t]he principal offences against the law of nations [that could be committed by private individuals and punished criminally] . . . [we]re of three kinds: 1. Violation of safe conducts; 2. Infringement of the rights of ambassadors; and, 3. Piracy." *Id.* Although the Supreme Court added counterfeiting of foreign currency and violations of the laws of war to this list . . . , those norms were also discussed in Vattel's influential treatise on the law of nations from that period. Vattel, Law of Nations §179 (1797).

Drug trafficking was not a matter of international concern in 1789, let alone a violation of customary international law. Vattel's Law of Nations contains no references to narcotics, opium, or drug trafficking. And the international community did not even begin its efforts to limit the drug trade until the turn of the twentieth century. Because violations of customary international law during the Founding Period were so limited, and narcotics then were not even a subject of international concern, we cannot conclude that drug trafficking was an offense against the law of nations when the Constitution was ratified.

Drug trafficking is also not a violation of contemporary customary international law. Although a number of specially affected States — States that benefit financially from the drug trade — have ratified treaties that address drug trafficking, they have failed to comply with the requirements of those treaties, and the international community has not treated drug trafficking as a violation of contemporary customary international law. Scholars also agree that drug trafficking is not a violation of contemporary customary international law.

The United States argues that the widespread ratification of the 1988 United Nations Convention Against Illicit Traffic in Narcotic Drugs and Psychotropic Substances establishes that drug trafficking violates a norm of customary international law, but we disagree. Treaties may constitute evidence of customary international law, but "will only constitute sufficient proof of a norm of customary international law if an overwhelming majority of States have ratified the treaty, and those States uniformly and consistently act in accordance with its principles." Flores v. S. Peru Copper Corp., 414 F.3d 233, 256 (2d Cir. 2003). . . . And as the International Court of Justice has explained, a customary international law norm will not form if specially affected States have not consented to its development through state practice consistent with the proposed norm. North Sea Continental Shelf Cases (Fed. Republic of Ger. v. Den.; Fed. Republic of Ger. v. Neth.), 1969 I.C.J. 3, 43 (Feb. 20).

The 1988 Convention was ratified by an overwhelming majority of States and currently has 188 States Parties, but the drug trade continues to flourish in many specially affected States despite their ratification of the Convention. . . . The practice of these specially affected States evidences that drug trafficking is not yet considered a violation of customary international law. Governments corrupted by the interests of drug traffickers are not simply unable to prosecute drug traffickers, but are often unwilling to do so because their economies are dependent upon the drug trade. The persistent failure of these specially affected States to comply with their treaty obligations suggests that they view the curtailment of drug trafficking as an aspirational goal, not a matter of mutual legal obligation under customary international law. . . .

Because drug trafficking is not a violation of customary international law, we hold that Congress exceeded its power, under the Offences Clause, when it proscribed the defendants' conduct in the territorial waters of Panama. And the United States has not offered us any alternative ground upon which the Act could be sustained as constitutional. As applied to these defendants, the Act is unconstitutional, and we must vacate their convictions.

Notes and Questions

1. Congress has an elaborate institutional machinery devoted to foreign relations. The principal committee in the Senate is the Committee on Foreign Relations, which has jurisdiction over an enormous array of foreign relations and related issues. Another important committee in the Senate is the Appropriations Committee, and its most important foreign relations subcommittee is the Subcommittee on State, Foreign Operations, and Related Programs, which handles the dispersion of funds for foreign operations (including various State Department programs). Another important subcommittee is the Judiciary Committee's Subcommittee on Border Security and Immigration (which, among other things, has jurisdiction over immigration and maintains oversight of the Department of Homeland Security's U.S. citizenship and immigration services). There is also the Armed Services Committee, which has jurisdiction over the U.S. armed forces and a variety of other military and defense matters. Finally, half a dozen committees and subcommittees in the Senate affect U.S. participation in international trade. In the House, the Committee on Foreign Affairs mirrors the Senate Foreign Relations Committee as the principal committee devoted to foreign relations. As in the Senate, there are also House committees or subcommittees on appropriations, immigration, the armed services, and international trade.

These committees and subcommittees have institutional experience and expertise that facilitate congressional influence in foreign relations. But while they can conduct oversight, they cannot set policy except through lawmaking, which requires majority approval of a bill by both houses of Congress and presentment of the bill to the President for signature. The decentralization of power in Congress, and the need for significant collective action to make law, may suggest a weakness in Congress's ability to conduct U.S. foreign relations. Recall that one reason for the foreign relations difficulties in the pre-constitutional period was that these relations were run by a committee (and later a department) in the Continental Congress. A decentralized, deliberative body like Congress has difficulty acting with dispatch. It also has difficulty speaking with the unified and coherent voice that may be needed in international communication and negotiation. Because its hall-mark is public deliberation, Congress also has difficulty maintaining secrecy, which is often crucial to the successful conduct of foreign relations. In addition, foreign relations problems arise on a daily basis, but Congress is not always in session. These are some of the reasons why, despite its broad powers and institutional expertise, Congress generally does not *conduct* U.S. foreign relations. Nevertheless, Congress exercises significant influence on U.S. foreign policy. It controls the power of the purse, its concurrence is needed in many foreign relations endeavors, and it can impose obstacles to Executive action even in areas where its affirmative participation is not required.

2. One of the most significant sources of congressional authority over foreign relations stems from its control over appropriations and spending. The Constitution provides that "no Money shall be drawn from the Treasury, but in Consequence of Appropriations made by Law" (Art. I, §9, cl. 7), and gives Congress the power to "provide for the common Defence and general Welfare of the United States" (Art. I, §8, cl. 1). In addition, the Constitution prohibits any appropriation of funds for the army "for a longer Term than two Years" (Art. I, §8, cl. 12). These provisions give Congress enormous discretion over when and how to spend money on the foreign relations activities of the United States, and thus enormous power over U.S. foreign relations. As Professor Henkin noted, "Congress decides the degree and detail of its support [for presidential foreign relations initiatives]: it determines ultimately the State Department's budget, how much money the President shall have to spend on the armed forces under his command, how much he can contrib-ute to United Nations programs." Louis Henkin, Foreign Affairs and the United States Constitution 74 (2d ed. 1996). In addition, "Congress and Congressional committees can use appropriations and the appropriations process to bargain also about other elements of Presidential policy in foreign affairs. Because the President usually cannot afford to veto appropriations acts, they are favorite vehicles for con-ditions and other 'riders' imposed on unwilling Presidents." *Id.* at 74-75.

Congress's appropriations power also gives it significant control over billions of dollars in U.S. foreign aid. Thus, for example, Congress often conditions foreign aid on the satisfaction of certain human rights practices in the donee country. In addition, the appropriations power can give Congress the final say in implement-ing the President's international initiatives. A famous early example was the dis-pute over whether Congress was required to issue appropriations needed to fund bilateral commissions contemplated by the Jay Treaty, which President Washington ratified in 1795. Although the House eventually authorized the needed appropri-ations, it did so after expressing the view that it retained the discretion not to do so. *See* David P. Currie, The Constitution in Congress: The Federalist Period, 1789-1801, at 214 (1997). Presidents have generally recognized the constraints imposed by Congress through its appropriations authority. *See, e.g.,* Expense of Presents to Foreign Governments—How Defrayed, 4 Op. Att'y Gen. 358, 359 (1845) (stating that in "the conduct of our foreign relations," the Executive "cannot exceed the amount . . . appropriated"). Nonetheless, "Congress ordinarily feels legally, polit-ically, or morally obligated to appropriate funds to maintain the President's for-eign affairs establishment and to implement his treaties and other undertakings." Henkin, *supra*, at 74. Below, in Section C, we consider possible constitutional limits on the conditions that Congress can impose on its appropriations. In Chapter 9, we consider the significance of Congress's control over appropriations and spending in the context of war.

3. Congress has the power under Article I, Section 8, Clause 3 of the Constitution to regulate both domestic and foreign commerce. What does *Clark* suggest about the relationship between Congress's domestic and foreign commerce powers? Why does the majority believe that concerns for state sovereignty and federalism are less applicable to the foreign rather than domestic commerce clause? Does the differential treatment of the two clauses stem from the text of the Constitution, or some other principle? Consider the following statement from a 1903 Supreme Court decision upholding a federal statute regulating interstate sale of lottery tickets:

> It is argued that the power to regulate commerce among the several states is the same as the power to regulate commerce with foreign nations, and with the Indian tribes. But is its scope the same? As in effect before observed, the power to regulate commerce with foreign nations and the power to regulate interstate commerce, are to be taken *diverso intuitu*, for the latter was intended to secure equality and freedom in commercial intercourse as between the states, not to permit the creation of impediments to such intercourse; while the former clothed Congress with that power over international commerce, pertaining to a sovereign nation in its intercourse with foreign nations, and subject, generally speaking, to no implied or reserved power in the states. The laws which would be necessary and proper in the one case would not be necessary or proper in the other.

Champion v. Ames (The "Lottery Case"), 188 U.S. 321, 373 (1903). According to *Ames*, why is the Foreign Commerce Clause not subject to implied or reserved powers? Because the states never had the power to regulate foreign commerce prior to the Constitution? Is this true? *Cf.* Japan Line, Ltd. v. County of Los Angeles, 441 U.S. 434, 448 (1979) ("Although the Constitution, Art. I, §8, cl. 3, grants Congress power to regulate commerce 'with foreign Nations' and 'among the several States' in parallel phrases, there is evidence that the Founders intended the scope of the foreign commerce power to be the greater."). In ascertaining the scope of the foreign commerce power, what is the relevance of the fact that states are prohibited under the Constitution from imposing duties on imports and exports without Congress's consent? *See* U.S. Const. art. I, §10, cl. 2. We return to potential federalism restrictions on the federal government's authority in foreign affairs in the discussion of the treaty power in Chapter 5.

4. In United States v. Clark, the Ninth Circuit, in concluding that the statute in that case "implicates foreign commerce to a constitutionally adequate degree," referred to two Supreme Court decisions that have imposed limitations on Congress's exercise of its domestic commerce power: United States v. Lopez, 514 U.S. 549 (1995), and United States v. Morrison, 529 U.S. 598 (2000). It also cited Gonzales v. Raich, 545 U.S. 1 (2005), in which the Supreme Court held that Congress could regulate the personal cultivation of marijuana for medicinal use under its domestic commerce power because it could rationally conclude that such personal cultivation could affect the (illegal) interstate market for marijuana. Are you convinced by the majority's treatment of these decisions? Or does the dissent have the better of the argument when it contends that those decisions require that statutes enacted pursuant to the Foreign Commerce Clause regulate commerce between the United States and another country, not commerce between a U.S. citizen and someone in a foreign country that has no substantial impact in the United States? Under the majority's analysis, what foreign conduct can Congress *not* regulate?

For a decision similar to *Clark*, see United States v. Baston, 818 F.3d 651 (11th Cir. 2016), in which the court concluded that Congress had the authority under the Foreign Commerce Clause to regulate the sex trafficking activities of a U.S. citizen overseas, because Congress had a rational basis for concluding that such conduct is "part of an economic class of activities that have a substantial effect on . . . commerce between the United States and other countries" (internal quotation marks omitted). The Supreme Court declined to review this decision. *See* Baston v. United States, 137 S. Ct. 850 (2017). Justice Thomas dissented from the denial of certiorari to question what he viewed as the courts of appeals' erroneous interpretation of the Foreign Commerce Clause "to permit Congress to regulate economic activity abroad if it has a substantial effect on this Nation's foreign commerce." Justice Thomas argued that the courts of appeals had read the original understanding of the Foreign Commerce Clause too broadly and that this reading "would permit Congress to regulate any economic activity anywhere in the world, so long as Congress had a rational basis to conclude that the activity has a substantial effect on commerce between this Nation and any other." He questioned this interpretation and urged the Court to grant certiorari to consider the Clause's proper scope. For an extensive consideration of the scope of the Foreign Commerce Clause, see Anthony J. Colangelo, *The Foreign Commerce Clause*, 96 Va. L. Rev. 949 (2010).

5. The statute at issue in *Clark* applies to "illicit sexual conduct" abroad by U.S. citizens. It defines such conduct to include not only commercial sex acts with minors, but also certain noncommercial sex acts with minors that would be criminal if they occurred in the United States. At the time of the decision in *Clark*, this statute applied to any U.S. citizen "who travels in foreign commerce, and engages in any illicit sexual conduct with another person." In 2013, however, Congress amended the statute so that it applies to any U.S. citizen "who travels in foreign commerce *or resides, either temporarily or permanently, in a foreign country,* and engages in any illicit sexual conduct with another person" (emphasis added). In light of this change, the court in United States v. Pepe, 895 F.3d 679 (9th Cir. 2018), concluded that, prior to the amendment, the statute must have applied only to defendants who had traveled to a foreign country for a temporary stay. It noted that this interpretation allowed it to avoid considering, for now, "the outer limits of Congress's power to regulate the conduct of U.S. citizens residing abroad." In that case, the defendant had been convicted of drugging and raping seven children in Cambodia, for which he was sentenced to 210 years imprisonment. The court remanded for an assessment of whether the defendant had been residing in Cambodia when the conduct occurred. If so, reasoned the court, he should not have been convicted under the pre-2013 version of the statute, because he would no longer have been traveling in foreign commerce at the time of the conduct.

6. An important independent congressional power is reflected in the Necessary and Proper Clause, also sometimes referred to as the "Sweeping Clause." This clause confers on Congress the authority "[t]o make all Laws which shall be necessary and proper for carrying into Execution the foregoing Powers, and all other Powers vested by this Constitution in the Government of the United States, or in any Department or Officer thereof." *See* U.S. Const. art. I, §8, cl. 18. By its terms, the Necessary and Proper Clause gives Congress not only the ability to enact laws to implement its own powers, but also the ability to enact laws to implement the powers of the other federal branches. Thus, for example, Congress can enact laws that are "necessary and proper" to implement the President's Article II foreign affairs powers.

In McCulloch v. Maryland, 17 U.S. (4 Wheat.) 316 (1819), the Supreme Court famously adopted an expansive construction of the Necessary and Proper Clause. In upholding the constitutionality of Congress's creation of a national bank, the Court stated: "Let the end be legitimate, let it be within the scope of the constitution; and all means which are appropriate, which are plainly adapted to that end, which are not prohibited, but consistent with the letter and spirit of the constitution, are constitutional." Despite the breadth of this power, it presumably is not unlimited. How are courts to determine whether a law falls within the scope of the Necessary and Proper Clause? Consider the following statement in *McCulloch*: "[W]here the law is not prohibited, and is really calculated to effect any of the objects intrusted to the government, to undertake here to inquire into the decree of its necessity, would be to pass the line which circumscribes the judicial department, and to tread on legislative ground. This court disclaims all pretensions to such a power." At first glance, this passage might suggest that the scope of Congress's necessary and proper authority is largely immune from judicial scrutiny. On the other hand, the passage could be read to require a judicial determination of whether a statute "is *really* calculated to effect . . . the objects intrusted to the government." If courts are to make that determination, what test should they use? *McCulloch* suggested two possibilities. First, the Court emphasized that a necessary and proper law was one whose means were "appropriate" and "plainly adapted" toward a legitimate end. Second, it suggested that courts should examine whether Congress acted with a proper purpose or merely under the "pretext" of exercising enumerated powers. Are courts competent to perform either this means-ends test or this purpose test? Is judicial competence in applying these tests a greater concern in the foreign affairs area?

For general discussion of the scope and meaning of the Necessary and Proper Clause, see Randy E. Barnett, *Necessary and Proper*, 44 UCLA L. Rev. 745 (1997); David E. Engdhal, *The Necessary and Proper Clause as an Intrinsic Restraint on Federal Lawmaking Power*, 22 Harv. J.L. & Pub. Pol'y 107 (1998); Stephen Gardbaum, *Rethinking Constitutional Federalism*, 74 Tex. L. Rev. 795 (1996); Gary Lawson & Patricia B. Granger, *The "Proper" Scope of Federal Power: A Jurisdictional Interpretation of the* Sweeping Clause, 43 Duke L.J. 267, 297 (1993); and William Van Alstyne, *The Role of Congress in Determining Incidental Powers of the President and of the Federal Courts: A Comment on the Horizontal Effect of "The Sweeping Clause,"* 36 Ohio St. L.J. 788 (1975).

7. Admiralty matters often implicate U.S. foreign policy; yet, the Constitution provides no explicit source of authority for Congress's regulation of admiralty. During the nineteenth century, the Supreme Court located the source in the Commerce Clause. *See, e.g.,* The Daniel Ball, 77 U.S. 557, 564 (1870). But during this period, the Court adhered to a narrow construction of the Commerce Clause, especially the interstate Commerce Clause, and sometimes construed congressional power over admiralty accordingly. *See, e.g.,* Moore v. American Transp. Co., 65 U.S. 1, 39 (1860) ("The act can apply to vessels only which are engaged in foreign commerce, and commerce between the States."). Later, the Court reasoned that Congress's power to regulate admiralty was "necessary and proper" to carry into execution the federal courts' Article III jurisdiction over admiralty matters. *See, e.g.,* Romero v. International Terminal Operating Co., 358 U.S. 354, 360-61 (1959); Southern Pacific Co. v. Jensen, 244 U.S. 205, 214-15 (1917). The Court has suggested two basic limits on this power: First, "there are boundaries to the maritime law and admiralty jurisdiction which inhere in those subjects and cannot be altered by legislation, as by excluding a thing falling clearly within them or including a thing falling clearly without." Panama R.R. Co. v. Johnson, 264 U.S. 375, 386 (1924). Second, the enactments, "when not relating to matters whose existence or influence is confined to a more restricted field . . . shall be coextensive with and operate uniformly in the whole of the United States." *Id.* at 387. *See also* United States v. Flores, 289 U.S. 137, 148 (1933) (referring to these "well recognized limitations"). For a discussion of the Court's changing interpretations of the source of congressional power over admiralty, see Note, *From Judicial Grant to Legislative Power: The Admiralty Clause in the Nineteenth Century,* 67 Harv. L. Rev. 1214, 1230-37 (1954).

8. Congress's power to define and punish offenses against the law of nations, discussed in *Bellaizac-Hurtado,* can be traced to the Founders' concern that the states might not adequately punish infractions of the law of nations (such as attacks on ambassadors), and might thereby implicate the international responsibility of the entire United States. This concern led the Continental Congress to pass a resolution in 1781 recommending that the states "provide expeditious, exemplary, and adequate punishment . . . for the infractions of the immunities of ambassadors and other public ministers authorized and received as such by the United States in Congress assembled." 21 Journals of the Continental Congress 1136 (1781); *see also* 29 Journals of the Continental Congress 654-66 (1785) (similar resolution). At the Constitutional Convention in 1787, Edmund Randolph stated that one of the defects of the Articles of Confederation was that Congress "could not cause infractions of treaties or of the law of nations, to be punished: that particular states might by their conduct provoke war without controul. . . ." 1 Records of the Federal Convention of 1787, at 19 (Max Farrand ed., 1911); *see also id.* at 25 (Randolph reported to have said, "If the rights of an ambassador be invaded by any citizen it is only in a few States that any laws exist to punish the offender.").

At the Constitutional Convention, James Wilson expressed concern about the implications of Congress's power to "define" the law of nations: "To pretend to *define* the law of nations which depended on the authority of all the Civilized Nations of the World, would have the look of arrogance, that would make us look ridiculous." Gouverneur Morris responded: "The word *define* is proper when applied to *offenses* in this case; the law of (nations) being often too vague and deficient to be a rule." 2 Records of the Federal Convention of 1787, at 614-15 (Max Farrand ed., 1911). *Cf.* United States v. Smith, 18 U.S. (5 Wheat.) 153, 159 (1820) ("Offences, too, against the law of nations, cannot, with any accuracy, be said to be completely ascertained and defined in any public code recognised by the common consent of nations.").

9. The Supreme Court discussed the Define and Punish Clause in United States v. Arjona, 120 U.S. 479 (1887). In that case, Ramon Arjona was being prosecuted for violating a federal statute that prohibited the counterfeiting of the bank notes, bonds, or other securities of foreign governments. In concluding that the statute fell within Congress's powers under the Define and Punish Clause and the Necessary and Proper Clause, the Court explained that:

> The national government is . . . made responsible to foreign nations for all violations by the United States of their international obligations, and because of this Congress is expressly authorized "to define and punish . . . offenses against the law of nations." Art. I, sec. 8, clause 10.
>
> The law of nations requires every national government to use "due diligence" to prevent a wrong being done within its own dominion to another nation with which it is

at peace, or to the people thereof, and because of this, the obligation of one nation to punish those who, within its own jurisdiction, counterfeit the money of another nation has long been recognized.

Id. at 483-84. The Court further reasoned that "[a] right secured by the law of nations to a nation or its people is one the United States, as the representatives of this nation, are bound to protect. Consequently, a law which is necessary and proper to afford this protection is one that Congress may enact, because it is one that is needed to carry into execution a power conferred by the Constitution on the government of the United States exclusively." *Id.* at 487. What does this analysis suggest about the Court's understanding of what it means for conduct to constitute an offense against the law of nations?

10. The court in *Bellaizac-Hurtado* identifies several potential limits on Congress's power under the Define and Punish Clause. First, it holds that the Define and Punish Clause "does not grant Congress the authority to punish conduct that is not a violation of the law of nations," and it conducts an independent review of whether the offense in question is really prohibited by the law of nations. Is that approach consistent with *Arjona*? In any event, doesn't the term "define" imply at least some congressional discretion to identify the content of international law and how it is made part of federal criminal law? And isn't Congress's power in this context amplified by the Necessary and Proper Clause? For an argument that Congress under the Define and Punish Clause "can define only offenses that already exist in international law," but that "congressional definitions should receive a fair degree of deference from the courts when, as will often be the case, the existence or details of the underlying international norms are substantially unclear," see Eugene Kontorovich, *Discretion, Delegation, and Defining in the Constitution's Law of Nations Clause*, 106 Nw. U. L. Rev. 1675, 1682 (2012).

Second, the court in *Bellaizac-Hurtado* interprets the phrase "law of nations" in Article I to mean that Congress can only define and punish offenses against customary international law, not treaties. We will discuss the distinction between these two forms of law in greater detail in Chapters 5, 6, and 7, but for now, it suffices to say that treaties are formal agreements among nations and customary international law consists of the general and consistent practice of nations followed out of a sense of legal obligation. Why would the Founders have omitted treaties from Congress's define and punish power? Does Congress have other authority for enacting federal criminal laws to define and punish offenses against treaties?

Third, the court raises the question whether Congress can only define and punish offenses that were offenses against the law of nations in 1789, when the Constitution was made. Does such a limitation make sense, or should modern customary international law also be a basis for legislation under the clause?

Keep in mind that, even if a criminal activity outside the United States does not fall within the scope of the Define and Punish Clause, it might fall under some other congressional power, such as the power to enact laws necessary and proper to implement treaties. *See, e.g.*, United States v. Noel, 893 F.3d 1294 (11th Cir. 2018).

For additional discussion of the Define and Punish Clause, see J. Andrew Kent, *Congress's Under-Appreciated Power to Define and Punish Offenses Against the Law of Nations*, 85 Tex. L. Rev. 843 (2007); Alex H. Loomis, *The Power to Define Offenses Against the Law of Nations*, 40 Harv. J. L. & Pub. Pol'y 417 (2017); Charles D. Siegal, *Deference and Its Dangers: Congress' Power to "Define . . . Offenses Against the Law of Nations,"* 21 Vand. J. Transnat'l L. 865, 874-79 (1988); and Note, *The Offences Clause After Sosa v. Alvarez-Machain*, 118 Harv. L. Rev. 2378 (2005).

11. One might also think that the Define and Punish Clause gives Congress only criminal enforcement authority, not the authority to regulate civil suits. However, Congress has invoked the Define and Punish Clause as a basis for enacting important civil legislation relating to foreign relations, including the Foreign Sovereign Immunities Act and the Torture Victim Protection Act (both of which are considered in Chapter 7). For an argument that the Clause authorizes civil as well as criminal enactments, see Beth Stephens, *Federalism and Foreign Affairs: Congress's Power to "Define and Punish . . . Offenses Against the Law of Nations,"* 42 Wm. & Mary L. Rev. 447 (2000). *But cf.* Siegal, *supra,* at 866-67 (stating that the Clause permits "Congress to define violations of customary international law as domestic crimes").

12. In addition to defining and punishing offenses against the law of nations, Congress has the power to define and punish felonies and piracies committed on the high seas. There has been a federal piracy statute since 1790. The current statute provides that, "Whoever, on the high seas, commits the crime of piracy as defined by the law of nations, and is afterwards brought into or found in the United States, shall be imprisoned for life." 18 U.S.C. §1651. In an early decision involving a predecessor to this statute, the Supreme Court held that Congress's definition of piracy by mere reference to the law of nations was sufficiently precise. *See* United States v. Smith, 18 U.S. (5 Wheat.) 153, 162 (1820). The Court reasoned that the crime of piracy had a definite meaning in international law and that "Congress may as well define by using a term of a known and determinate meaning, as by an express enumeration of all the particulars included in that term."

Piracy has not disappeared. In 2010, for example, a group of Somalis attacked a U.S. Navy frigate on the high seas, mistakenly thinking it was a merchant vessel. Their attack was unsuccessful, and they were captured and subsequently tried and convicted of piracy. The defendants argued that piracy, as defined by the law of nations when the piracy statute was first enacted in the early 1800s, requires a robbery of a vessel at sea. They further argued that they had not taken any property and had boarded the U.S. vessel only after being apprehended. The Fourth Circuit found this argument unpersuasive, concluding that the modern understanding of piracy encompasses acts of violence carried out against vessels for private gain, such as the acts in question in this case, and that the piracy statute implicitly incorporates this modern understanding. *See* United States v. Dire, 680 F.3d 446 (4th Cir. 2012). For discussion of this and other legal issues associated with prosecuting pirates in modern times, see Eugene Kontorovich, *"A Guantanamo on the Sea": The Difficulties of Prosecuting Pirates and Terrorists,* 98 Cal. L. Rev. 243 (2010). Chapter 8 of the casebook further considers piracy's status as an international crime.

13. The justifications for Congress's power to regulate various aspects of immigration have, as in the admiralty context, changed over the years. A possible basis for congressional regulation of immigration is the enumerated power to "establish an uniform Rule of Naturalization," U.S. Const. art. I, §8, cl. 4. The problem with this theory is that a power to regulate naturalization (the process by which a person becomes a U.S. citizen) is substantially narrower than a power to regulate immigration (a process that includes the admission, exclusion, and deportation of aliens, as well as the naturalization of aliens to become U.S. citizens). As a result, the Supreme Court has located the power to regulate immigration elsewhere. During most of the nineteenth century, the Court addressed Congress's power over immigration only indirectly, in the context of striking down state regulations relating to immigration under the dormant Commerce Clause. *See, e.g.,* The Passenger Cases, 48 U.S.

283 (1849).* The Court finally addressed the question directly in The Head Money Cases, 112 U.S. 580, 600 (1884), where the Court rejected a challenge to a congressional tax on ships for immigrants brought to U.S. ports, reasoning: "Congress having the power to pass a law regulating immigration as a part of the commerce of this country with foreign nations, we see nothing in the statute by which it has here exercised that power forbidden by any other part of the constitution."

Toward the end of the nineteenth century, the Court moved away from a Commerce Clause justification for congressional power over immigration, and began to embrace a more extensive source of power—inherent constitutional power based on national sovereignty. One of the first instances of this shift was the *Chinese Exclusion Case*, excerpted in Chapter 1. *Fong Yue Ting* extended this sovereignty rationale to cover the power to deport aliens living in the United States. Throughout the twentieth century, the Court continued to invoke the sovereignty rationale as a basis for Congress's power over immigration. *See, e.g.*, Miller v. Albright, 523 U.S. 420, 455-56 (1998); Landon v. Plasencia, 459 U.S. 21, 34 (1982); Galvan v. Press, 347 U.S. 522, 530 (1954). For articles analyzing the sources of congressional power over immigration, see Louis Henkin, *The Constitution and United States Sovereignty: A Century of* Chinese Exclusion *and Its Progeny*, 100 Harv. L. Rev. 853 (1987); Stephen Legomsky, *Immigration Law and the Principle of Plenary Congressional Power*, 1984 Sup. Ct. Rev. 255; Hiroshi Motomura, *Immigration Law After a Century of Plenary Power: Phantom Constitutional Norms and Statutory Interpretation*, 100 Yale L.J. 545 (1990); Gerald L. Neuman, *The Lost Century of American Immigration Law (1776-1875)*, 93 Colum. L. Rev. 1833 (1993).

14. The *Chinese Exclusion Case* and *Fong Yue Ting* are the founts of the "plenary power doctrine" in immigration law. This doctrine has two components. First is the idea, sketched above, that the source of congressional power over immigration is inherent constitutional power based on national sovereignty. Second, and a distinct concept, is the notion suggested in *Fong Yue Ting* that the validity of congressional regulations of immigration involve political questions committed to the political branches rather than the courts to resolve. (In accord with modern changes in the political question doctrine, more recent cases articulate this component of the plenary power doctrine in terms of "special judicial deference" to Congress, see Fiallo v. Bell, 430 U.S. 787, 793 (1977).) *Fong Yue Ting* and subsequent cases invoked the plenary power doctrine to reject aliens' due process claims. *See, e.g.*, United States ex rel. Knauff v. Shaughnessy, 338 U.S. 537, 544 (1950) ("Whatever the procedure authorized by Congress is, it is due process as far as an alien is concerned.").

The "deference" component of the plenary power doctrine has eroded in recent years. Beginning with Landon v. Plasencia, 459 U.S. 21 (1982), the Court began "to use mainstream procedural due process analysis in immigration law and made procedural due process claims potentially available to a wider circle of aliens." Hiroshi Motomura, *The Curious Evolution of Immigration Law: Procedural Surrogates for Substantive Constitutional Rights*, 92 Colum. L. Rev. 1625, 1656 (1992). More recent decisions have continued and expanded this trend. *See* Immigration and Naturalization Service v. St. Cyr, 533 U.S. 289 (2001) (upholding judicial review of deportation proceedings even though expulsion statute appeared to bar it); Zadvydas v. Davis, 533 U.S. 678 (2001) (holding that due process protects

---

* The first federal immigration statute was not enacted until 1875; prior to that time, several states played a major role in regulating immigration, primarily through police power. *See* Gerald L. Neuman, *The Lost Century of American Immigration Law (1776-1875)*, 93 Colum. L. Rev. 1833 (1993).

liberty of "all 'persons' in the United States, including aliens, whether their presence here is lawful, unlawful, temporary, or permanent"). *See also* Gabriel J. Chin, *Is There a Plenary Power Doctrine? A Tentative Apology and Prediction for Our Strange but Unexceptional Constitutional Immigration Law,* 14 Geo. Immigr. L.J. 257 (2000); Peter J. Spiro, *Explaining the End of Plenary Power,* 16 Geo. Immigr. L.J. 339 (2002).

15. To the extent that the plenary power doctrine survives, do you agree with the *Fong Yue Ting* dissents that the doctrine is (in Justice Brewer's words) "indefinite and dangerous" or (in Justice Field's words) "unlimited and despotic"? Why did Justice Field—the author of the majority opinion in The *Chinese Exclusion Case*—dissent in *Fong Yue Ting*? Was it because of the distinction between exclusion and deportation? Is this a difference that the Constitution recognizes? Why? Is Justice Brewer right to suggest, in dissent, that deportation is more problematic than exclusion because "[t]he constitution has no extraterritorial effect"? On the extraterritorial scope of constitutional rights, see Chapter 8.

16. Does Congress have a general foreign relations power? Recall from Chapter 2 that, in the Second Hickenlooper Amendment, Congress modified the act of state doctrine articulated in *Sabbatino* to permit courts greater leeway in judging the validity of certain acts of state. What was the constitutional basis for this statute? What is the constitutional basis for congressional assertions of U.S. sovereignty over U.S. airspace? (*See* 49 U.S.C. §40103.) For federal statutes authorizing extradition in the absence of a treaty? (*See* 18 U.S.C. §3186.) Professor Henkin, unable to find a clear basis in Article I for these and other enactments, grounded them in a general "Foreign Affairs Power" akin to powers inherent in sovereignty articulated in the *Chinese Exclusion Case* and *Fong Yue Ting. See* Henkin, *supra,* at 70-72; *cf.* Perez v. Brownell, 356 U.S. 44, 59 (1958) (referring to the "power of Congress to deal with foreign relations"). Do you agree? Is there some other constitutional basis for these statutes? If Congress does have a general foreign relations power, what are its limits? *Cf.* Louis Henkin, *The Treaty Makers and the Law Makers: The Law of the Land and Foreign Relations,* 107 U. Pa. L. Rev. 903, 920-30 (1959) (arguing that the Foreign Affairs Power supports legislation on any matter so related to foreign affairs that the United States might deal with it by treaty).

17. In the midst of the 1798-1800 undeclared war between France and the United States, George Logan, a Pennsylvania Quaker, traveled to France and attempted to work out a peace settlement. This effort indirectly led President Adams to dispatch negotiators to France and, eventually, to obtain peace. But the Federalists in Congress were furious, and responded in 1799 by enacting the Logan Act, which prohibited private correspondence with foreign governments. The modern version of the Act provides:

> Any citizen of the United States, wherever he may be, who, without authority of the United States, directly or indirectly commences or carries on any correspondence or intercourse with any foreign government or any officer or agent thereof, with intent to influence the measures or conduct of any foreign government or of any officer or agent thereof, in relation to any disputes or controversies with the United States, or to defeat the measures of the United States, shall be fined under this title or imprisoned not more than three years, or both.
>
> This section shall not abridge the right of a citizen to apply, himself or his agent, to any foreign government or the agents thereof for redress of any injury which he may have sustained from such government or any of its agents or subjects.

18 U.S.C. §953. What is the constitutional basis for this statute? The statute's supporters argued that it was necessary and proper to implement the President's

authority to negotiate with foreign nations. *See* David P. Currie, The Constitution in Congress: The Federalist Period, 1789-1801, at 262 n.208 (1997). Is this persuasive? Is there some other basis for congressional power to enact the Logan Act? The Foreign Affairs Power, perhaps? Does the Act violate the First Amendment? For discussions of the Act, see Detlev Vagts, *The Logan Act: Paper Tiger or Sleeping Giant?*, 60 Am. J. Int'l L. 268, 269-80 (1966); Kevin M. Kearney, Comment, *Private Citizens in Foreign Affairs: A Constitutional Analysis*, 36 Emory L.J. 285, 287-306 (1987); Curtis S. Simpson III, Comment, *The Logan Act of 1799: May It Rest in Peace*, 10 Cal. W. Int'l L.J. 365 (1980). For similar legislation, see The Johnson Act, 18 U.S.C. §955 (prohibiting private citizens from lending money to foreign nations in default on loans from the United States).

18. Other aspects of congressional power are explored throughout this casebook, including Congress's power to preempt state law (see Chapter 4), its power to override treaty obligations as a matter of U.S. domestic law (see Chapter 5), its power to violate customary international law (see Chapter 7), and its power related to war (see Chapters 9 and 10). *See also* Cecil V. Crabb, Jr., Glenn J. Antizzo, & Leila E. Sarieddine, Congress and the Foreign Policy Process (2000); James M. Lindsay, Congress and the Politics of U.S. Foreign Policy (1994); Thomas M. Franck & Edward Weisband, Foreign Policy by Congress (1979).

B. SOURCES OF EXECUTIVE POWER

This section explores the basic sources of Executive power in foreign affairs.* Unlike Article I's lengthy and detailed list of congressional foreign affairs powers, Article II grants relatively few enumerated foreign affairs powers to the President. Nevertheless, the President has always exercised enormous foreign relations power. Indeed, the President is often described as having the dominant role in the conduct of U.S. foreign relations. As we saw in Chapter 1, for example, the Supreme Court in United States v. Curtiss-Wright Export Corp., 299 U.S. 304 (1936), referred to "the very delicate, plenary and exclusive power of the President as the sole organ of the federal government in the field of international relations." The paradox of the relatively spare textual grants of power to the President and the reality of the President's broad foreign relations power is a recurring issue in this casebook. Before reading the materials that follow, carefully read Article II of the Constitution, in Appendix B, and review the Pacificus-Helvidius debate concerning the nature and scope of Executive power, in Chapter 1.

President Monroe's Annual Message to Congress, December 2, 1823

In 2 A Compilation of the Messages and Papers of the Presidents, 1789-1897, at 209, 218 (James D. Richardson ed., 1896)

[In the early 1820s, rumors circulated in the United States that Spain, supported by other continental European powers, was preparing to deploy a military force to

---

* One of the Executive Branch's most important powers—the "commander-in-chief" power—is discussed in Chapter 9. Another important set of presidential powers—treaty making and executive agreement making—is addressed in Chapters 5 and 6.

restore to Spain colonies that it had lost in revolutions in South and Central America during the previous decade. At the same time, Russia was threatening to extend its empire into northwestern North America. In August 1823, George Canning, the British foreign secretary, proposed that Great Britain and the United States form an alliance to oppose any such action by the continental powers. Secretary of War John Calhoun, along with former presidents Jefferson and Madison, supported the alliance with Britain. Secretary of State John Quincy Adams strenuously opposed it. He argued instead that the United States should issue a unilateral statement of policy about the inappropriateness of European meddling in the American hemisphere. President Monroe followed Adams's advice in his seventh annual message to Congress, excerpted below.]

[T]he American continents, by the free and independent condition which they have assumed and maintain, are henceforth not to be considered as subjects for future colonization by any European powers. . . .

We owe it . . . to candor and to the amicable relations existing between the United States and those powers to declare that we should consider any attempt on their part to extend their system to any portion of this hemisphere as dangerous to our peace and safety. With the existing colonies or dependencies of any European power we have not interfered and shall not interfere. But with the Governments who have declared their independence and maintain it, and whose independence we have, on great consideration and on just principles, acknowledged, we could not view any interposition for the purpose of oppressing them, or controlling in any other manner their destiny, by any European power in any other light than as the manifestation of an unfriendly disposition toward the United States.

Theodore Roosevelt, An Autobiography

388-89 (1914)

The most important factor in getting the right spirit in my Administration, next to insistence upon courage, honesty, and a genuine democracy of desire to serve the plain people, was my insistence upon the theory that the executive power was limited only by specific restrictions and prohibitions appearing in the Constitution or imposed by Congress under its Constitutional powers. My view was that every executive officer and above all every executive officer in high position was a steward of the people, bound actively and affirmatively to do all he could for the people and not to content himself with the negative merit of keeping his talents undamaged in a napkin. I declined to adopt this view that what was imperatively necessary for the Nation could not be done by the President unless he could find some specific authorization to do it. My belief was that it was not only his right but his duty to do anything that the needs of the Nation demanded unless such action was forbidden by the Constitution or by the laws. Under this interpretation of executive power, I did and caused to be done many things not previously done by the President and the heads of the departments. I did not usurp power, but I did greatly broaden the use of executive power. In other words, I acted for the public welfare, I acted for the common well-being of all our people, whenever and in whatever measure was necessary, unless prevented by direct constitutional or legislative prohibition.

William Howard Taft, Our Chief Magistrate and His Powers
139-40, 144-45 (1916)

The true view of the Executive functions is, as I conceive it, that the President can exercise no power which cannot be fairly and reasonably traced to some specific grant of power or justly implied and included within such express grant as proper and necessary to its exercise. Such specific grant must be either in the Federal Constitution or in an act of Congress passed in pursuance thereof. There is no undefined residuum of power which he can exercise because it seems to him to be in the public interest. . . . The grants of Executive power are necessarily in general terms in order not to embarrass the Executive within the field of action plainly marked for him, but his jurisdiction must be justified and vindicated by affirmative constitutional or statutory provision, or it does not exist. There have not been wanting, however, eminent men in high public office holding a different view and who have insisted upon the necessity for an undefined residuum of Executive power in the public interest. . . .

My judgment is that the view of Mr. Garfield and Mr. Roosevelt, ascribing an undefined residuum of power to the President is an unsafe doctrine and that it might lead under emergencies to results of an arbitrary character, doing irremediable injustice to private right. The mainspring of such a view is that the Executive is charged with responsibility for the welfare of all the people in a general way, that he is to play the part of a Universal Providence and set all things right, and that anything that in his judgement will help the people he ought to do, unless he is expressly forbidden not to do it. The wide field of action that this would give to the Executive one can hardly limit.

George W. Bush, The National Security Strategy of the United States of America (Sept. 2002)

. . . V. Prevent Our Enemies from Threatening Us, Our Allies, and Our Friends with Weapons of Mass Destruction . . .

The nature of the Cold War threat required the United States—with our allies and friends—to emphasize deterrence of the enemy's use of force, producing a grim strategy of mutual assured destruction. With the collapse of the Soviet Union and the end of the Cold War, our security environment has undergone profound transformation.

Having moved from confrontation to cooperation as the hallmark of our relationship with Russia, the dividends are evident: an end to the balance of terror that divided us; an historic reduction in the nuclear arsenals on both sides; and cooperation in areas such as counterterrorism and missile defense that until recently were inconceivable.

But new deadly challenges have emerged from rogue states and terrorists. None of these contemporary threats rival the sheer destructive power that was arrayed against us by the Soviet Union. However, the nature and motivations of these new adversaries, their determination to obtain destructive powers hitherto available only to the world's strongest states, and the greater likelihood that they will use weapons of mass destruction against us, make today's security environment more complex and dangerous. . . .

We must be prepared to stop rogue states and their terrorist clients before they are able to threaten or use weapons of mass destruction against the United States and our allies and friends. Our response must take full advantage of strengthened alliances, the establishment of new partnerships with former adversaries, innovation in the use of military forces, modern technologies, including the development of an effective missile defense system, and increased emphasis on intelligence collection and analysis. . . .

It has taken almost a decade for us to comprehend the true nature of this new threat. Given the goals of rogue states and terrorists, the United States can no longer solely rely on a reactive posture as we have in the past. The inability to deter a potential attacker, the immediacy of today's threats, and the magnitude of potential harm that could be caused by our adversaries' choice of weapons, do not permit that option. We cannot let our enemies strike first. . . .

For centuries, international law recognized that nations need not suffer an attack before they can lawfully take action to defend themselves against forces that present an imminent danger of attack. Legal scholars and international jurists often conditioned the legitimacy of preemption on the existence of an imminent threat—most often a visible mobilization of armies, navies, and air forces preparing to attack.

We must adapt the concept of imminent threat to the capabilities and objectives of today's adversaries. Rogue states and terrorists do not seek to attack us using conventional means. They know such attacks would fail. Instead, they rely on acts of terror and, potentially, the use of weapons of mass destruction—weapons that can be easily concealed, delivered covertly, and used without warning. . . .

The United States has long maintained the option of preemptive actions to counter a sufficient threat to our national security. The greater the threat, the greater is the risk of inaction—and the more compelling the case for taking anticipatory action to defend ourselves, even if uncertainty remains as to the time and place of the enemy's attack. To forestall or prevent such hostile acts by our adversaries, the United States will, if necessary, act preemptively.

Youngstown Sheet & Tube Co. v. Sawyer

343 U.S. 579 (1952)

[During the Korean War, a labor dispute arose in the U.S. steel industry, and the United Steelworkers threatened to go on strike. In an effort to avoid a disruption in steel production, President Truman issued an executive order directing the secretary of commerce to take possession of and operate some of the nation's steel mills. The executive order noted that the United States and other nations were engaged "in deadly combat with the forces of aggression in Korea" and that "the weapons and other materials needed by our armed forces and by those joined with us in the defense of the free world are produced to a great extent in this country, and steel is an indispensable component of substantially all of such weapons and materials." As support for the order, President Truman invoked "the authority vested in me by the Constitution and laws of the United States, and as President of the United States and Commander in Chief of the armed forces of the United States." The mill owners challenged the constitutionality of the President's order.]

MR. JUSTICE BLACK delivered the opinion of the Court. . . .

The President's power, if any, to issue the order must stem either from an act of Congress or from the Constitution itself. There is no statute that expressly authorizes the President to take possession of property as he did here. Nor is there any act of Congress to which our attention has been directed from which such a power can fairly be implied. Indeed, we do not understand the Government to rely on statutory authorization for this seizure. There are two statutes which do authorize the President to take both personal and real property under certain conditions. However, the Government admits that these conditions were not met and that the President's order was not rooted in either of the statutes. The Government refers to the seizure provisions of one of these statutes (§201(b) of the Defense Production Act) as "much too cumbersome, involved, and time-consuming for the crisis which was at hand."

Moreover, the use of the seizure technique to solve labor disputes in order to prevent work stoppages was not only unauthorized by any congressional enactment; prior to this controversy, Congress had refused to adopt that method of settling labor disputes. When the Taft-Hartley Act was under consideration in 1947, Congress rejected an amendment which would have authorized such governmental seizures in cases of emergency. Apparently it was thought that the technique of seizure, like that of compulsory arbitration, would interfere with the process of collective bargaining. Consequently, the plan Congress adopted in that Act did not provide for seizure under any circumstances. Instead, the plan sought to bring about settlements by use of the customary devices of mediation, conciliation, investigation by boards of inquiry, and public reports. In some instances temporary injunctions were authorized to provide cooling-off periods. All this failing, unions were left free to strike after a secret vote by employees as to whether they wished to accept their employers' final settlement offer.

It is clear that if the President had authority to issue the order he did, it must be found in some provision of the Constitution. And it is not claimed that express constitutional language grants this power to the President. The contention is that presidential power should be implied from the aggregate of his powers under the Constitution. Particular reliance is placed on provisions in Article II which say that "The executive Power shall be vested in a President . . ."; that "he shall take Care that the Laws be faithfully executed"; and that he "shall be Commander in Chief of the Army and Navy of the United States."

The order cannot properly be sustained as an exercise of the President's military power as Commander in Chief of the Armed Forces. The Government attempts to do so by citing a number of cases upholding broad powers in military commanders engaged in day-to-day fighting in a theater of war. Such cases need not concern us here. Even though "theater of war" be an expanding concept, we cannot with faithfulness to our constitutional system hold that the Commander in Chief of the Armed Forces has the ultimate power as such to take possession of private property in order to keep labor disputes from stopping production. This is a job for the Nation's lawmakers, not for its military authorities.

Nor can the seizure order be sustained because of the several constitutional provisions that grant executive power to the President. In the framework of our Constitution, the President's power to see that the laws are faithfully executed refutes the idea that he is to be a lawmaker. The Constitution limits his functions in the lawmaking process to the recommending of laws he thinks wise and the vetoing of laws he thinks bad. And the Constitution is neither silent nor equivocal about who shall make laws which the President is to execute. The first section of the first article says that "All legislative Powers herein granted shall be vested in a Congress of the United

States. . . ." After granting many powers to the Congress, Article I goes on to provide that Congress may "make all Laws which shall be necessary and proper for carrying into Execution the foregoing Powers, and all other Powers vested by this Constitution in the Government of the United States, or in any Department or Officer thereof." . . .

It is said that other Presidents without congressional authority have taken possession of private business enterprises in order to settle labor disputes. But even if this be true, Congress has not thereby lost its exclusive constitutional authority to make laws necessary and proper to carry out the powers vested by the Constitution "in the Government of the United States, or any Department or Officer thereof."

The Founders of this Nation entrusted the lawmaking power to the Congress alone in both good and bad times. It would do no good to recall the historical events, the fears of power and the hopes for freedom that lay behind their choice. Such a review would but confirm our holding that this seizure order cannot stand. . . .

MR. JUSTICE FRANKFURTER, concurring. . . .

Congress has frequently—at least 16 times since 1916—specifically provided for executive seizure of production, transportation, communications, or storage facilities. In every case it has qualified this grant of power with limitations and safeguards. This body of enactments . . . demonstrates that Congress deemed seizure so drastic a power as to require that it be carefully circumscribed whenever the President was vested with this extraordinary authority. . . .

Congress in 1947 was again called upon to consider whether governmental seizure should be used to avoid serious industrial shutdowns. Congress decided against conferring such power generally and in advance, without special Congressional enactment to meet each particular need. . . .

[N]othing can be plainer than that Congress made a conscious choice of policy in a field full of perplexity and peculiarly within legislative responsibility for choice. In formulating legislation for dealing with industrial conflicts, Congress could not more clearly and emphatically have withheld authority than it did in 1947. Perhaps as much so as is true of any piece of modern legislation, Congress acted with full consciousness of what it was doing and in the light of much recent history. . . .

It cannot be contended that the President would have had power to issue this order had Congress explicitly negated such authority in formal legislation. Congress has expressed its will to withhold this power from the President as though it had said so in so many words. . . .

Apart from his vast share of responsibility for the conduct of our foreign relations, the embracing function of the President is that "he shall take Care that the Laws be faithfully executed. . . ." Art. II, §3. The nature of that authority has for me been comprehensively indicated by Mr. Justice Holmes. "The duty of the President to see that the laws be executed is a duty that does not go beyond the laws or require him to achieve more than Congress sees fit to leave within his power." Myers v. United States, 272 U.S. 52, 177. The powers of the President are not as particularized as are those of Congress. But unenumerated powers do not mean undefined powers. The separation of powers built into our Constitution gives essential content to undefined provisions in the frame of our government.

To be sure, the content of the three authorities of government is not to be derived from an abstract analysis. The areas are partly interacting, not wholly disjointed. The Constitution is a framework for government. Therefore, the way the framework has consistently operated fairly establishes that it has operated according to its true nature. Deeply embedded traditional ways of conducting government cannot supplant the Constitution or legislation, but they give meaning to the words of a text or supply them. It is an inadmissibly narrow conception of American constitutional law to confine it to the words of the Constitution and to disregard the gloss which life has written upon them. In short, a systematic, unbroken, executive practice, long pursued to the knowledge of the Congress and never before questioned, engaged in by Presidents who have also sworn to uphold the Constitution, making as it were such exercise of power part of the structure of our government, may be treated as a gloss on "executive Power" vested in the President by §1 of Art. II. [Justice Frankfurter proceeded to examine prior presidential seizures and concluded that they "did not add up, either in number, scope, duration, or contemporaneous legal justification" to a systematic Executive practice in support of Truman's seizure, and did not "come to us sanctioned by long-continued acquiescence of Congress giving decisive weight to a construction by the Executive of its powers."]

MR. JUSTICE JACKSON, concurring in the judgment and opinion of the Court. . . .

A judge, like an executive adviser, may be surprised at the poverty of really useful and unambiguous authority applicable to concrete problems of executive power as they actually present themselves. Just what our forefathers did envision, or would have envisioned had they foreseen modern conditions, must be divined from materials almost as enigmatic as the dreams Joseph was called upon to interpret for Pharaoh. A century and a half of partisan debate and scholarly speculation yields no net result but only supplies more or less apt quotations from respected sources on each side of any question. They largely cancel each other.[1] And court decisions are indecisive because of the judicial practice of dealing with the largest questions in the most narrow way.

The actual art of governing under our Constitution does not and cannot conform to judicial definitions of the power of any of its branches based on isolated clauses or even single Articles torn from context. While the Constitution diffuses power the better to secure liberty, it also contemplates that practice will integrate the dispersed powers into a workable government. It enjoins upon its branches separateness but interdependence, autonomy but reciprocity. Presidential powers are not fixed but fluctuate, depending upon their disjunction or conjunction with those of Congress. We may well begin by a somewhat over-simplified grouping of practical situations in which a President may doubt, or others may challenge, his powers, and by distinguishing roughly the legal consequences of this factor of relativity.

1. When the President acts pursuant to an express or implied authorization of Congress, his authority is at its maximum, for it includes all that he possesses in his own right plus all that Congress can delegate.[2] In these circumstances, and in these

---

1. A Hamilton may be matched against a Madison. Professor Taft is counterbalanced by Theodore Roosevelt. It even seems that President Taft cancels out Professor Taft. Compare his "Temporary Petroleum Withdrawal No. 5" of September 27, 1909, United States v. Midwest Oil Co., 236 U.S. 459, 467, 468, with his appraisal of executive power in "Our Chief Magistrate and His Powers" 139-40.

2. It is in this class of cases that we find the broadest recent statements of presidential power, including those relied on here. United States v. Curtiss-Wright Corp., 299 U.S. 304, involved, not the question of the President's power to act without congressional authority, but the question of his right to act under and in accord with an Act of Congress. . . . That case does not solve the present controversy. It recognized internal and external affairs as being in separate categories, and held that the strict limitation upon congressional delegations of power to the President over internal affairs does not apply with respect to delegations of power in external affairs. It was intimated that the President might act in external affairs without congressional authority, but not that he might act contrary to an Act of Congress. . . .

only, may he be said (for what it may be worth) to personify the federal sovereignty. If his act is held unconstitutional under these circumstances, it usually means that the Federal Government as an undivided whole lacks power. A seizure executed by the President pursuant to an Act of Congress would be supported by the strongest of presumptions and the widest latitude of judicial interpretation, and the burden of persuasion would rest heavily upon any who might attack it.

2. When the President acts in absence of either a congressional grant or denial of authority, he can only rely upon his own independent powers, but there is a zone of twilight in which he and Congress may have concurrent authority, or in which its distribution is uncertain. Therefore, congressional inertia, indifference or quiescence may sometimes, at least as a practical matter, enable, if not invite, measures on independent presidential responsibility. In this area, any actual test of power is likely to depend on the imperatives of events and contemporary imponderables rather than on abstract theories of law.

3. When the President takes measures incompatible with the expressed or implied will of Congress, his power is at its lowest ebb, for then he can rely only upon his own constitutional powers minus any constitutional powers of Congress over the matter. Courts can sustain exclusive presidential control in such a case only by disabling the Congress from acting upon the subject. Presidential claim to a power at once so conclusive and preclusive must be scrutinized with caution, for what is at stake is the equilibrium established by our constitutional system.

Into which of these classifications does this executive seizure of the steel industry fit? It is eliminated from the first by admission, for it is conceded that no congressional authorization exists for this seizure. . . .

Can it then be defended under flexible tests available to the second category? It seems clearly eliminated from that class because Congress has not left seizure of private property an open field but has covered it by three statutory policies inconsistent with this seizure. . . .

This leaves the current seizure to be justified only by the severe tests under the third grouping, where it can be supported only by any remainder of executive power after subtraction of such powers as Congress may have over the subject. In short, we can sustain the President only by holding that seizure of such strike-bound industries is within his domain and beyond control by Congress. . . .

I did not suppose, and I am not persuaded, that history leaves it open to question, at least in the courts, that the executive branch, like the Federal Government as a whole, possesses only delegated powers. The purpose of the Constitution was not only to grant power, but to keep it from getting out of hand. However, because the President does not enjoy unmentioned powers does not mean that the mentioned ones should be narrowed by a niggardly construction. Some clauses could be made almost unworkable, as well as immutable, by refusal to indulge some latitude of interpretation for changing times. I have heretofore, and do now, give to the enumerated powers the scope and elasticity afforded by what seem to be reasonable, practical implications instead of the rigidity dictated by a doctrinaire textualism.

The Solicitor General seeks the power of seizure in three clauses of the Executive Article, the first reading, "The executive Power shall be vested in a President of the United States of America." Lest I be thought to exaggerate, I quote the interpretation which his brief puts upon it: "In our view, this clause constitutes a grant of all the executive powers of which the Government is capable." If that be true, it is difficult to see why the forefathers bothered to add several specific items, including some trifling ones.[9]

The example of such unlimited executive power that must have most impressed the forefathers was the prerogative exercised by George III, and the description of its evils in the Declaration of Independence leads me to doubt that they were creating their new Executive in his image. Continental European examples were no more appealing. And if we seek instruction from our own times, we can match it only from the executive powers in those governments we disparagingly describe as totalitarian. I cannot accept the view that this clause is a grant in bulk of all conceivable executive power but regard it as an allocation to the presidential office of the generic powers thereafter stated.

The clause on which the Government next relies is that "The President shall be Commander in Chief of the Army and Navy of the United States. . . ." These cryptic words . . . , undoubtedly put[ ] the Nation's armed forces under presidential command. Hence, this loose appellation is sometimes advanced as support for any presidential action, internal or external, involving use of force, the idea being that it vests power to do anything, anywhere, that can be done with an army or navy.

That seems to be the logic of an argument tendered at our bar—that the President having, on his own responsibility, sent American troops abroad derives from that act "affirmative power" to seize the means of producing a supply of steel for them. To quote, "Perhaps the most forceful illustration of the scope of Presidential power in this connection is the fact that American troops in Korea, whose safety and effectiveness are so directly involved here, were sent to the field by an exercise of the President's constitutional powers." Thus, it is said, he has invested himself with "war powers."

I cannot foresee all that it might entail if the Court should indorse this argument. Nothing in our Constitution is plainer than that declaration of a war is entrusted only to Congress. Of course, a state of war may in fact exist without a formal declaration. But no doctrine that the Court could promulgate would seem to me more sinister and alarming than that a President whose conduct of foreign affairs is so largely uncontrolled, and often even is unknown, can vastly enlarge his mastery over the internal affairs of the country by his own commitment of the Nation's armed forces to some foreign venture. I do not, however, find it necessary or appropriate to consider the legal status of the Korean enterprise to discountenance argument based on it. . . .

There are indications that the Constitution did not contemplate that the title Commander in Chief *of the Army and Navy* will constitute him also Commander in Chief of the country, its industries and its inhabitants. He has no monopoly of "war powers," whatever they are. While Congress cannot deprive the President of the command of the army and navy, only Congress can provide him an army or navy to command. It is also empowered to make rules for the "Government and Regulation of land and naval Forces," by which it may to some unknown extent impinge upon even command functions.

That military powers of the Commander in Chief were not to supersede representative government of internal affairs seems obvious from the Constitution and from elementary American history. . . .

9. "[H]e may require the Opinion, in writing, of the principal Officer in each of the executive Departments, upon any Subject relating to the Duties of their respective Offices. . . ." U.S. Const., Art. II, §2. He "shall Commission all the Officers of the United States." U.S. Const., Art. II, §3. Matters such as those would seem to be inherent in the Executive if anything is.

[Handwritten margin notes: "response to vesting clause" / "Hamilton's argument"]

We should not use this occasion to circumscribe, much less to contract, the lawful role of the President as Commander in Chief. I should indulge the widest latitude of interpretation to sustain his exclusive function to command the instruments of national force, at least when turned against the outside world for the security of our society. But, when it is turned inward, not because of rebellion but because of a lawful economic struggle between industry and labor, it should have no such indulgence. His command power is not such an absolute as might be implied from that office in a militaristic system but is subject to limitations consistent with a constitutional Republic whose law and policy-making branch is a representative Congress. The purpose of lodging dual titles in one man was to insure that the civilian would control the military, not to enable the military to subordinate the presidential office. No penance would ever expiate the sin against free government of holding that a President can escape control of executive powers by law through assuming his military role. What the power of command may include I do not try to envision, but I think it is not a military prerogative, without support of law, to seize persons or property because they are important or even essential for the military and naval establishment.

The third clause in which the Solicitor General finds seizure powers is that "he shall take Care that the Laws be faithfully executed. . . ." That authority must be matched against words of the Fifth Amendment that "No person shall be . . . deprived of life, liberty or property, without due process of law. . . ." One gives a governmental authority that reaches so far as there is law, the other gives a private right that authority shall go no farther. These signify about all there is of the principle that ours is a government of laws, not of men, and that we submit ourselves to rulers only if under rules.

The Solicitor General lastly grounds support of the seizure upon nebulous, inherent powers never expressly granted but said to have accrued to the office from the customs and claims of preceding administrations. The plea is for a resulting power to deal with a crisis or an emergency according to the necessities of the case, the unarticulated assumption being that necessity knows no law.

Loose and irresponsible use of adjectives colors all nonlegal and much legal discussion of presidential powers. "Inherent" powers, "implied" powers, "incidental" powers, "plenary" powers, "war" powers and "emergency" powers are used, often interchangeably and without fixed or ascertainable meanings. . . .

In the practical working of our Government we already have evolved a technique within the framework of the Constitution by which normal executive powers may be considerably expanded to meet an emergency. Congress may and has granted extraordinary authorities which lie dormant in normal times but may be called into play by the Executive in war or upon proclamation of a national emergency. . . . Under this procedure we retain Government by law—special, temporary law, perhaps, but law nonetheless. The public may know the extent and limitations of the powers that can be asserted, and persons affected may be informed from the statute of their rights and duties.

In view of the ease, expedition and safety with which Congress can grant and has granted large emergency powers, certainly ample to embrace this crisis, I am quite unimpressed with the argument that we should affirm possession of them without statute. Such power either has no beginning or it has no end. If it exists, it need submit to no legal restraint. I am not alarmed that it would plunge us straightway into dictatorship, but it is at least a step in that wrong direction.

As to whether there is imperative necessity for such powers, it is relevant to note the gap that exists between the President's paper powers and his real powers. The Constitution does not disclose the measure of the actual controls wielded by the modern presidential office. That instrument must be understood as an Eighteenth-Century sketch of a government hoped for, not as a blueprint of the Government that is. Vast accretions of federal power, eroded from that reserved by the States, have magnified the scope of presidential activity. Subtle shifts take place in the centers of real power that do not show on the face of the Constitution.

Executive power has the advantage of concentration in a single head in whose choice the whole Nation has a part, making him the focus of public hopes and expectations. In drama, magnitude and finality his decisions so far overshadow any others that almost alone he fills the public eye and ear. No other personality in public life can begin to compete with him in access to the public mind through modern methods of communications. By his prestige as head of state and his influence upon public opinion he exerts a leverage upon those who are supposed to check and balance his power which often cancels their effectiveness.

. . . I have no illusion that any decision by this Court can keep power in the hands of Congress if it is not wise and timely in meeting its problems. A crisis that challenges the President equally, or perhaps primarily, challenges Congress. If not good law, there was worldly wisdom in the maxim attributed to Napoleon that "The tools belong to the man who can use them." We may say that power to legislate for emergencies belongs in the hands of Congress, but only Congress itself can prevent power from slipping through its fingers. . . . With all its defects, delays and inconveniences, men have discovered no technique for long preserving free government except that the Executive be under the law, and that the law be made by parliamentary deliberations.

Such institutions may be destined to pass away. But it is the duty of the Court to be last, not first, to give them up.

[Justice Vinson, joined by Justices Reed and Minton, filed a 48-page dissent in *Youngstown*. The thrust of the dissent's argument was that Truman's action was consistent with his Article II duty to "take Care that the Laws be faithfully executed."

The dissent first tried to put the steel seizure in historical perspective. It began by characterizing the Korean War, and more generally the Cold War, as a "more terrifying threat" than World War II. It noted that Truman's actions in the Korean War were supported by the United Nations Security Council, and by congressional enactments that (a) dramatically increased defense spending (the bulk of which went to "military equipment and supplies — guns, tanks, ships, planes and ammunition — all of which require steel"), (b) established a new military draft, and (c) created organizations and programs (such as the Marshall Plan and the North Atlantic Treaty Organization (NATO)) designed to achieve victory in the Cold War. The dissent next reiterated the facts leading up to Truman's seizure of the steel mills, noting that the morning following the seizure, the President informed Congress of his actions and invited it to act otherwise if it "deem[s] some other course to be wiser," and that 12 days later, in the face of no congressional action, the President again sent a letter to Congress restating his position that "Congress can, if it wishes, reject the course of action I have followed in this matter." The dissent further noted the evidence in the record showing the importance of continued steel production to the war effort in Korea. It concluded: "Even ignoring for the moment whatever confidential information the President may possess as 'the Nation's organ for foreign affairs,' the uncontroverted affidavits in this record amply support the finding that 'a work stoppage would immediately jeopardize and imperil our national defense.'" Second, the dissent set forth its theory of Executive power. It argued that the constitutional Founders intended to establish "an office of power and independence" characterized by "initiative," "vigor," and "energy." It then cited a long list of Executive actions throughout U.S. history showing that "[w]ith or without explicit statutory authorization, Presidents have . . . dealt with national emergencies by acting promptly and resolutely to enforce legislative programs, at least to save those programs until Congress could act." It added that "Congress and the courts have responded to such executive initiative with consistent approval."

Third, the dissent turned to Truman's seizure of the steel mills, and argued "that the President was performing his duty under the Constitution to 'take Care that the Laws be faithfully executed. . . .'" The dissent reasoned:

> Much of the argument in this case has been directed at straw men. We do not now have before us the case of a President acting solely on the basis of his own notions of the public welfare. Nor is there any question of unlimited executive power in this case. The President himself closed the door to any such claim when he sent his Message to Congress stating his purpose to abide by any action of Congress, whether approving or disapproving his seizure action. Here, the President immediately made sure that Congress was fully informed of the temporary action he had taken only to preserve the legislative programs from destruction until Congress could act. . . . The absence of a specific statute authorizing seizure of the steel mills as a mode of executing the laws—both the military procurement program and the anti-inflation program—has not until today been thought to prevent the President from executing the laws. Unlike an administrative commission confined to the enforcement of the statute under which it was created, or the head of a department when administering a particular statute, the President is a constitutional officer charged with taking care that a "mass of legislation" be executed. Flexibility as to mode of execution to meet critical situations is a matter of practical necessity. This practical construction of the "Take Care" clause . . . was adopted by this Court in *In re Neagle*, . . . and other cases. . . . There is no statute prohibiting seizure as a method of enforcing legislative programs. Congress has in no wise indicated that its legislation is not to be executed by the taking of private property (subject of course to the payment of just compensation) if its legislation cannot otherwise be executed. . . . Whatever the extent of Presidential power on more tranquil occasions, and whatever the right of the President to execute legislative programs as he sees fit without reporting the mode of execution to Congress, the single Presidential purpose disclosed on this record is to faithfully execute the laws by acting in an emergency to maintain the status quo, thereby preventing collapse of the legislative programs until Congress could act. The President's action served the same purposes as a judicial stay entered to maintain the status quo in order to preserve the jurisdiction of a court.]

Notes and Questions

1. In contrast to Congress, the Executive Branch is organized hierarchically. The President sits atop, and exercises authority over, a massive bureaucracy devoted to foreign affairs. Within the White House, the National Security Council is charged with advising the President concerning foreign and military policies relating to national security. Outside the White House, the Department of State is the principal agent of the Executive Branch in the conduct of foreign relations. The State Department operates over 250 diplomatic and consular posts around the globe. It also negotiates treaties and other international agreements, represents the United

States at international conferences and other non-treaty international negotiations, monitors activities of foreign nations, makes policy recommendations, and implements Executive foreign policy in many contexts. The Department of Defense is responsible for military and security affairs, the Department of Treasury is responsible for international monetary affairs, and the Department of Commerce has jurisdiction over the expansion and protection of American business activities abroad. Other departments—especially Justice, Labor, Energy, and Agriculture—also have important foreign affairs responsibilities. Overseas intelligence operations are the responsibility of the Director of National Intelligence, a cabinet-level official who is the President's principal intelligence advisor and the coordinator of the entire intelligence community, including the Central Intelligence Agency. The Office of the United States Trade Representative manages U.S. trade policy. Dozens of additional agencies assist the President in conducting other aspects of U.S. foreign relations.

Institutionally, the Executive Branch has a number of advantages over Congress with respect to the conduct of foreign relations, including "the *unity* of the office, its capacity for *secrecy* and *dispatch,* and its superior sources of *information,* to which should be added the fact that it is always on hand and ready for action, whereas the houses of Congress are in adjournment much of the time." Edward S. Corwin, The President: Office and Powers 1787-1984, at 201 (Randall Bland et al. eds., 5th ed. 1984). Does the President have any other advantages? Are there drawbacks to the Executive Branch's organization? Given the size of the modern Executive Branch, and the differing institutional perspectives of its agencies, how unified is it in practice?

2. As noted at the outset of this section, the list of presidential foreign affairs powers in Article II is much less extensive than the list of congressional foreign affairs powers in Article I. Some aspects of Article II, such as the President's role as commander in chief of the army and navy and the power to make treaties with the advice and consent of two-thirds of the senators present, are explored in detail in subsequent chapters. In this section, we consider the "executive" power, the power to "take Care that the Laws be faithfully executed," the power to appoint U.S. ambassadors (subject to majority approval in the Senate) and to receive foreign ambassadors, and various possible inherent and implied powers.

3. Article II, Section 1 states that "[t]he executive Power shall be vested in a President of the United States of America." What is entailed by the phrase "executive Power"? Does this "vesting clause" convey authority to the President beyond the authority conveyed by the specific powers listed in Article II? Three important influences on the Founders—Blackstone, Locke, and Montesquieu—believed that foreign relations powers should be lodged in the Executive Branch of government, as was the case with the King of England. *See* 1 William Blackstone, Commentaries on the Laws of England 245-57 (1765); John Locke, Two Treatises of Government 383-84 (Peter Laslett ed., 1963) (1690); Baron de Montesquieu, The Spirit of Laws 185 (Thomas Nugent trans., 1994) (1751); *see generally* Saikrishna B. Prakash & Michael D. Ramsey, *The Executive Power over Foreign Affairs,* 111 Yale L.J. 231, 266-69 (2001) (summarizing these views). Recall from Chapter 1 that Alexander Hamilton, relying on the differences in the "vesting" clauses of Articles I and II, argued that the Founders incorporated these views of Executive power except to the extent that foreign relations powers were specifically allocated to another branch.

Professors Prakash and Ramsey reinvigorated the Hamiltonian view of Executive power in foreign affairs. They argue that Hamilton's view is consistent with both the original understanding of the Founders and the text of Article II. Their central contention is:

> [I]n 1787, when the Constitution provided that the President would have "the executive Power," that would have been understood to mean not only that the President would have the power to execute the laws (the primary and essential meaning of "executive power") but also that the President would have foreign affairs powers. As a result, the starting point is that foreign affairs powers are presidential, not from some shadowy implication of national sovereignty, per *Curtiss-Wright*, but from the ordinary eighteenth-century meaning of executive power.
>
> [T]he President's executive foreign affairs power is residual, encompassing only those executive foreign affairs powers not allocated elsewhere by the Constitution's text. The Constitution's allocation of specific foreign affairs powers or roles to Congress or the Senate are properly read as assignments away from the President. Absent these specific allocations, by Article II, Section 1, all traditionally executive foreign affairs powers would be presidential. . . . The Constitution's drafters believed that the English system afforded too much foreign affairs power to the monarch through the undivided possession of the executive power, and that some aspects of the traditional executive power over foreign affairs had legislative overtones (including the war and treaty-making powers). Accordingly, they divided the traditional executive power over foreign affairs by creating specific (but very substantial) exceptions to the general grant of executive power to the President. In the document they created, many key foreign affairs powers were either shared—such as the power to appoint ambassadors or make treaties—or allocated elsewhere—such as the power to declare war and issue letters of marque. As a result, once the drafting was complete, the President had a greatly diminished foreign affairs power as compared to the English monarchy. But the President retained a residual power—that is, the President, as the possessor of "the executive Power," had those executive foreign affairs powers not allocated elsewhere by the text. In short, far from suffering from huge gaps, the Constitution has a simple default rule that we call the "residual principle": Foreign affairs powers not assigned elsewhere belong to the President, by virtue of the President's executive power; while foreign affairs powers specifically allocated elsewhere are not presidential powers, in spite of the President's executive power.

Prakash & Ramsey, *supra*, at 253-54. Does this "Vesting Clause Thesis" make sense of the text of Article II? What is Justice Jackson's response in *Youngstown* to the Vesting Clause Thesis? If the Vesting Clause Thesis is right, why does Article II provide for a power to receive ambassadors? Wouldn't this power already be included within the "executive Power," as it is not assigned to another branch? Similarly, why, under the Vesting Clause Thesis, does Article II specifically allocate the commander-in-chief power to the President? Wouldn't this power also be included within the "executive Power"? Prakash and Ramsey maintain that because the Founders had given some military powers to Congress, they wanted to be clear that the President retained the commander-in-chief power. But in their view, wouldn't this result already follow from the default assumption about the meaning of "executive Power"? Also, this argument raises the question: under the Vesting Clause Thesis, is the only military-related presidential power the commander-in-chief power? Otherwise, wouldn't the Founders have specified the other powers (such as the power to declare peace)? War powers are discussed in more detail in Chapter 9.

For a critique of the Vesting Clause Thesis, see Curtis A. Bradley & Martin S. Flaherty, *Executive Power Essentialism and Foreign Affairs*, 102 Mich. L. Rev. 545 (2004). The Bradley/Flaherty article challenges the thesis on both textual and historical grounds:

> As for text, the difference in wording between the Article I and Article II Vesting Clauses can be explained in other plausible ways and need not be read as distinguishing

between a limited grant of legislative powers and a plenary grant of executive power. Familiar canons of construction, such as expressio unius, and other interpretive principles further cut against the Vesting Clause Thesis. That thesis, moreover, cannot explain some of Article II's specific grants of foreign affairs authority, and it sits uneasily with the Constitution's enumerated powers structure.

Given that the textual case for the Vesting Clause Thesis is at best uncertain, the persuasiveness of the thesis ultimately depends on history. Here there is a particular irony. Proponents of the Vesting Clause Thesis are often also advocates of a classically originalist approach to constitutional interpretation, pursuant to which the understanding of the Constitution's framers and ratifiers controls constitutional meaning. Yet, as we will show, the historical sources that are most relevant to the Founding, such as the records of the Federal Convention, the Federalist Papers, and the state ratification debates, contain almost nothing that supports the Vesting Clause Thesis, and much that contradicts it.

Supporters of the Vesting Clause Thesis attempt to compensate for the lack of direct Founding support by focusing on political theory and practice both before and after the ratification of the Constitution. Their historical narrative thus has two central features. First, it is a story of continuity, whereby European political theory is carried forward, relatively unblemished, into American constitutional design and practice. Second, the narrative relies on what could be called "executive power essentialism" — the proposition that the Founders had in mind, and intended the Constitution to reflect, a conception of what is "naturally" or "essentially" within executive power. We argue that this historical narrative is wrong on both counts. Among other things, the narrative fails to take account of complexity within eighteenth-century political theory, the experience of state constitutionalism before 1787, and the Founders' self-conscious rejection of the British model of government. The narrative also understates the degree to which the constitutional Founders were functionalists, willing to deviate from pure political theory and essentialist categories in order to design an effective government.

Moreover, as usually presented, the post-constitutional practice of the Washington Administration provides only half the story. Washington and his cabinet, perhaps unsurprisingly, tended to stake out pro-executive positions with respect to the management of U.S. diplomacy. To the extent that there was a consensus concerning these positions, that consensus was based on functional considerations related to specific constitutional grants, not the Vesting Clause. When other, more substantive issues arose—such as the power to remove executive officials (including the Secretary of State) and the power to declare neutrality—the consensus broke down and there was substantial disagreement about the sources and scope of executive power. Moreover, with the partial exception of Alexander Hamilton, neither Washington nor his cabinet actually articulated the Vesting Clause Thesis, preferring instead to make more specific and modest textual claims.

Bradley and Flaherty therefore argue that the Article II Vesting Clause should not be viewed as an independent source of foreign affairs authority, and that the President's foreign affairs powers are consequently limited to the powers expressly granted in Article II. They also note, however, that it might be appropriate to interpret those express grants broadly, and that their meaning might be informed by longstanding historical practice. For Prakash and Ramsey's reply to the Bradley/Flaherty article, see Saikrishna B. Prakash & Michael D. Ramsey, *Foreign Affairs and the Jeffersonian Executive: A Defense,* 89 Minn. L. Rev. 1591 (2005); *see also* Saikrishna Bangalore Prakash, Imperial from the Beginning: The Constitution of the Original Executive (2015) (comprehensive defense of the Vesting Clause Thesis with a particular focus on the Washington Administration). For additional critiques of the Vesting Clause Thesis, see Robert G. Natelson, *The Original Meaning of the Constitution's "Executive Vesting Clause": Evidence from Eighteenth-Century Drafting Practice,* 31 Whittier L. Rev.

1 (2009); Robert J. Reinstein, *The Limits of Executive Power,* 59 Am. U. L. Rev. 259 (2009); and Julian Davis Mortenson, *Article II Vests the Executive Power, Not the Royal Prerogative,* 119 Colum. L. Rev. 1169, 1173 (2019).

4. Article II, Section 3 of the Constitution provides that the President "shall take Care that the Laws be faithfully executed." The term "Laws" unquestionably includes the Constitution and federal statutes. In Chapter 9, we address whether the term also includes international laws, both treaty-based and customary. For now, the question is the meaning of the President's duty to "faithfully execute[ ]" the laws. Professor Monaghan notes that the text of Article II "seemingly contemplates only a 'law enforcement' Executive; that is, the President simply 'executes' the will of Congress." Henry P. Monaghan, *The Protective Power of the Presidency,* 93 Colum. L. Rev. 1, 11 (1993). Is this all that the "take care" power entails? As recounted in Chapter 1, Alexander Hamilton argued that the Take Care Clause supported President George Washington's issuance of the Neutrality Proclamation. Does this argument move beyond the "law enforcement" conception of the Take Care Clause?

The majority opinion in *Youngstown* provides what Professor Monaghan calls the "classic illustration" of the law enforcement conception of the "take care" power when it states that "[i]n the framework of our constitution, the President's power to see that the laws are faithfully executed refutes the idea that he is to be a lawmaker." Justice Jackson similarly states that the "take care" power only "gives a governmental authority that reaches so far as there is law," and concludes that this idea is central to the notion that "ours is a government of laws, not of men, and that we submit ourselves to rulers only if under rules." Justice Vinson's dissent, on the other hand, argues that Truman's action was consistent with, and indeed compelled by, his Article II duty to execute the laws. For this broader reading of the Take Care Clause, Vinson relied in part on In re Neagle, 135 U.S. 1 (1890). The question in that case was whether the U.S. Attorney General had lawfully assigned a federal marshal to guard Justice Field, whose life had been threatened. The Court held that he had, even though the government acknowledged that no "single specific statute" authorized him to do so. It reasoned that the President's duty to execute the laws was not "limited to the enforcement of acts of Congress or of treaties of the United States according to their express terms," but rather included "the rights, duties, and obligations growing out of the Constitution itself, our international relations, and all the protection implied by the nature of the government under the Constitution." For discussion of the facts and proceedings in *Neagle,* see John Harrison, *The Story of* In re Neagle*: Sex, Money, Politics, Perjury, Homicide, Federalism, and Executive Power,* in Presidential Power Stories 133 (Christopher H. Schroeder & Curtis A. Bradley eds., 2009).

Does *Neagle* support Vinson's broader reading of the "take care" power? In any event, won't the President always exercise discretion in deciding what steps are needed to faithfully execute the laws? How do courts police that discretion? Is the problem akin to the problem of judicial scrutiny of the Necessary and Proper Clause, discussed above in Section A? Should courts engage in means-ends scrutiny or purpose scrutiny in this context as well? Does Truman's action survive that scrutiny? How much incidental authority does the President possess in executing statutes and treaties?

In addition to the Take Care Clause, Article II also states that the President must take an oath or affirmation to "faithfully execute the Office of President." A recent historical examination of these two "faithful execution" clauses concludes that they "limit Presidents to exercise their power only when it is motivated in the public interest rather than in their private self-interest," and require "the President to follow the laws, instructions, and authorizations set in motion by the legislature." Andrew Kent, Ethan J. Leib & Jed Handelsman Shugerman, *Faithful Execution and Article II*, 132 Harv. L. Rev. 2111, 2120 (2019).

5. Whatever the proper conception of the Take Care and Oath Clauses, the majority in *Youngstown* seems to say that the President has no lawmaking powers. *See also* Medellin v. Texas, 552 U.S. 491, 532 (2008) ("[The Take Care Clause] authority allows the President to execute the laws, not make them."). As we shall see throughout this casebook, however, the President appears to make law related to foreign relations in a number of instances—for example, when concluding "sole" executive agreements with the force of domestic law, and when determining whether foreign heads of state are immune from suit in the United States. For analysis of the President's foreign affairs "lawmaking" powers, see Louis Henkin, Foreign Affairs and the United States Constitution 54-61 (2d ed. 1996); Monaghan, *supra*, at 47-56. For a more recent consideration of presidential lawmaking authority, see Michael Van Alstine, *Executive Aggrandizement in Foreign Affairs Lawmaking*, 54 UCLA L. Rev. 309 (2006).

6. How does President Roosevelt's "stewardship" theory of Executive power compare with the Vesting Clause Thesis and with the Vinson/*Neagle* conception of the Take Care Clause? Note that, although President Taft disagreed with Roosevelt's broad conception of presidential power, he

> did not think the president should construe his or her powers by a wooden, clause-by-clause exegesis of the constitutional text. In the area of foreign affairs, the president's diplomatic duties, powers as commander in chief, and duty under the take care clause to carry out the obligations of the United States to its citizens and to other nations come together to create broad authority to act independently of legislative authorization.

Editor's Introduction, in William Howard Taft, Our Chief Magistrate and His Powers xlii (H. Jefferson Powell ed., 2002). What difference is there between arguing that the President has broad residual foreign affairs authority and arguing that the President's express grants of authority in Article II should be interpreted broadly?

7. The steel seizure at issue in *Youngstown* took place in the midst of, and in alleged furtherance of, the Korean War. How does the origin and presence of the war influence the different opinions in *Youngstown*? Note in particular the differences between Justice Jackson's concurrence (which views the manner in which the war was started as a reason to read Executive power narrowly) and Justice Vinson's dissent (which views the Cold War background of the war as a reason to read Executive power broadly). Which view is right?

8. Under the analysis in *Curtiss-Wright*, why isn't the Korean War an "external affair" regarding which the President has plenary power? How should a court determine which tasks concern external affairs? Why does the Court take such a different approach to constitutional limits in *Youngstown*, where the majority opinion does not even cite *Curtiss-Wright*? How would you characterize the interpretive methodologies in the different opinions in *Youngstown*? Are the holdings in *Curtiss-Wright* and *Youngstown* reconcilable, as Justice Jackson suggests in footnote 2 of his concurrence? For an effort to synthesize *Curtiss-Wright* and *Youngstown*, see

Roy E. Brownell II, *The Coexistence of* United States v. Curtiss-Wright Export Corp. *and* Youngstown Sheet & Tube v. Sawyer *in National Security Jurisprudence,* 16 J.L. & Pol. 1 (2000). For a symposium on *Youngstown,* which focuses on, among other things, the relevance of *Youngstown* to the post–September 11, 2001, war on terrorism, see Youngstown *at Fifty: A Symposium,* 19 Const. Commentary 1-259 (2002). *See also* Christopher Bryant & Carl Tobias, Youngstown *Revisited,* 29 Hastings Const. L.Q. 373 (2002).

9. How does Justice Frankfurter's concurrence in *Youngstown* differ from the majority opinion? Is Frankfurter's conception of presidential power broader than the majority's conception? If so, how? Does Frankfurter's analysis allow the Constitution to be informally amended by the practices of the political branches? *See also* United States v. Midwest Oil Co., 236 U.S. 459, 473 (1915) ("[I]n determining . . . the existence of a power, weight should be given to the usage itself—even when the validity of the practice is the subject of investigation."). For additional discussion of the role of historical practice in determinations of presidential authority, see Curtis A. Bradley & Trevor W. Morrison, *Historical Gloss and the Separation of Powers,* 126 Harv. L. Rev. 421 (2012).

10. Justice Jackson's concurrence in *Youngstown,* especially its articulation of three categories of presidential power, has been very influential. Indeed, courts and commentators often give more weight to Jackson's concurrence than to the majority opinion. Why do you think this is so? How much guidance does Jackson's framework provide in ascertaining the scope of presidential power? Is it clear that President Truman's actions in *Youngstown* fell within the third category, as Jackson argues? (The next section considers Jackson's three categories in more detail.)

11. Recall John Marshall's famous statement, quoted in *Curtiss-Wright,* that the President is the "sole organ of the nation in its external relations, and its sole representative with foreign nations." Marshall made this statement in 1800 as a member of the House of Representatives in defense of President John Adams. Adams had ordered the extradition to Great Britain of Thomas Nash, alias Jonathan Robbins, who was accused of murder while aboard a British ship. Although Adams acted pursuant to a treaty with Great Britain, he was criticized on the ground that the extradition request from Great Britain should have been processed by judicial action, not Executive action. It was in this context that Marshall, defending Adams, proclaimed:

> The case was in its nature a national demand made upon the nation. The parties were the two nations. They cannot come into court to litigate their claims, nor can a court decide on them. Of consequence, the demand is not a case for judicial cognizance. *The president is the sole organ of the nation in its external relations, and its sole representative with foreign nations.* Of consequence, the demand of a foreign nation can only be made on him. He possesses the whole executive power. He holds and directs the force of the nation. Of consequence, any act to be performed by the force of the nation is to be performed through him. He is charged to execute the laws. A treaty is declared to be a law. He must then execute a treaty, where he, and he alone, possesses the means of executing it.

10 Annals of Congress 596, 613 (1800) (emphasis added). In context, what did Marshall mean in describing the President as the "sole organ"? If nothing else, Marshall appears to be arguing that the President is the official head of

communication for the U.S. government in foreign affairs. Where does the President obtain that authority? Is such a role implied in the President's express powers, such as the power to receive and appoint ambassadors, the power to make treaties, and the power to execute the laws? Is it implied from the fact that the presidency is a unitary institution, whereas Congress is a plural institution? For additional discussion of the Jonathan Robbins case and Marshall's defense of Adams, see Ruth Wedgwood, *The Revolutionary Martyrdom of Jonathan Robbins,* 100 Yale L.J. 229 (1990).

12. In practice, the Executive Branch exercises a virtual monopoly over formal communications with foreign nations and also plays a lead role in announcing U.S. foreign policy. The Monroe and Bush Doctrines, excerpted and described above, are important examples of the exercise of this authority. Each of these doctrines announced a fundamental proposition of U.S. foreign policy without any prior consultation with Congress. What are the legal effects of these doctrines? The political effects? Is each doctrine anything more than (as Lord Clarendon said of the Monroe Doctrine) "merely the dictum of its distinguished author"? Thomas A. Bailey, A Diplomatic History of the American People 189 (6th ed. 1958). If so, why? Where did the presidents obtain the authority to announce these doctrines? In terms of presidential authority, how do these doctrines compare with Washington's Neutrality Proclamation, which we discussed in Chapter 1? Do these doctrines bind Congress or future presidents? If the answer is no, is the President's power to announce important foreign policy initiatives such as these nonetheless important? Why or why not? Note that, despite the Executive Branch's role as the organ of formal diplomatic communications, members of Congress regularly interact with foreign officials, both in the United States and through travel abroad. For an examination of this practice, and of presidential control over it, see Ryan Scoville, *Legislative Diplomacy,* 112 Mich. L. Rev. 331 (2013). *See also* Kristen E. Eichensehr, *Courts, Congress, and the Conduct of Foreign Relations,* 85 U. Chi. L. Rev. 609 (2018) (examining the related phenomenon of "nonexecutive conduct of foreign relations," which occurs when courts or Congress take actions "that result in the opening of a direct channel of official communications between the U.S. nonexecutive branch and a foreign executive branch").

13. Article II grants the President the power to appoint "Ambassadors" and "other public Ministers," with the advice and consent of the Senate. This language has traditionally been viewed to require Senate confirmation for the appointment of resident ambassadors and other diplomats of similar rank. However, presidents sometimes select other agents to conduct diplomacy without seeking Senate confirmation. For example, President Roosevelt selected his close aide, Harry Hopkins, as his special envoy for some of his most sensitive meetings with foreign leaders during World War II, and President Trump has relied on his son-in-law, Jared Kushner, to facilitate peace negotiations in the Middle East. For a comprehensive historical and legal analysis of such "ad hoc" diplomacy, see Ryan M. Scoville, *Ad Hoc Diplomats,* 68 Duke L.J. 907 (2019).

14. For additional commentary on the issues in this section, see Raoul Berger, *The Presidential Monopoly of Foreign Relations,* 71 Mich. L. Rev. 1 (1972); Michael J. Glennon, *Two Views of Presidential Foreign Affairs Power: Little v. Barreme or Curtiss-Wright?,* 13 Yale J. Int'l L. 5 (1988); H. Jefferson Powell, *The Founders and the President's Authority over Foreign Affairs,* 40 Wm. & Mary L. Rev. 1471 (1999); H. Jefferson Powell, *The President's Authority over Foreign Affairs: An Executive Branch Perspective,* 67 Geo.

Wash. L. Rev. 527 (1999); Phillip R. Trimble, *The President's Foreign Affairs Power*, 83 Am. J. Int'l L. 750 (1989).

C. RELATIONSHIP BETWEEN CONGRESS AND THE PRESIDENT

Congress and the Executive Branch both regulate foreign relations, and their regulations frequently interact. Often they act in harmony. At other times, one branch acquiesces in the other's actions, albeit sometimes grudgingly. And at still other times, the branches act in opposition to one another. How should courts construe these various interactions? Are there limits on the extent to which Congress can delegate its authority to the Executive? Does inaction by one branch constitute acquiescence in and possibly approval of the constitutionality of the actions of the other? How should courts resolve conflicts between the political branches? How should conflicts that fall outside the scope of judicial review be resolved? This section addresses these and related questions in two parts. First, it considers how courts determine and construe congressional authorizations of Executive action. Second, it considers how both courts and the Executive Branch treat conflicts of congressional and executive authority.

1. Congressional Support for Presidential Action

Dames & Moore v. Regan

453 U.S. 654 (1981)

[On November 4, 1979, Iranian militants seized the U.S. embassy in Tehran and began holding the U.S. diplomatic personnel there as hostages. The revolutionary Iranian government made no effort to stop the militants and soon sided with them in negotiations. The government also repudiated its predecessor government's contracts with U.S. companies. Acting pursuant to the International Emergency Economic Powers Act (IEEPA), President Carter declared a national emergency and then blocked the removal or transfer of Iranian assets held within the jurisdiction of the United States. Carter subsequently issued orders authorizing the initiation of judicial proceedings in U.S. courts against Iran. These orders allowed for the entry of a pre-judgment attachment in such proceedings, but not a final judgment. After the issuance of these orders, Dames & Moore filed suit against Iran and various Iranian entities seeking the recovery of money owed to its subsidiary under a service contract, and it obtained a pre-judgment attachment of the property of certain Iranian banks. On January 20, 1981, the U.S. hostages were released by Iran pursuant to the Algiers Accords, an executive agreement. Under the Accords, the United States agreed to "terminate all legal proceedings in United States courts involving claims of United States persons and institutions against Iran and its state enterprises, to nullify all attachments and judgments obtained therein, to prohibit all further litigation based on such claims, and to bring about the termination of such claims through binding arbitration [before a special tribunal to be established in the Hague]." Immediately before leaving office, President Carter issued executive orders implementing the terms of the Accords. President Reagan subsequently issued an executive order in which he reaffirmed Carter's orders and "suspended" all "claims which may be presented to the . . . Tribunal" and provided that such claims "shall have no legal effect in any action now pending in any court of the United States." Dames & Moore challenged the validity of the Carter and Reagan executive orders.]

JUSTICE REHNQUIST delivered the opinion of the Court. . . .

The parties and the lower courts, confronted with the instant questions, have all agreed that much relevant analysis is contained in Youngstown Sheet & Tube Co. v. Sawyer, 343 U.S. 579 (1952). . . .

Although we have in the past found and do today find Justice Jackson's classification of executive actions into three general categories analytically useful, we should be mindful of Justice Holmes' admonition, quoted by Justice Frankfurter in *Youngstown, supra,* at 597 (concurring opinion), that "[the] great ordinances of the Constitution do not establish and divide fields of black and white." Springer v. Philippine Islands, 277 U.S. 189, 209 (1928) (dissenting opinion). Justice Jackson himself recognized that his three categories represented "a somewhat oversimplified grouping," 343 U.S. at 635, and it is doubtless the case that executive action in any particular instance falls, not neatly in one of three pigeonholes, but rather at some point along a spectrum running from explicit congressional authorization to explicit congressional prohibition. This is particularly true as respects cases such as the one before us, involving responses to international crises the nature of which Congress can hardly have been expected to anticipate in any detail.

. . . The Government . . . has principally relied on §203 of the IEEPA, 50 U.S.C. §1702(a)(1), as authorization for these actions. Section 1702(a)(1) provides in part:

> At the times and to the extent specified in section 1701 of this title, the President may, under such regulations as he may prescribe, by means of instructions, licenses, or otherwise —
>
>   (A) investigate, regulate, or prohibit —
>
>   (i) any transactions in foreign exchange,
>
>   (ii) transfers of credit or payments between, by, through, or to any banking institution, to the extent that such transfers or payments involve any interest of any foreign country or a national thereof,
>
>   (iii) the importing or exporting of currency or securities, and
>
>   (B) investigate, regulate, direct and compel, nullify, void, prevent, or prohibit, any acquisition, holding, withholding, use, transfer, withdrawal, transportation, importation or exportation of, or dealing in, or exercising any right, power, or privilege with respect to, or transactions involving, any property in which any foreign country or a national thereof has any interest; by any person, or with respect to any property, subject to the jurisdiction of the United States.

The Government contends that the acts of "nullifying" the attachments and ordering the "transfer" of the frozen assets are specifically authorized by the plain language of the above statute. . . .

Petitioner contends that we should ignore the plain language of this statute because an examination of its legislative history as well as the history of §5(b) of the Trading With the Enemy Act (hereinafter TWEA), 40 Stat. 411, as amended, 50 U.S.C. App. §5(b) (1976 ed. and Supp. III), from which the pertinent language of §1702 is directly drawn, reveals that the statute was not intended to give the

President such extensive power over the assets of a foreign state during times of national emergency. According to petitioner, once the President instituted the November 14, 1979, blocking order, §1702 authorized him "only to continue the freeze or to discontinue controls."

We do not agree and refuse to read out of §1702 all meaning to the words "transfer," "compel," or "nullify." Nothing in the legislative history of either §1702 or §5(b) of the TWEA requires such a result. To the contrary, we think both the legislative history and cases interpreting the TWEA fully sustain the broad authority of the Executive when acting under this congressional grant of power. Although Congress intended to limit the President's emergency power in peacetime, we do not think the changes brought about by the enactment of the IEEPA in any way affected the authority of the President to take the specific actions taken here. We likewise note that by the time petitioner instituted this action, the President had already entered the freeze order. Petitioner proceeded against the blocked assets only after the Treasury Department had issued revocable licenses authorizing such proceedings and attachments. The Treasury Regulations provided that "unless licensed" any attachment is null and void, 31 CFR §535.203(e) (1980), and all licenses "may be amended, modified, or revoked at any time." §535.805. As such, the attachments obtained by petitioner were specifically made subordinate to further actions which the President might take under the IEEPA. Petitioner was on notice of the contingent nature of its interest in the frozen assets. . . .

Because the President's action in nullifying the attachments and ordering the transfer of the assets was taken pursuant to specific congressional authorization, it is "supported by the strongest of presumptions and the widest latitude of judicial interpretation, and the burden of persuasion would rest heavily upon any who might attack it." *Youngstown*, 343 U.S. at 637 (Jackson, J., concurring). Under the circumstances of this case, we cannot say that petitioner has sustained that heavy burden. A contrary ruling would mean that the Federal Government as a whole lacked the power exercised by the President, see *id.* at 636-37, and that we are not prepared to say.

. . . Although we have concluded that the IEEPA constitutes specific congressional authorization to the President to nullify the attachments and order the transfer of Iranian assets, there remains the question of the President's authority to suspend claims pending in American courts. Such claims have, of course, an existence apart from the attachments which accompanied them. In terminating these claims through Executive Order No. 12294, the President purported to act under authority of both the IEEPA and 22 U.S.C. §1732, the so-called Hostage Act.

We conclude that although the IEEPA authorized the nullification of the attachments, it cannot be read to authorize the suspension of the claims. The claims of American citizens against Iran are not in themselves transactions involving Iranian property or efforts to exercise any rights with respect to such property. . . . The terms of the IEEPA therefore do not authorize the President to suspend claims in American courts. This is the view of all the courts which have considered the question.

The Hostage Act, passed in 1868, provides:

Whenever it is made known to the President that any citizen of the United States has been unjustly deprived of his liberty by or under the authority of any foreign government, it shall be the duty of the President forthwith to demand of that government the reasons of such imprisonment; and if it appears to be wrongful and in violation of the rights of American citizenship, the President shall forthwith demand the release of such citizen, and if the release so demanded is unreasonably delayed or refused, the President shall use such means, not amounting to acts of war, as he may think necessary and proper to obtain or effectuate the release; and all the facts and proceedings relative thereto shall as soon as practicable be communicated by the President to Congress. Rev. Stat. §2001, 22 U.S.C. §1732.

We are reluctant to conclude that this provision constitutes specific authorization to the President to suspend claims in American courts. Although the broad language of the Hostage Act suggests it may cover this case, there are several difficulties with such a view. The legislative history indicates that the Act was passed in response to a situation unlike the recent Iranian crisis. Congress in 1868 was concerned with the activity of certain countries refusing to recognize the citizenship of naturalized Americans traveling abroad, and repatriating such citizens against their will. These countries were not interested in returning the citizens in exchange for any sort of ransom. This also explains the reference in the Act to imprisonment "in violation of the rights of American citizenship." Although the Iranian hostage-taking violated international law and common decency, the hostages were not seized out of any refusal to recognize their American citizenship—they were seized precisely *because of* their American citizenship. The legislative history is also somewhat ambiguous on the question whether Congress contemplated Presidential action such as that involved here or rather simply reprisals directed against the offending foreign country and *its* citizens.

Concluding that neither the IEEPA nor the Hostage Act constitutes specific authorization of the President's action suspending claims, however, is not to say that these statutory provisions are entirely irrelevant to the question of the validity of the President's action. We think both statutes highly relevant in the looser sense of indicating congressional acceptance of a broad scope for executive action in circumstances such as those presented in this case. As noted. . . , the IEEPA delegates broad authority to the President to act in times of national emergency with respect to property of a foreign country. The Hostage Act similarly indicates congressional willingness that the President have broad discretion when responding to the hostile acts of foreign sovereigns. . . .

Although we have declined to conclude that the IEEPA or the Hostage Act directly authorizes the President's suspension of claims for the reasons noted, we cannot ignore the general tenor of Congress' legislation in this area in trying to determine whether the President is acting alone or at least with the acceptance of Congress. As we have noted, Congress cannot anticipate and legislate with regard to every possible action the President may find it necessary to take or every possible situation in which he might act. Such failure of Congress specifically to delegate authority does not, "especially . . . in the areas of foreign policy and national security," imply "congressional disapproval" of action taken by the Executive. Haig v. Agee, 453 U.S. 280, 291 (1981). On the contrary, the enactment of legislation closely related to the question of the President's authority in a particular case which evinces legislative intent to accord the President broad discretion may be considered to "invite" "measures on independent presidential responsibility." *Youngstown,* 343 U.S. at 637 (Jackson, J., concurring). At least this is so where there is no contrary indication of legislative intent and when, as here, there is a history of congressional acquiescence in conduct of the sort engaged in by the President. It is to that history which we now turn.

Not infrequently in affairs between nations, outstanding claims by nationals of one country against the government of another country are "sources of friction" between the two sovereigns. United States v. Pink, 315 U.S. 203, 225 (1942). To resolve these difficulties, nations have often entered into agreements settling the claims of their respective nationals. . . . Consistent with that principle, the United States has repeatedly exercised its sovereign authority to settle the claims of its nationals against foreign countries. Though those settlements have sometimes been made by treaty, there has also been a longstanding practice of settling such claims by executive agreement without the advice and consent of the Senate.[8] Under such agreements, the President has agreed to renounce or extinguish claims of United States nationals against foreign governments in return for lump-sum payments or the establishment of arbitration procedures. To be sure, many of these settlements were encouraged by the United States claimants themselves, since a claimant's only hope of obtaining any payment at all might lie in having his Government negotiate a diplomatic settlement on his behalf. But it is also undisputed that the "United States has sometimes disposed of the claims of its citizens without their consent, or even without consultation with them, usually without exclusive regard for their interests, as distinguished from those of the nation as a whole." Louis Henkin, Foreign Affairs and the Constitution 262-63 (1972). . . . It is clear that the practice of settling claims continues today. Since 1952, the President has entered into at least 10 binding settlements with foreign nations, including an $80 million settlement with the People's Republic of China.

Crucial to our decision today is the conclusion that Congress has implicitly approved the practice of claim settlement by executive agreement. This is best demonstrated by Congress' enactment of the International Claims Settlement Act of 1949, as amended, 22 U.S.C. §1621 et seq. The Act had two purposes: (1) to allocate to United States nationals funds received in the course of an executive claims settlement with Yugoslavia, and (2) to provide a procedure whereby funds resulting from future settlements could be distributed. To achieve these ends Congress created the International Claims Commission, now the Foreign Claims Settlement Commission, and gave it jurisdiction to make final and binding decisions with respect to claims by United States nationals against settlement funds. 22 U.S.C. §1623(a). By creating a procedure to implement future settlement agreements, Congress placed its stamp of approval on such agreements. Indeed, the legislative history of the Act observed that the United States was seeking settlements with countries other than Yugoslavia and that the bill contemplated settlements of a similar nature in the future.

Over the years Congress has frequently amended the International Claims Settlement Act to provide for particular problems arising out of settlement agreements, thus demonstrating Congress' continuing acceptance of the President's claim settlement authority. . . .[10]

In addition to congressional acquiescence in the President's power to settle claims, prior cases of this Court have also recognized that the President does have some measure of power to enter into executive agreements without obtaining the

8. At least since the case of the "Wilmington Packet" in 1799, Presidents have exercised the power to settle claims of United States nationals by executive agreement. In fact, during the period of 1817-1917, "no fewer than eighty executive agreements were entered into by the United States looking toward the liquidation of claims of its citizens." W. McClure, International Executive Agreements 53 (1941). *See also* 14 M. Whiteman, Digest of International Law 247 (1970).

10. Indeed, Congress has consistently failed to object to this longstanding practice of claim settlement by executive agreement, even when it has had an opportunity to do so. . . .

advice and consent of the Senate. In United States v. Pink, 315 U.S. 203 (1942), for example, the Court upheld the validity of the Litvinov Assignment, which was part of an Executive Agreement whereby the Soviet Union assigned to the United States amounts owed to it by American nationals so that outstanding claims of other American nationals could be paid. . . .

In light of all of the foregoing . . . we conclude that the President was authorized to suspend pending claims pursuant to Executive Order No. 12294. As Justice Frankfurter pointed out in *Youngstown*, 343 U.S. at 610-11, "a systematic, unbroken, executive practice, long pursued to the knowledge of the Congress and never before questioned . . . may be treated as a gloss on 'Executive Power' vested in the President by §1 of Art. II." Past practice does not, by itself, create power, but "long-continued practice, known to and acquiesced in by Congress, would raise a presumption that the [action] had been [taken] in pursuance of its consent. . . ." United States v. Midwest Oil Co., 236 U.S. 459, 474 (1915). Such practice is present here and such a presumption is also appropriate. In light of the fact that Congress may be considered to have consented to the President's action in suspending claims, we cannot say that action exceeded the President's powers.

Our conclusion is buttressed by the fact that the means chosen by the President to settle the claims of American nationals provided an alternative forum, the Claims Tribunal, which is capable of providing meaningful relief. . . . The fact that the President has provided such a forum here means that the claimants are receiving something in return for the suspension of their claims, namely, access to an international tribunal before which they may well recover something on their claims. Because there does appear to be a real "settlement" here, this case is more easily analogized to the more traditional claim settlement cases of the past.

Just as importantly, Congress has not disapproved of the action taken here. Though Congress has held hearings on the Iranian Agreement itself, Congress has not enacted legislation, or even passed a resolution, indicating its displeasure with the Agreement. Quite the contrary, the relevant Senate Committee has stated that the establishment of the Tribunal is "of vital importance to the United States." We are thus clearly not confronted with a situation in which Congress has in some way resisted the exercise of Presidential authority.

Finally, we re-emphasize the narrowness of our decision. We do not decide that the President possesses plenary power to settle claims, even as against foreign governmental entities. As the Court of Appeals for the First Circuit stressed, "[the] sheer magnitude of such a power, considered against the background of the diversity and complexity of modern international trade, cautions against any broader construction of authority than is necessary." But where, as here, the settlement of claims has been determined to be a necessary incident to the resolution of a major foreign policy dispute between our country and another, and where, as here, we can conclude that Congress acquiesced in the President's action, we are not prepared to say that the President lacks the power to settle such claims.

. . . We do not think it appropriate at the present time to address petitioner's contention that the suspension of claims, if authorized, would constitute a taking of property in violation of the Fifth Amendment to the United States Constitution in the absence of just compensation. . . .[14]

---

14. Though we conclude that the President has settled petitioner's claims against Iran, we do not suggest that the settlement has terminated petitioner's possible taking claim against the United States. We express no views on petitioner's claims that it has suffered a taking.

Notes and Questions

1. Why are the foreign relations powers divided between the President and Congress? Wouldn't it have been more efficient to let the President make all foreign relations decisions and all foreign relations law? Why did the Founders give different powers to different branches? The generic response is that separation of federal powers secures liberty by diffusing authority, and increases the quality of political outcomes through an institutional division of labor and enhanced deliberation. Do these justifications apply in the foreign affairs context? Why were the Founders so unclear about the allocation of authority for so many foreign relations tasks? Is there virtue in ambiguity and silence? Did the Founders expect the branches to work out the optimal allocation of foreign relations power?

2. Uncertainty about the constitutional allocation of authority between the President and Congress has been resolved by two distinct, and somewhat incompatible, interpretive strategies. The first, known as "formalism," emphasizes constitutional text, rule-bound adjudication, and clear lines of demarcation between the branches. For formalists, the critical threshold question is whether a particular exercise of authority is essentially legislative, executive, or judicial. Once the characterization is made, the action is scrutinized for conformity to constitutional allocation. The second interpretive strategy is known as "functionalism." Functionalists believe that the exigencies of modern government demand a more flexible interpretation of separation of powers. They tend to employ balancing approaches to separation of powers disputes, to ask whether particular institutional practices further the purposes of separation of powers, and to countenance the participation of each branch in the decisionmaking processes of the other. For analysis of the distinction, see William N. Eskridge, Jr., *Relationships Between Formalism and Functionalism in Separation of Powers Cases*, 22 Harv. J.L. & Pub. Pol'y 21 (1998); Martin S. Flaherty, *The Most Dangerous Branch*, 105 Yale L.J. 1725 (1996); Thomas Merrill, *The Constitutional Principle of Separation of Powers*, 1991 Sup. Ct. Rev. 225; and Peter L. Strauss, *Formal and Functional Approaches to Separation of Powers Questions: A Foolish Inconsistency?*, 72 Cornell L. Rev. 488 (1987). For a critique of the formalist and functionalist perspectives, see M. Elizabeth Magill, *The Real Separation in Separation of Powers Law*, 86 Va. L. Rev. 1127 (2000).

3. Perhaps the most prominent formalist separation of powers decision in modern times is Immigration and Naturalization Service v. Chadha, 462 U.S. 919 (1983), which held unconstitutional the "legislative veto" provision in the Immigration and Nationality Act. Section 244(a)(1) of the Act authorized the Attorney General to suspend deportation of a deportable alien who met specified conditions and whose deportation would "result in extreme hardship to the alien" or his or her family. The Act also required the Attorney General to report such suspensions to Congress. Section 244(c)(2) of the Act, the provision challenged in this case, allowed one house of Congress to veto the Attorney General's decisions suspending deportations. Chadha was an East Indian whose deportation the Attorney General suspended. Over a year later, the House of Representatives passed a resolution under §244(c)(2) that vetoed the suspended deportations of Chadha and others. Chadha challenged his subsequent deportation, arguing that §244(c)(2) was unconstitutional.

The Supreme Court agreed. It explained that "[t]he Constitution sought to divide the delegated powers of the new Federal Government into three defined categories, Legislative, Executive and Judicial, to assure, as nearly as possible, that each branch of government would confine itself to its assigned responsibility." The

Court proceeded to conclude that §244(c)(2) was "essentially legislative in purpose and effect" and thus violated the requirements of presentment to the President and bicameralism specified in Article I of the Constitution for the enactment of legislation. In response to the argument that legislative veto provisions like this one are useful in the modern administrative state because they allow Congress to retain some supervisory control over its delegations to the Executive Branch, the Court stated that "the fact that a given law or procedure is efficient, convenient, and useful in facilitating functions of government, standing alone, will not save it if it is contrary to the Constitution."

Justice White dissented. He contended that the Court's decision "not only invalidates §244(c)(2) of the Immigration and Nationality Act, but also sounds the death knell for nearly 200 other statutory provisions in which Congress has reserved a 'legislative veto.'" 462 U.S. at 867. He also argued that "the legislative veto is more than 'efficient, convenient, and useful.' It is an important if not indispensable political invention that allows the President and Congress to resolve major constitutional and policy differences, assures the accountability of independent regulatory agencies, and preserves Congress' control over lawmaking." *Id.* at 972-73. Finally, he expressed the view that "the wisdom of the Framers was to anticipate that the nation would grow and new problems of governance would require different solutions. Accordingly, our Federal Government was intentionally chartered with the flexibility to respond to contemporary needs without losing sight of fundamental democratic principles." *Id.* at 978.

4. Which approach—formalist or functionalist—better reflects the proper understanding of the constitutional separation of powers? Which approach is most appropriate for a case such as *Youngstown?* In that case, the majority opinion deployed a formal conception of separation of powers, while Justice Jackson's celebrated concurrence reflected a more functional conception. Is it helpful, or simplistic, for the majority in *Youngstown* to ask simply whether the steel seizure was a legislative or executive action? Couldn't it have been some of both? Isn't it a question of degree?

Is Justice Jackson's concurrence any more helpful? Consider his first category—presidential action pursuant to an express or implied congressional authorization. How does a Court discern an implied authorization? (We return to this issue below.) And, assuming that there is such an authorization, is Jackson correct to assert that if an act is held unconstitutional in this context, "it usually means that the Federal government as an undivided whole lacks power"? What about constitutional limitations on excessive delegation?

Jackson's second category is presidential action in the face of legislative silence. Again, as we shall explore below, the ascertainment of true congressional silence is often a difficult interpretive question. But assuming Congress has been silent, is it helpful to assert that "there is a zone of twilight in which [the President] and Congress may have concurrent authority, or in which its distribution is uncertain"? What does Jackson mean by "concurrent authority"? Can the President act until Congress says otherwise? What is the source of Executive authority here? When Jackson says that such assertions of presidential power depend on "imperatives of events and contemporary imponderables," is he talking about politics? Is the validity of presidential action within the second category a political question? In the face of congressional silence, are there any limits on presidential power except *ex post* congressional disapproval? What incentives does Jackson's framework give to the Executive Branch with respect to seeking congressional approval of foreign relations activities? For consideration of that question, see Edward T. Swaine, *The Political Economy of* Youngstown, 83 S. Cal. L. Rev. 263 (2010).

Jackson's third category is presidential action incompatible with the express or implied will of Congress. Again the problem arises of ascertaining the implied will of Congress. Can this will be ascertained through measures other than legislation? Jackson himself viewed *Youngstown* as a case of presidential action inconsistent with the implied will of Congress. What was this conclusion based on? Had Congress explicitly prohibited this action? Was Jackson interpreting congressional silence, in the context of Congress's other actions, to mean disapproval?

5. Although the Supreme Court in *Dames & Moore* pointed to no particular statute that conferred on the President the authority to suspend the private claims against Iran pending in U.S. courts, it nonetheless concluded that the presidential action "was authorized" to suspend the claims. Why did the Court reach this conclusion? Was it appropriate for the Court to look at the "general tenor of Congress's legislation in this area in trying to determine whether the President is acting alone or at least with the acceptance of Congress"? Do the majority opinions in *Youngstown* and *Chadha* permit this inquiry? What was the Court's basis for its "crucial" conclusion that Congress had implicitly approved the practice of claims settlement by executive agreement? And why did the Court find it "important[ ]" that "Congress has not disapproved of the action taken here [by the President]"? Professor Koh states that the approach in *Dames & Moore* "elevat[es] the president's power from the twilight zone — Jackson's category two — to its height in Jackson's category one" and "effectively follow[s] the dissenting view in *Youngstown*, which had converted legislative silence into consent, thereby delegating to the President authority that Congress itself had arguably withheld." Harold Hongju Koh, The National Security Constitution: Sharing Power After the Iran-Contra Affair 139 (1990). He adds:

> [B]y finding legislative "approval" when Congress had given none, [*Dames & Moore*] not only inverted the Steel Seizure holding which had construed statutory nonapproval of the president's act to mean legislative disapproval but also condoned legislative inactivity at a time that demanded interbranch dialogue and bipartisan consensus. . . . *Dames & Moore* championed unguided executive activism and congressional acquiescence in foreign affairs over the constitutional principle of balanced institutional participation.

Id. at 140. Do you agree with these contentions? If so, why do you think the Court departed so drastically from the *Youngstown* approach? In stating in the passive voice that the President "was authorized" to suspend the claims, was the Court saying that it was Congress or Article II, or both, that authorized the President to suspend the claims in question? In other parts of the opinion, the Court described Congress as having "accepted" or "acquiesced in" the President's action. What difference might it make whether Congress authorized the suspension of claims or merely supported the suspension in a way that was less than authorization, but more than silence?

6. The executive order and regulations at issue in *Dames & Moore* followed upon President Carter's proclamation of an emergency under IEEPA. This statute was enacted in 1977 in response to abuses under the Trading with the Enemy Act (TWEA) of 1917, codified as amended, 50 U.S.C. app. §§1-6, 41-44. The TWEA essentially gave the President authority to freeze and seize assets and regulate all international transactions simply by declaring a national emergency or war, and presidents from Wilson to Nixon invoked it in a variety of ways as a basis for domestic and international emergency acts. IEEPA limited the President's powers under TWEA to wartime. But it also delegated broad emergency powers in peacetime upon a presidential finding of "any unusual and extraordinary threat, which has its source in whole or substantial part outside the United States, to the national security, foreign policy, or economy of the United States, if the President declares a national emergency with respect to such threat." 50 U.S.C. §1701. According to a Congressional Research Service report, "As of March 1, 2019, presidents had declared 54 national emergencies involving IEEPA, 29 of which are still ongoing." Congressional Research Service, *The International Emergency Economic Powers Act: Origins, Evolution, and Use* (Mar. 20, 2019). In May 2019, President Trump announced another emergency under IEEPA, concerning immigration across the U.S. southern border, and used it as a basis for imposing tariffs on Mexico. *See* Scott R. Anderson & Kathleen Claussen, *The Legal Authority Behind Trump's New Tariffs on Mexico*, Lawfare (June 3, 2019).

IEEPA is the most-frequently invoked fount of emergency power, but by one recent count, a total of 123 statutes delegate authorities to the President that are triggered by a presidential declaration of a national emergency. *See* Brennan Center for Justice, *A Guide to Emergency Powers and Their Use* (2019). The National Emergencies Act of 1976 (NEA), 50 U.S.C. §§1601-1651, establishes formal procedures for the exercise of these presidential emergency authorities, including a requirement of a public declaration for every emergency, subsequent reporting duties to Congress, and an automatic termination of the emergency unless the President publishes a notice of renewal in the Federal Register. (Note that the NEA originally allowed congressional termination of an emergency by concurrent resolution, but that provision is now unconstitutional under *Chadha*.)

As of August 2019, 33 declared national emergencies were in effect under the NEA, most of which were based on IEEPA. For example, the emergency declared by President Carter in 1979 that was at issue in *Dames & Moore* is still in effect. Presidents George W. Bush and Barack Obama each declared a dozen national emergencies, and, for both presidents, ten of their declarations remain in effect today. As of August 2019, President Trump had declared five new national emergencies, including one related to sanctions in the event of foreign interference in a U.S. election, Exec. Order No. 13,848, 83 Fed. Reg. 46843 (Sept. 12, 2018), one designed to allocate funding for a border wall with Mexico, Presidential Proclamation 9,844, 84 Fed. Reg. 4949-4950 (Feb. 15, 2019) ("Southern Border Proclamation"), and one related to securing the information and communications technology supply chain, Exec. Order No. 13,873, 84 Fed. Reg. 22689 (May 15, 2019).

The term "emergency" connotes a serious or dangerous situation that requires immediate action. However, the relevant statutes leave the determination of an emergency to the President, who has tended to construe these authorities broadly. For example, President Obama in 2015 declared an emergency relating to violence and political unrest in Burundi, Executive Order 13712 (Nov. 22, 2015); President George W. Bush declared an emergency in 2003 related to the sale of Iraqi oil, Executive Order 13303 (May 22, 2003); and President Clinton in 1996 declared an emergency to address a Cuban military shootdown that year, Presidential Proclamation 6867 (Mar. 1, 1996). One can debate whether these were emergencies in the ordinary-language sense at the time they were declared, but none of them seems like an emergency today, even though presidents in the intervening years have renewed all of them, and all remain in effect. As these examples suggest, a president has extraordinary discretion to proclaim emergencies and (under the NEA, in one-year intervals) to extend them indefinitely. And courts have typically upheld Congress's very broad delegations of emergency power. *See, e.g.,* United States v. Ali Amirnazmi, 645 F.3d 564 (3rd Cir. 2011); United States v. Arch Trading Co., 987 F.2d 1087 (4th Cir. 1993).

7. The most controversial emergency declaration in recent years was President Trump's 2019 Southern Border Proclamation. *See* Presidential Proclamation 9,844, *supra.* President Trump stated in December 2018 that he would not support any government budget that did not include at least $5.7 billion to build a wall on the southern U.S. border. A partial government shutdown ensued, and eventually, on February 14, 2019, Congress passed a government funding package that included only $1.375 billion for physical barriers at the southern border. The following day, President Trump issued the Southern Border Proclamation to trigger additional congressional funding for a border wall. The proclamation stated that the "current situation at the southern border presents a border security and humanitarian crisis that threatens core national security interests and constitutes a national emergency." In support of this claim, the President stated that the southern border was a "major entry point for criminals, gang members, and illicit narcotics," and for "large-scale unlawful migration" that "has worsened in certain respects in recent years." The proclamation also noted that the Department of Defense had previously "provided support and resources to the Department of Homeland Security at the southern border," and that because of the "gravity of the current emergency situation, it is necessary for the Armed Forces to provide additional support to address the crisis." Based on these predicates, the President "declare[d] that a national emergency exists at the southern border of the United States." He further declared that this emergency "requires use of the Armed Forces." He then claimed that he could access $3.6 billion in funds for border wall construction under 10 U.S.C. §2808, which, in the event of an emergency that "requires the use of the armed forces," allows the Secretary of Defense to undertake "military construction projects" to "support such use of the armed forces." (As we discuss below, President Trump also claimed authority to access funds based on predicates unrelated to the emergency declaration.)

Many commentators questioned the accuracy or sufficiency of the factual predicates for President Trump's emergency declaration, as well as his interpretation and invocation of 10 U.S.C. §2808 to access funds for the border wall. Eleven days after the Proclamation, on February 16, 2019, the House of Representatives passed a Joint Resolution that, pursuant to the NEA, would have "terminated" the national emergency declared by President Trump. The Republican-controlled Senate later approved the Joint Resolution by a narrow majority. President Trump vetoed the Joint Resolution, however, thus leaving the emergency declaration in place. Several lawsuits against the Southern Border Proclamation soon followed.

As of August 2019, none of these lawsuits had reached the merits of the emergency declaration, because the Defense Department had not yet announced a plan to redirect funds in connection with the emergency declaration and Section 2808. However, some of the lawsuits also challenged the Defense Department's efforts to rely on a different provision, Section 8005 of the Department of Defense Appropriations Act of 2019, to reprogram $2.5 billion from the Department of Defense to the Department of Homeland Security to construct a southern border barrier. Section 8005 authorizes the Secretary of Defense to transfer funds for military purposes, if the Secretary determines that the transfer is "for higher priority items, based on unforeseen military requirements" and "the item for which funds are requested has [not] been denied by the Congress." In the lawsuit that proceeded the furthest, the Sierra Club sued the Trump Administration to enjoin this repro-gramming. A federal district court preliminarily enjoined the Trump Administration from using redirected military funds for the border wall under Section 8005, and the Ninth Circuit denied an emergency stay. The Supreme Court, however, issued a stay of the injunction. The Court explained: "Among the reasons [for the stay] is that the Government has made a sufficient showing at this stage that the plaintiffs have no cause of action to obtain review of the Acting Secretary's compliance with Section 8005." Trump v. Sierra Club, 2019 U.S. LEXIS 4491 (Sup. Ct., July 26, 2019).

If the government also proceeds to seek border construction funds under the emergency declaration and Section 2808, how would a court assess whether there is an emergency? Could a court second-guess the President's emergency declaration, or is that issue a political question? In announcing his declaration of a national emergency, President Trump acknowledged that he "didn't need to do this," but wanted to "do it much faster." Does the admitted lack of necessity for the emer-gency declaration call into question its legality? Does it matter to the legality of President Trump's emergency declaration, or to the invocation of Section 2808, that the President claimed the power to secure through an emergency declaration what he was unable to get from Congress in budget negotiations?

A presidential declaration of emergency is largely, if not exclusively, a factual determination. It is but one example of the pervasive phenomenon of a President making factual findings as a predicate to exercising legal authorities. For a compre-hensive examination of presidential factfinding across a range of presidential pow-ers, including proposals for regulating presidential factfinding, see Shalev Roisman, *Presidential Factfinding*, 72 Vand. L. Rev. 825 (2019).

8. Although presidents initially used IEEPA to impose sanctions on foreign governments, they have increasingly invoked the statute to impose more targeted sanctions on individuals, groups, and non-state actors, including terrorists, pro-liferators, hackers, and narcotics traffickers. *See* Congressional Research Service, *The International Emergency Economic Powers Act: Origins, Evolution, and Use* (Mar. 20, 2019). For example, in late 2016, the Obama Administration declared an emer-gency under IEEPA to respond to "malicious cyber-enabled activities" and imposed sanctions against nine Russian entities and individuals found to be responsible for cyberattacks designed to interfere with the presidential election. In 2018, the Trump Administration imposed additional sanctions on Russian actors for the 2016 election interference and also designated for sanctions more than 100 Russian indi-viduals and entities related to Russia's annexation of Crimea and interference in Ukraine, human rights abuses, and international assassination attempts. *See* Press Release, U.S. Dep't of Treasury, *Treasury Sanctions Russian Cyber Actors for Interference with the 2016 U.S. Elections and Malicious Cyber-Attacks* (Mar. 15, 2018). For a discus-sion of the growing use of targeted sanctions, particularly by the United States, and some of the controversies surrounding their use, see *Symposium on Unilateral Targeted Sanctions* in Volume 113 of AJIL Unbound, at https://www.cambridge.org/core/journals/american-journal-of-international-law/ajil-unbound-by-symposium/unilateral-targeted-sanctions.

9. Emergency power is but one area where Congress has delegated a substantial amount of its foreign policy decisionmaking power to the President. Another exam-ple is the Export Administration Act, 50 U.S.C. app. §§2401-2420, which gives the President near-plenary authority over U.S. exports. Congress has also delegated sig-nificant amounts of its power to regulate foreign trade to the President. *See* Timothy Meyer & Ganesh Sitaraman, *Trade and the Separation of Powers*, 107 Cal. L. Rev. 583

(2019) (describing and criticizing this phenomenon). One example is Section 301 of the Trade Act of 1974, which gives the President the authority to impose tariffs on imports that the U.S. Trade Representative finds either to (a) violate or conflict with a trade agreement or (b) burden or restrict U.S. commerce unjustifiably. President Trump has used this authority to impose billions of dollars' worth of tariffs on imports from China. Another example is Section 232 of the Trade Expansion Act of 1962, which states that if the Secretary of Commerce "finds that an article is being imported into the United States in such quantities or under such circumstances as to threaten to impair the national security," the President is authorized to take "such other actions as the President deems necessary to adjust the imports of such article so that such imports will not threaten to impair the national security." President Trump has used this authority to impose tariffs on steel and aluminum and has threatened to use it to impose tariffs on other imports.

Why has Congress delegated so much of its foreign affairs power to the President? Consider this statement from Zemel v. Rusk, 381 U.S. 1, 17 (1965): "[B]ecause of the changeable and explosive nature of contemporary international relations, and the fact that the Executive is immediately privy to information which cannot be swiftly presented to, evaluated by, and acted upon by the legislature, Congress—in giving the Executive authority over matters of foreign affairs—must of necessity paint with a brush broader than that it customarily wields in domestic areas." What effect does *Chadha* have on such broad-brush delegations?

10. As Justice Jackson emphasizes in his *Youngstown* concurrence, the President possesses significant independent foreign relations authority under Article II in addition to the authority Congress delegates to him. The President's independent authority affects judicial construction of statutory foreign affairs delegations in at least two related ways.

First, courts worry less about the constitutionality of delegations in this context since the Constitution itself assigns the President a role. A strong version of this view is found in *Curtiss-Wright*. A somewhat more modest example can be found in Loving v. United States, 517 U.S. 748 (1996). In that case, an army private found guilty of murder by a general court martial challenged his conviction on the ground that the aggravating factors that informed his sentence were promulgated by executive order without any "intelligible principle to guide the President's discretion" from Congress, in violation of the nondelegation doctrine. The Supreme Court rejected this argument:

> We think . . . that the question to be asked is not whether there was any explicit principle telling the President how to select aggravating factors, but whether any such guidance was needed, given the nature of the delegation and the officer who is to exercise the delegated authority. . . . [T]he delegation here was to the President in his role as Commander in Chief. Perhaps more explicit guidance as to how to select aggravating factors would be necessary if delegation were made to a newly created entity without independent authority in the area. The President's duties as Commander in Chief, however, require him to take responsible and continuing action to superintend the military, including the courts martial. The delegated duty, then, is interlinked with duties already assigned to the President by express terms of the Constitution, and the same limitations on delegation do not apply "where the entity exercising the delegated authority itself possesses independent authority over the subject matter," United States v. Mazurie, 419 U.S. 544, 556-57 (1975).

Id. at 772-73.

Second, as this passage from *Loving* suggests, courts tend to construe delegations to the President broadly in areas in which he or she possesses independent authority. See, for example, Regan v. Wald, 468 U.S. 222 (1984) (finding statutory authority for restrictions on travel to Cuba), and Haig v. Agee, 453 U.S. 280 (1981) (finding statutory authority for revocation of passport). *Cf. Dames & Moore*, 453 U.S. at 678 (noting that "the enactment of legislation closely related to the question of the President's authority in a particular case which evinces legislative intent to accord the President broad discretion may be considered to 'invite' 'measures on independent presidential responsibility'"). In light of Congress's extensive delegations in this context and courts' generous interpretations of such delegations, will the President almost always be able to claim congressional authorization in the area of foreign affairs? If so, how does this affect the framework established by the majority and concurring opinions in *Youngstown?*

11. The Court in *Dames & Moore* relied heavily on the historical practice of Executive Branch claims settlement in support of its conclusion that Congress authorized the President to suspend claims. Especially in the foreign affairs field, historical practice plays a critical role in informing the allocation of power between the President and Congress. *See, e.g.,* American Insurance Ass'n v. Garamendi, 539 U.S. 396, 415 (2003) ("Given the fact that the practice goes back over 200 years to the first Presidential administration, and has received congressional acquiescence throughout its history, the conclusion that the President's control of foreign relations includes the settlement of claims is indisputable.") (internal quotations and citations omitted); Youngstown Sheet & Tube Co. v. Sawyer, 343 U.S. 579, 610-11 (1952) (Frankfurter, J., concurring) ("[A] systematic, unbroken executive practice, long pursued to the knowledge of Congress and never before questioned, . . . making as it were such exercise of power part of the structure of our government, may be treated as a gloss on 'executive Power' vested in the President by §1 of Art. II."). Why is this so? Because constitutional text and structure in the foreign relations context are unclear? Because the President has significant concurrent constitutional authority in the foreign affairs field? Because original understanding matters less, and practical considerations more, in this context? Some other reason? Why didn't the Court in *Chadha* defer to historical practice in support of the legislative veto? For discussion of these issues, see Curtis A. Bradley & Trevor W. Morrison, *Historical Gloss and the Separation of Powers*, 126 Harv. L. Rev. 421 (2012); Michael J. Glennon, *The Use of Custom in Resolving Separation of Powers Disputes*, 64 B.U. L. Rev. 109 (1984); Peter J. Spiro, *Treaties, Executive Agreements, and Constitutional Method*, 79 Tex. L. Rev. 961 (2001).

Historical practice also is relevant in the interpretation of statutes that authorize Executive Branch action. Congress is generally presumed to be aware of relevant Executive Branch practice when it legislates, and especially when this practice is longstanding, courts will often conclude that Congress has approved the practice when it enacts a related statute. A good example is United States v. Midwest Oil Co., 236 U.S. 459 (1915), a case relied on in *Dames & Moore*. There, the President suspended a statutory land grant program in a way that did not appear to be authorized by the statute. The Supreme Court nevertheless upheld the suspension, reasoning that the President had for many years prior to the enactment of the statute exercised the power to suspend similar land grant programs. The Court explained that, "in determining the meaning of a statute or the existence of a power, weight shall be given to the usage itself—even when the validity of the practice is the subject of investigation," and added that the past Executive Branch practice created a "presumption that unauthorized acts would not have been allowed to be so often repeated as to crystallize into a regular practice." *Id.* at 473.

Is it proper for courts to construe statutes to conform to past Executive Branch practice? As one commentator has noted, although courts do not always infer congressional intent to ratify prior Executive Branch practice in this way, the inference is normally "stronger in the foreign affairs arena" than in other contexts. William N. Eskridge, Jr., *Interpreting Legislative Inaction*, 87 Mich. L. Rev. 67, 74 (1988). Why might Executive Branch practice be more important in the interpretation of foreign relations statutes? One reason might be that Congress faces "practical limitations on [its] capacity to forge *ex ante* standards for executive national security action." Peter Raven-Hansen & William C. Banks, *Pulling the Purse Strings of the Commander in Chief*, 80 Va. L. Rev. 833, 848 (1994). Another might be that the Executive Branch has special fact-gathering and interpretive expertise in this context. *See, e.g.*, Chicago & S. Air Lines, Inc. v. Waterman S.S. Corp., 333 U.S. 103, 111 (1948). Still another reason might be one that matters in the constitutional context, namely, that the President has significant concurrent constitutional authority in the foreign affairs field. Does it make sense to extend this constitutional reasoning to the interpretation of foreign affairs statutes? Is this what the Supreme Court meant in *Dames & Moore* when it stated that "the enactment of legislation closely related to the question of the President's authority in a particular case which evinces legislative intent to accord the President broad discretion may be considered to 'invite' 'measures on independent presidential responsibility'"?

2. Conflicts Between Congress and the President

Zivotofsky v. Kerry (*Zivotofsky II*)

135 S. Ct. 2076 (2015)

[Although Israel has controlled the western portion of Jerusalem since Israel's founding in 1948 and has controlled the eastern portion since 1967, there is a long-standing dispute between Israel and the Palestinians concerning legal sovereignty over the city. In an effort to remain neutral in this dispute, the U.S. Executive Branch has refused to recognize any country's sovereignty over the city, insisting that the issue be resolved through negotiation. As part of this policy, when a U.S. citizen is born in Jerusalem, the State Department lists only "Jerusalem" as the place of birth when issuing passports and consular reports of births abroad. In 2002, however, Congress enacted the Foreign Relations Authorization Act for Fiscal Year 2003, §214 of which was titled "United States Policy with Respect to Jerusalem as the Capital of Israel." Subsection d provided that, "[f]or purposes of the registration of birth, certification of nationality, or issuance of a passport of a United States citizen born in the city of Jerusalem, the Secretary shall, upon the request of the citizen or the citizen's legal guardian, record the place of birth as Israel." President George W. Bush signed the Act into law, but when doing so, he issued a statement expressing the view that §214(d) would, "if construed as mandatory rather than advisory, impermissibly interfere with the President's constitutional authority to formulate the position of the United States, speak for the Nation in international affairs, and determine the terms on which recognition is given to foreign states." Neither his administration nor the subsequent Obama Administration complied with §214(d). Through his parents, Menachem Zivotofsky, who was born in Jerusalem a few weeks after §214(d)'s enactment, challenged the State Department's refusal to record "Israel" as the place of birth in his passport and in the consular report of his birth. The U.S.

court vision

Court of Appeals for the D.C. Circuit ordered the suit dismissed on the ground that the constitutionality of §214(d) presented a nonjusticiable political question. The Supreme Court reversed and remanded in Zivotofsky v. Clinton, 132 S. Ct. 1421 (2012), a decision excerpted in Chapter 2 of this casebook. On remand, the D.C. Circuit held that §214(d) was unconstitutional because it invaded the exclusive authority of the President to recognize foreign sovereigns.]

JUSTICE KENNEDY delivered the opinion of the Court. . . .

Pursuant to §214(d), Zivotofsky claims the right to have "Israel" recorded as his place of birth in his passport. The arguments in Zivotofsky's brief center on his passport claim, as opposed to the consular report of birth abroad. . . . .

II

Jackson concurrence (Youngstown)

In considering claims of Presidential power this Court refers to Justice Jackson's familiar tripartite framework from Youngstown Sheet & Tube Co. v. Sawyer, 343 U.S. 579, 635-38 (1952) (concurring opinion). . . .

In this case the Secretary contends that §214(d) infringes on the President's exclusive recognition power by "requiring the President to contradict his recognition position regarding Jerusalem in official communications with foreign sovereigns." Brief for Respondent 48. In so doing the Secretary acknowledges the President's power is "at its lowest ebb." Youngstown, 343 U.S. at 637. Because the President's refusal to implement §214(d) falls into Justice Jackson's third category, his claim must be "scrutinized with caution," and he may rely solely on powers the Constitution grants to him alone. Id. at 638.

To determine whether the President possesses the exclusive power of recognition the Court examines the Constitution's text and structure, as well as precedent and history bearing on the question.

A

Recognition is a "formal acknowledgement" that a particular "entity possesses the qualifications for statehood" or "that a particular regime is the effective government of a state." Restatement (Third) of Foreign Relations Law of the United States §203, Comment a, p. 84 (1986). It may also involve the determination of a state's territorial bounds. See 2 M. Whiteman, Digest of International Law §1, p. 1 (1963) (Whiteman) ("[S]tates may recognize or decline to recognize territory as belonging to, or under the sovereignty of, or having been acquired or lost by, other states"). Recognition is often effected by an express "written or oral declaration." 1 John Bassett Moore, Digest of International Law §27, p. 73 (1906) (Moore). It may also be implied — for example, by concluding a bilateral treaty or by sending or receiving diplomatic agents. Id.; Ian Brownlie, Principles of Public International Law 93 (7th ed. 2008) (Brownlie).

Legal consequences follow formal recognition. Recognized sovereigns may sue in United States courts, see Guaranty Trust Co. v. United States, 304 U.S. 126, 137 (1938), and may benefit from sovereign immunity when they are sued, see National City Bank of N.Y. v. Republic of China, 348 U.S. 356, 358-59 (1955). The actions of a recognized sovereign committed within its own territory also receive deference in domestic courts under the act of state doctrine. See Oetjen v. Central Leather Co., 246 U.S. 297, 302-03 (1918). Recognition at international law, furthermore, is a precondition of regular diplomatic relations. 1 Moore §27, at 72. Recognition is thus "useful, even necessary," to the existence of a state. Id.

Despite the importance of the recognition power in foreign relations, the Constitution does not use the term "recognition," either in Article II or elsewhere. The Secretary asserts that the President exercises the recognition power based on the Reception Clause, which directs that the President "shall receive Ambassadors and other public Ministers." Art. II, §3. As Zivotofsky notes, the Reception Clause received little attention at the Constitutional Convention. In fact, during the ratification debates, Alexander Hamilton claimed that the power to receive ambassadors was "more a matter of dignity than of authority," a ministerial duty largely "without consequence." The Federalist No. 69, p. 420 (Clinton Rossiter ed., 1961).

[At the time of the founding, however, prominent international scholars suggested that receiving an ambassador was tantamount to recognizing the sovereignty of the sending state.] . . It is a logical and proper inference, then, that a Clause directing the President alone to receive ambassadors would be understood to acknowledge his power to recognize other nations.

This in fact occurred early in the Nation's history when President Washington recognized the French Revolutionary Government by receiving its ambassador. . . . As a result, the Reception Clause provides support, although not the sole authority, for the President's power to recognize other nations.

The inference that the President exercises the recognition power is further supported by his additional Article II powers. It is for the President, "by and with the Advice and Consent of the Senate," to "make Treaties, provided two thirds of the Senators present concur." Art. II, §2, cl. 2. In addition, "he shall nominate, and by and with the Advice and Consent of the Senate, shall appoint Ambassadors" as well as "other public Ministers and Consuls." *Id.*

As a matter of constitutional structure, these additional powers give the President control over recognition decisions. At international law, recognition may be effected by different means, but each means is dependent upon Presidential power. In addition to receiving an ambassador, recognition may occur on "the conclusion of a bilateral treaty," or the "formal initiation of diplomatic relations," including the dispatch of an ambassador. Brownlie 93; *see also* 1 Moore §27, at 73. The President has the sole power to negotiate treaties, see United States v. Curtiss-Wright Export Corp., 299 U.S. 304, 319 (1936), and the Senate may not conclude or ratify a treaty without Presidential action. The President, too, nominates the Nation's ambassadors and dispatches other diplomatic agents. Congress may not send an ambassador without his involvement. Beyond that, the President himself has the power to open diplomatic channels simply by engaging in direct diplomacy with foreign heads of state and their ministers. The Constitution thus assigns the President means to effect recognition on his own initiative. Congress, by contrast, has no constitutional power that would enable it to initiate diplomatic relations with a foreign nation. Because these specific Clauses confer the recognition power on the President, the Court need not consider whether or to what extent the Vesting Clause, which provides that the "executive Power" shall be vested in the President, provides further support for the President's action here. Art. II, §1, cl. 1.

The text and structure of the Constitution grant the President the power to recognize foreign nations and governments. The question then becomes whether that power is exclusive. The various ways in which the President may unilaterally effect recognition—and the lack of any similar power vested in Congress—suggest that it is. So, too, do functional considerations. Put simply, the Nation must have a single policy regarding which governments are legitimate in the eyes of the United States and which are not. Foreign countries need to know, before entering into diplomatic relations or commerce with the United States, whether their ambassadors will be received; whether their officials will be immune from suit in federal court; and whether they may initiate lawsuits here to vindicate their rights. These assurances cannot be equivocal.

Recognition is a topic on which the Nation must "'speak . . . with one voice.'" Am. Ins. Ass'n v. Garamendi, 539 U.S. 396, 424 (2003) (quoting Crosby v. National Foreign Trade Council, 530 U.S. 363, 381 (2000)). That voice must be the President's. Between the two political branches, only the Executive has the characteristic of unity at all times. And with unity comes the ability to exercise, to a greater degree, "[d]ecision, activity, secrecy, and dispatch." The Federalist No. 70, p. 424 (A. Hamilton). The President is capable, in ways Congress is not, of engaging in the delicate and often secret diplomatic contacts that may lead to a decision on recognition. *See, e.g.,* United States v. Pink, 315 U.S. 203, 229 (1942). He is also better positioned to take the decisive, unequivocal action necessary to recognize other states at international law. 1 Oppenheim's International Law §50, p. 169 (R. Jennings & A. Watts eds., 9th ed. 1992) (act of recognition must "leave no doubt as to the intention to grant it"). These qualities explain why the Framers listed the traditional avenues of recognition—receiving ambassadors, making treaties, and sending ambassadors—as among the President's Article II powers.

As described in more detail below, the President since the founding has exercised this unilateral power to recognize new states—and the Court has endorsed the practice. Texts and treatises on international law treat the President's word as the final word on recognition. . . . In light of this authority all six judges who considered this case in the Court of Appeals agreed that the President holds the exclusive recognition power.

It remains true, of course, that many decisions affecting foreign relations—including decisions that may determine the course of our relations with recognized countries—require congressional action. Congress may "regulate Commerce with foreign Nations," "establish an uniform Rule of Naturalization," "define and punish Piracies and Felonies committed on the high Seas, and Offences against the Law of Nations," "declare War," "grant Letters of Marque and Reprisal," and "make Rules for the Government and Regulation of the land and naval Forces." U.S. Const., Art. I, §8. In addition, the President cannot make a treaty or appoint an ambassador without the approval of the Senate. Art. II, §2, cl. 2. The President, furthermore, could not build an American Embassy abroad without congressional appropriation of the necessary funds. Art. I, §8, cl. 1. Under basic separation-of-powers principles, it is for the Congress to enact the laws, including "all Laws which shall be necessary and proper for carrying into Execution" the powers of the Federal Government. §8, cl. 18.

In foreign affairs, as in the domestic realm, the Constitution "enjoins upon its branches separateness but interdependence, autonomy but reciprocity." *Youngstown*, 343 U.S. at 635 (Jackson, J., concurring). Although the President alone effects the formal act of recognition, Congress' powers, and its central role in making laws, give it substantial authority regarding many of the policy determinations that precede and follow the act of recognition itself. If Congress disagrees with the President's recognition policy, there may be consequences. Formal recognition may seem a hollow act if it is not accompanied by the dispatch of an ambassador, the easing of trade restrictions, and the conclusion of treaties. And those decisions require action by the Senate or the whole Congress.

In practice, then, the President's recognition determination is just one part of a political process that may require Congress to make laws. The President's exclusive recognition power encompasses the authority to acknowledge, in a formal sense, the legitimacy of other states and governments, including their territorial bounds. Albeit limited, the exclusive recognition power is essential to the conduct of Presidential duties. The formal act of recognition is an executive power that Congress may not qualify. If the President is to be effective in negotiations over a formal recognition determination, it must be evident to his counterparts abroad that he speaks for the Nation on that precise question.

A clear rule that the formal power to recognize a foreign government subsists in the President therefore serves a necessary purpose in diplomatic relations. All this, of course, underscores that Congress has an important role in other aspects of foreign policy, and the President may be bound by any number of laws Congress enacts. In this way, ambition counters ambition, ensuring that the democratic will of the people is observed and respected in foreign affairs as in the domestic realm. *See* The Federalist No. 51, p. 322 (J. Madison).

B

No single precedent resolves the question whether the President has exclusive recognition authority and, if so, how far that power extends. In part that is because, until today, the political branches have resolved their disputes over questions of recognition. The relevant cases, though providing important instruction, address the division of recognition power between the Federal Government and the States, see, e.g., *Pink*, 315 U.S. 203, or between the courts and the political branches, see, e.g., *Banco Nacional de Cuba*, 376 U.S. at 412, not between the President and Congress. As the parties acknowledge, some isolated statements in those cases lend support to the position that Congress has a role in the recognition process. In the end, however, a fair reading of the cases shows that the President's role in the recognition process is both central and exclusive. . . .

[D]uring the 1930's and 1940's, the Court addressed issues surrounding President Roosevelt's decision to recognize the Soviet Government of Russia. In *United States* v. *Belmont*, 301 U.S. 324 (1937), and *Pink*, 315 U.S. 203, New York state courts declined to give full effect to the terms of executive agreements the President had concluded in negotiations over recognition of the Soviet regime. In particular the state courts, based on New York public policy, did not treat assets that had been seized by the Soviet Government as property of Russia and declined to turn those assets over to the United States. The Court stated that it "may not be doubted" that "recognition, establishment of diplomatic relations, . . . and agreements with respect thereto" are "within the competence of the President." *Belmont*, 301 U.S. at 330. In these matters, "the Executive ha[s] authority to speak as the sole organ of th[e] government." *Id.* The Court added that the President's authority "is not limited to a determination of the government to be recognized. It includes the power to determine the policy which is to govern the question of recognition." *Pink*, *supra* at 229. . . . Thus, New York state courts were required to respect the executive agreements.

It is true, of course, that *Belmont* and *Pink* are not direct holdings that the recognition power is exclusive. Those cases considered the validity of executive agreements, not the initial act of recognition. The President's determination in those cases did not contradict an Act of Congress. And the primary issue was whether the executive agreements could supersede state law. Still, the language in *Pink* and

Belmont, which confirms the President's competence to determine questions of recognition, is strong support for the conclusion that it is for the President alone to determine which foreign governments are legitimate.

Banco Nacional de Cuba contains even stronger statements regarding the President's authority over recognition. There, the status of Cuba's Government and its acts as a sovereign were at issue. As the Court explained, "Political recognition is exclusively a function of the Executive." 376 U.S. at 410. Because the Executive had recognized the Cuban Government, the Court held that it should be treated as sovereign and could benefit from the "act of state" doctrine. . . . As these cases illustrate, the Court has long considered recognition to be the exclusive prerogative of the Executive.

The Secretary now urges the Court to define the executive power over foreign relations in even broader terms. He contends that under the Court's precedent the President has "exclusive authority to conduct diplomatic relations," along with "the bulk of foreign-affairs powers." Brief for Respondent 18, 16. In support of his submission that the President has broad, undefined powers over foreign affairs, the Secretary quotes *United States v. Curtiss-Wright Export Corp.*, which described the President as "the sole organ of the federal government in the field of international relations." 299 U.S. at 320. This Court declines to acknowledge that unbounded power. A formulation broader than the rule that the President alone determines what nations to formally recognize as legitimate—and that he consequently controls his statements on matters of recognition—presents different issues and is unnecessary to the resolution of this case. . . .

Th[e] description of the President's exclusive power [in *Curtiss-Wright*] was not necessary to the holding . . .—which, after all, dealt with congressionally authorized action, not a unilateral Presidential determination. Indeed, *Curtiss-Wright* did not hold that the President is free from Congress' lawmaking power in the field of international relations. The President does have a unique role in communicating with foreign governments, as then-Congressman John Marshall acknowledged. But whether the realm is foreign or domestic, it is still the Legislative Branch, not the Executive Branch, that makes the law.

In a world that is ever more compressed and interdependent, it is essential the congressional role in foreign affairs be understood and respected. For it is Congress that makes laws, and in countless ways its laws will and should shape the Nation's course. The Executive is not free from the ordinary controls and checks of Congress merely because foreign affairs are at issue. . . . It is not for the President alone to determine the whole content of the Nation's foreign policy.

That said, judicial precedent and historical practice teach that it is for the President alone to make the specific decision of what foreign power he will recognize as legitimate, both for the Nation as a whole and for the purpose of making his own position clear within the context of recognition in discussions and negotiations with foreign nations. Recognition is an act with immediate and powerful significance for international relations, so the President's position must be clear. Congress cannot require him to contradict his own statement regarding a determination of formal recognition. . . .

C

Having examined the Constitution's text and this Court's precedent, it is appropriate to turn to accepted understandings and practice. In separation-of-powers cases this Court has often "put significant weight upon historical practice." NLRB v. Noel Canning, 134 S. Ct. 2550, 2559 (2014) (emphasis deleted). Here, history is not all on one side, but on balance it provides strong support for the conclusion that the recognition power is the President's alone. As Zivotofsky argues, certain historical incidents can be interpreted to support the position that recognition is a shared power. But the weight of historical evidence supports the opposite view, which is that the formal determination of recognition is a power to be exercised only by the President. . . .

[E]ven a brief survey of the major historical examples, with an emphasis on those said to favor Zivotofsky, establishes no more than that some Presidents have chosen to cooperate with Congress, not that Congress itself has exercised the recognition power.

From the first Administration forward, the President has claimed unilateral authority to recognize foreign sovereigns. For the most part, Congress has acquiesced in the Executive's exercise of the recognition power. On occasion, the President has chosen, as may often be prudent, to consult and coordinate with Congress. . . .

The first debate over the recognition power arose in 1793, after France had been torn by revolution. [The Court describes how President Washington received Ambassador Genet from revolutionary France without consulting Congress.] Congress expressed no disagreement with this position, and Genet's reception marked the Nation's first act of recognition—one made by the President alone.

The recognition power again became relevant when yet another revolution took place—this time, in South America, as several colonies rose against Spain. In 1818, Speaker of the House Henry Clay announced he "intended moving the recognition of Buenos Ayres and probably of Chile." Julius Goebel, The Recognition Policy of the United States 121 (1915) (Goebel). Clay thus sought to appropriate money "'[f]or one year's salary'" for "'a Minister'" to present-day Argentina. 32 Annals of Cong. 1500 (1818). President Monroe, however, did not share that view. Although Clay gave "one of the most remarkable speeches of his career," his proposed bill was defeated. Goebel 123; 32 Annals of Cong. 1655. That action has been attributed, in part, to the fact that Congress agreed the recognition power rested solely with the President. Goebel 124. Four years later, after the President had decided to recognize the South American republics, Congress did pass a resolution, on his request, appropriating funds for "such missions to the independent nations on the American continent, as the President of the United States may deem proper." Act of May 4, 1822, ch. 52, 3 Stat. 678.

A decade later, President Jackson faced a recognition crisis over Texas. In 1835, Texas rebelled against Mexico and formed its own government. See Goebel 144-47. But the President feared that recognizing the new government could ignite a war. After Congress urged him to recognize Texas, the President delivered a message to the Legislature. He concluded there had not been a "deliberate inquiry" into whether the President or Congress possessed the recognition power. He stated, however, "on the ground of expediency, I am disposed to concur" with Congress' preference regarding Texas. In response Congress appropriated funds for a "diplomatic agent to be sent to the Republic of Texas, whenever the President of the United States . . . shall deem it expedient to appoint such minister." Act of Mar. 3, 1837, 5 Stat. 170. Thus, although he cooperated with Congress, the President was left to execute the formal act of recognition.

President Lincoln, too, sought to coordinate with Congress when he requested support for his recognition of Liberia and Haiti. In his first annual message to

Congress, he said he could see no reason "why we should persevere longer in withholding our recognition of the independence and sovereignty of Hayti and Liberia." Lincoln's First Annual Message to Congress (Dec. 3, 1861), in 6 Messages and Papers of the Presidents 44, 47. Nonetheless, he was "[u]nwilling" to "inaugurate a novel policy in regard to them without the approbation of Congress." *Id.* In response Congress concurred in the President's recognition determination and enacted a law appropriating funds to appoint diplomatic representatives to the two countries — leaving, as usual, the actual dispatch of ambassadors and formal statement of recognition to the President. Act of June 5, 1862, 12 Stat. 421.

Three decades later, the branches again were able to reach an accord, this time with regard to Cuba. In 1898, an insurgency against the Spanish colonial government was raging in Cuba. President McKinley determined to ask Congress for authorization to send armed forces to Cuba to help quell the violence. Although McKinley thought Spain was to blame for the strife, he opposed recognizing either Cuba or its insurgent government. At first, the House proposed a resolution consistent with McKinley's wishes. The Senate countered with a resolution that authorized the use of force but that did recognize both Cuban independence and the insurgent government. When the Senate's version reached the House, the House again rejected the language recognizing Cuban independence. The resolution went to Conference, which, after debate, reached a compromise. The final resolution stated "the people of the Island of Cuba are, and of right ought to be, free and independent," but made no mention of recognizing a new Cuban Government. Act of Apr. 20, 1898, 30 Stat. 738. Accepting the compromise, the President signed the joint resolution.

For the next 80 years, "[p]residents consistently recognized new states and governments without any serious opposition from, or activity in, Congress." *Id.*; *see* 2 Whiteman §§6-60, at 133-242 (detailing over 50 recognition decisions made by the Executive). The next debate over recognition did not occur until the late 1970's. It concerned China.

President Carter recognized the People's Republic of China (PRC) as the government of China, and derecognized the Republic of China, located on Taiwan. As to the status of Taiwan, the President "acknowledge[d] the Chinese position" that "Taiwan is part of China," but he did not accept that claim. The President proposed a new law defining how the United States would conduct business with Taiwan. After extensive revisions, Congress passed, and the President signed, the Taiwan Relations Act, 93 Stat. 14 (1979). The Act (in a simplified summary) treated Taiwan as if it were a legally distinct entity from China — an entity with which the United States intended to maintain strong ties.

Throughout the legislative process, however, no one raised a serious question regarding the President's exclusive authority to recognize the PRC — or to decline to grant formal recognition to Taiwan. Rather, Congress accepted the President's recognition determination as a completed, lawful act; and it proceeded to outline the trade and policy provisions that, in its judgment, were appropriate in light of that decision.

This history confirms the Court's conclusion in the instant case that the power to recognize or decline to recognize a foreign state and its territorial bounds resides in the President alone. For the most part, Congress has respected the Executive's policies and positions as to formal recognition. At times, Congress itself has defended the President's constitutional prerogative. Over the last 100 years, there has been scarcely any debate over the President's power to recognize foreign states. In this respect the

Legislature, in the narrow context of recognition, on balance has acknowledged the importance of speaking "with one voice." *Crosby*, 530 U.S. at 381. The weight of historical evidence indicates Congress has accepted that the power to recognize foreign states and governments and their territorial bounds is exclusive to the Presidency.

III

As the power to recognize foreign states resides in the President alone, the question becomes whether §214(d) infringes on the Executive's consistent decision to withhold recognition with respect to Jerusalem. . . .

Section 214(d) requires that, in a passport or consular report of birth abroad, "the Secretary shall, upon the request of the citizen or the citizen's legal guardian, record the place of birth as Israel" for a "United States citizen born in the city of Jerusalem." That is, §214(d) requires the President, through the Secretary, to identify citizens born in Jerusalem who so request as being born in Israel. But according to the President, those citizens were not born in Israel. As a matter of United States policy, neither Israel nor any other country is acknowledged as having sovereignty over Jerusalem. In this way, §214(d) "directly contradicts" the "carefully calibrated and longstanding Executive branch policy of neutrality toward Jerusalem." *Zivotofsky v. Secretary of State*, 725 F.3d 197, 216, 217 (D.C. Cir. 2013).

If the power over recognition is to mean anything, it must mean that the President not only makes the initial, formal recognition determination but also that he may maintain that determination in his and his agent's statements. This conclusion is a matter of both common sense and necessity. If Congress could command the President to state a recognition position inconsistent with his own, Congress could override the President's recognition determination. Under international law, recognition may be effected by "written or oral declaration of the recognizing state." 1 Moore §27, at 73. In addition an act of recognition must "leave no doubt as to the intention to grant it." 1 Oppenheim's International Law §50, at 169. Thus, if Congress could alter the President's statements on matters of recognition or force him to contradict them, Congress in effect would exercise the recognition power.

As Justice Jackson wrote in *Youngstown*, when a Presidential power is "exclusive," it "disabl[es] the Congress from acting upon the subject." 343 U.S. at 637-38. Here, the subject is quite narrow: The Executive's exclusive power extends no further than his formal recognition determination. But as to that determination, Congress may not enact a law that directly contradicts it. This is not to say Congress may not express its disagreement with the President in myriad ways. For example, it may enact an embargo, decline to confirm an ambassador, or even declare war. But none of these acts would alter the President's recognition decision.

If Congress may not pass a law, speaking in its own voice, that effects formal recognition, then it follows that it may not force the President himself to contradict his earlier statement. That congressional command would not only prevent the Nation from speaking with one voice but also prevent the Executive itself from doing so in conducting foreign relations.

Although the statement required by §214(d) would not itself constitute a formal act of recognition, it is a mandate that the Executive contradict his prior recognition determination in an official document issued by the Secretary of State. As a result, it is unconstitutional. This is all the more clear in light of the longstanding treatment of a passport's place-of-birth section as an official executive statement implicating recognition. The Secretary's position on this point has been consistent: He will not place information in the place-of-birth section of a passport that contradicts the

President's recognition policy. If a citizen objects to the country listed as sovereign over his place of birth, then the Secretary will accommodate him by listing the city or town of birth rather than the country. But the Secretary will not list a sovereign that contradicts the President's recognition policy in a passport. Thus, the Secretary will not list "Israel" in a passport as the country containing Jerusalem.

The flaw in §214(d) is further underscored by the undoubted fact that that the purpose of the statute was to infringe on the recognition power—a power the Court now holds is the sole prerogative of the President. The statute is titled "United States Policy with Respect to Jerusalem as the Capital of Israel." The House Conference Report proclaimed that §214 "contains four provisions related to the recognition of Jerusalem as Israel's capital." H.R. Conf. Rep. No. 107-671, p. 123 (2002). And, indeed, observers interpreted §214 as altering United States policy regarding Jerusalem—which led to protests across the region. From the face of §214, from the legislative history, and from its reception, it is clear that Congress wanted to express its displeasure with the President's policy by, among other things, commanding the Executive to contradict his own, earlier stated position on Jerusalem. This Congress may not do.

International perception

It is true, as Zivotofsky notes, that Congress has substantial authority over passports. The Court does not question the power of Congress to enact passport legislation of wide scope. . . .

The problem with §214(d), however, lies in how Congress exercised its authority over passports. . . . To allow Congress to control the President's communication in the context of a formal recognition determination is to allow Congress to exercise that exclusive power itself. As a result, the statute is unconstitutional.

concurrence

JUSTICE BREYER, concurring:

I continue to believe that this case presents a political question inappropriate for judicial resolution. *See* Zivotofsky v. Clinton, 132 S. Ct. 1421 (2012) (Breyer, J., dissenting). But because precedent precludes resolving this case on political question grounds, I join the Court's opinion.

concur + dissent (Thomas)

JUSTICE THOMAS, concurring in the judgment in part and dissenting in part. . . .

[T]he Vesting Clause of Article II provides that "[t]he executive Power shall be vested in a President of the United States." Art. II, §1. This Clause is notably different from the Vesting Clause of Article I, which provides only that "[a]ll legislative Powers *herein granted* shall be vested in a Congress of the United States," Art. I, §1 (emphasis added). By omitting the words "herein granted" in Article II, the Constitution indicates that the "executive Power" vested in the President is not confined to those powers expressly identified in the document. Instead, it includes all powers originally understood as falling within the "executive Power" of the Federal Government. . . .

In the Anglo-American legal tradition, passports have consistently been issued and controlled by the body exercising executive power—in England, by the King; in the colonies, by the Continental Congress; and in the United States, by President Washington and every President since. . . .

That the President has the power to regulate passports under his residual foreign affairs powers does not, however, end the matter, for Congress has repeatedly legislated on the subject of passports. . . .

As with any congressional action, however, such legislation is constitutionally permissible only insofar as it is promulgated pursuant to one of Congress' enumerated powers. I must therefore address whether Congress had constitutional authority to enact §214(d)'s regulation of passports. . . .

The Constitution contains no Passport Clause, nor does it explicitly vest Congress with "plenary authority over passports." Because our Government is one of enumerated powers, "Congress has no power to act unless the Constitution authorizes it to do so." United States v. Comstock, 560 U.S. 126, 159 (2010) (Thomas, J., dissenting). And "[t]he Constitution plainly sets forth the 'few and defined' powers that Congress may exercise." Ibid. A "passport power" is not one of them.

Section 214(d)'s passport directive fares no better under those powers actually included in Article I. To start, it does not fall within the power "[t]o regulate Commerce with foreign Nations." "At the time the original Constitution was ratified, 'commerce' consisted of selling, buying, and bartering, as well as transporting for these purposes." United States v. Lopez, 514 U.S. 549, 585 (1995) (Thomas, J., concurring). The listing of the place of birth of an applicant—whether born in Jerusalem or not—does not involve selling, buying, bartering, or transporting for those purposes.

True, a passport is frequently used by persons who may intend to engage in commerce abroad, but that use is insufficient to bring §214(d)'s passport directive within the scope of this power. The specific conduct at issue here—the listing of the birthplace of a U.S. citizen born in Jerusalem on a passport by the President—is not a commercial activity. Any commercial activities subsequently undertaken by the bearer of a passport are yet further removed from that regulation.

The power "[t]o establish an uniform Rule of Naturalization" is similarly unavailing. At the founding, the word "naturalization" meant "[t]he act of investing aliens with the privileges of native subjects." 2 S. Johnson, A Dictionary of the English Language 1293 (4th ed. 1773). A passport has never been issued as part of the naturalization process. It is—and has always been—a "travel document," Dept. of State, 7 Foreign Affairs Manual (or FAM) §1311(b) (2013), issued for the same purpose it has always served: a request from one sovereign to another for the protection of the bearer.

For similar reasons, the Necessary and Proper Clause gives Congress no authority here. That Clause provides, "The Congress shall have Power . . . [t]o make all Laws which shall be necessary and proper for carrying into Execution the foregoing Powers, and all other Powers vested by this Constitution in the Government of the United States, or in any Department or Officer thereof." U.S. Const., Art. I, §8, cl. 18. As an initial matter, "Congress lacks authority to legislate [under this provision] if the objective is anything other than 'carrying into Execution' one or more of the Federal Government's enumerated powers." Comstock, supra, at 161 (Thomas, J., dissenting). . . .

But even if the objective of a law is carrying into execution one of the Federal Government's enumerated powers, the law must be both necessary and proper to that objective. The "Clause is not a warrant to Congress to enact any law that bears some conceivable connection to the exercise of an enumerated power." Gonzales v. Raich, 545 U.S. 1, 60 (2005) (Thomas, J., dissenting). Instead, "there must be a necessary and proper fit between the 'means' (the federal law) and the 'end' (the enumerated power or powers) it is designed to serve." Comstock, supra, at 160 (Thomas, J., dissenting). The "means" chosen by Congress "will be deemed 'necessary' if they are 'appropriate' and 'plainly adapted' to the exercise of an enumerated power, and 'proper' if they are not otherwise 'prohibited' by the Constitution and not '[in]consistent' with its 'letter and spirit.'" Id. at 160-61 (alteration in original).

The argument that §214(d), as applied to passports, could be an exercise of Congress' power to carry into execution its foreign commerce or naturalization powers falters because this aspect of §214(d) is directed at neither of the ends served by these powers. Although at a high level of generality, a passport could be related to foreign commerce and naturalization, that attenuated relationship is insufficient. The law in question must be "directly link[ed]" to the enumerated power. *Id.* at 169 n. 8. As applied to passports, §214(d) fails that test because it does not "'carr[y] into Execution'" Congress' foreign commerce or naturalization powers. *Id.* at 160. At most, it bears a tertiary relationship to an activity Congress is permitted to regulate: It directs the President's formulation of a document, which, in turn, may be used to facilitate travel, which, in turn, may facilitate foreign commerce. And the distinctive history of the passport as a travel rather than citizenship document makes its connection to naturalization even more tenuous.

Nor can this aspect of §214(d) be justified as an exercise of Congress' power to enact laws to carry into execution the President's residual foreign affairs powers. Simply put, §214(d)'s passport directive is not a "proper" means of carrying this power into execution.

. . . First, a law could be "improper" if it purports to direct another branch's exercise of its power. Second, a law could be "improper" if it takes one of those actions *and* the branch to which the power is allocated objects to the action. . . .

I need not resolve that question today, as the application of §214(d) to passports would be improper under either approach. The President has made a determination that the "place of birth" on a passport should list the country of present sovereignty. And the President has determined that no country is presently exercising sovereignty over the area of Jerusalem. Thus, the President has provided that passports for persons born in Jerusalem should list "Jerusalem" as the place of birth in the passport. Section 214(d) directs the President to exercise his power to issue and regulate the content of passports in a particular way, and the President has objected to that direction. Under either potential mechanism for evaluating the propriety of a law under the separation-of-powers limitation, this law would be improper. . . .

Because the President has residual foreign affairs authority to regulate passports and because there appears to be no congressional power that justifies §214(d)'s application to passports, Zivotofsky's challenge to the Executive's designation of his place of birth on his passport must fail. . . .

The majority does not perform this analysis, but instead relies on a variation of the recognition power. That power is among the foreign affairs powers vested in the President by Article II's Vesting Clause, as is confirmed by Article II's express assignment to the President of the duty of receiving foreign Ambassadors, Art. II, §3. But I cannot join the majority's analysis because no act of recognition is implicated here. . . .

Assuming for the sake of argument that listing a non-recognized foreign sovereign as a citizen's place of birth on a U.S. passport could have the effect of recognizing that sovereign under international law, no such recognition would occur under the circumstances presented here. The United States has recognized Israel as a foreign sovereign since May 14, 1948. That the United States has subsequently declined to acknowledge Israel's sovereignty over Jerusalem has not changed its recognition of Israel as a sovereign state. And even if the United States were to acknowledge Israel's sovereignty over Jerusalem, that action would not change its recognition of Israel as a sovereign state. That is because the United States has already afforded Israel the rights and responsibilities attendant to its status as a sovereign State. Taking a different position on the Jerusalem question will have no effect on that recognition. . . .

Dissents

CHIEF JUSTICE ROBERTS, with whom JUSTICE ALITO joins, dissenting. . . .

For our first 225 years, no President prevailed when contradicting a statute in the field of foreign affairs. In this case, the President claims the exclusive and preclusive power to recognize foreign sovereigns. The Court devotes much of its analysis to accepting the Executive's contention. I have serious doubts about that position. The majority places great weight on the Reception Clause, which directs that the Executive "shall receive Ambassadors and other public Ministers." Art. II, §3. But that provision, framed as an obligation rather than an authorization, appears alongside the *duties* imposed on the President by Article II, Section 3, not the *powers* granted to him by Article II, Section 2. Indeed, the People ratified the Constitution with Alexander Hamilton's assurance that executive reception of ambassadors "is more a matter of dignity than of authority" and "will be without consequence in the administration of the government." The Federalist No. 69, p. 420 (Clinton Rossiter ed., 1961). . . .

The majority's other asserted textual bases are even more tenuous. The President does have power to make treaties and appoint ambassadors. Art. II, §2. But those authorities are *shared* with Congress, so they hardly support an inference that the recognition power is *exclusive*.

Precedent and history lend no more weight to the Court's position. The majority cites dicta suggesting an exclusive executive recognition power, but acknowledges contrary dicta suggesting that the power is shared. When the best you can muster is conflicting dicta, precedent can hardly be said to support your side.

As for history, the majority admits that it too points in both directions. Some Presidents have claimed an exclusive recognition power, but others have expressed uncertainty about whether such preclusive authority exists. Those in the skeptical camp include Andrew Jackson and Abraham Lincoln, leaders not generally known for their cramped conceptions of Presidential power. Congress has also asserted its authority over recognition determinations at numerous points in history. The majority therefore falls short of demonstrating that "Congress has accepted" the President's exclusive recognition power. In any event, we have held that congressional acquiescence is only "pertinent" when the President acts in the absence of express congressional authorization, not when he asserts power to disregard a statute, as the Executive does here. Medellin v. Texas, 552 U.S. 491, 528 (2008); *see* Dames & Moore v. Regan, 453 U.S. 654, 678-79 (1981).

In sum, although the President has authority over recognition, I am not convinced that the Constitution provides the "conclusive and preclusive" power required to justify defiance of an express legislative mandate. *Youngstown*, 343 U.S. at 638 (Jackson, J., concurring). . . .

But even if the President does have exclusive recognition power, he still cannot prevail in this case, because the statute at issue *does not implicate recognition*. The relevant provision, §214(d), simply gives an American citizen born in Jerusalem the option to designate his place of birth as Israel "[f]or purposes of" passports and other documents. The State Department itself has explained that "identification"—not recognition—"is the principal reason that U.S. passports require 'place of birth.'" Congress has not disputed the Executive's assurances that §214(d) does not alter the longstanding United States position on Jerusalem. And the annals of diplomatic history record no examples of official recognition accomplished via optional passport designation.

The majority acknowledges both that the "Executive's exclusive power extends no further than his formal recognition determination" and that §214(d) does "not itself constitute a formal act of recognition." Taken together, these statements come close to a confession of error. The majority attempts to reconcile its position by reconceiving §214(d) as a "mandate that the Executive contradict his prior recognition determination in an official document issued by the Secretary of State." But as just noted, neither Congress nor the Executive Branch regards §214(d) as a recognition determination, so it is hard to see how the statute could contradict any such determination.

At most, the majority worries that there may be a *perceived* contradiction based on a *mistaken* understanding of the effect of §214(d), insisting that some "observers interpreted §214 as altering United States policy regarding Jerusalem." To afford controlling weight to such impressions, however, is essentially to subject a duly enacted statute to an international heckler's veto.

Moreover, expanding the President's purportedly exclusive recognition power to include authority to avoid potential misunderstandings of legislative enactments proves far too much. Congress could validly exercise its enumerated powers in countless ways that would create more severe perceived contradictions with Presidential recognition decisions than does §214(d). If, for example, the President recognized a particular country in opposition to Congress's wishes, Congress could declare war or impose a trade embargo on that country. A neutral observer might well conclude that these legislative actions had, to put it mildly, created a perceived contradiction with the President's recognition decision. And yet each of them would undoubtedly be constitutional. So too would statements by nonlegislative actors that might be seen to contradict the President's recognition positions, such as the declaration in a political party platform that "Jerusalem is and will remain the capital of Israel." Landler, Pushed by Obama, Democrats Alter Platform Over Jerusalem, N.Y. Times, Sept. 6, 2012, p. A14.

Ultimately, the only power that could support the President's position is the one the majority purports to reject: the "exclusive authority to conduct diplomatic relations." Brief for Respondent 18. The Government offers a single citation for this allegedly exclusive power: United States v. Curtiss-Wright Export Corp., 299 U.S. 304, 319-20 (1936). But as the majority rightly acknowledges, *Curtiss-Wright* did not involve a claim that the Executive could contravene a statute; it held only that he could act pursuant to a legislative delegation.

The expansive language in *Curtiss-Wright* casting the President as the "sole organ" of the Nation in foreign affairs certainly has attraction for members of the Executive Branch. The Solicitor General invokes the case no fewer than ten times in his brief. But our precedents have never accepted such a sweeping understanding of executive power. . . .

Just a few Terms ago, this Court rejected the President's argument that a broad foreign relations power allowed him to override a state court decision that contradicted U.S. international law obligations. *Medellin*, 552 U.S. at 523-32. If the President's so-called general foreign relations authority does not permit him to countermand a State's lawful action, it surely does not authorize him to disregard an express statutory directive enacted by Congress, which—unlike the States—has extensive foreign relations powers of its own. Unfortunately, despite its protest to the contrary, the majority today allows the Executive to do just that.

Resolving the status of Jerusalem may be vexing, but resolving this case is not. Whatever recognition power the President may have, exclusive or otherwise, is not implicated by §214(d). It has not been necessary over the past 225 years to definitively resolve a dispute between Congress and the President over the recognition power. Perhaps we could have waited another 225 years. But instead the majority strains to reach the question based on the mere possibility that observers overseas might misperceive the significance of the birthplace designation at issue in this case. And in the process, the Court takes the perilous step—for the first time in our history—of allowing the President to defy an Act of Congress in the field of foreign affairs. . . .

JUSTICE SCALIA, with whom THE CHIEF JUSTICE and JUSTICE ALITO join, dissenting. . . .

Before turning to Presidential power under Article II, I think it well to establish the statute's basis in congressional power under Article I. Congress's power to "establish an uniform Rule of Naturalization," Art. I, §8, cl. 4, enables it to grant American citizenship to someone born abroad. United States v. Wong Kim Ark, 169 U.S. 649, 702-03 (1898). The naturalization power also enables Congress to furnish the people it makes citizens with papers verifying their citizenship—say a consular report of birth abroad (which certifies citizenship of an American born outside the United States) or a passport (which certifies citizenship for purposes of international travel). As the Necessary and Proper Clause confirms, every congressional power "carries with it all those incidental powers which are necessary to its complete and effectual execution." Cohens v. Virginia, 19 U.S. 264, 429 (1821). Even on a miserly understanding of Congress's incidental authority, Congress may make grants of citizenship "effectual" by providing for the issuance of certificates authenticating them.

One would think that if Congress may grant Zivotofsky a passport and a birth report, it may also require these papers to record his birthplace as "Israel." The birthplace specification promotes the document's citizenship-authenticating function by identifying the bearer, distinguishing people with similar names but different birthplaces from each other, helping authorities uncover identity fraud, and facilitating retrieval of the Government's citizenship records. To be sure, recording Zivotofsky's birthplace as "Jerusalem" rather than "Israel" would fulfill these objectives, but when faced with alternative ways to carry its powers into execution, Congress has the "discretion" to choose the one it deems "most beneficial to the people." McCulloch v. Maryland, 17 U.S. 316, 421 (1819). It thus has the right to decide that recording birthplaces as "Israel" makes for better foreign policy. Or that regardless of international politics, a passport or birth report should respect its bearer's conscientious belief that Jerusalem belongs to Israel.

No doubt congressional discretion in executing legislative powers has its limits; Congress's chosen approach must be not only "necessary" to carrying its powers into execution, but also "proper." Congress thus may not transcend boundaries upon legislative authority stated or implied elsewhere in the Constitution. But as we shall see, §214(d) does not transgress any such restriction. . . .

The Court holds that the Constitution makes the President alone responsible for recognition and that §214(d) invades this exclusive power. I agree that the Constitution *empowers* the President to extend recognition on behalf of the United States, but I find it a much harder question whether it makes that power exclusive. The Court tells us that "the weight of historical evidence" supports exclusive executive authority over "the formal determination of recognition." But even with its attention confined to formal recognition, the Court is forced to admit that "history is not all on one side." . . . Neither text nor history nor precedent yields a clear answer to these questions. Fortunately, I have no need to confront these matters today—nor does the Court—because §214(d) plainly does not concern recognition.

Recognition is more than an announcement of a policy. Like the ratification of an international agreement or the termination of a treaty, it is a formal legal act with effects under international law. It signifies acceptance of an international status, and it makes a commitment to continued acceptance of that status and respect for any attendant rights. . . . In order to extend recognition, a state must perform an act that unequivocally manifests that intention. That act can consist of an express conferral of recognition, or one of a handful of acts that by international custom imply recognition—chiefly, entering into a bilateral treaty, and sending or receiving an ambassador.

To know all this is to realize at once that §214(d) has nothing to do with recognition. Section 214(d) does not require the Secretary to make a formal declaration about Israel's sovereignty over Jerusalem. And nobody suggests that international custom infers acceptance of sovereignty from the birthplace designation on a passport or birth report, as it does from bilateral treaties or exchanges of ambassadors. Recognition would preclude the United States (as a matter of international law) from later contesting Israeli sovereignty over Jerusalem. But making a notation in a passport or birth report does not encumber the Republic with any international obligations. It leaves the Nation free (so far as international law is concerned) to change its mind in the future. That would be true even if the statute required *all* passports to list "Israel." But in fact it requires only those passports to list "Israel" for which the citizen (or his guardian) *requests* "Israel"; all the rest, under the Secretary's policy, list "Jerusalem." It is utterly impossible for this deference to private requests to constitute an act that unequivocally manifests an intention to grant recognition.

Section 214(d) performs a more prosaic function than extending recognition. Just as foreign countries care about what our Government has to say about their borders, so too American citizens often care about what our Government has to say about their identities. The State Department does not grant or deny recognition in order to accommodate these individuals, but it does make exceptions to its rules about how it records birthplaces. Although normal protocol requires specifying the bearer's country of birth in his passport, the State Department will, if the bearer protests, specify the city of birth instead—so that an Irish nationalist may have his birthplace recorded as "Belfast" rather than "United Kingdom." And although normal protocol requires specifying the country with *present* sovereignty over the bearer's place of birth, a special exception allows a bearer born before 1948 in what was then Palestine to have his birthplace listed as "Palestine." Section 214(d) requires the State Department to make a further accommodation. Even though the Department normally refuses to specify a country that lacks recognized sovereignty over the bearer's birthplace, it must suspend that policy upon the request of an American citizen born in Jerusalem. Granting a request to specify "Israel" rather than "Jerusalem" does not recognize Israel's sovereignty over Jerusalem, just as granting a request to specify "Belfast" rather than "United Kingdom" does not derecognize the United Kingdom's sovereignty over Northern Ireland.

The best indication that §214(d) does not concern recognition comes from the State Department's policies concerning Taiwan. According to the Solicitor General, the United States "acknowledges the Chinese position" that Taiwan is a part of China, but "does not take a position" of its own on that issue. Brief for Respondent 51-52. Even so, the State Department has for a long time recorded the birthplace of a citizen born in Taiwan as "China." It indeed *insisted* on doing so until Congress passed a law (on which §214(d) was modeled) giving citizens the option to have their birthplaces recorded as "Taiwan." The Solicitor General explains that the designation "China" "involves a geographic description, not an assertion that Taiwan is

. . . part of sovereign China." Brief for Respondent 51-52. Quite so. Section 214(d) likewise calls for nothing beyond a "geographic description"; it does not require the Executive even to assert, never mind formally recognize, that Jerusalem is a part of sovereign Israel. Since birthplace specifications in citizenship documents are matters within Congress's control, Congress may treat Jerusalem as a part of Israel when regulating the recording of birthplaces, even if the President does not do so when extending recognition. . . .

The Court complains that §214(d) requires the Secretary of State to issue official documents implying that Jerusalem is a part of Israel; that it appears in a section of the statute bearing the title "United States Policy with Respect to Jerusalem as the Capital of Israel"; and that foreign "observers interpreted [it] as altering United States policy regarding Jerusalem." But these features do not show that §214(d) recognizes Israel's sovereignty over Jerusalem. They show only that the law displays symbolic support for Israel's territorial claim. That symbolism may have tremendous significance as a matter of international diplomacy, but it makes no difference as a matter of constitutional law.

Even if the Constitution gives the President sole power to extend recognition, it does not give him sole power to make all decisions relating to foreign disputes over sovereignty. To the contrary, a fair reading of Article I allows Congress to decide for itself how its laws should handle these controversies. Read naturally, power to "regulate Commerce with foreign Nations," §8, cl. 3, includes power to regulate imports from Gibraltar as British goods or as Spanish goods. Read naturally, power to "regulate the Value . . . of foreign Coin," §8, cl. 5, includes power to honor (or not) currency issued by Taiwan. And so on for the other enumerated powers. . . .

The Constitution likewise does not give the President exclusive power to determine which claims to statehood and territory "are legitimate in the eyes of the United States." Congress may express its own views about these matters by declaring war, restricting trade, denying foreign aid, and much else besides. . . .

In the final analysis, the Constitution may well deny Congress power to recognize—the power to make an international commitment accepting a foreign entity as a state, a regime as its government, a place as a part of its territory, and so on. But whatever else §214(d) may do, it plainly does not make (or require the President to make) a commitment accepting Israel's sovereignty over Jerusalem.

The Court does not try to argue that §214(d) extends recognition; nor does it try to argue that the President holds the exclusive power to make all nonrecognition decisions relating to the status of Jerusalem. As just shown, these arguments would be impossible to make with a straight face.

The Court instead announces a rule that is blatantly gerrymandered to the facts of this case. It concludes that, in addition to the exclusive power to make the "formal recognition determination," the President holds an ancillary exclusive power "to control . . . formal statements by the Executive Branch acknowledging the legitimacy of a state or government and its territorial bounds." It follows, the Court explains, that Congress may not "requir[e] the President to contradict an earlier recognition determination in an official document issued by the Executive Branch." So requiring imports from Jerusalem to be taxed like goods from Israel is fine, but requiring Customs to issue an official invoice to that effect is not? Nonsense.

Recognition is a type of legal act, not a type of statement. It is a leap worthy of the Mad Hatter to go from exclusive authority over making legal commitments about sovereignty to exclusive authority over making statements or issuing documents about national borders. The Court may as well jump from power over issuing declaratory judgments to a monopoly on writing law-review articles. . . .

To the extent doubts linger about whether the United States recognizes Israel's sovereignty over Jerusalem, §214(d) leaves the President free to dispel them by issuing a disclaimer of intent to recognize. A disclaimer always suffices to prevent an act from effecting recognition. Restatement (Second) of Foreign Relations Law of the United States §104(1) (1965). Recall that an earlier law grants citizens born in Taiwan the right to have their birthplaces recorded as "Taiwan." The State Department has complied with the law, but states in its Foreign Affairs Manual: "The United States does not officially recognize Taiwan as a 'state' or 'country,' although passport issuing officers may enter 'Taiwan' as a place of birth." 7 FAM §1300, App. D, §1340(d)(6). Nothing stops a similar disclaimer here.

At other times, the Court seems concerned with Congress's failure to give effect to a recognition decision that the President has already made. The Court protests, for instance, that §214(d) "directly contradicts" the President's refusal to recognize Israel's sovereignty over Jerusalem. But even if the Constitution empowers the President alone to extend recognition, it nowhere obliges Congress to align its laws with the President's recognition decisions. Because the President and Congress are "perfectly coordinate by the terms of their common commission," The Federalist No. 49, p. 314 (Clinton Rossiter ed., 1961) (Madison), the President's use of the recognition power does not constrain Congress's use of its legislative powers. . . .

The Court elsewhere objects that §214(d) interferes with the autonomy and unity of the Executive Branch, setting the branch against itself. The Court suggests, for instance, that the law prevents the President from maintaining his neutrality about Jerusalem in "his and his agent's statements." That is of no constitutional significance. As just shown, Congress has power to legislate without regard to recognition, and where Congress has the power to legislate, the President has a duty to "take Care" that its legislation "be faithfully executed," Art. II, §3. It is likewise "the duty of the secretary of state to conform to the law"; where Congress imposes a responsibility on him, "he is so far the officer of the law; is amenable to the laws for his conduct; and cannot at his discretion sport away the vested rights of others." Marbury v. Madison, 5 U.S. 137, 158, 166 (1803). The Executive's involvement in carrying out this law does not affect its constitutionality; the Executive carries out every law.

The Court's error could be made more apparent by applying its reasoning to the President's power "to make Treaties," Art. II, §2, cl. 2. There is no question that Congress may, if it wishes, pass laws that openly flout treaties made by the President. Head Money Cases, 112 U.S. 580, 597 (1884). Would anyone have dreamt that the President may refuse to carry out such laws—or, to bring the point closer to home, refuse to execute federal courts' judgments under such laws—so that the Executive may "speak with one voice" about the country's international obligations? To ask is to answer. Today's holding puts the implied power to recognize territorial claims (which the Court infers from the power to recognize states, which it infers from the responsibility to receive ambassadors) on a higher footing than the express power to make treaties. And this, even though the Federalist describes the making of treaties as a "delicate and important prerogative," but the reception of ambassadors as "more a matter of dignity than of authority," "a circumstance which will be without consequence in the administration of the government." The Federalist No. 69, p. 420 (Hamilton).

In the end, the Court's decision does not rest on text or history or precedent. It instead comes down to "functional considerations"—principally the Court's perception that the Nation "must speak with one voice" about the status of Jerusalem. The vices of this mode of analysis go beyond mere lack of footing in the Constitution. Functionalism of the sort the Court practices today will *systematically* favor the unitary President over the plural Congress in disputes involving foreign affairs. It is possible that this approach will make for more effective foreign policy, perhaps as effective as that of a monarchy. It is certain that, in the long run, it will erode the structure of separated powers that the People established for the protection of their liberty.

Memorandum from Walter Dellinger, Assistant Attorney General, Office of Legal Counsel, to Abner J. Mikva, Counsel to the President, "Presidential Authority to Decline to Execute Unconstitutional Statutes" (Nov. 2, 1994)

. . . [T]here are circumstances in which the President may appropriately decline to enforce a statute that he views as unconstitutional.

First, there is significant judicial approval of this proposition. Most notable is the Court's decision in Myers v. United States, 272 U.S. 52 (1926). There, the Court sustained the President's view that the statute at issue was unconstitutional without any member of the Court suggesting that the President had acted improperly in refusing to abide by the statute. More recently, in Freytag v. Commissioner, 501 U.S. 868 (1991), all four of the Justices who addressed the issue agreed that the President has "the power to veto encroaching laws . . . or even to disregard them when they are unconstitutional." *Id.* at 906 (Scalia, J., concurring); *see also* Youngstown Sheet & Tube Co. v. Sawyer, 343 U.S. 579, 635-38 (1952) (Jackson, J., concurring) (recognizing existence of President's authority to act contrary to a statutory command).

Second, consistent and substantial executive practice also confirms this general proposition. Opinions dating to at least 1860 assert the President's authority to decline to effectuate enactments that the President views as unconstitutional. *See, e.g.*, Memorial of Captain Meigs, 9 Op. Att'y Gen. 462, 469-70 (1860) (asserting that the President need not enforce a statute purporting to appoint an officer). . . .

While the general proposition that in some situations the President may decline to enforce unconstitutional statutes is unassailable, it does not offer sufficient guidance as to the appropriate course in specific circumstances. To continue our conversation about these complex issues, I offer the following propositions for your consideration.

1. The President's office and authority are created and bounded by the Constitution; he is required to act within its terms. Put somewhat differently, in serving as the executive created by the Constitution, the President is required to act in accordance with the laws—including the Constitution, which takes precedence over other forms of law. This obligation is reflected in the Take Care Clause and in the President's oath of office.

2. When bills are under consideration by Congress, the executive branch should promptly identify unconstitutional provisions and communicate its concerns to Congress so that the provisions can be corrected. Although this may seem elementary, in practice there have been occasions in which the President has been presented with enrolled bills containing constitutional flaws that should have been corrected in the legislative process.

3. The President should presume that enactments are constitutional. There will be some occasions, however, when a statute appears to conflict with the

Constitution. In such cases, the President can and should exercise his independent judgment to determine whether the statute is constitutional. In reaching a conclusion, the President should give great deference to the fact that Congress passed the statute and that Congress believed it was upholding its obligation to enact constitutional legislation. Where possible, the President should construe provisions to avoid constitutional problems.

4. The Supreme Court plays a special role in resolving disputes about the constitutionality of enactments. As a general matter, if the President believes that the Court would sustain a particular provision as constitutional, the President should execute the statute, notwithstanding his own beliefs about the constitutional issue. If, however, the President, exercising his independent judgment, determines both that a provision would violate the Constitution and that it is probable that the Court would agree with him, the President has the authority to decline to execute the statute.

5. Where the President's independent constitutional judgment and his determination of the Court's probable decision converge on a conclusion of unconstitutionality, the President must make a decision about whether or not to comply with the provision. That decision is necessarily specific to context, and it should be reached after careful weighing of the effect of compliance with the provision on the constitutional rights of affected individuals and on the executive branch's constitutional authority. Also relevant is the likelihood that compliance or non-compliance will permit judicial resolution of the issue. . . .

6. The President has enhanced responsibility to resist unconstitutional provisions that encroach upon the constitutional powers of the Presidency. Where the President believes that an enactment unconstitutionally limits his powers, he has the authority to defend his office and decline to abide by it, unless he is convinced that the Court would disagree with his assessment. If the President does not challenge such provisions (i.e., by refusing to execute them), there often will be no occasion for judicial consideration of their constitutionality; a policy of consistent Presidential enforcement of statutes limiting his power thus would deny the Supreme Court the opportunity to review the limitations and thereby would allow for unconstitutional restrictions on the President's authority.

Some legislative encroachments on executive authority, however, will not be justiciable or are for other reasons unlikely to be resolved in court. If resolution in the courts is unlikely and the President cannot look to a judicial determination, he must shoulder the responsibility of protecting the constitutional role of the presidency. This is usually true, for example, of provisions limiting the President's authority as Commander in Chief. Where it is not possible to construe such provisions constitutionally, the President has the authority to act on his understanding of the Constitution. . . .

7. The fact that a sitting President signed the statute in question does not change this analysis. The text of the Constitution offers no basis for distinguishing bills based on who signed them; there is no constitutional analogue to the principles of waiver and estoppel. Moreover, every President since Eisenhower has issued signing statements in which he stated that he would refuse to execute unconstitutional provisions. . . . (Of course, the President is not obligated to announce his reservations in a signing statement; he can convey his views in the time, manner, and form of his choosing.) . . .

We recognize that these issues are difficult ones. When the President's obligation to act in accord with the Constitution appears to be in tension with his duty to execute laws enacted by Congress, questions are raised that go to the heart of our constitutional structure. In these circumstances, a President should proceed with caution and with respect for the obligation that each of the branches shares for the maintenance of constitutional government.

Notes and Questions

1. Congress cannot regulate the exercise of a power that the Constitution assigns exclusively to the President. *See, e.g.*, Myers v. United States, 272 U.S. 52 (1926) (holding that a statute that prevented the President from removing postmasters without Senate approval was an unconstitutional limitation on the President's removal power under Article II); *Youngstown Sheet & Tube Co.*, 343 U.S. at 635-38 (Jackson, J., concurring) (recognizing in his third category the existence of presidential authority that Congress cannot regulate). But what are the President's exclusive powers? The text of Article II does not answer that question, and the Supreme Court has provided very little guidance. Only in rare instances has the Court invalidated federal statutes for intruding on an exclusive presidential power. *See, e.g.*, *Myers, supra*; Buckley v. Valeo, 424 U.S. 1 (1976) (invalidating statute that purported to give Congress the authority to appoint commissioners to the Federal Election Commission). And prior to *Zivotofsky II*, as Chief Justice Roberts notes, it had never done so in the foreign affairs field.

2. The majority opinion in *Zivotofsky II* analyzed the President's power over recognition. That power has two components: recognition of statehood, and government recognition. Recognition of statehood is "a formal acknowledgment by another state that an entity possesses the qualifications for statehood," including a defined territory, permanent population, government control, and capacity to engage in international relations. Restatement (Third) of the Foreign Relations Law of the United States §202, cmt. a (1987). Recognition of a government is "a formal acknowledgment that a particular regime is the effective government of a state and implies a commitment to treat that regime as the government of that state." *Id.*, §203, cmt. a. President Truman's recognition of Israel as a state, George Washington's reception of Genet as the minister from France, and President Carter's recognition of the People's Republic of China all constituted recognition of governments. Both forms of recognition enable diplomatic and related benefits under domestic and international law and promote the legitimacy of the recognized state or government with third parties. For additional discussion of U.S. historical practice relating to recognition, see Julius Goebel, The Recognition Policy of the United States (1915); Clarence Bergdahl, *The Power of Recognition*, 14 Am. J. Int'l L. 519 (1920); and Robert J. Reinstein, *Is the President's Recognition Power Exclusive?*, 86 Temple L. Rev. 1 (2013).

3. *Zivotofsky II* has three distinct holdings. The first is that the President has an independent power of recognition under Article II. This is an unsurprising conclusion, given that presidents have recognized foreign states and governments without congressional authorization since the beginning of the nation. But what is the source of the President's power to recognize? Article II provides that the President "shall receive Ambassadors and other public Ministers." Art. II, §3. But as the Court in *Zivotofsky II* notes, during the ratification debates, Alexander Hamilton claimed that the power to receive ambassadors was "more a matter of dignity than of authority," a ministerial duty largely "without consequence." The Court goes on to ground the President's recognition power in the understandings of international law at the

Founding, and in the text and structure of Article II. Can you parse the Court's precise arguments from text and structure? Why does the Court conclude from these factors that "each means" of recognition "is dependent upon Presidential power" and thus "give[s] the President control over recognition decisions"? For an extensive textualist and originalist examination of these and related questions, see Robert J. Reinstein, *Recognition: A Case Study on the Original Understanding of Executive Power*, 45 U. Rich. L. Rev. 801 (2011).

4. The second holding in *Zivotofsky II* is that the President's recognition power is exclusive. The Court offers a number of reasons for this conclusion. With respect to constitutional text and structure, it says: "The various ways in which the President may unilaterally effect recognition—and the lack of any similar power vested in Congress—suggest" that the President's power to recognize is exclusive. Is this argument compelling? Is it any different than the argument that recognition is an independent presidential power? Is it odd that the Court concludes that Congress has no power to recognize without (at this point) having examined Article I? Another rationale for the holding was Supreme Court precedent. Do you agree with Chief Justice Roberts that the decisions cited by the Court are at best "conflicting dicta" because some suggest that the recognition power is shared and none involves an actual recognition dispute between the branches? A third rationale was historical practice. The Court acknowledges that history is "not all on one side," but it relies heavily on the fact that "over the last 100 years, there has scarcely been any debate over the President's power to recognize foreign states." Does this lack of debate show that Congress has accepted an exclusive presidential recognition power, or merely that it rarely disagrees with the President's recognition policy? Is Chief Justice Roberts right that congressional acquiescence should be relevant only when determining whether the President has authority to act in the absence of express congressional authorization, "not when [the President] asserts power to disregard a statute"? Finally, the Court relies heavily on what it calls "functional considerations." What are those considerations? Why are they proper components of constitutional interpretation? Is Justice Scalia right that a reliance on such considerations will systematically favor executive authority? Does the Court provide any guidance on the weight to be given to these various sources of law in determining the content of exclusive presidential power?

5. One functional consideration that the Court emphasizes is that "the Nation must have a single policy regarding which governments are legitimate in the eyes of the United States and which are not." Assuming that this is correct, why must the "single policy" be set by the President, rather than (in some instances) by Congress through legislation? Assuming that the President should set the single policy, does the Court's analysis ensure that he or she will succeed? The Court emphasizes that Congress has substantial authority to regulate in the area of foreign affairs and that "[t]he Executive is not free from the ordinary controls and checks of Congress merely because foreign affairs are at issue." Under the Court's analysis, what can Congress do if it disagrees with the President's recognition policy? For example, can it pass trade, customs, or tax laws that conflict with such policy? Also, why is having one voice more important with respect to recognition than for other issues in foreign affairs? As Justice Scalia notes, it is well settled that Congress can override a treaty for purposes of U.S. law. Why, then, is it disallowed from overriding a President's recognition decision?

6. The third holding in *Zivotofsky II* is that Congress in §214(d) infringed on the President's exclusive recognition power. The Court reasoned that "Congress cannot require [the President] to contradict his own statement regarding a determination of formal recognition." Did §214(d) in fact require the President to do that? Would the "contradiction" have stemmed from how enforcement of §214(d) would have been perceived abroad? If so, should the constitutionality of legislation turn on foreign perceptions? Is Chief Justice Roberts right that "[t]o afford controlling weight to such impressions . . . is essentially to subject a duly enacted statute to an international heckler's veto"? Could the Executive Branch have prevented such perceptions by issuing a disclaimer, as Justice Scalia contends?

For commentary on *Zivotofsky II*, see Jack Goldsmith, Zivotofsky II *as Precedent in the Executive Branch*, 129 Harv. L. Rev. 112 (2015); Saikrishna Bangalore Prakash, Zivotofsky *and the Separation of Powers*, 2015 Sup. Ct. Rev. 1 (2015); and the 2015 symposium in *AJIL Unbound* (published online in two parts), with contributions from Curtis Bradley, Harlan Cohen, Jean Galbraith, Campbell McLachlan, Julian Mortenson, Catherine Powell, Peter Spiro, and John Torpey.

7. In December 2017, President Trump officially recognized Jerusalem as the capital of Israel and set in motion a process, now complete, of moving the U.S. embassy from Tel Aviv to Jerusalem, actions that reversed longstanding Executive Branch policy. *See Presidential Proclamation Recognizing Jerusalem as the Capital of the State of Israel and Relocating the United States Embassy to Israel to Jerusalem* (Dec. 6, 2017). After *Zivotofsky II*, there was no dispute that President Trump had authority to take these actions. Moreover, his actions, unlike the presidential action at issue in *Zivotofsky II*, were in accord with congressional directives. Since 1995, the Jerusalem Embassy Act had called for these actions, while allowing presidents to waive its requirements every six months (which presidents before Trump had done). Trump referred to the Act in his proclamation. He also said that he "judged this course of action to be in the best interests of the United States of America and the pursuit of peace between Israel and the Palestinians." The implications of the proclamation for disputes between Israel and the Palestinians over Jerusalem were unclear, given that Trump also noted that the United States "continues to take no position on any final status issues" and that "specific boundaries of Israeli sovereignty in Jerusalem are subject to final status negotiations between the parties."

In March 2019, President Trump proclaimed that "the United States recognizes that the Golan Heights are part of the State of Israel." *See Proclamation on Recognizing the Golan Heights as Part of the State of Israel* (Mar. 25, 2019). The Golan Heights is an area on Israel's northeast border with Syria. Israel seized control of the territory from Syria in the 1967 six-day war and effectively annexed it in 1981. However, the status of the territory under international law has remained contested, and the U.N. Security Council has condemned Israel's de-facto annexation of the Golan Heights as a violation of the U.N. Charter. Prior presidents had declined to recognize Israel's sovereignty over the Golan Heights on the ground that its status should be determined in negotiations among the relevant parties. President Trump's change in U.S. policy almost certainly falls within his recognition power as articulated in *Zivotofsky II*, but it implicates questions about the relationship of international law to the President's recognition power. The U.N. Charter is, after all, a treaty, and treaties are part of "the supreme Law of the Land" under the Constitution. Did the President violate his constitutional obligation to "take Care that the Laws be faithfully executed" by acting in contravention of international law? Or does the President get to decide what international law requires for the United States in this context? Is it relevant that the provisions of the U.N. Charter in question are probably "non-self-executing"? (The distinction between self-executing and non-self-executing treaties is addressed in

Chapter 5.) For further analysis, see Scott R. Anderson, *Recognizing Israel's Claims to the Golan Heights: Trump's Decision in Perspective*, Lawfare (Mar. 22, 2019).

8. In December 2017, Congress passed the National Defense Authorization Act for Fiscal Year 2018. Section 1232 of the Act provides that none of the funds appropriated under the Act "may be obligated or expended to implement any activity that recognizes the sovereignty of the Russian Federation over Crimea." It further provides that the "Secretary of Defense, with the concurrence of the Secretary of State, may waive the restriction on the obligation or expenditure of funds" if they determine that such a waiver is in the national security interest of the United States and they submit notice of the waiver to appropriate congressional committees. Is Section 1232 constitutional under *Zivotofsky II*? President Trump in a signing statement expressed the view that this section and various other sections in the Act "could potentially dictate the position of the United States in external military and foreign affairs and, in certain instances, direct the conduct of international diplomacy" and that his administration "will treat these provisions consistent with the President's exclusive constitutional authorities as Commander in Chief and as the sole representative of the Nation in foreign affairs to determine the terms on which recognition is given to foreign sovereigns and conduct the Nation's diplomacy."

9. *Zivotofsky II* contains the Supreme Court's most extensive analysis to date of the President's exclusive constitutional authority in foreign relations. As noted above, it is also the first decision in which a President has prevailed in a separation of powers dispute analyzed under Justice Jackson's category 3. Did the Court follow Jackson's guidance that presidential action that contravenes a congressional command is "most vulnerable to attack and in the least favorable of possible constitutional postures," and thus "must be scrutinized with caution"? To what extent does the Court's analysis differ from the approach Jackson outlined?

10. What is the status of *United States v. Curtiss-Wright Export Corp.* after *Zivotofsky II*? The Court distanced itself from some of the broad presidential power dicta in *Curtiss-Wright*. It also "decline[d] to acknowledge" that the President had the "broad, undefined powers over foreign affairs" claimed by the Solicitor General in reliance on *Curtiss-Wright*, and it made clear that "[t]he Executive is not free from the ordinary controls and checks of Congress merely because foreign affairs are at issue." On the other hand, the Court relied throughout its opinion on Executive Branch functional advantages as support for upholding presidential defiance of a statute that the Court thought "would not only prevent the Nation from speaking with one voice but also prevent the Executive itself from doing so in conducting foreign relations." It also affirmed the President's "unique role in communicating with foreign governments" and explained this role by reference to *Curtiss-Wright*'s invocation of then-Congressman John Marshall's statement that the President "is the sole organ of the nation in its external relations, and its sole representative with foreign nations." Is *Zivotofsky II* a counterpoint to Executive Branch invocations of *Curtiss-Wright*, despite its holding in favor of executive authority in this case? Or is it the new *Curtiss-Wright*, with the difference that its functional analysis and pro-presidential one-voice rhetoric are not (as in *Curtiss-Wright*) extraneous to the holding of the case?

11. In Ganesh Sitaraman & Ingrid Wuerth, *The Normalization of Foreign Relations Law*, 128 Harv. L. Rev. 1897 (2015), the authors contend that the Court has treated foreign relations issues "as if they were run-of-the-mill domestic policy issues, suitable for judicial review and governed by ordinary separation of powers and statutory interpretation principles." One example they give is the Court's decision in

Zivotofsky I. Normatively, they argue that this "normalization" trend is desirable, because functional justifications for treating foreign relations cases differently than domestic cases (such as arguments about executive expertise, the need for speed and secrecy in decisionmaking, and the especially high costs of erroneous decisions) are overstated. *See also* Harlan Grant Cohen, *Formalism and Distrust: Foreign Affairs Law in the Roberts Court*, 83 Geo. Wash. L. Rev. 381 (2015) (similar account of the current Supreme Court's approach to foreign relations law that emphasizes its shift towards formalist legal analysis). Several commentators have questioned the validity of the normalization thesis. *See* Curtis A. Bradley, *Foreign Relations Law and the Purported Shift Away from "Exceptionalism,"* 128 Harv. L. Rev. F. 294 (2015); Carlos M. Vázquez, *The Abiding Exceptionalism of Foreign Relations Doctrine*, 128 Harv. L. Rev. F. 305 (2015); and Stephen I. Vladeck, *The Exceptionalism of Foreign Relations Normalization*, 128 Harv. L. Rev. F. 322 (2015). For an argument that *Zivotofsky II* defied the normalization thesis because it "made clear that the Court had not in fact rejected functional considerations as a basis for measuring presidential power in foreign relations, and could switch back to it on a dime," see Goldsmith, Zivotofsky II *as Precedent in the Executive Branch, supra.*

12. What are *Zivotofsky II*'s implications for exclusive presidential power in other foreign relations law contexts? How do the Court's textual, structural, historical, and functional arguments map on to other areas of presidential power? Might the answer depend on the scope of the President's recognition power? Professor Henkin described the President's power over recognition as including "the power to do all that is involved in relations with other nations: establishing and maintaining channels for intercourse and communication; instructing and informing our ambassadors and receiving their reports, inquiries and recommendations; exchanging information and views with foreign governments," and he noted that it might even entail the authority "to decide also the contents of his communications to ambassadors and to foreign governments, including the attitudes and intentions of the United States that constitute U.S. foreign policy." Louis Henkin, Foreign Affairs and the United States Constitution 38 (2d ed. 1996). Can the power to receive ambassadors be read this broadly? If so, is Congress disabled after *Zivotofsky II* from regulating in these contexts? How should courts determine whether Congress's exercise of its powers under Article I unduly infringes on the President's diplomatic powers? For a pre-*Zivotofsky II* Executive Branch opinion that "Congress is limited in its authority to regulate the President's conduct of diplomatic relations" and may not "place limits on the President's use of his preferred agents to engage in a category of important diplomatic relations, and thereby determine the form and manner in which the Executive engages in diplomacy," see David J. Barron, Acting Assistant Attorney General, Office of Legal Counsel, *Constitutionality of Section 7054 of the Fiscal Year 2009 Foreign Appropriations Act,* June 1, 2009, available at www.justice .gov/olc/2009/section7054.pdf.

13. Justice Thomas's concurrence in *Zivotofsky II* is the most extended explanation and defense of the Vesting Clause Thesis (discussed above in Section B) in the pages of the Supreme Court reports. Do you see how Justice Thomas uses the Vesting Clause argument, combined with what he claims is a lack of Article I power over the passport issue in this case, to reach a conclusion of exclusive presidential power through a route quite different than that of the majority? Which route is more persuasive?

14. Justice Breyer joined the majority opinion but noted that he continued to believe (as he argued in *Zivotofsky I*) that the case should have been dismissed under the political question doctrine. Does this decision illustrate a potential downside of narrowing the political question doctrine, at least from the perspective of those concerned about the growth of presidential power? After all, if the case had been dismissed on political question grounds, Congress would have remained free to assert that it had the constitutional authority to enact §214(d) and similar measures, whereas now the Court has made clear that it lacks that authority. The Court's formalistic rejection of the political question doctrine in the first *Zivotofsky* decision eschewed prudential considerations that might have favored judicial abstention. The Court's subsequent decision on the merits is more pragmatic and functional in its approach. Might a formalistic approach to justiciability merely shift functional considerations to the merits stage of a case? *See* Curtis Bradley, Zivotofsky *and Pragmatic Foreign Relations Law* (June 9, 2015), SCOTUSBLOG, at http://www.scotusblog.com/2015/06/symposium-zivotofsky-and-pragmatic-foreign-relations-law/.

15. The clash in *Zivotofsky II* between §214(d) and the President's recognition policy was unmistakable. What should courts do when the scope of the federal statute and the extent to which it impinges on a presidential power are unclear? This issue came up in Department of the Navy v. Egan, 484 U.S. 518 (1988). In that case, the question was whether the Merit Systems Protection Board's statutory authority to review the removal of Executive employees included the authority to review the related decision to deny the employee in question a security clearance. The Supreme Court held that the Board had no such authority, reasoning in part:

> [The President's] authority to classify and control access to information bearing on national security and to determine whether an individual is sufficiently trustworthy to occupy a position in the Executive Branch that will give that person access to such information flows primarily from this constitutional investment of power in the President and exists quite apart from any explicit congressional grant. . . . [U]nless Congress specifically has provided otherwise, courts traditionally have been reluctant to intrude upon the authority of the Executive in military . . . affairs.

Id. at 527, 530. In effect, the Court required a clear statement by Congress before it would construe the statute as intruding on Executive authority. In what circumstances should this clear statement requirement apply? When the alternate statutory construction would be unconstitutional? When it would raise important constitutional questions? Does the clear statement requirement apply only when the presidential authority in question is an exclusive one, or also when the presidential authority is merely an independent one (i.e., derived from Article II, but subject to the concurrent regulation of Congress)?

16. President Bush signed the law that included §214(d) but announced that he believed this section was unconstitutional and would not enforce it, a stance that the Obama Administration continued. As the Dellinger memorandum excerpted above suggests, presidents have long proclaimed such an authority to disregard a statute they deem unconstitutional. They have reasoned that since the President has a duty to take care to faithfully execute the "Laws," including the Constitution, and since statutes must conform to the Constitution, the President has the authority to disregard a statute that he believes violates Article II. The Supreme Court appears to agree that the President possesses the power to interpret and disregard unconstitutional statutes in some instances, *see Myers, supra;* Freytag v. Commissioner, 501 U.S. 868 (1991) (Scalia, J., concurring) (stating that the President has "the power to veto encroaching laws . . . or even to disregard them when they are unconstitutional").

The Court in *Zivotofsky II* vindicated the constitutional interpretation by Presidents Bush and Obama. Often, however, a President decides not to enforce a statute that he or she thinks impinges on an exclusive Executive prerogative, even though no court has declared it to be so and no court is likely to exercise judicial review over the matter. Can the President and the President's lawyers be trusted faithfully to interpret the law in these circumstances? What criteria should the President and legal advisors employ in determining whether to disregard a statute that they believe violates Article II? Should the President give deference to the fact that Congress passed the statute and that Congress believed it was upholding its obligation to enact constitutional legislation? Should the President, where possible, construe provisions to avoid constitutional problems? How, if at all, should the answers to the questions be affected by the likelihood of judicial review? Do you agree with the approach to these issues suggested in the Dellinger memorandum? Is the Dellinger memorandum correct in claiming that the President has enhanced responsibilities to resist unconstitutional encroachments on his or her own power?

17. The excerpted memorandum by Dellinger, the Barron memorandum referred to in note 12, and many other Executive Branch legal opinions reproduced or mentioned in this casebook were written by the Office of Legal Counsel (OLC), a branch of the Department of Justice. OLC plays a crucial role in the elaborate bureaucracy of lawyers throughout the Executive Branch who monitor executive action to ensure its compliance with the Constitution, federal statutes, and treaties. Atop this bureaucracy sits the President, who under Article II has a duty to "take Care that the Laws be faithfully executed." The Take Care Clause requires the President to abide by the law and to enforce the law, but it has also been interpreted since the beginning of the nation to include power to *interpret* the law for the Executive Branch on the theory that the President and the President's subordinates cannot enforce or comply with the law unless they first know, through interpretation, what it requires. (An early example of Executive Branch interpretation occurred during the neutrality crisis of 1793, which is discussed in Chapter 1.)

Presidents are obviously very busy and are often not lawyers, so they delegate their interpretive authority to the Attorney General, who in turn since the 1950s has delegated it to OLC. OLC thus determines the law for the Executive Branch, subject to rare reversals by the President or Attorney General. OLC sometimes answers legal questions from the White House, as occurred with Dellinger's memorandum to the White House Counsel. It also resolves interpretive disputes between departments and agencies in the Executive Branch, and it comments on the constitutionality of bills before Congress.

Executive Branch interpretation of and compliance with the law is a vital function, especially in the foreign affairs context, where many legal issues never or rarely come before courts and thus are interpreted for the first time, and sometimes for the last, by the Executive Branch. Note that the head of OLC is a political appointee nominated by the President, confirmed by the Senate, and subject to dismissal by the President. In this light, can OLC opinions reflect a neutral, detached interpretation of the law? Should they? Does Congress interpret law in a neutral, detached way when it enacts statutes? Do courts when they determine the scope of their authorities? Should the President be able to seek legal advice from an office that shares his or her legal philosophy and goals? Will such an office always approve presidential action as lawful? Why might it not and why might the President not want it to?

Professor Morrison has provided some empirical evidence relevant to these last two questions. On the basis of studying 245 publicly available OLC opinions issued to the White House between 1977 and 2009 and on which the White House had a stated preference, Professor Morrison concluded that 79 percent found in favor of the White House view, 8 percent provided a mixed answer, and 13 percent went predominantly against the White House. Morrison notes that these numbers probably understate the extent to which OLC declines to rubber-stamp a presidential policy, because its "facilitative approach"—the practice of working with the client to find a lawful way to pursue the client's desired ends—sometimes leads it to begin the consultation with the client with a "no" but then work with the client to find a lawful alternative that ends up in a published opinion as a "yes." *See* Trevor W. Morrison, *Constitutional Alarmism*, 124 Harv. L. Rev. 1688, 1717-20 (2011).

For various perspectives on the issues raised in this note, see Bruce Ackerman, The Decline and Fall of the American Republic (2010); Harold Bruff, Bad Advice: Bush's Lawyers in the War on Terror (2009); Robert F. Bauer, *The National Security Lawyer, In Crisis: When the "Best View" of the Law May Not Be the Best View*, Geo. J. Leg. Ethics 175 (2018); Jack Goldsmith, The Terror Presidency: Law and Judgment Inside the Bush Administration (2007); Goldsmith, Zivotofsky II *as Precedent in the Executive Branch, supra*; Dawn Johnsen, *Faithfully Executing the Laws: Internal Legal Constraints on Executive Power*, 54 UCLA L. Rev. 1559 (2007); Trevor W. Morrison, *Stare Decisis in the Office of Legal Counsel*, 110 Colum. L. Rev. 1448 (2010); Randolph D. Moss, *Executive Branch Legal Interpretation: A Perspective from the Office of Legal Counsel*, 52 Admin. L. Rev. 1303 (2000). *See also* Symposium, *Executive Branch Interpretation of the Law*, 15 Cardozo L. Rev. 21 (1993-1994) (articles by William Barr, Thomas Merrill, Michael Stokes Paulsen, David Strauss, Michel Rosenfeld, Geoffrey Miller, Michael Herz, Neal Devins, Frank Easterbrook, Michael Fitts, John McGinnis, Nelson Lund, Samuel Alito, and Harold Koh). In addition, OLC itself has described its conception of its role and limits. *See* Memorandum from David J. Barron to the Attorneys of the Office, "Best Practices for OLC Legal Advice and Written Opinions," July 16, 2010, available at https://www.justice.gov/sites/default/files/olc/legacy/2010/08/26/olc-legal-advice-opinions.pdf. For a consideration of the role that Congress plays in structuring the relative powers of actors within the Executive Branch and their processes of decisionmaking, see Rebecca Ingber, *Congressional Administration of Foreign Affairs*, 106 Va. L. Rev. (forthcoming).

18. President Bush's announcement that he believed §214(d) was unconstitutional came in a statement that he issued in conjunction with his signing a bill into law. The Executive Branch has long claimed the authority to issue such statements, and has argued that the statements properly serve at least three functions: "(1) explaining to the public, and particularly to constituencies interested in the bill, what the President believes to be the likely effects of its adoption, (2) directing subordinate officers within the Executive Branch how to interpret or administer the enactment, and (3) informing Congress and the public that the Executive believes that a particular provision would be unconstitutional in certain of its applications, or that it is unconstitutional on its face, and that the provision will not be given effect by the Executive Branch to the extent that such enforcement would create an unconstitutional condition." Memorandum from Walter Dellinger, Assistant Attorney General, Office of Legal Counsel, to Bernard Nussbaum, Counsel to the President, "Legal Significance of Presidential Signing Statements" (Nov. 3, 1993).

The third purpose—using a signing statement to question the constitutionality of newly signed laws—attracted sharp criticism under President Bush, in part because (as we explore in Chapter 10) his statements invoked controversial constitutional arguments to question the validity of laws related to the war on terrorism.

Candidate Obama criticized Bush's use of signing statements in this way, and he announced new principles designed to limit their use. *See* Memorandum for the Heads of Executive Departments and Agencies, "Presidential Signing Statements" (Mar. 9, 2009). But within days of this Memorandum's issuance, President Obama issued a signing statement that proclaimed that several congressional restrictions in a spending bill interfered with the President's constitutional powers, ordered executive officials to treat the objectionable restrictions as "advisory" or "precatory" (and thus non-binding), and pledged to ignore a congressional funding restriction on U.S. participation in United Nations' agencies chaired by a government that supports international terrorism. *See* Statement by the President (Mar. 11, 2009). President Trump continued the practice as well. For example, in August 2018, he issued an especially wide-ranging signing statement identifying "constitutional concerns" with over 50 provisions in the National Defense Authorization Act for 2019. *See* Statement by President Donald J. Trump on H.R. 5515 (Aug. 13, 2018).

If the President believes that a provision in a bill is unconstitutional, is the President obligated to veto the bill? What if the bill has numerous provisions on a variety of subjects, and the President's constitutional concerns relate only to one provision? What if the President's constitutional concerns depend on how the provision is applied? Is it better for the President to articulate constitutional concerns about a provision openly in a signing statement rather than articulating them only within the Executive Branch? For differing perspectives on these and related issues, *compare* Curtis A. Bradley & Eric A. Posner, *Presidential Signing Statements and Executive Power*, 23 Const. Comm. 307 (2006) (arguing that presidential signing statements are legal and provide a useful way for the president to disclose his or her views about the meaning and constitutionality of legislation), *with* American Bar Association, Task Force on Presidential Signing Statements and the Separation of Powers Doctrine (August 2006) (arguing that signing statements that announce an intention not to enforce all or part of a statute are "contrary to the rule of law and our constitutional system of separation of powers"). *See also* Symposium, *The Last Word? The Constitutional Implications of Presidential Signing Statements*, 16 Wm. & Mary Bill of Rts. J. 1-314 (2007) (articles by Phillip Cooper, Neal Devins, Louis Fisher, Michele Gilman, Christopher Kelley, Neil Kinkopf, Nelson Lund, and Saikrishna Prakash); William Baude, *Signing Unconstitutional Laws*, 86 Ind. L.J. 303 (2011). *See also* Daniel B. Rodriguez et al., *Executive Opportunism, Presidential Signing Statements, and the Separation of Powers*, 8 J. Leg. Analysis 95 (2016); Christopher S. Yoo, *Presidential Signing Statements: A New Perspective*, 164 U. Pa. L. Rev. 1801 (2016).

19. As a general matter, Congress has discretion not to spend or appropriate money for whatever reason it likes, and the President cannot expend unappropriated government monies, even if the result is that the President cannot carry out foreign relations activities. Matters are more complicated when Congress conditions a spending authorization or appropriation on some restriction on presidential foreign relations action, or on the achievement of a particular foreign relations goal that affects a presidential foreign relations power. It is generally accepted that Congress has the authority to spend and appropriate monies to accomplish results that it could not mandate directly through its enumerated powers, as long as it does so for the "general Welfare of the United States." *See* U.S. Const. Art. I, §8, cl. 1; South Dakota v. Dole, 483 U.S. 203, 207 (1987); United States v. Butler, 297 U.S. 1, 65-66 (1936). However, "other constitutional provisions [outside of Article I] may provide an independent bar to the conditional grant of federal funds." *Dole*, 483 U.S. at 208. The difficult question in the foreign relations context is determining when the President's powers under Article II amount to an independent bar to congressional conditions. As Professor Powell has noted, "[i]t is often unclear whether to interpret a conditional spending provision as a legislative assumption of authority the Constitution grants to the President, or as the legitimate use of a congressional power to express congressional views on foreign policy, or even to accomplish other proper legislative goals, in a manner that affects, without usurping, presidential authority." H. Jefferson Powell, *The President's Authority over Foreign Affairs: An Executive Branch Perspective*, 67 Geo. Wash. L. Rev. 527, 552 (1999). For additional discussion of Congress's ability to affect foreign relations through its appropriations and spending powers, see William C. Banks & Peter Raven-Hansen, National Security Law and the Power of the Purse (1994); Powell, *supra*; Louis Fisher, *Presidential Independence and the Power of the Purse*, 3 U.C. Davis J. Int'l L. & Pol'y 107 (1997); J. Gregory Sidak, *The President's Power of the Purse*, 1989 Duke L.J. 1162; Zachary S. Price, *Funding Restrictions and Separation of Powers*, 71 Vand. L. Rev. 357 (2018). We return to the issue of conditional appropriations in the discussion of war powers in Chapter 9.

20. In order to exercise its legislation and oversight authorities in foreign affairs, Congress often requests information in the possession of the Executive Branch. For a variety of reasons, the Executive Branch sometimes does not want to turn over such information. When the Executive Branch declines to accommodate Congress's requests, Congress has a variety of political tools at its disposal to pressure the President into compliance: it can hold hearings on the matter, decline to appropriate money for presidential initiatives, refuse to confirm presidential appointments, and so forth. Congress (or its committees) can also issue a subpoena, which is simply a legal order to turn over documents or appear to testify. Sometimes the Executive Branch declines to comply with a congressional subpoena on the grounds of "executive privilege," a doctrine that derives from Article II and is designed to protect internal Executive Branch deliberations thought to be important to the President's exercise of his or her constitutional authorities.

The most important Supreme Court decision on executive privilege is United States v. Nixon, 418 U.S. 683 (1974). In that case, a special prosecutor appointed by the Justice Department had obtained a subpoena for the production before trial of certain tapes and documents relating to conversations and meetings between the President and others in connection with the Watergate scandal. When the trial judge ordered an *in camera* examination of the subpoenaed material, President Nixon claimed executive privilege and filed a motion to quash the subpoena. The Supreme Court upheld the trial judge's order. It acknowledged the existence of the executive privilege, and explained that the privilege was needed to protect and encourage high-level government communications, and to protect "the independence of the Executive Branch within its own sphere. . . ." *Id.* at 706. The Court then rejected the notion that executive privilege was absolute. It held that the privilege could be overcome when, as in the *Nixon* case, the evidence sought "is demonstrably relevant" to a criminal trial and is "specific and central to the fair adjudication in a particular criminal case." *Id.* at 712-13. The Court noted, however, that there may be an absolute privilege when the issue involves "military or diplomatic secrets," for in "these areas of Art. II duties, the courts have traditionally shown the utmost deference to Presidential responsibilities." *Id.* at 710. The Court also observed that, "*[a]bsent a claim of need to protect military, diplomatic, or sensitive national security secrets,* we find it difficult to accept the argument that even the very important interest in confidentiality of Presidential communications is significantly diminished by production of such material for *in camera* inspection with all the protection that a district court will be obliged to provide." *Id.* at 706 (emphasis added).

Nixon is one of the few Supreme Court decisions on executive privilege. The paucity of relevant Supreme Court precedent makes the outcome of any executive privilege confrontation uncertain. The uncertainty is only heightened with respect to the many issues that were not implicated in *Nixon* and remain unresolved by the Court. For example, the Court has not ruled on how the *Nixon* framework applies to subpoenas from Congress, and one of the most important lower court decisions on executive privilege emphasized (without further explanation) that "the President's ability to withhold information from Congress implicates different constitutional considerations than the President's ability to withhold evidence in judicial proceedings." In re Sealed Case, 121 F.3d 729, 753 (D.C. Cir. 1997). Also, *Nixon* involved communications with the President himself, but often subpoenas seek documents concerning legal advice from the Justice Department to the White House that might have informed the President's decisionmaking. It is unclear whether executive privilege extends this far. *Cf. id.* at 752 (privilege applies to presidential advisers in the White House who prepare advice for the President for decisions that the President will make, but not "to staff outside the White House in executive branch agencies").

Another open question concerns who ultimately decides the proper scope of executive privilege and, relatedly, whether Congress can enforce its subpoena. There are very few precedents on this issue because Congress and the President usually reach an accommodation short of full-scale confrontation. *See* United States v. American Tel. & Tel. Co., 567 F.2d 121, 127 (D.C. Cir. 1977) (noting in context of clash between congressional subpoena and assertion of executive privilege that "each branch should take cognizance of an implicit constitutional mandate to seek optimal accommodation through a realistic evaluation of the needs of the conflicting branches in the particular fact situation"). If no accommodation is reached, Congress has the authority to issue a contempt citation and refer the matter to the United States Attorney for the District of Columbia, who has a statutory "*duty* . . . to bring the matter before the grand jury for its action." 2 U.S.C. §194 (emphasis added). It is unlikely that this enforcement route will work, however, because the Executive Branch has long taken the view that §194 is unconstitutional to the extent that it requires a U.S. Attorney to prosecute a contempt action when the noncompliance is based on an assertion of executive privilege. *See* Memorandum to the Attorney General from Theodore B. Olson, Prosecution for Contempt of Congress of an Executive Branch Official Who Has Asserted a Claim of Executive Privilege, 8 Op. O.L.C. 101, 102 (1984). Congress also might invoke older cases indicating that Congress itself can enforce its subpoena, *see* Jurney v. MacCracken, 294 U.S. 125 (1935); Anderson v. Dunn, 19 U.S. (6 Wheat.) 204 (1821), and the current Sergeant-in-Arms of the Senate proclaims the authority "to arrest and detain any person violating Senate rules, including the President of the United States," *see* http://www.senate.gov/reference/office/sergeant_at_arms.htm. Finally, Congress might attempt to file a suit for declaratory or injunctive relief. For a decision rejecting the argument that presidential advisors have absolute immunity from congressional subpoenas, see Committee on the Judiciary v. Miers, 558 F. Supp. 2d 53 (D.D.C. 2008).

4

States and Foreign Relations

As discussed in Chapter 1, state interference in foreign relations was a significant problem during the Articles of Confederation period. The Constitution addressed this problem by enhancing the foreign relations powers of the national government vis-à-vis the states in a number of significant ways: Article I, Section 10 bars states from performing certain foreign relations functions, such as making treaties and engaging in war; Article I, Section 8 and Article II broadly authorize the federal political branches to conduct foreign relations through the enactment of federal statutes and treaties; the Supremacy Clause in Article VI establishes that these federal enactments are supreme over state law; Article III extends the federal judicial power to cases involving these federal enactments and to other transnational controversies; and the Take Care Clause in Article II authorizes the President to enforce federal enactments.

Because of the national government's broad constitutional authority over foreign relations, the United States' system of federalism might seem irrelevant to an understanding of U.S. foreign relations law. In fact, as the materials in this chapter illustrate, states are far from irrelevant to U.S. foreign relations. State law regulates many aspects of a foreign national's activities in the United States, and state courts often decide cases involving foreign parties or events. In addition, although states and municipalities are precluded from entering into treaties with foreign nations, they often engage in less formal international relations, such as sending international missions to foreign countries and establishing sister-city relationships. States and municipalities also sometimes take positions on international economic and political issues — through, for example, their purchasing and investment decisions. Even when such foreign relations activities trigger complaints by foreign governments or international institutions, the federal political branches often decline to preempt them.

This chapter introduces the theme of federalism and foreign relations. It begins with cases involving statutory and treaty preemption. These cases raise interpretive questions concerning how courts should determine whether federal political branch enactments have in fact preempted state authority. Next, the chapter turns to preemption doctrines not tied to a statute or treaty, namely, "Executive Branch preemption" (the power of the Executive Branch to take action in a way that results in preemption of state law) and "dormant foreign affairs preemption" (the power of federal courts to preempt state activities related to foreign affairs in the absence of political branch action). Subsequent chapters consider other federalism issues, including possible federalism-based limitations on the treaty power (Chapter 5), the preemption of state law through executive agreements (Chapter 6), and the relationship between customary international law and state law (Chapter 7).

Although the focus of this chapter is on federalism, the reader should pay close attention to the separation of powers issues implicated in the materials that follow. One of the underlying questions in these materials is whether federal *courts* should, in the absence of clear guidance from the federal *political branches*, limit state authority in the name of a federal foreign relations interest. In light of this question, consider whether the doctrines developed in this chapter are consistent with what you learned in Chapter 2 concerning the relative competence and authority of federal courts and the federal political branches in the foreign relations field. Consider also how the separation of powers issues in Chapter 3 concerning presidential-congressional relations in foreign relations differ from the separation of powers issues in this chapter.

A. STATUTORY PREEMPTION

Crosby v. National Foreign Trade Council

530 U.S. 363 (2000)

[In June 1996, Massachusetts adopted a statute that generally barred state entities from buying goods or services from any person or organization identified on a state-compiled "restricted purchase list" as doing business with Burma (also called Myanmar). The statute contained three exceptions: for situations in which the procurement was essential and, in the absence of the restricted bid, there would be no bids or insufficient competition; when the procurement was for medical supplies; or when the procurement efforts elicited no bids or offers that were less than 10 percent greater than the restricted bid.

In September 1996, Congress passed a statute imposing a set of mandatory and conditional sanctions on Burma. The federal statute imposed several sanctions directly on Burma—banning most federal aid to the Burmese government, instructing U.S. representatives in international financial institutions to vote against loans or other assistance to or for Burma, and providing that no entry visa was to be issued to any Burmese government official unless required by treaty or to staff the Burmese mission to the United Nations. These sanctions were to remain in effect "until such time as the President determines and certifies to Congress that Burma has made measurable and substantial progress in improving human rights practices and implementing democratic government." The federal statute also authorized the President to prohibit "United States persons" from "new investment" in Burma, and directed him to do so if he determined and certified to Congress that the Burmese government had physically harmed, rearrested, or exiled Aung San Suu Kyi (the opposition leader selected to receive the Nobel Peace Prize), or had committed "large-scale repression of or violence against the Democratic opposition." The statute also directed the President to work to develop "a comprehensive, multilateral strategy to bring democracy to and improve human rights practices and the quality of life in Burma." The statute further required the President to report periodically to certain committee chairmen on the progress toward democratization and better living conditions in Burma, as well as on the development of the required strategy. Finally, the statute authorized the President "to waive, temporarily or permanently, any sanction [under the federal statute] . . . if he determines and certifies to Congress that the application of such sanction would be contrary to the national security interests of the United States."

In May 1997, President Bill Clinton issued an executive order certifying that the government of Burma had "committed large-scale repression of the democratic opposition in Burma" and finding that the Burmese government's actions and policies constituted "an unusual and extraordinary threat to the national security and foreign policy of the United States," a threat characterized as a national emergency. The order proceeded to prohibit new investment in Burma "by United States persons," any approval or facilitation by a United States person of such new investment by foreign persons, and any transaction meant to evade or avoid the ban. The order generally incorporated the exceptions and exemptions in the statute. Finally, the order delegated to the Secretary of State the tasks of working with the Association of Southeast Asian Nations (ASEAN) and other countries to develop a strategy for promoting democracy, human rights, and quality of life in Burma, and of making the required congressional reports.

In this case, a trade group challenged the validity of the Massachusetts statute based on a variety of preemption arguments.]

JUSTICE SOUTER delivered the opinion of the Court. . . .

A fundamental principle of the Constitution is that Congress has the power to preempt state law. Art. VI, cl. 2. Even without an express provision for preemption, we have found that state law must yield to a congressional Act in at least two circumstances. When Congress intends federal law to "occupy the field," state law in that area is preempted. And even if Congress has not occupied the field, state law is naturally preempted to the extent of any conflict with a federal statute. Hines v. Davidowitz, 312 U.S. 52, 66-67 (1941). We will find preemption where it is impossible for a private party to comply with both state and federal law, . . . and where "under the circumstances of [a] particular case, [the challenged state law] stands as an obstacle to the accomplishment and execution of the full purposes and objectives of Congress." Hines, supra, at 67. What is a sufficient obstacle is a matter of judgment, to be informed by examining the federal statute as a whole and identifying its purpose and intended effects:

> For when the question is whether a Federal act overrides a state law, the entire scheme of the statute must of course be considered and that which needs must be implied is of no less force than that which is expressed. If the purpose of the act cannot otherwise be accomplished—if its operation within its chosen field else must be frustrated and its provisions be refused their natural effect—the state law must yield to the regulation of Congress within the sphere of its delegated power. Savage v. Jones, 225 U.S. 501, 533 (1912), quoted in Hines, supra, at 67, n.20.

Applying this standard, we see the state Burma law as an obstacle to the accomplishment of Congress's full objectives under the federal Act. We find that the state law undermines the intended purpose and "natural effect" of at least three provisions of the federal Act, that is, its delegation of effective discretion to the President to control economic sanctions against Burma, its limitation of sanctions solely to United States persons and new investment, and its directive to the President to proceed diplomatically in developing a comprehensive, multilateral strategy towards Burma.[8]

First, Congress clearly intended the federal act to provide the President with flexible and effective authority over economic sanctions against Burma. Although Congress immediately put in place a set of initial sanctions (prohibiting bilateral aid, support for international financial assistance, and entry by Burmese officials into the United States), it authorized the President to terminate any and all of those measures upon determining and certifying that there had been progress in human rights and democracy in Burma. It invested the President with the further power to ban new investment by United States persons, dependent only on specific Presidential findings of repression in Burma. And, most significantly, Congress empowered the President "to waive, temporarily or permanently, any sanction [under the federal act] . . . if he determines and certifies to Congress that the application of such sanction would be contrary to the national security interests of the United States."

This express investiture of the President with statutory authority to act for the United States in imposing sanctions with respect to the government of Burma, augmented by the flexibility to respond to change by suspending sanctions in the interest of national security, recalls Justice Jackson's observation in Youngstown Sheet & Tube Co. v. Sawyer, 343 U.S. 579, 635 (1952): "When the President acts pursuant to an express or implied authorization of Congress, his authority is at its maximum, for it includes all that he possesses in his own right plus all that Congress can delegate." See also id. at 635-36, n.2 (noting that the President's power in the area of foreign relations is least restricted by Congress and citing United States v. Curtiss-Wright Export Corp., 299 U.S. 304 (1936)). Within the sphere defined by Congress, then, the statute has placed the President in a position with as much discretion to exercise economic leverage against Burma, with an eye toward national security, as our law will admit. And it is just this plenitude of Executive authority that we think controls the issue of preemption here. The President has been given this authority not merely to make a political statement but to achieve a political result, and the fullness of his authority shows the importance in the congressional mind of reaching that result. It is simply implausible that Congress would have gone to such lengths to empower the President if it had been willing to compromise his effectiveness by deference to every provision of state statute or local ordinance that might, if enforced, blunt the consequences of discretionary Presidential action.

And that is just what the Massachusetts Burma law would do in imposing a different, state system of economic pressure against the Burmese political regime. As will be seen, the state statute penalizes some private action that the federal Act (as administered by the President) may allow, and pulls levers of influence that the federal Act does not reach. But the point here is that the state sanctions are immediate, and perpetual, there being no termination provision. This unyielding application undermines the President's intended statutory authority by making it impossible

---

8. We leave for another day a consideration in this context of a presumption against preemption. Assuming, *arguendo,* that some presumption against preemption is appropriate, we conclude, based on our analysis below, that the state Act presents a sufficient obstacle to the full accomplishment of Congress's objectives under the federal Act to find it preempted. *See* Hines v. Davidowitz, 312 U.S. 52, 67 (1941). Because our conclusion that the state Act conflicts with federal law is sufficient to affirm the judgment below, we decline to speak to field preemption as a separate issue, . . . or to pass on the First Circuit's rulings addressing the foreign affairs power or the dormant Foreign Commerce Clause. *See* Ashwander v. TVA, 297 U.S. 288, 346-47 (1936) (concurring opinion).

↑ would change burden of proof to state

for him to restrain fully the coercive power of the national economy when he may choose to take the discretionary action open to him, whether he believes that the national interest requires sanctions to be lifted, or believes that the promise of lifting sanctions would move the Burmese regime in the democratic direction. Quite simply, if the Massachusetts law is enforceable the President has less to offer and less economic and diplomatic leverage as a consequence. In Dames & Moore v. Regan, 453 U.S. 654 (1981), we used the metaphor of the bargaining chip to describe the President's control of funds valuable to a hostile country; here, the state Act reduces the value of the chips created by the federal statute. It thus "stands as an obstacle to the accomplishment and execution of the full purposes and objectives of Congress." *Hines,* 312 U.S. at 67.

Congress manifestly intended to limit economic pressure against the Burmese Government to a specific range. The federal Act confines its reach to United States persons, imposes limited immediate sanctions, places only a conditional ban on a carefully defined area of "new investment," and pointedly exempts contracts to sell or purchase goods, services, or technology. These detailed provisions show that Congress's calibrated Burma policy is a deliberate effort "to steer a middle path," *Hines, supra,* at 73.[13]

The State has set a different course, and its statute conflicts with federal law at a number of points by penalizing individuals and conduct that Congress has explicitly exempted or excluded from sanctions. While the state Act differs from the federal in relying entirely on indirect economic leverage through third parties with Burmese connections, it otherwise stands in clear contrast to the congressional scheme in the scope of subject matter addressed. It restricts all contracts between the State and companies doing business in Burma, except when purchasing medical supplies and other essentials (or when short of comparable bids). It is specific in targeting contracts to provide financial services, and general goods and services, to the Government of Burma, and thus prohibits contracts between the State and United States persons for goods, services, or technology, even though those transactions are explicitly exempted from the ambit of new investment prohibition when the President exercises his discretionary authority to impose sanctions under the federal Act.

As with the subject of business meant to be affected, so with the class of companies doing it: the state Act's generality stands at odds with the federal discreteness. The Massachusetts law directly and indirectly imposes costs on all companies that do any business in Burma, save for those reporting news or providing international telecommunications goods or services, or medical supplies. It sanctions companies promoting the importation of natural resources controlled by the government of Burma, or having any operations or affiliates in Burma. The state Act thus penalizes companies with pre-existing affiliates or investments, all of which lie beyond the reach of the federal Act's restrictions on "new investment" in Burmese economic development. The state Act, moreover, imposes restrictions on foreign companies as well as domestic, whereas the federal Act limits its reach to United States persons.

---

13. The fact that Congress repeatedly considered and rejected targeting a broader range of conduct lends additional support to our view. Most importantly, the federal Act, as passed, replaced the original proposed [statute], which barred "any investment in Burma" by a United States national without exception or limitation. Congress also rejected a competing amendment, which similarly provided that "United States nationals shall not make any investment in Burma," and would have permitted the President to impose conditional sanctions on the importation of "articles which are produced, manufactured, grown, or extracted in Burma," and would have barred all travel by United States nationals to Burma. Congress had rejected an earlier amendment that would have prohibited all United States investment in Burma, subject to the President's power to lift sanctions.

The conflicts are not rendered irrelevant by the State's argument that there is no real conflict between the statutes because they share the same goals and because some companies may comply with both sets of restrictions. The fact of a common end hardly neutralizes conflicting means, and the fact that some companies may be able to comply with both sets of sanctions does not mean that the state Act is not at odds with achievement of the federal decision about the right degree of pressure to employ. *See Hines,* 312 U.S. at 61 ("The basic subject of the state and federal laws is identical"); *id.* at 67 (finding conflict preemption). " 'Conflict is imminent'" when " 'two separate remedies are brought to bear on the same activity.'" Wisconsin Dept. of Industry v. Gould, Inc., 475 U.S. 282 (1986) (quoting Garner v. Teamsters, 346 U.S. 485, 498-99 (1953)). Sanctions are drawn not only to bar what they prohibit but to allow what they permit, and the inconsistency of sanctions here undermines the congressional calibration of force.

Finally, the state Act is at odds with the President's intended authority to speak for the United States among the world's nations in developing a "comprehensive, multilateral strategy to bring democracy to and improve human rights practices and the quality of life in Burma." Congress called for Presidential cooperation with members of ASEAN and other countries in developing such a strategy, directed the President to encourage a dialogue between the government of Burma and the democratic opposition, and required him to report to the Congress on the progress of his diplomatic efforts. As with Congress's explicit delegation to the President of power over economic sanctions, Congress's express command to the President to take the initiative for the United States among the international community invested him with the maximum authority of the National Government, *cf. Youngstown Sheet & Tube Co.,* 343 U.S. at 635, in harmony with the President's own constitutional powers, U.S. Const., Art. II, §2, cl. 2 ("[The President] shall have Power, by and with the Advice and Consent of the Senate, to make Treaties" and "shall appoint Ambassadors, other public Ministers and Consuls"); §3 ("[The President] shall receive Ambassadors and other public Ministers"). This clear mandate and invocation of exclusively national power belies any suggestion that Congress intended the President's effective voice to be obscured by state or local action.

Again, the state Act undermines the President's capacity, in this instance for effective diplomacy. It is not merely that the differences between the state and federal Acts in scope and type of sanctions threaten to complicate discussions; they compromise the very capacity of the President to speak for the Nation with one voice in dealing with other governments. We need not get into any general consideration of limits of state action affecting foreign affairs to realize that the President's maximum power to persuade rests on his capacity to bargain for the benefits of access to the entire national economy without exception for enclaves fenced off willy-nilly by inconsistent political tactics. When such exceptions do qualify his capacity to present a coherent position on behalf of the national economy, he is weakened, of course, not only in dealing with the Burmese regime, but in working together with other nations in hopes of reaching common policy and "comprehensive" strategy.

While the threat to the President's power to speak and bargain effectively with other nations seems clear enough, the record is replete with evidence to answer any skeptics. First, in response to the passage of the state Act, a number of this country's allies and trading partners filed formal protests with the National Government. . . . Second, the EU and Japan have gone a step further in lodging formal complaints against the United States in the World Trade Organization (WTO), claiming that the state Act violates certain provisions of the Agreement on Government Procurement, and the consequence has been to embroil the National Government for some time now in international dispute proceedings under the auspices of the WTO. In their brief before this Court, EU officials point to the WTO dispute as threatening relations with the United States, and note that the state Act has become the topic of "intensive discussions" with officials of the United States at the highest levels, those discussions including exchanges at the twice yearly EU-U.S. Summit. Third, the Executive has consistently represented that the state Act has complicated its dealings with foreign sovereigns and proven an impediment to accomplishing objectives assigned it by Congress. . . .[22] This evidence in combination is more than sufficient to show that the state Act stands as an obstacle in addressing the congressional obligation to devise a comprehensive, multilateral strategy. . . .

The State's remaining argument is unavailing. It contends that the failure of Congress to preempt the state Act demonstrates implicit permission. The State points out that Congress has repeatedly declined to enact express preemption provisions aimed at state and local sanctions, and it calls our attention to the large number of such measures passed against South Africa in the 1980s, which various authorities cited have thought were not preempted. The State stresses that Congress was aware of the state Act in 1996, but did not preempt it explicitly when it adopted its own Burma statute. The State would have us conclude that Congress's continuing failure to enact express preemption implies approval, particularly in light of occasional instances of express preemption of state sanctions in the past.

The argument is unconvincing on more than one level. A failure to provide for preemption expressly may reflect nothing more than the settled character of implied preemption doctrine that courts will dependably apply, and in any event, the existence of conflict cognizable under the Supremacy Clause does not depend on express congressional recognition that federal and state law may conflict, *Hines*, 312 U.S. at 67. The State's inference of congressional intent is unwarranted here, therefore, simply because the silence of Congress is ambiguous. Since we never ruled on whether state and local sanctions against South Africa in the 1980s were preempted or otherwise invalid, arguable parallels between the two sets of federal and state Acts do not tell us much about the validity of the latter.

Arizona v. United States

132 S. Ct. 2492 (2012)

JUSTICE KENNEDY delivered the opinion of the Court.

To address pressing issues related to the large number of aliens within its borders who do not have a lawful right to be in this country, the State of Arizona in 2010 enacted a statute called the Support Our Law Enforcement and Safe Neighborhoods Act. The law is often referred to as S.B. 1070. . . .

The United States filed this suit against Arizona, seeking to enjoin S.B. 1070 as preempted. Four provisions of the law are at issue here. Two create new state offenses. Section 3 makes failure to comply with federal alien-registration requirements a state misdemeanor. Section 5, in relevant part, makes it a misdemeanor for an unauthorized alien to seek or engage in work in the State; this provision is

---

22. The United States, in its brief as *amicus curiae,* continues to advance this position before us. This conclusion has been consistently presented by senior United States officials.

referred to as §5(C). Two other provisions give specific arrest authority and investigative duties with respect to certain aliens to state and local law enforcement officers. Section 6 authorizes officers to arrest without a warrant a person "the officer has probable cause to believe . . . has committed any public offense that makes the person removable from the United States." Section 2(B) provides that officers who conduct a stop, detention, or arrest must in some circumstances make efforts to verify the person's immigration status with the Federal Government.

The United States District Court for the District of Arizona issued a preliminary injunction preventing the four provisions at issue from taking effect. The Court of Appeals for the Ninth Circuit affirmed. . . .

The Government of the United States has broad, undoubted power over the subject of immigration and the status of aliens. This authority rests, in part, on the National Government's constitutional power to "establish an uniform Rule of Naturalization," U.S. Const., Art. I, §8, cl. 4, and its inherent power as sovereign to control and conduct relations with foreign nations. . . .

The federal power to determine immigration policy is well settled. Immigration policy can affect trade, investment, tourism, and diplomatic relations for the entire Nation, as well as the perceptions and expectations of aliens in this country who seek the full protection of its laws. Perceived mistreatment of aliens in the United States may lead to harmful reciprocal treatment of American citizens abroad.

It is fundamental that foreign countries concerned about the status, safety, and security of their nationals in the United States must be able to confer and communicate on this subject with one national sovereign, not the 50 separate States. . . . This Court has reaffirmed that "[o]ne of the most important and delicate of all international relationships . . . has to do with the protection of the just rights of a country's own nationals when those nationals are in another country." Hines v. Davidowitz, 312 U.S. 52 (1941).

Federal governance of immigration and alien status is extensive and complex. Congress has specified categories of aliens who may not be admitted to the United States. Unlawful entry and unlawful reentry into the country are federal offenses. Once here, aliens are required to register with the Federal Government and to carry proof of status on their person. Failure to do so is a federal misdemeanor. Federal law also authorizes States to deny noncitizens a range of public benefits; and it imposes sanctions on employers who hire unauthorized workers.

Congress has specified which aliens may be removed from the United States and the procedures for doing so. Aliens may be removed if they were inadmissible at the time of entry, have been convicted of certain crimes, or meet other criteria set by federal law. Removal is a civil, not criminal, matter. A principal feature of the removal system is the broad discretion exercised by immigration officials. Federal officials, as an initial matter, must decide whether it makes sense to pursue removal at all. If removal proceedings commence, aliens may seek asylum and other discretionary relief allowing them to remain in the country or at least to leave without formal removal.

Discretion in the enforcement of immigration law embraces immediate human concerns. Unauthorized workers trying to support their families, for example, likely pose less danger than alien smugglers or aliens who commit a serious crime. The equities of an individual case may turn on many factors, including whether the alien has children born in the United States, long ties to the community, or a record of distinguished military service. Some discretionary decisions involve policy choices that bear on this Nation's international relations. Returning an alien to his own country may be deemed inappropriate even where he has committed a removable offense or fails to meet the criteria for admission. The foreign state may be mired in civil war, complicit in political persecution, or enduring conditions that create a real risk that the alien or his family will be harmed upon return. The dynamic nature of relations with other countries requires the Executive Branch to ensure that enforcement policies are consistent with this Nation's foreign policy with respect to these and other realities. . . .

The pervasiveness of federal regulation does not diminish the importance of immigration policy to the States. Arizona bears many of the consequences of unlawful immigration. Hundreds of thousands of deportable aliens are apprehended in Arizona each year. Unauthorized aliens who remain in the State comprise, by one estimate, almost six percent of the population. And in the State's most populous county, these aliens are reported to be responsible for a disproportionate share of serious crime. . . .

Federalism, central to the constitutional design, adopts the principle that both the National and State Governments have elements of sovereignty the other is bound to respect. . . . From the existence of two sovereigns follows the possibility that laws can be in conflict or at cross-purposes. The Supremacy Clause provides a clear rule that federal law "shall be the supreme Law of the Land; and the Judges in every State shall be bound thereby, any Thing in the Constitution or Laws of any State to the Contrary notwithstanding." Art. VI, cl. 2. Under this principle, Congress has the power to preempt state law. *See* Crosby v. National Foreign Trade Council, 530 U.S. 363, 372 (2000). There is no doubt that Congress may withdraw specified powers from the States by enacting a statute containing an express preemption provision.

State law must also give way to federal law in at least two other circumstances. First, the States are precluded from regulating conduct in a field that Congress, acting within its proper authority, has determined must be regulated by its exclusive governance. The intent to displace state law altogether can be inferred from a framework of regulation "so pervasive . . . that Congress left no room for the States to supplement it" or where there is a "federal interest . . . so dominant that the federal system will be assumed to preclude enforcement of state laws on the same subject." Rice v. Santa Fe Elevator Corp., 331 U.S. 218, 230 (1947).

Second, state laws are preempted when they conflict with federal law. This includes cases where "compliance with both federal and state regulations is a physical impossibility," Florida Lime & Avocado Growers, Inc. v. Paul, 373 U.S. 132, 142-43 (1963) and those instances where the challenged state law "stands as an obstacle to the accomplishment and execution of the full purposes and objectives of Congress," *Hines,* 312 U.S. at 67; *see also Crosby, supra,* at 373. In preemption analysis, courts should assume that "the historic police powers of the States" are not superseded "unless that was the clear and manifest purpose of Congress." *Rice, supra,* at 230.

The four challenged provisions of the state law each must be examined under these preemption principles.

SECTION 3

Section 3 of S. B. 1070 creates a new state misdemeanor. It forbids the "willful failure to complete or carry an alien registration document . . . in violation of 8 United States Code section 1304(e) or 1306(a)." In effect, §3 adds a state-law penalty for conduct proscribed by federal law. The United States contends that this state enforcement mechanism intrudes on the field of alien registration, a field in which Congress has left no room for States to regulate.

The Court discussed federal alien-registration requirements in Hines v. Davidowitz, 312 U.S. 52 (1941). In 1940, as international conflict spread, Congress added to federal immigration law a "complete system for alien registration." *Id.* at 70. The new federal law struck a careful balance. It punished an alien's willful failure to register but did not require aliens to carry identification cards. There were also limits on the sharing of registration records and fingerprints. The Court found that Congress intended the federal plan for registration to be a "single integrated and all-embracing system." *Id.* at 74. Because this "complete scheme . . . for the registration of aliens" touched on foreign relations, it did not allow the States to "curtail or complement" federal law or to "enforce additional or auxiliary regulations." *Id.* at 66-67. As a consequence, the Court ruled that Pennsylvania could not enforce its own alien-registration program. *See id.* at 59.

The present regime of federal regulation is not identical to the statutory framework considered in *Hines*, but it remains comprehensive. Federal law now includes a requirement that aliens carry proof of registration. Other aspects, however, have stayed the same. Aliens who remain in the country for more than 30 days must apply for registration and be fingerprinted. Detailed information is required, and any change of address has to be reported to the Federal Government. The statute continues to provide penalties for the willful failure to register.

The framework enacted by Congress leads to the conclusion here, as it did in *Hines*, that the Federal Government has occupied the field of alien registration. . . . The federal statutory directives provide a full set of standards governing alien registration, including the punishment for noncompliance. It was designed as a "harmonious whole." *Hines, supra*, at 72. Where Congress occupies an entire field, as it has in the field of alien registration, even complementary state regulation is impermissible. Field preemption reflects a congressional decision to foreclose any state regulation in the area, even if it is parallel to federal standards.

Federal law makes a single sovereign responsible for maintaining a comprehensive and unified system to keep track of aliens within the Nation's borders. If §3 of the Arizona statute were valid, every State could give itself independent authority to prosecute federal registration violations, "diminish[ing] the [Federal Government]'s control over enforcement" and "detract[ing] from the 'integrated scheme of regulation' created by Congress." Wisconsin Dept. of Industry v. Gould, Inc., 475 U.S. 282, 288-89 (1986). Even if a State may make violation of federal law a crime in some instances, it cannot do so in a field (like the field of alien registration) that has been occupied by federal law. . . .

Arizona contends that §3 can survive preemption because the provision has the same aim as federal law and adopts its substantive standards. This argument not only ignores the basic premise of field preemption—that States may not enter, in any respect, an area the Federal Government has reserved for itself—but also is unpersuasive on its own terms. Permitting the State to impose its own penalties for the federal offenses here would conflict with the careful framework Congress adopted. Were §3 to come into force, the State would have the power to bring criminal charges against individuals for violating a federal law even in circumstances where federal officials in charge of the comprehensive scheme determine that prosecution would frustrate federal policies. . . .

SECTION 5(C)

Unlike §3, which replicates federal statutory requirements, §5(C) enacts a state criminal prohibition where no federal counterpart exists. The provision makes it a state misdemeanor for "an unauthorized alien to knowingly apply for work, solicit work in a public place or perform work as an employee or independent contractor" in Arizona. Violations can be punished by a $2,500 fine and incarceration for up to six months. The United States contends that the provision upsets the balance struck by the Immigration Reform and Control Act of 1986 (IRCA) and must be preempted as an obstacle to the federal plan of regulation and control. . . .

Th[e] comprehensive framework [in IRCA] does not impose federal criminal sanctions on the employee side (i.e., penalties on aliens who seek or engage in unauthorized work). . . .

The legislative background of IRCA underscores the fact that Congress made a deliberate choice not to impose criminal penalties on aliens who seek, or engage in, unauthorized employment. A commission established by Congress to study immigration policy and to make recommendations concluded these penalties would be "unnecessary and unworkable." Proposals to make unauthorized work a criminal offense were debated and discussed during the long process of drafting IRCA. But Congress rejected them. In the end, IRCA's framework reflects a considered judgment that making criminals out of aliens engaged in unauthorized work—aliens who already face the possibility of employer exploitation because of their removable status—would be inconsistent with federal policy and objectives.

IRCA's express preemption provision, which in most instances bars States from imposing penalties on employers of unauthorized aliens, is silent about whether additional penalties may be imposed against the employees themselves. But the existence of an "express pre-emption provisio[n] does *not* bar the ordinary working of conflict pre-emption principles" or impose a "special burden" that would make it more difficult to establish the preemption of laws falling outside the clause. Geier v. American Honda Motor Co., 529 U.S. 861, 869-72 (2000).

The ordinary principles of preemption include the well-settled proposition that a state law is preempted where it "stands as an obstacle to the accomplishment and execution of the full purposes and objectives of Congress." *Hines*, 312 U.S. at 67. Under §5(C), Arizona law would interfere with the careful balance struck by Congress with respect to unauthorized employment of aliens. Although §5(C) attempts to achieve one of the same goals as federal law—the deterrence of unlawful employment—it involves a conflict in the method of enforcement. The Court has recognized that a "[c]onflict in technique can be fully as disruptive to the system Congress enacted as conflict in overt policy." Motor Coach Employees v. Lockridge, 403 U.S. 274, 287 (1971). The correct instruction to draw from the text, structure, and history of IRCA is that Congress decided it would be inappropriate to impose criminal penalties on aliens who seek or engage in unauthorized employment. It follows that a state law to the contrary is an obstacle to the regulatory system Congress chose. Section 5(C) is preempted by federal law.

SECTION 6

Section 6 of S. B. 1070 provides that a state officer, "without a warrant, may arrest a person if the officer has probable cause to believe . . . [the person] has committed any public offense that makes [him] removable from the United States." The

United States argues that arrests authorized by this statute would be an obstacle to the removal system Congress created.

As a general rule, it is not a crime for a removable alien to remain present in the United States. If the police stop someone based on nothing more than possible removability, the usual predicate for an arrest is absent. When an alien is suspected of being removable, a federal official issues an administrative document called a Notice to Appear. The form does not authorize an arrest. Instead, it gives the alien information about the proceedings, including the time and date of the removal hearing. If an alien fails to appear, an *in absentia* order may direct removal.

The federal statutory structure instructs when it is appropriate to arrest an alien during the removal process. For example, the Attorney General can exercise discretion to issue a warrant for an alien's arrest and detention "pending a decision on whether the alien is to be removed from the United States." 8 U.S.C. §1226(a). And if an alien is ordered removed after a hearing, the Attorney General will issue a warrant. In both instances, the warrants are executed by federal officers who have received training in the enforcement of immigration law. If no federal warrant has been issued, those officers have more limited authority. They may arrest an alien for being "in the United States in violation of any [immigration] law or regulation," for example, but only where the alien "is likely to escape before a warrant can be obtained." §1357(a)(2).

Section 6 attempts to provide state officers even greater authority to arrest aliens on the basis of possible removability than Congress has given to trained federal immigration officers. Under state law, officers who believe an alien is removable by reason of some "public offense" would have the power to conduct an arrest on that basis regardless of whether a federal warrant has issued or the alien is likely to escape. This state authority could be exercised without any input from the Federal Government about whether an arrest is warranted in a particular case. This would allow the State to achieve its own immigration policy. The result could be unnecessary harassment of some aliens (for instance, a veteran, college student, or someone assisting with a criminal investigation) whom federal officials determine should not be removed.

This is not the system Congress created. Federal law specifies limited circumstances in which state officers may perform the functions of an immigration officer. A principal example is when the Attorney General has granted that authority to specific officers in a formal agreement with a state or local government. Officers covered by these agreements are subject to the Attorney General's direction and supervision. There are significant complexities involved in enforcing federal immigration law, including the determination whether a person is removable. As a result, the agreements reached with the Attorney General must contain written certification that officers have received adequate training to carry out the duties of an immigration officer.

By authorizing state officers to decide whether an alien should be detained for being removable, §6 violates the principle that the removal process is entrusted to the discretion of the Federal Government. A decision on removability requires a determination whether it is appropriate to allow a foreign national to continue living in the United States. Decisions of this nature touch on foreign relations and must be made with one voice. . . .

In defense of §6, Arizona notes a federal statute permitting state officers to "cooperate with the Attorney General in the identification, apprehension, detention, or removal of aliens not lawfully present in the United States." 8 U.S.C. §1357(g)(10)(B). There may be some ambiguity as to what constitutes cooperation under the federal law; but no coherent understanding of the term would incorporate the unilateral decision of state officers to arrest an alien for being removable absent any request, approval, or other instruction from the Federal Government. . . .

Congress has put in place a system in which state officers may not make warrant-less arrests of aliens based on possible removability except in specific, limited circumstances. By nonetheless authorizing state and local officers to engage in these enforcement activities as a general matter, §6 creates an obstacle to the full purposes and objectives of Congress. Section 6 is preempted by federal law.

SECTION 2(B)

Section 2(B) of S.B. 1070 requires state officers to make a "reasonable attempt . . . to determine the immigration status" of any person they stop, detain, or arrest on some other legitimate basis if "reasonable suspicion exists that the person is an alien and is unlawfully present in the United States." [The Court declines to rule that this provision is preempted, because there is "a basic uncertainty about what the law means and how it will be enforced" and thus "it would be inappropriate" at this stage "to assume §2(B) will be construed in a way that creates a conflict with federal law."]

. . . The National Government has significant power to regulate immigration. With power comes responsibility, and the sound exercise of national power over immigration depends on the Nation's meeting its responsibility to base its laws on a political will informed by searching, thoughtful, rational civic discourse. Arizona may have understandable frustrations with the problems caused by illegal immigration while that process continues, but the State may not pursue policies that undermine federal law.

JUSTICE SCALIA, concurring in part and dissenting in part.

. . . As a sovereign, Arizona has the inherent power to exclude persons from its territory, subject only to those limitations expressed in the Constitution or constitutionally imposed by Congress. . . .

There is no doubt that "before the adoption of the constitution of the United States" each State had the authority to "prevent [itself] from being burdened by an influx of persons." Mayor of New York v. Miln, 11 Pet. 102, 132-33 (1837). And the Constitution did not strip the States of that authority. To the contrary, two of the Constitution's provisions were designed to enable the States to prevent "the intrusion of obnoxious aliens through other States." Letter from James Madison to Edmund Randolph (Aug. 27, 1782), *in* 1 The Writings of James Madison 226 (1900). The Articles of Confederation had provided that "the free inhabitants of each of these States, paupers, vagbonds and fugitives from justice excepted, shall be entitled to all privileges and immunities of free citizens in the several States." Articles of Confederation, Art. IV. This meant that an unwelcome alien could obtain all the rights of a citizen of one State simply by first becoming an *inhabitant* of another. To remedy this, the Constitution's Privileges and Immunities Clause provided that "[t]he *Citizens* of each State shall be entitled to all Privileges and Immunities of Citizens in the several States." Art. IV, §2, cl. 1 (emphasis added). But if one State had particularly lax citizenship standards, it might still serve as a gateway for the entry of "obnoxious aliens" into other States. This problem was solved "by authorizing the general government to establish a uniform rule of naturalization throughout the United States." The Federalist No. 42; *see* Art. I, §8, cl. 4. In other words, the naturalization power was given to Congress not to abrogate States' power to exclude those they did not want, but to vindicate it.

Two other provisions of the Constitution are an acknowledgment of the States' sovereign interest in protecting their borders. Article I provides that "[n]o State shall, without the Consent of the Congress, lay any Imposts or Duties on Imports or Exports, *except what may be absolutely necessary for executing its inspection Laws.*" Art. I, §10, cl. 2 (emphasis added). This assumed what everyone assumed: that the States could exclude from their territory dangerous or unwholesome goods. A later portion of the same section provides that "[n]o State shall, without the Consent of Congress, . . . engage in War, *unless actually invaded, or in such imminent Danger as will not admit of delay.*" Art. I, §10, cl. 3 (emphasis added). This limits the States' sovereignty (in a way not relevant here) but leaves intact their inherent power to protect their territory.

Notwithstanding "[t]he myth of an era of unrestricted immigration" in the first 100 years of the Republic, the States enacted numerous laws restricting the immigration of certain classes of aliens, including convicted criminals, indigents, persons with contagious diseases, and (in Southern States) freed blacks. Gerald L. Neuman, The Lost Century of American Immigration (1776-1875), 93 Colum. L. Rev. 1833, 1835, 1841-80 (1993). State laws not only provided for the removal of unwanted immigrants but also imposed penalties on unlawfully present aliens and those who aided their immigration. . . .

In light of the predominance of federal immigration restrictions in modern times, it is easy to lose sight of the States' traditional role in regulating immigration—and to overlook their sovereign prerogative to do so. I accept as a given that State regulation is excluded by the Constitution when (1) it has been prohibited by a valid federal law, or (2) it conflicts with federal regulation—when, for example, it admits those whom federal regulation would exclude, or excludes those whom federal regulation would admit.   .

Possibility (1) need not be considered here: there is no federal law prohibiting the States' sovereign power to exclude (assuming federal authority to enact such a law). The mere existence of federal action in the immigration area—and the so-called field preemption arising from that action, upon which the Court's opinion so heavily relies, cannot be regarded as such a prohibition. We are not talking here about a federal law prohibiting the States from regulating bubble-gum advertising, or even the construction of nuclear plants. We are talking about a federal law going to the *core* of state sovereignty: the power to exclude. Like elimination of the States' other inherent sovereign power, immunity from suit, elimination of the States' sovereign power to exclude requires that "Congress . . . unequivocally expres[s] its intent to abrogate," Seminole Tribe of Fla. v. Florida, 517 U.S. 44, 55 (1996). Implicit "field preemption" will not do. . . .

What this case comes down to, then, is whether the Arizona law conflicts with federal immigration law—whether it excludes those whom federal law would admit, or admits those whom federal law would exclude. It does not purport to do so. It applies only to aliens who neither possess a privilege to be present under federal law nor have been removed pursuant to the Federal Government's inherent authority. I proceed to consider the challenged provisions in detail.

§6

. . . Arizona is *entitled* to have "its own immigration policy"—including a more rigorous enforcement policy—so long as that does not conflict with federal law. The Court says, as though the point is utterly dispositive, that "it is not a crime for a removable alien to remain present in the United States." It is not a federal crime, to be sure. But there is no reason Arizona cannot make it a state crime for a removable alien (or any illegal alien, for that matter) to remain present in Arizona. . . .

The Government complains that state officials might not heed "federal priorities." Indeed they might not, particularly if those priorities include willful blindness or deliberate inattention to the presence of removable aliens in Arizona. The State's whole complaint—the reason this law was passed and this case has arisen—is that the citizens of Arizona believe federal priorities are too lax. The State has the sovereign power to protect its borders more rigorously if it wishes, absent any valid federal prohibition. The Executive's policy choice of lax federal enforcement does not constitute such a prohibition.

§3

It is beyond question that a State may make violation of federal law a violation of state law as well. We have held that to be so even when the interest protected is a distinctively federal interest, such as protection of the dignity of the national flag, or protection of the Federal Government's ability to recruit soldiers. . . . Much more is that so when, as here, the State is protecting its *own* interest, the integrity of its borders. . . .

In some areas of uniquely federal concern—*e.g.,* fraud in a federal administrative process or perjury in violation of a federally required oath—this Court has held that a State has no legitimate interest in enforcing a federal scheme. But the federal alien registration system is certainly not of uniquely federal interest. States, private entities, and individuals rely on the federal registration system (including the E-Verify program) on a regular basis. Arizona's legitimate interest in protecting (among other things) its unemployment-benefits system is an entirely adequate basis for making the violation of federal registration and carry requirements a violation of state law as well.

The Court points out, however, that in some respects the state law exceeds the punishments prescribed by federal law: It rules out probation and pardon, which are available under federal law. The answer is that it makes no difference. Illegal immigrants who violate §3 violate *Arizona* law. It is one thing to say that the Supremacy Clause prevents Arizona law from excluding those whom federal law admits. It is quite something else to say that a violation of Arizona law cannot be punished more severely than a violation of federal law. Especially where (as here) the State is defending its own sovereign interests, there is no precedent for such a limitation. The sale of illegal drugs, for example, ordinarily violates state law as well as federal law, and no one thinks that the state penalties cannot exceed the federal. As I have discussed, moreover, "field preemption" cannot establish a prohibition of additional state penalties in the area of immigration. . . .

§5(C)

. . . Congress's intent with regard to exclusion of state law need not be guessed at, but is found in the law's express pre-emption provision, which excludes "any State or local law imposing civil or criminal sanctions (other than through licensing and similar laws) upon *those who employ, or recruit or refer for a fee for employment,* unauthorized aliens." §1324a(h)(2) (emphasis added). Common sense, reflected in the canon *expressio unius est exclusio alterius,* suggests that the specification of preemption for laws punishing "those who employ" implies the lack of pre-emption for other laws, including laws punishing "those who seek or accept employment."

The Court has no credible response to this. . . .

The Court concludes that §5(C) "would interfere with the careful balance struck by Congress," but that is easy to say and impossible to demonstrate. The Court relies primarily on the fact that "[p]roposals to make unauthorized work a criminal offense were debated and discussed during the long process of drafting [the Immigration Reform and Control Act of 1986 (IRCA)]," "[b]ut Congress rejected them." There is no more reason to believe that this rejection was expressive of a desire that there be no sanctions on employees, than expressive of a desire that such sanctions be left to the States. To tell the truth, it was most likely expressive of what inaction ordinarily expresses: nothing at all. . . .

Arizona has moved to protect its sovereignty—not in contradiction of federal law, but in complete compliance with it. The laws under challenge here do not extend or revise federal immigration restrictions, but merely enforce those restrictions more effectively. If securing its territory in this fashion is not within the power of Arizona, we should cease referring to it as a sovereign State. I dissent.

[Justices Thomas and Alito separately concurred in part and dissented in part.]

Notes and Questions

1. The Supremacy Clause makes clear that federal statutes can preempt state law. Sometimes Congress expressly states its intent to preempt. For example, the Employee Retirement Income Security Act (ERISA) provides that it "shall supersede any and all State laws insofar as they . . . relate to any employee benefit plan" covered by the Act. 29 U.S.C. §1144(a). Similarly, the federal copyright statute expressly preempts "legal or equitable rights [under state law] that are equivalent to any of the exclusive rights within the general scope of copyright as specified by [the federal statute]." 17 U.S.C. §301(a).

Most federal statutes, however, do not contain express preemption provisions. In these situations, preemption can still be found in the following circumstances: *Conflict preemption* occurs when it is impossible to comply with a federal statute (which is otherwise silent about preemption) and a state law. In this context, preemption follows by necessary implication from the fact of conflict. *Obstacle preemption* first identifies the "purposes and objectives" of a federal statute that is silent about preemptive scope; preemption follows if the state statute "stands as an obstacle to the accomplishment" of these purposes and objectives. *Field preemption* can occur in one of two ways. First, a federal regulatory scheme can be "so pervasive" as to imply that "Congress left no room for the States to supplement it." *See* English v. General Electric Co., 496 U.S. 72, 79 (1990). Second, a "federal interest" in the field addressed by a federal statute may be "so dominant" that federal law "will be assumed to preclude enforcement of state laws on the same subject." *See* Rice v. Santa Fe Elevator Corp., 331 U.S. 218, 230 (1947). The Supreme Court applied obstacle preemption in both *Crosby* and *Arizona*. The Court in *Arizona* also applied field preemption.

2. Article I, Section 10 of the Constitution prohibits the states from engaging in certain foreign relations functions, such as making treaties and engaging in war. Congress also has broad authority to use its Article I powers, such as its power to regulate interstate and foreign commerce, to expressly preempt state law relating to foreign affairs. Moreover, even in the absence of an express preemption provision, courts will override state laws that conflict with the requirements of federal law. In light of this, why is there a need for field and obstacle preemption? Because Congress cannot always anticipate a need for preemption when it enacts statutes? Because it is logistically difficult for Congress to enact preemptive legislation to respond to problematic state laws? At the end of its opinion in *Crosby*, the Court notes that Congress's failure to expressly preempt the state law there might have been due to Congress's assumption that the courts would preempt it. But is the Court's reasoning circular: Courts should not require express preemption because Congress is assuming that express preemption is not required?

3. As illustrated by *Crosby* and *Arizona*, obstacle and field preemption require courts to identify a statute's purposes and objectives. *See also* Karen A. Jordan, *The Shifting Preemption Paradigm: Conceptual and Interpretive Issues*, 51 Vand. L. Rev. 1149 (1998); Caleb Nelson, *Preemption*, 86 Va. L. Rev. 225 (2000). What were the purported federal statutory purposes and objectives in the two cases? How did the Supreme Court discern those purposes and objectives? Do courts have the competence, or the authority, to speculate about Congress's goals in this way, and to determine the appropriate level of generality at which to describe those goals? In the context of foreign relations statutes, does such judicial speculation entail the exercise of foreign policy judgment?

Under obstacle preemption, even if a court has correctly identified a statute's objectives, it must also determine whether the state law in question interferes with those objectives. What evidence should a court look at in resolving this issue? What weight did the Court in *Crosby* and *Arizona* give to Congress's failure to preempt the relevant state laws? To the views of the Executive Branch? To the views and complaints of foreign governments? What weight, if any, should be given to these sources?

4. Courts sometimes invoke presumptions to assist them in deciding whether a statute, silent on its face about preemption, nonetheless preempts state law. In the domestic context, courts often presume that Congress does not intend to preempt state laws, especially laws involving historic police powers of the states, unless Congress makes its preemptive intent clear. *See, e.g.*, Gregory v. Ashcroft, 501 U.S. 452, 464 (1991). This presumption is grounded in structural constitutional principles of federalism. It is designed to ensure that Congress considers the federal-state balance when enacting legislation and that any preemption of state law is attributable to the policy judgments of Congress, where the states are represented. *See, e.g.*, Kenneth Starr et al., The Law of Preemption 40-55 (1991); Laurence H. Tribe, 1 American Constitutional Law 1174-75 (3d ed. 2000); Paul Wolfson, *Preemption and Federalism: The Missing Link*, 16 Hastings Const. L.Q. 69, 111-14 (1988).

In many foreign relations contexts, however, courts do not appear to apply any such presumption. In fact, they arguably apply something like a presumption in favor of preemption. A leading example is Hines v. Davidowitz, 312 US 52 (1941), which was cited in both *Crosby* and *Arizona*. In *Hines*, the Supreme Court held that a Pennsylvania law requiring aliens to register once a year for a small fee and carry an identification card was preempted, on both obstacle and field preemption grounds, by a federal alien registration law, which contained different requirements. In considering the preemptive effect of the federal law, the Court in *Hines* stated that "it is of importance that this legislation is in a field which affects international relations, the one aspect of our government that, from the first, has been most generally conceded imperatively to demand broad national authority," and the Court added that "[a]ny concurrent state power that may exist is restricted to the narrowest of limits." *See also* Maryland v. Louisiana, 451 U.S. 725, 746 (1981) (citing *Hines* for the proposition that an "Act of Congress may touch a field in which the federal interest is so dominant that the federal system will be assumed to preclude enforcement of state laws on the same subject").

Is there a sound basis for relaxing, and perhaps even reversing, the presumption against preemption in the foreign relations context? Is this phenomenon based on the intuition that states do not have a legitimate interest in regulating matters that relate to foreign affairs? If so, is that intuition accurate? *See also* United States v. Locke, 529 U.S. 89, 108 (2000) ("The state laws now in question bear upon national and international maritime commerce, and in this area there is no beginning assumption that concurrent regulation by the State is a valid exercise of its police powers.").

5. In support of its conclusion that the Massachusetts statute stood as an obstacle to Congress's desire for the President to establish a "comprehensive, multilateral strategy" for dealing with Myanmar, the Court in *Crosby* cited the formal complaints lodged by the European Union and Japan against the United States in the World Trade Organization (WTO). The Court also noted that "EU officials point to the WTO dispute as threatening relations with the United States." The petitioners in *Crosby,* however, argued that the WTO proceedings, taken in context, demonstrated that the political branches did *not* wish to preempt the state law. First, when the case before the WTO was first brought, the Executive Branch criticized the action and pledged to "defend the [state] measure." Second, when Congress enacted implementing legislation for the WTO, it specified that U.S. courts could only declare state laws inconsistent with the WTO "in an action brought by the United States for the purpose of declaring such law or application invalid," 19 U.S.C. §3512(b)(2)(A), something that never occurred with respect to the Massachusetts statute. Should the Court have given more weight to these actions by the Executive Branch and Congress?

Crosby provoked substantial academic commentary that was noteworthy for its widely differing interpretations of the opinion. *See, e.g.,* Sarah H. Cleveland, Crosby *and the "One-Voice" Myth in U.S. Foreign Relations,* 46 Vill. L. Rev. 975, 1013 (2001); Jack L. Goldsmith, *Statutory Foreign Affairs Preemption,* 2001 Sup. Ct. Rev. 175; Daniel Halberstam, *The Foreign Affairs of Federal Systems: A National Perspective on the Benefits of State Participation,* 46 Vill. L. Rev. 1015, 1066 (2001); Robert Stumberg & Matthew C. Porterfield, *Who Preempted the Massachusetts Burma Law?: Federalism and Political Accountability Under the Global Trade Rules,* 31 Publius 173, 175 (2001); Edward Swaine, Crosby *as Foreign Relations Law,* 41 Va. J. Int'l L. 481 (2001); Mark Tushnet, *Globalization and Federalism in a Post-*Printz *World,* 36 Tulsa L.J. 11 (2000); Carlos Manuel Vazquez, *W[h]ither* Zschernig*?,* 46 Vill. L. Rev. 1259, 1323 (2001); Ernest A. Young, *Dual Federalism, Concurrent Jurisdiction, and the Foreign Affairs Exception,* 69 Geo. Wash. L. Rev. 139 (2001). For a more general account of the role of the states in foreign affairs, see Michael J. Glennon & Robert D. Sloane, Foreign Affairs Federalism: The Myth of National Exclusivity (2016).

6. In *Arizona,* the preemption of §3, which penalized failure to complete or carry a federal registration document, seemed to follow from the conclusion in *Hines* that the federal government's regulation of alien registration preempted the field. By contrast, the Court's analysis of §5 did not rely on field preemption. The Court instead ruled that the state law created an impermissible obstacle to the federal plan in the Immigration Reform and Control Act of 1986 (IRCA). One hurdle to this conclusion was that IRCA contains an express preemption provision that disallows state punishment of employers who hire unauthorized aliens but is silent on whether states may impose penalties against employees. Is Justice Scalia right to conclude in his dissent that the canon of *expressio unius* leads to the conclusion that Congress did not want to preempt state regulation of employees in this context?

The Court in *Arizona* also ruled that §6 of the state law, which authorized state officers to arrest removable aliens, was an obstacle to the related but somewhat narrower federal scheme for the arrest of removable aliens. What did the Court identify as the precise federal purpose that would be undermined by the state law in this context? With regard to preemption in this context and the others in the case, was the Court implicitly adopting a presumption in favor of preemption? Should the Court have given more weight to what Justice Scalia described as the states' "traditional role in regulating immigration"?

7. Before *Arizona*, a decision that was frequently cited as being in tension with *Hines* was De Canas v. Bica, 424 U.S. 321 (1976). In that case, California law prohibited the employment of illegal aliens if it would have an adverse impact on lawful resident workers. In concluding that the law was not preempted by federal immigration law, the Court reasoned that "States possess broad authority under their police powers to regulate the employment relationship to protect workers within the State." The Court distinguished *Hines* on the ground that the federal statute there was "in the specific field" in which the state was regulating, "while here there is no indication that Congress intended to preclude state law in the area of employment regulation." In *Arizona*, the Court dismissed the relevance of *De Canas*, observing that, in light of the comprehensive framework established by Congress in the Immigration Reform and Control Act of 1986, "[c]urrent federal law is substantially different from the regime that prevailed when *De Canas* was decided."

8. One important locus of legal disagreement about federalism and immigration in recent years has concerned "sanctuary jurisdictions." Sanctuary jurisdictions exist where state and local governmental entities have chosen to limit their cooperation with federal immigration authorities. They grew up in part as a response to the legal duties imposed by 8 U.S.C §1373, which (among other things) provides that "a Federal, State, or local government entity or official may not prohibit, or in any way restrict, any government entity or official from sending to, or receiving from, the Immigration and Naturalization Service information regarding the citizenship or immigration status, lawful or unlawful, of any individual." Policies adopted by sanctuary jurisdictions typically fall into one of three baskets: First, so-called "don't enforce" policies generally bar state or local police from assisting federal immigration authorities. Second, "don't ask" policies generally bar certain state or local officials from inquiring into a person's immigration status. Third, "don't tell" policies typically restrict information sharing between state or local law enforcement and federal immigration authorities. Congressional Research Service, *"Sanctuary" Jurisdictions: Federal, State, and Local Policies and Related Litigation* (May 3, 2019).

Shortly after taking office, President Trump issued Executive Order 13768, *Enhancing Public Safety in the Interior of the United States.* Section 9(a) of the Order directs the Attorney General and Secretary of Homeland Security to "ensure that jurisdictions that willfully refuse to comply with 8 U.S.C. §1373 (sanctuary jurisdictions) are not eligible to receive Federal grants, except as deemed necessary for law enforcement purposes by the Attorney General or the Secretary." Executive Order 13768, 82 Fed. Reg. 8799, 8801 (Jan. 25, 2017). A number of courts have ruled the Order is unconstitutional because, as one court put it, "Congress has the exclusive power to spend and has not delegated authority to the Executive to condition new grants on compliance with §1373." City and County of San Francisco v. Trump, 897

F.3d 1225 (9th Cir. 2018). For similar rulings against the order based on separation of powers, see City of Chicago v. Sessions, 888 F.3d 272 (7th Cir. 2018); City
of Philadelphia v. Sessions, 309 F. Supp. 3d 289 (E.D. Pa. 2018); City & County of
San Francisco v. Sessions, 349 F. Supp. 3d 924 (N.D. Cal. 2018). Of more relevance
to this chapter, however, is whether federal immigration law preempts sanctuary
city policies. The U.S. government, relying heavily on Arizona v. United States,
argued that it did, in a suit against the state of California. The suit sought to enjoin
California laws that (a) require employers to alert employees prior to federal immigration inspections, (b) prohibit state and local law enforcement agencies from
providing information regarding a person's date of release from incarceration and
other personal information, and (c) impose inspection requirements on facilities
that house civil immigration detainees. The U.S. Court of Appeals for the Ninth
Circuit declined to issue a preliminary injunction with respect to most of these provisions. See United States v. California, 921 F.3d 865 (9th Cir. 2019). The court reasoned that preemption was inappropriate for the employee notice provision since it
did not concern the relationship of employers to the federal government and thus
did not "undermine or disrupt the activities of federal immigration authorities." It
further reasoned that the limit on information sharing did not directly conflict with
8 U.S.C §1373. But the court held that one aspect of the inspection provision, which
required that the California Attorney General examine the circumstances surrounding the apprehension and transfer of federal immigration detainees, was subject
to a preliminary injunction because it entailed the imposition of a discriminatory
burden by a state on the federal government's activities, in violation of the constitutional doctrine of intergovernmental immunity. The court noted that "[t]his is
a novel requirement, apparently distinct from any other inspection requirements
imposed by California law."

A number of commentators have analyzed these and other issues relating to the
legality of sanctuary jurisdictions in recent years. See, e.g., Spencer E. Amdur, The
Right of Refusal: Immigration Enforcement and the New Cooperative Federalism, 35 Yale L. &
Pol'y Rev. 87 (2016); Barbara E. Armacost, "Sanctuary" Laws: The New Immigration
Federalism, 2016 Mich. St. L. Rev. 1197 (2016); Andrew B. Coan, Commandeering,
Coercion, and the Deep Structure of American Federalism, 95 B.U. L. Rev. 1 (2015);
Stella Burch Elias, The Perils and Possibilities of Refugee Federalism, 66 Am. U. L. Rev.
353 (2016); Christopher N. Lasch et al., Understanding "Sanctuary Cities," 59 B.C.
L. Rev. 1703 (2018); Peter Margulies, Deconstructing "Sanctuary Cities": The Legality
of Federal Grant Conditions that Require State and Local Cooperation on Immigration
Enforcement, 75 Wash. & Lee L. Rev. 1508 (2018); Elizabeth M. McCormick, Federal
Anti-Sanctuary Law: A Failed Approach to Immigration Enforcement and Poor Substitute for
Real Reform, 20 Lewis & Clark L. Rev. 165 (2016); David S. Rubenstein & Pratheepan
Gulasekaram, Immigration Exceptionalism, 111 Nw. U. L. Rev. 583 (2017); Richard
C. Schragger, The Attack on American Cities, 96 Tex. L. Rev. 1163 (2018). See also
Symposium, Immigration Law & Resistance: Ensuring a Nation of Immigrants, 52 U.C.
Davis L. Rev. 1 (2017).

B. TREATY PREEMPTION

Chapter 5 will focus extensively on the domestic status of treaties, including the judicial application of treaties to preempt state law and the general relationship of treaties
to principles of federalism. This section briefly addresses treaty preemption simply to

illustrate another way in which state foreign relations activities may be constrained. As we learned in Chapter 1, the failure of states to comply with treaty obligations, and the inability of the federal government to compel state compliance, was a significant problem under the Articles of Confederation. The constitutional Framers attempted to address this problem by, among other things, creating a Supremacy Clause that made treaties, in addition to federal statutes and the Constitution, supreme over state law.

Clark v. Allen

331 U.S. 503 (1947)

MR. JUSTICE DOUGLAS delivered the opinion of the Court.

Alvina Wagner, a resident of California, died in 1942, leaving real and personal property situate there. By a will dated December 23, 1941, and admitted to probate in a California court in 1942, she bequeathed her entire estate to four relatives who are nationals and residents of Germany. Six heirs-at-law, residents of California, filed a petition for determination of heirship in the probate proceedings claiming that the German nationals were ineligible as legatees under California law.[1]

There has never been a hearing on that petition. For in 1943 the Alien Property Custodian, to whose functions the Attorney General has recently succeeded, vested in himself all right, title and interest of the German nationals in the estate of this decedent. He thereupon instituted this action in the District Court against the executor under the will and the California heirs-at-law for a determination that they had no interest in the estate and that he was entitled to the entire net estate, after payment of administration and other expenses. The District Court granted judgment for the Custodian on the pleadings. The Circuit Court of Appeals . . . held for respondents. The case is here again on a petition for a writ of certiorari which we granted because the issues raised are of national importance.

First. Our problem starts with the Treaty of Friendship, Commerce and Consular Rights with Germany, signed December 8, 1923, and proclaimed October 14, 1925. It has different provisions governing the testamentary disposition of realty and personalty, which we will treat separately. The one pertaining to realty, contained in Article IV, reads as follows:

> Where, on the death of any person holding real or other immovable property or interests therein within the territories of one High Contracting Party, such property or interests therein would, by the laws of the country or by a testamentary disposition, descend or pass to a national of the other High Contracting Party, whether resident or

---

1. Section 259, California Probate Code, in 1942 provided:

The rights of aliens not residing within the United States or its territories to take either real or personal property or the proceeds thereof in this State by succession or testamentary disposition, upon the same terms and conditions as residents and citizens of the United States is dependent in each case upon the existence of a reciprocal right upon the part of citizens of the United States to take real and personal property and the proceeds thereof upon the same terms and conditions as residents and citizens of the respective countries of which such aliens are inhabitants and citizens and upon the rights of citizens of the United States to receive by payment to them within the United States or its territories money originating from the estates of persons dying within such foreign countries.

Section 259.2 provided:

If such reciprocal rights are not found to exist and if no heirs other than such aliens are found eligible to take such property, the property shall be disposed of as escheated property.

non-resident, were he not disqualified by the laws of the country where such property or interests therein is or are situated, such national shall be allowed a term of three years in which to sell the same, this term to be reasonably prolonged if circumstances render it necessary, and withdraw the proceeds thereof, without restraint or interference, and exempt from any succession, probate or administrative duties or charges other than those which may be imposed in like cases upon the nationals of the country from which such proceeds may be drawn.

The rights secured are in terms a right to sell within a specified time plus a right to withdraw the proceeds and an exemption from discriminatory taxation. It is plain that those rights extend to the German heirs of "any person" holding realty in the United States. And though they are not expressed in terms of ownership or the right to inherit, that is their import and meaning.

If, therefore, the provisions of the treaty have not been superseded or abrogated, they prevail over any requirements of California law which conflict with them. . . .

[The Court concludes that the treaty has not been superseded or abrogated, either by statute, treaty, or the outbreak of war, and that it therefore preempts inconsistent state law.]

. . . So far as the right of inheritance of realty under Article IV of the present treaty is concerned, we find no incompatibility with national policy, for reasons already given. . . .

Third. The problem of the personalty raises distinct questions. Article IV of the treaty contains the following provision pertaining to it:

Nationals of either High Contracting Party may have full power to dispose of their personal property of every kind within the territories of the other, by testament, donation, or otherwise, and their heirs, legatees and donees, of whatsoever nationality, whether resident or non-resident, shall succeed to such personal property, and may take possession thereof, either by themselves or by others acting for them, and retain or dispose of the same at their pleasure subject to the payment of such duties or charges only as the nationals of the High Contracting Party within whose territories such property may be or belong shall be liable to pay in like cases.

A practically identical provision of the Treaty of 1844 with Wurttemburg, Art. III, 8 Stat. 588, was before the Court in Frederickson v. Louisiana, 23 How. 445. In that case the testator was a citizen of the United States, his legatees being citizens and residents of Wurttemberg. Louisiana, where the testator was domiciled, levied a succession tax of 10 per cent on legatees not domiciled in the United States. The Court held that the treaty did not cover the "case of a citizen or subject of the respective countries residing at home, and disposing of property there in favor of a citizen or subject of the other . . ." That decision was made in 1860. In 1917 the Court followed it in cases involving three other treaties. Petersen v. Iowa, 245 U.S. 170; Duus v. Brown, 245 U.S. 176; Skarderud v. Tax Commission, 245 U.S. 633.

The construction adopted by those cases is, to say the least, permissible when the syntax of the sentences dealing with realty and personalty is considered. So far as realty is concerned, the testator includes "any person"; and the property covered is that within the territory of either of the high contracting parties. In case of personality, the provision governs the right of "nationals" of either contracting party to dispose of their property within the territory of the "other" contracting party; and it is "such personal property" that the "heirs, legatees and donees" are entitled to take.

Petitioner, however, presents a detailed account of the history of the clause which was not before the Court in Frederickson v. Louisiana, and which bears out the construction that it grants the foreign heir the right to succeed to his inheritance or the proceeds thereof. But we do not stop to review that history. For the consistent judicial construction of the language since 1860 has given it a character which the treaty-making agencies have not seen fit to alter. And that construction is entirely consistent with the plain language of the treaty. We therefore do not deem it appropriate to change that construction at this late date, even though as an original matter the other view might have much to commend it.

We accordingly hold that Article IV of the treaty does not cover personalty located in this country and which an American citizen undertakes to leave to German nationals. We do not know from the present record the nationality of Alvina Wagner. But since the issue arises on the Government's motion for judgment on the pleadings, we proceed on the assumption less favorable to it, viz., that she was an American citizen.

Fourth. It is argued, however, that even though the provision of the treaty is inapplicable, the personalty may not be disposed of pursuant to the California statute because that statute is unconstitutional. . . . The challenge to the statute is that it is an extension of state power into the field of foreign affairs, which is exclusively reserved by the Constitution to the Federal Government. That argument is based on the fact that under the statute the right of nonresident aliens to take by succession or testamentary disposition is dependent upon the existence of a reciprocal right on the part of citizens of the United States to take personalty on the same terms and conditions as residents and citizens of the other nation. The argument is that by this method California seeks to promote the right of American citizens to inherit abroad by offering to aliens reciprocal rights of inheritance in California. Such an offer of reciprocal arrangements is said to be a matter for settlement by the Federal Government on a nation-wide basis.

In Blythe v. Hinckley, 180 U.S. 333, California had granted aliens an unqualified right to inherit property within its borders. The alien claimant was a citizen of Great Britain with whom the United States had no treaty providing for inheritance by aliens in this country. The argument was that a grant of rights to aliens by a State was, in absence of a treaty, a forbidden entry into foreign affairs. The Court rejected the argument as being an extraordinary one. The objection to the present statute is equally farfetched.

Rights of succession to property are determined by local law. Those rights may be affected by an overriding federal policy, as where a treaty makes different or conflicting arrangements. Then the state policy must give way. *Cf.* Hines v. Davidowitz, 312 U.S. 52. But here there is no treaty governing the rights of succession to the personal property. Nor has California entered the forbidden domain of negotiating with a foreign country, United States v. Curtiss-Wright Corp., 299 U.S. 304, 316-17, or making a compact with it contrary to the prohibition of Article I, Section 10 of the Constitution. What California has done will have some incidental or indirect effect in foreign countries. But that is true of many state laws which none would claim cross the forbidden line.

Notes and Questions

1. Treaties differ from statutes in important respects. To become law, statutes require the agreement of a majority of both Houses of Congress and the President, or two-thirds of both Houses in situations in which the President vetoes the statute.

Treaties, by contrast, are made by the President with the advice and consent of two-thirds of the Senate. Unlike statutes, which might or might not be classified as implicating foreign relations, all treaties by definition implicate relations with other nations. Also unlike statutes, treaties have a dual domestic law/international law nature. Furthermore, as discussed in Chapter 5, only "self-executing" treaties preempt inconsistent state law. Thus with treaties, unlike with statutes, courts must answer the prior interpretive question of whether the treaty is self-executing before addressing the preemption question. Finally, as also discussed in Chapter 5, the Supreme Court has held that the treaty power is not limited to the scope of Congress's legislative powers. How, if at all, should these differences be reflected in different doctrines of preemption under the Supremacy Clause?

2. The first decision to strike down a state statute as inconsistent with a federal treaty was Ware v. Hylton, 3 U.S. 199 (1796). The Supreme Court held that the 1783 Treaty of Peace with Great Britain, which provided that British "creditors . . . shall meet with no lawful impediment to recovery . . . of all bona fide debts," preempted a 1780 Virginia statute that precluded such a recovery if the debt had already been paid to the state. *Ware* is also important for another reason: it was the first Supreme Court decision to exercise judicial review over the validity of state law. As David Currie has noted:

> The most important constitutional holding of Ware v. Hylton was that the federal courts had the power to determine the constitutionality of state laws. This crucial point, so painstakingly established with respect to federal laws a few years later in Marbury v. Madison, passed almost unnoticed.

David P. Currie, The Constitution in the Supreme Court: The First Hundred Years, 1789-1888, at 39 (1985).

3. Which presumptive canon—in favor of preemption, against preemption, or no presumption at all—is appropriate in the treaty context? The Supreme Court has not provided a clear answer to this question. Sometimes the Court has suggested that the general presumption against preemption should apply to treaties. *See, e.g.,* Guaranty Trust Co. v. United States, 304 U.S. 126, 143 (1938) ("Even the language of a treaty wherever reasonably possible will be construed so as not to override state laws or to impair rights arising under them."); United States v. Pink, 315 U.S. 203, 230 (1942) ("Even treaties . . . will be carefully construed so as not to derogate from the authority and jurisdiction of the States of this Nation unless clearly necessary to effectuate the national policy."). At other times, the Court has suggested that the presumption against preemption may not apply with respect to treaties. *See* El Al Israel Airlines v. Tseng, 525 U.S. 155, 175 (1999) (asserting that because "the nation-state, not subdivisions within one nation, is the focus of the [Warsaw] Convention and the perspective of our treaty partners, . . . [o]ur home-centered preemption analysis [with its presumption against preemption] . . . should not be applied, mechanically, in construing our international obligations"). What is the right approach? *Cf.* Bond v. United States, 572 U.S. 844, 858 (2014) (referring, in a case involving the interpretation of a federal statute that implemented a treaty, to the "well-established principle that ' "it is incumbent upon the federal courts to be certain of Congress' intent before finding that federal law overrides" ' the 'usual constitutional balance of federal and state powers' " (citations omitted). (*Bond* is excerpted in Chapter 5.)

4. What presumption, if any, was applied in Clark v. Allen? To what extent was the preemption analysis in these decisions affected by the nature of the state activity in question? Why did the Court in *Clark* conclude that the treaty did not apply to personal property?

5. *Clark* involved conflict preemption. The Supreme Court's decision in *Garamendi*, excerpted below in Section C, suggests that treaties, like federal statutes, can also provide a basis for field or obstacle preemption (although *Garamendi* involved executive agreements rather than a treaty concluded pursuant to the two-thirds senatorial consent process specified in Article II of the Constitution). If so, should the analysis for such preemption differ when it is based on a treaty rather than a statute?

6. For another example of treaty preemption, see In re World War II Era Japanese Forced Labor Litigation, 114 F. Supp. 2d 939 (N.D. Cal. 2000). In that case, a group of former U.S. and Allied prisoners of war sued various Japanese companies under a California statute for forced labor during World War II. The 1952 Treaty of Peace between Japan and the United States and its allies waived "all" reparations and "other claims" of the "nationals" of Allied powers "arising out of any actions taken by Japan and its nationals during the course of the prosecution of the war." The court ruled that this unambiguous waiver provision, especially in light of the treaty negotiation records, ratification history, and subsequent treaty practice, required preemption of the California statute. The court further noted that its view accorded with the view of the Executive Branch, which it said "carries significant weight." Is this deference appropriate? Recall the discussion in Chapter 2 of deference to the Executive Branch in the treaty context.

7. A federal statute can preempt state law only if the statute is constitutionally valid. Is this also true of treaties? If so, to what extent are treaties subject to procedural or substantive constitutional limitations? These questions are considered in Chapter 5.

C. DORMANT AND EXECUTIVE BRANCH PREEMPTION

Zschernig v. Miller

389 U.S. 429 (1968)

MR. JUSTICE DOUGLAS delivered the opinion of the Court.

This case concerns the disposition of the estate of a resident of Oregon who died there intestate in 1962. Appellants are decedent's sole heirs and they are residents of East Germany. Appellees include members of the State Land Board that petitioned the Oregon probate court for the escheat of the net proceeds of the estate under the provisions of Ore. Rev. Stat. §111.070 (1957), which provides for escheat in cases where a nonresident alien claims real or personal property unless three requirements are satisfied:

> (1) the existence of a reciprocal right of a United States citizen to take property on the same terms as a citizen or inhabitant of the foreign country;
> (2) the right of United States citizens to receive payment here of funds from estates in the foreign country; and
> (3) the right of the foreign heirs to receive the proceeds of Oregon estates "without confiscation."

The Oregon Supreme Court held that the appellants could take the Oregon realty involved in the present case by reason of Article IV of the 1923 Treaty of

Friendship, Commerce and Consular Rights with Germany but that by reason of the same Article, as construed in Clark v. Allen, 331 U.S. 503 (1947), they could not take the personalty. We noted probable jurisdiction.

The Department of Justice, appearing as *amicus curiae*, submits that, although the 1923 Treaty is still in force, Clark v. Allen should be overruled insofar as it construed the personalty provision of Article IV. That portion of Article IV speaks of the rights of "nationals of either High Contracting Party" to dispose of "their personal property of every kind within the territories of the other." That literal language and its long consistent construction, we held in Clark v. Allen, "does not cover personalty located in this country and which an American citizen undertakes to leave to German nationals."

We do not accept the invitation to re-examine our ruling in Clark v. Allen. For we conclude that the history and operation of this Oregon statute make clear that §111.070 is an intrusion by the State into the field of foreign affairs which the Constitution entrusts to the President and the Congress. *See* Hines v. Davidowitz.

[O]ne of the conditions of inheritance under the Oregon statute requires "proof that such foreign heirs, distributees, devisees or legatees may receive the benefit, use or control of money or property from estates of persons dying in this state without confiscation, in whole or in part, by the governments of such foreign countries," the burden being on the nonresident alien to establish that fact.

This provision came into Oregon's law in 1951. Prior to that time the rights of aliens under the Oregon statute were defined in general terms of reciprocity, similar to the California Act which we had before us in Clark v. Allen. We held in Clark v. Allen that a general reciprocity clause did not on its face intrude on the federal domain. We noted that the California statute, then a recent enactment, would have only "some incidental or indirect effect in foreign countries."

Had that case appeared in the posture of the present one, a different result would have obtained. We were there concerned with the words of a statute on its face, not the manner of its application. State courts, of course, must frequently read, construe, and apply laws of foreign nations. It has never been seriously suggested that state courts are precluded from performing that function, albeit there is a remote possibility that any holding may disturb a foreign nation — whether the matter involves commercial cases, tort cases, or some other type of controversy. At the time Clark v. Allen was decided, the case seemed to involve no more than a routine reading of foreign laws. It now appears that in this reciprocity area under inheritance statutes, the probate courts of various States have launched inquiries into the type of governments that obtain in particular foreign nations — whether aliens under their law have enforceable rights, whether the so-called "rights" are merely dispensations turning upon the whim or caprice of government officials, whether the representation of consuls, ambassadors, and other representatives of foreign nations is credible or made in good faith, whether there is in the actual administration in the particular foreign system of law any element of confiscation. . . .

In its brief *amicus curiae*, the Department of Justice states that: "The government does not . . . contend that the application of the Oregon escheat statute in the circumstances of this case unduly interferes with the United States' conduct of foreign relations."

The Government's acquiescence in the ruling of Clark v. Allen certainly does not justify extending the principle of that case, as we would be required to do here to uphold the Oregon statute as applied; for it has more than "some incidental or indirect effect in foreign countries," and its great potential for disruption or embarrassment makes us hesitate to place it in the category of a diplomatic bagatelle.

As we read the decisions that followed in the wake of Clark v. Allen, we find that they radiate some of the attitudes of the "cold war," where the search is for the "democracy quotient" of a foreign regime as opposed to the Marxist theory. The Oregon statute introduces the concept of "confiscation," which is of course opposed to the Just Compensation Clause of the Fifth Amendment. And this has led into minute inquiries concerning the actual administration of foreign law, into the credibility of foreign diplomatic statements, and into speculation whether the fact that some received delivery of funds should "not preclude wonderment as to how many may have been denied 'the right to receive.'" *See* State Land Board v. Kolovrat, 220 Ore. 448, 461-62, 349 P.2d 255, 262, *rev'd sub nom.* Kolovrat v. Oregon, 366 U.S. 187, on other grounds. . . .

That kind of state involvement in foreign affairs and international relations — matters which the Constitution entrusts solely to the Federal Government — is not sanctioned by Clark v. Allen. Yet such forbidden state activity has infected each of the three provisions of §111.070, as applied by Oregon. . . . As one reads the Oregon decisions, it seems that foreign policy attitudes, the freezing or thawing of the "cold war," and the like are the real desiderata. Yet they of course are matters for the Federal Government, not for local probate courts. In short, it would seem that Oregon judges in construing §111.070 seek to ascertain whether "rights" protected by foreign law are the same "rights" that citizens of Oregon enjoy. . . . The statute as construed seems to make unavoidable judicial criticism of nations established on a more authoritarian basis than our own.

It seems inescapable that the type of probate law that Oregon enforces affects international relations in a persistent and subtle way. The practice of state courts in withholding remittances to legatees residing in Communist countries or in preventing them from assigning them is notorious. The several States, of course, have traditionally regulated the descent and distribution of estates. But those regulations must give way if they impair the effective exercise of the Nation's foreign policy. Where those laws conflict with a treaty, they must bow to the superior federal policy. Yet, even in absence of a treaty, a State's policy may disturb foreign relations. As we stated in Hines v. Davidowitz: "Experience has shown that international controversies of the gravest moment, sometimes even leading to war, may arise from real or imagined wrongs to another's subjects inflicted, or permitted, by a government." Certainly a State could not deny admission to a traveler from East Germany nor bar its citizens from going there. If there are to be such restraints, they must be provided by the Federal Government. The present Oregon law is not as gross an intrusion in the federal domain as those others might be. Yet, as we have said, it has a direct impact upon foreign relations and may well adversely affect the power of the central government to deal with those problems.

The Oregon law does, indeed, illustrate the dangers which are involved if each State, speaking through its probate courts, is permitted to establish its own foreign policy.

MR. JUSTICE HARLAN, concurring in the result. . . .

[Justice Harlan first argues that the Oregon statute is preempted by the 1923 treaty, even with respect to the inheritance of personal property.]

Upon my view of this case, it would be unnecessary to reach the issue whether Oregon's statute governing inheritance by aliens amounts to an unconstitutional infringement upon the foreign relations power of the Federal Government. However, since this is the basis upon which the Court has chosen to rest its decision, I feel that I should indicate briefly why I believe the decision to be wrong on that score, too. . . .

Prior decisions have established that in the absence of a conflicting federal policy or violation of the express mandates of the Constitution the States may legislate in areas of their traditional competence even though their statutes may have an incidental effect on foreign relations. Application of this rule to the case before us compels the conclusion that the Oregon statute is constitutional. Oregon has so legislated in the course of regulating the descent and distribution of estates of Oregon decedents, a matter traditionally within the power of a State. Apart from the 1923 treaty, which the Court finds it unnecessary to consider, there is no specific interest of the Federal Government which might be interfered with by this statute. The appellants concede that Oregon might deny inheritance rights to all nonresident aliens. Assuming that this is so, the statutory exception permitting inheritance by aliens whose countries permit Americans to inherit would seem to be a measure wisely designed to avoid any offense to foreign governments and thus any conflict with general federal interests: a foreign government can hardly object to the denial of rights which it does not itself accord to the citizens of other countries.

The foregoing would seem to establish that the Oregon statute is not unconstitutional on its face. And in fact the Court seems to have found the statute unconstitutional only as applied. Its notion appears to be that application of the parts of the statute which require that reciprocity actually exist and that the alien heir actually be able to enjoy his inheritance will inevitably involve the state courts in evaluations of foreign laws and governmental policies, and that this is likely to result in offense to foreign governments. There are several defects in this rationale. The most glaring is that it is based almost entirely on speculation. My Brother Douglas does cite a few unfortunate remarks made by state court judges in applying statutes resembling the one before us. However, the Court does not mention, nor does the record reveal, any instance in which such an occurrence has been the occasion for a diplomatic protest, or, indeed, has had any foreign relations consequence whatsoever. The United States says in its brief as *amicus curiae* that it

> does not . . . contend that the application of the Oregon escheat statute in the circumstances of this case unduly interferes with the United States' conduct of foreign relations.

At an earlier stage in this case, the Solicitor General told this Court:

> The Department of State has advised us . . . that State reciprocity laws, including that of Oregon, have had little effect on the foreign relations and policy of this country. . . . Appellants' apprehension of a deterioration in international relations, unsubstantiated by experience, does not constitute the kind of "changed conditions" which might call for re-examination of Clark v. Allen.

Essentially, the Court's basis for decision appears to be that alien inheritance laws afford state court judges an opportunity to criticize in dictum the policies of foreign governments, and that these dicta may adversely affect our foreign relations. In addition to finding no evidence of adverse effect in the record, I believe this rationale to be untenable because logically it would apply to many other types of litigation which come before the state courts. It is true that, in addition to the many state court judges who have applied alien inheritance statutes with proper judicial decorum, some judges have seized the opportunity to make derogatory remarks about foreign governments. However, judges have been known to utter dicta critical of foreign governmental policies even in purely domestic cases, so that the mere possibility of offensive utterances can hardly be the test.

If the flaw in the statute is said to be that it requires state courts to inquire into the administration of foreign law, I would suggest that that characteristic is shared by other legal rules which I cannot believe the Court wishes to invalidate. For example, the Uniform Foreign Money-Judgments Recognition Act provides that a foreign-country money judgment shall not be recognized if it "was rendered under a system which does not provide impartial tribunals or procedures compatible with the requirements of due process of law." When there is a dispute as to the content of foreign law, the court is required under the common law to treat the question as one of fact and to consider any evidence presented as to the actual administration of the foreign legal system. And in the field of choice of law there is a nonstatutory rule that the tort law of a foreign country will not be applied if that country is shown to be "uncivilized." Surely, all of these rules possess the same "defect" as the statute now before us. Yet I assume that the Court would not find them unconstitutional.

American Insurance Association v. Garamendi

539 U.S. 396 (2003)

[The proceeds of many life insurance policies issued to Jews in Europe before World War II were never paid to the policyholders or their heirs, either because the proceeds were confiscated by the Nazis, the insurance companies denied the existence of the policies or claimed that they had lapsed from unpaid premiums, or the German government would not provide heirs with documentation of the policyholder's death. In 1999, California enacted the Holocaust Victim Insurance Relief Act (HVIRA). This statute required any insurer doing business in California to disclose information about all policies sold in Europe between 1920 and 1945 by the company itself or by any company related to it. After the war, the United States entered into a number of reparations agreements to resolve claims against Germany. These agreements included, most recently, the German Foundation Agreement, signed by President Clinton and German Chancellor Schröder in July 2000. In this agreement, Germany agreed to enact legislation establishing a foundation funded with 10 billion deutsche marks, contributed equally by the German government and German companies, to be used to compensate all those "who suffered at the hands of German companies during the National Socialist era." The President entered into similar agreements with Austria and France. In the agreements, the United States promised that it would try to persuade its courts, and state and local governments, to respect the foundations as the exclusive means for resolving World War II-era claims against private companies. The agreements also provided that the foundations would work with a voluntary organization — the International Commission on Holocaust Era Insurance Claims (ICHEIC) — to determine and settle outstanding insurance claims. The petitioners in this case, American and European insurance companies, challenged the validity of HVIRA.]

JUSTICE SOUTER delivered the opinion of the Court. . . .

The principal argument for preemption made by petitioners and the United States as *amicus curiae* is that HVIRA interferes with foreign policy of the Executive Branch, as expressed principally in the executive agreements with Germany, Austria, and France. The major premises of the argument, at least, are beyond dispute. There is, of course, no question that at some point an exercise of state power that touches on foreign relations must yield to the National Government's policy, given the "concern for uniformity in this country's dealings with foreign nations" that animated the Constitution's allocation of the foreign relations power to the National Government in the first place. Banco Nacional de Cuba v. Sabbatino, 376 U.S. 398, 427, n.25 (1964). . . .

Nor is there any question generally that there is executive authority to decide what that policy should be. Although the source of the President's power to act in foreign affairs does not enjoy any textual detail, the historical gloss on the "executive Power" vested in Article II of the Constitution has recognized the President's "vast share of responsibility for the conduct of our foreign relations." Youngstown Sheet & Tube Co. v. Sawyer, 343 U.S. 579, 610-11 (1952) (Frankfurter, J., concurring). While Congress holds express authority to regulate public and private dealings with other nations in its war and foreign commerce powers, in foreign affairs the President has a degree of independent authority to act. . . .

At a more specific level, our cases have recognized that the President has authority to make "executive agreements" with other countries, requiring no ratification by the Senate or approval by Congress, this power having been exercised since the early years of the Republic. *See* Dames & Moore v. Regan, 453 U.S. 654, 679, 682-83 (1981); United States v. Pink, 315 U.S. 203, 223, 230 (1942); United States v. Belmont, 301 U.S. 324, 330-31 (1937). . . . Given the fact that the practice goes back over 200 years to the first Presidential administration, and has received congressional acquiescence throughout its history, the conclusion "that the President's control of foreign relations includes the settlement of claims is indisputable." *Pink, supra,* at 240 (Frankfurter, J., concurring). . . .

The executive agreements at issue here do differ in one respect from those just mentioned insofar as they address claims associated with formerly belligerent states, but against corporations, not the foreign governments. But the distinction does not matter. Historically, wartime claims against even nominally private entities have become issues in international diplomacy, and three of the postwar settlements dealing with reparations implicating private parties were made by the Executive alone.[8] Acceptance of this historical practice is supported by a good pragmatic reason for depending on executive agreements to settle claims against foreign corporations associated with wartime experience. As shown by the history of insurance confiscation mentioned earlier, untangling government policy from private initiative during war time is often so hard that diplomatic action settling claims against private parties may well be just as essential in the aftermath of hostilities as diplomacy to settle claims against foreign governments. While a sharp line between public and private acts works for many purposes in the domestic law, insisting on the same line in defining the legitimate scope of the Executive's international negotiations would hamstring the President in settling international controversies.

---

8. The Yalta and Potsdam Agreements envisioning dismantling of Germany's industrial assets, public and private, and the follow-up Paris Agreement aspiring to settle the claims of western nationals against the German Government and private agencies were made as executive agreements.

Generally, then, valid executive agreements are fit to preempt state law, just as treaties are,[9] and if the agreements here had expressly preempted laws like HVIRA, the issue would be straightforward. But petitioners and the United States as *amicus curiae* both have to acknowledge that the agreements include no preemption clause, and so leave their claim of preemption to rest on asserted interference with the foreign policy those agreements embody. Reliance is placed on our decision in Zschernig v. Miller, 389 U.S. 429 (1968). . . .

[The Court describes both the majority opinion and Justice Harlan's concurrence in *Zschernig*.]

It is a fair question whether respect for the executive foreign relations power requires a categorical choice between the contrasting theories of field and conflict preemption evident in the *Zschernig* opinions,[11] but the question requires no answer here. For even on Justice Harlan's view, the likelihood that state legislation will produce something more than incidental effect in conflict with express foreign policy of the National Government would require preemption of the state law. And since on his view it is legislation within "areas of . . . traditional competence" that gives a State any claim to prevail, it would be reasonable to consider the strength of the state interest, judged by standards of traditional practice, when deciding how serious a conflict must be shown before declaring the state law preempted. . . . Judged by these standards, we think petitioners and the Government have demonstrated a sufficiently clear conflict to require finding preemption here.

IV

A

To begin with, resolving Holocaust-era insurance claims that may be held by residents of this country is a matter well within the Executive's responsibility for foreign affairs. Since claims remaining in the aftermath of hostilities may be "sources of friction" acting as an "impediment to resumption of friendly relations" between the countries involved, *Pink, supra,* at 225, there is a "longstanding practice" of the national Executive to settle them in discharging its responsibility to maintain the Nation's relationships with other countries, *Dames & Moore,* 453 U.S. at 679. The issue of restitution for Nazi crimes has in fact been addressed in Executive Branch diplomacy and formalized in treaties and executive agreements over the last half century, and although resolution of private claims was postponed by the Cold War, securing private interests is an express object of diplomacy today, just as it

9. Subject, that is, to the Constitution's guarantees of individual rights. *See* Reid v. Covert, 354 U.S. 1, 15-19 (1957); Boos v. Barry, 485 U.S. 312, 324 (1988). Even Justice Sutherland's reading of the National Governments "inherent" foreign affairs power in United States v. Curtiss-Wright Export Corp., 299 U.S. 304 (1936), contained the caveat that the power, "like every other governmental power, must be exercised in subordination to the applicable provisions of the Constitution." *Id.* at 320.

11. The two positions can be seen as complementary. If a State were simply to take a position on a matter of foreign policy with no serious claim to be addressing a traditional state responsibility, field preemption might be the appropriate doctrine, whether the National Government had acted and, if it had, without reference to the degree of any conflict, the principle having been established that the Constitution entrusts foreign policy exclusively to the National Government. *See, e.g.,* Hines v. Davidowitz, 312 U.S. 52, 63 (1941). Where, however, a State has acted within what Justice Harlan called its "traditional competence," *Zschernig,* 389 U.S. at 459, but in a way that affects foreign relations, it might make good sense to require a conflict, of a clarity or substantiality that would vary with the strength or the traditional importance of the state concern asserted. Whether the strength of the federal foreign policy interest should itself be weighed is, of course, a further question. . . .

was addressed in agreements soon after the Second World War. Vindicating victims injured by acts and omissions of enemy corporations in wartime is thus within the traditional subject matter of foreign policy in which national, not state, interests are overriding, and which the National Government has addressed.

The exercise of the federal executive authority means that state law must give way where, as here, there is evidence of clear conflict between the policies adopted by the two. The foregoing account of negotiations toward the three settlement agreements is enough to illustrate that the consistent Presidential foreign policy has been to encourage European governments and companies to volunteer settlement funds in preference to litigation or coercive sanctions. . . . As for insurance claims in particular, the national position, expressed unmistakably in the executive agreements signed by the President with Germany and Austria, has been to encourage European insurers to work with the ICHEIC to develop acceptable claim procedures, including procedures governing disclosure of policy information. . . . This position, of which the agreements are exemplars, has also been consistently supported in the high levels of the Executive Branch, as mentioned already. . . .[12] The approach taken serves to resolve the several competing matters of national concern apparent in [the language of] the German Foundation Agreement: the national interest in maintaining amicable relationships with current European allies; survivors' interests in a "fair and prompt" but nonadversarial resolution of their claims so as to "bring some measure of justice . . . in their lifetimes"; and the companies' interest in securing "legal peace" when they settle claims in this fashion. As a way for dealing with insurance claims, moreover, the voluntary scheme protects the companies' ability to abide by their own countries' domestic privacy laws limiting disclosure of policy information.

California has taken a different tack of providing regulatory sanctions to compel disclosure and payment, supplemented by a new cause of action for Holocaust survivors if the other sanctions should fail. The situation created by the California legislation calls to mind the impact of the Massachusetts Burma law on the effective exercise of the President's power, as recounted in the statutory preemption case, Crosby v. National Foreign Trade Council, 530 U.S. 363 (2000). HVIRA's economic compulsion to make public disclosure, of far more information about far more policies than ICHEIC rules require, employs "a different, state system of economic pressure," and in doing so undercuts the President's diplomatic discretion and the choice he has made exercising it. *Id.* at 376. Whereas the President's authority to provide for settling claims in winding up international hostilities requires flexibility in wielding "the coercive power of the national economy" as a tool of diplomacy, *id.* at 377, HVIRA denies this, by making exclusion from a large sector of the American insurance market the automatic sanction for noncompliance with the State's own policies on disclosure. "Quite simply, if the [California] law is enforceable the President has less to offer and less economic and diplomatic leverage as a consequence." *Ibid.* (citing *Dames & Moore*, 453 U.S. at 673). The law thus "compromises the very capacity of the President to speak for the Nation with one voice in dealing

12. In Barclays Bank PLC v. Franchise Tax Bd. of Cal., 512 U.S. 298, 328-30 (1994), we declined to give policy statements by Executive Branch officials conclusive weight as against an opposing congressional policy in determining whether California's "worldwide combined reporting" tax method violated the Foreign Commerce Clause. The reason, we said, is that "the Constitution expressly grants Congress, not the President, the power to regulate Commerce with foreign Nations." *Id.* at 329 (quoting Art. I, §8, cl. 3). As we have discussed, however, in the field of foreign policy, the President has the "lead role." First Nat. City Bank v. Banco Nacional de Cuba, 406 U.S. 759, 767 (1972).

with other governments" to resolve claims against European companies arising out of World War II. 530 U.S. at 381.[14]

Crosby's facts are replicated again in the way HVIRA threatens to frustrate the operation of the particular mechanism the President has chosen. The letters from Deputy Secretary Eizenstat to California officials show well enough how the portent of further litigation and sanctions has in fact placed the Government at a disadvantage in obtaining practical results from persuading "foreign governments and foreign companies to participate voluntarily in organizations such as ICHEIC." Brief for United States as Amicus Curiae 15. . . . In addition to thwarting the Government's policy of repose for companies that pay through the ICHEIC, California's indiscriminate disclosure provisions place a handicap on the ICHEIC's effectiveness (and raise a further irritant to the European allies) by undercutting European privacy protections. It is true, of course, as it is probably true of all elements of HVIRA, that the disclosure requirement's object of obtaining compensation for Holocaust victims is a goal espoused by the National Government as well. But "the fact of a common end hardly neutralizes conflicting means," *Crosby, supra,* at 379, and here HVIRA is an obstacle to the success of the National Government's chosen "calibration of force" in dealing with the Europeans using a voluntary approach, 530 U.S. at 380.

B

The express federal policy and the clear conflict raised by the state statute are alone enough to require state law to yield. If any doubt about the clarity of the conflict remained, however, it would have to be resolved in the National Government's favor, given the weakness of the State's interest, against the backdrop of traditional state legislative subject matter, in regulating disclosure of European Holocaust-era insurance policies in the manner of HVIRA.

The commissioner would justify HVIRA's ambitious disclosure requirement as protecting "legitimate consumer protection interests" in knowing which insurers have failed to pay insurance claims. But, quite unlike a generally applicable "blue sky" law, HVIRA effectively singles out only policies issued by European companies, in Europe, to European residents, at least 55 years ago. Cal. Ins. Code Ann. §13804(a); *see also* §790.15(a) (mandating license suspension only for "failure to pay any valid claim from Holocaust survivors"). Limiting the public disclosure requirement to these policies raises great doubt that the purpose of the California law is an evaluation of corporate reliability in contemporary insuring in the State.

Indeed, there is no serious doubt that the state interest actually underlying HVIRA is concern for the several thousand Holocaust survivors said to be living in the State. §13801(d) (legislative finding that roughly 5,600 documented Holocaust survivors reside in California). But this fact does not displace general standards for evaluating a State's claim to apply its forum law to a particular controversy or transaction, under which the State's claim is not a strong one. "Even if a plaintiff evidences his desire for forum law by moving to the forum, we have generally accorded

---

14. It is true that the President in this case is acting without express congressional authority, and thus does not have the "plenitude of Executive authority" that "controlled the issue of preemption" in Crosby v. National Foreign Trade Council, 530 U.S. 363, 376 (2000). But in *Crosby* we were careful to note that the President possesses considerable independent constitutional authority to act on behalf of the United States on international issues, *id.* at 381, and conflict with the exercise of that authority is a comparably good reason to find preemption of state law.

such a move little or no significance." Phillips Petroleum Co. v. Shutts, 472 U.S. 797, 820 (1985); *see* Allstate Ins. Co. v. Hague, 449 U.S. 302, 311 (1981) ("[A] postoccurrence change of residence to the forum State—standing alone—is insufficient to justify application of forum law").

But should the general standard not be displaced, and the State's interest recognized as a powerful one, by virtue of the fact that California seeks to vindicate the claims of Holocaust survivors? The answer lies in recalling that the very same objective dignifies the interest of the National Government in devising its chosen mechanism for voluntary settlements, there being about 100,000 survivors in the country, only a small fraction of them in California. As against the responsibility of the United States of America, the humanity underlying the state statute could not give the State the benefit of any doubt in resolving the conflict with national policy.

C

The basic fact is that California seeks to use an iron fist where the President has consistently chosen kid gloves. We have heard powerful arguments that the iron fist would work better, and it may be that if the matter of compensation were considered in isolation from all other issues involving the European allies, the iron fist would be the preferable policy. But our thoughts on the efficacy of the one approach versus the other are beside the point, since our business is not to judge the wisdom of the National Government's policy; dissatisfaction should be addressed to the President or, perhaps, Congress. The question relevant to preemption in this case is conflict, and the evidence here is "more than sufficient to demonstrate that the state Act stands in the way of [the President's] diplomatic objectives." *Crosby, supra,* at 386. . . .

V

[The Court concludes in this part that Congress has not affirmatively authorized the California statute.]

JUSTICE GINSBURG, with whom JUSTICE STEVENS, JUSTICE SCALIA, and JUSTICE THOMAS join, dissenting. . . .

The President's primacy in foreign affairs, I agree with the Court, empowers him to conclude executive agreements with other countries. Our cases do not catalog the subject matter meet for executive agreement, but we have repeatedly acknowledged the President's authority to make such agreements to settle international claims. And in settling such claims, we have recognized, an executive agreement may preempt otherwise permissible state laws or litigation. The executive agreements to which we have accorded preemptive effect, however, warrant closer inspection than the Court today endeavors. . . .

[Justice Ginsburg discusses the facts of *Belmont* and *Pink,* which are covered in Chapter 6 of this casebook, and *Dames & Moore,* which is excerpted in Chapter 3. In those decisions, the Court enforced executive agreements that resolved U.S. claims against foreign governments and treated the agreements as preemptive federal law.]

Together, *Belmont, Pink,* and *Dames & Moore* confirm that executive agreements directed at claims settlement may sometimes preempt state law. The Court states that if the executive "agreements here had expressly preempted laws like HVIRA, the issue would be straightforward." One can safely demur to that statement, for, as the Court acknowledges, no executive agreement before us expressly preempts the HVIRA. Indeed, no agreement so much as mentions the HVIRA's sole concern: public disclosure.

B

Despite the absence of express preemption, the Court holds that the HVIRA interferes with foreign policy objectives implicit in the executive agreements. I would not venture down that path. . . .

We have not relied on *Zschernig* since it was decided, and I would not resurrect that decision here. The notion of "dormant foreign affairs preemption" with which *Zschernig* is associated resonates most audibly when a state action "reflects a state policy critical of foreign governments and involves 'sitting in judgment' on them." L. Henkin, Foreign Affairs and the United States Constitution 164 (2d ed. 1996). The HVIRA entails no such state action or policy. It takes no position on any contemporary foreign government and requires no assessment of any existing foreign regime. It is directed solely at private insurers doing business in California, and it requires them solely to disclose information in their or their affiliates' possession or control. I would not extend *Zschernig* into this dissimilar domain.[4]

Neither would I stretch *Belmont, Pink,* or *Dames & Moore* to support implied preemption by executive agreement. In each of those cases, the Court gave effect to the express terms of an executive agreement. In *Dames & Moore,* for example, the Court addressed an agreement explicitly extinguishing certain suits in domestic courts. Here, however, none of the executive agreements extinguish any underlying claim for relief. The United States has agreed to file precatory statements advising courts that dismissing Holocaust-era claims accords with American foreign policy, but the German Foundation Agreement confirms that such statements have no legally binding effect. It remains uncertain, therefore, whether even *litigation* on Holocaust-era insurance claims must be abated in deference to the German Foundation Agreement or the parallel agreements with Austria and France. Indeed, ambiguity on this point appears to have been the studied aim of the American negotiating team.

If it is uncertain whether insurance *litigation* may continue given the executive agreements on which the Court relies, it should be abundantly clear that those agreements leave *disclosure* laws like the HVIRA untouched. The contrast with the Litvinov Assignment at issue in *Belmont* and *Pink* is marked. That agreement spoke directly to claim assignment in no uncertain terms; *Belmont* and *Pink* confirmed that state law could not invalidate the very assignments accomplished by the agreement. Here, the Court invalidates a state disclosure law on grounds of conflict with foreign policy "embodied" in certain executive agreements, although those agreements do not refer to state disclosure laws specifically, or even to information disclosure generally. It therefore is surely an exaggeration to assert that the "HVIRA threatens to frustrate the operation of the particular mechanism the President has chosen" to resolve Holocaust-era claims. If that were so, one might expect to find some reference to laws like the HVIRA in the later-in-time executive agreements. There is none.

---

4. The Court also places considerable weight on Crosby v. National Foreign Trade Council, 530 U.S. 363 (2000). As the Court acknowledges, however, *Crosby* was a statutory preemption case. The state law there at issue posed "an obstacle to the accomplishment of Congress's full objectives under the [relevant] federal Act." 530 U.S. at 373. That statutory decision provides little support for preempting a state law by inferring preclusive foreign policy objectives from precatory language in executive agreements.

To fill the agreements' silences, the Court points to statements by individual members of the Executive Branch. . . . But we have never premised foreign affairs preemption on statements of that order. *Cf.* Barclays Bank PLC v. Franchise Tax Bd. of Cal., 512 U.S. 298, 329-30 (1994) ("Executive Branch actions—press releases, letters, and *amicus* briefs" that "express federal policy but lack the force of law" cannot render a state law unconstitutional under the Foreign Commerce Clause.). We should not do so here lest we place the considerable power of foreign affairs preemption in the hands of individual sub-Cabinet members of the Executive Branch. Executive officials of any rank may of course be expected "faithfully [to] represent the President's policy," but no authoritative text accords such officials the power to invalidate state law simply by conveying the Executive's views on matters of federal policy. The displacement of state law by preemption properly requires a considerably more formal and binding federal instrument.

Sustaining the HVIRA would not compromise the President's ability to speak with one voice for the Nation. To the contrary, by declining to invalidate the HVIRA in this case, we would reserve foreign affairs preemption for circumstances where the President, acting under statutory or constitutional authority, has spoken clearly to the issue at hand. . . . And judges should not be the expositors of the Nation's foreign policy, which is the role they play by acting when the President himself has not taken a clear stand. As I see it, courts step out of their proper role when they rely on no legislative or even executive text, but only on inference and implication, to preempt state laws on foreign affairs grounds.

Notes and Questions

1. Is *Zschernig* consistent with Clark v. Allen, excerpted above in Section B? What did *Clark* suggest about the validity of state inheritance laws that are not preempted by a federal statute or treaty?

2. Prior to *Zschernig*, courts did not preempt state foreign relations activities in the absence of controlling enacted federal law, even though states frequently caused foreign relations controversies. *See* Louis Henkin, Foreign Affairs and the United States Constitution 162 (2d ed. 1996) (describing *Zschernig* as "new" constitutional doctrine); Jack L. Goldsmith, *Federal Courts, Foreign Affairs, and Federalism*, 83 Va. L. Rev. 1617, 1643-58 (1997). In addition, at least two pre-*Zschernig* Supreme Court decisions were dismissive of the idea of dormant foreign affairs preemption. *See* Clark v. Allen, 331 U.S. 503, 516-17 (1947) (rejecting dormant foreign relations challenge to a state anti-alien inheritance statute as "farfetched"); Blythe v. Hinckley, 180 U.S. 333, 340 (1901) (rejecting as "extraordinary" the argument that a California statute permitting aliens to inherit real property invaded the unexercised treaty power).

Nonetheless, *Zschernig* did have precursors. Prior to 1968, the closest the Court came to a dormant foreign affairs preemption doctrine was in Holmes v. Jennison, 39 U.S. 540 (1840), a case involving Vermont's attempted extradition of an alleged criminal to Canada. Writing for a plurality of four Justices, Chief Justice Taney maintained that federal power in "foreign intercourse" was exclusive, and that a concurrent state power to extradite was "incompatible and inconsistent with the powers conferred on the federal government." The four other participating Justices, by contrast, all rejected a dormant preemption argument. On remand from the Supreme Court's 4-4 decision, the Vermont Supreme Court held that the extradition constituted "an agreement between the governor of this state, in behalf of the state, and the governor of Canada" in violation of Article I, Section 10 of the U.S. Constitution. *See* Ex parte Holmes, 12 Vt. 631, 640 (1840). Although most commentators today believe that the extradition power is an exclusive federal power, and the Court has suggested this in dicta, see Valentine v. United States, 299 U.S. 5, 8 (1936) (stating that "it cannot be doubted that the power to provide for extradition is a national power; it pertains to the national government and not to the States"), the Court has never expressly held this.

Another area in which the Court has hinted at dormant foreign affairs preemption is immigration. In the nineteenth century, states exercised control over many immigration matters. *See* Gerald L. Neuman, *The Lost Century of American Immigration Law (1776-1875)*, 93 Colum. L. Rev. 1833 (1993). This practice abated in the last half of the nineteenth century after the Supreme Court invoked the dormant Commerce Clause to invalidate certain state laws regulating the migration of aliens, and the federal political branches began to enact immigration statutes and enter into treaties that regulated the issue. One prominent early dormant Commerce Clause decision concerning immigration was Chy Lung v. Freeman, 92 U.S. 275 (1875). There, the Court invalidated a California state commissioner's power to demand indemnification bonds for certain vaguely described classes of immigrants disembarking at California ports. The Court reasoned that because the Constitution "has forbidden the States to hold negotiations with any foreign nations . . . and has taken the whole subject of these relations [as reserved for the federal government]," the Framers could not be held to have "done so foolish a thing as to leave it in the power of the States to pass laws whose enforcement renders the general government liable to just recriminations that it must answer, while it does not prohibit to the States the acts for which it is held responsible." The Court added: "If [the United States] should get into a difficulty which would lead to war, or to suspension of intercourse, would California alone suffer, or all the Union?"

Although the reasoning in *Chy Lung* is similar to the reasoning in *Zschernig*, *Chy Lung* did not establish a stand-alone doctrine of dormant foreign affairs preemption. After *Chy Lung*, states enacted numerous anti-alien statutes that produced stormy diplomatic controversy, but no court or commentator hinted that the statutes could be preempted in the absence of a controlling federal treaty, statute, or textual constitutional prohibition. *See* Goldsmith, *supra*, at 1653-54; Dennis James Palumbo, The States and American Foreign Relations 147-92 (1960) (unpublished Ph.D. dissertation, University of Chicago). And, even as late as Hines v. Davidowitz, the Court stated that it was still an open question whether "federal power in [immigration], whether exercised or unexercised, is exclusive." Many post-*Hines* decisions refer to an exclusive federal immigration power, but no Supreme Court decision has clearly rested on this ground. For an argument that dormant preemption is not appropriate in the area of immigration, and that "federal exclusivity in the admission and removal of non-citizens is better understood to rest on ordinary statutory preemption," see Clare Huntington, *The Constitutional Dimension of Immigration Federalism*, 61 Vand. L. Rev. 787 (2008).

3. What is the constitutional source for dormant foreign affairs preemption? Read Article I, Section 10 of the Constitution. Among other things, this Section excludes state authority in a defined set of "high" foreign relations functions, such as treaty making and war making. Now read the foreign relations powers conferred on the federal government in Article I, Section 8 and in Article II, Sections 2-3. Are these powers *exclusive* (which means that they can be exercised only by the federal government)? Or are they, like most other powers conferred on the federal government, *concurrent* (which means that they can be exercised by both state and federal governments until the federal government affirmatively acts to preempt state authority)? Now consider the Tenth Amendment, which provides that the "powers not delegated to the United States by the Constitution, nor prohibited by it to the States, are reserved to the States respectively, or to the people." What implications, if any, can one draw from these textual provisions? *Compare* Goldsmith, *supra*, at 1642 (arguing that the "most natural inference . . . is that all foreign relations matters not excluded by Article I, Section 10 fall within the concurrent power of the state and federal governments until preempted by federal statute or treaty"), *with* Brannon P. Denning & Jack H. McCall, Jr., *The Constitutionality of State and Local "Sanctions" Against Foreign Countries: Affairs of State, States' Affairs, or a Sorry State of Affairs?*, 26 Hastings Const. L.Q. 307, 337 (1999) ("[T]he various provisions related to foreign affairs can be read to contain a structural or 'penumbral' restriction on state actions affecting foreign affairs, even in the absence of a congressional enactment.").

4. Another justification for dormant foreign affairs preemption is a functional one. Even if federal courts are not as well suited as the federal political branches to perform the foreign relations inquiries in support of dormant preemption, the federal political branches cannot redress every state foreign relations activity. Moreover, the federal courts are at least in a better position than states to identify and police U.S. foreign relations interests, and any errors the courts might make in inappropriately preempting state law can always be corrected by subsequent federal legislation. Is this argument persuasive? Do the federal political branches need the assistance of federal courts in policing states for harmful foreign relations activity? Are courts well suited to assist in this task? What effect does dormant foreign affairs preemption have on the political branches that are primarily responsible for conducting U.S. foreign relations? Are there any other costs to dormant foreign affairs preemption?

5. What is the scope of the prohibition on state activity announced in *Zschernig?* What matters in answering this question? Foreign relations effects? The state's purpose in engaging in the activity? Both? Neither? *See, e.g.,* Gingery v. City of Glendale, 831 F.3d 1222, 1231 (9th Cir. 2016) (rejecting dormant preemption challenge to a city's establishment of a monument to Korean "comfort women" from the World War II era, despite possibility of creating friction with Japan, in part because the city "has taken no action that would affect the legal rights and responsibilities of any individuals or foreign government"); Faculty Senate of Fla. Int'l Univ. v. Winn, 616 F.3d 1206 (11th Cir. 2010) (rejecting dormant preemption challenge to Florida statute that restricted the use of state money for travel by state employees to countries that the federal government had listed as "State Sponsors of Terrorism" because, "unlike the Oregon statute and practice in *Zschernig*, Florida is not asking in its Act—even in the Act's application—for proof about the conduct of any foreign government or making a judgment about that conduct which is apart from the federal government's own announced judgment").

6. There is a substantial literature on dormant foreign affairs preemption in addition to the sources cited above. *See, e.g.,* Louis Henkin, Foreign Affairs and the United States Constitution ch. VI (2d ed. 1996); Ryan Baasch & Saikrishna Bangalore Prakash, *Congress and the Reconstruction of Foreign Affairs Federalism,* 115 Mich. L. Rev. 47, 51 (2016); Richard B. Bilder, *The Role of Cities and States in Foreign Relations,* 83 Am. J. Int'l L. 821 (1989); Sarah H. Cleveland, Crosby *and the "One-Voice" Myth in U.S. Foreign Relations,* 46 Vill. L. Rev. 975 (2001); Howard N. Fenton, III, *The Fallacy of Federalism in Foreign Affairs: State and Local Foreign Policy Trade Restrictions,*

13 Nw. J. Int'l L. & Bus. 563 (1993); Harold G. Maier, *Preemption of State Law: A Recommended Analysis*, 83 Am. J. Int'l L. 832 (1989); Michael D. Ramsey, *The Power of the States in Foreign Affairs: The Original Understanding of Foreign Policy Federalism*, 75 Notre Dame L. Rev. 341 (1999); Michael H. Shuman, *Dateline Main Street: Courts v. Local Foreign Policies*, 86 Foreign Policy 158(1992); Peter J. Spiro, *Foreign Relations Federalism*, 70 U. Colo. L. Rev. 1223 (1999); Arthur Weisburd, *State Courts, Federal Courts, and International Cases*, 20 Yale J. Int'l L. 1 (1995). For an argument in favor of a "dormant treaty power" that would preclude states from "direct or indirect negotiating . . . with foreign powers on matters of national concern," see Edward T. Swaine, *Negotiating Federalism: State Bargaining and the Dormant Treaty Power*, 49 Duke L.J. 1127 (2000).

7. What is the relationship between statutory preemption and dormant foreign affairs preemption? At first glance, it might appear that the presence of a congressional statute makes the judicial decision whether to preempt more straightforward, or at least easier from a policy perspective. But is this true? As the federal Burma statute in *Crosby* and the immigration laws in *Arizona* illustrate, Congress often provides no concrete guidance about the preemptive scope of its statutes. Does this mean that courts deciding whether a statute preempts state law are effectively in the same position as they are in dormant preemption cases? Or does the presence of the federal statute provide courts with guidance about preemption, even though the statute is silent regarding preemptive scope? Is one method of preemption more legitimate than the other? Why?

8. Should courts always consider statutory preemption before dormant preemption? In explaining why it addressed statutory preemption and not dormant preemption, footnote 8 in *Crosby* cited Justice Brandeis's celebrated concurring opinion in Ashwander v. Tennessee Valley Authority, 297 U.S. 288, 341 (1936), which provides in pertinent part:

> The Court will not pass upon a constitutional question although properly presented by the record, if there is also present some other ground upon which the case may be disposed of. . . . Thus, if a case can be decided on either of two grounds, one involving a constitutional question, the other a question of statutory construction or general law, the Court will decide only the latter.

If a court considers and rejects a statutory preemption argument (i.e., if it concludes that there is no conflict between the federal and state enactments and that Congress did not intend to preempt), is it appropriate to strike down the state law nonetheless on the basis of a judicially developed preemption doctrine?

9. After *Zschernig*, the Supreme Court began to invoke a doctrine akin to dormant foreign affairs preemption in the context of applying the dormant Foreign Commerce Clause. Article I, Section 8, Clause 3 of the Constitution gives Congress the power to regulate commerce "among the several States" and "with foreign Nations." Even in the absence of affirmative congressional regulation, the Supreme Court has long invoked the "dormant" Commerce Clause as a basis for judicial preemption of state laws that unduly burden interstate or foreign commerce. The Court has devised a number of tests for such preemption.

With respect to the regulation of *interstate* commerce, the Court performs essentially a two-step inquiry. First, state laws that facially discriminate against interstate commerce are subject to strict scrutiny, and are "virtually per se invalid." Oregon Waste Systems, Inc. v. Department of Environmental Quality, 511 U.S. 93, 99 (1994).

Second, even a nondiscriminatory state law can be invalidated under the dormant Commerce Clause if "the burden imposed on [interstate] commerce is clearly excessive in relation to the putative local benefits." Pike v. Bruce Church, Inc., 397 U.S. 137, 142 (1970).

With respect to the regulation of *foreign* commerce, courts apply similar discrimination and balancing tests, with two differences. First, they apply the discrimination and balancing tests in a more searching manner with respect to foreign commerce. *See, e.g.,* Kraft General Foods v. Iowa Dep't of Revenue & Finance, 505 U.S. 71, 79 (1992) ("The constitutional prohibition against state taxation of foreign commerce is broader than the protection afforded to interstate commerce . . . in part because matters of concern to the entire Nation are implicated."). Second, beginning in Japan Line Ltd. v. County of Los Angeles, 441 U.S. 434 (1979), the Supreme Court imposed a new, and independent, prohibition under the dormant Foreign Commerce Clause: the state law must not prevent the federal government from speaking with "one voice" in foreign relations. The one-voice test under the dormant Foreign Commerce Clause requires courts to analyze the extent to which state law will "offend" a foreign nation, and to distinguish a state law that "merely has foreign resonances" from one that "implicates foreign affairs." Container Corp. of America v. Franchise Tax Board, 463 U.S. 159, 194 (1983).

In Barclays Bank v. Franchise Tax Board of California, 512 U.S. 298 (1994), the Supreme Court appeared to back away from the "one-voice test" for dormant Foreign Commerce Clause preemption. *Barclays Bank* involved a challenge to California's method of taxing foreign multinational corporations. The taxation method was different from the federal government's method and had drawn extensive international protest, and numerous countries filed *amicus curiae* briefs urging the Supreme Court to invalidate it. The Court nevertheless rejected the challenge because it could "discern no 'specific indications of congressional intent' to bar the state action." Emphasizing that "the Constitution does 'not make the judiciary the overseer of our government,'" the Court decided to "leave it to Congress—whose voice, in this area, is the Nation's—to evaluate whether the national interest is best served by tax uniformity, or state autonomy." *Id.* at 330-31. Is the reasoning in *Barclays Bank* consistent with *Zschernig?* Is the Court's conception of the judicial role in *Barclays Bank* consistent with *Zschernig?* What does *Garamendi* suggest about *Barclays Bank*'s effect on *Zschernig?* Does *Barclays Bank* survive *Garamendi?*

10. The Court's preemption analysis in *Garamendi* was influenced by the presence of a "sole" executive agreement—i.e., an agreement between the United States and another country that the President entered into on his own constitutional authority, without recourse to the Senate or Congress. As discussed in detail in Chapter 6, the Supreme Court, beginning in United States v. Belmont, 301 U.S. 324 (1937), determined that such sole executive agreements could, at least in some circumstances, preempt state law. Did the Court in *Garamendi* hold that the California statute was preempted by the executive agreement? If not, how did the executive agreement influence the Court's decision? How does the Court's analysis in *Garamendi* differ from its analysis in *Crosby* (also authored by Justice Souter), where a statute was in issue? What is the relevance, in this connection, of footnote 11 of the Court's opinion? Under the analysis in *Garamendi*, does the Executive Branch even need an executive agreement to preempt state law under *Garamendi?* Could the mere unilateral announcement of a foreign policy by the President be enough to preempt state law?

11. In thinking about the idea of Executive Branch foreign affairs preemption, consider these three post-*Garamendi* decisions by the federal courts of appeals:

a. In Movsesian v. Victoria Versicherung AG, 578 F.3d 1052 (9th Cir. 2009), the Ninth Circuit initially invalidated another California statute that extended the statute of limitations for claims under insurance policies held by "Armenian genocide victim[s]." The court reasoned that the statute did not concern an area of genuine state interest, conflicted with a federal policy (embodied in statements and letters of two presidents and other executive officials) against legislative recognition of an Armenian genocide, impermissibly impaired the President's ability to speak with one voice for the nation in foreign affairs, and undermined the President's diplomatic authority.

The Ninth Circuit panel subsequently granted rehearing, however, and overturned its prior decision, reasoning that "[t]here is no clearly established, express federal policy forbidding state references to the Armenian Genocide" and that "California's effort to regulate the insurance industry is well within the realm of its traditional interests." Movsesian v. Victoria Versicherung AG, 629 F.3d 901 (9th Cir. 2010). One judge dissented, arguing that "there is an express Presidential foreign policy, as acquiesced in by Congress, prohibiting legislative recognition of the 'Armenian Genocide,'" and that "[b]y formally recognizing the 'Armenian Genocide,' [the California law] directly conflicts with this foreign policy."

The rehearing decision was itself vacated by the Ninth Circuit sitting en banc, which invalidated the state law based on dormant foreign affairs preemption. *See* Movsesian v. Victoria Versicherung AG, 670 F.3d 1067 (9th Cir. 2012). The court reasoned that the state insurance law did not concern an area of traditional state responsibility (because it was directed at a foreign policy concern) and intruded on the federal government's exclusive power to conduct foreign affairs because it "expresses a distinct point of view on a specific matter of foreign policy" and had a distinct impact on U.S. foreign relations.

b. In In re Assicurazioni Generali, 592 F.3d 113 (2d Cir. 2010), the plaintiffs brought various state law claims seeking to recover under insurance policies purchased by their ancestors before the Holocaust from Assicurazioni Generali, S.p.A., an Italian insurance company. In concluding that the claims were preempted, the Second Circuit acknowledged that, unlike in *Garamendi* where the President had entered into executive agreements with Germany, Austria, and France, the President had not entered into an executive agreement with Italy concerning the processing of Holocaust-era insurance claims. The court reasoned, however, that the key factor in the preemption analysis in *Garamendi* was not the executive agreement, but rather the U.S. policy of encouraging the resolution of Holocaust-era claims through the International Commission on Holocaust Era Insurance Claims (ICHEIC). The court found preemption notwithstanding the fact that the time for the plaintiffs to file a claim with the ICHEIC had passed. The U.S. government policy was that the ICHEIC was the exclusive remedy, the court noted, adding that if the "ICHEIC door has closed on plaintiffs, it is because they chose to allow it to close."

c. In Philipp v. Federal Republic of Germany, 894 F. 3d 406 (D.C. Cir. 2018), heirs of Jewish art dealers doing business in Frankfurt, Germany in the 1930s sought to recover an art collection allegedly taken by the Nazis. The heirs first filed claims in Germany before an Advisory Commission that was set up pursuant to the 1998 State Department-sponsored Washington Conference Principles on Nazi-Confiscated Art, which had "encouraged" nations "to develop . . . alternative dispute resolution mechanisms for resolving ownership issues" related to such art. When the Advisory Commission denied the heirs' claim, the heirs brought state common law causes of action against Germany and one of its agencies in U.S. federal court. The D.C. Circuit rejected the defendants' argument that these claims were preempted. It reasoned that, "[u]nlike in *Garamendi*, where the President promised to seek 'dismissal on any valid legal ground,' or in *Crosby*, where the state law at issue 'blunt[ed]' the force of discretion Congress had explicitly granted the President, here there was no "direct conflict between the property-based common law claims raised by Plaintiffs and [United States] foreign policy." In support of this conclusion, the court noted that the plaintiffs' claims did not fall within the policy expressed in the executive agreements at issue in *Garamendi* and that Congress had demonstrated that it favored litigation of this sort by, among other things, enacting the Holocaust Expropriated Art Recovery Act of 2016, which extended federal and state statutes of limitation for Nazi art-looting claims. (The court also concluded that Germany did not have immunity from the suit because the case fell within the "expropriation exception" to immunity in the Foreign Sovereign Immunities Act. The Act is considered in Chapter 7 of this casebook.)

What do these decisions suggest about the circumstances under which Executive Branch policy will be found to have preemptive effect? How predictable is the law in this area?

12. Professors Ku and Yoo sharply distinguish *Garamendi* from *Zschernig*:

> Although *Garamendi* might be understood as a defeat for "foreign relations federalism" and state participation in matters relating to foreign affairs, it is hardly an unqualified endorsement of *Zschernig*'s reliance on federal courts to police state activities. Rather, *Garamendi*'s reliance on the statements and actions of executive branch officials to discern a "consistent Presidential foreign policy" in conflict with the state law affirms that the federal executive, rather than the federal courts, holds the primary responsibility for determining which state laws and policies unduly interfere with national policies.

Julian Ku & John Yoo, *Beyond Formalism in Foreign Affairs: A Functional Approach to the Alien Tort Statute*, 2004 Sup. Ct. Rev. 153, 210. Do you agree with this analysis? Since the courts and not the Executive will have the final say on the content of the relevant policy and whether it is sufficiently weighty for preemption, and since courts decide when and whether to rely on Executive Branch policy statements, could one argue instead that the real effect of *Garamendi* is to enhance judicial (as opposed to Executive) power over foreign relations?

Some commentators agree that *Garamendi* enhances Executive power, but they argue that it does so in a constitutionally problematic way. Consider this analysis:

> The Constitution's Article VI places the power of preemption in the legislative branch by making laws and treaties, but not executive decrees, the supreme law of the land. In unusual cases, state laws might be displaced by the judiciary, or by the President pursuant to executive agreements with foreign nations. Giving mere executive policy preemptive effect, as the Court did in *Garamendi*, bypasses these constitutional processes and concentrates power in the executive branch. That is particularly problematic in foreign affairs, where the President's substantial authority over the military and the organs of diplomacy already gives rise to broad independent power. The President's lack of lawmaking authority balances these other great executive powers, because without lawmaking authority, the President needs the support of other branches to fully effectuate foreign policy. This highlights an often overlooked way that federalism reinforces checks and balances at the national level. A robust foreign affairs federalism

promotes a cooperative approach to foreign affairs, because the President will need the support of Congress to oust disruptive state laws; as a result, more foreign affairs decision making will be done by Congress (or the Senate). In contrast, allowing the President unilaterally to oust states from foreign affairs, as the Court did in *Garamendi*, means that more foreign affairs disputes may be decided only by the President, through a concentration of executive and lawmaking power that is contrary to the first principles of separation of powers.

Michael D. Ramsey & Brannon P. Denning, American Association v. Garamendi *and Executive Preemption in Foreign Affairs*, 46 Wm. & Mary L. Rev. 825, 829-30 (2004). Do you agree with this analysis?

13. Does the Supreme Court have a coherent view of the proper role of the Executive Branch in its various preemption doctrines? In *Zschernig*, the Court appeared to ignore Department of Justice statements denying that the Oregon escheat statute interfered with the conduct of U.S. foreign relations. In *Barclays Bank* the Court similarly discounted Executive Branch statements. In *Garamendi*, by contrast, the Court relied on Executive Branch statements. Similarly, in the context of statutory preemption in *Crosby* (excerpted in the last section), the Court appeared to give great weight to Executive Branch representations about the foreign relations difficulties caused by the Massachusetts statute. Is there any way to reconcile these decisions?

14. To what extent can Congress authorize states to engage in foreign relations activities that might otherwise be subject to dormant or Executive Branch preemption? This issue is implicated by the Sudan Accountability and Divestment Act of 2007. The Act provides that notwithstanding any other provision of law, "a State or local government may adopt and enforce [certain] measures . . . to divest the assets of the State or local government from, or prohibit investment of the assets of the State or local government in, persons that the State or local government determines, using credible information available to the public, are conducting or have direct investments in business operations . . . in Sudan that include power production activities, mineral extraction activities, oil-related activities, or the production of military equipment." President Bush issued a signing statement when approving this Act, asserting that, "as the Constitution vests the exclusive authority to conduct foreign relations with the Federal Government, the executive branch shall construe and enforce this legislation in a manner that does not conflict with that authority."

It is well settled that Congress can authorize state activities that would otherwise be subject to dormant Commerce Clause preemption. *See, e.g.*, White v. Massachusetts Council of Construction Employers, Inc., 460 U.S. 204, 213 (1983) ("Where state or local government action is specifically authorized by Congress, it is not subject to the Commerce Clause even if it interferes with interstate commerce."). In addition, since Congress can modify earlier statutes, it can authorize state activities that would otherwise be subject to statutory preemption. In light of this, what (if any) constitutional issues are raised by the above Act?

15. In November 2010, Oklahoma voters approved a referendum that provides in relevant part:

> [Oklahoma courts], when exercising their judicial authority, shall uphold and adhere to the law as provided in the United States Constitution, the Oklahoma Constitution, the United States Code, federal regulations promulgated pursuant thereto, established common law, the Oklahoma Statutes and rules promulgated pursuant thereto, and if necessary the law of another state of the United States provided the law of the other state does not include Sharia law, in making judicial decisions. The courts shall not

look to the legal precepts of other nations or cultures. Specifically, the courts shall not consider international law or Sharia law.

Is this provision consistent with the Supremacy Clause of the Constitution? A federal district judge quickly enjoined application of the portion of this referendum that relates to Sharia law, on the ground that it discriminated against religion. A number of other states, however, have considered adopting similar legislation that would limit the use of foreign and international law by state courts. *See* Aaron Fellmeth, *International Law and Foreign Laws in the U.S. State Legislatures*, ASIL Insight (May 26, 2011), at https://www.asil.org/insights/volume/15/issue/13/international-law-and-foreign-laws-us-state-legislatures. What explains the sudden interest in such limitations?

16. In 2016, the Obama Administration ratified the Paris agreement on climate change, an action that is discussed in detail in Chapter 6 of the casebook. In early June 2017, President Trump announced that he would withdraw the United States from the agreement. In response to this announcement, a number of states and localities pledged to continue to pursue efforts to address climate change under state law. Hawaii subsequently passed legislation committing the state to meet the emissions reduction goals in the Paris agreement, and California entered into a non-binding agreement with China to cut emissions. It was further reported that "[r]epresentatives of American cities, states and companies are preparing to submit a plan to the United Nations pledging to meet the United States' greenhouse gas emissions targets under the Paris climate accord." Hiroko Tabuchi & Henry Fountain, *Bucking Trump, These Cities, States and Companies Commit to Paris Accord*, N.Y. Times (June 1, 2017). Are these various efforts preempted?

17. As discussed in Chapter 2, the lower federal courts can hear only those cases that (a) fall within the bounds of their Article III judicial power and (b) are authorized by a statutory grant of subject matter jurisdiction. For federal question jurisdiction under 28 U.S.C. §1331, a federal law issue must appear on the face of the well-pleaded complaint. This is true regardless of whether the case is originally filed in federal court or removed to federal court from state court. One gloss on the well-pleaded complaint rule is that, in situations in which federal law completely preempts a cause of action, any claim that comes within the scope of the preemption necessarily arises under federal law. *See, e.g.*, Beneficial National Bank v. Anderson, 539 U.S. 1 (2003). A few lower courts have held that state law claims relating to foreign affairs, even if not preempted by the Constitution or a federal statute, will sometimes implicate a "federal common law of foreign relations," such that cases raising such claims can be removed from state to federal court on federal question grounds. *See, e.g.*, Torres v. Southern Peru Copper, 113 F.3d 540 (5th Cir. 1997); Republic of the Philippines v. Marcos, 806 F.2d 344 (2d Cir. 1986). For a rejection of this idea, see Patrickson v. Dole Food Co., 251 F.3d 795 (9th Cir. 2001). For additional discussion, see Jack L. Goldsmith, *Federal Courts, Foreign Affairs, and Federalism*, 83 Va. L. Rev. 1617 (1997); and Ernest A. Young, *Stalking the Yeti: Protective Jurisdiction, Foreign Affairs Removal, and Complete Preemption*, 95 Cal. L. Rev. 1775 (2007).

PART III

INTERNATIONAL LAW IN THE U.S. LEGAL SYSTEM

5

Treaties

Article II of the Constitution grants the President the power "by and with the Advice and Consent of the Senate, to make Treaties, provided two thirds of the Senators present concur." The U.S. treaty-making process operates essentially as follows: Representatives of the President negotiate the terms of the treaty with foreign nations, and the President or a representative of the President signs the completed draft. The President then transmits the treaty to the Senate for its advice and consent. The treaty is first considered by the Senate Foreign Relations Committee, which decides whether to report it to the full Senate. If it does so, the full Senate votes on whether to give its advice and consent to the treaty. Typically, a President will not risk the defeat of a treaty when it appears that there are insufficient votes in the Senate. As a result, the Senate has rarely voted to reject a treaty.*

If the treaty receives the required two-thirds vote, the Senate sends a resolution to the President approving the treaty. Sometimes the resolution will contain conditions, such as "reservations," declining to consent to particular treaty provisions; "understandings," setting forth the Senate's view about the meaning of certain treaty terms; or "declarations," concerning how the treaty should be applied domestically. The President has the discretion at this point to ratify or not ratify the treaty. Ratification is the act by which a nation formally declares its intent to be bound by a treaty. When the President signs the instrument of ratification and the secretary of state affixes the Seal of the United States, the U.S. ratification process is complete. Even at this point, however, the United States is not bound by the terms of the treaty. The treaty becomes binding on the United States only after the instrument of ratification is either exchanged (as is usually the process with respect to bilateral treaties) or deposited at a specified place (as is usually the process with respect to multilateral treaties). In addition, the treaty will not become binding on the United States until it has taken effect internationally, which will sometimes occur only at a specified date or after a certain number of ratifications have been received.

The materials that follow explore the domestic status and scope of treaties. The chapter focuses only on "Article II treaties"—that is, treaties concluded pursuant to the two-thirds senatorial advice and consent process. Chapter 6

---

* The most famous example of such a rejection was of the Versailles Treaty that established the League of Nations after World War I. Other examples include the Senate's rejection in 1999 (during the Clinton Administration) of the Comprehensive Nuclear Test Ban Treaty, and the Senate's rejection in 2012 (during the Obama Administration) of the U.N. Convention on the Rights of Persons with Disabilities.

will consider "executive agreements," which are binding agreements concluded outside of the Article II process, and it will also discuss non-binding political commitments.

A. SELF-EXECUTION

Foster v. Neilson

27 U.S. (2 Pet.) 253 (1829)

[This case involved an 1819 treaty between the United States and Spain that ceded certain disputed territory east of the Mississippi River to the United States. The petitioners claimed title to a tract of land within the territory based on an 1804 grant from Spain, and on that basis sought to eject the respondent from the tract. The treaty provided in relevant part that all grants of land made by Spain in the ceded territory prior to the treaty "shall be ratified and confirmed to the persons in possession of the lands to the same extent that the same grants would be valid if the territories had remained under the dominion" of Spain. Before concluding this treaty, however, the U.S. government had taken the position that the area encompassing the tract had been ceded by Spain to France in 1800, and that France had conveyed it to the United States in 1803 as part of the Louisiana Purchase, and this view was reflected in several federal statutes enacted prior to the treaty.]

MR. CHIEF JUSTICE MARSHALL delivered the opinion of the Court. . . .

A treaty is, in its nature, a contract between two nations, not a legislative act. It does not generally effect, of itself, the object to be accomplished, especially so far as its operation is infra-territorial, but is carried into execution by the sovereign power of the respective parties to the instrument.

In the United States, a different principle is established. Our Constitution declares a treaty to be the law of the land. It is consequently to be regarded in courts of justice as equivalent to an act of the Legislature whenever it operates of itself, without the aid of any legislative provision. But when the terms of the stipulation import a contract, when either of the parties engages to perform a particular act, the treaty addresses itself to the political, not the Judicial Department, and the Legislature must execute the contract before it can become a rule for the Court.

The article [of the treaty] under consideration does not declare that all the grants made by [Spain] before the [treaty] shall be valid to the same extent as if the ceded territories had remained under [its] dominion. It does not say that those grants are hereby confirmed. Had such been its language, it would have acted directly on the subject, and would have repealed those acts of Congress which were repugnant to it; but its language is that those grants shall be ratified and confirmed to the persons in possession, &c. By whom shall they be ratified and confirmed? This seems to be the language of contract; and if it is, the ratification and confirmation which are promised must be the act of the Legislature. Until such act shall be passed, the Court is not at liberty to disregard the existing laws on the subject.

Asakura v. City of Seattle

265 U.S. 332 (1924)

[A Seattle ordinance required pawnbrokers to obtain licenses, but prohibited the granting of such licenses to noncitizens. Asakura, a pawnbroker who was a citizen of Japan, sued in state court to enjoin enforcement of the ordinance on the ground that it violated a treaty between the United States and Japan that granted "national treatment" (i.e., equal treatment with U.S. citizens) to Japanese citizens who engaged in trade in the United States.]

MR. JUSTICE BUTLER delivered the opinion of the Court. . . .

Does the ordinance violate the treaty? Plaintiff in error invokes and relies upon the following provisions: "The citizens or subjects of each of the High Contracting Parties shall have liberty to enter, travel and reside in the territories of the other to carry on trade, wholesale and retail, to own or lease and occupy houses, manufactories, warehouses and shops, to employ agents of their choice, to lease land for residential and commercial purposes, and generally to do anything incident to or necessary for trade upon the same terms as native citizens or subjects, submitting themselves to the laws and regulations there established. . . . The citizens or subjects of each . . shall receive, in the territories of the other, the most constant protection and security for their persons and property, ..."

A treaty made under the authority of the United States "shall be the supreme law of the land; and the judges in every State shall be bound thereby, any thing in the constitution or laws of any State to the contrary notwithstanding." Constitution, Art. VI, §2.

The treaty-making power of the United States is not limited by any express provision of the Constitution, and, though it does not extend "so far as to authorize what the Constitution forbids," it does extend to all proper subjects of negotiation between our government and other nations. Geofroy v. Riggs, 133 U.S. 258, 266, 267. . . . The treaty is binding within the State of Washington. The rule of equality established by it cannot be rendered nugatory in any part of the United States by municipal ordinances or state laws. It stands on the same footing of supremacy as do the provisions of the Constitution and laws of the United States. It operates of itself without the aid of any legislation, state or national; and it will be applied and given authoritative effect by the courts. . . .

It remains to be considered whether the business of pawnbroker is "trade" within the meaning of the treaty. Treaties are to be construed in a broad and liberal spirit, and, when two constructions are possible, one restrictive of rights that may be claimed under it and the other favorable to them, the latter is to be preferred. . . . The ordinance defines "pawnbroker" to "mean and include every person whose business or occupation [it] is to take and receive by way of pledge, pawn or exchange, goods, wares or merchandise, or any kind of personal property whatever, for the repayment or security of any money loaned thereon, or to loan money on deposit of personal property"; and defines "pawnshop" to "mean and include every place at which the business of pawnbroker is carried on." The language of the treaty is comprehensive. The phrase "to carry on trade" is broad. That it is not to be given a restricted meaning is plain. The clauses "to own or lease . . . shops, . . . to lease land for . . . commercial purposes, and generally to do anything incident to or necessary for trade," and "shall receive . . . the most constant protection and security for their . . . property . . ." all go to show the intention of the parties that the citizens or subjects to either shall have liberty in the territory of the other to engage in all kinds and classes of business that are or reasonably may be embraced within the meaning of the word "trade" as used in the treaty. . . . The ordinance violates the treaty.

Medellin v. Texas

552 U.S. 491 (2008)

[The United States joined the United Nations Charter in 1945. Among other things, the Charter established the International Court of Justice (ICJ), a 15-member Court that sits in The Hague and serves as the principal judicial organ of the United Nations. Article 94(1) of the Charter provides that "[e]ach Member of the United Nations undertakes to comply with the decision of the [ICJ] in any case to which it is a party."

In 1969, the United States ratified the Vienna Convention on Consular Relations, Article 36 of which provides that if a person detained by a foreign country "so requests, the competent authorities of the receiving State shall, without delay, inform the consular post of the sending State" of such detention, and that "[t]he said authorities shall inform the person concerned without delay of [this] right[]." Also in 1969, the United States ratified an Optional Protocol to the Vienna Convention, which provides that "[d]isputes arising out of the interpretation or application of the Convention shall lie within the compulsory jurisdiction of the International Court of Justice and may accordingly be brought before the Court by an application made by any party to the dispute being a Party to the present Protocol."

In 2003, Mexico brought a case against the United States in the ICJ, arguing that authorities in the United States had failed to comply with Article 36 of the Vienna Convention when arresting a number of Mexican nationals who were now on death row in various states. In a 2004 decision, *Case Concerning Avena and Other Mexican Nationals*, 2004 I.C.J. No. 128 (Judgment of Mar. 31) (*Avena*), the ICJ agreed with Mexico and held that 51 named Mexican nationals were entitled to review and reconsideration of their state-court convictions and sentences in the United States. This was the case, reasoned the ICJ, even if these nationals had failed to comply with generally applicable state rules governing challenges to criminal convictions.

In February 2005, President George W. Bush sent a memorandum to his Attorney General stating:

> I have determined, pursuant to the authority vested in me as President by the Constitution and the laws of the United States of America, that the United States will discharge its international obligations under the decision of the International Court of Justice in [*Avena*], by having State courts give effect to the decision in accordance with general principles of comity in cases filed by the 51 Mexican nationals addressed in that decision.

One of the individuals named in the ICJ's *Avena* decision was Jose Ernesto Medellin, who had been convicted of murder in a Texas state court in 1993 and sentenced to death. Relying on both *Avena* and the President's memorandum, Medellin filed an application for a writ of habeas corpus in state court. The state court rejected the application, reasoning that Medellin had failed to raise his Vienna Convention claim in a timely manner, as required by state law.]

CHIEF JUSTICE ROBERTS delivered the opinion of the Court. . . .

II. . . .

No one disputes that the *Avena* decision—a decision that flows from the treaties through which the United States submitted to ICJ jurisdiction with respect to Vienna Convention disputes—constitutes an *international* law obligation on the part of the United States. But not all international law obligations automatically constitute binding federal law enforceable in United States courts. The question we confront here is whether the *Avena* judgment has automatic *domestic* legal effect such that the judgment of its own force applies in state and federal courts.

This Court has long recognized the distinction between treaties that automatically have effect as domestic law, and those that—while they constitute international law commitments—do not by themselves function as binding federal law. . . . [W]hile treaties "may comprise international commitments . . . they are not domestic law unless Congress has either enacted implementing statutes or the treaty itself conveys an intention that it be 'self-executing' and is ratified on these terms." Igartua-De La Rosa v. United States, 417 F.3d 145, 150 (1st Cir. 2005) (en banc) (Boudin, C.J.).[2]

A treaty is, of course, "primarily a compact between independent nations." Head Money Cases, 112 U.S. 580, 598 (1884). It ordinarily "depends for the enforcement of its provisions on the interest and the honor of the governments which are parties to it." *Ibid.* . . . Only "[i]f the treaty contains stipulations which are self-executing, that is, require no legislation to make them operative, [will] they have the force and effect of a legislative enactment." [Whitney v. Robertson, 124 U.S. 190, 194 (1888)].[3]

Medellin and his *amici* nonetheless contend that the Optional Protocol, United Nations Charter, and ICJ Statute supply the "relevant obligation" to give the *Avena* judgment binding effect in the domestic courts of the United States. Because none of these treaty sources creates binding federal law in the absence of implementing legislation, and because it is uncontested that no such legislation exists, we conclude that the *Avena* judgment is not automatically binding domestic law.

The interpretation of a treaty, like the interpretation of a statute, begins with its text. Air France v. Saks, 470 U.S. 392, 396-97 (1985). Because a treaty ratified by the United States is "an agreement among sovereign powers," we have also considered as "aids to its interpretation" the negotiation and drafting history of the treaty as well as "the postratification understanding" of signatory nations. Zicherman v. Korean Air Lines Co., 516 U.S. 217, 226 (1996). . . .

The obligation on the part of signatory nations to comply with ICJ judgments derives . . . from Article 94 of the United Nations Charter—the provision that specifically addresses the effect of ICJ decisions. Article 94(1) provides that "[e]ach

2. The label "self-executing" has on occasion been used to convey different meanings. What we mean by "self-executing" is that the treaty has automatic domestic effect as federal law upon ratification. Conversely, a "non-self-executing" treaty does not by itself give rise to domestically enforceable federal law. Whether such a treaty has domestic effect depends upon implementing legislation passed by Congress.

3. Even when treaties are self-executing in the sense that they create federal law, the background presumption is that "international agreements, even those directly benefiting private persons, generally do not create private rights or provide for a private cause of action in domestic courts." 2 Restatement (Third) of Foreign Relations Law of the United States §907, Comment *a*, p. 395 (1986). . . .

Member of the United Nations *undertakes to comply* with the decision of the [ICJ] in any case to which it is a party." (Emphasis added.) The Executive Branch contends that the phrase "undertakes to comply" is not "an acknowledgement that an ICJ decision will have immediate legal effect in the courts of U.N. members," but rather "a *commitment* on the part of U.N. Members to take *future* action through their political branches to comply with an ICJ decision."

We agree with this construction of Article 94. The Article is not a directive to domestic courts. It does not provide that the United States "shall" or "must" comply with an ICJ decision, nor indicate that the Senate that ratified the U.N. Charter intended to vest ICJ decisions with immediate legal effect in domestic courts. Instead, "[t]he words of Article 94 . . . call upon governments to take certain action." Committee of United States Citizens Living in Nicaragua v. Reagan, 859 F.2d 929, 938 (D.C. Cir. 1988) (quoting Diggs v. Richardson, 555 F.2d 848, 851 (D.C. Cir. 1976); internal quotation marks omitted). In other words, the U.N. Charter reads like "a compact between independent nations" that "depends for the enforcement of its provisions on the interest and the honor of the governments which are parties to it." *Head Money Cases*, 112 U.S. at 598.

The remainder of Article 94 confirms that the U.N. Charter does not contemplate the automatic enforceability of ICJ decisions in domestic courts. Article 94(2) — the enforcement provision — provides the sole remedy for noncompliance: referral to the United Nations Security Council by an aggrieved state.

The U.N. Charter's provision of an express diplomatic — that is, nonjudicial — remedy is itself evidence that ICJ judgments were not meant to be enforceable in domestic courts. *See* Sanchez-Llamas [v. Oregon, 548 U.S. 331, 347 (2006)]. And even this "quintessentially *international* remed[y]," *id.* at 355, is not absolute. First, the Security Council must "dee[m] necessary" the issuance of a recommendation or measure to effectuate the judgment. Second, as the President and Senate were undoubtedly aware in subscribing to the U.N. Charter and Optional Protocol, the United States retained the unqualified right to exercise its veto of any Security Council resolution. . . .

If ICJ judgments were instead regarded as automatically enforceable domestic law, they would be immediately and directly binding on state and federal courts pursuant to the Supremacy Clause. Mexico or the ICJ would have no need to proceed to the Security Council to enforce the judgment in this case. Noncompliance with an ICJ judgment through exercise of the Security Council veto — always regarded as an option by the Executive and ratifying Senate during and after consideration of the U.N. Charter, Optional Protocol, and ICJ Statute — would no longer be a viable alternative. There would be nothing to veto. In light of the U.N. Charter's remedial scheme, there is no reason to believe that the President and Senate signed up for such a result.

In sum, Medellin's view that ICJ decisions are automatically enforceable as domestic law is fatally undermined by the enforcement structure established by Article 94. His construction would eliminate the option of noncompliance contemplated by Article 94(2), undermining the ability of the political branches to determine whether and how to comply with an ICJ judgment. Those sensitive foreign policy decisions would instead be transferred to state and federal courts charged with applying an ICJ judgment directly as domestic law. And those courts would not be empowered to decide whether to comply with the judgment — again, always regarded as an option by the political branches — any more than courts may consider whether to comply with any other species of domestic law. This result would be particularly anomalous in light of the principle that "[t]he conduct of the foreign relations of our Government is committed by the Constitution to the Executive and Legislative — 'the political' — Departments." Oetjen v. Central Leather Co., 246 U.S. 297, 302 (1918). . . .

It is, moreover, well settled that the United States' interpretation of a treaty "is entitled to great weight." Sumitomo Shoji America, Inc. v. Avagliano, 457 U.S. 176, 184-85 (1982). The Executive Branch has unfailingly adhered to its view that the relevant treaties do not create domestically enforceable federal law. . . .

The interpretive approach employed by the Court today — resorting to the text — is hardly novel. . . .

As against this time-honored textual approach, the dissent proposes a multi-factor, judgment-by-judgment analysis that would "jettiso[n] relative predictability for the open-ended rough-and-tumble of factors." Jerome B. Grubart, Inc. v. Great Lakes Dredge & Dock Co., 513 U.S. 527, 547 (1995). The dissent's novel approach to deciding which (or, more accurately, when) treaties give rise to directly enforceable federal law is arrestingly indeterminate. Treaty language is barely probative. Determining whether treaties themselves create federal law is sometimes committed to the political branches and sometimes to the judiciary. Of those committed to the judiciary, the courts pick and choose which shall be binding United States law — trumping not only state but other federal law as well — and which shall not. They do this on the basis of a multifactor, "context-specific" inquiry. Even then, the same treaty sometimes gives rise to United States law and sometimes does not, again depending on an ad hoc judicial assessment.

Our Framers established a careful set of procedures that must be followed before federal law can be created under the Constitution — vesting that decision in the political branches, subject to checks and balances. They also recognized that treaties could create federal law, but again through the political branches, with the President making the treaty and the Senate approving it. The dissent's understanding of the treaty route, depending on an ad hoc judgment of the judiciary without looking to the treaty language — the very language negotiated by the President and approved by the Senate — cannot readily be ascribed to those same Framers.

The dissent's approach risks the United States' involvement in international agreements. It is hard to believe that the United States would enter into treaties that are sometimes enforceable and sometimes not. Such a treaty would be the equivalent of writing a blank check to the judiciary. Senators could never be quite sure what the treaties on which they were voting meant. Only a judge could say for sure and only at some future date. This uncertainty could hobble the United States' efforts to negotiate and sign international agreements. . . .

Our prior decisions identified by the dissent as holding a number of treaties to be self-executing stand only for the unremarkable proposition that some international agreements are self-executing and others are not. It is well settled that the "[i]nterpretation of [a treaty] . . . must, of course, begin with the language of the Treaty itself." *Sumitomo Shoji America, Inc.*, 457 U.S. at 180. As a result, we have held treaties to be self-executing when the textual provisions indicate that the President and Senate intended for the agreement to have domestic effect. . . .

The dissent worries that our decision casts doubt on some 70-odd treaties under which the United States has agreed to submit disputes to the ICJ according to "roughly similar" provisions. Again, under our established precedent, some treaties are self-executing and some are not, depending on the treaty. . . .

Further, that an ICJ judgment may not be automatically enforceable in domestic courts does not mean the particular underlying treaty is not. Indeed, we have held that a number of the "Friendship, Commerce, and Navigation" Treaties cited by the dissent are self-executing—based on "the language of the[se] Treat[ies]." *See Sumitomo Shoji America, Inc., supra*, at 180, 189-90. . . . Contrary to the dissent's suggestion, neither our approach nor our cases require that a treaty provide for self-execution in so many talismanic words; that is a caricature of the Court's opinion. Our cases simply require courts to decide whether a treaty's terms reflect a determination by the President who negotiated it and the Senate that confirmed it that the treaty has domestic effect.

In addition, Congress is up to the task of implementing non-self-executing treaties, even those involving complex commercial disputes. The judgments of a number of international tribunals enjoy a different status because of implementing legislation enacted by Congress. . . . Such language [in the relevant statutes] demonstrates that Congress knows how to accord domestic effect to international obligations when it desires such a result. . . .

III

Medellin next argues that the ICJ's judgment in *Avena* is binding on state courts by virtue of the President's February 28, 2005 Memorandum. The United States contends that while the *Avena* judgment does not of its own force require domestic courts to set aside ordinary rules of procedural default, that judgment became the law of the land with precisely that effect pursuant to the President's Memorandum and his power "to establish binding rules of decision that preempt contrary state law." . . .

The United States maintains that the President's Memorandum is authorized by the Optional Protocol and the U.N. Charter. That is, because the relevant treaties "create an obligation to comply with *Avena*," they "*implicitly* give the President authority to implement that treaty-based obligation." As a result, [the United States argues,] the President's Memorandum is well grounded in the first category of the *Youngstown* framework.

We disagree. The President has an array of political and diplomatic means available to enforce international obligations, but unilaterally converting a non-self-executing treaty into a self-executing one is not among them. The responsibility for transforming an international obligation arising from a non-self-executing treaty into domestic law falls to Congress. As this Court has explained, when treaty stipulations are "not self-executing they can only be enforced pursuant to legislation to carry them into effect." *Whitney, supra*, at 194. . . .

The requirement that Congress, rather than the President, implement a non-self-executing treaty derives from the text of the Constitution, which divides the treaty-making power between the President and the Senate. The Constitution vests the President with the authority to "make" a treaty. If the Executive determines that a treaty should have domestic effect of its own force, that determination may be implemented "in mak[ing]" the treaty, by ensuring that it contains language plainly providing for domestic enforceability. If the treaty is to be self-executing in this respect, the Senate must consent to the treaty by the requisite two-thirds vote, consistent with all other constitutional restraints.

Once a treaty is ratified without provisions clearly according it domestic effect, however, whether the treaty will ever have such effect is governed by the fundamental constitutional principle that "'[t]he power to make the necessary laws is in Congress; the power to execute in the President.'" *Hamdan v. Rumsfeld*, 548 U.S. 557, 591 (2006) (quoting *Ex parte Milligan*, 71 U.S. 2, 139 (1866) (opinion of Chase, C.J.)); *see* U.S. Const., Art. I, §1 ("All legislative Powers herein granted shall be vested in a Congress of the United States"). As already noted, the terms of a non-self-executing treaty can become domestic law only in the same way as any other law—through passage of legislation by both Houses of Congress, combined with either the President's signature or a congressional override of a Presidential veto. *See* Art. I, §7. Indeed, "the President's power to see that the laws are faithfully executed refutes the idea that he is to be a lawmaker." *Youngstown*, 343 U.S. at 587.

A non-self-executing treaty, by definition, is one that was ratified with the understanding that it is not to have domestic effect of its own force. That understanding precludes the assertion that Congress has implicitly authorized the President—acting on his own—to achieve precisely the same result. We therefore conclude, given the absence of congressional legislation, that the non-self-executing treaties at issue here did not "express[ly] or implied[ly]" vest the President with the unilateral authority to make them self-executing. *See id.* at 635 (Jackson, J., concurring). Accordingly, the President's Memorandum does not fall within the first category of the *Youngstown* framework.

Indeed, the preceding discussion should make clear that the non-self-executing character of the relevant treaties not only refutes the notion that the ratifying parties vested the President with the authority to unilaterally make treaty obligations binding on domestic courts, but also implicitly prohibits him from doing so. When the President asserts the power to "enforce" a non-self-executing treaty by unilaterally creating domestic law, he acts in conflict with the implicit understanding of the ratifying Senate. His assertion of authority, insofar as it is based on the pertinent non-self-executing treaties, is therefore within Justice Jackson's third category, not the first or even the second.

The United States nonetheless maintains that the President's Memorandum should be given effect as domestic law because "this case involves a valid Presidential action in the context of Congressional 'acquiescence.'" Brief for United States as *Amicus Curiae* 11, n. 2. Under the *Youngstown* tripartite framework, congressional acquiescence is pertinent when the President's action falls within the second category—that is, when he "acts in absence of either a congressional grant or denial of authority." 343 U.S. at 637 (Jackson, J., concurring). Here, however, as we have explained, the President's effort to accord domestic effect to the *Avena* judgment does not meet that prerequisite.

In any event, even if we were persuaded that congressional acquiescence could support the President's asserted authority to create domestic law pursuant to a non-self-executing treaty, such acquiescence does not exist here. The United States first locates congressional acquiescence in Congress's failure to act following the President's resolution of prior ICJ controversies. A review of the Executive's actions in those prior cases, however, cannot support the claim that Congress acquiesced in this particular exercise of Presidential authority, for none of them remotely involved transforming an international obligation into domestic law and thereby displacing state law.

The United States also directs us to the President's "related" statutory responsibilities and to his "established role" in litigating foreign policy concerns as support for the President's asserted authority to give the ICJ's decision in *Avena* the force of domestic law. Congress has indeed authorized the President to represent the United

States before the United Nations, the ICJ, and the Security Council, but the authority of the President to represent the United States before such bodies speaks to the President's *international* responsibilities, not any unilateral authority to create domestic law. The authority expressly conferred by Congress in the international realm cannot be said to "invite" the Presidential action at issue here. *See Youngstown, supra,* at 637 (Jackson, J., concurring). At bottom, none of the sources of authority identified by the United States supports the President's claim that Congress has acquiesced in his asserted power to establish on his own federal law or to override state law.

None of this is to say, however, that the combination of a non-self-executing treaty and the lack of implementing legislation precludes the President from acting to comply with an international treaty obligation. It is only to say that the Executive cannot unilaterally execute a non-self-executing treaty by giving it domestic effect. That is, the non-self-executing character of a treaty constrains the President's ability to comply with treaty commitments by unilaterally making the treaty binding on domestic courts. The President may comply with the treaty's obligations by some other means, so long as they are consistent with the Constitution. But he may not rely upon a non-self-executing treaty to "establish binding rules of decision that preempt contrary state law." Brief for United States as *Amicus Curiae* 5. . . .

[The Court also concluded that "[t]he Executive's narrow and strictly limited authority to settle international claims disputes pursuant to an executive agreement cannot stretch so far as to support the current Presidential Memorandum," and it observed that the President's Article II authority to "take Care that the Laws be faithfully executed" "allows the President to execute the laws, not make them."]

[Justice Stevens concurred on the ground that the phrase "undertakes to comply" in Article 94 of the U.N. Charter, "while not the model of either a self-executing or a non-self-executing commitment," is best read as "contemplat[ing] future action by the political branches." He also suggested that, although the federal courts would not force it to do so, the State of Texas should take appropriate action to comply with *Avena.*]

JUSTICE BREYER, with whom JUSTICE SOUTER and JUSTICE GINSBURG join, dissenting. . . .

Supreme Court case law stretching back more than 200 years helps explain what, for present purposes, the Founders meant when they wrote that "all Treaties . . . shall be the supreme Law of the Land." Art. VI, cl. 2. . . .

[T]his Court has frequently held or assumed that particular treaty provisions are self-executing, automatically binding the States without more. . . . As far as I can tell, the Court has held to the contrary only in two cases: *Foster, supra,* which was later reversed, and Cameron Septic Tank Co. v. Knoxville, 227 U.S. 39 (1913), where specific congressional actions indicated that Congress thought further legislation necessary. The Court has found "self-executing" provisions in multilateral treaties as well as bilateral treaties. And the subject matter of such provisions has varied widely. . . .

All of these cases make clear that self-executing treaty provisions are not uncommon or peculiar creatures of our domestic law; that they cover a wide range of subjects; that the Supremacy Clause itself answers the self-execution question by applying many, but not all, treaty provisions directly to the States; and that the Clause answers the self-execution question differently than does the law in many other nations. The cases also provide criteria that help determine *which* provisions automatically so apply—a matter to which I now turn.

The case law provides no simple magic answer to the question whether a particular treaty provision is self-executing. But the case law does make clear that, insofar as today's majority looks for language about "self-execution" in the treaty itself and insofar as it erects "clear statement" presumptions designed to help find an answer, it is misguided. . . .

The many treaty provisions that this Court has found self-executing contain no textual language on the point. . . . These many Supreme Court cases finding treaty provisions to be self-executing cannot be reconciled with the majority's demand for textual clarity. . . .

The majority correctly notes that the treaties do not explicitly state that the relevant obligations are self-executing. But given the differences among nations [concerning self-execution], why would drafters write treaty language stating that a provision about, say, alien property inheritance, is self-executing? How could those drafters achieve agreement when one signatory nation follows one tradition and a second follows another? Why would such a difference matter sufficiently for drafters to try to secure language that would prevent, for example, Britain's following treaty ratification with a further law while (perhaps unnecessarily) insisting that the United States apply a treaty provision without further domestic legislation? Above all, what does the absence of specific language about "self-execution" prove? It may reflect the drafters' awareness of national differences. It may reflect the practical fact that drafters, favoring speedy, effective implementation, conclude they should best leave national legal practices alone. It may reflect the fact that achieving international agreement on *this* point is simply a game not worth the candle.

In a word, for present purposes, the absence or presence of language in a treaty about a provision's self-execution proves nothing at all. At best the Court is hunting the snark. At worst it erects legalistic hurdles that can threaten the application of provisions in many existing commercial and other treaties and make it more difficult to negotiate new ones.

The case law also suggests practical, context-specific criteria that this Court has previously used to help determine whether, for Supremacy Clause purposes, a treaty provision is self-executing. The provision's text matters very much. But that is not because it contains language that explicitly refers to self-execution. For reasons I have already explained, one should not expect *that* kind of textual statement. Drafting history is also relevant. But, again, that is not because it will explicitly address the relevant question. Instead text and history, along with subject matter and related characteristics will help our courts determine whether, as Chief Justice Marshall put it, the treaty provision "addresses itself to the political . . . department[s]" for further action or to "the judicial department" for direct enforcement. Foster v. Neilson, 27 U.S. 253, 314 (1829).

In making this determination, this Court has found the provision's subject matter of particular importance. Does the treaty provision declare peace? Does it promise not to engage in hostilities? If so, it addresses itself to the political branches. Alternatively, does it concern the adjudication of traditional private legal rights such as rights to own property, to conduct a business, or to obtain civil tort recovery? If so, it may well address itself to the Judiciary. Enforcing such rights and setting their boundaries is the bread-and-butter work of the courts.

One might also ask whether the treaty provision confers specific, detailed individual legal rights. Does it set forth definite standards that judges can readily enforce? Other things being equal, where rights are specific and readily enforceable, the treaty provision more likely "addresses" the judiciary. . . .

Alternatively, would direct enforcement require the courts to create a new cause of action? Would such enforcement engender constitutional controversy? Would it create constitutionally undesirable conflict with the other branches? In such circumstances, it is not likely that the provision contemplates direct judicial enforcement.

Such questions, drawn from case law stretching back 200 years, do not create a simple test, let alone a magic formula. But they do help to constitute a practical, context-specific judicial approach, seeking to separate run-of-the-mill judicial matters from other matters, sometimes more politically charged, sometimes more clearly the responsibility of other branches, sometimes lacking those attributes that would permit courts to act on their own without more ado. And such an approach is all that we need to find an answer to the legal question now before us.

Applying the approach just described, I would find the relevant treaty provisions self-executing as applied to the ICJ judgment before us (giving that judgment domestic legal effect) for the following reasons, taken together.

First, the language of the relevant treaties strongly supports direct judicial enforceability, at least of judgments of the kind at issue here. . . .

True, neither the Protocol nor the Charter explicitly states that the obligation to comply with an ICJ judgment automatically binds a party *as a matter of domestic law* without further domestic legislation. *But how could the language of those documents do otherwise?* The treaties are multilateral. And . . . some signatories follow British further-legislation-always-needed principles, others follow United States Supremacy Clause principles, and still others, *e.g.,* the Netherlands, can directly incorporate treaty provisions into their domestic law in particular circumstances. Why, given national differences, would drafters, seeking as strong a legal obligation as is practically attainable, use treaty language that *requires* all signatories to adopt uniform domestic-law treatment in this respect?

The absence of that likely unobtainable language can make no difference. We are considering the language for purposes of applying the Supremacy Clause. And for that purpose, this Court has found to be self-executing multilateral treaty language that is far less direct or forceful (on the relevant point) than the language set forth in the present treaties. . . . The language here in effect tells signatory nations to make an ICJ compulsory jurisdiction judgment "as binding as you can." Thus, assuming other factors favor self-execution, the language *adds,* rather than *subtracts,* support. . . .

I recognize, as the majority emphasizes, that the U.N. Charter uses the words "undertakes to comply," rather than, say, "shall comply" or "must comply." But what is inadequate about the word "undertak[e]"? A leading contemporary dictionary defined it in terms of "lay[ing] oneself under obligation . . . to perform or to execute." Webster's New International Dictionary 2770 (2d ed. 1939). And that definition is just what the equally authoritative Spanish version of the provision (familiar to Mexico) says directly: The words "*compromete a cumplir*" indicate a present obligation to execute, without any tentativeness of the sort the majority finds in the English word "undertakes." . . .

Second, the Optional Protocol here applies to a dispute about the meaning of a Vienna Convention provision that is itself self-executing and judicially enforceable. The Convention provision is about an individual's "rights," namely, his right upon being arrested to be informed of his separate right to contact his nation's consul. The provision language is precise. The dispute arises at the intersection of an individual right with ordinary rules of criminal procedure; it consequently concerns the kind of matter with which judges are familiar. The provisions contain judicially enforceable standards. . . .

Third, logic suggests that a treaty provision providing for "final" and "binding" judgments that "settl[e]" treaty-based disputes is self-executing insofar as the judgment in question concerns the meaning of an underlying treaty provision that is itself self-executing. . . .

Fourth, the majority's very different approach has seriously negative practical implications. The United States has ratified approximately 70 treaties with ICJ dispute resolution provisions roughly similar to those contained in the Optional Protocol; many of those treaties contemplate ICJ adjudication of the sort of substantive matters (property, commercial dealings, and the like) that the Court has found self-executing, or otherwise appear addressed to the judicial branch. None of the ICJ provisions in these treaties contains stronger language about self-execution than the language at issue here. . . .

Fifth, other factors, related to the particular judgment here at issue, make that judgment well suited to direct judicial enforcement. The specific issue before the ICJ concerned "'review and reconsideration'" of the "possible prejudice" caused in each of the 51 affected cases by an arresting State's failure to provide the defendant with rights guaranteed by the Vienna Convention. This review will call for an understanding of how criminal procedure works, including whether, and how, a notification failure may work prejudice. As the ICJ itself recognized, "it is the judicial process that is suited to this task." . . .

Sixth, to find the United States' treaty obligations self-executing as applied to the ICJ judgment (and consequently to find that judgment enforceable) does not threaten constitutional conflict with other branches; it does not require us to engage in nonjudicial activity; and it does not require us to create a new cause of action. The only question before us concerns the application of the ICJ judgment as binding law applicable to the parties in a particular criminal proceeding that Texas law creates independently of the treaty. . . .

Seventh, neither the President nor Congress has expressed concern about direct judicial enforcement of the ICJ decision. To the contrary, the President favors enforcement of this judgment. Thus, insofar as foreign policy impact, the interrelation of treaty provisions, or any other matter within the President's special treaty, military, and foreign affairs responsibilities might prove relevant, such factors *favor*, rather than militate against, enforcement of the judgment before us.

Notes and Questions

1. Article VI of the Constitution provides that "all Treaties made, or which shall be made, under the Authority of the United States, shall be the supreme Law of the Land; and the Judges in every State shall be bound thereby, any Thing in the Constitution or Laws of any State to the Contrary notwithstanding." This language could be read to suggest that every treaty ratified by the United States has the status of judicially enforceable federal law. Since Foster v. Neilson, however, it has been settled that some treaties are "non-self-executing," and thus do not by themselves provide a rule of decision for U.S. courts. What reasons did the Court give in *Foster* for finding the treaty provision there to be non-self-executing? What purposes are served by the distinction between self-executing and non-self-executing treaties? What problems, if any, would be created if courts deemed all treaties self-executing? Can the distinction between self-executing and non-self-executing treaties be reconciled with the text of the Supremacy Clause?

2. As discussed below in Section B, it is reasonably well settled that a self-executing treaty can override an earlier federal statute. Nevertheless, do you think the Court was reluctant in *Foster* to apply the treaty to override federal statutes? If so, why?

Several years after *Foster*, the Supreme Court changed its mind about the effect of the treaty provision at issue there. After examining the Spanish version of the provision, the English translation of which provided that the grants of land "shall remain ratified and confirmed," the Court concluded that the provision was in fact self-executing. *See* United States v. Percheman, 32 U.S. (7 Pet.) 51, 88-89 (1833). Unlike the land at issue in *Foster*, the land at issue in *Percheman* was indisputably within Spanish territory at the time of the 1819 treaty and thus the grant in question did not pose a potential conflict with preexisting statutes.

3. The Court in *Asakura* did not use the term "self-executing," but it found the treaty provision in that case to be judicially enforceable. Why? Because it was a bilateral treaty? A commercial treaty? Because language in the treaty suggested that it was directly enforceable by U.S. courts? *See also* Clark v. Allen, 331 U.S. 503 (1947) (applying property inheritance provision in a treaty with Germany to preempt state law).

4. *Medellin* is the most significant Supreme Court decision concerning treaty self-execution since *Foster*. Why does the Court in *Medellin* find the treaty provisions there to be non-self-executing? What evidence does the Court look at in reaching its conclusion? Is the Court's approach to self-execution in *Medellin* consistent with its approach in *Foster* and *Asakura*? Is the Court too focused on the treaty text? Do you agree with the Court that the phrase "undertakes to comply" in Article 94(1) of the U.N. Charter is suggestive of non-self-execution? What do you make of the dissent's argument that the majority is "hunting the snark" (i.e., something fictional) when looking for language of self-execution in the text?

5. In determining whether a treaty is self-executing, should courts attempt to discern what the treaty drafters or ratifiers intended? Or should courts look only for objective indications of self-execution or non-self-execution in the text of the treaty? If so, what would constitute such indications? Are there such indications to be discovered? What does *Medellin* suggest about this?

If intent does matter, should courts look to the intent of all the parties to the treaty, or just the intent of the U.S. treatymakers? What does *Foster* suggest? What does *Medellin* suggest? In deciding whose intent to consider, does it matter whether the treaty is bilateral or multilateral? Of what significance is the fact that in many countries, such as the United Kingdom, all treaties are considered non-self-executing? Is it likely that treaties with numerous parties will have a single intent concerning self-execution?

Here is how the Restatement (Fourth) of Foreign Relations Law describes the test for whether a treaty provision is self-executing:

> Courts will evaluate whether the text and context of the provision, along with other treaty materials, are consistent with an understanding by the U.S. treatymakers that the provision would be directly enforceable in courts in the United States. Relevant considerations include:
>
> (a) whether the treaty provision is sufficiently precise or obligatory to be suitable for direct application by the judiciary; and

(b) whether the provision was designed to have immediate effect, as opposed to contemplating additional measures by the political branches.

Restatement (Fourth) of the Foreign Relations Law of the United States §310 (2018). Is this approach consistent with *Medellin?* With the Supremacy Clause? How easy is it for courts to apply?

6. Recall from Chapter 2 that courts often give deference to the views of the Executive Branch concerning the meaning of treaties. Should courts similarly defer to Executive Branch views concerning whether a treaty is self-executing? What does *Medellin* suggest? *See also* Doe v. Holder, 763 F.3d 251, 257 (2d Cir. 2014) (reciting statements by both the Executive Branch and Congress suggesting that they viewed an article of a treaty as non-self-executing and noting that this was "a conclusion to which we are obligated to give great weight"); More v. Intelcom Support Services, Inc., 960 F.2d 466 (5th Cir. 1992) (deferring to the Executive Branch on the issue of self-execution and analogizing to the *Chevron* deference doctrine in administrative law).

7. Should there be a presumption in favor of self-execution, a presumption against self-execution, or no presumption at all? Which default rule is more consistent with the Supremacy Clause? With separation of powers principles? With federalism principles? What are the institutional consequences of each of the default rules? Which default rule is more likely to spur the treatymakers to address the question of non-self-execution? Of what significance is the fact that non-self-executing treaties are still binding on the United States on the international plane?

The Restatement (Third) of Foreign Relations Law endorsed a strong presumption in favor of self-execution that was supported by a number of commentators. *See, e.g.,* Restatement (Third) of Foreign Relations Law, §111, reporters' note 5; Louis Henkin, Foreign Affairs and the United States Constitution 201 (2d ed. 1996); Carlos M. Vazquez, *Laughing at Treaties,* 99 Colum. L. Rev. 2154 (1999). Did the Court in *Medellin* implicitly reject such a presumption? Did it implicitly adopt a presumption *against* self-execution? *See* ESAB Group, Inc. v. Zurich Ins. PLC, 685 F.3d 376, 387 (4th Cir. 2012) (noting "an emerging presumption against finding treaties to be self-executing").

Part of the Restatement (Third)'s reasoning was that if no implementing legislation is sought in connection with a treaty, it is likely that the Senate and the President would have expected the treaty to be self-executing, because otherwise they would potentially have been placing the United States in breach of its obligations under the treaty. Is this reasoning persuasive? Isn't it possible that the Senate and President would have expected compliance with a treaty to be achieved through preexisting law or nonjudicial action, rather than through either self-execution or new implementing legislation? In contrast to the Restatement (Third), the Restatement (Fourth) of Foreign Relations Law concluded that "case law has not established a general presumption for or against self-execution, in the sense of a clear statement or default rule that dictates a result in the absence of contrary evidence." Restatement (Fourth) of the Foreign Relations Law of the United States §310, Comment d (2018).

8. Starting in the 1970s, some lower courts adopted multifactored tests for evaluating whether treaty provisions were self-executing. The following list of factors is illustrative:

the purposes of the treaty and the objectives of its creators, the existence of domestic procedures and institutions appropriate for direct implementation, the availability and feasibility of alternative enforcement methods, and the immediate and long-range consequences of self- or non-self-execution.

United States v. Postal, 589 F.2d 862, 877 (5th Cir. 1979) (quoting People of Saipan v. United States Dep't of Interior, 502 F.2d 90, 97 (9th Cir. 1974)).

How much guidance do you think these factors give to courts and litigants? Why did the Court in *Medellin* reject the multifactored approach to self-execution suggested by the dissent? Might some of the factors recited by the dissent nevertheless be relevant under the majority's approach to self-execution? What is the majority's response to the dissent's argument that the ICJ judgment at issue in *Medellin* was "well suited to direct judicial enforcement"?

9. As a general matter, it does not violate separation of powers for the President and Senate to enter into a treaty that regulates a subject falling within Congress's powers. Thus, for example, the United States has throughout its history entered into treaties regulating international trade, even though Congress has the power to regulate international trade through its foreign commerce power. *See also* Edwards v. Carter, 580 F.2d 1055 (D.C. Cir. 1978) (holding that Congress's power to dispose of U.S. property, set forth in Article IV, §3, cl. 2 of the Constitution, is not exclusive and that the Panama Canal could therefore be transferred to Panama pursuant to a treaty).

Separation of powers problems can arise, however, if a treaty regulates a matter *exclusively* assigned to Congress. In that situation, the treaty will be deemed to be non-self-executing to avoid usurping Congress's authority. Matters commonly assumed to fall within Congress's exclusive authority include the appropriation of money, the imposition of taxes or tariffs, the declaration of war, and the creation of criminal liability. *See* Restatement (Third) of the Foreign Relations Law of the United States §111, cmt. i and reporters' note 6 (1987). Why do you think those actions are thought to require the participation of the full Congress? Does the language of Article I, §9, cl. 7 — "No Money shall be drawn from the Treasury, but in Consequence of Appropriations made by Law" — show that the appropriations power is exclusive? Does the language of Article I, Section 7 — "All Bills for raising Revenue shall originate in the House of Representatives" — show that the taxing power is exclusive? Is there a textual explanation for concluding that the powers to declare war and create criminal liability are exclusive? If not, is there an alternate explanation? *See also* Rebecca M. Kysar, *On the Constitutionality of Tax Treaties*, 38 Yale J. Int'l L. 1 (2013) (arguing that it is constitutionally problematic to treat tax treaties as self-executing because they directly affect government revenues without involving the House of Representatives, contrary to the constitutional requirement that "[a]ll Bills for raising Revenue shall originate in the House of Representatives").

10. Professor Yoo has argued that, as an original matter, treaties that touched on subjects within Congress's Article I powers could not be self-executing, but rather needed domestic implementing legislation before having domestic force. Treaties that regulated areas that would be beyond Congress's legislative powers, by contrast, did not impinge upon the legislative power and could apply as self-executing federal law even in the absence of implementing legislation. Professor Yoo concludes from this argument that, at the very least, the Constitution requires treaties to be non-self-executing unless the treatymakers clearly specify the contrary. *See* John C. Yoo, *Globalism and the Constitution: Treaties, Non-Self-Execution, and the Original Understanding*, 99 Colum. L. Rev. 1955 (1999). For a challenge to Professor Yoo's views based on historical materials, see Martin S. Flaherty, *History Right? Historical Scholarship, Original Understanding, and "Supreme Law of the Land,"* 99 Colum. L. Rev. 2095 (1999). For a challenge to his views based on structural constitutional arguments, and in particular the implications of the Supremacy Clause, see Carlos

M. Vazquez, *Laughing at Treaties*, 99 Colum. L. Rev. 2154 (1999). For Professor Yoo's reply, see John C. Yoo, *Treaties and Public Lawmaking: A Textual and Structural Defense of Non-Self-Execution*, 99 Colum. L. Rev. 2218 (1999).

How does Professor Yoo's theory fit with the text of the Supremacy Clause? With the reasons the Founders included treaties in that Clause? With *Foster*? With *Asakura*?

11. What, precisely, is a self-executing treaty? At the most general level, it is a treaty that can be enforced by courts without domestic implementing legislation. Is a self-executing treaty the same thing as a treaty that gives private parties a right to sue in U.S. courts? Can a non-self-executing treaty ever be enforced by a court—for example, as a defense to a state criminal charge, or when the federal government is suing to enforce the treaty? Is there a single non-self-execution "doctrine" that answers these and related questions? Consider the following analysis by Professor Vazquez:

> Bringing coherence and analytical clarity to this area of the law requires recognition that the self-execution "doctrine" addresses at least four distinct types of reasons why a treaty might be judicially unenforceable. First, a treaty might be judicially unenforceable because the parties (or perhaps the U.S. treatymakers unilaterally) made it judicially unenforceable. This is primarily a matter of intent. Second, a treaty might be judicially unenforceable because the obligation it imposes is of a type that, under our system of separated powers, cannot be enforced directly by the courts. This branch of the doctrine calls for a judgment concerning the allocation of treaty-enforcement power as between the courts and the legislature. Third, a treaty might be judicially unenforceable because the treatymakers lack the constitutional power to accomplish by treaty what they purported to accomplish. This branch of the doctrine calls for a judgment about the allocation of legislative power between the treatymakers and the lawmakers. Finally, a treaty provision might be judicially unenforceable because it does not establish a private right of action and there is no other legal basis for the remedy being sought by the party relying on the treaty. Unlike the first three categories of non-self-executing treaties, a treaty that is non-self-executing in the fourth sense will be judicially unenforceable only in certain contexts. These four issues are sufficiently distinct and require sufficiently differing analyses that they should be thought of as four distinct doctrines.

Carlos Manuel Vazquez, *The Four Doctrines of Self-Executing Treaties*, 89 Am. J. Int'l L. 695, 722-23 (1995). Is this helpful?

12. Sometimes the non-self-execution analysis will overlap with the justiciability limitations considered in Chapter 2. Consider, for example, Republic of the Marshall Islands v. United States, 865 F.3d 1187 (9th Cir. 2017). In that case, the Marshall Islands sued the United States, seeking to compel it to comply with Article VI of the Treaty on the Non-Proliferation of Nuclear Weapons, which provides that "[e]ach of the Parties to the Treaty undertakes to pursue negotiations in good faith on effective measures relating to cessation of the nuclear arms race at an early date and to nuclear disarmament, and on a treaty on general and complete disarmament under strict and effective international control." In directing dismissal of the case, the U.S. Court of Appeals for the Ninth Circuit stated: "Whether examined under the rubric of treaty self-execution, the redressability prong of standing, or the political question doctrine, the analysis stems from the same separation-of-powers principle—enforcement of this treaty provision is not committed to the judicial branch." The court emphasized, among other things, that Article VI "is addressed to the executive, urging further steps only the executive can take—negotiation with other nations."

13. Even if a treaty is self-executing and thus potentially subject to direct judicial enforcement, a court may conclude that it does not confer a private right to sue for relief, such as for damages. This was the court's conclusion with respect to the bilateral treaty at issue in McKesson v. Islamic Republic of Iran, 539 F.3d 485 (D.C. Cir. 2008). In that case, a U.S. company was suing Iran for its alleged expropriation of the company's ownership interest in an Iranian dairy firm. In support of its claim, the company relied on a 1955 Treaty of Amity, Economic Relations, and Consular Rights between the United States and Iran, Article IV(2) of which declares that "property shall not be taken except for a public purpose, nor shall it be taken without the prompt payment of just compensation." Although the court concluded that the treaty was self-executing, the court quoted footnote 3 of *Medellin* for the proposition that "the background presumption is that '[i]nternational agreements, even those directly benefiting private persons, generally do not create private rights or provide for a private cause of action in domestic courts.'" The court further noted that the treaty here did not explicitly call for domestic judicial enforcement, and the court said that "[i]n the absence of a textual invitation to judicial participation, we conclude the President and the Senate intended to enforce the Treaty of Amity through bilateral interaction between its signatories." The court also gave "great weight" to the Executive Branch's view that the treaty did not convey a private right of action. *See also* Restatement (Fourth) of the Foreign Relations Law of the United States §311(1) (2018) ("A treaty provision, even if it is self-executing, does not by virtue of that fact alone establish a private right of action or confer a right to seek particular remedies such as damages.").

14. Even if a self-executing treaty does not confer a private right of action, litigants may be able to invoke the treaty *defensively* to argue that it displaces a law being applied against them. *Cf.* Sanchez-Llamas v. Oregon, 548 U.S. 331, 346 (2006) ("Of course, it is well established that a self-executing treaty binds the States pursuant to the Supremacy Clause, and that the States therefore must recognize the force of the treaty in the course of adjudicating the rights of litigants."). On the other hand, even if a self-executing treaty confers some individually enforceable rights, a litigant might not be entitled, under either the treaty or other law, to the particular remedy that he or she is seeking. In *Sanchez-Llamas* (which is excerpted below in Section F), for example, the Supreme Court held that Article 36 of the Vienna Convention on Consular Relations did not confer a right to have evidence excluded as a remedy for its violation, in part because the exclusionary rule is "an entirely American legal creation," and "[i]t is implausible that other signatories to the Convention thought it to require a remedy that nearly all refuse to recognize as a matter of domestic law." Similarly, a number of circuit courts have held that even if Article 36 confers enforceable individual rights, it does not confer a right to have an indictment dismissed as a remedy for its violation. *See, e.g.,* United States v. Duarte-Acero, 296 F.3d 1277, 1281-82 (11th Cir. 2002); United States v. Page, 232 F.3d 536, 540-41 (6th Cir. 2000); United States v. Li, 206 F.3d 56, 61-62 (1st Cir. 2000) (en banc).

15. What does the Court in *Medellin* suggest about the domestic status of non-self-executing treaties? Are non-self-executing treaties simply judicially unenforceable, or do they more broadly lack the status of domestic law? Is it consistent with the Supremacy Clause to conclude that some treaties ratified by the United States lack the status of supreme law of the land? For a discussion of these issues, see Curtis A. Bradley, *Intent, Presumptions, and Non-Self-Executing Treaties,* 101 Am. J. Int'l L. 540 (2008).

Medellin was executed by the State of Texas in August 2008. In denying a stay of execution, the Supreme Court stated in a *per curiam* order that "[i]t is up to Congress whether to implement obligations undertaken under a treaty which (like this one) does not itself have the force and effect of domestic law sufficient to set aside the judgment or the ensuing sentence." What does that statement suggest about the domestic status of the treaty?

The domestic status of a non-self-executing treaty may also be relevant to whether a federal court has subject matter jurisdiction to hear a treaty claim. In particular, if a non-self-executing treaty does not have the status of federal law, a dispute relating to the treaty might not fall within federal question jurisdiction. *But cf.* Sluss v. U.S. Dep't of Justice, 898 F.3d 1242, 1248 (D.C. Cir. 2018) (holding that "whether a treaty is self-executing does not present a jurisdictional issue regarding the court's power to hear a case; rather, that inquiry relates to whether the plaintiff has a cause of action").

16. Can the President take actions to enforce a non-self-executing treaty within the United States, or must he or she await implementation of the treaty by Congress? In *Medellin,* the Supreme Court held that the President did not have the unilateral authority to preempt state law in order to enforce a non-self-executing treaty obligation. Is this conclusion consistent with American Insurance Association v. Garamendi, which is excerpted in Chapter 4? The Court in *Medellin* further expressed the view that, when the President attempts to enforce a non-self-executing treaty by unilaterally creating domestic law, "he acts in conflict with the implicit understanding of the ratifying Senate," and thus his actions fall within the lowest tier of Justice Jackson's framework from *Youngstown.* Do you agree? Does a decision by the Senate not to allow for direct judicial enforcement of a treaty necessarily mean that the Senate wanted to preclude the President from being able to implement the treaty? Did the Court in *Medellin* rule out all presidential enforcement of non-self-executing treaties? If not, what actions can a president still take to enforce such a treaty? For a challenge to "the assumption that Congress is the only appropriate intermediary between the courts and treaty provisions that are not directly enforceable" and an argument that "actors in the executive branch can serve this intermediary role, at least when certain conditions are met," see Jean Galbraith, *Making Treaty Implementation More Like Statutory Implementation,* 115 Mich. L. Rev. 1309, 1312-13 (2017).

17. The Supreme Court's self-execution analysis in *Medellin* has generated substantial academic debate, both over the soundness of the Court's legal reasoning and over what the Court's analysis suggests for future cases. *Compare, for example,* Carlos Manuel Vazquez, *Treaties as Law of the Land: The Supremacy Clause and the Judicial Enforcement of Treaties,* 122 Harv. L. Rev. 599 (2008) (generally critical of *Medellin*'s self-execution analysis), *with* Curtis A. Bradley, *Self-Execution and Treaty Duality,* 2009 Sup. Ct. Rev. 131 (generally supportive of the analysis). *See also* David H. Moore, *Law(makers) of the Land: The Doctrine of Treaty Non-Self-Execution,* 122 Harv. L. Rev. F. 32 (2009) (response to Vazquez article); Ernest A. Young, *Treaties as "Part of Our Law,"* 88 Tex. L. Rev. 91 (2009) (discussing *Medellin* and arguing that "[t]aking treaties seriously as part of our law—that is, treating them the same way we treat federal statutes and constitutional provisions—actually supports a number of conclusions generally advanced by nationalists"); John T. Parry, *Rewriting the Roberts Court's Law of Treaties,* 88 Tex. L. Rev. 65 (2010) (response to Young's article). For symposia discussions of *Medellin,* see "Agora: *Medellin*," 102 Am. J. Int'l L. 529-72 (2008) (articles by David Bederman, Curtis Bradley, Steve

Charnovitz, and Carlos Vazquez); and "Treaties and Domestic Law After Medellin v. Texas," 13 Lewis & Clark L. Rev. (2009) (articles by Scott Lyons, John Parry, Paul Stephan, and Ingrid Wuerth). *See also* William M. Carter, Jr., *Treaties as Law and the Rule of Law: The Judicial Power to Compel Domestic Treaty Implementation*, 69 Md. L. Rev. 344 (2010); Julian Ku, Medellin's *Clear Statement Rule: A Search for International Delegations*, 77 Fordham L. Rev. 609 (2008); Jane Koven Levit, *Does* Medellin *Matter?*, 77 Fordham L. Rev. 617 (2008); D. A. Jeremy Telman, Medellin *and Originalism*, 68 Md. L. Rev. 377 (2009).

For other scholarship on self-execution, see Edwin Dickinson, *Are the Liquor Treaties Self-Executing?*, 20 Am. J. Int'l L. 444 (1926); Yuji Iwasawa, *The Doctrine of Self-Executing Treaties in the United States: A Critical Analysis*, 26 Va. J. Int'l L. 627 (1986); Jordan J. Paust, *Self-Executing Treaties*, 82 Am. J. Int'l L. 760 (1988); David H. Moore, *Do U.S. Courts Discriminate Against Treaties?: Equivalence, Duality, and Non-Self-Execution*, 110 Colum. L. Rev. 2228 (2010); Stefan A. Riesenfeld, *The Doctrine of Self-Executing Treaties and U.S. v. Postal: Win at Any Price?*, 74 Am. J. Int'l L. 892 (1980); and Tim Wu, *Treaties' Domains*, 93 Va. L. Rev. 571 (2007). For a detailed consideration of early debates in Congress over the domestic status of treaties, see John T. Parry, *Congress, the Supremacy Clause, and the Implementation of Treaties*, 32 Fordham Int'l L.J. 1209 (2009).

B. CONFLICTS BETWEEN TREATIES AND FEDERAL STATUTES

The Constitution provides that both treaties and federal statutes are part of the supreme law of the land and thus preempt inconsistent state law. The Constitution does not specify, however, the relationship between treaties and statutes. If there is a conflict between a non-self-executing treaty and a statute, courts will apply the statute, since the treaty will not be judicially enforceable. But what should a court do if confronted with a conflict between a self-executing treaty and a federal statute? The decisions below consider this question.

Whitney v. Robertson

124 U.S. 190 (1888)

MR. JUSTICE FIELD delivered the opinion of the Court.

The plaintiffs are merchants, doing business in the city of New York, and in August, 1882, they imported a large quantity of "centrifugal and molasses sugars," the produce and manufacture of the island of San Domingo. These goods were similar in kind to sugars produced in the Hawaiian Islands, which are admitted free of duty under the treaty with the king of those islands, and the act of Congress, passed to carry the treaty into effect. They were duly entered at the custom house at the port of New York, the plaintiffs claiming that by the treaty with the Republic of San Domingo [the Dominican Republic] the goods should be admitted on the same terms, that is, free of duty, as similar articles, the produce and manufacture of the Hawaiian Islands. The defendant, who was at the time collector of the port, refused to allow this claim, treated the goods as dutiable articles under the acts of Congress, and exacted duties on them to the amount of $21,936. The plaintiffs appealed from the collector's decision to the Secretary of the Treasury, by whom the appeal was denied. They then paid under protest the duties exacted, and brought the present action to recover the amount. . . .

[The Court first holds that the "most favored nation" provision in the treaty with the Dominican Republic precluded discrimination but did not require the United States to extend to the Republic special concessions given to other countries for valuable consideration.]

But, independently of considerations of this nature, there is another and complete answer to the pretensions of the plaintiffs. The act of Congress under which the duties were collected authorized their exaction. It is of general application, making no exception in favor of goods of any country. It was passed after the treaty with the Dominican Republic, and, if there be any conflict between the stipulations of the treaty and the requirements of the law, the latter must control. A treaty is primarily a contract between two or more independent nations, and is so regarded by writers on public law. For the infraction of its provisions a remedy must be sought by the injured party through reclamations upon the other. When the stipulations are not self-executing they can only be enforced pursuant to legislation to carry them into effect, and such legislation is as much subject to modification and repeal by Congress as legislation upon any other subject. If the treaty contains stipulations which are self-executing, that is, require no legislation to make them operative, to that extent they have the force and effect of a legislative enactment. Congress may modify such provisions, so far as they bind the United States, or supersede them altogether. By the Constitution a treaty is placed on the same footing, and made of like obligation, with an act of legislation. Both are declared by that instrument to be the supreme law of the land, and no superior efficacy is given to either over the other. When the two relate to the same subject, the courts will always endeavor to construe them so as to give effect to both, if that can be done without violating the language of either; but if the two are inconsistent, the one last in date will control the other, provided always the stipulation of the treaty on the subject is self-executing. If the country with which the treaty is made is dissatisfied with the action of the legislative department, it may present its complaint to the executive head of the government, and take such other measures as it may deem essential for the protection of its interests. The courts can afford no redress. . . .

It follows, therefore, that when a law is clear in its provisions, its validity cannot be assailed before the courts for want of conformity to stipulations of a previous treaty not already executed. Considerations of that character belong to another department of the government. The duty of the courts is to construe and give effect to the latest expression of the sovereign will.

Cook v. United States

288 U.S. 102 (1933)

[The Eighteenth Amendment, which took effect in 1920, outlawed (among other things) the importation of intoxicating liquor into the United States. This Prohibition Amendment was repealed by the Twenty-First Amendment in 1933. In 1922, Congress enacted a statute, §581 of the Tariff Act, authorizing the Coast Guard to stop and inspect vessels within 12 miles of the U.S. coast to determine if any violation of law had been committed. This statute was reenacted in 1930. Pursuant to the statute, the Coast Guard stopped a British ship that was about 11 miles from the coast and found liquor on board. The Customs Service subsequently imposed a fine on the master of the ship for failing to disclose the liquor on the ship's manifest. The master of the ship, Cook, argued that a 1924 treaty between the United States and Great Britain modified the earlier statute and precluded the United States from exercising jurisdiction over the ship. The treaty gave the United States jurisdiction only over British vessels that could reach the U.S. coast within one hour. The vessel in this case could not go over 10 miles an hour and was more than 10 miles from the coast. The Government responded that the treaty did not modify §581 of the 1922 statute, and that if it did, the reenactment of §581 without change in 1930 removed the alleged modification.]

MR. JUSTICE BRANDEIS delivered the opinion of the Court. . . .

Second. The Treaty, being later in date than the Act of 1922, superseded, so far as inconsistent with the terms of the Act, the authority which had been conferred by §581 upon officers of the Coast Guard to board, search and seize beyond our territorial waters. Whitney v. Robertson, 124 U.S. 190, 194. For in a strict sense the Treaty was self-executing, in that no legislation was necessary to authorize executive action pursuant to its provisions.

The purpose of the provisions for seizure in §581, and their practical operation, as an aid in the enforcement of the laws prohibiting alcoholic liquors, leave no doubt that the territorial limitations there established were modified by the Treaty. This conclusion is supported by the course of administrative practice. Shortly after the Treaty took effect, the Treasury Department issued amended instructions for the Coast Guard which pointed out, after reciting the provisions of §581, that "in cases of special treaties, the provisions of those treaties shall be complied with"; and called attention particularly to the recent treaties dealing with the smuggling of intoxicating liquors. The Commandant of the Coast Guard, moreover, was informed in 1927, as the Solicitor General states, that all seizures of British vessels captured in the rum-smuggling trade should be within the terms of the Treaty and that seizing officers should be instructed to produce evidence, not that the vessel was found within the four-league limit, but that she was apprehended within one hour's sailing distance from the coast.

Third. The Treaty was not abrogated by re-enacting §581 in the Tariff Act of 1930 in the identical terms of the Act of 1922. A treaty will not be deemed to have been abrogated or modified by a later statute unless such purpose on the part of Congress has been clearly expressed. Here, the contrary appears. The committee reports and the debates upon the Act of 1930, like the re-enacted section itself, make no reference to the Treaty of 1924. Any doubt as to the construction of the section should be deemed resolved by the consistent departmental practice existing before its reenactment. . . .

Searches and seizures in the enforcement of the laws prohibiting alcoholic liquors are governed, since the 1930 Act, as they were before, by the provisions of the Treaty. Section 581, with its scope narrowed by the Treaty, remained in force after its reenactment in the Act of 1930. The section continued to apply to the boarding, search and seizure of all vessels of all countries with which we had no relevant treaties. It continued also, in the enforcement of our customs laws not related to the prohibition of alcoholic liquors, to govern the boarding of vessels of those countries with which we had entered into treaties like that with Great Britain.

Notes and Questions

1. As illustrated by *Whitney*, Congress's ability to override treaties, for purposes of U.S. domestic law, is well settled. *See also, e.g.,* Breard v. Greene, 523 U.S. 371, 376 (1998) (*per curiam*); Chae Chan Ping v. United States (*Chinese Exclusion Case*), 130 U.S. 581, 600-01 (1889); Edye v. Robertson (*Head Money Cases*), 112 U.S. 580, 597-98 (1884). In one of the earliest articulations of this proposition, a court explained the basis for it as follows:

> To refuse to execute a treaty, for reasons which approve themselves to the conscientious judgment of the nation, is a matter of the utmost gravity and delicacy; but the power to do so, is prerogative, of which no nation can be deprived, without deeply affecting its independence. That the people of the United States have deprived their government of this power in any case, I do not believe. That it must reside somewhere, and be applicable to all cases, I am convinced. I feel no doubt that it belongs to congress. That, inasmuch as treaties must continue to operate as part of our municipal law, and be obeyed by the people, applied by the judiciary and executed by the president, while they continue unrepealed, and inasmuch as the power of repealing these municipal laws must reside somewhere, and no body other than congress possesses it, then legislative power is applicable to such laws whenever they relate to subjects, which the constitution has placed under that legislative power.

Taylor v. Morton, 23 F. Cas. 784, 786 (C.C.D. Mass. 1855). How does this explanation for why statutes can override treaties compare with the explanation given in *Whitney*?

2. Today, the proposition that Congress can override treaties for purposes of U.S. domestic law is referred to as a component of the "later-in-time rule" or "last-in-time rule," pursuant to which treaties and statutes are given equal weight in the U.S. legal system. What is the basis for giving statutes and treaties equal weight? Treaties and statutes are both mentioned in the Supremacy Clause, but is every form of law mentioned in the Clause equal in status? Given that two-thirds of the Senate must consent in order for the United States to enter into a treaty, why should a simple majority of Congress have the ability to override a treaty? Given that the President is granted the power to make treaties (with the advice and consent of the Senate), why should Congress (if it passes a veto-proof statute) have the ability to override a treaty against the wishes of the President? Would U.S. treaty practice change if statutes could not override treaties? Would it change if treaties could not override statutes? In considering these questions, keep in mind that when Congress overrides a treaty as a matter of U.S. domestic law, the treaty still binds the United States under international law until validly terminated.

3. In *Whitney*, the later-in-time rule was applied to override an earlier treaty. As illustrated by *Cook*, the later-in-time rule can work the other way as well. That is, later-in-time treaties can, at least in theory, override earlier federal statutes. *See also* Opinion of Caleb Cushing, Copyright Convention with Great Britain (Feb. 16, 1854), 6 Op. Atty. Gen. 291 (1854) (expressing the view that a treaty could override an earlier federal statute). This is relatively rare, however, and *Cook* is the only modern Supreme Court decision recognizing such an override. Courts have allowed treaties to supersede the requirements of federal statutes in the area of income taxation, but that is in part because the Internal Revenue Code specifically provides that the income tax laws are to be applied "with due regard to any treaty obligation of the United States which applies to such taxpayer." 26 U.S.C. §894(a)(1); *cf.* 26 U.S.C. §7852(d)(1) ("For purposes of determining the relationship between a provision of a treaty and any law of the United States affecting revenue, neither the treaty nor the law shall have preferential status by reason of its being a treaty or law."). Why are there not more decisions allowing treaties to override statutes? Are the justifications the same for allowing later treaties to supersede earlier statutes as they are for allowing later statutes to supersede earlier treaties? What is the relationship between the self-execution doctrine and the ability of treaties to override statutes? *See also* Restatement (Fourth) of the Foreign Relations Law of the United States §309 (2018) ("When there is a conflict between a self-executing treaty provision and a federal statute, courts in the United States will apply whichever reflects the latest expression of the will of the U.S. political branches.").

4. As noted in *Cook,* courts will not apply a later-in-time statute to override an earlier treaty absent a clear conflict between the two. That is, courts will interpret statutes, where possible, to avoid treaty violations. At times, the Supreme Court has suggested that a statute will not be applied to displace a treaty unless there is evidence that Congress specifically intended this result. At other times, the Court has indicated that if there is a conflict between a clear statute and an earlier treaty, the statute will be applied regardless of whether there is evidence that Congress specifically intended to override the treaty. For discussion of these conflicting lines of authority, see Owner-Operator Independent Drivers Association v. United States Department of Transportation, 724 F.3d 230 (D.C. Cir. 2013). Which approach makes more sense—a clear statement requirement for overriding a treaty, or a mere presumption against treaty violations?

Whatever its precise content, this interpretive canon is based in part on the assumption that Congress does not lightly violate the international obligations established by a treaty. *See, e.g., Chew Heong,* 112 U.S. at 539 ("[T]he court should be slow to assume that congress intended to violate the stipulations of a treaty."). The canon is therefore related to the *Charming Betsy* canon of construction (which is considered in Chapter 7), pursuant to which "an act of congress ought never to be construed to violate the law of nations, if any other possible construction remains...." Murray v. Schooner Charming Betsy, 6 U.S. (2 Cranch) 64, 118 (1804). As such, it probably applies even to potential conflicts with non-self-executing treaties. *See, e.g.,* Ma v. Ashcroft, 257 F.3d 1095, 1114 (9th Cir. 2001) (applying the canon to avoid a violation of the International Covenant on Civil and Political Rights (ICCPR), which the Senate had declared to be non-self-executing). *But see* The Fund for Animals, Inc. v. Kempthorne, 472 F.3d 872, 880 (D.C. Cir. 2006) (Kavanaugh, J., concurring) ("There is little authority squarely analyzing whether those interpretive principles should extend to *non-self-executing* treaties, which have no force as a matter of domestic law."). This interpretive canon may also be related to the general presumption against implied repeals of domestic law, at least when applied to potential conflicts with self-executing treaties. *See, e.g.,* Chew Heong v. United States, 112 U.S. 536, 549 (1884) (noting that, "even in the case of statutes, whose repeal or modification involves no question of good faith with the government or people of other countries, the rule is well settled that repeals by implication are not favored, and are never admitted where the former can stand with the new act"). For a discussion of the interpretive issues raised by statutes that expressly incorporate treaty terms, see John F. Coyle, *Incorporative Statutes and the Borrowed Treaty Rule,* 50 Va. J. Int'l L. 655 (2010) (proposing that when a statute incorporates language or concepts from a treaty, the statute should be read to conform to the treaty, regardless of whether the statute is ambiguous).

5. Can Congress make an otherwise self-executing treaty non-self-executing? For a decision holding that it can, see Noriega v. Pastrana, 564 F.3d 1290 (11th Cir. 2009). That case concerned General Manuel Noriega, who was apprehended in Panama in 1989 by the U.S. military and then tried and convicted in the United States on drug and money laundering charges. When he was about to complete his prison sentence, the United States began proceedings to extradite him to France. Noriega filed a habeas corpus action, arguing that he was a prisoner of war and that the Third Geneva Convention obligated the United States to repatriate him to Panama rather than extradite him. In rejecting this argument, the court held that Noriega's claim was precluded by §5 of the Military Commissions Act of 2006 (MCA), which provides that "[n]o person may invoke the Geneva Conventions or any protocols thereto in any habeas corpus or other civil action or proceeding to which the United States, or . . . agent of the United States is a party as a source of rights in any court of the United States or its States or territories." The court reasoned that it was "unnecessary to resolve the question of whether the Geneva Conventions are self-executing, because it is within Congress' power to change domestic law, even if the law originally arose from a self-executing treaty." The court concluded that "while the United States' international obligations under the Geneva Conventions are not altered by the enactment of §5 of the MCA, Congress has superseded whatever domestic effect the Geneva Conventions may have had in actions such as this." For academic debate over Congress's authority to render a treaty non-self-executing, *compare* Curtis A. Bradley, *The Military Commissions Act, Habeas Corpus, and the Geneva Conventions*, 101 Am. J. Int'l L. 322, 339-41 (2007) (arguing that Congress has this authority), *with* Carlos Manuel Vazquez, *The Military Commissions Act, the Geneva Conventions, and the Courts: A Critical Guide*, 101 Am. J. Int'l L. 73, 89-91 (2007) (arguing that Congress does not have this authority).

6. For academic discussion of the later-in-time rule, see, for example, Louis Henkin, *The Constitution and United States Sovereignty: A Century of Chinese Exclusion and Its Progeny*, 100 Harv. L. Rev. 853 (1987); Julian Ku, *Treaties as Laws: A Defense of the Last-in-Time Rule for Treaties and Federal Statutes*, 80 Ind. L.J. 319 (2005); Jules Lobel, *The Limits of Constitutional Power: Conflicts Between Foreign Policy and International Law*, 71 Va. L. Rev. 1071 (1985); Detlev Vagts, *The United States and Its Treaties: Observance and Breach*, 95 Am. J. Int'l L. 313 (2001); and Peter Westen, *The Place of Foreign Treaties in the Courts of the United States: A Reply to Louis Henkin*, 101 Harv. L. Rev. 511 (1987). For an argument (based on Founding intent) that statutes should always take precedence in U.S. courts over treaties, and that treaties that conflict with statutes should be treated as non-self-executing, see Vasan Kesavan, *The Three Tiers of Federal Law*, 100 Nw. U. L. Rev. 1479 (2006). *See also* Akhil Reed Amar, America's Constitution 303 (2005) (similar conclusion).

C. THE TREATY POWER AND FEDERALISM

The Constitution makes clear that treaties are the supreme law of the land and therefore preempt inconsistent state law, at least if the treaties are self-executing.* The Supreme Court confirmed the supremacy of treaties over state law in an early decision, Ware v. Hylton, 3 U.S. (3 Dall.) 199 (1796), which held that the treaty

---

* Various grounds for preemption of state law are discussed in Chapter 4.

between the United States and Great Britain ending the Revolutionary War pre-empted a Virginia statute providing for the discharge of debts owed to British creditors. Despite the settled supremacy of treaties over state law, questions remain about the relationship between the treaty power and U.S. federalism. Are there any limits to the subject matters that can be regulated by treaty? Can treaties create domestic law that is beyond the scope of Congress's legislative powers? Does Congress have the authority under the Necessary and Proper Clause to enact legislation to implement treaties if the legislation would otherwise fall outside the scope of its legislative powers? Is the treaty power subject to any Tenth Amendment limitations? Can treaties "commandeer" state legislatures or executive branches? Can treaties override the sovereign immunity of the states? These and other federalism issues are considered below.

Geofroy v. Riggs

133 U.S. 258 (1890)

MR. JUSTICE FIELD, after stating the case, delivered the opinion of the Court. . . .

The question presented for solution . . . is whether the complainants, being citizens and residents of France, inherit an interest in the real estate in the District of Columbia of which their uncle, a citizen of the United States and a resident of the District, died seized. In more general terms the question is: can citizens of France take land in the District of Columbia by descent from citizens of the United States? . . .

[The Court explained that Congress in 1801 had declared the laws of Maryland to apply to the District of Columbia and that these laws restricted the ability of foreigners to inherit real property from U.S. citizens.]

On the 30th of September, 1800, a convention of peace, commerce and navigation was concluded between France and the United States, the 7th article of which provided that "the citizens and inhabitants of the United States shall be at liberty to dispose by testament, donation or otherwise, of their goods, movable and immovable, holden in the territory of the French Republic in Europe, and the citizens of the French Republic shall have the same liberty with regard to goods movable and immovable, holden in the territory of the United States, in favor of such persons as they shall think proper. The citizens and inhabitants of either of the two countries, who shall be heirs of goods, movable or immovable, in the other, shall be able to succeed *ab intestato*, without being obliged to obtain letters of naturalization, and without having the effect of this provision contested or impeded under any pretext whatever."

This article, by its terms, suspended, during the existence of the treaty, the provisions of the common law of Maryland and of the statutes of that state of 1780 and of 1791, so far as they prevented citizens of France from taking by inheritance from citizens of the United States, property, real or personal, situated therein.

That the treaty power of the United States extends to all proper subjects of negotiation between our government and the governments of other nations, is clear. It is also clear that the protection which should be afforded to the citizens of one country owning property in another, and the manner in which that property may be transferred, devised or inherited, are fitting subjects for such negotiation and of regulation by mutual stipulations between the two countries. As commercial intercourse increases between different countries the residence of citizens of one country within the territory of the other naturally follows, and the removal of their disability from alienage to hold, transfer and inherit property in such cases tends to promote amicable relations. Such removal has been within the present century the frequent subject of treaty arrangement. The treaty power, as expressed in the Constitution, is in terms unlimited except by those restraints which are found in that instrument against the action of the government or of its departments, and those arising from the nature of the government itself and of that of the States. It would not be contended that it extends so far as to authorize what the Constitution forbids, or a change in the character of the government or in that of one of the States, or a cession of any portion of the territory of the latter, without its consent. But with these exceptions, it is not perceived that there is any limit to the questions which can be adjusted touching any matter which is properly the subject of negotiation with a foreign country.

Article 7 of the convention of 1800 was in force when the act of Congress adopting the laws of Maryland, February 27, 1801, was passed. That law adopted and continued in force the law of Maryland as it then existed. It did not adopt the law of Maryland as it existed previous to the treaty; for that would have been in effect to repeal the treaty so far as the District of Columbia was affected. In adopting it as it then existed, it adopted the law with its provisions suspended during the continuance of the treaty so far as they conflicted with it—in other words, the treaty, being part of the supreme law of the land, controlled the statute and common law of Maryland whenever it differed from them. The treaty expired by its own limitation in eight years, pursuant to an article inserted by the Senate. During its continuance citizens of France could take property in the District of Columbia by inheritance from citizens of the United States. But after its expiration that right was limited as provided by the statute and common law of Maryland, as adopted by Congress on the 27th of February, 1801, until the convention between the United States and France was concluded, February 23, 1853. The 7th article of that convention is as follows:

> In all the States of the Union, whose existing laws permit it, so long and to the same extent as the said laws shall remain in force, Frenchmen shall enjoy the right of possessing personal and real property by the same title and in the same manner as the citizens of the United States. They shall be free to dispose of it as they may please, either gratuitously or for value received, by donation, testament, or otherwise, just as those citizens themselves; and in no case shall they be subjected to taxes on transfer, inheritance, or any others different from those paid by the latter, or to taxes which shall not be equally imposed.
>
> As to the States of the Union, by whose existing laws aliens are not permitted to hold real estate, the President engages to recommend to them the passage of such laws as may be necessary for the purpose of conferring this right.
>
> In like manner, but with the reservation of the ulterior right of establishing reciprocity in regard to possession and inheritance, the government of France accords to the citizens of the United States the same rights within its territory in respect to real and personal property, and to inheritance, as are enjoyed there by its own citizens.

This article is not happily drawn. It leaves in doubt what is meant by "States of the Union." Ordinarily these terms would be held to apply to those political communities exercising various attributes of sovereignty which compose the United States, as distinguished from the organized municipalities known as Territories and the District of Columbia. And yet separate communities, with an independent local government, are often described as states, though the extent of their political sovereignty be limited by relations to a more general government or to other countries. The term is used in general jurisprudence and by writers on public law as denoting organized political societies with an established government. Within this definition the District of Columbia, under the government of the United States, is as much a State as any of those political communities which compose the United States. . . .

Aside from the question in which of these significations the terms are used in the convention of 1853, we think the construction of article 7 is free from difficulty. In some States aliens were permitted to hold real estate, but not to take by inheritance. To this right to hold real estate in some States reference is had by the words "permit it" in the first clause, and it is alluded to in the second clause as not permitted in others. This will be manifest if we read the second clause before the first. This construction, as well observed by counsel, gives consistency and harmony to all the provisions of the article, and comports with its character as an agreement intended to confer reciprocal rights on the citizens of each country with respect to property held by them within the territory of the other. To construe the first clause as providing that Frenchmen shall enjoy the right of possessing personal and real property by the same title and in the same manner as citizens of the United States, in States, so long as their laws permit such enjoyment, is to give a meaning to the article by which nothing is conferred not already possessed, and leaves no adequate reason for the concession by France of rights to citizens of the United States, made in the third clause. We do not think this construction admissible. It is a rule, in construing treaties as well as laws, to give a sensible meaning to all their provisions if that be practicable. . . . As we read the article it declares that in all the States of the Union by whose laws aliens are permitted to hold real estate, so long as such laws remain in force, Frenchmen shall enjoy the right of possessing personal and real property by the same title and in the same manner as citizens of the United States. They shall be free to dispose of it as they may please — by donation, testament, or otherwise — just as those citizens themselves. But as to the States by whose existing laws aliens are not permitted to hold real estate, the treaty engages that the President shall recommend to them the passage of such laws as may be necessary for the purpose of conferring that right. . . .

. . . Our conclusion is, that the complainants are entitled to take by inheritance an interest in the real property in the District of Columbia of which their uncle died seized.

Missouri v. Holland

252 U.S. 416 (1920)

MR. JUSTICE HOLMES delivered the opinion of the Court.

This is a bill in equity brought by the State of Missouri to prevent a game warden of the United States from attempting to enforce the Migratory Bird Treaty Act of July 3, 1918, c. 128, 40 Stat. 755, and the regulations made by the Secretary of Agriculture in pursuance of the same. The ground of the bill is that the statute is an unconstitutional interference with the rights reserved to the States by the Tenth Amendment, and that the acts of the defendant done and threatened under that authority invade the sovereign right of the State and contravene its will manifested in statutes. . . . A motion to dismiss was sustained by the District Court on the ground that the act of Congress is constitutional. . . . The State appeals.

On December 8, 1916, a treaty between the United States and Great Britain was proclaimed by the President. It recited that many species of birds in their annual migrations traversed certain parts of the United States and of Canada, that they were of great value as a source of food and in destroying insects injurious to vegetation, but were in danger of extermination through lack of adequate protection. It therefore provided for specified close seasons and protection in other forms, and agreed that the two powers would take or propose to their law-making bodies the necessary measures for carrying the treaty out. The above mentioned Act of July 3, 1918, entitled an act to give effect to the convention, prohibited the killing, capturing or selling any of the migratory birds included in the terms of the treaty except as permitted by regulations compatible with those terms, to be made by the Secretary of Agriculture. Regulations were proclaimed on July 31, and October 25, 1918. It is unnecessary to go into any details, because, as we have said, the question raised is the general one whether the treaty and statute are void as an interference with the rights reserved to the States.

To answer this question it is not enough to refer to the Tenth Amendment, reserving the powers not delegated to the United States, because by Article II, §2, the power to make treaties is delegated expressly, and by Article VI treaties made under the authority of the United States, along with the Constitution and laws of the United States made in pursuance thereof, are declared the supreme law of the land. If the treaty is valid there can be no dispute about the validity of the statute under Article I, §8, as a necessary and proper means to execute the powers of the Government. The language of the Constitution as to the supremacy of treaties being general, the question before us is narrowed to an inquiry into the ground upon which the present supposed exception is placed.

It is said that a treaty cannot be valid if it infringes the Constitution, that there are limits, therefore, to the treaty-making power, and that one such limit is that what an act of Congress could not do unaided, in derogation of the powers reserved to the States, a treaty cannot do. An earlier act of Congress that attempted by itself and not in pursuance of a treaty to regulate the killing of migratory birds within the States had been held bad in the District Court. United States v. Shauver, 214 Fed. Rep. 154. United States v. McCullagh, 221 Fed. Rep. 288. Those decisions were supported by arguments that migratory birds were owned by the States in their sovereign capacity for the benefit of their people, and that under cases like Geer v. Connecticut, 161 U.S. 519, this control was one that Congress had no power to displace. The same argument is supposed to apply now with equal force.

Whether the two cases cited were decided rightly or not they cannot be accepted as a test of the treaty power. Acts of Congress are the supreme law of the land only when made in pursuance of the Constitution, while treaties are declared to be so when made under the authority of the United States. It is open to question whether the authority of the United States means more than the formal acts prescribed to make the convention. We do not mean to imply that there are no qualifications to the treaty-making power; but they must be ascertained in a different way. It is obvious that there may be matters of the sharpest exigency for the national well being that an act of Congress could not deal with but that a treaty followed by such an act could, and it is not lightly to be assumed that, in matters requiring national action, "a power which must belong to and somewhere reside in every civilized government" is not to be found. Andrews v. Andrews, 188 U.S. 14, 33. What was said in that case with regard to the powers of the States applies with equal force to the powers of the nation in cases where the States individually are incompetent to act. We are not yet discussing the particular case before us but only are considering the validity of the test proposed. With regard to that we may add that when we are dealing with words that also are a constituent act, like the Constitution of the United States, we must realize that they have called into life a being the development of which could not have been foreseen completely by the most gifted of its begetters. It was enough for them to realize or to hope that they had created an organism; it has taken a century and has cost their successors much sweat and blood to prove that they created a nation. The case before us must be considered in the light of our whole experience and not merely in that of what was said a hundred years ago. The treaty in question does not contravene any prohibitory words to be found in the Constitution. The only question is whether it is forbidden by some invisible radiation from the general terms of the Tenth Amendment. We must consider what this country has become in deciding what that Amendment has reserved.

The State, as we have intimated, founds its claim of exclusive authority upon an assertion of title to migratory birds, an assertion that is embodied in statute. No doubt it is true that as between a State and its inhabitants the State may regulate the killing and sale of such birds, but it does not follow that its authority is exclusive of paramount powers. To put the claim of the State upon title is to lean upon a slender reed. Wild birds are not in the possession of anyone; and possession is the beginning of ownership. The whole foundation of the State's rights is the presence within their jurisdiction of birds that yesterday had not arrived, tomorrow may be in another State and in a week a thousand miles away. If we are to be accurate we cannot put the case of the State upon higher ground than that the treaty deals with creatures that for the moment are within the state borders, that it must be carried out by officers of the United States within the same territory, and that but for the treaty the State would be free to regulate this subject itself.

As most of the laws of the United States are carried out within the States and as many of them deal with matters which in the silence of such laws the State might regulate, such general grounds are not enough to support Missouri's claim. Valid treaties of course "are as binding within the territorial limits of the States as they are elsewhere throughout the dominion of the United States." Baldwin v. Franks, 120 U.S. 678, 683. No doubt the great body of private relations usually fall within the control of the State, but a treaty may override its power. We do not have to invoke the later developments of constitutional law for this proposition; it was recognized as early as Hopkirk v. Bell, 3 Cranch, 454, with regard to statutes of limitation, and even earlier, as to confiscation, in Ware v. Hylton, 3 Dall. 199. It was assumed by Chief Justice Marshall with regard to the escheat of land to the State in Chirac v. Chirac, 2 Wheat. 259, 275. Hauenstein v. Lynham, 100 U.S. 483. Geofroy v. Riggs, 133 U.S. 258. Blythe v. Hinckley, 180 U.S. 333, 340. So as to a limited jurisdiction of foreign consuls within a State. Wildenhus's Case, 120 U.S. 1. *See* Ross v. McIntyre,140 U.S. 453. Further illustration seems unnecessary, and it only remains to consider the application of established rules to the present case.

Here a national interest of very nearly the first magnitude is involved. It can be protected only by national action in concert with that of another power. The subject-matter is only transitorily within the State and has no permanent habitat therein. But for the treaty and the statute there soon might be no birds for any powers to deal with. We see nothing in the Constitution that compels the Government to sit by while a food supply is cut off and the protectors of our forests and our crops are destroyed. It is not sufficient to rely upon the States. The reliance is vain, and were it otherwise, the question is whether the United States is forbidden to act. We are of opinion that the treaty and statute must be upheld.

Bond v. United States

572 U.S. 844 (2014)

[In 1997, the United States ratified the Convention on the Prohibition of the Development, Production, Stockpiling, and Use of Chemical Weapons and on Their Destruction. The Convention prohibits the development, stockpiling, or use of chemical weapons by any state party or person within a state party's jurisdiction, and it defines "chemical weapons" as "[t]oxic chemicals and their precursors, except where intended for purposes not prohibited under this Convention, as long as the types and quantities are consistent with such purposes." The "Purposes Not Prohibited Under this Convention" are defined as "[i]ndustrial, agricultural, research, medical, pharmaceutical, or other peaceful purposes." In 1998, Congress implemented the Convention by passing the Chemical Weapons Convention Implementation Act. The Act closely tracks the text of the treaty. Section 229 of the Act forbids any person knowingly "to develop, produce, otherwise acquire, transfer directly or indirectly, receive, stockpile, retain, own, possess, or use, or threaten to use, any chemical weapon." The Act defines "chemical weapon" in relevant part as "[a] toxic chemical and its precursors, except where intended for a purpose not prohibited under this chapter as long as the type and quantity is consistent with such a purpose." "Toxic chemical" is in turn defined in general as "any chemical which through its chemical action on life processes can cause death, temporary incapacitation or permanent harm to humans or animals."

Carol Anne Bond was a microbiologist in Pennsylvania who worked for a chemical manufacturer there. In 2006, her closest friend, Myrlinda Haynes, announced that she was pregnant. Bond subsequently discovered that her own husband was the father of Haynes's child. Seeking revenge against Haynes, Bond stole an arsenic-based compound (10-chloro-10H-phenoxarsine) from her employer and purchased on the Internet a vial of a chemical used in printing photographs and cleaning laboratory equipment. She then applied these chemicals to surfaces around the outside of Haynes's home, mailbox, and car in an effort to cause her injury. Haynes realized what was happening and generally avoided contact with the chemicals, although in one instance, she received a minor contact burn on her thumb. The local police were slow to act, so Haynes eventually contacted federal authorities, and they proceeded to charge Bond with two counts of violating §229 of the Chemical Weapons Convention Implementation Act. She entered into a conditional plea bargain that accepted guilt while preserving her right to appeal, and she was sentenced to six years in prison. On appeal, she argued that the application of the Act to her conduct exceeded the federal government's authority to regulate state and local matters, in violation of the Tenth Amendment to the Constitution. In 2011, the Supreme Court held that Bond had standing to raise this federalism argument. *See* Bond v. United States, 131 S. Ct. 2355 (2011) (*Bond I*). On remand, the U.S. Court of Appeals for the Third Circuit upheld her conviction, and she appealed again to the Supreme Court.]

CHIEF JUSTICE ROBERTS delivered the opinion of the Court. . . .

II

In our federal system, the National Government possesses only limited powers; the States and the people retain the remainder. The States have broad authority to enact legislation for the public good—what we have often called a "police power." United States v. Lopez, 514 U.S. 549, 567 (1995). The Federal Government, by contrast, has no such authority and "can exercise only the powers granted to it," McCulloch v. Maryland, 17 U.S. (4 Wheat.) 316, 405 (1819), including the power to make "all Laws which shall be necessary and proper for carrying into Execution" the enumerated powers, U.S. Const., Art. I, §8, cl. 18. For nearly two centuries it has been "clear" that, lacking a police power, "Congress cannot punish felonies generally." Cohens v. Virginia, 19 U.S. 264 (6 Wheat.) 428 (1821). A criminal act committed wholly within a State "cannot be made an offence against the United States, unless it have some relation to the execution of a power of Congress, or to some matter within the jurisdiction of the United States." United States v. Fox, 95 U.S. 670, 672 (1878).

The Government frequently defends federal criminal legislation on the ground that the legislation is authorized pursuant to Congress's power to regulate interstate commerce. In this case, however, the Court of Appeals held that the Government had explicitly disavowed that argument before the District Court. As a result, in this Court the parties have devoted significant effort to arguing whether section 229, as applied to Bond's offense, is a necessary and proper means of executing the National Government's power to make treaties. Bond argues that the lower court's reading of *Missouri v. Holland* would remove all limits on federal authority, so long as the Federal Government ratifies a treaty first. She insists that to effectively afford the Government a police power whenever it implements a treaty would be contrary to the Framers' careful decision to divide power between the States and the National Government as a means of preserving liberty. To the extent that *Holland* authorizes such usurpation of traditional state authority, Bond says, it must be either limited or overruled.

The Government replies that this Court has never held that a statute implementing a valid treaty exceeds Congress's enumerated powers. To do so here, the Government says, would contravene another deliberate choice of the Framers: to avoid placing subject matter limitations on the National Government's power to make treaties. And it might also undermine confidence in the United States as an international treaty partner.

Notwithstanding this debate, it is "a well-established principle governing the prudent exercise of this Court's jurisdiction that normally the Court will not decide a constitutional question if there is some other ground upon which to dispose of the case." Escambia County v. McMillan, 466 U.S. 48, 51 (1984) (per curiam); *see also* Ashwander v. TVA, 297 U.S. 288, 347 (1936) (Brandeis, J., concurring). Bond argues that section 229 does not cover her conduct. So we consider that argument first.

III

Section 229 exists to implement the Convention, so we begin with that international agreement. . . . [T]he Convention's drafters intended for it to be a comprehensive ban on chemical weapons. But even with its broadly worded definitions, we have doubts that a treaty about *chemical weapons* has anything to do with Bond's conduct.

The Convention, a product of years of worldwide study, analysis, and multinational negotiation, arose in response to war crimes and acts of terrorism. There is no reason to think the sovereign nations that ratified the Convention were interested in anything like Bond's common law assault.

Even if the treaty does reach that far, nothing prevents Congress from implementing the Convention in the same manner it legislates with respect to innumerable other matters — observing the Constitution's division of responsibility between sovereigns and leaving the prosecution of purely local crimes to the States. The Convention, after all, is agnostic between enforcement at the state versus federal level: It provides that "[e]ach State Party shall, *in accordance with its constitutional processes*, adopt the necessary measures to implement its obligations under this Convention." Art. VII(1) (emphasis added) . . . .

Fortunately, we have no need to interpret the scope of the Convention in this case. Bond was prosecuted under section 229, and the statute — unlike the Convention — must be read consistent with principles of federalism inherent in our constitutional structure.

In the Government's view, the conclusion that Bond "knowingly" "use[d]" a "chemical weapon" in violation of section 229(a) is simple: The chemicals that Bond placed on Haynes's home and car are "toxic chemical[s]" as defined by the statute, and Bond's attempt to assault Haynes was not a "peaceful purpose." The problem with this interpretation is that it would "dramatically intrude[] upon traditional state criminal jurisdiction," and we avoid reading statutes to have such reach in the absence of a clear indication that they do. United States v. Bass, 404 U.S. 336, 350 (1971).

Part of a fair reading of statutory text is recognizing that "Congress legislates against the backdrop" of certain unexpressed presumptions. EEOC v. Arabian American Oil Co., 499 U.S. 244, 248 (1991). As Justice Frankfurter put it in his famous essay on statutory interpretation, correctly reading a statute "demands awareness of certain presuppositions." Felix Frankfurter, *Some Reflections on the Reading of Statutes*, 47 Colum. L. Rev. 527, 537 (1947). . . . The notion that some things "go without saying" applies to legislation just as it does to everyday life.

Among the background principles of construction that our cases have recognized are those grounded in the relationship between the Federal Government and the States under our Constitution. It has long been settled, for example, that we presume federal statutes do not abrogate state sovereign immunity, Atascadero State Hospital v. Scanlon, 473 U.S. 234, 243 (1985), impose obligations on the States pursuant to section 5 of the Fourteenth Amendment, Pennhurst State School and Hospital v. Halderman, 451 U.S. 1, 16-17 (1981), or preempt state law, Rice v. Santa Fe Elevator Corp., 331 U.S. 218, 230 (1947).

Closely related to these is the well-established principle that "'it is incumbent upon the federal courts to be certain of Congress' intent before finding that federal law overrides'" the "usual constitutional balance of federal and state powers." Gregory v. Ashcroft, 501 U.S. 452, 460 (1991) (quoting *Atascadero, supra*, at 243). To quote Frankfurter again, if the Federal Government would "'radically readjust[ ] the balance of state and national authority, those charged with the duty of legislating [must be] reasonably explicit'" about it. BFP v. Resolution Trust Corporation, 511 U.S. 531, 544 (1994) (quoting *Some Reflections, supra*, at 539-40; second alteration in original). Or as explained by Justice Marshall, when legislation "affect[s] the federal balance, the requirement of clear statement assures that the legislature has in fact faced, and intended to bring into issue, the critical matters involved in the judicial decision." *Bass, supra*, at 349.

We have applied this background principle when construing federal statutes that touched on several areas of traditional state responsibility. . . . Perhaps the clearest example of traditional state authority is the punishment of local criminal activity. United States v. Morrison, 529 U.S. 598, 618 (2000). Thus, "we will not be quick to assume that Congress has meant to effect a significant change in the sensitive relation between federal and state criminal jurisdiction." *Bass*, 404 U.S. at 349. . . .

These precedents make clear that it is appropriate to refer to basic principles of federalism embodied in the Constitution to resolve ambiguity in a federal statute. In this case, the ambiguity derives from the improbably broad reach of the key statutory definition given the term—"chemical weapon"—being defined; the deeply serious consequences of adopting such a boundless reading; and the lack of any apparent need to do so in light of the context from which the statute arose—a treaty about chemical warfare and terrorism. We conclude that, in this curious case, we can insist on a clear indication that Congress meant to reach purely local crimes, before interpreting the statute's expansive language in a way that intrudes on the police power of the States. *See Bass, supra*, at 349.

We do not find any such clear indication in section 229. "Chemical weapon" is the key term that defines the statute's reach, and it is defined extremely broadly. But that general definition does not constitute a clear statement that Congress meant the statute to reach local criminal conduct.

In fact, a fair reading of section 229 suggests that it does not have as expansive a scope as might at first appear. To begin, as a matter of natural meaning, an educated user of English would not describe Bond's crime as involving a "chemical weapon." Saying that a person "used a chemical weapon" conveys a very different idea than saying the person "used a chemical in a way that caused some harm." The natural meaning of "chemical weapon" takes account of both the particular chemicals that the defendant used and the circumstances in which she used them.

When used in the manner here, the chemicals in this case are not of the sort that an ordinary person would associate with instruments of chemical warfare. . . . More to the point, the use of something as a "weapon" typically connotes "[a]n instrument of offensive or defensive combat," Webster's Third New International Dictionary 2589 (2002), or "[a]n instrument of attack or defense in combat, as a gun, missile, or sword," American Heritage Dictionary 2022 (3d ed. 1992). But no speaker in natural parlance would describe Bond's feud-driven act of spreading irritating chemicals on Haynes's door knob and mailbox as "combat." Nor do the other circumstances of Bond's offense—an act of revenge born of romantic jealousy, meant to cause discomfort, that produced nothing more than a minor thumb burn—suggest that a chemical weapon was deployed in Norristown, Pennsylvania. Potassium dichromate and 10-chloro-10H-phenoxarsine might be chemical weapons if used, say, to poison a city's water supply. But Bond's crime is worlds apart from such hypotheticals, and covering it would give the statute a reach exceeding the ordinary meaning of the words Congress wrote. . . .

The Government would have us brush aside the ordinary meaning and adopt a reading of section 229 that would sweep in everything from the detergent under the kitchen sink to the stain remover in the laundry room. Yet no one would ordinarily describe those substances as "chemical weapons." The Government responds that because Bond used "specialized, highly toxic" (though legal) chemicals, "this case presents no occasion to address whether Congress intended [§229] to apply to common household substances." Brief for United States 13, n. 3. That the statute *would* apply so broadly, however, is the inescapable conclusion of the Government's position: Any parent would be guilty of a serious federal offense—possession of a chemical weapon—when, exasperated by the children's repeated failure to clean the goldfish tank, he considers poisoning the fish with a few drops of vinegar. We are reluctant to ignore the ordinary meaning of "chemical weapon" when doing so would transform a statute passed to implement the international Convention on Chemical Weapons into one that also makes it a federal offense to poison goldfish. . . .

In light of all of this, it is fully appropriate to apply the background assumption that Congress normally preserves "the constitutional balance between the National Government and the States." *Bond I*, 131 S. Ct. at 2364. That assumption is grounded in the very structure of the Constitution. And as we explained when this case was first before us, maintaining that constitutional balance is not merely an end unto itself. Rather, "[b]y denying any one government complete jurisdiction over all the concerns of public life, federalism protects the liberty of the individual from arbitrary power." *Ibid.*

The Government's reading of section 229 would "'alter sensitive federal-state relationships,'" convert an astonishing amount of "traditionally local criminal conduct" into "a matter for federal enforcement," and "involve a substantial extension of federal police resources." *Bass*, 404 U.S. at 349-50. It would transform the statute from one whose core concerns are acts of war, assassination, and terrorism into a massive federal anti-poisoning regime that reaches the simplest of assaults. . . . Of course Bond's conduct is serious and unacceptable—and against the laws of Pennsylvania. But the background principle that Congress does not normally intrude upon the police power of the States is critically important. In light of that principle, we are reluctant to conclude that Congress meant to punish Bond's crime with a federal prosecution for a chemical weapons attack.

In fact, with the exception of this unusual case, the Federal Government itself has not looked to section 229 to reach purely local crimes. The Government has identified only a handful of prosecutions that have been brought under this section. Most of those involved either terrorist plots or the possession of extremely dangerous substances with the potential to cause severe harm to many people. . . . The Federal Government undoubtedly has a substantial interest in enforcing criminal laws against assassination, terrorism, and acts with the potential to cause mass suffering. Those crimes have not traditionally been left predominantly to the States, and nothing we have said here will disrupt the Government's authority to prosecute such offenses.

It is also clear that the laws of the Commonwealth of Pennsylvania (and every other State) are sufficient to prosecute Bond. Pennsylvania has several statutes that would likely cover her assault. And state authorities regularly enforce these laws in poisoning cases.

The Government objects that Pennsylvania authorities charged Bond with only a minor offense based on her "harassing telephone calls and letters," and declined to prosecute her for assault. But we have traditionally viewed the exercise of state officials' prosecutorial discretion as a valuable feature of our constitutional system. And nothing in the Convention shows a clear intent to abrogate that feature. Prosecutorial discretion involves carefully weighing the benefits of a prosecution against the evidence needed to convict, the resources of the public fisc, and the public policy of the State. Here, in its zeal to prosecute Bond, the Federal Government has "displaced" the "public policy of the Commonwealth of Pennsylvania, enacted in its capacity as sovereign," that Bond does not belong in prison for a chemical weapons offense.

As we have explained, "Congress has traditionally been reluctant to define as a federal crime conduct readily denounced as criminal by the States." *Bass*, 404 U.S. at 349. There is no clear indication of a contrary approach here. Section 229 implements the Convention, but Bond's crime could hardly be more unlike the uses of mustard gas on the Western Front or nerve agents in the Iran-Iraq war that form the core concerns of that treaty. . . . [T]here are no apparent interests of the United States Congress or the community of nations in seeing Bond end up in federal prison, rather than dealt with (like virtually all other criminals in Pennsylvania) by the State. The Solicitor General acknowledged as much at oral argument. *See* Tr. of Oral Arg. 47 ("I don't think anybody would say [that] whether or not Ms. Bond is prosecuted would give rise to an international incident").

This case is unusual, and our analysis is appropriately limited. Our disagreement with our colleagues reduces to whether section 229 is "utterly clear." (Scalia, J., concurring in judgment). We think it is not, given that the definition of "chemical weapon" in a particular case can reach beyond any normal notion of such a weapon, that the context from which the statute arose demonstrates a much more limited prohibition was intended, and that the most sweeping reading of the statute would fundamentally upset the Constitution's balance between national and local power. This exceptional convergence of factors gives us serious reason to doubt the Government's expansive reading of section 229, and calls for us to interpret the statute more narrowly.

In sum, the global need to prevent chemical warfare does not require the Federal Government to reach into the kitchen cupboard, or to treat a local assault with a chemical irritant as the deployment of a chemical weapon. There is no reason to suppose that Congress—in implementing the Convention on Chemical Weapons—thought otherwise. . . .

JUSTICE SCALIA, with whom JUSTICE THOMAS joins, and with whom JUSTICE ALITO joins as to Part I, concurring in the judgment. . . .

I. THE STATUTORY QUESTION

The meaning of the Act is plain. No person may knowingly "develop, produce, otherwise acquire, transfer directly or indirectly, receive, stockpile, retain, own, possess, or use, or threaten to use, any chemical weapon." A "chemical weapon" is "[a] toxic chemical and its precursors, except where intended for a purpose not prohibited under this chapter as long as the type and quantity is consistent with such a purpose." A "toxic chemical" is "any chemical which through its chemical action on life processes can cause death, temporary incapacitation or permanent harm to humans or animals. The term includes all such chemicals, regardless of their origin or of their method of production, and regardless of whether they are produced in facilities, in munitions or elsewhere." A "purpose not prohibited" is "[a]ny peaceful purpose related to an industrial, agricultural, research, medical, or pharmaceutical activity or other activity."

Applying those provisions to this case is hardly complicated. Bond possessed and used "chemical[s] which through [their] chemical action on life processes can cause death, temporary incapacitation or permanent harm." Thus, she possessed "toxic chemicals." And, because they were not possessed or used only for a "purpose not prohibited," they were "chemical weapons." Ergo, Bond violated the Act. End of statutory analysis, I would have thought.

The Court does not think the interpretive exercise so simple. But that is only because its result-driven antitextualism befogs what is evident. . . .

The Court *starts* with the federalism-related consequences of the statute's meaning and reasons backwards, holding that, if the statute has what the Court considers a disruptive effect on the "federal-state balance" of criminal jurisdiction, that effect causes the text, even if clear on its face, to be ambiguous. . . . Imagine what future courts can do with that judge-empowering principle: Whatever has improbably broad, deeply serious, and apparently unnecessary consequences . . . *is ambiguous!* . . .

In this case, the ordinary meaning of the term being defined is irrelevant, because the statute's own definition—however expansive—is utterly clear: any "chemical which through its chemical action on life processes can cause death, temporary incapacitation or permanent harm to humans or animals," unless the chemical is possessed or used for a "peaceful purpose." The statute parses itself. There is no opinion of ours, and none written by any court or put forward by any commentator since Aristotle, which says, or even suggests, that "dissonance" between ordinary meaning and the unambiguous words of a definition is to be resolved in favor of ordinary meaning. If that were the case, there would hardly be any use in providing a definition. . . .

I suspect the Act will not survive today's gruesome surgery. A criminal statute must clearly define the conduct it proscribes. If it does not "'give a person of ordinary intelligence fair notice'" of its scope, United States v. Batchelder, 442 U.S. 114, 123 (1979), it denies due process.

The *new* §229(a)(1) fails that test. Henceforward, a person "shall be fined . . . , imprisoned for any term of years, or both,"—or, if he kills someone, "shall be punished by death or imprisoned for life,"—whenever he "develop[s], produce[s], otherwise acquire[s], transfer[s] directly or indirectly, receive[s], stockpile[s], retain[s], own[s], possess[es], or use[s], or threaten[s] to use," any chemical "*of the sort that an ordinary person would associate with instruments of chemical warfare*" (emphasis added). Whether that test is satisfied, the Court unhelpfully (and also illogically) explains, depends not only on the "particular chemicals that the defendant used" but also on "the circumstances in which she used them." The "detergent under the kitchen sink" and "the stain remover in the laundry room" are apparently out—but what if they are deployed to poison a neighborhood water fountain? Poisoning a goldfish tank is also apparently out, but what if the fish belongs to a Congressman or Governor and the act is meant as a menacing message, a small-time equivalent of leaving a severed horse head in the bed? . . . Moreover, the Court's illogical embellishment seems to apply only to the "use" of a chemical, but "use" is only 1 of *11* kinds of activity that the statute prohibits. What, one wonders, makes something a "chemical weapon" when it is merely "stockpile[d]" or "possess[ed]?" To these questions and countless others, one guess is as bad as another.

No one should have to ponder the totality of the circumstances in order to determine whether his conduct is a felony. Yet that is what the Court will now require of all future handlers of harmful toxins—that is to say, all of us. Thanks to the Court's revisions, the Act, which before was merely broad, is now broad and unintelligible. . . . Before long, I suspect, courts will be required to say so.

Since the Act is clear, the *real* question this case presents is whether the Act is constitutional as applied to petitioner. An unreasoned and citation-less sentence from our opinion in Missouri v. Holland, 252 U.S. 416 (1920), purported to furnish the answer: "If the treaty is valid"—and no one argues that the Convention is not—"there can be no dispute about the validity of the statute under Article I, §8, as a necessary and proper means to execute the powers of the Government." *Id.* at 432. Petitioner and her *amici* press us to consider whether there is anything to this *ipse dixit.* The Constitution's text and structure show that there is not.

II. THE CONSTITUTIONAL QUESTION

Under Article I, §8, cl. 18, Congress has the power "[t]o make all Laws which shall be necessary and proper for carrying into Execution the foregoing Powers and all other Powers vested by this Constitution in the Government of the United States, or in any Department or Officer thereof." One such "other Powe[r]" appears in Article II, §2, cl. 2: "[The President] shall have Power, by and with the Advice and Consent of the Senate, to make Treaties, provided two thirds of the Senators present concur." Read together, the two Clauses empower Congress to pass laws "necessary and proper for carrying into Execution . . . [the] Power . . . to make Treaties."

It is obvious what the Clauses, read together, do *not* say. They do not authorize Congress to enact laws for carrying into execution "Treaties," even treaties that do not execute themselves, such as the Chemical Weapons Convention. Surely it makes sense, the Government contends, that Congress would have the power to carry out the obligations to which the President and the Senate have committed the Nation. The power to "carry into Execution" the "Power . . . to make Treaties," it insists, *has to* mean the power to execute the treaties themselves. . . .

How might Congress have helped "carr[y]" the power to make the treaty—here, the Chemical Weapons Convention—"into Execution"? In any number of ways. It could have appropriated money for hiring treaty negotiators, empowered the Department of State to appoint those negotiators, formed a commission to study the benefits and risks of entering into the agreement, or paid for a bevy of spies to monitor the treaty-related deliberations of other potential signatories. . . .

But a power to help the President *make* treaties is not a power to *implement* treaties already made. *See generally* Nicholas Quinn Rosenkranz, *Executing the Treaty Power,* 118 Harv. L. Rev. 1867 (2005). Once a treaty has been made, Congress's power to do what is "necessary and proper" to assist the making of treaties drops out of the picture. To legislate compliance with the United States' treaty obligations, Congress must rely upon its independent (though quite robust) Article I, §8, powers.

"[T]he Constitutio[n] confer[s] upon Congress . . . not all governmental powers, but only discrete, enumerated ones." Printz v. United States, 521 U.S. 898, 919 (1997). And, of course, "enumeration presupposes something not enumerated." Gibbons v. Ogden, 22 U.S. (9 Wheat.) 1, 195 (1824). But in *Holland,* the proponents of unlimited congressional power found a loophole: "By negotiating a treaty and obtaining the requisite consent of the Senate, the President . . . may endow Congress with a source of legislative authority independent of the powers enumerated in Article I." Laurence H. Tribe, American Constitutional Law §4-4, pp. 645-46 (3d ed. 2000). Though *Holland*'s change to the Constitution's text appears minor (the power to carry into execution the *power to make treaties* becomes the power to carry into execution *treaties*), the change to its structure is seismic.

To see why vast expansion of congressional power is not just a remote possibility, consider two features of the modern practice of treaty making. In our Nation's early history, and extending through the time when *Holland* was written, treaties were typically bilateral, and addressed only a small range of topics relating to the obligations of each state to the other, and to citizens of the other—military neutrality, for example, or military alliance, or guarantee of most-favored-nation trade treatment. *See* Curtis A. Bradley, *The Treaty Power and American Federalism*, 97 Mich. L. Rev. 390, 396 (1998). But beginning in the last half of the last century, many treaties were "detailed multilateral instruments negotiated and drafted at international conferences," *ibid.*, and they sought to regulate states' treatment of their own citizens, or even "the activities of individuals and private entities," Abram Chayes & Antonia Chandler Chayes, The New Sovereignty: Compliance with International Regulatory Agreements 14 (1995). "[O]ften vague and open-ended," such treaties "touch on almost every aspect of domestic civil, political, and cultural life." Curtis A. Bradley & Jack L. Goldsmith, *Treaties, Human Rights, and Conditional Consent*, 149 U. Pa. L. Rev. 399, 400 (2000).

Consider also that, at least according to some scholars, the Treaty Clause comes with no implied subject-matter limitations. On this view, "[t]he Tenth Amendment . . . does not limit the power to make treaties or other agreements," Restatement (Third) of Foreign Relations Law of the United States §302, Comment *d*, p. 154 (1986), and the treaty power can be used to regulate matters of strictly domestic concern.

If that is true, then the possibilities of what the Federal Government may accomplish, with the right treaty in hand, are endless and hardly farfetched. It could begin, as some scholars have suggested, with abrogation of this Court's constitutional rulings. For example, the holding that a statute prohibiting the carrying of firearms near schools went beyond Congress's enumerated powers, United States v. Lopez, 514 U.S. 549, 551 (1995), could be reversed by negotiating a treaty with Latvia providing that neither sovereign would permit the carrying of guns near schools. Similarly, Congress could reenact the invalidated part of the Violence Against Women Act of 1994 that provided a civil remedy for victims of gender-motivated violence, just so long as there were a treaty on point—and some authors think there already is . . . .

The Necessary and Proper Clause cannot bear such weight. . . . No law that flattens the principle of state sovereignty, whether or not "necessary," can be said to be "proper." . . .

The Government raises a functionalist objection: If the Constitution does not limit a *self-executing treaty* to the subject matter delineated in Article I, §8, then it makes no sense to impose that limitation upon a statute implementing a *non-self-executing treaty*. The premise of the objection (that the power to make self-executing treaties is limitless) is, to say the least, arguable. But even if it is correct, refusing to extend that proposition to non-self-executing treaties makes a great deal of sense. Suppose, for example, that the self-aggrandizing Federal Government wishes to take over the law of intestacy. If the President and the Senate find in some foreign state a ready accomplice, they have two options. First, they can enter into a treaty with "stipulations" specific enough that they "require no legislation to make them operative," Whitney v. Robertson, 124 U.S. 190, 194 (1888), which would mean in this example something like a comprehensive probate code. But for that to succeed, the President and a supermajority of the Senate would need to reach agreement on all the details—which, when once embodied in the treaty, could not be altered or superseded by ordinary legislation. The second option—far the better one—is for

Congress to gain lasting and flexible control over the law of intestacy by means of a non-self-executing treaty. "[Implementing] legislation is as much subject to modification and repeal by Congress as legislation upon any other subject." *Ibid.* And to make such a treaty, the President and Senate would need to agree only that they desire power over the law of intestacy. . . .

We have here a supposedly "narrow" opinion which, in order to be "narrow," sets forth interpretive principles never before imagined that will bedevil our jurisprudence (and proliferate litigation) for years to come. The immediate product of these interpretive novelties is a statute that should be the envy of every lawmaker bent on trapping the unwary with vague and uncertain criminal prohibitions. All this to leave in place an ill-considered *ipse dixit* that enables the fundamental constitutional principle of limited federal powers to be set aside by the President and Senate's exercise of the treaty power. We should not have shirked our duty and distorted the law to preserve that assertion; we should have welcomed and eagerly grasped the opportunity — nay, the obligation — to consider and repudiate it.

JUSTICE THOMAS, with whom JUSTICE SCALIA joins, and with whom JUSTICE ALITO joins as to Parts I, II, and III, concurring in the judgment. . . .

I write separately to suggest that the Treaty Power is itself a limited federal power. *Cf.* United States v. Lopez, 514 U.S. 549, 584 (1995) (Thomas, J., concurring) ("[W]e *always* have rejected readings of . . . the scope of federal power that would permit Congress to exercise a police power"). The Constitution empowers the President, "by and with the Advice and Consent of the Senate, to make Treaties, provided two thirds of the Senators present concur." Art. II, §2. The Constitution does not, however, comprehensively define the proper bounds of the Treaty Power, and this Court has not yet had occasion to do so. As a result, some have suggested that the Treaty Power is boundless — that it can reach any subject matter, even those that are of strictly domestic concern. *See, e.g.*, Restatement (Third) of Foreign Relations Law of the United States, §302, Comment *c* (1986). A number of recent treaties reflect that suggestion by regulating what appear to be purely domestic affairs. *See, e.g.*, Curtis A. Bradley, *The Treaty Power and American Federalism*, 97 Mich. L. Rev. 390, 402-09 (1998) (citing examples).

Yet to interpret the Treaty Power as extending to every conceivable domestic subject matter — even matters without any nexus to foreign relations — would destroy the basic constitutional distinction between domestic and foreign powers. *See* United States v. Curtiss-Wright Export Corp., 299 U.S. 304, 319 (1936) ("[T]he federal power over external affairs [is] in origin and essential character different from that over internal affairs . . ."). It would also lodge in the Federal Government the potential for "a 'police power' over all aspects of American life." *Lopez, supra*, at 584 (Thomas, J., concurring). A treaty-based power of that magnitude — no less than a plenary power of legislation — would threaten "the liberties that derive from the diffusion of sovereign power." Bond v. United States, 131 S. Ct. 2355, 2364 (2011). And a treaty-based police power would pose an even greater threat when exercised through a self-executing treaty because it would circumvent the role of the House of Representatives in the legislative process. *See* The Federalist No. 52, p. 355 (J. Cooke ed. 1961) (J. Madison) (noting that the House has a more "immediate dependence on, & an intimate sympathy with the people").

I doubt the Treaty Power creates such a gaping loophole in our constitutional structure. Although the parties have not challenged the constitutionality of the particular treaty at issue here, in an appropriate case I believe the Court should address the scope of the Treaty Power as it was originally understood. Today, it is enough to highlight some of the structural and historical evidence suggesting that the Treaty Power can be used to arrange intercourse with other nations, but not to regulate purely domestic affairs. . . .

[In parts I and II, Justice Thomas reviews various historical materials and argues that the treaty power was originally understood as applying only to matters of international intercourse. He acknowledges that the Founders decided not to enumerate limitations on the treaty power, but he contends that this was done in order to ensure that the federal government had the "ability to respond to unforeseeable varieties of intercourse with other nations," not because they wanted to "permit the President and the Senate to exercise domestic authority commensurate with their substantial power over external affairs."]

III

The original understanding that the Treaty Power was limited to international intercourse has been well represented in this Court's precedents. Although we have not had occasion to define the limits of the power in much detail, we have described treaties as dealing in some manner with intercourse between nations. *See, e.g.,* Holmes v. Jennison, 39 U.S. (14 Pet.) 540, 569 (1840) ("The power to make treaties . . . was designed to include all those subjects, which in the ordinary intercourse of nations had usually been made subjects of negotiation and treaty"); Holden v. Joy, 84 U.S. (17 Wall.) 211, 242-43 (1872) ("[T]he framers of the Constitution intended that [the Treaty Power] should extend to all those objects which in the intercourse of nations had usually been regarded as the proper subjects of negotiation and treaty, if not inconsistent with the nature of our government and the relation between the States and the United States"). *Cf.* Power Auth. of N.Y. v. Federal Power Comm'n, 247 F.2d 538, 542-43 (D.C. Cir. 1957) (Bazelon, J.) ("No court has ever said . . . that the treaty power can be exercised without limit to affect matters which are of purely domestic concern and do not pertain to our relations with other nations"), *vacated as moot*, 355 U.S. 64 (1957) (*per curiam*).

A common refrain in these cases is that the Treaty Power "extends to all proper subjects of negotiation with foreign governments." Those cases identified certain paradigmatic instances of "intercourse" that were "proper negotiating subjects" fit for treaty. . . . Nothing in our cases, on the other hand, suggests that the Treaty Power conceals a police power over domestic affairs.

Whatever its other defects, Missouri v. Holland, 252 U.S. 416 (1920), is consistent with that view. There, the Court addressed the constitutionality of a treaty that regulated the capture of birds that migrated between Canada and the United States. Although the Court upheld a statute implementing that treaty based on an improperly broad view of the Necessary and Proper Clause, *Holland* did not conclude that the Treaty Power itself was unlimited. To the contrary, the holding in *Holland* is consistent with the understanding that treaties are limited to matters of international intercourse. The Court observed that the treaty at issue addressed *migratory* birds that were "only transitorily within the State and ha[d] no permanent habitat therein." *Id.* at 435 ("[T]he treaty deals with creatures that [only] for the moment are within the state borders"). As such, the birds were naturally a matter of international intercourse because they were creatures in international transit.

At least until recently, the original understanding that the Treaty Power is limited was widely shared outside the Court as well. . . . The Second Restatement on the Foreign Relations Law of the United States, for example, opined that the Treaty Power is available only if the subject matter of the treaty "is of international concern." §117(1)(a) (1964-1965). The Second Restatement explained that a treaty "must relate to the external concerns of the nation as distinguished from matters of a purely internal nature." *Id.*, Comment *b*; *see also* Treaties and Executive Agreements: Hearings on S. J. Res. 1 before a Subcommittee of the Senate Committee on the Judiciary, 84th Cong., 1st Sess., 183 (1955) (Secretary of State Dulles) (Treaties cannot regulate matters "which do not essentially affect the actions of nations in relation to international affairs, but are purely internal"); Proceedings of the American Society of International Law 194-96 (1929) (C. Hughes) ("[The Treaty Power] is not a power intended to be exercised . . . with respect to matters that have no relation to international concerns"). *But see* Restatement (Third) of Foreign Relations Law of the United States §302, Comment *c* ("Contrary to what was once suggested, the Constitution does not require that an international agreement deal only with 'matters of international concern'"). At a minimum, the Second Restatement firmly reflects the understanding shared by the Framers that the Treaty Power has substantive limits. Only in the latter part of the past century have treaties challenged that prevailing conception by addressing "matters that in the past countries would have addressed wholly domestically" and "purport[ing] to regulate the relationship between nations and their own citizens," Bradley at 396. But even the Solicitor General in this case would not go that far; he acknowledges that "there may well be a line to be drawn" regarding "whether the subject matter of [a] treaty is a proper subject for a treaty." Tr. of Oral Arg. 43:10-15.

In an appropriate case, I would draw a line that respects the original understanding of the Treaty Power. I acknowledge that the distinction between matters of international intercourse and matters of purely domestic regulation may not be obvious in all cases. But this Court has long recognized that the Treaty Power is limited, and hypothetical difficulties in line-drawing are no reason to ignore a constitutional limit on federal power.

The parties in this case have not addressed the proper scope of the Treaty Power or the validity of the treaty here. The preservation of limits on the Treaty Power is nevertheless a matter of fundamental constitutional importance, and the Court ought to address the scope of the Treaty Power when that issue is presented. Given the increasing frequency with which treaties have begun to test the limits of the Treaty Power, that chance will come soon enough.

Notes and Questions

1. Article II of the Constitution states that the President and Senate have the power to make treaties, but it does not define the word "treaty." Can a treaty regulate "internal" or "domestic" matters? In order to be valid under U.S. law, must a treaty obligation be reciprocal? Must it be of mutual concern to the parties to the treaty?

When discussing treaties, the Founders appeared to have had in mind particular treaty subjects such as "war, peace, and commerce." *Federalist No. 64* (Jay). This does not necessarily mean, however, that the Founders intended to preclude treaty making on other subjects. Indeed, their decision not to specify subject matter limitations on the treaty power might have reflected a desire to preserve flexibility for the treatymakers. Given the lack of any express constitutional limitations on the treaty power, how should a court determine the scope of that power? What does Geofroy v. Riggs suggest? *See also* Santovincenzo v. Egan, 284 U.S. 30, 40 (1931) ("The treaty-making power is broad enough to cover all subjects that properly pertain to our foreign relations. . . ."); Asakura v. City of Seattle, 265 U.S. 332, 341 (1924) ("The treaty-making power . . . extends to all proper subjects of negotiation with foreign governments."). Interestingly, *Santovincenzo* was authored by Chief Justice Hughes, who two years earlier had suggested in a speech to the American Society of International Law that the treaty power might be limited to "matters of international concern." *See* 1929 Proc. Am. Soc. Int'l L. 194. What treaties, if any, would be precluded by the language in *Geofroy* or these other decisions? By Hughes's suggested "matters of international concern" test? What do you make of the Court's emphasis in Missouri v. Holland on the fact that the case involved "a national interest of very nearly the first magnitude" that could "be protected only by national action in concert with that of another power"? In the court of appeals' decision in the *Bond* case that preceded the Supreme Court decision excerpted above, the court expressed the view that "[t]hroughout much of American history, . . . including when *Holland* was handed down, it was understood that the Treaty Power was impliedly limited to certain subject matters." Bond v. United States, 681 F.3d 149, 159 (3d Cir. 2012).

The Restatement (Second) of Foreign Relations Law, published in 1965, states that the United States has the constitutional power to enter into international agreements as long as "the matter is of international concern." Restatement (Second) of the Foreign Relations Law of the United States §117(1)(a) (1965). The comments to this provision explain that an international agreement of the United States "must relate to the external concerns of the nation as distinguished from matters of a purely internal nature." *Id.,* cmt. b. The Restatement (Third), published in 1987, rejected the Restatement (Second)'s subject matter limitation. The Restatement (Third) stated that "[c]ontrary to what was once suggested, the Constitution does not require that an international agreement deal only with 'matters of international concern.' . . . The United States may make an agreement on any subject suggested by its national interests in relations with other nations." Restatement (Third) of the Foreign Relations Law of the United States §302, cmt. c (1987). Why do you think the Restatement changed its position?

The Restatement (Fourth) of Foreign Relations Law takes no position on this issue in its black-letter provisions, and makes the following observations in its reporters' notes:

> Presumably there must be an actual international agreement with another state (or with an entity, such as a public international organization, that has been given capacity to enter into an international agreement) that is intended to be legally binding. It is unclear whether there is any additional limitation on the subject matters that can constitutionally be addressed by the President and the Senate in a treaty. . . .
>
> It is [also] unclear whether, even if there is some sort of subject-matter limitation on the treaty power, there are sufficient judicially manageable standards to make it justiciable. . . . [N]o court has ever found a treaty to exceed constitutional limitations on the treaty power.

Restatement (Fourth) of the Foreign Relations Law of the United States §312, reporters' note 4 (2018).

2. One important difference between treaties and ordinary federal statutes is that treaties bind the United States to international obligations. In that sense, treaties (and executive agreements, see Chapter 6) can accomplish something that cannot be accomplished by legislation. Nevertheless, prior to *Holland*, the Supreme Court had never expressly held that the federal government has broader power to make changes to U.S. laws and entitlements through the use of treaties than it has through the enactment of federal statutes. There were a number of treaties before *Holland*, however, that arguably did exceed the scope of Congress's legislative powers. One notable example is the 1803 treaty between the United States and France for the Louisiana Purchase. In addition to providing for the acquisition by the United States of a vast amount of new territory, the treaty provided that the territory would be "incorporated into the Union of the United States." President Jefferson had doubts that the treaty was constitutional, explaining to a senator that "[t]he Constitution has made no provision for our holding foreign territory, still less for incorporating foreign nations into our Union." Although Jefferson initially suggested that a constitutional amendment be passed to give the federal government this power, he changed his mind and urged ratification and implementation of the treaty in the absence of such an amendment. *See* David P. Currie, The Constitution in Congress: The Jeffersonians, 1801-1829, at 95-107 (2001). Despite Jefferson's constitutional doubts, is a power to acquire territory implied from Congress's power in Article IV, §3, cl. 2, to "dispose of and make all needful Rules and Regulations respecting the Territory or other Property belonging to the United States"? And is a power to admit such acquired territory into the Union implied from the statement in Article IV, §3, cl. 1, that "New States may be admitted by the Congress into this Union"? For an argument that Jefferson's constitutional concerns about the Louisiana Purchase were valid, and that the incorporation of the Louisiana Territory into the federal union exceeded the federal government's treaty power, see Robert Knowles, *The Balance of Forces and the Empire of Liberty: States' Rights and the Louisiana Purchase*, 88 Iowa L. Rev. 343 (2003).

3. Even before *Holland*, the Supreme Court had never invalidated a treaty on federalism grounds. Moreover, as illustrated by *Geofroy*, the Court often referred to the treaty power in broad and general terms, and it applied treaties in a number of cases to displace contrary state law, even when the law concerned a matter traditionally regulated at the state level, such as the property or inheritance rights of foreign citizens within the state. *See, e.g.*, Hauenstein v. Lynham, 100 U.S. 483 (1879); Orr v. Hodgson, 17 U.S. (4 Wheat.) 221 (1819); Chirac v. Chirac, 15 U.S. (2 Wheat.) 259 (1817).

The Court nevertheless suggested at times that the treaty power was limited by the United States' federal structure. *See, e.g.*, Holmes v. Jennison, 39 U.S. (14 Pet.) 540, 569 (1840) (stating that the exercise of the treaty power must be "consistent with . . . the distribution of powers between the general and state governments"); New Orleans v. United States, 35 U.S. (10 Pet.) 662, 736 (1836) (noting that the federal government is "one of limited powers" and that its authority cannot be "enlarged under the treaty-making power"). U.S. officials also sometimes expressed this view. An 1831 Attorney General opinion, for example, stated that the federal government was "under a constitutional obligation to respect [the reserved powers of the states] in the formation of treaties." 2 Op. Att'y Gen. 437 (1831). In addition, in a number of instances in the late nineteenth and early twentieth centuries, U.S. officials declined to enter into negotiations concerning private international law treaties because of a purported concern that the treaties would infringe on the reserved powers of the states. *See* Kurt H. Nadelmann, *Ignored State Interests: The Federal Government and International Efforts to Unify Rules of Private Law*, 102 U. Pa. L. Rev. 323 (1923). Similarly, U.S. representatives insisted a few years before *Holland* that they could not agree to a treaty regulating certain labor conditions because those matters were within the reserved powers of the states. *See* James T. Shotwell, *Historical Significance of the International Labour Conference,* in Labour as an International Problem 41 (E. John Salano ed., 1920). These states' rights concerns continued to inhibit U.S. participation in private international law, labor, and other treaty regimes even after *Holland. See* Pittman B. Potter, *Inhibitions on the Treaty-Making Power of the United States,* 29 Am. J. Int'l L. 456 (1934).

4. Since the 1990s, the Supreme Court has imposed a number of federalism restraints on Congress's domestic lawmaking powers. In particular, it has imposed limits on the scope of Congress's powers under the Commerce Clause and Fourteenth Amendment, *see, e.g.,* United States v. Morrison, 529 U.S. 598 (2000); City of Boerne v. Flores, 521 U.S. 507 (1997); United States v. Lopez, 514 U.S. 549 (1995); prohibited Congress from "commandeering" state legislatures and executive officials, *see, e.g.,* Printz v. United States, 521 U.S. 898 (1997); New York v. United States, 505 U.S. 144 (1992); and limited the ability of Congress to override the immunity of states from private lawsuits, *see, e.g.,* Alden v. Maine, 527 U.S. 706 (1999); Seminole Tribe of Florida v. Florida, 517 U.S. 44 (1996). To what extent should these limitations apply to the treaty power? For example, in *City of Boerne,* the Supreme Court held that the Religious Freedom Restoration Act exceeded Congress's powers under the Fourteenth Amendment. Could Congress validly enact this statute as an implementation of the religious freedom provision in the International Covenant on Civil and Political Rights, a treaty ratified by the United States in 1992? For an argument that it could, see Gerald L. Neuman, *The Global Dimension of RFRA,* 14 Const. Commentary 33 (1997).

5. The Tenth Amendment provides that "[t]he powers not delegated to the United States by the Constitution, nor prohibited to it by the States, are reserved to the States respectively, or to the people." Article II of the Constitution clearly delegates the power to enter into treaties to the national government, and in Article I, Section 10, it expressly prohibits states from entering into treaties. Does this make the Tenth Amendment irrelevant to the treaty power? Consider this argument from Professor Louis Henkin: "Since the Treaty Power was delegated to the federal government, whatever is within its scope is not reserved to the states: the Tenth Amendment is not material." Louis Henkin, Foreign Affairs and the United States Constitution 191 (2d ed. 1996). By contrast, consider the following argument in an article published in 1909:

> This argument indeed proves that the states did not reserve the power to make treaties and hence have no such power even in the exercise of their reserved powers. But it fails to prove that the federal government in the exercise of its undoubted treaty-making power is not limited by those restrictions which the first ten amendments have placed on the power of the federal government. It proves that the federal power to make treaties is exclusive, but it does not prove that it is unlimited, or that [it] is not limited by the tenth amendment.

William E. Mikell, *The Extent of the Treaty-Making Power of the President and Senate of the United States* (pt. 2), 57 U. Pa. L. Rev. 528, 539-40 (1909). Which view is more persuasive?

6. The Supreme Court sometimes uses the label "Tenth Amendment" as a shorthand phrase for "any implied constitutional limitations on [the national government's] authority to regulate state activities, whether grounded in the Tenth Amendment itself or in principles of federalism derived generally from the Constitution." South Carolina v. Baker, 485 U.S. 505, 511 n.5 (1988). Does *Holland* address the relationship between that broader "Tenth Amendment" and the treaty power? For example, does *Holland* immunize the treaty power from anti-commandeering restrictions? State sovereign immunity limitations? *Compare, for example,* Martin Flaherty, *Are We to Be a Nation? Federal Power vs. "States' Rights" in Foreign Affairs,* 70 U. Colo. L. Rev. 1277, 1279 (1999) (arguing that the anti-commandeering restrictions do not limit the treaty power), *with* Louis Henkin, Foreign Affairs and the United States Constitution 467 (2d ed. 1996) (assuming that the restrictions do limit the treaty power). Note that the Supreme Court has indicated, albeit in a brief *per curiam* decision, that the treaty power is subject to state sovereign immunity limitations. *See* Breard v. Greene, 523 U.S. 371, 376-77 (1998). *See also* Carlos Manuel Vazquez, *Treaties and the Eleventh Amendment,* 42 Va. J. Int'l L. 713 (2002) (concluding that state sovereign immunity limitations apply to the treaty power).

7. The central holding of *Holland* is that the treaty power can be used to regulate matters beyond the scope of Congress's legislative powers. As a textual matter, this conclusion might seem obvious: Congress's legislative powers are referred to in Article I, whereas the treaty power is referred to in Article II. This structure might suggest that the limitations in Article I apply only to Congress's enactments, not treaties. On the other hand, as we saw above in the separation of powers materials, some provisions of Article I are thought to limit the treaty power—for example, the requirement in Article I, Section 9 that an appropriations statute be passed in order to draw money from the treasury, and the requirement in Article I, Section 7 that all revenue bills originate in the House of Representatives. Furthermore, it is now settled that the treaty power is limited by the First Amendment, yet that Amendment refers only to Congress, not the treatymakers ("Congress shall make no law . . ."). Although the First Amendment has been held to apply to the *states* by virtue of the Fourteenth Amendment Due Process Clause, there is no equivalent textual basis for applying the First Amendment to the federal treatymakers. Nevertheless, as discussed below in Note 13, the Supreme Court has made clear that the federal government may not use the treaty power to subvert the First Amendment and other individual rights protections. Can it similarly be argued that the federal treatymakers should be disallowed from subverting the general federalism structure of the Constitution?

8. One common argument for not imposing judicially enforced federalism limitations in the domestic arena is that there are sufficient political safeguards to protect federalism. This argument was first developed by Professor Herbert Wechsler in the 1950s and then further developed by Professor Jesse Choper in the 1970s. *See* Herbert Wechsler, *The Political Safeguards of Federalism: The Role of the States in the Composition and Selection of the National Government,* 54 Colum. L. Rev. 543 (1954); Jesse H. Choper, *The Scope of the National Power vis-à-vis the States: The Dispensability of Judicial Review,* 86 Yale L.J. 1552 (1977). The Supreme Court relied heavily on this political safeguards theory in its 1985 *Garcia* decision, in which a 5-4 majority of the Court largely abandoned judicial enforcement of the Tenth Amendment. *See* Garcia v. San Antonio Metro. Transit Auth., 469 U.S. 528 (1985). In recent years, the Supreme Court has arguably backed away from *Garcia*, although the decision has not yet been overruled. *See* John C. Yoo, *The Judicial Safeguards of Federalism,* 70 S. Cal. L. Rev. 1311 (1997).

The political safeguards theory was developed with domestic legislation in mind. How well does the theory apply in the context of the treaty power? On the one hand, it would seem that there are more federalism safeguards in the treaty process than in the domestic legislative process, because a treaty requires the approval of two-thirds of the Senate. Moreover, the Senate often has acted to protect state interests in the treaty process — for example, by attaching "federalism understandings" to its consent to human rights treaties. On the other hand, the treaty negotiation process is dominated by the President, who may not be particularly sensitive to state (as opposed to majoritarian) interests. The treaty process is also more opaque than the domestic legislative process, which might make it less open to state influence and input. Perhaps more important, most international agreements concluded by the United States in recent years have been in the form of congressional-executive agreements rather than Article II treaties and thus have not been subject to the two-thirds senatorial consent requirement. Some commentators have asserted that congressional-executive agreements are *completely interchangeable* with Article II treaties. These agreements are discussed in Chapter 6.

9. The Executive Branch sometimes takes federalism into account when negotiating, implementing, and enforcing treaties. For example, in submitting the Convention Against Transnational Organized Crime to the Senate in 2004, the Bush Administration suggested (and the Senate accepted) various conditions that effectively avoided the need to rely on Missouri v. Holland. *See* Letter of Submittal from Secretary of State Colin L. Powell (Jan. 22, 2004), S. Treaty Doc. 108-16, at vii (recommending reservation stating, among other things: "There are a small number of conceivable situations involving such rare offenses of a purely local character where U.S. federal and state criminal law may not be entirely adequate to satisfy an obligation under the Convention. The Government of the United States of America therefore reserves to the obligations set forth in the Convention to the extent they address conduct which would fall within this narrow category of highly localized activity."). At other times, the Executive Branch has suggested relying in part on existing state (and federal) law to fulfill treaty obligations rather than seeking to displace state law through either a self-executing treaty or new implementing legislation. *See, e.g.,* Letter of Submittal from Secretary of State Condoleezza Rice, U.N. Convention Against Corruption (Sept. 23, 2005), S. Treaty Doc. 109-6, at 3 (recommending inclusion of understanding stating that "the United States will rely on existing federal law and applicable state law to meet its obligations under the Convention"). For additional discussion of this phenomenon, see Duncan B. Hollis, *Executive Federalism: Forging New Federalist Constraints on the Treaty Power,* 79 S. Cal. L. Rev. 1327 (2006). As the author explains, "[t]he executive has largely addressed the treaty power question ad hoc. On occasion, it has taken advantage of [Missouri v. Holland's] import and insisted on a nationalist conception of the treaty power. But, just as often, it has invoked federalism as a continuing brake on its exercise of that power, even if only as a matter of policy." Assuming this is a correct description of Executive Branch practice, what do you think explains this phenomenon? *See also* Peter J. Spiro, *Resurrecting Missouri v. Holland,* 73 Mo. L. Rev. 1029 (2008) (describing how "the federal government failed to assimilate that version of the Treaty Power" reflected in *Holland,* and arguing that "*Holland*'s reversal would not be welcomed by those who work to advance global governance . . . [b]ut it would have the silver lining of redirecting advocacy to the subfederal level").

10. Consider the provision in the 1853 treaty, discussed in *Geofroy*, in which the President merely pledged to recommend certain measures to the states. Similar to this provision, the United States and other federal nations such as Canada have sometimes negotiated "federal-state" clauses to be included in treaties. These clauses typically limit the obligations of the federal nation to matters within its national legislative jurisdiction, and call upon it merely to recommend adoption of these obligations by its constituent states. Article 11 of the U.N. Convention on the Recognition and Enforcement of Foreign Arbitral Awards, for example, provides in relevant part:

> In the case of a federal or non-unitary State, the following provisions shall apply:
>   (a) With respect to those articles of this Convention that come within the legislative jurisdiction of the federal authority, the obligations of the federal Government shall to this extent be the same as those of Contracting States which are not federal States;
>   (b) With respect to those articles of this Convention that come within the legislative jurisdiction of constituent states or provinces which are not, under the constitutional system of the federation, bound to take legislative action, the federal Government shall bring such articles with a favourable recommendation to the notice of the appropriate authorities of constituent states or provinces at the earliest possible moment. . . .

Similarly, Article 28 of the American Convention on Human Rights (which the United States has signed but not ratified), provides in relevant part:

> 1. Where a State Party is constituted as a federal state, the national government of such State Party shall implement all the provisions of the Convention over whose subject matter it exercises legislative and judicial jurisdiction.
> 2. With respect to the provisions over whose subject matter the constituent units of the federal state have jurisdiction, the national government shall immediately take suitable measures, in accordance with its constitution and its laws, to the end that the competent authorities of the constituent units may adopt appropriate provisions for the fulfillment of this Convention.

What, if anything, do these clauses suggest about the relationship between the treaty power and American federalism?

11. The least controversial holding of *Holland* has been the proposition that, if a treaty is constitutionally valid, Congress can use its authority under the Necessary and Proper Clause to enact legislation to implement the treaty, even if Congress would lack the authority to such legislation in the absence of the treaty. This proposition appears to have been settled before *Holland. See* Neely v. Henkel, 180 U.S. 109, 121 (1901) ("The power of Congress to make all laws necessary and proper . . . includes the power to enact such legislation as is appropriate to give efficacy to any stipulations which it is competent for the President by and with the advice and consent of the Senate to insert in a treaty with a foreign power."). For modern lower court decisions applying this holding, see United States v. Shi, 525 F.3d 709, 721 (9th Cir. 2008); United States v. Belfast, 611 F.3d 783, 804-05 (11th Cir. 2010); United States v. Ferreira, 275 F.3d 1020, 1027-28 (11th Cir. 2001); and United States v. Lue, 134 F.3d 79, 82, 84 (2d Cir. 1998).

Professor Rosenkranz, however, has challenged this proposition. *See* Nicholas Quinn Rosenkranz, *Executing the Treaty Power,* 118 Harv. L. Rev. 1867 (2005). He points out that the Necessary and Proper Clause gives Congress the authority to make laws necessary and proper for carrying into execution "Powers" vested in other parts of the government, and he argues that, when applied to the "Power . . . to make Treaties" in Article II, it gives Congress only the authority to enact legislation to facilitate the *making* of treaties, not legislation to implement particular treaties. Consequently, he contends that, when a treaty is not self-executing, Congress can enact legislation to implement the treaty only if the legislation falls within its independent legislative powers. However, Professor Rosenkranz accepts the principal holding of *Holland*—i.e., that the treaty power is not itself limited to the scope of Congress's legislative powers—and thus under his analysis a self-executing treaty could create domestic law that exceeded Congress's legislative powers. Are you persuaded by his construction of the Necessary and Proper Clause? Does his distinction between self-executing and non-self-executing treaties make sense? If the U.S. treatymakers have the authority to change domestic law directly through a self-executing treaty, why is it constitutionally problematic for them to make the treaty non-self-executing and leave the details of implementation to Congress? For a defense of *Holland*'s holding concerning the Necessary and Proper Clause, see Carlos Manuel Vazquez, *Missouri v. Holland's Second Holding,* 73 Mo. L. Rev. 939 (2008). For additional discussion of the issue, see Edward T. Swaine, *Putting* Missouri v. Holland *on the Map,* 73 Mo. L. Rev. 1007 (2008). *See also* Jean Galbraith, *Congress's Treaty-Implementing Power in Historical Practice,* 56 Wm. & Mary L. Rev. 59 (2014) (arguing that historical practice supports Congress's authority to use the Necessary and Proper Clause to implement treaties).

In order for legislation to fall within Congress's Necessary and Proper Clause authority to implement a treaty, it will presumably need to relate to the terms of the treaty. Outside the treaty context, the Supreme Court has construed the phrase "necessary and proper" to require only that legislation be "rationally related to the implementation of a constitutionally enumerated power." United States v. Comstock, 560 U.S. 126, 134 (2010). Lower courts have generally assumed that the rational relationship test applies to legislation implementing a treaty. *See, e.g.,* United States v. Belfast, 611 F.3d 783, 804-05 (11th Cir. 2010); United States v. Lue, 134 F.3d 79, 84 (2d Cir. 1998).

12. In 1996, Congress enacted a law making female genital mutilation (FGM) a federal criminal offense. *See* 18 U.S.C. §116(a) ("whoever knowingly circumcises, excises, or infibulates the whole or any part of the labia majora or labia minora or clitoris of another person who has not attained the age of 18 years shall be fined under this title or imprisoned not more than 5 years, or both"). In United States v. Nagarwala, 350 F. Supp. 3d 316 (E.D. Mich. 2018), the district court held that this statute is unconstitutional because it exceeds Congress's legislative authority. The court rejected the government's argument that the statute could be justified as a necessary and proper implementation of the International Covenant on Civil and Political Rights (ICCPR). The government pointed to two provisions in the ICCPR: Article 3, which calls on the parties to "ensure the equal right of men and women to the enjoyment of all civil and political rights set forth in the present Covenant"; and Article 24, which states that "[e]very child shall have, without any discrimination as to race, colour, sex, language, religion, national or social origin, property or birth, the right to such measures of protection as are required by his status as a minor, on the part of his family, society and the State." The court concluded that the statute was not sufficiently related to either of these provisions to qualify as a necessary and proper implementation. The court further reasoned that, "even accepting the government's contention that the criminal punishment of FGM is rationally related to the cited articles of the ICCPR, federalism concerns and the Supreme Court's statements regarding state sovereignty in the area of punishing crime—and the federal government's lack of a general police power—prevent Congress from criminalizing FGM."

The U.S. Justice Department decided not to appeal this ruling. In a letter to Senator Dianne Feinstein, the ranking member of the Senate Judiciary Committee, the Department stated that it had concluded that it lacked a reasonable defense of the constitutionality of the statute. The Department explained that, "even maintaining the full continuing validity of *Holland*," the Department had "determined that it does not have an adequate argument that Section 116(a) is within Congress's authority to enact legislation to implement the ICCPR, which does not address FGM." The Department noted, however, that Congress could address the constitutional problem by revising the statute to ground it in Congress's Commerce Clause authority. It suggested in particular that the statute be revised to be limited to circumstances in which "(1) the defendant or victim travels in or uses a channel or instrumentality of interstate or foreign commerce in furtherance of the FGM; (2) the defendant uses a means, channel, facility, or instrumentality of interstate commerce in connection with the FGM; (3) a payment is made in or affecting interstate or foreign commerce in furtherance of the FGM; (4) an offer or other communication is made in or affecting interstate or foreign commerce in furtherance of the FGM; (5) the conduct occurs within the United States' special maritime and territorial jurisdiction, or within the District of Columbia or a U.S. territory; or (6) the FGM otherwise occurs in or affects interstate or foreign commerce." *See* Letter from Noel J. Francisco, Solicitor General, to Sen. Dianne Feinstein (Apr. 10, 2019), *at* https://www.justice.gov/oip/foia-library/osg-530d-letters/4_10_2019/download.

   13. What does *Holland* suggest about the relationship between the treaty power and individual rights? Some commentators feared that the analysis in *Holland* would allow the treatymakers the power to override the individual rights protections in the Bill of Rights. *See, e.g.,* Thomas Reed Powell, *Constitutional Law in 1919-20*, 19 Mich. L. Rev. 1, 13 (1920) (noting that the Court's "hint that there may be no other test to be applied than whether the treaty has been duly concluded indicates that the Court might hold that specific constitutional limitations in favor of individual liberty and property are not applicable to deprivations wrought by treaties"). Was that a fair concern? The Supreme Court largely dispelled this concern in Reid v. Covert, 354 U.S. 1 (1957), in which it held that Fifth Amendment guarantees to a grand jury indictment and trial by jury applied to trials conducted overseas pursuant to an executive agreement. A plurality of the Court distinguished *Holland* as follows:

> There is nothing in Missouri v. Holland, 252 U.S. 416, which is contrary to the position taken here. There the Court carefully noted that the treaty involved was not inconsistent with any specific provision of the Constitution. The Court was concerned with the Tenth Amendment which reserves to the States or the people all power not delegated to the National Government. To the extent that the United States can validly make treaties, the people and the States have delegated their power to the National Government and the Tenth Amendment is no barrier.

Id. at 18. Is that a valid distinction? In Boos v. Barry, 485 U.S. 312 (1988), the Court confirmed that the treaty power is subject to individual rights limitations. There, the Court held that legislation prohibiting the display of any sign within 500 feet of a foreign embassy if that sign tends to bring that foreign government into "public odium" or "public disrepute" violated the First Amendment, notwithstanding the fact that the legislation implemented a treaty. *See also* Restatement (Fourth) of the Foreign Relations Law of the United States §307 (2018) ("A treaty provision will not be given effect as law in the United States to the extent that giving it this effect would violate any individual constitutional rights.").

   14. In the 1950s, there were a number of proposals to amend the Constitution to limit the treaty power. One of the key supporters of these proposed amendments was Senator John Bricker of Ohio, and the proposals are often referred to collectively as the "Bricker Amendment." In general, the proposed amendments were intended to preclude treaties from being self-executing and to make clear that treaties could not override the reserved powers of the states. Some versions also would have restricted the use of executive agreements. One of the proposed amendments fell only one vote short of obtaining the necessary two-thirds vote in the Senate. As part of its efforts to defeat the Bricker Amendment, the Eisenhower Administration promised the Senate that it would not enter into any of the human rights treaties being developed at that time and would not attempt to use the treaty power to regulate domestic matters. For additional discussion of the Bricker Amendment controversy, see Duane Tananbaum, The Bricker Amendment Controversy: A Test of Eisenhower's Political Leadership (1988). What, if anything, does the Bricker Amendment controversy suggest about the scope of the treaty power?

15. In *Bond v. United States*, the Court concludes that, properly construed, the Chemical Weapons Convention Implementation Act does not apply to Bond's conduct. Was it appropriate for the Court to rely on the "natural meaning" of the term "chemical weapons" when both the Convention and the implementing legislation define that term? What was it about the statutory language that was ambiguous? What was the source of that ambiguity? Who has the better of the argument about the statute's purported ambiguity — Chief Justice Roberts or Justice Scalia?

The Court in *Bond* applies a clear statement requirement that it had developed in cases involving purely domestic statutes. Part of the justification for this requirement is that it forces Congress to specifically consider the federalism implications of intruding on state and local authority. Does this rationale apply to treaty-implementing legislation? Does this decision suggest that other federalism-based presumptions, such as the presumption against preemption of state law, also apply to treaty-implementing legislation? If so, does this mean that such presumptions also apply to foreign affairs legislation that does not implement a treaty?

The Court states that the clear statement rule applies to the interpretation of treaty-implementing legislation, but not to the interpretation of the treaty itself. Why not? Does this mean that the government can avoid the specificity required by the clear statement rule by making a treaty self-executing? Even if so, this may not be an option for treaty provisions that call for the criminalization of conduct: As mentioned above in Section A, it is generally assumed that such treaty provisions cannot be self-executing in the U.S. legal system.

After this decision, what conduct does §229 cover? Does the Court's "natural meaning" approach to construing the statute mean that the statute will now fail to provide sufficient notice of what it criminalizes, as Justice Scalia suggests? If so, does this mean that the Court erred in applying the clear statement requirement? Or does it mean that Congress should have drafted more precisely when it enacted the statute in the first place? In enacting the statute, why did Congress use language that was substantially similar to the language in the Convention? Is it likely that the Convention was drafted with the precision that is desirable in a criminal code? On the other hand, if Congress uses more precise language in the implementing legislation, might this cause the United States to be out of compliance with the requirements of the Convention?

16. Consider the constitutional analysis in Justice Scalia's concurrence in *Bond*. He would adopt the interpretation of the relationship between the treaty power and the Necessary and Proper Clause that Professor Rosenkranz advocated, as discussed above in Note 11. Does it make sense to conclude that if the Senate and President decide to make a treaty non-self-executing and thereby involve the full Congress in the internal implementation of the treaty, the national government has less authority to regulate than if the Senate and President decide to make the treaty self-executing, and thereby leave the House of Representatives out of the picture? How does Justice Scalia answer this question?

Consider Justice Thomas's concurrence. He would apply a subject matter limitation to the treaty power, something discussed above in Note 1. If treaties must concern "international intercourse," as Thomas argues, what types of treaties could the Senate and President *not* constitutionally conclude? Do human rights treaties concern international intercourse?

17. The Hostage Taking Act, 18 U.S.C. §1203, implements the International Convention Against the Taking of Hostages, which the United States joined in 1984. The Act makes it a federal crime for anyone to kidnap and threaten to kill, injure, or continue detaining another person "in order to compel a third person or a governmental organization to do or abstain from doing any act as an explicit or implicit condition for the release of the person detained." The Act applies to kidnappings in the United States as long as either the offender or the victim is an alien. By its terms, the Act appears to cover even local kidnappings that are designed to extract money from the victim's family, as long as an alien is involved. In decisions prior to *Bond*, lower courts had concluded that the Act applied in such local kidnapping cases, and that even if such an application of the Act exceeded Congress's normal legislative authority, it was valid under *Missouri v. Holland*. *See* United States v. Ferreira, 275 F.3d 1020 (11th Cir. 2001); United States v. Lue, 134 F.3d 79 (2d Cir. 1997). Will the clear statement requirement applied in *Bond* make a difference in future cases brought under the Hostage Taking Act? For a post-*Bond* decision holding that the Act does not require proof of a nexus to international terrorism, see United States v. Mikhel, 899 F.3d 1003 (D.C. Cir. 2018). For a decision upholding a prosecution under the Biological Weapons Anti-Terrorism Act, a statute similar to the Chemical Weapons Convention Implementation Act, see United States v. Levenderis, 806 F.3d 390 (6th Cir. 2015). In that case, the defendant was found to have developed ricin and stored it in his freezer for possible use in an elaborate suicide plot, pursuant to which first responders would be exposed to the chemical. The court reasoned that "[t]he type of substance defendant used is significantly more dangerous than the chemicals used in Bond," that the substance "is listed in Schedule 1 of the Annex on Chemicals in the Chemical Weapons Convention," and that "defendant possessed enough ricin to be lethal to hundreds of people exposed to the substance through inhalation."

18. For commentary on *Bond*, see, for example, Curtis A. Bradley, *Federalism, Treaty Implementation, and Political Process:* Bond v. United States, 108 Am. J. Int'l L. 486 (2014); Heather K. Gerken, *The Supreme Court, 2013 Term — Comment: Slipping the Bonds of Federalism*, 128 Harv. L. Rev. 85 (2014); and Alison L. LaCroix, *Redeeming* Bond*? The Court's Quiet Transformation of Federalism Doctrine*, 128 Harv. L. Rev. F. 31 (2014). See also the symposium on *Bond* in Volume 99, Issue 4 of the *Notre Dame Law Review*, with contributions from Roger Alford, Duncan Hollis, Julian Ku, John Yoo, Saikrishna Prakash, Michael Ramsey, David Sloss, Paul Stephan, and Edward Swaine. The articles in the symposium that are of particular relevance to the constitutional scope of the treaty power include: Duncan B. Hollis, *An Intersubjective Treaty Power*, 90 Notre Dame L. Rev. 1415 (2015); Michael D. Ramsey, *Congress's Limited Power to Enforce Treaties*, 90 Notre Dame L. Rev. 1539 (2015); and Saikrishna Bangalore Prakash, *The Boundless Treaty Power Within a Bounded Constitution*, 90 Notre Dame L. Rev. 1499 (2015). For an argument that *Bond* "gutted [*Missouri v. Holland*] by rejecting at least two indispensable predicates of Holmes's analysis: first, that a treaty and its implementing legislation must be considered together; and, second, that a treaty's validity under the Tenth Amendment immunizes that treaty's implementing legislation against a generic federalism challenge," see Michael J. Glennon & Robert D. Sloane *The Sad, Quiet Death of* Missouri v. Holland: *How* Bond *Hobbled the Treaty Power,* 41 Yale J. Int'l L. 51, 54 (2016).

For additional discussion of whether the treaty power should be subject to federalism limitations, compare Curtis A. Bradley, *The Treaty Power and American Federalism,* 97 Mich. L. Rev. 390 (1998) (arguing that it should), and Curtis A. Bradley, *The Treaty Power and American Federalism, Part II,* 99 Mich. L. Rev. 98 (2000) (same), with David M. Golove, *Treaty-Making and the Nation: The Historical Foundations of the Nationalist Conception of the Treaty Power,* 98 Mich. L. Rev. 1075 (2000) (arguing against federalism limitations). *See also* Robert Anderson IV, *"Ascertained in a Different Way": The Treaty Power at the Crossroads of Contract, Compact, and Constitution,* 69 Geo. Wash. L. Rev. 189 (2001); Audrey I. Benison, *International Criminal Tribunals: Is There a Substantive Limitation on the Treaty Power?,* 37 Stan. J. Int'l L. 75 (2001); Oona A. Hathaway et al., *The Treaty Power: Its History, Scope, and Limits,* 98 Cornell L. Rev. 239 (2013); Edward T. Swaine, *Does Federalism Constrain the Treaty Power?,* 103 Colum. L. Rev. 403 (2003); Janet R. Carter, Note, *Commandeering Under the Treaty Power,* 76 N.Y.U. L. Rev. 598 (2001); Note, *Restructuring the Modern Treaty Power,* 114 Harv. L. Rev. 2478 (2001). For additional discussion of the historical background and context of *Holland,* see Charles A. Lofgren, Missouri v. Holland *in Historical Perspective,* 1975 Sup. Ct. Rev. 77. For a symposium on *Holland,* see "Return to *Missouri v. Holland:* Federalism and International Law," 73 Mo. L. Rev. (2008) (articles by Robert Ahdieh, Paul Berman, Duncan Hollis, Julian Ku, Peggy McGuinness, Michael Ramsey, Judith Resnik, Ilya Somin, Peter Spiro, Paul Stephan, Edward Swaine, and Carlos Vazquez).

D. CONDITIONAL CONSENT

The Senate sometimes includes conditions with its advice and consent to treaties. At times, the President suggests these conditions when seeking the Senate's advice and consent, and at other times, the Senate adds them on its own initiative when considering the treaty. A variety of labels have been used for treaty conditions, including "reservation," "understanding," "condition," "proviso," and "declaration." Although the Senate and President have not been entirely consistent in their use of the labels, in general, the label "reservation" has been used when seeking to opt the United States out of a treaty provision or change its legal effect; "understanding" when setting forth the U.S. interpretation of a treaty provision; "condition" or "proviso" when specifying something about the process by which the President makes the treaty or the way it is implemented within the United States; and "declaration" when making a policy statement about the treaty or specifying its domestic status. *See* Congressional Research Service, Treaties and Other International Agreements: The Role of the United States Senate, S. Prt. 106-71, 106th Cong., 2d Sess. 126-27 (2001) ("CRS Study"). Although the President is not obligated to ratify a treaty after the Senate has given its advice and consent, if the President proceeds to do so, it is understood that the ratification is subject to the conditions.

Power Authority of New York v. Federal Power Commission

247 F.2d 538 (D.C. Cir. 1957)

[Petitioner, an agency of the State of New York, applied to the Federal Power Commission for a license to construct a power project utilizing all of the Niagara River water which, under a 1950 treaty between the United States and Canada, was available for American exploitation. In consenting to the treaty, the Senate had attached the following, which it called a "reservation":

> The United States on its part expressly reserves the right to provide by Act of Congress for redevelopment, for the public use and benefit, of the United States' share of the waters of the Niagara River made available by the provisions of the Treaty, and no project for redevelopment of the United States' share of such waters shall be undertaken until it be specifically authorized by Act of Congress.

The Commission dismissed petitioner's application on the ground that it lacked authority to issue the license. It reasoned that "[s]ince the reservation here was intended by the Senate as part of the treaty and was intended to prevent our jurisdiction attaching to the water made available by the treaty, it is entirely authoritative with us as the Supreme Law of the Land under Article VI of the Constitution." Petitioner then brought this review proceeding.]

BAZELON, CIRCUIT JUDGE. . . .

The parties agree that, if the reservation to the 1950 treaty is not "Law of the Land," the order should be set aside. Since the reservation did not have the concurrence of the House of Representatives, it is not "Law of the Land" by way of legislation. The question is whether it became "Law of the Land" as part of the treaty.

The Commission argues that the reservation is an effective part of the treaty because: (1) it was a condition of the Senate's consent to the ratification of the Treaty; (2) the condition was sanctioned by the President, was "accepted" by Canada, and was included in the exchange of ratifications; and (3) it "thus became a part of the Treaty." Simple as this argument seems, we cannot agree with it.

The treaty was signed on behalf of the United States and Canada on February 27, 1950. It defined the quantity of Niagara River water which was to be available for power purposes and provided that it "shall be divided equally between the United States of America and Canada." How each party was to exploit its share of the water was left for that party to decide. In transmitting the treaty to the Senate on May 2, 1950, the President pointed out that the treaty did not determine how the United States was to exploit its share of the water. . . .

The Foreign Relations Committee of the Senate agreed that the question was "domestic in nature" and "concerns the United States constitutional process alone." It recommended the reservation because, without it, "the redevelopment for power purposes would be governed by the Federal Power Act. The Committee intends by the reservation to retain that power in the hands of Congress." The Senate accepted the Committee's recommendation and consented to the ratification of the treaty with the reservation on August 9, 1950.

Meanwhile, the Canadian Parliament had approved the treaty as signed, without the reservation. . . . [W]ithout waiting for Canadian reaction to the reservation, the President ratified the treaty subject to the reservation. On September 21, 1951, the Canadian Ambassador . . . advised that his government accepted the reservation and would indicate its acceptance "by a statement to be included in the Protocol of exchange of ratifications." Two weeks later, without resubmitting the treaty to Parliament for approval of the reservation, the Canadian Government ratified the treaty. In the Protocol, on October 10, 1950, Canada inserted the following statement: "Canada accepts the above-mentioned reservation because its provisions relate only to the internal application of the Treaty within the United States and do not affect Canada's rights or obligations under the Treaty." . . .

Unquestionably the Senate may condition its consent to a treaty upon a variation of its terms. The effect of such a "consent," by analogy to contract law, is to reject the offered treaty and to propose the variation as a counter-offer which will become a binding agreement only if accepted by the other party. But, if what the Senate seeks to add was implicit in the original offer, the purported "conditional acceptance" is an acceptance and the contract arises without a further acceptance by the other party being required. The disposition of the United States share of the water covered by this treaty was, even apart from the reservation, something "which we in the United States must settle under our own procedures and laws." The reservation, therefore, made no change in the treaty. It was merely an expression of domestic policy which the Senate attached to its consent. It was not a counter-offer requiring Canadian acceptance before the treaty could become effective. That Canada did "accept" the reservation does not change its character. The Canadian acceptance, moreover, was not so much an acceptance as a disclaimer of interest. It is of some significance in this regard that the Canadian Government, although it had submitted the original treaty to the Parliament for its approval, found it unnecessary to resubmit the treaty to Parliament after the reservation was inserted. Also significant is the fact that the President ratified the treaty with the reservation without even waiting for Canada to "accept."

A true reservation which becomes a part of a treaty is one which alters "the effect of the treaty in so far as it may apply in the relations of (the) State with the other State or States which may be parties to the treaty." Report of the Harvard Research in International Law 29 Am. J. Int'l L. Supp. 843, 857 (1935). It creates "a different relationship between" the parties and varies "the obligations of the party proposing it. . . ." 2 Hyde, International Law, Chiefly As Interpreted and Applied by the United States (2d revised ed. 1945) 1435. The purported reservation to the 1950 treaty makes no change in the relationship between the United States and Canada under the treaty and has nothing at all to do with the rights or obligations of either party. . . . The Senate could, of course, have attached to its consent a reservation to the effect that the rights and obligations of the signatory parties should not arise until the passage of an act of Congress. Such a reservation, if accepted by Canada, would have made the treaty executory. But the Senate did not seek to make the treaty executory. By the terms of its consent, the rights and obligations of both countries arose at once on the effective date of the treaty. All that the Senate sought to make executory was the purely municipal matter of how the American share of the water was to be exploited.

A party to a treaty may presumably attach to it a matter of purely municipal application, neither affecting nor intended to affect the other party. But such matter does not become part of the treaty. . . .

The constitutionality of the reservation as a treaty provision was extensively argued by the parties. The respondent merely suggests that "there is no apparent limit" to what may be done under the treaty power, citing State of Missouri v. Holland, 252 U.S. 416 (1920). . . .

In State of Missouri v. Holland, 252 U.S. at 433, Mr. Justice Holmes questioned, but did not decide, whether there was any constitutional limitation on the treaty-making power other than the formal requirements prescribed for the making of treaties. The treaty he sustained related to a "national interest of very nearly the first magnitude" which "can be protected only by national action in concert with that of another power." And it conferred rights and imposed obligations upon both signatories. The treaty power's relative freedom from constitutional restraint, so far as it attaches to "any matter which is properly the subject of negotiation with a foreign country," Ware v. Hylton, 3 Dall. 199 (1796), is a long-established fact. No court has ever said, however, that the treaty power can be exercised without limit to affect matters which are of purely domestic concern and do not pertain to our relations with other nations.

Our present Secretary of State [Dulles] has said that the treaty power may be exercised with respect to a matter which "reasonably and directly affects other nations in such a way that it is properly a subject for treaties which become contracts between nations as to how they should act"; and not with respect to matters "which do not essentially affect the actions of nations in relation to international affairs, but are purely internal." He had earlier said:

> I do not believe that treaties should, or lawfully can, be used as a device to circumvent the constitutional procedures established in relation to what are essentially matters of domestic concern.

Charles Evans Hughes, just before he became Chief Justice and after he had been Secretary of State, addressing himself to the question whether there is any constitutional limitation of the treaty power, said:

> . . . The power is to deal with foreign nations with regard to matters of international concern. It is not a power intended to be exercised, it may be assumed, with respect to matters that have no relation to international concerns. . . . The nation has the power to make any agreement whatever in a constitutional manner that relates to the conduct of our international relations, unless there can be found some express prohibition in the Constitution, and I am not aware of any which would in any way detract from the power as I have defined it in connection with our relations with other governments. But if we attempted to use the treaty-making power to deal with matters which did not pertain to our external relations but to control matters which normally and appropriately were within the local jurisdiction of the States, then I again say there might be ground for implying a limitation upon the treaty-making power that it is intended for the purpose of having treaties made relating to foreign affairs and not to make laws for the people of the United States in their internal concerns through the exercise of the asserted treaty-making power.

In the Dulles view, this reservation, if part of the treaty, would be an invalid exercise of the treaty power. In the Hughes view, its constitutionality would be a matter of grave doubt. "The path of constitutional concern in this situation is clear." United States v. Witkovich, 353 U.S. 194 (1957). We construe the reservation as an expression of the Senate's desires and not a part of the treaty. We do not decide the constitutional question. . . .

BASTIAN, CIRCUIT JUDGE (dissenting). . . .

I must disagree with the implication in the majority opinion that this reservation, if a part of the treaty, would be invalid. . . . We are told that the reservation is void because it is regarded as of "purely domestic concern" and therefore not a valid subject matter for a treaty reservation. It is elementary law that treaties may and frequently do affect domestic concerns. Indeed, treaties may repeal previous municipal law passed by the Congress or by state legislatures. Therefore, if this reservation is void, it is not because it affects domestic law to the extent that it requires that the Federal Power Act not apply to the additional water power made available by the treaty.

If void, it must be because the reservation is not only of domestic concern, but is also remote from the valid subject matter of the treaty, and is not inspired by consideration of or pertinent to international relations or policy. While it is true that the President and officials of the Department of State have referred to the question of how the water power made available by the treaty was to be exploited as a matter of domestic concern, certainly that question is not remote from but is germane to the subject matter of the treaty. At the time the treaty was submitted to the Senate for ratification, the question of how and by whom water-power resources of the Niagara River would be exploited was a controversial issue in the Congress. With this controversy in mind, the Senate Foreign Relations Committee, in its report on the treaty, pointed out that extensive public hearings on implementing legislation would probably be necessary. The Committee recognized that it would take considerable time to complete such hearings and to obtain final Congressional action on the pending legislation. Yet the Committee and the Senate as a whole were reluctant to jeopardize the rights which this country would receive under the proposed treaty by delaying its ratification until after Congress had acted upon the pending legislation concerning Niagara River power development. . . .

Because of the possibility that the Canadians might in the absence of the treaty be compelled to take some unilateral action in harnessing the Niagara power, because undue delay might prejudice our good relations with Canada, and in view of an asserted acute power shortage in Canada requiring speedy ratification, this reservation was intimately and inseparably bound up in international questions. In this context it is not purely a domestic concern. If the subject matter of the reservation is domestic in nature, it was nonetheless inspired by, an outgrowth of, and inextricably connected with, an admittedly valid subject matter of a treaty. It is not required as a condition to validity that the reservation be in and of itself, treated in artificial isolation or detachment, a domestic matter properly a subject of contract between sovereigns. It is sufficient if it is directly related to a general subject which is properly a matter for contract between sovereigns, and if international policies and considerations are the raison d'etre of the reservation. As no properly negotiated and ratified treaty of the United States has ever been held invalid there can be no binding judicial authority in support of petitioner's argument for unconstitutionality. . . .

My colleagues recognize that the Senate could have made the treaty executory by providing in its consent that the rights and obligations of both signatory parties take effect only after passage of an act of Congress. They say, however, that the Senate did not do so. While I agree with this, I cannot agree that the Senate has no power to make the treaty executory as to this country alone.

There are many instances where the Senate has extended to the House of Representatives a voice in determining how treaties will be implemented. The Senate has on many occasions done this by insisting that a treaty not be effective until approved or implemented by an act of Congress. This is particularly so as regards treaties affecting revenues. It is also worthy of note that denial of House participation in domestic legislation effectuated by treaty has been one of the most common causes of controversy over the treaty power.

It is my view that recognition of the Senate's power to condition its consent to a treaty upon its remaining executory on both sides until Congress passes legislation to give the treaty operative effect carries with it recognition that the Senate may condition its consent upon the treaty not having an operative effect in this country alone until Congress acts. In either event the treaty rights and duties are the same. In one instance both parties are bound to await an act of Congress before exercising their rights under the treaty, whereas in the second instance, which is the case here, only this country is bound to await an act of Congress before availing itself of the rights allotted by the treaty. Why cannot the Senate make the reduction to use of the treaty rights by the United States await an act of Congress?

International Covenant on Civil and Political Rights
999 U.N.T.S. 171, 6 I.L.M. 368

Opened for Signature, December 19, 1966,
Ratified by the United States on June 5, 1992

ARTICLE 4

1. In time of public emergency which threatens the life of the nation and the existence of which is officially proclaimed, the States Parties to the present Covenant may take measures derogating from their obligations under the present Covenant to the extent strictly required by the exigencies of the situation, provided that such measures are not inconsistent with their other obligations under international law and do not involve discrimination solely on the ground of race, colour, sex, language, religion or social origin.

2. No derogation from articles 6, 7, 8 (paragraphs 1 and 2), 11, 15, 16 and 18 may be made under this provision.

3. Any State Party to the present Covenant availing itself of the right of derogation shall immediately inform the other States Parties to the present Covenant, through the intermediary of the Secretary-General of the United Nations, of the provisions from which it has derogated and of the reasons by which it was actuated. A further communication shall be made, through the same intermediary, on the date on which it terminates such derogation. . . .

ARTICLE 6

1. Every human being has the inherent right to life. This right shall be protected by law. No one shall be arbitrarily deprived of his life. . . .

4. Anyone sentenced to death shall have the right to seek pardon or commutation of the sentence. Amnesty, pardon or commutation of the sentence of death may be granted in all cases.

5. Sentence of death shall not be imposed for crimes committed by persons below eighteen years of age and shall not be carried out on pregnant women.

6. Nothing in this article shall be invoked to delay or to prevent the abolition of capital punishment by any State Party to the present Covenant.

ARTICLE 7

No one shall be subjected to torture or to cruel, inhuman or degrading treatment or punishment. In particular, no one shall be subjected without his free consent to medical or scientific experimentation. . . .

ARTICLE 9

1. Everyone has the right to liberty and security of person. No one shall be subjected to arbitrary arrest or detention. No one shall be deprived of his liberty except on such grounds and in accordance with such procedures as are established by law.

2. Anyone who is arrested shall be informed, at the time of arrest, of the reasons for his arrest and shall be promptly informed of any charges against him.

3. Anyone arrested or detained on a criminal charge shall be brought promptly before a judge or other officer authorized by law to exercise judicial power and shall be entitled to trial within a reasonable time or to release. It shall not be the general rule that persons awaiting trial shall be detained in custody, but release may be subject to guarantees to appear for trial, at any other stage of the judicial proceedings, and, should occasion arise, for execution of the judgement.

4. Anyone who is deprived of his liberty by arrest or detention shall be entitled to take proceedings before a court, in order that court may decide without delay on the lawfulness of his detention and order his release if the detention is not lawful.

5. Anyone who has been the victim of unlawful arrest or detention shall have an enforceable right to compensation. . . .

ARTICLE 17

1. No one shall be subjected to arbitrary or unlawful interference with his privacy, family, home or correspondence, nor to unlawful attacks on his honour and reputation.

2. Everyone has the right to the protection of the law against such interference or attacks.

ARTICLE 18

1. Everyone shall have the right to freedom of thought, conscience and religion. This right shall include freedom to have or to adopt a religion or belief of his choice, and freedom, either individually or in community with others and in public or private, to manifest his religion or belief in worship, observance, practice and teaching.

2. No one shall be subject to coercion which would impair his freedom to have or to adopt a religion or belief of his choice.

3. Freedom to manifest one's religion or beliefs may be subject only to such limitations as are prescribed by law and are necessary to protect public safety, order, health, or morals or the fundamental rights and freedoms of others.

4. The States Parties to the present Covenant undertake to have respect for the liberty of parents and, when applicable, legal guardians to ensure the religious and moral education of their children in conformity with their own convictions. . . .

ARTICLE 20

1. Any propaganda for war shall be prohibited by law.

2. Any advocacy of national, racial or religious hatred that constitutes incitement to discrimination, hostility or violence shall be prohibited by law. . . .

ARTICLE 26

All persons are equal before the law and are entitled without any discrimination to the equal protection of the law. In this respect, the law shall prohibit any discrimination and guarantee to all persons equal and effective protection against discrimination on any ground such as race, colour, sex, language, religion, political or other opinion, national or social origin, property, birth or other status.

U.S. Reservations, Declarations, and Understandings, International Covenant on Civil and Political Rights

138 Cong. Rec. S4781-01 (Daily ed., Apr. 2, 1992)

I. The Senate's advice and consent is subject to the following reservations:

(1) That Article 20 does not authorize or require legislation or other action by the United States that would restrict the right of free speech and association protected by the Constitution and laws of the United States.

(2) That the United States reserves the right, subject to its Constitutional constraints, to impose capital punishment on any person (other than a pregnant woman) duly convicted under existing or future laws permitting the imposition of capital punishment, including such punishment for crimes committed by persons below eighteen years of age.

(3) That the United States considers itself bound by Article 7 to the extent that "cruel, inhuman or degrading treatment or punishment" means the cruel and unusual treatment or punishment prohibited by the Fifth, Eighth and/or Fourteenth Amendments to the Constitution of the United States. . . .

II. The Senate's advice and consent is subject to the following understandings, which shall apply to the obligations of the United States under this Covenant:

(1) That the Constitution and laws of the United States guarantee all persons equal protection of the law and provide extensive protections against discrimination. The United States understands distinctions based upon race, color, sex, language, religion, political or other opinion, national or social origin, property, birth or any other status—as those terms are used in Article 2, paragraph 1 and Article 26—to be permitted when such distinctions are, at minimum, rationally related to a legitimate governmental objective. The United States further understands the prohibition in paragraph 1 of Article 4 upon discrimination, in time of public emergency, based "solely" on the status of race, color, sex, language, religion or social origin not to bar distinctions that may have a disproportionate effect upon persons of a particular status. . . .

(5) That the United States understands that this Covenant shall be implemented by the Federal Government to the extent that it exercises legislative and judicial jurisdiction over the matters covered therein, and otherwise by the state and local governments; to the extent that state and local governments exercise jurisdiction over such matters, the Federal Government shall take measures appropriate to the Federal system to the end that the competent authorities of the state or local governments may take appropriate measures for the fulfillment of the Covenant.

III. The Senate's advice and consent is subject to the following declarations:

(1) That the United States declares that the provisions of Articles 1 through 27 of the Covenant are not self-executing. . . .

IV. The Senate's advice and consent is subject to the following proviso, which shall not be included in the instrument of ratification to be deposited by the President:

Nothing in this Covenant requires or authorizes legislation, or other action, by the United States of America prohibited by the Constitution of the United States as interpreted by the United States.

Notes and Questions

1. According to a study in the 1990s, approximately 15 percent of all Article II treaties since the Founding have been ratified subject to conditions. *See* Kevin C. Kennedy, *Conditional Approval of Treaties by the U.S. Senate*, 19 Loy. L.A. Int'l & Comp. L.J. 89, 91, 97 (1996). As mentioned in the introduction to this chapter, although these conditions are formally adopted by the Senate as part of its advice and consent, they are sometimes proposed in the first instance by the President when the treaty is transmitted to the Senate. The Senate's power to give its conditional consent has two justifications. First, conditional consent is viewed as a component of the Senate's larger power to withhold consent altogether. Second, conditional consent is viewed as a substitute for the Senate's envisioned *ex ante* advice role that was effectively repudiated by the Washington Administration in the early 1790s. In order to preserve its ability to "advise" (as well as consent) regarding treaty terms, the Senate has since the 1790s asserted the power to condition its consent on amendments to the negotiated treaty. *See* CRS Study, *supra*; Samuel B. Crandall, Treaties, Their Making and Enforcement 70 (1904); Ralston Hayden, The Senate and Treaties, 1789-1817, at 110-11 (1920).

2. The first example of conditional consent by the Senate was a reservation made in connection with the Jay Treaty. A bare two-thirds of the Senate gave its advice and consent to the treaty in 1795, but only on the condition that an article of the treaty relating to trade between the United States and the British West Indies be suspended. Britain accepted this condition without complaint, and the treaty was eventually ratified. *See* Hayden, *supra*, at 87; George H. Haynes, The Senate of the United States 607-08 (1938). A few years later, the Senate gave its advice and consent to a treaty with Tunisia on the condition that an article in the treaty be suspended and renegotiated, and the article was in fact renegotiated prior to ratification. Treaty of Amity, Commerce, and Navigation, Aug. 28, 1797, U.S.-Tunis., T.S. No. 360, at 1088 n.1. The Senate again exercised its conditional consent power in connection with an 1800 treaty between the United States and France. Hayden, *supra*, at 121.

The United States' treaty partners did not always respond favorably to the Senate's conditions. In negotiating an 1803 boundary treaty with the United States, Great Britain would not accept the amendment proposed by the Senate, and the treaty was never ratified. The head of the British Foreign Office at that time criticized the United States' conditional consent practice, calling it "new, unauthorized, and not to be sanctioned." *Id.* at 150. Great Britain similarly complained about conditions proposed by the Senate in connection with an 1824 treaty concerning the African slave trade. *See* 5 John Bassett Moore, A Digest of International Law 748, at 200 (1906). Over time, however, this practice became generally accepted by the international community. The United States engaged in this practice in connection with numerous treaties during the nineteenth and early twentieth centuries, generally without controversy, as did many of its treaty partners. *See generally* David Hunter Miller, Reservations to Treaties: Their Effect and the Procedure in Regard Thereto (1919).

3. Was what the Senate called a "reservation" in the U.S.-Canada Treaty at issue in *Power Authority* really a reservation? Did it, like the reservations to the ICCPR, in any way qualify the United States' international obligations? Should courts defer to the Senate's characterization of its conditional consent, or should it, as the *Power Authority* court did, look behind the labels to determine how the condition operates in practice? Whatever the condition is called, isn't it clear that the President and the Senate intended to qualify U.S. ratification of the treaty on the condition of having binding domestic effect? Should courts second-guess such clear political branch wishes in the treaty context?

4. Why did the court in *Power Authority* view the "reservation" as precatory and not part of the treaty? Because it did not impose reciprocal obligations on Canada? Because the President ratified the treaty without waiting for Canada to accept the reservation? Because the reservation concerned a matter of purely domestic concern?

5. If valid, the "reservation" in *Power Authority* would have abrogated the preexisting domestic statute that, by its terms, governed the development of the Niagara River waters. The court in *Power Authority* thus might have believed that the Senate was attempting, through its conditional consent power, to change existing law without the involvement of the House of Representatives. *See* Opinion of Phillip C. Jessup & Oliver J. Lissitzyn for the Power Authority of the State of New York (Dec. 1955), quoted in William W. Bishop, Jr., Reservations to Treaties, II Receuil des Cours at 319-20 (1961). What would have been wrong with the Senate doing this? We know from the later-in-time rule that treaties can supersede prior statutes, so why wouldn't the Senate and President have had that authority here? Does *Power Authority* apply an interpretive presumption against overriding federal legislation by means of treaty conditions? Would such a presumption be any different than the general presumption against repealing federal statutes, which applies even in the later-in-time rule context? Professor Henkin contested the Jessup/Lissitzyn characterization of the Niagara reservation, arguing that "[t]he President and Senate have merely refused to throw new and valuable resources into an old established system of development which Congress may not have intended and may not now desire." Louis Henkin, *The Treaty Makers and the Law Makers: The Niagara Reservation,* 56 Colum. L. Rev. 1151, 1174 (1956). How would Henkin's characterization affect the validity of the reservation?

6. The majority in *Power Authority* acknowledges that the Senate could have conditioned its consent in a way that precluded the international obligation with Canada from coming into effect until passage of an Act of Congress. In a number of instances in the nineteenth and early twentieth centuries, the Senate consented to treaties on the condition that the treaties, or particular articles in the treaties, would take effect only after Congress passed legislation implementing them. For example, a provision in an 1875 trade treaty with Hawaii stated that the treaty would not take effect "until a law to carry it into operation shall have been passed by the Congress of the United States of America." Convention between the United States of America and His Majesty the King of the Hawaiian Islands, Jan. 30, 1875, U.S.-Hawaii, art. V, 19 Stat. 625, 627. Relatedly, the Senate has often reserved certain implementation duties for Congress. For example, in an 1899 treaty with Spain concerning the acquisition of Puerto Rico and the Philippines, the U.S. treatymakers included a provision stating that "the civil rights and political status of the native inhabitants of the territories hereby ceded to the United States shall be determined by the Congress." Treaty of Peace Between the United States of America and the Kingdom of Spain, Dec. 10, 1898, U.S.-Spain, art. IX, 30 Stat. 1754, 1759. *See also* Fourteen Diamond Rings v. United States, 183 U.S. 176, 182, 184-85 (1901) (Brown, J., concurring) (stating that there was "no doubt" that the U.S. treatymakers could provide that customs relations between territories ceded by treaty and the United States "should remain unchanged until legislation had been had upon the subject").

How did the reservation in *Power Authority* differ from these well-settled practices? Why did the majority believe these differences had constitutional significance?

7. When giving its advice and consent to human rights treaties, it has been common for the Senate to insist on a package of reservations, understandings, and declarations (collectively known as "RUDs"). The ICCPR RUDs, excerpted above, are typical. Such RUDs were first proposed by President Carter in 1978 as a way of overcoming decades-long opposition in the Senate—including, most famously, the Bricker Amendment debate—to ratification of human rights treaties. There were many reasons for this opposition, including concerns that (a) provisions in the human rights treaties might conflict with U.S. constitutional guarantees; (b) the vaguely worded terms in the treaties would, if self-executing, sow confusion in the law by superseding inconsistent state law and prior inconsistent federal legislation; (c) even if courts ultimately decided that each of the differently worded provisions in the ICCPR did not require a change in domestic law, litigation of these issues would be costly and would generate substantial legal uncertainty; and (d) the human rights treaties would affect the balance of power between state and federal governments. *See* Four Treaties Relating to Human Rights, Hearings before the Comm. on Foreign Relations, 96th Cong. 21 (1979) (testimony of Deputy Secretary of State Warren Christopher concerning ICCPR). RUDs were a response to these concerns that made it possible for the United States to ratify not only the ICCPR, but also the Genocide Convention, the Torture Convention, and the Convention on the Elimination of All Forms of Racial Discrimination. For a consideration of the historical and constitutional factors that help explain the qualified U.S. embrace of human rights treaties, see Curtis A. Bradley, *The United States and Human Rights Treaties: Race Relations, the Cold War, and Constitutionalism*, 9 Chinese J. Int'l L. 321 (2010).

8. Unlike the "reservation" in *Power Authority*, the reservations to the ICCPR were included in the original treaty ratification instruments and clearly constitute non-consent to particular treaty terms in the ICCPR. Are such reservations constitutional? The examples of conditional consent outlined in Note 2 were all reservations, and thus the practice of reservations goes back to the beginning of the nation. Some commentators, however, have argued that reservations are in tension with separation of powers principles, either because they violate the President's constitutional prerogatives in making treaties, or because they constitute an improper "line-item veto," whereby the Senate is in effect trying to change the terms of the treaty. Do these arguments apply to RUDs to human rights treaties, which have largely been proposed by presidents? Assuming they do, is it relevant that the Senate must attach a RUD before, and not after, ratification, *see* Fourteen Diamond Rings v. United States, 183 U.S. 176, 180 (1901) ("The meaning of the treaty cannot be controlled by subsequent explanations of some of those who may have voted to ratify it."); and that the President always retains the discretion to refuse to ratify a treaty that the Senate has consented to conditionally? As for the line-item veto argument, the Supreme Court struck down a line-item veto statute in Clinton v. New York, 524 U.S. 417 (1998), because the Court found that it gave "the President the unilateral power to change the text of duly enacted statutes." Do RUDs give the Senate unilateral power to change the text of duly ratified treaties? Or are they analogous to a bill passed by both Houses of Congress in the sense that the President retains the discretion to decline to make them binding U.S. law?

9. The ICCPR established a Human Rights Committee (HRC) that is charged with receiving reports submitted by nations under the ICCPR's self-reporting provisions and issuing "such general comments as it may consider appropriate." The HRC technically has no official power to issue binding legal interpretations of the ICCPR. Nonetheless, the HRC has declared itself to be the definitive interpreter of whether a reservation to the ICCPR is consistent with the international law rule that a reservation cannot violate the treaty's "object and purpose." *See* ICCPR Human Rights Comm., General Comment 24(52), 52d Sess., 1382d mtg. P 10, U.N. Doc. CCPR/C/21/Rev.1/Add. 6 (1994), at 18. The HRC also has stated that the execution of juvenile offenders violates the object and purpose test, and that the remedy for this violation is that the entire treaty, including the provision to which the United States reserved, remains binding on the United States. *See id.*; Human Rights Committee, Comments on United States of America, U.N. Doc. CCPR/C/79/Add. 50 (1995). In short, the HRC appears to have maintained that the U.S. reservation with respect to the juvenile death penalty is invalid under international law and that the United States is bound by the ICCPR's prohibition on the juvenile death penalty even though it specifically declined to consent to it.

In "Observations" responding to the HRC, the United States government contested these conclusions. It disagreed with the legal analysis supporting the view that the reservation to the death penalty provision violates the ICCPR's object and purpose, and it maintained that it is inconsistent with the principle of state consent to bind a nation to a term to which it had attached a reservation. *See* Observations by the United States on General Comment 24, 3 Int'l Hum. Rts. Rep. 265 (1996). France and Great Britain also objected to the HRC's conclusion that a nation could be bound to a treaty provision that it had expressly declined to accept. *See* Observations by France on General Comment 24 on Reservations to the ICCPR, 4 Int'l Hum. Rts. Rep. 6, 6-8 (1997); Observations by the United Kingdom on General Comment 24, 3 Int'l Hum. Rts. Rep. 261, 261-69 (1996). The United States, reservation with respect to the juvenile death penalty no longer has practical significance in light of the Supreme Court's decision in Roper v. Simmons, 543 U.S. 551 (2005), which declared the juvenile death penalty unconstitutional. But the HRC position nonetheless raises the more general question about the implications for domestic U.S. law of the possible invalidity of reservations under international law. If a reservation were invalid under international law, would it nonetheless bind U.S. courts?

This issue arises in connection with the United States' ratification of the Chemical Weapons Convention (CWC) in 1994. Article 22 of the CWC prohibits States Parties from attaching reservations to its Articles. Nonetheless, the United States ratified the CWC subject to 28 "conditions." Some of these conditions—such as the one providing the President with the power to refuse a contemplated CWC inspection on the grounds of protecting national security, and the one asserting a congressional right to make reservations to the Convention despite the no reservation clause—appear to amount to non-consent to particular treaty terms, and thus to be "reservations" as that term is typically understood. Assuming that the "conditions" violate the treaty, are they nevertheless legal under domestic law? When the President "takes care" to faithfully execute the treaty, does his constitutional duty require him, or prohibit him, from giving effect to the "conditions"?

10. When giving its advice and consent to human rights treaties, the Senate has often included a federalism understanding. An example is understanding (5) for the ICCPR. What is the legal effect, if any, of such an understanding? If it does not change the domestic legal effect of the treaty, what is its purpose?

11. The RUDs attached to the Senate's advice and consent to human rights treaties also typically include a declaration that the treaty is non-self-executing, and such declarations are often used today for other treaties as well. These declarations are supported by, and indeed are commonly proposed by, the Executive Branch. Why does the government want such declarations? The State Department's Legal Adviser offered this answer: "[T]he decision to make the treaty 'non-self-executing' reflects a strong preference, both within the Administration and in the Senate, not to use the unicameral treaty power of the U.S. Constitution to effect direct changes in the domestic law of the United States." Statement by Conrad K. Harper, USUN Press Release #49-(95), at 3 (Mar. 29, 1995).

Are declarations of non-self-execution constitutional? They do not have the same historical pedigree as reservations, but they are analogous to the longstanding practice, recounted in Note 6, of conditioning consent on subsequent congressional action. Does the term "shall" in the Supremacy Clause suggest an irrebuttable presumption that otherwise self-executing treaties be treated as self-executing? In answering this question, is it relevant that Congress frequently specifies that federal *statutes* do not preempt state law, do not invalidate prior federal law, or do not create a private cause of action? Does it matter that it is widely believed that Congress can declare congressional-executive agreements—which are equivalent to treaties on the international plane (these are discussed in Chapter 6)—to be non-self-executing? Does it matter that it has long been settled that, notwithstanding the Supremacy Clause, some treaties are non-self-executing? Does it matter that the non-self-execution declaration for the ICCPR was included within the U.S. instrument of ratification that defines the nature of the U.S. obligations to other countries? To date, courts have treated declarations of non-self-execution as authoritative. *See, e.g.,* Renkel v. United States, 456 F.3d 640, 644 (6th Cir. 2006) (discussing relevant case law).

Does *Power Authority* suggest that the domestic enforcement of treaties is a domestic rather than an international matter? If so, would this support the view that non-self-execution declarations exceed the scope of the treaty power? For arguments to this effect, see Malvina Halberstam, *United States Ratification of the Convention on the Elimination of All Forms of Discrimination Against Women,* 31 Geo. Wash. J. Int'l L. & Econ. 49, 69 (1997); John Quigley, *The International Covenant on Civil and Political Rights and the Supremacy Clause,* 42 DePaul L. Rev. 1287, 1303-05 (1993); Stefan A. Riesenfeld & Frederick M. Abbott, *The Scope of U.S. Senate Control over the Conclusion and Operation of Treaties,* 67 Chi.-Kent L. Rev. 571, 590-600 (1991). *But see* Curtis A. Bradley & Jack L. Goldsmith, *Treaties, Human Rights, and Conditional Consent,* 149 U. Pa. L. Rev. 399, 452-53 (2000) (arguing that *Power Authority* and the treaty power do not affect the validity of non-self-execution declarations).

One commentator has argued that the non-self-execution declarations merely preclude the implication of a private cause of action under the treaties and do not preclude courts from applying the treaties in situations not requiring the implication of a private cause of action—for example, as a defense to a criminal prosecution, or in a civil suit in which some other law provides a right to sue. *See* David Sloss, *The Domestication of International Human Rights: Non-Self-Executing Declarations and Human Rights Treaties*, 24 Yale J. Int'l L. 129 (1999). *But see* Bradley & Goldsmith, *supra*, at 421-22 (contesting that construction of the declarations). To date, courts have treated the non-self-execution declarations as precluding all judicial enforcement of the treaties, not just the implication of a private cause of action.

What about a Senate declaration stating that a treaty provision *is* self-executing? Is such a declaration valid? Binding on the courts? After the Supreme Court's decision in *Medellin v. Texas* (excerpted in Section A above), the Senate began issuing such declarations in connection with its provision of advice and consent to ratification of some treaties. What, if anything, does the Court's analysis in *Medellin* suggest about the validity of self-execution declarations? Are such declarations (like the presidential memorandum considered in *Medellin*) an improper attempt to create law without going through the full lawmaking process? For an argument that these declarations are valid and enforceable as long as the treaty provision in question is otherwise subject to judicial application, see Curtis A. Bradley, *Self-Execution and Treaty Duality*, 2009 Sup. Ct. Rev. 131, 154-55. For a contrary view, see Carlos Manuel Vazquez, *Treaties as Law of the Land: The Supremacy Clause and the Judicial Enforcement of Treaties*, 122 Harv. L. Rev. 599, 687-88 (2008).

12. A number of commentators have criticized the RUDs practice of the United States, especially in connection with human rights treaties. Consider, for example, Professor Henkin's critique:

> By its reservations, the United States apparently seeks to assure that its adherence to a convention will not change, or require change, in U.S. laws, policies or practices, even where they fall below international standards. . . .
>
> Reservations designed to reject any obligation to rise above existing law and practice are of dubious propriety: if states generally entered such reservations, the convention would be futile. The object and purpose of the human rights conventions, it would seem, are to promote respect for human rights by having countries—mutually—assume legal obligations to respect and ensure recognized rights in accordance with international standards. . . .
>
> By adhering to human rights conventions subject to these reservations, the United States, it is charged, is pretending to assume international obligations but in fact is undertaking nothing. It is seen as seeking the benefits of participation in the convention (e.g., having a U.S. national sit on the Human Rights Committee established pursuant to the Covenant) without assuming any obligations or burdens. The United States, it is said, seeks to sit in judgment on others but will not submit its human rights behavior to international judgment. . . .

Louis Henkin, *U.S. Ratification of Human Rights Conventions: The Ghost of Senator Bricker*, 89 Am. J. Int'l L. 341 (1995).

Supporters of RUDs have argued, in contrast, that RUDs have had wide bipartisan support and were crucial in breaking the logjam in domestic politics that had prevented U.S. ratification of any of the major human rights treaties. They also note that the RUDs do not make U.S. ratification of human rights treaties empty promises. The United States has in fact enacted domestic criminal, civil, and immigration laws to implement the Genocide and Torture Conventions. *See* 18 U.S.C. §1091 (1994) (genocide); 18 U.S.C. §2340A (1994) (torture). Furthermore, even with the RUDs, the United States has bound itself to almost all of the obligations in each of the four major human rights treaties it has ratified, and thus has promised not to retreat from those protections. In addition, the United States has opened its domestic human rights practices to official international scrutiny by filing with international bodies associated with the treaties reports that describe and defend U.S. human rights practices. Finally, supporters of RUDs note that there is no evidence linking U.S. RUDs practice with a diminution of human rights protections around the world, and indeed that international human rights law has flourished during the period that U.S. RUDs were introduced. *See generally* Bradley & Goldsmith, *supra*, at 456-68.

Which view is more persuasive?

13. To date, every court to have considered the issue has given effect to the U.S. RUDs to human rights treaties. Many of these cases have involved the legality under the ICCPR of the juvenile death penalty, an issue that, as noted above, is now essentially moot in light of the *Roper* decision. *See, e.g.,* Beazley v. Johnson, 242 F.3d 248 (5th Cir. 2001); Domingues v. Nevada, 114 Nev. 783, 961 P.2d 1279 (1998). For similar conclusions in other contexts, *see, for example,* Oxygene v. Lynch, 831 F.3d 541, 546 (4th Cir. 2016) (applying understanding relating to provision in Torture Convention); Flores v. S. Peru Copper Corp., 343 F.3d 140, 164 (2d Cir. 2003) (enforcing ICCPR non-self-execution declaration in context of environmental tort suit under the Alien Tort Statute); Bannerman v. Snyder, 325 F.3d 722, 724 (6th Cir. 2003) (enforcing ICCPR non-self-execution declaration in criminal context). *See also* Eric Chung, Note, *The Judicial Enforceability and Legal Effects of Treaty Reservations, Understandings, and Declarations,* 126 Yale L.J. 170, 176 (2016) (finding that "U.S. courts and international courts consistently enforce RUDs, except for international courts reviewing treaties that expressly prohibit their use").

14. The Restatement (Fourth) of Foreign Relations Law states that "[t]he Senate may attach reservations or other conditions to its advice and consent to a treaty as long as they relate to the treaty and are not inconsistent with the Constitution," and that "[i]f the President ratifies a treaty after obtaining the Senate's advice and consent, he or she is deemed to have accepted any conditions attached by the Senate to its advice and consent." Restatement (Fourth) of the Foreign Relations Law of the United States §305 (2018). When would a condition attached by the Senate not be consistent with the Constitution? The comments to this section of the Restatement observe that the conditions "may not, for example, infringe on individual constitutional rights, or usurp the exclusive constitutional authority of the President or the House of Representatives."

15. After ratifying a treaty, must the President obtain the Senate's advice and consent in order to withdraw a condition? There is very little practice relating to this question, since the United States has almost never sought to withdraw a condition. In 1984, however, President Reagan sought the Senate's advice and consent for the withdrawal of a reservation that had previously been included with the U.S. ratification of the Patent Cooperation Treaty. *See* Letter of Transmittal from President Ronald Reagan, July 27, 1984, in Treaty Doc. 98-20. The Senate gave its advice and consent to the withdrawal two years later. *See* 132 Cong. Rec. 29884-85 (Oct. 9, 1986). Soon thereafter, Congress amended the U.S. patent laws to take account of the obligations that the United States would have in the absence of the reservation. *See* Act of Nov. 6, 1986, Pub. L. No. 96-616, 100 Stat. 3485.

E. TREATY INTERPRETATION AND REINTERPRETATION

1. Treaty Interpretation

El Al Israel Airlines v. Tseng

525 U.S. 155 (1999)

[The Convention for the Unification of Certain Rules Relating to International Transportation by Air, popularly known as the Warsaw Convention, governs air carrier liability for "all international transportation of persons, baggage, or goods performed by aircraft for hire," Ch. I, Art. 1(1). The Warsaw Convention imposes liability for, among other things, bodily injuries suffered as a result of an "accident . . . on board the aircraft or in the course of any of the operations of embarking or disembarking," Ch. III, Art. 17. In a prior decision, the Supreme Court had held that liability could not be imposed under this provision for mental or psychic injuries unaccompanied by physical injuries. In this case, Tsui Yuan Tseng sued El Al Israel Airlines under New York state law for psychic tort damages that allegedly resulted from an intrusive security search at John F. Kennedy International Airport. The Second Circuit Court of Appeals held that the Warsaw Convention did not preempt such state-law tort claims. The Supreme Court granted certiorari to address the question whether the Convention precludes a passenger from maintaining an action for damages under state law when the Convention itself allows no recovery.]

JUSTICE GINSBURG delivered the Opinion of the Court. . . .

Our inquiry begins with the text of Article 24, which prescribes the exclusivity of the Convention's provisions for air carrier liability. "It is our responsibility to give the specific words of the treaty a meaning consistent with the shared expectations of the contracting parties." Air France v. Saks, 470 U.S. 392, 399 (1985). "Because a treaty ratified by the United States is not only the law of this land, see U.S. Const., Art. II, §2, but also an agreement among sovereign powers, we have traditionally considered as aids to its interpretation the negotiating and drafting history (*travaux preparatoires*) and the postratification understanding of the contracting parties." Zicherman v. Korean Air Lines Co., 516 U.S. 217, 226 (1996).

Article 24 provides that "cases covered by article 17"—or in the governing French text, "les cas prevus a l'article 17"—may "only be brought subject to the conditions and limits set out in the Convention." . . . In Tseng's view, and in the view of the Court of Appeals, "les cas prevus a l'article 17" means those cases in which a passenger could actually maintain a claim for relief under Article 17. So read, Article 24 would permit any passenger whose personal injury suit did not satisfy the liability conditions of Article 17 to pursue the claim under local law.

In El Al's view, on the other hand, and in the view of the United States as *amicus curiae*, "les cas prevus a l'article 17" refers generically to all personal injury cases stemming from occurrences on board an aircraft or in embarking or disembarking, and simply distinguishes that class of cases (Article 17 cases) from cases involving damaged luggage or goods, or delay (which Articles 18 and 19 address). So read, Article 24 would preclude a passenger from asserting any air transit personal injury claims under local law, including claims that failed to satisfy Article 17's liability conditions, notably, because the injury did not result from an "accident," see *Saks*, 470

U.S. at 405, or because the "accident" did not result in physical injury or physical manifestation of injury, see Eastern Airlines v. Floyd, 499 U.S. 530, 552 (1991).

Respect is ordinarily due the reasonable views of the Executive Branch concerning the meaning of an international treaty. *See* Sumitomo Shoji America, Inc. v. Avagliano, 457 U.S. 176, 184-85 (1982) ("Although not conclusive, the meaning attributed to treaty provisions by the Government agencies charged with their negotiation and enforcement is entitled to great weight."). We conclude that the Government's construction of Article 24 is most faithful to the Convention's text, purpose, and overall structure.

The cardinal purpose of the Warsaw Convention, we have observed, is to "achieve uniformity of rules governing claims arising from international air transportation." *Floyd*, 499 U.S. at 552. The Convention signatories, in the treaty's preamble, specifically "recognized the advantage of regulating in a uniform manner the conditions of . . . the liability of the carrier." To provide the desired uniformity, Chapter III of the Convention sets out an array of liability rules which, the treaty declares, "apply to all international transportation of persons, baggage, or goods performed by aircraft." In that Chapter, the Convention describes and defines the three areas of air carrier liability (personal injuries in Article 17, baggage or goods loss, destruction, or damage in Article 18, and damage occasioned by delay in Article 19), the conditions exempting air carriers from liability (Article 20), the monetary limits of liability (Article 22), and the circumstances in which air carriers may not limit liability (Articles 23 and 25). Given the Convention's comprehensive scheme of liability rules and its textual emphasis on uniformity, we would be hard put to conclude that the delegates at Warsaw meant to subject air carriers to the distinct, nonuniform liability rules of the individual signatory nations. . . .

A complementary purpose of the Convention is to accommodate or balance the interests of passengers seeking recovery for personal injuries, and the interests of air carriers seeking to limit potential liability. Before the Warsaw accord, injured passengers could file suits for damages, subject only to the limitations of the forum's laws, including the forum's choice of law regime. This exposure inhibited the growth of the then-fledgling international airline industry. Many international air carriers at that time endeavored to require passengers, as a condition of air travel, to relieve or reduce the carrier's liability in case of injury. The Convention drafters designed Articles 17, 22, and 24 of the Convention as a compromise between the interests of air carriers and their customers worldwide. In Article 17 of the Convention, carriers are denied the contractual prerogative to exclude or limit their liability for personal injury. In Articles 22 and 24, passengers are limited in the amount of damages they may recover, and are restricted in the claims they may pursue by the conditions and limits set out in the Convention.

Construing the Convention, as did the Court of Appeals, to allow passengers to pursue claims under local law when the Convention does not permit recovery could produce several anomalies. Carriers might be exposed to unlimited liability under diverse legal regimes, but would be prevented, under the treaty, from contracting out of such liability. Passengers injured physically in an emergency landing might be subject to the liability caps of the Convention, while those merely traumatized in the same mishap would be free to sue outside of the Convention for potentially unlimited damages. The Court of Appeals' construction of the Convention would encourage artful pleading by plaintiffs seeking to opt out of the Convention's liability scheme when local law promised recovery in excess of that prescribed by the treaty. Such a reading would scarcely advance the predictability that adherence to the treaty has achieved worldwide. . . .

The drafting history of Article 17 is consistent with our understanding of the preemptive effect of the Convention. The preliminary draft of the Convention submitted to the conference at Warsaw made air carriers liable "in the case of death, wounding, or any other bodily injury suffered by a traveler." In the later draft that prescribed what is now Article 17, airline liability was narrowed to encompass only bodily injury caused by an "accident." It is improbable that, at the same time the drafters narrowed the conditions of air carrier liability in Article 17, they intended, in Article 24, to permit passengers to skirt those conditions by pursuing claims under local law.

Inspecting the drafting history, the Court of Appeals stressed a proposal made by the Czechoslovak delegation to state in the treaty that, in the absence of a stipulation in the Convention itself, "'the provisions of laws and national rules relative to carriage in each [signatory] State shall apply.'" That proposal was withdrawn upon amendment of the Convention's title to read: "CONVENTION FOR THE UNIFICATION OF *CERTAIN* RULES RELATING TO INTERNATIONAL TRANSPORTATION BY AIR." The Second Circuit saw in this history an indication "that national law was intended to provide the passenger's remedy where the Convention did not expressly apply."

The British House of Lords, in Sidhu v. British Airways Plc, [1997] 1 All E.R. 193, considered the same history, but found it inconclusive. Inclusion of the word "certain" in the Convention's title, the Lords reasoned, accurately indicated that "the Convention is concerned with certain rules only, not with all the rules relating to international carriage by air." *Id.* at 204. For example, the Convention does not say "anything . . . about the carrier's obligations of insurance, and in particular about compulsory insurance against third party risks." *Ibid.* The Convention, in other words, is "a partial harmonization, directed to the particular issues with which it deals," *ibid.,* among them, a carrier's liability to passengers for personal injury. As to those issues, the Lords concluded, "the aim of the Convention is to unify." *Ibid.* Pointing to the overall understanding that the Convention's objective was to "ensure uniformity," *id.* at 209, the Lords suggested that the Czechoslovak delegation may have meant only to underscore that national law controlled "chapters of law relating to international carriage by air with which the Convention was not attempting to deal." *Ibid.* In light of the Lords' exposition, we are satisfied that the withdrawn Czechoslovak proposal will not bear the weight the Court of Appeals placed on it. . . .

Tseng urges that federal preemption of state law is disfavored generally, and particularly when matters of health and safety are at stake. Tseng overlooks in this regard that the nation-state, not subdivisions within one nation, is the focus of the Convention and the perspective of our treaty partners. Our home-centered preemption analysis, therefore, should not be applied, mechanically, in construing our international obligations.

Decisions of the courts of other Convention signatories corroborate our understanding of the Convention's preemptive effect. In *Sidhu,* the British House of Lords considered and decided the very question we now face concerning the Convention's exclusivity when a passenger alleges psychological damages, but no physical injury, resulting from an occurrence that is not an "accident" under Article 17. *See* 1 All E.R. at 201, 207. Reviewing the text, structure, and drafting history of the Convention, the Lords concluded that the Convention was designed to "ensure that, in all questions relating to the carrier's liability, it is the provisions of the Convention which apply and that the passenger does not have access to any other remedies, whether under the common law or otherwise, which may be available within the particular country where he chooses to raise his action." *Ibid.* Courts of other nations bound by the Convention have also recognized the treaty's encompassing preemptive effect. The "opinions of our sister signatories," we have observed, are "entitled to considerable weight." *Saks*, 470 U.S. at 404. The text, drafting history, and underlying purpose of the Convention, in sum, counsel us to adhere to a view of the treaty's exclusivity shared by our treaty partners.

JUSTICE STEVENS, dissenting. . . .

Everyone agrees that the literal text of the treaty does not preempt claims of personal injury that do not arise out of an accident. It is equally clear that nothing in the drafting history requires that result. On the contrary, the amendment to the title of the Convention made in response to the proposal advanced by the Czechoslovak delegation, suggests that the parties assumed that local law would apply to all non-accident cases. I agree with the Court that that inference is not strong enough, in itself, to require that the ambiguity be resolved in the plaintiff's favor. It suffices for me, however, that the history is just as ambiguous as the text. I firmly believe that a treaty, like an Act of Congress, should not be construed to preempt state law unless its intent to do so is clear. For this reason, I respectfully dissent.

Abbott v. Abbott

560 U.S. 1 (2010)

[The United States is a party to the Hague Convention on the Civil Aspects of International Child Abduction, which Congress has implemented in the International Child Abduction Remedies Act (ICARA), 42 U.S.C. §11601 *et seq.* The issue in this case was whether a Chilean father's "*ne exeat*" right under Chilean law, which required his former wife to obtain his consent before taking their son out of Chile, constituted a "right of custody" under the Convention. If so, it would trigger a duty on the part of the country to which the child was removed (in this case, the United States) to "order the return of the child forthwith" unless certain exceptions applied. ICARA authorizes a person who seeks a child's return to file a petition in state or federal court and instructs that the court "shall decide the case in accordance with the Convention."]

JUSTICE KENNEDY delivered the opinion of the Court. . . .

"The interpretation of a treaty, like the interpretation of a statute, begins with its text." Medellin v. Texas, 552 U.S. 491, 506 (2008). This Court consults Chilean law to determine the content of Mr. Abbott's right, while following the Convention's text and structure to decide whether the right at issue is a "righ[t] of custody."

Chilean law granted Mr. Abbott a joint right to decide his child's country of residence, otherwise known as a *ne exeat* right. . . .

The Convention recognizes that custody rights can be decreed jointly or alone, and Mr. Abbott's joint right to determine his son's country of residence is best classified as a joint right of custody, as the Convention defines that term. The Convention defines "rights of custody" to "include rights relating to the care of the person of the child and, in particular, the right to determine the child's place of residence."

Art. 5(a). Mr. Abbott's *ne exeat* right gives him both the joint "right to determine the child's place of residence" and joint "rights relating to the care of the person of the child." . . .

That a *ne exeat* right does not fit within traditional notions of physical custody is beside the point. The Convention defines "rights of custody," and it is that definition that a court must consult. This uniform, text-based approach ensures international consistency in interpreting the Convention. It forecloses courts from relying on definitions of custody confined by local law usage, definitions that may undermine recognition of custodial arrangements in other countries or in different legal traditions, including the civil-law tradition. . . .

Ms. Abbott gets the analysis backwards in claiming that a *ne exeat* right is not a right of custody because the Convention requires that any right of custody must be capable of exercise. The Convention protects rights of custody when "at the time of removal or retention those rights were actually exercised, either jointly or alone, or would have been so exercised but for the removal or retention." Art. 3(b). In cases like this one, a *ne exeat* right is by its nature inchoate and so has no operative force except when the other parent seeks to remove the child from the country. If that occurs, the parent can exercise the *ne exeat* right by declining consent to the exit or placing conditions to ensure the move will be in the child's best interests. When one parent removes the child without seeking the *ne exeat* holder's consent, it is an instance where the right would have been "exercised but for the removal or retention."

The Court of Appeals' conclusion that a breach of a *ne exeat* right does not give rise to a return remedy would render the Convention meaningless in many cases where it is most needed. The Convention provides a return remedy when a parent takes a child across international borders in violation of a right of custody. The Convention provides no return remedy when a parent removes a child in violation of a right of access but requires contracting states "to promote the peaceful enjoyment of access rights." Art. 21. . . . But unlike rights of access, *ne exeat* rights can only be honored with a return remedy because these rights depend on the child's location being the country of habitual residence.

Any suggestion that a *ne exeat* right is a "righ[t] of access" is illogical and atextual. The Convention defines "rights of access" as "includ[ing] the right to take a child for a limited period of time to a place other than the child's habitual residence," Art. 5(b), and ICARA defines that same term as "visitation rights," §11602(7). The joint right to decide a child's country of residence is not even arguably a "right to take a child for a limited period of time" or a "visitation righ[t]." Reaching the commonsense conclusion that a *ne exeat* right does not fit these definitions of "rights of access" honors the Convention's distinction between rights of access and rights of custody. . . .

This Court's conclusion that Mr. Abbott possesses a right of custody under the Convention is supported and informed by the State Department's view on the issue. The United States has endorsed the view that *ne exeat* rights are rights of custody. In its brief before this Court the United States advises that "the Department of State, whose Office of Children's Issues serves as the Central Authority for the United States under the Convention, has long understood the Convention as including *ne exeat* rights among the protected 'rights of custody.'" Brief for United States as *Amicus Curiae* 21; *see* Sumitomo Shoji America, Inc. v. Avagliano, 457 U.S. 176, 184, n. 10 (1982) (deferring to the Executive's interpretation of a treaty as memorialized in a brief before this Court). It is well settled that the Executive Branch's interpretation of a treaty "is entitled to great weight." *Id.* at 185. There is no reason to doubt that this well-established canon of deference is appropriate here. The Executive is well informed concerning the diplomatic consequences resulting from this Court's interpretation of "rights of custody," including the likely reaction of other contracting states and the impact on the State Department's ability to reclaim children abducted from this country.

This Court's conclusion that *ne exeat* rights are rights of custody is further informed by the views of other contracting states. In interpreting any treaty, "[t]he 'opinions of our sister signatories' . . . are 'entitled to considerable weight.' El Al Israel Airlines, Ltd. v. Tsui Yuan Tseng, 525 U.S. 155, 176 (1999) (quoting Air France v. Saks, 470 U.S. 392, 404 (1985)). The principle applies with special force here, for Congress has directed that "uniform international interpretation of the Convention" is part of the Convention's framework. *See* §11601(b)(3)(B).

A review of the international case law confirms broad acceptance of the rule that *ne exeat* rights are rights of custody. . . . [The court reviews decisions from Great Britain, Israel, Austria, South Africa, and Germany.]

It is true that some courts have stated a contrary view, or at least a more restrictive one. . . . [The court reviews decisions from Canada and France.] . . . .

Scholars agree that there is an emerging international consensus that *ne exeat* rights are rights of custody, even if that view was not generally formulated when the Convention was drafted in 1980. . . .

A history of the Convention, known as the Perez-Vera Report, has been cited both by the parties and by Courts of Appeals that have considered this issue. We need not decide whether this Report should be given greater weight than a scholarly commentary. It suffices to note that the Report supports the conclusion that *ne exeat* rights are rights of custody. The Report explains that rather than defining custody in precise terms or referring to the laws of different nations pertaining to parental rights, the Convention uses the unadorned term "rights of custody" to recognize "*all* the ways in which custody of children can be exercised" through "a flexible interpretation of the terms used, which allows the greatest possible number of cases to be brought into consideration." Thus the Report rejects the notion that because *ne exeat* rights do not encompass the right to make medical or some other important decisions about a child's life they cannot be rights of custody. Indeed, the Report is fully consistent with the conclusion that *ne exeat* rights are just one of the many "ways in which custody of children can be exercised."

Adopting the view that the Convention provides a return remedy for violations of *ne exeat* rights accords with its objects and purposes. The Convention is based on the principle that the best interests of the child are well served when decisions regarding custody rights are made in the country of habitual residence. *See* Convention Preamble. Ordering a return remedy does not alter the existing allocation of custody rights, Art. 19, but does allow the courts of the home country to decide what is in the child's best interests. It is the Convention's premise that courts in contracting states will make this determination in a responsible manner.

Custody decisions are often difficult. Judges must strive always to avoid a common tendency to prefer their own society and culture, a tendency that ought not interfere with objective consideration of all the factors that should be weighed in determining the best interests of the child. This judicial neutrality is presumed from the mandate of the Convention, which affirms that the contracting states are "[f]irmly convinced that the interests of children are of paramount importance in matters relating to their custody." Convention Preamble. International law serves a high purpose when it underwrites the determination by nations to rely upon their domestic courts to enforce just laws by legitimate and fair proceedings.

To interpret the Convention to permit an abducting parent to avoid a return remedy, even when the other parent holds a *ne exeat* right, would run counter to the Convention's purpose of deterring child abductions by parents who attempt to find a friendlier forum for deciding custodial disputes. . . .

Requiring a return remedy in cases like this one helps deter child abductions and respects the Convention's purpose to prevent harms resulting from abductions. . . .

JUSTICE STEVENS, with whom JUSTICE THOMAS and JUSTICE BREYER join, dissenting. . . .

The Court's interpretation depends entirely on a broad reading of the phrase "relating to" in the Convention's definition of "rights of custody." It is, undeniably, broad language. But, as the Court reads the term, it is so broad as to be utterly unhelpful in interpreting what "rights of custody" means. . . . I suppose it could be said that Mr. Abbott's ability to decide whether [the child] spends the night with one of his friends during a Saturday visit is also a "right relating to the care of the child." Taken in the abstract—and to its most absurd—*any* decision on behalf of a child could be construed as a right "relating to" the care of a child.

Such a view of the text obliterates the careful distinction the drafters drew between the rights of custody and the rights of access. Undoubtedly, they were aware of the concept of joint custody. But just because rights of custody can be shared by two parents, it does not follow that the drafters intended this limited veto power to be a right of custody. And yet this, it seems, is how the Court understands the case: Because the drafters intended to account for joint custodial arrangements, they intended for *this* travel restriction to be joint custody because it could be said, in some abstract sense, to relate to care of the child. I fail to understand how the Court's reading is faithful to the Convention's text and purpose, given that the text expressly contemplates two distinct classes of parental rights. Today's decision converts every noncustodial parent with access rights—least in Chile—into a custodial parent for purposes of the Convention. . . .

[I]n my view, the Convention's language is plain and that language precludes the result the Court reaches. . . . To support its reading of the text, however, the Court turns to authority we utilize to aid us in interpreting ambiguous treaty text: the position of the Executive Branch and authorities from foreign jurisdictions that have confronted the question before the Court. Were I to agree with the Court that it is necessary turn to these sources to resolve the question before us, I would not afford them the weight the Court does in this case.

Views of the Department of State. Without discussing precisely why, we have afforded "great weight" to "the meaning given [treaties] by the departments of government particularly charged with their negotiation and enforcement." Kolovrat v. Oregon, 366 U.S. 187, 194 (1961). We have awarded "great weight" to the views of a particular government department even when the views expressed by the department are newly memorialized, and even when the views appear contrary to those expressed by the department at the time of the treaty's signing and negotiation.. In this case, it appears that both are true: The Department of State's position, which supports the Court's conclusion, is newly memorialized, and is possibly inconsistent with the Department's earlier position.

Putting aside any concerns arising from the fact that the Department's views are newly memorialized and changing, I would not in this case abdicate our responsibility to interpret the Convention's language. This does not seem to be a matter in which deference to the Executive on matters of foreign policy would avoid international conflict; the State Department has made no such argument. Nor is this a case in which the Executive's understanding of the treaty's drafting history is particularly rich or illuminating. Finally, and significantly, the State Department, as the Central Authority for administering the Convention in the United States, has failed to disclose to the Court whether it has facilitated the return of children to America when the shoe is on the other foot. Thus, we have no informed basis to assess the Executive's postratification conduct, or the conduct of other signatories, to aid us in understanding the accepted meaning of potentially ambiguous terms.

Instead, the Department offers us little more than its own reading of the treaty's text. Its view is informed by no unique vantage it has, whether as the entity responsible for enforcing the Convention in this country or as a participating drafter. The Court's perfunctory, one-paragraph treatment of the Department's judgment of this matter only underscores this point. I see no reason, therefore, to replace our understanding of the Convention's text with that of the Executive Branch.

Views of foreign jurisdictions. The Court believes that the views of our sister signatories to the Convention deserve special attention when, in a case like this, "Congress has directed that 'uniform international interpretation' of the Convention is part of the Convention's framework." This may well be correct, but we should not substitute the judgment of other courts for our own. And the handful of foreign decisions the Court cites, provide insufficient reason to depart from my understanding of the meaning of the Convention, an understanding shared by many U.S. Courts of Appeals. . . . Indeed, the interest in having our courts correctly interpret the Convention may outweigh the interest in having the *ne exeat* clause issue resolved in the same way that it is resolved in other countries.

2. Treaty Reinterpretation

In the 1972 Treaty on the Limitation of Anti-Ballistic Missile Systems (ABM Treaty) between the United States and the Soviet Union, each party agreed "not to develop, test, or deploy ABM systems or components" and to restrict land-based ABM systems to two sites. In March 1983, President Reagan initiated the Strategic Defense Initiative (SDI) that sought to establish a space-based method to render incoming ballistic missile warheads "impotent and obsolete." Two years later, the Reagan Administration announced a new interpretation of the ABM Treaty that permitted research and development of ABM systems that, like the SDI system, used technologies not in existence in 1972. This new interpretation departed from prior Executive Branch interpretations of the ABM Treaty that were presented to the Senate during the ratification process, and some argued that the Executive was bound by the earlier interpretations. In response to this claim, Abraham Sofaer, then-Legal Adviser to the State Department, argued that Executive Branch representations to the Senate were binding on the Executive after ratification only if they were "generally understood," "clearly intended," and "relied upon" by the Senate during the ratification process. *See* David A. Koplow, *Constitutional Bait and Switch: Executive Reinterpretation of Arms Control Treaties*, 137 U. Pa. L. Rev. 153, 1374 (1989) (deriving this position from various sources, including Sofaer's testimony before the Senate). Below is an Executive Branch legal analysis in support of Sofaer's view.

Memorandum from Charles J. Cooper, Assistant Attorney General, Office of Legal Counsel, to Abraham D. Sofaer, Legal Adviser, Department of State, "Relevance of Senate Ratification History to Treaty Interpretation"

11 Op. Off. Legal Counsel 28 (Apr. 9, 1987)

This memorandum responds to your request for the views of this Office concerning the relevance of the Senate's deliberations on ratification of a treaty to subsequent interpretations of ambiguous treaty language by the Executive Branch. We use the term "deliberations" or "ratification record" to encompass sources such as hearings, committee reports, and floor debates, which are generally analogous to the "legislative history" of domestic statutes. Our focus is on the relevance of those sources to interpretation of a treaty as domestic law, i.e., their relevance to the President's constitutional responsibility to "take Care that the Laws be faithfully executed." U.S. Const. art. II, §3. We understand that you are reviewing separately the relevance that would be ascribed under international law to the Senate's ratification record.

The question you raise does not lend itself to any clear or easy answer. . . .

Under [the] separation of powers, the President has a dual role with respect to treaties. First, the President is responsible for "making" treaties, i.e., entering into negotiations with foreign governments and reaching agreement on specific provisions. U.S. Const. art. II, §2, cl. 2. Second, as part of his responsibility to "take Care that the Laws be faithfully executed," and as the "sole organ of the federal government in the field of international relations," the President is responsible for enforcing and executing international agreements, a responsibility that necessarily "involves also the obligation and authority to interpret what the treaty requires." L. Henkin, Foreign Affairs and the Constitution 167 (1972).[4]

The President's authority to make treaties is shared with the Senate, which must consent by a two-thirds vote. . . . This "JOINT AGENCY of the Chief Magistrate of the Union, and of two-thirds of the members of [the Senate]"[6] reflects the Framers' recognition that the negotiation and acceptance of treaties incorporates both legislative and executive responsibilities. . . . Rather than vest either Congress or the President with the sole power to make treaties, the Framers sought to combine the judgment of both, providing that the President shall make the treaties, but subject to the "advice and consent" of the Senate. Thus, the Framers included the Senate in the treaty-making process because the result of that process, just as the result of the legislative process, is essentially a law that has "the effect of altering the legal rights, duties and relations of persons . . . outside the Legislative Branch." INS v. Chadha, 462 U.S. 919, 952 (1983). [H]owever, conceptually the constitutional division of treaty-making responsibility between the Senate and the President is essentially the reverse of the division of law-making authority, with the President being the draftsman of the treaty and the Senate holding the authority to grant or deny approval.

In practice, the Senate's formal participation in the treaty-making process begins after negotiation of the treaty. At that time, the President transmits the treaty to the Senate, with a detailed description and analysis of the treaty, and any

---

4. The President's interpretation of a treaty is, of course, subject to review by the courts in a case or controversy that meets Article III requirements. *See* U.S. Const. art. III, §2 ("The judicial Power shall extend to all Cases, . . . arising under this Constitution, the Laws of the United States, and Treaties made, or which shall be made, under their Authority.").

6. *The Federalist No. 66*, at 406 (A. Hamilton) (C. Rossiter ed. 1961).

protocols, annexes, or other documents that the President considers to be integral parts of the proposed treaty. Under the Senate's rules, treaties are referred to the Senate Foreign Relations Committee, which may hold hearings to develop a record explaining the purposes, provisions, and significance of the agreement. Typically, the principal witnesses at such hearings are representatives of the Executive Branch. The Foreign Relations Committee then issues a report to the full Senate, with its recommendation on approval of the treaty.

The Senate's practice has been to approve, to disapprove, or to approve with conditions, treaties negotiated by the Executive Branch. Express conditions imposed by the Senate may include "understandings," which interpret or clarify the obligations undertaken by the parties to the treaty but do not change those obligations, or "reservations" and "amendments," which condition the Senate's consent on amendment or limitation of the substantive obligations of the parties under the agreement. On occasion, the Senate has accompanied its consent by "declarations," which state the Senate's position, opinion, or intention on issues raised by the treaty, although not on the provisions of the specific treaty itself.

When the Senate includes express conditions as part of its resolution of consent to ratification, the President may, if he objects, either refuse to ratify the treaty or resubmit it to the Senate with the hope that it will be approved unconditionally the second time. If the President proceeds with ratification, however, such understandings or other conditions expressly imposed by the Senate are generally included by the President with the treaty documents deposited for ratification or communicated to the other parties at the same time the treaty is deposited for ratification. Because such conditions are considered to be part of the United States' position in ratifying the treaty, they are generally binding on the President, both internationally and domestically, in his subsequent interpretation of the treaty.

The more difficult question is what relevance, if any, the President must give to less formal, contemporaneous indications of the Senate's understanding of the treaty, i.e., statements in committee reports, hearings, and debates which may reflect an understanding of certain treaty provisions by some Senators, but which were not embodied in any formal understanding or condition approved by the entire Senate.[14] With the not insubstantial exception of representations made or confirmed by the Executive Branch (discussed below), we believe such statements have only limited probative value and therefore are entitled to little weight in subsequent interpretations of the treaty.

First, it must be observed that a treaty is fundamentally a "contract between or among sovereign nations," and the primary responsibility—whether of the executive or the courts—is "to give the specific words of the treaty a meaning consistent with the shared expectations of the contracting parties." Air France v. Saks, 470 U.S. 392, 399 (1985). International agreements, like "other contracts . . . are to be read in the light of the conditions and circumstances existing at the time they were entered into, with a view to effecting the objects and purposes of the States thereby contracting." Rocca v. Thompson, 223 U.S. 317, 331-32 (1912). Necessarily,

---

14. It is clear that post hoc expressions of legislative intent, after the treaty has been duly ratified, cannot change the legal effect of an international agreement to which the Senate has given its approval. *See* Fourteen Diamond Rings v. United States, 183 U.S. 176, 179-80 (1901) (resolution adopted by Congress after the Senate had consented to ratification of a treaty is "absolutely without legal significance"). Congress may, of course, in effect validate an Executive Branch interpretation of a treaty by passing legislation consistent with that view.

the best evidence of the intent of the parties is the language and structure of the treaty and, secondarily, direct evidence of the understanding reached by the parties, as reflected in the negotiating record and subsequent administrative construction, rather than unilateral, post-negotiation statements made during the Senate ratification debates.

Moreover, the constitutional role of the Senate is limited to approval or disapproval of the treaty, much as the President's constitutional role in enacting domestic legislation is limited to his veto power. The Senate may, if it chooses, amend or interpret the treaty by attaching explicit conditions to its consent, which are then transmitted to, and either accepted or rejected by, the other parties. Absent such conditions, the Senate does not participate in setting the terms of the agreement between the parties, and therefore statements made by Senators, whether individually in hearings and debates or collectively in committee reports, should be accorded little weight unless confirmed by the Executive. . . .

Indeed, profound foreign policy implications would be raised if the United States were to supplement or alter treaty obligations to foreign governments based on statements made by members of the Senate during its consideration of the treaty that were not communicated to those governments in the form of express conditions. "Foreign governments dealing with us must rely upon the official instruments of ratification as an expression of the full intent of the government of the United States, precisely as we expect from foreign governments." Coplin v. United States, 6 Ct. Cl. 115, 145 (1984). . . .

On the other hand, statements made to the Senate by representatives of the Executive Branch as to the meaning of a treaty should have considerably more weight in subsequent interpretations of ambiguous terms of the treaty. Such statements do not present as substantial a threat to the reliance interests of foreign governments, because the Executive Branch negotiated the treaty and is therefore in a position to represent authoritatively the meaning of the agreement that emerged from the negotiating process. Moreover, given that the Senate's constitutional role is limited to approving a treaty already negotiated by the Executive Branch and that much of the extra-textual evidence of a treaty's meaning remains in the control of the Executive Branch, we believe the Senate itself has a substantial reliance interest in statements made by the Executive Branch officials seeking that approval.

Accordingly, consistent with the President's role as the nation's exclusive negotiator of treaties with foreign governments, we believe that statements made to the Senate by the Executive Branch during the ratification debates are relevant in much the same way that contemporaneous statements by congressional draftsmen or sponsors of domestic legislation are relevant to any subsequent interpretation of the statute. We note that because of the primary role played by the Executive Branch in the negotiation of treaties and the implementation of foreign policy, courts generally accord substantial deference—albeit not conclusive effect—to interpretations advanced by the Executive Branch. Although the courts often rely on interpretative statements made by the Executive Branch prepared well after negotiation and ratification of the treaty,[21] they find particularly persuasive a consistent pattern of Executive Branch interpretation, reflected in the application of the treaty by the Executive and the course of conduct of the parties in implementing

---

21. On occasion, the State Department makes specific suggestions to the court about the interpretation of an agreement. . . . The courts in fact often invite the United States to file *amicus* briefs giving the views of the Executive Branch in cases to which the United States is not a party.

the agreement. Much as contemporaneous administrative construction of domestic statutes by agencies charged with their implementation is generally accorded considerable deference by the courts, particularly when those agencies have made explicit representations to Congress during consideration of the legislation, statements made to the Senate by members of the Executive Branch about the scope and meaning of a treaty would be relevant evidence of the Executive Branch's view, and therefore would be accorded deference by a court in assessing the domestic effect of the treaty.

The weight to be given to an interpretative statement made by an Executive Branch official to the Senate during the ratification process will likely depend upon such factors as the formality of the statement, the identity and position of the Executive Branch official making the statement, the level of attention and interest focused on the meaning of the relevant treaty provision, and the consistency with which members of the Executive Branch adhered at the time to the view of the treaty provision reflected in the statement. All of these factors affect the degree to which the Senate could reasonably have relied upon the statement and, in turn, the weight that courts will attach to it. At one extreme, a single statement made by a middle-level Executive Branch official in response to a question at a hearing would not be regarded as definitive. Rather, in interpreting the domestic effect of a treaty, the courts would likely accord such a statement in the ratification record a degree of significance subordinate to more direct evidence of the mutual intent of the parties, such as the language and context of the treaty, diplomatic exchanges between the President and the other treaty parties, the negotiating record, and the practical construction of the provision reflected in the parties' course of dealings under the treaty. Moreover, courts often give substantial weight to the Executive Branch's current interpretation of the treaty, in recognition of the President's unique role in shaping foreign policy and communicating with foreign governments, and, accordingly, would be unlikely to bind future chief executives on the basis of an isolated remark of an Executive Branch official in a previous administration. In general, therefore, less formal statements made by the Executive Branch before the Senate (such as the one described in the preceding hypothetical) will be but one source of relevant evidence to be considered in interpreting an ambiguous treaty provision.

In contrast, in a case in which the statements by the Executive Branch amount to a formal representation by the President concerning the meaning of a particular treaty provision, the ratification record may be conclusive. If, for example, the ratification record unequivocally shows that the President presented the treaty to the Senate based on specific, official representations regarding the meaning of an ambiguous provision, that the Senate regarded that understanding as important to its consent, and that the Senate relied on the representations made by the Executive Branch in approving the treaty (and thus in refraining from attaching a formal reservation setting forth the understanding), we believe the President would, in effect, be estopped from taking a contrary position in his subsequent interpretation of the treaty, just as he would be bound by a formal reservation or understanding passed by the Senate to the same effect. Obviously, a President could not negotiate a treaty with other nations on the basis of one understanding of its import, submit the treaty to the Senate on a wholly different understanding, and then, in implementing the treaty, rely solely on the understanding he had reached with the other parties. Similarly, he could not reach a secret agreement with the other party that substantially modifies the obligations and authorities created by the text of the treaty submitted to the Senate, and then seek to use the secret agreement as a basis for actions inconsistent with the text of the treaty. Such results would essentially eviscerate the Senate's constitutional advice and consent role, because it would deprive the Senate of a fair opportunity to determine whether, or with what conditions, the treaty should become the "supreme Law of the Land." Accordingly, in such extreme cases, we have little doubt that, as a matter of domestic law, the courts would construe the treaty as presented to and accepted by the Senate, even if as a matter of international law the treaty might have a different meaning.[25]

The "Sofaer doctrine" excerpted above generated substantial criticism and debate—in Congress, among academic commentators, and in the international community. Congress subsequently imposed conditions on Defense Department appropriations forbidding the testing of new technologies that would violate the original, narrower construction of the Treaty. The Reagan Administration subsequently announced that, while it considered its broad interpretation of the Treaty "fully justified," it would follow a narrower interpretation in practice.

Several years later, the Senate gave its consent to the Intermediate-Range Nuclear Forces Treaty ("INF Treaty"), a treaty with the Soviet Union that called for the elimination of ground-based missiles capable of reaching distances between 300 and 3,500 miles. The Senate attached the following condition—the so-called Byrd-Biden Condition—to its advice and consent:

> The Senate's advice and consent to ratification of the I.N.F. Treaty is subject to the condition, based on the treaty clauses of the Constitution, that:
>
> 1. The United States shall interpret the treaty in accordance with the common understanding of the treaty shared by the President and the Senate at the time the Senate gave its advice and consent to ratification;
>
> 2. Such common understanding is based on: a) first, the text of the treaty and the provisions of this resolution of ratification; and b) second, the authoritative representations which were provided by the President and his representatives to the Senate and its committees, in seeking Senate consent to ratification, insofar as such representations were directed to the meaning and legal effect of the text of the treaty; and
>
> 3. The United States shall not agree to or adopt an interpretation different from that common understanding except pursuant to Senate advice and consent to a subsequent treaty or protocol, or the enactment of a statute; and
>
> 4. If, subsequent to ratification of the treaty, a question arises as to the interpretation of a provision of the treaty on which no common understanding was reached in accordance with paragraph 2, that provision shall be interpreted in accordance with applicable United States law.

134 Cong. Rec. S6724 (daily ed. May 26, 1988). The condition was adopted by the Senate by a vote of 72 to 27. During the 1990s, the Senate incorporated the Byrd-Biden Condition by reference in its resolutions of advice and consent to other major arms control treaties. The condition was also routinely included in resolutions of advice and consent for other treaties in the late 1990s and early 2000s.

----

25. Although courts generally seek to construe treaties consistent with their international import, on occasion courts have adopted constructions of particular treaties that conflict with the President's view of the international obligations created by the treaty. Moreover, Congress can enact domestic legislation that is inconsistent with existing treaty obligations, and thus has the effect of tying the President's hands domestically, while leaving the international obligations intact. It would not be unprecedented, therefore, for a court to construe a treaty more narrowly—or more broadly—as a matter of domestic law than the President construes the treaty as a matter of international law.

Notes and Questions

1. As both *El Al* and *Abbott* illustrate, when interpreting a treaty, the Supreme Court sometimes looks beyond the treaty's text to its purpose and drafting history and to the post-ratification practices of the treaty parties. In other cases, however, the Court relies on the treaty's text to the exclusion of these other factors. An example of the latter approach can be found in Chan v. Korean Airlines, 490 U.S. 122 (1989). The issue in *Chan* was whether an airline forfeited the Warsaw Convention's liability limitation by failing to provide notice of the limitation to passengers in the 10-point type required by a private accord among air carriers. The Court determined that the text of the Convention clearly limited liability in this context, and that, in the absence of textual ambiguity, recourse to drafting history or other evidence of what the drafters intended was inappropriate.

When should courts look beyond the treaty's text to other materials? Is the drafting history of a treaty like the legislative history of a statute? Is it more relevant or less relevant to the treaty's meaning than legislative history is to a statute's meaning? Does the contractual nature of treaties distinguish them from statutes for purposes of interpretation? Does it matter whether the treaty is bilateral or multilateral? For a discussion of these and related issues, see Curtis J. Mahoney, Note, *Treaties as Contracts: Textualism, Contract Theory, and the Interpretation of Treaties*, 116 Yale L.J. 824 (2007). *See also* Air France v. Saks, 470 U.S. 392, 396-97 (1985) ("'[T]o ascertain [treaty] meaning we may look beyond the written words to the history of the treaty, the negotiations, and the practical construction adopted by the parties.' The analysis must begin, however, with the text of the treaty and the context in which the written words are used.") (quoting Choctaw Nation of Indians v. United States, 318 U.S. 423, 431-32 (1943)).

2. The Restatement (Fourth) of Foreign Relations Law states that "[a] treaty is to be interpreted in good faith in accordance with the ordinary meaning to be given to its terms in their context and in light of its object and purpose." Restatement (Fourth) of the Foreign Relations Law of the United States §306(1) (2018). This standard is drawn from Article 31 of the Vienna Convention on the Law of Treaties. This section of the Restatement also provides that "[r]ecourse may be had to supplementary means of interpretation, including the treaty's negotiating history and the circumstances of its conclusion, in order to confirm the meaning" resulting from the application of this standard "or to determine the meaning when that application: (a) leaves the meaning ambiguous or obscure; or (b) leads to a result that is manifestly absurd or unreasonable." *Id.* §306(5). This provision is drawn from Article 32 of the Vienna Convention. In explaining its reliance on the Convention, the Restatement observes:

> Although the United States has not ratified the Vienna Convention on the Law of Treaties, these articles are now generally accepted as reflecting customary international law, including by the United States. As a result, the articles set forth principles that one would expect any interpreter to apply in construing obligations under a treaty.

Id. §306, Comment a. The reporters' notes to this section also contend that, "[i]n interpreting treaties, the Supreme Court generally has considered the same interpretive sources as those addressed in the Vienna Convention on the Law of Treaties, without necessarily invoking that Convention's precise ordering or methodology." *Id.* §306, reporters' note 3. Is the Supreme Court's approach to treaty interpretation in fact consistent with Articles 31 and 32 of the Vienna Convention? For discussion of tensions between the Convention and U.S. interpretation practice, see Evan Criddle, *The Vienna Convention on the Law of Treaties in U.S. Treaty Interpretation*, 44 Va. J. Int'l L. 431 (2004).

3. The Vienna Convention does not address how nations are to allocate interpretive authority over treaties within their legal systems. As discussed in Chapter 2, the Supreme Court has long stated that it will give "great weight" to the views of the Executive Branch concerning the meaning of a treaty. What are the Court's justifications for giving such deference? Is deference to the Executive likely to lead courts to adopt an interpretation different from the one that would result if courts simply applied the interpretive standards in the Vienna Convention? Or will the Executive Branch already have taken account of those standards in formulating its interpretation? In an effort to reconcile deference to the Executive with the Vienna Convention standards, the Restatement (Fourth) points out that, "[a]s a practical matter, the executive branch can be a helpful source of information to courts in the United States regarding the materials relevant to interpretation of a treaty, including the treaty's negotiating history and the interpretations of other treaty partners." *Id.* §306, reporters' note 10. To what extent does this observation reconcile the two approaches?

Consider Justice Stevens' critique of the majority's deference to the Executive Branch in *Abbott*. Should deference to Executive Branch treaty interpretations be more context-specific, as Justice Stevens argues? Or are there advantages to having a general policy of judicial deference?

4. The majority in both *El Al* and *Abbott* looked to the decisions of courts in other countries. Why is this so? Is the deference in this context stronger or weaker than the deference courts pay to Executive Branch interpretation of treaties? What happens if foreign court interpretations conflict with the Executive's interpretation? Should the Supreme Court prefer accuracy of interpretation over consistency with foreign court interpretations, as Justice Stevens argues in *Abbott*?

In Olympic Airways v. Husain, 541 U.S. 644 (2004), there was disagreement among the Supreme Court Justices over the degree of deference owed to foreign court decisions in the interpretation of treaties. *Husain* involved the question whether an airline's failure to move a passenger away from a smoking area, resulting in the passenger's death, could be an "accident" under Article 17 of the Warsaw Convention. Relying largely on earlier Supreme Court decisions and dictionary definitions, the majority concluded that it could. The majority rejected reliance on two contrary intermediate appellate courts from the United Kingdom and Australia on the ground that "there are substantial factual distinctions between these cases," and "the respective courts of last resort—the House of Lords and High Court of Australia—have yet to speak." *Id.* at 655 n.9. In dissent, Justice Scalia disagreed, reasoning:

> We can, and should, look to decisions of other signatories when we interpret treaty provisions. Foreign constructions are evidence of the original shared understanding of the contracting parties. Moreover, it is reasonable to impute to the parties an intent that their respective courts strive to interpret the treaty consistently. . . . Finally, even if we disagree, we surely owe the conclusions reached by appellate courts of other signatories the courtesy of respectful consideration. . . . To the extent the Court implies that [the foreign court decisions] merit only slight consideration because they were not decided by courts of last resort, I note that our prior Warsaw Convention cases have looked to decisions of intermediate appellate foreign courts as well as supreme courts.

Id. at 661-62 & n.2. Are you convinced by Justice Scalia's reasons for deferring to foreign judicial treaty interpretations? What if the Supreme Court relied on the lower court decisions and they were overturned on appeal? If there are just a few foreign decisions on point, does deference to those decisions run the risk of entrenching a possibly wrong initial decision?

5. One difference between a U.S. statute and a treaty is that the latter can be written in more than one authoritative language. Recall from Section A of this chapter that Chief Justice Marshall changed his mind about the meaning of the treaty at issue in Foster v. Neilson after consulting the Spanish language version of the treaty in United States v. Percheman. Which version — English, or some other language — is dispositive for U.S. courts? Article 33 of the Vienna Convention on the Law of Treaties states that in the event of a discrepancy between two or more authoritative languages that is not clarified by the normal rules of interpretation, "the meaning which best reconciles the texts, having regard to the object and purpose of the treaty, shall be adopted." To the extent that the Vienna Convention binds the United States, must a U.S. court take into account and reconcile non-English versions of the treaty when they conflict on a particular point with the English version? Does *Percheman* support this view? Are federal judges generally equipped to do this? Does it matter that the Senate considered and consented to only the English-language version?

6. The majority and dissent in *El Al* disagree over whether the presumption against preemption of state law that applies to statutes also applies to treaties. In light of the analysis of these issues in Chapter 4, which side has the better of the argument here? When Justice Ginsburg says that "our home-centered preemption analysis . . . should not be applied, mechanically, in construing our international obligations," does she mean that it has no relevance in the treaty context, or that it has less relevance?

7. Of what relevance to the interpretation of a treaty are statements made, either by the Senate or the Executive Branch, during the Senate advice and consent process? Why should a statement by a Senator, or even a Senate Foreign Relations Committee report, matter to the interpretation of a treaty? Do such statements and reports have more weight, or less, than they would for the interpretation of statutes? What about presidential statements to the Senate? If these statements can form part of the meaning of a treaty, then isn't it possible that the President could make a representation to the Senate on an interpretation of the treaty that does not accord with the understanding of the country or countries with which the President negotiated? As noted in the Cooper memorandum (excerpted above), foreign governments do not monitor hearings before the Senate Foreign Relations Committee and must rely on the official instruments of ratification, including any express formal conditions on consent, as an expression of the United States' intent. Is this why the Cooper memorandum suggests that certain representations by the President can form part of the meaning of the treaty under *domestic* law, but not under *international* law? Does it make sense to conclude that a treaty might have different meanings under domestic and international law? Is the Cooper memorandum's conclusion on this point consistent with the aim of the constitutional Founders to ensure that the United States had adequate domestic mechanisms to ensure compliance with treaties?

8. In connection with the ABM reinterpretation controversy, where does the President obtain the authority to reinterpret treaties? Does it flow from his Article II power to "take Care that the Laws be faithfully executed"? From his role as the "sole organ" of the United States with respect to foreign affairs? From his role in making treaties? From the Article II Vesting Clause, since the power to reinterpret is not expressly placed anywhere else? Note that Executive Branch agencies are permitted to change their interpretations of statutes that they are charged with administering, and that such changed interpretations, if reasonable, receive deference from courts. *See, e.g.,* FDA v. Brown & Williamson Tobacco Corp., 529 U.S. 120, 156-57 (2000); Chevron, U.S.A., Inc. v. NRDC, Inc., 467 U.S. 837, 863 (1984). Are treaties comparable to statutes administered by agencies? How does this issue of treaty reinterpretation relate to the deference that courts often give to the Executive Branch with respect to treaty interpretation issues, which we considered in Chapter 2?

9. Under what circumstances will Executive representations to the Senate preclude the President from reinterpreting a treaty? Does the formality of the representation matter? Whether the Executive Branch representative is a Cabinet secretary as opposed to a mid-level official? Whether the Executive Branch has been consistent in its view? The Cooper memorandum says that these factors inform the degree to which the Senate reasonably relies on the representation in consenting to the treaty. Why does that matter to the President's authority to reinterpret a treaty? Should it be the words of the treaty, and any formal conditions on consent, that matter? Why should the representations of one administration limit the reasonable interpretations of a treaty's text by another administration?

10. As the materials above make clear, the Reagan Administration's attempt to reinterpret the ABM Treaty failed because of substantial political opposition. What does this say about the tools that the Senate and, more broadly, Congress have for dealing with Executive Branch reinterpretation of treaties? How does this effectiveness inform your view of the legitimacy of Executive reinterpretation?

11. Is the Byrd-Biden Condition, excerpted above, constitutional? Is it like a conditional consent to the treaty that alters the treaty's terms, or does it purport to affect how other constitutional interpreters must construe the treaty's language? Professor Glennon takes the former view:

> The Senate well might have insisted that the INF Treaty actually be changed. Instead, the Senate chose a more restrained course; one that did not endanger the Treaty's ratification. It conditioned its consent upon adherence to a canon of construction tailored to this specific agreement. Rather than inject the Senate into the process of interpretation that occurs after the Senate's consent, therefore, the Condition simply shaped the meaning of the document to which the Senate consented. The President remains free, as he is with all other treaties, to interpret the INF Treaty to which the Senate consented. But he cannot interpret a treaty other than the one to which the Senate consented—subject to the Biden Condition—for to do so would be to make a new treaty.

Michael J. Glennon, *The Constitutional Power of the United States Senate to Condition Its Consent to Treaties,* 67 Chi.-Kent. L. Rev. 533, 552 (1991). President Reagan, by contrast, took the latter view, and had this response: "I cannot accept the proposition that a condition in a resolution to ratification can alter the allocation of rights and duties under the Constitution; nor could I . . . accept any diminution claimed to be effected by such a condition in the constitutional powers and responsibilities of the Presidency." 24 Weekly Comp./Pres. Doc. 779, 780 (June 13, 1988). Which characterization of the Byrd-Biden Condition is right? If Reagan was correct in his construction of what the Byrd-Biden Condition purports to do, is it an unconstitutional intrusion on presidential or judicial power? If Glennon is correct, does this make it constitutional?

12. For additional discussion of the issue of treaty interpretation, see Michael P. Van Alstine, *Dynamic Treaty Interpretation,* 146 U. Pa. L. Rev. 687 (1998); Michael P. Van Alstine, *Federal Common Law in an Age of Treaties,* 89 Cornell L. Rev. 892 (2004); David J. Bederman, *Revivalist Canons and Treaty Interpretation,* 41 UCLA L. Rev. 953 (1994); Alex Glashausser, *Difference and Deference in Treaty Interpretation,* 50 Vill. L. Rev. 25 (2005); John Norton Moore, *Treaty Interpretation, the Constitution and the Rule of Law,* 42 Va. J. Int'l L. 163 (2001).

For additional discussion of the issue of treaty reinterpretation, see Raymond L. Garthoff, Policy Versus Law: The Reinterpretation of the ABM Treaty (1987); Joseph R. Biden, Jr. & John B. Ritch III, *The Treaty Power: Upholding a Constitutional Partnership,* 137 U. Pa. L. Rev. 1529 (1989); Abram Chayes & Antonia Handler Chayes, *Testing and Development of "Exotic" Systems Under the ABM Treaty: The Great Reinterpretation Caper,* 99 Harv. L. Rev. 1956 (1986); Kevin C. Kennedy, *Treaty Interpretation by the Executive Branch: The ABM Treaty and "Star Wars" Testing and Development,* 80 Am. J. Int'l L. 854 (1986); David A. Koplow, *Constitutional Bait and Switch: Executive Reinterpretation of Arms Control Treaties,* 137 U. Pa. L. Rev. 1353 (1989); Eugene V. Rostow, *The Reinterpretation Debate and Constitutional Law,* 137 U. Pa. L. Rev. 1451 (1989); Abraham D. Sofaer, *The ABM Treaty and the Strategic Defense Initiative,* 99 Harv. L. Rev. 1972 (1986); Phillip R. Trimble, *The Constitutional Common Law of Treaty Interpretation: A Reply to the Formalists,* 137 U. Pa. L. Rev. 1461 (1989); John Yoo, *Politics as Law?: The Anti-Ballistic Missile Treaty, the Separation of Powers, and Treaty Interpretation,* 89 Cal. L. Rev. 851 (2001). For a response to Professor Yoo's article, and Professor Yoo's reply, see Michael P. Van Alstine, *The Judicial Power and Treaty Delegation,* 90 Cal. L. Rev. 1263 (2002), and John C. Yoo, *Treaty Interpretation and the False Sirens of Delegation,* 90 Cal. L. Rev. 1305 (2002).

F. DELEGATION OF AUTHORITY TO INTERNATIONAL INSTITUTIONS

Sanchez-Llamas v. Oregon

548 U.S. 331 (2006)

CHIEF JUSTICE ROBERTS delivered the opinion of the Court. . . .

The Vienna Convention [on Consular Relations] was drafted in 1963 with the purpose, evident in its preamble, of "contribut[ing] to the development of friendly relations among nations, irrespective of their differing constitutional and social systems." The Convention consists of 79 articles regulating various aspects of consular activities. At present, 170 countries are party to the Convention. The United States, upon the advice and consent of the Senate, ratified the Convention in 1969.

Article 36 of the Convention concerns consular officers' access to their nationals detained by authorities in a foreign country. The article provides that "if he so requests, the competent authorities of the receiving State shall, without delay, inform the consular post of the sending State if, within its consular district, a national of that State is arrested or committed to prison or to custody pending trial or is detained in any other manner." In other words, when a national of one country is detained by authorities in another, the authorities must notify the consular officers of the detainee's home country if the detainee so requests. Article 36(1)(b) further states that "[t]he said authorities shall inform the person concerned [*i.e.,* the detainee] without delay of his rights under this sub-paragraph." The Convention also provides guidance regarding how these requirements, and the other requirements of Article 36, are to be implemented:

> The rights referred to in paragraph 1 of this Article shall be exercised in conformity with the laws and regulations of the receiving State, subject to the proviso, however, that the said laws and regulations must enable full effect to be given to the purposes for which the rights accorded under this Article are intended. Art. 36(2).

Along with the Vienna Convention, the United States ratified the Optional Protocol Concerning the Compulsory Settlement of Disputes (Optional Protocol or Protocol). The Optional Protocol provides that "[d]isputes arising out of the interpretation or application of the Convention shall lie within the compulsory jurisdiction of the International Court of Justice [(ICJ)]," and allows parties to the Protocol to bring such disputes before the ICJ. The United States gave notice of its withdrawal from the Optional Protocol on March 7, 2005. . . .

Petitioner Mario Bustillo, a Honduran national, was with several other men at a restaurant in Springfield, Virginia, on the night of December 10, 1997. That evening, outside the restaurant, James Merry was struck in the head with a baseball bat as he stood smoking a cigarette. He died several days later. Several witnesses at the scene identified Bustillo as the assailant. Police arrested Bustillo the morning after the attack and eventually charged him with murder. Authorities never informed him that he could request to have the Honduran Consulate notified of his detention.

At trial, the defense pursued a theory that another man, known as "Sirena," was responsible for the attack. Two defense witnesses testified that Bustillo was not the killer. One of the witnesses specifically identified the attacker as Sirena. In addition, a third defense witness stated that she had seen Sirena on a flight to Honduras the day after the victim died. In its closing argument before the jury, the prosecution dismissed the defense theory about Sirena. A jury convicted Bustillo of first-degree murder, and he was sentenced to 30 years in prison. His conviction and sentence were affirmed on appeal.

After his conviction became final, Bustillo filed a petition for a writ of habeas corpus in state court. There, for the first time, he argued that authorities had violated his right to consular notification under Article 36 of the Vienna Convention. He claimed that if he had been advised of his right to confer with the Honduran Consulate, he "would have done so without delay." Moreover, the Honduran Consulate executed an affidavit stating that "it would have endeavoured to help Mr. Bustillo in his defense" had it learned of his detention prior to trial. Bustillo insisted that the consulate could have helped him locate Sirena prior to trial. His habeas petition also argued, as part of a claim of ineffective assistance of counsel, that his attorney should have advised him of his right to notify the Honduran Consulate of his arrest and detention. . . .

The Virginia courts denied petitioner Bustillo's Article 36 claim on the ground that he failed to raise it at trial or on direct appeal. The general rule in federal habeas cases is that a defendant who fails to raise a claim on direct appeal is barred from raising the claim on collateral review. There is an exception if a defendant can demonstrate both "cause" for not raising the claim at trial, and "prejudice" from not having done so. Like many States, Virginia applies a similar rule in state post-conviction proceedings, and did so here to bar Bustillo's Vienna Convention claim. Normally, in our review of state-court judgments, such rules constitute an adequate and independent state-law ground preventing us from reviewing the federal claim.

Bustillo contends, however, that state procedural default rules cannot apply to Article 36 claims. He argues that the Convention requires that Article 36 rights be given "'full effect'" and that Virginia's procedural default rules "prevented any effect (much less 'full effect') from being given to" those rights.

This is not the first time we have been asked to set aside procedural default rules for a Vienna Convention claim. Respondent . . . and the United States persuasively argue that this question is controlled by our decision in Breard v. Greene, 523 U.S. 371 (1998) (*per curiam*). In *Breard*, the petitioner failed to raise an Article 36 claim in state court—at trial or on collateral review—and then sought to have the claim heard in a subsequent federal habeas proceeding. He argued that "the Convention is the 'supreme law of the land' and thus trumps the procedural default doctrine." We rejected this argument as "plainly incorrect," for two reasons. First, we observed, "it has been recognized in international law that, absent a clear and express statement to the contrary, the procedural rules of the forum State govern the implementation of the treaty in that State." Furthermore, we reasoned that while treaty protections such as Article 36 may constitute supreme federal law, this is "no less true of provisions of the Constitution itself, to which rules of procedural default apply." In light of *Breard*'s holding, Bustillo faces an uphill task in arguing that the Convention requires States to set aside their procedural default rules for Article 36 claims.

Bustillo offers two reasons why *Breard* does not control his case. He first argues that *Breard*'s holding concerning procedural default was "unnecessary to the result," because the petitioner there could not demonstrate prejudice from the default and because, in any event, a subsequent federal statute—the Antiterrorism and Effective Death Penalty Act of 1996—superseded any right the petitioner had under the Vienna Convention to have his claim heard on collateral review. We find Bustillo's contention unpersuasive. Our resolution of the procedural default question in *Breard* was the principal reason for the denial of the petitioner's claim, and the discussion of the issue occupied the bulk of our reasoning. It is no answer to argue, as Bustillo does, that the holding in *Breard* was "unnecessary" simply because the petitioner in that case had several ways to lose.

Bustillo's second reason is less easily dismissed. He argues that since *Breard*, the ICJ has interpreted the Vienna Convention to preclude the application of procedural default rules to Article 36 claims. The *LaGrand Case (F.R.G. v. U.S.)*, 2001 I.C.J. 466 (Judgment of June 27) (*LaGrand*), and the *Case Concerning Avena and other Mexican Nationals (Mex. v. U.S.)*, 2004 I.C.J. No. 128 (Judgment of Mar. 31) (*Avena*), were brought before the ICJ by the governments of Germany and Mexico, respectively, on behalf of several of their nationals facing death sentences in the United States. The foreign governments claimed that their nationals had not been informed of their right to consular notification. They further argued that application of the procedural default rule to their nationals' Vienna Convention claims failed to give "full effect" to the purposes of the Convention, as required by Article 36. The ICJ agreed, explaining that the defendants had procedurally defaulted their claims "because of the failure of the American authorities to comply with their obligation under Article 36." Application of the procedural default rule in such circumstances, the ICJ reasoned, "prevented [courts] from attaching any legal significance" to the fact that the violation of Article 36 kept the foreign governments from assisting in their nationals' defense.

Bustillo argues that *LaGrand* and *Avena* warrant revisiting the procedural default holding of *Breard*. In a similar vein, several *amici* contend that "the United

States is *obligated* to comply with the Convention, *as interpreted by the ICJ.*" We dis-agree. Although the ICJ's interpretation deserves "respectful consideration," *Breard, supra,* we conclude that it does not compel us to reconsider our understanding of the Convention in *Breard.*

Under our Constitution, "the judicial Power of the United States" is "vested in one supreme Court, and in such inferior Courts as the Congress may from time to time ordain and establish." Art. III, §1. That "judicial Power . . . extends to . . . Treaties." *Id.,* §2. And, as Chief Justice Marshall famously explained, that judicial power includes the duty "to say what the law is." Marbury v. Madison, 5 U.S. 137, 177 (1803). If treaties are to be given effect as federal law under our legal system, determining their meaning as a matter of federal law "is emphatically the province and duty of the judicial department," headed by the "one supreme Court" established by the Constitution. It is against this background that the United States ratified, and the Senate gave its advice and consent to, the various agreements that govern referral of Vienna Convention disputes to the ICJ.

Nothing in the structure or purpose of the ICJ suggests that its interpretations were intended to be conclusive on our courts. The ICJ's decisions have "*no binding force* except between the parties and in respect of that particular case," Statute of the International Court of Justice, Art. 59 (emphasis added). Any interpretation of law the ICJ renders in the course of resolving particular disputes is thus not binding precedent *even as to the ICJ itself*; there is accordingly little reason to think that such interpretations were intended to be controlling on our courts. The ICJ's principal purpose is to arbitrate particular disputes between national governments. While each member of the United Nations has agreed to comply with decisions of the ICJ "in any case to which it is a party," United Nations Charter, Art. 94(1), the Charter's procedure for noncompliance—referral to the Security Council by the aggrieved state—contemplates quintessentially *international* remedies, Art. 94(2).

In addition, "while courts interpret treaties for themselves, the meaning given them by the departments of government particularly charged with their negoti-ation and enforcement is given great weight." Kolovrat v. Oregon, 366 U.S. 187, 194 (1961). Although the United States has agreed to "discharge its international obligations" in having state courts give effect to the decision in *Avena,* it has not taken the view that the ICJ's interpretation of Article 36 is binding on our courts. President Bush, Memorandum for the Attorney General (Feb. 28, 2005). Moreover, shortly after *Avena,* the United States withdrew from the Optional Protocol concern-ing Vienna Convention disputes. Whatever the effect of *Avena* and *LaGrand* before this withdrawal, it is doubtful that our courts should give decisive weight to the interpretation of a tribunal whose jurisdiction in this area is no longer recognized by the United States.

LaGrand and *Avena* are therefore entitled only to the "respectful consider-ation" due an interpretation of an international agreement by an international court. Even according such consideration, the ICJ's interpretation cannot over-come the plain import of Article 36. As we explained in *Breard,* the procedural rules of domestic law generally govern the implementation of an international treaty. In addition, Article 36 makes clear that the rights it provides "shall be exercised in conformity with the laws and regulations of the receiving State" pro-vided that "full effect . . . be given to the purposes for which the rights accorded under this Article are intended." Art. 36(2). In the United States, this means that the rule of procedural default—which applies even to claimed violations of our Constitution—applies also to Vienna Convention claims. Bustillo points to nothing in the drafting history of Article 36 or in the contemporary practice of other signatories that undermines this conclusion.

The ICJ concluded that where a defendant was not notified of his rights under Article 36, application of the procedural default rule failed to give "full effect" to the purposes of Article 36 because it prevented courts from attaching "legal significance" to the Article 36 violation. This reasoning overlooks the importance of procedural default rules in an adversary system, which relies chiefly on the *parties* to raise significant issues and present them to the courts in the appropriate manner at the appropriate time for adjudication. . . . The consequence of failing to raise a claim for adjudication at the proper time is generally forfeiture of that claim. As a result, rules such as procedural default routinely deny "legal significance" — in the *Avena* and *LaGrand* sense — to otherwise viable legal claims.

Procedural default rules generally take on greater importance in an adversary system such as ours than in the sort of magistrate-directed, inquisitorial legal system characteristic of many of the other countries that are signatories to the Vienna Convention. . . . In an inquisitorial system, the failure to raise a legal error can in part be attributed to the magistrate, and thus to the state itself. In our system, however, the responsibility for failing to raise an issue generally rests with the parties themselves.

The ICJ's interpretation of Article 36 is inconsistent with the basic framework of an adversary system. Under the ICJ's reading of "full effect," Article 36 claims could trump not only procedural default rules, but any number of other rules requiring parties to present their legal claims at the appropriate time for adjudication. If the State's failure to inform the defendant of his Article 36 rights generally excuses the defendant's failure to comply with relevant procedural rules, then presumably rules such as statutes of limitations and prohibitions against filing successive habeas petitions must also yield in the face of Article 36 claims. This sweeps too broadly, for it reads the "full effect" proviso in a way that leaves little room for Article 36's clear instruction that Article 36 rights "shall be exercised in conformity with the laws and regulations of the receiving State." . . .

[Justice Breyer issued a dissent, which was joined by Justice Stevens and Justice Souter. With respect to the weight to be given to the ICJ's reasoning concerning procedural default, Justice Breyer argued as follows:

> I will assume that the ICJ's interpretation does not bind this Court in this case. But as the majority points out, the ICJ's decisions on this issue nonetheless warrant our "respectful consideration." That "respectful consideration" reflects the understanding that uniformity is an important goal of treaty interpretation. And the ICJ's position as an international court specifically charged with the duty to interpret numerous international treaties (including the Convention) provides a natural point of reference for national courts seeking that uniformity.
>
> That "respectful consideration" also reflects an understanding of the ICJ's expertise in matters of treaty interpretation, a branch of international law. . . .
>
> Thus, this Court has repeatedly looked to the ICJ for guidance in interpreting treaties and in other matters of international law. . . .
>
> The lower courts have done the same. . . .
>
> Today's decision interprets an international treaty in a manner that conflicts not only with the treaty's language and history, but also with the ICJ's interpretation of the same treaty provision. In creating this last-mentioned conflict, as far as I can tell, the Court's decision is unprecedented.]

Natural Resources Defense Council v. EPA

464 F.3d 1 (D.C. Cir. 2006)

[In 1988, the United States ratified the Montreal Protocol on Substances that Deplete the Ozone Layer, a treaty that requires nations to reduce and ultimately eliminate the use of certain substances that degrade the ozone layer, in accordance with agreed-upon timetables. Congress incorporated the terms of the Protocol into domestic law in the Clean Air Act Amendments of 1990. The Protocol allows "adjustments" to be made to its terms without formal amendment and ratification. In incorporating the Protocol into domestic law, Congress defined the Protocol to include "adjustments adopted by the Parties thereto and amendments that have entered into force." In 1997, the parties "adjusted" the Protocol to require developed-country parties to cease production and consumption of methyl bromide by 2005, except "to the extent that the Parties decide to permit the level of production or consumption that is necessary to satisfy uses agreed by them to be critical uses." The Protocol provides that the parties are to meet annually to decide on critical-use levels. At one of these meetings, the parties issued a decision setting general guidelines for implementing critical-use exemptions ("Decision IX/6"), and at another meeting they issued a decision approving exemptions for 2005 ("Decision Ex.I/3"). The EPA then promulgated rules to implement the critical-uses exemptions. The Natural Resources Defense Council (NRDC) challenged the rules as inconsistent with Decision IX/6 and Decision Ex.I/3 "because EPA failed to disclose the full amount of existing stocks [of methyl bromide], failed to offset new production and consumption by the full amount of these stocks, and failed to reserve the stocks for critical uses, and because the total amount of methyl bromide critical use [authorized by the EPA] is not the technically and economically feasible minimum."]

RANDOLPH, CIRCUIT JUDGE. . . .
. . . NRDC argues that because the Clean Air Act requires EPA to abide by the Protocol, and because the Protocol authorizes future agreements concerning the scope of the critical-use exemption, those future agreements must "define the scope of EPA's Clean Air Act authority."

NRDC's interpretation raises significant constitutional problems. If the "decisions" are "law" — enforceable in federal court like statutes or legislative rules — then Congress either has delegated lawmaking authority to an international body or authorized amendments to a treaty without presidential signature or Senate ratification, in violation of Article II of the Constitution. The Supreme Court has not determined whether decisions of an international body created by treaty are judicially enforceable. But there is a close analogy in this court. The United States is a party to a treaty establishing the International Court of Justice (ICJ). In Committee of United States Citizens Living in Nicaragua v. Reagan, 859 F.2d 929 (D.C. Cir. 1988), we held that rulings of the ICJ do not provide "substantive legal standards for reviewing agency actions," *id.* at 942, because the rulings, though authorized by the ratified treaty, were not themselves self-executing treaties. *Id.* at 937-38; *see, e.g.,* Medellin v. Dretke, 544 U.S. 660, 682-84 (2005) (O'Connor, J., dissenting).

Although *Committee of United States Citizens* is highly suggestive of the outcome in this case, several features of the Montreal Protocol "decisions" may distinguish them from ICJ "adjudications." For one thing, Congress implemented the Montreal

Protocol with a direction to EPA to abide by its terms. *See* 42 U.S.C. §§7671c(d)(6), 7671m(b). For another, Montreal Protocol "decisions" are not adjudications between parties; instead, they purport to set rules for implementing ongoing treaty commitments.

The legal status of "decisions" of this sort appears to be a question of first impression. There is significant debate over the constitutionality of assigning lawmaking functions to international bodies. . . . A holding that the Parties' post-ratification side agreements were "law" would raise serious constitutional questions in light of the nondelegation doctrine, numerous constitutional procedural requirements for making law, and the separation of powers.

We need not confront the "serious likelihood that the statute will be held unconstitutional." Almendarez-Torres v. United States, 523 U.S. 224, 238 (1998); *see also id.* at 250 (Scalia, J., dissenting). It is far more plausible to interpret the Clean Air Act and Montreal Protocol as creating an ongoing international political commitment rather than a delegation of lawmaking authority to annual meetings of the Parties. *Cf.* Mistretta v. United States, 488 U.S. 361, 373 n.7 (1989).

Nowhere does the Protocol suggest that the Parties' post-ratification consensus agreements about how to implement the critical-use exemption are binding in domestic courts. The only pertinent language in Article 2H(5) states that the Parties will "decide to permit" production and consumption necessary to satisfy those uses that they "agree[]" to be critical uses. The Protocol is silent on any specific conditions accompanying the critical-use exemption. Post-ratification agreements setting these conditions are not the Protocol.

To illustrate, suppose the President signed and the Senate ratified a treaty with Germany and France to conserve fossil fuel. How this is to be accomplished the treaty does not specify. In a later meeting of representatives of the signatory countries at the United Nations, a consensus is reached to lower the speed limits on all major highways of the signatory nations to a maximum of 45 miles per hour. No one would say that United States law has thus been made.

EPA characterizes the decisions as "subsequent consensus agreements of the Parties that address the interpretation and application of the critical use provision. . . ." This may be so. Like any interpretive tool, however, the "decisions" are useful only to the extent they shed light on ambiguous terms in the Protocol. But the details of the critical-use exemption are not ambiguous. They are nonexistent. The "decisions" do not interpret treaty language. They fill in treaty gaps.

Article 2H(5) thus constitutes an "agreement to agree." The parties agree in the Protocol to reach an agreement concerning the types of uses for which new production and consumption will be permitted, and the amounts that will be permitted. "Agreements to agree" are usually not enforceable in contract. . . . And the fruits of those agreements are enforceable only to the extent that they themselves are contracts. There is no doubt that the "decisions" are not treaties.

The Parties' post-ratification actions suggest their common understanding that the decisions are international political commitments rather than judicially enforceable domestic law. . . . The Parties met to decide the 2006 critical-use exemptions well after EPA's rule went into effect. Yet they did not invoke the Protocol's internal noncompliance procedure against the United States, nor did they admonish the United States to change its interpretation of the previous decisions. This course of dealing suggests that the Parties intended the side agreements to be enforceable as a political matter at the negotiating table.

Our holding in this case in no way diminishes the power of the Executive to enter into international agreements that constrain its own behavior within the confines of statutory and treaty law. The Executive has the power to implement ongoing collective endeavors with other countries. Without congressional action, however, side agreements reached after a treaty has been ratified are not the law of the land; they are enforceable not through the federal courts, but through international negotiations.

Notes and Questions

1. Since World War II, there has been a vast growth in the number and importance of international institutions, many of which possess adjudicative, regulatory, or enforcement authority. In committing itself to these institutions (usually by treaty or congressional-executive agreement), the United States has consented to have these institutions make certain decisions and take certain actions that can affect the United States' rights and duties under international law and, in some instances, the enforceability of U.S. domestic law. There is significant debate over the extent to which U.S. delegations of authority to international institutions raise constitutional issues. What types of arrangements with international institutions do you think are most likely to raise constitutional issues? What types of arrangements are least likely to raise these issues? For example, is a delegation of adjudicative authority more or less likely to raise constitutional issues than a delegation of regulatory or executive authority?

2. Delegations of adjudicative authority to international institutions may raise issues under Article III of the Constitution. This Article provides that "[t]he judicial Power of the United States, shall be vested in one supreme Court, and in such inferior Courts as the Congress may from time to time ordain and establish," and it also specifies that the federal judicial power is to be exercised by judges who "shall hold their Offices during good Behaviour, and [who] shall, at stated Times, receive for their Services a Compensation, which shall not be diminished during their Continuance in Office." This language has been interpreted as at least sometimes precluding the vesting of the judicial power of the United States in domestic tribunals that are not ordained and established by Congress and that do not have the Article III tenure and salary protections. *See, e.g.,* Stern v. Marshall, 564 U.S. 462 (2011) (holding that non-Article III bankruptcy courts could not constitutionally adjudicate certain state-law counterclaims); Northern Pipeline Construction Co. v. Marathon Pipe Line Co., 458 U.S. 50 (1982) (holding that bankruptcy courts could not adjudicate certain state law contract claims). The Supreme Court has stated:

> When a suit is made of "the stuff of the traditional actions at common law tried by the courts at Westminster in 1789," *Northern Pipeline,* 458 U.S. at 90 (Rehnquist, J., concurring in judgment), and is brought within the bounds of federal jurisdiction, the responsibility for deciding that suit rests with Article III judges in Article III courts. The Constitution assigns that job—resolution of "the mundane as well as the glamorous, matters of common law and statute as well as constitutional law, issues of fact as well as issues of law"—to the Judiciary. *Id.* at 86-87.

Stern, 564 U.S. at 484.

3. *Sanchez-Llamas* concerns the U.S. relationship to the International Court of Justice (ICJ), a 15-judge international tribunal that sits in The Hague and has jurisdiction to resolve certain international law disputes between nations. In Article 94(1) of the United Nations Charter, each member (including the United States) "undertakes to comply with the decision of the International Court of Justice in any case to which it is a party." The Court can only hear cases, however, in which both parties have consented in some fashion to the Court's jurisdiction. For many years, the United States consented generally to the Court's jurisdiction over any international law question. But in 1985, after the Court exercised jurisdiction over a suit brought against the United States by Nicaragua, the United States withdrew its general consent. As a result, it can now be sued in the Court only if it has consented to the Court's jurisdiction in a particular treaty with the complaining party, or if it gives its specific consent to jurisdiction at the time the suit is filed. The United States continues to be a party, however, to a number of treaties that contain clauses authorizing the Court to resolve disputes arising under the treaties.

4. Article 36 of the Vienna Convention on Consular Relations requires party countries, when they arrest nationals of other party countries, to advise them of their right to have their consulate notified of the arrest and their right to communicate with the consulate. State and local authorities in the United States, however, have often failed to provide this notice when arresting foreign nationals. Until 2005, the United States was a party to an optional protocol to the Vienna Convention that gave the ICJ jurisdiction over disputes arising under the Convention. Starting in the 1990s, several nations brought cases against the United States in the ICJ on behalf of foreign nationals on death row who had been arrested and tried without receiving their consular notice under Article 36 of the Vienna Convention. The first case, *Breard,* was brought by Paraguay on behalf of a Paraguayan national, Angel Breard, who was on death row in Virginia. Despite the ICJ's issuance of a preliminary order requesting that the United States "take all measures at its disposal" to stay Breard's execution while the ICJ heard the case, his execution was carried out on schedule. In declining to stay the execution, the U.S. Supreme Court found that Breard had procedurally defaulted his Vienna Convention claim by failing to raise it in state courts. The Court explained:

> [W]hile we should give respectful consideration to the interpretation of an international treaty rendered by an international court with jurisdiction to interpret such, it has been recognized in international law that, absent a clear and express statement to the contrary, the procedural rules of the forum State govern the implementation of the treaty in that State. This proposition is embodied in the Vienna Convention itself, which provides that the rights expressed in the Convention "shall be exercised in conformity with the laws and regulations of the receiving State," provided that "said laws and regulations must enable full effect to be given to the purposes for which the rights accorded under this Article are intended." It is the rule in this country that assertions of error in criminal proceedings must first be raised in state court in order to form the basis for relief in habeas. Claims not so raised are considered defaulted. By not asserting his Vienna Convention claim in state court, Breard failed to exercise his rights under the Vienna Convention in conformity with the laws of the United States and the Commonwealth of Virginia. Having failed to do so, he cannot raise a claim of violation of those rights now on federal habeas review.

Breard v. Greene, 523 U.S. 371, 375 (1998). The subsequent ICJ cases, *LaGrand* and *Avena,* are described in *Sanchez-Llamas.*

5. Why did the Court in *Sanchez-Llamas* give only "respectful consideration" to the ICJ's reasoning in *LaGrand* and *Avena*? In referring to the "judicial power" and Marbury v. Madison, is the Court suggesting that it would violate Article III of the

Constitution for the United States to treat the reasoning of the ICJ as dispositive in domestic litigation? Why did the Court disagree with the ICJ's reasoning with respect to the procedural default issue? Although the dissent in *Sanchez-Llamas* purports to accept the "respectful consideration" standard, does its analysis in effect call for giving more deference to the ICJ? If so, on what basis? The dissent contends that the majority's decision is "unprecedented"; do you agree? For additional discussion of *Sanchez-Llamas*, see Curtis A. Bradley, *The Federal Judicial Power and the International Legal Order*, 2007 Sup. Ct. Rev. 59; Mark L. Movsesian, *Judging International Judgments*, 48 Va. J. Int'l L. 65 (2007); Paper Symposium, *Domestic Enforcement of Public International Law After Sanchez-Llamas v. Oregon*, Lewis & Clark L. Rev. 1-98 (2007) (articles by Julian Ku, Janet Levit, Margaret McGuinness, John Parry, Paul Stephan, and Melissa Waters).

6. In Medellin v. Texas, which is excerpted above in Section A, the Court considered whether Article 94(1) of the U.N. Charter was self-executing. Article 94(1) provides that "[e]ach Member of the United Nations undertakes to comply with the decision of the [ICJ] in any case to which it is a party." In resisting Medellin's claim that this treaty provision made ICJ judgments directly enforceable in U.S. courts, the Court expressed concern about the implications of such a delegation of authority:

> Moreover, the consequences of Medellin's argument give pause. An ICJ judgment, the argument goes, is not only binding domestic law but is also unassailable. As a result, neither Texas nor this Court may look behind a judgment and quarrel with its reasoning or result. (We already know, from *Sanchez-Llamas*, that this Court disagrees with both the reasoning and result in *Avena*.) Medellin's interpretation would allow ICJ judgments to override otherwise binding state law; there is nothing in his logic that would exempt contrary federal law from the same fate. See, e.g., Cook v. United States, 288 U. S. 102, 119 (1933) (later-in-time self-executing treaty supersedes a federal statue if there is a conflict). And there is nothing to prevent the ICJ from ordering state courts to annul criminal convictions and sentences, for any reason deemed sufficient by the ICJ. Indeed, that is precisely the relief Mexico requested.

The Court did note, however, that "[w]e do not suggest that treaties can never afford binding domestic effect to international tribunal judgments—only that the U.N. Charter, the Optional Protocol, and the ICJ Statute do not do so," and it observed that "[o]ur holding does not call into question the ordinary enforcement of foreign judgments or international arbitral agreements."

Would it have been unconstitutional if the Senate and President had delegated to the ICJ the authority that the Court thought was entailed by Medellin's argument? As noted in Chapter 2, federal and state courts in the United States often enforce foreign court civil judgments as a matter of comity. How is the enforcement of an ICJ judgment different from the enforcement of a foreign civil judgment?

For a state court decision granting an evidentiary hearing to determine whether a foreign national was prejudiced by the lack of consular notification, see Gutierrez v. Nevada, 2012 Nev. Unpub. LEXIS 1317 (Nev. Sup. Ct. Sept. 19, 2012). While noting that "*Avena* does not obligate the states to subordinate their post-conviction review procedures to the ICJ ruling," the court concluded that the record in this case, unlike the record in *Medellin* and other cases in which a hearing had been denied, showed that the defendant "arguably suffered actual prejudice due to the lack of consular assistance." *See also* Torres v. State, No. PCD-04-442, 2004 WL 3711623 (Okla. Crim. App. May 13, 2004) (granting evidentiary hearing to comply with *Avena*).

7. In 1993, the United States became a party, along with Canada and Mexico, to the North American Free Trade Agreement (NAFTA). At least two aspects of NAFTA raise potential constitutional issues. First, Chapter 19 of NAFTA allows certain import decisions of the member countries to be reviewed by binational arbitral panels. These panels apply the substantive law of the importing country, and their decisions are binding and final. Thus, in the case of the United States, the panels can exercise final review over the application of U.S. trade law by the International Trade Commission (a federal administrative agency). In situations in which a matter is referred by a panel back to the Commission, the Commission is bound by statute to "take action not inconsistent with the decision" of the panel. The panel members, however, will not necessarily be Article III judges. Nor is their selection subject to the Article II appointments process. Does this scheme raise constitutional issues? In particular, does it violate the limits on non-Article III courts? The scheme has been challenged in court on various constitutional grounds, but the challenges have to date been dismissed for lack of standing, see American Coalition for Competitive Trade v. Clinton, 128 F.3d 761 (D.C. Cir. 1997), and for lack of jurisdiction, see Coalition for Fair Lumber Imports v. United States, 471 F.3d 1329 (D.C. Cir. 2006). For a discussion of constitutional issues associated with the binational review system established under the predecessor to NAFTA (the United States-Canada Free Trade Agreement), see Jim C. Chen, *Appointments with Disaster: The Unconstitutionality of Binational Arbitral Review Under the United States-Canada Free Trade Agreement*, 49 Wash. & Lee L. Rev. 1455 (1992).

For an argument that arbitration panels like those used under NAFTA "raise no serious problems under Article III and are sanctioned by an ancient lineage," and that the Supreme Court is unlikely more generally to find that the Constitution places significant limits on supranational judicial review, see Henry Paul Monaghan, *Article III and Supranational Judicial Review*, 107 Colum. L. Rev. 833 (2007). Among other things, Professor Monaghan contends:

> While in the beginning of our constitutional history it was quite possible to claim that Our Federalism invested our national government with less legal authority in the international sphere than that possessed by other nation-states, any such conception has no purchase now. Indeed, the Court insists that the national government possesses an apparently freestanding "foreign affairs" power. That being the case, *and assuming here the general validity of supranational lawmaking*, it seems unlikely that the Court will understand the Constitution to seriously impede the manner by which supranational disputes are resolved.

Id. at 842-43 (emphasis in original). Do you agree with this assessment? Is it consistent with the reasoning in *Sanchez-Llamas?* Can you conceive of a scenario in which a court would be likely to find a delegation of adjudicative authority to an international tribunal to be unconstitutional?

8. A second feature of NAFTA that may raise constitutional issues is its provision for challenges by investors to the practices of the member countries. Chapter 11 of NAFTA requires each country to accord investors of the other two countries certain minimum standards of treatment, including protection against uncompensated expropriation. Investors who allege a violation of Chapter 11 may submit claims to a panel of three private arbitrators who can award monetary damages but not injunctive relief. (Under U.S. law, however, an award against the U.S. government by a foreign court or tribunal is paid only after the Attorney General certifies that it is in the interest of the United States to make the payment. *See* 28 U.S.C. §2414.) These provisions make it possible for NAFTA Chapter 11 arbitration panels to sit in judgment on U.S. judicial decisions that are procedurally irregular or otherwise grossly unfair. In *The Loewen Group, Inc. and United States of America*, Case No. ARB(AF)/ 98/3 (June 26, 2003), for example, a NAFTA arbitration panel seriously considered the possibility that the combination of an excessive punitive damages award in a Mississippi state trial court and a burdensome requirement for posting a bond in order to appeal constituted an expropriation of property, unequal treatment of a foreign company, and a denial of justice, all in violation of the NAFTA treaty. The *Loewen* panel ultimately rejected the claim on technical jurisdiction grounds and because the claimant did not fully exhaust its state court appellate remedies, but in taking the claims on the merits seriously it raised the possibility of a NAFTA tribunal sitting in judgment on the validity of U.S. judicial proceedings. Does such scrutiny raise any constitutional concerns—for example, concerns relating to federalism? For a general consideration of what *Loewen* and other cases suggest about the proper relationship between U.S. courts and international tribunals, see Ernest A. Young, *Institutional Settlement in a Globalizing Judicial System*, 54 Duke L.J. 1143 (2005).*

9. Delegations of regulatory authority to international institutions may raise issues under the "nondelegation doctrine." The Supreme Court has stated that "Congress generally cannot delegate its legislative power to another Branch." Mistretta v. United States, 488 U.S. 361, 372 (1989). At least in theory, this doctrine "forces a politically accountable Congress to make the policy choices, rather than leave this to unelected administrative officials." Erwin Chemerinsky, Constitutional Law: Principles and Policies 328 (3d ed. 2006). Under this doctrine, when Congress delegates power, it must "lay down by legislative act an intelligible principle to which the person or body authorized to [act] is directed to conform." J. W. Hampton, Jr. & Co. v. United States, 276 U.S. 394, 409 (1928). This "intelligible principle" requirement "seeks to enforce the understanding that Congress may not delegate the power to make laws and so may delegate no more than the authority to make policies and rules that implement its statutes." Loving v. United States, 517 U.S. 748, 758 (1996).

The Supreme Court has nevertheless allowed Congress to delegate substantial interpretive and regulatory authority to the Executive Branch and the Judiciary, and it has not found a violation of the "intelligible principle" requirement since the mid-1930s. The Court has explained that its nondelegation doctrine "has been driven by a practical understanding that in our increasingly complex society, replete with ever changing and more technical problems, Congress simply cannot do its job absent an ability to delegate power under broad general directives." *Mistretta*, 488 U.S. at 372. Although some Supreme Court Justices and academic commentators have called for reinvigorating the nondelegation doctrine, the Court has not yet shown an inclination to do so. *See, e.g.*, Gundy v. United States, 139 S. Ct. 2116 (2019) (rejecting nondelegation doctrine challenge to sex offender registration statute that delegated authority to the Attorney General to apply the statute's registration requirements to individuals convicted prior to the statute's enactment); Whitman v. American Trucking Associations, 531 U.S. 457 (2001) (finding that broad delegation of authority to the EPA satisfied the "intelligible principle" requirement).

---

* The Trump Administration has sought to replace NAFTA with a new U.S.-Mexico-Canada Agreement (USMCA). The USMCA, which as of August 2019 had not been approved by Congress, would largely leave in place the binational panel system from Chapter 19 of NAFTA, but would phase out the Chapter 11 investor-state dispute resolution system between Canada and the United States.

Furthermore, as we saw in Chapter 1, the Court has applied the nondelegation doctrine even less strictly in the foreign affairs area, explaining that "congressional legislation which is to be made effective through negotiation and inquiry within the international field must often accord to the President a degree of discretion and freedom from statutory restriction which would not be admissible were domestic affairs alone involved." United States v. Curtiss-Wright Export Corp., 299 U.S. 304, 320 (1936).

10. Regulatory delegations might also raise constitutional process issues analogous to those raised in INS v. Chadha, 462 U.S. 919 (1983). In that decision, the Supreme Court held that a legislative veto provision was unconstitutional because it allowed for legislative changes without going through the bicameralism and presentment process for legislation specified in Article I of the Constitution. If an international institution is allowed to make changes to U.S. treaty obligations without obtaining the advice and consent of the Senate, does that pose an analogous process issue under Article II of the Constitution? This issue is complicated by the fact that, as addressed in Chapter 6, the United States concludes many of its international agreements today as "executive agreements" rather than as Article II treaties.

11. The court in *NRDC* states that a "holding that the Parties' post-ratification side agreements were 'law' would raise serious constitutional questions in light of the nondelegation doctrine, numerous constitutional procedural requirements for making law, and the separation of powers." Is this view consistent with the materials described in Note 9? Is there an argument that courts should apply the nondelegation and related structural constitutional doctrines more aggressively with respect to international delegations than they do with respect to delegations to U.S. administrative agencies? Are there relevant differences between international institutions and U.S. administrative agencies—for example, with respect to accountability to and oversight by the American people?

Note that the court in *NRDC* avoided what it described as the "serious likelihood that the statute will be held unconstitutional" by interpreting the Clean Air Act and Montreal Protocol to establish a political commitment rather than a delegation of lawmaking authority. Is this the best reading of those instruments? Did the court's interpretation of them place the United States in breach of international law? Note that in the domestic regulatory context, courts have increasingly accommodated the values of the nondelegation and related structural constitutional doctrines not by invalidating statutes that raise these concerns, but rather by employing various canons—an express nondelegation canon, the canon of constitutional avoidance, federalism canons, and the like—that construe delegations narrowly and require Congress to legislate plainly in order to delegate more broadly. These canons are said to serve the main purpose of the nondelegation and related doctrines— government accountability—while at the same time respecting the government's need for flexibility and the limits of judicial competence in this area. *See generally* Cass R. Sunstein, *Nondelegation Canons,* 67 U. Chi. L. Rev. 315 (2000); John F. Manning, *The Nondelegation Doctrine as a Canon of Avoidance,* 2000 Sup. Ct. Rev. 233. Does this explain the court's approach in *NRDC?* What do you think of employing nondelegation canons in this context? For additional discussion of these and related issues, see Kristina Daugirdas, *International Delegations and Administrative Law,* 66 Md. L. Rev. 707 (2007).

12. The United States is a party to the World Trade Organization (WTO), which was established in 1995 to administer the General Agreement on Tariffs and Trade (GATT) and related treaties. This organization includes a Dispute

Settlement Body (DSB), which adjudicates trade disputes between the member countries. The DSB's decisions are binding, and, if the losing party does not comply with a decision, the DSB may authorize the prevailing party to impose trade sanctions on the losing party. The United States regularly participates in cases before the DSB, both as a plaintiff and as a defendant. As defendant, the United States has lost a number of significant cases, including a case challenging clean air regulations issued by the Environmental Protection Agency, a case challenging U.S. limits on shrimp imports designed to protect sea turtles, and a case challenging U.S. tax treatment of foreign sales corporations. Does U.S. participation in the World Trade Organization raise constitutional issues? Note that the legislation implementing the U.S. commitment to the WTO provides that (a) "No provision of [the GATT], nor the application of any such provision to any person or circumstance, that is inconsistent with any law of the United States shall have effect"; and (b) the GATT may not be enforced in a U.S. court *against a state* "except in an action brought by the United States for the purpose of declaring such law or application invalid." Do these limitations remove constitutional concerns?

In addition to its dispute settlement powers, the WTO has the power to adopt binding interpretations of the GATT and related treaties. These interpretations require the vote of only a three-fourths' majority of the WTO members. Thus, at least in theory, the WTO has the power to adopt interpretations of the treaties that are contrary to the views of the United States. In agreeing to give this interpretive authority to the WTO, has the United States effectively delegated away some of its treaty-making, or treaty-interpreting, power? If so, is such a delegation constitutional? Note that the United States has the right to withdraw from the WTO upon giving six months' notice. Does that right eliminate constitutional concerns?

13. Enforcement delegations may raise issues under the Appointments Clause in Article II of the Constitution. This Clause gives the President the power to appoint, with the advice and consent of the Senate, ambassadors, other public ministers and consuls, Supreme Court Justices, and all other "Officers of the United States" whose appointment is not otherwise provided for in the Constitution. It also states that Congress may vest the appointment of "inferior Officers" in either the President, the courts, or in the heads of departments. The Supreme Court has made clear that "[u]nless their selection is elsewhere provided for [in the Constitution], all officers of the United States are to be appointed in accordance with the Clause." Buckley v. Valeo, 424 U.S. 1, 132 (1976). The Court also has stated that "any appointee exercising significant authority pursuant to the laws of the United States is an 'Officer of the United States,' and must, therefore, be appointed in the manner prescribed" by the Clause. *Id.* at 126. The Clause does not apply, however, to "lesser functionaries subordinate to officers of the United States." *Id.* at 126 n.162. These requirements, the Court has explained, are designed both to prevent aggrandizement of power by one branch at the expense of another and to ensure public accountability in the appointments process.

The Chemical Weapons Convention, discussed in the notes in Sections C and D above, establishes an international organization, the Organization for the Prohibition of Chemical Weapons (OPCW), which has the power to verify Convention compliance by ordering inspections of public and private facilities in the United States. Inspections are conducted by the organization's Technical Secretariat, members of which are not appointed by or removable by U.S. officials. Is the authority exercised by these officials consistent with the Appointments Clause? Do these officials exercise "significant federal authority"? Does the delegation of authority to the OPCW undermine the principles of accountability served by the Appointments Clause? Should Appointments Clause limitations even apply in the context of U.S. participation in international institutions? Is it possible to argue, using *Curtiss-Wright* by analogy, that the treaty power is not subject to the same Appointments Clause restrictions as domestic legislation? For a consideration of these and related questions, see John C. Yoo, *The New Sovereignty and the Old Constitution: The Chemical Weapons Convention and the Appointments Clause,* 15 Const. Commentary 87 (1998).

14. The U.N. Security Council, established by the U.N. Charter, consists of five permanent members (the United States, Russia, Great Britain, France, and China) and ten rotating nonpermanent members. Under the Charter, the Council is charged with "primary responsibility for the maintenance of international peace and security." If the Security Council determines "the existence of any threat to the peace, breach of the peace, or act of aggression," it may call upon member states to take measures "not involving the use of armed force," such as "complete or partial interruption of economic relations and of rail, sea, air, postal, telegraphic, radio, and other means of communication, and the severance of diplomatic relations." If it determines that nonmilitary measures "would be inadequate or have proved to be inadequate," the Council can authorize "such action by air, sea, or land forces as may be necessary to maintain or restore international peace and security." Such actions "may include demonstrations, blockade, and other operations by air, sea, or land forces of Members of the United Nations."

The United States has promised in the Charter to "accept and carry out the decisions of the Security Council." Does this commitment raise constitutional issues? Does the U.S. veto power on the Security Council remove such issues? The D.C. Circuit faced these issues in Diggs v. Richardson, 555 F.2d 848 (D.C. Cir. 1976). In that case, the Security Council had issued a resolution calling upon all nations to cease certain relationships with South Africa, because of its occupation of the former U.N. trust territory of Namibia. Relying on this resolution, a group of plaintiffs sought declaratory and injunctive relief prohibiting the U.S. government from continuing to deal with South Africa concerning the importation of seal furs from Namibia. The D.C. Circuit upheld dismissal of the lawsuit, concluding that the U.N. resolution was not self-executing. The court noted, among other things, that the resolution was not addressed to the judicial branch, did not by its terms confer individual rights, addressed foreign relations issues within the discretion of the Executive Branch, and did not provide specific standards. Does treating Security Council resolutions as non-self-executing eliminate constitutional concerns? For a general argument that constitutional concerns posed by international delegations can be reduced or eliminated by treating the decisions or resolutions of international institutions as non-self-executing, thus requiring Congress to implement the actions and decisions of international institutions before they have domestic effect, see Curtis A. Bradley, *International Delegations, the Structural Constitution, and Non-Self-Execution,* 55 Stan. L. Rev. 1557 (2003). For additional discussion of the status of Security Council resolutions in the United States, see James A. R. Nafziger & Edward M. Wise, *The Status in United States Law of Security Council Resolutions Under Chapter VII of the United Nations Charter,* 46 Am. J. Comp. L. 421 (1998).

Another way in which the U.S. relationship with the Security Council might raise constitutional issues is with respect to the use of military force. Can the U.S. treatymakers delegate to the Security Council the decision of when to use military force? Can they delegate command authority over U.S. forces to the Council and its agents?

These and related questions are explored in Chapter 9. *See also* Michael J. Glennon & Allison R. Hayward, *Collective Security and the Constitution: Can the Commander in Chief Power Be Delegated to the United Nations?*, 82 Geo. L.J. 1573 (1994).

15. Delegations of authority to international institutions might also raise federalism issues, since these delegations will in some instances limit state and local authority. The ICJ decisions at issue in *Sanchez-Llamas* and *Medellin*, for example, directly concerned state law enforcement and judicial authority. Professor Swaine, however, argues that federalism values can actually be promoted by international delegations:

> International delegations are troubling precisely because they are constitutional in character: That is, legislative authority conferred on international institutions is difficult to reclaim. By the same token, however, this kind of commitment indirectly promotes a more specific constitutional value: the diffusion of political authority prized by federalism. While delegating national power to international institutions redistributes national legislative authority (including that which might otherwise fall to the states), it provides a bulwark against the concentration of political power in the national government that is consistent with the ambitions of federalism.
>
> Viewed this way, international delegations are constitutional in an important—and neglected—regard: They advance a constitutional value that deserves to be measured against any harm to constitutional values that they may risk. This does not, of course, amount to a concrete finding that international delegations should always withstand constitutional scrutiny, even in terms of the nondelegation and federalism doctrines. It does, however, warrant resisting a preemptive, undifferentiated constitutional objection to such activities, particularly any that would condemn them outright. It is also a small step toward a more sophisticated analysis, one particularly relevant to Congress and the President, for distinguishing types of delegations that are most problematic.

Edward T. Swaine, *The Constitutionality of International Delegations*, 104 Colum. L. Rev. 1492, 1501 (2004). Do you agree that international delegations can promote the values of U.S. federalism by diluting the power of the national government? Or do they simply move power even further away from U.S. states and localities? For a critique of Swaine's analysis, see Neil S. Siegel, *International Delegations and the Values of Federalism*, 70 Law & Contemp. Probs. 93 (2008).

16. For additional discussion of the constitutionality of U.S. delegations of authority to international institutions, see David M. Golove, *The New Confederalism: Treaty Delegations of Legislative, Executive, and Judicial Authority*, 55 Stan. L. Rev. 1697 (2003); Andrew T. Guzman & Jennifer Landsidle, *The Myth of International Delegation*, 96 Cal. L. Rev. 1693 (2008); Julian G. Ku, *The Delegation of Federal Power to International Organizations: New Problems with Old Solutions*, 85 Minn. L. Rev. 71 (2000); Jenny S. Martinez, *Towards an International Judicial System*, 56 Stan. L. Rev. 429 (2003); John O. McGinnis, *Medellin and the Future of International Delegation*, 118 Yale L.J. 1712, 1714 (2009); Ernest A. Young, *The Trouble with Global Constitutionalism*, 38 Tex. Int'l L.J. 527 (2003); and A. Mark Weisburd, *International Courts and American Courts*, 21 Mich. J. Int'l L. 877 (2000). *See also* Kristina Daugirdas, *Congress Underestimated: The Case of the World Bank*, 107 Am. J. Int'l L. 517, 520 (2013) (arguing that, with respect to the World Bank, "Congress can and does protect its institutional prerogatives, and its active involvement in this especially important international organization has been ongoing—the rule rather than the exception").

For a symposium on the phenomenon of national delegations of authority to international institutions, from the perspectives of both law and political science, see *The Law and Politics of International Delegation*, 71 Law & Contemp. Probs. 1-312

(2008) (articles by Karen Alter, Curtis Bradley, Tim Buthe, David Epstein, Judith Goldstein, Oona Hathaway, Laurence Helfer, Judith Kelley, Barbara Koremenos, Sharyn O'Halloran, Neil Siegel, Richard Steinberg, and Michael Tierney). For interesting early U.S. perspectives on the issue of international delegation, relating to proposed nineteenth-century international courts to adjudicate issues concerning the slave trade, see Eugene Kontorovich, *The Constitutionality of International Courts: The Forgotten Precedent of Slave Trade Tribunals*, 158 U. Pa. L. Rev. 39 (2009). For a broader examination of these courts as "the first successful international human rights campaign," see Jenny S. Martinez, *Antislavery Courts and the Dawn of International Human Rights Law*, 117 Yale L.J. 550 (2008). For a critique of Kontorovich's historical account, see Jenny S. Martinez, *International Courts and the U.S. Constitution: Reexamining the History*, 159 U. Pa. L. Rev. 1069 (2011).

G. SUSPENSION, TERMINATION, AND "UNSIGNING" OF TREATIES

This section considers the scope of the President's domestic authority to suspend or terminate treaties, as well as the issues raised by presidential "unsigning" of a treaty.

Goldwater v. Carter

617 F.2d 697 (D.C. Cir. 1979)

[This case concerned the constitutional validity of President Carter's termination of a defense treaty with Taiwan, which he announced in conjunction with his decision to recognize mainland China. In Chapter 2, there is an excerpt of the Supreme Court's decision in this case, in which the Court dismissed the case based on justiciability considerations and did not reach the merits. The lower courts had reached the merits, however, with the district court holding that the termination would not be effective unless approved by either two-thirds of the Senate or a majority of both Houses of Congress, and the court of appeals holding that the termination was effective without further senatorial or congressional action. The court of appeals decision is excerpted below.]

Opinion for the court PER CURIAM. . . .

[W]e think it important at the outset to stress that the Treaty, as it was presented to the Senate in 1954 and consented to by it, contained an explicit provision for termination by either party on one year's notice. The Senate, in the course of giving its consent, exhibited no purpose and took no action to reserve a role for itself by amendment, reservation, or condition in the effectuation of this provision. Neither has the Senate, since the giving of the notice of termination, purported to take any final or decisive action with respect to it, either by way of approval or disapproval. The constitutional issue we face, therefore, is solely and simply the one of whether the President in these precise circumstances is, on behalf of the United States, empowered to terminate the Treaty in accordance with its terms. It is our view that he is, and that the limitations which the District Court purported to place on his action in this regard have no foundation in the Constitution. . . .

Various considerations enter into our determination that the President's notice of termination will be effective on January 1, 1980. The result we reach draws upon their totality, but in listing them hereinafter we neither assign them hierarchical values nor imply that any one factor or combination of factors is determinative.

1. We turn first to the argument, embraced by the District Court, drawn from the language of Article II, §2, of the Constitution. It is that, since the President clearly cannot enter into a treaty without the consent of the Senate, the inference is inescapable that he must in all circumstances seek the same senatorial consent to terminate that treaty. As a matter of language alone, however, the same inference would appear automatically to obtain with respect to the termination by the President of officers appointed by him under the same clause of the Constitution and subject to Senate confirmation. But the Supreme Court has read that clause as not having such an inevitable effect in any and all circumstances. *Compare* Myers v. United States, 272 U.S. 52 (1926) *with* In re Humphrey's Executor v. United States, 295 U.S. 602 (1935). In the area of foreign relations in particular, where the constitutional commitment of powers to the President is notably comprehensive, it has never been suggested that the services of Ambassadors appointed by the President, confirmed by the Senate, and of critical importance as they are to the successful conduct of our foreign relations may not be terminated by the President without the prior authorization of that body.

Expansion of the language of the Constitution by sequential linguistic projection is a tricky business at best. Virtually all constitutional principles have unique elements and can be distinguished from one another. As the Supreme Court has recognized with respect to the clause in question, it is not abstract logic or sterile symmetry that controls, but a sensible and realistic ascertainment of the meaning of the Constitution in the context of the specific action taken.

2. The District Court's declaration, in the alternative, that the necessary authority in this instance may be granted by a majority of each house of Congress presumably has its source in the Supremacy Clause of Article VI. The argument is that a treaty, being a part of the "supreme Law of the Land," can only be terminated at the least by a subsequent federal statute. The central purpose of the Supremacy Clause has been accepted to be that of causing each of the designated supreme laws—Constitution, statute, and treaty to prevail, for purposes of domestic law, over state law in any form. Article VI speaks explicitly to the judges to assure that this is so. But these three types of supreme law are not necessarily the same in their other characteristics, any more than are the circumstances and terms of their creation the same. Certainly the Constitution is silent on the matter of treaty termination. And the fact that it speaks to the common characteristic of supremacy over state law does not provide any basis for concluding that a treaty must be unmade either by (1) the same process by which it was made, or (2) the alternative means by which a statute is made or terminated.

3. The constitutional institution of advice and consent of the Senate, provided two-thirds of the Senators concur, is a special and extraordinary condition of the exercise by the President of certain specified powers under Article II. It is not lightly to be extended in instances not set forth in the Constitution. Such an extension by implication is not proper unless that implication is unmistakably clear.

The District Court's absolutist extension of this limitation to termination of treaties, irrespective of the particular circumstances involved, is not sound. The making of a treaty has the consequences of an entangling alliance for the nation. Similarly, the amending of a treaty merely continues such entangling alliances, changing only their character, and therefore also requires the advice and consent of the Senate. It does not follow, however, that a constitutional provision for a special concurrence (two-thirds of the Senators) prior to entry into an entangling alliance necessarily applies to its termination in accordance with its terms.

4. The Constitution specifically confers no power of treaty termination on either the Congress or the Executive. We note, however, that the powers conferred upon Congress in Article I of the Constitution are specific, detailed, and limited, while the powers conferred upon the President by Article II are generalized in a manner that bespeaks no such limitation upon foreign affairs powers. "Section 1. The executive Power shall be vested in a President. . . ." Although specific powers are listed in Section 2 and Section 3, these are in many instances not powers necessary to an Executive, while "The executive Power" referred to in Section 1 is nowhere defined. There is no required two-thirds vote of the Senate conditioning the exercise of any power in Section 1.

In some instances, this difference is reflective of the origin of the particular power in question. In general, the powers of the federal government arise out of specific grants of authority delegated by the states hence the enumerated powers of Congress in Article I, Section 8. The foreign affairs powers, however, proceed directly from the sovereignty of the Union. "(I)f they had never been mentioned in the Constitution, (they) would have vested in the federal government as necessary concomitants of nationality." United States v. Curtiss-Wright Export Corp., 299 U.S. 304, 318 (1936).

The President is the constitutional representative of the United States with respect to external affairs. It is significant that the treaty power appears in Article II of the Constitution, relating to the executive branch, and not in Article I, setting forth the powers of the legislative branch. It is the President as Chief Executive who is given the constitutional authority to enter into a treaty; and even after he has obtained the consent of the Senate it is for him to decide whether to ratify a treaty and put it into effect. Senatorial confirmation of a treaty concededly does not obligate the President to go forward with a treaty if he concludes that it is not in the public interest to do so.

Thus, in contrast to the lawmaking power, the constitutional initiative in the treaty-making field is in the President, not Congress. It would take an unprecedented feat of judicial construction to read into the Constitution an absolute condition precedent of congressional or Senate approval for termination of all treaties, similar to the specific one relating to initial approval. And it would unalterably affect the balance of power between the two Branches laid down in Articles I and II.

5. Ultimately, what must be recognized is that a treaty is *sui generis*. It is not just another law. It is an international compact, a solemn obligation of the United States and a "supreme Law" that supersedes state policies and prior federal laws. For clarity of analysis, it is thus well to distinguish between treaty-making as an international act and the consequences which flow domestically from such act. In one realm the Constitution has conferred the primary role upon the President; in the other, Congress retains its primary role as lawmaker. The fact that the Constitution, statutes, and treaties are all listed in the Supremacy Clause as being superior to any form of state law does not mean that the making and unmaking of treaties can be analogized to the making and unmaking of domestic statutes any more than it can be analogized to the making or unmaking of a constitutional amendment.

The recognized powers of Congress to implement (or fail to implement) a treaty by an appropriation or other law essential to its effectuation, or to supersede for all practical purposes the effect of a treaty on domestic law, are legislative powers, not treaty-making or treaty termination powers. The issue here, however, is not Congress' legislative powers to supersede or affect the domestic impact of a treaty; the issue is whether the Senate (or Congress) must in this case give its prior consent to discontinue a treaty which the President thinks it desirable to terminate in the national interest and pursuant to a provision in the treaty itself. The existence, in practical terms, of one power does not imply the existence, in constitutional terms, of the other.

6. If we were to hold that under the Constitution a treaty could only be terminated by exactly the same process by which it was made, we would be locking the United States into all of its international obligations, even if the President and two-thirds of the Senate minus one firmly believed that the proper course for the United States was to terminate a treaty. Many of our treaties in force, such as mutual defense treaties, carry potentially dangerous obligations. These obligations are terminable under international law upon breach by the other party or change in circumstances that frustrates the purpose of the treaty. In many of these situations the President must take immediate action. The creation of a constitutionally obligatory role in all cases for a two-thirds consent by the Senate would give to one-third plus one of the Senate the power to deny the President the authority necessary to conduct our foreign policy in a rational and effective manner.

7. Even as to the formal termination of treaties, as the District Court pointed out, "a variety of means have been used to terminate treaties." There is much debate among the historians and scholars as to whether in some instances the legislature has been involved at all; they are agreed that, when involved, that involvement with the President has taken many different forms. . . .

The District Court concluded that the diversity of historical precedents left an inconclusive basis on which to decide the issue of whether the President's power to terminate a treaty must always be "shared" in some way by the Senate or Congress. We agree. Yet we think it is not without significance that out of all the historical precedents brought to our attention, in no situation has a treaty been continued in force over the opposition of the President.

There is on the other hand widespread agreement that the President has the power as Chief Executive under many circumstances to exercise functions regarding treaties which have the effect of either terminating or continuing their vitality. Prominent among these is the authority of the President as Chief Executive (1) to determine whether a treaty has terminated because of a breach, Charlton v. Kelly, 229 U.S. 447, 473-76 (1913); and (2) to determine whether a treaty is at an end due to changed circumstances.

In short, the determination of the conduct of the United States in regard to treaties is an instance of what has broadly been called the "foreign affairs power" of the President. We have no occasion to define that term, but we do take account of its vitality. The *Curtiss-Wright* opinion, written by a Justice who had served in the United States Senate, declares in oft-repeated language that the President is "the sole organ of the federal government in the field of international relations." That status is not confined to the service of the President as a channel of communication, as the District Court suggested, but embraces an active policy determination as to the conduct of the United States in regard to a treaty in response to numerous problems and circumstances as they arise.

8. How the vital functions of the President in implementing treaties and in deciding on their viability in response to changing events can or should interact with Congress' legitimate concerns and powers in relating to foreign affairs is an

area into which we should not and do not prematurely intrude. History shows us that there are too many variables to lay down any hard and fast constitutional rules.

We cannot find an implied role in the Constitution for the Senate in treaty termination for some but not all treaties in terms of their relative importance. There is no judicially ascertainable and manageable method of making any distinction among treaties on the basis of their substance, the magnitude of the risk involved, the degree of controversy which their termination would engender, or by any other standards. We know of no standards to apply in making such distinctions. The facts on which such distinctions might be drawn may be difficult of ascertainment; and the resolution of such inevitable disputes between the two Branches would be an improper and unnecessary role for the courts. To decide whether there was a breach or changed circumstances, for example, would involve a court in making fundamental decisions of foreign policy and would create insuperable problems of evidentiary proof. This is beyond the acceptable judicial role. All we decide today is that two-thirds Senate consent or majority consent in both houses is not necessary to terminate this treaty in the circumstances before us now.

9. The circumstances involved in the termination of the Mutual Defense Treaty with the Republic of China include a number of material and unique elements. Prominent is assertion by the officials of both the Republic of China and the People's Republic of China that each of them is the government of China, intending the term China to comprehend both the mainland of China and the island of Taiwan. In the 1972 Shanghai Communique, the United States acknowledged that position and did not challenge it. It is in this context that the recent Joint Communique set forth as of January 1, 1979 that the United States recognizes the People's Republic of China as "the sole legal government of China." This action made reference to "the people of Taiwan," stating that the peoples of the United States and Taiwan "will maintain cultural, commercial and other unofficial relations." This formulation was confirmed by the Taiwan Relations Act.

It is undisputed that the Constitution gave the President full constitutional authority to recognize the PRC and to derecognize the ROC. What the United States has evolved for Taiwan is a novel and somewhat indefinite relationship, namely, of unofficial relations with the people of Taiwan. The subtleties involved in maintaining amorphous relationships are often the very stuff of diplomacy a field in which the President, not Congress, has responsibility under our Constitution. The President makes a responsible claim that he has authority as Chief Executive to determine that there is no meaningful vitality to a mutual defense treaty when there is no recognized state. That is not to say that the recognition power automatically gives the President authority to take any action that is required or requested by the state being recognized. We do not need to reach this question. Nevertheless, it remains an important ingredient in the case at bar that the President has determined that circumstances have changed so as to preclude continuation of the Mutual Defense Treaty with the ROC; diplomatic recognition of the ROC came to an end on January 1, 1979, and now there exists only "cultural, commercial and other unofficial relations" with the "people on Taiwan."

10. Finally, and of central significance, the treaty here at issue contains a termination clause. The existence of Article X of the ROC treaty, permitting termination by either party on one year's notice, is an overarching factor in this case, which in effect enables all of the other considerations to be knit together.

Without derogating from the executive power of the President to decide to act contrary to the wording of a treaty for example, because of a breach by the other party (Charlton v. Kelly, supra), or because of a doctrine of fundamental change of circumstances (rebus sic stantibus) the President's authority as Chief Executive is at its zenith when the Senate has consented to a treaty that expressly provides for termination on one year's notice, and the President's action is the giving of notice of termination.

As already noted, we have no occasion to decide whether this factor would be determinative in a case lacking other factors identified above, e.g., under a notice of withdrawal from the NATO treaty unaccompanied by derecognition of the other signatories. No specific restriction or condition on the President's action is found within the Constitution or this treaty itself. The termination clause is without conditions and without designation as to who shall act to terminate it. No specific role is spelled out in either the Constitution or this treaty for the Senate or the Congress as a whole. That power consequently devolves upon the President, and there is no basis for a court to imply a restriction on the President's power to terminate not contained in the Constitution, in this treaty, or in any other authoritative source.

WITHDRAWAL FROM THE ABM TREATY

In December 2001, President Bush determined that the United States would terminate its obligations under the ABM treaty that was the subject of the reinterpretation debate recounted above. Here is the text of the December 13, 2001, Diplomatic Notes sent to Russia, Belarus, Kazakhstan, and Ukraine. (The notes were sent to these countries because the Soviet Union had disintegrated in the interim, and these were the resulting countries that had nuclear weapons.):

> The Embassy of the United States of America has the honor to refer to the Treaty between the United States of America and the Union of Soviet Socialist Republics (USSR) on the Limitation of Anti-Ballistic Missile Systems signed at Moscow May 26, 1972.
>
> Article XV, paragraph 2, gives each Party the right to withdraw from the Treaty if it decides that extraordinary events related to the subject matter of the treaty have jeopardized its supreme interests.
>
> The United States recognizes that the Treaty was entered into with the USSR, which ceased to exist in 1991. Since then, we have entered into a new strategic relationship with Russia that is cooperative rather than adversarial, and are building strong relationships with most states of the former USSR.
>
> Since the Treaty entered into force in 1972, a number of state and non-state entities have acquired or are actively seeking to acquire weapons of mass destruction. It is clear, and has recently been demonstrated, that some of these entities are prepared to employ these weapons against the United States. Moreover, a number of states are developing ballistic missiles, including long-range ballistic missiles, as a means of delivering weapons of mass destruction. These events pose a direct threat to the territory and security of the United States and jeopardize its supreme interests. As a result, the United States has concluded that it must develop, test, and deploy anti-ballistic missile systems for the defense of its national territory, of its forces outside the United States, and of its friends and allies.
>
> Pursuant to Article XV, paragraph 2, the United States has decided that extraordinary events related to the subject matter of the Treaty have jeopardized its supreme interests. Therefore, in the exercise of the right to withdraw from the Treaty provided in Article XV, paragraph 2, the United States hereby gives notice of its withdrawal from the Treaty. In accordance with the terms of the Treaty, withdrawal will be effective six months from the date of this notice.

The White House also issued the following Fact Sheet related to the ABM treaty withdrawal:

> The circumstances affecting U.S. national security have changed fundamentally since the signing of the ABM Treaty in 1972. The attacks against the U.S. homeland on September 11 vividly demonstrate that the threats we face today are far different from those of the Cold War. During that era, now fortunately in the past, the United States and the Soviet Union were locked in an implacably hostile relationship. Each side deployed thousands of nuclear weapons pointed at the other. Our ultimate security rested largely on the grim premise that neither side would launch a nuclear attack because doing so would result in a counter-attack ensuring the total destruction of both nations.
>
> Today, our security environment is profoundly different. The Cold War is over. The Soviet Union no longer exists. Russia is not an enemy, but in fact is increasingly allied with us on a growing number of critically important issues. The depth of United States-Russian cooperation in counterterrorism is both a model of the new strategic relationship we seek to establish and a foundation on which to build further cooperation across the broad spectrum of political, economic and security issues of mutual interest.
>
> Today, the United States and Russia face new threats to their security. Principal among these threats are weapons of mass destruction and their delivery means wielded by terrorists and rogue states. A number of such states are acquiring increasingly longer-range ballistic missiles as instruments of blackmail and coercion against the United States and its friends and allies. The United States must defend its homeland, its forces and its friends and allies against these threats. We must develop and deploy the means to deter and protect against them, including through limited missile defense of our territory.
>
> Under the terms of the ABM Treaty, the United States is prohibited from defending its homeland against ballistic missile attack. We are also prohibited from cooperating in developing missile defenses against long-range threats with our friends and allies. Given the emergence of these new threats to our national security and the imperative of defending against them, the United States is today providing formal notification of its withdrawal from the ABM Treaty. As provided in Article XV of that Treaty, the effective date of withdrawal will be six months from today.
>
> At the same time, the United States looks forward to moving ahead with Russia in developing elements of a new strategic relationship. . . .

"UNSIGNING" OF THE ROME STATUTE

On December 31, 2000, shortly before leaving office, President Clinton signed the Rome Statute, which is the treaty that established the International Criminal Court (ICC). Under that treaty, an international court, based in The Hague, Netherlands, has jurisdiction to try the offenses of genocide, crimes against humanity, war crimes, and the crime of aggression. In signing the treaty, President Clinton stated that:

> In signing . . . , we are not abandoning our concerns about significant flaws in the treaty.
>
> In particular, we are concerned that when the court comes into existence, it will not only exercise authority over personnel of states that have ratified the treaty, but also claim jurisdiction over personnel of states that have not.
>
> With signature, however, we will be in a position to influence the evolution of the court. Without signature, we will not.

In May 2002, at President Bush's direction, the Under Secretary of State for Arms Control, John Bolton, sent the following letter to the Secretary-General of the United Nations:

> Dear Mr. Secretary-General:
>
> This is to inform you, in connection with the Rome Statute of the International Criminal Court adopted on July 17, 1998, that the United States does not intend to become a party to the treaty. Accordingly, the United States has no legal obligations arising from its signature on December 31, 2000. The United States requests that its intention not to become a party, as expressed in this letter, be reflected in the depository's status lists relating to this treaty.

Press Statement, International Criminal Court: Letter from John Bolton to U.N. Secretary-General Kofi Annan (May 6, 2002), at https://2001-2009.state.gov/r/pa/prs/ps/2002/9968.htm. The sending of this letter was described by some commentators as "unsigning" the International Criminal Court treaty, although the Administration did not attempt to physically remove the U.S. signature.

In explaining the Administration's action, Marc Grossman, the Under Secretary of State for Political Affairs, stated:

> Here's what America believes in:
>
> - We believe in justice and the promotion of the rule of law.
> - We believe those who commit the most serious crimes of concern to the international community should be punished.
> - We believe that states, not international institutions are primarily responsible for ensuring justice in the international system.
> - We believe that the best way to combat these serious offenses is to build domestic judicial systems, strengthen political will and promote human freedom.
>
> We have concluded that the International Criminal Court does not advance these principles. Here is why:
>
> - We believe the ICC undermines the role of the United Nations Security Council in maintaining international peace and security.
> - We believe in checks and balances. The Rome Statute creates a prosecutorial system that is an unchecked power.
> - We believe that in order to be bound by a treaty, a state must be party to that treaty. The ICC asserts jurisdiction over citizens of states that have not ratified the treaty. This threatens US sovereignty.
> - We believe that the ICC is built on a flawed foundation. These flaws leave it open for exploitation and politically motivated prosecutions.
>
> President Bush has come to the conclusion that the United States can no longer be a party to this process. In order to make our objections clear, both in principle and philosophy, and so as not to create unwarranted expectations of U.S. involvement in the Court, the President believes that he has no choice but to inform the United Nations, as depository of the treaty, of our intention not to become a party to the Rome Statute of the International Criminal Court. This morning, at the instruction of the President, our mission to the United Nations notified the UN Secretary-General in his capacity as the depository for the Rome Statute of the President's decision. These actions are consistent with the Vienna Convention on the Law of Treaties.

Marc Grossman, Under Secretary for Political Affairs, Remarks to the Center for Strategic and International Studies, Washington, D.C. (May 6, 2002), at https://2001-2009.state.gov/p/us/rm/9949.htm.

Notes and Questions

1. The Vienna Convention on the Law of Treaties sets forth the conditions under which nations can suspend or terminate treaties. Although the United States has not ratified the Vienna Convention, it accepts that most of its provisions reflect binding customary international law. The Vienna Convention specifies a variety of circumstances, such as fraud or coercion, in which a treaty will be considered either void or voidable. It also describes the circumstances under which a party to a treaty may suspend or terminate its obligations going forward, such as in response to a material breach by another party. In addition, the Convention makes clear that a party may withdraw from a treaty that expressly provides for a right of withdrawal. If a treaty does not expressly provide for a right of withdrawal, the Vienna Convention states that no such right will be implied unless either (a) it is established that the parties intended to admit the possibility of denunciation or withdrawal, or (b) the right of denunciation or withdrawal may be implied by the nature of the treaty. When there is an implied right of withdrawal, the Vienna Convention provides that the party seeking to withdraw from the treaty must give at least 12 months' notice.

2. What is the source of the President's power to suspend or terminate a treaty? Article II of the Constitution requires that, in order to make a treaty, presidents must obtain the advice and consent of two-thirds of the Senate. Does this requirement imply that presidents must also obtain two-thirds Senate consent before they can suspend or terminate a treaty? Or does the Constitution's silence about this issue mean that the President possesses the authority to suspend or terminate a treaty, on a Hamiltonian Vesting Clause rationale? Is the analogy in *Goldwater* to the President's power to remove appointed officials persuasive?

If the President lacks the authority to suspend or terminate a treaty, who has it? We know from Section B that Congress can, with presidential consent or by overriding a veto, effectively abrogate a U.S. treaty commitment with a subsequent federal statute. Even that action, however, will not necessarily suspend or terminate the treaty under international law. In any event, does it make sense to make this the only mechanism to suspend or terminate treaties? What about a requirement that the President and two-thirds of the Senate must agree before a treaty is suspended or terminated? Does it make sense to give 34 Senators veto power over the issue? To enact a federal statute, Congress must either obtain presidential consent or override a presidential veto, and it is well settled that the same limitation applies to congressional repeal of a federal statute. Is the suspension or termination of a treaty analogous to the repeal of a statute for these purposes? Does the answer to this question depend on whether the treaty is self-executing?

In answering these questions, what is the significance of the fact that many constitutional Founders believed that it should be difficult for the United States to enter into treaties? Gouverneur Morris remarked at the Federal Convention, for example, that "[t]he more difficulty in making treaties, the more value will be set on them," and James Madison observed that it had been too easy to make treaties in the pre-constitutional period. As a practical matter, does the United States need more flexibility in the termination of its treaty commitments than in the making of such commitments?

3. The historical practice concerning U.S. treaty termination is contested, in part because each action is in some respects unique. In many instances, presidents have sought and obtained congressional consent for treaty terminations. The earliest example of this was Congress's termination of treaties with France in 1798, at the request of President Adams. Another example was a joint resolution passed by Congress in 1846 authorizing President Polk to terminate a treaty with Great Britain relating to the Oregon territory. In other instances, presidents have sought and obtained the consent of the Senate. President Buchanan terminated a commercial treaty with Denmark in 1858, for example, after receiving Senate authorization. In still other instances, presidents have acted unilaterally, as President Carter did in terminating the Taiwan treaty. In the *Goldwater* case, the Executive Branch cited 13 other such instances in which the President had unilaterally terminated a treaty. In a dissent in *Goldwater* that is not excerpted above, Judge MacKinnon challenged the Executive Branch's assertion after canvassing the historical record in detail. After concluding that "Congressional participation in termination has been the over-whelming historical practice," he had this to say about the 13 examples of unilateral Executive termination:

> In five instances Congress by direct authorization, or inconsistent legislation supplied the basis for the President's action; in two instances the putative abrogation was with-drawn and no termination resulted; one treaty was already terminated by the demise of the country; one treaty had become void by a change in the basic facts upon which the treaty was grounded; four treaties had already been abrogated by the other party; and [one] was not terminated.

What is at stake over the historical record of treaty terminations? If the President had terminated many treaties unilaterally in the past, why would that support an authority to do so with respect to the Taiwan treaty? Premised on the belief that history did not provide significant support for unilateral presidential termination of treaties, Judge MacKinnon expressed this view about the role of historical practice in constitutional interpretation: "Practice may not make perfect a constitutional power. Yet a prevailing practice, especially when begun in the light provided by the dawn of the Constitution, emanates a precedential aura of constitutional significance." Do you agree? Does the truth of this statement depend on how obviously "prevailing" the practice is? On whether the practice has or has not been controversial? For an account of the practice of treaty termination throughout U.S. history that finds that it was generally assumed during the nineteenth century that presidents needed congressional or senatorial approval to terminate a treaty, but that this understanding changed during the twentieth century, see Curtis A. Bradley, *Treaty Termination and Historical Gloss*, 92 Tex. L. Rev. 773 (2014).

Since the termination of the Taiwan treaty, the United States has acted to terminate dozens of treaties, and almost all of these terminations have been carried out by unilateral presidential action. *See* Office of the Legal Adviser, U.S. Dep't of State, 2002 Digest of United States Practice in International Law, at 202-06 (Sally J. Cummins & David P. Stewart eds., 2002) (listing 23 bilateral treaties and seven multilateral treaties terminated by presidential action since the termination of the Taiwan treaty). As discussed below, the Trump Administration has added to this historical practice.

4. Might the President have the authority to suspend or terminate treaties under some circumstances but not others? For example, both the Taiwan treaty and the ABM Treaty contained termination clauses. Would it matter to the President's power if a treaty lacked such a clause? Would the reason for the suspension or termination matter? Would it matter, for example, if the President's suspension or termination was (a) consistent with international law and was based on a material breach of the treaty by the other party, (b) consistent with international law, but based merely on policy reasons, or (c) contrary to international law? Might the President have a power of suspension of treaties (e.g., until a breach of the treaty is remedied), but not a power of termination?

5. The Restatement (Fourth) of Foreign Relations Law observes that, "[a]ccording to established practice, the President has the authority to act on behalf of the United States in suspending or terminating U.S. treaty commitments and in withdrawing the United States from treaties, either on the basis of terms in the treaty allowing for such action (such as a withdrawal clause) or on the basis of international law that would justify such action." Restatement (Fourth) of the Foreign Relations Law of the United States §313(1) (2018). For a challenge to this conventional wisdom, and an argument that, "absent exceptional circumstances, the degree of congressional participation constitutionally required to exit any particular agreement should mirror the degree of congressional participation that was required to enter that agreement in the first place," see Harold Hongju Koh, *Presidential Power to Terminate International Agreements*, 128 Yale L.J.F. 432, 435-36 (2018). *See also* Catherine Amirfar & Ashika Singh, *The Trump Administration and the "Unmaking" of International Agreements*, 59 Harv. Int'l L.J. 443, 444 (2018) (arguing that "it is too simplistic to say either that the President always or never can unilaterally withdraw from international agreements more generally").

6. In June 2002, 32 members of the House of Representatives brought suit in federal district court against President Bush and other Executive Branch officials, challenging the Bush Administration's authority to withdraw from the ABM Treaty. The House members argued that because the Constitution classifies treaties, like federal statutes, as the "supreme law of the land," the President does not have the authority to terminate a treaty without congressional consent, just as the President cannot terminate a statute without congressional consent. In December 2002, the district court dismissed the suit. Relying on Raines v. Byrd (discussed in Chapter 2), the court concluded that the House members lacked standing. The court also held that the case raised a nonjusticiable political question, for reasons similar to those articulated by then-Justice Rehnquist in his plurality opinion in Goldwater v. Carter (excerpted in Chapter 2). *See* Kucinich v. Bush, 236 F. Supp. 2d 1 (D.D.C. 2002).

7. Recall the controversy, discussed above in Sections A and F, over the International Court of Justice's holdings that the United States had violated the Vienna Convention on Consular Relations, and its instructions for relief within the U.S. legal system. The ICJ had jurisdiction in these cases pursuant to the Optional Protocol to the Vienna Convention, which the United States ratified in 1969. In March 2005, in the same month in which the President announced that the United States would comply with the ICJ's *Avena* decision through state court proceedings, Secretary of State Rice sent a letter to the Secretary-General of the United Nations informing him that the United States "hereby withdraws" from the Optional Protocol. Unlike the Taiwan defense treaty and the ABM Treaty, the Protocol does not specifically provide for withdrawal, and some have argued that under international law the United States either lacks the right to withdraw from the Protocol, or at least has an obligation to provide a year's notice prior to its withdrawal, which it apparently did not do. Does the absence of a termination provision in the Optional Protocol, or possible international law problems with the termination, affect the President's domestic authority to terminate the treaty?

8. The Trump Administration has acted to withdraw the United States from a number of international agreements. Some of these agreements were concluded outside of the Article II process for making treaties and thus are addressed in the next chapter, but several of them were Article II treaties:

(A) In July 2018, Iran brought suit against the United States in the International Court of Justice (ICJ) concerning the United States' re-imposition of sanctions relating to Iran's nuclear program, and the ICJ subsequently issued a provisional measures order requiring that the United States ensure that its sanctions exempt certain humanitarian goods. The Trump Administration responded in early October 2018 by giving notice that the United States was withdrawing from the Treaty of Amity, Economic Relations, and Consular Rights between Iran and the United States, which was the basis for Iran's suit. The Treaty of Amity is an Article II treaty approved by the Senate in 1956 and ratified by the United States that same year. Pursuant to the terms of the treaty, the withdrawal will take effect one year after the U.S. announcement. The U.S. withdrawal does not, however, affect pending ICJ cases implicating the treaty.

(B) Many countries recognize Palestine as a nation, but the United States does not. After Palestine brought suit against the United States in the ICJ challenging the relocation of the U.S. embassy in Israel from Tel Aviv to Jerusalem, the Trump Administration announced that it was withdrawing from the Optional Protocol to the Vienna Convention on Diplomatic Relations, which Palestine had invoked as the basis for the Court's jurisdiction. The Optional Protocol is an Article II treaty approved by the Senate in 1965 and ratified by the United States in 1972, and it provides that disputes "arising out of the interpretation or application of the [Vienna] Convention shall lie within the compulsory jurisdiction of the International Court of Justice and may accordingly be brought before the Court by an application made by any party to the dispute being a Party to the present Protocol." The announcement of withdrawal was made on the same day as the announcement of withdrawal from the Treaty of Amity with Iran. Unlike the Treaty of Amity, the Protocol does not have a withdrawal clause and thus does not specify a notice period, and the Trump Administration appeared to view the U.S. withdrawal as effective immediately. It is not clear, however, that international law allows for such an immediate withdrawal. The Vienna Convention on the Law of Treaties, which the United States has not ratified, but which is thought to reflect customary international law in at least many respects, provides for a default period of a year's notice when a treaty does not specify a withdrawal period.

(C) In late October 2018, President Trump announced that he intended to withdraw the United States from the Intermediate-Range Nuclear Forces (INF) Treaty with Russia. The INF Treaty is an Article II treaty approved by the Senate in 1988 and ratified by the United States that same year. It allows either party to withdraw "if it decides that extraordinary events related to the subject matter of this Treaty have jeopardized its supreme interests," but requires that the party give six months' notice of the withdrawal and provide "a statement of the extraordinary events the notifying Party regards as having jeopardized its supreme interests." In December 2018, Secretary of State Mike Pompeo declared that Russia had been in material breach of the treaty for years. He gave notice that the United States would suspend its obligations under the treaty unless Russia returned to compliance. On February 1, 2019, Pompeo announced that the United States was suspending its obligations under the treaty, beginning on February 2, in light of Russia's continued non-compliance. He further stated that the United States was giving Russia and other treaty parties formal notice of the U.S. withdrawal from the INF Treaty, which, pursuant to Article 15 of the Treaty, would take effect in six months. *See Remarks by Secretary of State Michael R. Pompeo* (Feb. 1, 2019), *at* https://ee.usembassy.gov/remarks-by-secretary-pompeo/.

––––––––––––––––

Do these actions by the Trump Administration, by adding to the historical practice of treaty terminations, further strengthen the argument that the President has the constitutional authority to act unilaterally in terminating treaties? In answering this question, how, if at all, might it matter that Congress as an institution has not objected to the President's legal authority to terminate these treaties? President Trump has also claimed that he has the authority to withdraw the United States from the North Atlantic Treaty, which established NATO, although he has not done so. The United States ratified this treaty in 1949 after the Senate gave its advice and consent. It allows any party to withdraw by giving a year's notice. If presidents generally can withdraw the United States from Article II treaties, is there any reason to conclude that this is not true for a significant security agreement like the NATO treaty?

For discussion of the first two treaty withdrawals, see Scott R. Anderson, *Walking Away from the World Court,* Lawfare (Oct. 5, 2018); John Bellinger, *Thoughts on the ICJ's Decision in Iran v. United States and the Trump Administration's Treaty Withdrawals,* Lawfare (Oct. 5, 2018); and Chimène Keitner, *What are the Consequences of the Trump Administration's Recent Treaty Withdrawals?,* Just Security (Oct. 17, 2018). For discussion of the contemplated withdrawal from the INF Treaty, see Hilary Hurd & Elena Chachko, *U.S. Withdrawal from the INF Treaty: The Facts and the Law,* Lawfare (Oct. 25, 2018).

9. Can Congress or the Senate take steps to prevent the President from withdrawing from treaties? This question has arisen in light of President Trump's many treaty withdrawals and especially in light of news reports in 2018 and 2019 that he had contemplated the possibility of withdrawing from the North Atlantic Treaty. In response to this possibility, several bills were proposed in Congress to prevent Trump from achieving this end.

For example, in January 2019, Senator Tim Kaine introduced a bill, S.J. Res. 4, that provided: "The President shall not suspend, terminate, or withdraw the United States from the North Atlantic Treaty, . . . except by and with the advice and consent of the Senate, provided that two thirds of the Senators present concur, or pursuant to an Act of Congress." The bill also barred the use of appropriated funds to suspend, terminate, or withdraw the United States from the treaty, absent approval by the Senate or Congress, and it required the President to notify the congressional foreign relations committees about "any effort" to suspend, terminate, or withdraw the United States from the treaty. If this bill became law, would it be constitutional? Of what relevance, if any, is *Zivotofsky II?* For commentary, see Scott R. Anderson, *Saving NATO,* Lawfare (July 25, 2018); Curtis A. Bradley & Jack Goldsmith, *Constitutional Issues Relating to the NATO Support Act,* Lawfare (Jan. 28, 2019). *See also* Kristen E. Eichensehr, *Treaty Termination and the Separation of Powers,* 53 Va. J. Int'l L. 247 (2013).

10. Throughout its history, the United States has signed numerous treaties that it has not subsequently ratified. This phenomenon has been especially evident in the last several decades. During this period, the United States has signed, but has not yet ratified, a variety of important multilateral treaties. These treaties include significant human rights agreements such as the International Covenant on Economic, Social, and Cultural Rights (signed in 1977); the American Convention on Human Rights (signed in 1977); the Convention on the Elimination of All Forms of Discrimination Against Women (signed in 1980); the Convention on the Rights of the Child (signed in 1995); and the Convention on the Rights of Persons with Disabilities (2009). They also include important environmental treaties such as the Kyoto Protocol on Global Warming (signed in 1998) and the Rio Convention on Biological Diversity (signed in 1993). Two other examples of signed but unratified treaties, much discussed in connection with the war on terrorism, are the First and Second Additional Protocols to the Geneva Conventions (signed in 1977).

A long delay in ratification does not necessarily mean that the United States will not become a party to a treaty. At least since World War I, it has not been uncommon for a significant period of time to elapse between U.S. signature and ratification of a treaty. Two particularly dramatic examples are the Geneva Protocol for the Prohibition of the Use in War of Asphyxiating, Poisonous or Other Gases, and of Bacteriological Methods of Warfare, which the United States signed in 1925 but did not ratify until 1975, 50 years later, and the Convention on the Prevention and Punishment of the Crime of Genocide, which the United States signed in 1948 but did not ratify until 1989, 41 years later.

What do you think explains the phenomenon of signed but unratified treaties? Why might a President sign a treaty knowing that there is little prospect that the Senate will give its consent to the treaty? Why might a President sign a treaty without any present plan to move forward with ratification? Why did President Clinton sign the treaty establishing the International Criminal Court knowing that the incoming Bush Administration was likely to oppose the treaty?

For an argument that the Constitution requires some degree of "synchronicity" in acts of federal lawmaking and that this means that presidents must conclude treaties within a reasonable time after receiving the Senate's advice and consent, see Saikrishna Bangalore Prakash, *Of Synchronicity and Supreme Law*, 132 Harv. L. Rev. 1220 (2019). Drawing on an analogy to the time that it took the states to ratify the Articles of Confederation, Professor Prakash contends that, "as a constitutional matter, treaties generally may be made within the scope of seven years from Senate consent" and that "[p]eriods appreciably longer would vitiate the sense that the Senate consented to the treaty in the context in which the treaty ultimately purported to become a valid international contract and supreme federal law." Assuming that there should be some sort of synchronicity requirement, should courts treat it as a political question?

11. Under contemporary treaty practice, a nation's signing of a treaty, especially a multilateral treaty, will often not make the nation a party to the treaty. Rather, nations typically become parties to treaties by an act of ratification—either by depositing an instrument of ratification with a depository (for multilateral treaties) or exchanging instruments of ratification (for bilateral treaties). According to Article 18 of the Vienna Convention on the Law of Treaties, however, a nation that signs a treaty is "obliged to refrain from acts which would defeat the object and purpose" of the treaty "until it shall have made its intention clear not to become a party to the treaty." Although the United States has not ratified the Vienna Convention, Executive Branch officials have stated on a number of occasions that they view at least much of the Convention as reflecting binding customary international law.

Assuming Article 18 reflects customary international law, does the President have the constitutional authority to impose this sort of obligation on the United States based merely on his signature of a treaty? If so, what is the source of this authority? Are there any constitutional limits on this authority? If these signing obligations are treated as non-self-executing, does that eliminate any potential constitutional problems? Did President Clinton's signature of the Rome Statute, which created the International Criminal Court, impose obligations on the United States?

12. Does the President have the constitutional authority to terminate the effects of a prior presidential signature of a treaty, as President Bush did with respect to the treaty establishing the International Criminal Court? If so, what is the source of that authority? Is it implied from the President's authority to sign the treaty in the first place? From the fact that the United States cannot ratify a treaty without presidential agreement? From the President's role as chief spokesperson for the United States in foreign affairs? How does this issue compare with the issue of the President's authority to terminate treaties?

Although the Bush Administration's announcement concerning the Rome Statute was described by some commentators as unprecedented, there have been other instances in which an administration has announced an intention not to ratify a treaty signed by its predecessor, although not through a formal letter to the United Nations. For example, President Carter signed the SALT II nuclear reduction treaty in 1979, but the Reagan Administration announced in 1982 that the United States had no intention of ratifying that treaty. Secretary of State Alexander Haig explained to the Senate Foreign Relations Committee that "[t]his proposal has been abandoned by this administration," and that "we consider SALT II dead and have so informed the Soviets." Similarly, the Reagan Administration announced in 1987 that it would not ratify the First Additional Protocol to the Geneva Conventions on the laws of war, which President Carter had signed in 1977. President Reagan explained in a message to the Senate that the Protocol was "fundamentally and irreconcilably flawed," that the problems with the Protocol were "so fundamental in character that they cannot be remedied through reservations," and that he therefore had "decided not to submit the Protocol to the Senate in any form."

13. How, if at all, is the President's authority to eliminate the legal effects of a signed but unratified treaty affected once the treaty has been submitted to the Senate? Consider the Arms Trade Treaty, which President Obama signed in 2013 and transmitted to the Senate in 2016. In April 2019, President Trump sent a "Message" to the Senate stating that he had "concluded that it is not in the interest of the United States to become a party" to the treaty and thus had "decided to withdraw the aforementioned treaty from the Senate and accordingly request that it be returned to [him]." *Presidential Message to the Senate of the United States on the Withdrawal of the Arms Trade Treaty* (Apr. 29, 2019), *at* https://www.whitehouse.gov/briefings-statements/presidential-message-senate-united-states-withdrawal-arms-trade-treaty/. Does the Senate have an obligation to return the treaty to the President? What would the effect be if, after the President's request, the Senate provided advice and consent to the treaty? The President can always refuse to ratify a treaty that the Senate has consented to, but what steps, if any, can a President take at that point to prevent a *future* president from ratifying the treaty? For an examination of these and related questions in connection with earlier treaties, see David C. Scott, Comment, *Presidential Power to "Unsign" Treaties*, 69 U. Chi. L. Rev. 1447 (2002). In July 2019, the Trump Administration sent a letter to the United Nations stating that "the United States does not intend to become a party to the treaty. Accordingly, the United States has no legal obligations arising from its signature."

14. For additional discussion of the issue of treaty termination, see David Gray Adler, The Constitution and the Termination of Treaties (1986); Victoria Maria Kraft, The U.S. Constitution and Foreign Policy: Terminating the Taiwan Treaty

(1991); Raoul Berger, *The President's Unilateral Termination of the Taiwan Treaty*, 75 Nw. U. L. Rev. 577 (1980); Louis Henkin, *Litigating the President's Power to Terminate Treaties*, 73 Am. J. Int'l L. 647 (1979); Daniel J. Hessel, Note, *Founding-Era Jus Ad Bellum and the Domestic Law of Treaty Withdrawal*, 125 Yale L.J. 2394 (2016); James J. Moriarty, *Congressional Claims for Treaty Termination Powers in the Age of the Diminished Presidency*, 14 Conn. J. Int'l L. 123 (1999); Randall H. Nelson, *The Termination of Treaties and Executive Agreements by the United States: Theory and Practice*, 42 Minn. L. Rev. 879 (1958); Anna Mamalakis Pappas, *The Constitutional Allocation of Competence in the Termination of Treaties*, 13 N.Y.U. J. Int'l L. & Pol. 473 (1981); David J. Scheffer, Comment, *The Law of Treaty Termination as Applied to the United States De-Recognition of the Republic of China*, 19 Harv. Int'l L.J. 931 (1978); Jonathan York Thomas, *The Abuse of History: A Refutation of the State Department Analysis of Alleged Instances of Independent Presidential Treaty Termination*, 6 Yale Studies in World Pub. Ord. 27 (1979).

For additional discussion of issues associated with the signing and unsigning of treaties, see Michael J. Glennon, Constitutional Diplomacy 169-75 (1990); Curtis A. Bradley, *Unratified Treaties, Domestic Politics, and the U.S. Constitution*, 48 Harv. Int'l L.J. 307 (2007); David H. Moore, *The President's Unconstitutional Treatymaking*, 59 UCLA L. Rev. 598 (2012); Edward T. Swaine, *Unsigning*, 55 Stan. L. Rev. 2061, 2064-65 (2003); David C. Scott, Note, *Presidential Power to "Un-Sign" Treaties*, 69 U. Chi. L. Rev. 1447 (2002); *see also* Curtis A. Bradley, *ASIL Insight: U.S. Announces Intent Not to Ratify International Criminal Court Treaty* (May 2002), at https://www.asil.org/insights/volume/7/issue/7/us-announces-intent-not-ratify-international-criminal-court-treaty.

6

Executive Agreements

Executive agreements are international agreements concluded by the United States without resort to the two-thirds senatorial advice and consent process specified in Article II. Presidents make many more executive agreements than treaties, and these agreements cover a wide array of topics and serve many different aims. In this chapter, we focus on three common forms of executive agreements. Section A discusses congressional-executive agreements, which are agreements authorized or approved by majority votes in both houses of Congress. Section B discusses "sole" executive agreements, which are agreements presidents make on their own authority under Article II. Section C discusses political commitments made by presidents and their subordinates. In contrast to congressional-executive agreements and sole executive agreements, political commitments do not create binding international legal obligations and thus impose no legal duty on the United States.

A. CONGRESSIONAL-EXECUTIVE AGREEMENTS

Congressional-executive agreements are international agreements that, like Article II treaties, are fully binding on the United States under international law, but unlike Article II treaties are authorized or approved in a statute passed by a majority of both houses of Congress. *Ex ante* congressional-executive agreements are those that Congress authorizes the President to make in advance. Presidents then negotiate, conclude, and ratify the agreement without returning to Congress. *Ex post* congressional-executive agreements are ones that the President negotiates and then sends to Congress for its approval before ratification.

The materials below focus on constitutional concerns raised with respect to two important trade agreements concluded pursuant to the *ex post* congressional-executive agreement process—the 1992 North American Free Trade Agreement (NAFTA) and the 1994 General Agreement on Tariffs and Trade (GATT). These materials are followed by a letter from two leading members of the Senate Foreign Relations Committee, arguing that significant arms control agreements must be concluded pursuant to the Article II treaty process.

Made in the USA Foundation v. United States

56 F. Supp. 2d 1226 (N.D. Ala. 1999), *aff'd on other grounds,*
242 F.3d 1300 (11th Cir. 2001)

ROBERT B. PROPST, DISTRICT JUDGE. . . .

In 1990, the United States, Mexico, and Canada initiated negotiations with the intention of creating a "free trade zone" through the elimination or reduction of tariffs and other barriers to trade. After two years of negotiations, the leaders of the three countries signed the North American Free Trade Agreement ("NAFTA" or the "Agreement") on December 17, 1992. Congress approved and implemented NAFTA on December 8, 1993 with the passage of NAFTA Implementation Act ("Implementation Act"), which was passed by a vote of 234 to 200 in the House and 61 to 38 in the Senate. The Implementation Act served two purposes, to "approve" NAFTA and to provide a series of laws to "locally" enforce NAFTA's provisions. The enactment of the Implementation Act brought to a close a lengthy period of rancorous debate over NAFTA. The instant suit seeks to reopen that debate by pulling back NAFTA's coat and demonstrating that the Agreement and Implementation Act stand on sand rather than on firm Constitutional ground. Brought to bear in this case is an almost century-long bout of Constitutional theorizing about whether the Treaty Clause, contained in Article II, Section 2 of the United States Constitution (the "Treaty Clause"), creates the exclusive means of making certain types of international agreements.

Neither NAFTA nor the Implementation Act were subjected to the procedures outlined in the Treaty Clause. The President purportedly negotiated and concluded NAFTA pursuant to his constitutional responsibility for conducting the foreign affairs of the United States and in accordance with the Omnibus Trade and Competitiveness Act of 1988, 19 U.S.C. §2901, et seq. ("Trade Act of 1988"), and the Trade Act of 1974, 19 U.S.C. §2101, et seq. ("Trade Act of 1974"), under the so-called fast track procedure. Congress then approved and implemented NAFTA by enacting the Implementation Act, allegedly pursuant to its power to legislate in the areas of tariffs and domestic and foreign commerce.

The plaintiffs contend that this failure to go through the Article II, Section 2, prerequisites renders the Agreement and, apparently, the Implementation Act, unconstitutional. The Government denies this. . . .

The Government argues that the Treaty Clause of Article II is not the exclusive means for entering into an international agreement such as NAFTA or for adopting legislation implementing such an agreement. To begin with, the Government notes that the plaintiffs concede the existence of some kinds of valid and binding international agreements that do not constitute Article II treaties. This concession, comments the Government, is unsurprising in light of the fact that there exist several types of non-Article II treaty international agreements that have been well-established as valid under United States law. Such agreements include: (1) congressional-executive agreements — agreements negotiated by the President that are either pre- or post-approved by a simple majority of Congress; (2) executive agreements authorized expressly or implicitly by an existing treaty; and (3) presidential or sole executive agreements — agreements concluded unilaterally by the President pursuant to his constitutional authority. The Government notes that nothing in the Constitutional text elevates the Article II treaty ratification process over Article I's lawmaking powers. Plaintiffs' claims represent, according to the

Government, nothing more than an attempt to engraft an artificial and illegitimate hierarchy onto the Constitution.

The plaintiffs argue that the Government's argument as to exclusivity is persuasive only to the extent that it promotes the position that some international agreements do not rise to the level of treaties and do not require approval of two-thirds of the Senate. They argue that acceptance of the executive agreement and/or the congressional-executive agreement as all-purpose alternatives to the Treaty Clause represents an acceptance of the principle that the Constitution may be amended without reference to Article V of the Constitution. They note that in the 1930's and 1940's, when advocates of the congressional-executive agreement first garnered significant support for their use, there was a widespread recognition of the fact that in order to make the practice constitutional an amendment would be necessary. A movement in favor of such an amendment took place in 1943-45, but was abandoned when advocates decided that it was "ridiculous to suppose that two-thirds of the Senate would voluntarily surrender its treaty-making prerogatives by supporting a formal constitutional amendment." Thus, according to [Laurence H. Tribe, *Taking Text and Structure Seriously: Reflections on the Free-Form Method in Constitutional Interpretation*, 108 Harv. L. Rev. 1221 (1995)], rather than properly amending the Constitution, politicians and academics chose to ignore the intent of the Framers and historical precedent in favor of political prudence and "strategic compromise." Tribe at 1280-86.

The plaintiffs reject the Government's characterization of the broad powers of the President and Congress with respect to international agreement-making. They claim that the Government's description of the powers of the President is so broad as to leave nothing beyond the scope of unilateral executive agreements as long as such agreements deal with "foreign affairs." Similarly, the Government's characterization of Congress's power lacks any defined boundaries, and, in effect, amounts to a total interchangeability argument. . . .

According to the Government, the text of the Constitution, as interpreted by the Supreme Court, allows for the utilization of executive agreements whenever there exists constitutional authority outside of the Treaty Clause allowing the President to negotiate and conclude an international agreement and allowing Congress to enact the legislation required for a given agreement's implementation. The Government, citing the Constitutional authority granted to both the President and Congress, and noting that the Supreme Court has characterized Congress's power to regulate "Commerce with foreign Nations" as "broad," "comprehensive," "plenary," and "complete," argues that NAFTA and the Implementation Act fall squarely within the combined enumerated powers of the two political branches. Further, it argues that the Agreement and the Act stand at the intersection of Congress's and the President's power over foreign commerce and foreign affairs, respectively, and that each provision of the Implementation Act could, therefore, have been enacted in the absence of any agreement with Mexico and Canada.

While acknowledging that NAFTA could have been ratified as a treaty, the Government contends that the congressional-executive agreement process was certainly acceptable, that the Treaty Clause does not expressly prohibit the employment of an alternative procedure, and that the congressional-executive agreement method may have been the Constitutionally preferable method by which to approve of and implement NAFTA. Thus, the Supreme Court, in holding that a later act of Congress may override a treaty, stated that the House's action with respect to such legislation "does not render it less entitled to respect in the matter of its repeal or modification than a treaty. . . . If there be any difference in this regard, it would seem to be in favor of an act in which all three of the bodies [the President, House, and Senate] participate."[269]

The plaintiffs argue that the text of the Constitution supports their contention that international agreements that have the substance of a treaty cannot be adopted without the approval of two-thirds of the Senate. In doing so, they begin by contending that the most "natural" reading of the Treaty Clause is one that reads the clause as creating the exclusive method by which to conclude that certain class of international agreements called "treaties." They, like Tribe, argue that basic provisions of the Constitution that define the locus of power for certain governmental actions are properly construed as creating the exclusive means by which to exercise those powers. Both the plaintiffs and Tribe assert that the Treaty Clause represents such a provision. They therefore argue that any other reading of the Treaty Clause renders it a "dead letter," and allows the corruption of one of the Constitution's fundamental provisions.

The plaintiffs argue that the language of the Compacts Clause, U.S. Const., Art. I, §10, clauses 1 and 3, is perfectly consistent with the contention that the Treaty Clause represents the exclusive method by which to conclude certain international agreements. The Compacts Clause was, as noted above, meant to represent an absolute bar with respect to the States' ability to enter into treaties with foreign powers. However, the Clause permits the States to enter into other international agreements with the consent of Congress. The plaintiffs argue that to the extent the Compact Clause evidences the Framers' recognition of a distinction between treaties and other international agreements, the Treaty Clause indicates that they intended to limit the federal government's method of concluding those things called treaties, while leaving open the question of how the federal government is to make other international agreements. Thus, the plaintiffs argue that in addressing "treaties" and not those other international agreements termed "agreements" and "compacts," the Treaty Clause clearly establishes that those agreements that do constitute treaties must be subjected to its more rigorous procedural requirements in order to be considered valid. . . .

The most significant issue before the court is whether the Treaty Clause is an exclusive means of making an international agreement under the circumstances of this case. It is clear that there is no explicit language in the Constitution which makes the Treaty Clause exclusive as to all international agreements. On the other hand, the broad breadth of the Commerce Clause, particularly the Foreign Commerce Clause, has been repeatedly emphasized. The inability of the Congress under the Articles of Confederation to regulate commerce was one of the main weaknesses which led to the call of the Constitutional Convention. The Annapolis Convention of 1786 was called to discuss problems which had resulted from this weakness. This meeting, in turn, led to the Constitutional Convention. The Commerce Clause was clearly intended to address this concern. The "Power" to regulate commerce, foreign and interstate and with Indian Tribes, was specifically given to Congress. The Treaty Clause makes no specific reference to commerce of any type. . . .

In the absence of specific limiting language in or relating to the Treaty Clause, I am led to conclude that the Foreign Commerce power of Congress is at least concurrent with the Treaty Clause power when an agreement, as is the case here,

---

269. Head Money Cases, 112 U.S. 580, 599 (1884).

is dominated by provisions specifically related to foreign commerce and has other provisions which are reasonably "necessary and proper" for "carrying all others into execution." . . . Further, I note that the President, in negotiating the Agreement in connection with the fast track legislation, was acting pursuant to his constitutional responsibility for conducting the Nation's foreign affairs and pursuant to a grant of authority from Congress.[352] The foregoing, considered in light of at least some degree of presumption of constitutionality to which the Agreement is entitled, leads me to ultimately conclude that NAFTA and the Implementation Act were made and approved in a constitutional manner.[354] One thing is clear. This court does not have jurisdiction to review the wisdom of NAFTA or to determine whether it is in the best interest of the Nation. . . .

In 1994, after years of negotiation, the "Uruguay Round" of the General Agreement on Tariffs and Trade (GATT) was concluded, and over 100 nations, including the United States, signed a "Final Act" that encompassed a variety of agreements. These agreements included detailed provisions concerning free trade of goods and services and the protection of intellectual property, as well as an agreement calling for the establishment of a World Trade Organization (WTO) that would adjudicate international trade disputes and formulate trade policy. The Clinton Administration's decision to ratify this treaty through the congressional-executive agreement process rather than through the Article II senatorial consent process prompted a written debate between Professor Laurence Tribe of the Harvard Law School and Assistant Attorney General Walter Dellinger. Here is an excerpt from a memorandum in which Dellinger responds to some of Professor Tribe's arguments.

Memorandum from Walter Dellinger, Assistant Attorney General, to Michael Kantor, U.S. Trade Representative

July 29, 1994

In a recent letter to Senator Robert Byrd, Professor Laurence H. Tribe took the position that "if there is any category of international agreement or accord that must surely be submitted to the Senate for approval under the usually rigorous two-thirds rule of the Treaty Clause, that category must include agreements like the Uruguay Round, which represents not merely a traditional trade agreement but a

---

352. Again, according to *Youngstown*, the President's power is at its pinnacle when he acts in concert with Congress. . . .

354. In reaching my conclusion, I do not accept a theory of total interchangeability. As the Supreme Court has stated, "it is obvious that there may be matters of the sharpest exigency for the national well being that an act of Congress could not deal with but that a treaty followed by such an act could." Missouri v. Holland, 252 U.S. 416, 433 (1920). Further, the Justice Department has stated that it does not disagree with the premise that some agreements with foreign nations "may have to be ratified as treaties." Memorandum, Walter Dellinger, Asst. Atty. Gen. to Ambassador Michael Kantor, November 22, 1994. Similarly, while purportedly speaking on behalf of the Senate Judiciary Committee, Senator Dirksen, in 1956, rejected the "doctrine that treaties and executive agreements are wholly interchangeable." Senate Rep. No. 1716, 84th Congress, 2nd Session 9 (1956). Thus, there may exist circumstances where the procedures outlined in the Treaty Clause must be adhered to in order to adopt an international agreement. However, it is not entirely clear what those circumstances are. In any case, in light of Congress's enumerated powers in the areas dealt with by NAFTA, I conclude that such circumstances are not present in this case. My opinion is limited to the area of foreign commerce and related enumerated powers coupled with Presidential power(s) and the powers under the Necessary and Proper Clause.

significant restructuring of the power alignment between the National Government and the States." Professor Tribe contends that the legal regime that would ensue from the enactment of the GATT implementing legislation "would entail a significant shift of sovereignty from state and local governments to the proposed World Trade Organization (WTO), in which the interests of these entities would be represented exclusively by the U.S. Trade Representative." Professor Tribe concludes that "the legal regime put in place by the Uruguay Round represents a structural rearrangement of state-federal relations of the sort that requires ratification by two-thirds of the Senate as a Treaty."

We disagree. . . . Congress has frequently enacted major international trade agreements that apply to the States, including agreements that raise the possibility that State law might be challenged as inconsistent with our international obligations. . . .

The Constitution itself recognizes the possibility of international agreements other than "treaties" in the sense of Art. II, §2, cl. 2. . . . [W]hile a state may not enter into a "Treaty" with a foreign power, it may (with Congress's approval) enter into an "Agreement or Compact" with one. . . . Accordingly, from the beginning of the Republic to the present, Presidents and Congresses have elected to enter into international agreements in preference to formal treaties. . . .

We do not understand Professor Tribe to be arguing that trade agreements in all cases must be approved by two-thirds of the Senate. Rather, he appears to be claiming that the GATT Uruguay Round has some specific feature that requires that *it*—unlike other trade agreements—be ratified in the manner prescribed by the Treaty Clause. . . . We are hard pressed, however, to identify with any certainty what this assertedly distinguishing feature of the GATT Uruguay Round is, or why it should entail the constitutional consequences that Professor Tribe seeks to draw from it.

Conceivably, Professor Tribe might mean only that the GATT Uruguay Round will change the relative balance of control over various trade-related matters between federal and state governments. But such a shift would in itself raise no substantive constitutional issues: it has long been settled that if federal legislation is within the substantive scope of a delegated power, it is constitutional, even though its purpose is to reconfigure state-federal relations. To deny that GATT Uruguay Round falls within the substantive scope of Congress's combined powers under the Interstate and Foreign Commerce Clause would be a radical attack upon the modern understanding of federal power: it would be an attempt to carve out of the scope of the Commerce Clause matters that are part of or are closely related to that Clause's core meaning, which is that Congress can control the conditions of all trade and commerce that affect more states than one. We doubt that Professor Tribe is taking so extreme a stance.

While Professor Tribe says little about the specific nature of "restructuring of the power alignment as between the National Government and the States" that, in his view, triggers the application of the Treaty Clause, he does claim that enactment of the GATT implementing legislation "would entail a significant shift of sovereignty from state and local governments to the proposed World Trade Organization (WTO), in which the interests of those entities would be represented exclusively by" [the U.S. Trade Representative]. We assume, therefore, that it is this particular feature of the GATT Uruguay Round that, in Professor Tribe's opinion, implicates the requirement for Senate approval under the Treaty Clause. Professor Tribe thus appears to be arguing that because the GATT Uruguay Round would diminish state sovereignty while augmenting the authority of the WTO—a foreign forum in which the states would be unable to represent themselves—that agreement can only be adopted in accordance with a procedure that provides maximum protection to the states. That procedure is found in the treaty ratification process, in which the states, by virtue of their equal representation in the Senate, are peculiarly well positioned to defend their own interests.

We do not dispute that the "the Constitution's federal structure imposes limitations on the Commerce Clause." Garcia v. San Antonio Metro. Transit Auth., 469 U.S. 528, 547 (1985). We also agree that state sovereignty within the federal system is "protected by procedural safeguards inherent in the structure of the federal system." *Id.* at 552. Finally, we agree that among the procedural devices in the Constitution for protecting the rights and interests of the states, the equal representation of the states in the Senate is particularly important.

We do not understand, however, why the asserted transfer of state authority to the WTO (even were this the case) should require the approval of two-thirds of the Senate, rather than a majority of both Houses of Congress. . . . Congress's powers vis-à-vis the States are no less "broad" under the Foreign Commerce Clause than they are under the Interstate Commerce Clause. If the Constitution permits Congress, when acting under the Interstate Commerce Clause, to affect the scope of state authority by majority votes of both Houses (together, of course, with Presidential approval), we see no reason why the states should be entitled to a different and more protective procedure when Congress affects them by acting under the Foreign Commerce Clause. In both contexts, the states may rely on their influence on the legislative process.

Letter from Senators Biden and Helms to Secretary of State Powell

March 15, 2002

[In November 2001, President Bush suggested that he and Russian President Vladimir Putin could achieve large cuts in nuclear weapons through an informal "handshake," but added that "if we need to write it down on a piece of paper, I'll be glad to do that." Presidential News Conference, November 19, 2001, in 37 Public Papers of the President No. 46 (2001). Some commentators interpreted this statement to be a proposal to achieve arms control through some kind of an executive agreement rather than through the Article II treaty process. During testimony before the Senate Foreign Relations Committee in February 2002, Secretary of State Colin Powell announced that the President did in fact intend to negotiate a legally binding agreement with Russia. One month later, the senior Democratic and Republican members of the Senate Foreign Relations Committee sent Secretary of State Powell the following letter.]

Dear Mr. Secretary:

Your February 5 testimony before the Committee on Foreign Relations indicates that the Administration has decided to negotiate a legally-binding agreement with the Russian Federation on further strategic arms reductions. Various subsequent reports left the same impression.

Clearly, any such agreement would most likely include significant obligations by the United States regarding deployed U.S. strategic nuclear warheads. We are therefore convinced that such an agreement would constitute a treaty subject to the advice and consent of the Senate.

With the exception of the SALT I agreement,* every significant arms control agreement during the past three decades has been transmitted to the Senate pursuant to the Treaty Clause of the Constitution. Mr. Secretary, we see no reason whatsoever to alter this practice, especially since it clearly appears that a legally binding bilateral agreement with Russia would in all likelihood incorporate (or continue) certain aspects of the START I Treaty.

Indeed, the question of Senate prerogative regarding international arms control agreements has been previously addressed by the Senate. In Declaration (5) of the START I Treaty resolution of ratification, the Senate stated its intent to consider for approval all international agreements obligating the United States to reduce or limit its military power in a significant manner, pursuant to the treaty power set forth in Article II, Section 2, Clause 2 of the Constitution.

Mr. Secretary, it is therefore clear that no Constitutional alternative exists to transmittal of the concluded agreement to the Senate for its advice and consent. . . .

Joseph R. Biden, Jr. (Chairman)
Jesse Helms (Ranking Member)

[President Bush subsequently made clear that he would submit the referenced arms reduction treaty with Russia to the Senate for its advice and consent. He and President Putin signed this treaty in May 2002, the Senate unanimously gave its advice and consent to the treaty in March 2003, and the treaty was formally ratified in June 2003.]

Notes and Questions

1. The U.S. government has made congressional-executive agreements since early in U.S. history. In 1792, for example, Congress authorized the Postmaster General to conclude international agreements concerning the exchange of mail. *See* Act of Feb. 20, 1792, ch. 7, §26, 1 Stat. 232, 239. This statute was the basis for U.S. international postal agreements for over a century. In 1890, Solicitor General William Howard Taft explained that "[f]rom the foundation of the Government to the present day . . . the Constitution has been interpreted to mean that the power vested in the President to make treaties, with the concurrence of two-thirds of the Senate, does not exclude the right of Congress to vest in the Postmaster-General power to conclude conventions with foreign governments for the cheaper, safer, and more convenient carriage of foreign mails." *Postal Conventions with Foreign Countries,* 19 Op. Att'y Gen. 513, 520 (1890).

2. Over the course of American history, the U.S. government has grown to rely much more on executive agreements (a category that includes congressional-executive agreements and sole executive agreements) than on treaties. From 1789-1839, the United States entered into 60 treaties and 27 executive agreements. The period from 1839-1889 saw a roughly equal split between treaties and executive agreements. Between 1889 and 1939, the United States concluded 524 treaties and 917 executive agreements. The balance swung sharply beginning around World War II. During

---

* [The 1972 SALT I arms control agreement was approved as a congressional-executive agreement rather than as an Article II treaty. *See* Strategic Arms Limitation I Agreement, Pub. L. No. 79-448, 86 Stat. 746.—EDS.]

the period 1939-1989, the United States concluded 702 treaties and 12,880 executive agreements. Congressional Research Service, *Treaties and Other International Agreements: The Role of the United States Senate*, S. Prt. 106-71, 106th Cong., 2d Sess. 39 (2001). This trend has continued and even accelerated in recent years. *See* Oona A. Hathaway, *Treaties' End: The Past, Present, and Future of International Lawmaking in the United States*, 117 Yale L.J. 1236, 1287 (2008) (249 treaties and 2,857 executive agreements from 1990 to 2000); Jeffrey Peake, *The Decline of Treaties? Obama, Trump, and the Politics of International Agreements*, Annual Meeting of the American Political Science Association 40 (Apr. 6, 2018) (111 treaties and 2,652 executive agreements between 2001 and 2012).

Although estimates vary, a large majority of modern executive agreements are congressional-executive agreements rather than sole executive agreements. Why has there been such a substantial increase in the relative use of congressional-executive agreements? Is this related to the mid-century rise in Executive Branch power in foreign affairs? Might it reflect the increasing number and complexity of U.S. government activities abroad? What, if anything, does the frequent use of congressional-executive agreements suggest about their constitutionality? Is it relevant that congressional-executive agreements have not usually generated interbranch conflict?

3. Most congressional-executive agreements are *ex ante* congressional-executive agreements. These agreements cover every conceivable topic, but the most common ones are defense and trade. For example, since 1949, presidents have, without returning to Congress, made dozens of international agreements with foreign nations pursuant to the Mutual Defense Assistance Act of 1949. That law states that the President shall "conclude agreements . . . to effectuate the policies and purposes of this Act," which include providing various forms of military assistance to support individual and collective self-defense in order to maintain and achieve peace and security. Similarly, presidents have made over a dozen international trade agreements pursuant to the Reciprocal Trade Agreements Act of 1934. That law states that the President "is authorized . . . to enter into foreign trade agreements with foreign governments or instrumentalities" if (among other things) the President finds that doing so would expand foreign markets for U.S. products.

The executive agreements made pursuant to these latter two statutes are expressly authorized by Congress. Not all congressional-executive agreements have such an explicit statutory basis. To take just one example, some congressional-executive agreements rest on the Act for International Development of 1961, which authorizes the President merely to "furnish military assistance on such terms and conditions as he may determine, to any friendly country or international organization, [by] acquiring from any source and providing (by loan, lease, sale, exchange, grant, or any other means) any defense article or defense service." Does the authorizing statute need to mention its support for an agreement explicitly, even if it does not specify the agreement's content? Or does a general authorization of executive action suffice because, under the principles laid down in *Curtiss-Wright* and other cases, statutory delegations of authority to the President in foreign affairs should be read generously?

4. *Ex post* congressional-executive agreements are rarer than *ex ante* agreements but tend to involve more significant commitments. Famous examples of important *ex post* congressional-executive agreements after World War II include the Bretton Woods Agreement (which established the International Monetary Fund and the World Bank), the GATT and NAFTA trade agreements, the SALT I arms control agreement, and the U.N. Headquarters Agreement. To give you a sense of the statutory basis for these agreements, the one for NAFTA stated that "Congress approves . . . the North American Free Trade Agreement entered into on December 17, 1992, with the Governments of Canada and Mexico." And the statute for SALT I stated, "The President is hereby authorized to approve on behalf of the United States the interim agreement between the United States of America and the Union of Soviet Socialist Republics on certain measures with respect to the limitation of strategic offensive arms . . . signed at Moscow on May 26, 1972."

5. Notice how much more discretion an *ex ante* congressional-executive agreement gives the President compared to a treaty or an *ex post* congressional-executive agreement. With the latter forms of agreement, the President brings a negotiated document with specific terms to the Senate or Congress for its approval or rejection. But with an *ex ante* congressional-executive agreement, Congress in advance and in general terms authorizes the President to make an agreement (or many agreements) that Congress never formally reviews before ratification. The authorization gives the President enormous discretion about how to craft the agreement. And very often an *ex ante* congressional-executive agreement is based on a statute that was enacted long before—perhaps even many decades before—the agreement. Professor Hathaway concludes from these factors that *ex ante* agreements "possess the form of congressional-executive cooperation without true collaboration." Oona A. Hathaway, *Presidential Power Over International Law: Restoring the Balance*, 119 Yale L. J. 140, 212-13 (2009). Do you agree? Does this conclusion detract from the constitutional legitimacy of *ex ante* congressional-executive agreements compared to the *ex post* version or a treaty? Why is an *ex ante* congressional-executive agreement any less legitimate than a domestic regulation based on an open-ended authorizing statute? Does it matter that, in contrast to an *ex ante* congressional-executive agreement, such a domestic regulation is governed by the procedural rules of the Administrative Procedure Act and may be subject to judicial review before promulgation?

6. Although the Supreme Court has never directly addressed the constitutionality of congressional-executive agreements, it has appeared to assume their validity in several decisions. In Weinberger v. Rossi, 456 U.S. 25 (1982), for example, the Court interpreted the word "treaty" in an employment discrimination statute as referring not only to Article II treaties, but also to congressional-executive agreements. The Court noted that the United States has entered into numerous such agreements, that they are binding on the United States, and that Congress sometimes uses the word "treaty" to refer to them. *See also* B. Altman & Co. v. United States, 224 U.S. 583 (1912) (construing the word "treaty" in a jurisdictional statute as including congressional-executive agreements); Field v. Clark, 143 U.S. 649 (1892) (upholding congressional delegation of tariff authority to the Executive Branch and citing, among other things, the history of congressional authorizations of executive trade agreements).

7. What is the precise constitutional basis on which the court in *Made in the USA Foundation* upholds the legality of NAFTA? Does the Article II Treaty Clause indicate that all international agreements entered into by the United States must go through the two-thirds senatorial advice and consent process? Does it indicate that at least *some* international agreements must go through this process? Do Congress's Article I powers provide a basis for congressional-executive agreements? Is Congress's power to make legislation on certain subjects tantamount to a power to approve international agreements on those subjects? Of what relevance to this issue is Congress's Necessary and Proper power?

Of what relevance is Article I, Section 10 of the Constitution? It precludes states from ever entering into a "treaty, alliance, or confederation," but it allows them to enter into an "agreement or compact . . . with a foreign power" if they obtain Congress's consent. This suggests that the Founders knew of international agreements other than what they called "treaties." But does this cut for or against the validity of congressional-executive agreements? On the one hand, it suggests that "treaties" are not the exclusive way to make international agreements. On the other hand, the fact that Article II of the constitution refers only to a federal government power to make "treaties" might cut against the validity of congressional-executive agreements. Or is it absurd to attribute to the Founders the view that there were certain international agreements that the federal government could not enter into?

8. The plaintiffs in *Made in the USA Foundation* appealed to the U.S. Court of Appeals for the Eleventh Circuit, which held that the constitutional challenge to NAFTA was nonjusticiable. While noting that "certain international agreements may well require Senate ratification as treaties through the constitutionally-mandated procedures of Art. II, §2," the court concluded that, at least in the context of that case, "the issue of what kinds of agreements require Senate ratification pursuant to the Art. II, §2 procedures presents a nonjusticiable political question." Made in the USA Foundation v. United States, 242 F.3d 1300, 1302, 1319 (11th Cir. 2001). Was this a proper application of the political question doctrine? Was this case more like Goldwater v. Carter, where the Supreme Court declined to exercise judicial review, or INS v. Chadha, where the Court exercised judicial review? (The political question doctrine is considered in detail in Chapter 2.) *Cf.* Star-Kist Foods, Inc. v. United States, 275 F.2d 472 (C.C.P.A. 1959) (holding that it was constitutional for the government to conclude a trade agreement with Iceland as a congressional-executive agreement).

9. Are congressional-executive agreements interchangeable with treaties? In other words, could any U.S. international agreement be entered into by either method? The Restatement (Third) of Foreign Relations Law maintains that "the prevailing view is that the Congressional-Executive agreement can be used as an alternative to the treaty method in every instance," and adds that "which procedure should be used is a political judgment, made in the first instance by the President." Restatement (Third) of the Foreign Relations Law of the United States §303 cmt. e (1987); *see also* Louis Henkin, Foreign Affairs and the United States Constitution 218 (2d ed. 1996); Bruce Ackerman & David Golove, *Is NAFTA Constitutional?*, 108 Harv. L. Rev. 799 (1995). Several scholars have questioned this conventional wisdom, arguing in various (and not always consistent) ways that treaties and congressional-executive agreements are not, and should not be, perfectly interchangeable. *See, e.g.*, John C. Yoo, *Laws as Treaties?: The Constitutionality of Congressional-Executive Agreements*, 99 Mich. L. Rev. 757 (2001); Peter J. Spiro, *Constitutional Method and the Great Treaty Debate*, 79 Tex. L. Rev. 961 (2001); and Joel R. Paul, *The Geopolitical Constitution: Executive Expediency and Executive Agreements*, 86 Cal. L. Rev. 671 (1998).

In considering the substitutability of treaties and congressional-executive agreements, what is the relevance, if any, of the fact that arms control agreements (with the exception of SALT I), human rights agreements, and extradition agreements are almost always concluded through the Article II process? *See* Yoo, *supra*, at 803-13; Spiro, *supra*, at 996-1002. Why have presidents consistently submitted these types of international agreements to the Senate? Does this practice have constitutional significance?

10. Professor Hathaway argues that the historical practice should not count against the interchangeability of treaties and congressional-executive agreements.

See Oona A. Hathaway, *Treaties' End: The Past, Present, and Future of International Lawmaking in the United States,* 117 Yale L.J. 1236 (2008). Based on an empirical analysis of international agreements concluded by the United States between 1980 and 2000, she finds that although the U.S. treaty practice does not show full interchangeability, it also (in her view) does not conform to any rational constitutional or normative pattern. Thus, as she explains:

> [M]ost free trade agreements are concluded through congressional-executive agreements. By contrast, agreements on investment and commercial matters—issues no less critical to the smooth operation of the global economy—are concluded through both treaties and congressional-executive agreements. The Law of the Sea Convention . . . was brought to the Senate under the Treaty Clause. But most other fisheries and maritime agreements are concluded through congressional-executive agreements. Human rights agreements are concluded as treaties. Meanwhile, the vast majority of education, health, and debt-restructuring agreements with developing countries—issues that can be just as important to human dignity—are concluded as congressional-executive agreements. Compared with agreements authorized as congressional-executive agreements, a higher share of agreements considered under the Treaty Clause are multilateral. Nevertheless, the vast majority of multilateral agreements are concluded through congressional-executive agreements.

Id. at 1240. Hathaway contends that the lack of full interchangeability of Article II treaties and congressional-executive agreements is the product of outdated regional conflicts at the Founding (some of which were related to slavery) and the opposition to human rights treaties in the 1950s (some of which came from segregationists in the South). She also argues that congressional-executive agreements are more democratically legitimate than Article II treaties because they include the House of Representatives in the process and because they require only majority approval. For these and other reasons, she concludes that almost all types of agreements currently concluded as Article II treaties should now be concluded as congressional-executive agreements.

Even if the historical practice is not fully rational or logical, might it nevertheless affect institutional expectations? Might the existence of specific constitutional text in Article II have an effect on the practice? Is it likely that the Senate will voluntarily cede what is left of its supermajority role in the process of making international agreements? Does the mere fact that a constitutional rule or process is not majoritarian mean that it should be abandoned?

11. Hathaway also finds that the United States "is unusual in requiring a supermajority legislative vote to approve treaties, it is in the distinct minority in excluding a part of the legislature that is usually involved in domestic lawmaking from international lawmaking, and it is among a small handful of countries that combine the latter feature with a rule that makes treaties automatically a part of domestic law." Hathaway, *Treaties' End,* at 1274. Is this comparative analysis relevant to how the U.S. Constitution should be interpreted? Is the unusual nature of the U.S. treaty process surprising, given the age of the U.S. Constitution and its unique version of federalism?

12. In 1997, President Bill Clinton agreed to submit the Flank Agreement, an update of the Treaty on Armed Conventional Forces in Europe (CFE Treaty), to the Senate for its Article II consent. This action marked an abandonment of an earlier decision to seek only a congressional majority approval for the Flank Agreement. *See* Phillip R. Trimble & Alexander W. Koff, *All Fall Down: The Treaty*

Power in the Clinton Administration, 16 Berkeley J. Int'l L. 55 (1998). In connection with the original CFE Treaty, the Senate had attached, as a condition of its consent, a declaration stating that international agreements that "reduce or limit the armed forces or armaments of the United States in a militarily significant manner" can be approved only pursuant to the Article II treaty process. *See* 137 Cong. Rec. S17846 (daily ed. Nov. 23, 1991). In a letter to the Senate, a presidential advisor noted that submission of the Flank Agreement for Senate approval was "without prejudice to its legal position vis-à-vis the approval options we believe are available to us." Letter from Samuel R. Berger, Assistant to the President for National Security Affairs, to Trent Lott, Majority Leader of the Senate, dated March 25, 1997, quoted in The Arms Control Reporter 1997 at 603.D.45. What does this episode suggest about the validity of congressional-executive agreements? About the limits on those agreements? About how the Senate's treaty prerogatives can be enforced?

13. What is the significance of the Biden-Helms letter to President Bush, excerpted above? Do you think this letter influenced the President to submit the arms control agreement with Russia to the Senate? Is the letter an indication that the President would face political difficulties with the Senate if he or she decided not to submit the agreement there? Does the letter have *legal* significance?

14. Consider these remarks by Harold Koh, then-Legal Adviser to the State Department, explaining why the Executive Branch sometimes seeks to conclude international agreements as Article II treaties rather than as congressional-executive agreements:

> I am sometimes asked, why don't we just ratify a particular convention by congressional-executive agreement, rather than Article II treaty? If it is so hard to get sixty-seven votes for a treaty, why don't we just accede to it by statute? The short answer, which you will understand sitting here less than a mile from the Capitol, is that a particular nontreaty route might be legally available to the Executive for entering into certain kinds of international agreements but may not be politically advisable as a matter of comity to Congress. Congress has its own strong views on how certain types of agreements should be entered into and will fight for those outcomes as a matter of institutional and political prerogative. That does not mean that the Executive's hands are tied in any given case. But what it does mean is that a key part of being an Executive Branch lawyer is accurately forecasting to your clients when choosing a particular legal route—even if lawful—may foster bitter political conflict and invite unnecessary trouble.

Harold Hongju Koh, *Twenty-First-Century International Lawmaking,* 101 Geo. L.J. 725, 728 (2013). Does this suggest that any constraints on the use of congressional-executive agreements as an alternative to Article II treaties are entirely political rather than legal? Why does "Congress ha[ve] its own strong views on how certain types of agreements should be entered into"?

15. Does interchangeability mean that if an international agreement fails to obtain the required two-thirds senatorial consent in the Article II process, the President can simply resubmit it to Congress for a majority vote? Or must the President choose one method and stick to it? Consider the fate of the Comprehensive Nuclear Test Ban Treaty. In October 1999, the Senate declined to give the requisite two-thirds consent to the treaty; 51 Senators voted against the treaty, 48 in its favor. If President Clinton could have persuaded two "no" voters to switch (thereby giving him a majority of support in the Senate), could he have resubmitted the treaty to the House and Senate as a congressional-executive agreement?

16. Assuming that every type of international agreement that could be done by treaty could also be done by congressional-executive agreement, are the two forms of international agreement treated alike for other purposes? For example, does the analysis of Missouri v. Holland, excerpted in Section C of Chapter 5, apply to congressional-executive agreements? That is, can congressional-executive agreements be used to regulate domestic matters that fall outside of Congress's legislative authority? *See, e.g.,* Hathaway, *Treaties' End,* at 1339 ("In contrast with Article II treaties, congressional-executive agreements cannot exceed the bounds placed by the Constitution on congressional authority."). Do congressional-executive agreements warrant the same degree of judicial deference to Executive Branch interpretation as treaties? Do the same rules of self-execution that apply to treaties also apply to congressional-executive agreements? How about the later-in-time rule? Do the same separation of powers limitations that apply to treaties (such as the bar on creating domestic criminal law by treaty) apply to congressional-executive agreements?

17. Congress can override presidential vetoes and enact legislation by two-thirds approval of both Houses. Does it follow that both houses of Congress could, through a two-thirds vote, enter into a congressional-executive agreement without the President's approval? If not, what does this tell us about the validity of congressional-executive agreements?

18. Assuming that the President generally has the authority to act unilaterally in withdrawing the United States from Article II treaties (see Section G of Chapter 5), can he or she withdraw from a congressional-executive agreement? For example, President Trump has threatened to withdraw the United States from the NAFTA agreement, which in Section 2205 states that "[a] Party may withdraw from this Agreement six months after it provides written notice of withdrawal to the other Parties." Could he withdraw the United States from the agreement on his own authority? Note that when Congress approved NAFTA, it in the same law passed extensive implementing legislation. Some parts of this legislation delegate discretionary authority to the President (for example, to lower tariffs), which presumably a President could choose not to exercise. Other parts appear to be premised on continued U.S. participation in the agreement—for example, provisions relating to dispute resolution. If Trump invoked the NAFTA withdrawal clause, would he in effect be terminating the statute, which a President normally cannot do? Or would he simply be withdrawing the nation from an international agreement, leaving the domestic implementing legislation intact but otiose? Might the answer to this question be different for *ex ante* congressional-executive agreements than for *ex post* congressional-executive agreements?

For competing views on these issues, compare, for example, Curtis A. Bradley, *Exiting Congressional-Executive Agreements,* 67 Duke L.J. 1615 (2018) (arguing that presidential termination authority is the same for Article II treaties and congressional-executive agreements), with Joel Trachtman, *Power to Terminate U.S. Trade Agreements: The Presidential Dormant Commerce Clause Versus an Historical Gloss Half Empty,* 51 Int'l Law. 445 (2018) (arguing that presidents cannot unilaterally terminate congressional-executive agreements relating to trade). *See also* Alison Peck, *Withdrawing from NAFTA,* 107 Geo. L.J. 647 (2019) (concluding that the President does not have statutory or constitutional authority to withdraw the United States from NAFTA).

19. As of October 2019, the Trump Administration had acted to withdraw the United States from two *ex ante* congressional-executive agreements:

(1) In October 2017, the administration announced that it was withdrawing the United States from the United Nations Educational, Scientific and Cultural Organization (UNESCO), due to alleged anti-Israel bias. The United States joined UNESCO in 1946 pursuant to an authorization from Congress. The Trump Administration's action is not unprecedented: The Reagan administration withdrew the United States from UNESCO in 1984 without seeking congressional authorization. The George W. Bush administration later had the United States rejoin UNESCO, also without seeking congressional authorization. Pursuant to the terms of the UNESCO Constitution, the Trump Administration's withdrawal became effective on December 31, 2018.

(2) In October 2018, the Trump Administration announced that the United States was withdrawing from the Universal Postal Union (UPU), contending that the "current international postal practices in the UPU do not align with United States economic and national security interests." According to Article 12 of the UPU Constitution, the U.S. withdrawal becomes effective one year after its notice is received. The United States first joined the UPU in the 1870s pursuant to an *ex ante* congressional-executive agreement. Subsequent statutes have continued to delegate to the Executive Branch the authority to conclude postal agreements and amendments to such agreements, although these statutes do not mention authority to terminate the agreements. *See, e.g.*, Postal Accountability and Enhancement Act, Pub. L. No. 109-435, §405, 120 Stat. 3198, 3230 (2006) (codified at 39 U.S.C. §407). For discussion of the U.S. decision to withdraw from the UPU, see Eliot Kim, *Withdrawal from the Universal Postal Union: A Guide for the Perplexed*, Lawfare (Oct. 31, 2018). (In September 2019, an agreement was reached that averted the U.S. withdrawal.)

These announced withdrawals attracted relatively little congressional attention. Does congressional silence in the face of such withdrawals count in favor of their legality?

20. Scholars have engaged in a lively debate about the legitimacy and proper scope of congressional-executive agreements. *See, e.g.*, Ackerman & Golove, *supra*; David M. Golove, *Against Free-Form Formalism*, 73 N.Y.U. L. Rev. 1791 (1998); Hathaway, *Treaties' End*, *supra*; Paul, *supra*; Spiro, *supra*; Tribe, *supra*; Yoo, *supra*. For an earlier debate, see Edwin Borchard, *Shall the Executive Agreement Replace the Treaty?*, 53 Yale L.J. 664 (1944); Edwin Borchard, *Treaties and Executive Agreements—A Reply*, 54 Yale L.J. 616 (1945); Myres McDougal & Asher Lans, *Treaties and Congressional-Executive or Presidential Agreements: Interchangeable Instruments of National Policy* (pt. 1), 54 Yale L.J. 184 (1945); and Myres McDougal & Asher Lans, *Treaties and Congressional-Executive or Presidential Agreements: Interchangeable Instruments of National Policy* (pt. 2), 54 Yale L.J. 534 (1945).

B. SOLE EXECUTIVE AGREEMENTS

"Sole executive agreements" are executive agreements concluded by the President on the basis of his or her Article II authority and without congressional approval. The Supreme Court has upheld the validity of sole executive agreements in several decisions. In addition to the materials excerpted below, review Dames & Moore v. Regan, which is excerpted in Chapter 3, and American Insurance Association v. Garamendi, which is excerpted in Chapter 4.

United States v. Belmont

301 U.S. 324 (1937)

MR. JUSTICE SUTHERLAND delivered the opinion of the Court.

This is an action at law brought by petitioner against respondents in a federal district court to recover a sum of money deposited by a Russian corporation (Petrograd Metal Works) with August Belmont, a private banker doing business in New York City under the name of August Belmont & Co. August Belmont died in 1924; and respondents are the duly-appointed executors of his will. . . .

The corporation had deposited with Belmont, prior to 1918, the sum of money which petitioner seeks to recover. In 1918, the Soviet Government duly enacted a decree by which it dissolved, terminated and liquidated the corporation (together with others), and nationalized and appropriated all of its property and assets of every kind and wherever situated, including the deposit account with Belmont. As a result, the deposit became the property of the Soviet Government, and so remained until November 16, 1933, at which time the Soviet Government released and assigned to petitioner all amounts due to that government from American nationals, including the deposit account of the corporation with Belmont. Respondents failed and refused to pay the amount upon demand duly made by petitioner.

The assignment was effected by an exchange of diplomatic correspondence between the Soviet Government and the United States. The purpose was to bring about a final settlement of the claims and counterclaims between the Soviet Government and the United States; and it was agreed that the Soviet Government would take no steps to enforce claims against American nationals; but all such claims were released and assigned to the United States, with the understanding that the Soviet Government was to be duly notified of all amounts realized by the United States from such release and assignment. The assignment and requirement for notice are parts of the larger plan to bring about a settlement of the rival claims of the high contracting parties. The continuing and definite interest of the Soviet Government in the collection of assigned claims is evident; and the case, therefore, presents a question of public concern, the determination of which well might involve the good faith of the United States in the eyes of a foreign government. The court below held that the assignment thus effected embraced the claim here in question; and with that we agree.

That court, however, took the view that the situs of the bank deposit was within the State of New York; that in no sense could it be regarded as an intangible property right within Soviet territory; and that the nationalization decree, if enforced, would put into effect an act of confiscation. And it held that a judgment for the United States could not be had, because, in view of that result, it would be contrary to the controlling public policy of the State of New York. The further contention is made by respondents that the public policy of the United States would likewise be infringed by such a judgment. The two questions thus presented are the only ones necessary to be considered.

First. We do not pause to inquire whether in fact there was any policy of the State of New York to be infringed, since we are of opinion that no state policy can prevail against the international compact here involved. . . .

We take judicial notice of the fact that coincident with the assignment set forth in the complaint, the President recognized the Soviet Government, and normal diplomatic relations were established between that government and the Government of the United States, followed by an exchange of ambassadors. The effect of this was to validate, so far as this country is concerned, all acts of the Soviet Government here involved from the commencement of its existence. The recognition, establishment of diplomatic relations, the assignment, and agreements with respect thereto, were all parts of one transaction, resulting in an international compact between the two governments. That the negotiations, acceptance of the assignment and agreements and understandings in respect thereof were within the competence of the President may not be doubted. Governmental power over internal affairs is distributed between the national government and the several states. Governmental power over external affairs is not distributed, but is vested exclusively in the national government. And in respect of what was done here, the Executive had authority to speak as the sole organ of that government. The assignment and the agreements in connection therewith did not, as in the case of treaties, as that term is used in the treaty making clause of the Constitution (Art. II, §2), require the advice and consent of the Senate.

A treaty signifies "a compact made between two or more independent nations with a view to the public welfare." Altman & Co. v. United States, 224 U.S. 583, 600. But an international compact, as this was, is not always a treaty which requires the participation of the Senate. There are many such compacts, of which a protocol, a modus vivendi, a postal convention, and agreements like that now under consideration are illustrations. The distinction was pointed out by this court in the *Altman* case, *supra,* which arose under §3 of the Tariff Act of 1897, authorizing the President to conclude commercial agreements with foreign countries in certain specified matters. We held that although this might not be a treaty requiring ratification by the Senate, it was a compact negotiated and proclaimed under the authority of the President, and as such was a "treaty" within the meaning of the Circuit Court of Appeals Act, the construction of which might be reviewed upon direct appeal to this court.

Plainly, the external powers of the United States are to be exercised without regard to state laws or policies. The supremacy of a treaty in this respect has been recognized from the beginning. Mr. Madison, in the Virginia Convention, said that if a treaty does not supersede existing state laws, as far as they contravene its operation, the treaty would be ineffective. "To counteract it by the supremacy of the state laws, would bring on the Union the just charge of national perfidy, and involve us in war." 3 Elliot's Debates 515. *And see* Ware v. Hylton, 3 Dall. 199, 236-37. And while this rule in respect of treaties is established by the express language of cl. 2, Art. VI, of the Constitution, the same rule would result in the case of all international compacts and agreements from the very fact that complete power over international affairs is in the national government and is not and cannot be subject to any curtailment or interference on the part of the several states. *Compare* United States v. Curtiss-Wright Export Corp., 299 U.S. 304, 316, et seq. In respect of all international negotiations and compacts, and in respect of our foreign relations generally, state lines disappear. As to such purposes the State of New York does not exist. Within the field of its powers, whatever the United States rightfully undertakes, it necessarily has warrant to consummate. And when judicial authority is invoked in aid of such consummation, state constitutions, state laws, and state policies are irrelevant to the inquiry and decision. It is inconceivable that any of them can be interposed as an obstacle to the effective operation of a federal constitutional power. *Cf.* Missouri v. Holland, 252 U.S. 416; Asakura v. Seattle, 265 U.S. 332, 341.

U.S. State Department, Foreign Affairs Manual

11 FAM 723.3: Considerations for Selecting among Constitutionally
Authorized Procedures

In determining a question as to the procedure which should be followed for any
particular international agreement, due consideration is given to the following
factors. . . .

    (1) The extent to which the agreement involves commitments or risks
        affecting the nation as a whole;

    (2) Whether the agreement is intended to affect State laws;

    (3) Whether the agreement can be given effect without the enactment of
        subsequent legislation by the Congress;

    (4) Past U.S. practice as to similar agreements;

    (5) The preference of the Congress as to a particular type of agreement;

    (6) The degree of formality desired for an agreement;

    (7) The proposed duration of the agreement, the need for prompt conclu-
        sion of the agreement, and the desirability of conducting a routine or
        short-term agreement; and

    (8) The general international practice as to similar agreements.

In determining whether any international agreement should be brought into
force as a treaty or as an international agreement other than a treaty, the utmost
care is to be exercised to avoid any invasion or compromise of the constitutional
powers of the Senate, the Congress as a whole, or the President.

Case-Zablocki Act

1 U.S.C. §112b (first enacted in 1972)

(a) The Secretary of State shall transmit to the Congress the text of any international
agreement (including the text of any oral international agreement, which agreement shall be reduced to writing), other than a treaty, to which the United States is a
party as soon as practicable after such agreement has entered into force with respect
to the United States but in no event later than sixty days thereafter. However, any
such agreement the immediate public disclosure of which would, in the opinion of
the President, be prejudicial to the national security of the United States shall not
be so transmitted to the Congress but shall be transmitted to the Committee on
Foreign Relations of the Senate and the Committee on [International Relations]
of the House of Representatives under an appropriate injunction of secrecy to be
removed only upon due notice from the President. Any department or agency of
the United States Government which enters into any international agreement on
behalf of the United States shall transmit to the Department of State the text of such
agreement not later than twenty days after such agreement has been signed.

Notes and Questions

1. Presidents have entered into "sole" executive agreements since the beginning of the nation. *See* Wilfred McClure, International Executive Agreements 53

(1941); Michael D. Ramsey, *Executive Agreements and the (Non)Treaty Power,* 77 N.C. L. Rev. 133 (1998). These agreements bind the United States on the international plane just as would a treaty with Senate participation. Most sole executive agreements have concerned relatively insignificant or short-term matters. But they also have included important matters, such as the Litvinov agreement at issue in *Belmont* and the Algiers Accords at issue in Dames & Moore v. Regan (excerpted in Chapter 3). What is the constitutional authority for sole executive agreements? Are there any limits on sole executive agreements? How would limits be discerned? How would they be enforced?

2. The asserted basis for the Litvinov Agreement was the President's power to recognize foreign governments. This power, in turn, purportedly stems from the President's power in Article II to "receive Ambassadors and other public Ministers." Does the recognition power flow from this Article II provision? In any event, does the power to recognize include the power to make international agreements relating to recognition? If so, how closely related must the agreements be to the recognition?

3. As both Dames & Moore v. Regan and American Insurance Association v. Garamendi (excerpted in Chapter 4) suggest, a prominent subject of sole executive agreements concerns the settlement of claims of American nationals against foreign governments. This practice dates back to the founding of the nation. *See* Evan T. Bloom, Note, *The Executive Claims Settlement Power: Constitutional Authority and Foreign Affairs Applications,* 85 Colum. L. Rev. 155 (1985) (recounting this history). As the Court noted in *Garamendi,* the first example was "as early as 1789, when the Washington administration settled demands against the Dutch Government by American citizens who lost their cargo when Dutch privateers overtook the schooner *Wilmington Packet.*" Traditionally, these executive agreements resolved claims against foreign sovereigns, and were practically the only recourse that U.S. citizens had to recovering property and related losses from foreign governments. But as the litigation in *Garamendi* shows, beginning in the 1990s, President Clinton extended such agreements to include claims by U.S. citizens against private parties where there may have been alternate mechanisms of redress. *See generally* Ingrid Brunk Wuerth, *The Dangers of Deference: International Claim Settlement by the President,* 44 Harv. Int'l L.J. 1 (2003) (describing and criticizing this trend).

Why exactly does the President have the power to enter into international agreements that settle claims between U.S. citizens and foreign governments? Some settlements occur when the U.S. victims have little alternate recourse and thus might be said to be grounded in the consent or acquiescence of the claimants, in which case the President would be exercising his or her authority as diplomatic representative of the nation in espousing their claims. Other settlements occur in the context of recognition (such as in *Belmont*) or in emergency or war situations where the President is arguably exercising commander-in-chief authority (such as in *Dames & Moore*). But where does the President obtain the authority to settle claims outside these contexts? From his or her role as the "sole organ" of communication in foreign relations? From the Article II Vesting Clause?

4. Consider Article I, Section 10 of the Constitution, which prohibits states from entering into "any Treaty," and requires that they obtain congressional consent before entering into "any Agreement or Compact . . . with a foreign Power." What is the difference between a "Treaty" and an "Agreement or Compact"? Is this distinction relevant to the validity of sole executive agreements? The Supreme Court discussed this distinction in Holmes v. Jennison, 39 U.S. (14 Pet.) 540 (1840). In that case, the issue was whether Vermont was precluded by Article I, Section 10 from extraditing an individual to Canada. A plurality of the Court concluded that, although Vermont's agreement with Canada to extradite the individual was not a "treaty," it was an "agreement" and thus required congressional authorization. The Court stated:

> But it may be said, that here is no treaty; and, undoubtedly, in the sense in which that word is generally understood, there is no treaty between Vermont and Canada. For when we speak of "a treaty," we mean an instrument written and executed with the formalities customary among nations; and as no clause in the Constitution ought to be interpreted differently from the usual and fair import of the words used, if the decision of this case depended upon the word above mentioned, we should not be prepared to say that there was any express prohibition of the power exercised by the state of Vermont.
>
> But the question does not rest upon the prohibition to enter into a treaty. In the very next clause of the Constitution, the states are forbidden to enter into any "agreement" or "compact" with a foreign nation; and as these words could not have been idly or superfluously used by the framers of the Constitution, they cannot be construed to mean the same thing with the word treaty. They evidently mean something more, and were designed to make the prohibition more comprehensive.
>
> A few extracts from an eminent writer on the laws of nations, showing the manner in which these different words have been used, and the different meanings sometimes attached to them, will, perhaps, contribute to explain the reason for using them all in the Constitution; and will prove that the most comprehensive terms were employed in prohibiting to the states all intercourse with foreign nations[:]
>
>> Vattel, page 192, sec. 152, says: "A treaty, in Latin faedus, is a compact made with a view to the public welfare, by the superior power, either for perpetuity, or for a considerable time."
>>
>> Section 153. "The compacts which have temporary matters for their object, are called agreements, conventions, and pactions. They are accomplished by one single act, and not by repeated acts. These compacts are perfected in their execution once for all; treaties receive a successive execution, whose duration equals that of the treaty."
>>
>> Section 154. Public treaties can only be made by the "supreme power, by sovereigns who contract in the name of the state. Thus conventions made between sovereigns respecting their own private affairs, and those between a sovereign and a private person, are not public treaties."
>>
>> Section 206, page 218. "The public compacts called conventions, articles of agreement, &c., when they are made between sovereigns, differ from treaties only in their object."

Id. at 571-72. Does this distinction between treaties and agreements and compacts suggest possible limits on the sole executive agreement power? Does it help explain the historical practice of presidential settlement of claims? For a thorough examination of compacts between states and foreign governments, see Duncan B. Hollis, *Unpacking the Compact Clause*, 88 Tex. L. Rev. 741 (2010). Professor Hollis challenges the view that such "foreign-state agreements (FSAs)" are infrequent, unimportant, or otherwise identical to those interstate compacts for which congressional consent is, despite the language of the Compacts Clause, generally unnecessary. He shows that over 340 FSAs have been concluded by 41 U.S. states since 1955, with over 200 of these coming in the last decade, and he concludes that FSAs are increasing in number and importance. He then argues that FSAs require more federal scrutiny than interstate compacts because of their foreign relations implications, and he proposes that Congress rather than courts take the lead, through a notification requirement if not something more stringent, such as express congressional consent.

5. Even assuming that presidents have the power to make executive agreements that bind the United States on the international plane, does it follow that these agreements preempt state law? The *Belmont* decision was the first decision to hold that a sole executive agreement preempts state law. *See also* United States v. Pink, 315 U.S. 203 (1942) (reaffirming *Belmont*). What does the language of the Supremacy Clause suggest about the preemptive power of executive agreements? Assuming, as stated in *Belmont,* that "in respect of our foreign relations generally, . . . the State of New York does not exist," does it follow that there are no limits on the power of the President to make executive agreements that preempt state law? What about separation of powers concerns, such as a concern with undermining the Senate's constitutional role in treaty making or Congress's constitutional role in creating federal legislation?

6. Take another look at Dames & Moore v. Regan. Most of that decision focuses on the domestic sources of authority for President Carter's and President Reagan's executive orders nullifying and transferring attached Iranian funds, and suspending claims in U.S. courts. Why didn't the Court rely more heavily on the Algiers Accords, the executive agreement that ended the hostage crisis? After all, this agreement obligated the United States to "terminate all legal proceedings" in U.S. courts, to "nullify all attachments . . . obtained therein," and to "prohibit all further litigation based on such claims." Does the Court's failure to rely more heavily on the Algiers Accords as the source of presidential power suggest a retrenchment from *Belmont*? Or does it reflect the fact that the executive orders at issue in *Dames & Moore* argu-ably limited the effect of a federal statute (the Foreign Sovereign Immunities Act)?

7. Consider this view expressed by Professor Clark:

> Our constitutional history suggests that the President has incidental power to make nontreaty agreements as a means of implementing his independent constitutional and statutory authority, although the precise line between proper and improper agree-ments may be difficult to draw under the Treaty Clause. . . . [C]ourts should permit a sole executive agreement to override preexisting legal rights only when the President has independent authority to do so. In such instances, it is the President's exercise of his underlying power—rather than the agreement itself—that alters preexisting legal rights and duties. Permitting the President to expand his authority unilaterally by the simple expedient of making a sole executive agreement has little constitutional or his-torical support and would circumvent the carefully crafted checks and balances built into the constitutional structure.

Bradford R. Clark, *Domesticating Sole Executive Agreements*, 93 Va. L. Rev. 1573, 1575, 1577 (2007). Do you agree? Is this view consistent with the Supreme Court decisions that have enforced sole executive agreements?

8. In Medellin v. Texas, 552 U.S. 491 (2008), which is excerpted in Chapter 5, the Supreme Court described its sole executive agreement decisions as simply "[upholding] the authority of the President to settle foreign claims pursuant to an executive agreement," and the Court emphasized that those cases "involve[d] a narrow set of circumstances: the making of executive agreements to settle civil claims between American citizens and foreign governments or foreign nationals." *Id.* at 530. The Court concluded that "[t]he Executive's narrow and strictly limited authority to settle international claims disputes pursuant to an executive agreement cannot stretch so far as to support the [memorandum through which President Bush attempted to implement the ICJ's decision in *Avena*]." *Id.* at 532. What do these statements suggest about the scope of the President's authority to enter into sole executive agreements?

9. In November 2007, the governments of Iraq and the United States announced that they intended to "negotiate arrangements" based upon a range of principles, including the principle that the United States would "support the Iraqi government in training, equipping, and arming the Iraqi Security Forces so they can provide security and stability to all Iraqis; support the Iraqi government in contributing to the international fight against terrorism by confronting terrorists such as Al Qaeda, its affiliates, other terrorist groups, as well as all other outlaw groups, such as criminal remnants of the former regime; and to provide security assurances to the Iraqi Government to deter any external aggression and to ensure the integrity of Iraq's territory." *See* Fact Sheet: U.S.-Iraq Declaration of Principles for Friendship and Cooperation, available at https://2001-2009.state.gov/p/nea/rls/95640.htm.

Many commentators interpreted this announcement as an indication that the Bush Administration was planning to enter into a sole executive agreement committing the United States to indefinite security guarantees in Iraq that would outlast the Bush Administration. Could President Bush enter into such an agreement consistent with the U.S. Constitution? Would the Commander-in-Chief Clause be the constitutional basis for entering into such an agreement? Might the President draw additional authority for such an agreement from various U.N. Security Council Resolutions calling on the world community to contribute to stability and security in Iraq? Would such an agreement bind the next President under international law? Under domestic constitutional law? Could the next President unilaterally terminate the agreement consistent with the Constitution? If you were arguing against the constitutionality of such an agreement, how would you distinguish *Belmont* and *Dames & Moore*? What do the answers to these questions suggest about the status of sole executive agreements as "Laws" within the meaning of the Take Care Clause of Article II or the Supremacy Clause of Article VI?

10. How much guidance do the factors listed in the State Department's manual, excerpted above, provide in deciding whether an international agreement should go through the Article II treaty process? Do these factors adequately protect the constitutional powers of the Senate? Of the full Congress? Assuming it were proper for a court to evaluate the validity of an executive agreement, how much weight, if any, should it give to these factors?

11. What is the significance of Congress's enactment of the Case-Zablocki Act, excerpted above, for the validity of executive agreements? Is the Act constitutional? Judicially enforceable? A Senate study concludes that the Act "has been helpful in apprising Congress of executive agreements as defined by the Act," and that the Act "has contributed to improved relations between Congress and the executive branch in the area of executive agreements." Congressional Research Service, Treaties and Other International Agreements: The Role of the United States Senate, S. Prt. 106-71, 106th Cong., 2d Sess. 225 (2001). Between 1978 and 1999, more than 7,000 agreements were transmitted to Congress pursuant to the Act. *See id.* at 226-27.

12. The Anti-Counterfeiting Trade Agreement (ACTA) is a legally binding international agreement that establishes standards for the enforcement of intellectual property rights. In December 2010, the Obama Administration announced that it had concluded ACTA, and it indicated that it intended to join the agreement without seeking congressional or senatorial approval. Most observers at that point assumed that the administration was planning to conclude ACTA as a sole executive agreement, and a number of scholars objected that this would be unconstitutional. Whatever the scope of the sole executive agreement power, they argued, it did not extend to the conclusion of an intellectual property agreement, which was not connected to the President's independent constitutional powers, was not a settlement of claims, and was not a short-term or temporary arrangement. *See, e.g.,* Oona A. Hathaway & Amy Kapczynski, *Going It Alone: The Anti-Counterfeiting Trade Agreement as a Sole Executive Agreement,* ASIL Insights (Aug. 24, 2011). Senator Ron Wyden similarly raised questions about the administration's authority to conclude ACTA as a sole executive agreement, contending that "regardless of whether the agreement requires changes in U.S. law, a point that is contested with respect to ACTA, the executive branch lacks constitutional authority to *enter* a binding international agreement covering issues delegated by the Constitution to Congress' authority, absent congressional approval." Letter from Senator Ron Wyden to President Barack Obama (Oct. 12, 2011), at https://www.wyden.senate.gov/download/?id=f20e3fd3-f2f1-4fc2-a387-570a575700d6&download=1.

In response to a subsequent set of questions that Senator Wyden raised about ACTA, State Department Legal Adviser Harold Koh contended that ACTA "was negotiated in response to express Congressional calls for international cooperation to enhance enforcement of intellectual property rights." Letter from Harold Hongju Koh, State Department Legal Adviser, to Senator Ron Wyden (Mar. 6, 2012), at http://www.state.gov/documents/organization/211889.pdf. Koh cited in particular the Prioritizing Resources and Information for Intellectual Property Act of 2008 (the Pro-IP Act). The Pro-IP Act called on the Executive Branch to develop a Joint Strategic Plan against counterfeiting and infringement, and it stated that the objectives of the Plan should include "international standards and policies for the effective protection and enforcement of intellectual property rights." 5 U.S.C. §8113(a)(6). In a letter sent to the Senate, dozens of law scholars responded to the administration's reliance on the Pro-IP Act, arguing that nothing in the text of the statute specifically authorized the administration to conclude a binding international agreement and that, when the relevant language was read in context, it "does no more than require a multi-agency plan to provide technical assistance to foreign governments." The letter also pointed out that the statutory provision in question was not even directed at the Office of the U.S. Trade Representative (USTR), the agency that negotiated ACTA, and that it was enacted after USTR had already started negotiating ACTA. *See* Letter from Scholars to Members of Senate Committee on Finance (May 6, 2012), at http://infojustice.org/wp-content/uploads/2012/05/Law-Professor-Letter-to-Senate-Finance-Committee-May-16-20122.pdf.

Addressing this controversy, Koh stated:

Academics like to put things in boxes, and they tend to treat this area of law as divided into three. First, you have your treaty box. Second, you have your congressional-executive-agreement box, which is subdivided into ex ante agreements, where Congress first authorizes the agreement by statute, and the Executive then negotiates and concludes it; and ex post agreements, where the Executive first negotiates an agreement and then brings it to Congress for subsequent approval. Third, you have your sole-executive-agreement box, covering those areas where the President makes international law based on his independent constitutional authority.

But in the real world, this tidy framework grossly oversimplifies reality. There are a wealth of international agreements that are consistent with, and can be implemented under, existing law, but that do not fall neatly into any of these boxes. Many of these agreements may not even be intended to affect legal interests at the domestic level (e.g., by being judicially enforceable like in the *Pink* and *Belmont* cases). For example, recently, we in the Legal Adviser's Office were surprised to find controversy surrounding the Executive's authority to enter into the Anti-Counterfeiting Trade Agreement (ACTA), a multilateral agreement on enforcing intellectual property rights. Certainly, some of that controversy may have derived from policy disagreements with the goals of the ACTA, but a surprisingly large number of law professors questioned the Executive's legal authority even to enter the agreement. They said, in effect, "I don't see an express ex ante congressional authorization, so it can't fit into the congressional-executive agreement box, nor does this look like a traditional topic for a sole executive agreement. Since it falls between the stools, that must mean the U.S. lacks any authority to enter the agreement!"

What this misses is that legislative authority in the foreign affairs area sits not on isolated stools, but rather runs along a spectrum of congressional approval, as Justice Jackson suggested in his landmark concurrence in the Steel Seizure case. Why was entering the agreement a legally available option? First, while Congress did not expressly pre-authorize this particular agreement, it did pass legislation calling on the Executive to "work[] with other countries to establish international standards and policies for the effective protection and enforcement of intellectual property rights." Further, we and the United States Trade Representative (USTR) determined that the agreement negotiated fit within the fabric of existing law; it was fully consistent with existing law and did not require any further legislation to implement. We also surveyed how the political branches have dealt with similar agreements in the past and found that Congress's call for executive action to protect intellectual property rights arose against the background of a long series of agreements on the specific question of intellectual property protection done in a similar fashion. What we saw in practice resembles a phenomenon I called in my book *The National Security Constitution* "quasi-constitutional custom," a widespread and consistent practice of Executive Branch activity that Congress, by its conduct, has essentially accepted. In this respect, the ACTA resembled the Algiers Accords that ended the Iranian Hostage Crisis, whose constitutionality was broadly upheld by the Supreme Court thirty-one years ago in *Dames & Moore v. Regan.*

Koh, *Twenty-First-Century International Lawmaking, supra,* at 732-33. For additional elaboration by Koh on this theme, see Harold Hongju Koh, *Triptych's End: A Better Framework to Evaluate 21st Century International Lawmaking,* 126 Yale L.J. Forum 338 (2017). Does the "spectrum" approach suggested by Koh give the Executive Branch too much discretion to conclude international agreements without adequate attention to the basis of congressional authorization?

13. Building on Professor Koh's remarks, Professors Bodansky and Spiro argue for a type of agreement that they describe as "Executive Agreements+." Daniel Bodansky & Peter Spiro, *Executive Agreements+,* 49 Vand. J. Transnat'l L. 885 (2016). An executive agreement+, in their view, is one that is "supported, but not specifically authorized, by congressional action." They maintain that such agreements require even less specific authorization from Congress than a congressional-executive agreement in that they merely need to "complement" existing statutes. In addition to ACTA, they cite as an example of an executive agreement+ the Minamata Convention on Mercury, a comprehensive international agreement concerning the production, use, and disposal of the chemical. The Obama Administration joined the Convention in 2013 without seeking congressional authorization or approval, and Bodanksy and Spiro defend the constitutionality of this action on the ground that the Convention would complement existing U.S. law relating to mercury. As Bodansky and Spiro observe, "Under the [executive agreements+]

approach, presidents would be enabled to enter into agreements in furtherance of any congressionally-validated policy, at least where the agreements did not require a change in U.S. law." But won't it be easy for the Executive Branch to maintain that an agreement would further a "congressionally-validated policy"? Why does a policy reflected in a domestic statute give the Executive Branch sanction to conclude a binding international agreement without congressional approval? When Congress enacts laws to further a domestic policy, does it necessarily want or invite the Executive Branch to make an international agreement on the topic? Bodansky and Spiro, following Professor Koh, purport to find judicial support for such agreements in *Dames & Moore.* Is that a fair reading of the decision? Wasn't there a much stronger basis in *Dames & Moore* for a claim of independent presidential authority to settle the Iranian hostage crisis than there is, for example, to regulate intellectual property or the environment? For an argument that the Executive Agreements+ idea is inconsistent with standard separation of powers principles and is not supported by *Dames & Moore,* see Curtis A. Bradley & Jack L. Goldsmith, *Presidential Control Over International Law,* 131 Harv. L. Rev. 1201, 1259-67 (2018).

14. For an overview of the sole executive agreement power, see Louis Henkin, Foreign Affairs and the United States Constitution 219-26 (2d ed. 1996). For articles critical of this power, see Clark, *supra;* Joel R. Paul, *The Geopolitical Constitution: Executive Expediency and Executive Agreements,* 86 Cal. L. Rev. 671 (1998); Ramsey, *supra.* For a good historical account of the context and significance of *Belmont,* see G. Edward White, *The Transformation of the Constitutional Regime of Foreign Relations,* 85 Va. L. Rev. 1, 111-34 (1999). For an argument that, as a result of gradual accretions, Congress has ceded too much authority to the President to make international agreements, and that this development is at odds with with principles of democratic governance, see Oona A. Hathaway, *Presidential Power over International Law: Restoring the Balance,* 119 Yale L.J. 140 (2009). To address this problem, Professor Hathaway proposes a comprehensive reform statute that would (among other things) provide a separate, administrative review track for agreements made solely by the President. *Compare* Bradley & Goldsmith, *Presidential Control, supra* (analyzing various difficulties in assessing whether the President has too much control over the making of international agreements).

C. POLITICAL COMMITMENTS

The instruments analyzed thus far—Article II treaties, congressional-executive agreements, and sole executive agreements—have different names, legal bases, and procedures under U.S. domestic law. But they all create obligations between the United States and other nations (or with international institutions) that are governed by international law. In that sense, these instruments are "treaties" on the international plane, since international law defines a "treaty" generically as "an international agreement concluded between States in written form and *governed by international law, . . . whatever its particular designation.*" Vienna Convention on the Law of Treaties, Art. 2(a), 1155 U.N.T.S. 331, 8 I.L.M. 679 (emphasis added). Such treaties are "binding upon the parties to it and must be performed by them in good faith." *Id.* at Art. 26.

The United States also makes international agreements on many topics that are *not* binding under international law. We refer to these agreements as "political commitments," but they are also called "soft law agreements," "memoranda of understanding," "gentlemen's agreements," or "legally non-binding agreements." *See generally* Anthony Aust, Modern Treaty Law and Practice ch. 3 (3d ed. 2013). In contrast to a treaty under international law (and thus to Article II treaties, congressional-executive agreements, and sole executive agreements), a political commitment imposes no obligation under international law between the parties to the agreement. The main criterion for distinguishing between a treaty governed by international law and a political commitment not governed by international law is party intent. *See id.* at 29. One important indication of intent is the terms the parties use in the agreement. Typically, an international treaty "enters into force," and its obligations are expressed in mandatory terms such as "shall," "undertake," "rights," and "obligations." By contrast, political commitments typically "come into operation" or "come into effect," and express softer obligations such as "should" or "will." *Id.* at 31.

Presidents make political commitments primarily on their own authority, without *ex ante* or *ex post* approval by Congress or the Senate. The materials below focus on political commitments related to two important presidential initiatives.

1. The Atlantic Charter

In August 1941, in the midst of World War II but before the United States had formally entered it, President Franklin D. Roosevelt met British Prime Minister Winston Churchill in Placentia Bay, Newfoundland. During the previous twelve months, Germany had rained down bombs on Great Britain and invaded Russia, and the United States had given significant support to Great Britain in the Destroyers for Bases deal of 1940 and the Lend-Lease Act of 1941. Churchill tried but failed in Newfoundland to convince Roosevelt to enter the war, but the two men did issue the following famous joint declaration of general principles and war aims.

Joint Declaration by the President and Prime Minister (The Atlantic Charter)

Signed in Placentia Bay, Newfoundland, August 14, 1941

The President of the United States of America and the Prime Minister, Mr. Churchill, representing His Majesty's Government in the United Kingdom, being met together, deem it right to make known certain common principles in the national policies of their respective countries on which they base their hopes for a better future for the world.

First, their countries seek no aggrandizement, territorial or other;

Second, they desire to see no territorial changes that do not accord with the freely expressed wishes of the peoples concerned;

Third, they respect the right of all peoples to choose the form of government under which they will live; and they wish to see sovereign rights and self government restored to those who have been forcibly deprived of them;

Fourth, they will endeavor, with due respect for their existing obligations, to further the enjoyment by all States, great or small, victor or vanquished, of access, on equal terms, to the trade and to the raw materials of the world which are needed for their economic prosperity;

Fifth, they desire to bring about the fullest collaboration between all nations in the economic field with the object of securing, for all, improved labor standards, economic advancement and social security;

Sixth, after the final destruction of the Nazi tyranny, they hope to see established a peace which will afford to all nations the means of dwelling in safety within their own boundaries, and which will afford assurance that all the men in all lands may live out their lives in freedom from fear and want;

Seventh, such a peace should enable all men to traverse the high seas and oceans without hindrance;

Eighth, they believe that all of the nations of the world, for realistic as well as spiritual reasons must come to the abandonment of the use of force. Since no future peace can be maintained if land, sea, or air armaments continue to be employed by nations which threaten, or may threaten, aggression outside of their frontiers, they believe, pending the establishment of a wider and permanent system of general security, that the disarmament of such nations is essential. They will likewise aid and encourage all other practicable measure which will lighten for peace-loving peoples the crushing burden of armaments.

Franklin D. Roosevelt
Winston S. Churchill

2. Agreement with Iran Concerning Production of Nuclear Weapons Material

Dating back to the Iran hostage crisis of 1979, Congress has enacted a series of laws that impose economic sanctions on Iran. *See* Dianne E. Rennack, Congressional Research Service, Iran: U.S. Economic Sanctions and the Authority to Lift Restrictions (Jan. 22, 2016). These sanctions are directed at different aspects of Iran's behavior, including nuclear proliferation, human rights abuses, and state-sponsored terrorism. Almost all of these statutory sanctions provisions empower the President to waive the sanctions, at the President's discretion and for various periods of time, if the President determines that certain statutory criteria are satisfied. In addition, for decades, the United Nations Security Council has voted to impose sanctions on Iran related to (among other things) its nuclear weapons development program.

On July 14, 2015, the United States, along with the other four permanent members of the U.N. Security Council plus Germany ("the P5+1"), announced a legally non-binding agreement with Iran to curtail Iran's nuclear weapons program in exchange for relief for Iran from certain national and international sanctions. The basic agreement, excerpted below, provides that Iran will reduce its nuclear weapons production capabilities with verification assurances, and in exchange the major global powers will vote in the Security Council to lift sanctions against Iran and will lift their domestic sanctions as well.

Joint Comprehensive Plan of Action

Signed in Vienna, Austria, July 14, 2015

The E3/EU+3 (China, France, Germany, the Russian Federation, the United Kingdom, and the United States, with the High Representative of the European

Union for Foreign Affairs and Security Policy) and the Islamic Republic of Iran welcome this historic Joint Comprehensive Plan of Action (JCPOA), which will ensure that Iran's nuclear programme will be exclusively peaceful, and mark a fundamental shift in their approach to this issue. . . .

PREAMBLE AND GENERAL PROVISIONS

   i.   The Islamic Republic of Iran and the E3/EU+3 . . . have decided upon this long-term Joint Comprehensive Plan of Action (JCPOA). This JCPOA, reflecting a step-by-step approach, includes the reciprocal commitments as laid down in this document and the annexes hereto and is to be endorsed by the United Nations (UN) Security Council.

   ii. The full implementation of this JCPOA will ensure the exclusively peaceful nature of Iran's nuclear programme.

   iii. Iran reaffirms that under no circumstances will Iran ever seek, develop, or acquire any nuclear weapons. . . .

   v.   This JCPOA will produce the comprehensive lifting of all UN Security Council sanctions, as well as multilateral and national sanctions related to Iran's nuclear programme . . . .

   ix. A Joint Commission consisting of the E3/EU+3 and Iran will be established to monitor the implementation of this JCPOA and will carry out the functions provided for in this JCPOA. . . .

   x.   The International Atomic Energy Agency (IAEA) will be requested to monitor and verify the voluntary nuclear-related measures as detailed in this JCPOA. The IAEA will be requested to provide regular updates to the Board of Governors, and as provided for in this JCPOA, to the UN Security Council. . . .

   xiv. The E3+3 will submit a draft resolution to the UN Security Council endorsing this JCPOA affirming that conclusion of this JCPOA marks a fundamental shift in its consideration of this issue and expressing its desire to build a new relationship with Iran. . . .

Iran and E3/EU+3 will take the following voluntary measures within the timeframe as detailed in this JCPOA and its Annexes

NUCLEAR

A. Enrichment, Enrichment R&D, Stockpiles

1. Iran's long-term plan includes certain agreed limitations on all uranium enrichment and uranium enrichment-related activities including certain limitations on specific research and development (R&D) activities for the first 8 years, to be followed by gradual evolution, at a reasonable pace, to the next stage of its enrichment activities for exclusively peaceful purposes. . . .

5. Based on its own long-term plan, for 15 years, Iran will carry out its uranium enrichment-related activities, including safeguarded R&D exclusively in the Natanz Enrichment facility, keep its level of uranium enrichment at up to 3.67% [which is down from 20% prior to the JCPOA]. . . .

C. Transparency and Confidence Building Measures

. . .

15. Iran will allow the IAEA to monitor the implementation of the voluntary measures for their respective durations, as well as to implement transparency measures, as set out in this JCPOA and its Annexes. . . .

16. Iran will not engage in activities, including at the R&D level, that could contribute to the development of a nuclear explosive device, including uranium or plutonium metallurgy activities. . . .

SANCTIONS

. . .

21. The United States will cease the application, and will continue to do so, in accordance with this JCPOA, of the [domestic law] sanctions specified in Annex II, to take effect simultaneously with the IAEA-verified implementation of the agreed nuclear-related measures by Iran as specified in Annex V. . . .

22. The United States will, as specified in Annex II and in accordance with Annex V, allow for the sale of commercial passenger aircraft and related parts and services to Iran; license non-U.S. persons that are owned or controlled by a U.S. person to engage in activities with Iran consistent with this JCPOA; and license the importation into the United States of Iranian-origin carpets and foodstuffs.

23. Eight years after Adoption Day or when the IAEA has reached the Broader Conclusion that all the nuclear material in Iran remains in peaceful activities, whichever is earlier, the United States will seek such legislative action as may be appropriate to terminate or modify to effectuate the termination of the sanctions specified in Annex II. . . .

DISPUTE RESOLUTION MECHANISM

. . .

36. If Iran believed that any or all of the E3/EU+3 were not meeting their commitments under this JCPOA, Iran could refer the issue to the Joint Commission for resolution; similarly, if any of the E3/EU+3 believed that Iran was not meeting its commitments under the JCPOA, any of the E3/EU+3 could do the same. . . .

Notes and Questions

1. Political commitments and other non-binding international agreements are as old as diplomacy. The Atlantic Charter, excerpted above, is widely considered to be an example of a political commitment. *See, e.g.,* Memorandum by Robert E. Dalton, Assistant Legal Adviser for Treaty Affairs, *International Documents of a Non-Legally Binding Character*, March 18, 1994 (citing the Atlantic Charter as one of the "better known" twentieth century examples of a non-binding political commitment). But why is this so? Because the document merely states "common principles"? Because it uses hortatory language about what the two nations "desire" or "hope" to happen? Because it was not formally ratified? Could President Roosevelt have made the Atlantic Charter as a legally binding sole executive agreement?

2. Another famous political commitment is the Helsinki Accords of 1975, Conference on Security and Cooperation in Europe: Final Act, Aug. 1, 1975, 14

I.L.M. 1292. The Helsinki Accords was a Cold War document signed by 35 nations, including the United States, that aimed to improve relations between the democratic West and Communist bloc countries, and that contained various commitments to respect human rights and freedoms, to pursue the peaceful resolution of disputes and refrain from using force or threatening the use of force, and to avoid interfering in the internal affairs of other nations. In explaining the United States' signature of the Accords, President Gerald Ford said: "I would emphasize that the document I will sign is neither a treaty, nor is it legally binding on any particular state. The Helsinki documents involve political and moral commitments aimed at lessening tension and opening further the lines of communication between the peoples of East and West. . . . We are not committing ourselves to anything beyond what we are already committed to by our own moral and legal standards and by more formal treaty agreements such as the United Nations Charter and Declaration of Human Rights." 73 Dept. of State Bull. 204, 205 (1975). For a court of appeals decision holding that the Accords did not confer judicially enforceable rights, see Frolova v. Union of Soviet Socialist Republics, 761 F.2d 370 (7th Cir. 1985).

3. Less prominent but more typical examples of political commitments are the hundreds of memoranda of understanding made by federal agencies with their counterparts abroad concerning cooperation on every conceivable regulatory topic. These regulatory political commitments fall into six general categories: information sharing and scientific collaboration; development and use of international standards; equivalency agreements that recognize that foreign regulations meet U.S. standards; regulatory capacity strengthening agreements; resource-sharing agreements; and coordination and voluntary programs. *See* U.S. Government Accountability Office, GAO-13-588, International Regulatory Cooperation 10 (2013). For discussion of how these regulatory commitments relate to foreign relations law and administrative law generally, see Jean Galbraith & David Zaring, *Soft Law as Foreign Relations Law*, 99 Cornell L. Rev. 735 (2014), and David Zaring, *Sovereignty Mismatch and the New Administrative Law*, 91 Wash. U. L. Rev. 59 (2013).

4. The Supreme Court has never ruled on the scope or legality of political commitments, and the constitutional basis for political commitments is uncertain. Scholars have offered various perspectives. Duncan Hollis and Joshua Newcomer argue that constitutional text and original understanding provide little guidance, and they instead locate the power to make political commitments primarily in the "[l]ongstanding customary practice by the Executive branch." *See* Duncan B. Hollis & Joshua J. Newcomer, *"Political" Commitments and the Constitution*, 49 Va. J. Int'l L. 507, 547 (2009). They note that "the executive branch has demonstrated a consistent practice of concluding political commitments," and add that Congress has largely acquiesced in this power with respect to the commitments it knows about, even though it has asserted its own authority to "facilitate, condone, resist, or supersede" particular ones. *Id.* at 562-69. They also argue that political commitments find structural constitutional support in the general delegation of foreign relations power to the federal government, the Compacts Clause, and "[t]he president's role as the dominant interlocutor with foreign states." *Id.* at 569-72. Is this latter basis for political commitments bolstered by *Zivotofsky II* (excerpted in Chapter 3) — in particular, its affirmation of the President's "unique role in communicating with foreign governments" and its invocation of John Marshall's statement that the President "is the sole organ of the nation in its external relations, and its sole representative with foreign nations"? By contrast, Professor Ramsey locates the power to enter into political commitments in the Article II Vesting Clause. Michael D. Ramsey, *Evading* *the Treaty Power?: The Constitutionality of Nonbinding Agreements,* 11 FIU L. Rev. 371, 374-75 (2016) (arguing that the Vesting Clause entails that "diplomacy and the management of foreign affairs are powers of the President, and those powers would likely include a general constitutional power to make nonbinding agreements"). *See also* Jack Goldsmith, *The Contributions of the Obama Administration to the Practice and Theory of International Law,* 57 Harv. Int'l L.J. 1, 11 (2016) (noting that political commitments are "closely tied to the President's power over diplomacy, since at the margins they blur into diplomatic discourse").

5. One difficulty in ascertaining the extent of congressional acquiescence in the President's political commitment practices is that Congress is not fully informed about political commitments. Hollis & Newcomer, *supra,* at 568. Note that the Executive Branch's duty under the Case-Zablocki Act to inform Congress about international agreements that the Executive enters into outside the Treaty Clause does not extend to political commitments. *See* 22 C.F.R. §181.2 (a)(1) (Case-Zablocki Act requires reporting only for agreements in which "[t]he parties must intend their undertaking to be legally binding, and not merely of political or personal effect"). For an argument that "the Case Act should be applied to political commitments as it is applied to other forms of international agreements," see Ryan Harrington, *A Remedy for Congressional Exclusion from Contemporary International Agreement Making,* 118 W. Va. L. Rev. 1211, 1227 (2016).

6. Political commitments are generally easier for presidents to negotiate and implement than a legally binding agreement, in part because they do not require domestic legislative approval. Moreover, because a political commitment is legally non-binding, it technically lasts only as long as the President, or one of the President's successors, voluntarily agrees to continue to abide by it. Note also that a political commitment by itself has no legal status in domestic federal law. How might these characteristics of political commitments affect compliance with political commitments? Because of these characteristics, political commitments have traditionally not been the basis for international agreements that require changes in domestic law to effectuate international cooperation. For such agreements, the President has typically needed the Senate or the full Congress, since the Senate (through self-executing treaties) or Congress (through statutes) can change domestic law at the same time that it approves an international agreement.

The JCPOA, however, illustrates that presidents can combine political commitments with existing domestic authorities to change domestic law and effectuate deep international cooperation without new legislative approval. President Obama claimed the authority to make commitments in the JCPOA without the approval of Congress or the Senate because the JCPOA was legally non-binding. On the JCPOA's "Implementation Day," January 16, 2016, the International Atomic Energy Agency (IAEA) verified that Iran had satisfied its key nuclear-related commitments described in the JCPOA, and the U.S. Secretary of State confirmed the IAEA's verification. Iran's compliance with the JCPOA triggered the United States' commitment to vote in the U.N. Security Council to lift international sanctions against Iran, and to lift its own domestic sanctions related to nuclear proliferation. President Obama claimed the power to effectuate these commitments because Congress had previously delegated to him the authority to direct the U.S. vote in the Security Council, *see* 22 U.S.C. §§287, 287a, and had also previously given him the discretion to lift the U.S. sanctions against Iran related to nuclear proliferation in certain circumstances.

7. One limitation on the innovative approach to making the JCPOA is the ease in reversing it. The bulk of the pertinent Iran sanctions waivers needed to implement the JCPOA had to be renewed after a period—typically, one year. President Obama thus could only ensure that the United States would lift its sanctions through his term and a bit into the next presidency. Moreover, as noted above, because the JCPOA is a political commitment, it is not binding under international law, and nothing in the Security Council's subsequent endorsement of the JCPOA changed this conclusion, since it did not impose an international law obligation on the United States to lift its domestic sanctions on Iran. *See* John Bellinger, *The New UNSCR on Iran: Does It Bind the United States (and Future Presidents)?*, Lawfare (July 18, 2015). Finally, since neither the Senate nor the Congress voted on the JCPOA, the agreement lacked the wide democratic sanction that might give a future president pause in altering the agreement.

President Trump came to office in 2017 as a critic of the JCPOA. On May 8, 2018, he announced that the United States was withdrawing from the Iran deal, and he signed a Presidential Memorandum that instructed federal agencies to re-impose the sanctions lifted or waived pursuant to the Iran deal within 180 days of the announcement. *See* Presidential Memorandum, *Ceasing U.S. Participation in the JCPOA and Taking Additional Action to Counter Iran's Malign Influence and Deny Iran All Paths to a Nuclear Weapon* (May 8, 2018), *at* https://www.whitehouse.gov/presidential-actions/ceasing-u-s-participation-jcpoa-taking-additional-action-counter-irans-malign-influence-deny-iran-paths-nuclear-weapon/. The administration subsequently reinstated all sanctions lifted under the agreement. *See* Exec. Order No. 13,846, 83 Fed. Reg. 38939 (Aug. 6, 2018). It declined to renew waivers of Iran sanctions under a number of statutes and reinstated most of the sanctions provided for in executive orders that the Obama Administration had rescinded under the nuclear deal. The administration also blocked the assets of hundreds of Iran-related individuals and entities and banned U.S. actors from transacting with them, which had the effect of triggering secondary sanctions that essentially closed the U.S. market to third parties that do business with the designated individuals and entities. The reinstated U.S. sanctions have had a severe effect on the Iranian economy and have led Iran to resume certain activities it pledged to suspend under the nuclear deal. In response, the Trump Administration has periodically added new sanctions against Iran. *See, e.g.*, Edward Wong, *Trump Imposes New Sanctions on Iran, Adding to Tensions*, N.Y. Times (June 24, 2019).

How did the way in which President Obama concluded the JCPOA inform President Trump's options for backing out of it? Note that the JCPOA was, in the span of three years, made by one President unilaterally, without contemporary input from Congress or the Senate, and then terminated by a different President unilaterally, without contemporary input from Congress or the Senate. Is the making and terminating of such an important international agreement by the President alone consistent with the Framers' vision for the conduct of U.S. foreign relations? What effect does such presidential unilateralism have on the effectiveness of U.S. foreign policy?

8. On May 22, 2015, almost two months before the JCPOA was finalized, President Obama signed into law the Iran Nuclear Agreement Review Act of 2015 (Iran Review Act), Pub. L. 114-17. The statute requires the President to transmit to Congress any agreement with Iran relating to its nuclear program, and it restricts the President from waiving sanctions against Iran during a specified period (30-85 days, depending on when the agreement is reached), during which time Congress could approve or reject the agreement, or take no action at all. The law also provides that if the President does eventually waive sanctions against Iran, he must report to Congress periodically on Iran's compliance with the nuclear agreement, and it provides for an expedited schedule for Congress to re-impose sanctions if Iran fails to comply with the agreement. In accordance with the Iran Review Act, Congress held hearings on the JCPOA in the months after it was announced. On September 11, 2015, the House voted against a resolution approving the deal by a vote of 247-186. The day before, the Senate failed to overcome a filibuster by Democrats that prevented a resolution of disapproval from reaching the Senate floor. Because Congress did not reject the JCPOA during the time period specified by the Iran Review Act, the President retained his pre-existing discretionary authorities to lift domestic sanctions against Iran, which he eventually did.

Where did Congress get the authority to delay implementation of a non-binding agreement negotiated by the president? Did it flow from its authority to impose the underlying sanctions? Note that President Obama had originally opposed an earlier but similar version of the Iran review legislation, and threatened to veto it, on the following grounds (as explained by his Chief of Staff):

> However, the legislation you have introduced in the Senate goes well beyond ensuring that Congress has a role to play in any deal with Iran. Instead, the legislation would potentially prevent any deal from succeeding by suggesting that Congress must vote to "approve" any deal, and by removing existing sanctions waiver authorities that have already been granted to the President. We believe that the legislation would likely have a profoundly negative impact on the ongoing negotiations—emboldening Iranian hard-liners, inviting a counter-productive response from the Iranian *majiles*; differentiating the U.S. position from our allies in the negotiations; and once again calling into question our ability to negotiate this deal. This would therefore complicate the possibility of achieving a peaceful resolution to the Iranian nuclear issue if legislative action is taken before a deal is completed. Moreover, if congressional action is perceived as preventing us from reaching a deal, it will create divisions within the international community, putting at risk the very international cooperation that has been essential to our ability to pressure Iran. Put simply, it would potentially make it impossible to secure international cooperation for additional sanctions, while putting at risk the existing multilateral sanctions regime.
>
> In addition to its impact on the negotiations, this legislation would also set a potentially damaging precedent for constraining future Presidents of either party from pursuing the conduct of essential diplomatic negotiations, making it much harder for future Presidents to negotiate similar political commitments. These factors have led the President to determine that he would veto this legislation, were it to pass the Congress.

See Letter from Denis McDonough, Assistant to the President and Chief of Staff, to Senator Bob Corker, Chairman, Senate Foreign Relations Committee (Mar. 14, 2015). McDonough does not quite claim here that the legislation would be unconstitutional. But under the reasoning of the Supreme Court's recent decision in *Zivotofsky II* (see Chapter 3), might the Executive Branch have plausibly argued that the proposed legislation unconstitutionally interfered with the President's negotiations with Iran?

9. President Obama's authority to conclude the JCPOA without the approval of Congress or the Senate turned on the claim that the JCPOA is a non-binding political commitment. Professor Ramsey has argued that the "main potential constitutional problem with the JCPOA is that its nonbindingness is not entirely clear." Michael D. Ramsey, *Evading the Treaty Power?: The Constitutionality of Nonbinding Agreements*, 11 FIU L. Rev. 371, 380 (2016). What language in the agreement indicates whether the JCPOA is a political commitment rather than a binding legal obligation? Note that the State Department has stated unambiguously that the JCPOA "is not a treaty or an executive agreement, and is not a signed document," but rather "reflects political commitments." Letter from Julia Frifield, Assistant Sec'y for Legislative Affairs, U.S. Dep't of State, to Mike Pompeo, U.S. House of Representatives (Nov. 19, 2015). It added that the "success of the JCPOA will depend not on whether it is legally binding or signed, but rather on the extensive verification measures we have put in place, as well as Iran's understanding that we have the capacity to re-impose—and ramp up—our sanctions if Iran does not meet its commitments." *Id.*

10. President Obama used a strategy similar to the JCPOA when he committed the United States in September 2016 to the Paris Agreement on climate change. *See* Framework Convention on Climate Change, Adoption of the Paris Agreement, U.N. Doc. FCCC/CP/2015/L.9/Rev.1 (Dec. 12, 2015). The Paris Agreement itself was a binding international obligation, at least some of which the President could commit the nation to as an executive agreement pursuant to a 1992 framework treaty consented to by the Senate. *See* United Nations Framework Convention on Climate Change, opened for signature June 4, 1992, S. Treaty Doc. No. 102-38, 1771 U.N.T.S. 164. *See also* Bradley & Goldsmith, *Presidential Control, supra,* at 1268-69 (explaining why the Paris Agreement should be conceptualized as an executive agreement made pursuant to a treaty). But the President probably could *not* commit the United States under international law to any specific emissions reductions targets. *See* David A. Wirth, *Cracking the American Climate Negotiators' Hidden Code: United States Law and the Paris Agreement,* 6 Climate L. 152, 158, 161-62 (2016). One reason that the President could not do this is that the substantive obligation to lower greenhouse gas emissions would be difficult to ground in the Framework Convention. Another reason is that the "Senate Foreign Relations Committee, in its report on the resolution of ratification for the [Framework Convention], expressed the expectation that future actions that would require legally binding emission reductions would require the Senate's advice and consent." *Id.* at 162.

Because the President could not make a binding agreement to commit to specific emissions reductions on his own authority, and because consent from the Senate or Congress looked unlikely, the administration insisted that the key emissions reduction provision in the Paris Agreement be expressed as a political commitment rather than a binding obligation. *See* Bradley & Goldsmith, *Presidential Control, supra,* at 1251 n.10 (collecting authorities). But to fulfill this commitment, the President then exercised independent, pre-existing domestic regulatory authorities to reduce emissions. Most notably, the administration invoked the Clean Air Act to promulgate a regulation, known as the Clean Power Plan, that required significant emission reductions from power plants to further the goals of the political commitment. Thus, in a fashion similar to the Iran deal, the President combined the power to make a political commitment with a pre-existing and independent delegated power from Congress to make an important international agreement without the consent of the Senate or the Congress.

One important difference between the Paris Agreements and the JCPOA, however, concerns the type of domestic regulation that implement the two agreements. In contrast to the statutory waiver provisions that implemented the JCPOA, which the President could invoke unilaterally, the domestic regulations the President made to implement the Paris Agreement — for example, the Clean Power Plan — are, like almost all domestic regulations, subject to domestic judicial review. (Judicial review of agency rulemaking is typically required either by particular regulatory statutes, or by the Administrative Procedure Act (APA), 5 U.S.C. §§551-559, 701-706.) Judicial review imposes significantly more accountability and constraint on the President than he has in most agreement-making contexts; and indeed, although the Clean Power Plan was promulgated in August 2015, it did not come into force during the Obama Administration, since the Supreme Court stayed the implementation pending an opportunity to review it. *See* West Virginia v. EPA, No. 15-1363 (D.C. Cir. filed Oct. 23, 2015), *stay order granted*, Feb. 9, 2016 (No. 15A773). Such review never occurred, since the Trump Administration came into office shortly thereafter and announced its intent to repeal and replace the Clean Power Plan. As a result, President Obama was unable while in office to carry out an important domestic regulatory initiative in support of his Paris Agreement pledge.

11. President Trump has taken two steps on the international and domestic planes to reverse Obama Administration initiatives related to the Paris Agreement.

First, in August 2017, Trump communicated to the United Nations that the United States intended to withdraw from the Paris Agreement. *See* U.S. Dep't of State, *Communication of Intent to Withdraw from Paris Agreement* (Aug. 4, 2017). Article 28.1 of the Agreement provides that a Party "may withdraw from this Agreement by giving written notification to the Depositary" at "any time after three years from the date on which this Agreement has entered into force for a Party," and that the withdrawal "shall take effect" one year later. As we learned in Section G of Chapter 5, there is a long historical tradition of presidents terminating U.S. treaties pursuant to withdrawal clauses (and sometimes even in the absence of such clauses). And as discussed in Section C of Chapter 2, a majority of the Court in *Goldwater v. Carter* ruled that a treaty termination in the context of a treaty with a withdrawal clause was non-justiciable, albeit under differing rationales, none of which garnered majority support. Assuming that the logic of treaty termination extends to withdrawal clauses in executive agreements made pursuant to treaties, it would appear that President Trump has the authority to terminate the Paris Agreement in accordance with its terms. Some commentators have noted, however, that the earliest that the withdrawal could take effect under Article 28.1 is on November 4, 2020, the day after the next U.S. presidential election. *See* Harold Hongju Koh et al., *Trump's So-Called Withdrawal from Paris: Far from Over,* Just Security (June 2, 2017). In withdrawing the United States from the Agreement, is President Trump bound by the terms of Article 28.1? In answering that question, does it matter that President Obama acted unilaterally in accepting the Paris Agreement for the United States (albeit ostensibly with authority derived from the Framework Convention)? In any event, it appears that the Trump Administration has accepted these limitations on withdrawal, since its August 2017 notice to the United Nations states that the United States will withdraw "as soon as it is eligible to do so, consistent with the terms of the Agreement."

Second, the Trump Administration has moved to repeal or modify the domestic regulatory actions the Obama Administration took to implement its Paris Agreement pledge. Most notably, on June 19, 2019, the Environmental Protection Agency repealed the Clean Power Plan and replaced it with a regulation, dubbed the Affordable Clean Energy rule, that contained far fewer restrictions on power plant carbon emissions. In addition, the EPA has proposed to roll back emissions restrictions on motor vehicles, and other agencies, such as the U.S. Department of Energy and the U.S. Department of Interior, have loosened Obama-era actions aimed at curbing emissions. The Trump Administration faces all of the normal administrative law requirements for repealing agency regulations and implementing new ones.

12. The JCPOA and the Paris Agreement are both very consequential international agreements. There are reasons to believe that Congress or the Senate, if asked, would *not* have consented to them. Majorities in both houses of Congress actually voted against approving the Iran deal in the context of the Iran Review Act. And the Senate has long been opposed to hard requirements on carbon emission reductions, and in recent years, it has consented to a historically low number of treaties. Is it troubling that the President made these historic agreements without the consent of the legislative branch? Consider this assessment:

> [T]he President in both examples made political commitments that did not require legislative approval and then exercised independent domestic authorities to effectuate the changes in domestic law that were needed to make the pledges in the two commitments credible and efficacious. There is nothing innovative about either prong of this approach. Presidents make political commitments all the time, and they exercise delegated authority from Congress all the time. What was innovative was bringing the two prongs together in one initiative to forge deep international cooperation supported by significant changes in U.S. domestic law without recourse to a congressional vote. In both cases the administration secured pledges of coordinated change from foreign countries through a political commitment and then delivered the U.S. side of the bargain by exercising extant delegated authority from Congress that Congress had no idea would lead to such international cooperation.

Goldsmith, *Contributions of the Obama Administration, supra,* at 12-13. What legal concerns might these powers, which are relatively unproblematic when exercised independently, raise when combined?

13. For a comprehensive assessment of presidential control over international law, including the making, interpretation, and terminating of the forms of binding international agreements and political commitments discussed in this chapter, see Bradley & Goldsmith, *Presidential Control, supra.* Among other things, this article argues that in the United States the President has come to control the making, interpretation, and termination of international agreements (including political commitments), without meaningful congressional input. The article also sets forth a framework for analyzing the legality of such agreements and for assessing larger normative questions about whether presidents are adequately accountable for their control over international agreements. For an argument that the various pathways for making international agreements are affected not only by constitutional law, but also by international law and administrative law, and that the latter two types of law impose constraints on presidential power, see Jean Galbraith, *From Treaties to International Commitments: The Changing Landscape of Foreign Relations Law,* 84 U. Chi. L. Rev. 1675 (2017).

7

Customary International Law

Customary international law is the law of the international community that "results from a general and consistent practice of states followed by them from a sense of legal obligation." Restatement (Third) of the Foreign Relations Law of the United States §102(2) (1987). Like treaties, customary international law binds the United States on the international plane. At the time of the Founding, customary international law was referred to as the "law of nations," a term that in its broadest sense included not only what we today call customary international law, but also the "law merchant" (general principles applicable to cross-border commerce), maritime law, and the law of conflict of laws.

As we learned in Chapter 1, the Founders hoped to establish a federal government that would be able to ensure that the United States (and its constituent parts, the States) carried out international obligations under both treaties and customary international law. Nonetheless, the Constitution mentions treaties more often than customary international law. Article I, Section 10 denies states the ability to enter into treaties. Article II grants the President the power to make treaties, with the advice and consent of two-thirds of the Senate. Article III grants the federal courts the power to hear cases arising under treaties. And Article VI states that treaties are part of the supreme law of the land. By contrast, the only reference to customary international law is in Article I, Section 8, clause 10, which authorizes Congress to "define and punish . . . Offences against the Law of Nations."

We know from Chapter 3 that Congress has significant authority, under the Define and Punish Clause and other clauses of Article I, to incorporate customary international law into U.S. federal law. This chapter explores additional issues concerning the role of customary international law in the U.S. legal system. Section A begins by examining the status of customary international law in the U.S. legal system in the absence of its incorporation by Congress into federal law. The next three sections examine concrete instances in which Congress has in fact incorporated customary international law into the domestic legal system or authorized the federal courts to do so. Sections B and C discuss the Alien Tort Statute (ATS), the principal statutory basis for human rights litigation. Those sections also examine the Torture Victim Protection Act (TVPA), in which Congress expressly incorporated specific international human rights norms into federal statutory law. Section D provides an overview of the immunity that foreign governments are accorded in civil suits brought against them in U.S. courts, something that implicates customary international law, but that since 1976 has been regulated in the United States by a comprehensive federal statute. Section E analyzes the immunity accorded to individual foreign officials, which is currently regulated in the United States not by statute, but rather by judicially developed common law informed to an uncertain degree by customary international law. Section F discusses the relevance of customary international law to the interpretation of federal statutes. Section G addresses an issue related to customary international law but that also builds on other issues explored in this book—judicial reliance on foreign and international materials in constitutional interpretation.

A. "PART OF OUR LAW"

The Paquete Habana

175 U.S. 677 (1900)

[During the Spanish-American War, a U.S. naval squadron was enforcing a blockade around Cuba. In doing so, it seized two Cuban vessels while they were engaged in catching and transporting fish off the coast of Cuba. A federal district court, exercising its admiralty jurisdiction, condemned the fishing vessels as prizes of war. The masters and owners of the vessels appealed directly to the Supreme Court pursuant to an 1891 jurisdictional statute that allowed appeals to the Court "[f]rom the final sentences and decrees in prize causes."]

MR. JUSTICE GRAY delivered the opinion of the court. . . .

By an ancient usage among civilized nations, beginning centuries ago, and gradually ripening into a rule of international law, coast fishing vessels, pursuing their vocation of catching and bringing in fresh fish, have been recognized as exempt, with their cargoes and crews, from capture as prize of war.

This doctrine, however, has been earnestly contested at the bar; and no complete collection of the instances illustrating it is to be found, so far as we are aware, in a single published work, although many are referred to and discussed by the writers on international law. . . . It is therefore worth the while to trace the history of the rule, from the earliest accessible sources, through the increasing recognition of it, with occasional setbacks, to what we may now justly consider as its final establishment in our own country and generally throughout the civilized world. . . .

[The Court proceeds to look at statements and practices by various European countries, especially England and France, starting in the 1400s. This evidence included instructions by these governments to their admirals, as well as various treaty provisions. This evidence was not uniform—in the late 1700s, for example, France stopped following the practice because of its perception that French fishing vessels were not receiving the same treatment.]

The doctrine which exempts coast fishermen with their vessels and cargoes from capture as prize of war has been familiar to the United States from the time of the War of Independence. . . .

[The Court notes, among other things, that England and France had abstained from interfering with coastal fishing during the Revolutionary War. The Court admitted, however, that those two countries had failed to exempt fishing vessels from capture during the period of the French Revolution. The Court also notes that the United States had recognized the exemption of coastal fishing boats from capture in its war with Mexico.]

International law is part of our law, and must be ascertained and administered by the courts of justice of appropriate jurisdiction, as often as questions of right depending upon it are duly presented for their determination. For this purpose, where there is no treaty, and no controlling executive or legislative act or judicial decision, resort must be had to the customs and usages of civilized nations; and, as evidence of these, to the works of jurists and commentators, who by years of labor, research and experience, have made themselves peculiarly well acquainted with the subjects of which they treat. Such works are resorted to by judicial tribunals, not for the speculations of their authors concerning what the law ought to be, but for trustworthy evidence of what the law really is. Hilton v. Guyot, 159 U.S. 113, 163, 164, 214, 215. . . .

[The Court then refers to the views of leading European commentators on international law. This evidence also was not uniform. Two English commentators, for example, although noting that the exemption was common practice, did not believe that it had become a settled rule of customary international law.]

This review of the precedents and authorities on the subject appears to us abundantly to demonstrate that at the present day, by the general consent of the civilized nations of the world, and independently of any express treaty or other public act, it is an established rule of international law, founded on considerations of humanity to a poor and industrious order of men, and of the mutual convenience of belligerent States, that coast fishing vessels, with their implements and supplies, cargoes and crews, unarmed, and honestly pursuing their peaceful calling of catching and bringing in fresh fish, are exempt from capture as prize of war.

The exemption, of course, does not apply to coast fishermen or their vessels, if employed for a warlike purpose, or in such a way as to give aid or information to the enemy; nor when military or naval operations create a necessity to which all private interests must give way.

Nor has the exemption been extended to ships or vessels employed on the high sea in taking whales or seals, or cod or other fish which are not brought fresh to market, but are salted or otherwise cured and made a regular article of commerce.

This rule of international law is one which prize courts, administering the law of nations, are bound to take judicial notice of, and to give effect to, in the absence of any treaty or other public act of their own government in relation to the matter. . . .

The position taken by the United States during the recent war with Spain was quite in accord with the rule of international law, now generally recognized by civilized nations, in regard to coast fishing vessels.

On April 21, 1898, the Secretary of the Navy gave instructions to Admiral Sampson, commanding the North Atlantic Squadron, to "immediately institute a blockade of the north coast of Cuba, extending from Cardenas on the east to Bahia Honda on the west." The blockade was immediately instituted accordingly. On April 22, the President issued a proclamation, declaring that the United States had instituted and would maintain that blockade, "in pursuance of the laws of the United States, and the law of nations applicable to such cases." And by the act of Congress of April 25, 1898, c. 189, it was declared that the war between the United States and Spain existed on that day, and had existed since and including April 21.

On April 26, 1898, the President issued another proclamation, which, after reciting the existence of the war, as declared by Congress, contained this further recital: "It being desirable that such war should be conducted upon principles in harmony with the present views of nations and sanctioned by their recent practice." This recital was followed by specific declarations of certain rules for the conduct of the war by sea, making no mention of fishing vessels. But the proclamation clearly manifests the general policy of the Government to conduct the war in accordance with the principles of international law sanctioned by the recent practice of nations.

On April 28, 1898, (after the capture of the two fishing vessels now in question,) Admiral Sampson telegraphed to the Secretary of the Navy as follows: "I find that a large number of fishing schooners are attempting to get into Havana from their fishing grounds near the Florida reefs and coasts. They are generally manned by excellent seamen, belonging to the maritime inscription of Spain, who have already served in the Spanish navy, and who are liable to further service. As these trained men are naval reserves, have a semi-military character, and would be most valuable to the Spaniards as artillerymen, either afloat or ashore, I recommend that they should be detained prisoners of war, and that I should be authorized to deliver them to the commanding officer of the army at Key West." To that communication the Secretary of the Navy, on April 30, 1898, guardedly answered: "Spanish fishing vessels attempting to violate blockade are subject, with crew, to capture, and any such vessel or crew considered likely to aid enemy may be detained." The Admiral's despatch assumed that he was not authorized, without express order, to arrest coast fishermen peaceably pursuing their calling; and the necessary implication and evident intent of the response of the Navy Department were that Spanish coast fishing vessels and their crews should not be interfered with, so long as they neither attempted to violate the blockade, nor were considered likely to aid the enemy. . . .

Upon the facts proved in either case, it is the duty of this court, sitting as the highest prize court of the United States, and administering the law of nations, to declare and adjudge that the capture was unlawful, and without probable cause. . . .

MR. CHIEF JUSTICE FULLER, with whom concurred MR. JUSTICE HARLAN and MR. JUSTICE MCKENNA, dissenting:

The district court held these vessels and their cargoes liable because not "satisfied that, as a matter of law, without any ordinance, treaty, or proclamation, fishing vessels of this class are exempt from seizure."

This Court holds otherwise not because such exemption is to be found in any treaty, legislation, proclamation, or instruction granting it, but on the ground that the vessels were exempt by reason of an established rule of international law applicable to them which it is the duty of the court to enforce.

I am unable to conclude that there is any such established international rule, or that this Court can properly revise action which must be treated as having been taken in the ordinary exercise of discretion in the conduct of war. . . .

[I]t is admitted [by the Court] that the alleged exemption [from seizure] does not apply

> to coast fishermen or their vessels if employed for a warlike purpose or in such a way as to give aid or information to the enemy, nor when military or naval operations create a necessity to which all private interests must give way,

and further that the exemption has not

> been extended to ships or vessels employed on the high sea in taking whales or seals, or cod or other fish which are not brought fresh to market, but are salted or otherwise cured and made a regular article of commerce.

It will be perceived that the exceptions reduce the supposed rule to very narrow limits, requiring a careful examination of the facts in order to ascertain its applicability, and the decision appears to me to go altogether too far in respect of dealing with captures directed or ratified by the officer in command.

But were these two vessels within the alleged exemption? They were of twenty-five and thirty-five tons burden, respectively. They carried large tanks in which the fish taken were kept alive. They were owned by citizens of Havana, and the owners and the masters and crew were to be compensated by shares of the catch. One of them had been two hundred miles from Havana, off Cape San Antonio, for twenty-five days, and the other for eight days off the coast of Yucatan. They belonged, in short, to the class of fishing or coasting vessels of from five to twenty tons burden, and from twenty tons upwards, which, when licensed or enrolled as prescribed by the Revised Statutes, are declared to be vessels of the United States, and the shares of whose men, when the vessels are employed in fishing, are regulated by statute. They were engaged in what were substantially commercial ventures, and the mere fact that the fish were kept alive by contrivances for that purpose—a practice of considerable antiquity—did not render them any the less an article of trade than if they had been brought in cured.

I do not think that, under the circumstances, the considerations which have operated to mitigate the evils of war in respect of individual harvesters of the soil can properly be invoked on behalf of these hired vessels as being the implements of like harvesters of the sea. Not only so as to the owners, but as to the masters and crews. The principle which exempts the husbandman and his instruments of labor exempts the industry in which he is engaged, and is not applicable in protection of the continuance of transactions of such character and extent as these.

In truth, the exemption of fishing craft is essentially an act of grace, and not a matter of right, and it is extended or denied as the exigency is believed to demand. . . .

In my judgment, the rule is that exemption from the rigors of war is in the control of the Executive. He is bound by no immutable rule on the subject. It is for him to apply, or to modify, or to deny altogether such immunity as may have been usually extended. . . .

Filartiga v. Pena-Irala

630 F.2d 876 (2d Cir. 1980)

[Joel Filartiga and his daughter Dolly, citizens of Paraguay, sued Pena-Irala, also a citizen of Paraguay, for torturing and wrongfully killing Joelito Filartiga, Joel's son and Dolly's brother, in Paraguay. The complaint alleged that the torture and killing took place while Pena-Irala was inspector-general of police in Asuncion, Paraguay. The Filartigas served Pena-Irala with process while he was living in the United States beyond the terms of his visa. Following this service, but before trial, the federal immigration service deported Pena-Irala to Paraguay. The district court dismissed the Filartigas' complaint for lack of subject matter jurisdiction.]

KAUFMAN, CIRCUIT JUDGE. . . .

[Appellants'] cause of action is stated as arising under "wrongful death statutes; the U.N. Charter; the Universal Declaration on Human Rights; the U.N. Declaration Against Torture; the American Declaration of the Rights and Duties of Man; and other pertinent declarations, documents and practices constituting the customary international law of human rights and the law of nations," as well as

28 U.S.C. §1350, Article II, §2 and the Supremacy Clause of the U.S. Constitution. Jurisdiction is claimed under the general federal question provision, 28 U.S.C. §1331 and, principally on this appeal, under the Alien Tort Statute, 28 U.S.C. §1350. . . .

Appellants rest their principal argument in support of federal jurisdiction upon the Alien Tort Statute, 28 U.S.C. §1350, which provides: "The district courts shall have original jurisdiction of any civil action by an alien for a tort only, committed in violation of the law of nations or a treaty of the United States." Since appellants do not contend that their action arises directly under a treaty of the United States,[7] a threshold question on the jurisdictional issue is whether the conduct alleged violates the law of nations. In light of the universal condemnation of torture in numerous international agreements, and the renunciation of torture as an instrument of official policy by virtually all of the nations of the world (in principle if not in practice), we find that an act of torture committed by a state official against one held in detention violates established norms of the international law of human rights, and hence the law of nations.

The Supreme Court has enumerated the appropriate sources of international law. The law of nations "may be ascertained by consulting the works of jurists, writing professedly on public law; or by the general usage and practice of nations; or by judicial decisions recognizing and enforcing that law." United States v. Smith, 18 U.S. (5 Wheat.) 153, 160-61 (1820). In *Smith*, a statute proscribing "the crime of piracy (on the high seas) as defined by the law of nations," 3 Stat. 510(a) (1819), was held sufficiently determinate in meaning to afford the basis for a death sentence. The *Smith* Court discovered among the works of Lord Bacon, Grotius, Bochard and other commentators a genuine consensus that rendered the crime "sufficiently and constitutionally defined." *Smith, supra*, at 162. . . .

[The Paquete] Habana is particularly instructive for present purposes, for it held that the traditional prohibition against seizure of an enemy's coastal fishing vessels during wartime, a standard that began as one of comity only, had ripened over the preceding century into "a settled rule of international law" by "the general assent of civilized nations." *Id.* at 694; *accord, id.* at 686. Thus it is clear that courts must interpret international law not as it was in 1789, but as it has evolved and exists among the nations of the world today. *See* Ware v. Hylton, 3 U.S. (3 Dall.) 199 (1796) (distinguishing between "ancient" and "modern" law of nations).

The requirement that a rule command the "general assent of civilized nations" to become binding upon them all is a stringent one. Were this not so, the courts of one nation might feel free to impose idiosyncratic legal rules upon others, in the name of applying international law. Thus, in Banco Nacional de Cuba v. Sabbatino, 376 U.S. 398 (1964), the Court declined to pass on the validity of the Cuban government's expropriation of a foreign-owned corporation's assets, noting the sharply conflicting views on the issue propounded by the capital-exporting, capital-importing, socialist and capitalist nations.

The case at bar presents us with a situation diametrically opposed to the conflicted state of law that confronted the *Sabbatino* Court. Indeed, to paraphrase that

---

7. Appellants "associate themselves with" the argument of some of the *amici curiae* that their claim arises directly under a treaty of the United States, but nonetheless primarily rely upon treaties and other international instruments as evidence of an emerging norm of customary international law, rather than independent sources of law.

Court's statement, *id.* at 428, there are few, if any, issues in international law today on which opinion seems to be so united as the limitations on a state's power to torture persons held in its custody.

The United Nations Charter (a treaty of the United States, see 59 Stat. 1033 (1945)) makes it clear that in this modern age a state's treatment of its own citizens is a matter of international concern. It provides:

> With a view to the creation of conditions of stability and well-being which are necessary for peaceful and friendly relations among nations . . . the United Nations shall promote . . . universal respect for, and observance of, human rights and fundamental freedoms for all without distinctions as to race, sex, language or religion.

Id. Art. 55. And further:

> All members pledge themselves to take joint and separate action in cooperation with the Organization for the achievement of the purposes set forth in Article 55.

Id. Art. 56.

While this broad mandate has been held not to be wholly self-executing, . . . this observation alone does not end our inquiry. For although there is no universal agreement as to the precise extent of the "human rights and fundamental freedoms" guaranteed to all by the Charter, there is at present no dissent from the view that the guaranties include, at a bare minimum, the right to be free from torture. This prohibition has become part of customary international law, as evidenced and defined by the Universal Declaration of Human Rights, General Assembly Resolution 217(III) (A) (Dec. 10, 1948) which states, in the plainest of terms, "no one shall be subjected to torture." The General Assembly has declared that the Charter precepts embodied in this Universal Declaration "constitute basic principles of international law."

Particularly relevant is the Declaration on the Protection of All Persons from Being Subjected to Torture, General Assembly Resolution 3452, 30 U.N. GAOR Supp. (No. 34) 91, U.N. Doc. A/1034 (1975). . . . The Declaration expressly prohibits any state from permitting the dastardly and totally inhuman act of torture. Torture, in turn, is defined as "any act by which severe pain and suffering, whether physical or mental, is intentionally inflicted by or at the instigation of a public official on a person for such purposes as . . . intimidating him or other persons." The Declaration goes on to provide that "(w)here it is proved that an act of torture or other cruel, inhuman or degrading treatment or punishment has been committed by or at the instigation of a public official, the victim shall be afforded redress and compensation, in accordance with national law." This Declaration, like the Declaration of Human Rights before it, was adopted without dissent by the General Assembly. . . .

These U.N. declarations are significant because they specify with great precision the obligations of member nations under the Charter. Since their adoption, "(m)embers can no longer contend that they do not know what human rights they promised in the Charter to promote." Sohn, "A Short History of United Nations Documents on Human Rights," in The United Nations and Human Rights, 18th Report of the Commission (Commission to Study the Organization of Peace ed. 1968). Moreover, a U.N. Declaration is, according to one authoritative definition, "a formal and solemn instrument, suitable for rare occasions when principles of great and lasting importance are being enunciated." 34 U.N. ESCOR, Supp. (No. 8) 15, U.N. Doc. E/cn.4/1/610 (1962) (memorandum of Office of Legal Affairs, U.N. Secretariat). Accordingly, it has been observed that the Universal Declaration of Human Rights "no longer fits into the dichotomy of 'binding treaty' against 'non-binding pronouncement,' but is rather an authoritative statement of the international community." E. Schwelb, Human Rights and the International Community 70 (1964). Thus, a Declaration creates an expectation of adherence, and "insofar as the expectation is gradually justified by State practice, a declaration may by custom become recognized as laying down rules binding upon the States." 34 U.N. ESCOR, *supra.* Indeed, several commentators have concluded that the Universal Declaration has become, in toto, a part of binding, customary international law.

Turning to the act of torture, we have little difficulty discerning its universal renunciation in the modern usage and practice of nations. *Smith, supra,* at 160-61. The international consensus surrounding torture has found expression in numerous international treaties and accords. . . . The substance of these international agreements is reflected in modern municipal—i.e., national—law as well. Although torture was once a routine concomitant of criminal interrogations in many nations, during the modern and hopefully more enlightened era it has been universally renounced. According to one survey, torture is prohibited, expressly or implicitly, by the constitutions of over fifty-five nations, including both the United States and Paraguay. . . . We have been directed to no assertion by any contemporary state of a right to torture its own or another nation's citizens. Indeed, United States diplomatic contacts confirm the universal abhorrence with which torture is viewed:

> In exchanges between United States embassies and all foreign states with which the United States maintains relations, it has been the Department of State's general experience that no government has asserted a right to torture its own nationals. Where reports of torture elicit some credence, a state usually responds by denial or, less frequently, by asserting that the conduct was unauthorized or constituted rough treatment short of torture.[15]

Memorandum of the United States as *Amicus Curiae* at 16 n.34.

Having examined the sources from which customary international law is derived—the usage of nations, judicial opinions and the works of jurists—we conclude that official torture is now prohibited by the law of nations. . . . The treaties and accords cited above, as well as the express foreign policy of our own government, all make it clear that international law confers fundamental rights upon all people vis-à-vis their own governments. While the ultimate scope of those rights will be a subject for continuing refinement and elaboration, we hold that the right to be free from torture is now among them. We therefore turn to the question whether the other requirements for jurisdiction are met.

Appellee submits that even if the tort alleged is a violation of modern international law, federal jurisdiction may not be exercised consistent with the dictates of Article III of the Constitution. The claim is without merit. Common law courts of general jurisdiction regularly adjudicate transitory tort claims between individuals over whom they exercise personal jurisdiction, wherever the tort occurred. Moreover, as part of an articulated scheme of federal control over external affairs,

---

15. The fact that the prohibition of torture is often honored in the breach does not diminish its binding effect as a norm of international law. As one commentator has put it, "The best evidence for the existence of international law is that every actual State recognizes that it does exist and that it is itself under an obligation to observe it. States often violate international law, just as individuals often violate municipal law; but no more than individuals do States defend their violations by claiming that they are above the law." J. Brierly, The Outlook for International Law 4-5 (Oxford 1944).

Congress provided, in the first Judiciary Act, §9(b), 1 Stat. 73, 77 (1789), for federal jurisdiction over suits by aliens where principles of international law are in issue. The constitutional basis for the Alien Tort Statute is the law of nations, which has always been part of the federal common law.

It is not extraordinary for a court to adjudicate a tort claim arising outside of its territorial jurisdiction. A state or nation has a legitimate interest in the orderly resolution of disputes among those within its borders, and where the *lex loci delicti commissi* is applied, it is an expression of comity to give effect to the laws of the state where the wrong occurred. . . .

During the eighteenth century, it was taken for granted on both sides of the Atlantic that the law of nations forms a part of the common law. 1 Blackstone, Commentaries 263-64 (1st ed. 1765-69); 4 *id.* at 67. Under the Articles of Confederation, the Pennsylvania Court of Oyer and Terminer at Philadelphia, per McKean, Chief Justice, applied the law of nations to the criminal prosecution of the Chevalier de Longchamps for his assault upon the person of the French Consul-General to the United States, noting that "(t)his law, in its full extent, is a part of the law of this state. . . ." Respublica v. DeLongchamps, 1 U.S. (1 Dall.) 113, 119 (1784). . . .

[O]ne of the principal defects of the Confederation that our Constitution was intended to remedy was the central government's inability to "cause infractions of treaties or of the law of nations, to be punished." 1 Farrand, Records of the Federal Convention 19 (Rev. ed. 1937) (Notes of James Madison). . . .

As ratified, the judiciary article contained no express reference to cases arising under the law of nations. Indeed, the only express reference to that body of law is contained in Article I, §8, cl. 10, which grants to the Congress the power to "define and punish . . . offenses against the law of nations." Appellees seize upon this circumstance and advance the proposition that the law of nations forms a part of the laws of the United States only to the extent that Congress has acted to define it. This extravagant claim is amply refuted by the numerous decisions applying rules of international law uncodified in any act of Congress. *E.g.*, Ware v. Hylton, 3 U.S. (3 Dall.) 199, (1796); *The Paquete Habana, supra,* 175 U.S. 677; *Sabbatino, supra,* 376 U.S. 398 (1964). A similar argument was offered to and rejected by the Supreme Court in United States v. Smith, *supra,* at 158-60, and we reject it today. As John Jay wrote in The Federalist No. 3, at 22 (1 Bourne ed. 1901), "Under the national government, treaties and articles of treaties, as well as the laws of nations, will always be expounded in one sense and executed in the same manner, whereas adjudications on the same points and questions in the thirteen states will not always accord or be consistent." Federal jurisdiction over cases involving international law is clear.

Thus, it was hardly a radical initiative for Chief Justice Marshall to state in The Nereide, 13 U.S. (9 Cranch) 388, 422 (1815), that in the absence of a congressional enactment,[20] United States courts are "bound by the law of nations, which is a part of the law of the land." These words were echoed in *The Paquete Habana, supra,* 175 U.S. at 700: "international law is part of our law, and must be ascertained and

---

20. The plainest evidence that international law has an existence in the federal courts independent of acts of Congress is the long-standing rule of construction first enunciated by Chief Justice Marshall: "an act of congress ought never to be construed to violate the law of nations, if any other possible construction remains. . . . " The Charming Betsy, 6 U.S. (2 Cranch) 64, 67 (1804), quoted in Lauritzen v. Larsen, 345 U.S. 571, 578 (1953).

administered by the courts of justice of appropriate jurisdiction, as often as questions of right depending upon it are duly presented for their determination."

The Filartigas urge that 28 U.S.C. §1350 be treated as an exercise of Congress's power to define offenses against the law of nations. While such a reading is possible, see Lincoln Mills v. Textile Workers, 353 U.S. 448 (1957) (jurisdictional statute authorizes judicial explication of federal common law), we believe it is sufficient here to construe the Alien Tort Statute, not as granting new rights to aliens, but simply as opening the federal courts for adjudication of the rights already recognized by international law. The statute nonetheless does inform our analysis of Article III, for we recognize that questions of jurisdiction "must be considered part of an organic growth — part of the evolutionary process," and that the history of the judiciary article gives meaning to its pithy phrases. Romero v. International Terminal Operating Co., 358 U.S. 354, 360 (1959). The Framers' overarching concern that control over international affairs be vested in the new national government to safeguard the standing of the United States among the nations of the world therefore reinforces the result we reach today.

Although the Alien Tort Statute has rarely been the basis for jurisdiction during its long history, in light of the foregoing discussion, there can be little doubt that this action is properly brought in federal court.[22] This is undeniably an action by an alien, for a tort only, committed in violation of the law of nations. The paucity of suits successfully maintained under the section is readily attributable to the statute's requirement of alleging a "*violation* of the law of nations" (emphasis supplied) at the jurisdictional threshold. Courts have, accordingly, engaged in a more searching preliminary review of the merits than is required, for example, under the more flexible "arising under" formulation. *Compare* O'Reilly de Camara v. Brooke, 209 U.S. 45, 52 (1907) (question of Alien Tort Statute jurisdiction disposed of "on the merits") (Holmes, J.), *with* Bell v. Hood, 327 U.S. 678 (1946) (general federal question jurisdiction not defeated by the possibility that the averments in the complaint may fail to state a cause of action). Thus, the narrowing construction that the Alien Tort Statute has previously received reflects the fact that earlier cases did not involve such well-established, universally recognized norms of international law that are here at issue. . . .

Pena argues that the customary law of nations, as reflected in treaties and declarations that are not self-executing, should not be applied as rules of decision in this case. In doing so, he confuses the question of federal jurisdiction under the Alien Tort Statute, which requires consideration of the law of nations, with the issue of the choice of law to be applied, which will be addressed at a later stage in the proceedings. The two issues are distinct. Our holding on subject matter jurisdiction decides only whether Congress intended to confer judicial power, and whether it is authorized to do so by Article III. . . .

. . . [F]or purposes of civil liability, the torturer has become like the pirate and slave trader before him *hostis humani generis*, an enemy of all mankind. Our holding today, giving effect to a jurisdictional provision enacted by our First Congress, is a small but important step in the fulfillment of the ageless dream to free all people from brutal violence.

---

22. We recognize that our reasoning might also sustain jurisdiction under the general federal question provision, 28 U.S.C. §1331. We prefer, however, to rest our decision upon the Alien Tort Statute, in light of that provision's close coincidence with the jurisdictional facts presented in this case.

Notes and Questions

1. In *The Paquete Habana*, what explains the differing views of the majority and dissent about whether the U.S. Navy had violated customary international law? What evidence did the majority cite in support of its conclusion that customary international law prohibited the seizures in question? Under the majority's analysis, what does it take in order for customary practices to become legally binding?

2. What differences are there between the sources and content of the customary international law at issue in *The Paquete Habana* and the sources and content of the customary international law at issue in *Filartiga*? Do both decisions satisfy the Restatement (Third) definition of customary international law set forth at the beginning of this chapter?

The Paquete Habana and *Filartiga* represent different conceptions of customary international law. *The Paquete Habana* reflects a traditional conception of customary international law that emphasized the importance of state consent as embodied in state practice that developed slowly over a substantial period of time. By contrast, *Filartiga* represents a modern conception of customary international law that focuses less on state practice and state consent and instead emphasizes General Assembly Resolutions (which in themselves are technically not a source of international law, but which nonetheless may have normative force as representing the views of the nations of the world); positions taken at multilateral treaty conferences, regardless of whether the treaties have been ratified; and the pronouncements of international bodies, such as human rights committees and the International Law Commission. For more elaborate descriptions of the differences outlined in this paragraph, see Restatement (Third) of the Foreign Relations Law of the United States §102, reporters' note 2 (1987); Jeffrey M. Blum & Ralph G. Steinhardt, *Federal Jurisdiction over International Human Rights Claims: The Alien Tort Claims Act After* Filartiga v. Pena-Irala, 22 Harv. Int'l L.J. 53, 98-102 (1981); and Curtis A. Bradley & Jack L. Goldsmith, *Customary International Law as Federal Common Law: A Critique of the Modern Position*, 110 Harv. L. Rev. 815, 838-42 (1997).

The differences between these conceptions of customary international law raise at least two sets of questions. The first concerns the significance of these differences for the legitimacy of international law *per se*. Is one conception of customary international law more legitimate than the other? For various perspectives, see Jack L. Goldsmith & Eric A. Posner, The Limits of International Law 132-33 (2005); Blum & Steinhardt, *supra*, at 98-102; and J. Patrick Kelly, *The Twilight of Customary International Law*, 40 Va. J. Int'l L. 449 (2000).

The second set of questions concerns the relevance of the distinction between traditional and modern customary international law for purposes of the *domestic* status of this law in the U.S. legal system. Consider the distinction as you work through the questions below.

3. Although the Constitution does not mention customary international law in either Article III or Article VI, those Articles do refer to the "Laws of the United States," and some scholars have argued that the Founders intended that phrase to encompass customary international law. Isn't this argument undermined by the express reference to the law of nations in Article I? Is it likely that the Founders would have wanted *all* of the law of nations to be included within Articles III and VI, including the law merchant? Would the Founders have considered customary international law to be "made in Pursuance [of the Constitution]," as required by the Supremacy Clause? If not, is it likely that they intended the phrase "Laws of the

United States" in Article III to be broader than the similar phrase in Article VI? For a discussion of these and related issues, *compare* Curtis A. Bradley, *The Alien Tort Statute and Article III*, 42 Va. J. Int'l L. 587 (2002) (arguing that the phrase "Laws of the United States" was not intended to encompass the law of nations in either Article III or Article VI), *with* William S. Dodge, *The Constitutionality of the Alien Tort Statute: Some Observations on Text and Context*, 42 Va. J. Int'l L. 687 (2002) (arguing that the phrase "Laws of the United States" in Article III was intended to encompass the law of nations). For a recent article concluding that the Founders understood references to the "Laws of the United States" in the Constitution as encompassing only federal statutes and thus as not including the law of nations, see John Harrison, *The Constitution and the Law of Nations*, 106 Geo. L.J. 1659 (2018). For an argument that the phrase "Laws of the United States" in Article III encompassed the law of nations, but that the same phrase in Article VI did not, see Michael D. Ramsey, *The Constitution's Text and Customary International Law*, 106 Geo. L.J. 1747 (2018).

4. In England, as noted by Blackstone, "the law of nations . . . is here adopted in its full extent by the common law, and is held to be a part of the law of the land." 4 William Blackstone, Commentaries on The Laws of England 67 (1769); *see also* Triquet v. Bath, 3 Burr. 1478, 1481, 97 Eng. Rep. 936, 938 (K.B. 1764) (Mansfield, J.) (stating that "[t]he law of nations, in its full extent was part of the law of England"). Prior to the Constitution, state courts in the United States applied customary international law as part of state common law. A prominent example was the Pennsylvania Supreme Court's decision in Respublica v. DeLongchamps, 1 U.S. (1 Dall.) 113 (1784), a case discussed in *Filartiga*. *DeLongchamps* involved the prosecution of a French citizen for his assault upon the French consul-general to the United States, an offense considered at that time to be a violation of the law of nations. The Pennsylvania court explained that the law of nations, "in its full extent, is part of the law of this State, and is to be collected from the practice of different Nations, and the authority of writers." *Id.* at 119.

It is unclear to what extent this understanding changed after the adoption of the Constitution. As noted in Chapter 1, several Founders, in connection with neutrality prosecutions in the 1790s, stated that the law of nations was part of the laws of the United States. *See, e.g.*, Henfield's Case, 11 F. Cas. 1099, 1100-01 (C.C.D. Pa. 1793) (No. 6360) (Grand Jury charge of Jay, C.J.); *id.* at 1117 (Grand Jury charge of Wilson, J.); *see also* Charge to the Grand Jury for the District of New York (Apr. 4, 1790), in New Hampshire Gazette (Portsmouth 1790) (Chief Justice Jay instructs that the law of nations was "part of the laws of this, and of every other civilized nation"). In another Grand Jury charge, Justice Iredell explained:

> The Common Law of England, from which our own is derived, fully recognizes the principles of the Law of Nations, and applies them in all cases falling under its jurisdiction, where the nature of the subject requires it. . . . In whatever manner the Law of Nations is violated, it is a subject of national, not personal complaint.

Charge to the Grand Jury for the District of South Carolina (May 12, 1794), in Gazette of the United States (Philadelphia 1794). Attorneys General Edmund Randolph and Charles Lee made similar statements in official legal opinions in the 1790s. Randolph specifically noted that this conclusion was unaffected by the fact that the law of nations was "not specially adopted by the Constitution or any municipal act." 1 Op. Att'y Gen. 26, 27 (1792) (Attorney General Randolph); *see also id.* at 68 (1797) (Attorney General Lee).

What did these statements mean? For the view that these statements show that customary international law was viewed as federal law, see Jordan J. Paust, International

Law as Law of the United States 5-8 (1996); Edwin Dickinson, *The Law of Nations as Part of the National Law of the United States,* 101 U. Pa. L. Rev. 26 (1952); Douglas J. Sylvester, *International Law as Sword or Shield? Early American Foreign Policy and the Law of Nations,* 32 N.Y.U. J. Int'l L. & Pol. 1 (1999). For the view that these statements meant simply that customary international law provided a non-federal rule of decision in cases otherwise within the federal courts' jurisdiction, see Bradley, *The Alien Tort Statute and Article III, supra;* Stewart Jay, *The Status of the Law of Nations in Early American Law,* 42 Vand. L. Rev. 819, 832 (1989); Arthur Weisburd, *The Executive Branch and International Law,* 41 Vand. L. Rev. 1205, 1222-23 (1988); *cf.* Robert C. Palmer, *The Federal Common Law of Crime,* 4 L. & Hist. Rev. 267, 294-96 (1986) (arguing that these statements meant that customary international law was state law). For a historical account that contends that "there was a broad consensus in the Founding period that the law of nations was incorporated into federal law and bound not only the states and the judiciary, but also the executive branch and, in the view of at least some, Congress as well," see David M. Golove & Daniel J. Hulsebosch, *The Law of Nations and the Constitution: An Early Modern Perspective,* 106 Geo. L.J. 1593, 1597 (2018).

5. Whatever its status at the Founding, it appears that by the late 1790s and early 1800s, customary international law was not viewed as federal law within the meaning of Articles III and VI. In Ware v. Hylton, 3 U.S. 199, 281 (1796), the Court considered whether Virginia's confiscation of debts owed to British creditors was consistent with the Treaty of Peace with Great Britain and the law of nations. As to the latter point, Justices Chase and Iredell concluded (without disagreement from the other Justices) that customary international law did not preempt inconsistent state law. *See id.* at 229 (Chase, J.); *id.* at 265-66 (Iredell, J.); *see generally* David P. Currie, The Constitution in the Supreme Court: The First Hundred Years, 1789-1888, at 38 & n.46 (1985). In the early nineteenth century, the Supreme Court held that nonwritten common law (including, presumably, customary international law) could not serve as the basis for a criminal prosecution in the federal courts. *See* United States v. Hudson & Goodwin, 11 U.S. (7 Cranch) 32, 34 (1812); United States v. Coolidge, 14 U.S. (1 Wheat.) 415, 416-17 (1816). In a legal opinion in 1802, Jefferson's Attorney General, Levi Lincoln, wrote that "an aggravated violation against the law of nations" did not contravene any "provision in the Constitution [or] any law of the United States," and that the "law of nations is considered as a part of the municipal law of each State." 5 Op. Att'y Gen. 691, 692 (1802).

6. In the nineteenth and early twentieth centuries, the law of nations was treated as an element of "general common law," a body of law most famously identified with Swift v. Tyson, 41 U.S. 1 (1842). General common law was a type of customary law that U.S. courts applied as "rules of decision in particular cases without insisting that the law be attached to any particular sovereign." William A. Fletcher, *The General Common Law and Section 34 of the Judiciary Act of 1798: The Example of Marine Insurance,* 97 Harv. L. Rev. 1513, 1517 (1984). General common law was not considered part of the "Laws of the United States" within the meaning of Articles III and VI of the Constitution; federal court interpretations of general common law were not binding on the states; and a case "arising under" general common law did not by that fact alone establish federal question jurisdiction. *See* Bradford R. Clark, *Federal Common Law: A Structural Reinterpretation,* 144 U. Pa. L. Rev. 1245, 1276-92 (1996); Fletcher, *supra,* at 1521-27. The Supreme Court expressly referred to customary international law as "general law" or "common law" during this period, and in several cases it declined to review state court determinations of customary international law because of the lack of a federal question. *See, e.g.,* Oliver Am. Trading

Co. v. Mexico, 264 U.S. 440, 442-43 (1924) (foreign sovereign immunity); New York Life Ins. Co. v. Hendren, 92 U.S. 286, 286-87 (1875) ("laws of war"). Was customary international law's status as non-federal general common law consistent with the Founders' commitment to federal control over U.S. foreign relations? If so, how? If not, why did courts treat customary international law in this fashion?

7. In light of this historical background, what is the meaning of the statement in *The Paquete Habana* that "international law is part of our law"? Does the Court view customary international law as federal law or general common law? In answering this question, what is the significance of the Court's statements that customary international law applies "where there is no treaty, and no controlling executive or legislative act," and that courts must "give effect to" customary international law "in the absence of any treaty or other public act of [the] government in relation to the matter"?

8. The Supreme Court overruled Swift v. Tyson in Erie Railroad Co. v. Tompkins, 304 U.S. 64 (1938), stating that "there is no federal general common law," and holding that "[e]xcept in matters governed by the Federal Constitution or by Act of Congress, the law to be applied in any case is the law of the State." One reason the Court in *Erie* rejected the notion of a general common law in the federal courts was the Court's belief that "law in the sense in which courts speak of it today does not exist without some definite authority behind it." *Erie* did not, however, eliminate the lawmaking powers of federal courts. *Erie* ruled that federal court development of general common law was illegitimate not because it was a form of judicial lawmaking per se, but rather because it was *unauthorized* lawmaking not grounded in a sovereign source. Federal courts thus retain some power to make federal common law when authorized to do so in some fashion by the Constitution or a federal statute or treaty. *See, e.g.,* Larry Kramer, *The Lawmaking Power of the Federal Courts,* 12 Pace L. Rev. 263, 268-88 (1992); Thomas Merrill, *The Common Law Powers of Federal Courts,* 52 U. Chi. L. Rev. 1, 17 (1985). This grounding of federal common lawmaking in a federal sovereign source makes the new federal common law, unlike the pre-*Erie* general common law, federal law within the meaning of Article II (Take Care Clause), Article III (arising under jurisdiction), and Article VI (the Supremacy Clause). What are the implications of *Erie* and post-*Erie* federal common law for the domestic status of customary international law? In the absence of congressional incorporation, should its applicability now be treated as matter of state law? Or did it become federal common law in the post-*Erie* sense? Alternatively, is it possible that customary international law survived as general common law?

9. Professor Philip Jessup, who later served as a judge on the International Court of Justice (ICJ), was the first commentator to recognize the need for an examination of *Erie*'s implications for the domestic status of customary international law. One year after *Erie,* Jessup acknowledged in a brief essay that if *Erie* were "applied broadly, it would follow that hereafter a state court's determination of a rule of international law would be a finding regarding the law of the state and would not be reviewed by the Supreme Court of the United States." Philip C. Jessup, *The Doctrine of* Erie Railroad v. Tompkins *Applied to International Law,* 33 Am. J. Int'l L. 740, 742 (1939). However, Jessup argued against this construction of *Erie.* He reasoned that the Court in *Erie* was not thinking about international law, and that it "would be as unsound as it would be unwise" to bind federal courts to state court interpretations of customary international law.

The first judicial decision to consider the domestic legal status of customary international law after *Erie,* Bergman v. De Sieyes, 170 F.2d 360 (2d Cir. 1948), appeared to conclude, contrary to Jessup, that the applicability of customary international law was to be determined by state law. In *Bergman*, a diversity case removed to New York federal court, the issue was whether an ambassador in transit to another country was entitled under customary international law to immunity from service of process. The court, in an opinion by Judge Learned Hand, explained that "[the New York state courts'] interpretation of international law is controlling upon us, and we are to follow them so far as they have declared themselves." After analyzing three New York decisions and a variety of international sources, Hand concluded that "the courts of New York would today hold" that an ambassador in transit is immune under customary international law from service of process in New York. *Id.* Judge Hand added the following caveat: "Whether an avowed refusal to accept a well-established doctrine of international law, or a plain misapprehension of it, would present a federal question we need not consider, for neither is present here." Does Hand's approach make sense? What is the significance of his caveat? What are the consequences of the view that customary international law is state law? Is this what the Founders would have wanted?

10. Consider the Supreme Court's 1964 decision in *Sabbatino*, excerpted in Chapter 2. Does the logic of *Sabbatino*'s federal common law analysis entail the conclusion that customary international law is post-*Erie* federal common law? Does the holding of *Sabbatino*—barring judicial review of the validity of certain acts of state under customary international law—support or weaken the view that customary international law is federal common law? What is the significance of the Court's favorable reference in *Sabbatino* to Jessup's article and the Court's statement that Jessup's "basic rationale is equally applicable to the act of state doctrine"? As a contrast, here is what the Second Circuit in *Sabbatino* had to say about the federal common law issue:

> We mention one further problem related to this case which we find unnecessary to settle but which may arise to torment some future court with a case similar to the present one. That problem is whether the law governing this case involves elements of federal law or whether the case is governed solely by New York law. *Cf.* Bergman v. De Sieyes, 170 F.2d 360 (2d Cir. 1948). It has been said that the act of state doctrine is part of the law of conflict of laws. If that is so, it would seem that under the rule in Klaxon Co. v. Stentor Elec. Mfg. Co., 313 U.S. 487 (1941), it is New York law which we are applying. On the other hand, certain cases have indicated that international law is part of the body of federal law. *See, e.g.*, The Lusitania, 251 F. 715, 732 (S.D.N.Y. 1918). Perhaps Erie R. R. v. Tompkins has changed the rule in these latterly mentioned cases. . . . For our purposes here we do not have to resolve these questions because it appears to us that a New York court would reach the same result we reach.

Banco Nacional de Cuba v. Sabbatino, 307 F.2d 845, 869 n.16 (2d Cir. 1962).

11. *Filartiga* was the first decision in the post-*Erie* period to squarely hold that customary international law has the status of federal common law. *Filartiga* itself makes clear one implication of this holding: a case arising under customary international law "arises under" federal law for purposes of Article III federal jurisdiction. Is this a proper construction of Article III? Is the court in *Filartiga* correct in stating that customary international law has "always been part of the federal common law"? Does a case under customary international law also "arise under" federal law for purposes of statutory federal question jurisdiction, 28 U.S.C. §1331?

12. A second possible consequence of *Filartiga*'s holding is that customary international law binds the President under Article II, which provides that the President "shall take Care that the Laws be faithfully executed." *See* U.S. Const., Art.

II, §3. Is customary international law included within the "Laws" that the President must faithfully execute? Recall from Chapter 1 that Hamilton, writing as Pacificus, argued that customary international law was included within the "Laws." He made this argument as support for an *enhancement* of presidential power, contending that President Washington's power to execute the laws included an ability to issue the Neutrality Proclamation and thereby execute customary international law rules relating to neutrality. But does the President have the domestic authority to *violate* customary international law? Most courts that have considered this question have held that he does. *See, e.g.,* Barrera-Echavarria v. Rison, 44 F.3d 1441, 1451 (9th Cir. 1995); Gisbert v. United States Attorney General, 988 F.2d 1437, 1448 (5th Cir. 1993); Garcia-Mir v. Meese, 788 F.2d 1446, 1454-55 (11th Cir. 1986). These decisions rely heavily on the statement from *The Paquete Habana* that customary international law is to be applied by U.S. courts "only 'where there is no treaty and no controlling executive or legislative act or judicial decision. . . .'" *Garcia-Mir,* 788 F.2d at 1454 (quoting *The Paquete Habana,* 175 U.S. at 700). The President normally cannot violate a federal statute; so why can the President violate federal law in the form of customary international law? If the President can violate customary international law, does this suggest that perhaps it is not federal law after all? Is it possible that customary international law is part of the "Laws of the United States" within the meaning of Article VI but not part of "the Laws" in the Article II Take Care Clause? In answering these questions, what is the significance of the observation in *Sabbatino* that "[w]hen articulating principles of international law in its relations with other states, the Executive Branch speaks not only as an interpreter of generally accepted and traditional rules, as would the courts, but also as an advocate of standards it believes desirable for the community of nations and protective of national concerns"?

For discussion of these and other issues concerning the relationship between customary international law and the Executive Branch, see Essays, *Agora: May the President Violate Customary International Law?,* 80 Am. J. Int'l L. 913 (1986); Essays, *Agora: May the President Violate Customary International Law? (Cont'd),* 81 Am. J. Int'l L. 371 (1987); *The Authority of the United States Executive to Interpret, Articulate or Violate the Norms of International Law,* 80 Am. Soc'y Int'l L. Proc. 297 (1986); Michael J. Glennon, *Raising* The Paquete Habana: *Is Violation of Customary International Law by the Executive Unconstitutional?,* 80 Nw. U. L. Rev. 321 (1985); Arthur M. Weisburd, *The Executive Branch and International Law,* 41 Vand. L. Rev. 1205 (1988).

13. A third possible consequence of the view that customary international law is federal common law is that it preempts inconsistent state law pursuant to the Supremacy Clause. This is the view of the Restatement and of a number of international law scholars. *See, e.g.,* Restatement (Third), *supra,* §111(1); Jordan J. Paust, International Law as Law of the United States 6-7 (1996); Lea Brilmayer, *Federalism, State Authority, and the Preemptive Power of International Law,* 1994 Sup. Ct. Rev. 295, 302-04; Louis Henkin, *International Law as Law in the United States,* 82 Mich. L. Rev. 1555, 1560-62 (1984); Harold Hongju Koh, *Is International Law Really State Law?,* 111 Harv. L. Rev. 1824 (1998).

Is the view that customary international law is preemptive federal law consistent with the text of the Supremacy Clause? The Supremacy Clause states that the Constitution, treaties, and "Laws of the United States which shall be made in Pursuance [*of the Constitution*]" are supreme over state law. As Professor Henkin noted:

> Customary international law, it will be argued, is the law of the international community of which the United States is a member, not a law of the United States directly. Strictly, customary international law is not "made" it results from the practice of states.

If it is "made," not all of it was made "pursuant" to the Constitution, since much of it antedated the Constitution. If it is made, it is not made by the United States and through its governmental institutions alone but by them together with many foreign governments in a process to which the United States contributes only in an uncertain way and to an indeterminate degree.

Louis Henkin, Foreign Affairs and the United States Constitution 508 n.16 (2d ed. 1996). Is this argument persuasive? How might customary international law be made to fit within the text of the Supremacy Clause?

There is little precedent for the proposition that customary international law can preempt an inconsistent state law. One state court decision, however, might be read to support this proposition: In Republic of Argentina v. City of New York, 250 N.E.2d 698 (Ct. App. N.Y. 1969), the New York Court of Appeals held that the City of New York could not assess taxes against Argentina's consulate property because the assessment would violate customary international law. The court did not explain its views about the precise status of customary international law, but the court might have implicitly been accepting Argentina's argument that customary international law had the status of preemptive federal law.

14. A final possibility is that customary international law, as federal common law, binds Congress. Lower courts have consistently held that Congress can violate customary international law. *See, e.g.,* United States v. Yousef, 327 F.3d 56, 93 (2d Cir. 2003); United States v. Yunis, 924 F.2d 1086, 1091 (D.C. Cir. 1991); *Garcia-Mir, supra.* However, as discussed in Chapter 5, the Supreme Court has held that self-executing treaties and federal statutes are essentially equal in status, such that the later in time prevails as a matter of U.S. domestic law. This invites the argument that a newly developed norm of customary international law, like a new treaty, could supersede a prior inconsistent federal statute. As the Restatement (Third) explains: "Since international customary law and an international agreement have equal authority in international law, and both are law of the United States, arguably later customary law should be given effect as law of the United States, even in the face of an earlier law or agreement, just as a later international agreement of the United States is given effect in the face of an earlier law or agreement." Restatement (Third) of Foreign Relations Law, §115, reporters' note 4. Is this argument persuasive? Can courts exercise other federal common law powers to invalidate a federal statute? For a rare decision suggesting that customary international law can supersede a federal statute if it develops after the enactment of the statute, see Beharry v. Reno, 183 F. Supp. 2d 584 (E.D.N.Y. 2002), *rev'd on other grounds,* 329 F.3d 51 (2d Cir. 2003). *But see* Guaylupo-Moya v. Gonzales, 423 F.3d 121 (2d Cir. 2005) ("[T]o the extent that *Beharry* purports to declare that international law should override the plain language and effect of the relevant statutes, that reasoning was in error; clear congressional action trumps customary international law and previously enacted treaties.").

15. Even if Congress is not bound by customary and other forms of international law, it often takes account of such law when enacting statutes, in part because of the influence of the Executive Branch during the legislative process. For an extensive analysis of this phenomenon, see Ashley Deeks, *Statutory International Law,* 57 Va. J. Int'l L. 263 (2018):

Congress . . . employs international law in a wide variety of ways, some of which express a congressional objection to international law, but many of which embrace that law. These international law-utilizing statutes (which this Article calls "statutory international law" or "SIL") operate like capillaries throughout the corpus of the U.S. Code, delivering small doses of international law to help minimize conflicts between U.S. law and behavior, on the one hand, and foreign behavior and expectations, on the other. Statutory international law addresses a wide variety of subjects, including tax, trade, maritime, criminal, military, human rights, and foreign relations issues. . . .

In at least some examples of SIL, the Executive has helped identify the relevance of international legal concepts to particular pieces of draft legislation and persuaded Congress to include those concepts in the statute. Congress has independent strategic reasons to enact SIL, to be sure, including because Congress agrees substantively with the rule, wishes to reduce its drafting costs, or hopes to use SIL to shift interpretive burdens to the other branches. However, executive pressure is an important exogenous reason for the production of SIL.

16. There is a great deal of commentary concerning the domestic status of customary international law in the absence of political branch incorporation of such law. The leading academic view following *Filartiga* was that all of customary international law has the status of self-executing federal common law that courts were bound to apply even in the absence of congressional authorization. See, for example, Restatement (Third) of Foreign Relations Law, §111; Lea Brilmayer, *Federalism, State Authority, and the Preemptive Power of International Law*, 1994 Sup. Ct. Rev. 295; Louis Henkin, *International Law as Law in the United States*, 82 Mich. L. Rev. 1555 (1984).

This conventional wisdom that customary international law has the status of federal common law became the subject of significant academic debate beginning in the mid-1990s. Articles challenging this conventional wisdom include Curtis A. Bradley & Jack L. Goldsmith, *Customary International Law as Federal Common Law: A Critique of the Modern Position*, 110 Harv. L. Rev. 815 (1997); Arthur M. Weisburd, *State Courts, Federal Courts, and International Cases*, 20 Yale J. Int'l L. 1 (1995); and Phillip R. Trimble, *A Revisionist View of Customary International Law*, 33 UCLA L. Rev. 665 (1986).

Articles defending the conventional wisdom include Ryan Goodman & Derek P. Jinks, Filartiga*'s Firm Footing: International Human Rights and Federal Common Law*, 66 Fordham L. Rev. 463 (1997); Harold Hongju Koh, *Is International Law Really State Law?*, 111 Harv. L. Rev. 1824 (1998); Gerald L. Neuman, *Sense and Nonsense About Customary International Law: A Response to Professors Bradley and Goldsmith*, 66 Fordham L. Rev. 371 (1997); Beth Stephens, *The Law of Our Land: Customary International Law as Federal Law After* Erie, 66 Fordham L. Rev. 393 (1997); and, more recently, Carlos M. Vazquez, *Customary International Law as U.S. Law: A Critique of the Revisionist and Intermediate Positions and a Defense of the Modern Position*, 86 Notre Dame L. Rev. 1495 (2011).

As the title of the last article suggests, scholars have staked out various middle-ground positions on the domestic legal status of customary international law. Some argue that federal courts should apply customary international law as non-federal common law of the sort that was applied prior to *Erie. See* Ernest A. Young, *Sorting Out the Debate over Customary International Law*, 42 Va. J. Int'l L. 365 (2002); T. Alexander Aleinikoff, *International Law, Sovereignty, and American Constitutionalism: Reflections on the Customary International Law Debate*, 98 Am. J. Int'l L. 91 (2004). *See also* David J. Bederman, *Law of the Land, Law of the Sea: The Lost Link Between Customary International Law and the General Maritime Law*, 51 Va. J. Int'l L. 299 (2011) (arguing that CIL should have the same domestic status today as "general maritime law"). Under the intermediate approach offered by Professors Bellia and Clark, by contrast, "the best reading of Supreme Court precedent . . . is that the law of nations does not apply as preemptive federal law by virtue of any general Article III power to fashion federal common law, but only when necessary to preserve and implement distinct Article I and Article II powers to recognize foreign nations, conduct foreign relations, and decide momentous questions of war and peace." Anthony J. Bellia, Jr. & Bradford R. Clark, *The Federal Common Law of Nations*, 109 Colum. L. Rev. 1 (2009). *See also* Anthony J. Bellia, Jr. & Bradford R. Clark, *The Law of Nations as Constitutional Law*, 98 Va. L. Rev. 729 (2012) (arguing that customary international law can properly be applied by U.S. courts to help implement the Constitution's allocation of foreign affairs powers). Professors Bellia and Clark have now published a book, *The Law of Nations and the United States Constitution* (2017), reflecting their views on the domestic status of the law of nations. This book was the subject of a 2018 symposium in the Georgetown Law Journal featuring articles by William S. Dodge, David M. Golove & Daniel J. Hulsebosch, John Harrison, Thomas H. Lee, Michael D. Ramsey, Paul B. Stephan, and Ingrid Wuerth. For an argument that "the text, structure, and objectives of the Constitution, and the weight of judicial authority, require treating all rules of customary international law as rules of federal law, but that such rules will be directly applicable in U.S. courts only when the federal political branches have expressly or impliedly provided for judicial application of a particular rule," see Gary Born, *Customary International Law in United States Courts*, 92 Wash. L. Rev. 1641, 1643 (2017).

B. ALIEN TORT STATUTE: NATURE AND SOURCE OF THE CAUSE OF ACTION

The Alien Tort Statute (ATS), at issue in *Filartiga*, provides that "[t]he district courts shall have original jurisdiction of any civil action by an alien for a tort only, committed in violation of the law of nations or a treaty of the United States." 28 U.S.C. §1350. The ATS was, in a slightly different form, part of the Judiciary Act of 1789 that first created and organized the U.S. federal court system. There is little mention of the ATS in the legislative history of the Judiciary Act, and its original purposes are uncertain. As Judge Henry Friendly once stated, "This old but little used section is a kind of legal Lohengrin; although it has been with us since the first Judiciary Act . . . no one seems to know whence it came." IIT v. Vencap, Ltd., 519 F.2d 1001, 1015 (2d Cir. 1975).

Filartiga breathed new life into the ATS with its holding that federal courts had jurisdiction under the statute and Article III to adjudicate lawsuits between aliens concerning violations of international human rights standards committed in other countries. The *Filartiga* holding solely concerned subject matter jurisdiction in ATS cases, however, and did not identify the source of the plaintiffs' cause of action. An important court of appeals decision four years after *Filartiga* focused on this question. In Tel-Oren v. Libyan Arab Republic, 726 F.2d 774 (D.C. Cir. 1984), aliens who were victims of a terrorist attack in Israel sued the Palestine Liberation Organization and others under the ATS, alleging violations of customary international law prohibitions on torture and summary execution. The court dismissed the suit, but the judges could not agree on the reason for dismissal. Judge Robb reasoned that the case raised nonjusticiable political questions. Judge Edwards reasoned that, although the ATS implicitly created a cause of action for violations of customary international law, such a cause of action was limited to suits against state actors. Judge Bork argued that neither the ATS nor customary international law created a cause of action. He also argued that judicial implication of a cause of action would impermissibly interfere with political branch control of U.S. foreign relations, and that courts should wait for "affirmative action by Congress" before allowing the ATS to be used as the vehicle for international human rights litigation.

In 1992, Congress provided "affirmative action" with regard to the international human rights violations of torture and extrajudicial killing by enacting the Torture Victim Protection Act (TVPA), excerpted below.

Torture Victim Protection Act

Pub. L. No. 102-256, §2, 106 Stat. 73 (Mar. 12, 1992)

(a) Liability. An individual who, under actual or apparent authority, or color of law, of any foreign nation—

(1) subjects an individual to torture shall, in a civil action, be liable for damages to that individual; or

(2) subjects an individual to extrajudicial killing shall, in a civil action, be liable for damages to the individual's legal representative, or to any person who may be a claimant in an action for wrongful death.

(b) Exhaustion of remedies. A court shall decline to hear a claim under this section if the claimant has not exhausted adequate and available remedies in the place in which the conduct giving rise to the claim occurred.

(c) Statute of limitations. No action shall be maintained under this section unless it is commenced within 10 years after the cause of action arose.

SEC. 3. DEFINITIONS

(a) Extrajudicial killing. For the purposes of this Act, the term "extrajudicial killing" means a deliberated killing not authorized by a previous judgment pronounced by a regularly constituted court affording all the judicial guarantees which are recognized as indispensable by civilized peoples. Such term, however, does not include any such killing that, under international law, is lawfully carried out under the authority of a foreign nation.

(b) Torture. For the purposes of this Act—

(1) the term "torture" means any act, directed against an individual in the offender's custody or physical control, by which severe pain or suffering (other than pain or suffering arising only from or inherent in, or incidental to, lawful sanctions), whether physical or mental, is intentionally inflicted on that individual for such purposes as obtaining from that individual or a third person information or a confession, punishing that individual for an act that individual or a third person has committed or is suspected of having committed, intimidating or coercing that individual or a third person, or for any reason based on discrimination of any kind; and

(2) mental pain or suffering refers to prolonged mental harm caused by or resulting from—

(A) the intentional infliction or threatened infliction of severe physical pain or suffering;

(B) the administration or application, or threatened administration or application, of mind altering substances or other procedures calculated to disrupt profoundly the senses or the personality;
　　(C) the threat of imminent death; or
　　(D) the threat that another individual will imminently be subjected to death, severe physical pain or suffering, or the administration or application of mind altering substances or other procedures
calculated to disrupt profoundly the senses or personality.

Twenty-four years after *Filartiga*, the Supreme Court addressed the meaning
and implications of the ATS in the following decision.

Sosa v. Alvarez-Machain

542 U.S. 692 (2004)

[The United States Drug Enforcement Administration (DEA) recruited petitioner
Sosa and other Mexican nationals to abduct respondent Alvarez-Machain (Alvarez),
also a Mexican national, from Mexico to stand trial in the United States for allegedly
assisting in the murder and torture of a DEA agent. Following his acquittal, Alvarez
sued Sosa and others under the ATS for violating customary international law prohibitions on arbitrary arrest and detention.]

JUSTICE SOUTER delivered the opinion of the Court. . . .
　　The parties and *amici* here advance radically different historical interpretations
of [the ATS]. Alvarez says that the ATS was intended not simply as a jurisdictional
grant, but as authority for the creation of a new cause of action for torts in violation
of international law. We think that reading is implausible. As enacted in 1789, the
ATS gave the district courts "cognizance" of certain causes of action, and the term
bespoke a grant of jurisdiction, not power to mold substantive law. The fact that the
ATS was placed in §9 of the Judiciary Act, a statute otherwise exclusively concerned
with federal-court jurisdiction, is itself support for its strictly jurisdictional nature.
Nor would the distinction between jurisdiction and cause of action have been elided
by the drafters of the Act or those who voted on it. . . . In sum, we think the statute
was intended as jurisdictional in the sense of addressing the power of the courts to
entertain cases concerned with a certain subject.
　　But holding the ATS jurisdictional raises a new question, this one about the
interaction between the ATS at the time of its enactment and the ambient law of
the era. Sosa would have it that the ATS was stillborn because there could be no
claim for relief without a further statute expressly authorizing adoption of causes of
action. *Amici* professors of federal jurisdiction and legal history take a different tack,
that federal courts could entertain claims once the jurisdictional grant was on the
books, because torts in violation of the law of nations would have been recognized
within the common law of the time. We think history and practice give the edge to
this latter position.
　　"When the United States declared their independence, they were bound to
receive the law of nations, in its modern state of purity and refinement." Ware

v. Hylton, 3 Dall. 199, 281 (1796) (Wilson, J.). In the years of the early Republic, this law of nations comprised two principal elements, the first covering the general norms governing the behavior of national states with each other: "the science which teaches the rights subsisting between nations or states, and the obligations correspondent to those rights," E. de Vattel, The Law of Nations, Preliminaries §3 (J. Chitty et al. transl. and ed. 1883) (hereinafter Vattel) (footnote omitted), or "that code of public instruction which defines the rights and prescribes the duties of nations, in their intercourse with each other," 1 James Kent Commentaries *1. This aspect of the law of nations thus occupied the executive and legislative domains, not the judicial. See 4 W. Blackstone, Commentaries on the Laws of England 68 (1769) (hereinafter Commentaries) ("Offenses against" the law of nations are "principally incident to whole states or nations").

The law of nations included a second, more pedestrian element, however, that did fall within the judicial sphere, as a body of judge-made law regulating the conduct of individuals situated outside domestic boundaries and consequently carrying an international savor. To Blackstone, the law of nations in this sense was implicated "in mercantile questions, such as bills of exchange and the like; in all marine causes, relating to freight, average, demurrage, insurances, bottomry . . . ; [and] in all disputes relating to prizes, to shipwrecks, to hostages, and ransom bills." Id. at 67. The law merchant emerged from the customary practices of international traders and admiralty required its own transnational regulation. And it was the law of nations in this sense that our precursors spoke about when the Court explained the status of coast fishing vessels in wartime grew from "ancient usage among civilized nations, beginning centuries ago, and gradually ripening into a rule of international law. . . ." The Paquete Habana, 175 U.S. 677, 686 (1900).

There was, finally, a sphere in which these rules binding individuals for the benefit of other individuals overlapped with the norms of state relationships. Blackstone referred to it when he mentioned three specific offenses against the law of nations addressed by the criminal law of England: violation of safe conducts, infringement of the rights of ambassadors, and piracy. 4 Commentaries 68. An assault against an ambassador, for example, impinged upon the sovereignty of the foreign nation and if not adequately redressed could rise to an issue of war. See Vattel 463-64. It was this narrow set of violations of the law of nations, admitting of a judicial remedy and at the same time threatening serious consequences in international affairs, that was probably on minds of the men who drafted the ATS with its reference to tort.

Before there was any ATS, a distinctly American preoccupation with these hybrid international norms had taken shape owing to the distribution of political power from independence through the period of confederation. The Continental Congress was hamstrung by its inability to "cause infractions of treaties, or of the law of nations to be punished," J. Madison, Journal of the Constitutional Convention 60 (E. Scott ed. 1893), and in 1781 the Congress implored the States to vindicate rights under the law of nations. In words that echo Blackstone, the congressional resolution called upon state legislatures to "provide expeditious, exemplary, and adequate punishment" for "the violation of safe conducts or passports, . . . of hostility against such as are in amity, . . . with the United States, . . . infractions of the immunities of ambassadors and other public ministers . . . [and] infractions of treaties and conventions to which the United States are a party." 21 Journals of the Continental Congress 1136-37 (G. Hunt ed. 1912) (hereinafter Journals of the Continental Congress). The resolution recommended that the States "authorise suits . . . for damages by the party injured, and for compensation to the United

States for damage sustained by them from an injury done to a foreign power by a citizen." *Id.* at 1137. . . . Apparently only one State acted upon the recommendation, . . . but Congress had done what it could to signal a commitment to enforce the law of nations.

Appreciation of the Continental Congress's incapacity to deal with this class of cases was intensified by the so-called Marbois incident of May 1784, in which a French adventurer, Longchamps, verbally and physically assaulted the Secretary of the French Legion in Philadelphia. Congress called again for state legislation addressing such matters, and concern over the inadequate vindication of the law of nations persisted through the time of the constitutional convention. During the Convention itself, in fact, a New York City constable produced a reprise of the Marbois affair and Secretary Jay reported to Congress on the Dutch Ambassador's protest, with the explanation that "the federal government does not appear . . . to be vested with any judicial Powers competent to the Cognizance and Judgment of such Cases." William R. Casto, The Federal Courts' Protective Jurisdiction Over Torts Committed in Violation of the Law of Nations, 18 Conn. L. Rev. 467, 494 & n.152 (1986).

The Framers responded by vesting the Supreme Court with original jurisdiction over "all Cases affecting Ambassadors, other public ministers and Consuls," U.S. Const., Art. III, §2, and the First Congress followed through. The Judiciary Act reinforced this Court's original jurisdiction over suits brought by diplomats, see 1 Stat. 80, ch. 20, §13, created alienage jurisdiction, §11 and, of course, included the ATS, §9. . . .

[D]espite considerable scholarly attention, it is fair to say that a consensus understanding of what Congress intended has proven elusive.

Still, the history does tend to support two propositions. First, there is every reason to suppose that the First Congress did not pass the ATS as a jurisdictional convenience to be placed on the shelf for use by a future Congress or state legislature that might, some day, authorize the creation of causes of action or itself decide to make some element of the law of nations actionable for the benefit of foreigners. The anxieties of the preconstitutional period cannot be ignored easily enough to think that the statute was not meant to have a practical effect. . . .

The second inference to be drawn from the history is that Congress intended the ATS to furnish jurisdiction for a relatively modest set of actions alleging violations of the law of nations. Uppermost in the legislative mind appears to have been offenses against ambassadors; violations of safe conduct were probably understood to be actionable; and individual actions arising out of prize captures and piracy may well have also been contemplated. But the common law appears to have understood only those three of the hybrid variety as definite and actionable, or at any rate, to have assumed only a very limited set of claims. . . .

We think it is correct, then, to assume that the First Congress understood that the district courts would recognize private causes of action for certain torts in violation of the law of nations, though we have found no basis to suspect Congress had any examples in mind beyond those torts corresponding to Blackstone's three primary offenses: violation of safe conducts, infringement of the rights of ambassadors, and piracy. We assume, too, that no development in the two centuries from the enactment of §1350 to the birth of the modern line of cases beginning with Filartiga v. Pena-Irala, 630 F.2d 876 (2d Cir. 1980), has categorically precluded federal courts from recognizing a claim under the law of nations as an element of common law; Congress has not in any relevant way amended §1350 or limited civil common law power by another statute. Still, there are good reasons for a restrained conception of the discretion a federal court should exercise in considering a new cause of action of this kind. Accordingly, we think courts should require any claim based on the present-day law of nations to rest on a norm of international character accepted by the civilized world and defined with a specificity comparable to the features of the 18th-century paradigms we have recognized. This requirement is fatal to Alvarez's claim.

A series of reasons argue for judicial caution when considering the kinds of individual claims that might implement the jurisdiction conferred by the early statute. First, the prevailing conception of the common law has changed since 1789 in a way that counsels restraint in judicially applying internationally generated norms. When §1350 was enacted, the accepted conception was of the common law as "a transcendental body of law outside of any particular State but obligatory within it unless and until changed by statute." Black and White Taxicab & Transfer Co. v. Brown and Yellow Taxicab & Transfer Co., 276 U.S. 518, 533 (1928) (Holmes, J., dissenting). Now, however, in most cases where a court is asked to state or formulate a common law principle in a new context, there is a general understanding that the law is not so much found or discovered as it is either made or created. . . .

Second, along with, and in part driven by, that conceptual development in understanding common law has come an equally significant rethinking of the role of the federal courts in making it. Erie R. Co. v. Tompkins, 304 U.S. 64 (1938), was the watershed in which we denied the existence of any federal "general" common law, which largely withdrew to havens of specialty, some of them defined by express congressional authorization to devise a body of law directly. Elsewhere, this Court has thought it was in order to create federal common law rules in interstitial areas of particular federal interest. And although we have even assumed competence to make judicial rules of decision of particular importance to foreign relations, such as the act of state doctrine, see Banco Nacional de Cuba v. Sabbatino, 376 U.S. 398, 427 (1964), the general practice has been to look for legislative guidance before exercising innovative authority over substantive law. It would be remarkable to take a more aggressive role in exercising a jurisdiction that remained largely in shadow for much of the prior two centuries.

Third, this Court has recently and repeatedly said that a decision to create a private right of action is one better left to legislative judgment in the great majority of cases. The creation of a private right of action raises issues beyond the mere consideration whether underlying primary conduct should be allowed or not, entailing, for example, a decision to permit enforcement without the check imposed by prosecutorial discretion. Accordingly, even when Congress has made it clear by statute that a rule applies to purely domestic conduct, we are reluctant to infer intent to provide a private cause of action where the statute does not supply one expressly. While the absence of congressional action addressing private rights of action under an international norm is more equivocal than its failure to provide such a right when it creates a statute, the possible collateral consequences of making international rules privately actionable argue for judicial caution.

Fourth, the subject of those collateral consequences is itself a reason for a high bar to new private causes of action for violating international law, for the potential implications for the foreign relations of the United States of recognizing such causes should make courts particularly wary of impinging on the discretion of the Legislative and Executive Branches in managing foreign affairs. It is one thing for

American courts to enforce constitutional limits on our own State and Federal Governments' power, but quite another to consider suits under rules that would go so far as to claim a limit on the power of foreign governments over their own citizens, and to hold that a foreign government or its agent has transgressed those limits. Yet modern international law is very much concerned with just such questions, and apt to stimulate calls for vindicating private interests in §1350 cases. Since many attempts by federal courts to craft remedies for the violation of new norms of international law would raise risks of adverse foreign policy consequences, they should be undertaken, if at all, with great caution. *Cf.* Tel-Oren v. Libyan Arab Republic, 726 F.2d 774, 813 (D.C. Cir. 1984) (Bork, J., concurring) (expressing doubt that §1350 should be read to require "our courts [to] sit in judgment of the conduct of foreign officials in their own countries with respect to their own citizens").

The fifth reason is particularly important in light of the first four. We have no congressional mandate to seek out and define new and debatable violations of the law of nations, and modern indications of congressional understanding of the judicial role in the field have not affirmatively encouraged greater judicial creativity. It is true that a clear mandate appears in the Torture Victim Protection Act of 1991, providing authority that "establishes an unambiguous and modern basis for" federal claims of torture and extrajudicial killing, H.R. Rep. No. 102-367, pt. 1, p. 3 (1991). But that affirmative authority is confined to specific subject matter, and although the legislative history includes the remark that §1350 should "remain intact to permit suits based on other norms that already exist or may ripen in the future into rules of customary international law," Congress as a body has done nothing to promote such suits. Several times, indeed, the Senate has expressly declined to give the federal courts the task of interpreting and applying international human rights law, as when its ratification of the International Covenant on Civil and Political Rights declared that the substantive provisions of the document were not self-executing.

These reasons argue for great caution in adapting the law of nations to private rights. . . .

Whereas Justice Scalia sees these developments as sufficient to close the door to further independent judicial recognition of actionable international norms, other considerations persuade us that the judicial power should be exercised on the understanding that the door is still ajar subject to vigilant doorkeeping, and thus open to a narrow class of international norms today. *Erie* did not in terms bar any judicial recognition of new substantive rules, no matter what the circumstances, and post-*Erie* understanding has identified limited enclaves in which federal courts may derive some substantive law in a common law way. For two centuries we have affirmed that the domestic law of the United States recognizes the law of nations. It would take some explaining to say now that federal courts must avert their gaze entirely from any international norm intended to protect individuals.

We think an attempt to justify such a position would be particularly unconvincing in light of what we know about congressional understanding bearing on this issue lying at the intersection of the judicial and legislative powers. The First Congress, which reflected the understanding of the framing generation and included some of the Framers, assumed that federal courts could properly identify some international norms as enforceable in the exercise of §1350 jurisdiction. We think it would be unreasonable to assume that the First Congress would have expected federal courts to lose all capacity to recognize enforceable international norms simply because the common law might lose some metaphysical cachet on the road to modern realism. Later Congresses seem to have shared our view. The position we take today has been assumed by some federal courts for 24 years, ever since the Second Circuit decided Filartiga v. Pena-Irala, 630 F.2d 876 (2d Cir. 1980), and for practical purposes the point of today's disagreement has been focused since the exchange between Judge Edwards and Judge Bork in Tel-Oren v. Libyan Arab Republic, 726 F.2d 774 (D.C. Cir. 1984), Congress, however, has not only expressed no disagreement with our view of the proper exercise of the judicial power, but has responded to its most notable instance by enacting legislation supplementing the judicial determination in some detail. *See supra* (discussing the Torture Victim Protection Act).

While we agree with Justice Scalia to the point that we would welcome any congressional guidance in exercising jurisdiction with such obvious potential to affect foreign relations, nothing Congress has done is a reason for us to shut the door to the law of nations entirely. It is enough to say that Congress may do that at any time (explicitly, or implicitly by treaties or statutes that occupy the field) just as it may modify or cancel any judicial decision so far as it rests on recognizing an international norm as such.[19]

We must still, however, derive a standard or set of standards for assessing the particular claim Alvarez raises, and for this case it suffices to look to the historical antecedents. Whatever the ultimate criteria for accepting a cause of action subject to jurisdiction under §1350, we are persuaded that federal courts should not recognize private claims under federal common law for violations of any international law norm with less definite content and acceptance among civilized nations than the historical paradigms familiar when §1350 was enacted. *See, e.g.,* United States v. Smith, 18 U.S. 153, 163-80 (1820) (illustrating the specificity with which the law of nations defined piracy). This limit upon judicial recognition is generally consistent with the reasoning of many of the courts and judges who faced the issue before it reached this Court. *See Filartiga, supra,* at 890 ("[F]or purposes of civil liability, the torturer has become—like the pirate and slave trader before him—*hostis humani generis,* an enemy of all mankind"); *Tel-Oren, supra,* at 781 (Edwards, J., concurring) (suggesting that the "limits of section 1350's reach" be defined by "a handful of heinous actions—each of which violates definable, universal and obligatory norms"); *see also* In re Estate of Marcos Human Rights Litigation, 25 F.3d 1467, 1475 (9th Cir. 1994) ("Actionable violations of international law must be of a norm that is specific, universal, and obligatory"). And the determination whether a norm is sufficiently definite to support a cause of action[20] should (and, indeed, inevitably must) involve an element of judgment about the practical consequences of making that cause available to litigants in the federal courts.[21] . . .

19. Our position does not . . . imply that every grant of jurisdiction to a federal court carries with it an opportunity to develop common law (so that the grant of federal-question jurisdiction would be equally as good for our purposes as §1350). Section 1350 was enacted on the congressional understanding that courts would exercise jurisdiction by entertaining some common law claims derived from the law of nations; and we know of no reason to think that federal-question jurisdiction was extended subject to any comparable congressional assumption. Further, our holding today is consistent with the division of responsibilities between federal and state courts after *Erie,* as a more expansive common law power related to 28 U.S.C. §1331 might not be.

20. A related consideration is whether international law extends the scope of liability for a violation of a given norm to the perpetrator being sued, if the defendant is a private actor such as a corporation or individual. *Compare* Tel-Oren v. Libyan Arab Republic, 726 F.2d 774, 791-95 (D.C. Cir. 1984) (Edwards, J., concurring) (insufficient consensus in 1984 that torture by private actors violates international law), *with* Kadic v. Karadzic, 70 F.3d 232, 239-41 (2d Cir. 1995) (sufficient consensus in 1995 that genocide by private actors violates international law).

21. This requirement of clear definition is not meant to be the only principle limiting the availability of relief in the federal courts for violations of customary international law, though it disposes of

Thus, Alvarez's detention claim must be gauged against the current state of international law, looking to those sources we have long, albeit cautiously, recognized....

To begin with, Alvarez cites two well-known international agreements that, despite their moral authority, have little utility under the standard set out in this opinion. He says that his abduction by Sosa was an "arbitrary arrest" within the meaning of the Universal Declaration of Human Rights (Declaration). And he traces the rule against arbitrary arrest not only to the Declaration, but also to article nine of the International Covenant on Civil and Political Rights (Covenant), to which the United States is a party, and to various other conventions to which it is not. But the Declaration does not of its own force impose obligations as a matter of international law. And, although the Covenant does bind the United States as a matter of international law, the United States ratified the Covenant on the express understanding that it was not self-executing and so did not itself create obligations enforceable in the federal courts. Accordingly, Alvarez cannot say that the Declaration and Covenant themselves establish the relevant and applicable rule of international law. He instead attempts to show that prohibition of arbitrary arrest has attained the status of binding customary international law.

Here, it is useful to examine Alvarez's complaint in greater detail. As he presently argues it, the claim does not rest on the cross-border feature of his abduction. Although the District Court granted relief in part on finding a violation of international law in taking Alvarez across the border from Mexico to the United States, the Court of Appeals rejected that ground of liability for failure to identify a norm of requisite force prohibiting a forcible abduction across a border. Instead, it relied on the conclusion that the law of the United States did not authorize Alvarez's arrest, because the DEA lacked extraterritorial authority under 21 U.S.C. §878, and because Federal Rule of Criminal Procedure 4(d)(2) limited the warrant for Alvarez's arrest to "the jurisdiction of the United States." It is this position that Alvarez takes now: that his arrest was arbitrary and as such forbidden by international law not because it infringed the prerogatives of Mexico, but because no applicable law authorized it.

Alvarez thus invokes a general prohibition of "arbitrary" detention defined as officially sanctioned action exceeding positive authorization to detain under the domestic law of some government, regardless of the circumstances. Whether or not this is an accurate reading of the Covenant, Alvarez cites little authority that a

---

this case. For example, the European Commission argues as *amicus curiae* that basic principles of international law require that before asserting a claim in a foreign forum, the claimant must have exhausted any remedies available in the domestic legal system, and perhaps in other fora such as international claims tribunals. *Cf.* Torture Victim Protection Act of 1991, §2(b) (exhaustion requirement). We would certainly consider this requirement in an appropriate case. Another possible limitation that we need not apply here is a policy of case-specific deference to the political branches. For example, there are now pending in federal district court several class actions seeking damages from various corporations alleged to have participated in, or abetted, the regime of apartheid that formerly controlled South Africa. *See* In re South African Apartheid Litigation, 238 F. Supp. 2d 1379 (JPML 2002) (granting a motion to transfer the cases to the Southern District of New York). The Government of South Africa has said that these cases interfere with the policy embodied by its Truth and Reconciliation Commission, which "deliberately avoided a 'victors' justice' approach to the crimes of apartheid and chose instead one based on confession and absolution, informed by the principles of reconciliation, reconstruction, reparation and goodwill." The United States has agreed. In such cases, there is a strong argument that federal courts should give serious weight to the Executive Branch's view of the case's impact on foreign policy. *Cf.* Republic of Aus. v. Altmann, 541 U.S. 677 (2004) (discussing the State Department's use of statements of interest in cases involving the Foreign Sovereign Immunities Act of 1976, 28 U.S.C. §1602 *et seq.*).

rule so broad has the status of a binding customary norm today.[27] He certainly cites nothing to justify the federal courts in taking his broad rule as the predicate for a federal lawsuit, for its implications would be breathtaking. His rule would support a cause of action in federal court for any arrest, anywhere in the world, unauthorized by the law of the jurisdiction in which it took place, and would create a cause of action for any seizure of an alien in violation of the Fourth Amendment, supplanting the actions under 42 U.S.C. §1983 and Bivens v. Six Unknown Fed. Narcotics Agents, 403 U.S. 388 (1971), that now provide damages remedies for such violations. It would create an action in federal court for arrests by state officers who simply exceed their authority; and for the violation of any limit that the law of any country might place on the authority of its own officers to arrest. And all of this assumes that Alvarez could establish that Sosa was acting on behalf of a government when he made the arrest, for otherwise he would need a rule broader still.

Alvarez's failure to marshal support for his proposed rule is underscored by the Restatement (Third) of Foreign Relations Law of the United States (1987), which says in its discussion of customary international human rights law that a "state violates international law if, as a matter of state policy, it practices, encourages, or condones . . . prolonged arbitrary detention." *Id.*, §702. Although the Restatement does not explain its requirements of a "state policy" and of "prolonged" detention, the implication is clear. Any credible invocation of a principle against arbitrary detention that the civilized world accepts as binding customary international law requires a factual basis beyond relatively brief detention in excess of positive authority. Even the Restatement's limits are only the beginning of the enquiry, because although it is easy to say that some policies of prolonged arbitrary detentions are so bad that those who enforce them become enemies of the human race, it may be harder to say which policies cross that line with the certainty afforded by Blackstone's three common law offenses. In any event, the label would never fit the reckless policeman who botches his warrant, even though that same officer might pay damages under municipal law.

Whatever may be said for the broad principle Alvarez advances, in the present, imperfect world, it expresses an aspiration that exceeds any binding customary rule having the specificity we require.[29] Creating a private cause of action to further that aspiration would go beyond any residual common law discretion we think it appropriate to exercise. It is enough to hold that a single illegal detention of less than a day, followed by the transfer of custody to lawful authorities and a prompt arraignment, violates no norm of customary international law so well defined as to support the creation of a federal remedy. . . .

---

27. Specifically, he relies on a survey of national constitutions; a case from the International Court of Justice; and some authority drawn from the federal courts. None of these suffice. The [national constitution survey] does show that many nations recognize a norm against arbitrary detention, but that consensus is at a high level of generality. The [ICJ] case . . . involved a different set of international norms and mentioned the problem of arbitrary detention only in passing; the detention in that case was, moreover, far longer and harsher than Alvarez's. And the authority from the federal courts, to the extent it supports Alvarez's position, reflects a more assertive view of federal judicial discretion over claims based on customary international law than the position we take today.

29. It is not that violations of a rule logically foreclose the existence of that rule as international law. *Cf.* Filartiga v. Pena-Irala, 630 F.2d 876, 884 n.15 (2d Cir. 1980) ("The fact that the prohibition of torture is often honored in the breach does not diminish its binding effect as a norm of international law"). Nevertheless, that a rule as stated is as far from full realization as the one Alvarez urges is evidence against its status as binding law; and an even clearer point against the creation by judges of a private cause of action to enforce the aspiration behind the rule claimed.

JUSTICE SCALIA, with whom THE CHIEF JUSTICE and JUSTICE THOMAS join, concurring in part and concurring in the judgment. . . .

The analysis in the Court's opinion departs from my own in this respect: After concluding . . . that "the ATS is a jurisdictional statute creating no new causes of action," the Court addresses at length . . . the "good reasons for a restrained conception of the *discretion* a federal court should exercise in considering a new cause of action" under the ATS. (Emphasis added.) By framing the issue as one of "discretion," the Court skips over the antecedent question of authority. This neglects the "lesson of *Erie*," that "grants of jurisdiction alone" (which the Court has acknowledged the ATS to be) "are not themselves grants of law-making authority." Daniel J. Meltzer, *Customary International Law, Foreign Affairs, and Federal Common Law*, 42 Va. J. Int'l L. 513, 541 (2002). On this point, the Court observes only that no development between the enactment of the ATS (in 1789) and the birth of modern international human rights litigation under that statute (in 1980) "has categorically *precluded* federal courts from recognizing a claim under the law of nations as an element of common law." (Emphasis added.) This turns our jurisprudence regarding federal common law on its head. The question is not what case or congressional action prevents federal courts from applying the law of nations as part of the general common law; it is what *authorizes* that peculiar exception from *Erie*'s fundamental holding that a general common law *does not exist.*

The Court would apparently find authorization in the understanding of the Congress that enacted the ATS, that "district courts would recognize private causes of action for certain torts in violation of the law of nations." But as discussed above, that understanding rested upon a notion of general common law that has been repudiated by *Erie.*

The Court recognizes that *Erie* was a "watershed" decision heralding an avulsive change, wrought by "conceptual development in understanding common law . . . [and accompanied by an] equally significant rethinking of the role of the federal courts in making it." The Court's analysis, however, does not follow through on this insight, interchangeably using the unadorned phrase "common law" . . . to refer to pre-*Erie* general common law and post-*Erie* federal common law. This lapse is crucial, because the creation of post-*Erie* federal common law is rooted in a positivist mindset utterly foreign to the American common-law tradition of the late 18th century. Post-*Erie* federal common lawmaking (all that is left to the federal courts) is so far removed from that general-common-law adjudication which applied the "law of nations" that it would be anachronistic to find authorization to do the former in a statutory grant of jurisdiction that was thought to enable the latter.* Yet that is precisely what the discretion-only analysis . . . suggests.

---

* The Court conjures the illusion of common lawmaking continuity between 1789 and the present by ignoring fundamental differences. The Court's approach places the law of nations on a federal law footing unknown to the First Congress. At the time of the ATS's enactment, the law of nations, being part of general common law, was *not* supreme federal law that could displace state law. By contrast, a judicially created federal rule based on international norms *would be* supreme federal law. Moreover, a federal common law cause of action of the sort the Court reserves discretion to create would "arise under" the laws of the United States, not only for purposes of Article III, but also for purposes of *statutory* federal-question jurisdiction. The lack of genuine continuity is thus demonstrated by the fact that today's opinion renders the ATS unnecessary for federal jurisdiction over so-called law of nations claims. If the law of nations can be transformed into federal law on the basis of (1) a provision that merely grants jurisdiction, combined with (2) some residual judicial power (from whence nobody knows) to create federal causes of action in cases implicating foreign relations, then a grant of federal question jurisdiction would give rise to a power to create international law-based federal common law just as effectively as would the ATS. This would mean that the ATS became largely superfluous as of 1875, when Congress granted general federal

Because today's federal common law is not our Framers' general common law, the question presented by the suggestion of discretionary authority to enforce the law of nations is not whether to extend old-school general-common-law adjudication. Rather, it is whether to create new federal common law. The Court masks the novelty of its approach when it suggests that the difference between us is that we would "close the door to further independent judicial recognition of actionable international norms," whereas the Court would permit the exercise of judicial power "on the understanding that the door is still ajar subject to vigilant doorkeeping." The general common law was the old door. We do not close that door today, for the deed was done in *Erie*. Federal common law is a *new* door. The question is not whether that door will be left ajar, but whether this Court will open it. . . .

To be sure, today's opinion does not itself precipitate a direct confrontation with Congress by creating a cause of action that Congress has not. But it invites precisely that action by the lower courts, even while recognizing (1) that Congress understood the difference between granting jurisdiction and creating a federal cause of action in 1789, (2) that Congress understands that difference today, and (3) that the ATS itself supplies only jurisdiction. In holding open the possibility that judges may create rights where Congress has not authorized them to do so, the Court countenances judicial occupation of a domain that belongs to the people's representatives. One does not need a crystal ball to predict that this occupation will not be long in coming, since the Court endorses the reasoning of "many of the courts and judges who faced the issue before it reached this Court," including the Second and Ninth Circuits.

The Ninth Circuit brought us the judgment that the Court reverses today. Perhaps its decision in this particular case, like the decisions of other lower federal courts that receive passing attention in the Court's opinion, "reflects a more assertive view of federal judicial discretion over claims based on customary international law than the position we take today." But the verbal formula it applied is the same verbal formula that the Court explicitly endorses. Endorsing the very formula that led the Ninth Circuit to its result in this case hardly seems to be a recipe for restraint in the future. . . .

Though it is not necessary to resolution of the present case, one further consideration deserves mention: Despite the avulsive change of *Erie*, the Framers who included reference to "the Law of Nations" in Article I, §8, cl. 10, of the Constitution would be entirely content with the post-*Erie* system I have described, and quite terrified by the "discretion" endorsed by the Court. That portion of the general common law known as the law of nations was understood to refer to the accepted practices of nations in their dealings with one another (treatment of ambassadors, immunity of foreign sovereigns from suit, etc.) and with actors on the high seas hostile to all nations and beyond all their territorial jurisdictions (pirates). Those accepted practices have for the most part, if not in their entirety, been enacted into United States statutory law, so that insofar as they are concerned the demise of the general common law is inconsequential. The notion that a law of nations, redefined to mean the consensus of states on *any* subject, can be used by a private citizen to control a sovereign's treatment of *its own citizens* within *its own territory* is a 20th-century invention of internationalist law professors and human-rights advocates. The Framers would,

---

question jurisdiction subject to a $500 amount-in-controversy requirement, and entirely superfluous as of 1980, when Congress eliminated the amount-in-controversy requirement.

I am confident, be appalled by the proposition that, for example, the American peoples' democratic adoption of the death penalty could be judicially nullified because of the disapproving views of foreigners.

We Americans have a method for making the laws that are over us. We elect representatives to two Houses of Congress, each of which must enact the new law and present it for the approval of a President, whom we also elect. For over two decades now, unelected federal judges have been usurping this lawmaking power by converting what they regard as norms of international law into American law. Today's opinion approves that process in principle, though urging the lower courts to be more restrained.

Notes and Questions

1. As the Court in *Sosa* suggests, the original purposes of the ATS are uncertain. By its terms, the ATS provides a basis for federal court jurisdiction in certain international tort cases. Do you think the ATS was, as the Court speculates, a response to the Continental Congress's inability to ensure compliance with U.S. international obligations? Does the Marbois affair recounted by the Court support this conclusion? Do you agree with the Court that, in enacting the ATS, Congress probably had in mind the three individual offenses against the law of nations recited by Blackstone (i.e., violations of safe conducts, infringements of the rights of ambassadors, and piracy)? To the extent that the pre-constitutional events cited by the Court suggest a desire to comply with international law obligations, and to avoid conflicts with foreign nations, is the use of the ATS since *Filartiga* consistent with these purposes?

For various perspectives on the original meaning and scope of the ATS, see Anthony J. Bellia, Jr. & Bradford R. Clark, *The Alien Tort Statute and the Law of Nations*, 78 U. Chi. L. Rev. 445 (2011); Curtis A. Bradley, *The Alien Tort Statute and Article III*, 42 Va. J. Int'l L. 587 (2002); Anne-Marie Burley, *The Alien Tort Statute and the Judiciary Act of 1789: A Badge of Honor*, 83 Am. J. Int'l L. 461 (1989); William R. Casto, *The Federal Courts' Protective Jurisdiction over Torts Committed in Violation of the Law of Nations*, 18 Conn. L. Rev. 467 (1986); William S. Dodge, *The Historical Origins of the Alien Tort Statute: A Response to the "Originalists,"* 19 Hastings Int'l & Comp. L. Rev. 221 (1996); Thomas H. Lee, *The Safe Conduct Theory of the Alien Tort Statute*, 106 Colum. L. Rev. 830 (2006); William J. Moon, *The Original Meaning of the Law of Nations*, 56 Va. J. Int'l L. 51 (2016); John M. Rogers, *The Alien Tort Statute and How Individuals "Violate" International Law*, 21 Vand. J. Transnat'l L. 47 (1988); Joseph Modeste Sweeney, *A Tort Only in Violation of the Law of Nations*, 18 Hastings Int'l & Comp. L. Rev. 445 (1995); Arthur Weisburd, *The Executive Branch and International Law*, 41 Vand. L. Rev. 1205 (1988).

2. The ATS requires that the plaintiff be an alien, and, since *Filartiga*, the ATS has often been used by aliens to sue other aliens. Would the First Congress have envisioned that the ATS would be a vehicle for alien-versus-alien suits concerning violations of the law of nations? If so, into which category of Article III jurisdiction would they have thought these cases would fall? What, if anything, does the Court in *Sosa* suggest about the relationship between the ATS and Article III? *Cf.* Mossman v. Higginson, 4 U.S. (4 Dall.) 12 (1800) (holding that the alien diversity provision in Article III does not extend to suits between aliens and therefore construing Section 11 of the Judiciary Act, which gave the circuit courts jurisdiction over suits "where an alien is a party," as "confined to suits between citizens and foreigners"). *See also*

Bradley, *The Alien Tort Statute and Article III, supra* (arguing that the drafters of the ATS probably had in mind suits against U.S. citizens); Bellia & Clark, *The Alien Tort Statute and the Law of Nations, supra* (same).

3. From the time of the ATS's enactment in 1789 to the *Filartiga* decision in 1980, only two decisions had relied on the ATS as a basis for jurisdiction. *See* Adra v. Clift, 195 F. Supp. 857 (D. Md. 1961) (holding that a mother's concealment of her half-Lebanese child's name and nationality, resulting in the child being given a falsified Iraqi passport, was a tort in violation of the law of nations for purposes of the ATS); Bolchos v. Darrell, 3 F. Cas. 810 (D.S.C. 1795) (No. 1607) (finding jurisdiction under both an admiralty statute and the ATS in a case involving dispute about ownership of slaves on board a captured Spanish vessel). Why did the ATS not serve as a basis for jurisdiction in more cases?

Part of the answer is that, before *Filartiga*, courts generally held that the law of nations did not regulate the ways in which nations treated their own citizens. *See, e.g.,* Dreyfus v. Von Finck, 534 F.2d 24, 31 (2d Cir. 1976) ("[V]iolations of international law do not occur when the aggrieved parties are nationals of the acting state."). This view reflected a pre-World War II conception of customary international law, in which "it was thought to be antithetical for there to be international legal rights that individuals could assert against states, especially against their own governments." Mark W. Janis, International Law 268 (6th ed. 2012). But after World War II, several developments—most notably the Nuremberg trials, the United Nations General Assembly's 1948 Universal Declaration of Human Rights, and a series of international human rights agreements—led to the view that "how a state treats individual human beings . . . is a matter of international concern and a proper subject for regulation by international law." Restatement (Third) of Foreign Relations Law of the United States, pt. VII introductory note at 144-45 (1987). As noted in the previous section, beginning with *Filartiga*, courts began to view a customary international human rights law based on these and related sources as cognizable in cases brought under the ATS.

4. To succeed in an ATS suit, it is not enough for plaintiffs to establish that the court has jurisdiction. The plaintiffs must also have a cause of action that allows them to seek their requested relief (such as damages). With the exception of Judge Bork's concurrence in *Tel-Oren*, most courts after *Filartiga* and before the Supreme Court's decision in *Sosa* concluded that the ATS itself provided a cause of action. *See, e.g.,* In re Estate of Ferdinand Marcos, Human Rights Litigation, 25 F.3d 1467, 1474-75 (9th Cir. 1994); *cf.* Abebe-Jira v. Negewo, 72 F.3d 844, 848 (11th Cir. 1996) (interpreting ATS as delegating to the federal courts the task of fashioning remedies, including causes of action, to give effect to the federal policies underlying the ATS).

In *Sosa*, the Court unanimously rejected this view, holding that the ATS is merely a jurisdictional statute that does not itself confer any causes of action. Nevertheless, a majority of the Court also ruled that in limited circumstances judges could create causes of action in ATS cases. What justifications does the majority give for doing so? Does the fact that Congress in 1789 would have expected some causes of action for violations of international law to be available as a matter of general common law compel the conclusion that, after the abolition of general common law and the adoption of much stricter standards for finding causes of action, courts may create federal common law causes of action when applying the ATS? In applying a statute, is a court obligated not only to apply what Congress enacted but also to attempt to recreate the jurisprudential landscape that Congress legislated against?

5. The Court in *Sosa* describes a number of reasons for judicial caution in recognizing new claims under the ATS, and it states that ATS litigation should be "subject to vigilant doorkeeping" by the lower federal courts. After *Sosa*, when is it appropriate for courts to recognize a cause of action in a case brought under the ATS? How specific must the international consensus be in order to support a cause of action? What evidence would show that a norm of international law has been "accepted by the civilized world and defined with a specificity comparable to the features of the 18th-century paradigms [discussed by the Court]"? For example, what weight should be given to non-binding U.N. resolutions or treaties that have not been ratified by the United States, or that have been ratified subject to a declaration stating that the treaty is not self-executing? Are these materials irrelevant sources of law, or merely insufficient by themselves to support a cause of action? Why, precisely, did the Court decline to find a cause of action for Alvarez's claim of arbitrary arrest?

6. What are the implications of *Sosa* for the domestic status of customary international law outside the context of the ATS? Is it possible to maintain, after *Sosa*, that *all* of customary international law is self-executing federal common law? That *none* of it is? For a discussion of these and related questions, see Curtis A. Bradley, Jack L. Goldsmith, & David H. Moore, Sosa, *Customary International Law, and the Continuing Relevance of* Erie, 120 Harv. L. Rev. 869 (2007). In this article, the authors argue that the Court's reasoning and conclusions in *Sosa* "are incompatible with the modern position claim that [customary international law] is automatically part of U.S. federal law," and that "[c]ommentators who construe *Sosa* as embracing the modern position have confounded the automatic incorporation of [customary international law] as domestic federal law in the absence of congressional authorization (that is, the modern position) with the entirely different issue of whether and to what extent a particular statute, the Alien Tort Statute (ATS), authorizes courts to apply [customary international law] as domestic federal law." *Id.* at 873, 935. For commentary on this article, see William S. Dodge, *Customary International Law and the Question of Legitimacy*, 120 Harv. L. Rev. F. 19 (2007); and Ernest A. Young, Sosa *and the Retail Incorporation of International Law*, 120 Harv. L. Rev. F. 28 (2007).

7. Can customary international law serve as a basis for federal court jurisdiction under the federal question jurisdiction statute, 28 U.S.C. §1331? What does footnote 22 of *Filartiga* suggest? Footnote 19 of *Sosa*? Of what relevance is *Sosa*'s footnote 19 to the questions in the previous note? Prior to *Sosa*, several lower courts rejected the claim that customary international law could be a basis for federal question jurisdiction under §1331. *See, e.g.,* Princz v. Federal Republic of Germany, 26 F.3d 1166, 1176 (D.C. Cir. 1994); Xuncax v. Gramajo, 886 F. Supp. 162, 193-94 (D. Mass. 1995); Handel v. Artukovic, 601 F. Supp. 1421, 1426 (C.D. Cal. 1985). Since *Sosa*, a number of courts have concluded that jurisdiction must be based on the ATS, and not §1331, in order to support judicial application of the international law-based causes of action allowed by the Supreme Court in *Sosa*. *See, e.g.,* Mohamad v. Rajoub, 634 F.3d 604, 609-10 (D.C. Cir. 2011); Serra v. Lappin, 600 F.3d 1191, 1197 & n. 7 (9th Cir. 2010). *See also* Sarei v. Rio Tinto, PLC, 671 F.3d 736, 751 (9th Cir. 2011) (en banc) (observing that "§1331 did not make the ATS superfluous, because only the ATS carries with it the Congressional assumption that the judiciary would use it to develop the common law in an area of particular federal interest: international relations").

8. Are there circumstances short of wholesale incorporation of customary international law, but outside the ATS context, in which courts can nonetheless apply customary international law as federal common law? In First National City Bank v. Banco Para El Comercio Exterior De Cuba, 462 U.S. 611 (1983), the Supreme Court looked to federal common law, which it viewed to be informed both by "international law principles and by articulated congressional policies," to determine when to pierce the corporate veil of separate juridical entities in suits under the Foreign Sovereign Immunities Act (FSIA). Customary international law might be similarly relevant to filling in gaps in the FSIA. *See* Curtis A. Bradley & Jack L. Goldsmith, *Pinochet and International Human Rights Litigation*, 97 Mich. L. Rev. 2129, 2166-67 (1999). One might also think that to the extent that federal courts apply principles of treaty interpretation from the Vienna Convention on the Law of Treaties, which binds the United States at most as customary international law, such principles would also apply as federal common law to bind state courts in their interpretation of treaties. *Cf.* Chubb & Son, Inc. v. Asiana Airlines, 214 F.3d 301 (2d Cir. 2000) (looking to principles of customary international law as embodied in the Vienna Convention on the Law of Treaties to ascertain whether a treaty existed between United States and Korea).

9. In footnote 21, the Court in *Sosa* refers to the possibility of "case-specific deference to the political branches," and, after describing the State Department's involvement in an ATS case involving South Africa, states that "[i]n such cases, there is a strong argument that federal courts should give serious weight to the Executive Branch's view of the case's impact on foreign policy." How much weight should courts give to the views of the Executive Branch about whether to recognize a particular cause of action under the ATS? Does case-specific deference to the Executive create a danger of politicizing ATS litigation?

10. In addition to the cause of action and Executive suggestion issues addressed in *Sosa*, the Court mentions in footnote 21 that another possible limitation in ATS cases is that the plaintiff may need to exhaust remedies available outside the United States. What would be the source of this limitation? For a decision suggesting that an exhaustion requirement should be applied in some ATS cases, see Sarei v. Rio Tinto, PLC, 550 F.3d 822 (9th Cir. 2008) (en banc). The lead plurality opinion in that case reasoned that, as a prudential matter, "where the United States 'nexus' is weak, courts should carefully consider the question of exhaustion, particularly—but not exclusively—with respect to claims that do not involve matters of 'universal concern.'" For additional discussion of the issue of exhaustion in ATS cases, see Note, *The Alien Tort Statute, Forum Shopping, and the Exhaustion of Local Remedies Norm*, 121 Harv. L. Rev. 2110 (2008). For an extension of the exhaustion idea outside the ATS context to a case brought under the FSIA involving an alleged expropriation of property, see Cassirer v. Kingdom of Spain, 580 F.3d 1048 (9th Cir. 2009).

11. As the Court notes in *Sosa*, the legislative history of the TVPA expresses support for the *Filartiga* approach to human rights litigation under the ATS. Despite this legislative history, is the text of the TVPA in fact consistent with the *Filartiga* approach to human rights litigation? Note that the TVPA, unlike the ATS, is limited to two specifically defined violations of international law and contains a statute of limitations and an exhaustion requirement. Note also that *Sosa* implied that Congress can shape the scope of the ATS "explicitly, or implicitly by treaties or statutes that occupy the field." *Sosa*, 542 U.S. at 731. In this light, does the TVPA narrow ATS-style human rights litigation with respect to torture and extrajudicial killing? Or can plaintiffs avoid the limitations of the TVPA by bringing their torture or extrajudicial claim under the ATS?

These questions were addressed in Enahoro v. Abubakar, 408 F.3d 877 (7th Cir. 2005), which held that a suit for torture and extrajudicial killing could not be brought under the ATS because the TVPA "occupied the field" of civil human rights lawsuits for these causes of action. The court reasoned that it would make no sense for Congress to codify a cause of action for torture and extrajudicial killing with the procedural restrictions in the TVPA if plaintiffs could simply plead these causes of action under the ATS alone and avoid the TVPA's procedural requirements. The court reasoned that this conclusion was consistent with the Supreme Court's insistence in *Sosa* on "vigilant doorkeeping" in developing private rights of action in human rights cases. Do you agree with this analysis? Other courts have held, by contrast, that plaintiffs may plead claims of torture under either the ATS or the TVPA. *See, e.g.,* Romero v. Drummond Co., 552 F.3d 1303, 1316 (11th Cir. 2008); Aldana v. Del Monte Fresh Produce, 416 F.3d 1242, 1250-51 (11th Cir. 2005).

A related question is whether the TVPA's procedural requirements apply to plaintiffs bringing suit under the ATS. For example, should the TVPA's exhaustion requirement apply in ATS suits not involving torture and extrajudicial killing? Some courts have held that it does not. *See, e.g.,* Jean v. Dorelien, 431 F.3d 776 (11th Cir. 2005); Doe v. Saravia, 348 F. Supp. 2d 1112, 1157-58 (E.D. Cal. 2004). *Compare* Sarei v. Rio Tinto, PLC, 550 F.3d 822, 832 (9th Cir. 2008) (en banc) ("While the TVPA is not dispositive of the question of whether exhaustion is required by the ATS, the TVPA nonetheless provides a useful, congressionally-crafted template to guide our adoption of an exhaustion principle for the ATS."). Why would Congress want an exhaustion requirement for torture and extrajudicial killing suits, but not, say, for suits involving prolonged and arbitrary detention? Another procedural limitation in the TVPA is a ten-year statute of limitations. Does it apply to ATS claims? Most courts have held that it does, reasoning that the ATS does not specify a statute of limitations and the TVPA is the closest analogy. *See, e.g.,* Chavez v. Carranza, 559 F.3d 486, 492 (6th Cir. 2009); Arce v. Garcia, 400 F.3d 1340, 1345-46 (11th Cir. 2005); Papa v. United States, 281 F.3d 1004, 1012-13 (9th Cir. 2002). Are these decisions correct? Does it make sense to apply the TVPA's statute of limitations but not its exhaustion requirement in ATS cases?

12. The first President Bush expressed the following concerns upon signing the TVPA:

> With rare exceptions, the victims of [acts covered by the TVPA] will be foreign citizens. There is thus a danger that U.S. courts may become embroiled in difficult and sensitive disputes in other countries, and possibly ill-founded or politically motivated suits, which have nothing to do with the United States and which offer little prospect of successful recovery. Such potential abuse of this statute undoubtedly would give rise to serious frictions in international relations and would also be a waste of our own limited and already overburdened judicial resources.

Statement by President George Bush Upon Signing H.R. 2092, 28 Weekly Comp. Pres. Doc. 465, March 16, 1992, reprinted in 1992 U.S.C.C.A.N. 91. Are these concerns justified? Do you think the cases covered in this section were politically motivated? Assuming they were, what's wrong with politically motivated lawsuits to redress gross human rights abuses? If President Bush was worried about problematic cases brought under the TVPA, why did he sign the legislation?

13. What is the constitutional authority for Congress to enact the TVPA? The Majority Senate Report explained congressional authority as follows:

Congress clearly has authority to create a private right of action for torture and extra-judicial killings committed abroad. Under article III of the Constitution, the Federal judiciary has the power to adjudicate cases "arising under" the "law of the United States." . . . The law of nations is "part of our law, and must be ascertained and administered by the courts of justice of appropriate jurisdiction, as often as questions of right depending upon it are duly presented for their determination." The Paquete Habana, 175 U.S. 677, 700 (1900).

S. Rep. No. 249, 102d Cong., 1st Sess. (1991). The Minority Senate Report disagreed:

> [The TVPA] appears to over-extend Congress' constitutional authority. Congress has the power to "define and punish Piracies and Felonies committed on the high Seas, and Offenses against the Law of Nations." But as the Department of Justice has noted, (t)he reference in the constitutional text to "punish(ing) Piracies and Felonies . . . and Offenses" suggests that the Founders intended that Congress use this power to define crimes. It is a difficult and unresolved question, therefore, whether that power extends to creating a civil cause of action in this country for disputes that have no factual nexus with the United States or its citizens.

Id. Who has the better of this argument? Does Congress's power here depend, as the Majority Report suggests, on whether the law of nations is automatically part of the laws of the United States? Does the Define and Punish Clause in fact have a penal law limitation and a nexus requirement, as the Minority Report suggests?

14. Can the TVPA be justified on some basis in Article I other than the Define and Punish Clause? How about the Commerce Clause? Can the TVPA be justified as an implementation of the Convention Against Torture and Other Cruel, Inhuman or Degrading Treatment or Punishment, ratified by the United States in 1994, which requires that nations "prosecute or extradite" torturers found in their territory? With regard to this latter question, the Majority Report states that the TVPA

> will carry out the intent of the Convention Against Torture and Other Cruel, Inhuman or Degrading Treatment or Punishment, ... The convention obligates state parties to adopt measures to ensure that torturers within their territories are held legally accountable for their acts. This legislation will do precisely that—by making sure that torturers and death squads will no longer have a safe haven in the United States.

S. Rep. No. 249, 102d Cong., 1st Sess. 4 (1991). The Minority Report took a somewhat different view:

> The Department of Justice noted, and we agree, that "(s)uch a unilateral assertion of extraterritorial jurisdiction would be in tension with the framework of the (U.N. Convention Against Torture and other Cruel, Inhuman or Degrading Treatment or Punishment)." According to the administration, the convention requires countries to provide remedies for acts of torture which took place only within their own territory. In fact the convention specifically declined to extend coverage to acts committed outside the country in which the lawsuit is brought. We do not wish to second-guess the experts who drafted this treaty, and believe it is unwise to do explicitly what its drafters chose not to do—extend the coverage to extraterritorial actions.

Id. Does the Convention Against Torture authorize the TVPA, or is the TVPA in tension with the Convention? Who decides this legal question—a majority of Congress, or courts?

15. The Supreme Court has held that, because the TVPA refers to suits against "individuals," only natural persons may be sued under the statute. *See* Mohamad

v. Palestinian Authority, 566 U.S. 449 (2012). As will become apparent, that holding is relevant to the materials in the next section.

16. For additional discussion of *Sosa* and its implications, see William S. Dodge, *Bridging* Erie: *Customary International Law in the U.S. Legal System After Sosa v. Alvarez-Machain*, 12 Tulsa J. Comp. & Int'l L. 87 (2004); Eugene Kontorovich, *Implementing Sosa v. Alvarez-Machain: What Piracy Teaches About the Limits of the Alien Tort Statute*, 80 Notre Dame L. Rev. 111 (2004); Julian Ku & John C. Yoo, *Beyond Formalism in Foreign Affairs: A Functional Approach to the Alien Tort Statute*, 2004 Sup. Ct. Rev. 153; David H. Moore, *An Emerging Uniformity for International Law*, 75 Geo. Wash. L. Rev. 1 2006); Ralph G. Steinhardt, *Laying One Bankrupt Critique to Rest:* Sosa v. Alvarez-Machain *and the Future of International Human Rights Litigation in U.S. Courts*, 57 Vand. L. Rev. 2241 (2004). For an article contesting the Supreme Court's premise in *Sosa* that when the ATS was enacted, Congress would have assumed that the common law supplied a cause of action for ATS cases, see Anthony J. Bellia Jr. & Bradford R. Clark, *The Original Source of the Cause of Action in Federal Courts: The Example of the Alien Tort Statute*, 101 Va. L. Rev. 609 (2015).

C. ALIEN TORT STATUTE: EXTRATERRITORIALITY AND CORPORATE LIABILITY

Kiobel v. Royal Dutch Petroleum Co.

569 U.S. 108 (2013)

[Residents of the Ogoni region of Nigeria, who were now living in the United States, sued Dutch, British, and Nigerian corporations engaged in oil exploration and production in that country under the ATS. The plaintiffs alleged that during the 1990s, the corporations had aided and abetted the Nigerian police and military in committing a variety of human rights abuses, including extrajudicial killing, crimes against humanity, torture, and arbitrary detention, in order to suppress opposition to the corporations' activities.]

CHIEF JUSTICE ROBERTS delivered the opinion of the Court. . . .

The Second Circuit dismissed the entire complaint, reasoning that the law of nations does not recognize corporate liability. We granted certiorari to consider that question. After oral argument, we directed the parties to file supplemental briefs addressing an additional question: "Whether and under what circumstances the [ATS] allows courts to recognize a cause of action for violations of the law of nations occurring within the territory of a sovereign other than the United States." We heard oral argument again and now affirm the judgment below, based on our answer to the second question. . . .

The question here is not whether petitioners have stated a proper claim under the ATS, but whether a claim may reach conduct occurring in the territory of a foreign sovereign. Respondents contend that claims under the ATS do not, relying primarily on a canon of statutory interpretation known as the presumption against extraterritorial application. That canon provides that "[w]hen a statute gives no clear indication of an extraterritorial application, it has none," Morrison v. National Australia Bank Ltd., 130 S. Ct. 2869, 2878 (2010), and reflects the "presumption that United States law governs domestically but does not rule the world," Microsoft Corp. v. AT&T Corp., 550 U.S. 437, 454 (2007).

This presumption "serves to protect against unintended clashes between our laws and those of other nations which could result in international discord." EEOC v. Arabian American Oil Co., 499 U.S. 244, 248 (1991). . . .

We typically apply the presumption to discern whether an Act of Congress regulating conduct applies abroad. . . . The ATS, on the other hand, is "strictly jurisdictional." Sosa v. Alvarez-Machain, 542 U.S. 692, 713 (2004). It does not directly regulate conduct or afford relief. It instead allows federal courts to recognize certain causes of action based on sufficiently definite norms of international law. But we think the principles underlying the canon of interpretation similarly constrain courts considering causes of action that may be brought under the ATS.

Indeed, the danger of unwarranted judicial interference in the conduct of foreign policy is magnified in the context of the ATS, because the question is not what Congress has done but instead what courts may do. This Court in *Sosa* repeatedly stressed the need for judicial caution in considering which claims could be brought under the ATS, in light of foreign policy concerns. . . . These concerns, which are implicated in any case arising under the ATS, are all the more pressing when the question is whether a cause of action under the ATS reaches conduct within the territory of another sovereign.

These concerns are not diminished by the fact that *Sosa* limited federal courts to recognizing causes of action only for alleged violations of international law norms that are "'specific, universal, and obligatory.'" 542 U.S. at 732 (quoting In re Estate of Marcos Human Rights Litigation, 25 F.3d 1467, 1475 (9th Cir. 1994)). As demonstrated by Congress's enactment of the Torture Victim Protection Act, note following 28 U.S.C. §1350, identifying such a norm is only the beginning of defining a cause of action. *See id.* §3 (providing detailed definitions for extrajudicial killing and torture); *id.* §2 (specifying who may be liable, creating a rule of exhaustion, and establishing a statute of limitations). Each of these decisions carries with it significant foreign policy implications.

The principles underlying the presumption against extraterritoriality thus constrain courts exercising their power under the ATS.

Petitioners contend that even if the presumption applies, the text, history, and purposes of the ATS rebut it for causes of action brought under that statute. It is true that Congress, even in a jurisdictional provision, can indicate that it intends federal law to apply to conduct occurring abroad. *See, e.g.,* 18 U.S.C. §1091(e) (providing jurisdiction over the offense of genocide "regardless of where the offense is committed" if the alleged offender is, among other things, "present in the United States"). But to rebut the presumption, the ATS would need to evince a "clear indication of extraterritoriality." *Morrison*, 130 S. Ct. at 2883. It does not.

To begin, nothing in the text of the statute suggests that Congress intended causes of action recognized under it to have extraterritorial reach. The ATS covers actions by aliens for violations of the law of nations, but that does not imply extraterritorial reach—such violations affecting aliens can occur either within or outside the United States. Nor does the fact that the text reaches "*any* civil action" suggest application to torts committed abroad; it is well established that generic terms like "any" or "every" do not rebut the presumption against extraterritoriality. . . .

Petitioners make much of the fact that the ATS provides jurisdiction over civil actions for "torts" in violation of the law of nations. They claim that in using that word, the First Congress "necessarily meant to provide for jurisdiction over extra-territorial transitory torts that could arise on foreign soil." For support, they cite the common-law doctrine that allowed courts to assume jurisdiction over such "transi-tory torts," including actions for personal injury, arising abroad. . . .

Under the transitory torts doctrine, however, "the only justification for allowing a party to recover when the cause of action arose in another civilized jurisdiction is a well founded belief that it was a cause of action in that place." Cuba R. Co. v. Crosby, 222 U.S. 473, 479 (1912) (majority opinion of Holmes, J.). The question under *Sosa* is not whether a federal court has jurisdiction to entertain a cause of action provided by foreign or even international law. The question is instead whether the court has authority to recognize a cause of action under U.S. law to enforce a norm of international law. The reference to "tort" does not demonstrate that the First Congress "necessarily meant" for those causes of action to reach conduct in the ter-ritory of a foreign sovereign. In the end, nothing in the text of the ATS evinces the requisite clear indication of extraterritoriality.

Nor does the historical background against which the ATS was enacted over-come the presumption against application to conduct in the territory of another sovereign. We explained in *Sosa* that when Congress passed the ATS, "three princi-pal offenses against the law of nations" had been identified by Blackstone: violation of safe conducts, infringement of the rights of ambassadors, and piracy. The first two offenses have no necessary extraterritorial application. . . .

Two notorious episodes involving violations of the law of nations occurred in the United States shortly before passage of the ATS. Each concerned the rights of ambassadors, and each involved conduct within the Union. In 1784, a French adventurer verbally and physically assaulted Francis Barbe Marbois—the Secretary of the French Legion—in Philadelphia. The assault led the French Minister Plenipotentiary to lodge a formal protest with the Continental Congress and threaten to leave the country unless an adequate remedy were provided. And in 1787, a New York constable entered the Dutch Ambassador's house and arrested one of his domestic servants. At the request of Secretary of Foreign Affairs John Jay, the Mayor of New York City arrested the constable in turn, but cautioned that because "'neither Congress nor our [State] Legislature have yet passed any act respecting a breach of the privileges of Ambassadors,'" the extent of any available relief would depend on the common law. *See* Curtis A. Bradley, *The Alien Tort Statute and Article III*, 42 Va. J. Int'l L. 587, 641-42 (2002) (quoting 3 Dept. of State, The Diplomatic Correspondence of the United States of America 447 (1837)). The two cases in which the ATS was invoked shortly after its passage also concerned con-duct within the territory of the United States. *See* Bolchos v. Darrell, 3 F. Cas. 810 (D.S.C. 1795) (No. 1607) (wrongful seizure of slaves from a vessel while in port in the United States); Moxon v. The Fanny, 17 F. Cas. 942 (D.C. Pa. 1793) (No. 9895) (wrongful seizure in United States territorial waters).

These prominent contemporary examples—immediately before and after pas-sage of the ATS—provide no support for the proposition that Congress expected causes of action to be brought under the statute for violations of the law of nations occurring abroad.

The third example of a violation of the law of nations familiar to the Congress that enacted the ATS was piracy. Piracy typically occurs on the high seas, beyond the territorial jurisdiction of the United States or any other country. . . . This Court has generally treated the high seas the same as foreign soil for purposes of the presumption against extraterritorial application. . . . Petitioners contend that because Congress surely intended the ATS to provide jurisdiction for actions against pirates, it necessarily anticipated the statute would apply to conduct occurring abroad.

Applying U.S. law to pirates, however, does not typically impose the sovereign will of the United States onto conduct occurring within the territorial jurisdiction of another sovereign, and therefore carries less direct foreign policy consequences. Pirates were fair game wherever found, by any nation, because they generally did not operate within any jurisdiction. We do not think that the existence of a cause of action against them is a sufficient basis for concluding that other causes of action under the ATS reach conduct that does occur within the territory of another sovereign; pirates may well be a category unto themselves. . . .

Finally, there is no indication that the ATS was passed to make the United States a uniquely hospitable forum for the enforcement of international norms. As Justice Story put it, "No nation has ever yet pretended to be the *custos morum* of the whole world. . . . " United States v. The La Jeune Eugenie, 26 F. Cas. 832, 847 (No. 15,551) (CC Mass. 1822). It is implausible to suppose that the First Congress wanted their fledgling Republic—struggling to receive international recognition—to be the first. Indeed, the parties offer no evidence that any nation, meek or mighty, presumed to do such a thing.

The United States was, however, embarrassed by its potential inability to provide judicial relief to foreign officials injured in the United States. Bradley, 42 Va. J. Int'l L., at 641. Such offenses against ambassadors violated the law of nations, "and if not adequately redressed could rise to an issue of war." *Sosa*, 542 U.S. at 715. . . . The ATS ensured that the United States could provide a forum for adjudicating such incidents. Nothing about this historical context suggests that Congress also intended federal common law under the ATS to provide a cause of action for conduct occurring in the territory of another sovereign.

Indeed, far from avoiding diplomatic strife, providing such a cause of action could have generated it. Recent experience bears this out. *See* Doe v. Exxon Mobil Corp., 654 F.3d 11, 77-78 (D.C. Cir. 2011) (Kavanaugh, J., dissenting in part) (listing recent objections to extraterritorial applications of the ATS by Canada, Germany, Indonesia, Papua New Guinea, South Africa, Switzerland, and the United Kingdom). Moreover, accepting petitioners' view would imply that other nations, also applying the law of nations, could hale our citizens into their courts for alleged violations of the law of nations occurring in the United States, or anywhere else in the world. The presumption against extraterritoriality guards against our courts triggering such serious foreign policy consequences, and instead defers such decisions, quite appropriately, to the political branches.

We therefore conclude that the presumption against extraterritoriality applies to claims under the ATS, and that nothing in the statute rebuts that presumption. "[T]here is no clear indication of extraterritoriality here," *Morrison*, 130 S. Ct. at 2883, and petitioners' case seeking relief for violations of the law of nations occurring outside the United States is barred.

On these facts, all the relevant conduct took place outside the United States. And even where the claims touch and concern the territory of the United States, they must do so with sufficient force to displace the presumption against extraterritorial application. Corporations are often present in many countries, and it would reach too far to say that mere corporate presence suffices. If Congress were to determine otherwise, a statute more specific than the ATS would be required.

JUSTICE KENNEDY, concurring.

The opinion for the Court is careful to leave open a number of significant questions regarding the reach and interpretation of the Alien Tort Statute. In my view that is a proper disposition. Many serious concerns with respect to human rights abuses committed abroad have been addressed by Congress in statutes such as the Torture Victim Protection Act of 1991 (TVPA), and that class of cases will be determined in the future according to the detailed statutory scheme Congress has enacted. Other cases may arise with allegations of serious violations of international law principles protecting persons, cases covered neither by the TVPA nor by the reasoning and holding of today's case; and in those disputes the proper implementation of the presumption against extraterritorial application may require some further elaboration and explanation.

[Justice Alito concurred and was joined by Justice Thomas. He sought to elaborate on the Court's observation that "even where the claims touch and concern the territory of the United States, they must do so with sufficient force to displace the presumption against extraterritorial application." In his view, "a putative ATS cause of action will fall within the scope of the presumption against extraterritoriality—and will therefore be barred—unless the domestic conduct is sufficient to violate an international law norm that satisfies *Sosa*'s requirements of definiteness and acceptance among civilized nations."]

JUSTICE BREYER, with whom JUSTICE GINSBURG, JUSTICE SOTOMAYOR, and JUSTICE KAGAN join, concurring in the judgment. . . .

Recognizing that Congress enacted the ATS to permit recovery of damages from pirates and others who violated basic international law norms as understood in 1789, *Sosa* essentially leads today's judges to ask: Who are today's pirates? We provided a framework for answering that question by setting down principles drawn from international norms and designed to limit ATS claims to those that are similar in character and specificity to piracy.

In this case we must decide the extent to which this jurisdictional statute opens a federal court's doors to those harmed by activities belonging to the limited class that *Sosa* set forth *when those activities take place abroad*. To help answer this question here, I would refer both to *Sosa* and, as in *Sosa*, to norms of international law.

In my view the majority's effort to answer the question by referring to the "presumption against extraterritoriality" does not work well. That presumption "rests on the perception that Congress ordinarily legislates with respect to domestic, not foreign matters." Morrison v. National Australia Bank Ltd., 130 S. Ct. 2869, 2877 (2010). The ATS, however, was enacted with "foreign matters" in mind. The statute's text refers explicitly to "alien[s]," "treat[ies]," and "the law of nations." The statute's purpose was to address "violations of the law of nations, admitting of a judicial remedy and at the same time threatening serious consequences in international affairs." *Sosa*, 542 U.S. at 715. And at least one of the three kinds of activities that we found to fall within the statute's scope, namely piracy, normally takes place abroad.

The majority cannot wish this piracy example away by emphasizing that piracy takes place on the high seas. That is because the robbery and murder that make up piracy do not normally take place in the water; they take place on a ship. And a ship is like land, in that it falls within the jurisdiction of the nation whose flag it flies. . . .

The majority nonetheless tries to find a distinction between piracy at sea and similar cases on land. It writes, "Applying U.S. law to pirates . . . does not typically impose the sovereign will of the United States onto conduct occurring within the *territorial* jurisdiction of another sovereign and therefore carries less direct foreign policy consequences." But, as I have just pointed out, "[a]pplying U.S. law to pirates" *does* typically involve applying our law to acts taking place within the jurisdiction of another sovereign. Nor can the majority's words "territorial jurisdiction" sensibly distinguish land from sea for purposes of isolating adverse foreign policy risks, as the Barbary Pirates, the War of 1812, the sinking of the *Lusitania,* and the Lockerbie bombing make all too clear.

The majority also writes, "Pirates were fair game wherever found, by any nation, because they generally did not operate within any jurisdiction." I very much agree that pirates were fair game "wherever found." Indeed, that is the point. That is why we asked, in *Sosa,* who are today's pirates? Certainly today's pirates include torturers and perpetrators of genocide. And today, like the pirates of old, they are "fair game" where they are found. . . . And just as a nation that harbored pirates provoked the concern of other nations in past centuries, so harboring "common enemies of all mankind" provokes similar concerns today. . . .

In applying the ATS to acts "occurring within the territory of a[nother] sovereign," I would assume that Congress intended the statute's jurisdictional reach to match the statute's underlying substantive grasp. That grasp, defined by the statute's purposes set forth in *Sosa,* includes compensation for those injured by piracy and its modern-day equivalents, at least where allowing such compensation avoids "serious" negative international "consequences" for the United States. 542 U.S. at 715. And just as we have looked to established international substantive norms to help determine the statute's substantive reach, so we should look to international jurisdictional norms to help determine the statute's jurisdictional scope.

The Restatement (Third) of Foreign Relations Law is helpful. Section 402 recognizes that, subject to §403's "reasonableness" requirement, a nation may apply its law (for example, federal common law, not only (1) to "conduct" that "takes place [or to persons or things] within its territory" but also (2) to the "activities, interests, status, or relations of its nationals outside as well as within its territory," (3) to "conduct outside its territory that has or is intended to have substantial effect within its territory," and (4) to certain foreign "conduct outside its territory . . . that is directed against the security of the state or against a limited class of other state interests." In addition, §404 of the Restatement explains that a "state has jurisdiction to define and prescribe punishment for certain offenses recognized by the community of nations as of universal concern, such as piracy, slave trade," and analogous behavior.

Considering these jurisdictional norms in light of both the ATS's basic purpose (to provide compensation for those injured by today's pirates) and *Sosa's* basic caution (to avoid international friction), I believe that the statute provides jurisdiction where (1) the alleged tort occurs on American soil, (2) the defendant is an American national, or (3) the defendant's conduct substantially and adversely affects an important American national interest, and that includes a distinct interest in preventing the United States from becoming a safe harbor (free of civil as well as criminal liability) for a torturer or other common enemy of mankind.

I would interpret the statute as providing jurisdiction only where distinct American interests are at issue. Doing so reflects the fact that Congress adopted the present statute at a time when, as Justice Story put it, "No nation ha[d] ever yet pretended to be the *custos morum* of the whole world." United States v. La Jeune Eugenie, 26 F. Cas. 832, 847 (No. 15,551) (CC Mass. 1822). That restriction also should help to minimize international friction. Further limiting principles such as exhaustion, *forum non conveniens*, and comity would do the same. So would a practice of courts giving weight to the views of the Executive Branch. . . .

As I have indicated, we should treat this Nation's interest in not becoming a safe harbor for violators of the most fundamental international norms as an important jurisdiction-related interest justifying application of the ATS in light of the statute's basic purposes—in particular that of compensating those who have suffered harm at the hands of, e.g., torturers or other modern pirates. . . .

International norms have long included a duty not to permit a nation to become a safe harbor for pirates (or their equivalent). . . .

More recently two lower American courts have, in effect, rested jurisdiction primarily upon that kind of concern. In Filartiga v. Pena-Irala, 630 F.2d 876 (2d Cir. 1980), an alien plaintiff brought a lawsuit against an alien defendant for damages suffered through acts of torture that the defendant allegedly inflicted in a foreign nation, Paraguay. Neither plaintiff nor defendant was an American national and the actions underlying the lawsuit took place abroad. The defendant, however, "had . . . resided in the United States for more than ninth months" before being sued, having overstayed his visitor's visa. *Id.* at 878-79. Jurisdiction was deemed proper because the defendant's alleged conduct violated a well-established international law norm, and the suit vindicated our Nation's interest in not providing a safe harbor, free of damages claims, for those defendants who commit such conduct.

In *Marcos*, the plaintiffs were nationals of the Philippines, the defendant was a Philippine national, and the alleged wrongful act, death by torture, took place abroad. . . . A month before being sued, the defendant, "his family, . . . and others loyal to [him] fled to Hawaii," where the ATS case was heard. In re Estate of Marcos, Human Rights Litigation, 25 F.3d 1467, 1469 (9th Cir. 1994). As in *Filartiga*, the court found ATS jurisdiction.

And in *Sosa* we referred to both cases with approval, suggesting that the ATS allowed a claim for relief in such circumstances. . . . Not surprisingly, both before and after *Sosa*, courts have consistently rejected the notion that the ATS is categorically barred from extraterritorial application. . . .

Application of the statute in the way I have suggested is consistent with international law and foreign practice. Nations have long been obliged not to provide safe harbors for their own nationals who commit such serious crimes abroad. . . .

Many countries permit foreign plaintiffs to bring suits against their own nationals based on unlawful conduct that took place abroad. . . .

Other countries permit some form of lawsuit brought by a foreign national against a foreign national, based upon conduct taking place abroad and seeking damages. Certain countries, which find "universal" criminal "jurisdiction" to try perpetrators of particularly heinous crimes such as piracy and genocide, see Restatement §404, also permit private persons injured by that conduct to pursue *"actions civiles,"* seeking civil damages in the criminal proceeding. . . .

At the same time Congress has ratified treaties obliging the United States to find and punish foreign perpetrators of serious crimes committed against foreign persons abroad. . . .

And Congress has sometimes authorized civil damages in such cases. See generally note following 28 U.S.C. §1350 (Torture Victim Protection Act of 1991 (TVPA) (private damages action for torture or extrajudicial killing committed under authority of a foreign nation). . . .

Congress, while aware of the award of civil damages under the ATS—including cases such as *Filartiga* with foreign plaintiffs, defendants, and conduct—has not sought to limit the statute's jurisdictional or substantive reach. Rather, Congress has enacted other statutes, and not only criminal statutes, that allow the United States to prosecute (or allow victims to obtain damages from) foreign persons who injure foreign victims by committing abroad torture, genocide, and other heinous acts. *See, e.g.*, 18 U.S.C. §2340A(b)(2) (authorizing prosecution of torturers if "the alleged offender is present in the United States, irrespective of the nationality of the victim or alleged offender"); §1091(e)(2)(D) (genocide prosecution authorized when, "regardless of where the offense is committed, the alleged offender is . . . present in the United States"); note following 28 U.S.C. §1350, §2(a) (private right of action on behalf of individuals harmed by an act of torture or extrajudicial killing committed "under actual or apparent authority, or color of law, of any foreign nation"). . . .

Applying these jurisdictional principles to this case, however, I agree with the Court that jurisdiction does not lie. The defendants are two foreign corporations. Their shares, like those of many foreign corporations, are traded on the New York Stock Exchange. Their only presence in the United States consists of an office in New York City (actually owned by a separate but affiliated company) that helps to explain their business to potential investors. The plaintiffs are not United States nationals but nationals of other nations. The conduct at issue took place abroad. And the plaintiffs allege, not that the defendants directly engaged in acts of torture, genocide, or the equivalent, but that they helped others (who are not American nationals) to do so.

Under these circumstances, even if the New York office were a sufficient basis for asserting general jurisdiction . . . it would be farfetched to believe, based solely upon the defendants' minimal and indirect American presence, that this legal action helps to vindicate a distinct American interest, such as in not providing a safe harbor for an "enemy of all mankind." Thus I agree with the Court that here it would "reach too far to say" that such "mere corporate presence suffices."

I consequently join the Court's judgment but not its opinion.

Jesner v. Arab Bank

138 S. Ct. 1386 (2018)

[This case involved ATS suits brought against a Jordanian corporation, Arab Bank, PLC, on behalf of thousands of individuals who were injured or killed as the result of terrorist attacks abroad. The plaintiffs alleged that officers of the bank facilitated the terrorist attacks by allowing the bank to be used to transfer funds to terrorist groups in the Middle East, in part through electronic transfers passing through the bank's offices in New York City. These connections to the United States were sufficient, the plaintiffs argued, to meet the "touch and concern" test in *Kiobel*.]

JUSTICE KENNEDY announced the judgment of the Court and delivered the opinion of the Court with respect to Parts I, II-B-1, and II-C, and an opinion with respect to Parts II-A, II-B-2, II-B-3, and III, in which THE CHIEF JUSTICE and JUSTICE THOMAS join. . . .

I

A

. . . During the pendency of this litigation, there was an unrelated case that also implicated the issue whether the ATS is applicable to suits in this country against foreign corporations. *See* Kiobel v. Royal Dutch Petroleum Co., 621 F.3d 111 (2d Cir. 2010). That suit worked its way through the trial court and the Court of Appeals for the Second Circuit. The *Kiobel* litigation did not involve banking transactions. Its allegations were that holding companies incorporated in the Netherlands and the United Kingdom had, through a Nigerian subsidiary, aided and abetted the Nigerian Government in human-rights abuses. In *Kiobel*, the Court of Appeals held that the ATS does not extend to suits against corporations. . . .

[W]hile this Court in *Kiobel* affirmed the ruling that the action there could not be maintained, it did not address the broader holding of the Court of Appeals that dismissal was required because corporations may not be sued under the ATS. Still, the courts of the Second Circuit deemed that broader holding to be binding precedent. As a consequence, in the instant case the District Court dismissed petitioners' ATS claims based on the earlier *Kiobel* holding in the Court of Appeals; and on review of the dismissal order the Court of Appeals, also adhering to its earlier holding, affirmed. This Court granted certiorari in the instant case.

Since the Court of Appeals relied on its *Kiobel* holding in the instant case, it is instructive to begin with an analysis of that decision. The majority opinion in *Kiobel*, written by Judge Cabranes, held that the ATS does not apply to alleged international-law violations by a corporation. Judge Cabranes relied in large part on the fact that international criminal tribunals have consistently limited their jurisdiction to natural persons.

Judge Leval filed a separate opinion. He concurred in the judgment on other grounds but disagreed with the proposition that the foreign corporation was not subject to suit under the ATS. Judge Leval conceded that "international law, of its own force, imposes no liabilities on corporations or other private juridical entities." But he reasoned that corporate liability for violations of international law is an issue of "civil compensatory liability" that international law leaves to individual nations. Later decisions in the Courts of Appeals for the Seventh, Ninth, and District of Columbia Circuits agreed with Judge Leval and held that corporations can be subject to suit under the ATS. The respective opinions by Judges Cabranes and Leval are scholarly and extensive, providing significant guidance for this Court in the case now before it.

With this background, it is now proper to turn to the history of the ATS and the decisions interpreting it. . . .

II

[The Court reviews the history of the ATS as recounted in Sosa v. Alvarez-Machain, 542 U.S. 692 (2004), as well as the evolution of ATS litigation from *Filartiga* to *Kiobel*.]

. . . . Before recognizing a common-law action under the ATS, federal courts must apply the test announced in *Sosa*. An initial, threshold question is whether a plaintiff can demonstrate that the alleged violation is "of a norm that is specific, universal, and obligatory." 542 U.S. at 732. And even assuming that, under international law, there is a specific norm that can be controlling, it must be determined further whether allowing this case to proceed under the ATS is a proper exercise of judicial discretion, or instead whether caution requires the political branches to grant specific authority before corporate liability can be imposed. *See id.* at 732-33 and nn. 20-21. "[T]he potential implications for the foreign relations of the United States of recognizing such causes should make courts particularly wary of impinging on the discretion of the Legislative and Executive Branches in managing foreign affairs." *Id.* at 727.

It must be said that some of the considerations that pertain to determining whether there is a specific, universal, and obligatory norm that is established under international law are applicable as well in determining whether deference must be given to the political branches. For instance, the fact that the charters of some international tribunals and the provisions of some congressional statutes addressing international human-rights violations are specifically limited to individual wrongdoers, and thus foreclose corporate liability, has significant bearing both on the content of the norm being asserted and the question whether courts should defer to Congress. The two inquiries inform each other and are, to that extent, not altogether discrete. . . .

A

Petitioners and Arab Bank disagree as to whether corporate liability is a question of international law or only a question of judicial authority and discretion under domestic law. . . .

[The Court considers various materials relating to corporate liability under international law.]

[T]he Court need not resolve the questions whether corporate liability is a question that is governed by international law, or, if so, whether international law imposes liability on corporations. There is at least sufficient doubt on the point to turn to *Sosa*'s second question—whether the Judiciary must defer to Congress, allowing it to determine in the first instance whether that universal norm has been recognized and, if so, whether it is prudent and necessary to direct its enforcement in suits under the ATS.

B

1

Sosa is consistent with this Court's general reluctance to extend judicially created private rights of action. The Court's recent precedents cast doubt on the authority of courts to extend or create private causes of action even in the realm of domestic law, where this Court has "recently and repeatedly said that a decision to create a private right of action is one better left to legislative judgment in the great majority of cases." *Sosa*, 542 U.S. at 727 (citations omitted). . . .

This caution extends to the question whether the courts should exercise the judicial authority to mandate a rule that imposes liability upon artificial entities like corporations. . . .

Neither the language of the ATS nor the precedents interpreting it support an exception to these general principles in this context. In fact, the separation-of-powers concerns that counsel against courts creating private rights of action apply with particular force in the context of the ATS. The political branches, not the Judiciary, have the responsibility and institutional capacity to weigh foreign-policy concerns. That the ATS implicates foreign relations "is itself a reason for a high bar to new private causes of action for violating international law." *Sosa*, supra, at 727.

In *Sosa*, the Court emphasized that federal courts must exercise "great caution" before recognizing new forms of liability under the ATS. In light of the foreign-policy and separation-of-powers concerns inherent in ATS litigation, there is an argument that a proper application of *Sosa* would preclude courts from ever recognizing any new causes of action under the ATS. But the Court need not resolve that question in this case. Either way, absent further action from Congress it would be inappropriate for courts to extend ATS liability to foreign corporations.

2

Even in areas less fraught with foreign-policy consequences, the Court looks to analogous statutes for guidance on the appropriate boundaries of judge-made causes of action. . . .

Here, the logical place to look for a statutory analogy to an ATS common-law action is the [Torture Victim Protection Act (TVPA)]—the only cause of action under the ATS created by Congress rather than the courts. . . .

The key feature of the TVPA for this case is that it limits liability to "individuals," which, the Court has held, unambiguously limits liability to natural persons. Mohamad v. Palestinian Authority, 566 U.S. 449, 453-56 (2012). Congress' decision to exclude liability for corporations in actions brought under the TVPA is all but dispositive of the present case. That decision illustrates that significant foreign-policy implications require the courts to draw a careful balance in defining the scope of actions under the ATS. It would be inconsistent with that balance to create a remedy broader than the one created by Congress. Indeed, it "would be remarkable to take a more aggressive role in exercising a jurisdiction that remained largely in shadow for much of the prior two centuries." *Sosa*, supra, at 726. . . .

Petitioners contend that, instead of the TVPA, the most analogous statute here is the Anti-Terrorism Act. That Act does permit suits against corporate entities. See 18 U.S.C. §§2331(3), 2333(d)(2). In fact, in these suits some of the foreign plaintiffs joined their claims to those of United States nationals suing Arab Bank under the Anti-Terrorism Act. But the Anti-Terrorism Act provides a cause of action only to "national[s] of the United States," and their "estate, survivors, or heirs." §2333(a). In contrast, the ATS is available only for claims brought by "an alien." 28 U.S.C. §1350. A statute that excludes foreign nationals (with the possible exception of foreign survivors or heirs) is an inapt analogy for a common-law cause of action that provides a remedy for foreign nationals only.

To the extent, furthermore, that the Anti-Terrorism Act is relevant it suggests that there should be no common-law action under the ATS for allegations like petitioners'. Otherwise, foreign plaintiffs could bypass Congress' express limitations on liability under the Anti-Terrorism Act simply by bringing an ATS lawsuit. The Anti-Terrorism Act . . . is part of a comprehensive statutory and regulatory regime that prohibits terrorism and terrorism financing. The detailed regulatory structures prescribed by Congress and the federal agencies charged with oversight of financial institutions reflect the careful deliberation of the political branches on when, and how, banks should be held liable for the financing of terrorism. It would be inappropriate for courts to displace this considered statutory and regulatory structure by holding banks subject to common-law liability in actions filed under the ATS. . . .

3

Other considerations relevant to the exercise of judicial discretion also counsel against allowing liability under the ATS for foreign corporations, absent instructions from Congress to do so. It has not been shown that corporate liability under the ATS is essential to serve the goals of the statute. As to the question of adequate remedies, the ATS will seldom be the only way for plaintiffs to hold the perpetrators liable. *See, e.g.*, 18 U.S.C. §1091 (criminal prohibition on genocide); §1595 (civil remedy for victims of slavery). And plaintiffs still can sue the individual corporate employees responsible for a violation of international law under the ATS. If the Court were to hold that foreign corporations have liability for international-law violations, then plaintiffs may well ignore the human perpetrators and concentrate instead on multinational corporate entities.

. . . [I]n the context of criminal tribunals international law itself generally limits liability to natural persons. Although the Court need not decide whether the seeming absence of a specific, universal, and obligatory norm of corporate liability under international law by itself forecloses petitioners' claims against Arab Bank, or whether this is an issue governed by international law, the lack of a clear and well-established international-law rule is of critical relevance in determining whether courts should extend ATS liability to foreign corporations without specific congressional authorization to do so. That is especially so in light of the TVPA's limitation of liability to natural persons, which parallels the distinction between corporations and individuals in international law.

If, moreover, the Court were to hold that foreign corporations may be held liable under the ATS, that precedent-setting principle "would imply that other nations, also applying the law of nations, could hale our [corporations] into their courts for alleged violations of the law of nations." *Kiobel*, 569 U.S. at 124. This judicially mandated doctrine, in turn, could subject American corporations to an immediate, constant risk of claims seeking to impose massive liability for the alleged conduct of their employees and subsidiaries around the world, all as determined in foreign courts, thereby "hinder[ing] global investment in developing economies, where it is most needed." Brief for United States as Amicus Curiae in *American Isuzu Motors, Inc. v. Ntsebeza*, O.T. 2007, No. 07-919, p. 20.

In other words, allowing plaintiffs to sue foreign corporations under the ATS could establish a precedent that discourages American corporations from investing abroad, including in developing economies where the host government might have a history of alleged human-rights violations, or where judicial systems might lack the safeguards of United States courts. And, in consequence, that often might deter the active corporate investment that contributes to the economic development that so often is an essential foundation for human rights.

It is also true, of course, that natural persons can and do use corporations for sinister purposes, including conduct that violates international law. That the corporate form can be an instrument for inflicting grave harm and suffering poses serious and complex questions both for the international community and for Congress. So there are strong arguments for permitting the victims to seek relief from corporations themselves. Yet the urgency and complexity of this problem make it all the more important that Congress determine whether victims of human-rights abuses may sue foreign corporations in federal courts in the United States. Congress, not the Judiciary, is the branch with "the facilities necessary to make fairly such an important policy decision where the possibilities of international discord are so evident and retaliative action so certain." *Kiobel*, 569 U.S. at 116. As noted further below, there are many delicate and important considerations that Congress is in a better position to examine in determining whether and how best to impose corporate liability. And, as the TVPA illustrates, Congress is well aware of the necessity of clarifying the proper scope of liability under the ATS in a timely way.

C

The ATS was intended to promote harmony in international relations by ensuring foreign plaintiffs a remedy for international-law violations in circumstances where the absence of such a remedy might provoke foreign nations to hold the United States accountable. Brief for United States as *Amicus Curiae* 7. But here, and in similar cases, the opposite is occurring.

Petitioners are foreign nationals seeking hundreds of millions of dollars in damages from a major Jordanian financial institution for injuries suffered in attacks by foreign terrorists in the Middle East. The only alleged connections to the United States are [electronic currency clearance] transactions in Arab Bank's New York branch and a brief allegation regarding a charity in Texas. The Court of Appeals did not address, and the Court need not now decide, whether these allegations are sufficient to "touch and concern" the United States under *Kiobel.*

At a minimum, the relatively minor connection between the terrorist attacks at issue in this case and the alleged conduct in the United States well illustrates the perils of extending the scope of ATS liability to foreign multinational corporations like Arab Bank. For 13 years, this litigation has "caused significant diplomatic tensions" with Jordan, a critical ally in one of the world's most sensitive regions. Brief for United States as *Amicus Curiae* 30. "Jordan is a key counterterrorism partner, especially in the global campaign to defeat the Islamic State in Iraq and Syria." *Id.* at 31. The United States explains that Arab Bank itself is "a constructive partner with the United States in working to prevent terrorist financing." Id. at 32 (internal quotation marks omitted). Jordan considers the instant litigation to be a "grave affront" to its sovereignty. See Brief for Hashemite Kingdom of Jordan as *Amicus Curiae* 3.

This is not the first time, furthermore, that a foreign sovereign has appeared in this Court to note its objections to ATS litigation. . . . These are the very foreign-relations tensions the First Congress sought to avoid.

Petitioners insist that whatever the faults of this litigation—for example, its tenuous connections to the United States and the prolonged diplomatic disruptions it has caused—the fact that Arab Bank is a foreign corporate entity, as distinct from a natural person, is not one of them. That misses the point. As demonstrated by this litigation, foreign corporate defendants create unique problems. And courts are not well suited to make the required policy judgments that are implicated by corporate liability in cases like this one.

Like the presumption against extraterritoriality, judicial caution under *Sosa* "guards against our courts triggering . . . serious foreign policy consequences, and instead defers such decisions, quite appropriately, to the political branches." *Kiobel,* 569 U.S. at 124. If, in light of all the concerns that must be weighed before imposing liability on foreign corporations via ATS suits, the Court were to hold that it has the discretion to make that determination, then the cautionary language of *Sosa* would be little more than empty rhetoric. Accordingly, the Court holds that foreign corporations may not be defendants in suits brought under the ATS.

III

With the ATS, the First Congress provided a federal remedy for a narrow category of international-law violations committed by individuals. Whether, more than two centuries on, a similar remedy should be available against foreign corporations is similarly a decision that Congress must make.

The political branches can determine, referring to international law to the extent they deem proper, whether to impose liability for human-rights violations upon foreign corporations in this Nation's courts, and, conversely, that courts in other countries should be able to hold United States corporations liable. Congress might determine that violations of international law do, or should, impose that liability to ensure that corporations make every effort to deter human-rights violations, and so that, even when those efforts cannot be faulted, compensation for injured persons will be a cost of doing business. If Congress and the Executive were to determine that corporations should be liable for violations of international law, that decision would have special power and force because it would be made by the branches most immediately responsive to, and accountable to, the electorate.

It is still another possibility that, in the careful exercise of its expertise in the field of foreign affairs, Congress might conclude that neutral judicial safeguards may not be ensured in every country; and so, as a reciprocal matter, it could determine that liability of foreign corporations under the ATS should be subject to some limitations or preconditions. Congress might deem this more careful course to be the best way to encourage American corporations to undertake the extensive investments and foreign operations that can be an important beginning point for creating the infrastructures that allow human rights, as well as judicial safeguards, to emerge. These delicate judgments, involving a balance that it is the prerogative of the political branches to make, especially in the field of foreign affairs, would, once again, also be entitled to special respect, especially because those careful distinctions might themselves advance the Rule of Law. All this underscores the important separation-of-powers concerns that require the Judiciary to refrain from making these kinds of decisions under the ATS. The political branches, moreover, surely are better positioned than the Judiciary to determine if corporate liability would, or would not, create special risks of disrupting good relations with foreign governments.

Finally, Congress might find that corporate liability should be limited to cases where a corporation's management was actively complicit in the crime. *Cf.* ALI, Model Penal Code §2.07(1)(c) (1985) (a corporation may be held criminally liable where "the commission of the offense was authorized, requested, commanded, performed or recklessly tolerated by the board of directors or by a high managerial agent acting on behalf of the corporation within the scope of his office or employment"). Again, the political branches are better equipped to make the preliminary findings and consequent conclusions that should inform this determination.

These and other considerations that must shape and instruct the formulation of principles of international and domestic law are matters that the political branches are in the better position to define and articulate. For these reasons, judicial deference requires that any imposition of corporate liability on foreign corporations for violations of international law must be determined in the first instance by the political branches of the Government. . . .

JUSTICE THOMAS, concurring.

I join the Court's opinion in full because it correctly applies our precedents. I also agree with the points raised by my concurring colleagues. Courts should not be in the business of creating new causes of action under the Alien Tort Statute (Gorsuch, J., concurring in part and concurring in judgment), especially when it risks international strife (Alito, J., concurring in part and concurring in judgment). And the Alien Tort Statute likely does not apply to suits between foreign plaintiffs and foreign defendants (opinion of Gorsuch, J.).

JUSTICE ALITO, concurring in part and concurring in the judgment.

Creating causes of action under the Alien Tort Statute against foreign corporate defendants would precipitate exactly the sort of diplomatic strife that the law was enacted to prevent. As a result, I agree with the Court that we should not take that step, and I join Parts I, II-B-1, and II-C of the opinion of the Court. I write separately to elaborate on why that outcome is compelled not only by "judicial caution," but also by the separation of powers. . . .

For the reasons articulated by Justice Scalia in *Sosa* and by Justice Gorsuch today, I am not certain that *Sosa* was correctly decided. But even taking that decision on its own terms, this Court should not create causes of action under the ATS against foreign corporate defendants. As part of *Sosa*'s second step, a court should decline to create a cause of action as a matter of federal common law where the result would be to further, not avoid, diplomatic strife. Properly applied, that rule easily resolves the question presented by this case.*

Sosa interpreted the ATS to authorize the federal courts to create causes of action as a matter of federal common law. We have repeatedly emphasized that "in fashioning federal [common law] principles to govern areas left open by Congress, our function is to effectuate congressional policy." United States v. Kimbell Foods, Inc., 440 U.S. 715, 738 (1979). Fidelity to congressional policy is not only prudent but necessary: Going beyond the bounds of Congress's authorization would mean unconstitutionally usurping part of the "legislative Powers." U.S. Const., Art. I, §1. Accordingly, the objective for courts in every case requiring the creation of federal common law must be "to find the rule that will best effectuate the federal policy." Textile Workers v. Lincoln Mills of Ala., 353 U.S. 448, 457, (1957).

The ATS was meant to help the United States avoid diplomatic friction. The First Congress enacted the law to provide a forum for adjudicating that "narrow set of violations of the law of nations" that, if left unaddressed, "threaten[ed] serious consequences" for the United States. Sosa v. Alvarez-Machain, 542 U.S. 692, 715 (2004). Specifically, the First Congress was concerned about offenses like piracy, violation of safe conducts, and infringement of the rights of ambassadors, each of which "if not adequately redressed could rise to an issue of war." *Sosa*, supra, at 715. . . . To minimize the danger, the First Congress enacted the ATS, "ensur[ing] that the United States could provide a forum for adjudicating such incidents" and thus helping the Nation avoid further diplomatic imbroglios. Kiobel v. Royal Dutch Petroleum Co., 569 U.S. 108, 114, 124 (2013).

Putting that objective together with the rules governing federal common law generally, the following principle emerges: Federal courts should decline to create federal common law causes of action under *Sosa*'s second step whenever doing so would not materially advance the ATS's objective of avoiding diplomatic strife. And applying that principle here, it is clear that federal courts should not create causes of action under the ATS against foreign corporate defendants. All parties agree that

---

* Because this case involves a foreign corporation, we have no need to reach the question whether an alien may sue a United States corporation under the ATS. And since such a suit may generally be brought in federal court based on diversity jurisdiction, 28 U.S.C. §1332(a)(2), it is unclear why ATS jurisdiction would be needed in that situation.

customary international law does not *require* corporate liability as a general matter. But if customary international law does not require corporate liability, then declining to create it under the ATS cannot give other nations just cause for complaint against the United States.

To the contrary, ATS suits against foreign corporations may provoke—and, indeed, frequently *have* provoked—exactly the sort of diplomatic strife inimical to the fundamental purpose of the ATS. Some foreign states appear to interpret international law as foreclosing civil corporate liability for violations of the law of nations. Creating ATS causes of action against foreign corporate defendants would put the United States at odds with these nations. Even when states do not object to this sort of corporate liability as a *legal* matter, they may be concerned about ATS suits against their corporations for political reasons. For example, Jordan considers this suit "a direct affront" to its sovereignty and one that "risks destabilizing Jordan's economy and undercutting one of the most stable and productive alliances the United States has in the Middle East." Brief for Hashemite Kingdom of Jordan as *Amicus Curiae* 4. Courting these sorts of problems—which seem endemic to ATS litigation—was the opposite of what the First Congress had in mind.

In response, the dissent argues merely that any diplomatic friction "can be addressed with a tool more tailored to the source of the problem than a blanket ban on corporate liability." Even on its own terms, that argument is problematic: Many of the "more tailored" tools offered by the dissent will still be hotly litigated by ATS plaintiffs, and it may be years before incorrect initial decisions about their applicability can be reviewed by the courts of appeals.

In any event, the dissent misunderstands the relevant standard. The question before us is whether the United States would be embroiled in fewer international controversies if we created causes of action under the ATS against foreign corporate defendants. Unless corporate liability would actively *decrease* diplomatic disputes, we have no authority to act. On that score, the dissent can only speculate that declining to create causes of action against foreign corporate defendants "might" lead to diplomatic friction. But the dissent has no real-world examples to support its hunch, and that is not surprising; the ATS already goes further than any other statute in the world in granting aliens the right to sue civilly for violations of international law, especially in light of the many other avenues for relief available. It would be rather rich for any other nation to complain that the ATS does not go far enough. Indeed, no country has. . . .

JUSTICE GORSUCH, concurring in part and concurring in the judgment.

I am pleased to join the Court's judgment and Parts I, II-B-1, and II-C of its opinion. Respectfully, though, I believe there are two more fundamental reasons why this lawsuit must be dismissed. A group of foreign plaintiffs wants a federal court to invent a new cause of action so they can sue another foreigner for allegedly breaching international norms. In any other context, a federal judge faced with a request like that would know exactly what to do with it: dismiss it out of hand. Not because the defendant happens to be a corporation instead of a human being. But because the job of creating new causes of action and navigating foreign policy disputes belongs to the political branches. For reasons passing understanding, federal courts have sometimes treated the Alien Tort Statute as a license to overlook these foundational principles. I would end ATS exceptionalism. We should refuse invitations to create new forms of legal liability. And we should not meddle in disputes between foreign citizens over international norms. I write because I am hopeful that courts in the future might pause to consider both of these reasons for restraint before taking up cases like this one. Whatever powers courts may possess in ATS suits, they are powers judges should be doubly careful not to abuse.

First adopted in 1789, the current version of the ATS provides that "[t]he district courts shall have original jurisdiction of any civil action by an alien for a tort only, committed in violation of the law of nations or a treaty of the United States." 28 U.S.C. §1350. More than two hundred years later, the meaning of this terse provision has still "proven elusive." Sosa v. Alvarez-Machain, 542 U.S. 692, 719 (2004). At the same time, this Court has suggested that Congress enacted the statute to afford federal courts jurisdiction to hear tort claims related to three violations of international law that were already embodied in English common law: violations of safe conducts extended to aliens, interference with ambassadors, and piracy. *Id.* at 715; 4 W. Blackstone, Commentaries on the Laws of England 68 (1769) (Blackstone); *see also* Anthony J. Bellia Jr. & Bradford R. Clark, *The Alien Tort Statute and the Law of Nations*, 78 U. Chi. L. Rev. 445 (2011) (arguing that the ATS meant to supply jurisdiction over a slightly larger set of claims involving intentional torts by Americans against aliens).

In this case, the plaintiffs seek much more. They want the federal courts to recognize a new cause of action, one that did not exist at the time of the statute's adoption, one that Congress has never authorized. While their request might appear inconsistent with *Sosa's* explanation of the ATS's modest origin, the plaintiffs say that a caveat later in the opinion saves them. They point to a passage where the Court went on to suggest that the ATS may *also* afford federal judges "discretion [to] conside[r] [creating] new cause[s] of action" if they "rest on a norm of international character accepted by the civilized world and defined with a specificity comparable to the features of the [three] 18th-century" torts the Court already described. *Sosa*, 542 U.S. at 725.

I harbor serious doubts about *Sosa's* suggestion. In our democracy the people's elected representatives make the laws that govern them. Judges do not. . . . Adopting new causes of action may have been a "proper function for common-law courts," but it is not appropriate "for federal tribunals" mindful of the limits of their constitutional authority. Alexander v. Sandoval, 532 U.S. 275, 287 (2001).

Nor can I see any reason to make a special exception for the ATS. As *Sosa* initially acknowledged, the ATS was designed as "a jurisdictional statute creating no new causes of action." 542 U.S. at 724. And I would have thought that the end of the matter. A statute that creates no new causes of action . . . creates no new causes of action. To the extent *Sosa* continued on to claim for federal judges the discretionary power to create new forms of liability on their own, it invaded terrain that belongs to the people's representatives and should be promptly returned to them. . . .

But even accepting *Sosa's* framework does not end the matter. As the Court acknowledges, there is a strong argument that "a proper application of *Sosa* would preclude courts from ever recognizing any new causes of action under the ATS." I believe that argument is correct. For the reasons just described, separation of powers considerations ordinarily require us to defer to Congress in the creation of new forms of liability. This Court hasn't yet used *Sosa's* assertion of discretionary authority to recognize a new cause of action, and I cannot imagine a sound reason, hundreds of years after the statute's passage, to start now. For a court inclined to claim the discretion to enter this field, it is a discretion best exercised by staying out of it. . . .

Another independent problem lurks here. This is a suit by foreigners against a foreigner over the meaning of international norms. Respectfully, I do not think the original understanding of the ATS or our precedent permits federal courts to hear cases like this. At a minimum, both those considerations and simple common sense about the limits of the judicial function should lead federal courts to require a domestic defendant before agreeing to exercise any *Sosa*-generated discretion to entertain an ATS suit.

. . . Like today's recodified version, 28 U.S.C. §1350, the original text of the ATS did not expressly call for a U.S. defendant. But I think it likely would have been understood to contain such a requirement when adopted.

That is because the First Congress passed the Judiciary Act in the shadow of the Constitution. The Act created the federal courts and vested them with statutory authority to entertain claims consistent with the newly ratified terms of Article III. Meanwhile, under Article III, Congress could not have extended to federal courts the power to hear just any suit between two aliens (unless, for example, one was a diplomat). Diversity of citizenship was required. So, because Article III's diversity-of-citizenship clause calls for a U. S. party, and because the ATS clause requires an alien plaintiff, it follows that an American defendant was needed for an ATS suit to proceed.

Precedent confirms this conclusion. In Mossman v. Higginson, 4 U.S. 12, 14, (1800), this Court addressed the meaning of a neighboring provision of the Judiciary Act. Section 11 gave the circuit courts power to hear, among other things, civil cases where "an alien is a party." 1 Stat. 78. As with §9, you might think §11's language could be read to permit a suit *between* aliens. Yet this Court held §11 must instead be construed to refer only to cases "where, indeed, an alien is one party, but a citizen is the other." *Mossman*, 4 Dall. at 14 (internal quotation marks omitted). That was necessary, *Mossman* explained, to give the statute a "constructio[n] consistent" with the diversity-jurisdiction clause of Article III. . . .

Nor does it appear the ATS meant to rely on any other head of Article III jurisdiction. You might wonder, for example, if the First Congress considered a "violation of the law of nations" to be a violation of, and thus "arise under," federal law. But that does not seem likely. . . . While this Court has called international law "part of our law," The Paquete Habana, 175 U.S. 677, 700 (1900), and a component of the "law of the land," The Nereide, 13 U.S. 388 (1815), that simply meant international law was no different than the law of torts or contracts—it "part of the so-called general common law," but *not* part of federal law. *Sosa*, 542 U.S. at 739-40 (opinion of Scalia, J.). *See* Curtis A. Bradley & Jack L. Goldsmith, *Customary International Law as Federal Common Law: A Critique of the Modern Position*, 110 Harv. L. Rev. 815, 824, 849-50 (1997); *see also* Ernest A. Young, *Sorting Out the Debate Over Customary International Law*, 42 Va. J. Int'l L. 365, 374-75 (2002). . . .

Any attempt to decipher a cryptic old statute is sure to meet with challenges. For example, one could object that this reading of the Act does not assign to the ATS the work of addressing assaults by aliens against foreign ambassadors on our soil, even though *Sosa* suggested the statute was enacted partly in response to precisely such a case: the "Marbois incident of May 1784, in which a French adventurer, De Longchamps, verbally and physically assaulted the Secretary of the French Legion in Philadelphia." 542 U.S. at 716. Many thought that the States' failure to provide a forum for relief to the foreign minister was a scandal and part of what prompted the framers of the Constitution to strengthen the national government. . . .

But worries along these lines may be misplaced. The ATS was never meant to serve as a freestanding statute, only as one clause in one section of the Judiciary Act. So even if you think *something* in the Judiciary Act must be interpreted to address the Marbois incident, that doesn't mean it must be the ATS clause. And, as it happens, a different provision of the Act *did* deal expressly with the problem of ambassadorial assaults: Section 13 conferred on this Court "original, but not exclusive jurisdiction of all suits brought by ambassadors, or other public ministers, or in which a consul, or vice consul shall be a party." 1 Stat. 80-81. That implemented Article III's provision empowering us to hear suits "affecting Ambassadors, other public ministers and Consuls." §2. And given that §13 deals with the problem of "ambassadors" so directly, it is unclear why we must read §9 to address that same problem. *See* Thomas H. Lee, *The Safe-Conduct Theory of the Alien Tort Statute*, 106 Colum. L. Rev. 830, 855-58 (2006).

Along different but similar lines, some might be concerned that requiring a U.S. defendant in ATS suits would leave the problem of piracy inadequately addressed, given that *Sosa* suggested that piracy was one of the three offenses the ATS may have meant to capture, and many pirates were foreigners. But here the response is much the same. A separate clause of §9 gave the district courts "exclusive original cognizance of all civil causes of admiralty and maritime jurisdiction." 1 Stat. 77. That statute has long been given a broad construction covering "all maritime contracts, torts and injuries," DeLovio v. Boit, 7 F. Cas. 418, 442 (No. 3,776) (CC Mass. 1815) (Story, J.), along with "prize jurisdiction, which probably included almost all 'piracy' cases after 1789," Lee, supra, at 867. So it is not clear why it's necessary to cram the problem of piracy into the ATS. If anything, it may be necessary *not* to do so. . . .

If doubt lingers on these historical questions, it is a doubt that should counsel restraint all the same. Even if the ATS might have meant to allow foreign *ambassadors* to sue foreign defendants, or foreign plaintiffs to sue foreign *pirates*, what would that prove about more mine-run cases like ours, where none of those special concerns are implicated? There are at least serious historical arguments suggesting the ATS was not meant to apply to suits like this one. And to the extent *Sosa* affords courts discretion to proceed, these arguments should inform any decision whether to exercise that discretion. . . .

Any consideration of *Sosa*'s discretion must also account for proper limits on the judicial function. As discussed above, federal courts generally lack the institutional expertise and constitutional authority to oversee foreign policy and national security, and should be wary of straying where they do not belong. Yet there are degrees of institutional incompetence and constitutional evil. It is one thing for courts to assume the task of creating new causes of action to ensure *our* citizens abide by the law of nations and *avoid* reprisals against this country. It is altogether another thing for courts to punish *foreign* parties for conduct that could not be attributed to the United States and thereby *risk* reprisals against this country. If a foreign state or citizen violates an "international norm" in a way that offends another foreign state or citizen, the Constitution arms the President and Congress with ample means to address it. Or, if they think best, the political branches may choose to look the other way. But in all events, the decision to impose sanctions in disputes between foreigners over international norms is not ours to make. It is a decision that belongs to those answerable to the people and assigned by the Constitution to defend this nation. If they wish our help, they are free to enlist it, but we should not ever be in the business of elbowing our way in.

JUSTICE SOTOMAYOR, with whom JUSTICE GINSBURG, JUSTICE BREYER, and JUSTICE KAGAN join, dissenting. . . .

Beginning "with the language of the statute itself," United States v. Ron Pair Enterprises, Inc., 489 U.S. 235, 241, two aspects of the text of the ATS make clear that the statute allows corporate liability. First, the text confers jurisdiction on federal district courts to hear "civil action[s]" for "tort[s]." 28 U.S.C. §1350. Where Congress uses a term of art like tort, "it presumably knows and adopts the cluster of ideas that were attached to [the] borrowed word in the body of learning from which it was taken and the meaning its use will convey to the judicial mind unless otherwise instructed." Morissette v. United States, 342 U.S. 246, 263 (1952).

Corporations have long been held liable in tort under the federal common law. . . . This Court "has assumed that, when Congress creates a tort action, it legislates against a legal background of ordinary tort-related . . . rules and consequently intends its legislation to incorporate those rules." Meyer v. Holley, 537 U.S. 280, 285 (2003). The presumption, then, is that, in providing for "tort" liability, the ATS provides for corporate liability.

Second, whereas the ATS expressly limits the class of permissible plaintiffs to "alien[s]," §1350, it "does not distinguish among classes of defendants," Argentine Republic v. Amerada Hess Shipping Corp., 488 U.S. 428, 438 (1989). That silence as to defendants cannot be presumed to be inadvertent. That is because in the same section of the Judiciary Act of 1789 as what is now the ATS, Congress provided the federal district courts with jurisdiction over "all suits against consuls or vice-consuls." §9, 1 Stat. 76-77. Where Congress wanted to limit the range of permissible defendants, then, it clearly knew how to do so. . . .

Nothing about the historical background against which the ATS was enacted rebuts the presumption that the statute incorporated the accepted principle of corporate liability for tortious conduct. Under the Articles of Confederation, the Continental Congress was unable to provide redress to foreign citizens for violations of treaties or the law of nations, which threatened to undermine the United States' relationships with other nations. The First Congress responded with, *inter alia*, the ATS. Although the two incidents that highlighted the need to provide foreign citizens with a federal forum in which to pursue their grievances involved conflicts between natural persons, . . . there is "no reason to conclude that the First Congress was supremely concerned with the risk that natural persons would cause the United States to be drawn into foreign entanglements, but was content to allow formal legal associations of individuals, i.e., corporations, to do so," Doe v. Exxon Mobil Corp., 654 F.3d 11, 47 (D.C. Cir. 2011), vacated on other grounds, 527 Fed. Appx. 7 (D.C. Cir. 2013) . . . . Indeed, foreclosing corporations from liability under the ATS would have been at odds with the contemporaneous practice of imposing liability for piracy on ships, juridical entities. . . .

[T]he concurrence suggests that federal courts may lack jurisdiction to entertain suits between aliens based solely on a violation of the law of nations. It contends that ATS suits between aliens fall under neither the federal courts' diversity jurisdiction nor our federal question jurisdiction. The Court was not unaware of this argument when it decided *Sosa*. . . . The Court nonetheless proceeded to decide the case, which it could not have done had it been concerned about its Article III power to do so. That decision forecloses the argument the concurrence now makes, as *Sosa* authorized courts to "recognize private claims *under federal common law* for violations of" certain international law norms. 542 U.S. at 732 (emphasis added) . . . .

Sosa was correct as a legal matter. Moreover, our Nation has an interest not only in providing a remedy when our own citizens commit law of nations violations, but also in preventing our Nation from serving as a safe harbor for today's pirates. . . . To the extent suits against foreign defendants may lead to international friction, that concern is better addressed under the presumption the Court established in *Kiobel* against extraterritorial application of the ATS than it is by relitigating settled precedent.

. . . Nothing about the corporate form in itself justifies categorically foreclosing corporate liability in all ATS actions. Each source of diplomatic friction that respondent Arab Bank and the plurality identify can be addressed with a tool more tailored to the source of the problem than a blanket ban on corporate liability. . . .

The majority also cites to instances in which other foreign sovereigns have "appeared in this Court to note [their] objections to ATS litigation," but none of those objections was about the availability of corporate liability as a general matter. . . .

As the United States urged at oral argument, when international friction arises, a court should respond with the doctrine that speaks directly to the friction's source. In addition to the presumption against extraterritoriality, federal courts have at their disposal a number of tools to address any foreign-relations concerns that an ATS case may raise. This Court has held that a federal court may exercise personal jurisdiction over a foreign corporate defendant only if the corporation is incorporated in the United States, has its principal place of business or is otherwise at home here, or if the activities giving rise to the lawsuit occurred or had their impact here. *See* Daimler AG v. Bauman, 571 U.S. 117 (2014). Courts also can dismiss ATS suits for a plaintiff's failure to exhaust the remedies available in her domestic forum, on *forum non conveniens* grounds, for reasons of international comity, or when asked to do so by the State Department. . . .

Several of these doctrines might be implicated in this case, and I would remand for the Second Circuit to address them in the first instance. The majority, however, prefers to use a sledgehammer to crack a nut. I see no need for such an ill-fitting and disproportionate response. Foreclosing foreign corporate liability in all ATS actions, irrespective of circumstance or norm, is simply too broad a response to case-specific concerns that can be addressed via other means. . . .

The plurality extrapolates from Congress' decision regarding the scope of liability under the TVPA a rule that it contends should govern all ATS suits. But there is no reason to think that because Congress saw fit to permit suits only against natural persons for two specific law-of-nations violations, Congress meant to foreclose corporate liability for all law-of-nations violations. . . .

To infer from the TVPA that no corporation may ever be held liable under the ATS for any violation of any international-law norm, moreover, ignores that Congress has elsewhere imposed liability on corporations for conduct prohibited by customary international law. For instance, the Antiterrorism Act of 1990 (ATA) created a civil cause of action for U.S. nationals injured by an act of international terrorism and expressly provides for corporate liability. 18 U.S.C. §2333. That Congress foreclosed corporate liability for torture and extrajudicial killing claims under the TVPA but permitted corporate liability for terrorism-related claims under the ATA is strong evidence that Congress exercises its judgment as to the appropriateness of corporate liability on a norm-by-norm basis, and that courts should do the same when considering whether to permit causes of action against corporations for law-of-nations violations under the ATS. . . .

Moreover, even if there are other grounds on which a suit alleging conduct constituting a law-of-nations violation can be brought, such as a state-law tort claim, the First Congress created the ATS because it wanted foreign plaintiffs to be able to bring their claims in federal court and sue for law-of-nations violations. A suit for state-law battery, even if based on the same alleged conduct, is not the equivalent of a federal suit for torture; the latter contributes to the uptake of international human rights norms, and the former does not.

Furthermore, holding corporations accountable for violating the human rights of foreign citizens when those violations touch and concern the United States may well be necessary to avoid the international tension with which the First Congress was concerned. Consider again the assault on the Secretary of the French Legation in Philadelphia by a French adventurer. Would the diplomatic strife that followed really have been any less charged if a corporation had sent its agent to accost the Secretary? Or, consider piracy. If a corporation owned a fleet of vessels and directed them to seize other ships in U.S. waters, there no doubt would be calls to hold the corporation to account. Finally, take, for example, a corporation posing as a job-placement agency that actually traffics in persons, forcibly transporting foreign nationals to the United States for exploitation and profiting from their abuse. Not only are the individual employees of that business less likely to be able fully to compensate successful ATS plaintiffs, but holding only individual employees liable does not impose accountability for the institution-wide disregard for human rights. Absent a corporate sanction, that harm will persist unremedied. Immunizing the corporation from suit under the ATS merely because it is a corporation, even though the violations stemmed directly from corporate policy and practice, might cause serious diplomatic friction. . . .

In categorically barring all suits against foreign corporations under the ATS, the Court ensures that foreign corporations—entities capable of wrongdoing under our domestic law—remain immune from liability for human rights abuses, however egregious they may be. . . .

Immunizing corporations that violate human rights from liability under the ATS undermines the system of accountability for law-of-nations violations that the First Congress endeavored to impose. It allows these entities to take advantage of the significant benefits of the corporate form and enjoy fundamental rights, without having to shoulder attendant fundamental responsibilities.

Notes and Questions

1. As discussed in Chapter 2, the Supreme Court has held that federal statutes should be presumed not to apply to conduct occurring outside the United States in the absence of a clear indication by Congress of extraterritorial application. In EEOC v. Arabian American Oil Co., 499 U.S. 244 (1991), the Court applied this presumption in holding that Title VII did not apply to a U.S. corporation's alleged discriminatory treatment of a U.S. citizen in Saudi Arabia. In Morrison v. National Australia Bank Ltd., 130 S. Ct. 2869 (2010), the Court applied the presumption in holding that Section 10(b) of the Securities Exchange Act did not apply to claims of alleged misconduct in connection with securities traded on foreign exchanges. The Court has explained that the presumption "rests on the perception that Congress ordinarily legislates with respect to domestic, not foreign matters," Morrison, 130 S. Ct. at 2877, and that it also "serves to protect against unintended clashes between our laws and those of other nations which could result in international discord," *Arabian American Oil*, 499 U.S. at 248. The Court has not applied the presumption to all federal statutes, however. Although it once applied the presumption in the area of antitrust law, it no longer does so. *See* Hartford Fire Insurance Co. v. California, 509 U.S. 764, 795-96 (1993) ("Although the proposition was perhaps not always free from doubt . . . it is well established by now that the Sherman Act applies to foreign conduct that was meant to produce and did in fact produce some substantial effect in the United States."). Moreover, the presumption does not apply to "criminal statutes which are, as a class, not logically dependent on their locality for the government's jurisdiction, but are enacted because of the right of the government to defend itself against obstruction, or fraud wherever perpetrated, especially if committed by its own citizens, officers, or agents." United States v. Bowman, 260 U.S. 94, 98 (1922).

2. Despite the presumption against extraterritoriality, most lower courts had assumed before the Supreme Court's decision in *Kiobel* that plaintiffs could bring claims under the ATS for foreign conduct. One reason they may have assumed this is that the ATS is limited to torts that violate international law. Since international law applies globally, it may not seem "extraterritorial" for a U.S. court to apply it to adjudicate a dispute concerning conduct abroad. In *Sosa*, however, the Supreme Court held that the cause of action in ATS cases derived from federal common law that in turn was authorized in some fashion by the ATS, a proposition confirmed by the Court in *Kiobel*. The issue in *Kiobel*, therefore, was whether the presumption against extraterritoriality applied to U.S. federal common law causes of action, not to international law. The majority contends that, if anything, the justifications for the presumption apply with greater force in the context of a judicially developed rather than statutory cause of action. Is that argument persuasive? If courts have been implicitly delegated the authority to develop common law causes of action, have they also been delegated the authority to determine the appropriate extraterritorial reach of the causes of action? Or is the initial delegation tenuous enough, and the subject matter potentially controversial enough, that courts should exercise special caution in extending judge-made ATS causes of action to foreign territory?

3. At the end of its opinion in *Kiobel*, the majority states that "where the claims touch and concern the territory of the United States, they must do so with sufficient force to displace the presumption against extraterritorial application" and that "mere corporate presence" in the United States is not enough. What, beyond mere corporate presence, might be enough? What answer was Justice Alito suggesting in his concurrence? If a U.S. corporation helps plan tortious activity that occurs abroad, is the case no longer extraterritorial for purposes of the presumption against extraterritoriality? What if the U.S. corporation simply has knowledge of the foreign tortious activity? What if an individual commits a tort in violation of international law abroad, but is now residing in the United States? For discussion of differing approaches to these questions by the lower courts, see Note, *Clarifying* Kiobel *'s Touch and Concern Test*, 130 Harv. L. Rev. 1902 (2017).

4. In arguing in *Kiobel* that the presumption against extraterritoriality had been overcome in that case, Justice Breyer contended in his concurrence that the ATS was designed in part to allow suits against pirates, whose conduct would typically take place outside the United States. What is the majority's response to this argument? What evidence is there, if any, that the ATS was in fact designed for suits against pirates? Even if pirates could have historically been sued under the ATS, is Justice Breyer right in describing egregious human rights abuses as "modern-day equivalents" of piracy? In any event, isn't Justice Breyer correct that the United States has an interest in not being a safe haven for human rights abusers? Is it a sufficient answer to Breyer that Congress has already addressed the issue to some extent through immigration and criminal laws and that it can provide for broader civil liability if it is dissatisfied with the decision in *Kiobel*?

5. The lower courts have developed differing approaches to applying *Kiobel*'s "touch and concern" test. In Mastafa v. Chevron Corp., 770 F.3d 170 (2d Cir. 2014), the Second Circuit relied heavily on Morrison v. National Australia Bank, a decision concerning extraterritorial application of the securities fraud statute (excerpted in Chapter 2), in which the Supreme Court looked to whether the U.S. activities of the defendant were within the "focus" of the statute. The Second Circuit then set forth the following principles that courts should consider:

> a. . . . the "focus" of the ATS—and, thus, the focus of the jurisdictional inquiry—is the conduct alleged to violate the law of nations (or alleged to aid and abet the violation of the law of nations), and where that conduct occurred.
> b. To establish our jurisdiction under the ATS, the complaint must plead: (1) conduct of the defendant that "touch[ed] and concern[ed]" the United States with sufficient force to displace the presumption against extraterritoriality, *and* (2) that the *same conduct*, upon preliminary examination, states a claim for a violation of the law of nations or aiding and abetting another's violation of the law of nations.
> c. In identifying the "relevant conduct" for jurisdictional purposes, . . . neither the U.S. citizenship of defendants, nor their mere presence in the United States, is relevant to a court's determination of its jurisdiction. . . .

Applying these principles, the court in *Mastafa* directed the dismissal of a case brought by Iraqi nationals in which they alleged that two corporations had facilitated the diversion of money to the Saddam Hussein regime in Iraq, thereby aiding and abetting human rights abuses committed by the regime. Although the plaintiffs had alleged sufficient domestic conduct to meet the "touch and concern" test, reasoned the court, they had failed to sufficiently allege that the defendants intended, by this conduct, to facilitate the human rights abuses.

In contrast with *Mastafa*, the Ninth Circuit in Doe v. Nestle USA, Inc., 766 F.3d 1013 (9th Cir. 2014) (*Nestle I*), ruled that *Kiobel* "did not incorporate *Morrison*'s focus test" for determining which ATS claims overcome the presumption against extraterritoriality. The court noted that the phrase "touch and concern" differed from the term "focus" and added that "since the focus test turns on discerning Congress's intent when passing a statute, it cannot sensibly be applied to ATS claims, which are common law claims based on international legal norms." Because the court did not want "to apply the amorphous touch and concern test on the record currently before us," however, it remanded the case to allow the plaintiffs, who were alleging that various corporations had aided and abetted child slavery in the Ivory Coast by providing assistance to farmers there who used child labor, to amend their complaint.

On remand from *Nestle I*, the district court granted the defendants' motion to dismiss the case. On appeal from that dismissal, however, the Ninth Circuit reversed its position on the applicability of the focus test to ATS litigation in light of the Supreme Court's 2016 decision in RJR Nabisco, Inc. v. European Community, 136 S. Ct. 2090 (2016), which is discussed in Section F of Chapter 2. *See* Doe v. Nestle, S.A., 906 F.3d 1120 (9th Cir. 2018) (*Nestle II*). The *Nestle II* court read *RJR Nabisco* as requiring the application of *Morrison*'s focus test to ATS litigation.

In *RJR Nabisco*, the Court applied the *Morrison* focus test to the Racketeer Influenced and Corrupt Organizations Act (RICO) and reiterated that *Morrison* reflects a two-step inquiry regarding extraterritoriality. The Court further stated that "*Morrison* and *Kiobel* [also] reflect a two-step framework for analyzing extraterritoriality issues."

Because *RJR Nabisco* has indicated that the two-step framework is required in the context of ATS claims, we apply it here. First, we determine "whether the [ATS] gives a clear, affirmative indication that it applies extraterritorially . . . . Because the ATS is not extraterritorial, then at the second step, we must ask whether this case involves "a domestic application of the statute, by looking to the statute's 'focus.'"

The court reversed and remanded to allow the plaintiffs another opportunity to amend their complaint.

For additional decisions applying *Kiobel*, see, for example:

Warfaa v. Ali, 811 F.3d 653 (4th Cir. 2016) (2-1 decision upholding dismissal of ATS claims based on torture and mistreatment in Somalia, even though the defendant was now residing in the United States, reasoning that "[m]ere happenstance of residency, lacking any connection to the relevant conduct, is not a cognizable consideration in the ATS context");

Balintulo v. Ford Motor Co., 796 F.3d 160 (2d Cir. 2015) (dismissing claims against Ford and IBM for allegedly aiding and abetting South Africa's historic apartheid practices because the pleadings "do not plausibly allege that the Companies themselves engaged in any 'relevant conduct' within the United States to overcome the presumption against extraterritorial application of the ATS");

Doe v. Drummond Co., 782 F.3d 576 (11th Cir. 2015) (concluding that the "touch and concern" standard from *Kiobel* was not met in a case involving a U.S. corporation's alleged aiding and abetting of human rights abuses by paramilitary forces (known as the Autodefensas Unidas de Colombia, or AUC) in Colombia because, although the plaintiffs alleged that "generally, Defendants made funding and policy decisions in the United States," they also alleged that "the agreements between Defendants and the perpetrators of the killings, the planning and execution of the extrajudicial killings and war crimes, the collaboration by Defendants' employees with the AUC, and the actual funding of the AUC all took place in Colombia");

Cardona v. Chiquita Brands Int'l, Inc., 760 F.3d 1185 (11th Cir. 2014) (dismissing ATS suit against a U.S. corporation because the tortious violations of international law that the corporation allegedly aided and abetted occurred outside the United States); and

Al Shimari v. CACI Premier Tech., Inc., 758 F.3d 516 (4th Cir. 2014) (allowing claims to proceed against a U.S. corporation for the torture and mistreatment of foreign nationals at the Abu Ghraib prison in Iraq because, among other things, the contract with the U.S. government pursuant to which the corporation carried out its activities in Iraq was issued in the United States and there were allegations that the corporation's managers in the United States had given tacit approval to the acts of torture and mistreatment and attempted to cover them up).

6. Does *Kiobel* suggest that *Filartiga* was wrongly decided? Importantly, the TVPA now provides an alternative basis for a case, like *Filartiga*, that involves acts of torture or "extrajudicial killing." Justice Kennedy noted this point in his concurrence. But he also observed that the decision left open "significant questions regarding the reach and interpretation of the Alien Tort Statute" and that "the presumption against extraterritorial application may require some further elaboration and explanation" in cases covered "neither by the TVPA nor by the reasoning and holding of today's case." What cases might he have had in mind?

7. Prior to Jesner v. Arab Bank, the lower courts had for many years allowed ATS suits against corporations and other non-state actors, although they had disagreed about the standards that should apply to these suits. Initially, the courts seemed reluctant to allow such suits. As noted at the beginning of Section B, four years after *Filartiga*, a panel of the D.C. Circuit, with three separate opinions and rationales, dismissed a case brought under the ATS against the Palestinian Liberation Organization (PLO) concerning that organization's involvement in a terrorist attack in Israel. *See* Tel-Oren v. Libyan Arab Republic, 726 F.2d 774 (D.C. Cir. 1984). The judge on the panel who was most supportive of *Filartiga*, Judge Edwards, reasoned that this case was distinguishable from *Filartiga* because the PLO was not a recognized state, and thus (unlike the Paraguayan official in *Filartiga*) could not commit official, or state-initiated, torture. *Id.* at 791.

8. In a case decided in the mid-1990s, the Second Circuit considered an ATS suit against the leader of a breakaway Bosnian-Serb republic for allegedly directing and overseeing egregious human rights violations by military forces under his command. *See* Kadic v. Karadzic, 70 F.3d 232 (2d Cir. 1995). Citing Judge Edwards's concurrence in *Tel-Oren*, the defendant argued that the case could not proceed because the breakaway republic was, like the PLO, not a recognized state. In rejecting this argument, the court first noted that some violations of international law, such as genocide, war crimes, and slavery, can be committed even by private actors. The court acknowledged that other human rights violations, including torture and summary execution, violate international law "only when committed by state officials or under color of law." But the court reasoned that, even if the breakaway republic was not a state, the defendant's actions could still be considered state action for purposes of liability under the ATS if he had "acted in concert" with the Yugoslav government.

Although *Karadzic* did not involve a corporate defendant, the court's conclusion that non-state actors could sometimes be sued under the ATS opened up the possibility of bringing ATS claims against a different type of non-state actor—private corporations. Litigants quickly realized this potential, and numerous ATS suits have since been brought against both foreign and U.S. corporations. These suits changed the character of ATS litigation because corporations often have deep pockets and assets within the United States, making the recovery of money (either through settlement or at trial) a much more realistic possibility. The heightened economic stakes also invited more sophisticated legal practice on both sides of these cases.

9. The Second Circuit considered a broader type of liability for non-state actors in Khulumani v. Barclay National Bank Ltd., 504 F.3d 254 (2d Cir. 2007). That case concerned a suit against numerous corporations for allegedly having "aided and abetted" racially restrictive and oppressive policies in South Africa during that country's apartheid era. In a 2-1 *per curiam* decision, the court concluded that the aiding and abetting claims could be brought under the ATS. The two judges in the majority disagreed, however, about the proper standard for aiding and abetting liability.

Judge Katzmann reasoned that the standard should be derived from international law, and that international law materials, especially the Rome Statute of the International Criminal Court, suggested that liability should be imposed only "when the defendant (1) provides practical assistance to the principal which has a substantial effect on the perpetration of the crime, and (2) does so with the purpose of facilitating the commission of that crime." Judge Hall, by contrast, reasoned that the standard should be derived from domestic federal common law, and that under such a standard (based on the Restatement (Second) of Torts), liability would be proper when the defendant

> (1) by knowingly and substantially assisting a principal tortfeasor, such as a foreign government or its proxy, to commit an act that violates a clearly established international law norm; (2) by encouraging, advising, contracting with, or otherwise soliciting a principal tortfeasor to commit an act while having actual or constructive knowledge that the principal tortfeasor will violate a clearly established customary international law norm in the process of completing that act; or (3) by facilitating the commission of human rights violations by providing the principal tortfeasor with the tools, instrumentalities, or services to commit those violations with actual or constructive knowledge that those tools, instrumentalities, or services will be (or only could be) used in connection with that purpose.

Id. at 288-89. Judge Korman dissented, arguing, among other things, that corporate liability was not sufficiently established under international law to meet the standard for ATS claims announced by the Supreme Court in *Sosa.* (*Khulumani* is the same case from South Africa discussed in footnote 21 of *Sosa.*)

10. A full panel of the Second Circuit subsequently endorsed Judge Katzmann's position with respect to the standard for aiding and abetting liability in Presbyterian Church of Sudan v. Talisman Energy, Inc., 582 F.3d 244 (2d Cir. 2009). In that case, a group of current and former residents of Sudan sued Talisman Energy, Inc., a Canadian corporation, under the Alien Tort Statute, alleging that Talisman had either aided and abetted or conspired with the Sudanese government in actions designed to facilitate the development of oil concessions in Sudan by Talisman affiliates, and that these actions constituted genocide, war crimes, and crimes against humanity. In upholding a dismissal of the case, the Second Circuit concluded that "*Sosa* and our precedents send us to international law to find the standard for accessorial liability," and it found that under international law, "the *mens rea* standard for aiding and abetting liability . . . is purpose rather than knowledge alone." Dismissal was therefore warranted, explained the court, because "[p]laintiffs have provided evidence that the Government violated customary international law; but they provide no evidence that Talisman acted with the purpose to support the Government's offenses." The court concluded:

> There is evidence that southern Sudanese were subjected to attacks by the Government, that those attacks facilitated the oil enterprise, and that the Government's stream of oil revenue enhanced the military capabilities used to persecute its enemies. But if ATS liability could be established by knowledge of those abuses coupled only with such commercial activities as resource development, the statute would act as a vehicle for private parties to impose embargos or international sanctions through civil actions in United States courts. Such measures are not the province of private parties but are, instead, properly reserved to governments and multinational organizations.

Id. at 264. For another decision adopting a purpose standard for aiding and abetting, see Aziz v. Alcolac, Inc., 658 F.3d 388 (4th Cir. 2011).

By contrast, the U.S. Court of Appeals for the D.C. Circuit concluded that a less stringent knowledge standard was appropriate, reasoning as follows:

> The court . . . looks to customary international law to determine the standard for assessing aiding and abetting liability. . . . Important sources are the international tribunals mandated by their charter to apply only customary international law. Two such

tribunals, the International Criminal Tribunals for the Former Yugoslavia and Rwanda, are considered authoritative sources of customary international law. . . .

The ICTY, in addressing whether the accomplice must "share the *mens rea* of the principal or whether mere knowledge" will suffice, concluded that "the latter will suffice." Prosecutor v. Furundzija, Case No. IT-95-17/1 Trial Chamber Judgement, ¶236 (Dec. 10, 1998). . . . The ICTR is in agreement. . . .

The Second Circuit, in Presbyterian Church of Sudan v. Talisman Energy, Inc., 582 F.3d 244 (2d Cir. 2009), nonetheless held that the aider and abettor must share the same purpose as the principal actor, relying on the Rome Statute of the International Criminal Court. . . .

Although we agree with the Second Circuit's premise that aiding and abetting must be embodied in a norm of customary international law . . . [t]he Rome Statute, which created the International Criminal Court, is properly viewed in the nature of a treaty and not as customary international law. . . . It specifically provides in Article 10 that it is not to "be interpreted as limiting or prejudicing in any way existing or developing rules of international law." This acknowledges that the Rome Statute was not meant to affect or amend existing customary international law. As a treaty, the Rome Statute binds only those countries that have ratified it, and the United States has not. . . .

Accordingly, we hold that aiding and abetting liability is available under the ATS because it involves a norm established by customary international law and that the *mens rea* and *actus reus* requirements are those established by the ICTY, the ICTR, and the Nuremberg tribunals, whose opinions constitute expressions of customary international law. The Rome Statute does not constitute customary international law. . . . The decisions of the ICTY and ICTR adopt a "knowledge" *mens rea* and a showing for *actus reus* of acts that have a substantial effect in bringing about the violation. . . .

Doe v. Exxon Mobil Corp., 654 F.3d 11, 33-39 (D.C. Cir. 2011).

11. Until the Second Circuit's decision in *Kiobel* in 2010, courts generally assumed that corporations could be sued under the ATS, and thus they focused (as in *Khulumani* and *Talisman*) on the relevant standards for such suits. The Second Circuit in *Kiobel* concluded that, in fact, corporations were not proper defendants in ATS cases. The Supreme Court declined to address this question in *Kiobel* in light of its extraterritoriality holding. The Second Circuit created a circuit conflict over the issue of corporate liability, and the conflict deepened after the decision. Both the D.C. Circuit in Doe v. Exxon Mobil Corp., 654 F.3d 11 (D.C. Cir. 2011), and the Seventh Circuit in Flomo v. Firestone Natural Rubber Co., 643 F.3d 1013 (7th Cir. 2011), expressly disagreed with the Second Circuit.

In *Jesner v. Arab Bank*, excerpted above, the Supreme Court held that foreign corporations cannot be sued under the ATS. Note that Justice Kennedy's opinion garnered a majority on two basic legal points. First, in Part II-B-1, he noted the Court's deep reluctance in recent cases outside the ATS context to extend or create private causes of action, and he concluded that nothing in the language of the ATS or in precedent supported an exception to these principles. After *Jesner*, when should courts recognize causes of action under the ATS? The Court observes that, in light of "the foreign-policy and separation-of-powers concerns inherent in ATS litigation," "there is an argument that a proper application of *Sosa* would preclude courts from ever recognizing any new causes of action under the ATS." Is that observation consistent with the reasoning in *Sosa*? Does the Court's statement that it need not "resolve" this question in this case portend an overruling of *Sosa*?

The second major point on which a majority of the Court agreed came in Part II-C, where Justice Kennedy reasoned that the international friction caused by suits against foreign corporations counseled against extending ATS causes of action to them. Is this argument persuasive? What about Justice Sotomayor's response that the danger of foreign relations friction can be adequately addressed through other doctrines? Note that the Executive Branch had filed an amicus brief in *Jesner*, opposing a categorical ban on corporate ATS liability, for reasons similar to those articulated by Justice Sotomayor. Should the Court have deferred to the Executive Branch's position?

12. Consider Justice Gorsuch's concurrence in *Jesner*. He suggests that the ATS might have been originally understood to be limited to suits against U.S. defendants. What reasons does he give for implying such a limitation? In any event, is it too late to argue this, given the various decisions (including *Sosa*) that have assumed that foreign citizens can be sued under the ATS?

13. After *Kiobel* and *Jesner*, what suits can still be brought under the ATS? Individuals, including individual officers of corporations, can still potentially be sued under the ATS. In addition to the extraterritoriality limitation imposed by *Kiobel*, what obstacles are such suits against individual defendants likely to encounter? The Court in *Jesner* did not decide whether U.S. corporations could be sued, but does its reasoning suggest an answer? For a recent decision allowing an ATS suit to proceed against U.S. corporate defendants, see Doe v. Nestle, S.A., 906 F.3d 1120 (9th Cir. 2018), which involved allegations that U.S. companies funded and otherwise supported child slave labor practices on cocoa farms in the Ivory Coast. As a policy matter, when corporate conduct has a connection to the United States that is sufficient to meet the territoriality requirement in *Kiobel*, does it make sense for U.S. law to impose liability only on U.S. but not foreign corporations? Will this place U.S. corporations at a competitive disadvantage?

14. In light of the Supreme Court's restriction of ATS litigation in *Kiobel* and *Jesner*, plaintiffs may attempt to use state tort law as a vehicle for litigating claims that they might otherwise have attempted to litigate under the ATS. Cases based on state law typically cannot be brought in federal court unless there is diversity jurisdiction, which will not be available in cases between foreign parties. Whether brought in federal or state court, cases based on state tort law are likely to raise difficult choice-of-law questions. Relevant to the choice-of-law question will be the fact that there are probably due process and other limitations on the extent to which states can apply their tort law to conduct in other countries, especially when the action has no connection to the state. *See* Home Ins. Co. v. Dick, 281 U.S. 397 (1930) (Due Process Clause precludes application of Texas contract law to event that occurred in Mexican waters and had little connection to Texas). Plaintiffs may also face more significant *forum non conveniens* limitations if they lack a federal cause of action, especially where both the plaintiffs and the defendants are non-U.S. citizens. In some instances, state causes of action might also be subject to federal preemption. (Preemption of state law that relates to foreign affairs is discussed in Chapter 4 of the casebook.) For discussion of alternatives to ATS litigation, see Donald Earl Childress III, *The Alien Tort Statute, Federalism, and the Next Wave of Transnational Litigation*, 100 Geo. L.J. 709 (2012). *See also* Seth Davis & Christopher A. Whytock, *State Remedies for Human Rights*, 98 B.U. L. Rev. 397, 405 (2018) (arguing in support of state remedies for international human rights violations, and contending that "[s]tate authority to provide redress is the default; the limits are what require justification").

15. For additional discussion of the extraterritoriality and corporate liability issues considered in this section, see Curtis A. Bradley, *Attorney General Bradford's Opinion and the Alien Tort Statute*, 106 Am. J. Int'l L. 509 (2012); Julian G. Ku, *The Curious Case of Corporate Liability Under the Alien Tort Statute: A Flawed System of Judicial*

Lawmaking, 51 Va. J. Int'l L. 353 (2011); Michael D. Ramsey, *International Law Limits on Investor Liability in Human Rights Litigation*, 50 Harv. Int'l L.J. 271 (2009); Beth Stephens, *The Amorality of Profit: Transnational Corporations and Human Rights*, 20 Berkeley J. Int'l L. 45 (2002); Carlos M. Vázquez, *Direct vs. Indirect Obligations of Corporations Under International Law*, 43 Colum. J. Transnat'l L. 927 (2005); *Developments in the Law: Corporate Liability for Violations of International Human Rights Law*, 114 Harv. L. Rev. 2025 (2001). For an effort to situate ATS litigation "within the traditional federal-courts framework of implied rights of action and federal common law," and an argument that this framework supports the Supreme Court's disallowance in *Kiobel* of "universal jurisdiction" under the ATS (that is, jurisdiction in cases in which the parties are not U.S. nationals and the relevant conduct took place outside the United States), see Ernest A. Young, *Universal Jurisdiction, the Alien Tort Statute, and Transnational Public Law Litigation After Kiobel*, 64 Duke L.J. 1023 (2015).

D. FOREIGN SOVEREIGN IMMUNITY

It has long been understood that, as a matter of customary international law, nations are entitled to a degree of immunity from suit in the courts of other countries. The adoption of foreign sovereign immunity in the United States is often traced to the Supreme Court's decision in The Schooner Exchange v. McFaddon, 11 U.S. (7 Cranch) 116 (1812). In *Schooner Exchange*, the Court directed the dismissal of an admiralty action brought against a French warship by individuals who claimed that the French navy had improperly seized the vessel from them. The Court referred to "a principle of public law"—presumably customary international law—whereby "national ships of war, entering the port of a friendly power open for their reception, are to be considered as exempted by the consent of that power from its jurisdiction." Over time, courts extended sovereign immunity to other foreign government ships, then to other foreign government property, and then to any suit against a foreign nation.

In the nineteenth century and early twentieth century, although courts sometimes considered the views of the Executive Branch in making sovereign immunity determinations, they did not feel obligated to accept those views. They deferred to the Executive Branch's decisions as to which governments should be recognized, but they felt free to make their own determinations regarding sovereign immunity, based on considerations of international law and comity. Consider, for example, the *Pesaro* litigation in the 1920s, which involved claims against an Italian government-owned steamship relating to its transportation of commercial cargo. The district court in that litigation solicited the views of the State Department, which argued that government-owned merchant vessels employed in commerce "should not be regarded as entitled to the immunities accorded public vessels of war." *See* The Pesaro, 277 F. 473 (S.D.N.Y. 1921). Although the district court did not treat the State Department's views as binding, it agreed with the State Department and held that the Italian ship was not entitled to immunity. Subsequently, this decision was vacated for reasons unrelated to the court's immunity analysis and reconsidered by a different district court judge. The new judge granted immunity based on his reading of prior sovereign immunity decisions, making no mention of the State Department's views. *See* The Pesaro, 13 F.2d 468 (S.D.N.Y. 1926). The Supreme Court affirmed, holding that merchant ships owned and operated by a foreign government have the same immunity as a government warship. *See* Berizzi Bros. Co. v. Steamship Pesaro, 271 U.S. 562 (1926).

This changed starting in the late 1930s. In Compania Espanola de Navegacion Maritima, S.A. v. The Navemar, 303 U.S. 68, 74 (1938), the Supreme Court suggested for the first time that Executive Branch suggestions of immunity were binding on the courts. Subsequently, in Ex parte Peru, 318 U.S. 578 (1943), and Mexico v. Hoffman, 324 U.S. 30 (1945), the Court made clear that, if the Executive Branch expressed its views regarding whether immunity should be granted, courts were bound to accept those views. Thus, the Court stated in *Hoffman* that "[i]t is therefore not for the courts to deny an immunity which our government has seen fit to allow, or to allow an immunity on new grounds which the government has not seen fit to recognize." Under this regime, "if the Executive announced a national policy in regard to immunity generally, or for the particular case, that policy was law for the courts and binding upon them, regardless of what international law might say about it." Louis Henkin, Foreign Affairs and the United States Constitution 56 (2d ed. 1996).

During the nineteenth century, this immunity was considered by the United States and other nations to be essentially absolute—if the defendant qualified as a foreign sovereign, then it would have immunity for all of its acts, even those that were purely commercial in nature. By the early twentieth century, however, a number of nations began moving away from an absolute approach to immunity toward a restrictive approach. Under the restrictive approach, foreign sovereigns are entitled to immunity for public or sovereign acts, but not for private or commercial acts. *See* Gamal Moursi Badr, State Immunity: An Analytical and Prognostic View (1984); Joseph M. Sweeney, The International Law of Sovereign Immunity (State Dept. 1963).

In 1952, in a letter to the Justice Department, the State Department formally announced that it would in all cases follow the restrictive theory of immunity. *See* Letter from Jack B. Tate, Acting Legal Adviser, U.S. Dept. of State, to Acting U.S. Attorney General Philip B. Perlman (May 19, 1952), *reprinted in* 26 Dept. State Bull. 984, 985 (1952). The letter cites a number of reasons for this policy, including the worldwide trend toward adoption of the restrictive theory and the "widespread and increasing practice on the part of governments of engaging in commercial activities."* After the issuance of the Tate Letter, foreign states sued in U.S. courts could seek relief in either of two ways. They could request immunity directly from the State Department, usually by submitting a diplomatic note. If the Department agreed that the foreign state should receive immunity, the Department would send a "Suggestion of Immunity" to the Attorney General with a request that it be transmitted to the court, and courts generally treated these suggestions as binding. Alternatively, foreign states could request immunity directly from the court, in which case the court would have to decide how to distinguish between sovereign and commercial acts, albeit often by reference to prior State Department determinations. This regime, under which the State Department made some immunity determinations and the courts made others, did not always produce consistent decisions. *Compare* Victory

---

* Earlier, in 1949, the State Department had prepared an extensive internal report reviewing the immunity law of other countries. *See* Memorandum from Conrad E. Snow to Members of the Committee on Sovereign Immunity, *Law of Sovereign Immunity* (Aug. 25, 1949). The cover memorandum circulating the report noted that, "[i]n view of the fundamental differences in basic concepts . . . it is important to give careful attention to the possibility of resolving the whole matter by multilateral convention." *Id.*

Transport, Inc. v. Comisaria General de Abastecimientos y Transportes, 336 F.2d 354 (2d Cir. 1964) (concluding, without input from the State Department, that ship chartered by Spanish government was engaged in commercial activity and thus not entitled to immunity), *with* Isbrandtsen Tankers v. President of India, 446 F.2d 1198, 1200-01 (2d Cir. 1971) (granting immunity in a factually similar suit brought against Indian government because, although the court was inclined to "find that the actions of the Indian government were . . . purely private commercial decisions," the State Department had determined otherwise).

Inconsistency in result was not the only problem with the Tate Letter regime. Other perceived inadequacies included the following:

> From a legal standpoint, if the [State] Department applies the restrictive principle in a given case, it is in the awkward position of a political institution trying to apply a legal standard to litigation already before the courts. Moreover, it does not have the machinery to take evidence, to hear witnesses, to afford appellate review.
>
> From a foreign relations standpoint, the initiative is often left to the foreign state. The foreign state chooses which sovereign immunity determinations it will leave to the courts, and which it will take to the State Department. The foreign state also decides when it will attempt to exert diplomatic influences, thereby making it more difficult for the State Department to apply the Tate letter criteria.
>
> From the standpoint of the private litigant, considerable uncertainty results. A private party who deals with a foreign government entity cannot be certain that his legal dispute with a foreign state will not be decided on the basis of nonlegal considerations through the foreign government's intercession with the Department of State.

H.R. Rep. No. 94-1487, at 8-9 (1976). For criticisms of the Tate Letter regime, see, for example, Monroe Leigh, *Sovereign Immunity — The Case of the "Imias,"* 68 Am. J. Int'l L. 280 (1974); and Andreas F. Lowenfeld, *Litigating a Sovereign Immunity Claim — The Haiti Case,* 49 N.Y.U. L. Rev. 377 (1974).

In 1976, after years of discussion and debate, Congress enacted the Foreign Sovereign Immunities Act (FSIA), 28 U.S.C. §§1330, 1602-11, the current text of which is printed in Appendix C of this casebook. According to its legislative history, the central purposes of the FSIA were to "[set] forth comprehensive rules governing sovereign immunity," to "codify the so-called 'restrictive' principle of sovereign immunity, as presently recognized in international law," and to "transfer the determination of sovereign immunity from the executive branch to the judicial branch, thereby reducing the foreign policy implications of immunity determinations and assuring litigants that these often crucial decisions are made on purely legal grounds and under procedures that insure due process." H.R. Rep. No. 94-1487, at 7, 12 (1976).

Saudi Arabia v. Nelson

507 U.S. 349 (1993)

JUSTICE SOUTER delivered the opinion of the Court.

The Foreign Sovereign Immunities Act of 1976 entitles foreign states to immunity from the jurisdiction of courts in the United States, subject to certain enumerated exceptions. One is that a foreign state shall not be immune in any case "in which the action is based upon a commercial activity carried on in the United States by the foreign state." We hold that respondents' action alleging personal injury resulting from unlawful detention and torture by the Saudi Government is not "based upon a commercial activity" within the meaning of the Act, which consequently confers no jurisdiction over respondents' suit.

Because this case comes to us on a motion to dismiss the complaint, we assume that we have truthful factual allegations before us, though many of those allegations are subject to dispute. Petitioner Kingdom of Saudi Arabia owns and operates petitioner King Faisal Specialist Hospital in Riyadh, as well as petitioner Royspec Purchasing Services, the hospital's corporate purchasing agent in the United States. The Hospital Corporation of America, Ltd. (HCA), an independent corporation existing under the laws of the Cayman Islands, recruits Americans for employment at the hospital under an agreement signed with Saudi Arabia in 1973.

In its recruitment effort, HCA placed an advertisement in a trade periodical seeking applications for a position as a monitoring systems engineer at the hospital. The advertisement drew the attention of respondent Scott Nelson in September 1983, while Nelson was in the United States. After interviewing for the position in Saudi Arabia, Nelson returned to the United States, where he signed an employment contract with the hospital, satisfied personnel processing requirements, and attended an orientation session that HCA conducted for hospital employees. In the course of that program, HCA identified Royspec as the point of contact in the United States for family members who might wish to reach Nelson in an emergency.

In December 1983, Nelson went to Saudi Arabia and began work at the hospital, monitoring all "facilities, equipment, utilities, and maintenance systems to insure the safety of patients, hospital staff, and others." He did his job without significant incident until March 1984, when he discovered safety defects in the hospital's oxygen and nitrous oxide lines that posed fire hazards and otherwise endangered patients' lives. Over a period of several months, Nelson repeatedly advised hospital officials of the safety defects and reported the defects to a Saudi Government commission as well. Hospital officials instructed Nelson to ignore the problems.

The hospital's response to Nelson's reports changed, however, on September 27, 1984, when certain hospital employees summoned him to the hospital's security office where agents of the Saudi Government arrested him.[1] The agents transported Nelson to a jail cell, in which they "shackled, tortured and beat" him, and kept him four days without food. Although Nelson did not understand Arabic, government agents forced him to sign a statement written in that language, the content of which he did not know; a hospital employee who was supposed to act as Nelson's interpreter advised him to sign "anything" the agents gave him to avoid further beatings. Two days later, government agents transferred Nelson to the Al Sijan Prison "to await trial on unknown charges."

At the prison, Nelson was confined in an overcrowded cell area infested with rats, where he had to fight other prisoners for food and from which he was taken only once a week for fresh air and exercise. Although police interrogators repeatedly questioned him in Arabic, Nelson did not learn the nature of the charges, if any, against him. For several days, the Saudi Government failed to advise Nelson's family of his whereabouts, though a Saudi official eventually told Nelson's wife,

---

1. Petitioners assert that the Saudi Government arrested Nelson because he had falsely represented to the hospital that he had received a degree from the Massachusetts Institute of Technology and had provided the hospital with a forged diploma to verify his claim. The Nelsons concede these misrepresentations, but dispute that they occasioned Scott Nelson's arrest.

respondent Vivian Nelson, that he could arrange for her husband's release if she provided sexual favors.

Although officials from the United States Embassy visited Nelson twice during his detention, they concluded that his allegations of Saudi mistreatment were "not credible" and made no protest to Saudi authorities. It was only at the personal request of a United States Senator that the Saudi Government released Nelson, 39 days after his arrest, on November 5, 1984. Seven days later, after failing to convince him to return to work at the hospital, the Saudi Government allowed Nelson to leave the country.

In 1988, Nelson and his wife filed this action against petitioners in the United States District Court for the Southern District of Florida seeking damages for personal injury. The Nelsons' complaint sets out 16 causes of action, which fall into three categories. Counts II through VII and counts X, XI, XIV, and XV allege that petitioners committed various intentional torts, including battery, unlawful detainment, wrongful arrest and imprisonment, false imprisonment, inhuman torture, disruption of normal family life, and infliction of mental anguish. Counts I, IX, and XIII charge petitioners with negligently failing to warn Nelson of otherwise undisclosed dangers of his employment, namely, that if he attempted to report safety hazards the hospital would likely retaliate against him and the Saudi Government might detain and physically abuse him without legal cause. Finally, counts VIII, XII, and XVI allege that Vivian Nelson sustained derivative injury resulting from petitioners' actions. Presumably because the employment contract provided that Saudi courts would have exclusive jurisdiction over claims for breach of contract, the Nelsons raised no such matters.

[The trial court dismissed for lack of subject-matter jurisdiction under the FSIA, the court of appeals reversed, and the Supreme Court granted certiorari.]

The Foreign Sovereign Immunities Act "provides the sole basis for obtaining jurisdiction over a foreign state in the courts of this country." Argentine Republic v. Amerada Hess Shipping Corp., 488 U.S. 428, 443 (1989). Under the Act, a foreign state is presumptively immune from the jurisdiction of United States courts; unless a specified exception applies, a federal court lacks subject-matter jurisdiction over a claim against a foreign state.

Only one such exception is said to apply here. The first clause of §1605(a)(2) of the Act provides that a foreign state shall not be immune from the jurisdiction of United States courts in any case "in which the action is based upon a commercial activity carried on in the United States by the foreign state." The Act defines such activity as "commercial activity carried on by such state and having substantial contact with the United States," §1603(e), and provides that a commercial activity may be "either a regular course of commercial conduct or a particular commercial transaction or act," the "commercial character of [which] shall be determined by reference to" its "nature," rather than its "purpose," §1603(d).

There is no dispute here that Saudi Arabia, the hospital, and Royspec all qualify as "foreign state[s]" within the meaning of the Act. For there to be jurisdiction in this case, therefore, the Nelsons' action must be "based upon" some "commercial activity" by petitioners that had "substantial contact" with the United States within the meaning of the Act. Because we conclude that the suit is not based upon any commercial activity by petitioners, we need not reach the issue of substantial contact with the United States.

We begin our analysis by identifying the particular conduct on which the Nelsons' action is "based" for purposes of the Act. . . . Although the Act contains no definition of the phrase "based upon," and the relatively sparse legislative history offers no assistance, guidance is hardly necessary. In denoting conduct that forms the "basis," or "foundation," for a claim, see Black's Law Dictionary 151 (6th ed. 1990) (defining "base"); Random House Dictionary 172 (2d ed. 1987) (same); Webster's Third New International Dictionary 180, 181 (1976) (defining "base" and "based"), the phrase is read most naturally to mean those elements of a claim that, if proven, would entitle a plaintiff to relief under his theory of the case. . . .

What the natural meaning of the phrase "based upon" suggests, the context confirms. Earlier, we noted that §1605(a)(2) contains two clauses following the one at issue here. The second allows for jurisdiction where a suit "is based . . . upon an act performed in the United States in connection with a commercial activity of the foreign state elsewhere," and the third speaks in like terms, allowing for jurisdiction where an action "is based . . . upon an act outside the territory of the United States in connection with a commercial activity of the foreign state elsewhere and that act causes a direct effect in the United States." Distinctions among descriptions juxtaposed against each other are naturally understood to be significant, . . . and Congress manifestly understood there to be a difference between a suit "based upon" commercial activity and one "based upon" acts performed "in connection with" such activity. The only reasonable reading of the former term calls for something more than a mere connection with, or relation to, commercial activity.[4]

In this case, the Nelsons have alleged that petitioners recruited Scott Nelson for work at the hospital, signed an employment contract with him, and subsequently employed him. While these activities led to the conduct that eventually injured the Nelsons, they are not the basis for the Nelsons' suit. Even taking each of the Nelsons' allegations about Scott Nelson's recruitment and employment as true, those facts alone entitle the Nelsons to nothing under their theory of the case. The Nelsons have not, after all, alleged breach of contract, but personal injuries caused by petitioners' intentional wrongs and by petitioners' negligent failure to warn Scott Nelson that they might commit those wrongs. Those torts, and not the arguably commercial activities that preceded their commission, form the basis for the Nelsons' suit.

Petitioners' tortious conduct itself fails to qualify as "commercial activity" within the meaning of the Act. . . . We have seen already that the Act defines "commercial activity" as "either a regular course of commercial conduct or a particular commercial transaction or act," and provides that "the commercial character of an activity shall be determined by reference to the nature of the course of conduct or particular transaction or act, rather than by reference to its purpose." 28 U.S.C. §1603(d). If this is a definition, it is one distinguished only by its diffidence; as we observed in our most recent case on the subject, it "leaves the critical term 'commercial' largely undefined." Republic of Argentina v. Weltover, Inc., 504 U.S. 607, 612 (1992). . . . We do not, however, have the option to throw up our hands. The term has to be given some interpretation, and congressional diffidence necessarily results in judicial responsibility to determine what a "commercial activity" is for purposes of the Act.

4. We do not mean to suggest that the first clause of §1605(a)(2) necessarily requires that each and every element of a claim be commercial activity by a foreign state, and we do not address the case where a claim consists of both commercial and sovereign elements. We do conclude, however, that where a claim rests entirely upon activities sovereign in character, as here, jurisdiction will not exist under that clause regardless of any connection the sovereign acts may have with commercial activity.

We took up the task just last Term in *Weltover, supra*, which involved Argentina's unilateral refinancing of bonds it had issued under a plan to stabilize its currency. Bondholders sued Argentina in federal court, asserting jurisdiction under the third clause of §1605(a)(2). In the course of holding the refinancing to be a commercial activity for purposes of the Act, we observed that the statute "largely codifies the so called 'restrictive' theory of foreign sovereign immunity first endorsed by the State Department in 1952." 504 U.S. at 612. We accordingly held that the meaning of "commercial" for purposes of the Act must be the meaning Congress understood the restrictive theory to require at the time it passed the statute. *See Weltover, supra*, at 612-13.

Under the restrictive, as opposed to the "absolute," theory of foreign sovereign immunity, a state is immune from the jurisdiction of foreign courts as to its sovereign or public acts (*jure imperii*), but not as to those that are private or commercial in character (*jure gestionis*). We explained in *Weltover* that a state engages in commercial activity under the restrictive theory where it exercises "only those powers that can also be exercised by private citizens," as distinct from those "powers peculiar to sovereigns." Put differently, a foreign state engages in commercial activity for purposes of the restrictive theory only where it acts "in the manner of a private player within" the market. . . .

We emphasized in *Weltover* that whether a state acts "in the manner of" a private party is a question of behavior, not motivation:

> [B]ecause the Act provides that the commercial character of an act is to be determined by reference to its "nature" rather than its "purpose," the question is not whether the foreign government is acting with a profit motive or instead with the aim of fulfilling uniquely sovereign objectives. Rather, the issue is whether the particular actions that the foreign state performs (whatever the motive behind them) are the *type* of actions by which a private party engages in "trade and traffic or commerce."

We did not ignore the difficulty of distinguishing "'purpose' (i.e., the *reason* why the foreign state engages in the activity) from 'nature' (i.e., the outward form of the conduct that the foreign state performs or agrees to perform)," but recognized that the Act "unmistakably commands" us to observe the distinction. Because Argentina had merely dealt in the bond market in the manner of a private player, we held, its refinancing of the bonds qualified as a commercial activity for purposes of the Act despite the apparent governmental motivation.

Unlike Argentina's activities that we considered in *Weltover*, the intentional conduct alleged here (the Saudi Government's wrongful arrest, imprisonment, and torture of Nelson) could not qualify as commercial under the restrictive theory. The conduct boils down to abuse of the power of its police by the Saudi Government, and however monstrous such abuse undoubtedly may be, a foreign state's exercise of the power of its police has long been understood for purposes of the restrictive theory as peculiarly sovereign in nature. . . . Exercise of the powers of police and penal officers is not the sort of action by which private parties can engage in commerce. . . .

The Nelsons and their *amici* urge us to give significance to their assertion that the Saudi Government subjected Nelson to the abuse alleged as retaliation for his persistence in reporting hospital safety violations, and argue that the character of the mistreatment was consequently commercial. One *amicus*, indeed, goes so far as to suggest that the Saudi Government "often uses detention and torture to resolve commercial disputes." But this argument does not alter the fact that the powers allegedly abused were those of police and penal officers. In any event, the argument is off the point, for it goes to purpose, the very fact the Act renders irrelevant to the question of an activity's commercial character. Whatever may have been the Saudi Government's motivation for its allegedly abusive treatment of Nelson, it remains the case that the Nelsons' action is based upon a sovereign activity immune from the subject-matter jurisdiction of United States courts under the Act.

In addition to the intentionally tortious conduct, the Nelsons claim a separate basis for recovery in petitioners' failure to warn Scott Nelson of the hidden dangers associated with his employment. The Nelsons allege that, at the time petitioners recruited Scott Nelson and thereafter, they failed to warn him of the possibility of severe retaliatory action if he attempted to disclose any safety hazards he might discover on the job. In other words, petitioners bore a duty to warn of their own propensity for tortious conduct. But this is merely a semantic ploy. For aught we can see, a plaintiff could recast virtually any claim of intentional tort committed by sovereign act as a claim of failure to warn, simply by charging the defendant with an obligation to announce its own tortious propensity before indulging it. To give jurisdictional significance to this feint of language would effectively thwart the Act's manifest purpose to codify the restrictive theory of foreign sovereign immunity. . . .

JUSTICE WHITE, with whom JUSTICE BLACKMUN joins, concurring in the judgment.

The majority concludes that petitioners enjoy sovereign immunity because respondents' action is not "based upon a commercial activity." I disagree. I nonetheless concur in the judgment because in my view the commercial conduct upon which respondents base their complaint was not "carried on in the United States." . . .

To run and operate a hospital, even a public hospital, is to engage in a commercial enterprise. The majority never concedes this point, but it does not deny it either, and to my mind the matter is self-evident. By the same token, warning an employee when he blows the whistle and taking retaliatory action, such as harassment, involuntary transfer, discharge, or other tortious behavior, although not prototypical commercial acts, are certainly well within the bounds of commercial activity. The House and Senate Reports accompanying the legislation virtually compel this conclusion, explaining as they do that "a foreign government's . . . employment or engagement of laborers, clerical staff or marketing agents . . . would be among those included within" the definition of commercial activity. H.R. Rep. No. 94-1487, p. 16 (1976) (House Report); S. Rep. No. 94-1310, p. 16 (1976) (Senate Report). Nelson alleges that petitioners harmed him in the course of engaging in their commercial enterprise, as a direct result of their commercial acts. His claim, in other words, is "based upon commercial activity."

Indeed, I am somewhat at a loss as to what exactly the majority believes petitioners have done that a private employer could not. As countless cases attest, retaliation for whistle-blowing is not a practice foreign to the marketplace. Congress passed a statute in response to such behavior, see Whistleblower Protection Act of 1989, 5 U.S.C. §1213 et seq. (1988 ed., Supp. III), as have numerous States. On occasion, private employers also have been known to retaliate by enlisting the help of police officers to falsely arrest employees. . . . More generally, private parties have been held liable for conspiring with public authorities to effectuate an arrest, . . . and for using private security personnel for the same purposes. . . .

Therefore, had the hospital retaliated against Nelson by hiring thugs to do the job, I assume the majority—no longer able to describe this conduct as "a foreign state's exercise of the power of its police"—would consent to calling it "commercial." For, in such circumstances, the state-run hospital would be operating as any private participant in the marketplace and respondents' action would be based on the operation by Saudi Arabia's agents of a commercial business.

At the heart of the majority's conclusion, in other words, is the fact that the hospital in this case chose to call in government security forces. I find this fixation on the intervention of police officers, and the ensuing characterization of the conduct as "peculiarly sovereign in nature," to be misguided. To begin, it fails to capture respondents' complaint in full. Far from being directed solely at the activities of the Saudi police, it alleges that agents of the hospital summoned Nelson to its security office because he reported safety concerns and that the hospital played a part in the subsequent beating and imprisonment. Without more, that type of behavior hardly qualifies as sovereign. Thus, even assuming for the sake of argument that the role of the official police somehow affected the nature of petitioners' conduct, the claim cannot be said to "rest entirely upon activities sovereign in character." At the very least it "consists of both commercial and sovereign elements," thereby presenting the specific question the majority chooses to elude. The majority's single-minded focus on the exercise of police power, while certainly simplifying the case, thus hardly does it justice.

Reliance on the fact that Nelson's employer enlisted the help of public rather than private security personnel is also at odds with Congress' intent. The purpose of the commercial exception being to prevent foreign states from taking refuge behind their sovereignty when they act as market participants, it seems to me that this is precisely the type of distinction we should seek to avoid. Because both the hospital and the police are agents of the state, the case in my mind turns on whether the sovereign is acting in a commercial capacity, not on whether it resorts to thugs or government officers to carry on its business. That, when the hospital calls in security to get even with a whistle-blower, it comes clothed in police apparel says more about the state-owned nature of the commercial enterprise than about the noncommercial nature of its tortious conduct. . . .

Contrary to the majority's suggestion, this conclusion does not involve inquiring into the purpose of the conduct. Matters would be different, I suppose, if Nelson had been recruited to work in the Saudi police force and, having reported safety violations, suffered retributive punishment, for there the Saudi authorities would be engaged in distinctly sovereign activities. The same would be true if Nelson was a mere tourist in Saudi Arabia and had been summarily expelled by order of immigration officials. In this instance, however, the state-owned hospital was engaged in ordinary commercial business. . . .

Nevertheless, I reach the same conclusion as the majority because petitioners' commercial activity was not "carried on in the United States." The Act defines such conduct as "commercial activity . . . having substantial contact with the United States." 28 U.S.C. §1603(e). Respondents point to the hospital's recruitment efforts in the United States, including advertising in the American media, and the signing of the employment contract in Miami. As I earlier noted, while these may very well qualify as commercial activity in the United States, they do not constitute the commercial activity upon which respondents' action is based. Conversely, petitioners' commercial conduct in Saudi Arabia, though constituting the basis of the Nelsons' suit, lacks a sufficient nexus to the United States. Neither the hospital's employment practices, nor its disciplinary procedures, has any apparent connection to this country. On that basis, I agree that the Act does not grant the Nelsons access to our courts.

Notes and Questions

1. The structure of the FSIA is complicated because issues of personal jurisdiction, subject matter jurisdiction, and immunity from suit are intertwined. Section 1330 of Title 28 provides in relevant part:

> (a) The district courts shall have original jurisdiction without regard to amount in controversy of any nonjury civil action against a foreign state . . . as to any claim for relief *in personam* with respect to which the foreign state is not entitled to immunity either under sections 1605–1607 of this title or under any applicable international agreement.
>
> (b) Personal jurisdiction over a foreign state shall exist as to every claim for relief over which the district courts have jurisdiction under subsection (a) where service has been made under section 1608 of this title.

The provisions of this section operate as follows: Under subsection (b), if proper service is made on a foreign state defendant, personal jurisdiction exists with respect to any claim for which there is federal subject matter jurisdiction. Federal subject matter jurisdiction, in turn, is available under subsection (a) for "any claim for relief *in personam* with respect to which the foreign state is not entitled to immunity." And as subsection (a) further states, the FSIA in §§1605-07 specifies various exceptions to sovereign immunity (in addition to any international agreement that might lift immunity). Under this structure, then, a court must determine whether the foreign state defendant is immune from suit in order to determine whether the court has personal and subject matter jurisdiction. If the court finds that the defendant is immune, the court lacks personal and subject matter jurisdiction. Conversely, if the court finds that an exception to immunity applies, and that proper service has been made, the court automatically has personal and subject matter jurisdiction (assuming no violation of due process requirements).

2. The first Supreme Court decision to consider the FSIA was Verlinden BV v. Central Bank of Nigeria, 461 U.S. 480 (1983). In that case, Verlinden, a Dutch corporation, was suing a Nigerian government-owned bank for breach of a letter of credit agreement, a claim that was governed by New York state law and was related to a supply contract governed by Dutch law. The bank argued that, even if the case fell within the commercial activity exception to immunity in the FSIA, it did not fall within the bounds of jurisdiction allowed to the federal courts in Article III of the Constitution. The Supreme Court disagreed, reasoning that the case arose under federal law for purposes of Article III "arising under" jurisdiction even though it did not involve a federal claim. The Court explained that the FSIA "codifies the standards governing foreign sovereign immunity as an aspect of substantive federal law" and that, because subject matter jurisdiction under the FSIA depends on finding a statutory exception to immunity, "every action against a foreign sovereign necessarily involves application of a body of substantive federal law, and accordingly 'arises under' federal law, within the meaning of Art. III."

3. In Argentine Republic v. Amerada Hess Shipping Corp., 488 U.S. 428, 443 (1989), the Supreme Court held that the FSIA provides the exclusive basis for U.S. court jurisdiction over suits against foreign states. In that case, Argentine military aircraft had bombed and destroyed an oil tanker in international waters during the 1982 Falkland Islands war between Great Britain and Argentina. The owner of the tanker and the company that had chartered it—both Liberian corporations—brought suit against Argentina in a New York federal court seeking compensation for the loss of the ship and its fuel. They alleged that Argentina's attack on the neutral tanker violated international law, and they argued that federal courts had jurisdiction over the suit pursuant to the Alien Tort Statute, 28 U.S.C. §1350, which provides that the federal district courts "shall have original jurisdiction of any civil action by an alien for a tort only, committed in violation of the law of nations or a treaty of the United States." The Supreme Court ordered dismissal of the suit, reasoning that "the text and structure of the FSIA demonstrate Congress' intention that the FSIA be the sole basis for obtaining jurisdiction over a foreign state in our courts." The Court also concluded that there were no applicable exceptions to immunity in that case.

4. The Supreme Court has also held that the FSIA applies retroactively to conduct that occurred prior to the enactment of the FSIA in 1976, and even conduct that occurred before the Executive Branch announced its shift to the restrictive theory of immunity in 1952. *See* Republic of Austria v. Altmann, 541 U.S. 677 (2004). In that case, Maria Altmann, a U.S. citizen, sued the government of Austria and an Austrian government-owned art gallery, pursuant to Section 1605(a)(3) of the FSIA, which allows certain claims for the taking of property in violation of international law. Altmann alleged that the Nazis had stolen six Gustav Klimt paintings from her uncle in the late 1930s and had subsequently sold them to the gallery, and that the gallery had unlawfully retained possession of the paintings by falsely stating in 1948 that her uncle's wife had donated the paintings to the gallery. In an opinion by Justice Stevens, the Supreme Court held that the suit was governed by the FSIA. Although statutes are normally presumed not to operate retroactively, the Court concluded that the presumption applied with less force here because the FSIA does not regulate substantive rights or duties. The Court also noted that the FSIA's preamble states that "[c]laims of foreign states to immunity should *henceforth* be decided by courts of the United States and of the States in conformity with the principles set forth in this chapter." 28 U.S.C. §1602 (emphasis added). This language suggests retroactivity, the Court reasoned. The Court also contended that retroactive application of the FSIA to all pending cases would be consistent with the purposes of the statute, by ensuring that the FSIA comprehensively addressed all suits brought against foreign states and by providing a clear rule about the FSIA's application that would be administered by the courts. Justice Breyer concurred, arguing that Austria could not have had a reasonable reliance interest in being protected from future lawsuits arising from a taking of property in violation of international law. Justice Kennedy dissented and was joined by Chief Justice Rehnquist and Justice Thomas. Kennedy argued that the FSIA should not be construed to alter retroactively the expectations that foreign states would have had in 1948, which is that there would have been absolute immunity subject to a possible Executive Branch override. The FSIA's preamble, Kennedy contended, "says no more than that the principles [in the FSIA] immediately apply from the point of the Act's effective date on." (After this decision, Ms. Altmann and Austria agreed to submit their dispute to arbitration in Austria. An arbitration panel subsequently ruled in favor of Altmann, and Austria returned the paintings to her. She later auctioned them off for large sums of money.)

5. The FSIA applies only to suits against "foreign states." "Foreign state" is defined to include not only the state itself but also "a political subdivision of a foreign state or an agency or instrumentality of a foreign state." *See* 28 U.S.C. §1603. The FSIA provides a definition of agencies or instrumentalities of foreign states, which includes, but is not limited to, corporations that have a majority of their shares owned by a foreign state. In Dole Food Co. v. Patrickson, 538 U.S. 468 (2003), the Supreme Court held that instrumentality status under the FSIA is to be determined based on the facts that exist at the time of the suit rather than at the time of the conduct in question. The Court reasoned, among other things, that foreign sovereign immunity "is not meant to avoid chilling foreign states or their instrumentalities in the conduct of their business but to give foreign states and their instrumentalities some protection from the inconvenience of suit as a gesture of comity between the United States and other sovereigns." What is the relationship between the Court's holding in *Dole* and its holding in *Altmann*?

6. Because of the holding in *Dole*, retroactive application of the FSIA may not always benefit plaintiffs. Consider Abrams v. Societe Nationale des Chemins de fer Francais, 389 F.3d 61 (2d Cir. 2004), which involved a suit by Holocaust victims and their heirs against a French government-owned railroad for allegedly having transported thousands of civilians to Nazi death and slave labor camps during World War II. The plaintiffs in this case argued against retroactive application of the FSIA, because, at the time of the events, the railroad was organized as a separate entity from the French government and thus might not have had immunity. Based on *Altmann*, however, the Second Circuit held that the suit was governed by the FSIA. The court reasoned that, "[w]hile [the French railroad] was predominately owned by civilians during World War II, it is now wholly-owned by the French government and . . . is an 'agent' or 'instrumentality' of France under the FSIA," and that, under *Dole* and *Altmann*, "its prior incarnation as a private entity does not bar the [FSIA's] retroactive application." The court also concluded that there was no applicable exception to immunity in that case.

7. Under the FSIA's waiver exception, a foreign state is not immune from suit if it "has waived its immunity either explicitly or by implication." 28 U.S.C. §1605(a)(1). Explicit waivers of immunity, such as a waiver in a treaty or contract, present relatively few problems. Such waiver provisions are commonly included in the legal documents when a foreign state borrows money from a bank or purchases goods or services from a sophisticated company. But what constitutes a waiver "by implication"? The legislative history of the FSIA states as follows:

> With respect to implicit waivers, the courts have found such waivers in cases where a foreign state has agreed to arbitration in another country or where a foreign state has agreed that the law of a particular country should govern a contract. An implicit waiver would also include a situation where a foreign state has filed a responsive pleading in an action without raising the defense of foreign sovereign immunity. H.R. Rep. No. 94-1487, at 18.

What does this statement suggest about the scope of the implicit waiver exception? In general, courts have construed the FSIA's implicit waiver exception narrowly, limiting it to situations in which the foreign state defendant has indicated a willingness to be sued in U.S. courts. The selection of U.S. law to govern a contract is generally treated as a waiver of FSIA immunity. *See, e.g.,* Eckert Int'l, Inc. v. Fiji, 32 F.3d 77 (4th Cir. 1994). But a selection of foreign law is generally not viewed as a waiver. *See, e.g.,* Maritime Int'l Nominees Establishment v. Republic of Guinea, 693 F.2d 1094, 1102 n.13 (D.C. Cir. 1982). Nor does a foreign state's waiver of immunity in its own courts typically constitute a waiver of immunity in U.S. courts. *See, e.g.,* Corzo v. Banco Cent. De Reserva del Peru, 243 F.3d 519, 523 (9th Cir. 2001). *See also* Blaxland v. Commonwealth Director of Public Prosecutions, 323 F.3d 1198 (9th Cir. 2003) (use of U.S. extradition procedures held not to constitute a waiver because the extradition process was political rather than judicial).

8. The "commercial activity" exception, 18 U.S.C. §1605(a)(2), is one of the most litigated provisions of the FSIA. It provides that "a foreign state shall not be immune from the jurisdiction" of a U.S. court in any case

> in which the action is based upon a commercial activity carried on in the United States by the foreign state; or upon an act performed in the United States in connection with a commercial activity of the foreign state elsewhere; or upon an act outside the territory of the United States in connection with a commercial activity of the foreign state elsewhere and that act causes a direct effect in the United States.

Section 1605(a)(2) thus can be satisfied by any one of three independent nexus requirements, and each nexus requirement uses the term "commercial activity." Section 1605(d), in turn, defines "commercial activity" to mean "either a regular course of commercial conduct or a particular commercial transaction or act," and adds that the "commercial character of an activity shall be determined by reference to the nature of the course of conduct or particular transaction or act, rather than by reference to its purpose."

The Supreme Court first interpreted the meaning of "commercial activity" in Republic of Argentina v. Weltover, Inc., 504 U.S. 607 (1992). In *Weltover*, foreign corporate holders of previously issued Argentine bonds declined to accept Argentina's attempted rescheduling of the maturity dates of the bonds, and sued Argentina to obtain payment. The Supreme Court held that the issuance of the bonds was a "commercial activity" and that the suit fell within the third clause of §1605(a)(2). As the Court recounts in *Nelson*, the Court in *Weltover*, drawing on §1605(d)'s definition of "commercial activity," reasoned that the commercial nature of an activity was to be determined by its nature rather than its purpose, and that a foreign state's activity is commercial when the foreign state acts "not as regulator of a market, but in the manner of a private player within it." Is the nature of an activity completely separate from its purpose? Can the nature of an activity be affected by who is doing it? How helpful is the *Weltover* "private player" test? For decisions applying that test, see, for example, Globe Nuclear Services & Supply GNSS, Ltd. v. AO Technsabexport, 376 F.3d 282 (4th Cir. 2004) (agreement to supply uranium hexafluoride that was extracted from nuclear weapons held to be commercial activity because "[t]he entrance into a contract to supply a private party with uranium hexafluoride is the very type of action by which private parties engage in 'trade and traffic or commerce'"), and Beg v. Islamic Republic of Pakistan, 353 F.3d 1323 (11th Cir. 2003) (expropriation of property held not to be a commercial activity because "private actors are not allowed to engage in 'takings' in the manner that governments are").

9. The plaintiffs in *Saudi Arabia v. Nelson* sued under the first clause of §1605(a)(2). Why did the Court in *Nelson* conclude that the suit was not "based upon" a commercial activity? What activities, according to the majority, was the plaintiffs' suit based upon? Why did the majority characterize false imprisonment and torture as "exercise of the powers of [Saudi Arabian] police" rather than (per Justice White's suggestion) as an activity, like retaliation for whistleblowing, that private entities sometimes engage in? Does the majority, in contravention of *Weltover*, improperly look to the purpose, as opposed to the nature, of the activity? Why didn't the plaintiffs in *Nelson* sue for breach of Mr. Nelson's employment contract, which would have made their case seem more commercial?

10. The Supreme Court applied *Nelson*'s "based upon" analysis in OBB Personenverkehr AG v. Sachs, 136 S. Ct. 390 (2015). In that case, a California resident purchased a Eurail pass over the Internet from a travel agent in Massachusetts that was authorized by the Eurail group to sell passes. When boarding an Austrian state-owned train in Austria, which is part of the network of trains recognizing the Eurail pass, the plaintiff was seriously injured. She sued the railway, alleging negligence, strict liability, and breach of implied warranty. In a divided en banc decision, the Ninth Circuit held that the plaintiff's claims were "based upon a commercial activity carried on in the United States by the foreign state" within the meaning of the first clause of the FSIA's commercial activity exception. The court reasoned that the actions of the travel agent could be attributed to the railway and that the sale of the ticket in the United States was an essential element of the plaintiff's claims.

The Supreme Court unanimously reversed, explaining that the Ninth Circuit had erred in its "essential element" approach to determining whether the plaintiff's claims were based upon commercial activity in the United States:

> The Ninth Circuit held that Sachs's claims were "based upon" the sale of the Eurail pass because the sale of the pass provide "*an element*" of each of her claims. Under *Nelson*, however, the mere fact that the sale of the Eurail pass would establish a single element of a claim is insufficient to demonstrate that the claim is "based upon" that sale for purposes of §1605(a)(2). . . .
>
> *Nelson* instead teaches that an action is "based upon" the "particular conduct" that constitutes the "gravamen" of the suit. . . .
>
> Under this analysis, the conduct constituting the gravamen of Sachs's suit plainly occurred abroad. All of her claims turn on the same tragic episode in Austria, allegedly caused by wrongful conduct and dangerous conditions in Austria, which led to injuries suffered in Austria.

11. The third clause of §1605(a)(2) creates an exception to immunity when "an act outside the territory of the United States in connection with a commercial activity of the foreign state elsewhere and that act causes a direct effect in the United States." Why didn't the plaintiffs in *Nelson* sue under that clause? *Cf.* Berkovitz v. Islamic Republic of Iran, 735 F.2d 329, 332 (9th Cir. 1984) (emotional suffering of family members held not to be a direct effect of tortious conduct abroad).

The Court in *Weltover* addressed the meaning of "direct effect" in the third clause of §1605(a)(2) and held that Argentina's unilateral rescheduling of its bonds satisfied this requirement because New York was a place of payment and Argentina had in fact made some interest payments on the bonds in New York. The Court concluded that "[b]ecause New York was thus the place of performance for Argentina's ultimate contractual obligations, the rescheduling of those obligations necessarily had a 'direct effect' in the United States: Money that was supposed to have been delivered to a New York bank for deposit was not forthcoming." The Court also rejected Argentina's argument that the "direct effect" requirement could not be satisfied where the plaintiffs are all foreign corporations with no other connections to the United States, reasoning that "[w]e expressly stated in *Verlinden* that the FSIA permits 'a foreign plaintiff to sue a foreign sovereign in the courts of the United States, provided the substantive requirements of the Act are satisfied.'" Courts are divided over how broadly to apply the *Weltover* test for "direct effects," with some requiring a "legally significant act" in the United States (such as failure to make a payment specified in the contract to be made in the United States), but others rejecting such a requirement. *See* Keller v. Central Bank of Nigeria, 277 F.3d 811, 817-18 (6th Cir. 2002) (describing division of authority).

12. Another exception to immunity under the FSIA is the so-called noncommercial tort exception. This exception removes immunity in any case, not otherwise covered by the commercial activity exception, "in which money damages are sought against a foreign state for personal injury or death, or damage to or loss of property, occurring in the United States and caused by the tortious act or omission of that foreign state or of any official or employee of that foreign state while acting within the scope of his office or employment." 28 U.S.C. §1605(a)(5). The plain language of the noncommercial tort exception requires that the injury or damage occur in the United States and thus by its terms excludes most foreign torts. Moreover, most courts to address the issue have also required that the tortious act or omission occur in the United States. *See, e.g.*, Persinger v. Islamic Republic of Iran, 729 F.2d 835, 842 (D.C. Cir. 1984). Why is the noncommercial tort exception so much narrower in its territorial application than the commercial activity exception?

13. The noncommercial tort exception does not apply to all torts. In particular, it does not apply to "any claim based upon the exercise or performance or the failure to exercise or perform a discretionary function regardless of whether the discretion be abused." In addition, it does not apply to "any claim arising out of malicious prosecution, abuse of process, libel, slander, misrepresentation, deceit, or interference with contract rights." 28 U.S.C. §1605(a)(5)(B). Why do you think Congress imposed these additional limitations on the noncommercial tort exception?

14. Section 1605(a)(3) of the FSIA states that a foreign state is not entitled to immunity with respect to claims

in which rights in property taken in violation of international law are in issue and that property or any property exchanged for such property is present in the United States in connection with a commercial activity carried on in the United States by the foreign state; or that property or any property exchanged for such property is owned or operated by an agency or instrumentality of the foreign state and that agency or instrumentality is engaged in a commercial activity in the United States.

This exception has been invoked in a number of recent cases, including in the *Altmann* case discussed above (although the Supreme Court addressed only the issue of the FSIA's retroactivity and did not address the scope of this particular exception). In considering this exception, courts have generally held that a foreign government's expropriation of its own citizens' property does not violate international law. *See, e.g.*, Fogade v. ENB Revocable Trust, 263 F.3d 1274, 1294 (11th Cir. 2001). For a decision holding that the takings exception applies to the taking of property of a state's own nationals if the taking is part of a campaign of genocide, see Simon v. Republic of Hungary, 812 F.3d 127 (D.C. Cir. 2016). *See also* Philipp v. Federal Republic of Germany, 894 F.3d 406 (D.C. Cir. 2018) (applying this principle); de Csepel v. Republic of Hungary, 859 F.3d 1094 (D.C. Cir. 2017) (same). In a later proceeding in the *Simon* case, the D.C. Circuit held that principles of comity did not require the plaintiffs to first exhaust remedies in Hungary, noting: "When Congress wanted to require the pursuit of foreign remedies as a predicate to FSIA jurisdiction, it said so explicitly." Simon v. Republic of Hungary, 911 F.3d 1172, 1181 (D.C. Cir. 2018). The court also concluded that the case should not be dismissed under the *forum non conveniens* doctrine.

15. In Bolivarian Republic of Venezuela v. Helmerich & Payne Int'l Drilling Co., 137 S. Ct. 1312 (2017), the Supreme Court held that a party's non-frivolous but ultimately erroneous assertion that property was taken in violation of international law is insufficient to sustain jurisdiction under Section 1605(a)(3). In that case, an American company and its Venezuelan subsidiary sued the Venezuelan government, arguing that the government had unlawfully expropriated the subsidiary's oil rigs. The U.S. Court of Appeals for the D.C. Circuit held that, although it was not clear that the expropriation actually violated international law, there was jurisdiction to hear the case because the plaintiffs had raised a non-frivolous argument that an international law violation had occurred. In disagreeing with this approach, the Supreme Court emphasized both the text of Section 1605(a)(3) as well as the FSIA's purpose of freeing foreign sovereigns from suit unless a case falls within a statutory exception to immunity. The Court also observed more generally that the FSIA was designed to codify the restrictive theory of immunity under international law, which generally preserves sovereign immunity for a sovereign's public acts within its own territory, and the Court said that it had "found nothing in the history of the statute that suggests Congress intended a radical departure from these basic principles." While a violation of international law might qualify as an exception to these principles, the Court said that this requires a finding that there actually has been such a violation, not merely a non-frivolous allegation. The Court therefore vacated the D.C. Circuit's opinion and remanded for further proceedings. (On remand, the D.C. Circuit dismissed the claims of the subsidiary company for failure to allege facts that would establish a taking in violation of international law.)

16. In 2016, Congress enacted the Foreign Cultural Exchange Jurisdictional Immunity Clarification Act, Pub. L. 114-319 (Dec. 16, 2016). This Act creates a new subsection (h) in 28 U.S.C. §1605 that exempts foreign art exhibitions in the United States from suit under Section 1605(a)(3) where (a) "a work is imported into the United States from any foreign state pursuant to an agreement that provides for the temporary exhibition or display of such work entered into between a foreign state that is the owner or custodian of such work and the United States or one or more cultural or educational institutions within the United States"; (b) "the President, or the President's designee, has determined . . . that such work is of cultural significance and the temporary exhibition or display of such work is in the national interest"; and (c) the notice has been published. When those conditions are met, "any activity in the United States of such foreign state, or of any carrier, that is associated with the temporary exhibition or display of such work shall not be considered to be commercial activity by such foreign state for purposes of subsection (a)(3)." There are exceptions for Nazi-era claims and other situations in which the work "was taken in connection with the acts of a foreign government against members of a targeted group as part of a systematic confiscation or misappropriation of works from members of a targeted and vulnerable group." One impetus for the legislation was the decision in Malewicz v. City of Amsterdam, 517 F. Supp. 2d 322 (D.D.C. 2007), in which the court had held that activity related to the loan of artwork to U.S. museums constituted "commercial activity" under Section 1605(a)(3)—a decision that generated significant concern and criticism from foreign state lenders of artwork. For discussion of the statute, see Ingrid Wuerth, *An Art Museum Amendment to the Foreign Sovereign Immunities Act*, Lawfare (Jan. 2, 2017).

17. There is also an exception to immunity in the FSIA for cases "in which rights in property in the United States acquired by succession or gift or rights in immovable property situated in the United States are in issue." 28 U.S.C. §1605(a)(4). The Supreme Court considered this exception in Permanent Mission of India to the United Nations v. City of New York, 551 U.S. 193 (2007). In that case, the Court held that a city could bring a declaratory judgment suit under the exception to establish the validity of tax liens imposed on property held by foreign governments for the purpose of housing diplomatic employees and their families. In addition to relying on the plain language of the exception, the Court reasoned that "property ownership is not an inherently sovereign function" for purposes of the restrictive theory of immunity that Congress intended to codify in the FSIA. In reaching its conclusion, the Court rejected a contrary interpretation of the FSIA advocated by the Executive Branch.

18. In 2008, Congress amended the FSIA to include a new §1605A. This section creates an express exception to the sovereign immunity of, and an express cause of action against, states that sponsor acts of terrorism. (The new statute fills in gaps identified by courts in earlier related statutes that sought to achieve the same ends. For an overview, see Congressional Research Service, *Suits Against States by Victims of Terrorism* (May 1, 2008), at http://fas.org/sgp/crs/terror/RL31258.pdf). Both the exception to immunity and the new cause of action against states apply to cases

> in which money damages are sought against a foreign state for personal injury or death that was caused by an act of torture, extrajudicial killing, aircraft sabotage, hostage taking, or the provision of material support or resources for such an act if such act or provision of material support or resources is engaged in by an official, employee, or agent of such foreign state while acting within the scope of his or her office, employment, or agency.

28 U.S.C. §1605A(a)(1), (c). Section 1605A applies only to countries included on the State Department's official list of terrorist states at the time of the terrorist acts in question, *id.* at §1605A(a)(2), which as of September 2019 was Iran, North Korea, Sudan, and Syria. The cause of action created by the statute is for personal injury or death and extends only to U.S. nationals, members of the armed forces, and employees of the U.S. Government. *Id.* at §1605(A)(c). For other details about the statute, see the Congressional Research Service report cited above.

Section 1605A delegates to the Executive Branch the task of deciding which nations lose their immunity and are subject to a cause of action by virtue of their involvement in terrorism. Is this delegation of authority consistent with the separation of powers structure of the Constitution, which assigns the power to regulate the jurisdiction of the federal courts to Congress rather than to the Executive? In Rein v. Socialist People's Libyan Arab Jamahiriya, 162 F.3d 748 (2d Cir. 1998), the court held that there was no violation of separation of powers in a suit against Libya, because Libya was listed as a state sponsor of terrorism in 1996 when Congress enacted the predecessor to Section 1605A that was at issue in that case. The court expressed no opinion about whether it would be constitutional to apply the statute's elimination of immunity to a nation added to the state sponsor list after Congress had enacted the relevant statute. For decisions reaching a similar conclusion, see Price v. Socialist People's Libyan Arab Jamahiriya, 110 F. Supp. 2d 10 (D.D.C. 2000); and Daliberti v. Republic of Iraq, 97 F. Supp. 2d 38 (D.D.C. 2000). If the Executive Branch changes the list of state sponsors of terrorism, is it improperly determining federal court jurisdiction? Does it matter whether the Executive is adding or deleting states from the list? How, if at all, is this Executive role different from the pre-FSIA regime, under which the Executive Branch could control the grant of immunity on a case-by-case basis?

What effect might §1605A have on future relations between the United States and the nations that are subject to suit? Does it create a risk of retaliation by these nations? Consider two examples. In November 2000, Iran's Parliament enacted a law that allows Iranian "victims of U.S. interference since the 1953 coup d'état" to sue the United States in Iranian courts. This law was reportedly enacted as a "measure of reciprocity" in response to the suits allowed in U.S. courts against Iran. And in 2003, Libya enacted a law that gave Libyan courts jurisdiction over foreign nationals and their government if that government allows lawsuits in its courts against Libya. It was reported in early 2004 that a suit had been brought under this law in Libya seeking billions of dollars in damages from the United States and the United Kingdom for air strikes that took place in 1986. Should the United States be concerned about such retaliatory measures?

19. In Bank Markazi v. Peterson, 136 S. Ct. 1310 (2016), the Supreme Court rejected a separation of powers challenge to 22 U.S.C. §8772, which was enacted as part of the Iran Threat Reduction and Syria Human Rights Act of 2012. Section 8772 designated certain Iranian government assets as eligible for post-judgment attachment to satisfy damage awards against Iran that had been obtained under the state sponsor of terrorism exception to immunity. The Act is unusual in that, in identifying the assets that can be attached, it refers specifically to pending litigation in which the assets are in dispute. Despite this provision, the Court concluded that the Act did not usurp the judicial role in violation of the separation of powers because it merely "provides a new standard clarifying that, if Iran owns certain assets, the victims of Iran-sponsored terrorist attacks will be permitted to execute against those assets," and because "[a]pplying laws implementing Congress' policy judgments, with fidelity to those judgments, is commonplace for the Judiciary." The Court also emphasized that the Act was "an exercise of congressional authority regarding foreign affairs, a domain in which the controlling role of the political branches is both necessary and proper." Historically, the Court noted, "Congress and the President have, time and again, as exigencies arose, exercised control over claims against foreign states and the disposition of foreign-state property in the United States." "Particularly pertinent," the Court observed, was the fact that "the Executive, prior to the enactment of the FSIA, regularly made case-specific determinations whether sovereign immunity should be recognized, and courts accepted those determinations as binding." Although Congress in the FSIA "transferred from the Executive to the courts the principal responsibility for determining a foreign state's amenability to suit," the Court said that "it remains Congress' prerogative to alter a foreign state's immunity and to render the alteration dispositive of judicial proceedings in progress."

After this decision, Iran initiated proceedings against the United States in the International Court of Justice, contending that the FSIA's state sponsor of terrorism exception to immunity violates customary international law.

20. In 2016, Congress enacted the Justice Against Sponsors of Terrorism Act (JASTA). *See* Pub. L. 114-222 (Sept. 28, 2016). JASTA creates a new exception to immunity, codified at 28 U.S.C. §1605B, for

> any case in which money damages are sought against a foreign state for physical injury to person or property or death occurring in the United States and caused by— (1) an act of international terrorism in the United States; and (2) a tortious act or acts of the foreign state, or of any official, employee, or agent of that foreign state while acting within the scope of his or her office, employment, or agency, regardless where the tortious act or acts of the foreign state occurred.

It also provides that "[a] court of the United States may stay a proceeding against a foreign state if the Secretary of State certifies that the United States is engaged in good faith discussions with the foreign state defendant concerning the resolution of the claims against the foreign state, or any other parties as to whom a stay of claims is sought." Such a stay may be granted for up to 180 days, and the stay can be extended based on a petition from the Attorney General, "if the Secretary of State recertifies that the United States remains engaged in good faith discussions with the foreign state defendant concerning the resolution of the claims against the foreign state, or any other parties as to whom a stay of claims is sought." Unlike the state sponsor of terrorism exception in §1605A, JASTA is not limited to suits against particular foreign nations. A central reason that it was enacted, however, was to facilitate litigation against Saudi Arabia that had been initiated by families of the victims of the 9/11 terrorist attacks.

In passing JASTA, Congress overrode a veto by President Obama. In his veto message, the President raised three concerns about JASTA: first, that it would improperly delegate to private litigants, their lawyers, and the courts the task of investigating and addressing potential connections between foreign governments and terrorism instead of keeping that task within the government; second, that it would potentially undermine longstanding principles of sovereign immunity and potentially lead to reciprocal actions by other countries to reduce U.S. sovereign immunity; and, third, that it would likely create friction with U.S. allies and other countries and thereby undermine cooperation on a variety of matters, including in combating terrorism. *See* Veto Message from the President—S. 2040 (Sept. 23, 2016), at https://www.whitehouse.gov/the-press-office/2016/09/23/veto-message-president-s2040. Echoing the President's concerns, other countries have criticized JASTA. For example, the European Union sent a letter to the U.S. State Department contending that JASTA was "in conflict with fundamental principles of international law." *See* Letter from European Union (Sept. 2016), at https://www.washingtonpost.com/news/powerpost/wp-content/uploads/sites/47/2016/09/EU-on-JASTA.pdf.

Although Congress voted overwhelmingly to override President Obama's veto (the vote was 97-1 in the Senate and 348-77 in the House), some members of Congress expressed concerns about the legislation. For example, 28 senators signed a letter worrying that "[i]f other nations respond to this bill by weakening U.S. sovereign immunity protections, then the United States could face private lawsuits in foreign courts as a result of important military or intelligence activities." *See* Letter to Sens. John Cornyn and Charles Schumer (Sept. 28, 2016), at https://www.scribd.com/document/ 325673727/Bipartisan-Senate-JASTA-Letter-092816.

Are the concerns expressed by President Obama, the EU, and the 28 senators valid? If so, are there modifications that Congress could make to JASTA that would address these concerns? Why did the executive and legislative branches have such different views about the desirability of this legislation?

21. In February 2012, the ICJ issued an important decision concerning sovereign immunity. In that case, Germany v. Italy, the ICJ held (by a vote of 12-3) that Italy had violated customary international law in allowing its courts to exercise jurisdiction over civil claims against Germany relating to Germany's violation of international humanitarian law during Germany's occupation of Italy in World War II. In the decision, the ICJ reasoned as follows:

(a) states have a right of sovereign immunity under customary international law, stemming from the sovereign equality of nations,

(b) the relevant international law of immunity is that which exists at the time of the proceedings rather than at the time of the underlying conduct,

(c) the acts of Germany in question constituted sovereign acts (*acta jure imperii*) for purposes of immunity, notwithstanding the illegality of the acts,

(d) states are generally entitled to immunity in other nations' courts for sovereign acts,

(e) even if there is an exception for tortious acts committed in the forum state, the exception does not apply to the sovereign acts of a state's armed forces and other organs of a state working with those forces during an armed conflict,

(f) this immunity applies even if the acts constituted serious violations of international human rights law or the law of armed conflict, and

(g) this is true even if the acts constituted *jus cogens* violations, and even if there are no other effective opportunities for relief.

In many respects, U.S. law is in accord with the decision. For example, U.S. courts have consistently rejected the argument that a violation of *jus cogens* norms constitutes an implicit waiver of sovereign immunity. In addition, as noted above, the U.S. Supreme Court has held, like the ICJ, that immunity is to be determined based on the law and circumstances at the time of the proceedings, not at the time of the acts.

The reasoning of the ICJ's decision raises questions, however, about the defensibility under customary international law of the FSIA's state sponsor of terrorism exception to immunity. The ICJ specifically noted that this exception "has no counterpart in the legislation of other States." (Canada, however, has enacted similar legislation. *See* Justice for Victims of Terrorism Act, S.C. 2012, c. 1, s. 2 (assented to March 13, 2012).) Moreover, if Germany's undisputed violations of international humanitarian law during World War II do not qualify for an exception to immunity, it is difficult to see how a state's sponsorship of terrorism would qualify. *But cf.* Restatement (Fourth) of the Foreign Relations Law of the United States §460, reporters' note 11 (2018) ("Given its focus on injuries to U.S. nationals resulting from acts that have been condemned as illegal by the international community, and the frequently repeated exhortation that states should provide relief and means of compensating victims of terrorism, it is not clear that §1605A contravenes any presumptive jurisdictional constraint under international law."). In any event, because the state sponsor of terrorism exception applies only to a small number of states with which the United States does not have close relations, the international consequences of the potential inconsistency with international law may be limited.

The ICJ's reasoning also may implicate the FSIA's property takings exception (28 U.S.C. §1605(a)(3)). Although the ICJ did not specifically mention this exception, it, like the state sponsor of terrorism exception, does not appear in the sovereign immunity law of other states. *See* Hazel Fox, The Law of State Immunity 350 (2d ed. 2008). While this exception applies only if the property at issue is either present in the United States in connection with a commercial activity or is owned or operated by an agency or instrumentality engaged in commercial activity in the United States, the exception does not require that the taking of property itself have been a non-sovereign act. It might be argued, however, that if a foreign state engages in conduct that meets the commercial nexus requirements of this exception, it has waived its immunity for these purposes. Nothing in the ICJ's decision speaks directly to that argument.

The FSIA's noncommercial tort exception (28 U.S.C. §1605(a)(5)) is easier to defend. As the ICJ noted, a number of states have an exception for torts committed in the forum state, and they do not specifically restrict the exception to private, commercial acts. While the U.S. exception does not contain an express carve-out for the conduct of foreign armed forces in the United States during an armed conflict, claims about such conduct are unlikely to arise in U.S. litigation. Moreover, such conduct might fall within the discretionary function limitation in the tort exception (a limitation that the ICJ observed "has no counterpart in the legislation of other States"). *But cf.* Letelier v. Republic of Chile, 486 F. Supp. 665, 673 (S.D.N.Y. 1980) (reasoning that a foreign state "has no 'discretion' to perpetrate conduct designed to result in the assassination of an individual or individuals, action that is clearly contrary to the precepts of humanity as recognized in both national and international law").

22. The Supreme Court construed the FSIA's provisions for sovereign immunity from *execution on a judgment* (as opposed to immunity from the exercise of jurisdiction) in Republic of Argentina v. NML Capital Ltd., 134 S. Ct. 2250 (2014). The case grew out of a default on Argentine bonds that Argentina later renegotiated, on less favorable terms, with "exchange bondholders." Respondent NML Capital, Ltd. refused the renegotiation and brought 11 lawsuits on debts owed under the original bonds. Argentina had waived its immunity from jurisdiction, and NML prevailed on the merits in each case. In an attempt to enforce judgments worth $2.5 billion, NML then issued subpoenas to two non-party banks, seeking information about Argentina's offshore financial transactions. Argentina objected that the discovery order violated the FSIA, but the Supreme Court disagreed.

The Court assumed that the Federal Rules of Civil Procedure permit discovery of third-party information related to a judgment debtor's extraterritorial assets and then considered whether the FSIA's provisions relating to immunity from execution, 28 U.S.C. §§1609-11, barred such discovery. Section 1609 states that "the property in the United States of a foreign state shall be immune from attachment[,] arrest[,] and execution," subject to exceptions in §1610, which include "property in the United States of a foreign state" that is "used for a commercial activity in the United States" (*see* §1610(a)), and that is also subject to another enumerated exception to immunity (such as waiver; *see* §1610(a)(1)-(7)). The FSIA also confers broader sovereign immunity from execution on certain designated property (such as property of a foreign central bank and foreign military property; *see* §1611). Because none of these provisions purports to provide immunity from discovery in aid of judgment execution, the Court concluded that the FSIA permits the discovery. The Court rejected the argument that §§1609-11 simply narrowed an otherwise still-applicable pre-FSIA rule of absolute immunity from execution that included a disallowance of discovery of extraterritorial assets. It doubted the existence of any such pre-FSIA immunity and ruled that the language of §1609 controlled in any event.

Perhaps more significant than the Court's holding were its more general statements about the interpretive principles that govern the FSIA. It noted that the FSIA replaced the "bedlam" of "executive-driven, factor-intensive" immunity determinations, which often turned on "diplomatic" and "political" factors, with the FSIA, which established a "comprehensive set of legal standards governing claims of immunity in every civil action against a foreign state." As a result, the Court concluded "*any sort of immunity defense* made by a foreign sovereign in an American court must stand on the Act's text," or "it must fall" (emphasis added). This sharp focus on the FSIA's text led the Court to reject claims by Argentina and the United States, as *amicus curiae*, that various foreign relations concerns should inform the interpretation of the FSIA and limit discovery:

> Discovery orders as sweeping as this one, the Government warns, will cause "a substantial invasion of [foreign states'] sovereignty," Brief for United States as Amicus Curiae 18, and will "[u]ndermin[e] international comity," *id.* at 19. Worse, such orders might provoke "reciprocal adverse treatment of the United States in foreign courts," *id.* at 20, and will "threaten harm to the United States' foreign relations more generally,"

id. at 21. These apprehensions are better directed to that branch of government with authority to amend the Act—which, as it happens, is the same branch that forced our retirement from the immunity-by-factor-balancing business nearly 40 years ago.

On the same day that it decided this case, the Supreme Court denied certiorari in a related case. In that case, the Second Circuit affirmed injunctions by the district court that had interpreted the equal treatment ("pari passu") clause in a different set of bonds to require Argentina to pay NML if it made payments to exchange bondholders who accepted the earlier renegotiation. *See* NML Capital, Ltd. v. Republic of Argentina, 699 F.3d 246 (2d Cir. 2012). Argentina argued that the injunctions violated the FSIA by ordering it to pay plaintiffs with immune property located outside the United States. The Second Circuit disagreed. The court noted that Argentina could comply with the injunction without the court exercising any dominion over sovereign property, including by paying both the exchange bondholders and the defaulted bondholders, or at least a proportionate amount to both. Because the injunctions "do not transfer any dominion or control over sovereign property to the court," the Second Circuit concluded they "do not violate §1609."

23. In 1997, the Palestinian organization Hamas carried out several suicide bombings on a pedestrian mall in Jerusalem, and among those injured were a number of U.S. citizens. The victims and their family members brought suit against Iran under the state sponsor of terrorism exception to immunity, 28 U.S.C. §1605A, alleging that Iran had provided material support and training to Hamas. The plaintiffs obtained a default judgment of $71.5 million. They then sought to enforce the judgment by attaching Persian artifacts owned by Iran that are currently held by a University of Chicago museum. The plaintiffs relied in particular on 28 U.S.C. §1610(g), which was enacted in 2008 and provides:

> (g) Property in Certain Actions.—
>
> (1) . . . [T]he property of a foreign state against which a judgment is entered under section 1605A, and the property of an agency or instrumentality of such a state, including property that is a separate juridical entity or is an interest held directly or indirectly in a separate juridical entity, is subject to attachment in aid of execution, and execution, upon that judgment as provided in this section, regardless of—
>
> > (A) the level of economic control over the property by the government of the foreign state;
> >
> > (B) whether the profits of the property go to that government;
> >
> > (C) the degree to which officials of that government manage the property or otherwise control its daily affairs;
> >
> > (D) whether that government is the sole beneficiary in interest of the property; or
> >
> > (E) whether establishing the property as a separate entity would entitle the foreign state to benefits in United States courts while avoiding its obligations.

In Rubin v. Islamic Republic of Iran, 138 S. Ct. 816 (2018), the Supreme Court unanimously held that the artifacts were not subject to attachment. In an opinion by Justice Sotomayor, the Court explained that Section 1610(g) was enacted to overturn First National City Bank v. Banco Para el Comercio Exterior de Cuba, 462 U.S. 611 (1983), in which the Court had held that judgments against foreign states could not normally be enforced against the foreign states' juridically-separate agencies and instrumentalities. Section 1610(g) does not, explained the Court, set forth an independent exception to attachment immunity: It "serves to identify property that will be available for attachment and execution in satisfaction of a §1605A judgment, but it does not in itself divest property of immunity." As a result, reasoned the Court, its reference to attachment "as provided in this section" means that an exception to immunity from attachment must be found elsewhere in Section 1610.

24. It is generally assumed that by shifting immunity determinations from the Executive Branch to the courts, the FSIA made these determinations less political. For a challenge to this assumption, see Adam S. Chilton & Christopher A. Whytock, *Foreign Sovereign Immunity and Comparative Institutional Competence*, 163 U. Pa. L. Rev. 411 (2015). Based on a statistical evaluation of foreign sovereign immunity determinations made before and after the enactment of the FSIA, the authors find "little evidence that political factors were systematically related to the State Department's foreign sovereign immunity decisions," and "significant evidence that political factors are related to the judiciary's immunity decisions."

25. For discussions of the history of foreign sovereign immunity in the United States, see Gary B. Born & Peter B. Rutledge, International Civil Litigation in United States Courts ch. 3 (6th ed. 2018); and Theodore R. Giuttari, The American Law of Sovereign Immunity (1970); *see also* G. Edward White, *The Transformation of the Constitutional Regime of Foreign Relations*, 85 Va. L. Rev. 1, 134-45 (1999) (discussing the treatment of foreign sovereign immunity by U.S. courts in the 1930s and 1940s). For discussions of the FSIA and its origins, see Joseph W. Dellapenna, Suing Foreign Governments and Their Corporations (2d ed. 2003); Mark B. Feldman, *The United States Foreign Sovereign Immunities Act of 1976 in Perspective: A Founder's View*, 35 Int'l & Comp. L.Q. 302 (1986); Robert B. von Mehren, *The Foreign Sovereign Immunities Act of 1976*, 17 Colum. J. Transnat'l L. 33 (1978); and Frederic Alan Weber, *The Foreign Sovereign Immunities Act of 1976: Its Origins, Meaning, and Effect*, 3 Yale J. World Pub. Ord. 1 (1976). *See also* Restatement (Fourth) of the Foreign Relations Law of the United States §§451-64 (2018).

Note on Diplomatic and Consular Immunity

Diplomatic and consular immunities were historically regulated by customary international law, but they are now codified in two treaties—the Vienna Convention on Diplomatic Relations ("Diplomatic Convention"), and the Vienna Convention on Consular Relations ("Consular Convention")—both of which the United States has ratified. Under these treaties, the nation that sends the diplomat or consular official is referred to as the "sending State," and the nation that receives the diplomat or consular official is referred to as the "receiving State."

Diplomatic agents have broad immunity from both criminal and civil jurisdiction. They are not subject to "any form of arrest or detention." Diplomatic Convention, art. 29. In addition, they have absolute immunity from the criminal jurisdiction of the receiving State. *Id.*, art. 31(1). Furthermore, they have immunity from civil and administrative proceedings, with exceptions for certain actions related to immovable property, succession, and non-official commercial activities. *Id.* Consular immunity is more qualified. Consular officials are not liable to arrest or detention "except in the case of a grave crime and pursuant to a decision by the competent judicial authority." Consular Convention, art. 41(1). They have immunity from criminal and civil jurisdiction, but only "in respect of acts performed in the exercise of consular functions." *Id.*, art. 43(1). Even this immunity does not apply with respect to civil actions for certain contract and tort claims where the consular official was not acting expressly in a public capacity. *Id.*, art. 43(2).

In addition to these individual immunities, diplomatic and consular properties are protected against interference by the receiving State. Although these properties are not, contrary to popular belief, treated as part of the sending State's territory, they are considered "inviolable" by the receiving State. For diplomatic missions, this means that they cannot be entered by officials of the receiving State "except with the consent of the head of the mission." Diplomatic Convention, art. 22(1). In addition, the receiving State has a duty "to take all appropriate steps to protect the premises of the mission against any intrusion or damage and to prevent any disturbance of the peace of the mission or impairment of its dignity." *Id.*, art. 22(2). For consular premises, officials of the receiving State cannot enter "that part of the consular premises which is used exclusively for the purpose of the work of the consular post except with the consent of the head of the consular post or of his designee or of the head of the diplomatic mission of the sending State." Consular Convention, art. 31(2). Consent is assumed, however, "in the case of fire or other disaster requiring prompt protective action." *Id.* As with diplomatic missions, the receiving State has a duty "to take all appropriate steps to protect the consular premises against any intrusion or damage and to prevent any disturbance of the peace of the consular post or impairment of its dignity." *Id.*, art. 31(3).

Despite these limitations on its jurisdiction, the receiving State may at any time declare a member of a diplomatic mission or consulate to be *persona non grata.* Once a person is declared *persona non grata,* the sending State must either recall the person or terminate his or her official functions. *See* Diplomatic Convention, art. 9(1); Consular Convention, art. 23(1).

Congress has further clarified the scope and domestic status of diplomatic immunity in the 1978 Diplomatic Relations Act, 22 U.S.C. §§254a-254e. This Act, among other things, authorizes the President, "on the basis of reciprocity and under such terms and conditions as he may determine, [to] specify privileges and immunities for the mission, the members of the mission, their families, and the diplomatic couriers which result in more favorable treatment or less favorable treatment than is provided under the Vienna Convention." *Id.*, §254c. It also provides that "[a]ny action or proceeding brought against an individual who is entitled to immunity with respect to such action or proceeding under the Vienna Convention on Diplomatic Relations . . . shall be dismissed," and that "[s]uch immunity may be established upon motion or suggestion by or on behalf of the individual, or as otherwise permitted by law or applicable rules of procedure." *Id.*, §254d.

Representatives of members of the United Nations and official invitees to the United Nations are also entitled to certain immunities. Under the 1947 Agreement Between the United Nations and the United States of America Regarding the Headquarters of the United Nations, also known as the "U.N. Headquarters Agreement," representatives of member states "shall, whether residing inside or outside the headquarters district, be entitled in the territory of the United States to the same privileges and immunities . . . as it accords to diplomatic envoys accredited to it." U.N. Headquarters Agreement, art. V, §15(4). The 1946 Convention on Privileges and Immunities of the United Nations states more specifically that representatives of member states shall "enjoy the following privileges and immunities: (a) immunity from personal arrest or detention . . . ; (b) inviolability for all papers and documents; . . . (g) such other privileges, immunities and facilities not inconsistent [with] the foregoing as diplomatic envoys enjoy." U.N. Convention, art. IV, §11. The U.N. Headquarters Agreement also prohibits the imposition of any impediments to transit to or from the headquarters district (a defined area around the United Nations headquarters) by a variety of individuals, including representatives of the U.N. members as well as "other persons invited to the headquarters district by the United Nations." U.N. Headquarters Agreement, art. IV, §11.

International organizations also have immunities from suit in U.S. courts. Under the 1945 International Organizations Immunities Act (IOIA), 22 U.S.C. §§288-288f-4, international organizations "shall enjoy the same immunity from suit and every form of judicial process as is enjoyed by foreign governments, except to the extent that such organizations may expressly waive their immunity for the purpose of any proceedings or by the terms of any contract." *Id.*, §288a(b). The Act defines "international organization" as "a public international organization in which the United States participates pursuant to any treaty or under the authority of any Act of Congress authorizing such participation or making an appropriation for such participation, and which shall have been designated by the President through appropriate Executive order as being entitled to enjoy the privileges, exemptions, and immunities herein provided." *Id.*, §288. The President, however, is authorized "at any time to revoke the designation of any international organization under this section, if in his judgment such action should be justified by reason of the abuse by an international organization or its officers and employees of the privileges, exemptions, and immunities herein provided or for any other reason." *Id.*

In Jam v. Int'l Finance Corp., 139 S. Ct. 759 (2019), a group of Indian nationals brought suit against the International Finance Corporation (IFC), an international organization based in Washington, D.C. that is part of the World Bank. The plaintiffs alleged that after the IFC loaned $450 million to an Indian company for the construction of a power plant in India, the company constructed the plant in a manner contrary to the funding agreement and IFC policy, and that the plant ended up causing environmental and social damage to the surrounding communities. The D.C. Circuit upheld dismissal of the suit under the IOIA. In concluding that the IFC was entitled to immunity in this case, the D.C. Circuit interpreted the IOIA as conferring essentially absolute immunity on international organizations, since that is the sort of immunity that foreign governments would have had when the IOIA was enacted.

The Supreme Court reversed in a 7-1 decision, holding that the IOIA affords international organizations only the same immunity from suit that foreign governments receive today under the FSIA. In an opinion by Chief Justice Roberts, the Court emphasized the plain language of the statute, reading the IOIA's "same . . . as" formulation as making international organization immunity and state immunity continuously equivalent. The Court confirmed this reading, using what it called the "reference canon" of interpretation, pursuant to which a statute that refers to a general subject is understood to adopt the law on that subject as it exists whenever a question arises under the statute. By contrast, the Court said that a statute that refers to another statute by specific title or section number adopts the referenced statute as it existed when the referring statute was enacted. The IOIA refers to an external body of potentially evolving law rather than a specific statute, and therefore, the Court reasoned, it requires reference to the rules governing foreign sovereign immunity as they evolve. In response to the IFC's argument that this outcome would open up international organizations such as international development banks to a host of litigation under the FSIA's commercial activities exception, the Court noted that the charters of international organizations could specify a different level of immunity from the FSIA and that there are other hurdles to litigation under the commercial activities exception. Justice Breyer dissented, invoking "the statute's history, its context, its purposes, and its consequences" to argue that international organizations should continue to have immunity for their commercial activities, subject to Executive Branch override, "just as foreign governments possessed that immunity when Congress enacted the statute in 1945."

Why is it important to give diplomats and consular officials immunity? Why is it important to treat diplomatic premises as inviolable? If the United States fails to respect diplomatic immunity or inviolability, what consequences is it likely to suffer abroad? What degree of immunity is needed to ensure the effective functioning of diplomatic missions and consulates? Do the reasons for diplomatic and consular immunity explain immunity for U.N. representatives and international organizations? What different reasons might there be for immunity in this latter context?

The American public and press are often surprised to learn that diplomats have absolute immunity from criminal prosecution, even for egregious crimes. In 1997, for example, a diplomat from the Republic of Georgia was involved in a fatal car crash in Washington, D.C., and many were shocked to learn that he was immune from prosecution in the United States. In an unusual development, the Republic of Georgia decided to waive the diplomat's immunity from prosecution in that case, and the diplomat pleaded guilty to involuntary manslaughter. Absent such a waiver, however, the only "remedy" would have been to declare the diplomat *persona non grata* and order him to leave the country.

Both the Diplomatic Convention and the Consular Convention make clear that the immunity of diplomats and consular officials can be waived by the sending State, as long as the waiver is "express." *See* Diplomatic Convention, art. 32; Consular Convention, art. 45. Why is the sending State allowed to waive immunity? Does a waiver of diplomatic immunity with respect to criminal prosecution also constitute a waiver of immunity with respect to civil liability for the same conduct? In the case described above regarding the Georgian diplomat, the court concluded that there was no waiver of civil liability. *See* Knab v. Republic of Georgia, 1998 U.S. Dist. LEXIS 8820 (D.D.C. 1998). The court noted, among other things, that the Diplomatic Convention confers criminal and civil immunity separately and with different scopes, and that the U.S. State Department had expressed the view that the diplomat's civil immunity remained intact. Is this persuasive? Note that diplomats and consular officials are deemed to waive their immunity with respect to counterclaims if they bring suit in a U.S. court. *See* Diplomatic Convention, art. 32(3); Consular Convention, art. 42(3).

Although diplomats have absolute immunity from criminal prosecution, their immunity from civil suits is subject to several exceptions. One of these exceptions is for "an action relating to any professional or commercial activity exercised by the diplomatic agent in the receiving State outside his official functions." How does this exception compare with the commercial activity exception in the Foreign Sovereign Immunities Act? To date, courts have read the diplomatic immunity exception much more narrowly, such that it applies only to the conduct of a trade or business, and not to commercial relationships that are incidental to daily life. *See, e.g.,* Tabion v. Mufti, 73 F.3d 535 (4th Cir. 1996); Logan v. Dupuis, 990 F. Supp. 26 (D.D.C. 1997). Why do you think courts have read this exception so narrowly? Should diplomats have broader immunity from civil suits than foreign governments?

What deference should courts give to the views of the Executive Branch in determining whether a defendant is protected by diplomatic immunity? Courts generally treat as conclusive State Department certifications of a diplomat's status. *See, e.g., Abdulaziz v. Metropolitan Dade County,* 741 F.3d 1328, 1331 (11th Cir. 1984). Courts give substantial but not dispositive weight to Executive Branch constructions of the Vienna Conventions. *See, e.g., Tabion,* 73 F.3d at 538. And, while courts give weight to the Executive Branch's views about whether immunity should be granted in a particular case, they do not typically treat those views as binding. *See, e.g., Knab,* 1998 U.S. Dist. LEXIS at *10 ("Although the Court is not obliged to defer to the State Department's opinion, it finds [the State Department's letter to the court] useful evidence.").

These deference issues were implicated in United States v. Al-Hamdi, 356 F.3d 564 (4th Cir. 2004). In that case, Al-Hamdi, the son of a Yemeni diplomat, appealed his conviction for possessing a firearm as a non-immigrant alien on the ground that he was entitled to diplomatic immunity. Article 37.1 of the Vienna Convention on Diplomatic Immunities provides that "members of the family of a diplomatic agent forming part of his household shall . . . enjoy the privileges and immunities" conferred on diplomats themselves. The Diplomatic Relations Act, which made the Vienna Convention applicable to the United States, provides that the phrase "members of the family" means the "members of the family of a member of a mission . . . who form part of his or her household." 22 U.S.C. §254a(2)(A). Despite these provisions, the State Department certified that Al-Hamdi, who was 25 years old at the time of his arrest, lost his diplomatic immunity in November 1998 when he turned 21. The State Department based its certification on a Circular Diplomatic Note that it had issued, of which the Yemeni government had notice, which interpreted the phrase "members of the family" as set forth in the Vienna Convention and the Diplomatic Relations Act to not include children over the age of 21. The Fourth Circuit agreed with the State Department that Al-Hamdi lacked immunity. The court first satisfied itself that the State Department's certification was not based on an impermissible interpretation of the Vienna Convention. After giving "substantial deference" to the State Department's interpretation of the Vienna Convention, and after noting that a receiving State always has had "broad discretion to classify diplomats," the court concluded that the State Department's interpretation was reasonable and, as a result, was binding on the court.

For additional discussion of diplomatic and consular immunity, see Restatement (Third) of the Foreign Relations Law of the United States §§464-66 (1987); Eileen Denza, Diplomatic Law: Commentary on the Vienna Convention on Diplomatic Relations (4th ed. 2016); Linda S. Frey & Marsha L. Frey, The History of Diplomatic Immunity (1999); Ivor Roberts, Satow's Diplomatic Practice (7th ed. 2017).

E. INDIVIDUAL OFFICIAL IMMUNITY

Samantar v. Yousuf

560 U.S. 305 (2010)

JUSTICE STEVENS delivered the opinion of the Court. . . .

Respondents are members of the Isaaq clan, which included well-educated and prosperous Somalis who were subjected to systematic persecution during the

1980's by the military regime then governing Somalia. They allege that petitioner exercised command and control over members of the Somali military forces who tortured, killed, or arbitrarily detained them or members of their families; that petitioner knew or should have known of the abuses perpetrated by his subordinates; and that he aided and abetted the commission of these abuses. Respondents' complaint sought damages from petitioner pursuant to the Torture Victim Protection Act of 1991, and the Alien Tort Statute. Petitioner, who was in charge of Somalia's armed forces before its military regime collapsed, fled Somalia in 1991 and is now a resident of Virginia. The United States has not recognized any entity as the government of Somalia since the fall of the military regime.

Respondents filed their complaint in November 2004, and petitioner promptly moved to dismiss. The District Court stayed the proceedings to give the State Department an opportunity to provide a statement of interest regarding petitioner's claim of sovereign immunity. Each month during the ensuing two years, petitioner advised the court that the State Department had the matter "still under consideration." In 2007, having received no response from the State Department, the District Court reinstated the case on its active docket. The court concluded that it did not have subject-matter jurisdiction and granted petitioner's motion to dismiss.

The District Court's decision rested squarely on the FSIA. The FSIA provides that a "foreign state shall be immune from the jurisdiction" of both federal and state courts except as provided in the Act, and the District Court noted that none of the parties had argued that any exception was applicable. Although characterizing the statute as silent on its applicability to the officials of a foreign state, the District Court followed appellate decisions holding that a foreign state's sovereign immunity under the Act extends to "an individual acting in his official capacity on behalf of a foreign state," but not to "an official who acts beyond the scope of his authority." (quoting Velasco v. Government of Indonesia, 370 F.3d 392, 398, 399 (4th Cir. 2004)). The court rejected respondents' argument that petitioner was necessarily acting beyond the scope of his authority because he allegedly violated international law.[3]

The Court of Appeals reversed, rejecting the District Court's ruling that the FSIA governs petitioner's immunity from suit. It acknowledged "the majority view" among the Circuits that "the FSIA applies to individual officials of a foreign state." It disagreed with that view, however, and concluded, "based on the language and structure of the statute, that the FSIA does not apply to individual foreign government agents like [petitioner]."[5] Having found that the FSIA does not govern whether petitioner enjoys immunity from suit, the Court of Appeals remanded the case for

3. Because we hold that the FSIA does not govern whether an individual foreign official enjoys immunity from suit, we need not reach respondents' argument that an official is not immune under the FSIA for acts of torture and extrajudicial killing. We note that in determining petitioner had not acted beyond the scope of his authority, the District Court afforded great weight to letters from the Somali Transitional Federal Government (TFG) to the State Department, in which the TFG supported petitioner's claim of immunity and stated "the actions attributed to [petitioner] in the lawsuit . . . would have been taken by [petitioner] in his official capacities." Although the District Court described the TFG as "recognized by the United States as the governing body in Somalia," the United States does not recognize the TFG (or any other entity) as the government of Somalia.

5. As an alternative basis for its decision, the Court of Appeals held that even if a current official is covered by the FSIA, a former official is not. Because we agree with the Court of Appeals on its broader ground that individual officials are not covered by the FSIA, petitioner's status as a former official is irrelevant to our analysis.

further proceedings, including a determination of whether petitioner is entitled to immunity under the common law. We granted certiorari. . . .

The FSIA provides that "a foreign state shall be immune from the jurisdiction of the courts of the United States and of the States" except as provided in the Act. . . . The question we face in this case is whether an individual sued for conduct undertaken in his official capacity is a "foreign state" within the meaning of the Act.

The Act defines "foreign state" in §1603 as follows:

> (a) A "foreign state" . . . includes a political subdivision of a foreign state or an agency or instrumentality of a foreign state as defined in subsection (b).
> (b) An "agency or instrumentality of a foreign state" means any entity—
> (1) which is a separate legal person, corporate or otherwise, and
> (2) which is an organ of a foreign state or political subdivision thereof, or a majority of whose shares or other ownership interest is owned by a foreign state or political subdivision thereof, and
> (3) which is neither a citizen of a State of the United States as defined in §1332(c) and (e) of this title, nor created under the laws of any third country.

The term "foreign state" on its face indicates a body politic that governs a particular territory. In §1603(a), however, the Act establishes that "foreign state" has a broader meaning, by mandating the inclusion of the state's political subdivisions, agencies, and instrumentalities. Then, in §1603(b), the Act specifically delimits what counts as an agency or instrumentality. Petitioner argues that either "foreign state," §1603(a), or "agency or instrumentality," §1603(b), could be read to include a foreign official. Although we agree that petitioner's interpretation is literally possible, our analysis of the entire statutory text persuades us that petitioner's reading is not the meaning that Congress enacted.

We turn first to the term "agency or instrumentality of a foreign state," §1603(b). It is true that an individual official could be an "agency or instrumentality," if that term is given the meaning of "any thing or person through which action is accomplished," In re Terrorist Attacks on Sept. 11, 2001, 538 F.3d 71, 83 (2d Cir. 2008). But Congress has specifically defined "agency or instrumentality" in the FSIA, and all of the textual clues in that definition cut against such a broad construction.

First, the statute specifies that " 'agency or instrumentality' . . . means any *entity*" matching three specified characteristics, §1603(b) (emphasis added), and "entity" typically refers to an organization, rather than an individual. Furthermore, several of the required characteristics apply awkwardly, if at all, to individuals. The phrase "separate legal person, corporate or otherwise," §1603(b)(1), could conceivably refer to a natural person, solely by virtue of the word "person." But the phrase "separate legal person" typically refers to the legal fiction that allows an entity to hold personhood separate from the natural persons who are its shareholders or officers. It is similarly awkward to refer to a person as an "organ" of the foreign state. And the third part of the definition could not be applied at all to a natural person. A natural person cannot be a citizen of a State "as defined in section 1332(c) and (e)," §1603(b)(3), because those subsections refer to the citizenship of corporations and estates. Nor can a natural person be "created under the laws of any third country." Thus, the terms Congress chose simply do not evidence the intent to include individual officials within the meaning of "agency or instrumentality."

Petitioner proposes a second textual route to including an official within the meaning of "foreign state." He argues that the definition of "foreign state" in §1603(a) sets out a nonexhaustive list that "includes" political subdivisions and agencies or instrumentalities but is not so limited. It is true that use of the word "include" can signal that the list that follows is meant to be illustrative rather than exhaustive. And, to be sure, there are fewer textual clues within §1603(a) than within §1603(b) from which to interpret Congress' silence regarding foreign officials. But even if the list in §1603(a) is merely illustrative, it still suggests that "foreign state" does not encompass officials, because the types of defendants listed are all entities.

Moreover, elsewhere in the FSIA Congress expressly mentioned officials when it wished to count their acts as equivalent to those of the foreign state, which suggests that officials are not included within the unadorned term "foreign state." For example, Congress provided an exception from the general grant of immunity for cases in which "money damages are sought against a foreign state" for an injury in the United States "caused by the tortious act or omission *of that foreign state or of any official* or employee of that foreign state while acting within the scope of his office." §1605(a)(5) (emphasis added). The same reference to officials is made in a similar, later enacted exception. *See* 28 U.S.C. §1605A(a)(1) (eliminating immunity for suits "in which money damages are sought against a foreign state" for certain acts "engaged in by an official, employee, or agent of such foreign state while acting within the scope of his or her office, employment, or agency"); *see also* §1605A(c) (creating a cause of action against the "foreign state" and "any official, employee, or agent" thereof). If the term "foreign state" by definition includes an individual acting within the scope of his office, the phrase "or of any official or employee . . ." in 28 U.S.C. §1605(a)(5) would be unnecessary.

Other provisions of the statute also point away from reading "foreign state" to include foreign officials. Congress made no express mention of service of process on individuals in §1608(a), which governs service upon a foreign state or political subdivision. Although some of the methods listed could be used to serve individuals—for example, by delivery "in accordance with an applicable international convention," §1608(a)(2)—the methods specified are at best very roundabout ways of serving an individual official. Furthermore, Congress made specific remedial choices for different types of defendants. *See* §1606 (allowing punitive damages for an agency or instrumentality but not for a foreign state); §1610 (affording a plaintiff greater rights to attach the property of an agency or instrumentality as compared to the property of a foreign state). By adopting petitioner's reading of "foreign state," we would subject claims against officials to the more limited remedies available in suits against states, without so much as a whisper from Congress on the subject. (And if we were instead to adopt petitioner's other textual argument, we would subject those claims to the different, more expansive, remedial scheme for agencies). The Act's careful calibration of remedies among the listed types of defendants suggests that Congress did not mean to cover other types of defendants never mentioned in the text. . . .

Petitioner argues that the FSIA is best read to cover his claim to immunity because of its history and purpose. As discussed at the outset, one of the primary purposes of the FSIA was to codify the restrictive theory of sovereign immunity, which Congress recognized as consistent with extant international law. We have observed that a related purpose was "codification of international law at the time of the FSIA's enactment," Permanent Mission of India to United Nations v. City of New York, 551 U.S. 193, 199 (2007), and have examined the relevant common law and international practice when interpreting the Act, *id.* at 200-01. Because of this relationship between the Act and the common law that it codified, petitioner argues that we should construe the FSIA consistently with the common law regarding individual immunity, which—in petitioner's view—was coextensive with the law of state immunity and always immunized a foreign official for acts taken on behalf of the foreign state. Even reading the Act in light of Congress' purpose of codifying *state* sovereign immunity, however, we do not think that the Act codified the common law with respect to the immunity of individual officials.

The canon of construction that statutes should be interpreted consistently with the common law helps us interpret a statute that clearly covers a field formerly governed by the common law. But the canon does not help us to decide the antecedent question whether, when a statute's coverage is ambiguous, Congress intended the statute to govern a particular field—in this case, whether Congress intended the FSIA to supersede the common law of official immunity.[14]

Petitioner argues that because state and official immunities are coextensive, Congress must have codified official immunity when it codified state immunity. But the relationship between a state's immunity and an official's immunity is more complicated than petitioner suggests, although we need not and do not resolve the dispute among the parties as to the precise scope of an official's immunity at common law. The very authority to which petitioner points us, and which we have previously found instructive, *see, e.g., Permanent Mission,* 551 U.S. at 200, states that the immunity of individual officials is subject to a caveat not applicable to any of the other entities or persons[15] to which the foreign state's immunity extends. The Restatement [(Second) of Foreign Relations Law of the United States] provides that the "immunity of a foreign state . . . extends to . . . any other public minister, official, or agent of the state with respect to acts performed in his official capacity *if the effect of exercising jurisdiction would be to enforce a rule of law against the state.*" Restatement §66 (emphasis added).[16] And historically, the Government sometimes suggested immunity under the common law for individual officials even when the foreign state did not qualify. *See, e.g.,* Greenspan v. Crosbie, No. 74 Civ. 4734 (GLG), 1976 U.S. Dist. LEXIS 12155 (SDNY, Nov. 23, 1976). There is therefore little reason to presume that when Congress set out to codify state immunity, it must also have, *sub silentio,* intended to codify official immunity.

Petitioner urges that a suit against an official must always be equivalent to a suit against the state because acts taken by a state official on behalf of a state are acts of the state. We have recognized, in the context of the act of state doctrine, that an

14. We find similarly inapposite petitioner's invocation of the canon that a statute should be interpreted in compliance with international law, see Murray v. Schooner Charming Betsy, 6 U.S. 64, 2 Cranch 64, 118 (1804), and his argument that foreign relations and the reciprocal protection of United States officials abroad would be undermined if we do not adopt his reading of the Act. Because we are not deciding that the FSIA bars petitioner's immunity but rather that the Act does not address the question, we need not determine whether declining to afford immunity to petitioner would be consistent with international law.

15. The *Restatement* does not apply this caveat to the head of state, head of government, or foreign minister. *See* Restatement §66. Whether petitioner may be entitled to head of state immunity, or any other immunity, under the common law is a question we leave open for remand. We express no view on whether Restatement §66 correctly sets out the scope of the common law immunity applicable to current or former foreign officials.

16. Respondents contend that this caveat refers to "the compulsive effect of the judgment on the state," but petitioner disputes that meaning. We need not resolve their dispute, as it is enough for present purposes that the Restatement indicates a foreign official's immunity may turn upon a requirement not applicable to any other type of defendant.

official's acts can be considered the acts of the foreign state, and that "the courts of one country will not sit in judgment" of those acts when done within the territory of the foreign state. *See* Underhill v. Hernandez, 168 U.S. 250, 252, 254 (1897). Although the act of state doctrine is distinct from immunity, and instead "provides foreign states with a substantive defense on the merits," [Republic of Austria v. Altmann, 541 U.S. 677, 700 (2004)], we do not doubt that in some circumstances the immunity of the foreign state extends to an individual for acts taken in his official capacity. But it does not follow from this premise that Congress intended to codify that immunity in the FSIA. It hardly furthers Congress' purpose of "clarifying the rules that judges should apply in resolving sovereign immunity claims," *id.* at 699, to lump individual officials in with foreign states without so much as a word spelling out how and when individual officials are covered.[17]

Petitioner would have a stronger case if there were any indication that Congress' intent to enact a comprehensive solution for suits against states extended to suits against individual officials. . . . [A]lthough questions of official immunity did arise in the pre-FSIA period, they were few and far between.[18] The immunity of officials simply was not the particular problem to which Congress was responding when it enacted the FSIA. . . . We have been given no reason to believe that Congress saw as a problem, or wanted to eliminate, the State Department's role in determinations regarding individual official immunity.[19]

Finally, our reading of the FSIA will not "in effect make the statute optional," as some Courts of Appeals have feared, by allowing litigants through "artful pleading . . . to take advantage of the Act's provisions or, alternatively, choose to proceed under the old common law," Chuidian v. Philippine Nat. Bank, 912 F.2d 1095, 1102 (9th Cir. 1990). Even if a suit is not governed by the Act, it may still be barred by foreign sovereign immunity under the common law. And not every suit can successfully be pleaded against an individual official alone.[20] Even when a plaintiff names only a foreign official, it may be the case that the foreign state itself, its political subdivision, or an agency or instrumentality is a required party, because that party has "an interest relating to the subject of the action" and "disposing of the action in the person's absence may . . . as a practical matter impair or impede the person's ability

---

17. The courts of appeals have had to develop, in the complete absence of any statutory text, rules governing when an official is entitled to immunity under the FSIA. For example, Courts of Appeals have applied the rule that foreign sovereign immunity extends to an individual official "for acts committed in his official capacity" but not to "an official who acts beyond the scope of his authority." *Chuidian*, 912 F.2d at 1103, 1106. That may be correct as a matter of common-law principles, but it does not derive from any clarification or codification by Congress. Furthermore, if Congress intended the FSIA to reach individuals, one would expect the Act to have addressed whether *former* officials are covered, an issue it settled with respect to instrumentalities, see Dole Food Co. v. Patrickson, 538 U.S. 468, 478 (2003) ("[I]nstrumentality status [must] be determined at the time suit is filed").

18. A study that attempted to gather all of the State Department decisions related to sovereign immunity from the adoption of the restrictive theory in 1952 to the enactment of the FSIA reveals only four decisions related to official immunity, and two related to head of state immunity, out of a total of 110 decisions. Sovereign Immunity Decisions of the Dept. of State, May 1952 to Jan. 1977 (M. Sandler, D. Vagts, & B. Ristau eds.), in Digest of U.S. Practice in Int'l Law 1020, 1080 (1977).

19. The FSIA was introduced in accordance with the recommendation of the State Department. The Department sought and supported the elimination of its role with respect to claims against foreign states and their agencies or instrumentalities. But the Department has from the time of the FSIA's enactment understood the Act to leave intact the Department's role in official immunity cases.

20. Furthermore, a plaintiff seeking to sue a foreign official will not be able to rely on the Act's service of process and jurisdictional provisions. Thus, a plaintiff will have to establish that the district court has personal jurisdiction over an official without the benefit of the FSIA provision that makes personal jurisdiction over a foreign state automatic when an exception to immunity applies and service of process has been accomplished in accordance with 28 U.S.C. §1608. . . .

to protect the interest." Fed. Rule Civ. Proc. 19(a)(1)(B). If this is the case, and the entity is immune from suit under the FSIA, the district court may have to dismiss the suit, regardless of whether the official is immune or not under the common law. *See* Republic of Philippines v. Pimentel, 553 U.S. 851, 867 (2008) ("[W]here sovereign immunity is asserted, and the claims of the sovereign are not frivolous, dismissal of the action must be ordered where there is a potential for injury to the interests of the absent sovereign."). Or it may be the case that some actions against an official in his official capacity should be treated as actions against the foreign state itself, as the state is the real party in interest. *Cf.* Kentucky v. Graham, 473 U.S. 159, 166 (1985) ("[A]n official-capacity suit is, in all respects other than name, to be treated as a suit against the entity. It is *not* a suit against the official personally, for the real party in interest is the entity" (citation omitted)).

We are thus not persuaded that our construction of the statute's text should be affected by the risk that plaintiffs may use artful pleading to attempt to select between application of the FSIA or the common law. And we think this case, in which respondents have sued petitioner in his personal capacity and seek damages from his own pockets, is properly governed by the common law because it is not a claim against a foreign state as the Act defines that term. Although Congress clearly intended to supersede the common-law regime for claims against foreign states, we find nothing in the statute's origin or aims to indicate that Congress similarly wanted to codify the law of foreign official immunity.

Yousuf v. Samantar (*Samantar II*)

699 F.3d 763 (4th Cir. 2012)

Traxler, Circuit Judge:

For the second time in this case, we are presented with the question of whether Appellant Mohamed Ali Samantar enjoys immunity from suit under the Torture Victim Protection Act of 1991 ("TVPA"), and the Alien Tort Statute ("ATS"). In the previous appeal, we rejected Samantar's claim to statutory immunity under the Foreign Sovereign Immunities Act ("FSIA"), but held open the possibility that Samantar could "successfully invoke an immunity doctrine arising under pre-FSIA common law." The Supreme Court affirmed our reading of the FSIA and likewise suggested Samantar would have the opportunity to assert common law immunity on remand. *See* Samantar v. Yousuf, 130 S. Ct. 2278, 2293 (2010).

On remand to the district court, Samantar sought dismissal of the claims against him based on common law immunities afforded to heads of state and also to other foreign officials for acts performed in their official capacity. . . .

The district court renewed its request to the State Department for a response to Samantar's immunity claims. Despite having remained silent during Samantar's first appeal, the State Department here took a position expressly opposing immunity for Samantar. The United States submitted to the district court a Statement of Interest (SOI) announcing that the Department of State, having considered "the potential impact of such a[n] [immunity] decision on the foreign relations interests of the United States," had determined that Samantar was not entitled to immunity from plaintiffs' lawsuit. The SOI indicated that two factors were particularly important to the State Department's determination that Samantar should not enjoy immunity. First, the State Department concluded that Samantar's claim for immunity was undermined by the fact that he "is a former official of a state with no currently recognized government to request immunity on his behalf," or to take a position as to "whether the acts in question were taken in an official capacity." Noting that "[t]he immunity protecting foreign officials for their official acts ultimately belongs to the sovereign rather than the official," the government reasoned that Samantar should not be afforded immunity "[i]n the absence of a recognized government . . . to assert or waive [Samantar's] immunity." Second, Samantar's status as a permanent legal resident was particularly relevant to the State Department's immunity determination. According to the SOI, "U.S. residents like Samantar who enjoy the protections of U.S. law ordinarily should be subject to the jurisdiction of our courts, particularly when sued by U.S. residents" or naturalized citizens such as two of the plaintiffs.

The district court denied Samantar's motion to dismiss, apparently viewing the Department of State's position as controlling and surrendering jurisdiction over the issue to the State Department: "The government has determined that the defendant does not have foreign official immunity. Accordingly, defendant's common law sovereign immunity defense is no longer before the Court, which will now proceed to consider the remaining issues in defendant's Motion to Dismiss." But, in denying Samantar's subsequent motion to reconsider, the district court implied that it performed its own analysis and merely took the State Department's view into account: "The Executive Branch has spoken on this issue and . . . [is] entitled to a great deal of deference. *They don't control but they are entitled to deference in this case.*" The district court noted that both "the residency of the defendant" and "the lack of a recognized government" were factors properly considered in the immunity calculus. . . .

Before proceeding further, we must decide the appropriate level of deference courts should give the Executive Branch's view on case-specific questions of individual foreign sovereign immunity. The FSIA displaced the common law regime for resolving questions of foreign *state* immunity and shifted the Executive's role as primary decision maker to the courts. After *Samantar*, it is clear that the FSIA did no such thing with respect to the immunity of *individual* foreign officials; the common law, not the FSIA, continues to govern foreign official immunity. And, in light of the continued viability of the common law for such claims, the Court saw "no reason to believe that Congress saw as a problem, or wanted to eliminate, the State Department's role in determinations regarding individual official immunity" under the common law. The extent of the State Department's role, however, depends in large part on what kind of immunity has been asserted.

In this case, Samantar claims two forms of immunity: (1) head-of-state immunity and (2) "foreign official" or "official acts" immunity. "Head-of-state immunity is a doctrine of customary international law" pursuant to which an incumbent "head of state is immune from the jurisdiction of a foreign state's courts." In re Grand Jury Proceedings, 817 F.2d 1108, 1110 (4th Cir. 1987). "Like the related doctrine of sovereign [state] immunity, the rationale of head-of-state immunity is to promote comity among nations by ensuring that leaders can perform their duties without being subject to detention, arrest or embarrassment in a foreign country's legal system." *Id.*

"A head-of-state recognized by the United States government is absolutely immune from personal jurisdiction in United States courts unless that immunity has been waived by statute or by the foreign government recognized by the United States." Lafontant v. Aristide, 844 F. Supp. 128, 131-32 (E.D.N.Y. 1994). Although all forms of individual immunity derive from the State, head-of-state immunity is tied closely to the sovereign immunity of foreign states.

Samantar also seeks immunity on the separate ground that all of the actions for which plaintiffs seek to hold him liable occurred during the course of his official duties within the Somali government. *See* Restatement (Second) of Foreign Relations Law §66(f) (stating that "[t]he immunity of a foreign state . . . extends to . . . any . . . public minister, official, or agent of the state with respect to acts performed in his official capacity if the effect of exercising jurisdiction would be to enforce a rule of law against the state"); Matar v. Dichter, 563 F.3d 9, 14 (2d Cir. 2009) ("At the time the FSIA was enacted, the common law of foreign sovereign immunity recognized an individual official's entitlement to immunity for acts performed in his official capacity."); *Samantar*, 130 S. Ct. at 2290-91 ("[W]e do not doubt that in some circumstances the immunity of the foreign state extends to an individual for acts taken in his official capacity."). This is a conduct-based immunity that applies to current and former foreign officials. *See Matar*, 563 F.3d at 14 ("An immunity based on acts—rather than status—does not depend on tenure in office.").

The United States, participating as *amicus curiae*, takes the position that federal courts owe absolute deference to the State Department's view of whether a foreign official is entitled to sovereign immunity on either ground. According to the government, under long-established Supreme Court precedent, the State Department's opinion on any foreign immunity issue is binding upon the courts. The State Department's position allows for the federal courts to function as independent decision makers on foreign sovereign immunity questions in only one instance: when the State Department remains silent on a particular case.[3] Thus, the United States contends that the State Department resolved the issues once it presented the district court with its view that Samantar was not entitled to immunity.

Samantar, by contrast, advocates the view that deference to the Executive's immunity determination is required *only when the State Department explicitly recommends that immunity be granted.* Samantar argues that when the State Department concludes, as it did in this case, that a foreign official is not entitled to immunity or remains silent on the issue, courts can and must decide independently whether to grant immunity. And, the plaintiffs offer yet a third view, suggesting that the State Department's position on foreign sovereign immunity does not completely control, but that courts must defer "to the reasonable views of the Executive Branch" regardless of whether the State Department suggests that immunity be granted or denied. In this case, plaintiffs contend the State Department's rationale for urging denial of immunity, as set forth in its SOI, was reasonable and that the district court properly deferred to it. . . .

It was not until the late 1930s—in the context of *in rem* actions against foreign ships—that judicial deference to executive foreign immunity determinations emerged as standard practice. . . . Citing a line of cases involving ships owned by foreign sovereigns, *Samantar* explained that

> a two-step procedure developed for resolving a foreign state's claim of sovereign immunity, typically asserted on behalf of seized vessels. . . . Under that procedure, the diplomatic representative of the sovereign could request a "suggestion of immunity" from the State Department. [Ex parte Peru, 318 U.S. 578, 581 (1943).] If the request was

---

3. Even then, however, the State Department insists that the courts must fashion a decision based on principles that it has articulated. *See Samantar*, 130 S. Ct. at 2284. In making this argument, the government fails to distinguish between status-based and conduct-based immunity.

granted, the district court surrendered its jurisdiction. . . . But "in the absence of recognition of the immunity by the Department of State," a district court "had authority to decide for itself whether all the requisites for such immunity existed." Ex parte Peru, 318 U.S. at 587 . . . .

Samantar, 130 S. Ct. at 2284. Subsequently, there was a shift in State Department policy from a theory of absolute immunity to restrictive immunity, but this shift "had little, if any, impact on federal courts' approach to immunity analyses . . . and courts continued to abide by that Department's suggestions of immunity." Republic of Austria v. Altmann, 541 U.S. 677, 690 (2004). Thus, at the time that Congress enacted the FSIA, the clearly established practice of judicial deference to executive immunity determinations had been expressed largely in admiralty cases.

In this pre-FSIA era, decisions involving claims of *individual* foreign sovereign immunity were scarce. *See Samantar*, 130 S. Ct. at 2291 (noting that "questions of official immunity . . . in the pre-FSIA period . . . were few and far between"). But, to the extent such individual claims arose, they generally involved status-based immunities such as head-of-state immunity, *see, e.g.*, Ye v. Zemin, 383 F.3d 620, 624-25 (7th Cir. 2004), or diplomatic immunity arising under international treaties. The rare cases involving immunity asserted by lower-level foreign officials provided inconsistent results.

The Constitution assigns the power to "receive Ambassadors and other public Ministers" to the Executive Branch, U.S. Const. art. II, §3, which includes, by implication, the power to accredit diplomats and recognize foreign heads of state. Courts have generally treated executive "suggestions of immunity" for heads of state as a function of the Executive's constitutional power and, therefore, as controlling on the judiciary. . . .

Accordingly, consistent with the Executive's constitutionally delegated powers and the historical practice of the courts, we conclude that the State Department's pronouncement as to head-of-state immunity is entitled to absolute deference. The State Department has never recognized Samantar as the head of state for Somalia; indeed, the State Department does not recognize the Transitional Federal Government or any other entity as the official government of Somalia, from which immunity would derive in the first place. The district court properly deferred to the State Department's position that Samantar be denied head-of-state immunity.

Unlike head-of-state immunity and other status-based immunities, there is no equivalent constitutional basis suggesting that the views of the Executive Branch control questions of foreign official immunity. Such cases do not involve any act of recognition for which the Executive Branch is constitutionally empowered; rather, they simply involve matters about the scope of defendant's official duties.

This is not to say, however, that the Executive Branch has no role to play in such suits. These immunity decisions turn upon principles of customary international law and foreign policy, areas in which the courts respect, but do not automatically follow, the views of the Executive Branch. . . . With respect to foreign official immunity, the Executive Branch still informs the court about the diplomatic effect of the court's exercising jurisdiction over claims against an official of a foreign state, and the Executive Branch may urge the court to grant or deny official-act immunity based on such considerations. . . .

In sum, we give absolute deference to the State Department's position on status-based immunity doctrines such as head-of-state immunity. The State Department's determination regarding conduct-based immunity, by contrast, is not controlling, but it carries substantial weight in our analysis of the issue. . . .

We turn to the remaining question of whether Samantar is entitled to foreign official immunity under the common law. In considering the contours of foreign official immunity, we must draw from the relevant principles found in both international and domestic immunity law, as well as the experience and judgment of the State Department, to which we give considerable, but not controlling, weight.

From the earliest Supreme Court decisions, international law has shaped the development of the common law of foreign sovereign immunity. . . . Indeed, an important purpose of the FSIA was the "codification of international law at the time of the FSIA's enactment." *Samantar*, 130 S. Ct. at 2289. Even after the FSIA was enacted, international law continued to be relevant to questions of foreign sovereign immunity as the Court interpreted the FSIA in light of international law.

As previously noted, customary international law has long distinguished between status-based immunity afforded to sitting heads-of-state and conduct-based immunity available to other foreign officials, including former heads-of-state. With respect to conduct-based immunity, foreign officials are immune from "claims arising out of their official acts while in office." Restatement (Third) of Foreign Relations Law §464, reprt. note 14; *Matar*, 563 F.3d at 14 ("An immunity based on acts—rather than status—does not depend on tenure in office."). This type of immunity stands on the foreign official's actions, not his or her status, and therefore applies whether the individual is currently a government official or not. . . . This conduct-based immunity for a foreign official derives from the immunity of the State: "The doctrine of the imputability of the acts of the individual to the State . . . in classical law . . . imputes the act solely to the state, who alone is responsible for its consequence. In consequence any act performed by the individual as an act of the State enjoys the immunity which the State enjoys." Hazel Fox, The Law of State Immunity at 455 (2d ed. 2008).

At least as early as its decision in Underhill v. Hernandez, 168 U.S. 250, 252 (1897), the Supreme Court embraced the international law principle that sovereign immunity, which belongs to a foreign *state*, extends to an individual *official* acting on behalf of that foreign state. By the time the FSIA was enacted, numerous domestic courts had embraced the notion, stemming from international law, that "[t]he immunity of a foreign state . . . extends to . . . any . . . public minister, official, or agent of the state with respect to acts performed in his official capacity if the effect of exercising jurisdiction would be to enforce a rule of law against the state." Restatement (Second) of Foreign Relations Law §66(f). Although the context for these cases was different—almost all involved the erroneous (pre-*Samantar*) application of the FSIA to individual foreign officials claiming immunity—these decisions are instructive for post-*Samantar* questions of common law immunity. . . .

These cases sketch out the general contours of official-act immunity: a foreign official may assert immunity for official acts performed within the scope of his duty, but not for private acts where "the officer purports to act as an individual and not as an official, [such that] a suit directed against that action is not a suit against the sovereign." [Chuidian v. Philippine National Bank, 912 F.2d 1095, 1106 (9th Cir. 1990).] A foreign official or former head-of-state will therefore not be able to assert this immunity for private acts that are not arguably attributable to the state, such as drug possession or fraud. *See, e.g.,* In re Doe, 860 F.2d 40, 45 (2d Cir. 1988) ("[W]ere we to reach the merits of the issue, we believe there is respectable authority for denying head-of-state immunity to a former head-of-state for private or criminal acts in violation of American law.").

In response, plaintiffs contend that Samantar cannot raise this immunity as a shield against atrocities such as torture, genocide, indiscriminate executions and prolonged arbitrary imprisonment or any other act that would violate a *jus cogens* norm of international law. . . . Unlike private acts that do not come within the scope of foreign official immunity, *jus cogens* violations may well be committed under color of law and, in that sense, constitute acts performed in the course of the foreign official's employment by the Sovereign. However, as a matter of international and domestic law, *jus cogens* violations are, by definition, acts that are not officially authorized by the Sovereign. . . .[6]

There has been an increasing trend in international law to abrogate foreign official immunity for individuals who commit acts, otherwise attributable to the State, that violate *jus cogens* norms—i.e., they commit international crimes or human rights violations. . . .

American courts have generally followed the foregoing trend, concluding that *jus cogens* violations are not legitimate official acts and therefore do not merit foreign official immunity but still recognizing that head-of-state immunity, based on status, is of an absolute nature and applies even against *jus cogens* claims. . . . We conclude that, under international and domestic law, officials from other countries are not entitled to foreign official immunity for *jus cogens* violations, even if the acts were performed in the defendant's official capacity.

Moreover, we find Congress's enactment of the TVPA, and the policies it reflects, to be both instructive and consistent with our view of the common law regarding these aspects of *jus cogens*. Plaintiffs asserted claims against Samantar under the TVPA which authorizes a civil cause of action against "[a]n individual who, under actual or apparent authority, or color of law, of any foreign nation . . . subjects an individual to torture" or "extrajudicial killing." "The TVPA thus recognizes explicitly what was perhaps implicit in the Act of 1789—that the law of nations is incorporated into the law of the United States and that a violation of the international law of human rights is (at least with regard to torture) *ipso facto* a violation of U.S. domestic law." Wiwa v. Royal Dutch Petroleum Co., 226 F.3d 88, 105 (2d Cir. 2000). Thus, in enacting the TVPA, Congress essentially created an express private right of action for individuals victimized by torture and extrajudicial killing that constitute violations of *jus cogens* norms. . . .

In its SOI, the State Department submitted a suggestion of non-immunity. The SOI highlighted the fact that Samantar "is a former official of a state with no currently recognized government to request immunity on his behalf" or to take a position as to "whether the acts in question were taken in an official capacity." Noting that "[t]he immunity protecting foreign officials for their official acts ultimately belongs to the sovereign rather than the official," the government reasoned that Samantar should not be afforded immunity "[i]n the absence of a recognized government . . . to assert or waive [Samantar's] immunity." The second major basis for the State Department's view that Samantar was not entitled to immunity was Samantar's status as a permanent legal resident. According to the SOI, "U.S. residents like Samantar who enjoy the protections of U.S. law ordinarily should be

---

6. In spite of this, allegations of *jus cogens* violations do not overcome head-of-state or any other status-based immunity. *See, e.g.,* Case Concerning the Arrest Warrant of 11 April 2000 (Democratic Republic of Congo v. Belgium) (2002) ICJ 3 (concluding that the sitting foreign minister of the Democratic Republic of Congo was entitled to status-based immunity against alleged *jus cogens* violations).

subject to the jurisdiction of the courts, particularly when sued by U.S. residents" or naturalized citizens such as two of the plaintiffs.

Both of these factors add substantial weight in favor of denying immunity. Because the State Department has not officially recognized a Somali government, the court does not face the usual risk of offending a foreign nation by exercising jurisdiction over the plaintiffs' claims. Likewise, as a permanent legal resident, Samantar has a binding tie to the United States and its court system.

Because this case involves acts that violated *jus cogens* norms, including torture, extrajudicial killings and prolonged arbitrary imprisonment of politically and ethnically disfavored groups, we conclude that Samantar is not entitled to conduct-based official immunity under the common law, which in this area incorporates international law. Moreover, the SOI has supplied us with additional reasons to support this conclusion. Thus, we affirm the district court's denial of Samantar's motion to dismiss based on foreign official immunity.

Notes and Questions

1. The FSIA applies to any suit against a "foreign state," which is defined to include "a political subdivision of a foreign state or an agency or instrumentality of a foreign state." 28 U.S.C. §1603(a). Prior to the Supreme Court's decision in *Samantar*, a number of federal circuit courts had interpreted these terms to include foreign officials sued for actions taken in their official capacity. The leading decision was Chuidian v. Philippine National Bank, 912 F.2d 1095 (9th Cir. 1990). In that case, a Philippine citizen brought suit against a member of a Philippine governmental commission, after the defendant had instructed a bank to dishonor a letter of credit that had been issued by a prior government of the Philippines. Noting that foreign officials received common law immunity before enactment of the FSIA, the court reasoned that it would be "illogical" to think that Congress in the FSIA eliminated the application of sovereign immunity to individuals "implicitly and without comment." The court added that "to allow unrestricted suits against individual foreign officials acting in their official capacities . . . [would allow] litigants to accomplish indirectly what the Act barred them from doing directly," and "would defeat the purposes of the Act." The court concluded that individual officials who act on behalf of the state can reasonably be considered "agencies or instrumentalities" of the state for purposes of the FSIA. Several other circuit courts subsequently adopted *Chuidian*'s interpretation of the FSIA.

2. *Chuidian* was not a human rights case, and human rights litigation under the *Filartiga* line of cases proceeded for many years, both before and after *Chuidian*, without much attention to the issue of individual official immunity. To the extent courts considered the issue, most concluded that, when officials committed human rights abuses, they were not acting in an official capacity, although the courts did not always explain why that was the case. Some of these courts referred to foreign law to determine the scope of the official's authority and found that the alleged human rights violations exceeded anything that could plausibly be considered within that authority. Other courts appear to have assumed that human rights abuses are *per se* unauthorized acts.

Eventually, greater conflict developed between the *Chuidian* line of decisions and human rights litigation. In several cases alleging war crimes and human rights violations by Israeli officials, courts held that suits against foreign officials for their official acts, even if those acts constituted human rights abuses, were covered by the FSIA. *See* Belhas v. Ya'alon, 515 F.3d 1279, 1284 (D.C. Cir. 2008); Matar v. Dichter, 500 F. Supp. 2d 284, 291 (S.D.N.Y. 2009), *aff'd on other grounds*, 563 F.3d 9 (2d Cir. 2009); Doe I v. State of Israel, 400 F. Supp. 2d 86, 104-05 (D.D.C. 2005). As one court explained, "[a]ll allegations stem from actions taken on behalf of the state and, in essence, the personal capacity suits amount to suits against the officers for being Israeli government officials." *Doe I*, 400 F. Supp. 2d at 105. Meanwhile, a conflict in the circuits developed over whether the FSIA applied to suits against individual foreign officials, a conflict resolved by the Supreme Court in *Samantar*.

3. Why does the Court in *Samantar* reject *Chuidian*'s "agency or instrumentality" construction of the FSIA? Should the Court have given more weight to the fact that Congress had been on notice of this construction of the statute for 20 years and had not overturned it? If the State Department had not objected to that construction, would the case have come out differently?

4. The petitioner's principal argument on appeal in *Samantar* was not that he was an "agency or instrumentality" of Somalia, although he argued that in the alternative. Rather, his principal argument was that a suit against a foreign official for actions taken in an official capacity should be treated as a suit "against the foreign state" for purposes of the FSIA. There were suggestions of this idea in some of the lower court decisions. *See, e.g.*, In re Terrorist Attacks on September 11, 2001, 538 F.3d 71, 84 (2d Cir. 2009) ("[A] claim against an agency of state power, including a state officer acting in his official capacity, can be in effect a claim against the state."); *Chuidian*, 912 F.2d at 1101 ("[A] suit against an individual acting in his official capacity is the practical equivalent of a suit against the sovereign directly.").

Why does the Court in *Samantar* reject this construction of the FSIA?

5. In *Samantar*, the Court places a lot of emphasis on the text of the FSIA. Which textual points do you find most persuasive? Which textual points do you find least persuasive? In footnote 17, one of the reasons the Court gives for not construing the FSIA to cover suits against foreign officials is the lack of statutory guidance on questions that these suits would implicate, such as the distinction between personal-capacity and official-capacity suits and whether immunity extends to former officials. After this decision, won't courts still be required to resolve those issues? If so, why is it better that they do so without reference to the FSIA?

6. The Court in *Samantar* concludes that the FSIA did not displace the common law of foreign official immunity, and it makes clear that "[e]ven if a suit is not governed by the Act, it may still be barred by foreign sovereign immunity under the common law." The Restatement (Second) of Foreign Relations Law of the United States, published in 1965, stated that under the common law a foreign state's immunity extended to an official or agent of a state "with respect to acts performed in his official capacity if the effect of exercising jurisdiction would be to enforce a rule of law against the state." (The Restatement (Third) does not address the topic.) The Court in *Samantar* does not take a position on whether the Restatement (Second)'s description of the common law is accurate. The Court does state, however, that "we do not doubt that in some circumstances the immunity of the foreign state extends to an individual for acts taken in his official capacity."

What is the significance of the qualification in the Restatement (Second) that the effect of the exercise of jurisdiction must "be to enforce a rule of law against the state"? The respondents in *Samantar* argued that this meant that a foreign official is protected by the state's immunity only when the judgment would be enforceable against the state. The petitioner argued, by contrast, that enforcing a rule of law against a state includes sitting in legal judgment on the state's official conduct.

7. What status does the common law of foreign official immunity have in the U.S. legal system? Is it *federal* common law? If so, what is the source of the courts' authority to develop this body of federal law? What materials should courts draw upon in developing it? International law? The policies reflected in the FSIA? The past practices and views of the Executive Branch? Something else? For a discussion of these and related issues, see Curtis A. Bradley & Laurence R. Helfer, *International Law and the U.S. Common Law of Foreign Official Immunity*, 2010 Sup. Ct. Rev. 213, and Ingrid Wuerth, *Foreign Official Immunity Determinations in U.S. Courts: The Case Against the State Department*, 51 Va. J. Int'l L. 915 (2011).

8. The petitioner in *Samantar* had argued that, under customary international law, a state's immunity covered a suit against a state official for actions taken in an official capacity, and the petitioner noted that the FSIA was designed in part to reflect the international law of sovereign immunity. Furthermore, the petitioner cited a well-settled canon of construction, known as the "*Charming Betsy* canon," whereby ambiguous statutes are to be construed so that they do not violate international law (this canon is discussed below in Section F). What is the Court's response to these international law arguments? The Court's approach can be contrasted with that of the British House of Lords in a 2006 decision, in which that court relied extensively on international law in construing the reference to "State" in the United Kingdom State Immunity Act as covering suits against foreign officials for actions taken in their official capacity. *See* Jones v. Ministry of the Interior of the Kingdom of Saudi Arabia, [2006] UKHL 26, [2007] 1 A.C. 270.

It is generally agreed that customary international law confers two types of immunity on individual officials—status immunity and conduct immunity. Status immunity protects particular types of government officials from civil suit or criminal prosecution in foreign courts, even for their private conduct, but only while the official is in office. This form of immunity applies to "heads of state" (a category that includes presidents, prime ministers, monarchs, and foreign ministers) as well as accredited diplomats. Conduct immunity protects all government officials who act on behalf of the state from civil suit or criminal prosecution in foreign courts, even after they leave office, but only for actions by the official in the discharge of his or her functions while in office. In a case involving a criminal arrest warrant issued against a sitting foreign minister, the International Court of Justice confirmed that *status* immunity for a head of state exists as a matter of customary international law, even for egregious human rights abuses. *See* Case Concerning the Arrest Warrant of 11 April 2000 (Democratic Republic of the Congo v. Belgium) (merits), 2002 ICJ Rep 3. There is more uncertainty, however, about whether and to what extent officials are entitled to *conduct* immunity when sued for human rights abuses. *See generally* Bradley & Helfer, *International Law and the U.S. Common Law of Foreign Official Immunity, supra.* Should the Court in *Samantar* have considered this question?

9. Most courts had concluded before *Samantar* that, even if the FSIA applied to lower-level foreign officials acting in an official capacity, it did not apply to heads of state. Nevertheless, almost every court to address the issue had recognized a doctrine of "head-of-state immunity." In addition, courts almost always granted head-of-state immunity when the Executive Branch suggested it. *See, e.g.*, Ye v. Zemin, 383 F.3d 620 (7th Cir. 2004) (granting immunity to China's president); Tachiona v. Mugabe, 169 F. Supp. 2d 259 (S.D.N.Y. 2001) (granting immunity to Zimbabwe's president and foreign minister); Lafontant v. Aristide, 844 F. Supp. 128 (E.D.N.Y.

1994) (granting immunity to exiled president of Haiti); Alicog v. Kingdom of Saudi Arabia, 860 F. Supp. 369, 382 (S.D. Tex. 1994) (granting immunity to king of Saudi Arabia); Saltany v. Reagan, 702 F. Supp. 319, 320 (D.D.C. 1988) (granting immunity to prime minister of Great Britain).

In cases in which the Executive Branch suggested it, courts also extended head-of-state immunity to certain other high-level officials and immediate family members of heads of state. *See, e.g.,* Kline v. Keneko, 535 N.Y.S.2d 303 (Sup. Ct. 1988) (granting immunity to the President's wife), *aff'd mem. sub nom.* Kline v. Cordero de la Madrid, 546 N.Y.S. 2d 506 (App. Div. 1989); Kilroy v. Windsor, No. C-78-291, slip op. (N.D. Ohio, Dec. 7, 1978) (unpublished) (granting immunity to Prince Charles of England); Chong Boon Kim v. Kim Yong Shik, 58 Am. J. Int'l L. 186 (Haw. Cir. Ct., Sept. 9, 1963) (granting immunity to foreign minister). *But see* El-Hadad v. Embassy of the U.A.E., 60 F. Supp. 2d 69, 82 n.10 (D.D.C. 1999) (reasoning that head-of-state immunity is limited to heads of state); Republic of Philippines v. Marcos, 665 F. Supp. 793, 797 (N.D. Cal. 1987) (refusing to grant immunity to Philippine solicitor general, despite suggestion of immunity from the State Department).

Some courts suggested that an Executive suggestion was a prerequisite for immunity. *See, e.g.,* Jungquist v. Nahyan, 940 F. Supp. 312, 321 (D.D.C. 1996). Other courts relied on the lack of an Executive suggestion simply as a factor weighing against immunity. *See, e.g.,* First American Corp. v. Al-Nahyan, 948 F. Supp. 1107, 1121 (D.D.C. 1996). Other courts reasoned that, when lacking guidance from the Executive, a court should decide for itself whether the head of state is entitled to immunity. *See* In re Doe, 860 F.2d 40, 45 (2d Cir. 1988); Abiola v. Abubakar, 267 F. Supp. 2d 907, 915 (N.D. Ill. 2003).

Courts also held that a foreign state may waive a head-of-state's immunity. *See, e.g.,* In re Doe, 860 F.2d 40, 44-45 (2d Cir. 1988); In re Grand Jury Proceedings, 817 F.2d 1108, 1111 (4th Cir. 1987); Paul v. Avril, 812 F. Supp. 207, 210 (S.D. Fla. 1992). These courts reasoned that "[b]ecause it is the state that gives the power to lead and the ensuing trappings of power—including immunity—the state may therefore take back that which it bestowed upon its erstwhile leaders." *Doe,* 860 F.2d at 45. *Cf. Lafontant,* 844 F. Supp. at 134 (declining to recognize waiver by ostensible new government of Haiti because the Executive Branch had not recognized the new government as legitimate).

In a number of instances, claims of immunity by former heads of state were resolved on the basis of a waiver by the ex-head of state's new government. Some courts suggested in dicta that former-head-of-state immunity does not extend to private (as opposed to official) acts. *See, e.g.,* In re Doe, 860 F.2d at 44; Republic of the Philippines v. Marcos, 806 F.2d 344, 360 (2d Cir. 1986); United States v. Noriega, 746 F. Supp. 1506, 1519 n.11 (S.D. Fla. 1990). At least one court questioned the availability of any immunity for former heads of state. *See* Roxas v. Marcos, 969 P.2d 1209, 1252 (Haw. 1998). *But cf.* Abiola v. Abubakar, 267 F. Supp. 2d 907, 916 (N.D. Ill. 2003) (reasoning that "the rationale for head-of-state-immunity is no less implicated when a former head of state is sued in a United States court for acts committed while head of state than it is when a sitting head of state is sued").

10. What if the Executive suggests that a court *deny* immunity to a head of state—is that suggestion also binding? There have not been many cases raising this question. Consider, however, United States v. Noriega, 117 F.3d 1206 (11th Cir. 1997). That case involved the criminal trial and prosecution of Manuel Noriega, a Panamanian general who had become the de facto leader of Panama after its democratically elected leader was ousted from power. In December 1989, the United

States sent troops to Panama, seized Noriega, and brought him to the United States. He was subsequently tried on various charges relating to cocaine trafficking. One of his defenses was that he had head-of-state immunity from prosecution. The U.S. Court of Appeals for the Eleventh Circuit rejected this argument, reasoning that "[t]he Executive Branch has not merely refrained from taking a position on this matter; to the contrary, by pursuing Noriega's capture and this prosecution, the Executive Branch has manifested its clear sentiment that Noriega should be denied head-of-state immunity."

11. After *Samantar*, will courts be bound by State Department suggestions of immunity in cases brought against foreign officials? What about State Department suggestions of non-immunity? Does allowing the Executive Branch to determine how courts resolve immunity determinations in pending cases raise separation of powers concerns? As discussed above in Section D, the Supreme Court had allowed the Executive Branch to exercise this authority prior to the enactment of the FSIA. But by the 1970s, this regime had become controversial, and Congress in the FSIA sought to make immunity determinations less political by shifting them to the courts and away from the Executive Branch. Is the decision in *Samantar* inconsistent with this purpose? The Court notes that there were not many cases prior to the FSIA's enactment that involved foreign official immunity, and the Court thinks this means that Congress had not "[seen] as a problem, or wanted to eliminate, the State Department's role in determinations regarding individual official immunity." But what about the fact that these individual official cases are now more common, in part because of the rise of ATS litigation after the 1980 decision in *Filartiga?* For an argument that courts should not treat State Department suggestions of immunity or non-immunity as binding, see Wuerth, *Foreign Official Immunity Determinations: The Case Against the State Department, supra.*

The Executive Branch has claimed since *Samantar* that courts should defer to it whenever it suggests individual official immunity, even for lower level officials and officials no longer in office. A number of courts have agreed, in cases involving current or former heads of state. *See, e.g.,* Manoharan v. Rajapaksa, 711 F.3d 178 (D.C. Cir. 2013) (sitting head of state of Sri Lanka); Habyarimana v. Kagame, 696 F.3d 1029 (10th Cir. 2012) (sitting head of state of Rwanda); Giraldo v. Drummond, 808 F. Supp. 2d 247 (D.D.C. 2011) (former head of state of Columbia).

12. Consider the Fourth Circuit's decision in *Samantar II*, excerpted above. Does the court's distinction between status immunity and conduct immunity make sense? Why does the Executive Branch's role in receiving ambassadors warrant absolute deference for the former but not the latter? What is the basis for the court's conclusion that conduct immunity does not apply to alleged *jus cogens* violations? Is the court saying that international law currently recognizes a *jus cogens* limitation on conduct immunity in civil cases, or simply that international law allows nations to adopt such a limitation if they choose to do so? If it is the latter, should this decision for the United States be made by the federal courts, or by the political branches of the government? Look at footnote 6 of the court's opinion. Why would there be a *jus cogens* limitation on conduct immunity but not status immunity? Does this decision, if accepted by other courts, mean that there will be no conduct immunity defense in, for example, a suit against an Israeli official for alleged war crimes in Gaza, or against a Chinese official for alleged torture of members of the Falun Gong?

13. As discussed in Section B, Congress enacted the TVPA in 1992. Even if courts should ordinarily confer immunity on foreign officials in ATS cases, such immunity might be less appropriate in cases brought under the TVPA. After all, in creating a cause of action for instances of torture and extrajudicial killing, the TVPA specifically requires that the defendant have acted "under actual or apparent authority, or color of law, of any foreign nation." The TVPA thus appears to be specifically targeted at the actions of foreign officials. On the other hand, the TVPA does not mention immunity. Should courts assume that Congress has not abrogated foreign official immunity absent an express statement to that effect from Congress? Why do you think Congress did not mention immunity in the TVPA? If foreign officials sued under the TVPA are entitled to immunity for official acts of torture and killing, would the TVPA be a dead letter? For a decision holding that the TVPA does not override head of state immunity, see Manoharan v. Rajapaksa, 711 F.3d 178 (D.C. Cir. 2013).

14. The following two court of appeals decisions illustrate contrasting views of the scope of foreign official immunity and its relationship to the TVPA:

a. In Lewis v. Mutond, 918 F.3d 142 (D.C. Cir. 2019), the D.C. Circuit considered a suit brought by a U.S. citizen against two officials of the Democratic Republic of the Congo (DRC). The plaintiff alleged that the defendants had subjected him to torture in the DRC, and he sought damages under the TVPA. Relying on the Restatement (Second) of the Foreign Relations Law of the United States, the court held that, absent a suggestion of immunity from the State Department, foreign officials have conduct immunity under U.S. common law only when exercising jurisdiction over them would have the effect of enforcing the rule of law against the foreign state. This standard requires, reasoned the court, that "a judgment against the official would bind (or be enforceable against) the foreign state." That was not true in this case, said the court: "Defendants have not proffered anything to show that Plaintiff seeks to draw on the DRC's treasury or force the state to take specific action, as would be the case if the judgment were enforceable against the state. Defendants in this case are being sued in their individual capacities and Plaintiff is not seeking compensation out of state funds." The court further stated: "In cases like this one, in which the plaintiff pursues an individual-capacity claim seeking relief against an official in a personal capacity, exercising jurisdiction does not enforce a rule against the foreign state." Two of the three judges on the panel also concluded that, in any event, the TVPA displaces the conduct immunity of foreign officials.

b. In Dogan v. Barak, 932 F.3d 888 (9th Cir. 2019), the Ninth Circuit considered a suit brought against a former Israeli Defense Minister under the TVPA. The suit concerned actions taken by the Israeli military as part of a naval blockade of the Gaza strip that resulted in the death of the plaintiffs' family member. The State Department had filed a Suggestion of Immunity in the case. The court reasoned that, even if the State Department's suggestion was not entitled to absolute deference, the defendant was entitled to immunity because exercising jurisdiction over him in this case would amount to enforcing a rule of law against Israel. This was so, the court explained, because the defendant's actions were alleged to have been carried out as part of official governmental policy: "The Complaint's claims for relief state—several times—that [the defendant's] actions were done under 'actual or apparent authority, or color of law, of the Israeli Ministry of Defense and the Government of the State of Israel.'" The court also held that the TVPA did not override foreign official immunity and that there was no exception to that immunity for *jus cogens* violations.

Is there any way of reconciling these decisions, or are they simply in conflict? Do you think courts are influenced in their immunity analysis by the particular country that the official is from, e.g., by whether the country is an ally of the United States? If so, might that be an argument in favor of deferring to the Executive Branch?

15. An increasing number of international human rights claims have been directed against the U.S. government and its officials. The U.S. government is immune from suit in U.S. courts, however, except to the extent that it has waived its immunity. Moreover, courts have held that any waiver of immunity must be explicit. The U.S. government's waiver of immunity for tort claims is set forth in the Federal Tort Claims Act (FTCA), 28 U.S.C. §1346(b)(1), §§2671-80. This waiver is subject to procedural requirements (such as exhaustion of administrative remedies) and various exceptions. The exceptions include the retention of immunity for "[a]ny claim arising in a foreign country." 28 U.S.C. §2680(k). In Sosa v. Alvarez-Machain, the Supreme Court (in a portion of the decision not excerpted above in Section B) rejected a "headquarters doctrine" limitation on this provision that had been adopted by some lower courts, whereby the U.S. government would have been subject to suit for acts or omissions in the United States that caused harm abroad. The FTCA also retains sovereign immunity for (a) "any claim . . . based upon the exercise or performance or the failure to exercise or perform a discretionary function or duty on the part of a federal agency or an employee of the Government, whether or not the discretion be abused," and (b) "any claim arising out of the combatant activities of the military or naval forces, or the Coast Guard, during time of war." 28 U.S.C. §2680(a), (j).

The Federal Employers Liability Reform and Tort Compensation Act of 1988 (also known as the "Westfall Act") further provides that, for civil actions arising out of the wrongful acts of an employee acting within the scope of his or her official duties, the U.S. government is to be substituted as the defendant and the action is to proceed only under the FTCA. See 28 U.S.C. §2679(b)(1), (d)(1). Although this provision does not apply to an action "which is brought for a violation of a statute of the United States under which such action against an individual is otherwise authorized," 28 U.S.C. §2679(b)(2)(B), courts have held that the ATS does not constitute such a statute, a holding that appears to be further supported by the Supreme Court's conclusion in Sosa that the ATS does not create a cause of action. The TVPA could arguably constitute such a statute, but it applies only to actions taken under color of foreign law and thus is normally inapplicable to actions by the U.S. government and its officials. In Saleh v. Bush, 848 F.3d 880 (9th Cir. 2017), the U.S. Court of Appeals for the Ninth Circuit held that the Westfall Act barred a suit against officials of the George W. Bush Administration for allegedly violating international law in waging war against Iraq.

Detainees at the Guantanamo Bay naval base have sued various U.S. military and civilian officials under the ATS for alleged torture and other mistreatment. In Rasul v. Bush, 542 U.S. 466 (2004), which as discussed in Chapter 10 held that U.S. courts could hear habeas corpus challenges filed on behalf of the Guantanamo detainees, the Supreme Court observed near the end of its opinion that aliens detained in military custody are not categorically excluded from the "privilege of litigation" in U.S. courts, and it noted that the ATS "explicitly confers the privilege of suing for an actionable 'tort . . . committed in violation of the law of nations or a treaty of the United States' on aliens alone." Nevertheless, courts have subsequently rejected such ATS claims against U.S. officials, based on the FTCA and Westfall Act. See, e.g., Rasul v. Myers, 512 F.3d 644 (D.C. Cir. 2008).

Suits against the U.S. government and its officials concerning their foreign affairs activities are also particularly likely to implicate the political question doctrine. See, e.g., Schneider v. Kissinger, 310 F. Supp. 2d 251 (D.D.C. 2004) (holding that political question doctrine barred judicial consideration of claims against the former national security advisor for allegedly having assisted in a failed coup attempt in Chile in 1970); Bancoult v. McNamara, 370 F. Supp. 2d 1 (D.D.C. 2004) (holding that political question doctrine barred judicial consideration of claims against the U.S. government for alleged forcible removal of indigenous population on islands in the Indian Ocean in the 1960s and 1970s).

Finally, while the Court once inferred implied rights of action under the Constitution in suits for damages against government officials, *see* Bivens v. Six Unknown Fed. Narcotics Agents, 403 U.S. 388 (1971) (persons injured by federal officers who violated the prohibition against unreasonable search and seizures can sue for damages under Fourth Amendment), in recent years the Court has been very reluctant to do so. Consider Ziglar v. Abbasi, 137 S. Ct. 1843 (2017), where the Court in a 4-2 decision (with Justices Sotomayor, Kagan, and Gorsuch not participating) held that illegal aliens detained in allegedly harsh conditions in the United States in the aftermath of the September 11 terrorist attacks could not sue officials of the federal government for damages under the Fourth and Fifth Amendments. The Court noted that *Bivens* was decided in an era in which implying causes of actions and judicial remedies was commonplace, but that this practice was now "disfavored," and that Congress should presumptively determine the availability of new causes of action. It then explained that a *Bivens* remedy should not be extended to new contexts and must, in any event, take into account "special factors counseling hesitation" in the creation of such a remedy. The Court concluded that detention policy after 9/11 was a new context that bore little resemblance to prior cases recognizing a *Bivens* remedy. It also ruled that there were a number of special factors that weighed against allowing a *Bivens* claim, including concerns about intruding into "sensitive functions of the Executive Branch" and inquiring into "sensitive issues of national security" that were the prerogative of Congress and the President. Note that although *Ziglar* concerned *constitutional* causes of action, it relied on separation of powers principles similar to ones invoked in cases that refuse to imply statutory causes of action. Note also that Jesner v. Arab Bank, excerpted above in Section C, relied heavily on *Ziglar* in concluding that courts should not recognize a cause of action in suits against foreign corporations under the Alien Tort Statute. *See Jesner*, 138 S. Ct. at 1402-03.

F. THE *CHARMING BETSY* CANON

The materials below consider the influence that customary international law can have on the interpretation of federal statutes.

Ma v. Reno

208 F.3d 815 (9th Cir. 2000), *reaffirmed and amended after remand*,
257 F.3d 1095 (9th Cir. 2001)

REINHARDT, CIRCUIT JUDGE. . . .

Petitioner Kim Ho Ma's family fled Cambodia in 1979 and took Ma, who was then two years old, with them. After spending over five years in refugee camps,

Ma's family lawfully entered the United States in 1985 as refugees. Ma's status was adjusted to that of a lawful permanent resident in 1987. In 1996, he was convicted, by a jury, of first degree manslaughter following a gang-related shooting. He was sentenced to 38 months in prison, but eventually served only 26 after receiving credit for good behavior. He was tried as an adult, although he was only seventeen years of age at the time of the crime. Although the Immigration and Naturalization Service (INS) repeatedly refers to Ma's criminal record, this was his only criminal conviction.

Ma's conviction made him removable as an alien convicted of certain crimes under 8 U.S.C. §1227(a)(2). Because he was released by the state authorities after April 1, 1997, the INS's authority to take him into custody was governed by the permanent custody rules of the Illegal Immigration Reform and Immigrant Responsibility Act of 1996 (IIRIRA) (codified at 8 U.S.C. §1231). The INS took Ma into custody following his release from prison and initiated removal proceedings against him. An immigration judge found Ma removable, and furthermore found him ineligible for asylum or withholding of deportation because of his conviction. Ma appealed this ruling to the Board of Immigration Appeals (BIA). The BIA affirmed the immigration judge's decision. Although Ma's order of removal became final on October 26, 1998, the INS could not remove him within the ninety day period during which it is authorized to do so because the United States had, and still has, no repatriation agreement with Cambodia. As a result, Ma remained in detention until he filed this petition for a writ of habeas corpus, which was granted by the district court on September 29, 1999. He is now twenty-two and has been in custody (and, but for the district court's decision, would have been incarcerated) for nearly five years, although his sentence accounts for only a little over two years of that period. . . .

Although the bulk of the parties' arguments, as well as the district court's ruling, address the constitutionality of the INS's detention policy, we must first determine whether Congress provided the INS with the authority to detain Ma indefinitely, as the Attorney General contends.

In general, after an alien is found removable, the Attorney General is required to remove that alien within ninety days after the removal order becomes administratively final. Many aliens, however, cannot be removed within the ninety day period for various reasons. First, some individual cases may simply require more time for processing. Second, there are cases involving aliens who have been ordered removed to countries with whom the United States does not have a repatriation agreement, such as Cambodia, Laos, and Vietnam. Finally, there may be those aliens whose countries refuse to take them for other reasons, and yet others who may be effectively "stateless" because of their race and/or place of birth. Ma falls in the second category.

Under the statute, aliens who cannot be removed at the end of ninety days fall into two groups. Those in the first group must be released subject to supervisory regulations that require them, among other things, to appear regularly before an immigration officer, provide information to that official, notify INS of any change in their employment or residence within 48 hours, submit to medical and psychiatric testing, and comply with substantial restrictions on their travel. 8 U.S.C. §1231(a)(3). Those in the second group "may be detained beyond the removal period" and, if released, shall be subject to the same supervisory provisions applicable to aliens in the first group. 8 U.S.C. §1231(a)(6). Aliens in the second group include, among others, persons removable because of criminal convictions (such as drug offenses, certain crimes of moral turpitude, "aggravated felonies," firearms offenses, and various other crimes). 8 U.S.C. §1227(a)(2). Ma's criminal conviction places him in the second group.

INS argues that its authority to "detain beyond the removal period" gives it the authority to detain indefinitely aliens who fall in the second group and who cannot be removed in the reasonably foreseeable future.[13] Ma argues the opposite—that the INS's authority to detain aliens beyond the removal period does not extend to cases in which removal is not likely in the reasonably foreseeable future. On its face, the statute's text compels neither interpretation: while §1231(a)(6) allows for the detention of group two aliens "beyond" ninety days, it is silent about how long beyond the ninety day period such detention is authorized. Thus, any construction of the statute must read in some provision concerning the length of time beyond the removal period detention may continue, whether it be "indefinitely," "for a reasonable time," or some other temporal measure.

We hold that Congress did not grant the INS authority to detain indefinitely aliens who, like Ma, have entered the United States and cannot be removed to their native land pursuant to a repatriation agreement. To the contrary, we construe the statute as providing the INS with authority to detain aliens only for a reasonable time beyond the statutory removal period. In cases in which an alien has already entered the United States and there is no reasonable likelihood that a foreign government will accept the alien's return in the reasonably foreseeable future, we conclude that the statute does not permit the Attorney General to hold the alien beyond the statutory removal period. Rather, the alien must be released subject to the supervisory authority provided in the statute.

We adopt our construction of the statute for several reasons. First, and most important, the result we reach allows us to avoid deciding whether or not INS's indefinite detention policy violates the due process guarantees of the Fifth Amendment. Second, our reading is the most reasonable one—it better comports with the language of the statute and permits us to avoid assuming that Congress intended a result as harsh as indefinite detention in the absence of any clear statement to that effect. Third, reading an implicit "reasonable time" limitation into the statute is consistent with our case law interpreting a similar provision in a prior immigration statute. Finally, the interpretation we adopt is more consonant with international law. . . .

[The court first addresses the various non-international law issues.]

In interpreting the statute to include a reasonable time limitation, we are also influenced by *amicus curiae* Human Rights Watch's argument that we should apply the well-established *Charming Betsy* rule of statutory construction which requires that we generally construe Congressional legislation to avoid violating international law. Weinberger v. Rossi, 456 U.S. 25, 32 (1982) (citing Murray v. The Schooner Charming Betsy, 6 U.S. (2 Cranch) 64, 117-118 (1804)). We have reaffirmed this rule on several occasions. . . .

---

13. Although we recognize that, in general, the Attorney General's interpretation of the immigration laws is entitled to substantial deference, INS v. Aguirre-Aguirre, 526 U.S. 415, 425 (1999), we have held that *Chevron* principles (Chevron U.S.A. v. Natural Resources Defense Council, 467 U.S. 837 (1984)) are not applicable where a substantial constitutional question is raised by an agency's interpretation of a statute it is authorized to construe. . . . As we explain *infra,* the agency's interpretation raises just such a substantial question.

We recently recognized that "a clear international prohibition" exists against prolonged and arbitrary detention.* Martinez v. City of Los Angeles, 141 F.3d 1373, 1384 (9th Cir. 1998).[28] Furthermore, Article 9 of the International Covenant on Civil and Political Rights (ICCPR), which the United States has ratified, provides that "no one shall be subjected to arbitrary arrest and detention." . . . ; *see also* Trans World Airlines, Inc. v. Franklin Mint Corp., 466 U.S. 243, 252 (1984) (holding that ambiguous Congressional action should not be construed to abrogate a treaty).

In the present case, construing the statute to authorize the indefinite detention of removable aliens might violate international law. . . . Given the strength of the rule of international law, our construction of the statute renders it consistent with the *Charming Betsy* rule.

Serra v. Lapin

600 F.3d 1101 (9th Cir. 2010)

CLIFTON, CIRCUIT JUDGE:

Current and former federal prisoners allege that the low wages they were paid for work performed in prison violated their rights under the Fifth Amendment and various sources of international law. Plaintiffs sued officials of the Bureau of Prisons for damages and injunctive and declaratory relief. We conclude that prisoners have no enforceable right to be paid for their work under the Constitution or international law, and we affirm the district court's dismissal of the action. . . .

[The court first concludes that the Constitution allows for even uncompensated labor as part of criminal punishment, and thus that the low wages here did not violate the prisoners' constitutional rights.]

Plaintiffs also cite sources of international law as a basis for the right they assert to higher wages for work performed in prison. The individual documents that Plaintiffs cite, however, do not confer judicially enforceable rights, and Plaintiffs are unable to bring a claim under the law of nations.

Plaintiffs fail to state a viable claim under the International Covenant on Civil and Political Rights. "For any treaty to be susceptible to judicial enforcement it must both confer individual rights and be self-executing." Cornejo v. County of San Diego, 504 F.3d 853, 856 (9th Cir. 2007). A treaty is self-executing when it is

---

* [In *Martinez*, the court had stated: "That prohibition [on arbitrary arrest and detention] can be found in treaties, the laws of nations and court opinions. For example, the Universal Declaration of Human Rights, article 9, states: 'No one shall be subjected to arbitrary arrest, detention or exile.' G.A. Res. 217A(III), 3 U.N. GAOR Supp. No. 16, U.N. Doc. A/810 (1948); *see also* International Covenant on Civil and Political Rights, art. 9, *adopted* Dec. 16, 1966, S. Treaty Doc. 95-2, 999 U.N.T.S. 171 (entered into force Mar. 23, 1976, entered into force for the United States Sept. 8, 1992). Additionally, at least 119 national constitutions recognize the right to be free from arbitrary detention."—EDS.]

28. This court has held that within the domestic legal structure, international law is displaced by "a properly enacted statute, provided it be constitutional, even if that statute violates international law." Alvarez-Mendez v. Stock, 941 F.2d 956, 963 (9th Cir. 1991) (involving prolonged detention of excludable aliens). Those rulings, however, do not suggest that courts should refrain from applying the *Charming Betsy* principle. Rather, they stand for the proposition that when Congress has clearly abrogated international law through legislation, that legislation nonetheless has the full force of law. *See* Restatement (Third) of [Foreign Relations] Law §115(1)(a) ("An Act of Congress supersedes an earlier rule of international law or a provision of an international agreement as law of the United States if the purpose of the act to supersede the earlier rule or provision is clear and if the act and the earlier rule or provision cannot be fairly reconciled."). Although Congress may override international law in enacting a statute, we do not presume that Congress had such an intent when the statute can reasonably be reconciled with the law of nations.

automatically enforceable in domestic courts without implementing legislation. *See* Medellin v. Texas, 552 U.S. 491, 504-05 (2008). The ICCPR fails to satisfy either requirement because it was ratified "on the express understanding that it was not self-executing and so did not itself create obligations enforceable in the federal courts." Sosa v. Alvarez-Machain, 542 U.S. 692, 735 (2004).

The Standard Minimum Rules for the Treatment of Prisoners ("Standard Minimum Rules") similarly fail as a source of justiciable rights. This document was adopted by the First United Nations Congress on the Prevention of Crime and the Treatment of Offenders in 1955 "to set out what is generally accepted as being good principle and practice in the treatment of prisoners and the management of institutions." It is not a treaty, and it is not binding on the United States. Even if it were a self-executing treaty, the document does not purport to serve as a source of private rights. The "Rules" themselves acknowledge that they are not all "capable of application in all places and at all times," and are "not intended to preclude experiment." Moreover, the specific rule identified by Plaintiffs as a source of rights declares only that "[t]here shall be a system of equitable remuneration of the work of prisoners" without specifying what wages would qualify.

Finally, Plaintiffs assert that "the customs and usages" of the nations of the world, as revealed in these and other sources, form customary international law entitling them to higher wages. This claim fails because customary international law is not a source of judicially enforceable private rights in the absence of a statute conferring jurisdiction over such claims. *See* Princz v. Federal Republic of Germany, 26 F.3d 1166, 1174 n.1 (D.C. Cir. 1994) ("While it is true that 'international law is part of our law,' it is also our law that a federal court is not competent to hear a claim arising under international law absent a statute granting such jurisdiction."); *see also Sosa*, 542 U.S. at 720 (" '[O]ffences against this law of nations are principally incident to whole states or nations,' and not individuals seeking relief in court." (quoting Blackstone, 4 Commentaries 68)). Plaintiffs can point to no statute that brings their claim within our purview.

The Alien Tort Statute ("ATS") is the only possible vehicle for a claim like Plaintiffs' because no other statute recognizes a general cause of action under the law of nations. The ATS grants to the district courts "original jurisdiction of any civil action by an alien for a tort only, committed in violation of the law of nations or a treaty of the United States." We need not decide whether Plaintiffs' proposed minimum wage for prison labor "rest[s] on a norm of international character accepted by the civilized world and defined with a specificity comparable to the features of [Blackstone's] 18th-century paradigms," *Sosa*, 542 U.S. at 725, because Plaintiffs have conceded that they are not aliens. The scope of the ATS is limited to suits "by an alien." The ATS admits no cause of action by non-aliens.

We have allowed ourselves a few sidelong glances at the law of nations in non-ATS cases by applying the canon of statutory construction that "[w]here fairly possible, a United States statute is to be construed as not to conflict with international law or with an international agreement with the U.S." Munoz v. Ashcroft, 339 F.3d 950, 958 (9th Cir. 2003) (quoting Restatement (Third) of Foreign Relations Law §114 (1987)). The canon is derived from Chief Justice Marshall's statement that

> an act of Congress ought never to be construed to violate the law of nations if any other possible construction remains, and consequently can never be construed to violate neutral rights, or to affect neutral commerce, further than is warranted by the law of nations as understood in this country.

Murray v. The Schooner Charming Betsy, 6 U.S. (2 Cranch) 64, 118 (1804). The *Charming Betsy* canon is not an inviolable rule of general application, but a principle of interpretation that bears on a limited range of cases. Mindful that "Congress has the power to legislate beyond the limits posed by international law," Cabrera-Alvarez v. Gonzales, 423 F.3d 1006, 1009 (9th Cir. 2005), we do not review federal law for adherence to the law of nations with the same rigor that we apply when we must review statutes for adherence to the Constitution. We invoke the *Charming Betsy* canon only where conformity with the law of nations is relevant to considerations of international comity, *see* Arc Ecology v. United States Dep't of the Air Force, 411 F.3d 1092, 1102-03 (9th Cir. 2005), and only "where it is possible to do so without distorting the statute." *Cabrera-Alvarez*, 423 F.3d at 1010. We decline to determine whether Plaintiffs' rates of pay were in violation of the law of nations because this case meets neither condition for applying the canon.

First, the purpose of the *Charming Betsy* canon is to avoid the negative "foreign policy implications" of violating the law of nations, Weinberger v. Rossi, 456 U.S. 25, 32 (1982), and Plaintiffs have offered no reason to believe that their low wages are likely to "embroil[ ] the nation in a foreign policy dispute." *Arc Ecology*, 411 F.3d at 1102. That the courts should ever invoke the *Charming Betsy* canon in favor of United States citizens is doubtful, because a violation of the law of nations as against a United States citizen is unlikely to bring about the international discord that the canon guards against. In *The Charming Betsy*, the status of the ship's owner as a Danish subject, and thus a neutral in the conflict between the United States and France, was critical to the Court's conclusion that the Non-Intercourse Act of 1800 should not be interpreted to permit the seizure and sale of his ship. We have never employed the *Charming Betsy* canon in a case involving exclusively domestic parties and domestic acts, nor has the Supreme Court. As a general rule, domestic parties must rely on domestic law when they sue each other over domestic injuries in federal court. We need not consider whether the statutory and regulatory regime of federal inmate compensation conflicts with the law of nations because Plaintiffs, as United States citizens and residents, have not demonstrated that their low wages have any possible ramifications for this country's foreign affairs.

Second, "[t]he *Charming Betsy* canon comes into play only where Congress's intent is ambiguous," United States v. Yousef, 327 F.3d 56, 92 (2d Cir. 2003), and there is nothing ambiguous about the complete discretion that Congress vested in the Attorney General with regard to inmate pay. Congress is not constrained by international law as it is by the Constitution. As a result, "we are bound by a properly enacted statute, provided it be constitutional, even if that statute violates international law." Alvarez-Mendez v. Stock, 941 F.2d 956, 963 (9th Cir. 1991). Because the statutes giving the Attorney General discretion over prisoner pay grades are unambiguous, there is no reason for this court to decide whether they accord with the law of nations. Thus, the district court did not err in dismissing Plaintiffs' complaint.

Notes and Questions

1. The Supreme Court has long sought to construe federal statutes so that they do not violate international law. In Talbot v. Seeman, 5 U.S. (1 Cranch) 1 (1801), the Court considered the amount of salvage that should be awarded to a U.S. navy captain for seizing, during the undeclared war between the United States and

France, a neutral ship that had been captured by the French. The captain cited a 1799 federal statute that allowed salvage in the amount of one-half the value of the ship and its cargo in the case of ships seized "belonging to . . . subjects of any nation in amity with the United States, if re-taken from the enemy . . . after ninety-six hours." The Court was concerned, however, that allowing such a large salvage for a neutral vessel would violate customary international law, given that neutral vessels were ordinarily not subject to *any* salvage under such law. In an opinion by Chief Justice Marshall, the Court acknowledged that the language of the statute could be read as supporting the captain's claim. Nevertheless, the Court said that "the laws of the United States ought not, if it be avoidable, so to be construed as to infract the common principles and usages of nations." The Court proceeded to construe the statute as applying only in the case of vessels from countries at war with the capturing country and thus as inapplicable in this case. The Court explained that, "[b]y this construction, the act of Congress will never violate those principles which we believe, and which it is our duty to believe, the legislature of the United States will always hold sacred."

The Court reaffirmed this canon of construction in Murray v. The Schooner Charming Betsy, 6 U.S. (2 Cranch) 64 (1804), albeit without citing back to the *Talbot* decision. Like *Talbot*, the *Charming Betsy* case concerned events relating to the undeclared war with France. During that war, the United States passed the Nonintercourse Act of 1800, which prohibited trade "between any person or persons resident within the United States or under their protection, and any person or persons resident within the territories of the French Republic, or any of the dependencies thereof." To enforce the statute, the U.S. Navy was under orders from President Adams to seize any vessel suspected of trading with the French. A Navy frigate subsequently seized the schooner *Charming Betsy* on the high seas, suspecting her of engaging in trade with Guadaloupe, a French dependency, in violation of the statute. The owner of the ship had been born in the United States but had moved as a child to St. Thomas, a Danish island, and had become a Danish citizen. He argued that, because he was a citizen of a neutral country, the seizure of his vessel violated international law rules of neutrality. The Court, again in an opinion by Chief Justice Marshall, recited among the "principles . . . believed to be correct" and "which ought to be kept in view in construing the act now under consideration," the following proposition: "an act of Congress ought never to be construed to violate the law of nations if any other possible construction remains. . . ." The Court proceeded to construe the Nonintercourse Act as not applying to the owner of the vessel, because he was not at the time of the seizure a resident of the United States or "under [its] protection." The canon of construction invoked by the Court is today commonly referred to as the "*Charming Betsy* canon."

2. The Restatement (Third) of Foreign Relations Law describes the *Charming Betsy* canon in somewhat softer terms than the language used by Chief Justice Marshall. The Restatement (Third) states that "[w]here fairly possible, a United States statute is to be construed so as not to conflict with international law or with an international agreement of the United States." Restatement (Third) of the Foreign Relations Law of the United States §114 (1987); *see also* Restatement (Fourth) of the Foreign Relations Law of the United States §309(1) (2018) ("Where fairly possible, courts in the United States will construe federal statutes to avoid a conflict with a treaty provision."); *id.* §406 ("Where fairly possible, courts in the United States construe federal statutes to avoid conflict with international law governing jurisdiction to prescribe."). Under either formulation of the canon, what evidence will be sufficient to show that Congress intended a result contrary to international law?

3. What are the purposes of the *Charming Betsy* canon? To capture likely congressional intent? To induce Congress to think carefully before taking action that might put the United States in breach of international law? To reduce the likelihood that courts will, through legal interpretation, cause foreign relations friction? What do the two decisions excerpted above suggest about the purposes of the canon? Do you agree with the court in Serra v. Lapin that it is "doubtful" that the canon applies to alleged violations of international law vis-à-vis U.S. citizens and nationals?

4. What, if anything, does the *Charming Betsy* canon tell us about the status of international law in U.S. courts? In Filartiga v. Pena-Irala, which we considered above in Section A, the court cited the *Charming Betsy* canon as "[t]he plainest evidence that international law has an existence in the federal courts independent of acts of Congress." *See* 630 F.2d 876, 887 n.20. When applying the *Charming Betsy* canon, are courts likely to require as much evidence of a purported customary international law rule as they would if they were applying customary international law directly?

5. Under the *Charming Betsy* canon, courts attempt to construe statutes to avoid violations of customary international law. As discussed in Chapter 5, courts similarly attempt to construe statutes to avoid violations of treaties (and they sometimes, but not always, cite the *Charming Betsy* decision when doing so). Are there differences between customary international law and treaties that should affect how courts apply the avoidance canon in the two contexts? Note that, in the treaty context, some courts have required evidence of a clear intent by Congress to override a treaty before a statute will be given this effect. *See, e.g.,* Owner-Operator Independent Drivers Association v. U.S. Dep't of Transportation, 724 F.3d 230 (D.C. Cir. 2013). Courts have not required such evidence, however, in order for statutes to displace customary international law. Why not?

6. The Supreme Court has long held that statutes should be construed, where reasonably possible, so that they do not violate the Constitution. *See* Edward J. DeBartolo Corp. v. Florida Gulf Coast Bldg. & Constr. Trades Council, 485 U.S. 568, 575 (1988); Ashwander v. TVA, 297 U.S. 288, 346 (1936) (Brandeis J., concurring). What relationship, if any, is there between this constitutional avoidance canon and the *Charming Betsy* canon? Why do you think the Court attempts to avoid finding statutes unconstitutional? Are there similar reasons for attempting to avoid finding statutes in violation of international law? What do the two decisions excerpted above suggest?

7. What is the relationship between the *Charming Betsy* canon and deference to the Executive Branch, either pursuant to the *Chevron* doctrine or, more generally, as a matter of "foreign affairs deference"? Should the canon override such deference? Does the answer depend on whether the international law violation involves a treaty or customary international law? What deference, if any, did the courts in the above decisions give to the Executive Branch? For discussion of the relationship between the *Charming Betsy* canon and *Chevron* deference, see Curtis A. Bradley, Chevron *Deference and Foreign Affairs*, 86 Va. L. Rev. 649, 685-90 (2000). Note that, as we have seen in other materials, the Executive Branch may receive deference in its interpretation of international law. As a result, it may be in a position to influence a court's determination of whether there is a potential conflict with international law, and thus whether to apply the *Charming Betsy* canon at all.

8. As discussed in Chapter 2, courts generally presume that federal statutes do not apply to conduct occurring in other countries. This "presumption against extraterritoriality" does not apply to all federal statutes, however, and even when it does apply it can be overcome by evidence that Congress intended to apply the statute abroad. Even after concluding that a statute has extraterritorial effect, courts sometimes invoke the *Charming Betsy* canon to avoid applications of the statute that would arguably violate customary international law norms on "prescriptive jurisdiction" (that is, on the authority of nations to regulate conduct). *See, e.g.,* F. Hoffman-La Roche Ltd. v. Empagran S.A., 542 U.S. 155, 164 (2004); Hartford Fire Insurance Co. v. California, 509 U.S. 764, 814-16 (1993) (Scalia, J., dissenting); McCulloch v. Sociedad Nacional de Marineros de Honduras, 372 U.S. 10, 21 (1962).

It is generally agreed that customary international law imposes limits on a nation's prescriptive jurisdiction. Under this view, a nation's exercise of prescriptive jurisdiction, in order to be lawful, must fall within one of five categories: territoriality; nationality; the protective principle; passive personality; or universality. Under the territoriality category, nations may regulate conduct that takes place within their territory or has substantial effects within their territory. Under the nationality category, nations may regulate the conduct of their citizens both inside and outside their territory. Under the protective principle, nations may regulate certain conduct outside their territory that threatens their national security or government operations. Under the passive personality category, nations may regulate certain conduct that harms their nationals abroad. Finally, under the universality category, nations may regulate certain egregious conduct committed anywhere in the world. *See* Restatement (Fourth) of the Foreign Relations Law of the United States §413 (2018); United States v. Pizzarusso, 388 F.2d 8 (2d Cir. 1968). Another "category" in which the exercise of prescriptive jurisdiction is permissible is when one nation specifically agrees with another nation (for example, in a treaty) to allow the other nation to regulate within the first nation's territory. If nothing else, this category follows from the proposition that nations can override customary international law between themselves by agreement. These categories of prescriptive jurisdiction are considered further in Chapter 8, in the materials on international criminal law.

9. In the extraterritoriality context and in other contexts where the *Charming Betsy* canon is most frequently applied, the statute in question regulates primary conduct. Does the canon also apply in the different context of a grant of discretionary enforcement authority to the President? One purpose of the canon is to avoid having judges, who are politically unaccountable and inexpert in foreign affairs, erroneously place the United States in violation of international law through their construction of a statute. Is this purpose served by applying it to authorizing statutes like the AUMF? *Cf.* United States v. Corey, 232 F.3d 1166, 1179 n.9 (9th Cir. 2000) ("These concerns [underlying the *Charming Betsy* canon] are obviously much less serious where the interpretation arguably violating international law is urged upon us by the Executive Branch of our government. When construing a statute with potential foreign policy implications, we must presume that the President has evaluated the foreign policy consequences of such an exercise of U.S. law and determined that it serves the interests of the United States."); *Authority of the Federal Bureau of Investigation to Override International Law in Extraterritorial Law Enforcement Activities,* 13 Op. Off. Legal Counsel 163, 171 (1989) (concluding that the *Charming Betsy* canon was not applicable to "broad authorizing statutes 'carrying into execution'" core Executive powers). For discussion of these issues, compare Ingrid Brunk Wuerth, *Authorizations for the Use of Force, International Law, and the* Charming Betsy *Canon,* 46 B.C. L. Rev. 293, 324-28 (2005) (arguing that canon does apply to authorizing statutes), with Curtis A. Bradley & Jack L. Goldsmith, *Congressional*

Authorization and the War on Terrorism, 118 Harv. L. Rev. 2047, 2097-98 (2005) (suggesting that it may not apply to such statutes).

10. Sometimes the issue is not whether a statute violates international law, but rather whether the statute extends as far as international law would allow. This issue has come up in connection with suits brought under the FSIA, which, as we have seen, provides that foreign states are immune from suit in U.S. courts unless the suit falls within one of the Act's specified exceptions to immunity. Although the FSIA does not contain an express exception to immunity for violations of *jus cogens* norms of international law, some litigants and scholars have argued that the FSIA's exception for situations in which a foreign state has "waived its immunity . . . by implication" should be construed to include situations in which a foreign state has acted contrary to *jus cogens* norms. Supporters of this construction sometimes invoke the *Charming Betsy* canon. They reason that foreign states are not entitled under international law to immunity from suit for violations of *jus cogens* norms, and that, pursuant to the *Charming Betsy* canon, the FSIA should be construed similarly to deny immunity in this situation.

Courts have consistently rejected this construction of the FSIA. *See, e.g.,* Sampson v. Federal Republic of Germany, 250 F.3d 1145 (7th Cir. 2001); Smith v. Socialist People's Libyan Arab Jamahiriya, 101 F.3d 239, 344-45 (2d Cir. 1996); Princz v. Federal Republic of Germany, 26 F.3d 1166 (D.C. Cir. 1994); Siderman de Blake v. Republic of Argentina, 965 F.2d 699, 718-19 (9th Cir. 1992). Consider one court's explanation of why this construction does not follow from the *Charming Betsy* canon:

> While the *Charming Betsy* canon directs courts to construe ambiguous statutes to avoid conflicts with international law, international law itself does not mandate Article III jurisdiction over foreign sovereigns. In other words, although *jus cogens* norms may address sovereign immunity in contexts where the question is whether international law itself provides immunity, e.g., the Nuremberg proceedings, *jus cogens* norms do not require Congress (or any government) to create jurisdiction. Because international law is silent on the grant of federal court jurisdiction at issue, we interpret the FSIA without reference to the *Charming Betsy* canon. . . .
>
> [A]lthough international law is "part of our law," it does not follow that federal statutes must be read to reflect the norms of international law. . . . Since customary international law in the modern era is often based on the contents of multi-lateral treaties to which the United States attaches reservations (or refuses to join at all), there is little reason to indulge in a presumption that Congress intends courts to mold ambiguous statutes into consistency with international law. Use of the canon so as to effectively incorporate customary international law into federal statutes when the political branches of our government may have rejected the international law at issue seems dubious at best.

Sampson, 250 F.3d at 1151-53. Is the court's analysis persuasive? For a more expansive view of the role of the *Charming Betsy* canon, in the context of federal immigration law, see Beharry v. Reno, 183 F. Supp. 2d 584, 591 (S.D.N.Y. 2002) (relying on *Charming Betsy* for the proposition that "[i]mmigration statutes must be woven into the seamless web of our national and international law"), *rev'd on other grounds,* 329 F.3d 51 (2d Cir. 2003).

11. For general discussions of the *Charming Betsy* canon, see Curtis A. Bradley, *The* Charming Betsy *Canon and Separation of Powers: Rethinking the Interpretive Role of International Law,* 86 Geo. L.J. 479 (1998); Ralph G. Steinhardt, *The Role of International Law as a Canon of Domestic Statutory Construction,* 43 Vand. L. Rev. 1103 (1990);

Jonathan Turley, *Dualistic Values in an Age of International Legisprudence*, 44 Hastings L.J. 185 (1993). *See also* Jane A. Restani & Ira Bloom, *Interpreting International Trade Statutes: Is the* Charming Betsy *Sinking?*, 24 Fordham Int'l L.J. 1533 (2001); Note, *The* Charming Betsy *Canon, Separation of Powers, and Customary International Law*, 121 Harv. L. Rev. 1215 (2008); Michael F. Williams, Note, Charming Betsy, Chevron, *and the World Trade Organization: Thoughts on the Interpretive Effect of International Trade Law*, 32 Law & Pol'y Int'l Bus. 677 (2001). For a historical description of the *Charming Betsy* case, see Frederick C. Leiner, *The* Charming Betsy *and the Marshall Court*, 14 Am. J. Leg. Hist. 1 (2001).

G. RELIANCE ON FOREIGN AND INTERNATIONAL MATERIALS IN CONSTITUTIONAL INTERPRETATION

Roper v. Simmons

543 U.S. 551 (2005)

[Simmons committed a gruesome murder at age 17 and was later convicted of capital murder and sentenced to death. He argued that the Eighth Amendment's ban on cruel and unusual punishments prohibits the execution of individuals who commit their capital offenses before the age of 18.]

JUSTICE KENNEDY delivered the opinion of the Court.

This case requires us to address, for the second time in a decade and a half, whether it is permissible under the Eighth and Fourteenth Amendments to the Constitution of the United States to execute a juvenile offender who was older than 15 but younger than 18 when he committed a capital crime. In Stanford v. Kentucky, 492 U.S. 361 (1989), a divided Court rejected the proposition that the Constitution bars capital punishment for juvenile offenders in this age group. We reconsider the question.

The Eighth Amendment provides: "Excessive bail shall not be required, nor excessive fines imposed, nor cruel and unusual punishments inflicted." The provision is applicable to the States through the Fourteenth Amendment. . . .

The prohibition against "cruel and unusual punishments," like other expansive language in the Constitution, must be interpreted according to its text, by considering history, tradition, and precedent, and with due regard for its purpose and function in the constitutional design. To implement this framework we have established the propriety and affirmed the necessity of referring to "the evolving standards of decency that mark the progress of a maturing society" to determine which punishments are so disproportionate as to be cruel and unusual. Trop v. Dulles, 356 U.S. 86, 100-01 (1958) (plurality opinion).

[After determining that there was a national consensus against the death penalty for juveniles, and that the death penalty is disproportionate punishment for offenders under 18, the Court turned to consider foreign and international law.]

Our determination that the death penalty is disproportionate punishment for offenders under 18 finds confirmation in the stark reality that the United States is the only country in the world that continues to give official sanction to the juvenile death penalty. This reality does not become controlling, for the task of interpreting the Eighth Amendment remains our responsibility. Yet at least from the time of the Court's decision in *Trop*, the Court has referred to the laws of other countries and to international authorities as instructive for its interpretation of the Eighth Amendment's prohibition of "cruel and unusual punishments." 356 U.S. at 102-03 (plurality opinion) ("The civilized nations of the world are in virtual unanimity that statelessness is not to be imposed as punishment for crime"); *see also* Atkins v. Virginia, 536 U.S. 304, 317, n.21 (2002) (recognizing that "within the world community, the imposition of the death penalty for crimes committed by mentally retarded offenders is overwhelmingly disapproved"); Thompson v. Oklahoma, 487 U.S. 815, 830-31 & n.31 (1988) (plurality opinion) (noting the abolition of the juvenile death penalty "by other nations that share our Anglo-American heritage, and by the leading members of the Western European community," and observing that "we have previously recognized the relevance of the views of the international community in determining whether a punishment is cruel and unusual"); Enmund v. Florida, 458 U.S. 782, 796-797, n.22 (1982) (observing that "the doctrine of felony murder has been abolished in England and India, severely restricted in Canada and a number of other Commonwealth countries, and is unknown in continental Europe"); Coker v. Georgia, 433 U.S. 584, 596, n.10 (1977) (plurality opinion) ("It is . . . not irrelevant here that out of 60 major nations in the world surveyed in 1965, only 3 retained the death penalty for rape where death did not ensue.").

As respondent and a number of *amici* emphasize, Article 37 of the United Nations Convention on the Rights of the Child, which every country in the world has ratified save for the United States and Somalia, contains an express prohibition on capital punishment for crimes committed by juveniles under 18. United Nations Convention on the Rights of the Child, Art. 37, Nov. 20, 1989, 1577 U.N.T.S. 3 (entered into force Sept. 2, 1990). No ratifying country has entered a reservation to the provision prohibiting the execution of juvenile offenders. Parallel prohibitions are contained in other significant international covenants. *See* International Covenant for Civil and Political Rights, Art. 6(5), 999 U.N.T.S., at 175 (prohibiting capital punishment for anyone under 18 at the time of offense) (signed and ratified by the United States subject to a reservation regarding Article 6(5)); American Convention on Human Rights: Pact of San Jose, Costa Rica, Art. 4(5), Nov. 22, 1969, 1144 U.N.T.S. 146 (entered into force July 19, 1978) (same); African Charter on the Rights and Welfare of the Child, Art. 5(3), OAU Doc. CAB/LEG/24.9/49 (1990) (entered into force Nov. 29, 1999) (same).

Respondent and his *amici* have submitted, and petitioner does not contest, that only seven countries other than the United States have executed juvenile offenders since 1990: Iran, Pakistan, Saudi Arabia, Yemen, Nigeria, the Democratic Republic of Congo, and China. Since then each of these countries has either abolished capital punishment for juveniles or made public disavowal of the practice. In sum, it is fair to say that the United States now stands alone in a world that has turned its face against the juvenile death penalty.

Though the international covenants prohibiting the juvenile death penalty are of more recent date, it is instructive to note that the United Kingdom abolished the juvenile death penalty before these covenants came into being. The United Kingdom's experience bears particular relevance here in light of the historic ties between our countries and in light of the Eighth Amendment's own origins. . . . As of now, the United Kingdom has abolished the death penalty in its entirety; but, decades before it took this step, it recognized the disproportionate nature of the juvenile death penalty; and it abolished that penalty as a separate matter. . . . In the 56 years that have passed since the United Kingdom abolished the juvenile death penalty, the weight of authority against it there, and in the international community, has become well established.

It is proper that we acknowledge the overwhelming weight of international opinion against the juvenile death penalty, resting in large part on the understanding that the instability and emotional imbalance of young people may often be a factor in the crime. The opinion of the world community, while not controlling our outcome, does provide respected and significant confirmation for our own conclusions.

Over time, from one generation to the next, the Constitution has come to earn the high respect and even, as Madison dared to hope, the veneration of the American people. The document sets forth, and rests upon, innovative principles original to the American experience, such as federalism; a proven balance in political mechanisms through separation of powers; specific guarantees for the accused in criminal cases; and broad provisions to secure individual freedom and preserve human dignity. These doctrines and guarantees are central to the American experience and remain essential to our present-day self-definition and national identity. Not the least of the reasons we honor the Constitution, then, is because we know it to be our own. It does not lessen our fidelity to the Constitution or our pride in its origins to acknowledge that the express affirmation of certain fundamental rights by other nations and peoples simply underscores the centrality of those same rights within our own heritage of freedom. . . .

JUSTICE O'CONNOR, dissenting. . . .

[Justice O'Connor disagreed with the majority's conclusion that the execution of juvenile offenders violates the Eighth Amendment, reasoning that neither the objective evidence of contemporary societal values, nor the Court's moral proportionality analysis, sufficed to justify the conclusion. She then had the following to say about the Court's discussion of foreign and international law.]

Without question, there has been a global trend in recent years towards abolishing capital punishment for under-18 offenders. Very few, if any, countries other than the United States now permit this practice in law or in fact. While acknowledging that the actions and views of other countries do not dictate the outcome of our Eighth Amendment inquiry, the Court asserts that "the overwhelming weight of international opinion against the juvenile death penalty . . . does provide respected and significant confirmation for [its] own conclusions." Because I do not believe that a genuine national consensus against the juvenile death penalty has yet developed, and because I do not believe the Court's moral proportionality argument justifies a categorical, age-based constitutional rule, I can assign no such confirmatory role to the international consensus described by the Court. In short, the evidence of an international consensus does not alter my determination that the Eighth Amendment does not, at this time, forbid capital punishment of 17-year-old murderers in all cases.

Nevertheless, I disagree with Justice Scalia's contention that foreign and international law have no place in our Eighth Amendment jurisprudence. Over the course of nearly half a century, the Court has consistently referred to foreign and international law as relevant to its assessment of evolving standards of decency. This inquiry reflects the special character of the Eighth Amendment, which, as the Court has long held, draws its meaning directly from the maturing values of civilized society. Obviously, American law is distinctive in many respects, not least where the specific provisions of our Constitution and the history of its exposition so dictate. But this Nation's evolving understanding of human dignity certainly is neither wholly isolated from, nor inherently at odds with, the values prevailing in other countries. On the contrary, we should not be surprised to find congruence between domestic and international values, especially where the international community has reached clear agreement—expressed in international law or in the domestic laws of individual countries—that a particular form of punishment is inconsistent with fundamental human rights. At least, the existence of an international consensus of this nature can serve to confirm the reasonableness of a consonant and genuine American consensus. The instant case presents no such domestic consensus, however, and the recent emergence of an otherwise global consensus does not alter that basic fact. . . .

JUSTICE SCALIA, with whom THE CHIEF JUSTICE and JUSTICE THOMAS join, dissenting. . . .

Though the views of our own citizens are essentially irrelevant to the Court's decision today, the views of other countries and the so-called international community take center stage.

The Court begins by noting that "Article 37 of the United Nations Convention on the Rights of the Child, which every country in the world has ratified save for the United States and Somalia, contains an express prohibition on capital punishment for crimes committed by juveniles under 18." The Court also discusses the International Covenant on Civil and Political Rights (ICCPR), which the Senate ratified only subject to a reservation that reads:

> The United States reserves the right, subject to its Constitutional restraints, to impose capital punishment on any person (other than a pregnant woman) duly convicted under existing or future laws permitting the imposition of capital punishment, including such punishment for crime committed by persons below eighteen years of age.

Senate Committee on Foreign Relations, International Covenant on Civil and Political Rights, S. Exec. Rep. No. 102-23 (1992).

Unless the Court has added to its arsenal the power to join and ratify treaties on behalf of the United States, I cannot see how this evidence favors, rather than refutes, its position. That the Senate and the President—those actors our Constitution empowers to enter into treaties, see Art. II, §2—have declined to join and ratify treaties prohibiting execution of under-18 offenders can only suggest that our country has either not reached a national consensus on the question, or has reached a consensus contrary to what the Court announces. That the reservation to the ICCPR was made in 1992 does not suggest otherwise, since the reservation still remains in place today. It is also worth noting that, in addition to barring the execution of under-18 offenders, the United Nations Convention on the Rights of the Child prohibits punishing them with life in prison without the possibility of release. If we are truly going to get in line with the international community, then the Court's reassurance that the death penalty is really not needed, since "the punishment of life imprisonment without the possibility of parole is itself a severe sanction," gives little comfort. . . .

[The] basic premise of the Court's argument—that American law should conform to the laws of the rest of the world—ought to be rejected out of hand. In fact the Court itself does not believe it. In many significant respects the laws of most other countries differ from our law—including not only such explicit provisions of our Constitution as the right to jury trial and grand jury indictment, but even many interpretations of the Constitution prescribed by this Court itself. The Court-pronounced exclusionary rule, for example, is distinctively American. When we adopted that rule in Mapp v. Ohio, 367 U.S. 643, 655 (1965), it was "unique to American Jurisprudence." Bivens v. Six Unknown Fed. Narcotics Agents, 403 U.S. 388, 415 (1971) (Burger, C.J., dissenting). Since then a categorical exclusionary rule has been "universally rejected" by other countries, including those with rules prohibiting illegal searches and police misconduct, despite the fact that none of these countries "appears to have any alternative form of discipline for police that is effective in preventing search violations." Bradley, Mapp *Goes Abroad*, 52 Case W. Res. L. Rev. 375, 399-400 (2001). England, for example, rarely excludes evidence found during an illegal search or seizure and has only recently begun excluding evidence from illegally obtained confessions. Canada rarely excludes evidence and will only do so if admission will "bring the administration of justice into disrepute." The European Court of Human Rights has held that introduction of illegally seized evidence does not violate the "fair trial" requirement in Article 6, §1, of the European Convention on Human Rights.

The Court has been oblivious to the views of other countries when deciding how to interpret our Constitution's requirement that "Congress shall make no law respecting an establishment of religion . . ." Amdt. 1. Most other countries—including those committed to religious neutrality—do not insist on the degree of separation between church and state that this Court requires. For example, whereas "we have recognized special Establishment Clause dangers where the government makes direct money payments to sectarian institutions," Rosenberger v. Rector and Visitors of Univ. of Va., 515 U.S. 819, 842 (1995) (citing cases), countries such as the Netherlands, Germany, and Australia allow direct government funding of religious schools on the ground that "the state can only be truly neutral between secular and religious perspectives if it does not dominate the provision of so key a service as education, and makes it possible for people to exercise their right of religious expression within the context of public funding." S. Monsma & J. Soper, The Challenge of Pluralism: Church and State in Five Democracies 207 (1997). England permits the teaching of religion in state schools. Even in France, which is considered "America's only rival in strictness of church-state separation," "the practice of contracting for educational services provided by Catholic schools is very widespread." C. Glenn, The Ambiguous Embrace: Government and Faith-Based Schools and Social Agencies 110 (2000).

And let us not forget the Court's abortion jurisprudence, which makes us one of only six countries that allow abortion on demand until the point of viability. Though the Government and *amici* in cases following Roe v. Wade, 410 U.S. 113 (1973), urged the Court to follow the international community's lead, these arguments fell on deaf ears.

The Court's special reliance on the laws of the United Kingdom is perhaps the most indefensible part of its opinion. It is of course true that we share a common history with the United Kingdom, and that we often consult English sources when asked to discern the meaning of a constitutional text written against the backdrop of 18th-century English law and legal thought. If we applied that approach today, our task would be an easy one. As we explained in Harmelin v. Michigan, 501 U.S. 957, 973-74 (1991), the "Cruell and Unusuall Punishments" provision of the English Declaration of Rights was originally meant to describe those punishments " 'out of [the Judges'] Power' "—that is, those punishments that were not authorized by common law or statute, but that were nonetheless administered by the Crown or the Crown's judges. Under that reasoning, the death penalty for under-18 offenders would easily survive this challenge. The Court has, however—I think wrongly—long rejected a purely originalist approach to our Eighth Amendment, and that is certainly not the approach the Court takes today. Instead, the Court undertakes the majestic task of determining (and thereby prescribing) our Nation's current standards of decency. It is beyond comprehension why we should look, for that purpose, to a country that has developed, in the centuries since the Revolutionary War—and with increasing speed since the United Kingdom's recent submission to the jurisprudence of European courts dominated by continental jurists—a legal, political, and social culture quite different from our own. If we took the Court's directive seriously, we would also consider relaxing our double jeopardy prohibition, since the British Law Commission recently published a report that would significantly extend the rights of the prosecution to appeal cases where an acquittal was the result of a judge's ruling that was legally incorrect. We would also curtail our right to jury trial in criminal cases since, despite the jury system's deep roots in our shared common law, England now permits all but the most serious offenders to be tried by magistrates without a jury.

The Court should either profess its willingness to reconsider all these matters in light of the views of foreigners, or else it should cease putting forth foreigners' views as part of the reasoned basis of its decisions. To invoke alien law when it agrees with one's own thinking, and ignore it otherwise, is not reasoned decisionmaking, but sophistry.[9]

The Court responds that "it does not lessen our fidelity to the Constitution or our pride in its origins to acknowledge that the express affirmation of certain fundamental rights by other nations and peoples simply underscores the centrality of those same rights within our own heritage of freedom." To begin with, I do not believe that approval by "other nations and peoples" should buttress our commitment to American principles any more than (what should logically follow) disapproval by "other nations and peoples" should weaken that commitment. More importantly, however, the Court's statement flatly misdescribes what is going on here. Foreign sources are cited today, not to underscore our "fidelity" to the Constitution, our "pride in its origins," and "our own [American] heritage." To the contrary, they are cited to set aside the centuries-old American practice—a practice still engaged in by a large majority of the relevant States—of letting a jury of 12 citizens decide whether, in the particular case, youth should be the basis for withholding the death penalty. What these foreign sources "affirm," rather than repudiate, is the Justices' own notion of how the world ought to be, and their diktat that it shall be so henceforth in America. The Court's parting attempt to downplay the significance of its extensive discussion of foreign law is unconvincing. "Acknowledgment" of foreign

---

9. . . . Justice O'Connor asserts that an international consensus can at least "serve to confirm the reasonableness of a consonant and genuine American consensus." Surely not unless it can also demonstrate the unreasonableness of such a consensus. Either America's principles are its own, or they follow the world; one cannot have it both ways. . . . Justice O'Connor finds it unnecessary to consult foreign law in the present case because there is "no . . . domestic consensus" to be confirmed. But since she believes that the Justices can announce their own requirements of "moral proportionality" despite the absence of consensus, why would foreign law not be relevant to that judgment? If foreign law is powerful enough to supplant the judgment of the American people, surely it is powerful enough to change a personal assessment of moral proportionality.

approval has no place in the legal opinion of this Court unless it is part of the basis for the Court's judgment—which is surely what it parades as today.

Notes and Questions

1. In addition to the majority opinion in *Roper*, the Supreme Court has in a number of modern constitutional decisions referred to foreign or international law materials. In Lawrence v. Texas, 539 U.S. 558 (2003), in striking down a Texas anti-sodomy law and overturning Bowers v. Hardwick, 478 U.S. 186 (1986), the Court cited to British law and to a decision by the European Court of Human Rights:

> The sweeping references by Chief Justice Burger [in his concurrence in *Bowers*] to the history of Western civilization and to Judeo-Christian moral and ethical standards did not take account of other authorities pointing in an opposite direction. A committee advising the British Parliament recommended in 1957 repeal of laws punishing homosexual conduct. Parliament enacted the substance of those recommendations 10 years later.
>
> Of even more importance, almost five years before *Bowers* was decided the European Court of Human Rights considered a case with parallels to *Bowers* and to today's case. An adult male resident in Northern Ireland alleged he was a practicing homosexual who desired to engage in consensual homosexual conduct. The laws of Northern Ireland forbade him that right. He alleged that he had been questioned, his home had been searched, and he feared criminal prosecution. The court held that the laws proscribing the conduct were invalid under the European Convention on Human Rights. Authoritative in all countries that are members of the Council of Europe (21 nations then, 45 nations now), the decision is at odds with the premise in *Bowers* that the claim put forward was insubstantial in our Western civilization.

In his dissent in that case (joined by two other Justices), Justice Scalia objected that these foreign law materials were not relevant to the constitutional analysis and were not responsive to the majority opinion in *Bowers*:

> Constitutional entitlements do not spring into existence because some States choose to lessen or eliminate criminal sanctions on certain behavior. Much less do they spring into existence, as the Court seems to believe, because *foreign nations* decriminalize conduct. The *Bowers* majority opinion *never* relied on "values we share with a wider civilization," but rather rejected the claimed right to sodomy on the ground that such a right was not "'deeply rooted in *this Nation's* history and tradition,'" 478 U.S. at 193-94 (emphasis added). *Bowers'* rational-basis holding is likewise devoid of any reliance on the views of a 'wider civilization,' see *id.* at 196. The Court's discussion of these foreign views (ignoring, of course, the many countries that have retained criminal prohibitions on sodomy) is therefore meaningless dicta. Dangerous dicta, however, since "this Court . . . should not impose foreign moods, fads, or fashions on Americans." Foster v. Florida, 537 U.S. 990 n. (2002) (Thomas, J., concurring in denial of *certiorari*).

In Grutter v. Bollinger, 539 U.S. 306 (2003), which upheld the University of Michigan law school's use of affirmative action in admissions, Justice Ginsburg began her concurrence by noting that "[t]he Court's observation that race-conscious programs 'must have a logical end point' accords with the international understanding of the office of affirmative action." She then proceeded to cite and quote from the Convention on the Elimination of All Forms of Racial Discrimination, and the Convention on the Elimination of All Forms of Discrimination Against Women.

In Atkins v. Virginia, 536 U.S. 304 (2002), the Court held that the execution of persons with mental retardation violated the Eighth Amendment, and it observed in a footnote that "within the world community, the imposition of the death penalty for crimes committed by mentally retarded offenders is overwhelmingly disapproved." In dissent, Justice Scalia argued that the practices of the world community are "irrelevant" and noted that the world community's "notions of justice are (thankfully) not always those of our people."

Finally, in Printz v. United States, 521 U.S. 898 (1997), Justice Breyer dissented from the majority's conclusion that the Brady Handgun Violence Prevention Act's provisions requiring the Attorney General to command the chief law enforcement officer of each local jurisdiction to conduct background checks for handgun purchasers exceeded Congress's power. Justice Breyer reasoned:

> [T]he United States is not the only nation that seeks to reconcile the practical need for a central authority with the democratic virtues of more local control. At least some other countries, facing the same basic problem, have found that local control is better maintained through application of a principle that is the direct opposite of the principle the majority derives from the silence of our Constitution. The federal systems of Switzerland, Germany, and the European Union, for example, all provide that constituent states, not federal bureaucracies, will themselves implement many of the laws, rules, regulations, or decrees enacted by the central "federal" body. They do so in part because they believe that such a system interferes less, not more, with the independent authority of the "state," member nation, or other subsidiary government, and helps to safeguard individual liberty as well.
>
> Of course, we are interpreting our own Constitution, not those of other nations, and there may be relevant political and structural differences between their systems and our own. *Cf. The Federalist No. 20*, pp. 134-38 (C. Rossiter ed. 1961) (J. Madison and A. Hamilton) (rejecting certain aspects of European federalism). But their experience may nonetheless cast an empirical light on the consequences of different solutions to a common legal problem — in this case the problem of reconciling central authority with the need to preserve the liberty-enhancing autonomy of a smaller constituent governmental entity. *Cf. id., No. 42*, p. 268 (J. Madison) (looking to experiences of European countries); *id., No. 43*, pp. 275, 276 (J. Madison) (same).

The majority, in an opinion by Justice Scalia, responded to this argument as follows:

> Justice Breyer's dissent would have us consider the benefits that other countries, and the European Union, believe they have derived from federal systems that are different from ours. We think such comparative analysis inappropriate to the task of interpreting a constitution, though it was of course quite relevant to the task of writing one. The Framers were familiar with many federal systems, from classical antiquity down to their own time; they are discussed in Nos. 18-20 of *The Federalist.* Some were (for the purpose here under discussion) quite similar to the modern "federal" systems that Justice Breyer favors. Madison's and Hamilton's opinion of such systems could not be clearer. *Federalist No. 20*, after an extended critique of the system of government established by the Union of Utrecht for the United Netherlands, concludes:
>
>> I make no apology for having dwelt so long on the contemplation of these federal precedents. Experience is the oracle of truth; and where its responses are unequivocal, they ought to be conclusive and sacred. The important truth, which it unequivocally pronounces in the present case, is that a sovereignty over sovereigns, a government over governments, a legislation for communities, as contra distinguished from individuals, as it is a solecism in theory, so in practice it is subversive of the order and ends of civil polity. . . .

Antifederalists, on the other hand, pointed specifically to Switzerland—and its then 400 years of success as a "confederate republic"—as proof that the proposed Constitution and its federal structure was unnecessary. The fact is that our federalism is not Europe's. It is "the unique contribution of the Framers to political science and political theory." United States v. Lopez, 514 U.S. 549, 575 (1995) (Kennedy, J., concurring) (citing Friendly, *Federalism: A Forward*, 86 Yale L. J. 1019 (1977)).

2. What legal force is the Court in *Roper* giving to foreign and international materials? Is it treating those materials like precedents? Persuasive authority? As a common law court in one U.S. state might treat a common law decision in another? Do these materials merely confirm the Court's judgment reached through independent means? Are they used as *factual* evidence of a consensus against the juvenile death penalty rather than as legal authority? How, if at all, do the majority opinion and Justice O'Connor's dissenting opinion differ regarding the use of these materials?

3. Under any of the theories in Note 2 about how the international and foreign materials might be used, why are they relevant to an analysis of the Eighth Amendment? Is it because of the term "unusual" in the Eighth Amendment? Did the Framers of the U.S. Constitution intend for the meaning of the prohibitions in the Eighth Amendment to change in accordance with changing global opinions as reflected in international and foreign law? Is that the relevant question? If we uncovered clear evidence that the Framers intended "unusual" to mean "unusual within the U.S. legal culture," or "unusual in 1791," would that rebut the analysis in *Roper*? Note, in this connection, that Justice Scalia, the leading critic of the Court's use of foreign and international materials, often relies on English precedents to help elucidate the original understanding of the Constitution. How does that differ from the *Roper* majority's use of foreign precedents?

4. The Court in *Roper* refers to both foreign court materials and international law materials. Do these two sets of materials have the same relevance to U.S. constitutional interpretation? Are foreign court interpretations of analogous constitutional provisions more relevant to U.S. constitutional law than what international instruments say? Or are international instruments more relevant to the extent that they reflect a broader consensus?

5. Under the Court's analysis in *Roper*, would it be appropriate to rely on foreign and international materials in the interpretation of every constitutional provision? Does the relevance of such materials depend on the constitutional clause in question? Consider, in this regard, some historical uses of foreign and international materials in Supreme Court adjudication:

> In the late nineteenth and early twentieth centuries, after the Civil War had vindicated the Union's claim to nationhood, the Supreme Court repeatedly invoked international law doctrines and writers in support of its elaboration of powers inherent in national sovereignty. The Court rationalized some of these inherent powers as interpretations of enumerated powers but implied others structurally as freestanding powers. The latter included the power to acquire new territory by discovery and occupation, the power to control the entry and residence of aliens, and the power to require citizens residing abroad to return. To the extent that these arguments relied on older publicists such as Vattel, they may be construed as imputing earlier international law doctrines to the framers; to the extent that they relied on current authors and later instances of state practice, their claims of necessary sovereign powers addressed the international regime of their own period.

Inherent sovereign powers construed as ancillary to enumerated powers included the power to govern overseas territories acquired by treaty as colonies, the power to conscript soldiers, the federal power of eminent domain, and even the federal power to make paper money legal tender. In some of these cases, no international obligation or relationship was implicated, and the publicists served less as guides to genuinely international law than as theorists of sovereignty and compilers of general principles of public law common to "civilized nations." Such usage blurs the distinction between employing international law as an interpretive aid and employing foreign law, but those two categories can be difficult to separate, given that patterns of state practice provide evidence of international law. . . .

The Supreme Court has also invoked international and foreign sources in construing other constitutional amendments, including the Thirteenth Amendment, the Eighteenth Amendment, and . . . the Eighth Amendment.

Gerald L. Neuman, *The Uses of International Law in Constitutional Interpretation*, 98 Am. J. Int'l L. 82 (2004).

6. Professor Alford is less sanguine about the trend of using foreign and international materials to inform constitutional interpretation:

The first misuse of international sources—particularly evident in death penalty litigation—occurs when the "global opinions of humankind" are ascribed constitutional value to thwart the domestic opinions of Americans. To the extent that value judgments are a source of constitutional understandings of community standards, in the hierarchical ranking of relative values domestic majoritarian judgments should hold sway over international majoritarian values. . . .

The second misuse of international sources occurs when treaties are elevated to a status they do not enjoy under our federal system. The entire edifice of constitutional law rests on the foundation that the acts of the political branches are subject to and limited by the Constitution. . . .

The third misuse of international sources occurs when the Court references them haphazardly, relying on only those materials that are readily at its fingertips. In the international legal arena, where the Court has little or no expertise, the Court is unduly susceptible to selective and incomplete presentations of the true state of international and foreign affairs. . .

A final misuse occurs when international and foreign materials are used selectively. In a country that "considers itself the world's foremost protector of civil liberties," what is perhaps most surprising about the enthusiasm for comparativism is the assumption that it will enhance rather than diminish basic human rights in this country. This assumption is either blind to our visionary leadership, deaf to the discord in the international instruments, or selectively mute in giving voice to only certain topics for comparison.

Roger P. Alford, *Misusing International Sources to Interpret the Constitution*, 98 Am. J. Int'l L. 57 (2004). Which, if any, of these "misuses" occurred in *Roper*? How can Professor Alford's concerns be reconciled with Professor Neuman's historical summary?

7. As Justice Scalia points out in his dissent in *Roper*, the Court has not yet invoked foreign and international materials as a basis for moving U.S. constitutional law in a less progressive direction. For example, the U.S. Constitution has been interpreted to protect abortion, free speech, and criminal procedure rights more vigorously than international or foreign law typically require. Should the Court rethink its doctrines in these areas? Or are international and foreign materials only potentially relevant when they are more rights-protecting, perhaps akin to the notion that state constitutional law can be more rights-protecting, but not less so, than U.S. constitutional rights? Relatedly, is the practice of relying on foreign and international materials to inform the meaning of the U.S. Constitution sufficiently respectful of the values of diversity? Are there unique practices in the United States, grounded in the United States' particular history and culture, that are worth preserving? For example, the United States has one of the most speech-protective constitutional doctrines in the world. How should courts determine which unique practices are and are not worth preserving?

8. Was it problematic for the Court in *Roper* to rely on a treaty that the United States has not ratified (the Convention on the Rights of the Child) and a treaty that the United States had made non-self-executing and to which the United States attached a reservation on the issue of the juvenile death penalty (the International Covenant on Civil and Political Rights) as a basis for interpreting the Eighth Amendment? Why wasn't the political branches' self-conscious effort not to eliminate the juvenile death penalty by treaty more relevant to the cruelty and unusualness of the juvenile death penalty than the views in other nations? What does the answer to this question suggest about answers to the questions in Note 2? Is the Court's use of treaties in *Roper* consistent with the respect that courts generally pay to U.S. reservations, understandings, and declarations when claims based on treaties are brought before them (see Chapter 5)? Is it consistent with the Court's restrictive conception of customary international law sources in *Sosa?*

9. What is the relationship between the Court's reliance in *Roper* on foreign and international materials and the *Charming Betsy* canon discussed in the previous section? Does the *Charming Betsy* canon apply to constitutional interpretation? How would it work in that context? For example, would it require interpreting the Eighth Amendment to prohibit criminal punishments that violate international law? If the Eighth Amendment did not prohibit such criminal punishments, would that mean that the Eighth Amendment was in violation of international law? Or is it the federal or state enactment of the criminal punishments that would violate international law? And, if those enactments were clear, would there be any role for the *Charming Betsy* canon? In any event, does the Court in *Roper* conclude that the execution of juvenile offenders in the United States violates international law?

10. Bills have been proposed in Congress in recent years that would restrict the Supreme Court's reliance on foreign and international materials in constitutional interpretation, but serious questions have been raised about their consistency with Article III of the Constitution, and none has been enacted. As noted in Chapter 4, however, some states have enacted legislation restricting the use of foreign and international law by state courts. *See* Aaron Fellmeth, *International Law and Foreign Laws in the U.S. State Legislatures*, ASIL Insight (May 26, 2011), at https://www.asil.org/insights/volume/15/issue/13/international-law-and-foreign-laws-us-state-legislatures.

11. As discussed in Chapter 10, the Supreme Court held in Hamdan v. Rumsfeld, 548 U.S. 557 (2006), that Common Article 3 of the Geneva Conventions applied to the conflict between the United States and the Al Qaeda terrorist organization. In the subsequent Military Commission Act of 2006 (MCA), Congress amended the War Crimes Act, 28 U.S.C. §2441 (excerpted in Chapter 9), in order to clarify what constitutes a grave breach of Common Article 3. The MCA states that the amended sections of the War Crimes Act "fully satisfy the obligation" under the Geneva Conventions to punish grave breaches under Common Article 3. The MCA then provides: "No foreign or international source of law shall supply a basis for a rule of decision in the courts of the United States in interpreting the prohibitions enumerated in" the amended portion of the War Crimes Act. What do you think

Congress was trying to accomplish in this provision? Is its attempt to prevent courts from consulting foreign or international materials constitutional?

12. The Supreme Court returned to the issue of the relevance of foreign and international law to constitutional interpretation in Graham v. Florida, 560 U.S. 48 (2010). In support of its holding that the Eighth Amendment prohibits life imprisonment of a juvenile for a non-homicide offense, the Court pointed to numerous foreign and international sources. The Court noted that "the United States is the only Nation that imposes life without parole sentences on juvenile nonhomicide offenders." It also noted that the Convention on the Rights of the Child, a treaty ratified by every nation except the United States and Somalia, prohibits the imposition of "life imprisonment without possibility of release . . . for offences committed by persons below eighteen years of age." While the Court acknowledged that this treaty is not binding on the United States, it explained that "[t]he question before us is not whether international law prohibits the United States from imposing the sentence at issue in this case," but rather "whether that punishment is cruel and unusual." In making that determination, said the Court, " 'the overwhelming weight of international opinion against' life without parole for nonhomicide offenses committed by juveniles 'provide[s] respected and significant confirmation for our own conclusions.' " (quoting Roper v. Simmons, 543 U.S. 551, 578 (2005)). The Court made clear that the laws and practices of foreign nations, as well as international agreements, were "relevant to the Eighth Amendment not because those norms are binding or controlling but because the judgment of the world's nations that a particular sentencing practice is inconsistent with basic principles of decency demonstrates that the Court's rationale has respected reasoning to support it."

In dissent, Justice Thomas, joined by Justices Scalia and Alito, observed that, "despite the Court's attempt to count the actual number of juvenile nonhomicide offenders serving life-without-parole sentences in other nations (a task even more challenging than counting them within our borders), the *laws* of other countries permit juvenile life-without-parole sentences." In addition, he noted that "democracies around the world remain free to adopt life-without-parole sentences for juvenile offenders tomorrow if they see fit," but "starting today, ours can count itself among the few in which judicial decree prevents voters from making that choice."

13. A large literature analyzes the use of foreign and international materials in constitutional interpretation. Representative examples include Jeremy Waldron, "Partly Laws Common to All Mankind": Foreign Law in American Courts (2012); *Agora: The United States Constitution and International Law*, 98 Am. J. Int'l L. 42 (2004); Roger Alford, *In Search of a Theory for Constitutional Comparativism*, 52 UCLA L. Rev. 639 (2005); Daniel Bodansky, *The Use of International Sources in Constitutional Opinion*, 32 Ga. J. Int'l & Comp. L. 421 (2004); Steven G. Calabresi & Stephanie Dotson Zimdahl, *The Supreme Court and Foreign Sources of Law: Two Hundred Years of Practice and the Juvenile Death Penalty Decision*, 47 Wm. & Mary L. Rev. 743 (2005); Sarah H. Cleveland, *Our International Constitution*, 31 Yale J. Int'l L. 1 (2006); Robert J. Delahunty & John Yoo, *Against Foreign Law*, 29 Harv. J.L. & Pub. Pol'y 291 (2005); Daniel A. Farber, *The Supreme Court, the Law of Nations, and Citations of Foreign Law: The Lessons of History*, 95 Cal. L. Rev. 1335 (2007); Vicki C. Jackson, *Constitutional Comparisons: Convergence, Resistance, Engagement*, 119 Harv. L. Rev. 109 (2005); Austen L. Parrish, *Storm in a Teacup: The U.S. Supreme Court's Use of Foreign Law*, 2007 U. Ill. L. Rev. 637 (2007); Eric A. Posner & Cass R. Sunstein, *The Law of Other States*, 59 Stan. L. Rev. 131 (2006); Nicholas Quinn Rosenkranz, *Condorcet and the Constitution: A Response to* The Law of Other States, 59 Stan. L. Rev. 1281 (2007); Ganesh Sitaraman,

The Use and Abuse of Foreign Law in Constitutional Interpretation, 32 Harv. J.L. & Pub. Pol'y 653 (2009); Mark Tushnet, *Transnational/Domestic Constitutional Law*, 37 Loy. L.A. L. Rev. 239 (2003); Michael Wells, *International Norms in Constitutional Law*, 32 Ga. J. Int'l & Comp. L. 429 (2004); Stephen Yeazell, *When and How U.S. Courts Should Cite Foreign Law*, 26 Const. Comm. 59 (2009); Ernest A. Young, *Foreign Law and the Denominator Problem*, 119 Harv. L. Rev. 148 (2005).

PART IV

CRIME, WAR, AND TERRORISM

8

International Crime

This chapter considers the application of U.S. criminal law and enforcement authority beyond the nation's borders. Section A examines the extent to which the U.S. Constitution's individual rights protections apply abroad, including in ways that might limit the extraterritorial application and enforcement of criminal law. Section B then explores general issues relating to the extraterritorial application of U.S. federal criminal statutes. Section C focuses on the criminal prosecution of acts of piracy, which raises particularly interesting questions about the relationship between U.S. law and international law. Section D describes various aspects of U.S. extradition law. Finally, Section E considers the legal consequences of the United States' extraterritorial abduction of criminal suspects.

A. THE CONSTITUTION ABROAD

Reid v. Covert

354 U.S. 1 (1957)

[Clarice Covert, a civilian, killed her husband, a sergeant in the United States Air Force, at an airbase in England. Dorothy Smith, also a civilian, killed her husband, an Army officer, at a post in Japan. Both women were tried by a court martial for murder—in England and Japan, respectively—under the Uniform Code of Military Justice (UCMJ), Article 2(11) of which provided:

> The following persons are subject to this code: . . .
>
> Subject to the provisions of any treaty or agreement to which the United States is or may be a party or to any accepted rule of international law, all persons serving with, employed by, or accompanying the armed forces without the continental limits of the United States. . . .

Both women claimed that they were insane at the time of the murder; both were found guilty and sentenced to life in prison; and both filed petitions for a writ of habeas corpus, arguing that the Constitution prohibited their trial by military authorities. One court granted the writ; another denied it. The Supreme Court consolidated the cases and initially held that the military trials were constitutional. The Court subsequently granted rehearing and issued the following decision.]

MR. JUSTICE BLACK announced the judgment of the Court and delivered an opinion, in which THE CHIEF JUSTICE, MR. JUSTICE DOUGLAS, and MR. JUSTICE BRENNAN join. . . .

At the beginning we reject the idea that when the United States acts against citizens abroad it can do so free of the Bill of Rights. The United States is entirely a creature of the Constitution. Its power and authority have no other source. It can only act in accordance with all the limitations imposed by the Constitution. When the Government reaches out to punish a citizen who is abroad, the shield which the Bill of Rights and other parts of the Constitution provide to protect his life and liberty should not be stripped away just because he happens to be in another land. This is not a novel concept. To the contrary, it is as old as government. . . .

The rights and liberties which citizens of our country enjoy are not protected by custom and tradition alone, they have been jealously preserved from the encroachments of Government by express provisions of our written Constitution.

Among those provisions, Art. III, §2 and the Fifth and Sixth Amendments are directly relevant to these cases. . . .

The language of Art. III, §2 manifests that constitutional protections for the individual were designed to restrict the United States Government when it acts outside of this country, as well as here at home. After declaring that *all* criminal trials must be by jury, the section states that when a crime is "not committed within any State, the Trial shall be at such Place or Places as the Congress may by Law have directed." If this language is permitted to have its obvious meaning, §2 is applicable to criminal trials outside of the States as a group without regard to where the offense is committed or the trial held. . . . The Fifth and Sixth Amendments, like Art. III, §2, are also all inclusive with their sweeping references to "no person" and to "all criminal prosecutions."

. . . While it has been suggested that only those constitutional rights which are "fundamental" protect Americans abroad, we can find no warrant, in logic or otherwise, for picking and choosing among the remarkable collection of "Thou shalt nots" which were explicitly fastened on all departments and agencies of the Federal Government by the Constitution and its Amendments. Moreover, in view of our heritage and the history of the adoption of the Constitution and the Bill of Rights, it seems peculiarly anomalous to say that trial before a civilian judge and by an independent jury picked from the common citizenry is not a fundamental right. . . .

The keystone of supporting authorities mustered by the Court's opinion last June to justify its holding that Art. III, §2, and the Fifth and Sixth Amendments did not apply abroad was In re Ross, 140 U.S. 453. The *Ross* case is one of those cases that cannot be understood except in its peculiar setting; even then, it seems highly unlikely that a similar result would be reached today. Ross was serving as a seaman on an American ship in Japanese waters. He killed a ship's officer, was seized and tried before a consular "court" in Japan. At that time, statutes authorized American consuls to try American citizens charged with committing crimes in Japan and certain other "non-Christian" countries. These statutes provided that the laws of the United States were to govern the trial except:

> where such laws are not adapted to the object, or are deficient in the provisions necessary to furnish suitable remedies, the common law and the law of equity and admiralty shall be extended in like manner over such citizens and others in those countries; and if neither the common law, nor the law of equity or admiralty, nor the statutes of the United States, furnish appropriate and sufficient remedies, the ministers in those countries, respectively, shall, by decrees and regulations which shall have the force of law, supply such defects and deficiencies.

The consular power approved in the *Ross* case was about as extreme and absolute as that of the potentates of the "non-Christian" countries to which the statutes applied. Under these statutes consuls could and did make the criminal laws, initiate charges, arrest alleged offenders, try them, and after conviction take away their liberty or their life — sometimes at the American consulate. Such a blending of executive, legislative, and judicial powers in one person or even in one branch of the Government is ordinarily regarded as the very acme of absolutism. Nevertheless, the Court sustained Ross' conviction by the consul. It stated that constitutional protections applied "only to citizens and others within the United States, or who are brought there for trial for alleged offences committed elsewhere, and not to residents or temporary sojourners abroad." Despite the fact that it upheld Ross' conviction under United States laws passed pursuant to asserted constitutional authority, the Court went on to make a sweeping declaration that "[t]he Constitution can have no operation in another country."

The *Ross* approach that the Constitution has no applicability abroad has long since been directly repudiated by numerous cases. That approach is obviously erroneous if the United States Government, which has no power except that granted by the Constitution, can and does try citizens for crimes committed abroad. Thus the *Ross* case rested, at least in substantial part, on a fundamental misconception and the most that can be said in support of the result reached there is that the consular court jurisdiction had a long history antedating the adoption of the Constitution. The Congress has recently buried the consular system of trying Americans. We are not willing to jeopardize the lives and liberties of Americans by disinterring it. At best, the *Ross* case should be left as a relic from a different era.

The Court's opinion last Term also relied on the "Insular Cases" to support its conclusion that Article III and the Fifth and Sixth Amendments were not applicable to the trial of Mrs. Smith and Mrs. Covert. We believe that reliance was misplaced. The "Insular Cases," which arose at the turn of the century, involved territories which had only recently been conquered or acquired by the United States. These territories, governed and regulated by Congress under Art. IV, §3, had entirely different cultures and customs from those of this country. This Court, although closely divided, ruled that certain constitutional safeguards were not applicable to these territories since they had not been "expressly or impliedly incorporated" into the Union by Congress. While conceding that "fundamental" constitutional rights applied everywhere, the majority found that it would disrupt long-established practices and would be inexpedient to require a jury trial after an indictment by a grand jury in the insular possessions.

The "Insular Cases" can be distinguished from the present cases in that they involved the power of Congress to provide rules and regulations to govern temporarily territories with wholly dissimilar traditions and institutions whereas here the basis for governmental power is American citizenship. None of these cases had anything to do with military trials and they cannot properly be used as vehicles to support an extension of military jurisdiction to civilians. Moreover, it is our judgment that neither the cases nor their reasoning should be given any further expansion. The concept that the Bill of Rights and other constitutional protections against arbitrary government are inoperative when they become inconvenient or when expediency dictates otherwise is a very dangerous doctrine and if allowed to flourish would destroy the benefit of a written Constitution and undermine the basis of our Government. If our foreign commitments become of such nature that the Government can no longer satisfactorily operate within the bounds laid down by the

Constitution, that instrument can be amended by the method which it prescribes. But we have no authority, or inclination, to read exceptions into it which are not there. . . .

MR. JUSTICE HARLAN, concurring in the result.

I concur in the result, on the narrow ground that where the offense is capital, Article 2(11) cannot constitutionally be applied to the trial of civilian dependents of members of the armed forces overseas in times of peace. . . .

Under the Constitution Congress has only such powers as are expressly granted or those that are implied as reasonably necessary and proper to carry out the granted powers. Hence the constitutionality of the statute here in question must be tested, not by abstract notions of what is reasonable "in the large," so to speak, but by whether the statute, as applied in these instances, is a reasonably necessary and proper means of implementing a power granted to Congress by the Constitution. To say that the validity of the statute may be rested upon the inherent "sovereign powers" of this country in its dealings with foreign nations seems to me to be no more than begging the question. As I now see it, the validity of this court-martial jurisdiction must depend upon whether the statute, as applied to these women, can be justified as an exercise of the power, granted to Congress by Art. I, §8, cl. 14 of the Constitution, "To make Rules for the Government and Regulation of the land and naval Forces." I can find no other constitutional power to which this statute can properly be related.

. . . We return, therefore, to the *Ross* question: to what extent do these provisions of the Constitution apply outside the United States?

As I have already stated, I do not think that it can be said that these safeguards of the Constitution are never operative without the United States, regardless of the particular circumstances. On the other hand, I cannot agree with the suggestion that every provision of the Constitution must always be deemed automatically applicable to American citizens in every part of the world. For *Ross* and the *Insular Cases* do stand for an important proposition, one which seems to me a wise and necessary gloss on our Constitution. The proposition is, of course, not that the Constitution "does not apply" overseas, but that there are provisions in the Constitution which do not *necessarily* apply in all circumstances in every foreign place. . . . In other words, what *Ross* and the *Insular Cases* hold is that the particular local setting, the practical necessities, and the possible alternatives are relevant to a question of judgment, namely, whether jury trial *should* be deemed a necessary condition of the exercise of Congress' power to provide for the trial of Americans overseas.

I think the above thought is crucial in approaching the cases before us. Decision is easy if one adopts the constricting view that these constitutional guarantees as a totality do or do not "apply" overseas. But, for me, the question is *which* guarantees of the Constitution *should* apply in view of the particular circumstances, the practical necessities, and the possible alternatives which Congress had before it. The question is one of judgment, not of compulsion. . . . [W]e have before us a question analogous, ultimately, to issues of due process; one can say, in fact, that the question of which specific safeguards of the Constitution are appropriately to be applied in a particular context overseas can be reduced to the issue of what process is "due" a defendant in the particular circumstances of a particular case.

On this basis, I cannot agree with the sweeping proposition that a full Article III trial, with indictment and trial by jury, is required in every case for the trial of a civilian dependent of a serviceman overseas. The Government, it seems to me, has made an impressive showing that at least for the run-of-the-mill offenses committed by dependents overseas, such a requirement would be . . . impractical and . . . anomalous. . . .

So far as capital cases are concerned, I think they stand on quite a different footing than other offenses. In such cases the law is especially sensitive to demands for that procedural fairness which inheres in a civilian trial where the judge and trier of fact are not responsive to the command of the convening authority. . . . The number of such cases would appear to be so negligible that the practical problems of affording the defendant a civilian trial would not present insuperable problems.

United States v. Verdugo-Urquidez

494 U.S. 259 (1990)

[Verdugo-Urquidez, a citizen and resident of Mexico, was believed by the United States Drug Enforcement Agency (DEA) to be a leader of an organization in Mexico that smuggled narcotics into the United States. In cooperation with U.S. officials, Mexican police officials apprehended Verdugo-Urquidez and brought him to the U.S. Border Patrol station in Calexico, California, where U.S. officials arrested him pursuant to a U.S. arrest warrant. U.S. officials subsequently searched Verdugo-Urquidez's home in Mexico without a U.S. search warrant, but with the authorization of Mexican officials. A U.S. district court suppressed the evidence of criminality discovered during this search, reasoning that the Fourth Amendment applied to the searches and that the DEA agents had failed to justify searching Verdugo-Urquidez's premises without a warrant. A divided panel of the Court of Appeals for the Ninth Circuit affirmed.]

CHIEF JUSTICE REHNQUIST delivered the opinion of the Court. . . .

Before analyzing the scope of the Fourth Amendment, we think it significant to note that it operates in a different manner than the Fifth Amendment, which is not at issue in this case. The privilege against self-incrimination guaranteed by the Fifth Amendment is a fundamental trial right of criminal defendants. Although conduct by law enforcement officials prior to trial may ultimately impair that right, a constitutional violation occurs only at trial. The Fourth Amendment functions differently. It prohibits "unreasonable searches and seizures" whether or not the evidence is sought to be used in a criminal trial, and a violation of the Amendment is "fully accomplished" at the time of an unreasonable governmental intrusion. United States v. Calandra, 414 U.S. 338, 354 (1974); United States v. Leon, 468 U.S. 897, 906 (1984). For purposes of this case, therefore, if there were a constitutional violation, it occurred solely in Mexico. Whether evidence obtained from respondent's Mexican residences should be excluded at trial in the United States is a remedial question separate from the existence vel non of the constitutional violation. . . .

That text [of the Fourth Amendment], by contrast with the Fifth and Sixth Amendments, extends its reach only to "the people." . . . "[T]he people" seems to have been a term of art employed in select parts of the Constitution. The Preamble declares that the Constitution is ordained and established by "the People of the United States." The Second Amendment protects "the right of the people to keep and bear Arms," and the Ninth and Tenth Amendments provide that certain rights and powers are retained by and reserved to "the people." While this textual exegesis is by no means conclusive, it suggests that "the people" protected by the Fourth Amendment, and by the First and Second Amendments, and to whom rights and powers are reserved in the Ninth and Tenth Amendments, refers to a class of persons who are part of a national community or who have otherwise developed sufficient connection with this country to be considered part of that community. The language of these Amendments contrasts with the words "person" and "accused" used in the Fifth and Sixth Amendments regulating procedure in criminal cases.

What we know of the history of the drafting of the Fourth Amendment also suggests that its purpose was to restrict searches and seizures which might be conducted by the United States in domestic matters. The Framers originally decided not to include a provision like the Fourth Amendment, because they believed the National Government lacked power to conduct searches and seizures. Many disputed the original view that the Federal Government possessed only narrow delegated powers over domestic affairs, however, and ultimately felt an Amendment prohibiting unreasonable searches and seizures was necessary. . . . The driving force behind the adoption of the Amendment . . . was widespread hostility among the former colonists to the issuance of writs of assistance empowering revenue officers to search suspected places for smuggled goods, and general search warrants permitting the search of private houses, often to uncover papers that might be used to convict persons of libel. The available historical data show, therefore, that the purpose of the Fourth Amendment was to protect the people of the United States against arbitrary action by their own Government; it was never suggested that the provision was intended to restrain the actions of the Federal Government against aliens outside of the United States territory. . . .

The global view taken by the Court of Appeals of the application of the Constitution is also contrary to this Court's decisions in the *Insular Cases,* which held that not every constitutional provision applies to governmental activity even where the United States has sovereign power. . . . If that is true with respect to territories ultimately governed by Congress, respondent's claim that the protections of the Fourth Amendment extend to aliens in foreign nations is even weaker. And certainly, it is not open to us in light of the *Insular Cases* to endorse the view that every constitutional provision applies wherever the United States Government exercises its power.

Indeed, we have rejected the claim that aliens are entitled to Fifth Amendment rights outside the sovereign territory of the United States. In Johnson v. Eisentrager, 339 U.S. 763 (1950), the Court held that enemy aliens arrested in China and imprisoned in Germany after World War II could not obtain writs of habeas corpus in our federal courts on the ground that their convictions for war crimes had violated the Fifth Amendment and other constitutional provisions. . . .

To support his all-encompassing view of the Fourth Amendment, respondent points to language from the plurality opinion in Reid v. Covert, 354 U.S. 1 (1957). . . .

Respondent urges that we interpret [*Reid*] to mean that federal officials are constrained by the Fourth Amendment wherever and against whomever they act. But the holding of *Reid* stands for no such sweeping proposition: it decided that United States citizens stationed abroad could invoke the protection of the Fifth and Sixth Amendments. The concurring opinions . . . in *Reid* resolved the case on much narrower grounds than the plurality and declined even to hold that United States citizens were entitled to the full range of constitutional protections in all overseas criminal prosecutions. Since respondent is not a United States citizen, he can derive no comfort from the *Reid* holding.

Verdugo-Urquidez also relies on a series of cases in which we have held that aliens enjoy certain constitutional rights. These cases, however, establish only that aliens receive constitutional protections when they have come within the territory of the United States and developed substantial connections with the country. Respondent is an alien who has had no previous significant voluntary connection with the United States, so these cases avail him not. . . .

[Respondent's current presence in the United States for trial] is not of the sort to indicate any substantial connection with our country. The extent to which respondent might claim the protection of the Fourth Amendment if the duration of his stay in the United States were to be prolonged—by a prison sentence, for example—we need not decide. When the search of his house in Mexico took place, he had been present in the United States for only a matter of days. We do not think the applicability of the Fourth Amendment to the search of premises in Mexico should turn on the fortuitous circumstance of whether the custodian of its nonresident alien owner had or had not transported him to the United States at the time the search was made. . . .

Not only are history and case law against respondent, but as pointed out in Johnson v. Eisentrager, 393 U.S. 763 (1950), the result of accepting his claim would have significant and deleterious consequences for the United States in conducting activities beyond its boundaries. The rule adopted by the Court of Appeals would apply not only to law enforcement operations abroad, but also to other foreign policy operations which might result in "searches or seizures." The United States frequently employs armed forces outside this country—over 200 times in our history—for the protection of American citizens or national security. Application of the Fourth Amendment to those circumstances could significantly disrupt the ability of the political branches to respond to foreign situations involving our national interest. Were respondent to prevail, aliens with no attachment to this country might well bring actions for damages to remedy claimed violations of the Fourth Amendment in foreign countries or in international waters. . . .

We think that the text of the Fourth Amendment, its history, and our cases discussing the application of the Constitution to aliens and extraterritorially require rejection of respondent's claim. At the time of the search, he was a citizen and resident of Mexico with no voluntary attachment to the United States, and the place searched was located in Mexico. Under these circumstances, the Fourth Amendment has no application.

For better or for worse, we live in a world of nation-states in which our Government must be able to "functio[n] effectively in the company of sovereign nations." Perez v. Brownell, 356 U.S. 44, 57 (1958). Some who violate our laws may live outside our borders under a regime quite different from that which obtains in this country. Situations threatening to important American interests may arise halfway around the globe, situations which in the view of the political branches of our Government require an American response with armed force. If there are to be restrictions on searches and seizures which occur incident to such American action, they must be imposed by the political branches through diplomatic understanding, treaty, or legislation. . . .

JUSTICE KENNEDY, concurring. . . .

The conditions and considerations of this case would make adherence to the Fourth Amendment's warrant requirement impracticable and anomalous. Just as the Constitution in the *Insular Cases* did not require Congress to implement all constitutional guarantees in its territories because of their "wholly dissimilar traditions and institutions," the Constitution does not require United States agents to obtain a warrant when searching the foreign home of a nonresident alien. If the search had occurred in a residence within the United States, I have little doubt that the full protections of the Fourth Amendment would apply. But that is not this case. The absence of local judges or magistrates available to issue warrants, the differing and perhaps unascertainable conceptions of reasonableness and privacy that prevail abroad, and the need to cooperate with foreign officials all indicate that the Fourth Amendment's warrant requirement should not apply in Mexico as it does in this country. For this reason, in addition to the other persuasive justifications stated by the Court, I agree that no violation of the Fourth Amendment has occurred in the case before us. The rights of a citizen, as to whom the United States has continuing obligations, are not presented by this case.

I do not mean to imply, and the Court has not decided, that persons in the position of the respondent have no constitutional protection. The United States is prosecuting a foreign national in a court established under Article III, and all of the trial proceedings are governed by the Constitution. All would agree, for instance, that the dictates of the Due Process Clause of the Fifth Amendment protect the defendant. Indeed, as Justice Harlan put it [in *Reid*], "the question of which specific safeguards . . . are appropriately to be applied in a particular context . . . can be reduced to the issue of what process is 'due' a defendant in the particular circumstances of a particular case." Nothing approaching a violation of due process has occurred in this case. . . .

JUSTICE BRENNAN, with whom JUSTICE MARSHALL joins, dissenting. . . .

The Court today creates an antilogy: the Constitution authorizes our Government to enforce our criminal laws abroad, but when Government agents exercise this authority, the Fourth Amendment does not travel with them. This cannot be. At the very least, the Fourth Amendment is an unavoidable correlative of the Government's power to enforce the criminal law.

What the majority ignores . . . is the most obvious connection between Verdugo-Urquidez and the United States: he was investigated and is being prosecuted for violations of United States law and may well spend the rest of his life in a United States prison. The "sufficient connection" is supplied not by Verdugo-Urquidez, but by the Government. Respondent is entitled to the protections of the Fourth Amendment because our Government, by investigating him and attempting to hold him accountable under United States criminal laws, has treated him as a member of our community for purposes of enforcing our laws. He has become, quite literally, one of the governed. Fundamental fairness and the ideals underlying our Bill of Rights compel the conclusion that when we impose "societal obligations," such as the obligation to comply with our criminal laws, on foreign nationals, we in turn are obliged to respect certain correlative rights, among them the Fourth Amendment.

By concluding that respondent is not one of "the people" protected by the Fourth Amendment, the majority disregards basic notions of mutuality. If we expect aliens to obey our laws, aliens should be able to expect that we will obey our Constitution when we investigate, prosecute, and punish them. . . .

Mutuality is essential to ensure the fundamental fairness that underlies our Bill of Rights. Foreign nationals investigated and prosecuted for alleged violations of United States criminal laws are just as vulnerable to oppressive Government behavior as are United States citizens investigated and prosecuted for the same alleged violations. Indeed, in a case such as this where the Government claims the existence of an international criminal conspiracy, citizens and foreign nationals may be codefendants, charged under the same statutes for the same conduct and facing the same penalties if convicted. They may have been investigated by the same agents pursuant to the same enforcement authority. When our Government holds these codefendants to the same standards of conduct, the Fourth Amendment, which protects the citizen from unreasonable searches and seizures, should protect the foreign national as well.

Mutuality also serves to inculcate the values of law and order. By respecting the rights of foreign nationals, we encourage other nations to respect the rights of our citizens. Moreover, as our Nation becomes increasingly concerned about the domestic effects of international crime, we cannot forget that the behavior of our law enforcement agents abroad sends a powerful message about the rule of law to individuals everywhere. . . . This principle is no different when the United States applies its rules of conduct to foreign nationals. If we seek respect for law and order, we must observe these principles ourselves. Lawlessness breeds lawlessness.

Finally, when United States agents conduct unreasonable searches, whether at home or abroad, they disregard our Nation's values. For over 200 years, our country has considered itself the world's foremost protector of liberties. The privacy and sanctity of the home have been primary tenets of our moral, philosophical, and judicial beliefs. Our national interest is defined by those values and by the need to preserve our own just institutions. We take pride in our commitment to a Government that cannot, on mere whim, break down doors and invade the most personal of places. We exhort other nations to follow our example. How can we explain to others — and to ourselves — that these long cherished ideals are suddenly of no consequence when the door being broken belongs to a foreigner? . . .

The majority's rejection of respondent's claim to Fourth Amendment protection is apparently motivated by its fear that application of the Amendment to law enforcement searches against foreign nationals overseas "could significantly disrupt the ability of the political branches to respond to foreign situations involving our national interest." The majority's doomsday scenario — that American Armed Forces conducting a mission to protect our national security with no law enforcement objective "would have to articulate specific facts giving them probable cause to undertake a search or seizure" — is fanciful. Verdugo-Urquidez is protected by the Fourth Amendment because our Government, by investigating and prosecuting him, has made him one of "the governed." Accepting respondent as one of "the governed," however, hardly requires the Court to accept enemy aliens in wartime as among "the governed" entitled to invoke the protection of the Fourth Amendment.

Moreover, with respect to non-law-enforcement activities not directed against enemy aliens in wartime but nevertheless implicating national security, doctrinal exceptions to the general requirements of a warrant and probable cause likely would be applicable more frequently abroad, thus lessening the purported tension between the Fourth Amendment's strictures and the Executive's foreign affairs power. Many situations involving sensitive operations abroad likely would involve exigent circumstances such that the warrant requirement would be excused.

Therefore, the Government's conduct would be assessed only under the reasonableness standard, the application of which depends on context.

Notes and Questions

1. The preamble to the Constitution provides: "We the People of the United States, in Order to . . . secure the Blessings of Liberty to ourselves and our Posterity, do ordain and establish this Constitution for the United States of America." The Supremacy Clause states that "[t]his Constitution . . . shall be the supreme Law of the Land." And Article III authorizes federal court jurisdiction over, among other things, suits involving foreign citizens, subjects, and ambassadors. What, if anything, do these provisions suggest about the geographical scope of the U.S. Constitution?

2. Constitutional rights apply with full force to U.S. citizens within the United States. Aliens within the United States are also considered persons entitled to constitutional protection. *See, e.g.,* Zadvydas v. Davis, 533 U.S. 678, 693 (2001); Yick Wo v. Hopkins, 118 U.S. 356 (1886). Even aliens not within the United States are entitled to some constitutional protection, at least with respect to governmental actions taken within the United States that affect their interests. *See, e.g.,* J. McIntyre Machinery, Ltd. v. Nicastro, 131 S. Ct. 2780 (2011) (applying due process limits on personal jurisdiction to claim against British corporation); Asahi Metal Indus. Co. v. Superior Court, 480 U.S. 102 (1987) (applying due process limits on personal jurisdiction to claim against Japanese corporation). With respect to governmental actions taken wholly outside the United States, constitutional protection has been less certain. In the nineteenth century, the Supreme Court expressed skepticism about the extent to which the Constitution applied in this situation. *See, e.g.,* In re Ross, 140 U.S. 453, 464 (1891) (reasoning that the Constitution did not apply to the trial of an American seaman by an American consular tribunal in Japan because "[t]he Constitution can have no operation in another country"). In the *Insular Cases*, the Court held that the United States need only confer "fundamental" constitutional rights on citizens and aliens alike in "unincorporated" possessions abroad over which the United States exercised sovereignty. *See, e.g.,* DeLima v. Bidwell, 182 U.S. 1 (1901). For a comprehensive discussion of this line of cases, see Gerald L. Neuman, *Whose Constitution?*, 100 Yale L.J. 909 (1991). What is the status of *Ross* and the *Insular Cases* after the decisions excerpted above?

3. There are at least four possible approaches to the application of constitutional rights. First, a "universalist" approach "require[s] that constitutional provisions that create rights with no express limitations as to the persons or places covered should be interpreted as applicable to every person and at every place." Second, a "membership" approach "legitimates government through the idea of an actual or hypothetical agreement embodying the consent of the governed who have established the state and empowered it to govern." On this view, "beneficiaries have rights based in the contract; nonbeneficiaries are relegated to whatever rights they may have independent of the contract." The only difficult issue is the identity of the parties to the contract. Third, under a "territorial" model, "the Constitution constrains the United States government only when it acts within the borders of the United States." Fourth, and finally, a "balancing" approach holds that "the government's reduced right to obedience [abroad] and reduced means of enforcement [abroad] may call for a reciprocal reduction in individual rights [abroad]." *See* Neuman, *supra*, at 916-21. Which of these four approaches is normatively most attractive? Which does the U.S. Constitution embrace? Which approach is embraced by each of the opinions excerpted above?

4. Are you convinced by the reasoning of the *Reid* plurality? Does the plurality's claim that the United States "can only act in accordance with all the limitations imposed by the Constitution" beg the question whether the Constitution limits federal action abroad? Are you convinced by the inferences of extraterritorial reach that the plurality draws from Article III, §2? Do you think the drafters of Article III had extraterritoriality in mind? Even if we accept the inference of extraterritoriality from Article III, should we draw the same conclusion from the Fifth and Sixth Amendments' "sweeping references to 'no person' and to 'all criminal prosecutions'"? In answering these questions, what is the relevance, if any, of Congress's Article I power to "make Rules for the Government and Regulation of the land and naval forces"?

5. What are the differences in reasoning between the *Reid* plurality and Justice Harlan's concurrence? Harlan disagrees with "the suggestion that every provision of the Constitution must always be deemed automatically applicable to American citizens in every part of the world." And yet he concludes that the United States must respect the right to trial by jury and indictment by grand jury when prosecuting civilians abroad for capital crimes. How does Harlan know the extent to which the Constitution applies abroad? What guidance does he provide for future cases? Because of Harlan's concurrence, the *Reid* holding was technically limited to capital cases. The Supreme Court extended *Reid*'s holding to noncapital cases in Kinsella v. United States ex rel. Singleton, 361 U.S. 234 (1960). For additional background on Reid v. Covert, and consideration more broadly of the phenomenon of prosecuting civilians in military courts-martial, see Captain Brittany Warren, *The Case of the Murdering Wives:* Reid v. Covert *and the Complicated Question of Civilians and Courts-Martial,* 212 Mil. L. Rev. 133 (2012).

6. Is *Verdugo-Urquidez* consistent with *Reid*? Do you agree with the *Verdugo-Urquidez* majority that the Fourth Amendment violation, if any, took place in Mexico rather than in the United States? In a trial within the United States, should the scope of constitutional protection turn on the characterization of where a violation occurs? What are the criteria for determining where a violation occurs? What about Justice Brennan's claim that, by making Verdugo-Urquidez the subject of a U.S. investigation, and by holding him accountable under U.S. law, the United States made him one of the "governed" for purposes of the Bill of Rights? *See also* United States v. Odeh, 548 F.3d 276 (2d Cir. 2008) (holding that searches of U.S. citizens abroad need only satisfy the Fourth Amendment's requirement of reasonableness and are not subject to the Fourth Amendment's warrant requirement); United States v. Stokes, 72 F.3d 880 (7th Cir. 2013) (same).

7. In Boumediene v. Bush, 553 U.S. 723 (2008) (excerpted in Chapter 10), the Supreme Court held that the constitutional right of habeas corpus, protected by the Suspension Clause in Article I, Section 9 of the Constitution, applied to aliens being detained by the U.S. military at the U.S. naval base at Guantanamo Bay, Cuba. The Court described three factors that are relevant to determining the reach of the Suspension Clause: "(1) the citizenship and status of the detainee and the adequacy of the process through which that status determination was made; (2) the nature of the sites where apprehension and then detention took place; and (3) the practical obstacles inherent in resolving the prisoner's entitlement to the writ." The Court added that, in light of the longstanding and complete control exercised by the United States over Guantanamo, "[i]n every practical sense Guantanamo is not abroad; it is within the constant jurisdiction of the United States." The Court also expressed concern that, if the Constitution is deemed inapplicable whenever the United States lacks formal sovereignty over an area, the government could enter into an arrangement with another country that would allow it "to govern without legal constraint," and concluded that "[o]ur basic charter cannot be contracted away like this." As discussed in Chapter 10, it is unclear what implications the decision has for the application of the Suspension Clause to places other than Guantanamo. It is also unclear what implications this decision has for the extraterritorial application of other constitutional rights, even to Guantanamo. For consideration of these and related questions, see, for example, Christina Duffy Burnett, *A Convenient Constitution? Extraterritoriality After* Boumediene, 109 Colum. L. Rev. 973 (2009); Andrew Kent, Boumediene, Munaf, *and the Supreme Court's Misreading of the* Insular Cases, 97 Iowa L. Rev. 101 (2011); and Gerald L. Neuman, *The Extraterritorial Constitution After* Boumediene v. Bush, 82 S. Cal. L. Rev. 2259 (2009).

8. In 2010, a U.S. border patrol agent standing on the U.S. side of the U.S.-Mexico border shot and killed Sergio Hernandez, a Mexican teenager, who was in Mexico. The teenager's parents sued the agent and his supervisors, contending that the shooting constituted a violation of Hernandez's Fourth and Fifth Amendment rights. Applying *Verdugo*, a federal appellate court concluded that "Hernandez lacked sufficient voluntary connections with the United States to invoke the Fourth Amendment." Hernandez v. United States, 757 F.2d 249, 266 (5th Cir. 2014). But, after considering the analysis in *Boumediene*, the court concluded that "a noncitizen injured outside the United States as a result of arbitrary official conduct by a law enforcement officer located in the United States may invoke the protections provided by the Fifth Amendment." The court reasoned that, "even though the United States has no formal control or de facto sovereignty over the Mexican side of the border, the heavy presence and regular activity of federal agents across a permanent border without any shared accountability weigh in favor of recognizing some constitutional reach." In a subsequent en banc ruling, however, the court vacated the portion of its decision concerning the Fifth Amendment and held that there was no need to decide the issue because any such Fifth Amendment right was not clearly established at the time of the shooting and that the defendant officials therefore had qualified immunity from the suit. *See* Hernandez v. United States, 785 F.3d 117 (5th Cir. 2015).

In 2017, the Supreme Court issued a per curiam decision, vacating the Fifth Circuit's decision and remanding for consideration of whether the plaintiff had a viable *Bivens* claims for damages in light of the Court's decision in *Ziglar v. Abbasi* (described in Chapter 7). It also held that the plaintiff's Fifth Amendment claim was not barred by qualified immunity. But it declined to resolve whether the plaintiff was protected by the Fourth Amendment when he was shot. On remand, the Fifth Circuit held that the "transnational aspects of the facts" presented a new context in which a *Bivens* remedy was inappropriate. The court also held that there were numerous "special factors" counselling restraint, including a concern that the extension of *Bivens* here would threaten "the political branches' supervision of national security" and would risk "interference with foreign affairs and diplomacy more generally." In May 2019, the Supreme Court agreed to review this ruling.

In Rodriguez v. Swartz, 899 F.3d 719 (9th Cir. 2018), the U.S. Court of Appeals for the Ninth Circuit considered another case involving a shooting by a U.S. border patrol agent of someone in Mexico. In that case, the agent allegedly fired numerous shots across the border at night and killed the victim, without any justification.

The court held (in a 2-1 decision) that, assuming the allegations were true, the agent violated clearly established Fourth Amendment rights and thus would not be protected from suit by qualified immunity, and the victim's mother could pursue a *Bivens* claim for damages against the agent. With respect to the extraterritorial application of the Fourth Amendment, the court reasoned:

> Applying the Constitution in this case would simply say that American officers must not shoot innocent, non-threatening people for no reason. Enforcing that rule would not unduly restrict what the United States could do either here or abroad. So under the particular circumstances of this case, [the victim] had a Fourth Amendment right to be free from the objectively unreasonable use of deadly force by an American agent acting on American soil, even though Swartz's bullets hit him in Mexico. *Verdugo-Urquidez* does not require a different conclusion.

Does the court persuasively distinguish the U.S. agent's actions in *Rodriguez* from those of the U.S. agents in *Verdugo-Urquidez?* Where did the Fourth Amendment violation occur in *Rodriguez?*

9. For general scholarship on the territorial reach of the U.S. Constitution, see, for example, J. Andrew Kent, *A Textual and Historical Case Against a Global Constitution,* 95 Geo. L.J. 463 (2007); Neuman, *Whose Constitution?, supra;* Kal Raustiala, *The Geography of Justice,* 73 Fordham L. Rev. 2501 (2005); and Kermit Roosevelt III, *Guantanamo and the Conflict of Laws: Rasul and Beyond,* 153 U. Pa. L. Rev. 2017 (2005). For an historical account of changing conceptions of territoriality in U.S. law and policy, including conceptions about the territorial reach of the Constitution, see Kal Raustiala, Does the Constitution Follow the Flag? The Evolution of Territoriality in American Law (2009).

B. EXTRATERRITORIAL APPLICATION OF FEDERAL CRIMINAL STATUTES

United States v. Yunis

924 F.2d 1086 (D.C. Cir. 1991)

[Fawaz Yunis was one of several men who hijacked a Royal Jordanian Airlines flight from Beirut, Lebanon. The plane took off and eventually landed back in Beirut, where the hijackers, including Yunis, released the hostages (including two Americans), blew up the plane, and fled. The FBI subsequently arrested Yunis on a yacht in international waters in the eastern Mediterranean. Yunis was brought to the United States, where he was convicted of conspiracy, 18 U.S.C. §371, hostage taking, 18 U.S.C. §1203, and air piracy, 49 U.S.C. App. §1472(n). Yunis appealed.]

MIKVA, CHIEF JUDGE . . .

Yunis appeals first of all from the district court's denial of his motion to dismiss for lack of subject matter and personal jurisdiction. Appellant's principal claim is that, as a matter of domestic law, the federal hostage taking and air piracy statutes do not authorize assertion of federal jurisdiction over him. Yunis also suggests that a contrary construction of these statutes would conflict with established principles of international law, and so should be avoided by this court. Finally, appellant claims that the district court lacked personal jurisdiction because he was seized in violation of American law.

The Hostage Taking Act provides, in relevant part:

> (a) Whoever, whether inside or outside the United States, seizes or detains and threatens to kill, to injure, or to continue to detain another person in order to compel a third person or a governmental organization to do or to abstain from any act . . . shall be punished by imprisonment by any term of years or for life.
>
> (b)(1) It is not an offense under this section if the conduct required for the offense occurred outside the United States unless—
>> (A) the offender or the person seized or detained is a national of the United States;
>> (B) the offender is found in the United States; or
>> (C) the governmental organization sought to be compelled is the Government of the United States.

18 U.S.C. §1203. Yunis claims that this statute cannot apply to an individual who is brought to the United States by force, since those convicted under it must be "found in the United States." But this ignores the law's plain language. Subsections (A), (B), and (C) of section 1203(b)(1) offer independent bases for jurisdiction where "the offense occurred outside the United States." Since two of the passengers on Flight 402 were U.S. citizens, section 1203(b)(1)(A), authorizing assertion of U.S. jurisdiction where "the offender or the person seized or detained is a national of the United States," is satisfied. The statute's jurisdictional requirement has been met regardless of whether or not Yunis was "found" within the United States under section 1203(b)(1)(B).

Appellant's argument that we should read the Hostage Taking Act differently to avoid tension with international law falls flat. Yunis points to no treaty obligations of the United States that give us pause. Indeed, Congress intended through the Hostage Taking Act to execute the International Convention Against the Taking of Hostages, which authorizes any signatory state to exercise jurisdiction over persons who take its nationals hostage "if that State considers it appropriate." International Convention Against the Taking of Hostages, opened for signature Dec. 18, 1979, art. 5, para. 1.

Nor is jurisdiction precluded by norms of customary international law. The district court concluded that two jurisdictional theories of international law, the "universal principle" and the "passive personal[ity] principle," supported assertion of U.S. jurisdiction to prosecute Yunis on hijacking and hostage-taking charges. Under the universal principle, states may prescribe and prosecute "certain offenses recognized by the community of nations as of universal concern, such as piracy, slave trade, attacks on or hijacking of aircraft, genocide, war crimes, and perhaps certain acts of terrorism," even absent any special connection between the state and the offense. See Restatement (Third) of the Foreign Relations Law of the United States §§404, 423 (1987). Under the passive personal[ity] principle, a state may punish non-nationals for crimes committed against its nationals outside of its territory, at least where the state has a particularly strong interest in the crime. See id. at §402 comment g.

Relying primarily on the Restatement, Yunis argues that hostage taking has not been recognized as a universal crime and that the passive personal[ity] principle authorizes assertion of jurisdiction over alleged hostage takers only where the victims were seized because they were nationals of the prosecuting state. Whatever merit appellant's claims may have as a matter of international law, they cannot prevail before this court. Yunis seeks to portray international law as a self-executing code that trumps domestic law whenever the two conflict. That effort misconceives the role of judges as appliers of international law and as participants in the federal system. Our duty is to enforce the Constitution, laws, and treaties of the United States, not to conform the law of the land to norms of customary international law. *See* U.S. Const. art. VI. As we said in Committee of U.S. Citizens Living in Nicaragua v. Reagan, 859 F.2d 929 (D.C. Cir. 1988): "Statutes inconsistent with principles of customary international law may well lead to international law violations. But within the domestic legal realm, that inconsistent statute simply modifies or supersedes customary international law to the extent of the inconsistency."

To be sure, courts should hesitate to give penal statutes extraterritorial effect absent a clear congressional directive. *See* Foley Bros. v. Filardo, 336 U.S. 281, 285 (1949); United States v. Bowman, 260 U.S. 94, 98 (1922). Similarly, courts will not blind themselves to potential violations of international law where legislative intent is ambiguous. *See* Murray v. The Schooner Charming Betsy, 6 U.S. (2 Cranch) 64, 118 (1804) ("[A]n act of congress ought never to be construed to violate the law of nations, if any other possible construction remains. . . ."). But the statute in question reflects an unmistakable congressional intent, consistent with treaty obligations of the United States, to authorize prosecution of those who take Americans hostage abroad no matter where the offense occurs or where the offender is found. Our inquiry can go no further. . . .

The Antihijacking Act provides for criminal punishment of persons who hijack aircraft operating wholly outside the "special aircraft jurisdiction" of the United States, provided that the hijacker is later "found in the United States." 49 U.S.C. App. §1472(n). Flight 402, a Jordanian aircraft operating outside of the United States, was not within this nation's special aircraft jurisdiction. Yunis urges this court to interpret the statutory requirement that persons prosecuted for air piracy must be "found" in the United States as precluding prosecution of alleged hijackers who are brought here to stand trial. But the issue before us is more fact-specific, since Yunis was indicted for air piracy while awaiting trial on hostage-taking and other charges; we must determine whether, once arrested and brought to this country on those other charges, Yunis was subject to prosecution under the Antihijacking Act as well.

The Antihijacking Act of 1974 was enacted to fulfill this nation's responsibilities under the Convention for the Suppression of Unlawful Seizure of Aircraft (the "Hague Convention"), which requires signatory nations to extradite or punish hijackers "present in" their territory. Convention for the Suppression of Unlawful Seizure of Aircraft, Dec. 16, 1970, art. 4, para. 2. This suggests that Congress intended the statutory term "found in the United States" to parallel the Hague Convention's "present in [a contracting state's] territory," a phrase which does not indicate the voluntariness limitation urged by Yunis. Moreover, Congress interpreted the Hague Convention as requiring the United States to extradite or prosecute "offenders in its custody," evidencing no concern as to how alleged hijackers came within U.S. territory. S. Rep. No. 13, 93d Cong., 1st Sess. at 3. From this legislative history we conclude that Yunis was properly indicted under section 1472(n) once in the United States and under arrest on other charges.

The district court correctly found that international law does not restrict this statutory jurisdiction to try Yunis on charges of air piracy. Aircraft hijacking may well be one of the few crimes so clearly condemned under the law of nations that states may assert universal jurisdiction to bring offenders to justice, even when the state has no territorial connection to the hijacking and its citizens are not involved. But in any event we are satisfied that the Antihijacking Act authorizes assertion of federal jurisdiction to try Yunis regardless of hijacking's status vel non as a universal crime. Thus, we affirm the district court on this issue.

United States v. Lawrence

727 F.3d 386 (5th Cir. 2013)

[Appellants Felicia Parker and Ade Lawrence, a U.S. citizen and a Nigerian citizen, respectively, living in the United States, participated in a plan to transport cocaine from South America to the United Kingdom on board commercial airplanes. They took a number of actions in the United States in support of the plan, including arranging for couriers who were U.S. citizens to travel from Texas to South America to pick up the cocaine. They were convicted of conspiracy to possess illicit substances aboard an aircraft with intent to distribute in violation of 21 U.S.C. §963.]

LEMELLE, DISTRICT JUDGE [sitting by designation]. . . .

On appeal, Appellants . . . argue that: (1) the substantive crime underlying the conspiracy charge—possession with intent to distribute in violation of 21 U.S.C. §959(b)—was not intended to apply to possession of illicit substances aboard a plane traveling between two foreign nations with intent to distribute in a foreign country and that extraterritorial application of §959(b) would violate due process and international law; [and] (2) if Congress enacted §959(b)(2) with the intent that it should apply extraterritorially, it went beyond its Constitutional authority in doing so. . . .

21 U.S.C. §959, entitled "Possession, manufacture, or distribution of controlled substance," is located under Subchapter II (Import and Export) of the Drug Abuse Prevention and Control Act ("DAPCA"). §959 states the following:

> (a) Manufacture or distribution for purpose of unlawful importation
> It shall be unlawful for any person to manufacture or distribute a controlled substance . . .
>> (1) intending that such substance or chemical will be unlawfully imported into the United States or into waters within a distance of 12 miles of the coast of the United States; or
>> (2) knowing that such substance or chemical will be unlawfully imported into the United States or into waters within a distance of 12 miles of the coast of the United States.
> (b) Possession, manufacture, or distribution by person on board aircraft
> It shall be unlawful for any United States citizen on board any aircraft, or any person on board any aircraft owned by a United States citizen or registered in the United States, to —
>> (1) manufacture or distribute a controlled substance or listed chemical; or
>> (2) possess a controlled substance or listed chemical with intent to distribute.
> (c) Acts committed outside territorial jurisdiction of the United States; venue

   This section is intended to reach acts of manufacture or distribution committed outside the territorial jurisdiction of the United States. Any person who
violates this section shall be tried in the United States district court at the point
of entry where such person enters the United States, or in the United States
District Court for the District of Columbia.

   . . . The phrase "*any* United States citizen on board *any aircraft*" used in subsection (b) of 21 U.S.C. §959 suggests that the entire subsection was meant to apply
extraterritorially. Appellants contend that the provision should be read to refer only
to aircrafts traveling within or to/from the United States. However, given the nature
of the international drug trade, possession of an illicit substance aboard an aircraft will often involve travel between foreign nations and consequently, implicates
extraterritoriality. . . .

   " 'It is a longstanding principle of American law that legislation of Congress,
unless a contrary intent appears, is meant to apply only within the territorial jurisdiction of the United States.' " United States v. Villanueva, 408 F.3d 193, 197 (5th
Cir. 2005) (citing Smith v. United States, 507 U.S. 197, 204 (1993)). However, this
presumption can be overcome where extraterritorial application can be "inferred
from the nature of the offenses and Congress' other legislative efforts to eliminate
the type of crime involved." *Id.* at 199 (citing United States v. Baker, 609 F.2d 134,
136 (5th Cir. 1980)). In United States v. Bowman, the Supreme Court articulated
when the presumption against extraterritoriality may be overcome in the context of
criminal statutes. 260 U.S. 94, 98 (1922). The presumption that Congress intends
to limit the jurisdiction of its statutes to the territorial United States "should not be
applied to criminal statutes which are, as a class, not logically dependent on their
locality for the government's jurisdiction, but are enacted because of the right of
the government to defend itself against obstruction, or fraud wherever perpetrated,
especially if committed by its own citizens, officers, or agents." *Id.* (emphasis added).
Furthermore, intent to extend jurisdiction beyond the territorial United States can
also be inferred where "to limit [the] locus [of the offense] to the strictly territorial
jurisdiction would be greatly to curtail the scope and usefulness of the statute." *Id.*
   Extraterritorial application of §959(b) is justified under *Bowman.* "In the context of drug smuggling laws, this Court has found the necessary congressional intent
to overcome the presumption against extraterritorial application," *Villanueva,* 408
F.3d at 199, and in evaluating DAPCA's statutory framework, this Court has previously commented that Congress intended that the statute "have a broad sweep in
dealing with all aspects of drug abuse." *Baker,* 609 F.2d at 137. However, previous
cases on extraterritorial application of drug statutes involved Defendants intending
to export illicit drugs from the United States or to import and distribute them within
the United States. Yet, other Circuits have asserted that the United States government may make efforts to stem the international drug trade "without any showing
of an actual effect on the United States" because of the threat that the international
drug trade presents to the nation's ability to function. United States v. Perlaza, 439
F.3d 1149, 1162 (9th Cir. 2006). In enacting DAPCA, Congress noted the United
States' status as a party to "international conventions designed to establish effective
control over *international* and domestic traffic in controlled substances." (emphasis
added). Explicit reference to this status supports Congressional intent for extraterritorial application of DAPCA. Thus, limiting the application of §959(b) to domestic possession of illicit drugs on an aircraft would greatly curtail the intended scope
and usefulness of DAPCA.

Having established Congressional intent to give §959(b) extraterritorial application, we must now consider whether international law permits the exercise of such jurisdiction. Rivard v. United States, 375 F.2d 882, 885 (5th Cir. 1967). "Under international law a state does not have jurisdiction to enforce a rule of law prescribed by it, unless it had jurisdiction to prescribe the rule." *Rivard*, 375 F.2d at 885 (citing Restatement, Second of Foreign Relations Law §7(2) (1965)). "The law of nations permits the exercise of criminal jurisdiction by a nation under five general principles. They are the territorial, national, protective, universality, and passive personality principles." *Id.* Under the nationality principle, "a country may supervise and regulate the acts of its citizens both within and without its territory." United States v. Columba-Colella, 604 F.2d 356, 358 (5th Cir. 1979). It is generally accepted that "the legislative authority of the United States over its citizens extends to conduct by Americans . . . even within the territory of other sovereigns." United States v. Mitchell, 553 F.2d 996, 1001 (5th Cir. 1977) (citing Steele v. Bulova Watch Co., 344 U.S. 280 (1952)). Under this theory, the exercise of jurisdiction over Appellant Parker's extraterritorial conduct is proper as she is a United States citizen.

"Under the protective theory . . . a country's legislature is competent to enact . . . [and] enforce criminal laws *wherever and by whomever* the act is performed that threatens the country's security or directly interferes with its governmental operations." *Columba-Colella*, 604 F.2d at 358 (emphasis added). As noted earlier, Congress has demonstrated, in enacting DAPCA and in ratifying various international conventions on the eradication of drug trafficking, that it considers the international drug trade to be a major threat to the safety of the United States. . . . Appellant Lawrence recruited drug couriers within the United States and organized a plan to traffic drugs internationally. Given Congressional efforts to halt the international drug trade, we find that criminalization of Appellant Lawrence's conduct is justified under the protective principle. The court notes that we do not, today, address the question of application of §959(b) to a crime where absolutely no actions related to the crime were committed in the United States or to a situation where the conduct at issue was lawful in the jurisdictions in which it occurred but unlawful in the United States. . . .

In *Blackmer v. United States*, the Supreme Court stated that U.S. citizens "owe allegiance to the United States [and that] [b]y virtue of the obligations of citizenship, the United States retain[s] its authority over [its citizens], and [its citizens are] bound by its laws made applicable to [them] in a foreign country." 284 U.S. 421, 437 (1932). In that case, the Court found that a U.S. citizen was still subject to punishment in the courts of the United States for violations of United States' laws through conduct perpetrated abroad. *Id.* Under *Blackmer,* application of §959(b) to Appellant Parker, a U.S. citizen, does not violate the Due Process Clause.

In the context of non-U.S. citizens, "due process requires the Government to demonstrate that there exists 'a sufficient nexus between the conduct condemned and the United States' such that application of the statute would not be arbitrary or fundamentally unfair to the defendant." *Perlaza*, 439 F.3d at 1160. Appellant Lawrence himself and his part in the conspiracy do have such a nexus to the United States: Lawrence resided in Houston, Texas, with his wife (who served as one of his couriers), recruited drug couriers, formulated the plan to traffic drugs, bought plane tickets, applied for his drug couriers' passports, and transferred some of the requisite cash to his couriers all in the United States. These contacts create a nexus sufficient to satisfy due process requirements.

The United States Constitution expressly empowers Congress "[t]o make all Laws which shall be necessary and proper for carrying into Execution [Congress's Article 1, §8] Powers and all other Powers vested by this Constitution in the Government of the United States." . . . The Supreme Court has "rejected the view that the Necessary and Proper Clause demands that an Act of Congress be '*absolutely necessary*' to the exercise of an enumerated power. . . . [I]t suffices that [a statute] is 'conducive to the administration of justice' in federal court, and is 'plainly adapted' to that end." *Id.* at 462 (citing McCulloch v. Maryland, 17 U.S. 316, 414, 417, 421 (1819)). "[I]n determining whether the Necessary and Proper Clause grants Congress the legislative authority to enact a particular federal statute, we look to see whether the statute constitutes a means that is rationally related to the implementation of a constitutionally enumerated power." United States v. Comstock, 560 U.S. 126 (2010). Congress possesses authority to criminalize conduct in the course of "carrying into Execution" the powers "vested by" the United States Constitution.

"[The President] shall have power, by and with the Advice and Consent of the Senate, to make Treaties." U.S. Const. art. II, §2, cl. 2. All treaties ratified by Congress become the supreme law of the land. U.S. Const. art. VI, cl. 2. At the time that DAPCA was enacted, the United States was party to the Single Convention on Narcotic Drugs (1961), to which Congress made explicit reference when it passed DAPCA, highlighting the Convention's relevance to the enactment of the legislation.

Article 36 of the Single Convention states that each Party to the Convention shall adopt such measures as will ensure that, *inter alia*, possession of drugs "contrary to the provisions of this Convention, and any other action which in the opinion of such Party may be contrary to the provisions of this Convention, shall be punishable offenses when committed intentionally." United Nations Single Convention on Narcotic Drugs, 1961, art. 36(1), Mar. 30, 1961. Appellants note that Art. 36(2)(a)(iv) of the Single Convention states that offenses "committed either by nationals or by foreigners shall be prosecuted by the Party in whose territory the offence was committed" and argue that allowing §959(b)(2) to have extraterritorial effect would violate the treaty. Appellants' reliance on this provision is unavailing. First, as previously noted, under the protective principle, it is accepted that a state may enforce its laws against its own citizens abroad without offending the sovereignty of foreign nations. *Columba-Colella*, 604 F.2d at 358. Thus, the prosecution of Appellant Parker, a U.S. citizen, comports with international law. Furthermore, the Single Convention states that "[i]ntentional participation in, *conspiracy to commit* and attempts to commit, any of such offences, and preparatory acts and financial operations" in connection with prohibited offenses will be punishable. *Id.* at art. 36(2)(a)(ii) (emphasis added). Both appellants were charged with conspiracy to possess with intent to distribute. As previously noted, Appellant Lawrence formed the conspiracy in the United States and took a multitude of actions in furtherance of the conspiracy in the United States. Thus, application of §§959(b)(2) and 963 to Appellant Lawrence is also consistent with U.S. treaty obligations.

Given the directives of the Single Convention, extraterritorial application of §959(b)(2) is rationally related to the implementation Congress's treaty-making power, "conducive to the administration of justice" in federal court, and "plainly adapted" to that end. Thus, we find that extraterritorial application of §959(b)(2) in this case is permissible as implementing Congress' treaty-making power under the Necessary and Proper Clause.

Notes and Questions

1. In order for a federal criminal statute to apply to foreign conduct, Congress must have constitutional authority to regulate the conduct. As discussed in Chapter 3, Congress can draw on a variety of constitutional provisions to support such authority, including the Foreign Commerce Clause and the Define and Punish Clause. Moreover, as discussed in Chapter 5, Congress has broad authority under the Necessary and Proper Clause to enact legislation to implement treaties. These and other provisions give Congress broad authority to regulate extraterritorially, but this authority is not unlimited. Which constitutional provisions supported the prosecutions in *Yunis* and *Lawrence?* What foreign criminal conduct can Congress *not* constitutionally regulate?

2. Even if Congress possesses the constitutional authority to apply criminal law extraterritorially, courts generally presume, as we learned in Chapter 2, that statutes do not apply to foreign conduct. *See, e.g.,* Morrison v. National Australia Bank Ltd., 561 U.S. 247 (2010). The Supreme Court articulated a somewhat special rule about the applicability of this presumption to criminal laws in United States v. Bowman, 260 U.S. 94 (1922). That case involved an indictment for a conspiracy to defraud a corporation owned by the United States, in which the predicate acts took place on the high seas. Although the statute in question (which criminalized fraud on the U.S. government and its corporations) did not expressly extend to the high seas, the Court nonetheless construed it as applying to the conduct in question, reasoning:

> We have in this case a question of statutory construction. The necessary *locus,* when not specially defined, depends upon the purpose of Congress as evinced by the description and nature of the crime and upon the territorial limitations upon the power and jurisdiction of a government to punish crime under the law of nations. Crimes against private individuals or their property, like assaults, murder, burglary, larceny, robbery, arson, embezzlement, and frauds of all kinds which affect the peace and good order of the community must, of course, be committed within the territorial jurisdiction of the government where it may properly exercise it. If punishment of them is to be extended to include those committed outside of the strict territorial jurisdiction, it is natural for Congress to say so in the statute, and failure to do so will negative the purpose of Congress in this regard. . . .
>
> But the same rule of interpretation should not be applied to criminal statutes which are, as a class, not logically dependent on their locality for the government's jurisdiction, but are enacted because of the right of the government to defend itself against obstruction or fraud wherever perpetrated, especially if committed by its own citizens, officers, or agents. Some such offenses can only be committed within the territorial jurisdiction of the government because of the local acts required to constitute them. Others are such that to limit their locus to the strictly territorial jurisdiction would be greatly to curtail the scope and usefulness of the statute, and leave open a large immunity for frauds as easily committed by citizens on the high seas and in foreign countries as at home. In such cases, Congress has not thought it necessary to make specific provision in the law that the *locus* shall include the high seas and foreign countries, but allows it to be inferred from the nature of the offense. . . .

Id. at 97-99.

How did the courts in *Yunis* and *Lawrence* apply *Bowman?* Did they apply it in the same way? Most federal appellate court decisions, like *Lawrence,* view *Bowman* as lowering the threshold for overcoming the presumption against extraterritoriality in the criminal context from something like a plain statement rule to a contextual inquiry that focuses on the nature of the offense and the aims of Congress. For decisions allowing for extraterritorial application under this reduced threshold, see, for example, United States v. Leija-Sanchez, 602 F.3d 797 (7th Cir. 2010) (murder in aid of racketeering activity); United States v. Frank, 599 F.3d 1221 (11th Cir. 2010) (purchasing of minors abroad by U.S. citizen for sexual conduct); United States v. Delgado-Garcia, 374 F.3d 1337 (D.C. Cir. 2004) (attempted smuggling of aliens into the United States); United States v. Plummer, 221 F.3d 1298 (11th Cir. 2000) (attempted cigar smuggling); United States v. Harvey, 2 F.3d 1318 (3d Cir. 1993) (sexual exploitation of children). For additional discussion of *Bowman,* see Zachary D. Clopton, Bowman *Lives: The Extraterritorial Application of U.S. Criminal Law After Morrison v. National Australia Bank,* 67 N.Y.U. Ann. Surv. Am. L. 137 (2011).

3. Even if the presumption against extraterritoriality is inapplicable or is overcome with respect to criminal statutes, international law can, as *Yunis* and *Lawrence* make clear, still be relevant to the interpretation of criminal statutes. It is generally agreed that customary international law imposes limits on a nation's ability to regulate conduct—that is, on its "prescriptive jurisdiction." Under this view, a nation's exercise of prescriptive jurisdiction, in order to be lawful, must fall within one of five categories: territoriality; nationality; the protective principle; passive personality; or universality. Under the territoriality category, nations may regulate conduct that takes place within their territory or has substantial effects within their territory. Under the nationality category, nations may regulate the conduct of their citizens both inside and outside their territory. Under the protective principle, nations may regulate certain conduct outside their territory that threatens their national security or government operations. Under the passive personality category, nations may regulate certain conduct that harms their nationals abroad. Finally, under the universality category, nations may regulate certain egregious conduct committed anywhere in the world. *See* Restatement (Fourth) of the Foreign Relations Law of the United States §§402, 413 (2018); United States v. Pizzarusso, 388 F.2d 8 (2d Cir. 1968). Another "category" in which the exercise of prescriptive jurisdiction is permissible is when one nation specifically agrees with another nation (for example, in a treaty) to allow the other nation to regulate within the first nation's territory. If nothing else, this category follows from the proposition that nations can override customary international law between themselves by agreement.

How did the courts in *Yunis* and *Lawrence* invoke international law in construing the criminal statutes before them? In *Yunis,* the court looked to international law in the course of applying the "*Charming Betsy*" canon, pursuant to which "an act of congress ought never to be construed to violate the law of nations, if any other possible construction remains." Murray v. Schooner Charming Betsy, 6 U.S. (2 Cranch) 64, 118 (1804). In *Lawrence,* in asking "whether international law permits the exercise of such jurisdiction," was the court applying the *Charming Betsy* canon or invoking international law in a different way?

4. Prescriptive jurisdiction over conduct or persons within a country's territorial boundaries has long been uncontroversial. This concept of territorial jurisdiction also includes conduct that occurs outside a country but has effects within that country. An early endorsement of this proposition came in the decision of the Permanent Court of International Justice in The Case of the S.S. Lotus, 1927 PCIJ, Ser. A, No. 10. In that case, a French steamship and a Turkish steamship collided on the high seas, causing eight Turkish nationals to die. The court held that Turkey could apply its criminal laws to a French officer on the French ship, on the theory that his negligence had caused the collision.

For conduct that occurs outside a nation's territory, what effects are sufficient to allow the nation to regulate the conduct? How, if at all, is the defendant's intent relevant to this analysis? Should this territorial category of jurisdiction also apply to situations in which a defendant engages in lawful conduct within the territory that has harmful effects outside the territory?

5. As noted above, under customary international law, nations have broad authority to regulate the conduct of their own nationals around the world. *See, e.g.,* Blackmer v. United States, 284 U.S. 421 (1932) (upholding application of a federal subpoena statute to a U.S. citizen living in France). What is the rationale for this nationality category of jurisdiction? What limits, if any, should there be for this category of prescriptive jurisdiction?

Consider 18 U.S.C. §2423(c), which provides that "[a]ny United States citizen or alien admitted for permanent residence who travels in foreign commerce or resides, either temporarily or permanently, in a foreign country, and engages in any illicit sexual conduct with another person shall be fined under this title or imprisoned not more than 30 years, or both." The phrase "illicit sexual contact" is defined to include commercial and other sexual acts with persons under 18 years of age. The statute as originally enacted in 2003 only reached individuals traveling in foreign commerce, but Congress amended the statute as part of the Violence Against Women Reauthorization Act of 2013 to reach individuals residing overseas. *See* Pub. L. No. 113-4 §1211(b), 127 Stat. 54 (2013). Is the statute consistent with international law? In United States v. Clark, 315 F. Supp. 2d 1127 (W.D. Wash. 2004), *aff'd*, 435 F.3d 1100 (9th Cir. 2006), the court concluded that the pre-amendment version of the statute was supported by both the nationality principle and the universality principle. In September 2019, in a case in which the U.S. government prosecuted a U.S. citizen for engaging in "illicit sexual conduct" while residing in Vietnam, the D.C. Circuit concluded that the current version of the statute was implementing legislation for the Optional Protocol to the U.N. Convention on the Rights of the Child, to which the United States and Vietnam are both parties. United States v. Park, 2019 WL 4383261 (D.C. Cir. 2019). The court therefore treated the statute as an effort by Congress to "give the treaty practical effect," and did not consider whether the statute would have been consistent with international law absent a relevant treaty.

6. The protective principle allows for the prosecution of "certain conduct outside its territory by persons not its nationals or residents that is directed against the security of the United States or against a limited class of other U.S. interests, including counterfeiting, espionage, and the murder of U.S. government officials." Restatement (Fourth) of the Foreign Relations Law of the United States §402 cmt. i (2018). Should this category of prescriptive jurisdiction extend to the prosecution of drug trafficking? Even the trafficking of drugs outside the United States, as in *Lawrence*? For a critique of such application of the protective principle, see Eugene Kontorovich, *Beyond the Article I Horizon: Congress's Enumerated Powers and Universal Jurisdiction Over Drug Crimes*, 93 Minn. L. Rev. 1191, 1229-31 (2009). *Cf.* United States v. Bellaizac-Hurtado, 700 F.3d 1245 (11th Cir. 2012) (concluding that drug trafficking is not an offense against the law of nations and that Congress therefore cannot use its Define and Punish Clause authority to regulate it in another nation's territorial waters).

The Drug Trafficking Vessel Interdiction Act of 2008 provides that:

> Whoever knowingly operates, or attempts or conspires to operate, by any means, or embarks in any submersible vessel or semi-submersible vessel that is without nationality

and that is navigating or has navigated into, through, or from waters beyond the outer limit of the territorial sea of a single country or a lateral limit of that country's territorial sea with an adjacent country, with the intent to evade detection, shall be fined under this title, imprisoned not more than 15 years, or both.

18 U.S.C. §2285(a). For a decision holding that Congress had the authority to enact this statute pursuant to its authority to "define and punish . . . Felonies committed on the high Seas," see United States v. Saac, 632 F.3d 1203 (11th Cir. 2011). *See also* United States v. Rojas, 812 F.3d 382 (5th Cir. 2016) (concluding that the prosecution of foreign citizens for conspiring to import drugs into the United States was consistent with both the territorial principle and the protective principle); United States v. Baston, 818 F.3d 651 (11th Cir. 2015) (holding that Congress's regulation of sex trafficking was consistent with the protective principle).

7. Somewhat less settled under international law is the passive personality category, which would allow nations to assert jurisdiction, especially criminal jurisdiction, over aliens who injure their nationals abroad. Historically, the United States disputed the validity of this category of jurisdiction. For example, in the *Cutting Case* in 1887, the Secretary of State protested when Mexico arrested a U.S. citizen for libeling a Mexican citizen in the United States. *See* 2 John Bassett Moore, International Law Digest 232-40 (1906). In recent years, however, the United States and other countries have increasingly relied upon this category of jurisdiction as a basis for regulating terrorist attacks on their citizens. In addition to the *Yunis* decision excerpted above, see, for example, United States v. Yousef, 327 F.3d 56 (2d Cir. 2003). What conduct should be covered by this category of prescriptive jurisdiction?

Consider United States v. Neil, 312 F.3d 419 (9th Cir. 2002). In that case, the court affirmed the conviction of a foreign citizen who, while working as an employee aboard a foreign cruise ship, engaged in sexual contact with a 12-year-old passenger, who was an American citizen, while the ship was in Mexican territorial waters. The cruise ship departed from and returned to one of California's harbors. Upon her return, the young female victim missed several days of school and underwent psychological counseling. The defendant had argued that the United States did not have extraterritorial jurisdiction over the crime. The applicable U.S. statute (18 U.S.C. §2344(a)) makes it a criminal offense to "knowingly engage in a sexual act with another person who has attained the age of 12 years but has not attained the age of 16 years." This statute applies in the "special maritime and territorial jurisdiction of the United States," which is defined elsewhere as including, "[t]o the extent permitted by international law, any foreign vessel during a voyage having a scheduled departure from or arrival in the United States with respect to an offense committed by or against a national of the United States." 18 U.S.C. §7(8). The court of appeals found that international law supported extraterritorial jurisdiction in this case under the territorial principle and the passive personality principle. Do you agree?

8. All but one of the five categories of prescriptive jurisdiction require a territorial or nationality connection between the regulating nation and the conduct, offender, or victim. The exception is the category of universal jurisdiction. What conduct is subject to universal jurisdiction? If a treaty confers universal jurisdiction over particular conduct, does it allow a nation to exercise such jurisdiction over citizens of countries that have not ratified the treaty?

In United States v. Yousef, 327 F.3d 56 (2d Cir. 2003), the Court disagreed with the suggestion in *Yunis* (and in the Restatement (Third) of Foreign Relations Law

(1987)) that certain acts of terrorism may fall within the category of universal jurisdiction. The court reasoned as follows:

> The class of crimes subject to universal jurisdiction traditionally included only piracy. . . . In modern times, the class of crimes over which States can exercise universal jurisdiction has been extended to include war crimes and acts identified after the Second World War as "crimes against humanity." . . .
>
> The concept of universal jurisdiction has its origins in prosecutions of piracy, which States and legal scholars have acknowledged for at least 500 years as a crime against all nations both because of the threat that piracy poses to orderly transport and commerce between nations and because the crime occurs statelessly on the high seas. . . .
>
> Universal jurisdiction over violations of the laws of war was not suggested until the Second World War. . . . Following the Second World War, the United States and other nations recognized "war crimes" and "crimes against humanity," including "genocide," as crimes for which international law permits the exercise of universal jurisdiction. . . .
>
> A commentator of the time explained that war crimes are "similar to piratical acts" because "in both situations there is . . . a lack of any adequate judicial system operating on the spot where the crime takes place — in the case of piracy it is because the acts are on the high seas and in the case of war crimes because of a chaotic condition or irresponsible leadership in time of war." Willard B. Cowles, Universality of Jurisdiction Over War Crimes, 33 Cal. L. Rev. 177, 194 (1945).
>
> The historical restriction of universal jurisdiction to piracy, war crimes, and crimes against humanity demonstrates that universal jurisdiction arises under customary international law only where crimes (1) are universally condemned by the community of nations, and (2) by their nature occur either outside of a State or where there is no State capable of punishing, or competent to punish, the crime (as in a time of war).
>
> Unlike those offenses supporting universal jurisdiction under customary international law — that is, piracy, war crimes, and crimes against humanity — that now have fairly precise definitions and that have achieved universal condemnation, "terrorism" is a term as loosely deployed as it is powerfully charged. . . . [T]he mere existence of the phrase "state-sponsored terrorism" proves the absence of agreement on basic terms among a large number of States that terrorism violates public international law. Moreover, there continues to be strenuous disagreement among States about what actions do or do not constitute terrorism, nor have we shaken ourselves free of the cliche that "one man's terrorist is another man's freedom fighter."

Id. at 104-07. Is this persuasive? Note that the court there proceeded to hold that the prosecution in question (for a conspiracy to bomb U.S. airliners abroad) was supported by a treaty, the Montreal Convention for the Suppression of Unlawful Acts Against the Safety of Civil Aviation, and also by the protective principle. The court also noted that, even if the prosecution did not comport with international law restrictions on prescriptive jurisdiction, Congress had the power to override those restrictions for purposes of U.S. law.

For a general discussion of universal jurisdiction, see Kenneth C. Randall, *Universal Jurisdiction Under International Law*, 66 Tex. L. Rev. 785 (1988). *See also* Symposium, *Universal Jurisdiction: Myths, Realities, and Prospects*, 35 New Eng. L. Rev. 227-469 (2001). For discussion of the costs and benefits of universal jurisdiction, compare Henry A. Kissinger, *The Pitfalls of Universal Jurisdiction*, 80 Foreign Aff. 86 (July/Aug. 2001), with Kenneth Roth, *The Case for Universal Jurisdiction*, 80 Foreign Aff. 150 (Sept./Oct. 2001).

9. Most U.S. criminal statutes expressly or implicitly require a connection to the United States or a U.S. national and thus do not assert universal jurisdiction.

This is true, for example, of the U.S. war crimes statute, which only applies where "the person committing such war crime or the victim of such war crime is a member of the Armed Forces of the United States or a national of the United States." *See* 18 U.S.C. §2441. Until recently, this was true even of the federal genocide statute, which required that the offense occur in the United States or that the offender be a U.S. national. In 2007, however, the statute was amended to allow for prosecution of non-U.S. citizens who commit genocide outside the United States and are "brought into, or found in" the United States. *See* 18 U.S.C. §1091(d)(5). The federal torture statute, enacted in 1994, also allows for universal jurisdiction over official acts of torture committed outside the United States. *See* 18 U.S.C. §2340A. However, this statute has almost never been used. In 2008, Congress enacted the Child Soldiers Accountability Act, making it a federal crime to knowingly recruit, enlist, or conscript a person under 15 years of age into an armed force or group or to knowingly use a person under 15 years of age to participate actively in hostilities. This Act applies even to conduct by non-U.S. nationals abroad as long as they are present in the United States when charged. *See* 18 U.S.C. §2442(c)(3). Why are there not more examples of universal jurisdiction in U.S. criminal law? (There is additional discussion of universal jurisdiction in the section below on piracy.) *See also* Curtis A. Bradley, *Universal Jurisdiction and U.S. Law*, 2001 U. Chi. Legal F. 323.

10. In December 2006, the U.S. government sought and obtained an indictment against Charles McArthur Emmanuel, the son of former Liberian president Charles Taylor, for violating the federal torture statute. The government alleged that Emmanuel, who was born in the United States, participated in the torture of a man in Liberia in 2002. This was apparently the first time the government had ever charged someone with violating the torture statute. Emmanuel, also known as "Chuckie Taylor," was subsequently convicted under the torture statute and sentenced to 97 years in prison. The U.S. Court of Appeals for the Eleventh Circuit upheld the conviction in United States v. Belfast, 611 F.3d 783 (11th Cir. 2010), and rejected the argument that the criminal torture statute exceeded Congress's authority. The court reasoned that the statute fell within Congress's authority under the Necessary and Proper Clause to implement treaties—in this case, the Convention Against Torture and Other Cruel, Inhuman or Degrading Treatment or Punishment.

11. As noted in Chapter 4, there are Fourteenth Amendment due process limits on the extent to which U.S. states may apply their laws to conduct occurring outside the state. It is not clear whether or to what extent there are also Fifth Amendment due process limits on the permissible application of federal law to conduct occurring outside the United States. *Lawrence* assumes that the Due Process Clause is relevant to the extraterritorial application of U.S. federal law, but finds sufficient contacts with the United States to satisfy due process. For discussion of this issue, see Lea Brilmayer & Charles Norchi, *Federal Extraterritoriality and Fifth Amendment Due Process*, 105 Harv. L. Rev. 1217 (1992), and A. Mark Weisburd, *Due Process Limits on Federal Extraterritorial Legislation*, 35 Colum. J. Transnat'l L. 379 (1997).

This due process issue has arisen in cases brought under the Maritime Drug Law Enforcement Act (MDLEA), which provides that "[w]hile on board a covered vessel, an individual may not knowingly or intentionally . . . manufacture or distribute, or possess with intent to manufacture or distribute, a controlled substance." A "covered vessel" is defined as "(1) a vessel of the United States or a vessel subject to the jurisdiction of the United States; or (2) any other vessel if the individual is a citizen of the United States or a resident alien of the United States," and the Act also defines a "vessel subject to the jurisdiction of the United States" to include a "vessel without nationality." *See* 46 U.S.C.A. §§70502-03. The MDLEA further provides that a "failure to comply with international law does not divest a court of jurisdiction and is not a defense to a proceeding" under the statute. *See id.* §70505. Courts have generally assumed that applications of this statute are subject to due process limitations but that these limitations simply require that the law not be applied in an "arbitrary or fundamentally unfair" manner. *See, e.g.,* United States v. Ballestas, 795 F.3d 138 (D.C. Cir. 2015); United States v. Suerte, 291 F.3d 366 (5th Cir. 2002); United States v. Cardales, 168 F.3d 548 (1st Cir. 1999). The U.S. Court of Appeals for the Ninth Circuit also requires a nexus between the defendant's activities and the United States. *See, e.g.,* United States v. Klimavicius-Viloria, 144 F.3d 1249 (9th Cir. 1998); United States v. Davis, 905 F.2d 245, 248-49 (9th Cir. 1990). Other circuit courts have expressly rejected this nexus requirement. *See Suerte,* 291 F.3d at 369-72 (summarizing decisions). Even the Ninth Circuit does not impose this requirement for stateless vessels, see United States v. Caicedo, 47 F.3d 370, 379 (9th Cir. 1995), and for situations in which international law allows for universal jurisdiction, see United States v. Shi, 525 F.3d 709, 723 (9th Cir. 2008).

In United States v. Brehm, 691 F.3d 547 (4th Cir. 2012), the Fourth Circuit considered this due process issue in the context of a prosecution under the Military Extraterritorial Jurisdiction Act (MEJA), which allows for the prosecution of individuals who commit serious crimes "while employed by or accompanying the Armed Forces outside the United States." In that case, a South African citizen stabbed a British citizen at Kandahar Airfield (KAF), a NATO-operated military base in Afghanistan, while both were employed with private contractors supporting the NATO war effort. In concluding that the assertion of extraterritorial criminal jurisdiction in that case did not violate due process, the court noted that "[the defendant's] actions affected significant American interests at KAF, not the least of which was the preservation of law and order on the base, the maintenance of military-related discipline, and the reallocation of DOD resources to confine [the defendant], provide care for [the victim], and investigate the incident."

C. PIRACY

United States v. Dire

680 F.3d 446 (4th Cir. 2012)

KING, CIRCUIT JUDGE:

In the early morning hours of April 1, 2010, on the high seas between Somalia and the Seychelles (in the Indian Ocean off the east coast of Africa), the defendants—Abdi Wali Dire, Gabul Abdullahi Ali, Abdi Mohammed Umar, Abdi Mohammed Gurewardher, and Mohammed Modin Hasan—imprudently launched an attack on the *USS Nicholas,* having confused that mighty Navy frigate for a vulnerable merchant ship. The defendants, all Somalis, were swiftly apprehended and then transported to the Eastern District of Virginia, where they were convicted of the crime of piracy, as proscribed by 18 U.S.C. §1651, plus myriad other criminal offenses. In this appeal, the defendants challenge their convictions and life-plus-eighty-year sentences on several grounds, including that their fleeting and fruitless strike on the *Nicholas* did not, as a matter of law, amount to a §1651 piracy offense. As explained below, we reject their contentions and affirm. . . .

[§1651] provides in full:

> Whoever, on the high seas, commits the crime of piracy as defined by the law of nations, and is afterwards brought into or found in the United States, shall be imprisoned for life.

According to the defendants, the crime of piracy has been narrowly defined for purposes of §1651 as robbery at sea, i.e., seizing or otherwise robbing a vessel. Because they boarded the *Nicholas* only as captives and indisputably took no property, the defendants contest their convictions on Count One, as well as the affixed life sentences. . . .

[A]rticle I of the Constitution accords Congress the power "[t]o define and punish Piracies and Felonies committed on the high Seas, and Offences against the Law of Nations." U.S. Const. art. I, §8, cl. 10. In its present form, the language of 18 U.S.C. §1651 can be traced to an 1819 act of Congress, which similarly provided, in pertinent part:

> That if any person or persons whatsoever, shall, on the high seas, commit the crime of piracy, as defined by the law of nations, and such offender or offenders, shall afterwards be brought into or found in the United States, every such offender or offenders shall, upon conviction thereof, . . . be punished. . . .

Whereas today's mandatory penalty for piracy is life imprisonment, however, the Act of 1819 commanded punishment "with death." Examining the Act of 1819 in its *United States v. Smith* decision of 1820, the Supreme Court recognized:

> There is scarcely a writer on the law of nations, who does not allude to piracy, as a crime of a settled and determinate nature; and whatever may be the diversity of definitions, in other respects, all writers concur, in holding, that robbery, or forcible depredations upon the sea, *animo furandi* [intent to steal], is piracy.

18 U.S. (5 Wheat.) 153, 161 (1820). Accordingly, the *Smith* Court, through Justice Story, articulated "no hesitation in declaring, that piracy, by the law of nations, is robbery upon the sea." . . .

As detailed [by the district court], "there are two prominent international agreements that have directly addressed, and defined, the crime of general piracy." The first of those treaties is the Geneva Convention on the High Seas (the "High Seas Convention"), which was adopted in 1958 and ratified by the United States in 1961, rendering the United States one of today's sixty-three parties to that agreement. . . .

Under the High Seas Convention,

> [p]iracy consists of any of the following acts:
>
> (1) Any illegal acts of violence, detention or any act of depredation, committed for private ends by the crew or the passengers of a private ship or a private aircraft, and directed:
>   (a) On the high seas, against another ship or aircraft, or against persons or property on board such ship or aircraft;
>   (b) Against a ship, aircraft, persons or property in a place outside the jurisdiction of any State;
> (2) Any act of voluntary participation in the operation of a ship or of an aircraft with knowledge of facts making it a pirate ship or aircraft;
> (3) Any act of inciting or of intentionally facilitating an act described in sub-paragraph 1 or subparagraph 2 of this article.

Geneva Convention on the High Seas, art. 15.

The second pertinent treaty is the United Nations Convention on the Law of the Sea (the "UNCLOS"), which has amassed 162 parties since 1982—albeit not the United States, which has not ratified the UNCLOS "but has recognized that its baseline provisions reflect customary international law." *See* United States v. Alaska, 503 U.S. 569, 588 n.10 (1992). Relevant here, the UNCLOS provides that

> [p]iracy consists of any of the following acts:
>
> (a) any illegal acts of violence or detention, or any act of depredation, committed for private ends by the crew or the passengers of a private ship or a private aircraft, and directed:
>
> > (i) on the high seas, against another ship or aircraft, or against persons or property on board such ship or aircraft;
> >
> > (ii) against a ship, aircraft, persons or property in a place outside the jurisdiction of any State;
>
> (b) any act of voluntary participation in the operation of a ship or of an aircraft with knowledge of facts making it a pirate-ship or aircraft;
>
> (c) any act of inciting or of intentionally facilitating an act described in subparagraph (a) or (b).

U.N. Convention on the Law of the Sea, art. 101. Upon comparing the High Seas Convention with the UNCLOS, the district court recognized that the latter treaty "defines piracy in exactly the same terms as the [former agreement], with only negligible stylistic changes." The court also observed that the UNCLOS "represents the most recent international statement regarding the definition . . . of piracy."

Turning to the contentions of the parties herein, the district court related the defendants' position "that the authoritative definition of piracy under the law of nations, and thus within the meaning of 18 U.S.C. §1651, is provided by the Supreme Court's decision in *Smith.*" According to the defendants, because their Indictment did not allege "that they committed any actual robbery on the high seas," the Count One piracy charge had to be dismissed. For its part, however, the government defended Count One on the premise "that *Smith* neither foreclosed the possibility that piracy included conduct other than robbery nor precluded the possibility that the definition of piracy under the law of nations might later come to include conduct other than robbery." In response, the district court recognized that "if the definition of piracy under the law of nations can evolve over time, such that the modern law of nations must be applied, rather than any recitation of the state of the law in the early Nineteenth Century," the court need not determine "[w]hether *Smith* was limited to its facts and not intended to be exhaustive, or whether its description of piracy was exhaustive but only represented the definition of piracy accepted at that time by the international community." The court then embarked on the relevant analysis.

First, the district court interpreted 18 U.S.C. §1651 as an unequivocal demonstration of congressional intent "to incorporate . . . any subsequent developments in the definition of general piracy under the law of nations." The court rationalized:

> The plain language of 18 U.S.C. §1651 reveals that, in choosing to define the international crime of piracy by [reference to the "law of nations"], Congress made a conscious decision to adopt a flexible—but at all times sufficiently precise—definition of general piracy that would automatically incorporate developing international norms regarding piracy. Accordingly, Congress necessarily left it to the federal courts to

determine the definition of piracy under the law of nations based on the international consensus at the time of the alleged offense.

. . . "Having concluded that Congress's proscription of 'piracy as defined by the law of nations' in 18 U.S.C. §1651 necessarily incorporates modern developments in international law," the district court next endeavored to "discern the definition of piracy under the law of nations at the time of the alleged offense in April 2010." In so doing, the court observed that the law of nations is ascertained today via the same path followed in 1820 by the Supreme Court in *Smith*: consultation of " 'the works of jurists, writing professedly on public law[s]' "; consideration of " 'the general usage and practice of nations' "; and contemplation of " 'judicial decisions recognising and enforcing that law.' " (quoting *Smith*, 18 U.S. at 160-61). Engaging in that analysis, the court concluded:

> As of April 1, 2010, the law of nations, also known as customary international law, defined piracy to *include* acts of violence committed on the high seas for private ends without an actual taking. More specifically, . . . the definition of general piracy under modern customary international law is, at the very least, reflected in Article 15 of the 1958 High Seas Convention and Article 101 of the 1982 UNCLOS.

Narrowing customary international law to one of those two treaties, the court chose the UNCLOS, which—in addition to "contain[-ing] a definition of general piracy that is, for all practical purposes, identical to that of the High Seas Convention"— "has many more states parties than the High Seas Convention" and "has been much more widely accepted by the international community than the High Seas Convention."

In the course of its discussion of the High Seas Convention and the UNCLOS, the district court recognized that " '[t]reaties are proper evidence of customary international law because, and insofar as, they create legal obligations akin to contractual obligations on the States parties to them.' " According to the court, "[w]hile all treaties shed some light on the customs and practices of a state, 'a treaty will only constitute sufficient proof of a norm of customary international law if an overwhelming majority of States have ratified the treaty, and those States uniformly and consistently act in accordance with its principles.' " "In this regard," the court emphasized, "it is also important to understand that a treaty can either 'embod[y] or create[] a rule of customary international law,' and such a rule 'applies beyond the limited subject matter of the treaty and *to nations that have not ratified it.*' " With those principles in mind, the court recognized:

> There were 63 states parties to the High Seas Convention as of June 10, 2010, including the United States, and there were 161 states parties to UNCLOS (including the European Union) as of October 5, 2010, including Somalia. The 161 states parties to UNCLOS represent the "overwhelming majority" of the 192 Member States of the United Nations, and the 194 countries recognized by the United States Department of State. UNCLOS's definition of piracy therefore represents a widely accepted norm, followed out of a sense of agreement (or, in the case of the states parties, treaty obligation), that has been recognized by an overwhelming majority of the world.

The status of UNCLOS as representing customary international law is enhanced by the fact that the states parties to it include all of the nations bordering the Indian Ocean on the east coast of Africa, where the incident in the instant case is alleged to have taken place: South Africa, Mozambique, Tanzania, Kenya, and Somalia. Also significant in determining whether UNCLOS constitutes sufficient proof of a norm of customary international law is the fact that both the United States and Somalia, two countries that clearly have an influence on the piracy issue, have each ratified, and thus accepted, a treaty containing the exact same definition of general piracy.

Moreover, although the definition of general piracy provided by the High Seas Convention and UNCLOS is not nearly as succinct as "robbery on the sea," the definitions are not merely general aspirational statements, but rather specific enumerations of the elements of piracy reflecting the modern consensus view of international law. Accordingly, UNCLOS's definition of general piracy has a norm-creating character and reflects an existing norm of customary international law that is binding on even those nations that are not a party to the Convention, including the United States.

. . . Additionally, the court recognized that "[c]ontemporary scholarly sources . . . appear to agree that the definition of piracy in UNCLOS represents customary international law." "While writers on the issue do present disagreements regarding the definition of general piracy," the court acknowledged, "such disagreements do not implicate the core definition provided in UNCLOS." . . .

The district court then reaffirmed that, as of the alleged offense date of April 2010, the definition of piracy under the law of nations was found in the substantively identical High Seas Convention and UNCLOS, the latter having "been accepted by the overwhelming majority of the world as reflecting customary international law." Mirroring those treaties, the court pronounced that "piracy within the meaning of §1651 consists of any of the following acts and their elements":

> (A) (1) any illegal act of violence or detention, or any act of depredation; (2) committed for private ends; (3) on the high seas or a place outside the jurisdiction of any state; (4) by the crew or the passengers of a private ship . . . ; (5) and directed against another ship . . . , or against persons or property on board such ship . . . ; or
> (B) (1) any act of voluntary participation in the operation of a ship . . . ; (2) with knowledge of the facts making it a pirate ship; or
> (C) (1) any act of inciting or of intentionally facilitating (2) an act described in subparagraph (A) or (B). . . .

[T]he district court instructed the jury on Count One, over the defendants' objection, that the Law of Nations defines the crime of piracy to [include] any of the three following actions:

> (A) any illegal acts of violence or detention or any act of depredation committed for private ends on the high seas or a place outside the jurisdiction of any state by the crew or the passengers of a private ship and directed against another ship or against persons or property on board such ship; or
> (B) any act of voluntary participation in the operation of a ship with knowledge of facts making it a pirate ship; or
> (C) any act of inciting or of intentionally facilitating an act described in (A) or (B) above.

The court also specified "that an assault with a firearm as alleged in the indictment in this case, if proven beyond a reasonable doubt, is an illegal act of violence." The jury found each of the defendants guilty of the Count One piracy offense by a general verdict. . . .

The crux of the defendants' position is now, as it was in the district court, that the definition of general piracy was fixed in the early Nineteenth Century, when Congress passed the Act of 1819 first authorizing the exercise of universal jurisdiction by United States courts to adjudicate charges of "piracy as defined by the law of nations." Most notably, the defendants assert that the "law of nations," as understood in 1819, is not conterminous with the "customary international law" of today. . . .

The defendants' view is thoroughly refuted, however, by a bevy of precedent, including the Supreme Court's 2004 decision in Sosa v. Alvarez-Machain. . . . Significantly, the [Alien Tort Statute ("ATS")] predates the criminalization of general piracy. . . . Yet the *Sosa* Court did not regard the ATS as incorporating some stagnant notion of the law of nations. Rather, the Court concluded that, while the first Congress probably understood the ATS to confer jurisdiction over only the three paradigmatic law-of-nations torts of the time—including piracy—the door was open to ATS jurisdiction over additional "claim[s] based on the present-day law of nations," albeit in narrow circumstances. . . .

Although, as the defendants point out, the ATS involves civil claims and the general piracy statute entails criminal prosecutions, there is no reason to believe that the "law of nations" evolves in the civil context but stands immobile in the criminal context. Moreover, if the Congress of 1819 had believed either the law of nations generally or its piracy definition specifically to be inflexible, the Act of 1819 could easily have been drafted to specify that piracy consisted of "piracy as defined *on March 3, 1819* [the date of enactment], by the law of nations," or solely of, as the defendants would have it, "robbery upon the sea." . . .

Additional theories posited by the defendants of a static piracy definition are no more persuasive. For example, the defendants contend that giving "piracy" an evolving definition would violate the principle that there are no federal common law crimes. See Br. of Appellants 32 (citing United States v. Hudson, 11 U.S. (7 Cranch) 32, 34 (1812), for the proposition "that federal courts have no power to exercise 'criminal jurisdiction in common-law cases'"). The 18 U.S.C. §1651 piracy offense cannot be considered a common law crime, however, because Congress properly "ma[de] an act a crime, affix[ed] a punishment to it, and declare[d] the court that shall have jurisdiction of the offence." *See Hudson*, 11 U.S. at 34. Moreover, in its 1820 *Smith* decision, the Supreme Court unhesitatingly approved of the piracy statute's incorporation of the law of nations, looking to various sources to ascertain how piracy was defined under the law of nations. *See Smith*, 18 U.S. at 159-61.

The defendants would have us believe that, since the *Smith* era, the United States' proscription of general piracy has been limited to "robbery upon the sea." But that interpretation of our law would render it incongruous with the modern law of nations and prevent us from exercising universal jurisdiction in piracy cases. At bottom, then, the defendants' position is irreconcilable with the noncontroversial notion that Congress intended in §1651 to define piracy as a universal jurisdiction crime. In these circumstances, we are constrained to agree with the district court that §1651 incorporates a definition of piracy that changes with advancements in the law of nations.

United States v. Ali

718 F.3d 929 (D.C. Cir. 2013)

[In November 2008, a group of Somalis seized the *CEC Future*, a Danish-owned merchant ship flying a Bahamian flag and carrying cargo owned by a U.S. corporation, on the high seas in the Gulf of Aden. They forced crew members at gunpoint to reroute the ship to Point Ras Binna, off the coast of Somalia, where defendant Ali Mohamed Ali, a Somali national, boarded the ship and began negotiating a ransom with the ship's owners. The negotiations lasted until mid-January 2009, when the pirates received a $1.7 million ransom and Ali and his colleagues left the ship. While Ali was on board, the ship was exclusively in territorial waters, except for a few minutes when it entered the high seas. In June 2010, Ali was appointed Director General of the Ministry of Education for the Republic of Somaliland, a self-proclaimed sovereign state within Somalia. In April 2011, he traveled to the United States to attend what he believed was an education conference, but which was actually an FBI ruse to lure him to U.S. territory. When Ali landed at Dulles International Airport to attend the sham conference, he was arrested.]

BROWN, CIRCUIT JUDGE . . . .

A grand jury issued a four-count superseding indictment against Ali, charging him first with conspiracy to commit piracy under the law of nations, in violation of 18 U.S.C. §371, which makes it a crime for "two or more persons" to "conspire . . . to commit any offense against the United States." Invoking aiding and abetting liability under 18 U.S.C. §2, Count Two charged Ali with committing piracy under the law of nations, in violation of 18 U.S.C. §1651, which provides, "Whoever, on the high seas, commits the crime of piracy as defined by the law of nations, and is afterwards brought into or found in the United States, shall be imprisoned for life." . . .

Ali filed a motion to dismiss the charges as legally defective, meeting with partial success. Beginning with the premise that the definition of piracy under international law does not encompass conspiratorial liability, the district court dismissed Count One in full, concluding §1651, which defines piracy in terms of "the law of nations," could not ground a conspiracy charge. The court similarly refused to interpret §371, the federal conspiracy statute, as applying to piracy under the law of nations. So read, the court said, the statute would contravene international law in a way Congress never intended. As for Count Two, the court reasoned piracy under §1651 and international law only concerns acts committed on the high seas and consequently limited Count Two to acts of aiding and abetting Ali committed while *he* was on the high seas. . . .

In most cases, the criminal law of the United States does not reach crimes committed by foreign nationals in foreign locations against foreign interests. Two judicial presumptions promote this outcome. The first is the presumption against the extraterritorial effect of statutes: "When a statute gives no clear indication of an extraterritorial application, it has none." Morrison v. Nat'l Austl. Bank Ltd., 130 S. Ct. 2869, 2878 (2010). The second is the judicial presumption that "an act of Congress ought never to be construed to violate the law of nations if any other possible construction remains," Murray v. Schooner Charming Betsy, 6 U.S. (2 Cranch) 64, 118 (1804) — the so-called *Charming Betsy* canon. Because international law itself limits a state's authority to apply its laws beyond its borders, see Restatement Third of Foreign Relations Law §§402–03, *Charming Betsy* operates alongside the presumption against extraterritorial effect to check the exercise of U.S. criminal jurisdiction. Neither presumption imposes a substantive limit on Congress's legislative authority, but they do constrain judicial inquiry into a statute's scope.

Piracy, however, is no ordinary offense. The federal piracy statute clearly applies extraterritorially to "[w]hoever, on the high seas, commits the crime of piracy as defined by the law of nations," even though that person is only "afterwards brought into or found in the United States." 18 U.S.C. §1651. Likewise, through the principle of universal jurisdiction, international law permits states to "define and prescribe punishment for certain offenses recognized by the community of nations as of universal concern." Restatement (Third) of Foreign Relations Law §404; . . . .

Universal jurisdiction is not some idiosyncratic domestic invention but a creature of international law. Unlike the average criminal, a pirate may easily find himself before an American court despite committing his offense on the other side of the globe. Ali's situation is a bit more complicated, though. His indictment contains no straightforward charge of piracy. Rather, the government accuses him of two inchoate offenses relating to piracy: conspiracy to commit piracy and aiding and abetting piracy.

On their face, both ancillary statutes apply generally and without exception: §2 to "[w]hoever . . . aids, abets, counsels, commands, induces or procures" the commission of "an offense against the United States," 18 U.S.C. §2(a) (emphasis added), and §371 to persons who "do any act to effect the object of the conspiracy" to "commit *any* offense against the United States," 18 U.S.C. §371 (emphasis added). But so powerful is the presumption against extraterritorial effect that even such generic language is insufficient rebuttal. *See* Small v. United States, 544 U.S. 385, 388 (2005). That leaves both statutes ambiguous as to their application abroad, requiring us to resort to interpretive canons to guide our analysis.

Given this ambiguity in the extraterritorial scope of the two ancillary statutes, we consider whether applying them to Ali's actions is consistent with international law. Conducting this *Charming Betsy* analysis requires parsing through international treaties, employing interpretive canons, and delving into drafting history. Likewise, because the two ancillary statutes are "not so broad as to expand the extraterritorial reach of the underlying statute," United States v. Yakou, 428 F.3d 241, 252 (D.C. Cir. 2005), we also conduct a separate analysis to determine the precise contours of §1651's extraterritorial scope. Ultimately, Ali's assault on his conspiracy charge prevails for the same reason the attack on the aiding and abetting charge fails.

We begin with Ali's charge of aiding and abetting piracy. Aiding and abetting is a theory of criminal liability, not a separate offense — one that allows a defendant who "aids, abets, counsels, commands, induces or procures" commission of a crime to be punished as a principal, 18 U.S.C. §2(a). "All that is necessary is to show some affirmative participation which at least encourages the principal offender to commit the offense, with all its elements, as proscribed by the statute." United States v. Raper, 676 F.2d 841, 850 (D.C. Cir. 1982). From Ali's perspective, it is not enough that acts of piracy were committed on the high seas and that he aided and abetted them. Rather, he believes any acts of aiding and abetting he committed must themselves have occurred in extraterritorial waters and not merely supported the capture of the *CEC Future* on the high seas.

Ali's argument involves two distinct (though closely related) inquiries. First, does the *Charming Betsy* canon pose any obstacle to prosecuting Ali for aiding and abetting piracy? For we assume, absent contrary indication, Congress intends its enactments to comport with international law. Second, is the presumption against extraterritoriality applicable to acts of aiding and abetting piracy not committed on the high seas?

Section 1651 criminalizes "the crime of piracy as defined by the law of nations." Correspondence between the domestic and international definitions is essential to exercising universal jurisdiction. Otherwise, invocation of the magic word "piracy" would confer universal jurisdiction on a nation and vest its actions with the authority of international law. As a domestic matter, doing so may be perfectly legal.

But because *Charming Betsy* counsels against interpreting federal statutes to contravene international law, we must satisfy ourselves that prosecuting Ali for aiding and abetting piracy would be consistent with the law of nations.

Though §1651's invocation of universal jurisdiction may comport with international law, that does not tell us whether §2's broad aider and abettor liability covers conduct neither within U.S. territory nor on the high seas. Resolving that difficult question requires examining precisely what conduct constitutes piracy under the law of nations. Luckily, defining piracy is a fairly straightforward exercise. Despite not being a signatory, the United States has recognized, via United Nations Security Council resolution, that the U.N. Convention on the Law of the Sea ("UNCLOS") "sets out the legal framework applicable to combating piracy and armed robbery at sea." S.C. Res. 2020, U.N. Doc. S/Res/2020, at 2 (Nov. 22, 2011). According to UNCLOS:

> Piracy consists of any of the following acts:
>
> (a) any illegal acts of violence or detention, or any act of depredation, committed for private ends by the crew or the passengers of a private ship . . . and directed:
>> (i) on the high seas, against another ship . . . or against persons or property on board such ship . . . ;
>> (ii) against a ship, . . . persons or property in a place outside the jurisdiction of any State;
>
> (b) any act of voluntary participation in the operation of a ship . . . with knowledge of facts making it a pirate ship . . . ;
>
> (c) any act of inciting or of intentionally facilitating an act described in subparagraph (a) or (b).

UNCLOS, art. 101. By including "intentionally facilitating" a piratical act within its definition of piracy, article 101(c) puts to rest any worry that American notions of aider and abettor liability might fail to respect the international understanding of piracy. One question remains: does international law require facilitative acts take place on the high seas?

Explicit geographical limits—"on the high seas" and "outside the jurisdiction of any state"—govern piratical acts under article 101(a)(i) and (ii). Such language is absent, however, in article 101(c), strongly suggesting a facilitative act need not occur on the high seas so long as its predicate offense has. So far, so good; *Charming Betsy* poses no problems. . . .

Thwarted by article 101's text, Ali contends that even if facilitative acts count as piracy, a nation's universal jurisdiction over piracy offenses is limited to high seas conduct. In support of this claim, Ali invokes UNCLOS article 105, which reads,

> On the high seas, or in any other place outside the jurisdiction of any State, every State may seize a pirate ship or aircraft, or a ship or aircraft taken by piracy and under the control of pirates and arrest the persons and seize the property on board. The courts of the State which carried out the seizure may decide upon the penalties to be imposed. . . .

Ali understands article 105's preface to govern the actual enforcement of antipiracy law—and, by extension, to restrict universal jurisdiction to the high seas—even if the definition of piracy is more expansive. In fact, Ali gets it backward. Rather than curtailing the categories of persons who may be prosecuted as pirates, the provision's reference to the high seas highlights the broad authority of nations to apprehend pirates even in international waters. His reading also proves too much, leaving nations incapable of prosecuting even those undisputed pirates they discover within their own borders—a far cry from "universal" jurisdiction. Article 105 is therefore no indication international law limits the liability of aiders and abettors to their conduct on the high seas. . . .

Ali next attempts to achieve through the presumption against extraterritoriality what he cannot with *Charming Betsy*. Generally, the extraterritorial reach of an ancillary offense like aiding and abetting or conspiracy is coterminous with that of the underlying criminal statute. And when the underlying criminal statute's extraterritorial reach is unquestionable, the presumption is rebutted with equal force for aiding and abetting. Ali admits the piracy statute must have some extraterritorial reach—after all, its very terms cover conduct outside U.S. territory—but denies that the extraterritorial scope extends to any conduct that was not itself perpetrated on the high seas. . . .

Ali claims the government seeks to use aider and abettor liability to expand the extraterritorial scope of the piracy statute beyond conduct on the high seas. Because §1651 expressly targets crimes committed on the high seas, he believes Congress intended its extraterritorial effect—and, by extension, that of the aiding and abetting statute—to extend to international waters and no further. . . .

[I]nstead of thwarting some clearly expressed Congressional purpose, extending aider and abettor liability to those who facilitate such conduct furthers the goal of deterring piracy on the high seas—even when the facilitator stays close to shore. . . . As UNCLOS art. 101(c) recognizes, it is self-defeating to prosecute those pirates desperate enough to do the dirty work but immunize the planners, organizers, and negotiators who remain ashore.

Nor does the Supreme Court's recent decision in Kiobel v. Royal Dutch Petroleum Co., 133 S. Ct. 1659 (2013), change the equation. Reiterating that "[w]hen a statute provides for some extraterritorial application, the presumption against extraterritoriality operates to limit that provision to its terms," the Court rejected the notion that "because Congress surely intended the [Alien Tort Statute] to provide jurisdiction for actions against pirates, it necessarily anticipated the statute would apply to conduct occurring abroad." *Id.* at 1667. Ali contends that §1651's high seas requirement is similarly limiting, and that the presumption against extraterritoriality remains intact as to acts done elsewhere.

Even assuming Ali's analogy to *Kiobel* is valid, he overlooks a crucial fact: §1651's high seas element is not the only evidence of the statute's extraterritorial reach, for the statute references not only "the high seas" but also "the crime of piracy as defined by the law of nations." As explained already, the law of nations specifically contemplates, within its definition of piracy, facilitative acts undertaken from within a nation's territory. By defining piracy in terms of the law of nations, §1651 incorporated this extraterritorial application of the international law of piracy and indicates Congress's intent to subject extraterritorial acts like Ali's to prosecution.

Why then does §1651 mention the high seas at all if "the law of nations," which has its own high seas requirements, is filling in the statute's content? Simply put, doing so fits the international definition of piracy—a concept that encompasses both crimes on the high seas and the acts that facilitate them—into the structure of U.S. criminal law. To be convicted as a principal under §1651 alone, one must commit piratical acts on the high seas, just as UNCLOS article 101(a) demands. But applying aider and abettor liability to the sorts of facilitative acts proscribed by UNCLOS article 101(c) requires using §1651 and §2 in tandem. That is not to say §1651's high seas requirement plays no role in prosecuting Ali for aiding and abetting piracy, for the government must prove *someone* committed piratical acts while on the high seas. That is an element the government must prove at trial, but not one it must show Ali perpetrated personally.

Of course, §1651's high seas language could also be read as Congress's decision to narrow the scope of the international definition of piracy to encompass only those actions committed on the high seas. But Ali's preferred interpretation has some problems. Most damningly, to understand §1651 as a circumscription of the law of nations would *itself* run afoul of *Charming Betsy*, requiring a construction in conflict with international law. Ultimately, we think it most prudent to read the statute the way it tells us to. It is titled "[p]iracy under law of nations," after all.

Like the *Charming Betsy* canon, the presumption against extraterritorial effect does not constrain trying Ali for aiding and abetting piracy. While the offense he aided and abetted must have involved acts of piracy committed on the high seas, his own criminal liability is not contingent on his having facilitated these acts while in international waters himself.

Though the aiding and abetting statute reaches Ali's conduct, his conspiracy charge is another matter. In many respects conspiracy and aiding and abetting are alike, which would suggest the government's ability to charge Ali with one implies the ability to charge him with both. . . .

Yet a crucial difference separates the two theories of liability. Because §371, like §2, fails to offer concrete evidence of its application abroad, we turn, pursuant to the *Charming Betsy* canon, to international law to help us resolve this ambiguity of meaning. Whereas UNCLOS, by including facilitative acts within article 101's definition of piracy, endorses aider and abettor liability for pirates, the convention is silent on conspiratorial liability. International law provides for limited instances in which nations may prosecute the crimes of foreign nationals committed abroad, and, in invoking universal jurisdiction here, the government predicates its prosecution of Ali on one of those theories. And although neither side disputes the applicability of universal jurisdiction to piracy as defined by the law of nations, UNCLOS's plain language does not include *conspiracy* to commit piracy. The government offers us no reason to believe otherwise, and at any rate, we are mindful that "imposing liability on the basis of a violation of 'international law' or the 'law of nations' or the 'law of war' generally must be based on norms *firmly* grounded in international law." Hamdan v. United States, 696 F.3d 1238, 1250 n.10 (D.C. Cir. 2012) (emphasis added). International law does not permit the government's abortive use of universal jurisdiction to charge Ali with conspiracy. Thus, the *Charming Betsy* doctrine, which was no impediment to Ali's aider and abettor liability, cautions against his prosecution for conspiracy.

The government hopes nonetheless to salvage its argument through appeal to §371's text. Though courts construe statutes, when possible, to accord with international law, Congress has full license to enact laws that supersede it. The government suggests Congress intended to do precisely that in §371, which provides that "[i]f two or more persons conspire . . . to commit any offense against the United States . . . and one or more of such persons do any act to effect the object of the conspiracy," each is subject to criminal liability. Homing in on the phrase "any offense against the United States," the government contends Congress intended the statute to apply to all federal criminal statutes, even when the result conflicts with international law. Yet, as we explained above, if we are to interpret §371 as supplanting international law, we need stronger evidence than this. Indeed, the Supreme Court recently rejected the notion that similar language of general application successfully rebuts the presumption against extraterritorial effect. *See Kiobel*, 133 S. Ct. at 1665 ("Nor does the fact that the text reaches '*any* civil action' suggest application to torts committed abroad; it is well established that generic terms like 'any' or 'every' do not rebut the presumption against extraterritoriality.").

Under international law, prosecuting Ali for conspiracy to commit piracy would require the United States to have universal jurisdiction over his offense. And such jurisdiction would only exist if the underlying charge actually falls within UNCLOS's definition of piracy. Because conspiracy, unlike aiding and abetting, is not part of that definition, and because §371 falls short of expressly rejecting international law, *Charming Betsy* precludes Ali's prosecution for conspiracy to commit piracy. The district court properly dismissed Count One.

Notes and Questions

1. Article I, §8, cl. 10 of the Constitution gives Congress the authority "[t]o define and punish Piracies and Felonies committed on the high Seas." The United States has had a statute criminalizing piracy since 1790. In its first incarnation, that statute provided:

> That if any person or persons shall commit upon the high seas, or in any river, haven, basin or bay, out of the jurisdiction of any particular state, murder or robbery, or any other offence which if committed within the body of a county, would by the laws of the United States be punishable with death; or if any captain or mariner of any ship or other vessel, shall piratically and feloniously run away with such ship or vessel, or any goods or merchandise to the value of fifty dollars, or yield up such ship or vessel voluntarily to any pirate; or if any seaman shall lay violent hands upon his commander, thereby to hinder and prevent his fighting in defence of his ship or goods committed to his trust, or shall make a revolt in the ship; every such offender shall be deemed, taken and adjudged to be a pirate and felon, and being thereof convicted, shall suffer death; and the trial of crimes committed on the high seas, or in any place out of the jurisdiction of any particular state, shall be in the district where the offender is apprehended, or into which he may first be brought.

Act of April 30, 1790, §8, 1 Stat. 112. The Supreme Court interpreted this statute as not authorizing "the courts of the Union to inflict its penalties on persons who are not citizens of the United States, nor sailing under their flag, nor offending particularly against them." United States v. Palmer, 16 U.S. (3 Wheat.) 610, 631 (1818).

The piracy statute was amended in 1819 to provide:

> That if any person or persons whatsoever, shall, on the high seas, commit the crime of piracy, as defined by the law of nations, and such offender or offenders, shall afterwards be brought into or found in the United States, every such offender or offenders shall, upon conviction thereof, before the circuit court of the United States for the district into which he or they may be brought, or in which he or they shall be found, be punished with death.

Act of March 3, 1819, §5, 3 Stat. 510. In United States v. Smith, 18 U.S. (5 Wheat.) 153, 161 (1820), the Supreme Court concluded that Congress had sufficiently defined the crime of piracy in this statute by referring to the law of nations, reasoning that "piracy, by the law of nations, is robbery upon the sea, and . . . it is sufficiently and constitutionally defined by the fifth section of the act of 1819." The current piracy statute is worded in similar terms, although it provides for life imprisonment rather than the death penalty: "Whoever, on the high seas, commits the crime of piracy as defined by the law of nations, and is afterwards brought into or found in the United States, shall be imprisoned for life." 18 U.S.C. §1651.

2. Piracy has long been considered a universal jurisdiction offense. That is, it has long been thought proper under international law for nations to exercise prescriptive jurisdiction over pirates regardless of their nationality or the location of their conduct. *See, e.g., Smith*, 18 U.S. at 161 (referring to piracy as "an offence against the universal law of society, a pirate being deemed an enemy of the human race"); United States v. Klintock, 18 U.S. (5 Wheat.) 144, 152 (1820) (stating that persons committing piracy "are proper subjects for the penal code of all nations"). *But see* Alfred P. Rubin, Ethics and Authority in International Law 84-110 (1997) (arguing that universal jurisdiction over pirates was more rhetoric than reality, because states rarely invoked universal jurisdiction as the basis for piracy prosecutions). For a useful discussion of early American piracy law, and its relationship to British piracy law, see Edwin D. Dickinson, *Is the Crime of Piracy Obsolete?*, 38 Harv. L. Rev. 334 (1925). Modern claims about universal jurisdiction sometimes involve analogies to piracy. Recall from Chapter 7, for example, the statement in *Filartiga v. Pena-Irala* (which concerned a claim of torture under the Alien Tort Statute) that the torturer had become "like the pirate and slave trader before him *hostis humani generis*, an enemy of all mankind." *See also* Kiobel v. Royal Dutch Petroleum Co., 133 S. Ct. 1659, 1672 (2013) (Breyer, J., concurring) (arguing that the Alien Tort Statute must operate extraterritorially because it historically would have been available for acts of piracy). For criticism of the analogy, see Eugene Kontorovich, *The Piracy Analogy: Modern Universal Jurisdiction's Hollow Foundation*, 45 Harv. Int'l L.J. 183 (2004).

3. Of what relevance is the presumption against extraterritoriality to piracy prosecutions? Piracy by definition takes place outside the United States, and 18 U.S.C. §1651 contains the phrase "on the high seas." Does that mean that the presumption should be inapplicable in this context? What do *Dire* and *Ali* suggest?

4. Even if the presumption against extraterritoriality is overcome with respect to the substantive crime of piracy, why is it also overcome in *Ali* with respect to aider and abettor liability? The court asserts that "the extraterritorial reach of an ancillary offense like aiding and abetting or conspiracy is coterminous with that of the underlying criminal statute." Why is that? Even if the court is right on that point, why should aiding and abetting liability extend beyond the extraterritorial scope of the underlying piracy statute, which is limited to actions "on the high seas"? What role does international law play in the court's analysis? For another decision holding that the aiding and abetting statute applies even to acts in a foreign country or its waters if the acts intentionally facilitate acts of piracy on the high seas, see United States v. Shibin, 722 F.3d 233 (4th Cir. 2013).

5. What role should the *Charming Betsy* canon play in piracy prosecutions? Note how *Dire* and *Ali* raise different issues in this regard. When might the prosecution of piracy violate customary international law limits on prescriptive jurisdiction? Are you convinced by the differential treatment in *Ali* between the extraterritorial scope of aiding and abetting liability and conspiracy liability?

6. Did the court in *Dire* properly conclude that it should look to modern international law on piracy in construing the piracy statute? Is this analogous to looking to modern customary international law when applying the Alien Tort Statute, a statute relating to civil causes of action, as the court suggests? As noted in Chapter 1, the Supreme Court early in its history held that there is no federal common law of crimes. Does *Dire* in effect nevertheless allow for a federal common law of piracy? What is the court's response to this question?

Consider, in answering these questions, the following passage from Ex Parte Quirin, 317 U.S. 1, 29-30 (1942), a decision upholding a World War II military commission prosecution of violations of the international laws of war:

> It is no objection [to the validity of military commissions] that Congress in providing for the trial of such offenses has not itself undertaken to codify that branch of international law or to mark its precise boundaries, or to enumerate or define by statute all the acts which that law condemns. An Act of Congress punishing "the crime of piracy as defined by the law of nations" is an appropriate exercise of its constitutional authority, Art. I, §8, cl. 10, "to define and punish" the offense since it has adopted by reference the sufficiently precise definition of international law. Similarly by the reference in the 15th Article of War to "offenders or offenses that . . . by the law of war may be triable by such military commissions," Congress has incorporated by reference, as within the jurisdiction of military commissions, all offenses which are defined as such by the law of war, and which may constitutionally be included within that jurisdiction. Congress had the choice of crystallizing in permanent form and in minute detail every offense against the law of war, or of adopting the system of common law applied by military tribunals so far as it should be recognized and deemed applicable by the courts. It chose the latter course.

Might there be relevant differences, in terms of what should be allowed, between a piracy prosecution in federal court and a wartime prosecution before a commission of military officers? (The *Quirin* decision is considered further in Chapter 10.)

7. In both *Dire* and *Ali*, the courts attempt to discern the content of customary international law. What evidence do they cite in support of their conclusions about this content? In identifying rules of customary international law, is it proper to look to treaties (such as the U.N. Convention on the Law of the Sea) that the United States has not ratified?

D. EXTRADITION

It is not uncommon for someone to commit a crime in one country and then flee to another. The normal process for obtaining custody of a criminal suspect located in another country is extradition. Extradition is "the surrender by one nation to another of an individual accused or convicted of an offense outside of its own territory, and within the territorial jurisdiction of the other, which, being competent to try and to punish him, demands his surrender." Terlinden v. Ames, 184 U.S. 270, 289 (1902).

Extradition from the United States to other countries is governed by the federal extradition statute, 18 U.S.C. §§3181-3196. The extradition process is ordinarily initiated by a request from a foreign nation to the Department of State. If the Department of State determines that the request is within the relevant extradition treaty, it will forward the request to the Department of Justice. If the Department of Justice similarly concludes that the extradition request is proper, it forwards the request to the U.S. Attorney for the judicial district where the person sought is located. The U.S. Attorney then files a complaint with an appropriate judicial officer, seeking an arrest warrant. The judicial officer will then hold a hearing to determine whether (a) the crime charged is an extraditable crime under the treaty, and

(b) there is probable cause to believe that the person committed the crime. If these requirements are met, the judicial officer will certify to the Secretary of State that the person is extraditable. Upon receiving such certification, the Secretary of State has the discretion to extradite but is not obligated to do so. The certification is not subject to direct appeal, but it is subject to collateral challenge through a habeas corpus action. If the judicial officer determines that the individual is *not* extraditable, the government may not appeal. It may, however, bring another extradition proceeding against the individual before a different judicial officer.

The United States not only extradites suspects to other countries, it also seeks extradition of suspects located abroad. Under international law, nations are not obligated to extradite a suspect to another country in the absence of an extradition treaty with that country, although some nations will do so as a matter of comity. *See* Factor v. Laubenheimer, 290 U.S. 276, 287 (1933). The United States currently has bilateral extradition treaties with over 110 nations.

Here is an excerpt of a fairly standard U.S. extradition treaty:

Treaty on Extradition Between the United States of America and Canada, 27 U.S.T. 983

Entered into force March 22, 1976; Amended by Protocol that entered into force November 26, 1991

ARTICLE 1

Each Contracting Party agrees to extradite to the other, in the circumstances and subject to the conditions described in this Treaty, persons found in its territory who have been charged with, or convicted of, any of the offenses covered by Article 2 of this Treaty committed within the territory of the other. . . .

ARTICLE 2

(1) Extradition shall be granted for conduct which constitutes an offense punishable by the laws of both Contracting Parties by imprisonment or other form of detention for a term exceeding one year or any greater punishment. . . .

ARTICLE 4

(1) Extradition shall not be granted in any of the following circumstances:

(i) When the person whose surrender is sought is being proceeded against, or has been tried and discharged or punished in the territory of the requested State for the offense for which his extradition is requested.

(ii) When the prosecution for the offense has become barred by lapse of time according to the laws of the requesting State.

(iii) When the offense in respect of which extradition is requested is of a political character, or the person whose extradition is requested proves that the extradition request has been made for the purpose of trying or punishing him for an offense of the above-mentioned character.

If any question arises as to whether a case comes within the provisions of this subparagraph, the authorities of the Government on which the requisition is made shall decide.

(2) For the purpose of this Treaty, the following offenses shall be deemed not to be offenses within subparagraph (iii) of paragraph 1 of this Article: . . .

(ii) Murder, manslaughter or other culpable homicide, malicious wounding or inflicting grievous bodily harm;

(iii) An offense involving kidnapping, abduction, or any form of unlawful detention, including taking a hostage;

(iv) An offense involving the placing or use of explosives, incendiaries or destructive devices or substances capable of endangering life or of causing grievous bodily harm or substantial property damage. . . .

ARTICLE 6

When the offense for which extradition is requested is punishable by death under the laws of the requesting State and the laws of the requested State do not permit such punishment for that offense, extradition may be refused unless the requesting State provides such assurances as the requested State considers sufficient that the death penalty shall not be imposed, or, if imposed, shall not be executed. . . .

ARTICLE 9

(1) The request for extradition shall be made through the diplomatic channel.

(2) The request shall be accompanied by a description of the person sought, a statement of the facts of the case, the text of the laws of the requesting State describing the offense and prescribing the punishment for the offense, and a statement of the law relating to the limitation of the legal proceedings.

(3) When the request relates to a person who has not yet been convicted, it must also be accompanied by a warrant of arrest issued by a judge or other judicial officer of the requesting State and by such evidence as, according to the laws of the requested State, would justify his arrest and committal for trial if the offense had been committed there, including evidence proving the person requested is the person to whom the warrant of arrest refers.

(4) When the request relates to a person already convicted, it must be accompanied by the judgment of conviction and sentence passed against him in the territory of the requesting State, by a statement showing how much of the sentence has not been served, and by evidence proving that the person requested is the person to whom the sentence refers.

ARTICLE 10

(1) Extradition shall be granted only if the evidence be found sufficient, according to the laws of the place where the person sought shall be found, either to justify his committal for trial if the offense of which he is accused had been committed in its territory or to prove that he is the identical person convicted by the courts of the requesting State.

(2) The documentary evidence in support of a request for extradition or copies of these documents shall be admitted in evidence in the examination of the request for extradition when, in the case of a request emanating from Canada, they are authenticated by an officer of the Department of Justice of Canada and are certified by the principal diplomatic or consular officer of the United States in Canada, or when, in the case of a request emanating from the United States, they are authenticated by an officer of the Department of State of the United States and are certified by the principal diplomatic or consular officer of Canada in the United States. . . .

ARTICLE 12

(1) A person extradited under the present Treaty shall not be detained, tried or punished in the territory of the requesting State for an offense other than that for which extradition has been granted nor be extradited by that State to a third State unless:

(i) He has left the territory of the requesting State after his extradition and has voluntarily returned to it;

(ii) He has not left the territory of the requesting State within thirty days after being free to do so; or

(iii) The requested State has consented to his detention, trial, punishment for an offense other than that for which extradition was granted or to his extradition to a third State, provided such other offense is covered by Article 2.

(2) The foregoing shall not apply to offenses committed after the extradition.

The above treaty contains a number of standard features, including:

Dual Criminality Requirement. As illustrated by Article 2(1) of the treaty, extradition treaties typically require "dual criminality"—that is, the conduct in question must be a crime in both the requesting state and the sending state. These treaties also typically require that the crime be a serious offense in both jurisdictions—for example, a crime punishable by at least one year in prison. Why do you think extradition treaties contain these requirements?

It is well settled that the two nations' laws need not be exactly the same in order to satisfy the dual criminality requirement. Rather, "[i]t is enough if the particular act charged is criminal in both jurisdictions." Collins v. Loisel, 259 U.S. 309, 312 (1922); *see also* Brauch v. Raiche, 618 F.2d 843 (1st Cir. 1980). What law should U.S. courts look to in determining whether the conduct in question would be a crime in the United States? Federal law? State law? If state law, which state's law? *See, e.g.,* DeSilva v. DiLeonardi, 125 F.3d 1110, 1113 (7th Cir. 1997) ("Acts are considered criminal 'in this country' if they would be unlawful under federal statutes, the law of the state where the accused is found, or the law of the preponderance of the states."); Yau-Leung v. Soscia, 649 F.2d 914, 918 (2d Cir. 1981) ("The phrase 'under the law of the United States of America' in an extradition treaty referring to American criminal law must be taken as including both state and federal law absent evidence that it was intended to the contrary."). What if the requesting state is seeking to try someone for conduct occurring outside the requesting state's borders, but the requested state would not apply its own laws extraterritorially to such conduct? *Compare* Demjanjuk v. Petrovsky, 776 F.2d 571 (6th Cir. 1985) (concluding that it was sufficient that the United States would prosecute the conduct if it had occurred within the United States), *with* Regina v. Bow Street Metropolitan Stipendiary Magistrate, Ex parte Pinochet Ugarte, 2 W.L.R. 827 (H.L. 1999) (requiring that the conduct have been an extraterritorial crime in Great Britain when committed).

Political Offense Exception. Another common provision in extradition treaties is a "political offense" exception, such as the one in Article 4(1)(iii) of the above treaty with Canada. What are the justifications for this exception? What factors should a court look at in evaluating the political offense exception? How much deference, if any, should it give to the views of the Executive Branch? For decisions considering these questions, see, for example, Quinn v. Robinson, 783 F.2d 776 (9th Cir. 1986); Eain v. Wilkes, 641 F.2d 504 (7th Cir. 1981); and In re Mackin, 668 F.2d 122 (2d Cir. 1981).

Some extradition treaties refer to a political offense exception without defining the term. Before 1985, this was the case with respect to the U.S. extradition treaty with Great Britain, which provided simply that "extradition shall not be granted if . . . the offense for which extradition is requested is regarded by the requested party as one of a political character." In this situation, courts have distinguished between "pure" and "relative" political offenses. Pure political offenses are acts, such as treason, sedition, and espionage, which are aimed directly at a government and do not violate the private rights of individuals. Courts typically have treated these offenses as non-extraditable. Relative political offenses are common crimes committed in connection with a political act. For those offenses, courts (applying a variety of tests) have examined whether the nexus between the crime and the political act is sufficiently close to warrant treating the crime as non-extraditable.

The political offense exception in the U.S.-British extradition treaty was successfully invoked in a number of cases in the 1970s and 1980s by alleged members of the Irish Republican Army. *See, e.g.,* In re McMullen, No. 3-78-1899 M.G. (N.D. Cal. 1979), *reprinted in* 132 Cong. Rec. 16,585 (1986); In re Mackin, No. 86 Cr. Misl., *app. denied*, 668 F.2d 122 (2d Cir. 1981); In re Doherty, 599 F. Supp. 270 (S.D.N.Y. 1984). These decisions drew protests from the British government, and the United States and Great Britain eventually negotiated a supplemental extradition treaty in 1985 that contained a long list of crimes that could not be deemed political offenses, but also provided that the judiciary had the authority to determine whether an extradition request was motivated by a desire to punish the person on account of factors such as religion or political opinions. In 2003, the United States and the United Kingdom renegotiated their extradition treaty, which continued to include a list of crimes that could not be deemed political offenses (including murder, manslaughter, malicious wounding, kidnapping, abduction, and using explosive devices capable of endangering life) but provided that it was for the U.S. Executive, not the courts, to determine whether a particular UK extradition request was politically motivated. The treaty entered into force in 2007. Does this provision improperly interfere with the role of the courts? Note that Article 4(2) of the above treaty with Canada similarly excludes certain offenses from the political offense exception.

Statute of Limitations. Another common restriction in extradition treaties is a statute of limitations. Many treaties allow the extraditee to invoke both the statute of limitations of the requested state and that of the requesting state. Some treaties, however (such as the above treaty with Canada), refer only to the statute of limitations of the requesting state. *See* Murphy v. United States, 199 F.3d 599 (2d Cir. 1999) (discussing treaty with Canada). Note that statutes of limitation are often tolled during the time a person is a fugitive or fighting extradition. *See, e.g.,* 18 U.S.C. §3290 ("No statute of limitations shall extend to any person fleeing from justice."). In determining the appropriate U.S. statute of limitations, should a court look to federal or state law? *See, e.g.,* Garcia-Guillern v. United States, 450 F.2d 1189, 1193 n.1 (5th Cir. 1971) ("A treaty is an agreement between two nations and the statutes of limitations of the various states of the United States should not be used to interfere with obligations under a treaty if the crime has not prescribed according to the federal statute of limitations.").

Specialty Doctrine. United States courts have long enforced the "specialty doctrine," which limits the charges that can be filed against suspects extradited to the United States. The Supreme Court first recognized this limitation in United States v. Rauscher, 119 U.S. 407 (1886). There, William Rauscher, the second mate on a ship, killed one of the crew members of the ship while on the high seas. A U.S. grand jury indicted Rauscher, but he fled to Great Britain before the United States could take him into custody. The United States requested extradition in order to try Rauscher for committing murder on the high seas, and Great Britain granted the request. The United States then attempted to try him for "inflicting cruel and unusual punishment." The Supreme Court held that this was improper. The Court explained that, "according to the doctrine of publicists and writers on international law, the country receiving the offender against its laws from another country had no right to proceed against him for any other offence than that for which he had been delivered up." The Court further concluded that the extradition treaty between the United States and Great Britain "did not intend to depart in this respect from the recognized public law which had prevailed in the absence of treaties." Finally, the Court noted that two U.S. extradition statutes implicitly assumed the specialty doctrine. Under the specialty doctrine, the Court stated, an individual extradited to the United States "shall be tried only for the offence with which he is charged in the extradition proceedings and for which he was delivered up, and that if not tried for that, or after trial and acquittal, he shall have a reasonable time to leave the country before he is arrested upon the charge of any other crime committed previous to his extradition." Chief Justice Waite dissented, arguing that any immunity that Rauscher might have from prosecution must stem from the extradition treaty, and that there was nothing in the extradition treaty with Great Britain requiring the specialty doctrine.

In the absence of a treaty provision incorporating the specialty doctrine, what is the legal source of this doctrine? Customary international law? Federal (or general) common law? International comity? What status does this doctrine have in U.S. courts? Should it supersede prosecutorial decisions made by the Executive Branch? Why have a specialty doctrine? What would happen to cooperative extradition among nations if one country started prosecuting extradited criminals for offenses other than the ones for which they were extradited? For a consideration of these and other questions, see Jacques Semmelman, *The Doctrine of Specialty in the Federal Courts: Making Sense of United States v. Rauscher,* 34 Va. J. Int'l L. 71 (1993).

Should a court apply the specialty doctrine when the sending state does not object to the prosecution? Most courts have held that the specialty doctrine does not apply if the sending state specifically consents to the prosecution. *See, e.g.,* United States v. Tse, 135 F.3d 200 (1st Cir. 1998); United States v. Puentes, 50 F.3d 1567 (11th Cir. 1995). Courts are divided over whether the extraditee can raise the specialty doctrine when the sending state is silent. Some courts have concluded that the extraditee cannot raise the doctrine unless the sending state affirmatively objects to the new prosecution. *See, e.g.,* United States v. Barinas, 865 F.3d 99, 105 (2d Cir. 2017); United States v. Kaufman, 874 F.2d 242, 243 (5th Cir. 1989). Other courts have held that, in the face of silence, the court must guess whether the sending state would object to the new prosecution. *See, e.g.,* United States v. Andonian, 29 F.3d 1432 (9th Cir. 1995). Still other courts have held that the extraditee may raise the specialty doctrine, but only if the sending state has not waived its right to object to the prosecution. *See, e.g., Puentes, supra.* What is the right approach? Note that many extradition treaties today expressly refer to the specialty doctrine. See, for example, Article 12 in the above treaty with Canada. For a decision holding that the specialty doctrine does not apply when a suspect is delivered to the United States as part of an informal agreement rather than pursuant to the terms of an extradition treaty, see United States v. Valencia-Trujillo, 573 F.3d 1171 (11th Cir. 2009). The court there reasoned, among other things, that "[u]nless extradition conditions or restrictions are grounded in self-executing provisions of a treaty, they do not have 'the force and effect of a legislative enactment' that the defendant has standing to assert in the courts of this country."

Limits Imposed by Sending States. When the United States requests extradition of a suspect from another country, the extradition process is governed not only by the relevant treaty, but also by the laws of the other country. Such laws may impose barriers to U.S. extradition requests. For example, some nations will not extradite their own citizens. This became an issue in the case of Samuel Sheinbein, who fled to Israel after committing a grisly murder in Maryland in 1997. Israel controversially refused to extradite Sheinbein to the United States, after determining that he qualified for Israeli citizenship (even though Sheinbein had never lived in Israel and his father had lived there only briefly). *See* Melinda Henneberger, *Israel Refuses to Extradite a Murder Suspect,* N.Y. Times, Oct. 1, 1997, at A12. Instead, Sheinbein was tried in Israel, where he was found guilty and sentenced to 24 years in prison. (Israel has since changed its law to allow extradition of Israeli citizens. If the citizen is also a resident of Israel at the time of the offense, the law requires that the requesting state agree that it will allow the person to serve his or her term of imprisonment, if any, in Israel.) Note that the United States will extradite its own nationals, as long as the extradition treaty with the requesting nation allows for such extradition. *See* Charlton v. Kelly, 229 U.S. 447, 467 (1913).

In addition, some nations will not extradite to the United States if the suspect is likely to face the death penalty. In most cases, extradition is allowed once the relevant state or federal authorities provide an assurance that they will not seek the death penalty. In one case from Italy in 1996, however, extradition was denied notwithstanding such assurances from state authorities (in Florida). *See* John Tagliabue, *Italian Court Blocks Extradition, Citing Death Penalty in Florida,* N.Y. Times, June 28, 1996, at A7. Interestingly, Italy subsequently allowed some of the trial to take place in Florida, albeit under Italian law and with Italian judges. In a case from Mexico in 1997, state authorities in California refused to provide an assurance that they would not seek the death penalty, so Mexico decided to try the suspect itself. *See* Nicholas Riccardi, *Mexico Will Try Fugitive Wanted in Slayings of 4,* L.A. Times, Oct. 2, 1997, at B1. More recently, concerns about the U.S. death penalty surfaced in connection with U.S. efforts to obtain custody of and try individuals suspected of involvement in the September 11, 2001, terrorist attacks. *See* T. R. Reid, *Europeans Reluctant to Send Terror Suspects to U.S.; Allies Oppose Death Penalty and Bush's Plan for Secret Military Tribunals,* Wash. Post, Nov. 29, 2001, at A23. Some extradition treaties expressly refer to a death penalty limitation. See, for example, Article 6 in the treaty with Canada excerpted above.

Even when extradition to the United States is approved, the extradition proceedings in the foreign country may take substantial time. This was the case, for example, with respect to Ira Einhorn, who was charged with killing his girlfriend in 1977 in Philadelphia. The United States requested his extradition from France in 1997, and, although French courts ultimately approved the extradition, Einhorn was able to delay extradition through court challenges and appeals to political officials. *See* Linda Lloyd, *Einhorn Will Appeal Extradition from France on 1977 Murder Charges,* Philadelphia Inquirer, Sept. 20, 2000. Einhorn was finally extradited to the United States in July 2001. *See* Francis X. Clines, *France Sending Fugitive Home to U.S. for New Trial,* N.Y. Times, July 20, 2001.

Extradition from the United States implicates a variety of constitutional issues, some of which are explored in the materials below.

Lo Duca v. United States

93 F.3d 1100 (2d Cir. 1996) (as amended)

[In 1993, Paolo Lo Duca, an Italian citizen living in New York, was convicted in Italy on drug charges. Italy subsequently submitted an application to the United States, pursuant to an extradition treaty between the two countries, asking for Lo Duca's extradition. Lo Duca was arrested, and a magistrate judge found that he was subject to extradition. Lo Duca then brought a habeas corpus action arguing that 18 U.S.C. §3184, which provides that when a justice, judge, or magistrate finds someone to be extraditable, the justice, judge, or magistrate is to "certify the same, together with a copy of all the testimony taken before him, to the Secretary of State," is unconstitutional.]

JON O. NEWMAN, CHIEF JUDGE. . . .

Lo Duca presents two alternative contentions, consideration of which depends upon our resolution of an initial question: do judicial officers acting pursuant to section 3184 exercise the "judicial power" of the United States under Article III of the Constitution? If an extradition officer does exercise Article III power, then Lo Duca contends that the statutory scheme is unconstitutional since it subjects Article III judgments to revision by the Executive Branch. On the other hand, if an extradition officer does not exercise Article III power, then Lo Duca contends that Congress has unconstitutionally authorized federal judges and magistrate judges to engage in extrajudicial activities.

This is not the first time that our Circuit has considered the question of whether extradition officers exercise Article III power. In *Austin,* we recently held that the function performed by an extradition officer is not an exercise of the judicial power of the United States. Austin [v. Healey, 5 F.3d 598, 603 (2d. Cir. 1993)]. This holding accords with the decisions of the First, Eleventh, and District of Columbia Circuits. . . .

This conclusion is bolstered by the fact that, although direct judicial review of an extradition proceeding is not available, there is the possibility for what has been called "executive revision," pursuant to the discretionary authority of the Executive Branch to refuse extradition. The first case involving executive revision arose in a different context in Hayburn's Case, 2 U.S. (2 Dall.) 409 (1792). . . . Congress had provided that the circuit courts should decide in the first instance whether individual veterans were eligible for disability pensions. These determinations, however, were subject to revision by the Secretary of War. Chief Justice Jay and Justice Cushing, sitting as members of the Circuit Court of the District of New York, held that "the [pension adjusting] duties assigned to the Circuit Courts . . . are not of [judicial] description . . . ; inasmuch as [the statute] subjects the decisions of these courts . . . to the consideration and suspension of the Secretary at War. . . ." Similar statements regarding the non-judicial nature of the power granted by Congress were made by Justices Wilson, Blair, and Iredell in their capacities as circuit judges. Thus, the various Justices held that the statute failed to accomplish a grant of judicial power under Article III, and in that regard, the fact that the statute contemplated executive revision was dispositive.

Chief Justice Jay and Justice Cushing additionally explained that the statute could be considered, not as a grant of Article III power, but "as appointing commissioners for the purposes mentioned in it. . . ." "[T]he Judges of this Court regard themselves as being the commissioners designated by the act, and therefore as being at liberty to accept or decline that office." The Justices concluded that "the Judges of this Court will . . . adjourn the court from day to day . . . and . . . proceed as commissioners to execute the business of this act in the same court room, or chamber." Notably, the Justices found no constitutional impediment to their rendering adjudicatory decisions under the statute, as long as those decisions were distinct from their judicial functions regarding cases and controversies under Article III.

In United States v. Ferreira, 54 U.S. (13 How.) 40 (1852) (1870), the Supreme Court considered a similar statute authorizing federal district judges in Florida to adjust certain claims made by the Spanish inhabitants of that state against the United States. Those determinations were subject to approval by the Secretary of the Treasury. *Id.* The Supreme Court held that "such a tribunal is not a judicial one. . . . The authority conferred on the respective judges was nothing more than that of a commissioner. . . ." As the Supreme Court elaborated:

> The powers conferred by these acts of Congress upon the judge . . . are, it is true, judicial in their nature. For judgment and discretion must be exercised by both of them. But it is nothing more than the power ordinarily given by law to a commissioner appointed to adjust claims to lands or money under a treaty. . . . [It] is not judicial . . . , in the sense in which judicial power is granted by the constitution to the courts of the United States.

Thus, the Supreme Court found it unexceptional that the judges, as commissioners, acted in an "adjudicatory" capacity.[5]

Instead of focusing on the misleading distinction between adjudicatory and non-adjudicatory functions, *Ferreira* relied on the fact that the decisions of the

---

5. The Constitution itself provides numerous situations where some form of adjudication is required outside the context of Article III. For example, the executive decision to grant a Presidential pardon may be based on a review of the law and facts that would normally be reserved to the province of courts. Similarly, the executive decision to veto legislation may be based on an opinion that such legislation is unconstitutional.

district judges were subject to executive revision. The Supreme Court found it "too evident for argument" that the statute did not confer Article III power since

> neither the evidence, nor [the judge's] award, are to be filed in the court in which he presides, nor recorded there; but he is required to transmit, both the decision and the evidence upon which he decided, to the Secretary of the Treasury; and the claim is to be paid if the Secretary thinks it just and equitable, but not otherwise.

Thus, the fact of executive revision led the Supreme Court in *Ferreira* to hold that those judges, acting as commissioners, did not exercise Article III power. Similarly, in this case, it is dispositive that, since the decisions of extradition officers are subject to revision by the Secretary of State, those officers do not exercise judicial power within the meaning of Article III.[6]

Lastly, we point out that, as a matter of statutory language, section 3184 closely tracks the holdings of . . . *Hayburn's Case* and *Ferreira* by granting jurisdiction over extradition complaints not to "courts" but to individual enumerated "justices," "judges," and "magistrates," including judges of state courts of general jurisdiction. . . . This distinction between "courts" and "judges" in the context of extradition proceedings has been long recognized. . . . We note that, traditionally, it is "courts" and not "judges" that exercise Article III power. *See* U.S. Const. art. III, §1 ("The judicial power of the United States shall be vested in one supreme Court, and in such inferior Courts as the Congress may from time to time ordain and establish."). The use of the word "judges" in section 3184 is more consistent with a statute appointing commissioners "by official, instead of personal descriptions." *Hayburn's Case*, 2 U.S. (2 Dall.) at 410 n.1.

Having examined the text of the statute, its structural correlation with Article III, and the relevant historical precedents, we conclude that our holding in *Austin* was correct—extradition officers do not exercise judicial power under Article III of the Constitution. *Austin*, 5 F.3d at 603. We therefore turn to Lo Duca's following arguments, which contend that section 3184 is unconstitutional precisely because it does not confer Article III power.

Lo Duca first argues that section 3184 violates the doctrine of separation of powers insofar as it seeks to require Article III courts to conduct non-Article III extradition proceedings. *See* National Mutual Insurance Co. v. Tidewater Transfer Co., 337 U.S. 582 (1949). In *Tidewater*, the Supreme Court confronted the question whether Congress could expand the jurisdiction of federal courts beyond the class of cases and controversies enumerated in Article III. In three separate opinions, six Justices reaffirmed the traditional view that federal courts are courts of limited jurisdiction whose judicial powers are bounded by Article III. *See id.* at 607 (Rutledge, J., joined by Murphy, J., concurring in the judgment); *id.* at 635 (Vinson, C.J., joined by Douglas, J., dissenting); *id.* at 647 (Frankfurter, J., joined by Reed, J., dissenting). Justice Jackson expressed a contrary view in his plurality opinion announcing the judgment of the Court. *Id.* at 583 (Jackson, J., joined by Black and Burton, JJ.). He

---

6. Lo Duca notes that, as a practical matter, extradition officers certainly appear to exercise judicial power—they issue arrest warrants, preside in courtrooms, and use other judicial resources. These actions, however, are not incompatible with their designation as commissioners acting in a non-Article III capacity. Their authority to issue arrest warrants derives not from any inherent judicial power, but rather from the text of section 3184 itself. *See* 18 U.S.C. §3184. Lo Duca does not contend that this task is such an "essential attribute of judicial power" that it can be exercised only within the confines of Article III.

wrote that, under Article I, Congress could grant jurisdiction for federal courts to hear non-Article III cases. *See Tidewater,* 337 U.S. at 592-93. Justices Rutledge and Murphy, who "strongly dissented" from that reasoning, nonetheless concurred in the result on other grounds. *See id.* at 604, 626 (Rutledge, J., concurring in the judgment) (calling the opinion of Justice Jackson a "dangerous doctrine").

In cases reaching as far back as Marbury v. Madison, 5 U.S. (1 Cranch) 137 (1803), the Supreme Court has held that Congress may not expand the jurisdiction of federal courts beyond the limits established by Article III. . . . Lo Duca relies on these cases to contend that the Constitution prevents Congress from vesting federal courts with jurisdiction over non-Article III extradition complaints.

Without questioning these cases, the Government responds that federal courts are not the subject of section 3184. Rather, "§3184 vests individual judges with jurisdiction over extradition requests." [In re Mackin, 668 F.2d 122, 130 n.11 (2d Cir. 1981).] This distinction between "courts" and "judges" is dispositive. . . . Only individual justices, judges, and magistrate judges are authorized to act under the statute. Since they function, as in *Hayburn's Case* and in *Ferreira,* as commissioners, they are not bound by the limits of Article III.

Lo Duca next argues that, insofar as section 3184 requires judges to act in an extrajudicial capacity, the statute runs afoul of Mistretta v. United States, 488 U.S. 361 (1989). In *Mistretta,* the Supreme Court was concerned with the possibility that Congress might compromise the independence of Article III judges by requiring them to participate in extrajudicial activities. This concern, however, does not apply with equal force to those who are not Article III judges. Thus, Lo Duca's claim founders at the outset since his extradition proceedings were conducted solely by federal magistrate judges. Then-Magistrate Judge Ross issued the warrant under which Lo Duca was arrested. Magistrate Judge Gold conducted the subsequent extradition hearing and granted the certificate of extraditability. Since federal magistrate judges are not Article III judges, the Constitution does not accord them the same protections against Congressional expansion of their duties. . . . Nothing in *Mistretta* suggests that federal magistrate judges would be precluded from conducting extradition proceedings.

Lo Duca argues nonetheless that, if Article III judges cannot act as extradition officers, then they lack the power to delegate those duties to a magistrate judge under the Federal Magistrates Act, 28 U.S.C. §636(b) (1994). This argument presupposes that magistrate judges serve as extradition officers in their capacity as "adjuncts" to Article III courts under section 636(b). Yet, as this Court has pointed out, magistrate judges acting under section 3184 do not rely on the Federal Magistrates Act for their authority. Rather, section 3184 contains its own independent grant of authority to allow magistrate judges to hear extradition complaints. 18 U.S.C. §3184. Once a magistrate judge is authorized to act under section 3184, that officer does not need subsequent permission from a supervising court on a case-by-case basis. A magistrate judge serving as an extradition officer pursuant to section 3184 acts as a commissioner, in the same capacity as any other enumerated justice or judge under section 3184.

In any event, even if Lo Duca's extradition proceedings had been conducted by a federal judge, there would be no violation of *Mistretta.* On the contrary, *Mistretta* expressly states that federal judges may participate in extrajudicial activities as long as two requirements are met. First, the judge must be acting "in an individual, not judicial, capacity." *Mistretta,* 488 U.S. at 404. Second, "a particular extrajudicial assignment [must not] undermine[] the integrity of the Judicial Branch." *Id.* We have already held that judges acting pursuant to section 3184 do so as commissioners in an individual capacity. We now consider whether the particular task of adjudicating extradition complaints might undermine the integrity of the Judicial Branch.

Mistretta was concerned with two possible subversions of judicial integrity. The first was the possibility that Congress might force federal judges to perform extrajudicial tasks. In this case, however, we have no reason to believe that any federal judge has been forced to conduct an extradition proceeding. Moreover, since we are instructed to construe federal statutes to avoid constitutional infirmity, we read section 3184 as merely authorizing federal judges to act as extradition officers. . . . Section 3184 states that an extradition officer "*may* . . . issue his warrant for the apprehension of the person so charged, that he *may* be brought before such justice, judge, or magistrate, to the end that the evidence of criminality *may* be heard and considered." 18 U.S.C. §3184 (emphasis added).

Mistretta was also concerned with the possibility that certain extrajudicial activities might undermine the integrity of the Judicial Branch by weakening public confidence. *See Mistretta,* 488 U.S. at 407-08. We believe that, in this particular context, history sufficiently allays this concern. For nearly 150 years, federal judges have adjudicated extradition complaints under section 3184 with no indication of any adverse consequences. Of course, this is hardly surprising since an extradition proceeding is "an essentially neutral endeavor and one in which judicial participation is peculiarly appropriate." *Id.* at 407. We conclude that the extrajudicial duties authorized by section 3184 do not undermine the integrity of the Judicial Branch, and *Mistretta* does not prohibit federal judges from hearing extradition complaints.

Lo Duca's final argument invokes the Appointments Clause of the Constitution. U.S. Const. art. II, §2, cl. 2. He contends that, insofar as judicial officers acting under section 3184 do not serve in their traditional capacity as "justice," "judge," or "magistrate," they must receive a second appointment to carry out their duties as "extradition officer." This argument might carry some weight if the description of extradition officers in section 3184 included persons who held no prior office, but extradition officers have already been appointed to one position—either justice, judge, or magistrate judge. Where Congress provides additional duties that are "germane" to an already existing position, the Appointments Clause does not require a second appointment. . . . The duties performed by an extradition officer are virtually identical to those performed every day by judges and magistrate judges in the course of preliminary criminal proceedings. This case is a far cry from *Mistretta,* where participation on the Sentencing Commission entailed duties that were substantially different from a judge's normal tasks. Since extradition proceedings are sufficiently germane to the traditional duties of judges and magistrate judges, under the Appointments Clause, these judicial officers do not require a second appointment to hear extradition complaints.[11]

---

11. Some might question whether the task of hearing extradition complaints, which is a non-judicial task for purposes of Article III, is nevertheless "germane" to the traditionally judicial task of determining probable cause. We think that this situation falls within a narrow (perhaps unique) set of circumstances where the function is technically non-judicial in nature, but sufficiently similar to judicial functions so as to satisfy the "germaneness" requirement.

Ntakirutimana v. Reno

184 F.3d 419 (5th Cir. 1999)

[In 1994, the U.N. Security Council created an international criminal tribunal (the International Criminal Tribunal for Rwanda or ICTR) to try individuals responsible for genocide in Rwanda. In 1995, President Clinton entered into an executive agreement with the ICTR committing the United States to extradite suspects to the tribunal, and Congress enacted legislation in 1996 to implement this agreement. The ICTR subsequently indicted Elizaphan Ntakirutimana, a Rwandan citizen living in Texas, on charges of genocide and other crimes. A magistrate judge refused to allow extradition of Ntakirutimana, concluding that suspects could not be extradited from the United States except pursuant to an extradition treaty approved by two-thirds of the Senate. A federal district court judge overturned this decision, holding that extradition was proper. Ntakirutimana then filed a petition for a writ of habeas corpus, which the district court denied.]

EMILIO M. GARZA, CIRCUIT JUDGE. . . .

To determine whether a treaty is required to extradite Ntakirutimana, we turn to the text of the Constitution. Ntakirutimana contends that Article II, Section 2, Clause 2 of the Constitution requires a treaty to extradite. This Clause, which enumerates the President's foreign relations power, provides in part that "[the President] shall have Power, by and with the Advice and Consent of the Senate, to make Treaties, provided two thirds of the Senators present concur; and he shall nominate, and by and with the Advice and Consent of the Senate, shall appoint Ambassadors, other public Ministers and Consuls. . . ." U.S. Const. art. II, §2, cl. 2. This provision does not refer either to extradition or to the necessity of a treaty to extradite. The Supreme Court has explained, however, that "the power to surrender is clearly included within the treaty-making power and the corresponding power of appointing and receiving ambassadors and other public ministers." Terlinden v. Ames, 184 U.S. 270, 289 (1902) (citation omitted).

Yet, the Court has found that the Executive's power to surrender fugitives is not unlimited. In Valentine v. United States, 299 U.S. 5 (1936), the Supreme Court considered whether an exception clause in the United States' extradition treaty with France implicitly granted to the Executive the discretionary power to surrender citizens. The Court first stated that the power to provide for extradition is a national power that "is not confided to the Executive in the absence of treaty or legislative provision." The Court explained:

[The power to extradite] rests upon the fundamental consideration that the Constitution creates no executive prerogative to dispose of the liberty of the individual. Proceedings against him must be authorized by law. There is no executive discretion to surrender him to a foreign government, unless that discretion is granted by law. It necessarily follows that as the legal authority does not exist save as it is given by act of Congress or by the terms of a treaty, it is not enough that the statute or treaty does not deny the power to surrender. It must be found that statute or treaty confers the power.

The Court then considered whether any statute authorized the Executive's discretion to extradite. The Court commented that:

Whatever may be the power of the Congress to provide for extradition independent of treaty, that power has not been exercised save in relation to a foreign country or territory "occupied by or under the control of the United States." Aside from that limited provision, the Act of Congress relating to extradition simply defines the procedure to carry out an existing extradition treaty or convention.

The Court concluded that no statutory basis conferred the power on the Executive to surrender a citizen to the foreign government. The Court subsequently addressed whether the treaty conferred the power to surrender, and found that it did not. The Court concluded that, "we are constrained to hold that [the President's] power, in the absence of statute conferring an independent power, must be found in the terms of the treaty and that, as the treaty with France fails to grant the necessary authority, the President is without the power to surrender the respondents." The Court added that the remedy for this lack of power "lies with the Congress, or with the treaty-making power wherever the parties are willing to provide for the surrender of citizens."

Valentine indicates that a court should look to whether a treaty *or statute* grants executive discretion to extradite. Hence, *Valentine* supports the constitutionality of using the Congressional-Executive Agreement to extradite Ntakirutimana. Ntakirutimana attempts to distinguish *Valentine* on the ground that the case dealt with a *treaty* between France and the United States. Yet, *Valentine* indicates that a statute suffices to confer authority on the President to surrender a fugitive. Ntakirutimana suggests also that *Valentine* expressly challenged the power of Congress, independent of treaty, to provide for extradition. *Valentine*, however, did not place a limit on Congress's power to provide for extradition. Thus, although some authorization by law is necessary for the Executive to extradite, neither the Constitution's text nor *Valentine* require that the authorization come in the form of a treaty.

Notwithstanding the Constitution's text or *Valentine*, Ntakirutimana argues that the intent of the drafters of the Constitution supports his interpretation. He alleges that the delegates to the Constitutional Convention intentionally placed the Treaty power exclusively in the President and the Senate. The delegates designed this arrangement because they wanted a single executive agent to negotiate agreements with foreign powers, and they wanted the senior House of Congress — the Senate — to review the agreements to serve as a check on the executive branch. Ntakirutimana also claims that the rejection of alternative proposals suggests that the framers believed that a treaty is the only means by which the United States can enter into a binding agreement with a foreign nation.

We are unpersuaded by Ntakirutimana's extended discussion of the Constitution's history. Ntakirutimana does not cite to any provision in the Constitution or any aspect of its history that requires a treaty to extradite. Ntakirutimana's argument, which is not specific to extradition, is premised on the assumption that a treaty is required for an international agreement. To the contrary, "the Constitution, while expounding procedural requirements for treaties alone, apparently contemplates alternate modes of international agreements." Laurence H. Tribe, American Constitutional Law §4-5, at 228-29 (2d ed. 1988). "The Supreme Court has recognized that of necessity the President may enter into certain binding agreements with foreign nations not strictly congruent with the formalities required by the Constitution's Treaty Clause." United States v. Walczak, 783 F.2d 852, 855 (9th Cir. 1986) (citations omitted) (executive agreement). More specifically, the Supreme Court has repeatedly stated that a treaty or statute may confer the power to extradite. . . .

Ntakirutimana next argues that historical practice establishes that a treaty is required to extradite. According to Ntakirutimana, the United States has never surrendered a person except pursuant to an Article II treaty, and the only involuntary transfers without an extradition treaty have been to "a foreign country or territory 'occupied by or under the control of the United States.'" *Valentine*, 299 U.S. at 9. This argument fails for numerous reasons. First, *Valentine* did not suggest that this "historical practice" limited Congress's power. Second, the Supreme Court's statements that a statute may confer the power to extradite also reflect a historical understanding of the Constitution. Even if Congress has rarely exercised the power to extradite by statute, a historical understanding exists nonetheless that it may do so. Third, in some instances in which a fugitive would not have been extraditable under a treaty, a fugitive has been extradited pursuant to a statute that "filled the gap" in the treaty. Thus, we are unconvinced that the President's practice of usually submitting a negotiated treaty to the Senate reflects a historical understanding that a treaty is required to extradite.

We are unpersuaded by Ntakirutimana's other arguments. First, he asserts that the failure to require a treaty violates the Constitution's separation of powers. He contends that if a treaty is not required, then "the President alone could make dangerous agreements with foreign governments" or "Congress could legislate foreign affairs." This argument is not relevant to an Executive-Congressional agreement, which involves neither the President acting unilaterally nor Congress negotiating with foreign countries. Second, Ntakirutimana argues that "statutes cannot usurp the Treaty making power of Article II." The Supreme Court, however, has held that statutes can usurp a treaty. This is confirmed by the "last in time" rule that, if a statute and treaty are inconsistent, then the last in time will prevail. This rule explicitly contemplates that a statute and a treaty may at times cover the same subject matter. Third, Ntakirutimana contends that not requiring a treaty reads the treaty-making power out of the Constitution. Yet, the treaty-making power remains unaffected, because the President may still elect to submit a negotiated treaty to the Senate, instead of submitting legislation to Congress. . . .

HAROLD R. DEMOSS, CIRCUIT JUDGE, dissenting. . . .

The "Congressional-Executive Agreement" method of ratifying the Surrender Agreement with the Tribunal runs afoul of the Constitution's Treaty Clause, and §1342 alone is constitutionally insufficient to ratify the Surrender Agreement which has been invoked to support the extradition. . . .

The Constitution's treaty procedure must be followed in order to ratify an extradition agreement which contractually binds our nation to respect obligations to another nation. The intent of the framers could not be clearer on this point. Our Founding Fathers were very concerned about the new nation becoming entangled in foreign alliances. The possibility of giving the President full authority for foreign affairs was considered and rejected. In *The Federalist No. 75*, Alexander Hamilton argued that it would be "utterly unsafe and improper" to completely entrust foreign affairs to a President, who is elected for only four years at a time. The Founders were especially concerned with the possibility that, in the conduct of foreign policy, American officials might become seduced by their foreign counterparts or a President might actually betray the country. Thus, while primary responsibility for foreign affairs was given to the President, a significant restraint and "check" on the use of the treaty power was created by requiring for treaties the advice and consent of two-thirds of the Senate. *See The Federalist No. 69* (Alexander Hamilton) (noting that this "check" is a major distinction between the presidency and England's monarchy, in which the king was "the sole and absolute representative of the nation in all foreign transactions"). The decision to require approval of two-thirds of Senators was controversial and hotly debated, but it was ultimately decided that sheer importance of the treaty power merited such a treatment. Treaties cannot be accomplished by any means other than the Article II treaty ratification procedure.

Of course, not all agreements with foreign countries require the full Article II "treaty" treatment in order to be effective. The Constitution implicitly recognizes a hierarchy of arrangements with foreign countries, of which treaties are the most sacrosanct. Compare U.S. Const. art. I, §10, cl. 1 ("No State shall enter into any Treaty, Alliance, or Confederation . . ."), with U.S. Const. art. I, §10, cl. 3 ("No State shall, without the Consent of Congress . . . enter into any Agreement or Compact with another State, or with a foreign Power. . . ."). The Attorney General's primary argument in defense of the enforceability of the extradition agreement with the Tribunal follows this line of thought. She has argued, and the majority echoes, that the Constitution contains no explicit reference to extradition.

But the fact of the matter is that while the Constitution has no provisions explicitly relating to extradition, it likewise has no provisions explicitly relating to executive agreements. It only mentions treaties. Our national government is one of limited, enumerated powers. All agree that the Surrender Agreement is not a treaty. We are therefore left to read between the lines to ascertain whether the President and Congress have wrongfully attempted by ordinary legislative procedures, to exercise a power governed by the Treaty Clause or whether some source of power other than the Treaty Clause enables the President and Congress to bind the country to the Surrender Agreement.

Our inquiry is significantly informed by a demonstration of what specific powers are encompassed by the Treaty Clause. "A treaty is in its nature a contract between two nations, not a legislative act." Foster v. Neilson, 27 U.S. (2 Pet.) 253, 314 (1829). . . . It is precisely the position of the Attorney General that the Surrender Agreement is a valid contract with a foreign authority and that it has the force of law. In Alexander's day, an agreement with those characteristics was called a treaty.

If the Treaty Clause is to have any meaning there is some variety of agreements which *must* be accomplished through the formal Article II process. Otherwise, the heightened consideration dictated by Article II could be avoided by the President and a majority of Congress simply by substituting the label of "executive agreement" for that of "treaty." The Supreme Court has recognized this principle:

> Express power is given to the President, by and with the advice and consent of the Senate, to make treaties, provided two-thirds of the senators present concur, and inasmuch as the power is given, in general terms, without any description of the objects intended to be embraced within its scope, *it must be assumed that the framers of the Constitution intended that it should extend to all those objects which in the intercourse of nations had usually been regarded as the proper subjects of negotiation and treaty,* if not inconsistent with the nature of our government and the relation between the States and the United States.

Holden v. Joy, 84 U.S. (17 Wall.) 211, 242-43 (1872) (emphasis supplied).

Plainly, an extradition agreement is a type of agreement historically found in a treaty and therefore governed by the Treaty Clause. Extradition, which is defined as "the surrender by one nation to another of an individual accused or convicted of an offense outside of its own territory, and within the territorial jurisdiction of the other, which, being competent to try and to punish him, demands the surrender," Terlinden v. Ames, 184 U.S. 270, 289 (1902), has usually been regarded as the proper subject of negotiation and treaty. Historically, the United States has not surrendered a person to a foreign authority (excluding countries or territories controlled by the United States) in the absence of a valid extradition treaty. Every extradition agreement ever entered into by the United States (before the advent of the new Tribunals) has been accomplished by treaty, including the Jay Treaty (1795) and the Webster Ashburton Treaty (1842). The original extradition statutes, enacted in 1848, required the existence of an extradition treaty, and there was no exception until §1342 was passed to accommodate the Tribunals for Rwanda and the former Yugoslavia. Furthermore, "the principles of international law recognize no *right* to extradition apart from treaty." Factor v. Laubenheimer, 290 U.S. 276, 287 (1933).

The insistence on the use of the treaty power for certain types of international agreements comports with the Founding Fathers' intention that the President not have unfettered discretion to enter agreements with foreign nations. *See* The Federalist No. 75 (Alexander Hamilton). Unless the Article II procedure is insisted upon, the President can exercise such plenary power simply by denominating his agreements as something other than "treaties."

Notably, the United States has publicly declared to the entire world that it can only enter into an extradition agreement through a treaty. In its fifth reservation to the Convention on the Prevention and Punishment of the Crime of Genocide, Dec. 9, 1948, 78 U.N.T.S. 277, the United States proclaimed to the international diplomatic community that it "reserves the right to effect its participation in any such tribunal only by a treaty entered into specifically for that purpose with the advice and consent of the Senate." There is no treaty which has been entered into "with the advice and consent of the Senate" which authorizes the participation in the Tribunal by the United States. This reservation clearly evidences the intent and expectation of the United States that the only way its participation in the Tribunal could take place was by a duly negotiated and ratified treaty on that subject. A reading of the Treaty Clause of the Constitution which permits the semantic shenanigans suggested by the Attorney General is an insult to the intricate structure of the Constitution, which seeks to avoid tyranny and ensure democracy through a deliberate separation of power and a delicate system of checks and balances. . . .

The Attorney General and my colleagues in the majority place great reliance on Valentine v. United States ex rel. Neidecker, 299 U.S. 5 (1936), in which the Court stated: "It cannot be doubted that the power to provide for extradition is a national power; it pertains to the national government and not to the states. But, albeit a national power, it is not confided to the Executive in the absence of treaty or legislative provision." *Valentine* was a case that did involve a treaty—its stray reference to "legislative provision" is pure dicta, and certainly not a plain holding that extradition may be accomplished by the President simply on the basis of congressional approval. Likewise, in Terlinden v. Ames, 184 U.S. 270 (1902), in which the Court noted that "in the United States, the general opinion and practice have been that extradition should be declined in the absence of a conventional or legislative provision," there was also a valid extradition treaty, and the reference to a "legislative provision" is again dicta.

The Attorney General insists that the President has the power to unilaterally enter an extradition agreement with foreign nations, the only distinction between that variety of agreement and an Article II treaty being that only a treaty will impose upon the President a duty to extradite. In defense of this principle, the Attorney General points to Factor v. Laubenheimer, 290 U.S. 276 (1933), which states:

> While a government may, if agreeable to its own constitution and laws, voluntarily exercise the power to surrender a fugitive from justice to the country from which he had fled, and it has been said that it is under a moral duty to do so, the legal right to demand his extradition and the correlative duty to surrender him to the demanding country exist only when created by treaty.

But these cases do not support the Attorney General's position. The quoted passage stands for the unremarkable propositions that a sovereign nation can (and perhaps should), if consistent with its own laws, surrender to another sovereign nation one of the surrendering nation's own citizens who is accused of crimes by that other sovereign nation, but that no such duty or legal obligation arises absent a treaty. Those propositions do not mean that the President, acting unilaterally, can enter non-binding executive agreements to extradite, or that Congress may ratify such an agreement. The Attorney General does not purport to act pursuant to some sort of sovereign power to surrender Ntakirutimana; she has consciously premised her argument on the validity and enforceability of the Surrender Agreement. This is plain from the briefs filed in this Court. Given that the Surrender Agreement is the authority invoked by the Attorney General, it is the authority which we must consider.

The executive and legislative branches of government erroneously disregarded their obligation to respect the structure provided by the Constitution when they purported to enter this extradition agreement.[14] We should issue a writ of habeas corpus, and Ntakirutimana should not be surrendered. The extradition agreement in place between the United States and the Tribunal is unenforceable, as it has not been properly ratified. The agreement's implementing legislation is unconstitutional insofar as it purports to ratify the Surrender Agreement by a means other than that prescribed by the Treaty Clause. The two acts seek impermissibly to evade the mandatory constitutional route for implementing such an agreement.[15] I therefore respectfully dissent.[16]

Notes and Questions

1. The first reported U.S. extradition case was United States v. Robbins, 27 F. Cas. 825 (D.S.C. 1799). In that case, Jonathan Robbins was extradited to Great Britain,

---

14. It is not true, as has been suggested in the media, that "[i]f Mr. Ntakirutimana's constitutional argument prevails, it will diminish the ability of the United States to cooperate in international war crimes prosecutions." *War Crimes and Extradition*, Wash. Post, Apr. 10, 1999, at A20. All that is required for participation is conformance with the Constitution. If the President wishes to bind the United States to an agreement such as the Surrender Agreement, he must obtain the advice and consent of two-thirds of the Senate as provided in Article II.

15. Whether executive and legislative actions such as those giving rise to this case reflect, as political commentator George Will has suggested, a disturbing trend of "dilution of American democracy," I leave for others to judge. George Will, *See You in Congress . . .* , Wash. Post, May 20, 1999, at A29.

16. Ntakirutimana challenges the Tribunal itself as an *ultra vires* creation of the United Nations Security Council. His is not a novel argument—the authority of the ad hoc Tribunals for Rwanda and the former Yugoslavia has been hotly debated in academia . . . , rejected by Rwanda's neighbors who refuse to accept the ICTR's process, and fully litigated in the Tribunal for the former Yugoslavia. To the extent that the viability of the Tribunal is a legitimate subject of foreign policy within the realm of the Executive, separation-of-powers concerns justify our Court in abstaining from the political question of the Tribunal's authority.

pursuant to the Jay Treaty, and hanged for participating in a violent mutiny aboard a British vessel. The extradition took place notwithstanding Robbins's claim that he was a U.S. citizen who had been impressed into service by the British. The case was very controversial and generated a number of debates relating to the scope of the treaty power, the foreign affairs powers of the Executive Branch, and the role of an independent judiciary. *See generally* Ruth Wedgwood, *The Revolutionary Martyrdom of Jonathan Robbins,* 100 Yale L.J. 229 (1990). It was in defending President John Adams's authority to extradite Jonathan Robbins pursuant to an extradition treaty that John Marshall (while in the House of Representatives) described the President as the "sole organ of the nation in its external relations." *See* John Marshall, Address Before the House of Representatives (Mar. 7, 1800), in 10 Annals of Cong. 596, 613 (Washington, Gales & Seaton 1851).

2. A version of the current extradition statute has been in place since 1848. In 1995, the U.S. District Court for the District of Columbia nevertheless held that this statutory scheme was unconstitutional. The court reasoned that the scheme violated Article III of the Constitution because it allowed the Executive Branch the power, in effect, to exercise appellate review over federal judicial decisions. *See* LoBue v. Christopher, 893 F. Supp. 65 (D.D.C. 1995). This decision was subsequently vacated by the D.C. Circuit for lack of jurisdiction. (The D.C. Circuit concluded that the petitioners should have brought their challenge in a habeas corpus action in the federal district in which they were being held, which was the Northern District of Illinois.) Needless to say, the district court's decision generated significant attention and controversy. At least for now, however, the *Lo Duca* decision excerpted above appears to have put the issue to rest. *See also* Lopez-Smith v. Hood, 121 F.3d 1322, 1327 (9th Cir. 1997) (agreeing with *Lo Duca*). Should the fact that the U.S. extradition process has operated without apparent constitutional deficiency for 150 years count in favor of the modern constitutionality of the practice? What is the relevance, if any, of the fact that, before 1848, extradition was committed to the discretion of the Executive Branch?

3. What is the strongest constitutional argument against the extradition statute? That the magistrate performs an extrajudicial function in issuing a certificate of extraditability? That it exercises a judicial function that is non-final in light of the Secretary of State's discretion? That the Secretary of State exercises a judicial function? Are you convinced by the court's conclusion in *Lo Duca* that extradition magistrates act in an individual rather than judicial capacity? Would the analysis in *Lo Duca* have been different if the extradition statute had allowed the Secretary of State to overturn findings of *non*-extraditability? Is there a connection between the constitutional issues in *Lo Duca* and the constitutional issues in *Ntakirutimana*?

4. Should the "congressional-executive agreement" power, which we considered in Chapter 6, extend to extradition? In resolving this question, what weight, if any, should be given to the fact that extradition has generally been conducted pursuant to Article II treaties? Are there special policy reasons in the extradition context for insisting on adherence to the Article II process? In answering this question, what is the relevance, if any, of the fact that extradition treaties are generally considered to be self-executing in U.S. courts? *See* Terlinden v. Ames, 184 U.S. 270, 288 (1902); United States v. Balsys, 119 F.3d 122, 138 n.14 (2d Cir. 1997), *rev'd on other grounds,* 524 U.S. 666 (1998). Assuming that a treaty is not the exclusive basis for extradition, what clause in Article I authorizes the congressional-executive agreement at issue in *Ntakirutimana*? Or is the agreement justified under an inherent congressional foreign affairs power? Could Congress have authorized the extradition by a statute that was not an international agreement? On the issues in this note, see generally Evan J. Wallach, *Extradition to the Rwandan War Crimes Tribunal: Is Another Treaty Required?*, 3 UCLA J. Int'l L. & For. Aff. 59 (1998). For an argument that an Article II treaty is "likely necessary" for extradition to another country, see Oona A. Hathaway, *Treaties' End: The Past, Present, and Future of International Lawmaking in the United States*, 117 Yale L.J. 1236, 1346-48 (2008).

5. In considering whether to extradite a suspect, U.S. courts apply a rule of "non-inquiry," a doctrine that counsels against judicial inquiry into the procedures or treatment that the suspect will face in the requesting state. The Supreme Court noted in Neely v. Henkel, 180 U.S. 109, 123 (1901), for example, that "[w]hen an American citizen commits a crime in a foreign country, he cannot complain if required to submit to such modes of trial and to such punishment as the laws of that country may prescribe for its own people, unless a different mode be provided for by treaty stipulations between that country and the United States." *See also* United States v. Smyth, 61 F.3d 711, 714 (9th Cir. 1995) ("Undergirding this principle is the notion that courts are ill-equipped as institutions and ill-advised as a matter of separation of powers and foreign relations policy to make inquiries into and pronouncements about the workings of foreign countries' justice systems."); United States v. Manzi, 888 F.2d 204, 206 (1st Cir. 1989) ("Courts have chosen to defer these questions to the executive branch because of its exclusive power to conduct foreign affairs."). Is it proper for courts to defer in this way?

Some courts have suggested in dicta that there may be a "humanitarian" exception to the rule of non-inquiry, pursuant to which courts could bar extradition if the suspect would likely face procedures or punishment "so antipathetic to a federal court's sense of decency" to compel relaxation of the rule. *See* Gallina v. Fraser, 278 F.2d 77, 79 (2d Cir. 1960); *see also, e.g.*, Emami v. U.S. District Court, 834 F.2d 1444, 1453 (9th Cir. 1987). By contrast, other courts have stated that humanitarian considerations relating to the likely treatment of the suspect are proper considerations only for the Secretary of State, not the courts. *See, e.g.*, Martin v. Warden, 993 F.2d 824, 830 (11th Cir. 1993); *see also* Ahmad v. Wigen, 910 F.2d 1063, 1067 (2d Cir. 1990) (stating that "it is the function of the Secretary of State to determine whether extradition should be denied on humanitarian grounds"). What is the right approach?

Article 3 of the United Nations Convention Against Torture and Other Cruel, Inhuman or Degrading Treatment or Punishment, which the United States has ratified, prohibits extradition of persons likely to face torture in the requesting nation. Although the Senate declared the Convention to be non-self-executing when it consented to ratification, Congress enacted legislation in 1998 implementing Article 3 of the Convention, as part of the Foreign Affairs Reform and Restructuring Act of 1998 (FARR Act). This legislation states that it is "the policy of the United States not to expel, extradite, or otherwise effect the involuntary return of any person to a country in which there are substantial grounds for believing the person would be in danger of being subjected to torture." The legislation also directs "the appropriate agencies" to "prescribe regulations to implement the obligations of the United States under Article 3" of the Torture Convention. The Department of State subsequently adopted regulations setting out a procedure for the Secretary of State to identify individuals who qualify for relief under the Torture Convention. Both the FARR Act and the regulations provided, however, that they did not provide courts with jurisdiction to review claims for breach of these provisions.

What are the implications of the Torture Convention, the FARR Act, and the regulations for the rule of non-inquiry? In a subsequently vacated decision, the U.S. Court of Appeals for the Ninth Circuit suggested that the legislation and regulations superseded the common law rule of non-inquiry, and thereby allowed judicial review of the Secretary of State's extradition decision on the ground that the Secretary is not complying with Article 3 of the Torture Convention. The court invoked, among other things, the *Charming Betsy* canon. *See* Cornejo-Barreto v. Seifert, 218 F.3d 1004, 1014 (9th Cir. 2000). In a later decision in that case, the Ninth Circuit disapproved the reasoning in its earlier decision and held that the rule of non-inquiry barred judicial review. *See* Cornejo-Barreto v. Siefert, 379 F.3d 1075 (9th Cir. 2004). That decision was also vacated, however, by a grant of rehearing en banc, and then by a determination of mootness when Mexico dropped its extradition request.

In Mironescu v. Costner, 480 F.3d 664 (4th Cir. 2007), the Fourth Circuit held that the rule of non-inquiry did not bar a district court from considering on habeas corpus whether someone would likely be tortured if extradited. The court reasoned that the habeas statute by its terms extends to individuals being held "in violation of the Constitution or laws or treaties of the United States," and the extradition of someone likely to be tortured would be in violation of a federal statute, the FARR Act. Nevertheless, the court concluded that a section of the FARR Act itself barred consideration of the habeas claim, since it provided that "nothing in this section shall be construed as providing any court jurisdiction to consider or review claims raised under the [Torture] Convention or this section" except in the context of a review of a final immigration removal order. Since the petitioner here was presenting his torture claim as part of a challenge to extradition rather than in the context of immigration proceedings, reasoned the court, this section of the FARR Act "clearly precluded the district court from exercising jurisdiction."

In Garcia v. Thomas, 683 F.3d 952 (9th Cir. 2012), the Ninth Circuit held, in an en banc decision, that a person being extradited could bring a habeas corpus challenge alleging that his extradition would violate the Convention Against Torture (CAT). Even though the CAT is not self-executing, the court reasoned that "[t]he CAT and its implementing regulations are binding domestic law, which means that the Secretary of State *must* make a torture determination before surrendering an extraditee who makes a CAT claim." The court further observed that:

> The process due here is that prescribed by the statute and implementing regulation: The Secretary must consider an extraditee's torture claim and find it not "more likely than not" that the extraditee will face torture before extradition can occur. An extraditee thus possesses a narrow liberty interest: that the Secretary comply with her statutory and regulatory obligations.

Id. at 957. The court remanded to the district court "so that the Secretary of State may augment the record by providing a declaration that she has complied with her obligations."

6. In Munaf v. Geren, 553 U.S. 674 (2008), two U.S. citizens being detained in Iraq by the U.S. military operating as part of a U.N.-authorized multinational force sought to file habeas corpus petitions in a U.S. federal court, and they also sought to enjoin the U.S. military from transferring them to Iraqi authorities for criminal prosecution. The Supreme Court unanimously held that the detainees had a statutory right to file habeas corpus petitions in a U.S. federal court. The Court also held, however, that U.S. courts exercising their habeas jurisdiction did not have the authority to enjoin the U.S. military from transferring the petitioners to

Iraqi custody. In explaining why this remedy was not available, the Court noted that the petitioners did not dispute that they had voluntarily traveled to Iraq and were alleged to have committed crimes there. "Given these facts," reasoned the Court, "our cases make clear that Iraq has a sovereign right to prosecute [the petitioners] for crimes committed on its soil." The Court also observed that "habeas is not a means of compelling the United States to harbor fugitives from the criminal justice system of a sovereign with undoubted authority to prosecute them."

The Court's conclusion was not altered by the petitioners' allegations that they might be tortured by Iraqi authorities. While such allegations "are of course a matter of serious concern," said the Court, "in the present context that concern is to be addressed by the political branches, not the judiciary." "The judiciary," the Court explained, "is not suited to second-guess such determinations—determinations that would require federal courts to pass judgment on foreign justice systems and undermine the Government's ability to speak with one voice in this area." The Court also noted that "[p]etitioners here allege only the possibility of mistreatment in a prison facility; this is not a more extreme case in which the Executive has determined that a detainee is likely to be tortured but decides to transfer him anyway."

Finally, the Court rejected the argument that a transfer of the petitioners to Iraqi authorities would constitute an "extradition" that would require authorization from a treaty or statute. The Court noted that:

> [The petitioners] voluntarily traveled to Iraq and are being held there. They are therefore subject to the territorial jurisdiction of that sovereign, not of the United States. Moreover, . . . the petitioners are being held by the United States, acting as part of [a multinational force], at the request of and on behalf of the Iraqi Government. It would be more than odd if the Government had no authority to transfer them to the very sovereign on whose behalf, and within whose territory, they are being detained.

What are the limits of this decision? What if the petitioners had been brought against their will into Iraq? What if there was evidence showing that the government knew that the petitioners were likely to be tortured? *See also* Omar v. McHugh, 646 F.3d 13 (D.C. Cir. 2011) (declining to allow dual Jordanian/U.S. national detained by the U.S. military in Iraq to challenge his transfer to Iraqi authorities).

7. Can one of the U.S. states extradite a criminal to a foreign country or tribunal, or is international extradition exclusively a federal function? If it is exclusively a federal function, is this so by virtue of the Constitution, the extradition statute, or particular extradition treaties?

Strange as it may now seem, during the first half of the nineteenth century, "extradition was practiced by some of the states, which made and granted demands for the surrender of fugitive criminals in international cases." 1 John Basset Moore, A Treatise on Extradition and Interstate Rendition 54 (1891); *see generally id.* at 53-71 (collecting state extradition statutes and extradition cases). In Holmes v. Jennison, 39 U.S. 540 (1840), the Supreme Court split 4-4 concerning the constitutionality of this practice. Chief Justice Taney authored an opinion for four Justices reasoning that Vermont's attempted extradition to Canada was a foreign compact prohibited by Article I, Section 10 of the Constitution. Taney also argued that the extradition power was exclusively federal, although he did not make clear whether this was because of dormant preemption or because the absence of federal extradition treaties constituted the affirmative "policy of the general government." In contrast, the four other participating Justices all rejected the dormant preemption argument.

By the turn of the century it appears that the extradition power was viewed as exclusive even in the absence of federal enactments, although it was never established whether this was so because of the Foreign Compacts Clause or because of dormant preemption. Thus, for example, in United States v. Rauscher, 119 U.S. 407 (1886), the Court in dicta approved of Taney's opinion in *Holmes* that the extradition power was exclusively federal without making clear whether this was because of Article I, §10 or dormant preemption. Moore's famous 1891 treatise viewed it as "settled doctrine" that the extradition power was exclusive, but emphasized that the issue "has by no means been free from controversy, and has never been actually decided by the Supreme Court of the United States." The issue became less important as the federal government began to regulate the issue by statute and treaty. *See Rauscher,* 119 U.S. at 414-15 (noting that the exclusivity of the extradition power "in the absence of treaties or acts of Congress on the subject, is now of very little importance, since, with nearly all the nations of the world with whom our relations are such that fugitives from justice may be found within their dominions or within ours, we have treaties which govern the rights and conduct of the parties in such cases" and "[t]hese treaties are also supplemented by acts of Congress, and both are in their nature exclusive"); *cf.* Valentine v. United States, 299 U.S. 5, 8 (1936) (stating, in case interpreting federal extradition treaty, that "[i]t cannot be doubted that the power to provide for extradition is a national power; it pertains to the national government and not to the States").

What would happen today if a foreign nation with which the United States did not have an extradition treaty requested extradition of a criminal from a state governor? Would the Constitution prevent the governor from responding? What about the federal extradition statute? In considering these questions, recall the cases and doctrines discussed in Chapter 4.

8. For general discussions of U.S. extradition law, see Restatement (Fourth) of the Foreign Relations Law of the United States §428 (2018); and M. Cherif Bassiouni, International Extradition: United States Law and Practice (6th ed. 2014).

E. EXTRATERRITORIAL ABDUCTION

United States v. Alvarez-Machain

504 U.S. 655 (1992)

[Humberto Alvarez-Machain, a Mexican citizen and a medical doctor, was indicted in a U.S. federal court for participating in the kidnap and murder of a U.S. Drug Enforcement Agency (DEA) agent in Mexico. DEA officials attempted to gain custody of Alvarez-Machain through informal negotiations with Mexico, but were unsuccessful. DEA officials then offered to pay a reward for the delivery of Alvarez-Machain to the United States. On April 2, 1990, Alvarez-Machain was kidnapped in Guadalajara, Mexico, and flown by private plane to El Paso, Texas, where DEA officials arrested him. The Mexican government officially protested the U.S. government's involvement in the abduction. Alvarez-Machain subsequently moved to dismiss the indictment against him on the ground that his abduction violated the extradition treaty between the United States and Mexico. The district court granted his motion and ordered that he be repatriated to Mexico, and the appeals court affirmed.]

CHIEF JUSTICE REHNQUIST delivered the opinion of the Court. . . .

Although we have never before addressed the precise issue raised in the present case, we have previously considered proceedings in claimed violation of an extradition treaty and proceedings against a defendant brought before a court by means of a forcible abduction. We addressed the former issue in United States v. Rauscher, 119 U.S. 407 (1886); more precisely, the issue whether the Webster-Ashburton Treaty of 1842, 8 Stat. 576, which governed extraditions between England and the United States, prohibited the prosecution of defendant Rauscher for a crime other than the crime for which he had been extradited. Whether this prohibition, known as the doctrine of specialty, was an intended part of the treaty had been disputed between the two nations for some time. Justice Miller delivered the opinion of the Court, which carefully examined the terms and history of the treaty; the practice of nations in regards to extradition treaties; the case law from the States; and the writings of commentators, and reached the following conclusion:

> [A] person who has been brought within the jurisdiction of the court *by virtue of proceedings under an extradition treaty,* can only be tried for one of the offences described in that treaty, and for the offence with which he is charged in the proceedings for his extradition, until a reasonable time and opportunity have been given him, after his release or trial upon such charge, to return to the country from whose asylum he had been forcibly taken under those proceedings.

([E]mphasis added).

In addition, Justice Miller's opinion noted that any doubt as to this interpretation was put to rest by two federal statutes which imposed the doctrine of specialty upon extradition treaties to which the United States was a party. Unlike the case before us today, the defendant in *Rauscher* had been brought to the United States by way of an extradition treaty; there was no issue of a forcible abduction.

In Ker v. Illinois, 119 U.S. 436 (1886), also written by Justice Miller and decided the same day as *Rauscher,* we addressed the issue of a defendant brought before the court by way of a forcible abduction. Frederick Ker had been tried and convicted in an Illinois court for larceny; his presence before the court was procured by means of forcible abduction from Peru. A messenger was sent to Lima with the proper warrant to demand Ker by virtue of the extradition treaty between Peru and the United States. The messenger, however, disdained reliance on the treaty processes, and instead forcibly kidnapped Ker and brought him to the United States. We distinguished Ker's case from *Rauscher,* on the basis that Ker was not brought into the United States by virtue of the extradition treaty between the United States and Peru, and rejected Ker's argument that he had a right under the extradition treaty to be returned to this country only in accordance with its terms. We rejected Ker's due process argument more broadly, holding in line with "the highest authorities" that "such forcible abduction is no sufficient reason why the party should not answer when brought within the jurisdiction of the court which has the right to try him for such an offence, and presents no valid objection to his trial in such court."

In Frisbie v. Collins, 342 U.S. 519 (1952), we applied the rule in *Ker* to a case in which the defendant had been kidnapped in Chicago by Michigan officers and brought to trial in Michigan. We upheld the conviction over objections based on the Due Process Clause and the federal Kidnapping Act and stated:

> This Court has never departed from the rule announced in [Ker] that the power of a court to try a person for crime is not impaired by the fact that he had been brought within the court's jurisdiction by reason of a "forcible abduction." No persuasive reasons are now presented to justify overruling this line of cases. They rest on the sound basis that due process of law is satisfied when one present in court is convicted of crime after having been fairly apprized of the charges against him and after a fair trial in accordance with constitutional procedural safeguards. There is nothing in the Constitution that requires a court to permit a guilty person rightfully convicted to escape justice because he was brought to trial against his will.

The only differences between *Ker* and the present case are that *Ker* was decided on the premise that there was no governmental involvement in the abduction; and Peru, from which Ker was abducted, did not object to his prosecution.[9] Respondent finds these differences to be dispositive, . . . contending that they show that respondent's prosecution, like the prosecution of Rauscher, violates the implied terms of a valid extradition treaty. The Government, on the other hand, argues that *Rauscher* stands as an "exception" to the rule in *Ker* only when an extradition treaty is invoked, and the terms of the treaty provide that its breach will limit the jurisdiction of a court. Therefore, our first inquiry must be whether the abduction of respondent from Mexico violated the Extradition Treaty between the United States and Mexico. If we conclude that the Treaty does not prohibit respondent's abduction, the rule in *Ker* applies, and the court need not inquire as to how respondent came before it.

In construing a treaty, as in construing a statute, we first look to its terms to determine its meaning. The Treaty says nothing about the obligations of the United States and Mexico to refrain from forcible abductions of people from the territory of the other nation, or the consequences under the Treaty if such an abduction occurs. Respondent submits that Article 22(1) of the Treaty, which states that it "shall apply to offenses specified in Article 2 [including murder] committed before and after this Treaty enters into force," evidences an intent to make application of the Treaty mandatory for those offenses. However, the more natural conclusion is that Article 22 was included to ensure that the Treaty was applied to extraditions requested after the Treaty went into force, regardless of when the crime of extradition occurred.

More critical to respondent's argument is Article 9 of the Treaty, which provides:

> 1. Neither Contracting Party shall be bound to deliver up its own nationals, but the executive authority of the requested Party shall, if not prevented by the laws of that Party, have the power to deliver them up if, in its discretion, it be deemed proper to do so.
> 2. If extradition is not granted pursuant to paragraph 1 of this Article, the requested Party shall submit the case to its competent authorities for the purpose of prosecution, provided that Party has jurisdiction over the offense.

According to respondent, Article 9 embodies the terms of the bargain which the United States struck: If the United States wishes to prosecute a Mexican national, it

---

9. Ker also was not a national of Peru, whereas respondent is a national of the country from which he was abducted. Respondent finds this difference to be immaterial.

may request that individual's extradition. Upon a request from the United States, Mexico may either extradite the individual or submit the case to the proper authorities for prosecution in Mexico. In this way, respondent reasons, each nation preserved its right to choose whether its nationals would be tried in its own courts or by the courts of the other nation. This preservation of rights would be frustrated if either nation were free to abduct nationals of the other nation for the purposes of prosecution. More broadly, respondent reasons, as did the Court of Appeals, that all the processes and restrictions on the obligation to extradite established by the Treaty would make no sense if either nation were free to resort to forcible kidnapping to gain the presence of an individual for prosecution in a manner not contemplated by the Treaty.

We do not read the Treaty in such a fashion. Article 9 does not purport to specify the only way in which one country may gain custody of a national of the other country for the purposes of prosecution. In the absence of an extradition treaty, nations are under no obligation to surrender those in their country to foreign authorities for prosecution. Extradition treaties exist so as to impose mutual obligations to surrender individuals in certain defined sets of circumstances, following established procedures. The Treaty thus provides a mechanism which would not otherwise exist, requiring, under certain circumstances, the United States and Mexico to extradite individuals to the other country, and establishing the procedures to be followed when the Treaty is invoked.

The history of negotiation and practice under the Treaty also fails to show that abductions outside of the Treaty constitute a violation of the Treaty. As the Solicitor General notes, the Mexican Government was made aware, as early as 1906, of the *Ker* doctrine, and the United States' position that it applied to forcible abductions made outside of the terms of the United States-Mexico Extradition Treaty.[11] Nonetheless, the current version of the Treaty, signed in 1978, does not attempt to establish a rule that would in any way curtail the effect of *Ker*. Moreover, although language which would grant individuals exactly the right sought by respondent had been considered and drafted as early as 1935 by a prominent group of legal scholars sponsored by the faculty of Harvard Law School, no such clause appears in the current Treaty.

Thus, the language of the Treaty, in the context of its history, does not support the proposition that the Treaty prohibits abductions outside of its terms. The remaining question, therefore, is whether the Treaty should be interpreted so as to include an implied term prohibiting prosecution where the defendant's presence is obtained by means other than those established by the Treaty.

---

11. In correspondence between the United States and Mexico growing out of the 1905 Martinez incident, in which a Mexican national was abducted from Mexico and brought to the United States for trial, the Mexican Charge wrote to the Secretary of State protesting that as Martinez' arrest was made outside of the procedures established in the extradition treaty, "the action pending against the man can not rest [on] any legal foundation." Letter of Balbino Davalos to Secretary of State, *reprinted in* Papers Relating to the Foreign Relations of the United States, H.R. Doc. No. 1, 59th Cong., 2d Sess., pt. 2, p. 1121 (1906). The Secretary of State responded that the exact issue raised by the Martinez incident had been decided by *Ker*, and that the remedy open to the Mexican Government, namely, a request to the United States for extradition of Martinez' abductor, had been granted by the United States. Letter of Robert Bacon to Mexican Charge, *reprinted in* Papers Relating to the Foreign Relations of the United States, H.R. Doc. No. 1, *supra*, at 1121-1122. Respondent and the Court of Appeals stress a statement made in 1881 by Secretary of State James Blaine to the Governor of Texas to the effect that the extradition treaty in its form at that time did not authorize unconsented to abductions from Mexico. This misses the mark, however, for the Government's argument is not that the Treaty authorizes the abduction of respondent, but that the Treaty does not prohibit the abduction.

Respondent contends that the Treaty must be interpreted against the backdrop of customary international law, and that international abductions are "so clearly prohibited in international law" that there was no reason to include such a clause in the Treaty itself. The international censure of international abductions is further evidenced, according to respondent, by the United Nations Charter and the Charter of the Organization of American States. Respondent does not argue that these sources of international law provide an independent basis for the right respondent asserts not to be tried in the United States, but rather that they should inform the interpretation of the Treaty terms.

The Court of Appeals deemed it essential, in order for the individual defendant to assert a right under the Treaty, that the affected foreign government had registered a protest. Respondent agrees that the right exercised by the individual is derivative of the nation's right under the Treaty, since nations are authorized, notwithstanding the terms of an extradition treaty, to voluntarily render an individual to the other country on terms completely outside of those provided in the treaty. The formal protest, therefore, ensures that the "offended" nation actually objects to the abduction and has not in some way voluntarily rendered the individual for prosecution. Thus the Extradition Treaty only prohibits gaining the defendant's presence by means other than those set forth in the Treaty when the nation from which the defendant was abducted objects.

This argument seems to us inconsistent with the remainder of respondent's argument. The Extradition Treaty has the force of law, and if, as respondent asserts, it is self-executing, it would appear that a court must enforce it on behalf of an individual regardless of the offensiveness of the practice of one nation to the other nation. In *Rauscher*, the Court noted that Great Britain had taken the position in other cases that the Webster-Ashburton Treaty included the doctrine of specialty, but no importance was attached to whether or not Great Britain had protested the prosecution of Rauscher for the crime of cruel and unusual punishment as opposed to murder.

More fundamentally, the difficulty with the support respondent garners from international law is that none of it relates to the practice of nations in relation to extradition treaties. In *Rauscher*, we implied a term in the Webster-Ashburton Treaty because of the practice of nations with regard to extradition treaties. In the instant case, respondent would imply terms in the Extradition Treaty from the practice of nations with regards to international law more generally. Respondent would have us find that the Treaty acts as a prohibition against a violation of the general principle of international law that one government may not "exercise its police power in the territory of another state." Brief for Respondent 16. There are many actions which could be taken by a nation that would violate this principle, including waging war, but it cannot seriously be contended that an invasion of the United States by Mexico would violate the terms of the Extradition Treaty between the two nations.[15]

_____

15. In the same category are the examples cited by respondent in which, after a forcible international abduction, the offended nation protested the abduction and the abducting nation then returned the individual to the protesting nation. These may show the practice of nations under customary international law, but they are of little aid in construing the terms of an extradition treaty, or the authority of a court to later try an individual who has been so abducted. More to the point for our purposes are cases such as *The Richmond*, 13 U.S. 102 (1815), and *The Merino*, 22 U.S. 391 (1824), both of which hold that a seizure of a vessel in violation of international law does not affect the jurisdiction of a United States court to adjudicate rights in connection with the vessel. . . .

In sum, to infer from this Treaty and its terms that it prohibits all means of gaining the presence of an individual outside of its terms goes beyond established precedent and practice. In *Rauscher,* the implication of a doctrine of specialty into the terms of the Webster-Ashburton Treaty, which, by its terms, required the presentation of evidence establishing probable cause of the crime of extradition before extradition was required, was a small step to take. By contrast, to imply from the terms of this Treaty that it prohibits obtaining the presence of an individual by means outside of the procedures the Treaty establishes requires a much larger inferential leap, with only the most general of international law principles to support it. The general principles cited by respondent simply fail to persuade us that we should imply in the United States-Mexico Extradition Treaty a term prohibiting international abductions.

Respondent and his *amici* may be correct that respondent's abduction was "shocking," and that it may be in violation of general international law principles. Mexico has protested the abduction of respondent through diplomatic notes, and the decision of whether respondent should be returned to Mexico, as a matter outside of the Treaty, is a matter for the Executive Branch. We conclude, however, that respondent's abduction was not in violation of the Extradition Treaty between the United States and Mexico, and therefore the rule of Ker v. Illinois is fully applicable to this case. The fact of respondent's forcible abduction does not therefore prohibit his trial in a court in the United States for violations of the criminal laws of the United States. . . .

JUSTICE STEVENS, with whom JUSTICE BLACKMUN and JUSTICE O'CONNOR join, dissenting. . . .

[This] case is unique for several reasons. It does not involve an ordinary abduction by a private kidnaper, or bounty hunter, as in Ker v. Illinois, 119 U.S. 436 (1886); nor does it involve the apprehension of an American fugitive who committed a crime in one State and sought asylum in another, as in Frisbie v. Collins, 342 U.S. 519 (1952). Rather, it involves this country's abduction of another country's citizen; it also involves a violation of the territorial integrity of that other country, with which this country has signed an extradition treaty. . . .

The extradition treaty with Mexico is a comprehensive document containing 23 articles and an appendix listing the extraditable offenses covered by the agreement. The parties announced their purpose in the preamble: The two governments desire "to cooperate more closely in the fight against crime and, to this end, to mutually render better assistance in matters of extradition." From the preamble, through the description of the parties' obligations with respect to offenses committed within as well as beyond the territory of a requesting party, the delineation of the procedures and evidentiary requirements for extradition, the special provisions for political offenses and capital punishment, and other details, the Treaty appears to have been designed to cover the entire subject of extradition. Thus, Article 22, entitled "Scope of Application," states that the "Treaty shall apply to offenses specified in Article 2 committed before and after this Treaty enters into force," and Article 2 directs that "extradition shall take place, subject to this Treaty, for willful acts which fall within any of [the extraditable offenses listed in] the clauses of the Appendix." Moreover, as noted by the Court, Article 9 expressly provides that neither contracting party is bound to deliver up its own nationals, although it may do so in its discretion, but if it does not do so, it "shall submit the case to its competent authorities for purposes of prosecution."

The Government's claim that the Treaty is not exclusive, but permits forcible governmental kidnapping, would transform these, and other, provisions into little more than verbiage. For example, provisions requiring "sufficient" evidence to grant extradition (Art. 3), withholding extradition for political or military offenses (Art. 5), withholding extradition when the person sought has already been tried (Art. 6), withholding extradition when the statute of limitations for the crime has lapsed (Art. 7), and granting the requested country discretion to refuse to extradite an individual who would face the death penalty in the requesting country (Art. 8), would serve little purpose if the requesting country could simply kidnap the person. As the Court of Appeals for the Ninth Circuit recognized in a related case, "each of these provisions would be utterly frustrated if a kidnapping were held to be a permissible course of governmental conduct." United States v. Verdugo-Urquidez, 939 F.2d 1341, 1349 (1991). In addition, all of these provisions "only make sense if they are understood as *requiring* each treaty signatory to comply with those procedures whenever it wishes to obtain jurisdiction over an individual who is located in another treaty nation." *Id.* at 1351.

It is true, as the Court notes, that there is no express promise by either party to refrain from forcible abductions in the territory of the other nation. Relying on that omission,[10] the Court, in effect, concludes that the Treaty merely creates an optional method of obtaining jurisdiction over alleged offenders, and that the parties silently reserved the right to resort to self-help whenever they deem force more expeditious than legal process.[11] If the United States, for example, thought it more expedient to torture or simply to execute a person rather than to attempt extradition, these options would be equally available because they, too, were not explicitly prohibited by the Treaty. That, however, is a highly improbable interpretation of a consensual agreement, which on its face appears to have been intended to set forth comprehensive and exclusive rules concerning the subject of extradition. In my opinion, "the manifest scope and object of the treaty itself," *Rauscher,* 119 U.S. at 422, plainly imply a mutual undertaking to respect the territorial integrity of the other contracting party. That opinion is confirmed by a consideration of the "legal context" in which the Treaty was negotiated. . . .

In *Rauscher,* the Court construed an extradition treaty that was far less comprehensive than the 1978 Treaty with Mexico. The 1842 treaty with Great Britain determined the boundary between the United States and Canada, provided for the suppression of the African slave trade, and also contained one paragraph authorizing the extradition of fugitives "in certain cases." In Article X, each nation agreed to "deliver up to justice all persons" properly charged with any one of seven specific crimes, including murder. After *Rauscher* had been extradited for murder, he was charged with the lesser offense of inflicting cruel and unusual punishment on a

---

10. The Court resorts to the same method of analysis as did the dissent in United States v. Rauscher, 119 U.S. 407 (1886). Chief Justice Waite would only recognize an explicit provision, and in the absence of one, he concluded that the treaty did not require that a person be tried only for the offense for which he had been extradited: "The treaty requires a delivery up to justice, on demand, of those accused of certain crimes, but says nothing about what shall be done with them after the delivery has been made. It might have provided that they should not be tried for any other offences than those for which they were surrendered, but it has not." *Id.* at 434. That approach was rejected by the Court in *Rauscher* and should also be rejected by the Court here.

11. To make the point more starkly, the Court has, in effect, written into Article 9 a new provision, which says: "Notwithstanding paragraphs 1 and 2 of this Article, either Contracting Party can, without the consent of the other, abduct nationals from the territory of one Party to be tried in the territory of the other."

member of the crew of a vessel on the high seas. Although the treaty did not purport to place any limit on the jurisdiction of the demanding state after acquiring custody of the fugitive, this Court held that he could not be tried for any offense other than murder. Thus, the treaty constituted the exclusive means by which the United States could obtain jurisdiction over a defendant within the territorial jurisdiction of Great Britain.

The Court noted that the treaty included several specific provisions, such as the crimes for which one could be extradited, the process by which the extradition was to be carried out, and even the evidence that was to be produced, and concluded that "the fair purpose of the treaty is, that the person shall be delivered up to be tried for that offence and for no other." The Court reasoned that it did not make sense for the treaty to provide such specifics only to have the person "pas[s] into the hands of the country which charges him with the offence, free from all the positive requirements and just implications of the treaty under which the transfer of his person takes place." To interpret the treaty in a contrary way would mean that a country could request extradition of a person for one of the seven crimes covered by the treaty, and then try the person for another crime, such as a political crime, which was clearly not covered by the treaty; this result, the Court concluded, was clearly contrary to the intent of the parties and the purpose of the treaty.

Rejecting an argument that the sole purpose of Article X was to provide a procedure for the transfer of an individual from the jurisdiction of one sovereign to another, the Court stated:

> No such view of solemn public treaties between the great nations of the earth can be sustained by a tribunal called upon to give judicial construction to them.
>
> The opposite view has been attempted to be maintained in this country upon the ground that there is no express limitation in the treaty of the right of the country in which the offence was committed to try the person for the crime alone for which he was extradited, and that once being within the jurisdiction of that country, no matter by what contrivance or fraud or by what pretence of establishing a charge provided for by the extradition treaty he may have been brought within the jurisdiction, he is, when here, liable to be tried for any offence against the laws as though arrested here originally. This proposition of the absence of express restriction in the treaty of the right to try him for other offences than that for which he was extradited, is met by the manifest scope and object of the treaty itself.

Thus, the Extradition Treaty, as understood in the context of cases that have addressed similar issues, suffices to protect the defendant from prosecution despite the absence of any express language in the Treaty itself purporting to limit this Nation's power to prosecute a defendant over whom it had lawfully acquired jurisdiction.

Although the Court's conclusion in *Rauscher* was supported by a number of judicial precedents, the holdings in these cases were not nearly as uniform as the consensus of international opinion that condemns one nation's violation of the territorial integrity of a friendly neighbor. It is shocking that a party to an extradition treaty might believe that it has secretly reserved the right to make seizures of citizens in the other party's territory. . . .

In the *Rauscher* case, the legal background that supported the decision to imply a covenant not to prosecute for an offense different from that for which extradition had been granted was far less clear than the rule against invading the territorial integrity of a treaty partner that supports Mexico's position in this case. If *Rauscher* was correctly decided—and I am convinced that it was—its rationale clearly dictates a comparable result in this case.[26]

A critical flaw pervades the Court's entire opinion. It fails to differentiate between the conduct of private citizens, which does not violate any treaty obligation, and conduct expressly authorized by the Executive Branch of the Government, which unquestionably constitutes a flagrant violation of international law, and in my opinion, also constitutes a breach of our treaty obligations. Thus, at the outset of its opinion, the Court states the issue as "whether a criminal defendant, abducted to the United States from a nation with which it has an extradition treaty, thereby acquires a defense to the jurisdiction of this country's courts." That, of course, is the question decided in Ker v. Illinois, 119 U.S. 436 (1886); it is not, however, the question presented for decision today. . . .

As the Court observes at the outset of its opinion, there is reason to believe that respondent participated in an especially brutal murder of an American law enforcement agent. That fact, if true, may explain the Executive's intense interest in punishing respondent in our courts. Such an explanation, however, provides no justification for disregarding the Rule of Law that this Court has a duty to uphold. That the Executive may wish to reinterpret[34] the Treaty to allow for an action that the Treaty in no way authorizes should not influence this Court's interpretation. Indeed, the desire for revenge exerts "a kind of hydraulic pressure . . . before which even well settled principles of law will bend," Northern Securities Co. v. United States, 193 U.S. 197, 401 (1904) (Holmes, J., dissenting), but it is precisely at such moments that we should remember and be guided by our duty "to render judgment evenly and dispassionately according to law, as each is given understanding to ascertain and apply it." United States v. Mine Workers, 330 U.S. 258, 342 (1947) (Rutledge, J., dissenting). The way that we perform that duty in a case of this kind sets an example that other tribunals in other countries are sure to emulate.

Notes and Questions

1. Did the United States have jurisdiction under international law to apply its laws to Alvarez-Machain—that is, did it have *prescriptive jurisdiction*? If Alvarez-Machain had voluntarily entered the United States, would it have been permissible under international law for the United States to try him under U.S. law? If so, why should the United States not also have the right to secure his arrest in Mexico?

---

26. Just as Rauscher had standing to raise the treaty violation issue, respondent may raise a comparable issue in this case. Certainly, if an individual who is not a party to an agreement between the United States and another country is permitted to assert the rights of that country in our courts, as is true in the specialty cases, then the same rule must apply to the individual who has been a victim of this country's breach of an extradition treaty and who wishes to assert the rights of that country in our courts after that country has already registered its protest.

34. Certainly, the Executive's view has changed over time. At one point, the Office of Legal Counsel advised the administration that such seizures were contrary to international law because they compromised the territorial integrity of the other nation and were only to be undertaken with the consent of that nation. 4B Op. Off. Legal Counsel 549, 556 (1980). More recently, that opinion was revised, and the new opinion concluded that the President did have the authority to override customary international law. Hearing before the Subcommittee on Civil and Constitutional Rights of the House Committee on the Judiciary, 101st Cong., 1st Sess., 4-5 (1989) (statement of William P. Barr, Assistant Attorney General, Office of Legal Counsel, U.S. Department of Justice).

2. As discussed earlier in this chapter, the international law of prescriptive jurisdiction is not strictly territorial. By contrast, enforcement jurisdiction is still widely considered to be territorial in nature. Under this view, nations have no authority to conduct an arrest in another country without that country's consent. *See, e.g.,* Restatement (Fourth) of Foreign Relations Law of the United States §432 (2018) ("Under customary international law: . . . a state may not exercise jurisdiction to enforce in the territory of another state without the consent of the other state."). Why is enforcement jurisdiction limited by territory? Should international law ever allow cross-border arrests?

3. What evidence does the majority in *Alvarez-Machain* cite to show that the extradition treaty is not violated? Is this evidence persuasive? Is it, as the majority contends, too great an inferential leap to conclude that the treaty forbids abductions? How does the Court's approach to treaty interpretation in this case compare with its approach in the *Rauscher* case, which is discussed in the majority and dissenting opinions?

4. It is widely accepted that customary international law prohibits a nation from apprehending someone in another country without that country's consent. *See* Michael Glennon, *State-Sponsored Abduction: A Comment on* Alvarez-Machain, 86 Am. J. Int'l L. 746 (1992). So, even assuming the Court was correct in *Alvarez-Machain* regarding the meaning of the extradition treaty, why was customary international law not a sufficient basis for relief? Note that, on remand, the Ninth Circuit expressed some uncertainty regarding whether the Supreme Court had addressed the customary international law argument. *See* United States v. Alvarez-Machain, 971 F.2d 310 (9th Cir. 1992). What do you think? Does *Alvarez-Machain* have any implications for the debate, discussed in Chapter 7, about whether customary international law is self-executing domestic federal law?

5. The *Alvarez-Machain* decision was heavily criticized by Mexico and other nations. *See* William J. Aceves, *The Legality of Transborder Abductions: A Study of United States v. Alvarez-Machain*, 3 Sw. J. L. & Trade Am. 101 (1996). It also was generally criticized by academic commentators. *See, e.g.,* Jonathan A. Bush, *How Did We Get Here? Foreign Abductions After* Alvarez-Machain, 45 Stan. L. Rev. 939 (1993); Andrew L. Strauss, *A Global Paradigm Shattered: The Jurisdictional Nihilism of the Supreme Court's Abduction Decision in* Alvarez-Machain, 4 Temp. L. Rev. 1209 (1994); Douglas J. Sylvester, *Customary International Law, Forcible Abductions, and America's Return to the "Savage State,"* 42 Buff. L. Rev. 555 (1994). For a rare defense of the decision, see Malvina Halberstam, *In Defense of the Supreme Court Decision in* Alvarez-Machain, 86 Am. J. Int'l L. 736 (1992).

In 1994, the Clinton Administration negotiated with Mexico a modification to the bilateral extradition treaty that would expressly prohibit "trans-border abductions" like the one in *Alvarez-Machain.* For reasons that are unclear, the Executive never submitted the treaty amendment to the Senate for its advice and consent.

6. In an ironic twist, the case against Alvarez-Machain was thrown out on remand for lack of evidence. *See* United States v. Alvarez-Machain, No. CR-87-422-(G)-ER (C.D. Cal. Dec. 14, 1992). Subsequently, Alvarez-Machain brought a civil suit against the U.S. government and the Mexican citizens involved in his abduction. After a number of decisions in the lower courts, Alvarez-Machain's claims were ordered dismissed by the Supreme Court in the Sosa v. Alvarez-Machain decision excerpted in Chapter 7. (The Court determined that Alvarez-Machain's claims against the U.S. government did not fall within an exception in the Federal Tort

Claims Act and thus were barred by the government's sovereign immunity, and that Alvarez-Machain did not have a cognizable claim under the Alien Tort Statute.)

7. For post-*Alvarez-Machain* decisions allowing the prosecution of abducted defendants because of the lack of a violation of the relevant extradition treaty, see, for example, United States v. Noriega, 117 F.3d 1206 (11th Cir. 1997) (seizure of general in Panama so that he could be tried on drug charges); and Kasi v. Angelone, 300 F.3d 487 (4th Cir. 2002) (seizure of individual in Pakistan so that he could be tried for shooting CIA employees in Virginia). The United States is not the only nation that has engaged in extraterritorial abductions. In 1960, for example, Israel abducted Nazi war criminal Adolf Eichmann from Argentina. In response, the U.N. Security Council passed a resolution condemning the abduction and requesting that Israel make "appropriate reparations" to Argentina in accordance with the U.N. Charter and rules of international law. *See* Question Relating to the Case of Adolf Eichmann, S.C. Res. 138, U.N. SCOR, 15th Sess., 868th mtg. at 4, U.N. Doc. S/4349 (1960).

8. In a decision predating *Alvarez-Machain,* the U.S. Court of Appeals for the Second Circuit suggested that a court could use its supervisory powers to dismiss a prosecution when an individual is severely mistreated by the government or its agents in connection with an abduction. *See* United States v. Toscanino, 500 F.2d 267, 275 (2d Cir. 1974). The Second Circuit subsequently held that this exception applies only where the defendant can prove "the use of torture, brutality and similar outrageous conduct." United States ex rel. Lujan v. Gengler, 510 F.2d 62, 65 (2d Cir. 1975). The precise scope of this mistreatment exception, and its viability after *Alvarez-Machain,* are uncertain. *See, e.g.,* United States v. Matta-Ballesteros, 71 F.3d 754 (9th Cir. 1995) (mere kidnapping by the government does not fall within this exception); *cf.* United States v. Best, 304 F.3d 308, 312 (3d Cir. 2002) ("Subsequent decisions of the Supreme Court indicate that there is reason to doubt the soundness of the *Toscanino* exception, even as limited to its flagrant facts.").

Jose Padilla, a U.S. citizen who was apprehended in the United States in 2002 and held by the U.S. military for several years as an "enemy combatant" before being turned over to civilian authorities for trial, attempted to invoke the purported mistreatment exception as a basis for dismissal of his prosecution, arguing that he had been mistreated while in military custody. The court rejected this argument, reasoning that any abuse Padilla may have suffered in military custody was separate from the circumstances of his criminal process, and also that potential suppression of evidence obtained as a result of coercion would be a sufficient remedy to ensure that the alleged mistreatment did not undermine the criminal process. *See* United States v. Padilla, 2007 U.S. Dist. LEXIS 26077 (S.D. Fla. 2007).

9. There has been uncertainty at times regarding the *statutory* authority of U.S. law enforcement officials to make arrests in foreign countries without those countries' consent. A federal statute provides that "[t]he Attorney General may appoint officials to detect and prosecute crimes against the United States." 28 U.S.C. §533(1). Another statute gives FBI agents the authority to "make arrests . . . for any felony cognizable under the laws of the United States if they have reasonable grounds to believe that the person to be arrested has committed or is committing such felony." 18 U.S.C. §3052. Neither statute contains an explicit geographic limitation or an explicit directive to comply with international law. Nevertheless, in a 1980 memorandum to the Attorney General, the Office of Legal Counsel (OLC) concluded that the FBI lacked the authority to make arrests in foreign countries without those countries' consent. *See* Extraterritorial Apprehension by the Federal

Bureau of Investigation, 4B Op. Off. Legal Counsel 543 (1980). Among other things, the 1980 memorandum reasoned that such an arrest would violate international law, and it relied on the *Charming Betsy* canon of construction. Nine years later, OLC reversed itself, concluding that the FBI did have statutory authority to make extraterritorial arrests, even if such arrests violate international law. *See* Authority of the Federal Bureau of Investigation to Override International Law in Extraterritorial Law Enforcement Activities, 13 Op. Off. Legal Counsel 164 (1989). The 1989 memorandum concluded that the *Charming Betsy* canon was "wholly inapposite" to the statutes in question, reasoning that the FBI is an agency through which the President carries out his constitutional law enforcement duties, that the President himself has the power to violate customary international law, and that "it must be presumed that Congress intended to grant the President's instrumentality the authority to act in contravention of international law when directed to do so." Which memorandum was correct? For a discussion of the OLC memoranda, see Curtis A. Bradley, Chevron *Deference and Foreign Affairs*, 86 Va. L. Rev. 649, 697-99 (2000). (These memoranda are also mentioned in footnote 34 of the dissent in *Alvarez-Machain*.)

9

War Powers

This chapter considers the constitutional authority of the United States to use military force. It begins in Sections A and B with an analysis of the respective war powers of Congress and the President. Section C then examines Congress's ability to regulate the President's use of force. Section D discusses the legal and policy issues implicated by covert action. Section E assesses the role of civil liberties during wartime. Issues specific to the post-September 11 "war on terrorism" and the conflict with the Islamic State are treated separately in Chapter 10.

A. CONGRESS'S ROLE IN AUTHORIZING WAR

Article I, Section 8 of the Constitution confers on Congress many war-related powers, including: the power to "declare War, grant Letters of Marque and Reprisal, and make Rules concerning Captures on Land and Water" (cl. 11); the power to appropriate money for the military, which, in the case of the army, is limited to two-year periods (cls. 12-13); the power to "make Rules for the Government and Regulation of the land and naval Forces" (cl. 14); the power to "provide for calling forth the Militia to execute the Laws of the Union, suppress Insurrections and repel Invasions" (cl. 15); and the power to "provide for organizing, arming, and disciplining, the Militia, and for governing such Part of them as may be employed in the Service of the United States" (cl. 16). This section examines the meaning and scope of these powers, and considers their implications for Congress's role in authorizing the United States to use military force.

1. Historical Background

In late eighteenth-century England, the power to wage war, like other foreign relations powers, rested exclusively with the king. As Blackstone explained in his Commentaries on the Laws of England, the king had "the sole prerogative of making war and peace," such that "in order to make a war completely effectual, it is necessary with use in England that it be publicly declared and duly proclaimed by the king's authority." 1 William Blackstone, Commentaries on the Laws of England 249-50 (1765).

Upon separating from England, the foreign affairs of the United States, including its management of the Revolutionary War, were handled by the Continental Congress. The First Continental Congress, which convened in September 1774, issued the Articles of Association, imposed an economic boycott of British goods, and threatened a ban on American exports to Britain. The Second Continental Congress, which convened in May 1775, appointed George Washington as commander in chief of the "United Colonies," as well as a dozen other generals. In November of that year, the Continental Congress established a Committee of Secret Correspondence that, primarily through Benjamin Franklin and John Adams, would later negotiate loans and gifts from France, Holland, and Spain. Following the Declaration of Independence in July 1776, the foreign affairs details of which are described in Chapter 1, the Continental Congress managed the war, continued to seek foreign assistance, and called up the state militia. The Continental Congress was a weak institution, however, with no legal authority to enact or enforce laws or to raise or finance an army, and thus was often dependent on the states for money, troops, and supplies. As a result, the Continental Army was chronically depleted, and the United States often relied for its defense on state militias that tended to be unreliable, undisciplined, and inefficient. As Washington once described the state militia during this period, "they come in you cannot tell how, go, you cannot tell when; and act, you Cannot tell where, consume your Provisions, exhaust your Stores, and leave you at last in a critical moment." Letter from George Washington to the President of the Continental Congress, December 20, 1776, *in* 6 The Writings of George Washington 403 (John C. Fitzpatrick ed., 1931-1944).

Under the Articles of Confederation, which took effect in 1781, the Continental Congress was given the "sole and exclusive right and power of determining on peace and war." In addition, states were prohibited from "engag[ing] in any war without the consent of the United States in Congress assembled" unless they were invaded, or threatened with imminent invasion by an Indian tribe. The Articles also provided that expenses incurred for defense would be paid out of a common treasury, financed by the states in proportion to the value of their land. These provisions worked better on paper than in practice. Congress still lacked the effective power to raise a standing national army or navy. It also lacked the power to draft individuals for military service. And states did not contribute their share to the public treasury. Thus, as Edmund Randolph explained at the Federal Convention in 1787, one of the principal defects of the Confederation had been that it did not provide "security agai[nst] foreign invasion; congress not being permitted to prevent a war nor to support it by th[eir] own authority." 1 The Records of the Federal Convention of 1787, at 19 (Max Farrand ed., 1911).

Not surprisingly, therefore, the text of the Constitution contains a number of provisions relating to the use of military force. Article I gives Congress the powers described above. Article II provides that the President "shall be Commander in Chief of the Army and Navy of the United States, and of the Militia of the several States, when called into the actual Service of the United States." Finally, Article I, Section 10 prohibits the states from engaging in war unless they are invaded or in imminent danger, and it prohibits them from keeping troops or ships of war during a time of peace without the consent of Congress.

At the Constitutional Convention, a draft of the Constitution would have given Congress the power to "make" war. The word "make" was changed during the Convention, however, to "declare." The following oft-discussed excerpt from James Madison's notes of the Convention debates reflects this change:

> Mr. Pinkney opposed the vesting this power [to make war] in the Legislature. Its proceedings were too slow. It wd. meet but once a year. The Hs. of Rps. would be too

numerous for such deliberations. The Senate would be the best depositary, being more acquainted with foreign affairs, and most capable of proper resolutions. If the States are equally represented in Senate, so as to give no advantage to large States, the power will notwithstanding be safe, as the small have their all at stake in such cases as well as the large States. It would be singular for one authority to make war, and another peace.

Mr. Butler. The Objections agst the Legislature lie in a great degree agst the Senate. He was for vesting the power in the President, who will have all the requisite qualities, and will not make war but when the Nation will support it.

Mr. Madison and Mr. Gerry moved to insert "*declare*," striking out "*make*" war; leaving to the Executive the power to repel sudden attacks.

Mr. Sharman thought it stood very well. The Executive shd. be able to repel and not to commence war. "Make" better than "declare" the latter narrowing the power too much.

Mr. Gerry never expected to hear in a republic a motion to empower the Executive alone to declare war.

Mr. Elseworth. there is a material difference between the cases of making *war*, and making *peace*. It shd. be more easy to get out of war, than into it. War also is a simple and overt declaration. peace attended with intricate & secret negociations.

Mr. Mason was agst giving the power of war to the Executive, because not safely to be trusted with it; or to the Senate, because not so constructed as to be entitled to it. He was for clogging rather than facilitating war; but for facilitating peace. He preferred "*declare*" to "*make*."

On the Motion to insert *declare* — in place of *Make*, it was agreed to.

[Connecticut originally voted against this motion, but] On the remark by Mr. King that "*make*" war might be understood to "conduct" it which was an Executive function, Mr. Elseworth gave up his objection and the vote of Con[necticut] was changed to — ay.

2 The Records of the Federal Convention of 1787, at 318-19 (Max Farrand ed., 1911).

The Constitution's assignment of war powers is discussed in *The Federalist Papers,* excerpted below.

Federalist No. 24 (Hamilton)

A stranger to our politics, who was to read our newspapers at the present juncture, without having previously inspected the plan reported by the convention, would be naturally led to one of two conclusions: either that it contained a positive injunction, that standing armies should be kept up in time of peace; or that it vested in the EXECUTIVE the whole power of levying troops, without subjecting his discretion, in any shape, to the control of the legislature.

If he came afterwards to peruse the plan itself, he would be surprised to discover, that neither the one nor the other was the case; that the whole power of raising armies was lodged in the LEGISLATURE, not in the EXECUTIVE; that this legislature was to be a popular body, consisting of the representatives of the people periodically elected; and that instead of the provision he had supposed in favor of standing armies, there was to be found, in respect to this object, an important qualification even of the legislative discretion, in that clause which forbids the appropriation of money for the support of an army for any longer period than two years a precaution which, upon a nearer view of it, will appear to be a great and real security against the keeping up of troops without evident necessity.

Federalist No. 25 (Hamilton)

[If, as some suggest, the Constitution were to prohibit] the RAISING of armies in time of peace, the United States would then exhibit the most extraordinary spectacle which the world has yet seen, that of a nation incapacitated by its Constitution to prepare for defense, before it was actually invaded. As the ceremony of a formal denunciation of war has of late fallen into disuse, the presence of an enemy within our territories must be waited for, as the legal warrant to the government to begin its levies of men for the protection of the State. We must receive the blow, before we could even prepare to return it. All that kind of policy by which nations anticipate distant danger, and meet the gathering storm, must be abstained from, as contrary to the genuine maxims of a free government. We must expose our property and liberty to the mercy of foreign invaders, and invite them by our weakness to seize the naked and defenseless prey, because we are afraid that rulers, created by our choice, dependent on our will, might endanger that liberty, by an abuse of the means necessary to its preservation.

Here I expect we shall be told that the militia of the country is its natural bulwark, and would be at all times equal to the national defense. This doctrine, in substance, had like to have lost us our independence. It cost millions to the United States that might have been saved. The facts which, from our own experience, forbid a reliance of this kind, are too recent to permit us to be the dupes of such a suggestion. The steady operations of war against a regular and disciplined army can only be successfully conducted by a force of the same kind. Considerations of economy, not less than of stability and vigor, confirm this position. The American militia, in the course of the late war, have, by their valor on numerous occasions, erected eternal monuments to their fame; but the bravest of them feel and know that the liberty of their country could not have been established by their efforts alone, however great and valuable they were. War, like most other things, is a science to be acquired and perfected by diligence, by perseverance, by time, and by practice.

Federalist No. 69 (Hamilton)

The President is to be the "commander-in-chief of the army and navy of the United States, and of the militia of the several States, when called into the actual service of the United States." . . . In most of these particulars, the power of the President will resemble equally that of the king of Great Britain and of the governor of New York. The most material points of difference are these: First. The President will have only the occasional command of such part of the militia of the nation as by legislative provision may be called into the actual service of the Union. The king of Great Britain and the governor of New York have at all times the entire command of all the militia within their several jurisdictions. In this article, therefore, the power of the President would be inferior to that of either the monarch or the governor. Secondly. The President is to be commander-in-chief of the army and navy of the United States. In this respect his authority would be nominally the same with that of the king of Great Britain, but in substance much inferior to it. It would amount to nothing more than the supreme command and direction of the military and naval forces, as first General and admiral of the Confederacy; while that of the British king extends to the declaring of war and to the raising and regulating of fleets and armies, all which, by the Constitution under consideration, would appertain to the legislature.

There was also discussion of the Constitution's assignment of war powers in the state debates over ratification of the U.S. Constitution. Perhaps the most frequently quoted statement from these debates is the following excerpt of a speech by James Wilson in the Pennsylvania convention:

> This [constitutional] system will not hurry us into war; it is calculated to guard against it. It will not be in the power of a single man, or a single body of men, to involve us in such distress, for the important power of declaring war is vested in the legislature at large; this declaration must be made with the concurrence of the House of Representatives. From this circumstance we may draw a certain conclusion, that nothing but our national interest can draw us into a war.

2 The Documentary History of the Ratification of the Constitution 583 (Merrill Jensen ed., 1976). Also frequently quoted is the following statement by James Iredell at the North Carolina ratifying convention:

> I believe most of the governors of the different states have powers similar to those of the President. In almost every country, the executive has command of the military forces. From the nature of the thing, the command of armies ought to be delegated to one person only. The secrecy, dispatch, and decision, which are necessary in military operations, can only be expected from one person. The President, therefore, is to command the military forces of the United States, and this power I think a proper one; at the same time it will be found to be sufficiently guarded. A very material difference may be observed between this power, and the authority of the king of Great Britain under similar circumstances. The king of Great Britain is not only the commander-in-chief of the land and naval forces, but has power, in time of war, to raise fleets and armies. He also has authority to declare war. The President has not the power of declaring war by his own authority, nor that of raising fleets and armies. These powers are vested in other hands. The power of declaring war is expressly given to Congress, that is, to the two branches of the legislature. . . . They have also expressly delegated to them the powers of raising and supporting armies, and of providing and maintaining a navy.

4 Jonathan Elliot, The Debates in the Several State Conventions on the Adoption of the Federal Constitution 107-08 (1888).

2. The Undeclared War with France

The United States engaged in an undeclared naval war against France early in its history. Recall from Chapter 1 that in 1793, following France's declaration of war on Great Britain and other countries, President Washington issued a proclamation of neutrality. Despite this proclamation, both England and France attacked U.S. commercial shipping. John Jay negotiated a treaty with Great Britain, ratified in 1795, that reduced the British attacks. The French, perceiving the Jay Treaty to be evidence of U.S. favoritism toward the British, increased their attacks on U.S. shipping. In 1797, Washington's successor, John Adams, sent three commissioners (including future Chief Justice John Marshall) to France to resolve the crisis. When it was later revealed that the French treated the U.S. commissioners rudely and asked them for a large bribe (an episode known as the "XYZ Affair"), public opinion in the United States turned against the French, and Congress enacted numerous statutes relating to war with France. These statutes enlarged the army and navy, empowered the President to raise troops, authorized the construction of forts and the purchase of weapons, barred commercial relations with France, declared treaties with France to be legally void, and, most important, gave the President the power to capture French warships and commission privateers. *See* David P. Currie, The Constitution in Congress: The Federalist Period, 1789-1801, at 243-44 (1997). Congress never declared war, however. This undeclared war with France is the subject of the Bas v. Tingy decision below, as well as the Little v. Barreme decision excerpted in Section C.

Bas v. Tingy

4 U.S. 37 (1800)

[During the undeclared war with France, Congress enacted two statutes concerning the recapture of American vessels. The first statute, enacted on June 28, 1798, provided:

> That whenever any vessel the property of, or employed by, any citizen of the United States, or person resident therein, or any goods or effects belonging to any such citizen, or resident, shall be re-captured by any public armed vessel of the United States, the same shall be restored to the former owner, or owners, upon due proof, he or they paying and allowing, as and for salvage to the re-captors, one-eighth part of the value of such vessel, goods and effects, free from all deduction and expenses.

The second statute, enacted the following year on March 2, 1799, differed slightly in wording:

> That for the ships or goods belonging to the citizens of the United States, or to the citizens, or subjects, of any nation in amity with the United States, if re-taken from the enemy within twenty-four hours, the owners are to allow one-eighth part of the whole value for salvage, &c. and if above ninety-six hours one-half, all of which is to be paid without any deduction whatsoever . . . that all the money accruing, of which has already accrued from the sale of prizes, shall be and remain forever a fund for the payment of the half-pay to the officers and seamen, who may be entitled to receive the same.

In this case, the commander of an American public vessel claimed that, based on the 1799 statute, he was entitled to an award of one-half of the value of an American merchant ship he had recaptured from the French. The owner of the merchant ship responded that, because Congress had not declared war on France, France was not an "enemy," and therefore the 1799 statute did not apply.]

The [Justices] delivered their opinions *seriatim* in the following manner:

JUSTICE MOORE.

This case depends on the construction of the [1799] act, for the regulation of the navy. It is objected, indeed, that the act applies only to future wars; but its provisions are obviously applicable to the present situation of things, and there is nothing to prevent an immediate commencement of its operation.

It is, however, more particularly urged, that the word "enemy" cannot be applied to the French; because the section in which it is used, is confined to such a state of war, as would authorise a re-capture of property belonging to a nation in amity with the United States, and such a state of war, it is said, does not exist between America and France. A number of books have been cited to furnish a glossary on the word enemy; yet, our situation is so extraordinary, that I doubt whether a parallel case can be traced in the history of nations. But, if words are the representatives of ideas, let me ask, by what other word the idea of the relative situation of America and France could be communicated, than by that of hostility, or war? And how can the characters of the parties engaged in hostility or war, be otherwise described than by the denomination of enemies? It is for the honour and dignity of both nations, therefore, that they should be called enemies; for, it is by that description alone, that either could justify or excuse, the scene of bloodshed, depredation and confiscation, which has unhappily occurred; and, surely, congress could only employ the language of the act of June 13, 1798, towards a nation whom she considered as an enemy. . . .

JUSTICE WASHINGTON. . . .

It may, I believe, be safely laid down, that every contention by force between two nations, in external matters, under the authority of their respective governments, is not only war, but public war. If it be declared in form, it is called solemn, and is of the perfect kind; because one whole nation is at war with another whole nation; and all the members of the nation declaring war, are authorised to commit hostilities against all the members of the other, in every place, and under every circumstance. In such a war all the members act under a general authority, and all the rights and consequences of war attach to their condition.

But hostilities may subsist between two nations more confined in its nature and extent; being limited as to places, persons, and things; and this is more properly termed imperfect war; because not solemn, and because those who are authorised to commit hostilities, act under special authority, and can go no farther than to the extent of their commission. Still, however, it is public war, because it is an external contention by force, between some of the members of the two nations, authorised by the legitimate powers. It is a war between the two nations, though all the members are not authorised to commit hostilities such as in a solemn war, where the government restrain the general power.

Now, if this be the true definition of war, let us see what was the situation of the United States in relation to France. In March 1799, congress had raised an army; stopped all intercourse with France; dissolved our treaty; built and equip ships of war; and commissioned private armed ships; enjoining the former, and authorising the latter, to defend themselves against the armed ships of France, to attack them on the high seas, to subdue and take them as prize, and to re-capture armed vessels found in their possession. Here, then, let me ask, what were the technical characters of an American and French armed vessel, combating on the high seas, with a view the one to subdue the other, and to make prize of his property? They certainly were not friends, because there was a contention by force; nor were they private enemies, because the contention was external, and authorised by the legitimate authority of the two governments. If they were not our enemies, I know not what constitutes an enemy.

But, secondly, it is said, that a war of the imperfect kind, is more properly called acts of hostility, or reprizal, and that congress did not mean to consider the hostility subsisting between France and the United States, as constituting a state of war.

In support of this position, it has been observed, that in no law prior to March 1799, is France styled our enemy, nor are we said to be at war. This is true; but neither of these things were necessary to be done: because as to France, she was sufficiently described by the title of the French republic; and as to America, the degree of hostility meant to be carried on, was sufficiently described without declaring war, or declaring that we were at war. Such a declaration by congress, might have constituted a perfect state of war, which was not intended by the government. . . .

Justice Chase. . . .

What, then, is the nature of the contest subsisting between America and France? In my judgment, it is a limited, partial, war. Congress has not declared war in general terms; but congress has authorised hostilities on the high seas by certain persons in certain cases. There is no authority given to commit hostilities on land; to capture unarmed French vessels, nor even to capture French armed vessels lying in a French port; and the authority is not given, indiscriminately, to every citizen of America, against every citizen of France; but only to citizens appointed by commissions, or exposed to immediate outrage and violence. So far it is, unquestionably, a partial war; but, nevertheless, it is a public war, on account of the public authority from which it emanates.

There are four acts, authorised by our government, that are demonstrative of a state of war. A belligerent power has a right, by the law of nations, to search a neutral vessel; and, upon suspicion of a violation of her neutral obligations, to seize and carry her into port for further examination. But by the acts of congress, an American vessel it authorised: 1st. To resist the search of a French public vessel; 2d. To capture any vessel that should attempt, by force, to compel submission to a search; 3d. To re-capture any American vessel seized by a French vessel; and 4th. To capture any French armed vessel wherever found on the high seas. This suspension of the law of nations, this right of capture and re-capture, can only be authorised by an act of the government, which is, in itself, an act of hostility. But still it is a restrained, or limited, hostility; and there are, undoubtedly, many rights attached to a general war, which do not attach to this modification of the powers of defence and aggression. . . . As there may be a public general war, and a public qualified war; so there may, upon correspondent principles, be a general enemy, and a partial enemy. The designation of "enemy" extends to a case of perfect war; but as a general designation, it surely includes the less, as well as the greater, species of warfare. If congress had chosen to declare a general war, France would have been a general enemy; having chosen to wage a partial war, France was, at the time of the capture, only a partial enemy; but still she was an enemy.

3. The War of 1812

When war broke out between Great Britain and France in 1803, American commercial shipping got caught in the crossfire. Great Britain enacted and enforced harsh neutrality laws, and on that basis seized U.S. merchant vessels for allegedly violating the British blockade of Europe. The British also impressed thousands of U.S. sailors into service for the Royal Navy. By 1811, so-called War Hawks in the U.S. House of Representatives (most notably Henry Clay of Kentucky and John Calhoun of South Carolina) began to clamor for war with Great Britain, in part because of continued British interference in American shipping, but also to redress alleged British instigation of Indians on the western frontier of the United States. On June 1, 1812, President James Madison asked Congress to declare war against Great Britain. Three days later, the House of Representatives voted (79 to 49) to declare war, and after much debate, on June 17, 1812, the U.S. Senate also voted for war, 19 to 13. On June 18, 1812, President Madison signed the following measure into law:

> An Act Declaring War Between the United Kingdom of Great Britain and Ireland and the Dependencies Thereof and the United States of America and Their Territories.

Be it enacted by the Senate and House of Representatives of the United States of America in Congress assembled, That war be and the same is hereby declared to exist between the United Kingdom of Great Britain and Ireland and the dependencies thereof, and the United States of America and their territories; and that the President of the United States is hereby authorized to use the whole land and naval force of the United States to carry the same into effect, and to issue to private armed vessels of the United States commissions or letters of marque and general reprisal, in such form as he shall think proper, and under the seal of the United States, against the vessels, goods, and effects of the government of the said United Kingdom of Great Britain and Ireland, and the subjects thereof.

Brown v. United States

12 U.S. (8 Cranch) 110 (1814)

[The issue in this case was whether Congress, in its act of June 18, 1812, had implicitly authorized the Executive Branch to confiscate enemy property (pine timber owned by a British citizen) located within the United States.]

MARSHALL, C.J. delivered the opinion of the Court, as follows. . . .

Respecting the power of government no doubt is entertained. That war gives to the sovereign full right to take the persons and confiscate the property of the enemy wherever found, is conceded. The mitigations of this rigid rule, which the humane and wise policy of modern times has introduced into practice, will more or less affect the exercise of this right, but cannot impair the right itself. That remains undiminished, and when the sovereign authority shall chuse to bring it into operation, the judicial department must give effect to its will. But until that will shall be expressed, no power of condemnation can exist in the Court. . . .

Since, in this country, from the structure of our government, proceedings to condemn the property of an enemy found within our territory at the declaration of war, can be sustained only upon the principle that they are instituted in execution of some existing law, we are led to ask, Is the declaration of war such a law? Does that declaration, by its own operation, so vest the property of the enemy in the government, as to support proceedings for its seizure and confiscation, or does it vest only a right, the assertion of which depends on the will of the sovereign power? . . .

The modern rule [under international law] would seem to be, that tangible property belonging to an enemy and found in the country at the commencement of war, ought not to be immediately confiscated; and in almost every commercial treaty an article is inserted stipulating for the right to withdraw such property. . . .

The constitution of the United States was framed at a time when this rule, introduced by commerce in favor of moderation and humanity, was received throughout the civilized world. In expounding that constitution, a construction ought not lightly to be admitted which would give to a declaration of war an effect in this country it does not possess elsewhere, and which would fetter that exercise of entire discretion respecting enemy property, which may enable the government to apply to the enemy the rule that he applies to us.

If we look to the constitution itself, we find this general reasoning much strengthened by the words of that instrument.

That the declaration of war has only the effect of placing the two nations in a state of hostility, of producing a state of war, of giving those rights which war confers; but not of operating, by its own force, any of those results, such as a transfer of property, which are usually produced by ulterior measures of government, is fairly deducible from the enumeration of powers which accompanies that of declaring war. "Congress shall have power"—"to declare war, grant letters of marque and reprisal, and make rules concerning captures on land and water."

It would be restraining this clause within narrower limits than the words themselves import, to say that the power to make rules concerning captures on land and water, is to be confined to captures which are exterritorial. If it extends to rules respecting enemy property found within the territory, then we perceive an express grant to congress of the power in question as an independent substantive power, not included in that of declaring war.

The acts of congress furnish many instances of an opinion that the declaration of war does not, of itself, authorize proceedings against the persons or property of the enemy found, at the time, within the territory.

War gives an equal right over persons and property: and if its declaration is not considered as prescribing a law respecting the person of an enemy found in our country, neither does it prescribe a law for his property. The act concerning alien enemies, which confers on the president very great discretionary powers respecting their persons, affords a strong implication that he did not possess those powers by virtue of the declaration of war.

The "act for the safe keeping and accommodation of prisoners of war," is of the same character.

The act prohibiting trade with the enemy, contains this clause:

> And be it further enacted, That the president of the United States be, and he is hereby authorized to give, at any time within six months after the passage of this act, passports for the safe transportation of any ship or other property belonging to British subjects, and which is now within the limits of the United States.

The phraseology of this law shows that the property of a British subject was not considered by the legislature as being vested in the United States by the declaration of war; and the authority which the act confers on the president, is manifestly considered as one which he did not previously possess.

The proposition that a declaration of war does not, in itself, enact a confiscation of the property of the enemy within the territory of the belligerent, is believed to be entirely free from doubt. Is there in the act of congress, by which war is declared against Great Britain, any expression which would indicate such an intention?

That act, after placing the two nations in a state of war, authorizes the president of the United States to use the whole land and naval force of the United States to carry the war into effect, and "to issue to private armed vessels of the United States, commissions or letters of marque and general reprisal against the vessels, goods and effects of the government of the united kingdom of Great Britain and Ireland, and the subjects thereof."

That reprisals may be made on enemy property found within the United States at the declaration of war, if such be the will of the nation, has been admitted; but it is not admitted that, in the declaration of war, the nation has expressed its will to that effect. . . .

It is urged that, in executing the laws of war, the executive may seize and the Courts condemn all property which, according to the modern law of nations, is subject to confiscation, although it might require an act of the legislature to justify the condemnation of that property which, according to modern usage, ought not to be confiscated.

This argument must assume for its basis the position that modern usage constitutes a rule which acts directly upon the thing itself by its own force, and not through the sovereign power. This position is not allowed. This usage is a guide which the sovereign follows or abandons at his will. The rule, like other precepts of morality, of humanity, and even of wisdom, is addressed to the judgment of the sovereign; and although it cannot be disregarded by him without obloquy, yet it may be disregarded. . . .

The rule which we apply to the property of our enemy, will be applied by him to the property of our citizens. Like all other questions of policy, it is proper for the consideration of a department which can modify it at will; not for the consideration of a department which can pursue only the law as it is written. It is proper for the consideration of the legislature, not of the executive or judiciary.

It appears to the Court, that the power of confiscating enemy property is in the legislature, and that the legislature has not yet declared its will to confiscate property which was within our territory at the declaration of war. . . .

STORY, J., dissenting. . . .

The act of 18th June, 1812, ch. 102, is in very general terms, declaring war against Great Britain, and authorizing the president to employ the public forces to carry it into effect. Independent of such express authority, I think that, as the executive of the nation, he must, as an incident of the office, have a right to employ all the usual and customary means acknowledged in war, to carry it into effect. And there being no limitation in the act, it seems to follow that the executive may authorize the capture of all enemies' property, wherever, by the law of nations, it may be lawfully seized. . . .

I will now consider what, in point of law, is the operation of the acts of Congress made in relation to the present war. . . . [Justice Story recounts the congressional acts referred to in the majority opinion.]

These are all the acts which confer powers, or make provisions touching the management of the war. In no one of them is there the slightest limitation upon the executive powers growing out of a state of war; and they exist, therefore, in their full and perfect vigor. By the constitution, the executive is charged with the faithful execution of the laws; and the language of the act declaring war authorizes him to carry it into effect. In what manner, and to what extent, shall he carry it into effect? What are the legitimate objects of the warfare which he is to wage? There is no act of the legislature defining the powers, objects or mode of warfare: by what rule, then, must he be governed? I think the only rational answer is by the law of nations as applied to a state of war. Whatever act is legitimate, whatever act is approved by the law, or hostilities among civilized nations, such he may, in his discretion, adopt and exercise; for with him the sovereignty of the nation rests as to the execution of the laws. If any of such acts are disapproved by the legislature, it is in their power to narrow and limit the extent to which the rights of war shall be exercised; but until such limit is assigned, the executive must have all the right of modern warfare vested in him, to be exercised in his sound discretion, or he can have none. Upon what principle, I would ask, can he have an implied authority to adopt one and not another? The best manner of annoying, injuring and pressing the enemy, must, from the nature of things, vary under different circumstances; and the executive is responsible to the nation for the faithful discharge of his duty, under all the changes of hostilities. . . .

It is also said that a declaration of war does not carry with it the right to confiscate property found in our country at the commencement of war, because the constitution itself, in giving congress the power "to declare war, grant letters of marque and reprisal, and make rules concerning captures on land and water," has clearly evinced that the power to declare war did not, *ex vi terminorum*, include a right to capture property every where, and that the power to make rules concerning captures on land and water, may well be considered as a substantive power as to captures of property within our own territory. . . . The power to declare war, in my opinion, includes all the powers incident to war, and necessary to carry it into effect. If the constitution had been silent as to letters of marque and captures, it would not have narrowed the authority of congress. The authority to grant letters of marque and reprisal, and to regulate captures, are ordinary and necessary incidents to the power of declaring war. It would be utterly ineffectual without them. The expression, therefore, of that which is implied in the very nature of the grant, cannot weaken the force of the grant itself. The words are merely explanatory, and introduced *ex abundanti cautela*. It might be as well contended that the power "to provide and maintain a navy," did not include the power to regulate and govern it, because there is in the constitution an express provision to this effect. And yet I suppose that no person would doubt that congress, independent of such express provision, would have the power to regulate and govern the navy; and if they should authorize the executive "to provide and maintain a navy," it seems to me as clear that he must have the incidental power to make rule for its government. In truth, it is by no means unfrequent in the constitution to add clauses of a special nature to general powers which embrace them, and to provide affirmatively for certain powers, without meaning thereby to negative the existence of powers of a more general nature.

My argument proceeds upon the ground, that when the legislative authority, to whom the right to declare war is confided, has declared war in its most unlimited manner, the executive authority, to whom the execution of the war is confided, is bound to carry it into effect. He has a discretion vested in him, as to the manner and extent; but he cannot lawfully transcend the rules of warfare established among civilized nations. He cannot lawfully exercise powers or authorize proceedings which the civilized world repudiates and disclaims. The sovereignty, as to declaring war and limiting its effects, rests with the legislature. The sovereignty, as to its execution, rests with the president. If the legislature do not limit the nature of the war, all the regulations and rights of general war attach upon it.

The War of 1812 was the first war in which Congress officially declared war. Subsequently, it declared war in only four other conflicts: the Mexican-American War of 1846-1848; the Spanish-American War of 1898; World War I (which the United States entered in 1917); and World War II (which the United States entered in December 1941). By contrast, the United States has utilized military force in hundreds of situations not involving declarations of war. In some but not all of these undeclared conflicts, Congress expressly approved the use of force even though it did not declare war. For example, the two major conflicts initiated during the administration of George W. Bush — the War on Terror and the Iraq War of 2003 — were both preceded by congressional authorizations for the use of military force, but not declarations of war. There have sometimes been questions, however, about what constitutes a sufficient congressional authorization and what authority a particular authorization confers. This was true, for example, during the Vietnam War.

4. The Vietnam War

American involvement in Vietnam began in the 1950s, when Presidents Truman and Eisenhower provided economic and military assistance and advisory support to the French government in Indochina, and later to the State of Vietnam in its conflict against Communist revolutionary forces. After the French decision to withdraw in 1954, the United States continued to provide support to Vietnam, which now controlled only the southern half of the country. Presidents Kennedy and Johnson expanded American involvement there. By 1962, there were approximately 9,000 U.S. military personnel in Vietnam, and that number expanded to over 20,000 by the summer of 1964, an escalation that took place without specific congressional authorization. In early August 1964, two American destroyers reported that they were under attack by North Vietnamese forces in the Gulf of Tonkin. There is evidence, still contested, suggesting that some of the attacks in the Gulf of Tonkin did not occur or may have been exaggerated by the Johnson Administration in order to prompt Congress to support the war.* In any event, on August 7, 1964, Congress passed the following resolution:

> ... Resolved by the Senate and House of Representatives of the United States of America in Congress assembled, That the Congress approves and supports the determination of the President, as Commander in Chief, to take all necessary measures to repel any armed attack against the forces of the United States and to prevent further aggression.
>
> Sec. 2. The United States regards as vital to its national interest and to world peace the maintenance of international peace and security in southeast Asia. Consonant with the Constitution of the United States and the Charter of the United Nations and in accordance with its obligations under the Southeast Asia Collective Defense Treaty, the United States is, therefore, prepared, as the President determines, to take all necessary steps, including the use of armed force, to assist any member or protocol state of the Southeast Asia Collective Defense Treaty requesting assistance in defense of its freedom.
>
> Sec. 3. This resolution shall expire when the President shall determine that the peace and security of the area is reasonably assured by international conditions created by action of the United Nations or otherwise, except that it may be terminated earlier by concurrent resolution of the Congress.

Joint Resolution of Congress, Pub. L. No. 88-408, 78 Stat. 384 (1964). After the Gulf of Tonkin Resolution, U.S. military involvement in Vietnam increased dramatically. In February 1965, the United States began a sustained bombing campaign in North Vietnam. In March 1965, it began to send combat troops to Vietnam; by early 1968, U.S. combat troops there numbered more than half a million. In addition to the Gulf of Tonkin Resolution, Congress repeatedly authorized the appropriation of money to finance the war and repeatedly renewed selective service provisions allowing for a military draft. The Vietnam War became increasingly controversial, however, and in December 1970, Congress passed legislation repealing the Gulf of Tonkin Resolution. President Nixon signed this legislation in January 1971, while

---

* For accounts of the origins of the Vietnam War and the escalating U.S. involvement in Vietnam, see, for example, David Kaiser, American Tragedy: Kennedy, Johnson, and the Origins of the Vietnam War (2000); Frederik Longevall, Embers of War: The Fall of an Empire and the Making of America's Vietnam (2012); and Frederik Longevall, Choosing War: The Lost Chance for Peace and the Escalation of War in Vietnam (1999). For an assessment of the Gulf of Tonkin incident, see Edwin E. Moise, Tonkin Gulf and the Escalation of the Vietnam War (1996).

maintaining that he retained authority as Commander in Chief to continue using military force in Vietnam.

Orlando v. Laird

443 F.2d 1039 (2d Cir. 1971)

[In 1970, before Congress repealed the Gulf of Tonkin Resolution, two enlistees in the U.S. Army sued to enjoin the Secretary of Defense, the Secretary of the Army, and certain commanding officers from enforcing orders directing the enlistees to report for transfer to Vietnam. Their principal claim was that these Executive Branch officials exceeded their constitutional authority by ordering the enlistees to participate in a war not properly authorized by Congress.]

ANDERSON, CIRCUIT JUDGE. . . .

We [have previously held] that the constitutional delegation of the war-declaring power to the Congress contains a discoverable and manageable standard imposing on the Congress a duty of mutual participation in the prosecution of war. Judicial scrutiny of that duty, therefore, is not foreclosed by the political question doctrine. As we see it, the test is whether there is any action by the Congress sufficient to authorize or ratify the military activity in question. The evidentiary materials produced at the hearings in the district court clearly disclose that this test is satisfied.

The Congress and the Executive have taken mutual and joint action in the prosecution and support of military operations in Southeast Asia from the beginning of those operations. The Tonkin Gulf Resolution, enacted August 10, 1964 (repealed December 31, 1970) was passed at the request of President Johnson and, though occasioned by specific naval incidents in the Gulf of Tonkin, was expressed in broad language which clearly showed the state of mind of the Congress and its intention fully to implement and support the military and naval actions taken by and planned to be taken by the President at that time in Southeast Asia, and as might be required in the future "to prevent further aggression." Congress has ratified the executive's initiatives by appropriating billions of dollars to carry out military operations in Southeast Asia and by extending the Military Selective Service Act with full knowledge that persons conscripted under that Act had been, and would continue to be, sent to Vietnam. Moreover, it specifically conscripted manpower to fill "the substantial induction calls necessitated by the current Vietnam buildup."

There is, therefore, no lack of clear evidence to support a conclusion that there was an abundance of continuing mutual participation in the prosecution of the war. Both branches collaborated in the endeavor, and neither could long maintain such a war without the concurrence and cooperation of the other.

Although appellants do not contend that Congress can exercise its war declaring power only through a formal declaration, they argue that congressional authorization cannot, as a matter of law, be inferred from military appropriations or other war-implementing legislation that does not contain an express and explicit authorization for the making of war by the President. Putting aside for a moment the explicit authorization of the Tonkin Gulf Resolution, we disagree with appellants' interpretation of the declaration clause for neither the language nor the purpose underlying that provision prohibits an inference of the fact of authorization from such legislative action as we have in this instance. The framers' intent to vest the war power in Congress is in no way defeated by permitting an inference of authorization from legislative action furnishing the manpower and materials of war for the protracted military operation in Southeast Asia.

The choice, for example, between an explicit declaration on the one hand and a resolution and war-implementing legislation, on the other, as the medium for expression of congressional consent involves "the exercise of a discretion demonstrably committed to the . . . legislature," Baker v. Carr, [369 U.S. 186, 211 (1962)], and therefore, invokes the political question doctrine.

Such a choice involves an important area of decision making in which, through mutual influence and reciprocal action between the President and the Congress, policies governing the relationship between this country and other parts of the world are formulated in the best interests of the United States. If there can be nothing more than minor military operations conducted under any circumstances, short of an express and explicit declaration of war by Congress, then extended military operations could not be conducted even though both the Congress and the President were agreed that they were necessary and were also agreed that a formal declaration of war would place the nation in a posture in its international relations which would be against its best interests. For the judicial branch to enunciate and enforce such a standard would be not only extremely unwise but also would constitute a deep invasion of the political question domain. As the Government says, ". . . decisions regarding the form and substance of congressional enactments authorizing hostilities are determined by highly complex considerations of diplomacy, foreign policy and military strategy inappropriate to judicial inquiry." It would, indeed, destroy the flexibility of action which the executive and legislative branches must have in dealing with other sovereigns. What has been said and done by both the President and the Congress in their collaborative conduct of the military operations in Vietnam implies a consensus on the advisability of not making a formal declaration of war because it would be contrary to the interests of the United States to do so. The making of a policy decision of that kind is clearly within the constitutional domain of those two branches and is just as clearly not within the competency or power of the judiciary.

Notes and Questions

1. How did the allocation of war powers under the Constitution differ from the allocation of war powers under the Articles of Confederation? What accounts for the differences? What were the inadequacies under the Articles of Confederation relating to war, and how were they dealt with in the Constitution? Why did the Founders substitute the word "declare" for the word "make"? Is it relevant that Article I, Section 10 of the Constitution provides that the states may not "engage" in war? Is engaging in a war different from declaring a war?

2. What is entailed by Congress's power to "declare war"? When, if ever, is a declaration of war constitutionally necessary in order for the United States to engage in war? As *Federalist No. 25* suggests, numerous wars in the eighteenth century began without a declaration, and a declaration often came, if at all, years after the initiation of direct armed conflict between two nations. *See, e.g.,* Louis Henkin, Foreign Affairs and the United States Constitution 76, 370 n.65 (2d ed. 1996); J. F. Maurice, Hostilities Without Declaration of War (1883); Clyde Eagleton, *The Form and Function of the Declaration of War,* 32 Am. J. Int'l L. 19 (1938). Moreover, as noted above, the United States has throughout its history engaged in hundreds of conflicts — of varying scope and duration — without a formal declaration of war. Does this practice suggest that a declaration of war is never constitutionally necessary in order for the United States to use military force? If so, what is the constitutional significance of Congress's power to "declare" war?

3. One historic function of a declaration of war was to give other nations legal notice under international law. At the time of the Founding, war was a "fundamental concept in public international law," sharply distinguishable from "peace," to which particular legal consequences attached. Henkin, *supra*, at 98. During war, elaborate rules of belligerency governed relations between warring states, and equally elaborate rules of neutrality governed relations between belligerent and neutral states. "War," so understood, was different from other uses of military force, which did not by themselves necessarily trigger all of the rules of belligerency and neutrality. As the opinions in Bas v. Tingy suggest, sometimes this distinction was framed in terms of the differences between "perfect" and "imperfect" war, or between "general" and "limited" war. On this understanding, a declaration of war was a method by which states could trigger the full array of international law rules governing neutral and belligerent states on issues such as rights to seizure of vessels, shipment of contraband, and institution of blockades, as well as domestic laws related to war and emergency powers. *See, e.g.,* 1 William Blackstone, Commentaries 250; 3 E. de Vattel, The Law of Nations or the Principles of Natural Law 255 (photo. reprint 1995) (James Brown Scott ed., Charles G. Fenwick trans., Carnegie Institute of Washington 1916) (1758).

Many commentators maintain that modern international law has largely eliminated this historic function for declarations of war. As Professor Kahn explains:

> Since the advent of the United Nations (UN) Charter, war has been abolished as a category of international law. A declaration of war serves no purpose under international law; it can have no bearing on the underlying legal situation. No longer a performative utterance, it is only a meaningless utterance — not even descriptive — from the perspective of international law. . . . War has disappeared from international law because force is no longer a legitimate means of changing state entitlements. The fundamental rule of postwar international law was the prohibition on the use or threat of force. This was enshrined in Article 2(4) of the UN Charter: "All members shall refrain in their international relations from the threat or use of force against the territorial integrity or political independence of any state."

Paul W. Kahn, *War Powers and the Millennium*, 34 Loy. L.A. L. Rev. 11, 16-17 (2000). Do these changes in international law explain why the United States has not issued a formal declaration of war since World War II? How do these changes in the international law effect of war declarations affect Congress's role in U.S. warmaking? Can changes in international law alter the scope or meaning of the U.S. Constitution?

4. Even if declarations of war have lost their function under international law, and even if a declaration of war is not a constitutional prerequisite for U.S. warmaking, the Declare War Clause may still be relevant to the constitutional distribution of war powers authority between Congress and the President. Many scholars believe that Congress has the exclusive power to authorize significant offensive military operations, and they often rely on the Declare War Clause as textual support for this position. *See, e.g.,* John Hart Ely, War and Responsibility: Constitutional Lessons of Vietnam and Its Aftermath 3-10 (1993); Louis Fisher, Presidential War Power 1-16 (2d ed. 2004); Henkin, *supra*, at 76, 97-101; Harold Hongju Koh, The National Security Constitution: Sharing Power after the Iran-Contra Affair 74-77 (1990);

Charles A. Lofgren, *War-making Under the Constitution: The Original Understanding*, 81 Yale L.J. 672, 695 (1972).

Does the text of the Declare War Clause support this view? The clause refers to a particular congressional action — declaring war — and does not state that Congress has the more general power to "authorize" or "initiate" war. Do either the Founding materials excerpted above, or Bas v. Tingy, support the view that only Congress can authorize war? Or do they merely show that Congress has the exclusive authority to declare war, and that it can authorize war without issuing a declaration, without addressing whether Congress's power to authorize war is exclusive? Would it be consistent with these materials for the President to possess the power to make war in all circumstances in which Congress has not authorized or declared it? Of what relevance is it that some statutes refer to declarations of war? For example, the Alien Enemy Act, first enacted in 1798, gives the President the power to detain and expel enemy aliens within the United States "[w]henever there is a declared war between the United States and any foreign nation or government, or any invasion or predatory incursion is perpetrated, attempted, or threatened against the territory of the United States by any foreign nation or government." 50 U.S.C. §21.

5. Post-Founding statements and practices provide clearer evidence than the constitutional text to support the view that congressional authorization is constitutionally required for some uses of force by the United States. When the United States faced attacks from Indians along the western frontier, George Washington consistently denied that he had the power to engage in offensive military actions in the absence of congressional authorization: "The Constitution vests the power of declaring war with Congress; therefore no offensive expedition of importance can be undertaken until after they have deliberated on the subject, and authorized such a measure." Letter from George Washington to Governor William Moultrie, August 28, 1793, in 33 The Writings of George Washington 73 (John C. Fitzpatrick ed., 1939). John Adams evinced a similar attitude toward presidential war power with respect to the undeclared war with France in 1798. *See* Dean Alfange, Jr., *The Quasi-War and Presidential Warmaking*, in David Gray Adler & Larry N. George eds., The Constitution and the Conduct of Foreign Policy 274-90 (1996). Jefferson took a similar view — at least in public — with respect to attacks by the Barbary Pirates in 1801-1802. *See* Currie, Federalist Period, *supra*, at 88; *but see id.* at 127-29 (describing how Jefferson took more aggressive offensive action than his public pronouncements deemed appropriate).

For other early statements in support of Congress's authority over the initiation of war, see Letter from Thomas Jefferson to James Madison, Sept. 6, 1789, in 15 The Papers of Thomas Jefferson 397 (Julian P. Boyd ed., 1958) ("We have already given in example one effectual check to the Dog of war by transferring the power of letting him loose from the Executive to the Legislative body. . . ."); Letter from James Madison to Thomas Jefferson, April 2, 1798, in 6 The Writings of James Madison 312 (Gaillard Hunt ed., 1906) ("The constitution supposes, what The History of all Gov[ernments] demonstrates, that the Ex[ecutive] is the branch of power most interested in war, & most prone to it. It has accordingly with studied care, vested the question of war in the Legisl[ature]."); *cf.* Talbot v. Seeman, 5 U.S. 1, 28 (1801) ("The whole powers of war being, by the constitution of the United States, vested in congress, the acts of that body can alone be resorted to as our guides in this enquiry. It is not denied, nor in the course of the argument has it been denied, that congress may authorize general hostilities, in which case the general laws of war apply to our situation; or partial hostilities, in which case the laws of war, so far as they actually apply to our situation, must be noticed."). In assessing the constitutional distribution of war authority, what weight should be given to these early statements?

6. Several scholars have challenged the view that the Declare War Clause gives Congress the exclusive power to authorize war. *See, e.g.,* Robert F. Turner, Repealing the War Powers Resolution: Restoring the Rule of Law in U.S. Foreign Policy 80-81 (1991); Henry P. Monaghan, *Presidential War-making,* 50 B.U. L. Rev. 19 (special issue 1970); Eugene V. Rostow, *Great Cases Make Bad Law: The War Powers Act,* 50 Tex. L. Rev. 833, 864-66 (1972); John C. Yoo, *The Continuation of Politics by Other Means: The Original Understanding of War Powers,* 84 Cal. L. Rev. 167 (1996). Professor Yoo has presented the most developed version of this position. He argues that constitutional text should be read in its eighteenth-century context to mean that Congress's war declaration power is limited to the notification and international law functions mentioned above. In his view, "interpreting 'declare war' to mean 'authorize' or 'commence' is a twentieth-century construct inconsistent with the eighteenth century understanding of the phrase." Yoo, *supra,* at 204. He concludes that the Constitution "demanded no constitutionally correct method of waging war," *id.* at 296, that the President has broad residual power to engage in offensive military action even in the absence of congressional authorization, and that Congress retains an ultimate check on presidential war power through its appropriations power. *Id.* at 295-305. This theory makes sense of the term "declare," and comports with modern war powers practice. But does it hold up in light of evidence that the Founders were trying to limit presidential war power, and were rejecting the English model? If Professor Yoo is right, why did Washington, Adams, and Jefferson believe, when each was President, that they lacked the power to initiate offensive military actions in the absence of congressional authorization?

Professor Ramsey has attempted to reconcile Professor Yoo's textual arguments with the evidence that the Founders thought that Congress must authorize offensive hostilities. *See* Michael D. Ramsey, *Textualism and War Powers,* 69 U. Chi. L. Rev. 1543 (2002). He argues that in the eighteenth century, war could, in the words of John Locke, be "declared by word or action." Thus Congress could "declare" war either by a formal declaration, or by authorizing the commencement of hostilities even in the absence of a declaration. If Professor Ramsey's premise about the meaning of "declare" is correct, does his theory successfully vindicate the "authorization" theory of congressional war powers? Does it matter that the "word or action" theory is nowhere mentioned in the Founding debates? For a response to Professor Ramsey's arguments, see John C. Yoo, *War and the Constitutional Text,* 69 U. Chi. L. Rev. 1639 (2002). For Professor Ramsey's rejoinder, see Michael D. Ramsey, *Text and History in the War Powers Debate: A Reply to Professor Yoo,* 69 U. Chi. L. Rev. 1685 (2002).

Professor Prakash takes Ramsey's analysis one step further. Relying on historical materials, Prakash contends that *any* action by the United States to begin waging war is a declaration of war and thus is within the control of Congress, even if another nation has already declared war against the United States by word or action. *See* Saikrishna Prakash, *Unleashing the Dogs of War: What the Constitution Means by "Declare War,"* 93 Cornell L. Rev. 45 (2007). Under this theory, "the President does not declare war by instructing the armed forces to act in self-defense," *id.* at 57, but the President would be declaring war, and thus would need congressional authorization, if he launched a counteroffensive in response to an attack. *See also* Saikrishna Bangalore Prakash, *Exhuming the Seemingly Moribund Declaration of War,* 77 Geo. Wash. L. Rev. 89 (2008) (arguing that, at the time of the constitutional Founding, "all manner of hostile actions and signals that indicated war would begin (or had begun) were declarations of war," and that, in that sense, "[n]ations continue to declare war and issue declarations of war quite often"). Professor Ramsey disagrees, arguing that "[l]aunching a counteroffensive in response to an attack, after first fighting defensively, in no eighteenth-century sense 'declared' war. War would already exist as a result of the attack and the defense; shifting from defense to offense would not affect its status." Michael D. Ramsey, *The President's Power to Respond to Attacks*, 93 Cornell L. Rev. 169, 194 (2007). Professors Delahunty and Yoo also disagree, arguing that the best reading of the Constitution's text and structure suggest that the Declare War Clause was designed to give Congress authority to regulate the U.S. relationship with other nations, not to check the authority of the Executive, and that Congress's ability to act as a check on the Executive was conferred instead through its power to create and fund the military. *See* Robert J. Delahunty & John Yoo, *Making War*, 93 Cornell L. Rev. 123 (2007).

7. If Congress must authorize "war," what does war encompass? For example, does it encompass the use of force against non-state actors, such as pirates? What about the use of force against unrecognized government entities? What if the use of force is carried out with the consent of the nation on whose territory it occurs? What about small-scale uses of force, such as a naval bombardment of a village to retaliate for an earlier attack on a U.S. ship? These and related questions generated significant uncertainty and debate during the nineteenth and early twentieth centuries, even among those who believed that Congress was required to authorize war. *See* Curtis A. Bradley & Jean Galbraith, *Presidential War Powers as a Two-Level Dynamic: International Law, Domestic Law, and Practice-Based Legal Change*, 91 N.Y.U. L. Rev. 689 (2016). This point is explored further in Section B of this chapter.

8. Congress's power to "grant Letters of Marque and Reprisal" might provide further support for the congressional authorization view. A letter of marque and reprisal is a governmental authorization to a private party to engage in hostile action against citizens or vessels of another nation. Some scholars have argued that the Marque and Reprisal Clause supplements the Declare War Clause, with the Declare War Clause covering perfect and large-scale wars, and the Marque and Reprisal Clause covering imperfect and smaller wars. *See, e.g.,* Lofgren, *War-Making, supra. But see* C. Kevin Marshall, *Putting Privateers in Their Place: The Applicability of the Marque and Reprisal Clause to Undeclared Wars*, 64 U. Chi. L. Rev. 953 (1997) (criticizing this argument). Why would a power to authorize private citizens to engage in hostilities give Congress the exclusive ability to authorize the U.S. military to engage in hostilities? Of what relevance is it that Congress has not granted a letter of marque and reprisal since the nineteenth century?

9. Congress also has the power to "make rules concerning Captures on Land and Water." What does Brown v. United States, excerpted above, suggest about the implications of this power? For an argument that the Captures Clause was designed to give Congress the authority to determine what property is subject to capture by both public and private forces of the United States, and that this assignment of authority "supports an expansive role for Congress in war initiation and prosecution," see Ingrid Wuerth, *The Captures Clause*, 76 U. Chi. L. Rev. 1683, 1690 (2009).

10. What does *Brown* suggest about the role of war declarations? Does it support or detract from the theory that war declarations serve notice and related functions under international law? What does it suggest about how authorizations to use force should be interpreted? Is its holding based on, and thus limited to, the Constitution's assignment to Congress of the power to make rules concerning captures on land and on the particular array of statutes associated with the War of 1812?

Or does it more broadly require Congress to specifically authorize the President to engage in each element of war? Is *Brown* limited to presidential seizures within the United States, or does it apply to seizure of enemy property everywhere, including the high seas? Is *Brown* consistent with the Constitution's assignment of the commander-in-chief power to the President? Why didn't the Court conclude that the 1812 authorization "to use the whole land and naval force of the United States to carry the [war with Great Britain] into effect" entailed the power to confiscate enemy property? Why did the Court reject Justice Story's position that in a declared war with an unqualified authorization to use force, Congress should be deemed to have conferred all of the authorities on the President permitted by the international laws of war?

11. What is the significance of Congress's power to appropriate money for the military, which, in the case of the army, the Constitution limits to two-year periods? In general, the two-year limit was a compromise procedural mechanism to allay concerns about a peacetime standing army. As Professor Kohn has noted, "[n]o principle of government was more widely understood or more completely accepted by the generation of Americans that established the United States than the danger of a standing army in peacetime." Richard H. Kohn, Eagle and Sword: The Beginnings of the Military Establishment in America, 1783-1802, at 2 (1975). Concerns about standing armies were reflected in the Declaration of Independence, which castigates King George for keeping a peacetime standing army "without the consent of our legislatures." This danger to liberty was not an abstraction — few forgot the Boston Massacre of 1770, where British troops killed five civilians and created "a cause celebre up and down the seacoast . . . [that] permanently embedded the prejudice against standing armies into the American political tradition." Lois G. Schwoerer, "No Standing Armies!": The Anti-Army Ideology in Seventeenth Century England 5-6 (1974).

In the Founding debates, the main arguments against a standing army were that they were a threat to liberty, they were unnecessary because America was isolated from its main threats, and state militias sufficed for defensive purposes. Largely for reasons articulated by Hamilton in the excerpt from *Federalist No. 25* — the inadequacy of the state militia system during the revolutionary war (and during the Articles of Confederation period), and the need to deter and meet foreign attacks — most of the Founders assumed that the new Constitution would provide for a standing army, and the main issue was how to set limits on it. *See* Kohn, *supra*, at 77-78. Some suggested capping the standing army at 1,000-2,000 troops, and others suggested a refunding requirement every year, but ultimately the two-year appropriations requirement was agreed upon. As Hamilton explained the rationale for the provision in *Federalist No. 26*, "The Legislature of the United States will be obliged by this provision, once at least in every two years, to deliberate upon the propriety of keeping a military force on foot; to come to a new resolution on the point; and to declare their sense of the matter, by a formal vote in the face of their constituents. They are not at liberty to vest in the executive department permanent funds for the support of an army."

Does the two-year appropriations limit for the army help explain the widespread early belief that Congress needed to authorize all offensive uses of U.S. military force? At the Founding, the United States had a tiny standing army (718 persons) and no standing navy, and many Founders believed that a larger standing military force was unnecessary or pernicious. In this context congressional participation — in the form of authorizing the raising of troops, and the financing of them — was literally necessary for the President to exercise military power abroad. As a result, the appropriations authority, along with Congress's authority to regulate the use of the militia, would have required — and in fact, did require — early presidents to seek and secure statutory authority to use military force for any extended period, regardless of whether war had been declared. Was this appropriation requirement the real check on presidential use of force without congressional authorization? *See* Philip Bobbitt, *War Powers: An Essay on John Hart Ely's War and Responsibility: Constitutional Lessons of Vietnam and Its Aftermath*, 92 Mich. L. Rev. 1364, 1385, 1392, 1396 (1994); Yoo, *Continuation of Politics, supra.*

If control over appropriations is an important check on the President's ability to use force abroad, what is the significance of the fact that over the course of U.S. history, the size of the standing army has dramatically increased — from 12,000 during the War of 1812, to 50,000 during the Spanish-American War, to 250,000 following World War I, to 12 million during World War II? Today this number is about 1.3 million, with almost 1 million more in the reserves. As one commentator noted in the 1960s, "America possesses a standing army, sufficiently large, sufficiently well-equipped, and sufficiently mobile to make possible, through presidential action alone and on very short notice, conflicts of unforeseeable dimensions anywhere in the world." Note, *Congress, the President, and the Power to Commit Forces to Combat*, 81 Harv. L. Rev. 1771, 1791 (1968). For an argument that Congress's ability to control war through its appropriations power has declined over the course of American history, and a proposal to reverse this trend, see Bruce Ackerman & Oona Hathaway, *Limited War and the Constitution: Iraq and the Crisis of Presidential Illegality*, 109 Mich. L. Rev. 447 (2011).

12. Every time that Congress has declared war, it has additionally authorized the President to use force against the enemy. The statute commencing the War of 1812, excerpted above, is one example. Another example is the World War II joint resolution concerning the war with Germany. The title of the joint resolution made clear that the resolution did two things: it both "declar[ed] that a state of war exists between the Government of Germany and the Government and the people of the United States" and "made provision to prosecute the same." The body of the resolution did precisely these two things:

> Therefore, be it Resolved by the Senate and House of Representatives of the United States of America in Congress assembled, That the state of war between the United States and the Government of Germany which has thus been thrust upon the United States is hereby formally declared; and the President is hereby authorized and directed to employ the entire naval and military forces of the United States and the resources of the Government to carry on war against the Government of Germany; and, to bring the conflict to a successful termination, all of the resources of the country are hereby pledged by the Congress of the United States.

The identical pattern of expressly distinguishing between Congress's war declaration and its authorization for the President to use force is evident in every other statute declaring war in U.S. history — the other World War II joint resolutions, the World War I joint resolutions, and the statutes declaring war in the Spanish-American War, and the Mexican-American War. *See* Curtis A. Bradley & Jack L. Goldsmith, *Congressional Authorization and the War on Terrorism*, 118 Harv. L. Rev. 2047, 2062-64 (2005).

What is the significance of this practice? Does it support the view that war declarations and war authorizations serve different aims? Does it show that congressional war authorizations, as opposed to war declarations, are what empower the President to use force abroad? Does this pattern suggest that Congress could declare war but not authorize the President to use force? What does Brown v. United States suggest about this issue?

13. Recall Justice Washington's distinction in Bas v. Tingy between an "imperfect" war that is "more confined in its nature and extent; being limited as to places, persons, and things," and a "perfect" one, in which "one whole nation is at war with another whole nation; and all the members of the nation declaring war, are authorised to commit hostilities against all the members of the other, in every place, and under every circumstance." One can group most conflicts in U.S. history into one or the other of these two categories. In addition to the quasi-war with France, examples of limited wars include Congress's authorization of the President to use various specified military resources and methods related to the repulsion, suppression, or protection of Indians, its authorization of the President to use limited force to occupy and control Florida, and its authorization of the President to use limited force against slave traders and pirates and against the Barbary states that had been preying on U.S. shipping. *See* Bradley & Goldsmith, *Congressional Authorization, supra,* at 2073-74 & nn.112-16. By contrast, the authorizations of force in declared wars have tended not to have any limits other than to indicate who the enemy is. So, for example, the authorization against Germany in World War I simply "authorized and directed" the President "to employ the entire naval and military forces of the United States and the resources of the Government," without restriction on the method of force or targets, "to carry on war against the Imperial German Government."

What is the significance of the distinction between imperfect wars with limited authorizations to use force, and perfect wars with broad and generally unlimited authorizations to use force? Do the limited authorizations in imperfect wars implicitly restrict presidential power? Are there any limits on presidential power in perfect wars with broad authorizations? Did the Gulf of Tonkin Resolution trigger a perfect or an imperfect war?

14. Assuming congressional authorization is sometimes required for U.S. warmaking, must this authorization take a particular form? Are there situations in which it must take the form of a declaration of war? Is the choice of the form of authorization a political question, as the court concludes in Orlando v. Laird? Assuming that the authorization need not take a particular form, what counts as authorization? Do military appropriations count? Selective service authorizations? General statutes regulating the armed services? Consider the Vietnam War. In addition to the Gulf of Tonkin Resolution, Congress repeatedly authorized the appropriation of money to finance the war and repeatedly renewed selective service provisions allowing for a military draft. Is the court correct in Orlando v. Laird that these provisions, taken together, constitute congressional authorization for the war in Vietnam? *Compare* Ely, *supra,* at 12-46 (analyzing question in detail and concluding that there was authorization), *with* William Van Alstyne, *Congress, the President, and the Power to Declare War: A Requiem for Vietnam,* 121 U. Pa. L. Rev. 1, 23-24 (1972) (concluding no authorization); Alexander M. Bickel, *Congress, the President and the Power to Wage War,* 48 Chi.-Kent L. Rev. 131, 136-38 (1971) (concluding no authorization or an excessive delegation of war power authority). If authorization can be inferred from appropriations and other measures, what, if any, limits are there on the President's use of the peacetime standing army? The Office of Legal Counsel in the Clinton Administration's Department of Justice argued that "in establishing and funding a military force that is capable of being projected anywhere around the globe, Congress has given the President, as Commander in Chief, considerable discretion in deciding how that force is to be deployed." Letter from Walter Dellinger, Assistant Attorney General, Office of Legal Counsel, to Senators Robert K. Dole, Alan K. Simpson, Strom Thurmond, and William S. Cohen (Sept. 27, 1994), at https://www.justice.gov/sites/default/files/olc/opinions/1994/09/31/op-olc-v018-p0173.pdf. Is this correct?

15. Are there any limits on Congress's ability to authorize the President to go to war? Must Congress specify the enemy? The purpose for the use of force? The location where force may be used? The duration of the use of force? What if Congress authorized the President to use military force against whomever he wanted, whenever and wherever he wanted? Some scholars have argued that the Gulf of Tonkin Resolution was unconstitutional because it failed to identify a particular enemy and failed to sufficiently channel the President's military discretion. *See, e.g.,* Bickel, *supra, at* 137-40; Francis D. Wormuth, *The Nixon Theory of the War Power: A Critique,* 60 Cal. L. Rev. 623, 692-700 (1972). John Hart Ely, by contrast, argued that to satisfy the nondelegation doctrine, a congressional authorization to use force need only specify an enemy, and the Gulf of Tonkin Resolution did so implicitly because of its preamble. Ely, *supra,* at 25-26. *Cf.* William H. Rehnquist, *The Constitutional Issues — Administration Position,* 45 N.Y.U. L. Rev. 628, 636-37 (1970) ("It has been suggested that there may be a question of unlawful delegation of powers here [with respect to the Gulf of Tonkin Resolution], and that Congress is not free to give a blank check to the President. Whatever may be the answer to that abstract question in the domestic field, I think it is plain from United States v. Curtiss-Wright Export Corp. . . . that the principle of unlawful delegation of powers does not apply to the field of external affairs." (footnotes omitted)). What, if any, constitutional limits are there on Congress's ability to delegate war-making authority to the President? We examine this question further in Section D, in the discussion of covert action. For a historically based argument that the Constitution "grants Congress broad power to safeguard the Constitution and its government from invasions and rebellions," including through delegation of extensive authority to the President, see Saikrishna Bangalore Prakash, *The Sweeping Domestic War Powers of Congress,* 113 Mich. L. Rev. 1337 (2015).

B. THE PRESIDENT'S INDEPENDENT MILITARY POWERS

Article II of the Constitution makes the President the "Commander in Chief of the armed forces." The President may also have military powers as a result of other provisions in Article II, including its vesting of "[t]he executive Power" in the President, and its requirement that the President "shall take Care that the Laws be faithfully executed." This section considers the scope of the President's independent military powers, as illustrated by a variety of conflicts throughout history.

1. The Mexican-American War

One of the United States' five declared wars was the Mexican-American War of 1846-1848, which stemmed in part from a dispute over the border between Texas and Mexico. After gaining its independence from Mexico, Texas was annexed by the

United States. The southern border of Texas was in dispute, with the United States claiming that it extended down to the Rio Grande River and Mexico claiming that it extended only down to the Nueces River. In June 1845, General Zachary Taylor, at the direction of President James Polk, moved his troops to the Rio Grande. This action prompted military clashes between U.S. and Mexican forces. President Polk then delivered the following message to Congress:

> The grievous wrongs perpetrated by Mexico upon our citizens throughout a long period of years, remain unredressed; and solemn treaties, pledging her public faith for this redress, have been disregarded. A Government either unable or unwilling to enforce the execution of such treaties, fails to perform one of its plainest duties.
>
> Our commerce with Mexico has been almost annihilated. It was formerly highly beneficial to both nations; but our merchants have been deterred from prosecuting it, by the system of outrage and extortion which the Mexican authorities have pursued against them; . . . . [N]ow, after reiterated menaces, Mexico has passed the boundary of the United States, has invaded our territory and shed American blood upon the American soil. She has proclaimed that hostilities have commenced, and that the two nations are now at war.
>
> As war exists, and, notwithstanding all our efforts to avoid it, exists by the act of Mexico herself, we are called upon, by every consideration of duty and patriotism, to vindicate, with decision the honor, the rights, and the interests of our country. . . .
>
> In further vindication of our rights and defense of our territory, I invoke the prompt action of Congress to recognize the existence of the war, and to place at the disposition of the Executive the means of prosecuting the war with vigor, and thus hastening the restoration of peace. To this end I recommend that authority should be given to call into the public service a large body of volunteers to serve for not less than six or twelve months unless sooner discharged. A volunteer force is, beyond question, more efficient than any other description of citizen soldiers; and it is not to be doubted that a number far beyond that required would readily rush to the field upon the call of their country. I further recommend that a liberal provision be made for sustaining our entire military force, and furnishing it with supplies and munitions of war.

President's Message to Congress, May 11, 1846, *reprinted in* Cong. Globe, 29th Cong., 1st Sess. 783 (1846).

Although some members of Congress expressed concern that the President was rushing the country into war, Congress acceded to Polk's request. On May 13, 1846, it recognized that "a state of war exists" between the United States and Mexico, and authorized the President, "for the purpose of enabling the government of the United States to prosecute said war to a speedy and successful termination," to "employ the militia, naval, and military forces of the United States, and to call for and accept the services of any number of volunteers, not exceeding fifty thousand." Act of May 13, 1846, ch. 16, 9 Stat. 9. After the war was concluded two years later, however, the House of Representatives adopted a resolution stating that the Mexican-American War was "a war unnecessarily and unconstitutionally begun by the President of the United States." Cong. Globe, 30th Cong., 1st Sess. 95 (1848). One of the House members who voted in favor of this resolution was Abraham Lincoln. Subsequently, he wrote the following letter to his friend William Herndon responding to Herndon's defense of Polk's actions:

> Let me first state what I understand to be your position. It is that if it shall become necessary to repel invasion, the President may, without violation of the Constitution, cross the line and invade the territory of another country, and that whether such necessity exists in any given case the President is the sole judge. . . .

Allow the President to invade a neighboring nation whenever he shall deem it necessary to repel an invasion, and you allow him to do so whenever he may choose to say he deems it necessary for such a purpose, and you allow him to make war at his pleasure. . . .

The provision of the Constitution giving the war-making power to Congress was dictated, as I understand it, by the following reasons: kings had always been involving and impoverishing their people in wars, pretending generally, if not always, that the good of the people was the object. This our convention understood to be the most oppressive of all kingly oppressions, and they resolved to so frame the Constitution that no one man should hold the power of bringing oppression upon us. But your view destroys the whole matter, and places our President where kings have always stood.

Letter from Abraham Lincoln to William H. Herndon (Feb. 15, 1848), *in* 2 The Writings of Abraham Lincoln 52 (Arthur Brooks Lapsley ed., 1905).

2. The Bombardment of Greytown

Durand v. Hollins

8 F. Cas. 111 (C.C.S.D.N.Y. 1860)

[In 1854, Captain George Hollins, of the *USS Cyane,* ordered the bombardment of Greytown, Nicaragua, in response to the theft and destruction of American property and an attack on an American minister. Durand, an American citizen living in Greytown, sued Hollins for destruction of his property caused by the bombardment. In defense, Hollins argued that his actions had been authorized by the Secretary of the Navy.]

NELSON, CIRCUIT JUSTICE.

The principal ground of objection to the pleas, as a defence of the action, is, that neither the president nor the secretary of the navy had authority to give the orders relied on to the defendant, and, hence, that they afford no ground of justification. . . .

As the executive head of the nation, the president is made the only legitimate organ of the general government, to open and carry on correspondence or negotiations with foreign nations, in matters concerning the interests of the country or of its citizens. It is to him, also, the citizens abroad must look for protection of person and of property, and for the faithful execution of the laws existing and intended for their protection. For this purpose, the whole executive power of the country is placed in his hands, under the constitution, and the laws passed in pursuance thereof; and different departments of government have been organized, through which this power may be most conveniently executed, whether by negotiation or by force — a department of state and a department of the navy.

Now, as it respects the interposition of the executive abroad, for the protection of the lives or property of the citizen, the duty must, of necessity, rest in the discretion of the president. Acts of lawless violence, or of threatened violence to the citizen or his property, cannot be anticipated and provided for; and the protection, to be effectual or of any avail, may, not unfrequently, require the most prompt and decided action. Under our system of government, the citizen abroad is as much entitled to protection as the citizen at home. The great object and duty of government is the protection of the lives, liberty, and property of the people composing it, whether abroad or at home; and any government failing in the accomplishment of the object, or the performance of the duty, is not worth preserving.

I have said, that the interposition of the president abroad, for the protection of the citizen, must necessarily rest in his discretion; and it is quite clear that, in all cases where a public act or order rests in executive discretion neither he nor his authorized agent is personally civilly responsible for the consequences. . . . The question whether it was the duty of the president to interpose for the protection of the citizens at Greytown against an irresponsible and marauding community that had established itself there, was a public political question, in which the government, as well as the citizens whose interests were involved, was concerned, and which belonged to the executive to determine; and his decision is final and conclusive, and justified the defendant in the execution of his orders given through the secretary of the navy.

3. The Civil War

Southern forces opened fire on Fort Sumter on April 12, 1861. In the following days and weeks, President Lincoln took a number of responsive actions without authorization or input from Congress, including calling up 75,000 militiamen from the states, seeking volunteers for the federal army and navy, and imposing a naval blockade on Southern ports. In his address to a special session of Congress on July 4, Lincoln explained the legal bases for these actions:

> Recurring to the action of the Government, it may be stated that at first a call was made for 75,000 militia, and rapidly following this a proclamation was issued for closing the ports of the insurrectionary districts by proceedings in the nature of blockade. So far all was believed to be strictly legal. . . .
>
> Other calls were made for volunteers to serve for three years, unless sooner discharged, and also for large additions to the Regular Army and Navy. These measures, whether strictly legal or not, were ventured upon under what appeared to be a popular demand and a public necessity, trusting then, as now, that Congress would readily ratify them. It is believed that nothing has been done beyond the constitutional competency of Congress. . . .
>
> It was with the deepest regret that the Executive found the duty of employing the war power, in defense of the Government, forced upon him. He could but perform this duty or surrender the existence of the Government. . . .
>
> As a private citizen the Executive could not have consented that these [U.S. governmental] institutions shall perish; much less could he in betrayal of so vast and so sacred a trust as these free people had confided to him. He felt that he had no moral right to shrink, nor even to count the chances of his own life, in what might follow. In full view of his great responsibility he has, so far, done what he has deemed his duty. You will now, according to your own judgment, perform yours.

Abraham Lincoln's Special Session Message, July 4, 1861. The next month, Congress passed a statute ratifying Lincoln's military actions:

> That all the acts, proclamations and orders of the President of the United States after the fourth of March, eighteen hundred and sixty-one, respecting the army and navy of the United States, and calling out or relating to the militia or volunteers from the States, are hereby approved and in all respects legalized and made valid, to the same

intent and with the same effect as if they had been issued and done under the previous express authority and direction of the Congress of the United States.

12 Stat. 326 (1861).

The Prize Cases

67 U.S. 635 (1863)

MR. JUSTICE GRIER. . . .

Had the President a right to institute a blockade of ports in possession of persons in armed rebellion against the Government, on the principles of international law, as known and acknowledged among civilized States? . . .

That a blockade de facto actually existed, and was formally declared and notified by the President on the 27th and 30th of April, 1861, is an admitted fact in these cases.

That the President, as the Executive Chief of the Government and Commander-in-chief of the Army and Navy, was the proper person to make such notification, has not been, and cannot be disputed.

The right of prize and capture has its origin in the "*jus belli*," and is governed and adjudged under the law of nations. To legitimate the capture of a neutral vessel or property on the high seas, a war must exist de facto, and the neutral must have a knowledge or notice of the intention of one of the parties belligerent to use this mode of coercion against a port, city, or territory, in possession of the other.

Let us enquire whether, at the time this blockade was instituted, a state of war existed which would justify a resort to these means of subduing the hostile force. . . .

By the Constitution, Congress alone has the power to declare a national or foreign war. It cannot declare war against a State, or any number of States, by virtue of any clause in the Constitution. The Constitution confers on the President the whole Executive power. He is bound to take care that the laws be faithfully executed. He is Commander-in-chief of the Army and Navy of the United States, and of the militia of the several States when called into the actual service of the United States. He has no power to initiate or declare a war either against a foreign nation or a domestic State. But by the Acts of Congress of February 28th, 1795, and 3d of March, 1807, he is authorized to call out the militia and use the military and naval forces of the United States in case of invasion by foreign nations, and to suppress insurrection against the government of a State or of the United States.

If a war be made by invasion of a foreign nation, the President is not only authorized but bound to resist force by force. He does not initiate the war, but is bound to accept the challenge without waiting for any special legislative authority. And whether the hostile party be a foreign invader, or States organized in rebellion, it is none the less a war, although the declaration of it be "unilateral." . . .

This greatest of civil wars was not gradually developed by popular commotion, tumultuous assemblies, or local unorganized insurrections. However long may have been its previous conception, it nevertheless sprung forth suddenly from the parent brain, a Minerva in the full panoply of war. The President was bound to meet it in the shape it presented itself, without waiting for Congress to baptize it with a name; and no name given to it by him or them could change the fact. . . .

Whether the President in fulfilling his duties, as Commander-in-chief, in suppressing an insurrection, has met with such armed hostile resistance, and a civil war of such alarming proportions as will compel him to accord to them the character of belligerents, is a question to be decided by him, and this Court must be governed by the decisions and acts of the political department of the Government to which this power was entrusted. "He must determine what degree of force the crisis demands." The proclamation of blockade is itself official and conclusive evidence to the Court that a state of war existed which demanded and authorized a recourse to such a measure, under the circumstances peculiar to the case. . . .

If it were necessary to the technical existence of a war, that it should have a legislative sanction, we find it in almost every act passed at the extraordinary session of the Legislature of 1861, which was wholly employed in enacting laws to enable the Government to prosecute the war with vigor and efficiency. And finally, in 1861, we find Congress "*ex major cautela*" and in anticipation of such astute objections, passing an act "approving, legalizing, and making valid all the acts, proclamations, and orders of the President, &c., as if they had been issued and done under the previous express authority and direction of the Congress of the United States."

Without admitting that such an act was necessary under the circumstances, it is plain that if the President had in any manner assumed powers which it was necessary should have the authority or sanction of Congress, that on the well known principle of law, "*omnis ratihabitio retrotrahitur et mandato equiparatur,*" this ratification has operated to perfectly cure the defect. . . .

The objection made to this act of ratification, that it is *ex post facto*, and therefore unconstitutional and void, might possibly have some weight on the trial of an indictment in a criminal Court. But precedents from that source cannot be received as authoritative in a tribunal administering public and international law.

On this first question therefore we are of the opinion that the President had a right, *jure belli*, to institute a blockade of ports in possession of the States in rebellion, which neutrals are bound to regard. . . .

Mr. Justice Nelson, dissenting. . . .

Upon the whole, after the most careful consideration of this case which the pressure of other duties has admitted, I am compelled to the conclusion that no civil war existed between this Government and the States in insurrection till recognized by the Act of Congress 13th of July, 1861; that the President does not possess the power under the Constitution to declare war or recognize its existence within the meaning of the law of nations, which carries with it belligerent rights, and thus change the country and all its citizens from a state of peace to a state of war; that this power belongs exclusively to the Congress of the United States, and, consequently, that the President had no power to set on foot a blockade under the law of nations, and that the capture of the vessel and cargo in this case, and in all cases before us in which the capture occurred before the 13th of July, 1861, for breach of blockade, or as enemies' property, are illegal and void, and that the decrees of condemnation should be reversed and the vessel and cargo restored.

Mr. Chief Justice Taney, Mr. Justice Catron, and Mr. Justice Clifford, concurred in the dissenting opinion of Mr. Justice Nelson.

4. The Korean War

The Korean War of 1950-1953 is the most extensive U.S. military campaign initiated and sustained by a President without express congressional authorization. It was also the first time that a President relied on the U.N. Charter as authority for sending U.S. troops into combat. We first describe the U.N. Charter and its U.S. implementing legislation, as well as the Cold War context, and then examine the legal aspects of the Korean War.

The United Nations Charter.   The U.N. Charter established a Security Council, which consists of five permanent members (the United States, Russia, Great Britain, France, and China) and ten rotating nonpermanent members. The Council is charged with "primary responsibility for the maintenance of international peace and security" under the Charter. U.N. Charter, Art. 24. If the Council determines "the existence of any threat to the peace, breach of the peace, or act of aggression," *id.* at Art. 39, and if it determines that nonmilitary measures "would be inadequate or have proved to be inadequate," *id.* at Art. 42, it can authorize "such action by air, sea, or land forces as may be necessary to maintain or restore international peace and security." *Id.* Such actions "may include demonstrations, blockade, and other operations by air, sea, or land forces of Members of the United Nations."

The Charter also provides for the establishment of military force agreements between the United Nations and member countries. In Article 43(1) of the Charter, all U.N. members "undertake to make available to the Security Council, on its call and in accordance with a special agreement or agreements, armed forces, assistance, and facilities, including rights of passage, necessary for the purpose of maintaining international peace and security." These agreements, which were to be "concluded between the Security Council and Members," and "subject to ratification by the signatory states in accordance with their respective constitutional processes," would govern "the numbers and types of forces, their degree of readiness and general location, and the nature of the facilities and assistance to be provided." *Id.* at Arts. 43(2)-(3).

Finally, several provisions of the Charter place obligations on member states with respect to the above provisions. Article 49 provides: "The Members of the United Nations shall join in affording mutual assistance in carrying out the measures decided upon by the Security Council." Similarly, Article 25 provides: "The Members of the United Nations agree to accept and carry out the decisions of the Security Council in accordance with the present Charter." *See also id.* at Art. 2(5), Art. 48(1), Art. 48(2).

The Senate gave its consent to the U.N. Charter in 1945 by a vote of 89-2. The dissenting senators (Bushfield and Wheeler) objected that, in ratifying the Charter, the United States was unconstitutionally delegating its war power to the Security Council, and to the Executive Branch's representative on the Council. Soon thereafter, Congress enacted the United Nations Participation Act, 22 U.S.C. §§287-287e, which authorizes the President to negotiate an agreement with the United Nations for the use of U.S. forces (as contemplated by Article 43 of the U.N. Charter), subject to congressional approval:

> The President is authorized to negotiate a special agreement or agreements with the Security Council which shall be subject to the approval of the Congress by appropriate Act or joint resolution, providing for the numbers and types of armed forces, their degree of readiness and general location, and the nature of facilities and assistance, including rights of passage, to be made available to the Security Council on its call for the purpose of maintaining international peace and security in accordance with article 43 of said Charter. The President shall not be deemed to require the authorization of the Congress to make available to the Security Council on its call in order to take action under article 42 of said Charter and pursuant to such special agreement or

agreements the armed forces, facilities, or assistance provided for therein: Provided, That, except as authorized in section 287d-1 of this title, nothing herein contained shall be construed as an authorization to the President by the Congress to make available to the Security Council for such purpose armed forces, facilities, or assistance in addition to the forces, facilities, and assistance provided for in such special agreement or agreements.

22 U.S.C. §287d. Despite this provision, the United States has never concluded an Article 43 agreement with the Security Council.

In 1949, the U.N. Participation Act was amended to provide in relevant part:

(a) Notwithstanding the provisions of any other law, the President, upon a request by the United Nations for cooperative action, and to the extent that he finds that it is consistent with the national interest to comply with such request may authorize, in support of such activities of the United Nations as are specifically directed to the peaceful settlement of disputes and not involving the employment of armed forces contemplated by chapter VII of the United Nations Charter —

(1) the detail to the United Nations, under such terms and conditions as the President shall determine, of personnel of the armed forces of the United States to serve as observers, guards, or in any noncombatant capacity, but in no event shall more than a total of one thousand of such personnel be so detailed at any one time. . . .

Cold War Context. The Cold War between the United States and the Soviet Union formed an important background context to the Korean War, and indeed to most military conflicts involving the United States in the period 1947-1991. The Cold War was "cold" because it did not involve direct military conflict between the world's two superpowers. But it was "war" because it involved heightened political and military tensions between the two nations combined with various proxy wars between them around the globe.

The Cold War is traditionally thought to have begun in 1947. By that year, the Soviet Union was far along in consolidating effective military, political, and economic control over the central and eastern European nations that became known as the Eastern bloc, and was attempting to assert its influence in Western Europe and the Middle East. In response, President Truman announced in 1947 what became known as the "Truman Doctrine," which pledged U.S. military and economic aid to Turkey and Greece, and which led later that year to the Marshall Plan, which provided massive amounts of such aid throughout Western Europe. Other important Cold War events preceding the Korean War include the Soviet Union's blockade of western Berlin in 1948, which led to the two-year "Berlin airlift" of food and other provisions by the United States and other western countries, and the establishment of the North Atlantic Treaty Organization (NATO) in 1949.

Legal Aspects of the Korean War. On June 24, 1950, North Korean forces, which had received support from both the Soviet Union and the People's Republic of China (i.e., Communist China), invaded South Korea. The following day, the Security Council issued a resolution denouncing the attack and calling for an immediate ceasefire and a withdrawal of North Korean forces to the 38th parallel. (The Soviet Union did not veto the resolution because it had been boycotting Council meetings since January 1950 on the ground that the People's Republic of China rather than the Republic of China (Taiwan) should hold the permanent seat in the U.N. Security Council.) The resolution also called upon members of the United

Nations "to render every assistance to the United Nations in the execution of this resolution." S.C. Res. 82, U.N. SCOR, 5th Sess., 473d mtg., at 4, U.N. Doc. S/INF/ 4/Rev.1 (1950). On June 26, President Truman, referring to the Security Council's resolution, publicly announced a commitment of U.S. air and naval forces to assist South Korean forces in repelling the North Korean attack. The next day, on June 27, the Security Council issued another resolution calling upon "[m]embers of the United Nations to furnish such assistance to the Republic of Korea as may be necessary to repel the armed attack and to restore international peace and security in the area." S.C. Res. 83, U.N. SCOR, 5th Sess., Res. & Dec., at 4, U.N. Doc. S/INF/ 5/Rev.1 (1950). The Council subsequently placed the forces of 15 countries under U.S. command, and Truman appointed General Douglas MacArthur to lead these forces.

There was widespread support in Congress for Truman's initial commitment of U.S. armed forces to Korea. Some members of Congress invoked the U.N. Charter in defending Truman's actions. Senator Knowland, for example, stated:

> [The President] has been authorized to do it under the terms of our obligations to the United Nations Charter. I believe he has the authority to do it under his constitutional power as Commander in Chief of the Armed Forces of the United States.
>
> Certainly the action which has been taken to date is not one which would have required, or one in which I believe it was desirable to have, a declaration of war, as such, by the Congress of the United States. What is being done is more in the nature of police action.

96 Cong. Rec. 9540 (1950).

A few senators, however, criticized Truman for failing to obtain congressional authorization. Senator Taft, for example, argued as follows:

> [President Truman's] action unquestionably has brought about a de facto war with the Government of northern Korea. He has brought that war without consulting Congress and without congressional approval. We have a situation in which in a far distant part of the world one nation has attacked another, and if the President can intervene in Korea without congressional approval, he can go to war in Malaya or Indonesia or Iran or South America. . . .
>
> It is claimed that the Korean situation is changed by the obligations into which we have entered under the Charter of the United Nations. I think this is true, but I do not think it justifies the President's present action without approval by Congress. . . .
>
> [In the U.N. Participation Act], we have enacted the circumstances under which the President may use armed forces in support of a resolution of the Security Council of the United Nations. The first requisite is that we negotiate an agreement to determine what forces shall be used, and in what quantity, and that the agreement be approved by Congress. No agreement has ever been negotiated, of course, and no agreement has ever been presented to Congress. So far as I can see, and so far as I have studied the matter, I would say that there is no authority to use armed forces in support of the United Nations in the absence of some previous action by Congress dealing with the subject and outlining the general circumstances and the amount of the forces that can be used.

96 Cong. Rec. 9322-23 (1950).

In defending against such criticism, Secretary of State Dean Acheson (like Senator Knowland) invoked the U.N. Charter:

> All actions taken by the United States to restore the peace in Korea have been under the aegis of the United Nations. . . .

We are confronted with a direct challenge to the United Nations. Whether this organization, which embodies our hopes for an international order based on peace with justice and freedom, can survive this test will depend upon the vigor with which it answers the challenge and the support which it receives from free nations.

. . . This action, pursuant to the Security Council resolutions, is solely for the purpose of restoring the Republic of Korea to its status prior to the invasion from the north and of reestablishing the peace broken by that aggression.

23 Dep't of State Bull. 43, 46 (July 10, 1950). The Truman Administration later justified its dispatch of troops to Korea without congressional authorization as follows: "The power to send troops abroad is certainly one of the powers which the President may exercise in carrying out such a treaty as . . . the United Nations Charter." Joint Comm. of the Comms. on Foreign Relations and on Armed Services, 82d Cong., 1st Sess., Powers of the President to Send the Armed Forces Outside the United States 20 (1951).

5. The U.S. Airstrikes Against Syria in 2017 and 2018

In March 2011, pro-democracy protests began in Syria against President Bashar al Assad. Syrian security forces fired on demonstrators, which triggered nation-wide protests. Opposition protesters took up arms to defend themselves and to expel security forces from their neighborhoods. Violence escalated into a civil war between Assad's forces and rebel groups. In 2012, the U.N. Security Council adopted Resolution 2042, condemning the "widespread violations of human rights by the Syrian authorities, as well as any human rights abuses by armed groups" and calling upon "all parties in Syria, including the opposition, immediately to cease all armed violence in all its forms." S.C. Res. 2042 (Apr. 14, 2012). Notwithstanding that resolution, fighting continued. In August 2013, hundreds of people were killed when rockets filled with a nerve agent were fired at Damascus suburbs. The United States assessed that the Assad government carried out the attack, although the Assad government blamed the rebels. White House, *Government Assessment of the Syrian Government's Use of Chemical Weapons on August 21, 2013*, at https://obamawhitehouse.archives.gov/the-press-office/2013/08/30/government-assessment-syrian-government-s-use-chemical-weapons-august-21.

President Obama prepared to use military force in response to Syria's actions, but decided at the last minute to seek congressional authorization. The issue soon became moot because, in September 2013, Russia and the United States concluded a "Framework for Elimination of Syrian Chemical Weapons." The Security Council welcomed the Framework and decided that Syria "shall not use, develop, produce, otherwise acquire, stockpile or retain chemical weapons," though it did not authorize any state to use force against Syria. S.C. Res. 2118 (Sept. 27, 2013).

Notwithstanding these developments, Syria continued to use chemical weapons in the conflict. In September 2014, a fact-finding mission of the Organisation for the Prohibition of Chemical Weapons (OPCW) found "compelling information" that chlorine gas was used "systematically and repeatedly" as a weapon in villages in northern Syria earlier that year. Although the OPCW report did not specifically attribute the use of chlorine to the Syrian government, Secretary of State John Kerry said that the use of helicopters to drop the chlorine gas "strongly point[ed]" to the Syrian government as the perpetrator. Newspapers reported a number of additional attacks using chlorine and mustard gas between 2014 and 2017.

On April 6, 2017, the United States, on orders from President Trump, launched 59 Tomahawk cruise missiles at the Shayrat airbase in Syria in response to an alleged chemical attack by forces associated with the Syrian government on civilians in the Syrian town of Khan Shayshun. In a letter to Congress, President Trump stated that he "acted in the vital national security and foreign policy interests of the United States, pursuant to my constitutional authority to conduct foreign relations and as Commander in Chief and Chief Executive." The Trump Administration did not provide an official public legal rationale, but it did circulate unsigned talking points "among representatives in various agencies about the strike's legal basis" that provide some insight into its thinking. Charlie Savage, *Watchdog Group Sues Trump Administration, Seeking Legal Rationale Behind Syria Strike*, N.Y. Times (May 8, 2017).

The rationale under domestic law in the talking points was as follows:

> As Commander in Chief, the President has the power under Article II of the Constitution to use this sort of military force overseas to defend important U.S. national interests. The United States has a strong national interest in preserving regional stability, averting a worsening of the humanitarian catastrophe in Syria, and deterring the use and proliferation of chemical weapons, especially in a region rife with international terrorist groups with long-standing interests in obtaining these weapons and using them to attack the United States and its allies and partners. This domestic law basis is very similar to the authority for the use of force in Libya in 2011, as set forth in an April 2011 opinion by the Department of Justice's Office of Legal Counsel.

Just over a year later, a similar operation occurred. On April 13, 2018, President Trump ordered the U.S. military to launch airstrikes against three facilities associated with the Syrian government's chemical weapons capability. The strikes came in response to the Syrian government's alleged deadly use of chemical weapons on civilians on April 7 in Douma, Syria. President Trump notified Congress of the planned strike beforehand, but did not seek or obtain congressional authorization. On May 31, 2018, the Justice Department's Office of Legal Counsel issued the following opinion, which memorialized its advice to the White House Counsel, prior to the 2018 strikes, that the strikes were lawful.

Memorandum Opinion from Steven A. Engel, Assistant Attorney General, Office of Legal Counsel, to the Attorney General, "April 2018 Airstrikes Against Syrian Chemical-Weapons Facilities"

At https://www.justice.gov/olc/opinion/file/1067551/download (May 31, 2018)

. . . When it comes to the war powers of the President, we do not write on a blank slate. The legal opinions of executive advisers and the still weightier precedents of history have established that the President, as Commander in Chief and Chief Executive, has the constitutional authority to deploy the military to protect American persons and interests without seeking prior authorization from Congress. *See, e.g., The President and the War Power: South Vietnam and the Cambodian Sanctuaries*, 1 Op. O.L.C. Supp. 321, 331 (May 22, 1970) (*"Cambodian Sanctuaries"*); *Training of British Flying Students in the United States*, 40 Op. Att'y Gen. 58, 62 (1941) (Jackson, A.G.) (*"British Flying Students"*). The President's authority in this area has been elucidated by dozens of occasions over the course of 230 years, quite literally running from the halls of Montezuma to the shores of Tripoli and beyond. Many of those actions were approved by opinions of this Office or of the Attorney General, and many involved engagements considerably broader than the April 2018 Syrian strikes. The Constitution reserves to Congress the authority to "declare War" and thereby to decide whether to commit the Nation to a sustained, full-scale conflict with another Nation. Yet Presidents have repeatedly engaged in more limited hostilities to advance the Nation's interests without first seeking congressional authorization. . . .

In evaluating the division of authority between the President and Congress, the Supreme Court has placed "significant weight" on "accepted understandings and practice." Zivotofsky v. Kerry, 135 S. Ct. 2076, 2091 (2015); *see* NLRB v. Noel Canning, 134 S. Ct. 2550, 2559 (2014) (noting that "long settled and established practice is a consideration of great weight in a proper interpretation of constitutional provisions regulating the relationship between Congress and the President" (internal quotation marks and alterations omitted)); Dames & Moore v. Regan, 453 U.S. 654, 678–86 (1981) (describing "a history of congressional acquiescence in conduct of the sort engaged in by the President"). We have recognized that "[s]ince judicial precedents are virtually non-existent" in defining the scope of the President's war powers, "the question is one which of necessity must be decided by historical practice." *Presidential Authority to Permit Incursion Into Communist Sanctuaries in the Cambodia-Vietnam Border Area*, 1 Op. O.L.C. Supp. 313, 317 (May 14, 1970) ("*Vietnam Border Area*").

And that history points strongly in one direction. While our Nation has sometimes debated the scope of the President's war powers under the Constitution, his authority to direct U.S. forces in hostilities without prior congressional authorization is supported by a "long continued practice on the part of the Executive, acquiesced in by the Congress." *Cambodian Sanctuaries*, 1 Op. O.L.C. Supp. at 326; *see also Deployment of United States Armed Forces to Haiti*, 28 Op. O.L.C. 30, 31 (2004) ("*Haiti Deployment II*") ("History offers ample evidence for the proposition that the President may take military action abroad, even, as here, in the absence of specific prior congressional authorization."); *Presidential Power to Use the Armed Forces Abroad Without Statutory Authorization*, 4A Op. O.L.C. 185, 187 (1980) ("*Presidential Power*") ("Our history is replete with instances of presidential uses of military force abroad in the absence of prior congressional approval."). . . .

Although "[t]he limits of the President's power as Commander in Chief are nowhere defined in the Constitution," we have recognized a "negative implication from the fact that the power to declare war is committed to Congress." *Cambodian Sanctuaries*, 1 Op. O.L.C. Supp. at 325. The Constitution reserves to Congress the power to "declare War," U.S. Const. art. I, §8, cl. 11, and the authority to fund military operations, *id.* art. I, §8, cl. 12. This was a deliberate choice of the Founders, who sought to prevent the President from bringing the Nation into a full-scale war without the authorization of Congress. . . . These legislative powers ensure that the use of force "cannot be sustained over time without the acquiescence, indeed the approval, of Congress, for it is Congress that must appropriate the money to fight a war or a police action." *Presidential Power*, 4A Op. O.L.C. at 188. These powers further oblige the President to seek congressional approval prior to contemplating military action that would bring the Nation into a war.

Not every military operation, however, rises to the level of a war. . . .

. . . In evaluating whether a proposed military action falls within the President's authority under Article II of the Constitution, we have distilled our precedents into two inquiries. First, we consider whether the President could reasonably determine that the action serves important national interests. *See, e.g., Somalia Deployment*, 16 O.L.C. at 9 ("At the core of this power is the President's authority to take military action to protect American citizens, property, and interests from foreign threats."); *British Flying Students*, 40 Op. Att'y Gen. at 62 ("[T]he President's authority has long been recognized as extending to the dispatch of armed forces outside of the United States, either on missions of good will or rescue, or for purposes of protecting American lives or property or American interests."). Second, we consider whether the "anticipated nature, scope and duration" of the conflict might rise to the level of a war under the Constitution. *See Authority to Use Military Force in Libya*, 35 Op. O.L.C. ___, at *9 (Apr. 1, 2011) ("*Libya Deployment*") (quoting *Deployment of United States Armed Forces into Haiti*, 18 Op. O.L.C. 173, 179 (1994) ("*Haiti Deployment I*"). Prior to the Syrian strikes, we applied this framework to conclude that the proposed Syrian operation would fall within the President's constitutional authority.

This Office has recognized that a broad set of interests would justify use of the President's Article II authority to direct military force. These interests understandably grant the President a great deal of discretion. The scope of U.S. involvement in the world, the presence of U.S. citizens across the globe, and U.S. leadership in times of conflict, crisis, and strife require that the President have wide latitude to protect American interests by responding to regional conflagrations and humanitarian catastrophes as he believes appropriate. The Commander in Chief bears great responsibility for the use of the armed forces and for putting U.S. forces in harm's way. We would not expect that any President would use this power without a substantial basis for believing that a proposed operation is necessary to advance important interests of the Nation. The aim of this inquiry is not to evaluate the worth of the interests at stake—a question more of policy than of law—but rather, to set forth the justifications for the President's use of military force and to situate those interests within a framework of prior precedents.

In our past opinions, this Office has identified a number of different interests that have supported sending U.S. forces into harm's way, including the following:

- the protection of U.S. persons and property, *see, e.g., Presidential Power*, 4A Op. O.L.C. at 187 ("Presidents have repeatedly employed troops abroad in defense of American lives and property."); *Haiti Deployment II*, 28 Op. O.L.C. at 31 ("The President has the authority to deploy the armed forces abroad in order to protect American citizens and interests from foreign threats.");
- assistance to allies, *see, e.g., Haiti Deployment I*, 18 Op. O.L.C. at 79 (approving of intervention "at the invitation of a fully legitimate government"); *Presidential Power*, 4A Op. O.L.C. at 187–88 (citing the Korean War as "precedent . . . for the commitment of United States armed forces, without prior congressional approval or declaration of war, to aid an ally in repelling an armed invasion");
- support for the United Nations, *see, e.g., Haiti Deployment II*, 28 Op. O.L.C. at 33 ("Another American interest in Haiti arises from the involvement of the United Nations in the situation there."); *Somalia Deployment*, 16 Op. O.L.C. at 11 ("[M]aintaining the credibility of United Nations Security Council decisions, protecting the security of United Nations and related relief efforts, and ensuring the effectiveness of United Nations peacekeeping operations can be considered a vital national interest[.]"); and
- promoting regional stability, *see, e.g., Haiti Deployment II*, 29 Op. O.L.C. at 32 ("The President also may determine that the deployment is necessary to protect American foreign policy interests. One such interest is the preservation of regional stability."); *Libya Deployment* at *12 ("[W]e believe the President

could reasonably find a significant national security interest in preventing Libyan instability from spreading elsewhere in this critical region.").

In recent years, we have also identified the U.S. interest in mitigating humanitarian disasters. *See* Memorandum Opinion for the Counsel to the President, from Karl R. Thompson, Principal Deputy Assistant Attorney General, Office of Legal Counsel, *Re: Authority to Use Military Force in Iraq* at 20–24 (Dec. 30, 2014) ("*Iraq Deployment*"). With respect to Syria, in April 2017, the President identified the U.S. interest in preventing the use and proliferation of chemical weapons, *see* Letter to Congressional Leaders on United States Military Operations in Syria, 2017 Daily Comp. Pres. Doc. 201700244, at 1 (Apr. 8, 2017) ("2017 Congressional Notification"). . . .

The President identified three interests in support of the April 2018 Syria strikes: the promotion of regional stability, the prevention of a worsening of the region's humanitarian catastrophe, and the deterrence of the use and proliferation of chemical weapons. *See* Letter to Congressional Leaders on United States Military Operations in Syria, 2018 Daily Comp. Pres. Doc. 201800243, at 1 (Apr. 15, 2018). Prior to the attack, we advised that the President could reasonably rely on these national interests to authorize air strikes against particular facilities associated with Syria's chemical-weapons program without congressional authorization. . . .

Here, the President could reasonably determine that Syria's use of chemical weapons in the ongoing civil war threatens to undermine further peace and security of the Near East, a region that remains critically important to our national security. Syria's possession and use of chemical weapons have increased the risk that others will gain access to them. . . . The proliferation of such weapons to other countries with fragile governments or to terrorist groups could further spread conflict and disorder within the region. . . . The United States has a direct interest in ensuring that others in the region not look to Syria's use of chemical weapons as a successful precedent for twenty-first-century conflicts.

Moreover, the regime's use of chemical weapons is a particularly egregious part of a broader destabilizing conflict. The civil war in Syria directly empowered the growth of the Islamic State of Iraq and Syria ("ISIS"), a terrorist threat that has required the deployment of over 2,000 U.S. troops. . . . The instability in Syria has had a direct and marked impact upon the national security of close American allies and partners, including Iraq, Israel, Jordan, Lebanon, and Turkey, all of which border Syria and have had to deal with unrest from the conflict. . . . In addition, the power vacuum in Syria has provided an opportunity for Russia and Iran to deepen their presence in the region and engage in activities that have had a directly adverse impact on the interests and security of the United States and its allies in the area. *See* President Donald J. Trump, National Security Strategy of the United States of America at 49 (Dec. 2017), https://www.whitehouse.gov/wp-content/uploads/2017/12/NSS-Final-12-18-2017-0905.pdf ("Rival states are filling vacuums created by state collapse and prolonged regional conflict.").

The Syrian regime's continued attacks on civilians have also contributed to the displacement of civilians and thus deepened the instability in the region. According to the Director of National Intelligence, as of October 2017, more than 5 million Syrian refugees had fled to neighboring countries and more than 6 million were displaced internally. . . . These large-scale population movements have added to unrest throughout the region. . . .

In directing the strikes, the President also relied on the national interest in mitigating a humanitarian crisis. In analyzing proposed military operations in Iraq designed to prevent genocidal acts against the Yazidis and otherwise to protect civilians at risk, we advised that humanitarian concerns could provide a basis for the President's use of force under his constitutional authority. *See Iraq Deployment* at 20–24. Given the role of the United States in the international community and the humanitarian interests of its people, Presidents have on many occasions deployed troops to prevent or mitigate humanitarian disasters. . . .

The Syrian regime's use of chemical weapons has contributed to the on-going humanitarian crisis in Syria. As discussed above, civilians fleeing from the strikes become refugees needing assistance. Internally displaced persons in Syria often lack access to basic services or medical care, difficulties that are heightened for victims of chemical-weapons attacks. But even where the attacks do not displace civilians, the nature of chemical weapons alone makes their use a humanitarian issue. . . .

In carrying out these strikes, the President also relied on the national interest in deterring the use and proliferation of chemical weapons. The President previously relied upon this interest in ordering the April 2017 airstrike in response to the attack on Khan Shaykhun. *See* 2017 Congressional Notification (stating that the President directed a strike on the Shayrat military airfield to "degrade the Syrian military's ability to conduct further chemical weapons attacks and to dissuade the Syrian regime from using or proliferating chemical weapons, thereby promoting the stability of the region and averting a worsening of the region's current humanitarian catastrophe"). While we are unaware of prior Presidents justifying U.S. military actions based on this interest as a matter of domestic law, we believe that it is consistent with those that have justified previous uses of force. . . . For nearly thirty years, Presidents have repeatedly declared the proliferation of chemical weapons to be a national emergency. In 1997, the United States ratified the Chemical Weapons Convention, which prohibits the use, development, production, and retention of chemical weapons. And Congress cited Iraq's development of chemical weapons as one of the reasons in support of authorizing the use of military force against Iraq in 2002. . . .

In sum, the President here was faced with a grave risk to regional stability, a serious and growing humanitarian disaster, and the use of weapons repeatedly condemned by the United States and other members of the international community. In such circumstances, the President could reasonably conclude that these interests provided a basis for airstrikes on facilities that support the regime's use of chemical weapons. We believe that these interests fall comfortably within those that our Office has previously relied upon in concluding that the President had appropriately exercised his authority under Article II, and we so advised prior to the Syrian strikes.

We next considered whether the President could expect the Syrian operations to rise to the level of a war requiring congressional authorization. Such a determination "requires a fact-specific assessment of the 'anticipated nature, scope, and duration' of the planned military operations." *Libya Deployment* at *8 (quoting *Haiti Deployment I*, 18 Op. O.L.C. at 179). As we have previously explained, military operations will likely rise to the level of a war only when characterized by "prolonged and substantial military engagements, typically involving exposure of U.S. military personnel to significant risk over a substantial period." *Id.*

We have found that previous military deployments did not rise to the level of a war even where the deployment was substantial. For example, the United States spent two years enforcing a no-fly zone, protecting United Nations ("UN") peacekeeping forces, and securing safe areas for civilians in Bosnia, all without congressional authorization. *See Proposed Deployment of United States Armed Forces into Bosnia*, 19 Op. O.L.C. 327, 329 & n.2 (1995) (*"Bosnia Deployment"*) (noting the plan to deploy 20,000 ground troops to Bosnia as well as additional troops to surrounding areas in a support capacity); *see also Libya Deployment* at *9; (noting "one two-week operation in which NATO attacked hundreds of targets and the United States alone flew over 2300 sorties"). Similarly, in 1994, we approved a plan to deploy as many as 20,000 troops to Haiti. *Haiti Deployment I*, 18 Op. O.L.C. at 179 n.10. We also approved a U.S.-led air campaign in Libya in 2011 that lasted for over a week and involved the use of over 600 missiles and precision-guided munitions. In none of these cases did we conclude that prior congressional authorization was necessary.

In reviewing these deployments, we considered whether U.S. forces were likely to encounter significant armed resistance and whether they were likely to "suffer or inflict substantial casualties as a result of the deployment." *Haiti Deployment I*, 18 Op. O.L.C. at 179. In this regard, we have looked closely at whether an operation will require the introduction of U.S. forces directly into the hostilities, particularly with respect to the deployment of ground troops. The deployment of ground troops "is an essentially different, and more problematic, type of intervention," given "the difficulties of disengaging ground forces from situations of conflict, and the attendant risk that hostilities will escalate." *Bosnia Deployment*, 19 Op. O.L.C. at 333. In such circumstances, "arguably there is a greater need for approval at the outset for the commitment of such troops to such situations." *Id.* . . .

With these precedents in mind, we concluded that the proposed Syrian operation, in its nature, scope, and duration, fell far short of the kinds of engagements approved by prior Presidents under Article II. First, in contrast with some prior deployments, the United States did not plan to employ any U.S. ground troops, and in fact, no U.S. airplanes crossed into Syrian airspace. Where, as here, the operation would proceed without the introduction of U.S. troops into harm's way, we were unlikely to be "confronted with circumstances in which the exercise of [Congress's] power to declare war is effectively foreclosed." *Bosnia Deployment*, 19 Op. O.L.C. at 333.

Second, the mission was sharply circumscribed. This was not a case where the military operation served an open-ended goal. Rather, the President selected three military targets with the aim of degrading and destroying the Syrian regime's ability to produce and use chemical weapons. . . . And the strikes were planned to minimize casualties, further demonstrating the limited nature of the operation. Those aspects both underscored the "limited mission" and the fact that the operation was not "aim[ed] at the conquest or occupation of territory nor even, as did the planned Haitian intervention, at imposing through military means a change in the character of a political régime." *Bosnia Deployment*, 19 Op. O.L.C. at 332.

Third, the duration of the planned operation was expected to be very short. In fact, the entire operation lasted several hours, and the actual attack lasted only a few minutes.

Standing on its own, the attack on three Syrian chemical-weapons facilities was not the kind of "prolonged and substantial military engagement" that would amount to a war. *Libya Deployment* at *8. We did not, however, measure the engagement based solely upon the contours of the first strike. Rather, in evaluating the expected scope of hostilities, we also considered the risk that an initial strike could escalate into a broader conflict against Syria or its allies, such as Russia and Iran. *See Haiti Deployment I*, 18 Op. O.L.C. at 179 ("In deciding whether prior Congressional authorization for the Haitian deployment was constitutionally necessary, the President was entitled to take into account . . . the limited antecedent risk that United States forces would encounter significant armed resistance or suffer or inflict substantial casualties as a result of the deployment."). But the fact that there is some risk to American personnel or some risk of escalation does not itself mean that the operation amounts to a war. *See Cambodian Sanctuaries*, 1 Op. O.L.C. Supp. at 331; *Bosnia Deployment*, 19 Op. O.L.C. at 332. We therefore considered the likelihood of escalation and the measures that the United States intended to take to minimize that risk.

We were advised that escalation was unlikely (and reviewed materials supporting that judgment), and we took note of several measures that had been taken to reduce the risk of escalation by Syria or Russia. The targets were selected because of their particular connections to the chemical-weapons program, underscoring that the strikes sought to address the extraordinary threat posed by the use of chemical weapons and did not seek to precipitate a regime change. The targets were chosen to minimize civilian casualties, and the strikes took place at a time that further reduced the threat to civilians, again reducing the likelihood that Syria would retaliate. The targets were also chosen to minimize risk to Russian soldiers, and deconfliction processes were used, two steps that reduced the possibility that Russia would respond militarily. Given the absence of ground troops, the limited mission and time frame, and the efforts to avoid escalation, the anticipated nature, scope, and duration of these airstrikes did not rise to the level of a "war" for constitutional purposes.

Notes and Questions

1. In *Federalist No. 69*, excerpted in Section A, Alexander Hamilton stated that the President's authority as Commander in Chief "would amount to nothing more than the Supreme command and direction of the military and naval forces." In practice, presidents have exercised a much broader array of military powers than this description might suggest. In any event, what is entailed by the "command and direction" of the armed forces? Does it include decisions about the use of particular weapons? The choice of military targets? The detention and trial of enemy prisoners? The termination of hostilities? What is the relationship between the President's Commander-in-Chief authority and Congress's war powers, such as its power to declare war and its power to "make Rules for the Government and Regulation of the land and naval Forces"?

2. There is general agreement that, in addition to his authority to direct the armed forces during a war, the President has the power to repel attacks on the United States. As stated in *The Prize Cases*, "If a war be made by invasion of a foreign nation, the President is not only authorized but bound to resist by force." Also, recall from Section A that, according to James Madison's Notes of the Federal Convention, the Constitution's conferral on Congress of the power to "declare" war would "leav[e] to the Executive the power to repel sudden attacks." What is the constitutional source of this power? How is this power reconciled with Congress's war declaration and other war-related powers?

3. What is encompassed by the President's power to repel attacks? Must the President wait for the attacks to occur, or can he act preemptively? Does the existence today of missiles and weapons of mass destruction affect the answer to this question? Once the United States is attacked, are there limits on what the President can do in response? Must the President's response be proportional to the attack?

Could the President wage a full war in response to a small-scale attack? Can the President carry the conflict into another country without congressional authorization? In 1801, President Jefferson instructed the naval force that it could respond to attacks by the Barbary Pirates by disarming captured ships, but that, because of the lack of congressional authorization, they were to release the crews of the ships and take no further offensive action. *See* 11 Annals of Congress 12 (1801) (Jefferson's message to Congress). Alexander Hamilton disagreed with this limitation, arguing that once the United States is attacked, the President has full power to respond with any force that he deems suitable. *See* 25 The Papers of Alexander Hamilton 453-57 (Harold C. Syrett ed., 1997). Do you agree? What do *The Prize Cases* suggest? Could Lincoln have fought the entire Civil War without congressional authorization?

4. While *The Prize Cases* are widely viewed as supporting a broad presidential authority to repel attacks, the decision also stated that the President "has no power to initiate or declare a war either against a foreign nation or a domestic State." In addition, the Court noted that Congress had by statute authorized the President to "call out the militia and use the military and naval forces of the United States in case of invasion by foreign nations, and to suppress insurrection against the government of a State or of the United States." Lincoln went beyond that statutory authorization by calling for volunteers for the U.S. Army and Navy, and by incurring debts on behalf of the United States to fund these forces. Were these acts constitutional? What was Lincoln's answer in his July 4, 1861, message to Congress? Why would it matter that, as Lincoln claimed, the actions he took were not beyond *Congress's* power? What was the legal significance of Congress's *ex post* ratification of Lincoln's acts in August 1861? Was this *ex post* ratification necessary? Did it imply a defect in the President's actions? Did it render constitutional acts that were until then unconstitutional? Or was Congress's action legally meaningless? For analysis of these issues, see Daniel Farber, Lincoln's Constitution (2003). We return to related issues about emergency power in Section E below.

5. When President Lincoln announced his blockade of southern ports, he stated that he was acting "in pursuance of the laws of the United States *and of the law of nations.*" Presidential Proclamation 81, April 19, 1861 (emphasis added). Under the prevailing international laws of war, certain requirements had to be met in order for a blockade to be lawful and thereby create a right to seize neutral vessels that attempted to run the blockade. What is the relationship between such international law requirements and the President's authority as Commander in Chief? What did the Court suggest about this in *The Prize Cases*? For discussion of various international law issues raised by the blockade, see John Fabian Witt, Lincoln's Code: The Laws of War in American History 142-63 (2012); Andrew Kent, *The Constitution and the Laws of War During the Civil War*, 85 Notre Dame L. Rev. 1839, 1893-1902 (2010); Thomas H. Lee & Michael D. Ramsey, *The Story of the Prize Cases: Executive Action and Judicial Review in Wartime*, in Presidential Power Stories (Christopher H. Schroeder & Curtis A. Bradley, eds., Foundation Press 2008); and Thomas H. Lee, *The Civil War in U.S. Foreign Relations Law: A Dress Rehearsal for Modern Transformations*, 53 St. Louis Univ. L. J. 53, 61-64 (2008).

6. What are the implications of *The Prize Cases* for the interpretation of congressional authorizations to the President to use military force abroad? Recall from Section A that the Supreme Court in Brown v. United States construed the 1812 declaration of war and authorization as not empowering the President to seize enemy property in the United States without specific congressional authorization. Does *Brown* survive *The Prize Cases*? Professor Henkin maintained that *Brown* was decided in an era in which the presidential war power was "still in its infancy," and he doubted that it survived the Civil War, in which both President Lincoln and the Supreme Court agreed that the President could seize both enemy property and neutral vessels operating in violation of a blockade, even in the absence of specific congressional authorization. *See* Henkin, *supra*, at 104; *see also* Curtis A. Bradley & Jack L. Goldsmith, *Congressional Authorization and the War on Terrorism*, 118 Harv. L. Rev. 2047, 2093-94 (2005). Do you agree? *Cf.* David Golove, *Military Tribunals, International Law, and the Constitution: A Franckian-Madisonian Approach*, 35 N.Y.U. J. Int'l L. & Pol. 363, 385 (2003) (suggesting that Lincoln's Emancipation Proclamation, in which Lincoln freed Southern slaves without any congressional authorization, and which he justified by reference to his Commander-in-Chief authority and the laws of war, is inconsistent with *Brown*).

7. Can presidents exercise their acknowledged foreign relations powers — for example, the power to dismiss an ambassador, break off diplomatic relations, or announce a new U.S. foreign policy — in a way that is likely to provoke an attack and thus trigger his defensive war powers? Is this what President Polk did with Mexico? *See also* Message from President Wilson to Congress, April 2, 1917, in 55 Cong. Rec. 103 (1917) (acknowledging that his order to U.S. merchant ships to arm themselves against attack by German submarines was "practically certain" to draw the United States into the first World War). Are there any legal limitations on the President's ability to provoke a war? For consideration of the President's authority to *threaten* war, see Matthew C. Waxman, *The Power to Threaten War*, 123 Yale L.J. 1626 (2014).

8. *Durand* concerned the U.S. military's bombardment of Greytown, Nicaragua. In justifying the military's action, President Pierce described Greytown as "a piratical resort of outlaws or a camp of savages" rather than a nation. *See* President Franklin Pierce, Second Annual Message to Congress (Dec. 4, 1854). Does the President have greater constitutional authority to use military force against entities and territories not recognized by the United States as nations than against recognized nations? The court in *Durand* does not rely on such a distinction, and instead states that the President has the discretionary authority to use force to protect the lives and property of U.S. citizens abroad. Presidents have often invoked the authority. In 1900, for example, President McKinley sent over 5,000 U.S. troops to China during the Boxer Rebellion, as part of a multinational coalition, without congressional authorization. In doing so, he emphasized that the U.S. action "involved no war against the Chinese nation" and was justified in part by the need to "secur[e] wherever possible the safety of American life and property in China." More recent examples include the U.S. invasion of Haiti in 1994, of Panama in 1989, of Grenada in 1983, and the failed attempt to rescue U.S. hostages in Iran in 1980. What is the constitutional source of this authority? Does it include protecting U.S. "interests" as well as persons and property? Does it extend to protecting *foreign* nationals and property? For an Executive Branch argument that it does extend in these latter two ways, see Timothy Flanigan, Memorandum Opinion for the Attorney General, Authority to Use United States Military Forces in Somalia, December 4, 1992, at https://www.justice.gov/sites/default/files/olc/opinions/1992/12/31/op-olc-v016-p0006.pdf. (See also the discussion of the Libya intervention, below.)

When acting to protect Americans abroad, does the President have greater constitutional authority to use military force against nations that lack the capacity to maintain law and order? A number of U.S. military interventions in Latin America in the early twentieth century appeared to be premised on this claim. During this period, the Executive Branch, first under Theodore Roosevelt and then under

William Howard Taft, began undertaking various "international police actions" ostensibly designed to restore order in Latin American countries. *See* David Gartner, *Foreign Relations, Strategic Doctrine, and Presidential Power*, 63 Ala. L. Rev. 499, 503 (2012). As Taft explained after he left the presidency, while using force to protect American citizens abroad was potentially an "act of war [as a matter of constitutional law] if committed in a country like England or Germany or France," this was not the case in countries where "law and order are not maintained, as in some Central and South American countries." William Howard Taft, *The Boundaries Between the Executive, the Legislative, and the Judicial Branches of the Government*, 25 Yale L.J. 599, 610-11 (1916). This distinction between "wars" and "police actions" was picked up, in a different context, in connection with the Korean War.

9. As noted above, the Truman Administration was the first to rely on the U.N. Charter as a source of authority for using force abroad. Are you convinced by the Truman Administration's arguments? Do these arguments amount to the claim that the Article II Take Care Clause permits the President to use military force to enforce the United States' international obligations? Is this claim valid? Professor Stromseth argues that it is not, reasoning that the Constitution's allocation of war powers cannot be changed by treaty. *See* Jane E. Stromseth, *Collective Force and Constitutional Responsibility: War Powers in the Post-Cold War Era*, 50 U. Miami L. Rev. 145 (1995). But does this response beg the question about what the Constitution authorizes? Isn't a treaty a "law" for purposes of the Take Care Clause? Even if it is, though, is the President's treaty enforcement authority under the Take Care Clause limited to domestic enforcement, or is international enforcement permitted as well? If the latter, is Congress's war declaration power a check on the President's take care power? Or vice-versa? Which power is more fundamental? Assuming that the Take Care Clause argument has some validity in theory, does it justify Truman's actions in Korea? In this connection, recall that Truman committed U.S. troops to Korea before the U.N. Security Council issued its authorization to use force. And note that the Security Council "recommended," and did not order, nations to "repel the armed attack" on South Korea. *See* S.C. Res. 83 (1950).

10. Consider Senator Knowland's suggested constitutional justification for Truman's actions in the Korean War. Is there really a distinction between a "war," which Congress must authorize before the President can send U.S. troops abroad, and a U.N.-authorized "police action" designed to prevent illegal uses of force, which Congress need not authorize? Professor Stromseth thinks not. She argues that legal uses of forces under the U.N. Charter might still be a "war" for U.S. constitutional purposes (and thus require congressional approval) because of the nature and circumstances of the operation and the magnitude of the combat risks involved. And she adds that the Security Council cannot substitute for the kind of check on unilateral presidential action that the Founders sought in Congress, because the Security Council does not represent the American people and is not politically accountable to them. *See* Stromseth, *supra*, at 157-58. Do you agree with this assessment? Professor Kahn offers a response to one of these concerns, maintaining that the "effective check on the abuse of force would come from the Security Council, not Congress." Kahn, *supra*, at 51. Is this right? Is the Security Council a democratic institution? Does the U.S. veto power in the Security Council ensure that no U.S. troops will be dispatched unless doing so is in U.S. interests? Does the Security Council provide a sufficient check on presidential action? Does the fact that "Congress . . . retains an ultimate authority to prohibit American participation in [U.N.] police actions," see Kahn, *supra*, at 51, constitute an effective check? Or does this reverse the burden of inertia that the constitutional Founders imposed on the large-scale commitment of U.S. troops abroad?

11. Consider Senator Taft's objection to Truman's commitment of troops in Korea. Is it true that the U.N. Participation Act prohibits the use of armed forces in support of a U.N.-authorized police action in the absence of a congressionally approved agreement under Article 43 of the U.N. Charter specifying the circumstances in which forces can be used? The question raises two issues. The first is: Does the U.N. Charter authorize the Security Council to call on member states to use force outside of Article 43 Agreements? Consider this answer:

> Just as Congress nowadays does not grant letters of marque and reprisal (Constitution, Article I, section 8(11)) or establish post roads (Article I, section 8(7)), so the Security Council has not made use of Article 43 of the Charter, which authorizes it to negotiate agreements with consenting member states that, preemptively, would have placed designated national military contingents at the Council's disposal. That no such agreements were made, owing to the Cold War, does not signify a lapse in the Organization's general police power, set out in Article 42, any more than the abstinence by Congress in matters of post roads signifies a lapse in its power to legislate on other matters pertaining to the Postal Service. Rather, the practice of the Security Council has evolved other means for taking coercive measures, including the use of police forces raised ad hoc in response to a specific threat to the peace. . . . [T]he central idea of a globally sanctioned police action was never abandoned; . . . the failure to implement Article 43 merely led to organic growth and the alternative creation of police action through invocation of Article 42, which does not require special agreements.

Franck & Patel, *supra*, at 66. Do you agree?

Assuming this assessment is correct, does the U.N. Participation Act nonetheless prohibit the President from sending U.S. troops abroad pursuant to a Security Council authorization in the absence of congressional authorization? Does the Participation Act make Article 43 Agreements a pre-condition to the presidential use of force pursuant to a Security Council request? How do you read the proviso at the end of 22 U.S.C. §287d, which states that "nothing herein contained shall be construed as an authorization to the President by the Congress to make available to the Security Council . . . armed forces, facilities, or assistance in addition to the forces, facilities, and assistance provided for in such special agreement or agreements"? Clearly Congress did not provide a separate authorization for Security Council-authorized presidential action, but did it affirmatively forbid it? Of what relevance is the 1949 amendment to the U.N. Participation Act, excerpted above? Can the President claim an independent power under the Take Care Clause to enforce Security Council actions even in the absence of an Article 43 Special Agreement or some other congressional authorization? In this connection, can we attribute any significance to Senator Wheeler's proposed amendment to the Participation Act, later defeated, which would have provided: "Wherever a decision to use United States armed forces arises in the Security Council, such a decision must be made by Congress."? *See* 91 Cong. Rec. 11,036 (1945).

12. As the materials in this section demonstrate, Presidents have often employed U.S. troops outside the United States in the absence of congressional authorization, especially in the modern era. This has been made possible in part by the dramatic increase in the size of the standing army, which in turn, reflects a two-century evolution in the nature of international affairs and the United States' role in those affairs. In particular, throughout the twentieth century, and especially following World War II, presidential foreign relations powers increased enormously in response to the possibility of nuclear war and the United States' more prominent role as a world superpower. It is no accident that during this period, presidents have asserted war-making powers more aggressively. The entire Korean War was initiated and fought without express congressional authorization. The United States' commitment of military force in Vietnam long predated the Gulf of Tonkin Resolution. Most uses of force abroad in the 1980s and 1990s — including the 1999 air campaign in Kosovo, the 1994 air strikes in Bosnia, the 1992-1993 operation in Somalia, the 1989 invasion of Panama, the 1986 air strikes against Libya, the 1983 invasion of Grenada, and the 1982 deployment of troops in Lebanon — took place without express congressional authorization.

13. The U.S. intervention in Libya in 2011 serves as a relatively recent example of significant military operations ordered by a President without congressional approval. In mid-February 2011, protests began in Libya against the autocratic government of Colonel Muammar al-Qadhafi. The Libyan government responded by violently attacking the protesters, many of whom fled to neighboring countries. By March 17, Qadhafi's forces were preparing to retake the city of Benghazi "house by house, room by room," and with "no mercy and no pity" to those who resisted, as Qadhafi stated in a radio address. Later the same day, the U.N. Security Council adopted Resolution 1973 by a vote of 10-0 (with five members abstaining). The Resolution "demand[ed] the immediate establishment of a cease-fire and a complete end to violence and all attacks against, and abuses of, civilians." It also authorized member states, acting individually or through regional organizations, "to take all necessary measures . . . to protect civilians and civilian populated areas under threat of attack in the Libyan Arab Jamahiriya, including Benghazi, while excluding a foreign occupation force of any form on any part of Libyan territory." It more specifically authorized member states to enforce "a ban on all [unauthorized] flights in the airspace of the Libyan Arab Jamahiriya in order to help protect civilians."

The Libyan government continued to conduct offensive operations, including attacks on civilians and civilian-populated areas. In response, on March 19, 2011, the United States, with the support of coalition partners, launched air strikes against Libyan targets to enforce Resolution 1973. President Obama explained in a report to Congress that he ordered these actions, "which are in the national security and foreign policy interests of the United States, pursuant to my constitutional authority to conduct U.S. foreign relations and as Commander in Chief and Chief Executive." He described the nature and purpose of the operations as follows:

> U.S. military forces commenced operations to assist an international effort authorized by the United Nations (U.N.) Security Council and undertaken with the support of European allies and Arab partners, to prevent a humanitarian catastrophe and address the threat posed to international peace and security by the crisis in Libya. As part of the multilateral response authorized under U.N. Security Council Resolution 1973, U.S. military forces, under the command of Commander, U.S. Africa Command, began a series of strikes against air defense systems and military airfields for the purposes of preparing a no-fly zone. These strikes will be limited in their nature, duration, and scope. Their purpose is to support an international coalition as it takes all necessary measures to enforce the terms of U.N. Security Council Resolution 1973. . . .
>
> The United States has not deployed ground forces into Libya. United States forces are conducting a limited and well-defined mission in support of international efforts to protect civilians and prevent a humanitarian disaster. ... We will seek a rapid, but responsible, transition of operations to coalition, regional, or international organizations that

are postured to continue activities as may be necessary to realize the objectives of U.N. Security Council Resolutions 1970 and 1973.

By March 31, the United States had transferred responsibility for ongoing coalition military operations in Libya to NATO. After that date, however, the United States continued to play a significant role in the Libya intervention under the NATO umbrella. In April, Secretary of Defense Robert Gates announced that the United States was using armed predator drones on targets in Libya. And on May 23, Secretary of State Hillary Clinton stated that "the United States continues to fly 25 percent of all sorties" and "to provide the majority of intelligence, surveillance and reconnaissance assets." Against that backdrop, the Justice Department's Office of Legal Counsel issued an opinion concerning the President's authority to use military force in Libya, which is cited several times in the OLC opinion on Syria excerpted above.

14. Courts have never resolved the scope of the President's unilateral power to use force in the absence of congressional authorization, and it is possible that justiciability doctrines will bar such a judicial resolution. In light of the lack of judicial precedent, it is unsurprising that the excerpted Office of Legal Counsel (OLC) opinion on the Syria strikes relies heavily on prior presidential uses of force abroad without congressional authorization, as well as Executive Branch analyses in support of the legality of those uses of force. OLC argues that " '[s]ince judicial precedents are virtually non-existent' in defining the scope of the President's war powers, 'the question is one which of necessity must be decided by historical practice' " and asserts "that history points strongly in one direction." The OLC opinion on Libya took a similar approach. For an argument along similar lines, see Peter J. Spiro, *War Powers and the Sirens of Formalism*, 68 N.Y.U. L. Rev. 1338, 1355 (1993) (book review) ("It is . . . the 'court of history,' an accretion of interactions among the branches, that gives rise to basic norms governing the branches' behavior in the [war powers] area."). But does this historical practice in fact reflect Congress's understanding of constitutional meaning? Congress is a corporate body that speaks officially through its statutes. During the long practice of unilateral presidential uses of force, Congress has continued to finance an enormous military and has placed few overt restrictions or conditions on the use of that military. Nevertheless, it did enact the War Powers Resolution of 1973, a statute that (as discussed in the next section) purports to restrict unilateral presidential uses of force. In addition, Congress sometimes responds to unilateral presidential uses of force by approving the action after the fact with specified limitations, including, sometimes, time limitations. *See* Curtis A. Bradley & Jack L. Goldsmith, *Congressional Authorization and the War on Terrorism*, 118 Harv. L. Rev. 2047, 2077 (2005). Furthermore, individual members of Congress have sometimes questioned the legality of unilateral presidential uses of force. Does this congressional pattern constitute agreement with presidents about the scope of their unilateral power to use force? Consider this response to the reliance on historical practice in the OLC opinion on the Libya intervention:

> A practice of constitutional dimension must be regarded by both political branches as a juridical norm; the incidents comprising the practice must be accepted, or at least acquiesced in, by the other branch. In many of the precedents that provide the "historical gloss" on which OLC so heavily relies, Congress objected. Furthermore, the precedents must be on point. Here, many are not: nearly all involved fights with pirates, clashes with cattle rustlers, trivial naval engagements, and other minor uses of force not directed at significant adversaries. In a number of the supposed "precedents,"

Congress actually approved of the executive's action by enacting authorizing legislation (as with the Barbary Wars).

Michael J. Glennon, *The Cost of "Empty Words": A Comment on the Justice Department's Libya Opinion*, Harv. Nat'l Sec. J., April 14, 2011, at http://harvardnsj.org/2011/04/the-cost-of-empty-words-a-comment-on-the-justice-departments-libya-opinion-2/. *See also* Michael Ramsey, *Declaring War and Libya: A Comment on Past Practice*, Opinio Juris, March 25, 2011, at http://opiniojuris.org/2011/03/25/declaring-war-and-libya-a-comment-on-past-practice (arguing that "there have not been all that many instances of Presidents unambiguously beginning military conflicts in the last 50 years (as opposed to sort-of-plausibly claiming to be responding to attacks or making deployments not involving actual hostilities) [and] most of those instances have been strongly contested by members of Congress and legal commentators"). Who is right as a legal matter? Does it matter who is right if the President uses force, Congress as an institution does nothing in response, and the courts decline to get involved? For additional discussion of how historical practice can inform understandings of presidential and congressional power, including with respect to the initiation of war, see Curtis A. Bradley & Trevor W. Morrison, *Historical Gloss and the Separation of Powers*, 126 Harv. L. Rev. 411 (2012).

15. Before the Trump Administration's airstrikes against Syria in 2017 and 2018, the Obama Administration had contemplated using force against Syria in response to its use of chemical weapons. In August 2012, early in the Syria conflict, President Obama announced that the use of chemical weapons by the Assad regime in Syria in its civil war would involve crossing a "red line" that would carry "enormous consequences." A year later, when it appeared that the regime had crossed that line by using sarin gas against a rebel-held suburb of Damascus, Obama began preparing a military response. At that point, it appeared that he would act without seeking authorization from Congress. Abruptly, however, he changed course and said that he would first seek congressional approval. This was a risky move, because it was far from clear that Congress would provide such authorization. Obama explained his decision as follows:

> [H]aving made my decision as Commander-in-Chief based on what I am convinced is our national security interests, I'm also mindful that I'm the President of the world's oldest constitutional democracy. I've long believed that our power is rooted not just in our military might, but in our example as a government of the people, by the people, and for the people. And that's why I've made a second decision: I will seek authorization for the use of force from the American people's representatives in Congress. . . .
>
> [W]hile I believe I have the authority to carry out this military action without specific congressional authorization, I know that the country will be stronger if we take this course, and our actions will be even more effective.

White House, *Statement by the President on Syria* (Aug. 31, 2013), *at* https://obamawhitehouse.archives.gov/the-press-office/2013/08/31/statement-president-syria. The issue of whether Congress would approve the use of force quickly became moot in light of a diplomatic resolution of the chemical weapons issue, facilitated by Russia.

Why did President Obama seek congressional authorization if he had concluded that he had the unilateral constitutional power to use force? He stated that "the country will be stronger if we take this course, and our actions will be even more effective," but what if Congress had denied him authorization? Would a congressional failure to authorize force after the President had sought it mean that Congress had disapproved the use of force? In other words, would a presidential invasion of Syria following a failure of congressional authorization be analyzed through the lens of the second category of Justice Jackson's framework in *Youngstown*, or the third category?

16. The Trump Administration's intervention in Syria was not a response to an actual or threatened attack on the United States, and it did not involve the protection of the lives or property of U.S. citizens. The intervention was designed, rather, "to degrade the Syrian military's ability to conduct further chemical weapons attacks and to dissuade the Syrian regime from using or proliferating chemical weapons, thereby promoting the stability of the region and averting a worsening of the region's current humanitarian catastrophe," as President Trump noted. Is this a legitimate basis for the President to use force without congressional authorization? The OLC opinion identified three "important national interests" that it claimed justified this particular use of military force: the promotion of regional stability, the prevention of a worsening of the region's humanitarian catastrophe, and the deterrence of the use and proliferation of chemical weapons. Are these the types of interests that warrant unilateral presidential uses of force? Can you imagine a plausible presidential use of force that would not implicate the first interest? As for the second interest, what is the connection between a humanitarian catastrophe in the Middle East and the national security of the United States? Humanitarian catastrophes are relatively common phenomena around the world. Would a President be able to rely on that interest, standing alone, as a justification for military intervention? Have we reached a point where, under the Executive Branch view of the law, Article II imposes no appreciable limits on relatively small-scale unilateral presidential uses of force in any plausible instance in which the President would want to use such force?

In the Libya intervention, the Security Council authorized member states to use force to protect civilians. In its Libya opinion, OLC concluded that "supporting the [Security Council]'s credibility and effectiveness" constituted one of the "national interests" that provided a sufficient basis for the President's action. In contrast, the Syrian intervention lacked U.N. Security Council authorization, and arguably violated the U.N. Charter. Does the absence of Security Council authorization for the Syrian strikes undermine presidential power under the OLC analysis because using force in possible violation of the U.N. Charter would harm rather than preserve the credibility and effectiveness of the Security Council?

More generally, why is an assessment of whether a military operation serves U.S. national interests part of the analysis of whether the President has the unilateral constitutional authority to conduct the operation? When deciding to use military force, won't presidents always believe that such use will serve U.S. national interests? Is the Office of Legal Counsel suggesting that it can second-guess the President's evaluation of the national interests? Or will it instead always defer to the President on this issue? For a discussion of how OLC's use of the "national interests" limitation has evolved over time and an argument that the limitation provides few meaningful constraints, see Curtis Bradley & Jack Goldsmith, *OLC's Meaningless "National Interests" Test for the Legality of Presidential Uses of Force*, Lawfare (June 5, 2018).

17. The OLC opinion for Syria acknowledges that "a planned military engagement that constitutes a 'war' within the meaning of the Declaration of War Clause may require prior congressional authorization." But, it concludes that such prior congressional authorization is generally necessary only for "prolonged and substantial military engagements, typically involving exposure of U.S. military personnel to significant risk over a substantial period." What is the OLC opinion's evidence for this interpretation of the War Declaration Clause? Is it based on, or consistent with, the original understanding? Is it based on a reading of historical practice? Wasn't the Korean War a "prolonged and substantial" military engagement? If that lengthy and bloody conflict did not require congressional authorization, what type of military intervention does? Does the OLC opinion for Syria suggest that if a war intended to be limited morphs into something more extensive in duration and scope, the Constitution requires the President to seek Congress's approval?

18. For commentary on the legality of the April 2017 Syria strike under domestic law, see Jack Goldsmith, *The Constitutionality of the Syria Strike Through the Eyes of OLC (and the Obama Administration)*, Lawfare (Apr. 7, 2016); Harold Koh, *Not Illegal: But Now the Hard Part Begins,* Just Security (Apr. 7, 2017); Marty Lederman, *Why the Strikes Against Syria Probably Violate the U.N. Charter and (therefore) the U.S. Constitution,* Just Security (Apr. 6, 2017); Charlie Savage, *Was Trump's Syria Strike Illegal? Explaining Presidential War Powers*, N.Y. Times (Apr. 7, 2017). For analysis of the strikes' international legality, see Ashley Deeks, *How Does the Syrian Situation Stack up to the "Factors" that Justified Intervention in Kosovo?*, Lawfare (Apr. 7, 2017); Charlie Dunlap, *Yes, the Attack on Syria was Justifiable, and International Law Will Benefit from It*, Lawfare (Apr. 7, 2017).

For analyses of the 2018 Syria strikes and the OLC opinion, see Curtis Bradley & Jack Goldsmith, *OLC's Meaningless "National Interests" Test for the Legality of Presidential Uses of Force*, Lawfare (June 5, 2018); Jack Goldsmith, *The New OLC Opinion on Syria Brings Obama Legal Rationales Out of the Shadows*, Lawfare (June 1, 2018); Deborah Pearlstein, *One More Thing About That New OLC Opinion on Syria*, Balkinization (June 4, 2018); Steve Vladeck, *OLC's Formal (and Remarkably Broad) Defense of the April Syria Strikes*, Just Security (June 1, 2018); Keith E. Whittington, *R.I.P. Congressional War Power*, Lawfare (April 20, 2018).

C. CONGRESS'S AUTHORITY TO REGULATE THE PRESIDENT'S USE OF FORCE

This section considers Congress's ability to regulate the President's use of force, with a particular focus on the War Powers Resolution. As shown in Sections A and B, Congress and the President both have a variety of war-related powers. In the absence of congressional restriction, presidents can exercise any powers they have that are derived from the Constitution. This is true even when their constitutional powers overlap with those of Congress. It is generally accepted, however, that the President is obligated to comply with congressional restrictions when a matter falls within Congress's and the President's *concurrent* authority. Only when a matter falls within the President's *exclusive* authority is it immune from congressional regulation. As Justice Jackson noted in *Youngstown*, "[w]hen the President takes measures incompatible with the expressed or implied will of Congress, his power is at its lowest ebb, for then he can rely only upon his own constitutional powers minus any constitutional powers of Congress over the matter."

Little v. Barreme

6 U.S. 170 (1804)

[In February 1799, in the midst of the undeclared war with France, Congress passed a "non-intercourse" statute prohibiting trade with France. Section 1 of the statute prohibited vessels "owned, hired, or employed, wholly or in part, by any person resident within the United States, and which shall depart therefrom" from traveling to "any port or place within the territory of the French republic, or the dependencies thereof, or to any place in the West Indies, or elsewhere under the acknowledged government of France." Vessels violating this law were "liable to be seized, and may be prosecuted and condemned, in any circuit or district court of the United States, which shall be holden within or for the district where the seizure shall be made." Section 5 of the statute provided that the President had the authority to direct the commanders of public armed ships of the United States to "stop and examine any ship or vessel of the United States on the high seas, which there may be reason to suspect to be engaged in any traffic or commerce contrary to the true tenor thereof; and if, upon examination, it shall appear that such ship or vessel is bound or sailing to any port or place within the territory of the French republic, or her dependencies, contrary to the intent of this act, it shall be the duty of the commander of such public armed vessel to seize every such ship or vessel engaged in such illicit commerce. . . ."]

MARSHALL, CHIEF JUSTICE . . . delivered the opinion of the Court.

The *Flying-Fish*, a Danish vessel having on board Danish and neutral property, was captured on the 2d of December 1799, on a voyage from Jeremie to St. Thomas's, by the United States frigate *Boston*, commanded by Captain Little, and brought into the port of Boston, where she was libelled as an American vessel that had violated the nonintercourse law.

The judge before whom the cause was tried, directed a restoration of the vessel and cargo as neutral property, but refused to award damages for the capture and detention, because in his opinion, there was probable cause to suspect the vessel to be American.

On an appeal to the circuit court this sentence was reversed, because the *Flying-Fish* was on a voyage from, not to, a French port, and was therefore, had she even been an American vessel, not liable to capture on the high seas. . . .

It is by no means clear that the president of the United States whose high duty it is to "take care that the laws be faithfully executed," and who is commander in chief of the armies and navies of the United States, might not, without any special authority for that purpose, in the then existing state of things, have empowered the officers commanding the armed vessels of the United States, to seize and send into port for adjudication, American vessels which were forfeited by being engaged in this illicit commerce. But when it is observed that the general clause of the first section of the "act, which declares that such vessels may be seized, and may be prosecuted in any district or circuit court, which shall be holden within or for the district where the seizure shall be made," obviously contemplates a seizure within the United States; and that the 5th section gives a special authority to seize on the high seas, and limits that authority to the seizure of vessels bound or sailing to a French port, the legislature seem to have prescribed that the manner in which this law shall be carried into execution, was to exclude a seizure of any vessel not bound to a French port. Of consequence, however strong the circumstances might be, which induced captain Little to suspect the *Flying-Fish* to be an American vessel, they could not excuse the detention of her, since he would not have been authorised to detain her had she been really American.

It was so obvious, that if only vessels sailing to a French port could be seized on the high seas, that the law would be very often evaded, that this act of congress appears to have received a different construction from the executive of the United States; a construction much better calculated to give it effect.

A copy of this act was transmitted by the secretary of the navy, to the captains of the armed vessels, who were ordered to consider the 5th section as a part of their instructions. The same letter contained the following clause.

> A proper discharge of the important duties enjoined on you, arising out of this act, will require the exercise of a sound and an impartial judgment. You are not only to do all that in you lies, to prevent all intercourse, whether direct or circuitous, between the ports of the United States, and those of France or her dependencies, where the vessels are apparently as well as really American, and protected by American papers only, but you are to be vigilant that vessels or cargoes really American, but covered by Danish or other foreign papers, and bound to or from French ports, do not escape you.

These orders given by the executive under the construction of the act of Congress made by the department to which its execution was assigned, enjoin the seizure of American vessels sailing from a French port. Is the officer who obeys them liable for damages sustained by this misconstruction of the act, or will his orders excuse him? If his instructions afford him no protection, then the law must take its course, and he must pay such damages as are legally awarded against him; if they excuse an act not otherwise excusable, it would then be necessary to inquire whether this is a case in which the probable cause which existed to induce a suspicion that the vessel was American, would excuse the captor from damages when the vessel appeared in fact to be neutral.

I confess the first bias of my mind was very strong in favour of the opinion that though the instructions of the executive could not give a right, they might yet excuse from damages. I was much inclined to think that a distinction ought to be taken between acts of civil and those of military officers; and between proceedings within the body of the country and those on the high seas. That implicit obedience which military men usually pay to the orders of their superiors, which indeed is indispensably necessary to every military system, appeared to me strongly to imply the principle that those orders, if not to perform a prohibited act, ought to justify the person whose general duty it is to obey them, and who is placed by the laws of his country in a situation which in general requires that he should obey them. I was strongly inclined to think that where, in consequence of orders from the legitimate authority, a vessel is seized with pure intention, the claim of the injured party for damages would be against that government from which the orders proceeded, and would be a proper subject for negotiation. But I have been convinced that I was mistaken, and I have receded from this first opinion. I acquiesce in that of my brethren, which is, that the instructions cannot change the nature of the transaction, or legalize an act which without those instructions would have been a plain trespass.

It becomes therefore unnecessary to inquire whether the probable cause afforded by the conduct of the *Flying-Fish* to suspect her of being an American, would excuse Captain Little from damages for having seized and sent her into port, since had she actually been an American, the seizure would have been unlawful.

Captain Little then must be answerable in damages to the owner of this neutral vessel.*

War Powers Resolution

Pub. L. No. 93-148, 87 Stat. 555 (1973), 50 U.S.C. §§1541-1548

PURPOSE AND POLICY

Sec. 2. (a) It is the purpose of this joint resolution to fulfill the intent of the framers of the Constitution of the United States and insure that the collective judgment of both the Congress and the President will apply to the introduction of United States Armed Forces into hostilities, or into situations where imminent involvement in hostilities is clearly indicated by the circumstances, and to the continued use of such forces in hostilities or in such situations. . . .

(c) The constitutional powers of the President as Commander-in-Chief to introduce United States Armed Forces into hostilities, or into situations where imminent involvement in hostilities is clearly indicated by the circumstances, are exercised only pursuant to (1) a declaration of war, (2) specific statutory authorization, or (3) a national emergency created by attack upon the United States, its territories or possessions, or its armed forces.

CONSULTATION

Sec. 3. The President in every possible instance shall consult with Congress before introducing United States Armed Forces into hostilities or into situations where imminent involvement in hostilities is clearly indicated by the circumstances, and after every such introduction shall consult regularly with the Congress until United States Armed Forces are no longer engaged in hostilities or have been removed from such situations.

REPORTING REQUIREMENT

Sec. 4. (a) In the absence of a declaration of war, in any case in which United States Armed Forces are introduced—

(1) into hostilities or into situations where imminent involvement in hostilities is clearly indicated by the circumstances;

(2) into the territory, airspace or waters of a foreign nation, while equipped for combat, except for deployments which relate solely to supply, replacement, repair, or training of such forces; or

(3) in numbers which substantially enlarge United States Armed Forces equipped for combat already located in a foreign nation; the President shall submit within 48 hours to the Speaker of the House of Representatives and to the President pro tempore of the Senate a report, in writing, setting forth —

(A) the circumstances necessitating the introduction of United States Armed Forces;

---

* [Congress subsequently indemnified Captain Little for the damage award. *See* James E. Pfander & Jonathan L. Hunt, *Public Wrongs and Private Bills: Indemnification and Government Accountability in the Early Republic*, 85 N.Y.U. L. Rev. 1862, 1878 (2010). — EDS.]

(B) the constitutional and legislative authority under which such introduction took place; and

(C) the estimated scope and duration of the hostilities or involvement. . . .

(c) Whenever United States Armed Forces are introduced into hostilities or into any situation described in subsection (a) of this section, the President shall, so long as such armed forces continue to be engaged in such hostilities or situation, report to the Congress periodically on the status of such hostilities or situation as well as on the scope and duration of such hostilities or situation, but in no event shall he report to the Congress less often than once every six months.

CONGRESSIONAL ACTION

Sec. 5. . . . (b) Within sixty calendar days after a report is submitted or is required to be submitted pursuant to section 4(a)(1), whichever is earlier, the President shall terminate any use of United States Armed Forces with respect to which such report was submitted (or required to be submitted), unless the Congress (1) has declared war or has enacted a specific authorization for such use of United States Armed Forces, (2) has extended by law such sixty-day period, or (3) is physically unable to meet as a result of an armed attack upon the United States. Such sixty-day period shall be extended for not more than an additional thirty days if the President determines and certifies to the Congress in writing that unavoidable military necessity respecting the safety of United States Armed Forces requires the continued use of such armed forces in the course of bringing about a prompt removal of such forces.

(c) Notwithstanding subsection (b), at any time that United States Armed Forces are engaged in hostilities outside the territory of the United States, its possessions or territories without a declaration of war or specific statutory authorization, such forces shall be removed by the President if the Congress so directs by concurrent resolution. . . .

INTERPRETATION OF JOINT RESOLUTION

Sec. 8. (a) Authority to introduce United States Armed Forces into hostilities or into situations wherein involvement in hostilities is clearly indicated by the circumstances shall not be inferred —

(1) from any provision of law (whether or not in effect before the date of the enactment of this joint resolution), including any provision contained in any appropriation Act, unless such provision specifically authorizes the introduction of United States Armed Forces into hostilities or into such situations and states that it is intended to constitute specific statutory authorization within the meaning of this joint resolution; or

(2) from any treaty heretofore or hereafter ratified unless such treaty is implemented by legislation specifically authorizing the introduction of United States Armed Forces into hostilities or into such situations and stating that it is intended to constitute specific statutory authorization within the meaning of this joint resolution. . . .

(d) Nothing in this joint resolution —

(1) is intended to alter the constitutional authority of the Congress or of the President, or the provision of existing treaties; or (2) shall be construed as granting any authority to the President with respect to the introduction of United States Armed Forces into hostilities or into situations wherein involvement in hostilities is clearly indicated by the circumstances which authority he would not have had in the absence of this joint resolution.

War Crimes Act of 1996 (as amended)

18 U.S.C. §2441

(a) Offense. Whoever, whether inside or outside the United States, commits a war crime, in any of the circumstances described in subsection (b), shall be fined under this title or imprisoned for life or any term of years, or both, and if death results to the victim, shall also be subject to the penalty of death.

(b) Circumstances. The circumstances referred to in subsection (a) are that the person committing such breach or the victim of such war crime is a member of the Armed Forces of the United States or a national of the United States (as defined in section 101 of the Immigration and Nationality Act).

(c) Definition. As used in this section, the term "war crime" means any conduct —

(1) defined as a grave breach in any of the international conventions signed at Geneva 12 August 1949, or any protocol to such convention to which the United States is a party;

(2) prohibited by Article 23, 25, 27, or 28 of the Annex to the Hague Convention IV, Respecting the Laws and Customs of War on Land, signed 18 October 1907;

(3) which constitutes a grave breach of common Article 3 (as defined in subsection (d)) when committed in the context of and in association with an armed conflict not of an international character; or

(4) of a person who, in relation to an armed conflict and contrary to the provisions of the Protocol on Prohibitions or Restrictions on the Use of Mines, Booby-Traps and Other Devices as amended at Geneva on 3 May 1996 (Protocol II as amended on 3 May 1996), when the United States is a party to such Protocol, willfully kills or causes serious injury to civilians.

(d) Common Article 3 violations.

(1) Prohibited conduct. In subsection (c)(3), the term "grave breach of common Article 3" means any conduct (such conduct constituting a grave breach of common Article 3 of the international conventions done at Geneva August 12, 1949), as follows:

(A) Torture. The act of a person who commits, or conspires or attempts to commit, an act specifically intended to inflict severe physical or mental pain or suffering (other than pain or suffering incidental to lawful sanctions) upon another person within his custody or physical control for the purpose of obtaining information or a confession, punishment, intimidation, coercion, or any reason based on discrimination of any kind.

(B) Cruel or inhuman treatment. The act of a person who commits, or conspires or attempts to commit, an act intended to inflict severe or serious physical or mental pain or suffering (other than pain or suffering incidental to lawful sanctions), including serious physical abuse, upon another within his custody or control.

(C) Performing biological experiments. The act of a person who subjects, or conspires or attempts to subject, one or more persons within his custody or physical control to biological experiments without a legitimate medical or dental purpose and in so doing endangers the body or health of such person or persons.

(D) Murder. The act of a person who intentionally kills, or conspires or attempts to kill, or kills whether intentionally or unintentionally in the course of committing any other offense under this subsection, one or more persons taking no active part in the hostilities, including those placed out of combat by sickness, wounds, detention, or any other cause.

(E) Mutilation or maiming. The act of a person who intentionally injures, or conspires or attempts to injure, or injures whether intentionally or unintentionally in the course of committing any other offense under this subsection, one or more persons taking no active part in the hostilities, including those placed out of combat by sickness, wounds, detention, or any other cause, by disfiguring the person or persons by any mutilation thereof or by permanently disabling any member, limb, or organ of his body, without any legitimate medical or dental purpose.

(F) Intentionally causing serious bodily injury. The act of a person who intentionally causes, or conspires or attempts to cause, serious bodily injury to one or more persons, including lawful combatants, in violation of the law of war.

(G) Rape. The act of a person who forcibly or with coercion or threat of force wrongfully invades, or conspires or attempts to invade, the body of a person by penetrating, however slightly, the anal or genital opening of the victim with any part of the body of the accused, or with any foreign object.

(H) Sexual assault or abuse. The act of a person who forcibly or with coercion or threat of force engages, or conspires or attempts to engage, in sexual contact with one or more persons, or causes, or conspires or attempts to cause, one or more persons to engage in sexual contact.

(I) Taking hostages. The act of a person who, having knowingly seized or detained one or more persons, threatens to kill, injure, or continue to detain such person or persons with the intent of compelling any nation, person other than the hostage, or group of persons to act or refrain from acting as an explicit or implicit condition for the safety or release of such person or persons.

Memorandum from Walter Dellinger, Assistant Attorney General, Office of Legal Counsel, to Alan J. Kreczko, Special Assistant to the President and Legal Adviser to the National Security Council, "Placing of United States Armed Forces Under United Nations Operational or Tactical Control"

At https://www.justice.gov/sites/default/files/olc/opinions/1996/05/31/op-olc-v020-p0182.pdf (May 8, 1996)

This memorandum responds to your request for our views as to the constitutionality of H.R. 3308, a bill that would limit the President's ability to place United States armed forces under the United Nations' ("U.N.") operational or tactical control.

Section 3 of H.R. 3308 would add a new section 405 to chapter 20 of title 10, United States Code, to read as follows:

> Except as provided in subsection (b) and (c), funds appropriated or otherwise made available for the Department of Defense may not be obligated or expended for activities of any element of the armed forces that after the date of the enactment of this section is placed under United Nations operational or tactical control, as defined in subsection (f).

Proposed subsection 405(f) provides that elements of the armed forces shall be considered to be placed under U.N. operational or tactical control if they are under the operational or tactical control of an individual who is acting on behalf of the U.N. in a peacekeeping, peacemaking or similar activity, and if the senior military commander of the U.N. force or operation is either a foreign national or a U.S. citizen other than an active duty U.S. military officer.

Proposed section 405 thus bars the President from placing U.S. armed forces participating in U.N. peacekeeping operations under the U.N. operational or tactical control, as so defined.

Two subsections set out exceptions to the prohibition. Subsection 405(c) provides that the limitation does not apply if Congress specifically authorizes a particular placement of U.S. forces under U.N. operational or tactical control, or if the U.S. forces involved in a placement are participating in operations conducted by the North Atlantic Treaty Organization.

Subsections 405(b) and (d) together provide that the President may waive the limitation if he certifies to Congress 15 days in advance of the placement that it is "in the national security interests of the United States to place any element of the armed forces under United Nations operational of tactical control," and provides a detailed report setting forth specific items of information within eleven distinct categories. If the President certifies that an "emergency" precluded compliance with the 15 day limitation, he must make the required certification and report in a timely manner, but no later than 48 hours after a covered operational or tactical control is initiated.

The proposed amendment unconstitutionally constrains the President's exercise of his constitutional authority as Commander-in-Chief. Further, it undermines his constitutional role as the United States' representative in foreign relations. . . .

Article II, §2, of the Constitution declares that the *President* "shall be Commander in Chief of the Army and Navy of the United States." Whatever the scope of this authority in other contexts, there can be no room to doubt that the Commander-in-Chief Clause commits to the President alone the power to select the particular personnel who are to exercise tactical and operational control over U.S. forces. *See* Fleming v. Page, 50 U.S. (9 How.) 603, 615 (1850) ("As commander-in-chief, [the President] is authorized to direct the movements of the naval and military forces placed by law at his command, and to employ them in the manner he may deem most effectual. . . ."). Indeed, the major object of the Clause is to "vest in the President the supreme command over all the military forces, — such supreme and undivided command as would be necessary to the prosecution of a successful war." United States v. Sweeny, 157 U.S. 281, 284 (1895). . . .

It is for the President alone, as Commander-in-Chief, to make the choice of the particular personnel who are to exercise operational and tactical command functions over the U.S. Armed Forces. True, Congress has the power to lay down general rules creating and regulating "the framework of the Military Establishment," Chappell v. Wallace, 462 U.S. 296, 301 (1983); but such framework rules may not unduly constrain or inhibit the President's authority to make and to implement the decisions that he deems necessary or advisable for the successful conduct of military missions in the field, including the choice of particular persons to perform specific command functions in those missions. . . . In the present context, the President may determine that the purposes of a particular U.N. operation in which U.S. Armed Forces participate would be best served if those forces were placed under the operational or tactical control of an agent of the U.N., as well as under a U.N. senior military commander who was a foreign national (or a U.S. national who is not an active duty military officer). Congress may not prevent the President from acting on such a military judgment concerning the choice of the commanders under whom the U.S. forces engaged in the mission are to serve.

Moreover, in seeking to impair the President's ability to deploy U.S. Armed Forces under U.N. operational and tactical command in U.N. operations in which the United States may otherwise lawfully participate, Congress is impermissibly undermining the President's constitutional authority with respect to the conduct of diplomacy. . . . U.N. peacekeeping missions involve multilateral arrangements that require delicate and complex accommodations of a variety of interests and concerns, including those of the nations that provide troops or resources, and those of the nation or nations in which the operation takes place. The success of the mission may depend, to a considerable extent, on the nationality of the commanding officers, or on the degree to which the operation is perceived as a *U.N.* activity (rather than that of a single nation or bloc of nations). Given that the United States may lawfully participate in such U.N. operations, we believe that Congress would be acting unconstitutionally if it were to tie the President's hands in negotiating agreements with respect to command structures for those operations.

It might be argued that section 405 does not impose a significant constraint on the President's constitutional authority because it grants the President the authority to waive the prohibition whenever he deems it in the "national security interest" of the United States to do so, provided he reports his decision to execute a waiver to Congress 15 days in advance. If he certifies that an emergency is present, he may avoid the 15 day limitation and make a report in a timely manner, but no later than 48 hours after troops are placed under U.N. command. Thus, functionally, section 405 effects only a conditional ban on the President's constitutional authority to control the tactical and operational deployment of U.S. forces. Congress cannot, however, burden or infringe the President's exercise of a core constitutional power by attaching conditions precedent to the exercise of that power. . . .

We are mindful that Congress has framed its restriction on placing troops under U.N. control as a prohibition on the obligation or expenditure of appropriated funds. That Congress has chosen to invade the President's authority indirectly, through a condition on an appropriation, rather than through a direct mandate, is immaterial. Broad as Congress' spending power undoubtedly is, it is clear that Congress may not deploy it to accomplish unconstitutional ends. . . .

Memorandum from Randolph D. Moss, Assistant Attorney General, to the Attorney General, "Authorization for Continuing Hostilities in Kosovo"

At https://www.justice.gov/sites/default/files/olc/opinions/2000/12/31/op-olc-v024-p0327.pdf (Dec. 19, 2000)

[On March 24, 1999, President Clinton announced the commencement of NATO air and cruise missile attacks against armed forces of Serbia in response to human rights abuses committed in Kosovo. Two days later, he submitted to Congress a report, "consistent with the War Powers Resolution," that explained the circumstances for the use of armed forces and the expected scope and duration of the action. He further explained that he had "taken these actions pursuant to [his] authority . . . as Commander in Chief and Chief Executive." On April 28, the House of Representatives voted on four resolutions related to the conflict. It defeated a proposed declaration of war against Serbia as well as a concurrent resolution directing the President to terminate the use of armed forces within 30 days. It also voted to block funding for ground troops without additional specific authorization from Congress. Finally, it defeated by a tie 213-213 vote a concurrent resolution stating that the President "is authorized to conduct military air operations and missile strikes" against Serbia. On May 21, however, the President signed into law a supplemental appropriations bill passed by Congress that funded continuing hostilities relating to Kosovo. Four days later, on May 25, the 60-day period set forth in §5(b) of the War Powers Resolution expired. The conflict subsequently ended on June 10, with Serbia's agreement to withdraw its forces from Kosovo and allow deployment of a NATO-led peacekeeping force.]

This Memorandum memorializes and explains advice we provided to you in May of 1999 regarding whether . . . the emergency supplemental appropriation for military operations in Kosovo constituted authorization for continuing hostilities after the expiration of sixty days under section 5(b) of the War Powers Resolution (the "WPR"). This Office advised that the appropriation did constitute such authorization. . . .

The Supreme Court has recognized that, as a general matter, appropriation statutes may "stand[] as confirmation and ratification of the action of the Chief Executive." Fleming v. Mohawk Wrecking & Lumber Co., 331 U.S. 111, 116 (1947). Congress may also "amend substantive law in an appropriations statute, as long as it does so clearly." Robertson v. Seattle Audubon Soc., 503 U.S. 429, 440 (1992). . . .

The notion that Congress can authorize hostilities through appropriation laws follows directly from this general principle. As Ely explains:

> Throughout the course of the [Vietnam] war, hundreds of billions of dollars were appropriated to support it, and the draft was repeatedly extended. Supporters understandably cited these measures as further congressional authorization.
>
> The law generally pertaining to authorization by appropriation is about what first-order common sense suggests it should be. If there is no reason to infer that Congress knew what the agency or program in question was about, the fact that it was buried in an appropriations measure is typically not taken to constitute authorization of it. If the program was conspicuous, it is. Indeed, assuming sufficient notice of what was going on, appropriations may in some ways constitute unusual evidence of approval, in that typically Congress acts twice — once to authorize the expenditure and again to appropriate the money.

[John Hart Ely, War and Responsibility 27 (1993).] Indeed, Congress has on numerous occasions authorized U.S. involvement in armed conflict at least in part through appropriation laws. . . .

Section 5(b) of the WPR permits continuation of hostilities when a congressional enactment represents "specific authorization for such use of United States Armed Forces." As has been discussed, courts, government officials, and scholars have repeatedly (although not uniformly) recognized that appropriation statutes may constitute authorization for conflict. Thus, if the WPR did not provide any further interpretive gloss on the question, it would appear that an appropriation statute — if enacted for the purpose of continuing hostilities — would be "specific authorization." Section 8(a) of the WPR, however, provides that authority "shall not be inferred . . . from any provision of law . . . including any provision contained in any appropriations Act, unless such provision specifically authorizes the introduction of United States Armed Forces into hostilities or into such situations and states that it is intended to constitute specific statutory authorization within the meaning of this chapter." In assessing whether an appropriation statute can constitute authorization, the critical question thus becomes how to understand section 8(a)(1). . . .

To the extent [an] interpretation [of section 8(a)(1)] would take from Congress a constitutionally permissible method of authorizing war, it runs afoul of the axiom that one Congress cannot bind a later Congress. *See, e.g.*, Marbury v. Madison, 5 U.S. (1 Cranch) 137, 177 (1803) (noting that, in contrast to a constitution, legislative acts are "alterable when the legislature shall please to alter [them]"). . . .

Applying this general principle to the issue of section 8(a)(1)'s constitutionality, Professor Philip Bobbitt has argued that, were section 8(a)(1) read to bind subsequent Congresses, it would be unconstitutional:

> [F]ramework statutes — like Gramm-Rudman, for example — cannot bind future Congresses. If Congress can constitutionally authorize the use of force through its appropriations and authorization procedures, an interpretive statute that denies this inference — as does . . . the original War Powers Resolution — is without legal effect. On the other hand, if one Congress could bind subsequent Congresses in this way, it would effectively enshrine itself in defiance of [an] electoral mandate. Imagine, for example, a statute that provided that no appropriations or authorization provision shall exceed a term of six months or an act that forbade the President from interpreting any subsequent statute as permitting him to issue regulations to enforce that statute unless specifically authorized to do so therein. A rule of interpretation, if it contravenes a valid constitutional power — in this case, . . . that a subsequent Congress could constitutionally endorse a war by an appropriations and authorization statute — would amount to a restriction on the ability of a Congress to repeal by inference preexisting law. Such a fresh hurdle to later legislation is nowhere authorized by the Constitution and is inconsistent with the notion of legitimacy derived through the mandate of each new Congress.

[Philip Bobbitt, *War Powers: An Essay on John Hart Ely's War and Responsibility: Constitutional Lessons of Vietnam and Its Aftermath*, 92 Mich. L. Rev. 1364, 1399 (1994).]

This argument is compelling. If section 8(a)(1) were read to block all possibility of inferring congressional approval of military action from any appropriation, unless that appropriation referred in terms to the WPR and stated that it was intended to constitute specific authority for the action under that statute, then it would be unconstitutional. As discussed in the previous section, under the Constitution, Congress can authorize or ratify presidential engagement in hostilities through an appropriation law. One statute, such as the WPR, cannot mandate that certain types of appropriation statutes that would otherwise constitute authorization for conflict cannot do so simply because a subsequent Congress does not use certain "magical passwords." Marcello v. Bonds, 349 U.S. 302, 310 (1955) (holding that detailed procedures established by the Immigration and Naturalization Act applied despite discrepancies between that Act and the Administrative Procedure Act ("APA") and despite the fact that the APA provided that exemptions from its requirements must be expressly indicated). . . .

In order to avoid this constitutional problem, we do not interpret section 8(a)(1) as binding future Congresses but instead as having the effect of establishing a background principle against which Congress legislates. In our view, section 8(a)(1) continues to have operative legal effect, but only so far as it operates to inform how an executive or judicial branch actor should interpret the intent of subsequent Congresses that enact appropriation statutes that do not specifically reference the WPR. On the question whether an appropriation statute enacted by a subsequent Congress constitutes authorization for continued hostilities, it is the intent of the subsequent Congress, as evidenced by the text and legislative history of the appropriation statute, that controls the analysis. The existence of section 8(a)(1) might affect this analysis. If the appropriation statute is entirely ambiguous as to whether it constitutes authorization for continuing hostilities, for example, it might be proper for a judicial or executive branch actor to conclude that, because the subsequent Congress was aware of the background principle established by section 8(a)(1), its failure to refer specifically back to the WPR evidences an intent not to authorize continuing hostilities. If, however, Congress, in enacting an appropriation statute, demonstrates a clear intent to authorize continuing hostilities, then it would be appropriate to conclude that the appropriation statute does authorize those hostilities, even though the statute does not specifically refer back to the WPR. Under these circumstances, the appropriation statute would supersede or work an implied partial repeal of section 8(a)(1). In other words, section 8(a)(1) establishes procedural requirements that, under the statute, Congress must follow to authorize hostilities; nonetheless, a subsequent Congress remains free to choose in a particular instance to enact legislation that clearly authorizes hostilities and, in so doing, it can decide not to follow the WPR's procedures. . . .

The determination of whether any particular appropriation statute that does not refer back to the WPR constitutes authorization for continuing hostilities will necessarily depend on the facts of each case. Certain types of evidence will be highly probative of an intent to authorize ongoing military operations. For example, evidence demonstrating that Congress was concerned with funding a specific military effort, as opposed to making general defense appropriations, would tend to show such an intention. Likewise, in a case where the President has requested an appropriation in order to continue military operations, evidence showing that Members of Congress were specifically aware of the purposes of the appropriation request will tend to show that Congress intended to authorize continuing military operations as required by the WPR. Finally, if Congress appropriates funds only for protection of troops already committed or prohibits the use of appropriated funds for the introduction of new troops, a presumption might arise that Congress did not intend to authorize continuing hostilities but instead intended simply to protect troops already on the ground. On the other hand, unlimited appropriations would tend to suggest an intent to authorize continuing hostilities. In short, where Congress, in passing an appropriations bill, clearly intends to authorize conflict, the WPR cannot be read to deny legal effect to that clear intent. . . .

[The opinion goes on to conclude that in passing the supplemental appropriations bill, "Congress clearly intended to authorize continuing military operations in Kosovo."]

Testimony by Legal Adviser Harold Hongju Koh, U.S. Department of State, on Libya and War Powers, Before Senate Foreign Relations Committee

At http://2009-2017.state.gov/s/l/releases/remarks/167250.htm (June 28, 2011)

[Recall from Section B that on March 19, 2011, the United States, in conjunction with other countries, began to launch air strikes in Libya to enforce U.N. Security Council Resolution 1973. On March 21, 2011, President Obama sent a letter to Congress, "consistent with the War Powers Resolution," informing it of the Libya action. On April 4, 2011, U.S. forces transferred responsibility for leading and conducting the mission to NATO. The United States continued to supply approximately 75 percent of NATO's intelligence, logistical, and refueling support for the Libya mission, and continued air strikes from its fighter planes and unmanned aerial vehicles (or "drones") on an intermittent basis. On May 20, 2011, 60 days after the Libya operation began, the United States was still providing intelligence and logistical assistance to NATO and still firing missiles at Libyan forces. On that date, President Obama wrote a new letter to Congress stating that congressional action in support of the Libya mission "would underline the U.S. commitment to this remarkable international effort" and "is also important in the context of our constitutional framework, as it would demonstrate a unity of purpose among the political branches on this important national security matter." The letter did not, however, mention the War Powers Resolution. The following testimony was given approximately 100 days after the Libya operation began, during which time Congress had not provided any authorization for the operation.]

[A] combination of four factors present in Libya suggests that the current situation does not constitute the kind of "hostilities" envisioned by the War Powers Resolution's 60-day automatic pullout provision.

First, the *mission* is limited: By Presidential design, U.S. forces are playing a constrained and supporting role in a NATO-led multinational civilian protection operation, which is implementing a U.N. Security Council Resolution tailored to that limited purpose. This is a very unusual set of circumstances, not found in any of the historic situations in which the "hostilities" question was previously debated, . . . Of course, NATO forces as a whole are more deeply engaged in Libya than are U.S. forces, but the War Powers Resolution's 60-day pullout provision was designed to address the activities of the latter.

Second, the *exposure* of our armed forces is limited: To date, our operations have not involved U.S. casualties or a threat of significant U.S. casualties. Nor do our current operations involve active exchanges of fire with hostile forces, and members of our military have not been involved in significant armed confrontations or sustained confrontations of any kind with hostile forces. . . . The Congress that adopted the War Powers Resolution was principally concerned with the safety of *U.S. forces*, and with the risk that the President would entangle them in an overseas conflict from which they could not readily be extricated. In this instance, the absence of U.S. ground troops, among other features of the Libya operation, significantly reduces both the risk to U.S. forces and the likelihood of a protracted entanglement that Congress may find itself practically powerless to end.

Third, the *risk of escalation* is limited: U.S. military operations have not involved the presence of U.S. ground troops, or any significant chance of escalation into a broader conflict characterized by a large U.S. ground presence, major casualties, sustained active combat, or expanding geographical scope. . . .

Fourth and finally, the *military means* we are using are limited: This situation does not present the kind of "full military engagement[] with which the [War Powers] Resolution is primarily concerned." (*Presidential Power to Use the Armed Forces Abroad Without Statutory Authorization*, 4A Op. O.L.C. 185, 194 (1980).) The violence that U.S. armed forces have directly inflicted or facilitated after the handoff to NATO has been modest in terms of its frequency, intensity, and severity. . . . [T]he bulk of U.S. contributions to the NATO effort has been providing intelligence capabilities and refueling assets. A very significant majority of the overall sorties are being flown by our coalition partners, and the overwhelming majority of strike sorties are being flown by our partners. American strikes have been confined, on an as-needed basis, to the suppression of enemy air defenses to enforce the no-fly zone, and to limited strikes by Predator unmanned aerial vehicles against discrete targets in support of the civilian protection mission; since the handoff to NATO, the total number of U.S. munitions dropped has been a tiny fraction of the number dropped in Kosovo. . . .

Had any of these elements been absent in Libya, or present in different degrees, a different legal conclusion might have been drawn. But the unusual confluence of these four factors, in an operation that was expressly designed to be limited — limited in mission, exposure of U.S. troops, risk of escalation, and military means employed — led the President to conclude that the Libya operation did not fall within the War Powers Resolution's automatic 60-day pullout rule.

Nor is this action inconsistent with the spirit of the Resolution. [We] are far from the core case that most Members of Congress had in mind in 1973. The Congress that passed the Resolution in that year had just been through a long, major, and searing war in Vietnam, with hundreds of thousands of boots on the ground, secret bombing campaigns, international condemnation, massive casualties, and no clear way out. In Libya, by contrast, we have been acting transparently and in close consultation with Congress for a brief period; with no casualties or ground troops; with international approval; and at the express request of and in cooperation with NATO, the Arab League, the Gulf Cooperation Council, and Libya's own Transitional National Council. We should not read into the 1973 Congress's adoption of what many have called a "No More Vietnams" resolution an intent to require the premature termination, nearly forty years later, of limited military force in support of an international coalition to prevent the resumption of atrocities in Libya. Given the limited risk of escalation, exchanges of fire, and U.S. casualties, we do not believe that the 1973 Congress intended that its Resolution be given such a rigid construction — absent a clear Congressional stance — to stop the President from directing supporting actions in a NATO-led, Security Council-authorized operation, for the narrow purpose of preventing the slaughter of innocent civilians.

Notes and Questions

1. The President has a constitutional duty to "take Care that the Laws are faithfully executed." When Congress enacts a statute that restricts presidential power, the Take Care Clause requires him to abide by the statute unless it conflicts with a higher law that the President also must execute, most notably the Constitution. It follows that congressional restrictions on presidential uses of force raise the following general questions: Does the Constitution give the President a core of exclusive military powers that Congress cannot limit? If so, what falls within those exclusive presidential powers? And who decides which presidential powers are exclusive?

2. Presidents have argued at times that they possess exclusive Commander-in-Chief authorities that are beyond Congress's power to regulate. Although it is generally accepted that some aspects of the Commander-in-Chief function are exclusive, the content of such exclusive authority remains contested. *See* Youngstown Sheet & Tube Co. v. Sawyer, 343 U.S. 579, 641 (1952) (Jackson, J., concurring) ("These cryptic words [of the Commander-in-Chief Clause] have given rise to some of the most persistent controversies in our constitutional history. Of course, they imply something more than an empty title. But just what authority goes with the name has plagued presidential advisers who would not waive or narrow it by nonassertion yet cannot say where it begins or ends."). The least controversial element of the exclusive Commander-in-Chief authority is that Congress cannot relieve the President of command of the armed force of the United States. *See id.* at 641 (noting that the Commander-in-Chief Clause "undoubtedly puts the Nation's armed forces under presidential command"). What is included within this command authority? What other Commander-in-Chief authorities should be considered exclusive? Decisions about troop movements? Enemy targets? Use of particular weapons? What materials should one look to in answering these questions?

3. In a pair of articles, Professors Barron and Lederman argue that (a) constitutional text and original understanding provide support only for an exclusive presidential power of "superintendence" over the military chain of command, not an exclusive power of managing military campaigns; (b) Congress has throughout history enacted regulations concerning the terms of battle and the conduct and composition of the armed forces; and (c) for the most part, presidential claims about a preclusive Commander-in-Chief authority that is not subject to regulation by Congress did not emerge until after World War II. *See* David J. Barron & Martin S. Lederman, *The Commander in Chief at the Lowest Ebb — Framing the Problem, Doctrine, and Original Understanding,* 121 Harv. L. Rev. 689 (2008); David J. Barron & Martin S. Lederman, *The Commander in Chief at the Lowest Ebb — A Constitutional History,* 121 Harv. L. Rev. 941 (2008). What follows from these claims? Should courts be involved in discerning the bounds of the President's exclusive Commander-in-Chief authority? Or should the determination be worked out in an evolutionary way through interactions between Congress and the President? Whether addressed in the courts or by the political branches, what influence will arguments about original understanding and historical practice likely have on determinations about the scope of the President's exclusive authority?

4. What does Little v. Barreme suggest about Congress's power to control presidential military power during wartime? Would the case have come out differently if Congress had been attempting to limit the President's power vis-à-vis an enemy ship rather than vis-à-vis a U.S. citizen engaged in commerce? What if Congress had declared war against France and authorized force without qualification except to say that the President could not fire on or seize enemy French ships found on the high seas? What does Brown v. United States, excerpted in Section A, suggest about these questions? Does the holding in *Barreme* concern the war power of the President or simply the liability of presidential subordinates? Why is the captain in *Barreme* liable for damages and the captain in *Durand* is not? Can Justice Nelson's opinion in *Durand,* excerpted in Section B, be reconciled with his dissent in *The Prize Cases*? For differing views about the significance of *Barreme,* compare Michael J. Glennon, Constitutional Diplomacy 3-8 (1991) (arguing that *Barreme* supports broad congressional authority to control the President during wartime), with J. Gregory Sidak, *The Quasi-War Cases,* 28 Harv. J.L. & Pub. Pol'y 465 (2004) (disputing that proposition).

5. As noted in Section A, Congress has the authority to "make Rules concerning Captures on Land and Water." Professor Wuerth argues that the constitutional Founders intended this "Captures Clause" to include the congressional power to authorize seizure of both public and private vessels during wartime. *See* Ingrid Wuerth, *The Captures Clause,* 76 Chi. L. Rev. 1683 (2009). Wuerth further argues that, consistent with this original design, Congress in the early years of the nation used the Captures Clause to make "important decisions about strategy and compliance with international law." She concludes that "any claim that the president, as a matter of constitutional text and history, controls all tactical decisions about how force is deployed, is put to rest by a careful reading of the Captures Clause."

6. The Vietnam War is discussed in Section A. As that war dragged on, Congress became increasingly resistant to U.S. involvement. In 1967, for example, it issued a "Statement of Congressional Policy" expressing "its support of efforts being made by the President of the United States and other men of good will throughout the world to prevent an expansion of the war in Vietnam and to bring that conflict to an end through a negotiated settlement which will preserve the honor of the United States, protect the vital interests of this country, and allow the people of South Vietnam to determine the affairs of that nation in their own way." In December 1970, it enacted the Cooper-Church Amendment to the U.S. defense appropriations bill, forbidding the use of any U.S. ground forces in Laos or Cambodia. In January 1971, it repealed the Gulf of Tonkin Resolution. The same year, it enacted the Mansfield Amendment, which provided:

> It is hereby declared to be the policy of the United States to terminate at the earliest practicable date all military operations of the United States in Indochina, and to provide for the prompt and orderly withdrawal of all United States military forces at a date certain, subject to the release of all American prisoners of war held by the Government of North Vietnam and forces allied with such Government and an accounting for all Americans missing in action who have been held by or known to such Government or such forces.

However, Congress also continued to appropriate funds for military activities in Southeast Asia, and to extend selective service statutes. Do these congressional actions, taken together, constitute a withdrawal of authorization for the war in Vietnam? *Compare* Francis D. Wormuth & Edwin B. Firmage, To Chain the Dog of War: The War Power of Congress in History and Law 231 (2d ed. 1989) (arguing that they did), *with* John Hart Ely, War and Responsibility: Constitutional Lessons of Vietnam and Its Aftermath 32-34 (1993) (arguing that they did not). What would it have taken for Congress to de-authorize the war? What practical hurdles might there have been to a more unambiguous de-authorization? What about the possibility of a presidential veto? Does it make sense that Congress would need a two-thirds majority in both Houses to de-authorize a war?

7. The War Powers Resolution was enacted in the wake of the Vietnam War and it represents Congress's boldest attempt to regulate the President's unilateral use of military force. It was enacted over the veto of President Nixon by a vote of 76 to 18 in the Senate and 284 to 135 in the House, despite Nixon's claim that it "would seriously undermine this Nation's ability to act decisively and convincingly in times of international crisis." The Resolution's basic structure is to provide Congress's interpretation of the constitutional allocation of war powers (in §2), to require the President to consult with Congress before and after engaging in hostilities abroad (§3), to require the President to report to Congress after engaging in hostilities and other military acts abroad in order to explain the basis for the President's action (§4), to require the President to remove the troops from hostilities after a specified period if Congress has not given its approval (§5(b)), and to provide interpretive clarity about the meaning of the Resolution and other federal statutes and treaties related to war (§8).

Does the War Powers Resolution meet its stated goal of "fulfill[ing] the intent of the framers of the Constitution"? To what extent does the Resolution simply express what the Constitution already requires? To what extent does it exceed what the

Constitution requires? To what extent, if at all, does it impinge upon the President's war powers?

8. Consider §2 of the War Powers Resolution. Based on what you learned in Sections A and B, is it an accurate statement of the constitutional distribution of war authority? What legal effect does this section have? If nothing else, doesn't this section complicate the notion that Congress has acquiesced or consented to a developing constitutional norm of presidential unilateralism in the initiation of war? The Executive Branch obviously does not believe that §2 exhausts the contexts in which it can use military force without congressional authorization, and it has described this section as merely an incomplete and non-binding expression of Congress's views.

9. Consider §5 of the War Powers Resolution. Is it in tension with §2? Does §5 in effect authorize the President to engage in short-term military conflicts without congressional authorization? That is how the Executive Branch has construed it:

> The WPR requires that, in the absence of a declaration of war, the President must report to Congress within 48 hours of introducing armed forces into such circumstances and must terminate the use of United States armed forces within 60 days (or 90 days, if military necessity requires additional time to effect a withdrawal) unless Congress permits otherwise. This structure makes sense only if the President may introduce troops into hostilities or potential hostilities without prior authorization by the Congress: the WPR regulates such action by the President and seeks to set limits to it. . . .
>
> The WPR was enacted against a background that was "replete with instances of presidential uses of military force abroad in the absence of prior congressional approval." While Congress obviously sought to structure and regulate such unilateral deployments, its overriding interest was to prevent the United States from being engaged, without express congressional authorization, in major, prolonged conflicts such as the wars in Vietnam and Korea, rather than to prohibit the President from using or threatening to use troops to achieve important diplomatic objectives where the risk of sustained military conflict was negligible.

Letter to Senator Robert Dole et al., from Walter Dellinger, Assistant Attorney General, Office of Legal Counsel, Deployment of United States Armed Forces into Haiti (Sept. 27, 1994), at https://www.justice.gov/sites/default/files/olc/opinions/1994/09/31/op-olc-v018-p0173.pdf. In a portion of its legal opinion on Libya in 2011, the Office of Legal Counsel relied on this reasoning to conclude that, "[b]y allowing United States involvement in hostilities to continue for 60 or 90 days, Congress signaled in the WPR that it considers congressional authorization most critical for 'major, prolonged conflicts such as the wars in Vietnam and Korea,' not more limited engagements." Memorandum Opinion from Caroline D. Krass, Principal Deputy Assistant Attorney General, Office of Legal Counsel, to the Attorney General, "Authority to Use Military Force in Libya" (April 1, 2011), at https://fas.org/irp/agency/doj/olc/libya.pdf.

Is this construction of the War Powers Resolution persuasive? If so, should Congress be allowed to delegate away its constitutional authority over the initiation of military conflicts (assuming it has that authority) in this blanket fashion? If such a delegation would raise constitutional concerns, is that a reason to avoid construing the War Powers Resolution in the manner suggested by the Executive Branch?

10. Is the War Powers Resolution well drafted to meet its aim of "ensur[ing] that the collective judgment of both the Congress and the President will apply to the introduction of United States Armed Forces into hostilities"? Writing in the 1980s, Professor Koh thought not. He pointed out that §3 requires the President to consult with Congress "in every possible instance" before sending troops into hostilities, but also allows the President to decide what is "possible," as well as how many and which members of Congress to consult. He also noted that §4 of the Resolution permits the President to file reports to Congress in three different but related situations involving the use of the U.S. military abroad, but only requires the removal of troops within 60 days from when the first of the three types of report is filed. Koh concluded that "simply by his choice of report, the President can satisfy the Resolution's procedural reporting obligation, while evading the Resolution's substantive obligation to remove those troops within sixty days." Harold Hongju Koh, *Why the President (Almost) Always Wins in Foreign Affairs: Lessons of the Iran-Contra Affair*, 97 Yale L.J. 1255 (1988). *See also* John Hart Ely, *Suppose Congress Wanted a War Powers Resolution That Worked*, 88 Colum. L. Rev. 1379, 1385-1400 (1988) (identifying many provisions in the WPR that "don't do any good and only give the President an excuse to flout the Resolution"). Why would Congress have enacted a statute that could be evaded in these ways? Might Congress have intended the President to have flexibility under the War Powers Resolution? If so, why?

11. Consider the Moss memorandum concerning Kosovo, excerpted above. Is its analysis of the effect of §8(a)(1) of the War Powers Resolution persuasive? Is it a fair reading of that section? Would a broader reading be unconstitutional, as suggested by the memorandum? Under the analysis in that memorandum, when can appropriations statutes constitute authorizations that satisfy the requirements of the War Powers Resolution? Congress is under enormous political pressure to "support the troops" that the President sends into combat, and therefore typically appropriates money for their operations, at least in the short run. In this light, does the analysis in the Moss memorandum effectively negate the effect of the War Powers Resolution? Or can Congress avoid this effect by specifying that the appropriation is not intended as an authorization?

12. Since the enactment of the War Powers Resolution, there have been at least 19 significant uses of U.S. force abroad: the 1975 rescue of the U.S. merchant ship *Mayaguez*; the 1980 Iran hostage rescue mission; the dispatch of troops to Lebanon in 1982; the 1983 invasion of Grenada; the 1986 air strikes against Libya; the 1987 escort operations to protect Persian Gulf shipping; the 1989 intervention in Panama; the 1991 Gulf War; the 1992-1993 humanitarian and combat mission in Somalia; the 1993 air strikes against Iraq in response to the attempted assassination of the first President Bush; the 1993 air strikes in Bosnia; the 1998 air strikes in Sudan and Afghanistan; the 1999 air strikes against Yugoslavia relating to Kosovo; the war begun in Afghanistan in 2001; the war begun in Iraq in 2003; the military operations against Libya in 2011; the conflict against the Islamic State initiated in 2014; and the airstrikes against Syria in 2017 and 2018. Only three of these actions — the 1991 Gulf War, the conflict in Afghanistan initiated in 2001, and the 2003 war in Iraq — were preceded by express congressional authorization. Two others — the Lebanon and Somalia missions — received *ex post* approval from Congress. The remaining 14 actions received no specific congressional approval, although some of them might be justified as responses to attacks or threatened attacks on U.S. citizens or property or, as with the conflict against the Islamic State, might be grounded in an earlier congressional authorization by interpreting that authorization broadly.

In all of these situations, and in scores of lesser military interventions, presidents justified their actions — in whole or in part — under the Commander-in-Chief and related presidential powers. In none of these situations did any president acknowledge an obligation to comply with the War Powers Resolution. Presidents have often stated that they are informing Congress of their actions "consistent with" the Resolution. In a number of instances, presidents have also sought congressional support for military operations — sometimes successfully (as in Iraq), and sometimes not (as in Kosovo) — without acknowledging any requirement that they do so. What do these patterns suggest about the effectiveness of the War Powers Resolution? If presidents do not feel obliged to comply with the War Powers Resolution, why do they note that their actions are consistent with the Resolution, and why do they often seek Congress's support?

13. One way that the War Powers Resolution could be given more bite would be for it to be enforced in the courts. To date, however, courts have dismissed challenges to presidential uses of force under the Resolution based on limiting doctrines such as standing, ripeness, equitable discretion, and the political question doctrine. *See, e.g.,* Smith v. Obama, 217 F. Supp. 3d 283 (D.D.C. 2016) (dismissing challenge to conflict against the Islamic State based on standing and political question grounds), *dismissed as moot,* 731 Fed. Appx. 8 (D.C. Cir. 2018); Whitney v. Obama, 845 F. Supp. 2d 136 (D.D.C. 2012) (dismissing challenge to intervention in Libya on mootness grounds); Kucinich v. Obama, 821 F. Supp. 2d 110 (D.D.C. 2011) (dismissing challenge to intervention in Libya on standing grounds); Campbell v. Clinton, 203 F.3d 19 (D.C. Cir. 2000) (dismissing challenge to Kosovo bombing campaign on standing grounds); Ange v. Bush, 752 F. Supp. 509 (D.D.C. 1990) (dismissing challenge to Gulf War on political question, equitable discretion, and ripeness grounds); Lowry v. Reagan, 676 F. Supp. 333 (D.D.C. 1987) (dismissing challenge to reflagging operations in the Persian Gulf on equitable discretion and political question grounds); Sanchez-Espinoza v. Reagan, 568 F. Supp. 596 (D.D.C. 1983) (dismissing challenge to covert assistance to Nicaraguan Contras on political question grounds), *aff'd on other grounds,* 770 F.2d 202 (D.C. Cir. 1985); Crockett v. Reagan, 558 F. Supp. 893 (D.D.C. 1982) (dismissing challenge to military aid to El Salvador on political question grounds), *aff'd without opinion,* 720 F.2d 1355 (D.C. Cir. 1983). *But cf. Campbell,* 203 F.3d at 37 (Tatel, J., concurring) ("In my view, were this case brought by plaintiffs with standing, we could determine whether the President, in undertaking the air campaign in Yugoslavia, exceeded his authority under the Constitution or the War Powers Resolution.").

Why do you think courts have been reluctant to become involved in enforcing the War Powers Resolution? Do courts have the expertise and access to information necessary to resolve challenges under the Resolution? Would judicial enforcement of the Resolution deprive the President of needed flexibility? What do Bas v. Tingy and *The Prize Cases* suggest about these questions? In the absence of judicial review, are the validity and scope of the Resolution merely academic questions? If courts were to enforce the Resolution, how much deference should they give to the President's views regarding whether a particular situation implicates the statutory restrictions?

14. Even though courts typically do not become involved, why isn't Congress more aggressive in insisting on presidential compliance with the War Powers Resolution? Why does Congress as an institution (as opposed to individual members) rarely express direct opposition to presidential commitments of U.S. armed forces? Why doesn't Congress do more before or after a President uses force — perhaps by putting conditional spending restraints on Defense Department authorizations — to check and shape unilateral presidential uses of force? What are Congress's institutional incentives, both before and after the President uses unilateral military force?

The possibility of a presidential veto may provide a partial answer to these questions. Congress can act with the force of law only through its statutes, and its statutes can be blocked by a presidential veto, unless the veto is overridden by two-thirds of both Houses of Congress. Section 5(c) of the War Powers Resolution was designed to address this veto limitation. It provides that "at any time that United States Armed Forces are engaged in hostilities outside the territory of the United States, its possessions or territories without a declaration of war or specific statutory authorization, such forces shall be removed by the President if the Congress so directs by concurrent resolution." Most scholars believe that such a concurrent resolution, if not presented to the President for signature and possible veto, is invalid under INS v. Chadha, 462 U.S. 919 (1983).

Another possible explanation for congressional passivity is that Congress is opportunistic. Professor Ely maintained, for example, that Congress's performance since the enactment of the War Powers Resolution "demonstrates that it may prove only too happy to have the monkey of accountability taken off its back — to settle back into the pattern of letting the President get out front and then, when the war begins not to play so well, making various feints in the direction of ending it, complaining that it is being stymied by the possibility of a veto and that there isn't much it can do about a *fait accompli.*" Ely, 88 Colum. L. Rev. at 1385. Is this description persuasive?

Note that Congress does sometimes act in response to presidential uses of force and on rare occasions uses political pressure to convince the President to agree to modest but legally binding limits on the President's unilateral military action. When U.S. forces involved in President Reagan's deployment of troops to Lebanon in 1982 began to suffer casualties, for example, Congress exercised political pressure that led to a compromise in which the President agreed by statute to a 180-day deadline on the mission. *See* Multinational Force in Lebanon Resolution, S.J. Res. 159, 97 Stat. 805 (1983). Similarly, after U.S. troops suffered casualties in 1993 in Somalia when operating as part of a U.N. mission, Congress in November 1993 approved the use of U.S. forces in Somalia but cut off funding for operations in Somalia for most purposes after March 31, 1994. *See* §8151 of the Department of Defense Appropriations Act for FY1994, Pub. L. No. 103-139.

Congress more recently tried but failed to impose legally binding limits on military activities in Yemen. Since 2015, the United States has been providing military and intelligence assistance to Saudi Arabia in its conflict in Yemen, without congressional authorization. In April 2019, Congress approved a joint resolution providing as follows:

> Congress hereby directs the President to remove United States Armed Forces from hostilities in or affecting the Republic of Yemen, except United States Armed Forces engaged in operations directed at al Qaeda or associated forces, by no later than the date that is 30 days after the date of the enactment of this joint resolution (unless the President requests and Congress authorizes a later date), and unless and until a declaration of war or specific authorization for such use of United States Armed Forces has been enacted.

In support of its authority to enact this provision, Congress referred to the War Powers Resolution as well as other statutes. President Trump vetoed the joint resolution, stating, among other things, that it:

> would interfere with the President's constitutional authority as Commander in Chief of the Armed Forces, and could endanger our service members by impairing their

ability to efficiently and effectively conduct military engagements and to withdraw in an orderly manner at the appropriate time.

Presidential Veto Message to the Senate to Accompany S.J. Res. 7 (Apr. 16, 2019). Congress failed to overturn Trump's veto, and it seems unlikely that Congress will be able to find another legislative avenue that would avoid a veto. What does this suggest about the War Powers Resolution's efficacy?

More often, the political pressure does not rise to the level of a legal enactment. For example, in June 2011, the House of Representatives approved a resolution in connection with the Libya intervention. The resolution stated as a matter of "policy" that U.S. armed forces shall only be used to defend U.S. interests, that the President failed to provide Congress with a convincing rationale for the intervention, and that the President "shall not deploy, establish, or maintain" ground troops in Libya. It also stated that the President was required to submit to the House several reports related to the Libya intervention, and it reaffirmed Congress's power to withhold funding for unauthorized uses of force, including the Libya campaign. This resolution was not legally binding, but it had bipartisan support, and many viewed it as a vote of no confidence in the President's Libya policy. An even less formal congressional action occurred in connection with President Obama's contemplated use of force against Syria in 2013: 116 members of the House of Representatives signed a letter to him stating that "[w]e strongly urge you to consult and receive authorization from Congress before ordering the use of U.S. military force in Syria. Your responsibility to do so is prescribed in the Constitution and the War Powers Resolution of 1973." How might these and other forms of "mere" political pressure (and anticipated political pressure) influence presidential war powers, either before or after force is deployed? How might they be relevant in discerning the constitutional distribution of war authority?

15. The Koh testimony on June 28, 2011, excerpted above, was the Obama Administration's official explanation of why it did not violate §5(b) of the War Powers Resolution when 60 days had passed after the initial intervention without congressional authorization for the Libya operation. Four days before this testimony, the House of Representatives voted on two measures related to the Libya operation. The first would have authorized the mission basically as the Obama Administration had conducted it, but would have ruled out ground forces. The second would have prohibited any air strikes in Libya but permitted continued logistical and related support. Both measures were defeated.

Are you convinced by Koh's argument that firing missiles from fighter jets and drones that kill people over an extended period of time pursuant to a U.N.-authorized use of force does not constitute "hostilities"? Would the absence of any of the four factors invoked in his testimony lead to a different conclusion about "hostilities"? Were the mission and the military means employed truly "limited"? Why does the relative absence of a threat to U.S. troops, or the small likelihood of escalation, matter to the definition of hostilities? One difficulty in assessing Koh's argument is that the War Powers Resolution does not define "hostilities." Isn't it a problem for Koh's argument that standard dictionary definitions of the term "hostilities" refer to acts or states of warfare or violence or unfriendliness without reference to the vulnerability of the aggressor or the reciprocity of the fighting? Note also that the House Report on the bill that became the War Powers Resolution states that the term "*hostilities*" "was substituted for the phrase *armed conflict* during the subcommittee drafting process because it was considered to be somewhat broader in scope." On the other hand, if the 60-day cutoff provision in the War Powers Resolution is of questionable constitutionality, as the Executive Branch has at various times suggested, perhaps it is proper for the Executive to interpret it more narrowly than ordinary interpretive principles might suggest?

16. The bill discussed in the Dellinger memorandum excerpted above, which would have limited the placement of U.S. troops under U.N. command, was never enacted. If it had been, would it have been constitutional? If the analysis in the memorandum is correct, what other presidential action is Congress barred from regulating? Even if Congress cannot directly regulate the placement of U.S. troops under foreign command, can it do so indirectly through its appropriations power? Do you think the President would have committed troops to U.N. command if Congress had succeeded in enacting legislation, over his veto, to cut off funds?

17. What if a treaty, as opposed to a statute, purports to limit the President's Commander-in-Chief power? For example, the four Geneva Conventions of 1949 place significant restrictions on what the United States can do in a war to prisoners of war, civilians, and others. Can the Geneva Conventions restrict the President on the battlefield? Is a treaty part of the "Laws" of the United States that the President must faithfully execute? Does it matter whether the treaty is self-executing (i.e., directly enforceable by U.S. courts) or non-self-executing (not directly enforceable by U.S. courts)? What if Congress has incorporated portions of the treaty into domestic law, as it has for the Geneva Conventions in the War Crimes Act of 1996, excerpted above? Does it matter whether the President, as opposed to one of the President's subordinates, makes the decision to disregard the treaty? For analysis of these issues, see Derek Jinks & David Sloss, *Is the President Bound by the Geneva Conventions?*, 90 Cornell L. Rev. 97 (2004).

18. For commentary on the War Powers Resolution, see, for example, Robert F. Turner, The War Powers Resolution: Its Implementation in Theory and Practice (1983); J. Brian Atwood, *The War Powers Resolution in the Age of Terrorism*, 52 St. Louis L.J. 57 (2007); Stephen L. Carter, *The Constitutionality of the War-Powers Resolution*, 70 Va. L. Rev. 101 (1984); Maj. Geoffrey S. Corn, *Clinton, Kosovo, and the Final Destruction of the War Powers Resolution*, 42 Wm. & Mary L. Rev. 1149 (2001); John Hart Ely, *Suppose Congress Wanted a War Powers Act That Worked*, 88 Colum. L. Rev. 1379 (1988); J. Terry Emerson, *The War Powers Resolution Tested: The President's Independent Defense Power*, 51 Notre Dame L. Rev. 187 (1975); Michael J. Glennon, *Too Far Apart: Repeal the War Powers Resolution*, 50 U. Miami L. Rev. 17 (1995); Eugene V. Rostow, *Great Cases Make Bad Law: The War Powers Act*, 50 Tex. L. Rev. 833 (1972); Eugene V. Rostow, *"Once More Unto the Breach": The War Powers Resolution Revisited*, 21 Val. U. L. Rev. 1 (1986); Peter M. Shane, *Learning McNamara's Lessons: How the War Powers Resolution Advances the Rule of Law*, 47 Case W. Res. L. Rev. 1281 (1997); Cyrus R. Vance, *Striking the Balance: Congress and the President Under the War Powers Resolution*, 133 U. Pa. L. Rev. 79 (1984). For a discussion of how psychological research concerning decisionmaking biases might have implications for war powers debates, including debates over possible reforms of the War Powers Resolution, see Ganesh Sitaraman & David Zionts, *Behavioral War Powers*, 90 N.Y.U. L. Rev. 516 (2015). For discussion of the Obama Administration's legacy relating to the domestic and international law of war powers, see *Agora, President Obama's War Powers Legacy*, Volume 110, Issue 4, American Journal of International Law (with essays by Curtis Bradley & Jack Goldsmith, Ashley Deeks, Ryan Goodman, Rebecca Ingber, and Michael Ramsey).

D. COVERT ACTION

"Intelligence" is the information that a nation needs to formulate and conduct foreign and military policy and to redress threats to its national security. The U.S. government has 17 agencies, known collectively as the "U.S. Intelligence Community," that collect, analyze, and distribute intelligence to achieve these goals. One of these agencies is the Central Intelligence Agency (CIA). The CIA collects intelligence outside the United States, primarily through human sources. It also evaluates and analyzes intelligence collected by it and other agencies and produces intelligence reports used by various components of the U.S. government. Separate from these intelligence collection and analysis tasks, the CIA also engages in covert actions. A covert action is one that seeks to influence foreign governments or groups outside the United States with the intent that the role of the U.S. government not be apparent or acknowledged. "The value of covert action to a President is that it offers a 'third way' or 'quiet option,' a middle ground between overt measures on the one hand (diplomacy, trade incentives or sanctions, foreign aid, etc.) and the use of military force on the other. Covert action gives the president an alternative that may be more effective than diplomacy and a bit less noisy than the overt use of force." William J. Daugherty, Executive Secrets: Covert Action and the Presidency 19 (2004). Covert actions range from providing financial assistance to a foreign government or candidate in a foreign election, to various forms of propaganda or disinformation, to sabotage, to paramilitary or other violent actions in a foreign country.

This last form of covert action — acts akin to ones that might otherwise be undertaken by U.S. military forces — is the subject of this section. Famous historical examples of this form of covert action include U.S. support for the failed Bay of Pigs invasion in Cuba, plots to assassinate Fidel Castro and others in the 1960s, assistance with the 1980 escape of American diplomats who had taken refuge in the Canadian embassy in Iran, American financial and military support for the Afghanistan mujahedeen in the 1970s and 1980s, and similar support for the Nicaraguan Contras in the 1980s. As these examples indicate, covert action can be a substitute for, or a component of, presidential war powers. We study covert action in a separate section, however, because it is governed by a different legal framework than the one thus far studied in this chapter. (Issues relating to covert action in the post-9/11 "War on Terror" are addressed in Chapter 10.)

1. Historical Background

The United States has engaged in covert actions since the Founding period. As the head of the American Commission in Paris during the Revolutionary War, Benjamin Franklin covertly planted propaganda and disinformation to build French support for the American cause, and coordinated the efforts of privateers against British shipping. President Thomas Jefferson ordered a covert action to overthrow the Pasha of Tripoli as part of his efforts to defeat threats from the Barbary States. President Grant sent a secret agent to Canada to influence public sentiment in favor of rebellion from Great Britain. President Theodore Roosevelt used covert American agents and financial support to help stoke a rebellion in Panama. In World War II, President Roosevelt created the Office of Strategic Services, which collected intelligence and ran numerous covert operations in Europe, Africa, and

Asia, including sabotage, guerilla operations, and killings. There are many other examples. *See generally* Christopher Andrew, For the President's Eyes Only: Secret Intelligence and the American Presidency from Washington to Bush (1995); John J. Carter, Covert Operations as a Tool of Presidential Foreign Policy in American History from 1800 to 1920: Foreign Policy in the Shadows (2000).

The CIA was created by the National Security Act of 1947. The same Act merged the War and Navy Departments into the Defense Department headed by the Secretary of Defense. It also created the National Security Council (NSC), the group of the President's senior foreign relations and national security advisors that today includes (among others) the Vice-President, the Secretaries of State, Treasury, and Defense, the Chairman of the Joint Chiefs of Staff, the Director of National Intelligence and, when relevant, the Attorney General. The original National Security Act charged the CIA, "under the direction of the National Security Council," with coordinating the intelligence activities of other government components, especially in the State Department and new Department of Defense. But the CIA, building on the legacy of the Office of Strategic Services, quickly became both the government's premier intelligence collection agency and the agency that conducted covert actions.

The arguable statutory basis for covert actions from the CIA's founding until the 1970s was a provision in the National Security Act that made it the "duty of the Agency . . . to perform such other functions and duties relating to intelligence affecting the national security as the National Security Council may from time to time direct." National Security Act of 1947, §102(d)(5). In its first meeting in December 1947, President Truman's NSC, alarmed by Soviet Union infiltration into Europe, invoked §102(d)(5) to authorize the CIA to conduct psychological operations in Eastern Europe. In June 1948, the NSC invoked the same provision to authorize the CIA to conduct "covert operations," which it defined as "all activities . . . conducted or sponsored by this Government against hostile foreign states or groups or in support of friendly foreign states or groups but which are so planned and executed that any U.S. Government responsibility for them is not evident to unauthorized persons and that if uncovered the U.S. Government can plausibly disclaim any responsibility for them," and which included "propaganda, economic warfare; preventive direct action, including sabotage, anti-sabotage, demolition and evacuation measures; subversion against hostile states, including assistance to underground resistance movements, guerrillas and refugee liberation groups, and support of indigenous anti-communist elements in threatened countries of the free world." By 1960, the CIA had conducted over 200 covert actions, including successful coups in Iran and Guatemala. Between 1961 and 1974, it conducted over 900 major covert actions and thousands of smaller ones, including various assassination plots and counterinsurgency operations in Latin America, Africa, and the Far East. *See generally* Daugherty, Executive Secrets, *supra*; Tim Weiner, Legacy of Ashes: The History of the CIA (2008); Amy B. Zegart, Flawed by Design: The Evolution of the CIA, JCS, and NSC (1999).

From its creation until the 1970s, the CIA had little oversight, either within the Executive Branch or by Congress. Within the Executive Branch, the CIA was loosely supervised by the NSC. But in practice the CIA engaged in numerous covert actions without full disclosure to or approval from the NSC or the President, and the White House largely acquiesced in this practice so that it could maintain the President's "plausible deniability" in case something went wrong with an operation. In Congress, oversight was technically done by subcommittees in the Senate and House Arms Services Committees, but Congress enacted few laws to govern the CIA and supervision of it was lax. The dominant congressional attitude during the first 30 years of the Cold War was that CIA activities "had to be taken on faith," as Senator Richard Russell said in 1956, because of the need for secrecy, discretion, and ruthlessness in confronting the Soviet Union. As a result, Congress was rarely told about covert actions before they were conducted and often was not told after they were conducted. "It is not a question of reluctance on the part of CIA officials to speak to us," said Senator Leverett Saltonstall in 1956. "Instead, it is a question of our reluctance . . . to seek information and knowledge on subjects which I personally, as a Member of Congress and as a citizen, would rather not have." This attitude persisted in Congress in the first quarter century of the Cold War. Congress would sometimes chastise the CIA for its mistakes after the fact, but meaningful oversight was, until the 1970s, absent. *See generally* Weiner, Legacy of Ashes, *supra*; David M. Barrett, The CIA and Congress: The Untold Story (2005); L. Britt Snider, The Agency and The Hill: CIA's Relationship with Congress, 1946-2004 (2008).

On May 8, 1973, in response to stories about CIA involvement in Watergate, CIA Director Schlesinger ordered every CIA employee to report to him any CIA activities at any time in the Agency's history "which might be construed to be outside" the National Security Act of 1947, as amended. The resulting 693-page report documented numerous illegal or inappropriate activities by the CIA, including politically motivated surveillance of American citizens, domestic break-in programs, non-consensual medical experiments, assassination plots, and illegal detentions. Starting in 1974, some of these activities began to leak into the press. So too did other illegal or abusive activities by other intelligence agencies. As a result, Congress established two committees to investigate thoroughly the entire Intelligence Community: The Senate Select Committee to Study Governmental Operations with Respect to Intelligence Activities, known as the Church Committee; and the House Select Committee on Intelligence, known as the Pike Committee. The Church Committee focused more on covert action. It concluded that covert action as practiced since 1947 had been undisciplined, non-accountable both inside and outside the Executive Branch, and often illegal or harmful to the United States. The Committee considered a recommendation to ban covert action altogether, but it ultimately determined that the practice remained necessary. It concluded:

> The Committee's review of covert action has underscored the necessity for a thorough-going strengthening of the Executive's internal review process for covert action and for the establishment of a realistic system of accountability, both within the Executive, and to Congress and to the American people. The requirement for a rigorous and credible system of control and accountability is complicated, however, by the shield of secrecy which must necessarily be imposed on any covert activity if it is to remain secret. The challenge is to find a substitute for the public scrutiny through congressional debate and press attention that normally attends governmental decisions.

Final Report of the Select Committee to Study Governmental Operations with Respect to Intelligence Activities 158 (1976).

Before the 1990s, Congress and the Executive Branch sought to meet this challenge in two laws. In 1974, before the Church Committee completed its Report, Congress enacted the Hughes-Ryan Amendment. It provided: "No funds appropriated under this or any other Act may be expended by or on behalf of the [CIA] for operation in foreign countries . . . unless and until the President finds that each such operation is important to the national security . . . and reports, in a timely fashion, a description and scope of such operation to the appropriate committees of the Congress." This provision is a roundabout reference to covert action. It was designed to end plausible deniability within the Executive Branch by ensuring that the President approved each covert action in a document called a "finding." It was also designed to ensure that the President reported each covert action to Congress, though its timing requirement is vague. The Intelligence Oversight Act of 1980 added additional reforms. It created two permanent intelligence committees to oversee the Intelligence Community — the House Permanent Select Committee on Intelligence and the Senate Select Committee on Intelligence — and limited CIA and Intelligence Community reporting requirements to these two committees. It required the President to keep these committees "fully and currently informed of all intelligence activities . . . , including any significant anticipated intelligence activity." And it required the President to "fully inform the intelligence committees in a timely fashion" of covert actions for which "prior notice" was not given, as well as a statement of reasons for the late notice.

The Iran-Contra scandal in the mid-1980s revealed the inadequacies in this system. The scandal grew out of two separate covert operations. One was President Reagan's efforts, through the CIA, to help the Nicaraguan "Contras" overthrow the government of Nicaragua. When Congress learned of CIA involvement in the Contras' efforts, it enacted numerous complex restrictions over many years, the most important of which provided that "no funds available to the Central Intelligence Agency . . . or any other agency or entity of the United States involved in intelligence activities may be obligated or expended for the purpose or which would have the effect of supporting, directly or indirectly, military or paramilitary operations in Nicaragua. . . ." Despite this ban, a group within the NSC, with the assistance of CIA Director William Casey, established a secret network of individuals and companies known as "the Enterprise" to raise funds from foreign governments and private parties to support the Contras. One source for funds for the Enterprise was a second and unrelated CIA covert operation to help sell arms purchased from Israel to Iran in order to improve relations with Iran and secure the release of American hostages in the Middle East. The proceeds generated by the sale of arms were channeled to the Contras through the Enterprise.

In addition to violating a number of substantive legal restrictions, the Reagan Administration in the Iran-Contra scandal violated the spirit if not the letter of the reporting laws. President Reagan did not make a presidential finding about the Contras operation and made haphazard and after-the-fact findings about the Iranian operation. In addition, he never reported the Contras operation to Congress, and reported the Iranian operation action ten months after it began. After studying the scandal, the Senate Intelligence Committee noted that congressional guidance on covert actions was "ambiguous, confusing and incomplete," that presidential approval procedures for covert actions "are not specified," that the "statutory requirements for informing the intelligence committees of covert actions are subject to misinterpretation," and that the "scope of [covert] activities covered by the law is undefined." S. Rep. 102-85, at 34 (June 19, 1991). In the Intelligence Authorization Act of 1991, Congress sought to fix these and related problems by expressly defining covert action by statute for the first time, by clarifying and tightening the requirement of a presidential finding and advanced notification to Congress of covert actions, and through other measures.

2. Statutory and Regulatory Framework

Section 3093 of Title 50 of the U.S. Code, which originated as §503 of the National Security Act of 1947, is the modern statutory framework for covert actions. It reflects the alterations of the Intelligence Authorization Act of 1991 and other statutory amendments. Every sentence of §3093 is important for understanding the legal structure of covert actions. Begin by studying the definition of "covert action" in §3093(e), and then go back to the beginning of the statute and read through it carefully.

50 U.S.C. §3093. Presidential Approval and Reporting of Covert Actions

(a) Presidential findings

The President may not authorize the conduct of a covert action by departments, agencies, or entities of the United States Government unless the President determines such an action is necessary to support identifiable foreign policy objectives of the United States and is important to the national security of the United States, which determination shall be set forth in a finding that shall meet each of the following conditions:

(1) Each finding shall be in writing, unless immediate action by the United States is required and time does not permit the preparation of a written finding, in which case a written record of the President's decision shall be contemporaneously made and shall be reduced to a written finding as soon as possible but in no event more than 48 hours after the decision is made.

(2) Except as permitted by paragraph (1), a finding may not authorize or sanction a covert action, or any aspect of any such action, which already has occurred.

(3) Each finding shall specify each department, agency, or entity of the United States Government authorized to fund or otherwise participate in any significant way in such action. Any employee, contractor, or contract agent of a department, agency, or entity of the United States Government other than the Central Intelligence Agency directed to participate in any way in a covert action shall be subject either to the policies and regulations of the Central Intelligence Agency, or to written policies or regulations adopted by such department, agency, or entity, to govern such participation.

(4) Each finding shall specify whether it is contemplated that any third party which is not an element of, or a contractor or contract agent of, the United States Government, or is not otherwise subject to United States Government policies and regulations, will be used to fund or otherwise participate in any significant way in the covert action concerned, or be used to undertake the covert action concerned on behalf of the United States.

(5) A finding may not authorize any action that would violate the Constitution or any statute of the United States.

(b) Reports to congressional intelligence committees; production of information

To the extent consistent with due regard for the protection from unauthorized disclosure of classified information relating to sensitive intelligence sources and methods or other exceptionally sensitive matters, the Director of National

Intelligence and the heads of all departments, agencies, and entities of the United States Government involved in a covert action —

(1) shall keep the congressional intelligence committees fully and currently informed of all covert actions which are the responsibility of, are engaged in by, or are carried out for or on behalf of, any department, agency, or entity of the United States Government, including significant failures; and

(2) shall furnish to the congressional intelligence committees any information or material concerning covert actions which is in the possession, custody, or control of any department, agency, or entity of the United States Government and which is requested by either of the congressional intelligence committees in order to carry out its authorized responsibilities.

(c) Timing of reports; access to finding

(1) The President shall ensure that any finding approved pursuant to subsection (a) of this section shall be reported to the congressional intelligence committees as soon as possible after such approval and before the initiation of the covert action authorized by the finding, except as otherwise provided in paragraph (2) and paragraph (3).

(2) If the President determines that it is essential to limit access to the finding to meet extraordinary circumstances affecting vital interests of the United States, the finding may be reported to the chairmen and ranking minority members of the congressional intelligence committees, the Speaker and minority leader of the House of Representatives, the majority and minority leaders of the Senate, and such other member or members of the congressional leadership as may be included by the President.

(3) Whenever a finding is not reported pursuant to paragraph (1) or (2) of this section, the President shall fully inform the congressional intelligence committees in a timely fashion and shall provide a statement of the reasons for not giving prior notice.

(4) In a case under paragraph (1), (2), or (3), a copy of the finding, signed by the President, shall be provided to the chairman of each congressional intelligence committee. When access to a finding is limited to the Members of Congress specified in paragraph (2), a statement of the reasons for limiting such access shall also be provided.

(d) Changes in previously approved actions

The President shall ensure that the congressional intelligence committees, or, if applicable, the Members of Congress specified in subsection (c)(2) of this section, are notified of any significant change in a previously approved covert action, or any significant undertaking pursuant to a previously approved finding, in the same manner as findings are reported pursuant to subsection (c) of this section.

(e) "Covert action" defined

As used in this subchapter, the term "covert action" means an activity or activities of the United States Government to influence political, economic, or military conditions abroad, where it is intended that the role of the United States Government will not be apparent or acknowledged publicly, but does not include —

(1) activities the primary purpose of which is to acquire intelligence, traditional counterintelligence activities, traditional activities to improve or maintain the operational security of United States Government programs, or administrative activities;

(2) traditional diplomatic or military activities or routine support to such activities;

(3) traditional law enforcement activities conducted by United States Government law enforcement agencies or routine support to such activities; or

(4) activities to provide routine support to the overt activities (other than activities described in paragraph (1), (2), or (3)) of other United States Government agencies abroad.

(f) Prohibition on covert actions intended to influence United States political processes, etc.

No covert action may be conducted which is intended to influence United States political processes, public opinion, policies, or media.

In 1981, the Reagan Administration issued Executive Order 12,333 to fill in the gaps of U.S. statutes in the regulation and oversight of the U.S. Intelligence Community. This executive order, which built on earlier executive orders by Presidents Ford and Carter related to intelligence and covert action, has been amended several times since the Reagan Administration. Below are excerpts pertaining to covert action in the most recent version of the executive order, which the second Bush Administration amended on July 30, 2008.

Executive Order 12,333: United States Intelligence Activities (as amended)

PART 1 Goals, Directions, Duties, and Responsibilities with Respect to United States Intelligence Efforts

. . .

1.2 The National Security Council

(a) Purpose. The National Security Council (NSC) shall act as the highest ranking executive branch entity that provides support to the President for review of, guidance for, and direction to the conduct of all foreign intelligence, counterintelligence, and covert action, and attendant policies and programs.

(b) Covert Action and Other Sensitive Intelligence Operations. The NSC shall consider and submit to the President a policy recommendation, including all dissents, on each proposed covert action and conduct a periodic review of ongoing covert action activities, including an evaluation of the effectiveness and consistency with current national policy of such activities and consistency with applicable legal requirements. The NSC shall perform such other functions related to covert action as the President may direct, but shall not undertake the conduct of covert actions. The NSC shall also review proposals for other sensitive intelligence operations.

1.3 Director of National Intelligence. Subject to the authority, direction, and control of the President, the Director of National Intelligence (Director) shall serve as the head of the Intelligence Community, act as the principal adviser to the President, to the NSC, and to the Homeland Security Council for intelligence matters related to national security, and shall oversee and direct the implementation of the National Intelligence Program and execution of the National Intelligence Program budget. The Director will lead a unified, coordinated, and effective intelligence effort. . . .

(b) In addition to fulfilling the obligations and responsibilities prescribed by the Act, the Director:

. . . (3) Shall oversee and provide advice to the President and the NSC with respect to all ongoing and proposed covert action programs; . . .

1.7 Intelligence Community Elements. Each element of the Intelligence Community shall have the duties and responsibilities specified below, in addition to those specified by law or elsewhere in this order. Intelligence Community elements within executive departments shall serve the information and intelligence needs of their respective heads of departments and also shall operate as part of an integrated Intelligence Community, as provided in law or this order.

(a) The Central Intelligence Agency. The Director of the Central Intelligence Agency shall: . . .

(4) Conduct covert action activities approved by the President. No agency except the Central Intelligence Agency (or the Armed Forces of the United States in time of war declared by the Congress or during any period covered by a report from the President to the Congress consistent with the War Powers Resolution, Public Law 93-148) may conduct any covert action activity unless the President determines that another agency is more likely to achieve a particular objective; . . .

PART 2 Conduct of Intelligence Activities . . .

2.11 Prohibition on Assassination. No person employed by or acting on behalf of the United States Government shall engage in or conspire to engage in assassination.

2.12 Indirect Participation. No element of the Intelligence Community shall participate in or request any person to undertake activities forbidden by this Order.

2.13 Limitation on Covert Action. No covert action may be conducted which is intended to influence United States political processes, public opinion, policies, or media. . . .

PART 3 General Provisions

3.5 Definitions. For the purposes of this Order, the following terms shall have these meanings: . . .

(b) Covert action means an activity or activities of the United States Government to influence political, economic, or military conditions abroad, where it is intended that the role of the United States Government will not be apparent or acknowledged publicly, but does not include:

(1) Activities the primary purpose of which is to acquire intelligence, traditional counterintelligence activities, traditional activities to improve or maintain the operational security of United States Government programs, or administrative activities;

(2) Traditional diplomatic or military activities or routine support to such activities;

(3) Traditional law enforcement activities conducted by United States Government law enforcement agencies or routine support to such activities; or

(4) Activities to provide routine support to the overt activities (other than activities described in paragraph (1), (2), or (3)) of other United States Government agencies abroad. . . .

3. The 1998 Covert Action Against Osama Bin Laden

Final Report of the National Commission on Terrorist Attacks Upon the United States

126-33 (2004)

[By 1997, the U.S. government had identified Osama Bin Laden (sometimes spelled "Bin Ladin"), the leader of Al Qaeda who was then living in Afghanistan, as a financier and organizer of terrorist activity against U.S. interests. By the spring of 1998, the CIA's "Bin Laden Unit" had developed plans for a possible covert action that would use friendly Afghanistan tribal groups ("Afghan Tribals" or "Tribal Assets") to capture Bin Laden at his compound near Kandahar, known as Tarnak Farms, and transfer him to the United States or an Arab country for trial. These plans were at the time deemed too risky and were temporarily shelved. However, interest in the covert action grew after the August 7, 1998, Al Qaeda bombings of U.S. embassies in Kenya and Tanzania. The United States' initial response to the embassy bombings was a Tomahawk cruise missile attack on Bin Laden camps in Afghanistan, as well as on the Al Shifa pharmaceutical plant in Sudan, which the United States claimed had links to Al Qaeda and was producing a deadly nerve agent.]

. . . As part of the response to the embassy bombings, President Clinton signed a Memorandum of Notification authorizing the CIA to let its tribal assets use force to capture Bin Ladin and his associates. CIA officers told the tribals that the plan to capture Bin Ladin, which had been "turned off" three months earlier, was back on. The memorandum also authorized the CIA to attack Bin Ladin in other ways. . . .

The counterterrorism staff at CIA thought it was gaining a better understanding of Bin Ladin and his network. In preparation for briefing the Senate Select Committee on Intelligence on September 2, [CIA director George Tenet] was told that the intelligence community knew more about Bin Ladin's network "than about any other top tier terrorist organization." . . .

Given the President's August Memorandum of Notification, the CIA had already been working on new plans for using the Afghan tribals to capture Bin Ladin. During September and October, the tribals claimed to have tried at least four times to ambush Bin Ladin. Senior CIA officials doubted whether any of these ambush attempts had actually occurred. But the tribals did seem to have success in reporting where Bin Ladin was. . . .

The CIA reported on December 18 that Bin Ladin might be traveling to Kandahar and could be targeted there with cruise missiles. . . '.

The principals considered a cruise missile strike to try to kill Bin Ladin. One issue they discussed was the potential collateral damage — the number of innocent bystanders who would be killed or wounded. . . . By the end of the meeting, the principals decided against recommending to the President that he order a strike. . . .

The principals began considering other, more aggressive covert alternatives using the tribals. CIA officers suggested that the tribals would prefer to try a raid rather than a roadside ambush because they would have better control, it would be less dangerous, and it played more to their skills and experience. But everyone knew that if the tribals were to conduct such a raid, guns would be blazing. The current Memorandum of Notification instructed the CIA to capture Bin Ladin and to use lethal force only in self-defense. Work now began on a new memorandum that would give the tribals more latitude. The intention was to say that they could use lethal force if the attempted capture seemed impossible to complete successfully.

Early drafts of this highly sensitive document emphasized that it authorized only a capture operation. The tribals were to be paid only if they captured Bin Ladin, not if they killed him. Officials throughout the government approved this draft. But on December 21, . . . the CIA's leaders urged strengthening the language to allow the tribals to be paid whether Bin Ladin was captured *or* killed. [National Security Advisor Samuel Berger] and Tenet then worked together to take this line of thought even further.

They finally agreed, as Berger reported to President Clinton, that an extraordinary step was necessary. The new memorandum would allow the killing of Bin Ladin if the CIA and the tribals judged that capture was not feasible (a judgment it already seemed clear they had reached). The Justice Department lawyer who worked on the draft told us that what was envisioned was a group of tribals assaulting a location, leading to a shoot-out. Bin Ladin and others would be captured if possible, but probably would be killed. The administration's position was that under the law of armed conflict, killing a person who posed an imminent threat to the United States would be an act of self-defense, not an assassination. On Christmas Eve 1998, Berger sent a final draft to President Clinton, with an explanatory memo. The President approved the document.[123]

Because the White House considered this operation highly sensitive, only a tiny number of people knew about this Memorandum of Notification. Berger arranged for the NSC's legal adviser to inform Albright, Cohen, Shelton, and Reno. None was allowed to keep a copy. Congressional leaders were briefed, as required by law. Attorney General Reno had sent a letter to the President expressing her concern: she warned of possible retaliation, including the targeting of U.S. officials. She did not pose any legal objection. A copy of the final document, along with the carefully crafted instructions that were to be sent to the tribals, was given to Tenet.

A message from Tenet to CIA field agents directed them to communicate to the tribals the instructions authorized by the President: the United States preferred that Bin Ladin and his lieutenants be captured, but if a successful capture operation was not feasible, the tribals were permitted to kill them. The instructions added that the tribals must avoid killing others unnecessarily and must not kill or abuse Bin Ladin or his lieutenants if they surrendered. Finally, the tribals would not be paid if this set of requirements was not met. . . .

Policymakers in the Clinton administration, including the President and his national security advisor, told us that the President's intent regarding covert action against Bin Ladin was clear: he wanted him dead. This intent was never well communicated or understood within the CIA. Tenet told the Commission that except in one specific case (discussed later), the CIA was authorized to kill Bin Ladin only in the context of a capture operation. CIA senior managers, operators, and lawyers confirmed this understanding. "We always talked about how much easier it would have been to kill him," a former chief of the Bin Ladin unit said.

In February 1999, another draft Memorandum of Notification went to President Clinton. It asked him to allow the CIA to give exactly the same guidance to the

---

123. Both [Office of Legal Counsel head Randolph] Moss and [National Security Council lawyer James] Baker told us they concluded that killing Bin Ladin did not violate the assassination ban contained in Executive Order 12,333.

Northern Alliance as had just been given to the tribals: they could kill Bin Ladin if a successful capture operation was not feasible. On this occasion, however, President Clinton crossed out key language he had approved in December and inserted more ambiguous language. No one we interviewed could shed light on why the President did this. President Clinton told the Commission that he had no recollection of why he rewrote the language.

Later in 1999, when legal authority was needed for enlisting still other collaborators and for covering a wider set of contingencies, the lawyers returned to the language used in August 1998, which authorized force only in the context of a capture operation. Given the closely held character of the document approved in December 1998, and the subsequent return to the earlier language, it is possible to understand how the former White House officials and the CIA officials might disagree as to whether the CIA was ever authorized by the President to kill Bin Ladin.

The dispute turned out to be somewhat academic, as the limits of available legal authority were not tested. [Richard Clarke, the chief counter-terrorism advisor on the National Security Council,] commented to Berger that "despite 'expanded' authority for CIA's sources to engage in direct action, they have shown no inclination to do so." He added that it was his impression that the CIA thought the tribals unlikely to act against Bin Ladin and hence relying on them was "unrealistic." Events seemed to bear him out, since the tribals did not stage an attack on Bin Ladin or his associates during 1999. . . .

Notes and Questions

1. Section 3093 of Title 50, excerpted above, defines "covert action" in subsection (e) to mean "an activity or activities of the United States Government to influence political, economic, or military conditions abroad, where it is intended that the role of the United States Government will not be apparent or acknowledged publicly." In addition, §3093(a) requires the President to determine for each covert action, in a document called a "Finding," that the "action is necessary to support identifiable foreign policy objectives of the United States and is important to the national security of the United States." The primary elements of a covert action are thus (a) an activity to influence conditions abroad, (b) designed not to be acknowledged by the United States, (c) that the President determines supports a foreign policy objective and is important to the national interest. That is an extremely broad and open-ended definition. Note that the covert action statute does not specify that only the CIA can conduct a covert action. Section 3093(a)(3) implies that other agencies besides the CIA can be involved in such an action, and Executive Order 12,333, §1.7(a)(4) states: "No agency except the Central Intelligence Agency (or the Armed Forces of the United States in time of war declared by the Congress or during any period covered by a report from the President to the Congress consistent with the War Powers Resolution) may conduct any covert action activity *unless the President determines that another agency is more likely to achieve a particular objective.*" (Emphasis added.) Nonetheless, the CIA is the primary agency that conducts covert actions.

2. Prior to 1947, no statute authorized covert actions, and thus presidents conducted them pursuant to their constitutional authorities under Article II. Which provisions of Article II confer authority to conduct covert actions? Since 1947, Congress has arguably authorized covert actions, at least implicitly, in various ways.

What provision of §3093 authorizes covert actions? Is the authorization implicit in the definition of and restrictions on covert action? To the extent that such covert actions involve secret paramilitary or other war-like actions, what in Article I of the Constitution gives Congress the authority to enact such provisions? The "Declare War" Clause? Congress's various authorities over U.S. armed forces? The Necessary and Proper Clause? Assuming that Congress can regulate in this area, does the Constitution permit such an open-ended congressional authorization insofar as the covert action is war-like? Should such an authorization be viewed as an excessive delegation? To what extent should the answer to these questions be informed by the fact that presidents engaged in covert actions prior to 1947 based on Article II? By the fact that the political branches have gone along with this basic arrangement since 1947? How do answers to these questions relate to the issues, discussed in previous sections, of whether and when presidents may use military force without congressional authorization?

3. Section 3093(a)(5) states that a covert action may not "violate the Constitution or any statute of the United States." Why did Congress specify that covert actions may not violate the Constitution? Isn't that true regardless of whether the statute says so? As for the prohibition on violating "any statute," difficult questions can arise when general criminal prohibitions on their face forbid activities that the CIA conducts. For example, when the CIA gives money or equipment to help one of its assets penetrate a terrorist organization, does it violate the criminal prohibition on material support to a terrorist organization, 18 U.S.C. §2339B? When it obtains secrets of foreign governments through a deceitful telephone call, does it violate the mail fraud statute, which makes it a crime to obtain property by means of false representation by telephone, 18 U.S.C. §1341? Does a non-U.S. citizen working for the CIA under the false "cover" of being a U.S. citizen violate the criminal prohibition on falsely representing oneself as a U.S. citizen, 18 U.S.C. §911? Does a violent covert action in a country with which United States is at peace violate the Neutrality Act's criminal prohibition on any "military or naval expedition or enterprise to be carried on . . . against the territory or dominion of any foreign prince or state," 18 U.S.C. §960? One possible way around these problems is to apply a canon of statutory construction that treats generally worded statutes, at least in some circumstances, as inapplicable to the government unless they state so clearly. The Supreme Court described this canon as follows:

> The cases in which [the canon that the general words of a statute do not include the government or affect its rights unless the construction is clear and indisputable upon the text of the act] has been applied fall into two classes. The first is where an act, if not so limited, would deprive the sovereign of a recognized or established prerogative title or interest. A classical instance is the exemption of the state from the operation of general statutes of limitation. The rule of exclusion of the sovereign is less stringently applied where the operation of the law is upon the agents or servants of the government, rather than on the sovereign itself.
>
> The second class — that where public officers are impliedly excluded from language embracing all persons — is where a reading which would include such officers would work obvious absurdity, as, for example, the application of a speed law to a policeman pursuing a criminal or the driver of a fire engine responding to an alarm.

Nardone v. United States, 302 U.S. 379, 384 (1937). Would it deprive the United States of an established prerogative of intelligence gathering and covert actions, or work an obvious absurdity, to apply the general criminal statutes described above to the CIA? Does it matter, in applying this canon, that Congress sometimes expressly extends criminal statutes to government officials, *see, e.g.*, 18 U.S.C. §§2340-2340A (defining federal crime of torture to apply to those "acting under the color of the law"), and sometimes expressly exempts the government from a criminal prohibition, *see, e.g.*, 18 U.S.C. §§2511(2)(e)-(f) (exempting certain forms of governmental electronic surveillance from the crime of intercepting electronic communications). On these questions, see Fred F. Manget, *Intelligence and the Criminal Law System*, 17 Stan. L. & Pol'y Rev. 415, 429-34 (2006).

4. Section 3093(a)(5) prohibits violations of the Constitution or any statute, but says nothing about violations of international law. Presumably, the ban extends to violations of international law if the international law is incorporated into a statute, such as the torture law mentioned above, which implements the obligations of the Torture Convention, and the War Crimes Act, 18 U.S.C. §2441, which implements the Geneva Conventions and other international obligations. But is the CIA in its covert actions bound by "non-self-executing international law" that has not been incorporated into domestic law? For example, must it comply with the U.N. Charter, which is not incorporated into domestic law, but which on the international plane requires nations to "refrain in their international relations from the threat or use of force against the territorial integrity or political independence of any state," unless acting in self-defense, or pursuant to a U.N. Security Council Resolution? Former legal advisor to the NSC James E. Baker maintains that §3093(a)(5) requires covert action to comply with "international law to the extent that such law is incorporated into U.S. law." *See* James E. Baker, In the Common Defense: National Security Law for Perilous Times 154 (2007). Does that mean that covert actions may violate the U.N. Charter? Isn't it obvious that many of them in fact do?

5. International law is potentially relevant to another substantive limit on covert actions: the federal assassination ban. The Church Commission condemned CIA involvement in assassination plots and was prepared to ban them by statute. But when President Gerald Ford proclaimed in Executive Order 11,905 that "[n]o employee of the United States Government shall engage in, or conspire to engage in, political assassination," Congress dropped the threatened legislation. The assassination ban remains in effect in Executive Order 12,333, §2.11, a successor to Executive Order 11,905, with essentially the same wording except that the Carter Administration eliminated the qualifier "political," a change all future presidents maintained. But what is "assassination"? The term is not defined in the executive order. Does it prohibit all state-sponsored killings? Politically motivated ones? Something beyond politically motivated killings (perhaps because of the elimination of the term "political")? State-sponsored killings that violate international law?

To understand how the Executive Branch construes the term, consider that Clinton Administration lawyers argued that a covert action order to kill Bin Laden would be consistent with the assassination ban because "under the law of armed conflict, killing a person who posed an imminent threat to the United States would be an act of self-defense, not an assassination." The "law of armed conflict" is another term for *jus in bello* or the laws of war — i.e., the international laws that govern how warfare is waged. The Clinton Administration legal theory appeared to be (a) the United States was in an "armed conflict" with Al Qaeda in 1998, probably because Al Qaeda declared war on it in as early as 1996 and attacked the United States several times in the 1990s; (b) targeting a legitimate "military objective" in an armed conflict is lawful under international law and thus not an assassination; and (c) Bin Laden was a legitimate military objective because he was the leader of Al Qaeda. *See also* Baker, In the Common Defense, *supra*, at 154-55 (arguing that "the targeting of legitimate military targets consistent with the law of armed conflict is not considered 'assassination' under the executive order"). Are you convinced by this theory? What other international laws might be relevant to the meaning of the assassination ban? What if the target of a killing is a legitimate military objective under the law of armed conflict but the attack would violate the U.N. Charter, which prohibits uses of force against another nation unless made in self-defense or pursuant to a U.N. Security Council Resolution? For various perspectives on the meaning of assassination in addition to Baker's, see W. Michael Reisman & James E. Baker, Regulating Covert Action: Practices, Contexts, and Policies of Covert Coercion Abroad in International and American Law (1992); Jonathan M. Fredman, *Covert Action, Loss of Life, and the Prohibition on Assassination*, No. 1 Studies in Intelligence 15 (1997); William C. Banks & Peter Raven-Hansen, *Targeted Killing and Assassination: The U.S. Legal Framework*, 37 U. Rich. L. Rev. 667 (2002-2003); W. Hays Parks, *Memorandum of Law: Executive Order 12,333 and Assassination*, Army Lawyer 4 (Dec. 1989); Michael N. Schmitt, *State-Sponsored Assassination in International and Domestic Law*, 17 Yale J. Int'l L. 609 (1992); Abraham Sofaer, *Terrorism, the Law, and National Defense*, 126 Mil. L. Rev. 89 (1989); Thomas C. Wingfield, *Taking Aim at Regime Elites: Assassination, Tyrannicide, and Regime Elites*, 22 Am. J. Int'l L. & Trade 287 (1998).

Note that the assassination ban is in an Executive Order that can in theory be changed at any time by the President. James Baker argues that this means that the ban is "subject like other executive orders to classified presidential interpretation, amendment, or suspension." Baker, In the Common Defense, *supra*, at 155. Does that mean that the President is permitted to assassinate someone under domestic law if the President waives or modifies the ban in secret? If so, what purpose might the ban serve? We return to the assassination ban in the next chapter, when we discuss "targeted killing" in the war on terrorism.

6. One justification for the relatively open-ended delegation of covert action authority to the President, and the relatively lax set of substantive controls on such actions, is that covert actions are closely regulated procedurally. Study carefully the various procedural requirements in §3093 and in Executive Order 12,333. How do they redress the problems that arose in the Iran-Contra scandal? Do they do so successfully?

The requirements of §3093 and Executive Order 12,333 have given rise to an elaborate bureaucratic procedure to support each covert action. This structure, hinted at in the excerpt about the Bin Laden operation, operates in general as follows. *See generally* William J. Daugherty, '*Approval and Review of Covert Action Programs Since Reagan*, 17 Int'l J. Intelligence and Counterintelligence 62 (2004). A request for covert action typically begins outside the CIA, in the National Security Council. The CIA has an extensive internal process to craft and vet each proposed covert action to ensure that it is likely to succeed, worth the risks, and lawful. The proposal takes the form of a draft "Finding" for the President's signature that satisfies the certification requirements of §3093(a), and a detailed supporting document that typically states the precise foreign policy objectives to be gained by the covert action, a plan of action, a risk assessment, and a list of required resources. The CIA coordinates the draft Finding through the Director of National Intelligence, which since 2004 has overseen the entire Intelligence Community (a task formerly performed by the Director of the CIA), and which under Executive Order 12,333 oversees all covert action programs. Once this process is complete, the proposal goes to the White House. There it is elaborately reviewed again by lawyers and policymakers from the National Security Council, and the Departments of Justice, State, and Defense. It is further vetted by the Deputies Committee (number two officials in the relevant Departments, including the Justice Department) and the Principals Committee" (the National Security Advisor and the heads of relevant Departments, including the Attorney General). If approved, the proposed Finding and supporting memorandum goes to the President for signature. Under §3093(c), Findings must be reported to the congressional intelligence committees "as soon as possible after such approval and before the initiation of the covert action authorized by the finding," §3093(c)(1). Any subsequent changes to a covert action or significant new activity pursuant to a previous covert action Finding must be reported to Congress as well, *see* §3093(c)(1). The document that accomplishes this is called a Memorandum of Notification.

The intelligence committees lack a formal mechanism to modify or veto the intelligence actions the President reports to them, but they do have significant power to do so. *See generally* Daugherty, *Approval and Review, supra*; Snider, *The Agency and the Hill, supra.* They can leak the proposed operation to the press. They can (despite executive secrecy) take the proposal to the full Congress and seek legislation to stop it, as happened when Congress curbed covert action in Angola in 1975. They can deny funding for the operation's implementation, as they have done at least a few times, most notably when Congress terminated funds for the Contras in the 1980s. Or they can take a more direct route by complaining to the President, either with a formal vote, or through informal channels. Not all of the evidence for presidential reversals is publicly available, but we do know that in several instances President Reagan signed but then rescinded proposed covert actions in response to committee unhappiness, and the first President Bush pulled back on at least one. More recently, in 2004, members of the intelligence committees reportedly objected strongly to a covert action Finding to support U.S.-friendly candidates in an upcoming Iraq election and President Bush rescinded the Finding. *See* Douglas Jehl & David Sanger, *Plan Called for Covert Aid in Iraq Vote*, N.Y. Times, July 17, 2005. Presidents often relent in the face of serious objections from the intelligence committees because they know that a covert or intelligence operation is politically much riskier, and its success less assured, if the committees are not on board, and that the committees will retaliate in other intelligence contexts if the President departs too sharply from their wishes.

7. Note that there are two exceptions to the President's duty to report covert actions. First, if the President "determines that it is essential to limit access to the finding to meet extraordinary circumstances affecting vital interests of the United States," the President may report the Finding only to the "Gang of Eight," which consists of the chairmen and ranking minority members of the congressional intelligence committees and the top two Democrats and top two Republicans in the Senate and House of Representatives, §3093(c)(2). Second, "[w]henever a finding is not reported to [the committees or the Gang of Eight], the President shall fully inform the congressional intelligence committees in a timely fashion and shall provide a statement of the reasons for not giving prior notice," §3093(c)(3). Does this latter exception, which was the subject of lengthy negotiation between President George H. W. Bush and Congress, implicitly authorize the President to withhold reporting to Congress? Why is it drafted the way it is? There are no known instances of Presidents invoking this provision, but there is an example of a President withholding notification for a covert action from Congress on a principled ground prior to the enactment of §3093(c)(3) that may explain why the provision exists. President

Carter withheld notification to Congress of a covert action to assist with the rescue of six Americans from the Canadian embassy in Iran in 1980 on the ground that Canada refused to cooperate in the operation unless he withheld notice. Is this a sound exercise of discretion to withhold notice from Congress? Would the statutory language limit non-reporting to circumstances such as these?

8. What is the relationship between the President's covert action authority and the President's war power authority under the Commander-in-Chief Clause? To answer this question, compare the 1998 Tomahawk cruise missile attack on Bin Laden camps in Afghanistan that was the initial U.S. response to the African embassy bombings, and the later 1998 covert action plan to capture or kill Bin Laden. The cruise missile strike rested on the President's constitutional authority, and President Clinton reported the strike to Congress after the fact, "consistent with the War Powers Resolution." President Clinton's covert action a few months later rested on his constitutional authority plus the statutory authority in §3093. President Clinton sent a Memorandum of Notification (which updated an earlier Finding) to the intelligence committees before the action. The action never came to fruition, but if it had, the President would not have needed to report it under the War Powers Resolution, which applies only to the "introduction of *United States Armed Forces*" into hostilities or potential hostilities, see War Powers Resolution §§2(a), 5(b), and thus does not apply to CIA covert actions. Recall, further, that in §2(c) of the War Powers Resolution, Congress stated the three circumstances in which it thought the President could use force unilaterally, and that §5(b) of the War Powers Resolution requires the President to terminate certain uses of military forces after 60 or 90 days in the absence of intervening congressional approval. By contrast, §3093 offers no concrete limits on the use of covert actions and contains no termination provision. Do these differences between the regulation of war powers and covert actions make sense? When and why might the President choose one form of action over the other? Are there any natural limits on the use of covert action, perhaps because the CIA lacks the military capacities of the U.S. armed forces? Might these relative capacities be changing in light of the fact that the "Special Activities Division" of the CIA, the component that runs paramilitary and lethal operations, has its own vehicles, airplanes, and military equipment, and that since September 11, 2001, the CIA has developed a capacity to launch missiles from its own unmanned aerial vehicles (colloquially known as "drones")?

9. Consider these questions further in light of the 2011 military operations in Libya. Recall from Section C that the overt military intervention began in March 2011; that President Obama justified this intervention on the basis of his constitutional powers; that he reported the intervention to Congress consistent with the War Powers Resolution and pledged that he would "not put ground troops into Libya"; that he halted U.S.-piloted air strikes in late March but continued U.S. air strikes from U.S. military drones in April; and that in May and June the military intervention became mired in legal controversy when it lasted more than 60 days without congressional authorization, in possible contravention of §5(b) of the War Powers Resolution.

Now consider the following facts about CIA activities in Libya: In late February 2011, before the U.N.-approved no-fly zone and authorization of force, President Obama sent CIA operatives (who are technically not "ground troops") into Libya to gather intelligence for future air strikes and to learn about the rebels. Then, sometime in March, the President signed a Finding authorizing a covert action to provide arms, money, trainers, and other support to Libyan rebels, if the need and occasion arose. *See* Mark Mazzetti & Eric Schmidt, *C.I.A. Agents in Libya Aid Airstrikes and Meet Rebels*, N.Y. Times, Mar. 30, 2011; Mark Hosenball, *U.S. Agents Were in Libya Before Secret Obama Order*, Reuters, Mar. 31, 2011; Karen DeYoung & Greg Miller, *In Libya, CIA Is Gathering Intelligence on Rebels*, Wash. Post, Mar. 30, 2011. Note that a Finding was probably not needed for the late-February intervention to the extent that it was primarily an intelligence-gathering operation or diplomatic initiative, both of which are excluded from the definition of "covert action" in §3093(e)(1) and (2). By contrast, when the CIA presence shifted beyond mere intelligence collection to acts designed "to influence political, economic, or military conditions abroad," §3093(e), the covert action requirements were triggered. Note further that while the mere intelligence-gathering activities that began in late February did not trigger the covert action requirements, the President still had a duty to report them, under a different notification scheme for intelligence activities, to the intelligence committees. *See* 50 U.S.C. §3092(a)(1) (imposing a duty on the Executive Branch to "keep the congressional intelligence committees fully and currently informed of all intelligence activities, other than a covert action . . . , including any significant anticipated intelligence activity and any significant intelligence failure").

Instead of using U.S. military forces to bomb Libyan targets, which raised difficult questions under the War Powers Resolution, could the President have skirted domestic legal controversy via a "covert action" in which the CIA dropped bombs in Libya from its own drones? What legal and political obstacles might have prevented him from taking this route? What does the answer to this question indicate about the substitutability of war powers and covert actions? Does the possibility of CIA drone attacks make the War Powers Resolution or the covert action statute, or both, seem outdated? Why?

10. The United States military often conducts secret operations of various sorts in the midst of or in preparation for war that are not "covert actions" within the meaning of §3093. As a general matter, these secret military activities would require authorization from the President exercising Article II authorities, or from Congress in an authorization to use military force. They would also need to comply with the general chain of command requirements as set forth in Title 10 of the U.S. Code. Many of these secret operations so authorized might be thought to satisfy the general definition of "covert actions" in §3093(e) because they are designed to influence political, economic, or military conditions abroad, and thus might trigger §3093's relatively strict procedural requirements. However, §3093(e)(2) contains an important exception for "traditional military activities." The covert action statute does not define "traditional military activities." But the legislative history to the Intelligence Authorization Act of 1991, where the definition and exception originated, contains an influential explanation:

> It is the intent of the conferees that "traditional military activities" include activities by military personnel under the direction and control of a United States military commander (whether or not the U.S. sponsorship of such activities is apparent or later to be acknowledged) preceding and related to hostilities which are either anticipated (meaning approval has been given by the National Command Authorities for the activities and for operational planning for hostilities) to involve U.S. military forces, or where such hostilities involving United States military forces are ongoing, and, where the fact of the U.S. role in the overall operation is apparent or to be acknowledged publicly. In this regard, the conferees intend to draw a line between activities that are and are not under the direction and control of the military commander. Activities that

are not under the direction and control of a military commander should not be considered as "traditional military activities."

See 3 Joint Explanatory Statement of the Committee of Conference, H.R. 1455, July 25, 1991. Whether a secret military activity constitutes a covert action, or whether it is excluded by the "traditional military activities" exception, can have important consequences. As a general matter, and in contrast to CIA covert actions, the Department of Defense does not have strict reporting requirements to its main oversight committees, the Senate and House Arms Services Committees. Moreover, some small-scale secret military activities in a foreign country might not rise to the level of threatened "hostilities" or other predicates that would trigger reporting requirements under the War Powers Resolution. In this scenario, the U.S. military might engage in secret military operations to which no reporting operations attach. We consider the complex relationship between covert actions and secret military activities, as well as what happens when the CIA and U.S. armed forces work together in secret operations, in the next chapter on the war on terrorism.

11. In the context of cyber operations, there is little historical precedent to inform the question of which acts constitute traditional military activities. This ambiguity has reportedly produced tensions among several executive agencies. The Defense Department apparently wanted the authority to conduct offensive cyber operations, including operations that destroy, disrupt, or degrade targeted computers or networks. It argued that those operations would constitute traditional military activities, even if undertaken outside war zones, and so were excluded from the procedural requirements of the covert action statute. In contrast, the CIA apparently argued that offensive cyber operations fell within the definition of covert action and should not be undertaken outside of that framework. *See* Ellen Nakashima, *Pentagon Is Debating Cyber-Attacks*, Wash. Post, Nov. 6, 2010. In the 2019 John S. McCain National Defense Authorization Act, Congress resolved the debate in favor of the Defense Department. 10 U.S.C. §394(c) provides: "A clandestine military activity or operation in cyberspace shall be considered a traditional military activity for the purposes of section 503(e)(2) of the National Security Act of 1947 (50 U.S.C. 3093(e)(2))." At the same time, the statute requires the Secretary of Defense to brief the congressional defense committees on a quarterly basis about "any military activities or operations in cyberspace," preserving a measure of congressional oversight over these operations. For a discussion of these provisions, see Robert Chesney, *The Law of Military Cyber Operations and the New NDAA*, Lawfare (July 26, 2018).

E. WAR AND INDIVIDUAL LIBERTIES

This section considers the issue of protecting individual liberties during wartime. To illustrate the types of issues that can arise, materials are presented from three conflicts — the Civil War, World War II, and the Vietnam War — followed by notes and questions. When reading these materials, consider (a) whether the purported infringement on individual liberties was the result of unilateral action by the Executive or joint action by the Executive and Congress, and (b) the extent to which the Supreme Court takes account of perceived national security interests in determining the scope of the individual right in question.

1. The Civil War

As we learned in Chapter 1, soon after the Civil War began in April 1861, President Lincoln suspended the writ of habeas corpus in various parts of the United States, and Chief Justice Taney, riding Circuit, declared this action unconstitutional in May 1861 in *Ex parte Merryman*. In his July 4, 1861, message to Congress, Lincoln defended his actions:

> [T]he legality and propriety of what has been done [pursuant to my authorization to military authorities to suspend the writ of habeas corpus] are questioned and the attention of the country has been called to the proposition that one who is sworn to "take care that the laws be faithfully executed" should not himself violate them. . . . The whole of the laws which were required to be faithfully executed were being resisted and failing of execution in nearly one-third of the States. Must they be allowed to finally fail of execution, even had it been perfectly clear that by the use of the means necessary to their execution some single law, made in such extreme tenderness of the citizen's liberty that practically it relieves more of the guilty than of the innocent, should to a very limited extent be violated? To state the question more directly, are all the laws but one to go unexecuted and the Government itself go to pieces lest that one be violated? Even in such a case would not the official oath be broken if the Government should be overthrown, when it was believed that disregarding the single law would tend to preserve it? But it was not believed that this question was presented. It was not believed that any law was violated. The provision of the Constitution that "the privilege of the writ of habeas corpus shall not be suspended unless when in cases of rebellion or invasion the public safety may require it," is equivalent to a provision — is a provision — that such privilege may be suspended when in cases of rebellion or invasion the public safety does require it. It was decided that we have a case of rebellion, and that the public safety does require the qualified suspension of the privilege of the writ which was authorized to be made. Now, it is insisted that Congress and not the Executive is vested with this power. But the Constitution itself is silent as to which, or who, is to exercise the power; and as the provision was plainly made for a dangerous emergency, it cannot be believed the framers of the instrument intended that in every case the danger should run its course until Congress could be called together, the very assembling of which might be prevented, as was intended in this case, by the rebellion.
>
> . . . Whether there shall be any legislation upon the subject, and if any, what, is submitted entirely to the better judgment of Congress.

More than a year and a half later, Congress enacted the Habeas Corpus Act of 1863. Section 1 of the Act provided that "during the present rebellion, the President of the United States, whenever, in his judgment the public safety may require it, is authorized to suspend the writ of *habeas corpus* in any case throughout the United States or any part thereof." Section 2 of the Act then qualified this authorization in an important way. It required the Executive Branch to furnish a list of persons other than "prisoners of war" who were imprisoned without trial in states "in which the administration of the laws has continued unimpaired in the . . . Federal courts," and required federal courts to release such persons if the grand jury did not indict them for a federal crime by the time the grand jury terminated its session.

Ex parte Milligan

71 U.S. 2 (1866)

[In October 1864, in the midst of the Civil War, the U.S. general commanding the military district of Indiana arrested Lambdin Milligan. Milligan, a U.S. citizen living in Indiana, was accused of conspiracy against the government, giving aid and comfort to the rebels, initiating insurrection, disloyal practices, and violating the laws of war. He was tried before a commission of U.S. military judges established by Lincoln, exercising his powers as Commander in Chief. The commission found Milligan guilty and sentenced him to be hanged. Milligan then petitioned a lower federal court for a writ of habeas corpus. He argued that because he was a citizen of Indiana who was not a prisoner of war, and because the grand jury of the district had met and convened without indicting him, §2 of the Habeas Corpus Act of 1863, which qualified the President's authority to suspend the writ of habeas corpus, was satisfied and required his release. The lower federal court certified the case to the Supreme Court.]

MR. JUSTICE DAVIS delivered the opinion of the court. . . .

The Constitution of the United States is a law for rulers and people, equally in war and in peace, and covers with the shield of its protection all classes of men, at all times, and under all circumstances. No doctrine, involving more pernicious consequences, was ever invented by the wit of man than that any of its provisions can be suspended during any of the great exigencies of government. Such a doctrine leads directly to anarchy or despotism, but the theory of necessity on which it is based is false; for the government, within the Constitution, has all the powers granted to it, which are necessary to preserve its existence; as has been happily proved by the result of the great effort to throw off its just authority.

Have any of the rights guaranteed by the Constitution been violated in the case of Milligan? and if so, what are they?

Every trial involves the exercise of judicial power; and from what source did the military commission that tried him derive their authority? Certainly no part of the judicial power of the country was conferred on them; because the Constitution expressly vests it "in one supreme court and such inferior courts as the Congress may from time to time ordain and establish," and it is not pretended that the commission was a court ordained and established by Congress. They cannot justify on the mandate of the President; because he is controlled by law, and has his appropriate sphere of duty, which is to execute, not to make, the laws; and there is "no unwritten criminal code to which resort can be had as a source of jurisdiction."

But it is said that the jurisdiction is complete under the "laws and usages of war."

It can serve no useful purpose to inquire what those laws and usages are, whence they originated, where found, and on whom they operate; they can never be applied to citizens in states which have upheld the authority of the government, and where the courts are open and their process unobstructed. This court has judicial knowledge that in Indiana the Federal authority was always unopposed, and its courts always open to hear criminal accusations and redress grievances; and no usage of war could sanction a military trial there for any offence whatever of a citizen in civil life, in nowise connected with the military service. Congress could grant no such power; and to the honor of our national legislature be it said, it has never been provoked by the state of the country even to attempt its exercise. One of the plainest constitutional provisions was, therefore, infringed when Milligan was tried by a court not ordained and established by Congress, and not composed of judges appointed during good behavior.

Why was he not delivered to the Circuit Court of Indiana to be proceeded against according to law? No reason of necessity could be urged against it; because

Congress had declared penalties against the offences charged, provided for their punishment, and directed that court to hear and determine them. . . .

Another guarantee of freedom was broken when Milligan was denied a trial by jury. . . . [T]his right — one of the most valuable in a free country — is preserved to every one accused of crime who is not attached to the army, or navy, or militia in actual service. The sixth amendment affirms that "in all criminal prosecutions the accused shall enjoy the right to a speedy and public trial by an impartial jury," language broad enough to embrace all persons and cases; but the fifth, recognizing the necessity of an indictment, or presentment, before any one can be held to answer for high crimes, "excepts cases arising in the land or naval forces, or in the militia, when in actual service, in time of war or public danger"; and the framers of the Constitution, doubtless, meant to limit the right of trial by jury, in the sixth amendment, to those persons who were subject to indictment or presentment in the fifth.

The discipline necessary to the efficiency of the army and navy, required other and swifter modes of trial than are furnished by the common law courts; and, in pursuance of the power conferred by the Constitution, Congress has declared the kinds of trial, and the manner in which they shall be conducted, for offences committed while the party is in the military or naval service. Every one connected with these branches of the public service is amenable to the jurisdiction which Congress has created for their government, and, while thus serving, surrenders his right to be tried by the civil courts. All other persons, citizens of states where the courts are open, if charged with crime, are guaranteed the inestimable privilege of trial by jury. This privilege is a vital principle, underlying the whole administration of criminal justice; it is not held by sufferance, and cannot be frittered away on any plea of state or political necessity. When peace prevails, and the authority of the government is undisputed, there is no difficulty of preserving the safeguards of liberty; for the ordinary modes of trial are never neglected, and no one wishes it otherwise; but if society is disturbed by civil commotion — if the passions of men are aroused and the restraints of law weakened, if not disregarded — these safeguards need, and should receive, the watchful care of those entrusted with the guardianship of the Constitution and laws. . . .

It is claimed that martial law covers with its broad mantle the proceedings of this military commission. The proposition is this: that in a time of war the commander of an armed force (if in his opinion the exigencies of the country demand it, and of which he is to judge), has the power, within the lines of his military district, to suspend all civil rights and their remedies, and subject citizens as well as soldiers to the rule of his will; and in the exercise of his lawful authority cannot be restrained, except by his superior officer or the President of the United States.

If this position is sound to the extent claimed, then when war exists, foreign or domestic, and the country is subdivided into military departments for mere convenience, the commander of one of them can, if he chooses, within his limits, on the plea of necessity, with the approval of the Executive, substitute military force for and to the exclusion of the laws, and punish all persons, as he thinks right and proper, without fixed or certain rules.

The statement of this proposition shows its importance; for, if true, republican government is a failure, and there is an end of liberty regulated by law. Martial law, established on such a basis, destroys every guarantee of the Constitution, and effectually renders the "military independent of and superior to the civil power" — the attempt to do which by the King of Great Britain was deemed by our fathers such an offence, that they assigned it to the world as one of the causes which impelled them to declare their independence. Civil liberty and this kind of martial law cannot endure together; the antagonism is irreconcilable; and, in the conflict, one or the other must perish. . . .

It is essential to the safety of every government that, in a great crisis, like the one we have just passed through, there should be a power somewhere of suspending the writ of habeas corpus. In every war, there are men of previously good character, wicked enough to counsel their fellow-citizens to resist the measures deemed necessary by a good government to sustain its just authority and overthrow its enemies; and their influence may lead to dangerous combinations. In the emergency of the times, an immediate public investigation according to law may not be possible; and yet, the peril to the country may be too imminent to suffer such persons to go at large. Unquestionably, there is then an exigency which demands that the government, if it should see fit in the exercise of a proper discretion to make arrests, should not be required to produce the persons arrested in answer to a writ of habeas corpus. The Constitution goes no further. It does not say after a writ of habeas corpus is denied a citizen, that he shall be tried otherwise than by the course of the common law; if it had intended this result, it was easy by the use of direct words to have accomplished it. The illustrious men who framed that instrument were guarding the foundations of civil liberty against the abuses of unlimited power; they were full of wisdom, and the lessons of history informed them that a trial by an established court, assisted by an impartial jury, was the only sure way of protecting the citizen against oppression and wrong. Knowing this, they limited the suspension to one great right, and left the rest to remain forever inviolable. But, it is insisted that the safety of the country in time of war demands that this broad claim for martial law shall be sustained. If this were true, it could be well said that a country, preserved at the sacrifice of all the cardinal principles of liberty, is not worth the cost of preservation. Happily, it is not so. . . .

It is difficult to see how the safety of the country required martial law in Indiana. If any of her citizens were plotting treason, the power of arrest could secure them, until the government was prepared for their trial, when the courts were open and ready to try them. It was as easy to protect witnesses before a civil as a military tribunal; and as there could be no wish to convict, except on sufficient legal evidence, surely an ordained and established court was better able to judge of this than a military tribunal composed of gentlemen not trained to the profession of the law.

It follows, from what has been said on this subject, that there are occasions when martial rule can be properly applied. If, in foreign invasion or civil war, the courts are actually closed, and it is impossible to administer criminal justice according to law, then, on the theatre of active military operations, where war really prevails, there is a necessity to furnish a substitute for the civil authority, thus overthrown, to preserve the safety of the army and society; and as no power is left but the military, it is allowed to govern by martial rule until the laws can have their free course. As necessity creates the rule, so it limits its duration; for, if this government is continued after the courts are reinstated, it is a gross usurpation of power. Martial rule can never exist where the courts are open, and in the proper and unobstructed exercise of their jurisdiction. It is also confined to the locality of actual war. Because, during the late Rebellion it could have been enforced in Virginia, where the national authority was overturned and the courts driven out, it does not follow that it should obtain in Indiana, where that authority was never disputed, and justice was always administered. And so in the case of a foreign invasion, martial rule may become a necessity in one state, when, in another, it would be "mere lawless violence." . . .

If the military trial of Milligan was contrary to law, then he was entitled, on the facts stated in his petition, to be discharged from custody by the terms of the act of Congress of March 3d, 1863. . . . Milligan avers he was a citizen of Indiana, not in the military or naval service, and was detained in close confinement, by order of the President, from the 5th day of October, 1864, until the 2d day of January, 1865, when the Circuit Court for the District of Indiana, with a grand jury, convened in session at Indianapolis; and afterwards, on the 27th day of the same month, adjourned without finding an indictment or presentment against him. If these averments were true (and their truth is conceded for the purposes of this case), the court was required to liberate him on taking certain oaths prescribed by the law, and entering into recognizance for his good behavior.

But it is insisted that Milligan was a prisoner of war, and, therefore, excluded from the privileges of the statute. It is not easy to see how he can be treated as a prisoner of war, when he lived in Indiana for the past twenty years, was arrested there, and had not been, during the late troubles, a resident of any of the states in rebellion. If in Indiana he conspired with bad men to assist the enemy, he is punishable for it in the courts of Indiana; but, when tried for the offence, he cannot plead the rights of war; for he was not engaged in legal acts of hostility against the government, and only such persons, when captured, are prisoners of war. If he cannot enjoy the immunities attaching to the character of a prisoner of war, how can he be subject to their pains and penalties? . . .

THE CHIEF JUSTICE [Chase] delivered the following opinion.

[Chase first argued that because Milligan satisfied the criteria of §2 of the Habeas Corpus Act of 1863 — i.e., that he was not a prisoner of war, was imprisoned in a state where the laws had continued unimpaired in the federal courts, and was not indicted by the grand jury during its term — the Habeas Statute required his release.]

But the [majority opinion] goes further; and as we understand it, asserts not only that the military commission held in Indiana was not authorized by Congress, but that it was not in the power of Congress to authorize it. . . .

We cannot agree to this. . . .

We think that Congress had power, though not exercised, to authorize the military commission which was held in Indiana. . . .

Congress has the power not only to raise and support and govern armies but to declare war. It has, therefore, the power to provide by law for carrying on war. This power necessarily extends to all legislation essential to the prosecution of war with vigor and success, except such as interferes with the command of the forces and the conduct of campaigns. That power and duty belong to the President as commander-in-chief. . . .

[W]hen the nation is involved in war, and some portions of the country are invaded, and all are exposed to invasion, it is within the power of Congress to determine in what states or districts such great and imminent public danger exists as justifies the authorization of military tribunals for the trial of crimes and offences against the discipline or security of the army or against the public safety. . . .

We cannot doubt that, in such a time of public danger, Congress had power, under the Constitution, to provide for the organization of a military commission, and for trial by that commission of persons engaged in this conspiracy. The fact that the Federal courts were open was regarded by Congress as a sufficient reason for not exercising the power; but that fact could not deprive Congress of the right to exercise it. Those courts might be open and undisturbed in the execution of their functions, and yet wholly incompetent to avert threatened danger, or to punish, with adequate promptitude and certainty, the guilty conspirators. . . .

We have confined ourselves to the question of power. It was for Congress to determine the question of expediency. And Congress did determine it. That body did not see fit to authorize trials by military commission in Indiana, but by the strongest implication prohibited them. . . .

MR. JUSTICE WAYNE, MR. JUSTICE SWAYNE, and MR. JUSTICE MILLER, concur with me in these views.

2. World War II

Korematsu v. United States

323 U.S. 214 (1944)

[Two months after the attack on Pearl Harbor in 1941, President Roosevelt issued the following executive order:

> WHEREAS the successful prosecution of the war requires every possible protection against espionage and against sabotage to national-defense material, national-defense premises, and national-defense utilities . . .
>
> NOW, THEREFORE, by virtue of the authority vested in me as President of the United States, and Commander in Chief of the Army and Navy, I hereby authorize and direct the Secretary of War, and the Military Commanders whom he may from time to time designate, whenever he or any designated Commander deems such actions necessary or desirable, to prescribe military areas in such places and of such extent as he or the appropriate Military Commanders may determine, from which any or all persons may be excluded, and with such respect to which, the right of any person to enter, remain in, or leave shall be subject to whatever restrictions the Secretary of War or the appropriate Military Commander may impose in his discretion. The Secretary of War is hereby authorized to provide for residents of any such area who are excluded therefrom, such transportation, food, shelter, and other accommodations as may be necessary, in the judgement of the Secretary of War or the said Military Commander, and until other arrangements are made, to accomplish the purpose of this order. . . .
>
> I hereby further authorize and direct the Secretary of War and the said Military Commanders to take such other steps as he or the appropriate Military Commander may deem advisable to enforce compliance with the restrictions applicable to each Military area hereinabove authorized to be designated, including the use of Federal troops and other Federal Agencies, with authority to accept assistance of state and local agencies.

Executive Order No. 9066, 7 Fed. Reg. 1407. Pursuant to this Order, the Commanding General of the Western Command excluded Japanese-Americans from the West Coast area and ordered them curfewed, and/or detained in relocation centers. In 1942, Congress enacted a statute that provided:

> . . . whoever shall enter, remain in, leave, or commit any act in any military area or military zone prescribed, under the authority of an Executive order of the President, by the Secretary of War, or by any military commander designated by the Secretary of War, contrary to the restrictions applicable to any such area or zone or contrary to the order of the Secretary of War or any such military commander, shall, if it appears that he knew or should have known of the existence and extent of the restrictions or order and that his act was in violation thereof, be guilty of a misdemeanor and upon

conviction shall be liable to a fine of not to exceed $5,000 or to imprisonment for not more than one year, or both, for each offense.

Act of Congress of March 21, 1942, 56 Stat. 173. Korematsu, an American citizen of Japanese descent, was convicted under this statute for remaining in San Leandro, California, a "Military Area," contrary to Civilian Exclusion Order No. 34 of the Commanding General of the Western Command, U.S. Army, which directed that after May 9, 1942, all persons of Japanese ancestry should be excluded from that area.]

MR. JUSTICE BLACK delivered the opinion of the Court. . . .

One of the series of orders and proclamations, a curfew order, which like the exclusion order here was promulgated pursuant to Executive Order 9066, subjected all persons of Japanese ancestry in prescribed West Coast military areas to remain in their residences from 8 p.m. to 6 a.m. As is the case with the exclusion order here, that prior curfew order was designed as a "protection against espionage and against sabotage." In Hirabayashi v. United States, 320 U.S. 81, we sustained a conviction obtained for violation of the curfew order. The *Hirabayashi* conviction and this one thus rest on the same 1942 Congressional Act and the same basic executive and military orders, all of which orders were aimed at the twin dangers of espionage and sabotage.

The 1942 Act was attacked in the *Hirabayashi* case as an unconstitutional delegation of power; it was contended that the curfew order and other orders on which it rested were beyond the war powers of the Congress, the military authorities and of the President, as Commander in Chief of the Army; and finally that to apply the curfew order against none but citizens of Japanese ancestry amounted to a constitutionally prohibited discrimination solely on account of race. To these questions, we gave the serious consideration which their importance justified. We upheld the curfew order as an exercise of the power of the government to take steps necessary to prevent espionage and sabotage in an area threatened by Japanese attack.

In the light of the principles we announced in the *Hirabayashi* case, we are unable to conclude that it was beyond the war power of Congress and the Executive to exclude those of Japanese ancestry from the West Coast war area at the time they did. True, exclusion from the area in which one's home is located is a far greater deprivation than constant confinement to the home from 8 p.m. to 6 a.m. Nothing short of apprehension by the proper military authorities of the gravest imminent danger to the public safety can constitutionally justify either. But exclusion from a threatened area, no less than curfew, has a definite and close relationship to the prevention of espionage and sabotage. The military authorities, charged with the primary responsibility of defending our shores, concluded that curfew provided inadequate protection and ordered exclusion. They did so, as pointed out in our *Hirabayashi* opinion, in accordance with Congressional authority to the military to say who should, and who should not, remain in the threatened areas.

In this case the petitioner challenges the assumptions upon which we rested our conclusions in the *Hirabayashi* case. He also urges that by May 1942, when Order No. 34 was promulgated, all danger of Japanese invasion of the West Coast had disappeared. After careful consideration of these contentions we are compelled to reject them.

Here, as in the *Hirabayashi* case, "we cannot reject as unfounded the judgment of the military authorities and of Congress that there were disloyal members of that population, whose number and strength could not be precisely and quickly ascertained. We cannot say that the war-making branches of the Government did not have ground for believing that in a critical hour such persons could not readily be isolated and separately dealt with, and constituted a menace to the national defense and safety, which demanded that prompt and adequate measures be taken to guard against it."

Like curfew, exclusion of those of Japanese origin was deemed necessary because of the presence of an unascertained number of disloyal members of the group, most of whom we have no doubt were loyal to this country. It was because we could not reject the finding of the military authorities that it was impossible to bring about an immediate segregation of the disloyal from the loyal that we sustained the validity of the curfew order as applying to the whole group. In the instant case, temporary exclusion of the entire group was rested by the military on the same ground. The judgment that exclusion of the whole group was for the same reason a military imperative answers the contention that the exclusion was in the nature of group punishment based on antagonism to those of Japanese origin. That there were members of the group who retained loyalties to Japan has been confirmed by investigations made subsequent to the exclusion. Approximately five thousand American citizens of Japanese ancestry refused to swear unqualified allegiance to the United States and to renounce allegiance to the Japanese Emperor, and several thousand evacuees requested repatriation to Japan.

We uphold the exclusion order as of the time it was made and when the petitioner violated it. In doing so, we are not unmindful of the hardships imposed by it upon a large group of American citizens. But hardships are part of war, and war is an aggregation of hardships. All citizens alike, both in and out of uniform, feel the impact of war in greater or lesser measure. Citizenship has its responsibilities as well as its privileges, and in time of war the burden is always heavier. Compulsory exclusion of large groups of citizens from their homes, except under circumstances of direst emergency and peril, is inconsistent with our basic governmental institutions. But when under conditions of modern warfare our shores are threatened by hostile forces, the power to protect must be commensurate with the threatened danger. . . .

It is said that we are dealing here with the case of imprisonment of a citizen in a concentration camp solely because of his ancestry, without evidence or inquiry concerning his loyalty and good disposition towards the United States. Our task would be simple, our duty clear, were this a case involving the imprisonment of a loyal citizen in a concentration camp because of racial prejudice. Regardless of the true nature of the assembly and relocation centers — and we deem it unjustifiable to call them concentration camps with all the ugly connotations that term implies — we are dealing specifically with nothing but an exclusion order. To cast this case into outlines of racial prejudice, without reference to the real military dangers which were presented, merely confuses the issue. Korematsu was not excluded from the Military Area because of hostility to him or his race. He *was* excluded because we are at war with the Japanese Empire, because the properly constituted military authorities feared an invasion of our West Coast and felt constrained to take proper security measures, because they decided that the military urgency of the situation demanded that all citizens of Japanese ancestry be segregated from the West Coast temporarily, and finally, because Congress, reposing its confidence in this time of war in our military leaders — as inevitably it must — determined that they should have the power to do just this. There was evidence of disloyalty on the part of some, the military authorities considered that the need for action was great, and time was short. We cannot — by availing ourselves of the calm perspective of hindsight — now say that at that time these actions were unjustified.

MR. JUSTICE FRANKFURTER, concurring. . . .

The provisions of the Constitution which confer on the Congress and the President powers to enable this country to wage war are as much part of the Constitution as provisions looking to a nation at peace. . . . Therefore, the validity of action under the war power must be judged wholly in the context of war. That action is not to be stigmatized as lawless because like action in times of peace would be lawless. To talk about a military order that expresses an allowable judgment of war needs by those entrusted with the duty of conducting war as "an unconstitutional order" is to suffuse a part of the Constitution with an atmosphere of unconstitutionality. The respective spheres of action of military authorities and of judges are of course very different. But within their sphere, military authorities are no more outside the bounds of obedience to the Constitution than are judges within theirs. . . . To recognize that military orders are "reasonably expedient military precautions" in time of war and yet to deny them constitutional legitimacy makes of the Constitution an instrument for dialectic subtleties not reasonably to be attributed to the hard-headed Framers, of whom a majority had had actual participation in war. If a military order such as that under review does not transcend the means appropriate for conducting war, such action by the military is as constitutional as would be any authorized action by the Interstate Commerce Commission within the limits of the constitutional power to regulate commerce. And being an exercise of the war power explicitly granted by the Constitution for safeguarding the national life by prosecuting war effectively, I find nothing in the Constitution which denies to Congress the power to enforce such a valid military order by making its violation an offense triable in the civil courts. To find that the Constitution does not forbid the military measures now complained of does not carry with it approval of that which Congress and the Executive did. That is their business, not ours.

MR. JUSTICE MURPHY, dissenting.

This exclusion of "all persons of Japanese ancestry, both alien and non-alien," from the Pacific Coast area on a plea of military necessity in the absence of martial law ought not to be approved. Such exclusion goes over "the very brink of constitutional power" and falls into the ugly abyss of racism.

In dealing with matters relating to the prosecution and progress of a war, we must accord great respect and consideration to the judgments of the military authorities who are on the scene and who have full knowledge of the military facts. . . .

At the same time, however, it is essential that there be definite limits to military discretion, especially where martial law has not been declared. Individuals must not be left impoverished of their constitutional rights on a plea of military necessity that has neither substance nor support. Thus, like other claims conflicting with the asserted constitutional rights of the individual, the military claim must subject itself to the judicial process of having its reasonableness determined and its conflicts with other interests reconciled. . . .

The main reasons relied upon by those responsible for the forced evacuation . . . do not prove a reasonable relation between the group characteristics of Japanese Americans and the dangers of invasion, sabotage and espionage. The reasons appear, instead, to be largely an accumulation of much of the misinformation, half-truths and insinuations that for years have been directed against Japanese Americans by people with racial and economic prejudices — the same people who have been among the foremost advocates of the evacuation. A military judgment based upon such racial and sociological considerations is not entitled to the great weight ordinarily given the judgments based upon strictly military considerations. Especially is this so when every charge relative to race, religion, culture, geographical location, and legal and economic status has been substantially discredited by independent studies made by experts in these matters.

The military necessity which is essential to the validity of the evacuation order thus resolves itself into a few intimations that certain individuals actively aided the enemy, from which it is inferred that the entire group of Japanese Americans could not be trusted to be or remain loyal to the United States. No one denies, of course, that there were some disloyal persons of Japanese descent on the Pacific Coast who did all in their power to aid their ancestral land. Similar disloyal activities have been engaged in by many persons of German, Italian and even more pioneer stock in our country. But to infer that examples of individual disloyalty prove group disloyalty and justify discriminatory action against the entire group is to deny that under our system of law individual guilt is the sole basis for deprivation of rights. . . .

MR. JUSTICE JACKSON, dissenting.

Korematsu was born on our soil, of parents born in Japan. The Constitution makes him a citizen of the United States by nativity and a citizen of California by residence. No claim is made that he is not loyal to this country. There is no suggestion that apart from the matter involved here he is not law-abiding and well disposed. Korematsu, however, has been convicted of an act not commonly a crime. It consists merely of being present in the state whereof he is a citizen, near the place where he was born, and where all his life he has lived. . . .

It would be impracticable and dangerous idealism to expect or insist that each specific military command in an area of probable operations will conform to conventional tests of constitutionality. When an area is so beset that it must be put under military control at all, the paramount consideration is that its measures be successful, rather than legal. The armed services must protect a society, not merely its Constitution. The very essence of the military job is to marshal physical force, to remove every obstacle to its effectiveness, to give it every strategic advantage. Defense measures will not, and often should not, be held within the limits that bind civil authority in peace. No court can require such a commander in such circumstances to act as a reasonable man; he may be unreasonably cautious and exacting. Perhaps he should be. But a commander in temporarily focusing the life of a community on defense is carrying out a military program; he is not making law in the sense the courts know the term. He issues orders, and they may have a certain authority as military commands, although they may be very bad as constitutional law.

But if we cannot confine military expedients by the Constitution, neither would I distort the Constitution to approve all that the military may deem expedient. That is what the Court appears to be doing, whether consciously or not. I cannot say, from any evidence before me, that the orders of General DeWitt were not reasonably expedient military precautions, nor could I say that they were. But even if they were permissible military procedures, I deny that it follows that they are constitutional. If, as the Court holds, it does follow, then we may as well say that any military order will be constitutional and have done with it.

The limitation under which courts always will labor in examining the necessity for a military order are illustrated by this case. How does the Court know that these orders have a reasonable basis in necessity? No evidence whatever on that subject has been taken by this or any other court. There is sharp controversy as to the credibility of the DeWitt report. So the Court, having no real evidence before it, has no choice but to accept General DeWitt's own unsworn, self-serving statement, untested by any cross-examination, that what he did was reasonable. And thus it will always be when courts try to look into the reasonableness of a military order.

In the very nature of things, military decisions are not susceptible of intelligent judicial appraisal. They do not pretend to rest on evidence, but are made on information that often would not be admissible and on assumptions that could not be proved. Information in support of an order could not be disclosed to courts without danger that it would reach the enemy. Neither can courts act on communications made in confidence. Hence courts can never have any real alternative to accepting the mere declaration of the authority that issued the order that it was reasonably necessary from a military viewpoint.

Much is said of the danger to liberty from the Army program for deporting and detaining these citizens of Japanese extraction. But a judicial construction of the due process clause that will sustain this order is a far more subtle blow to liberty than the promulgation of the order itself. A military order, however unconstitutional, is not apt to last longer than the military emergency. Even during that period a succeeding commander may revoke it all. But once a judicial opinion rationalizes such an order to show that it conforms to the Constitution, or rather rationalizes the Constitution to show that the Constitution sanctions such an order, the Court for all time has validated the principle of racial discrimination in criminal procedure and of transplanting American citizens. The principle then lies about like a loaded weapon ready for the hand of any authority that can bring forward a plausible claim of an urgent need. Every repetition imbeds that principle more deeply in our law and thinking and expands it to new purposes. . . .

I should hold that a civil court cannot be made to enforce an order which violates constitutional limitations even if it is a reasonable exercise of military authority. The courts can exercise only the judicial power, can apply only law, and must abide by the Constitution, or they cease to be civil courts and become instruments of military policy.

Of course the existence of a military power resting on force, so vagrant, so centralized, so necessarily heedless of the individual, is an inherent threat to liberty. But I would not lead people to rely on this Court for a review that seems to me wholly delusive. The military reasonableness of these orders can only be determined by military superiors. If the people ever let command of the war power fall into irresponsible and unscrupulous hands, the courts wield no power equal to its restraint. The chief restraint upon those who command the physical forces of the country, in the future as in the past, must be their responsibility to the political judgments of their contemporaries and to the moral judgments of history.

My duties as a justice as I see them do not require me to make a military judgment as to whether General DeWitt's evacuation and detention program was a reasonable military necessity. I do not suggest that the courts should have attempted to interfere with the Army in carrying out its task. But I do not think they may be asked to execute a military expedient that has no place in law under the Constitution. I would reverse the judgment and discharge the prisoner.

Ex parte Endo

323 U.S. 283 (1944)

[Appellant Mitsuye Endo, an American citizen of Japanese ancestry, was evacuated from Sacramento, California, in 1942, pursuant to the same military orders at issue in *Korematsu*, and was removed to the Tule Lake War Relocation Center located at Newell, Modoc County, California, an interim place of residence for Japanese evacuees. At such centers, the War Relocation Authority was supposed to segregate loyal from disloyal evacuees, detain only the disloyal ones, and relocate loyal ones in selected communities. In connection with such relocation, the War Relocation Authority established a procedure for obtaining leave from Relocation Centers that provided, so far as indefinite leave was concerned, as follows:

> Application for leave clearance is required. An investigation of the applicant is made for the purpose of ascertaining "the probable effect upon the war program and upon the public peace and security of issuing indefinite leave" to the applicant. The grant of leave clearance does not authorize departure from the Relocation Center. Application for indefinite leave must also be made. Indefinite leave may be granted under 14 specified conditions. For example, it may be granted (1) where the applicant proposes to accept an employment offer or an offer of support that has been investigated and approved by the Authority; or (2) where the applicant does not intend to work but has "adequate financial resources to take care of himself" and a Relocation Officer has investigated and approved "public sentiment at his proposed destination", or (3) where the applicant has made arrangements to live at a hotel or in a private home approved by a Relocation Officer while arranging for employment; or (4) where the applicant proposes to accept employment by a federal or local governmental agency; or (5) where the applicant is going to live with designated classes of relatives.

> Even if an applicant met these requirements, no leave was granted if the proposed place of residence or employment was within a locality where "community sentiment is unfavorable" or when the applicant planned to go to an area that had been closed by the Authority to the issuance of indefinite leave. Nor did such leave issue if the area where the applicant planned to reside or work was one that had not been cleared for relocation.

In July 1942, Endo filed a petition for a writ of habeas corpus in federal district court, alleging that she was a loyal and law-abiding citizen of the United States, that no charge had been made against her, that she was being unlawfully detained, and that she was confined in the Relocation Center under armed guard and held there against her will. Executive Branch officials acknowledged that she was a loyal and law-abiding citizen, but argued that her continued detention was nonetheless warranted because she planned to live and work in an area where community sentiment was unfavorable to the presence of even loyal Japanese-Americans who had been relocated.]

MR. JUSTICE DOUGLAS delivered the opinion of the Court.

We are of the view that Mitsuye Endo should be given her liberty. In reaching that conclusion we do not come to the underlying constitutional issues which have been argued. For we conclude that, whatever power the War Relocation Authority may have to detain other classes of citizens, it has no authority to subject citizens who are concededly loyal to its leave procedure.

It should be noted at the outset that we do not have here a question such as was presented in *Ex parte Milligan* . . . where the jurisdiction of military tribunals to try persons according to the law of war was challenged in habeas corpus proceedings. Mitsuye Endo is detained by a civilian agency, the War Relocation Authority, not by the military. Moreover, the evacuation program was not left exclusively to the military; the Authority was given a large measure of responsibility for its execution and Congress made its enforcement subject to civil penalties by the Act of March 21, 1942. Accordingly, no questions of military law are involved.

Such power of detention as the Authority has stems from Executive Order No. 9066. That order is the source of the authority delegated by General De Witt in his letter of August 11, 1942. And Executive Order No. 9102 which created the War Relocation Authority purported to do no more than to implement the program authorized by Executive Order No. 9066.

We approach the construction of Executive Order No. 9066 as we would approach the construction of legislation in this field. That Executive Order must indeed be considered along with the Act of March 21, 1942, which ratified and confirmed it as the Order and the statute together laid such basis as there is for participation by civil agencies of the federal government in the evacuation program. Broad powers frequently granted to the President or other executive officers by Congress so that they may deal with the exigencies of war time problems have been sustained. And the Constitution when it committed to the Executive and to Congress the exercise of the war power necessarily gave them wide scope for the exercise of judgment and discretion so that war might be waged effectively and successfully. At the same time, however, the Constitution is as specific in its enumeration of many of the civil rights of the individual as it is in its enumeration of the powers of his government. Thus it has prescribed procedural safeguards surrounding the arrest, detention and conviction of individuals. Some of these are contained in the Sixth Amendment, compliance with which is essential if convictions are to be sustained. And the Fifth Amendment provides that no person shall be deprived of liberty (as well as life or property) without due process of law. Moreover, as a further safeguard against invasion of the basic civil rights of the individual it is provided in Art. I, Sec. 9 of the Constitution that "The Privilege of the Writ of Habeas Corpus shall not be suspended, unless when in Cases of Rebellion or Invasion the public Safety may require it."

We mention these constitutional provisions not to stir the constitutional issues which have been argued at the bar but to indicate the approach which we think should be made to an Act of Congress or an order of the Chief Executive that touches the sensitive area of rights specifically guaranteed by the Constitution. This Court has quite consistently given a narrower scope for the operation of the presumption of constitutionality when legislation appeared on its face to violate a specific prohibition of the Constitution. We have likewise favored that interpretation of legislation which gives it the greater chance of surviving the test of constitutionality. Those analogies are suggestive here. We must assume that the Chief Executive and members of Congress, as well as the courts, are sensitive to and respectful of the liberties of the citizen. In interpreting a war-time measure we must assume that their purpose was to allow for the greatest possible accommodation between those liberties and the exigencies of war. We must assume, when asked to find implied powers in a grant of legislative or executive authority, that the law makers intended to place no greater restraint on the citizen than was clearly and unmistakably indicated by the language they used.

The Act of March 21, 1942, was a war measure. . . . The purpose and objective of the Act and of these orders are plain. Their single aim was the protection of the war effort against espionage and sabotage. It is in light of that one objective that the powers conferred by the orders must be construed.

Neither the Act nor the orders use the language of detention. . . . Moreover, unlike the case of curfew regulations the legislative history of the Act of March 21, 1942, is silent on detention. And that silence may have special significance in view of the fact that detention in Relocation Centers was no part of the original program of evacuation but developed later to meet what seemed to the officials in charge to be mounting hostility to the evacuees on the part of the communities where they sought to go.

We do not mean to imply that detention in connection with no phase of the evacuation program would be lawful. The fact that the Act and the orders are silent on detention does not of course mean that any power to detain is lacking. Some such power might indeed be necessary to the successful operation of the evacuation program. At least we may so assume. Moreover, we may assume for the purposes of this case that initial detention in Relocation Centers was authorized. But we stress the silence of the legislative history and of the Act and the Executive Orders on the power to detain to emphasize that any such authority which exists must be implied. If there is to be the greatest possible accommodation of the liberties of the citizen with this war measure, any such implied power must be narrowly confined to the precise purpose of the evacuation program.

A citizen who is concededly loyal presents no problem of espionage or sabotage. Loyalty is a matter of the heart and mind not of race, creed, or color. He who is loyal is by definition not a spy or a saboteur. When the power to detain is derived from the power to protect the war effort against espionage and sabotage, detention which has no relationship to that objective is unauthorized. . . .

Community hostility even to loyal evacuees may have been (and perhaps still is) a serious problem. But if authority for their custody and supervision is to be sought on that ground, the Act of March 21, 1942, Executive Order No. 9066, and Executive Order No. 9102, offer no support. And none other is advanced. To read them that broadly would be to assume that the Congress and the President intended that this discriminatory action should be taken against these people wholly on account of their ancestry even though the government conceded their loyalty to this country. We cannot make such an assumption. As the President has said of these loyal citizens: "Americans of Japanese ancestry, like those of many other ancestries, have shown that they can, and want to, accept our institutions and work loyally with the rest of us, making their own valuable contribution to the national wealth and well-being. In vindication of the very ideals for which we are fighting this war it is important to us to maintain a high standard of fair, considerate, and equal treatment for the people of this minority as of all other minorities."

3. Vietnam War

New York Times Co. v. United States

403 U.S. 713 (1971)

[The *New York Times* and the *Washington Post* obtained from Daniel Ellsberg, a former Defense Department official, portions of a secret Defense Department study popularly known as the "Pentagon Papers," and began to publish them on June

12 and 17, 1971. The Pentagon Papers analyzed in detail the formulation and execution of American diplomatic and military policy in Indochina. The Executive Branch sought to enjoin further publication of the Pentagon Papers on the ground that publication would jeopardize national security and diplomatic negotiations, would result in the death of Americans, and would prolong the Vietnam War. The lower courts declined to grant an injunction, but did order a stay of publication until June 25. On that date, the Supreme Court granted *certiorari* and continued the stay; on June 26, it heard oral arguments in the cases; and on June 30, it issued the following decision.]

Per Curiam. . . .

"Any system of prior restraints of expression comes to this Court bearing a heavy presumption against its constitutional validity." Bantam Books, Inc. v. Sullivan, 372 U.S. 58, 70 (1963). The Government "thus carries a heavy burden of showing justification for the imposition of such a restraint." Organization for a Better Austin v. Keefe, 402 U.S. 415, 419 (1971). The District Court for the Southern District of New York in the *New York Times* case and the District Court for the District of Columbia and the Court of Appeals for the District of Columbia Circuit in the *Washington Post* case held that the Government had not met that burden. We agree. . . .

Mr. Justice Black, with whom Mr. Justice Douglas joins, concurring. . . .

In the First Amendment the Founding Fathers gave the free press the protection it must have to fulfill its essential role in our democracy. The press was to serve the governed, not the governors. The Government's power to censor the press was abolished so that the press would remain forever free to censure the Government. The press was protected so that it could bare the secrets of government and inform the people. Only a free and unrestrained press can effectively expose deception in government. And paramount among the responsibilities of a free press is the duty to prevent any part of the government from deceiving the people and sending them off to distant lands to die of foreign fevers and foreign shot and shell. . . .

[W]e are asked to hold that despite the First Amendment's emphatic command, the Executive Branch, the Congress, and the Judiciary can make laws enjoining publication of current news and abridging freedom of the press in the name of "national security." The Government does not even attempt to rely on any act of Congress. Instead it makes the bold and dangerously far-reaching contention that the courts should take it upon themselves to "make" a law abridging freedom of the press in the name of equity, presidential power and national security, even when the representatives of the people in Congress have adhered to the command of the First Amendment and refused to make such a law. To find that the President has "inherent power" to halt the publication of news by resort to the courts would wipe out the First Amendment and destroy the fundamental liberty and security of the very people the Government hopes to make "secure." . . .

Mr. Justice Douglas, with whom Mr. Justice Black joins, concurring. . . .

[The First Amendment] leaves . . . no room for governmental restraint on the press.

There is, moreover, no statute barring the publication by the press of the material which the Times and the Post seek to use. . . .

So any power that the Government possesses must come from its "inherent power."

The power to wage war is "the power to wage war successfully." *See* Hirabayashi v. United States, 320 U.S. 81, 93. But the war power stems from a declaration of war. The Constitution by Art. I, §8, gives Congress, not the President, power "to declare War." Nowhere are presidential wars authorized. We need not decide therefore what leveling effect the war power of Congress might have.

These disclosures may have a serious impact. But that is no basis for sanctioning a previous restraint on the press. . . .

The dominant purpose of the First Amendment was to prohibit the widespread practice of governmental suppression of embarrassing information. It is common knowledge that the First Amendment was adopted against the widespread use of the common law of seditious libel to punish the dissemination of material that is embarrassing to the powers-that-be. The present cases will, I think, go down in history as the most dramatic illustration of that principle. A debate of large proportions goes on in the Nation over our posture in Vietnam. That debate antedated the disclosure of the contents of the present documents. The latter are highly relevant to the debate in progress. . . .

MR. JUSTICE BRENNAN, concurring. . . .

"The chief purpose of [the First Amendment's] guaranty [is] to prevent previous restraints upon publication." Near v. Minnesota, [283 U.S. 697, 713 (1931)]. Thus, only governmental allegation and proof that publication must inevitably, directly, and immediately cause the occurrence of an event kindred to imperiling the safety of a transport already at sea can support even the issuance of an interim restraining order. In no event may mere conclusions be sufficient: for if the Executive Branch seeks judicial aid in preventing publication, it must inevitably submit the basis upon which that aid is sought to scrutiny by the judiciary. And therefore, every restraint issued in this case, whatever its form, has violated the First Amendment — and not less so because that restraint was justified as necessary to afford the courts an opportunity to examine the claim more thoroughly. Unless and until the Government has clearly made out its case, the First Amendment commands that no injunction may issue.

MR. JUSTICE STEWART, with whom MR. JUSTICE WHITE joins, concurring. . . .

In the absence of the governmental checks and balances present in other areas of our national life, the only effective restraint upon executive policy and power in the areas of national defense and international affairs may lie in an enlightened citizenry — in an informed and critical public opinion which alone can here protect the values of democratic government. For this reason, it is perhaps here that a press that is alert, aware, and free most vitally serves the basic purpose of the First Amendment. For without an informed and free press there cannot be an enlightened people.

Yet it is elementary that the successful conduct of international diplomacy and the maintenance of an effective national defense require both confidentiality and secrecy. Other nations can hardly deal with this Nation in an atmosphere of mutual trust unless they can be assured that their confidences will be kept. And within our own executive departments, the development of considered and intelligent international policies would be impossible if those charged with their formulation could not communicate with each other freely, frankly, and in confidence. In the area of basic national defense the frequent need for absolute secrecy is, of course, self-evident.

I think there can be but one answer to this dilemma, if dilemma it be. The responsibility must be where the power is. If the Constitution gives the Executive a large degree of unshared power in the conduct of foreign affairs and the maintenance of our national defense, then under the Constitution the Executive must have the largely unshared duty to determine and preserve the degree of internal security necessary to exercise that power successfully. It is an awesome responsibility, requiring judgment and wisdom of a high order. . . .

This is not to say that Congress and the courts have no role to play. Undoubtedly Congress has the power to enact specific and appropriate criminal laws to protect government property and preserve government secrets. Congress has passed such laws, and several of them are of very colorable relevance to the apparent circumstances of these cases. . . .

But in the cases before us we are asked neither to construe specific regulations nor to apply specific laws. We are asked, instead, to perform a function that the Constitution gave to the Executive, not the Judiciary. We are asked, quite simply, to prevent the publication by two newspapers of material that the Executive Branch insists should not, in the national interest, be published. I am convinced that the Executive is correct with respect to some of the documents involved. But I cannot say that disclosure of any of them will surely result in direct, immediate, and irreparable damage to our Nation or its people. That being so, there can under the First Amendment be but one judicial resolution of the issues before us. I join the judgments of the Court.

MR. JUSTICE WHITE, with whom MR. JUSTICECE STEWART joins, concurring. . . .

At least in the absence of legislation by Congress, based on its own investigations and findings, I am quite unable to agree that the inherent powers of the Executive and the courts reach so far as to authorize remedies having such sweeping potential for inhibiting publications by the press. . . .

The Criminal Code contains numerous provisions potentially relevant to these cases. . . .

It is thus clear that Congress has addressed itself to the problems of protecting the security of the country and the national defense from unauthorized disclosure of potentially damaging information. *Cf.* Youngstown Sheet & Tube Co. v. Sawyer, 343 U.S. 579, 585-86 (1952); *see also id.* at 593-628 (Frankfurter, J., concurring). It has not, however, authorized the injunctive remedy against threatened publication. It has apparently been satisfied to rely on criminal sanctions and their deterrent effect on the responsible as well as the irresponsible press. I am not, of course, saying that either of these newspapers has yet committed a crime or that either would commit a crime if it published all the material now in its possession. That matter must await resolution in the context of a criminal proceeding if one is instituted by the United States. . . .

MR. JUSTICE MARSHALL, concurring. . . .

It would . . . be utterly inconsistent with the concept of separation of powers for this Court to use its power of contempt to prevent behavior that Congress has specifically declined to prohibit. There would be a similar damage to the basic concept of these coequal branches of Government if when the Executive Branch has adequate authority granted by Congress to protect "national security" it can choose instead to invoke the contempt power of a court to enjoin the threatened conduct. The Constitution provides that Congress shall make laws, the President execute laws, and courts interpret laws. Youngstown Sheet & Tube Co. v. Sawyer, 343 U.S. 579 (1952). It did not provide for government by injunction in which the courts and the Executive Branch can "make law" without regard to the action of Congress. It may be more convenient for the Executive Branch if it need only convince a judge to prohibit conduct rather than ask the Congress to pass a law, and it may be more convenient to enforce a contempt order than to seek a criminal conviction in a jury trial. . . .

MR. CHIEF JUSTICE BURGER, dissenting. . . .

[Chief Justice Burger stated that he "generally" agreed with Justices Harlan and Blackmun, but because the case was "conducted in unseemly haste," he would extend the stays, pending a full trial on the merits.]

MR. JUSTICE HARLAN, with whom THE CHIEF JUSTICE and MR. JUSTICE BLACKMUN join, dissenting. . . .

It is plain to me that the scope of the judicial function in passing upon the activities of the Executive Branch of the Government in the field of foreign affairs is very narrowly restricted. This view is, I think, dictated by the concept of separation of powers upon which our constitutional system rests. . . .

The power to evaluate the "pernicious influence" of premature disclosure is not, however, lodged in the Executive alone. I agree that, in performance of its duty to protect the values of the First Amendment against political pressures, the judiciary must review the initial Executive determination to the point of satisfying itself that the subject matter of the dispute does lie within the proper compass of the President's foreign relations power. Constitutional considerations forbid "a complete abandonment of judicial control." Moreover, the judiciary may properly insist that the determination that disclosure of the subject matter would irreparably impair the national security be made by the head of the Executive Department concerned — here the Secretary of State or the Secretary of Defense — after actual personal consideration by that officer. This safeguard is required in the analogous area of executive claims of privilege for secrets of state. But in my judgment the judiciary may not properly go beyond these two inquiries and redetermine for itself the probable impact of disclosure on the national security. . . .

Even if there is some room for the judiciary to override the executive determination, it is plain that the scope of review must be exceedingly narrow. I can see no indication in the opinions of either the District Court or the Court of Appeals in the *Post* litigation that the conclusions of the Executive were given even the deference owing to an administrative agency, much less that owing to a co-equal branch of the Government operating within the field of its constitutional prerogative.

Notes and Questions

1. As the materials in this section show, war tests a nation's commitment to individual liberties, for during war, the tradeoffs between liberty and security are most apparent. How should the United States reconcile its constitutional commitment to civil liberties with the need to protect national security and to wage war successfully? Cicero answered a similar question with the now-famous maxim "*inter arma silent leges*" ("in times of war, the law is silent"). The Court in *Ex parte Milligan*

answered the question quite differently when it stated that the Constitution operates "equally in war and in peace," protecting "all classes of men, at all times, and under all circumstances." 71 U.S. 2, 120-21 (1866). Former Chief Justice Rehnquist concluded a study of the question with an intermediate position: "The laws will . . . not be silent in time of war, but they will speak with a somewhat different voice." William H. Rehnquist, All the Laws But One: Civil Liberties in Wartime 225 (1998). Which of these three answers best describes the decisions excerpted in this section?

2. What do the opinions in this section suggest about the role that courts should play in the enforcement of civil liberties during wartime? Is the political question doctrine stronger or weaker when civil liberties are at stake? How are courts supposed to judge the validity of the President's claim of military necessity? Do the answers to these questions depend on whether Congress has declared war? On whether the Executive Branch acts with or without congressional authorization? On whether judicial review takes place during or after the war? How does the analysis from the majority and concurring opinions in *Youngstown* apply to cases involving the curtailment of civil liberties? Realistically, do courts have the ability to curb government restrictions on individual liberties during wartime?

3. Professor Pushaw argues that the Supreme Court's willingness to restrict the President during wartime is affected by several pragmatic considerations:

> First, the Court evaluates the gravity and immediacy of the military crisis, as well as the necessity for the President's responsive measure. Not surprisingly, the Court has granted the President far more latitude in addressing nation-threatening emergencies like the Civil War and World War II than lesser conflicts. . . .
>
> Second, the Justices consider the egregiousness and magnitude of the legal violation. For example, judges find unnecessary or arbitrary deprivations of bodily liberty more troublesome than temporary suppression of speech to protect our troops. Again, this factor has built-in subjectivity, and hindsight often reveals that the heat of the moment clouded judgment. . . .
>
> Third, the Court calculates the likelihood that its orders will be obeyed, which depends primarily upon the President's political strength and secondarily upon whether the crisis is ongoing or has passed. This last criterion is never articulated but often seems pivotal.

Robert J. Pushaw, Jr., *The "Enemy Combatant" Cases in Historical Context: The Inevitability of Pragmatic Judicial Review,* 82 Notre Dame L. Rev. 1005, 1014-15 (2007). Is this assessment consistent with the Supreme Court decisions in this Section?

4. The Suspension Clause of Article I, §9, cl. 2 of the Constitution provides that the "Privilege of the Writ of Habeas Corpus shall not be suspended, unless when in Cases of Rebellion or Invasion the public Safety may require it." Did Lincoln have the authority to suspend the writ of habeas corpus before Congress authorized him to do so in March 1863? Or was Chief Justice Taney right in *Ex parte Merryman,* excerpted in Chapter 1, that Congress has the exclusive power to suspend the writ? Does it matter that the Suspension Clause is written in the passive voice and thus does not name the entity that has the power to suspend? What is the significance of the fact that the Suspension Clause is in Article I, which regulates the powers of Congress, and that all of the other clauses of Article I, section 9 where the Suspension Clause appears contemplate qualifications on congressional power? What about Lincoln's argument that it would be absurd to assign the suspension power exclusively to a branch of government that might not be able to meet in an emergency? If a bomb in the Capitol killed every member of Congress, would the federal government lack the authority to suspend the writ until a new Congress could be elected? On the other hand, perhaps the Constitution does not contemplate such an extreme situation?

In a modern decision that we analyze in the next chapter, every Justice of the Supreme Court assumed, with little analysis and in dicta, that only Congress could suspend the writ of habeas corpus. *See* Hamdi v. Rumsfeld, 542 U.S. 507 (2004). For an argument that the President has a concurrent authority to suspend the writ of habeas corpus in the absence of contrary action by Congress, see Daniel Farber, Lincoln's Constitution 158-63 (2003).

5. Assuming that the Constitution permits only Congress to suspend the writ, can it be argued that Lincoln nonetheless acted appropriately because it was an emergency and the fate of the United States was at stake? This was the thrust of Lincoln's famous "all the laws but one" argument in his address to Congress. Are you persuaded? Can an emergency ever justify the President in disregarding the Constitution or otherwise not complying with the law?

Answers to this question divide into three groups. An "absolutist" perspective "contends that the government has no emergency power to deal with crisis other than that specifically provided by the Constitution." Jules Lobel, *Emergency Power and the Decline of Liberalism*, 98 Yale L.J. 1385, 1386-87 (1989). This approach is essentially represented by the *Milligan* majority opinion. A "relativist" perspective "argues that the Constitution is a flexible document that permits the President to take whatever measures are necessary in crisis situations." *Id.* at 1388. An example of the relativist perspective can be found in President Franklin Roosevelt's claim that the President has the constitutional power to ignore statutory provisions when "necessary to avert a disaster which would interfere with the winning of the war." *Id.* Professor Lobel notes:

> Both the relativist and absolutist views have an underlying philosophical unity, as both eviscerate the dichotomy between constitutional normalcy and extra-constitutional emergency. The first does so by denying the need for emergency power; the second does so by interpreting the Constitution to provide the Executive with the authority to use such extraordinary power.

98 Yale L.J. at 1388. By contrast, a third view, "liberal constitutionalism," preserves the distinction between normal and emergency power. On this view, "[n]ormalcy permit[s] a governmental structure based on separation of powers, respect for civil liberties and the rule of law, while emergencies require[] strong executive rule, premised not on law and respect for civil liberties, but rather on discretion to take a wide range of actions to preserve the government." *Id.* Lincoln's "all the laws but one" explanation for his suspension of the writ of habeas corpus, combined with his acknowledgment that Congress could judge his actions, is an example of liberal constitutionalism. Similarly, Jefferson wrote:

> A strict observance of the written laws is doubtless one of the high duties of a good citizen, but it is not the highest. The laws of necessity, of self-preservation, of saving our country when in danger, are of higher obligation. To lose our country by a scrupulous adherence to written law, would be to lose the law itself, with life, liberty, property and all those who are enjoying them with us; thus absurdly sacrificing the end to the means. . . . The officer who is called to act on this superior ground, does indeed risk himself on the justice of the controlling powers of the Constitution, and his station makes it his duty to incur that risk. . . . The line of discrimination between cases may be difficult; but the good officer is bound to draw it at his own peril, and throw himself on the justice of his country and the rectitude of his motives.

Letter from Thomas Jefferson to John B. Colvin, Sept. 20, 1810, in 11 The Works of Thomas Jefferson 146, 148-49 (Paul L. Ford ed., 1905).

Which of these three views is most persuasive? What are the advantages and dangers of each of these three views? Is the absolutist perspective practical? How can the relativist perspective be cabined to ensure that the President does not abuse emergency power? Under the liberal perspective, how are emergency situations distinguished from normal ones? Who decides? Which perspective gives a President the right incentives to act only in true emergencies?

In considering these questions, what is the relevance of the Oath Clause for the President, which requires him to "solemnly swear (or affirm) that [he] will faithfully execute the Office of President of the United States, and will to the best of [his] Ability, preserve, protect and defend the Constitution of the United States"? U.S. Const. art. II, §1, cl. 8. By contrast to the President's oath, all other federal and state officers are required merely to "support" the Constitution. U.S. Const. art. VI, cl. 3. Does the President's unique constitutional duty to "preserve, protect and defend the Constitution" entail a unique authority to disregard law, including the Constitution, when he deems an emergency threat to the Constitution to require it? For a critical analysis of this question in the context of Lincoln's actions, see Michael Stokes Paulsen, *The Constitution of Necessity*, 79 Notre Dame L. Rev. 1257 (2004).

6. Does a suspension of the writ broaden the government's substantive authority to arrest and detain during an invasion or rebellion, or merely preclude the particular remedy of a judicial order of discharge during the time of the suspension? Commentators are divided on the issue. *Compare* Trevor W. Morrison, *Suspension and the Extrajudicial Constitution*, 107 Colum. L. Rev. 1533 (2007) (arguing that the suspension power does not provide legal authority for any arrest or detention that could not be made in the absence of the suspension), *with* Amanda L. Tyler, *Suspension as an Emergency Power*, 118 Yale L.J. 600 (2009) (arguing that a congressional suspension of the writ overrides substantive rights that would otherwise restrict arrest and detention, and that subsequent civil suits relating to such conduct are thereby also precluded).

7. *Milligan* raises the question of the constitutional validity of military commissions. Such commissions have historically been used in three situations: (a) to try enemy belligerents for violations of the laws of war; (b) to administer justice in territory occupied by the military; and (c) to replace civilian courts where martial law has been declared. (A military commission should not be confused with a court martial, which tries members of the U.S. military forces under the Uniform Code of Military Justice, 10 U.S.C. §§801 et seq.) Military commissions typically try defendants before military judges rather than a jury, and typically feature more relaxed procedural and evidentiary rules than are found in civilian trials. Why are trials with these characteristics needed in the military context? Why not have all trials during war in civilian courts? We will return to the issue of military commissions in the war on terrorism materials in Chapter 10.

8. What is the holding of *Milligan*? What is the relationship between the majority opinion's constitutional analysis and its analysis of the Habeas Corpus Act of 1863? Why didn't the Court rely exclusively on the Habeas Act, like the concurrence? What is at stake in the disagreement between the majority and concurrence? Is the discussion of martial law in the last few paragraphs of the majority opinion consistent with its earlier unqualified statements about the applicability of the Constitution during wartime?

9. The Supreme Court's decisions in *Hirabayashi*, *Korematsu*, and *Endo* involved the legality, respectively, of World War II curfew orders for Japanese-Americans, exclusion orders for Japanese-Americans, and detentions of Japanese-Americans. Why did the Court uphold the first two and invalidate the third? Was it really because the detention order in *Endo* was not authorized by Congress or the President? Would *Endo* have come out differently if Congress in World War II had expressly authorized the detention of an admittedly loyal Japanese-American on the ground that community sentiment was unfavorable to her release? If not, why did the Court go out of its way to say that it was not reaching the constitutional question? Compare, in this regard, the analysis of the majority opinion in *Milligan*.

10. Most analysts today believe that the Japanese exclusion order at issue in *Korematsu* was a disproportionate response to the threat of sabotage, invasion, or espionage by Japanese agents. *See, e.g.*, Greg Robinson, By Order of the President: FDR and the Internment of Japanese Americans (2001). Is this *ex post* perspective — which Justice Black's majority opinion in *Korematsu* refers to as the "calm perspective of hindsight" — the proper perspective from which to determine the validity of military orders in response to perceived emergencies? Can judges second-guess military claims of emergency in the midst of a war in which the nation's security is threatened? In answering this question, is it relevant that most claims of emergency or necessity turn out, after the fact, to have been exaggerated? What do you make of Justice Jackson's proposed solution to this conundrum, and Justice Frankfurter's implicit response?

As discussed in Chapter 2, the Supreme Court in Trump v. Hawaii, 138 S. Ct. 2392 (2018), upheld President Trump's "travel ban" order that restricted entry into the United States by nationals of certain foreign countries — primarily but not exclusively countries with predominately Muslim populations. In upholding the order, a majority of the Court concluded that the government had put forward a sufficient national security justification for the restriction. In her dissent in that case, Justice Sotomayor wrote:

> Today's holding is all the more troubling given the stark parallels between the reasoning of this case and that of Korematsu v. United States, 323 U.S. 214 (1944). In *Korematsu*, the Court gave "a pass [to] an odious, gravely injurious racial classification" authorized by an executive order. Adarand Constructors, Inc. v. Peña, 515 U.S. 200, 275 (1995) (Ginsburg, J., dissenting). As here, the Government invoked an ill-defined national-security threat to justify an exclusionary policy of sweeping proportion. As here, the exclusion order was rooted in dangerous stereotypes about, *inter alia*, a particular group's supposed inability to assimilate and desire to harm the United States. As here, the Government was unwilling to reveal its own intelligence agencies' views of the alleged security concerns to the very citizens it purported to protect. And as here, there was strong evidence that impermissible hostility and animus motivated the Government's policy.

In response, the majority expressly repudiated *Korematsu*, stating: "The dissent's reference to *Korematsu*, however, affords this Court the opportunity to make express what is already obvious: *Korematsu* was gravely wrong the day it was decided, has been overruled in the court of history, and — to be clear — 'has no place in law under the Constitution.' 323 U.S. at 248 (Jackson, J., dissenting)." Is this repudiation anything more than symbolic? What do you think of Justice Sotomayor's charge that the Court "redeploys the same dangerous logic underlying *Korematsu* and merely replaces one 'gravely wrong' decision with another"? In what ways is *Trump v. Hawaii* like or unlike *Korematsu*?

11. The Court in *Endo* employs a canon of statutory construction of wartime congressional authorizations that is very protective of civil liberties and that appears to impose a clear statement requirement before civil liberties will be contracted. Is such a canon appropriate? Is it consistent with the principle, articulated in decisions like *Curtiss-Wright* and *Dames & Moore,* that congressional authorizations to the President should be construed broadly? Can these decisions be reconciled with *Endo?* For analysis of these issues, see Curtis A. Bradley & Jack L. Goldsmith, *Congressional Authorization and the War on Terrorism,* 118 Harv. L. Rev. 2047, 2102-07 (2005); Cass R. Sunstein, *Minimalism at War,* 2004 Sup. Ct. Rev. 47.

12. Can you discern a common rationale in the various opinions supporting the judgment in the *Pentagon Papers* case? Would the result have been different if Congress had prohibited publication of the information that the *New York Times* and *Washington Post* sought to publish? What is the relevance of *Youngstown* to this question? What was the relevance of the fact that the Vietnam War was not a *declared* war, or that at the time of the opinion in 1971, there was widespread national debate over the course and legitimacy of the war?

The *Pentagon Papers* case pits the First Amendment's prior restraint doctrine against the Executive's broad powers in foreign affairs and national security. Although the First Amendment prevailed in the *Pentagon Papers* case, it need not always do so. As the Court stated in Near v. Minnesota, 283 U.S. 697, 716 (1931):

> [The] protection even as to previous restraint is not absolutely unlimited. But the limitation has been recognized only in exceptional cases. . . . No one would question but that a government might prevent actual obstruction to its recruiting service or the publication of the sailing dates of transports or the number and location of troops. . . . The security of the community life may be protected against incitements to acts of violence and the overthrow by force of orderly government.

What do the various opinions in the *Pentagon Papers* case say about how courts should determine whether the threat to U.S. security is so overwhelming as to permit a prior restraint? What kind of showing could the government have made to demonstrate that national security would be undermined by the publication? Won't it always be necessary for courts to judge how convincing this showing is? Can courts do this with confidence?

Free speech rights have often been curtailed in wartime. An early example is the Sedition Act, enacted during the administration of John Adams on the eve of the undeclared war with France, which provided for fines and imprisonment for the publication of any "false, scandalous and malicious writing" against the government. Another example is the Espionage Act of 1917, which, among other things, provided for fines and imprisonment for speech intended to create resistance to the military draft during World War I. *See* Schenck v. United States, 249 U.S. 47 (1919) (upholding one of the many prosecutions under this statute). For an account of the treatment of free speech during wartime throughout U.S. history, see Geoffrey R. Stone, Perilous Times: Free Speech in Wartime (2004).

13. The next chapter of this casebook considers a variety of issues relating to the post-September 11 "war on terrorism," particularly issues relating to the military detention and trial of alleged terrorists. Efforts to address terrorism implicated free speech considerations in Holder v. Humanitarian Law Project, 561 U.S. 1 (2010). That case concerned the constitutionality of 18 U.S.C. §2339B, which makes it a federal crime to "knowingly provid[e] material support or resources to a foreign terrorist organization." The term "material support" is in turn defined to include, among other things, "training," "expert advice or assistance," "service," and "personnel." The plaintiffs sought to provide certain types of assistance to two groups that had been designated by the Secretary of State as foreign terrorist organizations. The assistance would have included political advocacy activities, teaching members how to petition representative bodies such as the United Nations for relief, and training members how to use humanitarian and international law to resolve disputes. In an opinion by Chief Justice Roberts, the Court held that the application of the statute to these activities would not violate the First Amendment. The Court described the government's interest in combating terrorism as "of the highest order," and it emphasized that "[t]he statute reaches only material support coordinated with or under the direction of a designated foreign terrorist organization." It also found that Congress was justified in concluding that "working in coordination with or at the command of the [terrorist groups] serves to legitimize and further their terrorist means." In addition, the Court accorded deference to the Executive Branch's assessment that the forms of assistance in question would facilitate terrorism. "Given the sensitive interests in national security and foreign affairs at stake," the Court concluded, "the political branches have adequately substantiated their determination that, to serve the Government's interest in preventing terrorism, it was necessary to prohibit providing material support in the form of training, expert advice, personnel, and services to foreign terrorist groups, even if the supporters meant to promote only the groups' nonviolent ends."

Justice Breyer dissented, joined by Justices Ginsburg and Sotomayor. Justice Breyer disputed whether the government's compelling interest in protecting the nation from terrorism "can justify the statute's criminal prohibition." He did not see how teaching groups, "say, how to petition the United Nations for political change is fungible with other resources that might be put to more sinister ends in the way that donations of money, food, or computer training are fungible." Nor did he believe that the concern about giving the groups "legitimacy" was sufficient to justify the restriction of speech. He explained:

> Speech, association, and related activities on behalf of a group will often, perhaps always, help to legitimate that group. Thus, were the law to accept a "legitimating" effect, in and of itself and without qualification, as providing sufficient grounds for imposing such a ban, the First Amendment battle would be lost in untold instances where it should be won. Once one accepts this argument, there is no natural stopping place. . . .
>
> Moreover, the risk that those who are taught will put otherwise innocent speech or knowledge to bad use is omnipresent, at least where that risk rests on little more than (even informed) speculation. Hence to accept this kind of argument without more and to apply it to the teaching of a subject such as international human rights law is to adopt a rule of law that, contrary to the Constitution's text and First Amendment precedent, would automatically forbid the teaching of any subject in a case where national security interests conflict with the First Amendment. The Constitution does not allow all such conflicts to be decided in the Government's favor.

Finally, Justice Breyer said that he would "concede that the Government's expertise in foreign affairs may warrant deference in respect to many matters," but he argued that "it remains for this Court to decide whether the Government has shown that such an interest justifies criminalizing speech activity otherwise protected by the First Amendment . . . [a]nd the fact that other nations may like us less for granting that protection cannot in and of itself carry the day."

10

Terrorism

On September 11, 2001, 19 men connected to the Al Qaeda terrorist network hijacked four commercial airplanes in the United States. The hijackers crashed two of the planes into the World Trade Center in New York, and another into the Pentagon in northern Virginia. The fourth plane crashed in Pennsylvania, apparently after a struggle between the passengers and the hijackers. The attacks killed thousands of people, the vast majority of whom were civilians, and caused billions of dollars in property and economic damage. The United States responded by, among other things, initiating combat operations in Afghanistan against Al Qaeda forces, as well as the forces of the Taliban government that ruled much of Afghanistan at that time and had been harboring Al Qaeda. The United States quickly defeated the Taliban as a ruling force in Afghanistan, although military conflict against remnants of Taliban forces continued. The United States also drove Al Qaeda forces out of Afghanistan into Pakistan and elsewhere. But U.S. military and paramilitary action persisted against Al Qaeda and especially against its growing affiliate organizations around the globe, and is still ongoing today. In 2014, a terrorist group called the Islamic State (also referred to as ISIS, the Islamic State of Iraq and the Levant, or ISIL), which had originated as an Al Qaeda affiliate, took over territory in Iraq and Syria as part of an effort to form a so-called "caliphate" (a form of Islamic government). Along with Iraq and other allies, the United States fought against ISIL in both Iraq and Syria. By March 2019, ISIL had been ousted from the territory it held, but the group still had geographically dispersed leaders, fighters, and resources.

The domestic legal regime that has regulated the conflicts with the Taliban and with Al Qaeda and its affiliates has gone through many changes since September 11, 2001, and currently combines elements of both war powers and criminal law. This chapter considers how this legal regime has evolved. It begins with potentially relevant World War II precedents and then focuses on individual rights and separation of powers issues concerning military detention, the trial of alleged terrorists by military commissions, access by alleged terrorists to U.S. courts, and the interrogation, surveillance, and targeted killing of alleged terrorists.

A. WORLD WAR II PRECEDENTS

Ex parte Quirin

317 U.S. 1 (1942)

[Eight agents of the German Nazi government, seven of whom were German citizens and one of whom (Haupt) was allegedly an American citizen, were arrested after they had surreptitiously entered the United States with explosives, intending to commit acts of sabotage. President Roosevelt convened a military commission of eight generals to try the accused for offenses against the laws of war, and prescribed the procedures for trial and for review of any sentence. Seven of the agents, including Haupt, sought habeas corpus relief in the Supreme Court.]

MR. CHIEF JUSTICE STONE delivered the opinion of the Court. . . .

Petitioners' main contention is that the President is without any statutory or constitutional authority to order the petitioners to be tried by military tribunal for offenses with which they are charged; that in consequence they are entitled to be tried in the civil courts with the safeguards, including trial by jury, which the Fifth and Sixth Amendments guarantee to all persons charged in such courts with criminal offenses. In any case it is urged that the President's Order, in prescribing the procedure of the Commission and the method for review of its findings and sentence, and the proceedings of the Commission under the Order, conflict with Articles of War adopted by Congress — particularly Articles 38, 43, 46, 50½ and 70 — and are illegal and void.

The Government challenges each of these propositions. But regardless of their merits, it also insists that petitioners must be denied access to the courts, both because they are enemy aliens or have entered our territory as enemy belligerents, and because the President's Proclamation undertakes in terms to deny such access to the class of persons defined by the Proclamation, which aptly describes the character and conduct of petitioners. It is urged that if they are enemy aliens or if the Proclamation has force, no court may afford the petitioners a hearing. But there is certainly nothing in the Proclamation to preclude access to the courts for determining its applicability to the particular case. And neither the Proclamation nor the fact that they are enemy aliens forecloses consideration by the courts of petitioners' contentions that the Constitution and laws of the United States constitutionally enacted forbid their trial by military commission. . . . We pass at once to the consideration of the basis of the Commission's authority.

We are not here concerned with any question of the guilt or innocence of petitioners. Constitutional safeguards for the protection of all who are charged with offenses are not to be disregarded in order to inflict merited punishment on some who are guilty. But the detention and trial of petitioners — ordered by the President in the declared exercise of his powers as Commander in Chief of the Army in time of war and of grave public danger — are not to be set aside by the courts without the clear conviction that they are in conflict with the Constitution or laws of Congress constitutionally enacted.

Congress and the President, like the courts, possess no power not derived from the Constitution. But one of the objects of the Constitution, as declared by its preamble, is to "provide for the common defence." [The Court lists various congressional and presidential powers relating to war.]

By the Articles of War, Congress has provided rules for the government of the Army. It has provided for the trial and punishment, by courts martial, of violations of the Articles by members of the armed forces and by specified classes of persons associated or serving with the Army. Arts. 1, 2. But the Articles also recognize the "military commission" appointed by military command as an appropriate tribunal for the trial and punishment of offenses against the law of war not ordinarily tried by court martial. See Arts. 12, 15. Articles 38 and 46 authorize the President, with certain limitations, to prescribe the procedure for military commissions. Articles 81 and 82 authorize trial, either by court martial or military commission, of those charged with relieving, harboring or corresponding with the enemy and those charged with spying. And Article 15 declares that "the provisions of these articles conferring jurisdiction upon courts martial shall not be construed as depriving military commissions . . . or other military tribunals of concurrent jurisdiction in respect of offenders or offenses that by statute or by the law of war may be triable by such military commissions . . . or other military tribunals." Article 2 includes among those persons subject to military law the personnel of our own military establishment. But this, as Article 12 provides, does not exclude from that class "any other person who by the law of war is subject to trial by military tribunals" and who under Article 12 may be tried by court martial or under Article 15 by military commission. . . .

From the very beginning of its history this Court has recognized and applied the law of war as including that part of the law of nations which prescribes, for the conduct of war, the status, rights and duties of enemy nations as well as of enemy individuals. By the Articles of War, and especially Article 15, Congress has explicitly provided, so far as it may constitutionally do so, that military tribunals shall have jurisdiction to try offenders or offenses against the law of war in appropriate cases. Congress, in addition to making rules for the government of our Armed Forces, has thus exercised its authority to define and punish offenses against the law of nations by sanctioning, within constitutional limitations, the jurisdiction of military commissions to try persons for offenses which, according to the rules and precepts of the law of nations, and more particularly the law of war, are cognizable by such tribunals. And the President, as Commander in Chief, by his Proclamation in time of war has invoked that law. By his Order creating the present Commission he has undertaken to exercise the authority conferred upon him by Congress, and also such authority as the Constitution itself gives the Commander in Chief, to direct the performance of those functions which may constitutionally be performed by the military arm of the nation in time of war.

An important incident to the conduct of war is the adoption of measures by the military command not only to repel and defeat the enemy, but to seize and subject to disciplinary measures those enemies who in their attempt to thwart or impede our military effort have violated the law of war. It is unnecessary for present purposes to determine to what extent the President as Commander in Chief has constitutional power to create military commissions without the support of Congressional legislation. For here Congress has authorized trial of offenses against the law of war before such commissions. We are concerned only with the question whether it is within the constitutional power of the National Government to place petitioners upon trial before a military commission for the offenses with which they are charged. We must therefore first inquire whether any of the acts charged is an offense against the law of war cognizable before a military tribunal, and if so whether the Constitution prohibits the trial. We may assume that there are acts regarded in other countries, or by some writers on international law, as offenses against the law of war which would not be triable by military tribunal here, either because they are not recognized by our courts as violations of the law of war or because they are of that class of offenses constitutionally triable only by a jury. It was upon such grounds that the Court denied the right to proceed by military tribunal in *Ex parte Milligan,* 71 U.S. (4 Wall.) 2 (1866). But as we shall show, these petitioners were charged with an offense against the law of war which the Constitution does not require to be tried by jury.

It is no objection that Congress in providing for the trial of such offenses has not itself undertaken to codify that branch of international law or to mark its precise boundaries, or to enumerate or define by statute all the acts which that law condemns. An Act of Congress punishing "the crime of piracy, as defined by the law of nations" is an appropriate exercise of its constitutional authority, Art. I, §8, cl. 10, "to define and punish" the offense, since it has adopted by reference the sufficiently precise definition of international law. Similarly, by the reference in the 15th Article of War to "offenders or offenses that . . . by the law of war may be triable by such military commissions," Congress has incorporated by reference, as within the jurisdiction of military commissions, all offenses which are defined as such by the law of war, and which may constitutionally be included within that jurisdiction. Congress had the choice of crystallizing in permanent form and in minute detail every offense against the law of war, or of adopting the system of common law applied by military tribunals so far as it should be recognized and deemed applicable by the courts. It chose the latter course.

By universal agreement and practice, the law of war draws a distinction between the armed forces and the peaceful populations of belligerent nations and also between those who are lawful and unlawful combatants. Lawful combatants are subject to capture and detention as prisoners of war by opposing military forces. Unlawful combatants are likewise subject to capture and detention, but in addition they are subject to trial and punishment by military tribunals for acts which render their belligerency unlawful. The spy who secretly and without uniform passes the military lines of a belligerent in time of war, seeking to gather military information and communicate it to the enemy, or an enemy combatant who without uniform comes secretly through the lines for the purpose of waging war by destruction of life or property, are familiar examples of belligerents who are generally deemed not to be entitled to the status of prisoners of war, but to be offenders against the law of war subject to trial and punishment by military tribunals.

Such was the practice of our own military authorities before the adoption of the Constitution, and during the Mexican and Civil Wars. . . .

Citizenship in the United States of an enemy belligerent does not relieve him from the consequences of a belligerency which is unlawful because in violation of the law of war. Citizens who associate themselves with the military arm of the enemy government, and with its aid, guidance and direction enter this country bent on hostile acts, are enemy belligerents within the meaning of the Hague Convention and the law of war. It is as an enemy belligerent that petitioner Haupt is charged with entering the United States, and unlawful belligerency is the gravamen of the offense of which he is accused. . . .

But petitioners insist that, even if the offenses with which they are charged are offenses against the law of war, their trial is subject to the requirement of the Fifth Amendment that no person shall be held to answer for a capital or otherwise infamous crime unless on a presentment or indictment of a grand jury, and that such trials by Article III, §2, and the Sixth Amendment must be by jury in a civil court. Before the Amendments, §2 of Article III, the Judiciary Article, had provided, "The

Trial of all Crimes, except in Cases of Impeachment, shall be by Jury," and had directed that "such Trial shall be held in the State where the said Crimes shall have been committed."

Presentment by a grand jury and trial by a jury of the vicinage where the crime was committed were, at the time of the adoption of the Constitution, familiar parts of the machinery for criminal trials in the civil courts. But they were procedures unknown to military tribunals, which are not courts in the sense of the Judiciary Article, . . . and which, in the natural course of events, are usually called upon to function under conditions precluding resort to such procedures. As this Court has often recognized, it was not the purpose or effect of §2 of Article III, read in the light of the common law, to enlarge the then existing right to a jury trial. . . .

The Fifth and Sixth Amendments, while guaranteeing the continuance of certain incidents of trial by jury which Article III, §2 had left unmentioned, did not enlarge the right to jury trial as it had been established by that Article. . . .

The fact that "cases arising in the land or naval forces" are excepted from the operation of the Amendments does not militate against this conclusion. Such cases are expressly excepted from the Fifth Amendment, and are deemed excepted by implication from the Sixth. It is argued that the exception, which excludes from the Amendment cases arising in the armed forces, has also, by implication, extended its guaranty to all other cases; that, since petitioners, not being members of the Armed Forces of the United States, are not within the exception, the Amendment operates to give to them the right to a jury trial. But we think this argument misconceives both the scope of the Amendment and the purpose of the exception.

We may assume, without deciding, that a trial prosecuted before a military commission created by military authority is not one "arising in the land . . . forces," when the accused is not a member of or associated with those forces. But even so, the exception cannot be taken to affect those trials before military commissions which are neither within the exception nor within the provisions of Article III, §2, whose guaranty the Amendments did not enlarge. No exception is necessary to exclude from the operation of these provisions cases never deemed to be within their terms. . . .

We cannot say that Congress, in preparing the Fifth and Sixth Amendments [for ratification], intended to extend trial by jury to the cases of alien or citizen offenders against the law of war otherwise triable by military commission, while withholding it from members of our own armed forces charged with infractions of the Articles of War punishable by death. It is equally inadmissible to construe the Amendments — whose primary purpose was to continue unimpaired presentment by grand jury and trial by petit jury in all those cases in which they had been customary — as either abolishing all trials by military tribunals, save those of the personnel of our own armed forces, or, what in effect comes to the same thing, as imposing on all such tribunals the necessity of proceeding against unlawful enemy belligerents only on presentment and trial by jury. We conclude that the Fifth and Sixth Amendments did not restrict whatever authority was conferred by the Constitution to try offenses against the law of war by military commission, and that petitioners, charged with such an offense not required to be tried by jury at common law, were lawfully placed on trial by the Commission without a jury.

Petitioners, and especially petitioner Haupt, stress the pronouncement of this Court in the *Milligan* case, that the law of war "can never be applied to citizens in states which have upheld the authority of the government, and where the courts are open and their process unobstructed." Elsewhere in its opinion, the Court was at pains to point out that Milligan, a citizen twenty years resident in Indiana, who had never been a resident of any of the states in rebellion, was not an enemy belligerent either entitled to the status of a prisoner of war or subject to the penalties imposed upon unlawful belligerents. We construe the Court's statement as to the inapplicability of the law of war to Milligan's case as having particular reference to the facts before it. From them the Court concluded that Milligan, not being a part of or associated with the armed forces of the enemy, was a non-belligerent, not subject to the law of war save as — in circumstances found not there to be present, and not involved here — martial law might be constitutionally established.

The Court's opinion is inapplicable to the case presented by the present record. We have no occasion now to define with meticulous care the ultimate boundaries of the jurisdiction of military tribunals to try persons according to the law of war. It is enough that petitioners here, upon the conceded facts, were plainly within those boundaries, and were held in good faith for trial by military commission, charged with being enemies who, with the purpose of destroying war materials and utilities, entered, or after entry remained in, our territory without uniform — an offense against the law of war. We hold only that those particular acts constitute an offense against the law of war which the Constitution authorizes to be tried by military commission.

Johnson v. Eisentrager

339 U.S. 763 (1950)

[On May 8, 1945, the German High Command unconditionally surrendered, thereby obligating all forces under German control to cease active hostilities. After that date, the U.S. Army captured the petitioners — 21 German nationals in China — and charged them with violating the laws of war by engaging in continued military activity against the United States (through assistance to the Japanese). The commanding U.S. general at Nanking, exercising authority granted by the Joint Chiefs of Staff, convened a military commission that tried and convicted the petitioners. After their transfer to the Landsberg Prison in the American-occupied part of Germany, petitioners sought habeas corpus review from U.S. federal courts, arguing that their trial, conviction, and imprisonment violated various constitutional provisions. The lower court held that the petitioners were entitled to seek habeas corpus relief.]

JUSTICE JACKSON delivered the opinion of the Court.

The ultimate question in this case is one of jurisdiction of civil courts of the United States vis-à-vis military authorities in dealing with enemy aliens overseas. . . .

We are cited to no instance where a court, in this or any other country where the writ is known, has issued it on behalf of an alien enemy who, at no relevant time and in no stage of his captivity, has been within its territorial jurisdiction. Nothing in the text of the Constitution extends such a right, nor does anything in our statutes. . . . We are here confronted with a decision whose basic premise is that these prisoners are entitled, as a constitutional right, to sue in some court of the United States for a writ of habeas corpus. To support that assumption we must hold that a prisoner of our military authorities is constitutionally entitled to the writ, even though he (a) is an enemy alien; (b) has never been or resided in the United States; (c) was captured outside of our territory and there held in military custody as a prisoner of war; (d) was tried and convicted by a Military Commission sitting outside the United States; (e) for offenses against laws of war committed outside the United States; (f) and is at all times imprisoned outside the United States. . . .

We have pointed out that the privilege of litigation has been extended to aliens, whether friendly or enemy, only because permitting their presence in the country implied protection. No such basis can be invoked here, for these prisoners at no relevant time were within any territory over which the United States is sovereign, and the scenes of their offense, their capture, their trial and their punishment were all beyond the territorial jurisdiction of any court of the United States. . . .

A basic consideration in habeas corpus practice is that the prisoner will be produced before the court. . . . To grant the writ to these prisoners might mean that our army must transport them across the seas for hearing. This would require allocation of shipping space, guarding personnel, billeting and rations. It might also require transportation for whatever witnesses the prisoners desired to call as well as transportation for those necessary to defend legality of the sentence. The writ, since it is held to be a matter of right, would be equally available to enemies during active hostilities as in the present twilight between war and peace. Such trials would hamper the war effort and bring aid and comfort to the enemy. They would diminish the prestige of our commanders, not only with enemies but with wavering neutrals. It would be difficult to devise more effective fettering of a field commander than to allow the very enemies he is ordered to reduce to submission to call him to account in his own civil courts and divert his efforts and attention from the military offensive abroad to the legal defensive at home. Nor is it unlikely that the result of such enemy litigiousness would be a conflict between judicial and military opinion highly comforting to enemies of the United States. . . .

The prisoners rely, however, upon two decisions of this Court to get them over the threshold — Ex parte Quirin, 317 U.S. 1, and In re Yamashita, 327 U.S. 1. Reliance on the *Quirin* case is clearly mistaken. Those prisoners were in custody in the District of Columbia. One was, or claimed to be, a citizen. They were tried by a Military Commission sitting in the District of Columbia at a time when civil courts were open and functioning normally. They were arrested by civil authorities and the prosecution was personally directed by the Attorney General, a civilian prosecutor, for acts committed in the United States. They waived arraignment before a civil court and it was contended that the civil courts thereby acquired jurisdiction and could not be ousted by the Military. None of the places where they were acting, arrested, tried or imprisoned were, it was contended, in a zone of active military operations, were not under martial law or any other military control, and no circumstances justified transferring them from civil to military jurisdiction. None of these grave grounds for challenging military jurisdiction can be urged in the case now before us.

Nor can the Court's decision in the *Yamashita* case aid the prisoners. This Court refused to receive Yamashita's petition for a writ of habeas corpus. For hearing and opinion, it was consolidated with another application for a writ of certiorari to review the refusal of habeas corpus by the Supreme Court of the Philippines over whose decisions the statute then gave this Court a right of review. By reason of our sovereignty at that time over these insular possessions, Yamashita stood much as did Quirin before American courts. Yamashita's offenses were committed on our territory, he was tried within the jurisdiction of our insular courts and he was imprisoned within territory of the United States. None of these heads of jurisdiction can be invoked by these prisoners.

Despite this, the doors of our courts have not been summarily closed upon these prisoners. Three courts have considered their application and have provided their counsel opportunity to advance every argument in their support and to show some reason in the petition why they should not be subject to the usual disabilities of non-resident enemy aliens. . . .

The Court of Appeals . . . gave our Constitution an extraterritorial application to embrace our enemies in arms. Right to the writ, it reasoned, is a subsidiary procedural right that follows from possession of substantive constitutional rights. These prisoners, it considered, are invested with a right of personal liberty by our Constitution and therefore must have the right to the remedial writ. . . .

If the Fifth Amendment confers its rights on all the world except Americans engaged in defending it, the same must be true of the companion civil-rights Amendments, for none of them is limited by its express terms, territorially or as to persons. Such a construction would mean that during military occupation irreconcilable enemy elements, guerrilla fighters, and "werewolves" could require the American Judiciary to assure them freedoms of speech, press, and assembly as in the First Amendment, right to bear arms as in the Second, security against "unreasonable" searches and seizures as in the Fourth, as well as rights to jury trial as in the Fifth and Sixth Amendments.

Such extraterritorial application of organic law would have been so significant an innovation in the practice of governments that, if intended or apprehended, it could scarcely have failed to excite contemporary comment. Not one word can be cited. No decision of this Court supports such a view. None of the learned commentators on our Constitution has even hinted at it. The practice of every modern government is opposed to it. We hold that the Constitution does not confer a right of personal security or an immunity from military trial and punishment upon an alien enemy engaged in the hostile service of a government at war with the United States. . . .

MR. JUSTICE BLACK, with whom MR. JUSTICE DOUGLAS and MR. JUSTICE BURTON concur, dissenting. . . .

If the [Court's] opinion thus means, and it apparently does, that these petitioners are deprived of the privilege of habeas corpus solely because they were convicted and imprisoned overseas, the Court is adopting a broad and dangerous principle. The range of that principle is underlined by the argument of the Government brief that habeas corpus is not even available for American citizens convicted and imprisoned in Germany by American military tribunals. While the Court wisely disclaims any such necessary effect for its holding, rejection of the Government's argument is certainly made difficult by the logic of today's opinion. Conceivably a majority may hereafter find citizenship a sufficient substitute for territorial jurisdiction and thus permit courts to protect Americans from illegal sentences. But the Court's opinion inescapably denies courts power to afford the least bit of protection for any alien who is subject to our occupation government abroad, even if he is neither enemy nor belligerent and even after peace is officially declared. It has always been recognized that actual warfare can be conducted successfully only if those in command are left the most ample independence in the theatre of operations. Our Constitution is not so impractical or inflexible that it unduly restricts such necessary independence. It would be fantastic to suggest that alien enemies could hail our military leaders into judicial tribunals to account for their day-to-day activities on the battlefront. Active fighting forces must be free to fight while hostilities are in progress. But that undisputable axiom has no bearing on this case or the general problem from which it arises.

When a foreign enemy surrenders, the situation changes markedly. If our country decides to occupy conquered territory either temporarily or permanently, it assumes the problem of deciding how the subjugated people will be ruled, what laws will govern, who will promulgate them, and what governmental agency of ours will see that they are properly administered. This responsibility immediately raises questions concerning the extent to which our domestic laws, constitutional and statutory, are transplanted abroad. Probably no one would suggest, and certainly I would not, that this nation either must or should attempt to apply every constitutional provision of the Bill of Rights in controlling temporarily occupied countries. But that does not mean that the Constitution is wholly inapplicable in foreign territories that we occupy and govern. The question here involves a far narrower issue. Springing from recognition that our government is composed of three separate and independent branches, it is whether the judiciary has power in habeas corpus proceedings to test the legality of criminal sentences imposed by the executive through military tribunals in a country which we have occupied for years. . . .

Though the scope of habeas corpus review of military tribunal sentences is narrow, I think it should not be denied to these petitioners and others like them. We control that part of Germany we occupy. These prisoners were convicted by our own military tribunals under our own Articles of War, years after hostilities had ceased. However illegal their sentences might be, they can expect no relief from German courts or any other branch of the German Government we permit to function. Only our own courts can inquire into the legality of their imprisonment. Perhaps, as some nations believe, there is merit in leaving the administration of criminal laws to executive and military agencies completely free from judicial scrutiny. Our Constitution has emphatically expressed a contrary policy.

Notes and Questions

1. On December 11, 1941, four days after the Pearl Harbor attacks and three days after the United States declared war against Japan, Germany declared war on the United States, and the United States responded by declaring war against Germany. The U.S. war declaration provided:

Whereas the Government of Germany has formally declared war against the Government and the people of the United States of America:

Therefore be it Resolved by the Senate and House of Representatives of the United States of America in Congress assembled, That the state of war between the United States and the Government of Germany which has thus been thrust upon the United States is hereby formally declared; and the President is hereby authorized and directed to employ the entire naval and military forces of the United States and the resources of the Government to carry on war against the Government of Germany; and, to bring the conflict to a successful termination, all of the resources of the country are hereby pledged by the Congress of the United States.

2. The cases in this section and in the subsequent sections came to the courts on petitions for writs of habeas corpus. A petition for a writ of habeas corpus is the traditional means by which someone being detained by the government can seek judicial review of the legality of the detention. Congress by statute has long regulated the scope and procedures for the writ of habeas corpus. But there are limits on Congress's power to restrict the writ. The Constitution provides, in Article I, Section 9, that "The Privilege of the Writ of Habeas Corpus shall not be suspended, unless when in Cases of Rebellion or Invasion the public Safety may require it." The Supreme Court has construed this clause as conferring a constitutional right of habeas corpus that applies unless Congress provides an adequate substitute for habeas or validly suspends the writ. Congress has rarely suspended the writ, although it did authorize presidential suspension of the writ during the Civil War.

3. The eight Nazi saboteurs whose military trial was at issue in *Quirin* were captured in late June 1942, and many of them were executed in early August of the same year. When FBI director J. Edgar Hoover announced the capture, there was an outcry in the country for "swift justice to the saboteurs." Felix Cotton, *Death Penalty Asked for 8 Captured Spies*, Wash. Post 2 (June 29, 1942). On July 2, Roosevelt issued two proclamations that together established a military commission to try the eight saboteurs. One established the jurisdiction of the military commission and purported to preclude judicial review of its decisions, providing that

> all persons who are subjects, citizens, or residents of any nation at war with the United States or who give obedience to or act under the direction of any such nation, and who during time of war enter or attempt to enter the United States or any territory or possession thereof, through coastal or boundary defenses, and are charged with committing or attempting or preparing to commit sabotage, espionage, hostile or warlike acts, or violations of the law or war, shall be subject to the law of war and to the jurisdiction of military tribunals; and that such persons shall not be privileged to seek any remedy or maintain any proceeding directly or indirectly, or to have any such remedy or proceeding sought on their behalf, in the courts of the United States, or of its States, territories, and possessions, except under such regulations as the Attorney General, with the approval of the Secretary of War, may from time to time prescribe.

7 Fed. Reg. 5101 (July 2, 1942). The other proclamation named the eight defendants, as well as the judges, prosecutors, and defense counsel. It also outlined the structure of the commission, in very general terms, as follows:

> The Commission shall have power to and shall, as occasion requires, make such rules for the conduct of the proceeding, consistent with the powers of military commissions under the Articles of War, as it shall deem necessary for a full and fair trial of the matters before it. Such evidence shall be admitted as would, in the opinion of the President of the Commission, have probative value to a reasonable man. The concurrence of at least two-thirds of the Members of the Commission present shall be necessary for a conviction or sentence. The record of the trial including any judgment or sentence, shall be transmitted directly to me for my action thereon.

7 Fed. Reg. 5103 (July 2, 1942).

The saboteurs' trial began on July 8, 1942, in the Justice Department and was entirely closed to the press and public. Three weeks into the trial, the saboteurs' military lawyer, having asked and received permission from the President, sought a writ of habeas corpus in the Supreme Court challenging the legality of the commission. The Court held an emergency oral argument and on July 31 announced its unanimous decision that the commission was legally constituted (though the Court would not issue its opinion in support of the decision for almost three months). Unbeknownst to the public, the military commission trial ended three days after the Supreme Court announcement, on August 3, 1942. The commission found all eight defendants guilty, recommended that they all be executed, and sent the 3,000-page record to the President for review. On August 8, President Roosevelt publicly announced that he had approved the commission's judgments but had commuted the sentences of two of the saboteurs who had cooperated with the authorities. By the time of the public announcement, the executions had been carried out. In their postmortems, the press praised the military commission for its fairness and integrity, the Supreme Court for its quick review and approval of the commission's legality, and the entire process as a victory for democracy and justice. The *New Republic* was typical in stating that the episode revealed that "even in wartime and even toward the enemy we do not abandon our basic protection of individual rights." Editorial, *The Saboteurs and the Court*, New Republic 159 (Aug. 10, 1942).

4. The Court in *Quirin* held that Congress in Article 15 of the 1916 Articles of War had authorized military commission trials. But both the language of Article 15 and the testimony of its sponsor suggest that Article 15 was simply meant to preserve and clarify the historical authority of the President to establish military commissions in the face of Congress's expansion of court-martial jurisdiction over the laws of war. *See* Testimony of the Judge Advocate General of the Army, S. Rep. No. 130, 64th Cong., 1st Sess. 40 (1916); *see also* In re Yamashita, 327 U.S. 1, 20 (1946). Why did the Court view Article 15 as congressional authorization? Where does Congress get the constitutional authority to create such commissions? From its power to declare war? To regulate the armed forces? To define and punish offenses against the law of nations?

5. Is Congress's authority to establish military commissions exclusive of the President, or is it concurrent? Could the President, in the absence of congressional approval, establish military commissions under the President's authority as Commander in Chief? What does Article 15 suggest? The Court in *Quirin* declined to address this question. But might one interpret Congress's recognition of a pre-existing authority, in combination with the historical practice of using military commissions and the idea that military tribunals are tools for meting out justice in times of war, to mean that the President can on his own establish the tribunals, at least in the absence of congressional disapproval of this practice? *See* Madsen v. Kinsella, 343 U.S. 341, 348 (1952) ("In the absence of attempts by Congress to limit the President's power, it appears that, as Commander-in-Chief of the Army and Navy of the United States, he may, in time of war, establish and prescribe the jurisdiction and procedure of military commissions, and of tribunals in the nature of such commissions, in the territory occupied by the United States by force of arms."); *cf.* Dames & Moore v. Regan, 453 U.S. 654, 677 (1981) (concluding that presidential power to suspend international claims was supported by congressional acquiescence).

Where might the President get the constitutional authority to create military commissions? The Commander in Chief Clause? The Executive Power clause? International law? *Cf.* Ex parte Vallandigham, 68 U.S. 243, 249 (1863) (stating that military commissions derive their authority from "the common law of war").

6. In addition to holding that Roosevelt's military commission was supported by congressional authorization, the Court in *Quirin* held that the commission was constitutional. Is this holding consistent with *Milligan*? The Court distinguished *Milligan* on two grounds: first, Milligan, unlike the Nazi saboteurs, was not part of or associated with the armed forces of the enemy, and thus was not an enemy belligerent entitled to the status of a prisoner of war (POW) or subject to the penalties imposed upon unlawful belligerents; and, second, the Constitution's jury trial provisions were intended only to preserve jury trial rights available at common law, and the common law did not extend jury trial rights to properly constituted military commissions. Are these arguments persuasive? Why is status as a belligerent, or the absence of that status, relevant to the constitutionality of military commissions? Turning to the Court's jury trial argument, can it be reconciled with the fact that "cases arising in the land or naval forces," which is presumably a reference to the trials of U.S. soldiers, is expressly excepted from the Fifth Amendment jury trial right?

7. *Quirin* is a case about military commissions, but its statement that lawful and unlawful belligerents are subject to "capture and detention" is also important. In World War II, the United States detained more than 400,000 enemy combatants in prisoner-of-war camps inside the United States. *See generally* Arnold Krammer, Nazi Prisoners of War in America (1996). A large majority of the prisoners were German, but some were Italian or Japanese, and a handful were U.S. citizens who had served with enemy forces. One such citizen captured in Italy while serving in the Italian army and held as a POW in the United States brought a habeas petition for release. The U.S. Court of Appeals for the Ninth Circuit denied relief, holding that the U.S. military could hold even a U.S. citizen as a prisoner of war until the end of hostilities. *See* In re Territo, 156 F.2d 142 (9th Cir. 1946). Citing *Quirin*, the court concluded that "all persons who are active in opposing an army in war may be captured and except for spies and other non-uniformed plotters and actors for the enemy are prisoners of war." The court further explained that "[t]he object of capture is to prevent the captured individual from serving the enemy. He is disarmed and from then on he must be removed as completely as practicable from the front, treated humanely and in time exchanged, repatriated or otherwise released." The court in *Territo* did not make clear whether it was denying habeas relief on the merits, or whether habeas relief was unavailable to a prisoner of war. But the decision was made easier by the fact that the petitioner acknowledged being an enemy soldier. Note that the same was true of the petitioners in *Quirin*. Might the cases have come out differently if there had been some doubt on this point?

8. What is the holding of *Eisentrager*? Did the Court deny the writ of habeas corpus because the prisoners were tried outside the United States? Because they were imprisoned outside the United States? Because of the practical problems associated with granting them the writ? Did the denial of habeas corpus depend on the fact that the petitioners had already received process in the military commission trial? Would the reasoning of *Eisentrager* apply to alien prisoners of war detained without trial in Germany? What if the prisoners of war were U.S. citizens detained in Germany?

9. Do you agree with Justice Black's claim in *Eisentrager* that the denial of habeas to the petitioners "solely because they were convicted and imprisoned overseas" is a "broad and dangerous principle"? What precisely is the danger? Why is Justice Black so careful to rule out judicial review of "day-to-day activities on the battlefront"?

10. The 1907 Hague Convention on the Laws and Customs of War on Land (and in particular its annex, the Hague Regulations Respecting the Laws and Customs of War on Land) and the Geneva Convention Relative to the Treatment of Prisoners of War of 1929, were relevant to the government's power to detain and try enemy soldiers in World War II. The Hague Regulations defined belligerent status, outlined prisoner-of-war rights, prescribed which weapons could be used and how, determined how a war could end, and specified the powers and limitations of occupying authorities. The 1929 Geneva Convention provided more elaborate rules for POWs, including prison conditions, minimal living standards, penal sanctions, and repatriation. Both treaties were updated and in some respects replaced by the Third

Geneva Convention Relative to the Treatment of Prisoners of War of 1949, which is discussed in the next section.

How are such treaty rights to be enforced? The Court in *Eisentrager*, in a portion of its opinion not excerpted above, expresses the view in a footnote that "[i]t is . . . the obvious scheme of the [Geneva Convention] that responsibility for observance and enforcement of these [treaty] rights is upon political and military authorities."

11. Another important World War II-era decision, mentioned in *Eisentrager*, is In re Yamashita, 327 U.S. 1 (1946). This case involved the trial of General Yamashita, the commander of the Japanese army in the Philippines, before a military commission of U.S. Army officers established in the Philippines by the commanding general of the U.S. Army in the western Pacific. The commission sentenced Yamashita to death after finding him guilty of violating the laws of war for failing to prevent his troops from committing atrocities against civilians and prisoners of war. On a petition for a writ of habeas corpus filed with the Supreme Court, Yamashita argued that, as summarized in Justice Murphy's dissent, he "was rushed to trial under an improper charge, given insufficient time to prepare an adequate defense, deprived of the benefits of some of the most elementary rules of evidence and summarily sentenced to be hanged," in violation of the Due Process Clause and the 1929 Geneva Convention.

The Supreme Court declined to set aside the military commission judgment. The Court was able to assert habeas corpus jurisdiction over the case, the Court in *Eisentrager* later explained, because the United States exercised sovereignty over the Philippines, and thus Yamashita "stood much as did Quirin before American courts," in the sense that his "offenses were committed on our territory . . . and he was imprisoned within territory of the United States." On the merits, the Court in *Yamashita*, relying on *Quirin*, reasoned that it possessed authority under the habeas corpus statute only to consider the legality of the military commission, not Yamashita's guilt or innocence. "If the military tribunals have lawful authority to hear, decide, and condemn, their action is not subject to judicial review merely because they have made a wrong decision on disputed facts." The only question, the Court reasoned, was whether Yamashita's alleged conduct violated the laws of war, and after reviewing the charges in detail it concluded that it did. With regard to Yamashita's claims that the evidentiary rules and other procedures were invalid, the Court held "that the commission's rulings on evidence and on the mode of conducting these proceedings against petitioner are not reviewable by courts, but only by reviewing military authorities."

12. A final significant decision growing out of World War II is Ludecke v. Watkins, 335 U.S. 160 (1948). The issue before the Court was whether the authority conveyed by the Alien Enemy Act, which allows the President to remove enemy aliens during a "declared war," see 50 U.S.C. §21, had expired because of Germany's unconditional surrender, the disintegration of the Nazi regime, and the general cessation of hostilities between the United States and Germany. The Court declined to rule that the war was over because the President had proclaimed that "a state of war still exists," and the United States had not concluded a peace treaty or issued an official proclamation of peace. The Court reasoned that war termination "is a political act" and that whether the war had terminated for purposes of continued authority to retain and remove a German citizen under the Alien Enemy Act turned on "matters of political judgment for which judges have neither technical competence nor official responsibility."

B. MILITARY DETENTION OF ALLEGED TERRORISTS

Authorization for Use of Military Force

Pub. L. No. 107-40 (Sept. 18, 2001)

JOINT RESOLUTION

To authorize the use of United States Armed Forces against those responsible for the recent attacks launched against the United States.

WHEREAS, on September 11, 2001, acts of treacherous violence were committed against the United States and its citizens; and

WHEREAS, such acts render it both necessary and appropriate that the United States exercise its right to self-defense and to protect United States citizens both at home and abroad; and

WHEREAS, in light of the threat to the national security and foreign policy of the United States posed by these grave acts of violence; and

WHEREAS, such acts continue to pose an unusual and extraordinary threat to the national security and foreign policy of the United States; and

WHEREAS, the President has authority under the Constitution to take action to deter and prevent acts of international terrorism against the United States: Now, therefore, be it

Resolved by the Senate and the House of Representatives of the United States of America in Congress assembled, . . .

Section 2 AUTHORIZATION FOR USE OF UNITED STATES ARMED FORCES

(a) IN GENERAL. — That the President is authorized to use all necessary and appropriate force against those nations, organizations, or persons he determines planned, authorized, committed, or aided the terrorist attacks that occurred on September 11, 2001, or harbored such organizations or persons, in order to prevent any future acts of international terrorism against the United States by such nations, organizations or persons.

(b) War Powers Resolution Requirements —

(1) SPECIFIC STATUTORY AUTHORIZATION. — Consistent with Section 8(a)(1) of the War Powers Resolution, the Congress declares that this section is intended to constitute specific statutory authorization within the meaning of Section 5(b) of the War Powers Resolution.

(2) APPLICABILITY OF OTHER REQUIREMENTS. — Nothing in this resolution supersedes any requirement of the War Powers Resolution.

Hamdi v. Rumsfeld

542 U.S. 507 (2004)

[Shortly after the September 11 attacks, Congress enacted an Authorization for Use of Military Force (AUMF), which is excerpted above. Subsequently, U.S. armed forces were sent to Afghanistan, where they engaged in combat with the Al Qaeda terrorist organization and the Taliban regime that ruled much of Afghanistan. During that conflict, the U.S. government acquired custody of Yaser Hamdi, a U.S. citizen who was seized in Afghanistan by members of the Northern Alliance (a coalition of Afghanistan groups opposed to the Taliban government) and turned over to the U.S. military. The military subsequently moved Hamdi to the U.S. naval base at Guantanamo Bay, Cuba. Upon learning that he was a U.S. citizen, the military transferred him to a naval brig in Norfolk, Virginia, and then subsequently to a brig in South Carolina. The U.S. government maintained that Hamdi was an "enemy combatant" who could be held without trial. Hamdi's father filed a petition on his behalf in a federal court in Virginia, seeking habeas corpus relief. In response to the petition, the government filed a short declaration (the "Mobbs Declaration"), stating that Hamdi had traveled to Afghanistan in the summer of 2001, had affiliated himself with the Taliban military, and had surrendered to Northern Alliance forces while carrying a rifle. The district court concluded that this declaration was insufficient to support Hamdi's detention, calling it "little more than the government's 'say-so.'" The Fourth Circuit reversed, holding that, because it was "undisputed that Hamdi was captured in a zone of active combat in a foreign theater of conflict," no factual inquiry or evidentiary hearing allowing Hamdi to be heard or to rebut the government's assertions was necessary or proper.]

JUSTICE O'CONNOR announced the judgment of the Court and delivered an opinion, in which THE CHIEF JUSTICE, JUSTICE KENNEDY, and JUSTICE BREYER join. . . .

The threshold question before us is whether the Executive has the authority to detain citizens who qualify as "enemy combatants." There is some debate as to the proper scope of this term, and the Government has never provided any court with the full criteria that it uses in classifying individuals as such. It has made clear, however, that, for purposes of this case, the "enemy combatant" that it is seeking to detain is an individual who, it alleges, was "'part of or supporting forces hostile to the United States or coalition partners'" in Afghanistan and who "'engaged in an armed conflict against the United States'" there. We therefore answer only the narrow question before us: whether the detention of citizens falling within that definition is authorized.

The Government maintains that no explicit congressional authorization is required, because the Executive possesses plenary authority to detain pursuant to Article II of the Constitution. We do not reach the question whether Article II provides such authority, however, because we agree with the Government's alternative position, that Congress has in fact authorized Hamdi's detention, through the AUMF. . . .

The AUMF authorizes the President to use "all necessary and appropriate force" against "nations, organizations, or persons" associated with the September 11, 2001, terrorist attacks. There can be no doubt that individuals who fought against the United States in Afghanistan as part of the Taliban, an organization known to have supported the al Qaeda terrorist network responsible for those attacks, are individuals Congress sought to target in passing the AUMF. We conclude that detention of individuals falling into the limited category we are considering, for the duration of the particular conflict in which they were captured, is so fundamental and accepted an incident to war as to be an exercise of the "necessary and appropriate force" Congress has authorized the President to use.

The capture and detention of lawful combatants and the capture, detention, and trial of unlawful combatants, by "universal agreement and practice," are "important incidents of war." Ex parte Quirin, [317 U.S. 1, 28 (1942)]. The purpose of detention is to prevent captured individuals from returning to the field of battle and taking up arms once again. . . .

There is no bar to this Nation's holding one of its own citizens as an enemy combatant. In *Quirin*, one of the detainees, Haupt, alleged that he was a naturalized

United States citizen. We held that "citizens who associate themselves with the military arm of the enemy government, and with its aid, guidance and direction enter this country bent on hostile acts, are enemy belligerents within the meaning of . . . the law of war." While Haupt was tried for violations of the law of war, nothing in *Quirin* suggests that his citizenship would have precluded his mere detention for the duration of the relevant hostilities. Nor can we see any reason for drawing such a line here. A citizen, no less than an alien, can be "part of or supporting forces hostile to the United States or coalition partners" and "engaged in an armed conflict against the United States," Brief for Respondents 3; such a citizen, if released, would pose the same threat of returning to the front during the ongoing conflict.

In light of these principles, it is of no moment that the AUMF does not use specific language of detention. Because detention to prevent a combatant's return to the battlefield is a fundamental incident of waging war, in permitting the use of "necessary and appropriate force," Congress has clearly and unmistakably authorized detention in the narrow circumstances considered here.

Hamdi objects, nevertheless, that Congress has not authorized the indefinite detention to which he is now subject. The Government responds that "the detention of enemy combatants during World War II was just as 'indefinite' while that war was being fought." We take Hamdi's objection to be not to the lack of certainty regarding the date on which the conflict will end, but to the substantial prospect of perpetual detention. We recognize that the national security underpinnings of the "war on terror," although crucially important, are broad and malleable. As the Government concedes, "given its unconventional nature, the current conflict is unlikely to end with a formal cease-fire agreement." The prospect Hamdi raises is therefore not far-fetched. If the Government does not consider this unconventional war won for two generations, and if it maintains during that time that Hamdi might, if released, rejoin forces fighting against the United States, then the position it has taken throughout the litigation of this case suggests that Hamdi's detention could last for the rest of his life.

It is a clearly established principle of the law of war that detention may last no longer than active hostilities. . . . [The Court cites various treaty provisions and other materials.]

Hamdi contends that the AUMF does not authorize indefinite or perpetual detention. Certainly, we agree that indefinite detention for the purpose of interrogation is not authorized. Further, we understand Congress' grant of authority for the use of "necessary and appropriate force" to include the authority to detain for the duration of the relevant conflict, and our understanding is based on longstanding law-of-war principles. If the practical circumstances of a given conflict are entirely unlike those of the conflicts that informed the development of the law of war, that understanding may unravel. But that is not the situation we face as of this date. Active combat operations against Taliban fighters apparently are ongoing in Afghanistan. . . . The United States may detain, for the duration of these hostilities, individuals legitimately determined to be Taliban combatants who "engaged in an armed conflict against the United States." If the record establishes that United States troops are still involved in active combat in Afghanistan, those detentions are part of the exercise of "necessary and appropriate force," and therefore are authorized by the AUMF.

Ex parte Milligan, 71 U.S. 2 (1866), does not undermine our holding about the Government's authority to seize enemy combatants, as we define that term today. In that case, the Court made repeated reference to the fact that its inquiry into whether the military tribunal had jurisdiction to try and punish Milligan turned in large part on the fact that Milligan was not a prisoner of war, but a resident of Indiana arrested while at home there. That fact was central to its conclusion. Had Milligan been captured while he was assisting Confederate soldiers by carrying a rifle against Union troops on a Confederate battlefield, the holding of the Court might well have been different. The Court's repeated explanations that Milligan was not a prisoner of war suggest that had these different circumstances been present he could have been detained under military authority for the duration of the conflict, whether or not he was a citizen. . . .

Even in cases in which the detention of enemy combatants is legally authorized, there remains the question of what process is constitutionally due to a citizen who disputes his enemy-combatant status. . . .

Though they reach radically different conclusions on the process that ought to attend the present proceeding, the parties begin on common ground. All agree that, absent suspension, the writ of habeas corpus remains available to every individual detained within the United States. U.S. Const., Art. I, §9, cl. 2 ("The Privilege of the Writ of Habeas Corpus shall not be suspended, unless when in Cases of Rebellion or Invasion the public Safety may require it"). Only in the rarest of circumstances has Congress seen fit to suspend the writ. At all other times, it has remained a critical check on the Executive, ensuring that it does not detain individuals except in accordance with law. All agree suspension of the writ has not occurred here. Thus, it is undisputed that Hamdi was properly before an Article III court to challenge his detention under [the habeas statute,] 28 U.S.C. §2241. Further, all agree that §2241 and its companion provisions provide at least a skeletal outline of the procedures to be afforded a petitioner in federal habeas review. Most notably, §2243 provides that "the person detained may, under oath, deny any of the facts set forth in the return or allege any other material facts," and §2246 allows the taking of evidence in habeas proceedings by deposition, affidavit, or interrogatories.

The simple outline of §2241 makes clear both that Congress envisioned that habeas petitioners would have some opportunity to present and rebut facts and that courts in cases like this retain some ability to vary the ways in which they do so as mandated by due process. The Government recognizes the basic procedural protections required by the habeas statute, but asks us to hold that, given both the flexibility of the habeas mechanism and the circumstances presented in this case, the presentation of the Mobbs Declaration to the habeas court completed the required factual development. It suggests two separate reasons for its position that no further process is due.

First, the Government urges the adoption of the Fourth Circuit's holding below — that because it is "undisputed" that Hamdi's seizure took place in a combat zone, the habeas determination can be made purely as a matter of law, with no further hearing or factfinding necessary. This argument is easily rejected. As the dissenters from the denial of rehearing en banc noted, the circumstances surrounding Hamdi's seizure cannot in any way be characterized as "undisputed," as "those circumstances are neither conceded in fact, nor susceptible to concession in law, because Hamdi has not been permitted to speak for himself or even through counsel as to those circumstances." . . .

The Government's second argument requires closer consideration. This is the argument that further factual exploration is unwarranted and inappropriate in light of the extraordinary constitutional interests at stake. Under the Government's most extreme rendition of this argument, "respect for separation of powers and the limited institutional capabilities of courts in matters of military decision-making in connection with an ongoing conflict" ought to eliminate entirely any individual process, restricting the courts to investigating only whether legal authorization exists for the broader detention scheme. At most, the Government argues, courts should review its determination that a citizen is an enemy combatant under a very deferential "some evidence" standard. Under this review, a court would assume the accuracy of the Government's articulated basis for Hamdi's detention, as set forth in the Mobbs Declaration, and assess only whether that articulated basis was a legitimate one.

In response, Hamdi emphasizes that this Court consistently has recognized that an individual challenging his detention may not be held at the will of the Executive without recourse to some proceeding before a neutral tribunal to determine whether the Executive's asserted justifications for that detention have basis in fact and warrant in law. He argues that the Fourth Circuit inappropriately "ceded power to the Executive during wartime to define the conduct for which a citizen may be detained, judge whether that citizen has engaged in the proscribed conduct, and imprison that citizen indefinitely," and that due process demands that he receive a hearing in which he may challenge the Mobbs Declaration and adduce his own counter evidence. . . .

Both of these positions highlight legitimate concerns. And both emphasize the tension that often exists between the autonomy that the Government asserts is necessary in order to pursue effectively a particular goal and the process that a citizen contends he is due before he is deprived of a constitutional right. The ordinary mechanism that we use for balancing such serious competing interests, and for determining the procedures that are necessary to ensure that a citizen is not "deprived of life, liberty, or property, without due process of law," U.S. Const., Amdt. 5, is the test that we articulated in Mathews v. Eldridge, 424 U.S. 319 (1976). *Mathews* dictates that the process due in any given instance is determined by weighing "the private interest that will be affected by the official action" against the Government's asserted interest, "including the function involved" and the burdens the Government would face in providing greater process. The *Mathews* calculus then contemplates a judicious balancing of these concerns, through an analysis of "the risk of an erroneous deprivation" of the private interest if the process were reduced and the "probable value, if any, of additional or substitute safeguards." We take each of these steps in turn.

It is beyond question that substantial interests lie on both sides of the scale in this case. Hamdi's "private interest . . . affected by the official action," is the most elemental of liberty interests — the interest in being free from physical detention by one's own government. . . .

Nor is the weight on this side of the *Mathews* scale offset by the circumstances of war or the accusation of treasonous behavior, for "it is clear that commitment for *any* purpose constitutes a significant deprivation of liberty that requires due process protection," Jones v. United States, 463 U.S. 354, 361 (1983) (emphasis added), and at this stage in the *Mathews* calculus, we consider the interest of the erroneously detained individual. . . . Moreover, as critical as the Government's interest may be in detaining those who actually pose an immediate threat to the national security of the United States during ongoing international conflict, history and common sense teach us that an unchecked system of detention carries the potential to become a means for oppression and abuse of others who do not present that sort of threat. . . .

On the other side of the scale are the weighty and sensitive governmental interests in ensuring that those who have in fact fought with the enemy during a war do not return to battle against the United States. As discussed above, the law of war and the realities of combat may render such detentions both necessary and appropriate, and our due process analysis need not blink at those realities. Without doubt, our Constitution recognizes that core strategic matters of warmaking belong in the hands of those who are best positioned and most politically accountable for making them.

The Government also argues at some length that its interests in reducing the process available to alleged enemy combatants are heightened by the practical difficulties that would accompany a system of trial-like process. In its view, military officers who are engaged in the serious work of waging battle would be unnecessarily and dangerously distracted by litigation half a world away, and discovery into military operations would both intrude on the sensitive secrets of national defense and result in a futile search for evidence buried under the rubble of war. To the extent that these burdens are triggered by heightened procedures, they are properly taken into account in our due process analysis.

Striking the proper constitutional balance here is of great importance to the Nation during this period of ongoing combat. But it is equally vital that our calculus not give short shrift to the values that this country holds dear or to the privilege that is American citizenship. It is during our most challenging and uncertain moments that our Nation's commitment to due process is most severely tested; and it is in those times that we must preserve our commitment at home to the principles for which we fight abroad. . . .

With due recognition of these competing concerns, we believe that neither the process proposed by the Government nor the process apparently envisioned by the District Court below strikes the proper constitutional balance when a United States citizen is detained in the United States as an enemy combatant. That is, "the risk of erroneous deprivation" of a detainee's liberty interest is unacceptably high under the Government's proposed rule, while some of the "additional or substitute procedural safeguards" suggested by the District Court are unwarranted in light of their limited "probable value" and the burdens they may impose on the military in such cases.

We therefore hold that a citizen-detainee seeking to challenge his classification as an enemy combatant must receive notice of the factual basis for his classification, and a fair opportunity to rebut the Government's factual assertions before a neutral decisionmaker. . . .

At the same time, the exigencies of the circumstances may demand that, aside from these core elements, enemy combatant proceedings may be tailored to alleviate their uncommon potential to burden the Executive at a time of ongoing military conflict. Hearsay, for example, may need to be accepted as the most reliable available evidence from the Government in such a proceeding. Likewise, the Constitution would not be offended by a presumption in favor of the Government's evidence, so long as that presumption remained a rebuttable one and fair opportunity for rebuttal were provided. Thus, once the Government puts forth credible evidence that the habeas petitioner meets the enemy-combatant criteria, the onus could shift to the petitioner to rebut that evidence with more persuasive evidence that he falls outside the criteria. A burden-shifting scheme of this sort would meet the goal of ensuring that the errant tourist, embedded journalist, or local aid worker has a chance to prove military error while giving due regard to the Executive once it has put forth meaningful support for its conclusion that the detainee is in fact an enemy combatant. In the words of *Mathews,* process of this sort would sufficiently address the "risk of erroneous deprivation" of a detainee's liberty interest while eliminating certain procedures that have questionable additional value in light of the burden on the Government. . . .

In so holding, we necessarily reject the Government's assertion that separation of powers principles mandate a heavily circumscribed role for the courts in such circumstances. Indeed, the position that the courts must forgo any examination of the individual case and focus exclusively on the legality of the broader detention scheme cannot be mandated by any reasonable view of separation of powers, as this approach serves only to condense power into a single branch of government. We have long since made clear that a state of war is not a blank check for the President when it comes to the rights of the Nation's citizens. Youngstown Sheet & Tube Co. v. Sawyer, 343 U.S. 579, 587 (1952). Whatever power the United States Constitution envisions for the Executive in its exchanges with other nations or with enemy organizations in times of conflict, it most assuredly envisions a role for all three branches when individual liberties are at stake. Likewise, we have made clear that, unless Congress acts to suspend it, the Great Writ of habeas corpus allows the Judicial Branch to play a necessary role in maintaining this delicate balance of governance, serving as an important judicial check on the Executive's discretion in the realm of detentions. Thus, while we do not question that our due process assessment must pay keen attention to the particular burdens faced by the Executive in the context of military action, it would turn our system of checks and balances on its head to suggest that a citizen could not make his way to court with a challenge to the factual basis for his detention by his government, simply because the Executive opposes making available such a challenge. Absent suspension of the writ by Congress, a citizen detained as an enemy combatant is entitled to this process.

Because we conclude that due process demands some system for a citizen detainee to refute his classification, the proposed "some evidence" standard is inadequate. Any process in which the Executive's factual assertions go wholly unchallenged or are simply presumed correct without any opportunity for the alleged combatant to demonstrate otherwise falls constitutionally short. As the Government itself has recognized, we have utilized the "some evidence" standard in the past as a standard of review, not as a standard of proof. That is, it primarily has been employed by courts in examining an administrative record developed after an adversarial proceeding — one with process at least of the sort that we today hold is constitutionally mandated in the citizen enemy-combatant setting. This standard therefore is ill suited to the situation in which a habeas petitioner has received no prior proceedings before any tribunal and had no prior opportunity to rebut the Executive's factual assertions before a neutral decisionmaker.

Today we are faced only with such a case. Aside from unspecified "screening" processes, and military interrogations in which the Government suggests Hamdi could have contested his classification, Hamdi has received no process. An interrogation by one's captor, however effective an intelligence-gathering tool, hardly constitutes a constitutionally adequate factfinding before a neutral decisionmaker. . . . Plainly, the "process" Hamdi has received is not that to which he is entitled under the Due Process Clause.

There remains the possibility that the standards we have articulated could be met by an appropriately authorized and properly constituted military tribunal.

Indeed, it is notable that military regulations already provide for such process in related instances, dictating that tribunals be made available to determine the status of enemy detainees who assert prisoner-of-war status under the Geneva Convention. In the absence of such process, however, a court that receives a petition for a writ of habeas corpus from an alleged enemy combatant must itself ensure that the minimum requirements of due process are achieved. Both courts below recognized as much, focusing their energies on the question of whether Hamdi was due an opportunity to rebut the Government's case against him. The Government, too, proceeded on this assumption, presenting its affidavit and then seeking that it be evaluated under a deferential standard of review based on burdens that it alleged would accompany any greater process. As we have discussed, a habeas court in a case such as this may accept affidavit evidence like that contained in the Mobbs Declaration, so long as it also permits the alleged combatant to present his own factual case to rebut the Government's return. We anticipate that a District Court would proceed with the caution that we have indicated is necessary in this setting, engaging in a factfinding process that is both prudent and incremental. We have no reason to doubt that courts faced with these sensitive matters will pay proper heed both to the matters of national security that might arise in an individual case and to the constitutional limitations safeguarding essential liberties that remain vibrant even in times of security concerns. . . .

[Justice Souter, joined by Justice Ginsburg, concurred in part, dissented in part, and concurred in the judgment. He argued that the AUMF was focused on military power and thus could fairly be read to authorize the use of armies and weapons against the named enemy, but could not be read in the absence of clearer congressional guidance to authorize detention. Justice Souter further argued that the government should not be able to rely on international law in construing the AUMF since it was not complying with international law in its detention operations (such as the requirement in the Third Geneva Convention that detainees in a conflict be given individual hearings to determine whether they qualify as prisoners of war when there is any doubt about their status). Nonetheless, Justice Souter joined the plurality's call for a hearing at which Hamdi could present evidence to contest his status as an enemy combatant, in order "to give practical effect to the conclusions of eight members of the Court rejecting the Government's position."]

[Justice Scalia dissented and was joined by Justice Stevens. Relying on *Ex parte Milligan*, Scalia argued that a U.S. citizen could not be held by the government in the United States without trial absent a suspension of the writ of habeas corpus. He also criticized the plurality for its "Mr. Fix-it Mentality" and for "view[ing] it as its mission to Make Everything Come Out Right, rather than merely to decree the consequences, as far as individual rights are concerned, of the other two branches' actions and omissions." "The problem with this approach," Scalia said, "is not only that it steps out of the courts' modest and limited role in a democratic society; but that by repeatedly doing what it thinks the political branches ought to do it encourages their lassitude and saps the vitality of government by the people."]

[Justice Thomas separately dissented. He agreed with the plurality that the AUMF constituted a congressional authorization of the detention. He disagreed, however, with the plurality's due process analysis. Citing decisions such as *The Prize Cases*, *Curtiss-Wright*, and *Dames & Moore*, he argued that, "[b]y detaining Hamdi, the

President, in the prosecution of a war and authorized by Congress, has acted well within his authority. Hamdi thereby received all the process to which he was due under the circumstances. I therefore believe that this is no occasion to balance the competing interests, as the plurality unconvincingly attempts to do."]

Notes and Questions

1. Since the September 11 terrorist attacks, the U.S. military has detained thousands of foreign Al Qaeda and Taliban prisoners in Afghanistan and at the U.S. naval base at Guantanamo Bay, Cuba. In addition, the CIA held a smaller number of "high-level detainees" at secret prisons around the globe (all of which President Obama closed in 2009), and the U.S. military has sometimes detained terrorists, temporarily, on U.S. ships. The U.S. military has also detained some individuals within the United States, including two U.S. citizens — Yaser Hamdi and Jose Padilla. The U.S. government maintained that both the foreign detainees and the U.S. citizen detainees qualified as "enemy combatants" who could be held without trial until the end of hostilities. This section focuses on the basic principles of detention with special reference to detentions within the United States and at the Guantanamo Bay detention center. In Section D we consider the special issues raised by detentions in Afghanistan, in secret prisons, and elsewhere.

2. How relevant are the World War II-era precedents and practices, outlined in the previous section, to the post-September 11 detentions? How is the post-September 11 conflict different from World War II? In applying the World War II precedents, does it matter that Congress did not declare war after the September 11 attacks? That Al Qaeda is not a nation-state? That the conflict with Al Qaeda, and against international terrorists more generally, may last indefinitely? That the vast majority of enemy soldiers in World War II wore uniforms while no one in Al Qaeda does so? What exactly is the scope of the war on terrorism? Is it limited to the conflict between the United States and Al Qaeda and its affiliates? Is it a broader conflict with Islamist terrorists? With terrorists of global reach?

What is the relevance of the Authorization for Use of Military Force (AUMF), excerpted above, to these questions? Why didn't Congress declare war? How does the AUMF compare with past authorizations of force? To use the language of Bas v. Tingy (excerpted in Section A of Chapter 9), is the AUMF a limited authorization triggering an imperfect war, or a broad authorization triggering a perfect war? How does it define the enemy? What limitations does it contain? What is encompassed by the phrase "all necessary and appropriate force"? To what extent should courts defer to presidential interpretations of the AUMF?

3. The *Hamdi* plurality concludes that Congress in the AUMF provided statutory authority for Hamdi's detention, but its analysis raises a number of issues.

First, the plurality looks to the "incidents of war" to give content to the "force" authorized by the AUMF. How does the plurality identify incidents of war? What other incidents of war are authorized by the AUMF, other than detention? Military targeting? Trial by military commission? Surveillance of the enemy? In considering what the "incidents of war" include, of what relevance is international law? The plurality suggests that the AUMF should be construed to authorize presidential military actions permitted under the international laws of war. If so, does it follow that the AUMF should be construed as not authorizing presidential actions that would violate the international laws of war? Should courts assume that Congress has affirmatively prohibited violations of the international laws of war? Should the President be able to receive the benefits of the international laws of war (such as detention authority) while avoiding the burdens imposed by those laws (such as the protections given to prisoners of war in the Third Geneva Convention, described in the next note)? For discussion of the relationship between the AUMF and international law, see Curtis A. Bradley & Jack L. Goldsmith, *Congressional Authorization and the War on Terrorism*, 118 Harv. L. Rev. 2047, 2087-2102 (2005); Ryan Goodman & Derek Jinks, *International Law, U.S. War Powers, and the Global War on Terrorism*, 118 Harv. L. Rev. 2653 (2005); and Ingrid Brunk Wuerth, *Authorizations for the Use of Force, International Law, and the* Charming Betsy *Canon*, 46 B.C. L. Rev. 293 (2005).

Second, what is the class of persons who can be detained under the AUMF? Hamdi was a member of the Taliban captured in Afghanistan, and the plurality limits its analysis to "enemy combatants," a term defined for purposes of the case as persons who are part of or supporting forces hostile to the United States or its coalition partners and who have engaged in armed conflict against the United States in Afghanistan. Would the plurality's analysis support detention of members of Al Qaeda captured in Afghanistan? Members of Al Qaeda captured outside Afghanistan? Terrorists loosely associated with Al Qaeda? Terrorists who threaten the United States, but who are not associated with Al Qaeda? (We explore some of these questions below in Section E, in the context of targeted killing.)

Third, the plurality observes that enemy combatants can be held until the end of hostilities. If the war on terrorism lasts indefinitely, does this mean that the President has the authority to detain alleged terrorists indefinitely without trial? What is the significance of the plurality's statement that, "[i]f the practical circumstances of a given conflict are entirely unlike those of the conflicts that informed the development of the law of war, [our understanding that Congress' grant of authority for the use of 'necessary and appropriate force' includes the authority to detain for the duration of the relevant conflict] may unravel"?

4. The plurality in *Hamdi* did not address the scope of the President's independent constitutional authority in the war on terrorism, but rather considered only the authority conferred by the AUMF. What independent powers do you think the President has in the war on terrorism, beyond those conferred by the AUMF? For example, can the President use force against terrorists who threaten the United States but who do not have a connection to the September 11 attacks? Under what circumstances? In considering this question, what is the significance of the "whereas" clause in the AUMF that states "the President has authority under the Constitution to take action to deter and prevent acts of international terrorism against the United States"?

In a memorandum prepared shortly after September 11, the Justice Department's Office of Legal Counsel concluded that "the President has the constitutional power not only to retaliate against any person, organization, or State suspected of involvement in terrorist attacks on the United States, but also against foreign States suspected of harboring or supporting such organizations," and that the President "may deploy military force preemptively against terrorist organizations or the States that harbor or support them, whether or not they can be linked to the specific terrorist incidents of September 11." Memorandum from John C. Yoo, Deputy Assistant Attorney General, to the Deputy Counsel to the President, "The President's Constitutional Authority to Conduct Military Operations Against Terrorists and Nations Supporting Them" (Sept. 25, 2001), at https://www.justice.gov/sites/default/files/olc/opinions/2001/09/31/op-olc-v025-p0188.pdf. Does this conclusion follow from the generally accepted principles of independent presidential war power explored in Chapter 9? If this conclusion is correct, did the AUMF add anything to the President's authority? If not, why did the President seek its enactment?

5. The Third Geneva Convention applies "to all cases of declared war or of any other armed conflict which may arise between two or more of the High Contracting Parties." Both the United States and Afghanistan are parties to the Convention. Article 4 of the Convention defines POWs as follows:

> Prisoners of war, in the sense of the present Convention, are persons belonging to one of the following categories, who have fallen into the power of the enemy:
>
> 1. Members of the armed forces of a Party to the conflict as well as members of militias or volunteer corps forming part of such armed forces.
>
> 2. Members of other militias and members of other volunteer corps, including those of organized resistance movements, belonging to a Party to the conflict and operating in or outside their own territory, even if this territory is occupied, provided that such militias or volunteer corps, including such organized resistance movements, fulfill the following conditions:
>
> > (a) That of being commanded by a person responsible for his subordinates;
> >
> > (b) That of having a fixed distinctive sign recognizable at a distance;
> >
> > (c) That of carrying arms openly;
> >
> > (d) That of conducting their operations in accordance with the laws and customs of war.
>
> 3. Members of regular armed forces who profess allegiance to a government or an authority not recognized by the Detaining Power.

Article 5 of the Convention further provides that, "Should any doubt arise as to whether persons, having committed a belligerent act and having fallen into the hands of the enemy, belong to any of the categories enumerated in Article 4, such persons shall enjoy the protection of the present Convention until such time as their status has been determined by a competent tribunal." If a captured prisoner warrants the status as a POW, he receives numerous rights under the Convention, including the right, when interrogated, to give only his name, rank, and a few other pieces of information (Article 17); the right to be "quartered under conditions as favorable as those for the forces of the Detaining Power who are billeted in the same area" (Article 25); the right to send and receive letters and cards (Article 71); the right not to be "sentenced by the military authorities and courts of the Detaining Power to any penalties except those provided for in respect of members of the armed forces of the said Power who have committed the same acts" (Article 87); the right to be sentenced "only if the sentence has been pronounced by the same courts according to the same procedure as in the case of members of the armed forces of the Detaining Power" (Article 102); and the right to "be released and repatriated without delay after the cessation of active hostilities" (Article 118).

Although the Third Geneva Convention generally applies only to an armed conflict between states, Article 3 of the Convention (called "Common Article 3" since each of the four 1949 Geneva Conventions contains the same article) governs an "armed conflict not of an international character occurring in the territory of one of the High Contracting Parties." Common Article 3 prohibits each party in such a conflict from committing (among other things) acts of "mutilation, cruel treatment and torture," the "[t]aking of hostages," "[o]utrages upon personal dignity, in particular, humiliating and degrading treatment," and the "passing of sentences and the carrying out of executions without previous judgment pronounced by a regularly constituted court affording all the judicial guarantees which are recognized as indispensable by civilized peoples."

6. On February 7, 2002, President Bush issued a memorandum interpreting the Third Geneva Convention in the conflict against Al Qaeda and the Taliban. The memorandum stated that "the war against terrorism ushers in a new paradigm . . . . that requires new thinking in the law of war, but thinking that should nevertheless be consistent with the principles of Geneva." It then announced the President's legal determinations that Al Qaeda was not entitled to Geneva Convention POW protections because it was not a state party to the Convention, that Taliban fighters were not entitled to the protections because they did not satisfy the provisions of Article 4 of Geneva and thus were unlawful combatants, and that neither group was entitled to the protections of Common Article 3 because the conflict was an international one. Memorandum from the President to the Vice-President et al., *Humane Treatment of al Qaeda and Taliban Detainees* (Feb. 7, 2002), *at* http://www.washingtonpost.com/wp-srv/nation/documents/020702bush.pdf.

The Supreme Court rejected the President's conclusion about Common Article 3 in Hamdan v. Rumsfeld, 548 U.S. 557 (2006), a decision excerpted in Section C of this chapter. In the course of ruling that President Bush's military commissions violated congressional restrictions that implicitly incorporated the Geneva Conventions, the Court in *Hamdan* concluded that Common Article 3 is applicable to the armed conflict with Al Qaeda because the conflict is not "of an international character" within the meaning of that provision. Following *Hamdan*, the Bush Administration announced that it would abide by Common Article 3 at Guantanamo Bay and elsewhere. The Obama Administration similarly pledged that it would follow Common Article 3, and, like its predecessor, did not extend POW status under Article 4 of the Third Geneva Convention to Al Qaeda or Taliban fighters.

7. In addition to Yaser Hamdi, the U.S. military after September 11 detained two other individuals inside the United States, both of whom were (unlike Hamdi) initially apprehended within the United States.

The first, Jose Padilla, was a U.S. citizen suspected of ties to Al Qaeda and of planning to develop and use a "dirty bomb" (i.e., a radiological bomb) in the United States. The U.S. government arrested Padilla on his arrival from Pakistan at a Chicago airport and transferred him to New York, but it later designated him an "enemy combatant" and transferred him to military custody in South Carolina. Padilla subsequently filed a habeas petition in the district court in South Carolina. The U.S. Court of Appeals for the Fourth Circuit eventually concluded that the AUMF authorized the President to detain Padilla because he had allegedly taken up arms against the United States in Afghanistan and subsequently received directions from Al Qaeda to travel to the United States to blow up apartment buildings. *See* Padilla v. Hanft, 423 F.3d 386 (4th Cir. 2005). The fact that Padilla was seized on U.S. soil did not affect this conclusion, ruled the court, because "Padilla poses the same threat of returning to the battlefield as Hamdi posed at the time of the Supreme Court's adjudication of Hamdi's petition." The court also noted that the plurality in *Hamdi* relied on *Ex parte Quirin*, which involved the capture of a U.S. citizen on U.S. soil. Two months after the Fourth Circuit's decision, the government transferred Padilla to civilian custody, thereby mooting his effort to obtain Supreme Court review of the Fourth Circuit's decision. Padilla was subsequently tried in a federal court in Miami. He was not charged with anything relating to the original allegations about a dirty bomb or blowing up apartment buildings, but rather was charged with violating 18 U.S.C. §956(a), a statute that criminalizes conspiracies to commit acts of murder or kidnapping in a foreign country. He was sentenced to 17 years' imprisonment.

The other individual held in military detention in the United States was Ali Saleh Kahlah al-Marri, a citizen of Qatar who entered the country on September 10, 2001. The government arrested al-Marri in December 2001, and charged him in an Illinois federal court with credit card fraud and related false statements. Al-Marri pleaded not guilty to these charges. In June 2003, about a month before al-Marri's trial was scheduled to begin, President Bush signed an order in which he "determined" that al-Marri was an enemy combatant. The Illinois federal court dismissed the indictment and transferred al-Marri to military custody in Charleston, South Carolina. In response to al-Marri's habeas corpus petition in South Carolina, the U.S. government alleged that he had trained with Al Qaeda in Afghanistan, met Bin Laden there and volunteered for a "martyr mission" on behalf of Al Qaeda, entered the United States to serve as a "sleeper agent" to facilitate terrorist activities, and met and later communicated with Al Qaeda financiers. An en banc panel of the Fourth Circuit ruled that, assuming the government's allegations were true, al-Marri's detention was lawful. *See* Al-Marri v. Pucciarelli, 534 F.3d 213 (4th Cir. 2008) (en banc). The judgment was announced in a short *per curiam* opinion, and individual judges wrote separately to explain their vote. In support of the judgment, Judge Traxler argued that "[t]here is nothing in the language of the AUMF that suggests that Congress intended to limit the military response or the presidential authorization to acts occurring in foreign territories, and it strains reason to believe that Congress, in enacting the AUMF in the wake of [the 9/11] attacks, did *not* intend for it to encompass al Qaeda operatives standing in the exact position as the attackers who brought about its enactment." Judge Motz disagreed. She argued that *Ex parte Milligan* stood for the proposition that "our Constitution does not permit the Government to subject *civilians* within the United States to military jurisdiction." She also maintained that the case was distinguishable from *Hamdi* and *Padilla* because al-Marri never took up arms on the Afghan battlefield and had not engaged in combat with United States forces anywhere in the world. The Supreme Court agreed to review this decision in 2008, but in 2009, the new Obama Administration transferred al-Marri to civilian custody and tried him in a federal court in Illinois, where he was convicted, pursuant to a plea bargain, of conspiring to provide material support to a foreign terrorist organization and sentenced to eight and a half years' imprisonment. The Supreme Court had earlier granted the government's request to dismiss al-Marri's case in the Court and to direct the Fourth Circuit to vacate its decision.

Did the Fourth Circuit correctly rule that the U.S. military could detain Padilla and al-Marri as enemy combatants? To what extent is *Ex parte Milligan* relevant to these detentions? Is al-Marri's detention harder to justify under *Hamdi* than Padilla's detention? What do the convictions of Padilla and Hamdi in a federal criminal court suggest about the need for or appropriateness of enemy combatant detentions of alleged terrorists? The government moved both Padilla and al-Marri back and forth between the criminal justice and military detention systems. Should the government have the discretion to move alleged terrorists among legal systems, seemingly at will, in this manner?

8. During the Bush Administration, approximately 800 alleged terrorists were brought to the detention facility at Guantanamo Bay and held there for some period of time, and more than 500 of those detainees were eventually released or transferred. When Barack Obama took office as President on January 20, 2009, he issued an executive order directing that the Guantanamo detention facility be closed within one year and calling for an Executive Branch review of the status of each of the detainees still at Guantanamo to determine whether they should be transferred, released, or prosecuted. The task force charged with the review concluded that, of the 240 individuals in detention when Obama became President, 156 could be (and some had been) transferred to another country, 44 should be prosecuted in civilian trials or military commissions, and 48 were "too dangerous to transfer but not feasible for prosecution" and thus should continue to be held in military detention pursuant to the AUMF. *See* Final Report, Guantanamo Bay Task Force Review (Jan. 22, 2010), *at* http://www.fas.org/irp/eprint/gtmo-review.pdf. For a variety of reasons, Obama was not able to close the Guantanamo detention facility in a year, and indeed the facility was still functioning near the end of his presidency, in fall 2016, although Obama did manage to substantially reduce the number of detainees there by transferring them to other countries. Among other things, for a number of years his administration had trouble finding a suitable foreign location for many of the transferrable detainees, and (for reasons explored below in Section C) the civilian trial and military commission options proved more challenging than the administration anticipated. Another reason why Obama could not close the Guantanamo detention center was that Congress had since 2009 placed legal restrictions on the building of a detention facility for Guantanamo detainees in the United States, and on the transfer of Guantanamo detainees to the United States or to other countries.

9. In the National Defense Authorization Act (NDAA) for Fiscal Year 2014, Congress continued the restrictions on building a U.S. detention facility (§1033) and on transferring Guantanamo detainees to the United States (§1034). But in §1035, Congress loosened restrictions on detainee transfers. Section 1035 of the NDAA authorized the Secretary of Defense to "transfer or release any individual detained at Guantanamo" if he made certain determinations. It also provided that "[t]he Secretary of Defense shall notify the appropriate committees of Congress of a determination [to release or transfer a detainee] not later than 30 days before the transfer or release of the individual," and it specified the information that "[e]ach notification shall include, at minimum." When signing this Act into law in December 2013, President Obama issued a signing statement that expressed the view that §1035, while an improvement over restrictions in earlier legislation, "in certain circumstances would violate constitutional separation of powers principles." Obama further observed that "[t]he executive branch must have the flexibility, among other things, to act swiftly in conducting negotiations with foreign countries regarding the circumstances of detainee transfers."

On May 31, 2014, the United States released to the government of Qatar five senior Taliban detainees held at the Guantanamo detention center in exchange for the lone American prisoner of war from the Afghan conflict, Sergeant Bowe Bergdahl. The Obama Administration did not provide the 30-day notice to Congress specified in §1035. The administration's most elaborate legal explanation for not giving this notice came in an unsigned, undated analysis from the Defense Department to Congress's General Accounting Office (GAO):

> The transfer was necessary to secure the release of a captive U.S. soldier, and the Administration had determined that providing notice as specified in the statute could jeopardize negotiations to secure the soldier's release and endanger the soldier's life. In those circumstances, providing notice would have interfered with the Executive's performance of two related functions that the Constitution assigns to the President: protecting the lives of Americans abroad and protecting U.S. service members. Such interference would "significantly alter the balance between Congress and

the President," and could even raise constitutional concerns; and courts have required a "clear statement" from Congress before they will interpret a statute to have such an effect. Armstrong v. Bush, 924 F.2d 282, 289 (D.C. Cir. 1991). Congress may not have spoken with sufficient clarity in section 1035(d) because the notice requirement does not in its terms apply to a time-sensitive prisoner exchange designed to save the life of a U.S. soldier. Cf. Bond v. United States, 134 S. Ct. 2077, 2090-93 (2014). . . .

[I]f section 1035(d) were construed as applicable to the transfer, the statute would be unconstitutional as applied because requiring 30 days' notice of the transfer would have violated the constitutionally-mandated separation of powers. Compliance with a 30 days' notice requirement in these circumstances would have "prevent[ed] the Executive Branch from accomplishing its constitutionally assigned functions," Morrison v. Olson, 487 U.S. 654, 695 (1988), without being "justified by an overriding need" to promote legitimate objectives of Congress, Nixon v. Administrator of General Servs., 433 U.S. 425, 443 (1977). As just discussed, the Administration had determined that providing notice as specified in the statute would undermine the Executive's efforts to protect the life of a U.S. soldier. Congress's desire to have 30 days to weigh in on the determination that the Secretary had already made, in accordance with criteria specified by Congress, that the transfer did not pose the risks that Congress was seeking to avoid, was not a sufficiently weighty interest to justify this frustration of the Executive's ability to carry out these constitutionally assigned functions. Thus, even though, as a general matter, Congress had authority under its constitutional powers related to war and the military to enact section 1035(d), that provision would have been unconstitutional to the extent it applied to the unique circumstances of this transfer.

See Jack Goldsmith, *Was the Bergdahl Swap Lawful?*, Lawfare (Mar. 25, 2015) (reproducing document). The GAO responded to these arguments by concluding that the Defense Department had violated §1035, but it failed to engage the administration's legal arguments fully because it said it lacked authority to "offer any opinion on the constitutionality of section 1035." *See* Memorandum from Susan A. Poling, General Counsel, Government Accountability Office, to the Honorable Mitch McConnell et al., *Department of Defense — Compliance with Statutory Notification Requirement* (Aug. 21, 2014), at http://www.gao.gov/assets/670/665390.pdf.

Are you convinced by the Defense Department's arguments? The first argument is that because the notice requirement would raise constitutional concerns, the statute should be read not to require notice in the emergency context presented by the Bergdahl transfer. Typically, the canon of constitutional avoidance requires the statute under interpretation to be ambiguous. But note the citation to *Bond v. United States*, which (as discussed in Chapter 5) applied an avoidance canon in the federalism context to statutory language that was arguably clear on its face. Is this form of argument legitimate when the statute seems so clearly to require notice? The second argument is that the notice is "unconstitutional as applied." Presumably, the "constitutionally assigned functions" that the notice requirement frustrated are "protecting the lives of Americans abroad and protecting U.S. service members." Do these presidential functions flow from the President's designation as Commander in Chief? Why was Congress's desire to consider the appropriateness of the transfer within the 30-day period "not a sufficiently weighty interest to justify this frustration of the Executive's ability to carry out these constitutionally assigned functions"? Can the President disregard any statutory restrictions that would jeopardize negotiations to secure a soldier's release? Could the President, for example, disregard the substantive determinations that Congress requires the President to make before releasing or transferring a detainee?

10. In January 2018, President Trump signed an executive order relating to the Guantanamo Bay detention facility. *See Executive Order on Protecting America Through Lawful Detention of Terrorists* (Jan. 30, 2018), *at* https://www.whitehouse .gov/presidential-actions/presidential-executive-order-protecting-america-lawful-detention-terrorists/. The order replaced the Obama executive order relating to Guantanamo, but was otherwise largely symbolic. It reaffirmed the need for the detention facility and restated the legal basis for it. In May 2018, President Trump transferred a Guantanamo detainee to Saudi Arabia. That was the first and, to date, the only detainee transfer from the detention facility during the Trump Administration. As of September 2019, the Trump Administration had not brought any new detainees to the detention facility, and there were 40 detainees there.

11. Although the Obama Administration sought to close the Guantanamo detention facility, brought no newly captured detainees there, and transferred or repatriated many of the detainees who were being held there, it asserted the legal authority to hold alleged terrorists in military detention at Guantanamo. In particular, it claimed (in briefs filed in various habeas cases) the following detention authority:

> The president . . . has the authority to detain persons who were part of, or substantially supported, Taliban or al-Qaida forces or associated forces that are engaged in hostilities against the United States or its coalition partners, including any person who has committed a belligerent act, or has directly supported hostilities, in aid of such enemy armed forces.

The Obama Administration also claimed in briefs that the President's detention power is "not limited to persons captured on the battlefields of Afghanistan" and that courts "should defer to the President's judgment" about the meaning of the AUMF. These were the same positions advocated by the Bush Administration, with two exceptions. First, the Obama Administration position required that individuals detained based on their support of (rather than affiliation with) the Taliban or Al Qaeda must have provided "substantial" support. In addition, while the Bush Administration, especially in its early years, grounded its detention authority in the President's Commander-in-Chief power in addition to the AUMF, the Obama Administration grounded its detention authority solely in the AUMF.

The Obama Administration also asserted that this military detention authority applied on the high seas. In April 2011, for example, U.S. forces captured Ahmed Warsame, a Somali national, aboard a fishing vessel in the Gulf of Aden in international waters between Yemen and Somalia. Warsame was a member of Al Shabbab, a terrorist organization affiliated with Al Qaeda and that has connections to other terrorist organizations associated with Al Qaeda. The United States held Warsame in military detention for two months on a U.S. Navy ship on the high seas, where he was interrogated. At the end of the interrogation, the government transferred Warsame to New York, where he pleaded guilty to several terrorism-related crimes and became a cooperating witness in other terrorism trials. For an extensive analysis of executive, congressional, and judicial decisionmaking concerning Guantanamo detainees during the Obama Administration and an explanation for why the detention facility there persisted despite President Obama's efforts to close it, see Aziz Z. Huq, *The President and the Detainees*, 165 U. Pa. L. Rev. 499 (2017).

12. In the NDAA for Fiscal Year 2012, Congress for the first time expressly addressed detention authority under the AUMF. Sections 1021(a) and (b) of the 2012 NDAA stated that "the authority of the President to use all necessary and appropriate force pursuant to the [2001 AUMF] *includes the authority for the Armed Forces of the United States to detain*" a person who "planned, authorized, committed, or aided the terrorist attacks that occurred on September 11, 2001, or harbored those responsible for those attacks," and a "person who was a part of or substantially supported al-Qaeda, the Taliban, or associated forces that are engaged in hostilities against the United States or its coalition partners, including any person who has committed a belligerent act or has directly supported such hostilities in aid of such enemy forces" (emphasis added). Section 1021(d) further provided that "[n]othing in this section is intended to limit or expand the authority of the President or the scope of the [AUMF]." And §1021(e) stated that "[n]othing in this section shall be construed to affect existing law or authorities relating to the detention of United States citizens, lawful resident aliens of the United States, or any other persons who are captured or arrested in the United States." How, if at all, does §1021 affect the President's detention authority under the AUMF?

13. The *Hamdi* plurality suggested that review by a body of military officials might satisfy its due process analysis, and shortly after the decision the Department of Defense created "Combatant Status Review Tribunals" (CSRTs) to review challenges by detainees at Guantanamo to their designation as enemy combatants. These CSRTs were superseded in practice, however, by habeas corpus review in federal district court following the Supreme Court's decision in Boumediene v. Bush, 553 U.S. 723 (2008), which held that individuals detained by the U.S. military at Guantanamo have a constitutional right to seek habeas corpus review in U.S. courts. (*Boumediene* is considered below in Section D.)

After *Boumediene*, dozens of detainees filed habeas corpus petitions in the federal district courts in the District of Columbia (where the habeas cases were consolidated), and those courts, as well as the D.C. Circuit court of appeals, issued numerous decisions that fleshed out the nature and scope of the President's detention authority. The following are some of the most important issues addressed in these cases, as well as related Executive Branch developments:

a. *Extension of Detention Authority to Al Qaeda.* The *Hamdi* decision concerned the detention of an enemy combatant who was a member of the Taliban, and some aspects of the decision might be read to suggest that extending AUMF detention authority to members of Al Qaeda, or to alleged terrorists picked up outside of Afghanistan, was a more difficult issue. The post-*Boumediene* lower court decisions in the District of Columbia, however, concluded that the detention authority conferred by the AUMF extends to the detention of Al Qaeda members captured both inside Afghanistan, *see, e.g.,* Al Adahi v. Obama, 613 F.3d 1102 (D.C. Cir. 2010), and outside Afghanistan, *see, e.g.,* Bensayah v. Obama, 610 F.3d 718 (D.C. Cir. 2010) (capture in Bosnia).

b. *Other Issues Concerning the Scope of Detention Authority.* The federal courts in the District of Columbia largely agreed with the scope of detention authority proposed by the Bush and Obama Administrations. The courts concluded that the President's military detention authority under the AUMF extended to those who (1) are *part of* Al Qaeda or the Taliban, (2) are part of forces *associated with* Al Qaeda or the Taliban, or (3) *purposefully and materially support* Al Qaeda, the Taliban, or associated forces in hostilities against the United States or coalition partners. This definition, which is more robust than the one used in *Hamdi* but is close to the one confirmed in the NDAA of 2012, raises a number of interpretive issues.

First, what does it mean to be a "part of" a diffuse organization such as Al Qaeda? The D.C. Circuit described the test this way:

Although it is clear al Qaeda has, or at least at one time had, a particular organizational structure, the details of its structure are generally unknown, but it is thought to be somewhat amorphous. As a result, it is impossible to provide an exhaustive list of criteria for determining whether an individual is "part of" al Qaeda. That determination must be made on a case-by-case basis by using a functional rather than a formal approach and by focusing upon the actions of the individual in relation to the organization. That an individual operates within al Qaeda's formal command structure is surely sufficient but is not necessary to show he is "part of" the organization; there may be other indicia that a particular individual is sufficiently involved with the organization to be deemed part of it, but the purely independent conduct of a freelancer is not enough.

Bensayah v. Obama, 610 F.3d 718, 725 (D.C. Cir. 2010). Applying this test, courts viewed attendance at an Al Qaeda training camp or guesthouse as powerful evidence of functional membership in these groups. *See, e.g.,* Al Adahi v. Obama, 613 F.3d 1102 (D.C. Cir. 2010). Other factors relevant to the functional test include the location of capture, association with other Al Qaeda members, attendance at religious schools where others were recruited to fight for Al Qaeda, or travel to Afghanistan along a path used by other Al Qaeda members.

Second, how should a court determine which organizations or forces are sufficiently "associated" with Al Qaeda to be included under the AUMF? One district court drew on the law-of-war concept of "co-belligerency" to flesh out this category:

In addition to members of al Qaeda and the Taliban, the government's detention authority also reaches those who were members of "associated forces." For purposes of these habeas proceedings, the Court interprets the term "associated forces" to mean "co-belligerents" as that term is understood under the law of war. The government itself advocates this reading of the language. A "co-belligerent" in an international armed conflict context is a state that has become a fully fledged belligerent fighting in association with one or more belligerent powers. One only attains co-belligerent status by violating the law of neutrality — *i.e.,* the duty of non-participation and impartiality. If those duties are violated, then the adversely affected belligerent is permitted to take reprisals against the ostensibly neutral party. This is also consistent with historical practice in the United States. Accordingly, the government has the authority to detain members of "associated forces" as long as those forces would be considered co-belligerents under the law of war.

Hamlily v. Obama, 616 F. Supp. 2d 63, 75 (D.D.C. 2009). The court added that " 'associated forces' do not include terrorist organizations who merely share an abstract philosophy or even a common purpose with al Qaeda — there must be an actual association in the current conflict with al Qaeda or the Taliban." Does this mean that a copycat terrorist organization that is inspired by Al Qaeda but that does not act in coordination with it is not covered by the AUMF?

Third, courts have not specified what types of "purposeful and material support" to Al Qaeda can render someone detainable under the AUMF. What types of support should count? Provision of arms? Intelligence? Financing? Logistical support? Need these and other forms of support be large-scale in order to qualify? Must the person providing support know how it will be used? What sources should courts look to in answering these questions? What do the AUMF and *Hamdi* suggest? What are the dangers of extending detention authority to those who support Al Qaeda?

  c. *Relevance of International Law.* The plurality in *Hamdi* looked to the international laws of war to give meaning to the "force" authorized by the AUMF. But can the laws of war provide limitations on what the AUMF authorizes, or, stronger yet, be read into the AUMF as an affirmative limitation on presidential power?

The D.C. Circuit addressed these issues in Al-Bihani v. United States, 590 F.3d 866 (D.C. Cir. 2010). The petitioner in that case, who had served in a paramilitary force allied with the Taliban, argued that he could not be detained under the AUMF because international law for a variety of reasons prohibited his detention. In rejecting these arguments, the court noted that "all of them rely heavily on the premise that the war powers granted by the AUMF and other statutes are limited by the international laws of war," and the court said that "[t]his premise is mistaken." The court explained:

> The international laws of war as a whole have not been implemented domestically by Congress and are therefore not a source of authority for U.S. courts. Even assuming Congress had at some earlier point implemented the laws of war as domestic law through appropriate legislation, Congress had the power to authorize the President in the AUMF and other later statutes to exceed those bounds. Further weakening their relevance to this case, the international laws of war are not a fixed code. Their dictates and application to actual events are by nature contestable and fluid. Therefore, while the international laws of war are helpful to courts when identifying the general set of war powers to which the AUMF speaks, [see Hamdi v. Rumsfeld, 542 U.S. 507, 520 (2004) (plurality opinion)], their lack of controlling legal force and firm definition render their use both inapposite and inadvisable when courts seek to determine the limits of the President's war powers. Therefore, putting aside that we find Al-Bihani's reading of international law to be unpersuasive, we have no occasion here to quibble over the intricate application of vague treaty provisions and amorphous customary principles. The sources we look to for resolution of Al-Bihani's case are the sources courts always look to: the text of relevant statutes and controlling domestic caselaw.

Based on domestic law sources, the court concluded that the AUMF authorized Al-Bihani's detention because he was part of and supported a group that affiliated with Al Qaeda and the Taliban. Judge Williams concurred in the judgment but noted that the majority's dismissal of international law's relevance to the interpretation of the AUMF "appears hard to square" with *Hamdi*. Al-Bihani sought rehearing of the panel's ruling on the relevance of the laws of war. The D.C. Circuit unanimously rejected his request. The seven judges not on the original panel, concurring in the denial of the rehearing petition, stated that the panel's discussion of international law's relevance to the AUMF "is not necessary to the disposition of the merits." But the panel judges filed lengthy concurrences about the relevance of international law to interpreting the AUMF. Judge Brown, the author of the panel opinion, denied that the law-of-war discussion in the opinion was dicta. Judge Williams argued that it was appropriate to use the laws of war not only to interpret what Congress affirmatively authorized in the AUMF but also to interpret the outer limits of that authorization. He maintained that using international law in this way is similar to using a dictionary to inform the meaning of a statute in the sense that it is an extraneous source that, based on plausible assumptions, indicates congressional intent. Judge Kavanaugh — in an 87-page concurrence that discussed numerous issues concerning the relationship between international law and domestic law — argued that Judge Williams's use of the laws of war was "radical" because it implied that international law has the status of domestic federal law and "trumps the President in resolving statutory ambiguities."

Is the original panel's conclusion that the AUMF is not limited by the international laws of war consistent with the plurality opinion in *Hamdi*? What is the difference between using international law to interpret the scope of a congressional authorization and using it to impose constraints on what is authorized? What is at stake in the debate between Judge Williams and Judge Kavanaugh? Do you think Congress had international law in mind when it enacted the AUMF?

d. *Length of Detention.* The plurality in *Hamdi* stated that the AUMF authorizes detention of covered persons "for the duration of the relevant conflict." How does this concept apply in a war against terrorist organizations? Building on Ludecke v. Watkins, discussed above in note 12 of Section A, the D.C. Circuit concluded in 2010 that the determination of when hostilities have ceased under the AUMF "is a political decision, and we defer to the Executive's opinion on the matter, at least in the absence of an authoritative congressional declaration purporting to terminate the war." Al-Bihani v. Obama, 590 F.3d 866, 874 (D.C. Cir. 2010); *see also* Al Maqaleh v. Hagel, 738 F.3d 312, 330 (D.C. Cir. 2013) ("Whether an armed conflict has ended is a question left exclusively to the political branches.").

This issue took on renewed importance after President Obama stated on December 28, 2014, that "our combat mission in Afghanistan is ending, and the longest war in American history is coming to a responsible conclusion." Based on this and similar statements by the President, a Guantanamo detainee named Mukhtar Yahia Naji al Warafi argued in a habeas action that, because he was detained on the basis of his membership in the Taliban, and because the United States and the Taliban are no longer in armed conflict, the government's authority to detain him has expired. In a brief responding to Warafi's argument, the government maintained (based on significant documentary evidence) that hostilities in Afghanistan continued, and that President Obama was stating only that the combat mission in Afghanistan, and not hostilities, had ended. The government further argued, based on *Ludecke* and *Al-Bihani*, that the determination of whether hostilities have ended "is a question for the political branches." The district court disagreed with this latter claim and concluded that in a habeas action it was appropriate for the judiciary to make its own determination about whether hostilities have ended. *See* Al Warafi v. Obama, 2015 U.S. Dist. LEXIS 99781 (D.D.C. 2015), *vacated as moot*, 2016 U.S. App. LEXIS 4227 (D.C. Cir. 2016). The court reasoned that the Supreme Court's assertion of judicial review in *Hamdi* over the power to detain on a "record" that "establishes that United States troops are still involved in active combat in Afghanistan" implied "that a court can and must examine . . . the issue of whether active hostilities continue." The court further concluded, however, that the government had provided sufficient evidence that this had not yet occurred in Afghanistan. Finally, the court reasoned that the President's speeches, which lack the force of law, do not by themselves establish that hostilities have ended. *See also* Al-Alwi v. Trump, 901 F.3d 294 (D.C. Cir. 2018) (concluding that the hostilities encompassed by the AUMF are ongoing).

To what extent, if at all, should courts determine the proper length of detention in the war on terrorism? Isn't the length of detention at least as significant for purposes of individual liberty as the initial authority to detain? On the other hand, what standards would the courts use to determine the proper length of detention? In answering these questions, consider the Executive Branch procedures for regular review of individual detentions. In 2011, President Obama issued an executive order establishing Periodic Review Boards (PRBs) that determine, for each detainee at Guantanamo, whether continued detention "is necessary to protect against a significant threat to the security of the United States." *See* Executive Order: Periodic Review of Individuals Detained at Guantanamo Bay Naval Station Pursuant to the Authorization for Use of Military Force (Mar. 7,

2011), *at* https://obamawhitehouse.archives.gov/the-press-office/2011/03/07/executive-order-13567-periodic-review-individuals-detained-guant-namo-ba. The Trump Administration continued the use of PRBs in Executive Order 13823. *See* Executive Order: Protecting America Through Lawful Detention of Terrorists (Jan. 30, 2018), *at* https://www.whitehouse.gov/presidential-actions/presidential-executive-order-protecting-america-lawful-detention-terrorists/. What effect, if any, should these Executive Branch review procedures have on whether the courts address the length of detention issue?

14. Even when the conflict with the Taliban is determined to be over, there will be a separate question of when the conflict with Al Qaeda and associated forces will end. Jeh Johnson, a former Defense Department General Counsel, had the following to say on this question in 2012:

> In the current conflict with al Qaeda, I can offer no prediction about when this conflict will end, or whether we are, as Winston Churchill described it, near the "beginning of the end."
>
> I do believe that on the present course, there will come a tipping point — a tipping point at which so many of the leaders and operatives of al Qaeda and its affiliates have been killed or captured, and the group is no longer able to attempt or launch a strategic attack against the United States, such that al Qaeda as we know it, the organization that our Congress authorized the military to pursue in 2001, has been effectively destroyed.
>
> At that point, we must be able to say to ourselves that our efforts should no longer be considered an "armed conflict" against al Qaeda and its associated forces; rather, a counterterrorism effort against individuals who are the scattered remnants of al Qaeda, or are parts of groups unaffiliated with al Qaeda, for which the law enforcement and intelligence resources of our government are principally responsible, in cooperation with the international community — with our military assets available in reserve to address continuing and imminent terrorist threats.
>
> At that point we will also need to face the question of what to do with any members of al Qaeda who still remain in U.S. military detention without a criminal conviction and sentence. In general, the military's authority to detain ends with the "cessation of active hostilities." For this particular conflict, all I can say today is that we should look to conventional legal principles to supply the answer, and that both our Nations faced similar challenging questions after the cessation of hostilities in World War II, and our governments delayed the release of some Nazi German prisoners of war.[23]

Jeh Charles Johnson, *The Conflict Against Al Qaeda and its Affiliates: How Will It End?* (Nov. 30, 2012), *at* http://www.lawfareblog.com/2012/11/jeh-johnson-speech-at-the-oxford-union. Under Johnson's view, how will the United States know when Al Qaeda and its affiliates can no longer "attempt" a "strategic attack"? Does Johnson imply that even if the United States defeats Al Qaeda, the armed conflict authorized by the AUMF continues until it also defeats all "associated forces"? Consistent with Justice O'Connor's plurality opinion in *Hamdi,* Johnson acknowledges that military authority to detain ends with the "cessation of active hostilities." But he adds that "conventional legal principles" should inform the duty to release, and in a footnote he notes that the United States "delayed the release of some Nazi German prisoners of war . . . for over six years after the fighting with Germany had ended." Is Johnson right to imply that the United States could continue to detain alleged terrorists at

---

23. Regarding post-hostilities detention during the conclusion of World War II, see Ludecke v. Watkins, 335 U.S. 160 (1948) (holding that the President's authority to detain German nationals continued for over six years after the fighting with Germany had ended). . . .

Guantanamo Bay and elsewhere after the armed conflict with Al Qaeda and associates ends? For how long, and under what rationale? On these questions, see David Simon, *Ending Perpetual War? Constitutional War Termination Powers and the Conflict Against Al Qaeda*, 41 Pepperdine L. Rev. 685 (2014); Adam Klein, Note, *The End of Al Qaeda? Rethinking the Legal End of the War on Terror*, 110 Colum. L. Rev. 1865 (2010). For a comprehensive analysis of how the AUMF became "a protean foundation for indefinite war against an assortment of terrorist organizations in numerous countries" during the Obama Administration, including an assessment of the role that international law played in informing the content of the AUMF during this period, see Curtis A. Bradley & Jack L. Goldsmith, *Obama's AUMF Legacy*, 110 Am. J. Int'l L. 628 (2016).

In 2019, Justice Breyer commented on the question of the conflict's duration in a statement respecting a denial of certiorari. In Al-Alwi v. Trump, No. 18-740 (June 10, 2019), Justice Breyer wrote:

> In Hamdi v. Rumsfeld, a majority of this Court understood the AUMF to permit the President to detain certain enemy combatants for the duration of the relevant conflict. Justice O'Connor's plurality opinion cautioned that "[i]f the practical circumstances" of that conflict became "entirely unlike those of the conflicts that informed the development of the law of war," the Court's "understanding" of what the AUMF authorized "may unravel." Indeed, in light of the "unconventional nature" of the "war on terror," there was a "substantial prospect" that detention for the "duration of the relevant conflict" could amount to "perpetual detention." But as that was "not the situation we face[d] as of th[at] date," the plurality reserved the question whether the AUMF or the Constitution would permit such a result. In my judgment, it is past time to confront the difficult question left open by *Hamdi*.

15. The most contested issue relating to the 2001 AUMF in recent years has concerned the statute's extension to ISIL. ISIL emerged from the remnants of Al Qaeda in Iraq (AQI), an Al Qaeda affiliate led by Abu Mu'sab al-Zarqawi that the United States fought in Iraq in the 2000s as part of the Sunni insurgency there. In 2013, AQI changed its name to ISIL, and in 2014, after a power struggle with Al Qaeda and some of its associates, ISIL cut all ties with Al Qaeda. ISIL fought in the Syrian civil war, occupied significant territory in Iraq and Syria in the spring and summer of 2014, and declared a "caliphate" in June 2014. As part of its operations, it committed a variety of atrocities, including beheadings of a number of individuals it had captured, including several Americans.

a. *Extension of AUMF to ISIL.* In August 2014, U.S. military forces initiated air strikes in Iraq against ISIL. In his War Powers Resolution notification to Congress, President Obama explained that the military operations were "limited in their scope and duration" and were justified on the basis of self-defense ("to protect American personnel in Iraq by stopping the current advance on Erbil") and humanitarian grounds ("to help forces in Iraq as they fight to break the siege of Mount Sinjar and protect the civilians trapped there"). The President stated that he took these actions "pursuant to my constitutional authority to conduct U.S. foreign relations and as Commander in Chief and Chief Executive." For the next month, the President authorized additional air strikes in Iraq, for both self-defense and humanitarian purposes, and continued to justify those strikes based solely on his authority under Article II of the Constitution.

On September 10, 2014, President Obama addressed the nation and explained that ISIL posed a threat to Iraq, Syria, the Middle East, U.S. persons in those places, and potentially the United States itself. He announced a campaign to "degrade, and ultimately destroy, ISIL through a comprehensive and sustained counterterrorism strategy" that included a "systematic campaign of air strikes against these terrorists." U.S. air strikes against ISIL subsequently expanded in number and extended geographically to Syria. In a War Powers Resolution letter to Congress on September 23, 2014, President Obama stated that he was taking the measures "pursuant to my constitutional *and statutory* authority as Commander in Chief" (emphasis added). He explained that his statutory authority included the 2001 AUMF (which authorized the use of force against the "nations, organizations, or persons" responsible for the 9/11 attacks) and the 2002 AUMF (which authorized the President to use force to "defend the national security of the United States against the continuing threat posed by Iraq"). The Obama Administration never published an official legal opinion explaining why these statutes applied to ISIL in Iraq and Syria. But the General Counsel of the Defense Department offered this explanation in April 2015:

> The 2001 AUMF has authorized the use of force against the group now called ISIL since at least 2004, when bin Laden and al-Zarqawi brought their groups together. The recent split between ISIL and current al-Qa'ida leadership does not remove ISIL from coverage under the 2001 AUMF, because ISIL continues to wage the conflict against the United States that it entered into when, in 2004, it joined bin Laden's al-Qa'ida organization in its conflict against the United States. As AQI, ISIL had a direct relationship with bin Laden himself and waged that conflict in allegiance to him while he was alive. ISIL now claims that it, not al-Qa'ida's current leadership, is the true executor of bin Laden's legacy. There are rifts between ISIL and parts of the network bin Laden assembled, but some members and factions of al-Qa'ida-aligned groups have publicly declared allegiance to ISIL. At the same time, ISIL continues to denounce the United States as its enemy and to target U.S. citizens and interests.
>
> In these circumstances, the President is not divested of the previously available authority under the 2001 AUMF to continue protecting the country from ISIL — a group that has been subject to that AUMF for close to a decade — simply because of disagreements between the group and al-Qa'ida's current leadership. A contrary interpretation of the statute would allow the enemy — rather than the President and Congress — to control the scope of the AUMF by splintering into rival factions while continuing to prosecute the same conflict against the United States.
>
> Some initially greeted with skepticism the President's reliance on the 2001 AUMF for authority to renew military operations against ISIL last year. To be sure, we would be having a different conversation if ISIL had emerged out of nowhere a year ago, having no history with bin Laden and no more connection to current al-Qa'ida leadership than it has today, or if the group once known as AQI had, for example, renounced terrorist violence against the United States at some point along the way. But ISIL did not spring fully formed from the head of Zeus a year ago, and the group certainly has never laid down its arms in its conflict against the United States.
>
> The name may have changed, but the group we call ISIL today has been an enemy of the United States within the scope of the 2001 AUMF continuously since at least 2004. A power struggle may have broken out within bin Laden's jihadist movement, but this same enemy of the United States continues to plot and carry out violent attacks against us to this day. Viewed in this light, reliance on the AUMF for counter-ISIL operations is hardly an expansion of authority. After all, how many new terrorist groups have, by virtue of this reading of the statute, been determined to be among the groups against which military force may be used? The answer is zero.

Stephen Preston, *The Legal Framework for the United States' Use of Military Force Since 9/11*, Annual Meeting of the American Society of International Law, Washington, D.C., Apr. 10, 2015.

Under the legal framework described by Preston, could the United States interpret the AUMF to extend to "associated forces" of ISIL, such as ISIL affiliates in Pakistan, Libya, and Egypt? For a discussion of U.S. uses of force against groups affiliated with ISIL, see Harleen Gambhir, *The Next Wave of AUMF Expansion? The Islamic State's Global Affiliates*, Lawfare (Nov. 13, 2017).

b. *Scope of the Conflict Against ISIL.* The Obama Administration used force against ISIL in Iraq, Syria, and Libya. This included a U.S. ground presence in connection with the conflict against ISIL in Iraq and Syria. By the fall of 2016, the United States had approximately 4,500 soldiers in Iraq to protect U.S. property and persons in those countries, to train and assist Iraqi forces battling ISIL, and in some instances to engage in combat against ISIL. By early 2019, during the Trump Administration, there were approximately 2,000 U.S. troops in Syria to provide training, planning, and guidance to local forces battling ISIL there. In February 2019, President Trump ordered the Defense Department to draw down those forces to a few hundred troops.

c. *A New AUMF for ISIL?* On November 5, 2014, President Obama stated that he was "going to begin engaging Congress over a new authorization to use military force against ISIL" because the world "needs to know we are united behind this effort and the men and women of our military deserve our clear and unified support." He also stated that he wanted to "right-size and update" the 2001 AUMF to "suit the current fight, rather than previous fights." On February 11, 2015, he submitted the following draft to Congress:

JOINT RESOLUTION To authorize the limited use of the United States Armed Forces against the Islamic State of Iraq and the Levant. . . .
Resolved by the Senate and House of Representatives of the United States of America in Congress assembled, That

SECTION 1. SHORT TITLE.
This joint resolution may be cited as the "Authorization for Use of Military Force against the Islamic State of Iraq and the Levant."

SEC. 2. AUTHORIZATION FOR USE OF UNITED STATES ARMED FORCES.
(a) AUTHORIZATION. — The President is authorized, subject to the limitations in subsection (c), to use the Armed Forces of the United States as the President determines to be necessary and appropriate against ISIL or associated persons or forces as defined in section 5.
(b) WAR POWERS RESOLUTION REQUIREMENTS. —
(1) SPECIFIC STATUTORY AUTHORIZATION. — Consistent with section 8(a)(1) of the War Powers Resolution (50 U.S.C. 1547(a)(1)), Congress declares that this section is intended to constitute specific statutory authorization within the meaning of section 5(b) of the War Powers Resolution (50 U.S.C. 1544(b)).
(2) APPLICABILITY OF OTHER REQUIREMENTS. — Nothing in this resolution supersedes any requirement of the War Powers Resolution (50 U.S.C. 1541 et seq.).
(c) LIMITATIONS. —
The authority granted in subsection (a) does not authorize the use of the United States Armed Forces in enduring offensive ground combat operations.

SEC. 3. DURATION OF THIS AUTHORIZATION.
This authorization for the use of military force shall terminate three years after the date of the enactment of this joint resolution, unless reauthorized.

SEC. 4. REPORTS.
The President shall report to Congress at least once every six months on specific actions taken pursuant to this authorization.

SEC. 5. ASSOCIATED PERSONS OR FORCES DEFINED.
In this joint resolution, the term "associated persons or forces" means individuals and organizations fighting for, on behalf of, or alongside ISIL or any closely-related successor entity in hostilities against the United States or its coalition partners.

SEC. 6. REPEAL OF AUTHORIZATION FOR USE OF MILITARY FORCE AGAINST IRAQ.
The Authorization for Use of Military Force Against Iraq Resolution of 2002 (Public Law 107–243; 116 Stat. 1498; 50 U.S.C. 1541 note) is hereby repealed.

After the President submitted this proposal, some members of Congress from both parties spoke out about the need for Congress to authorize the conflict against ISIL. But President Obama's draft AUMF received no serious institutional consideration, and as of fall 2019, President Trump had not taken up the issue.

   d. *Legality of the Conflict Against ISIL.* Has the Executive's use of force against ISIL since August 2014 been consistent with U.S. domestic law? Did President Obama have authority under Article II of the Constitution to authorize the air strikes in August and September 2014 for purely humanitarian purposes? How does the humanitarian situation in Iraq differ legally from the situations in Kosovo (1999) and Libya (2011)? Is the claim that the 2001 AUMF authorizes force against ISIL persuasive? Does it matter that Congress has enacted appropriations for the conflict with ISIL for several years? How could the AUMF extend to ISIL if that organization was no longer part of or associated with Al Qaeda? Is the reliance on the 2002 AUMF for Iraq more or less persuasive? For a decision dismissing a challenge to the military campaign against ISIL on standing and political question grounds, see Smith v. Obama, 217 F. Supp. 3d 282 (D.D.C. 2016), *vacated as moot,* Smith v. Trump, 731 Fed. Appx. 8 (Mem) (D.C. Cir. 2018).

   Why did President Obama propose an AUMF for ISIL if he thought that he already had full authority to use force against it under some combination of the 2001 and 2002 AUMFs and Article II? If President Obama's proposal passed, would it have enlarged or contracted his overall military powers? Did the limit on ground forces in §2(c) of the President's draft leave the President free to order ground troops, either under Article II or under a prior interpretation of the 2001 AUMF that contains no ground troops limitation, given that President Obama's draft would have left in place the 2001 AUMF?

   e. *Military Strikes.* In May and June 2017, the Trump Administration carried out various military strikes against the Syrian government and pro-Syrian government forces. Senator Bob Corker, then-Chairman of the Senate Foreign Relations Committee, sought an explanation from the administration of its legal authority to conduct such operations. In a letter dated August 2, 2017, the State Department responded to Corker by contending that the 2001 AUMF "provides authority to use force to defend U.S., Coalition, and partner forces engaged in the campaign to defeat ISIS to the extent such use of force is a necessary and appropriate measure in support of counter-ISIS operations." The letter further explained that "[t]he strikes taken by the United States in May and June 2017 against the Syrian government and pro-Syrian-Government forces were limited and lawful measures to counter immediate threats to U.S. or partner forces engaged in that campaign." Finally, the letter noted that "the Administration is not seeking revisions to the 2001 AUMF or additional authorizations to use force." *See* Letter from Charles Faulkner, Bureau of Legislative Affairs, Department of State, to Sen. Bob Corker (Aug. 2, 2017), *at* https://www.justsecurity.org/wp-content/uploads/2017/08/8-2-17-Corker-Response.pdf.

C. MILITARY COMMISSION TRIALS

Hamdan v. Rumsfeld

548 U.S. 557 (2006)

[On November 13, 2001, President Bush issued a military order concerning the "Detention, Treatment, and Trial of Certain Non-Citizens in the War Against Terrorism" pursuant to his powers as Commander in Chief and the AUMF. The order authorized the use of military commissions against aliens who (a) were present and former members of Al Qaeda, (b) "engaged in, aided or abetted, or conspired to commit, acts of international terrorism, or acts in preparation therefore, that have caused, threatened to cause, or have as their aim to cause, injury to or adverse effects on the United States, its citizens, national security, foreign policy, or economy," or (c) knowingly harbored any of these individuals. Under the order, the military commissions are authorized to try these various individuals for "any and all offenses triable by military commission that such individual is alleged to have committed." The November 13 order directed the Secretary of Defense to issue whatever regulations were necessary to establish the commissions, and the Department of Defense subsequently issued numerous orders and instructions relating to the commissions. These orders and instructions, among other things, established extensive procedures for the commissions and defined the crimes that could be tried before the commissions.

During hostilities in Afghanistan, in 2001, Afghan militia forces captured Salim Hamdan, a Yemeni national, and turned him over to the U.S. military, which, in 2002, transported him to a detention facility in Guantanamo Bay, Cuba. President Bush subsequently deemed Hamdan eligible for trial by military commission, and Hamdan was eventually charged with conspiracy "to commit . . . offenses triable by military commission," including attacking civilians, attacking civilian objects, murder, and terrorism. He challenged the validity of the military commission system on a variety of grounds.]

JUSTICE STEVENS announced the judgment of the Court and delivered the opinion of the Court [except as to] Parts V and VI-D-iv, in which JUSTICE SOUTER, JUSTICE GINSBURG, and JUSTICE BREYER joined. . . .

[The Court first concludes that the Detainee Treatment Act of 2005 (DTA), which restricted habeas corpus jurisdiction over challenges brought by detainees at Guantanamo Bay, does not apply to cases, like this one, that were pending on the date of the DTA's enactment. The Court also rejects the government's arguments for abstention. It then turns to the merits.]

IV

The military commission, a tribunal neither mentioned in the Constitution nor created by statute, was born of military necessity. Though foreshadowed in some respects by earlier tribunals like the Board of General Officers that General Washington convened to try British Major John Andre for spying during the Revolutionary War, the commission "as such" was inaugurated in 1847. As commander of occupied Mexican territory, and having available to him no other tribunal, General Winfield Scott that year ordered the establishment of both " '*military commissions*' " to try ordinary crimes committed in the occupied territory and a "*council of war*" to try offenses against the law of war.

When the exigencies of war next gave rise to a need for use of military commissions, during the Civil War, the dual system favored by General Scott was not adopted. Instead, a single tribunal often took jurisdiction over ordinary crimes, war crimes, and breaches of military orders alike. As further discussed below, each aspect of that seemingly broad jurisdiction was in fact supported by a separate military exigency. Generally, though, the need for military commissions during this period — as during the Mexican War — was driven largely by the then very limited jurisdiction of courts-martial: "The *occasion* for the military commission arises principally from the fact that the jurisdiction of the court-martial proper, in our law, is restricted by statute almost exclusively to members of the military force and to certain specific offences defined in a written code." [William Winthrop, Military Law and Precedents 831 (rev. 2d ed. 1920).]

Exigency alone, of course, will not justify the establishment and use of penal tribunals not contemplated by Article I, §8 and Article III, §1 of the Constitution unless some other part of that document authorizes a response to the felt need. And that authority, if it exists, can derive only from the powers granted jointly to the President and Congress in time of war.

The Constitution makes the President the "Commander in Chief" of the Armed Forces, Art. II, §2, cl. 1, but vests in Congress the powers to "declare War . . . and make Rules concerning Captures on Land and Water," Art. I, §8, cl. 11, to "raise and support Armies," *id.*, cl. 12, to "define and punish . . . Offences against the Law of Nations," *id.*, cl. 10, and "To make Rules for the Government and Regulation of the land and naval Forces," *id.*, cl. 14. The interplay between these powers was described by Chief Justice Chase in the seminal case of *Ex parte Milligan*:

> The power to make the necessary laws is in Congress; the power to execute in the President. Both powers imply many subordinate and auxiliary powers. Each includes all authorities essential to its due exercise. But neither can the President, in war more than in peace, intrude upon the proper authority of Congress, nor Congress upon the proper authority of the President. . . . Congress cannot direct the conduct of campaigns, nor can the President, or any commander under him, without the sanction of Congress, institute tribunals for the trial and punishment of offences, either of soldiers or civilians, unless in cases of a controlling necessity, which justifies what it compels, or at least insures acts of indemnity from the justice of the legislature.

Whether Chief Justice Chase was correct in suggesting that the President may constitutionally convene military commissions "without the sanction of Congress" in cases of "controlling necessity" is a question this Court has not answered definitively, and need not answer today. For we held in *Quirin* that Congress had, through Article of War 15, sanctioned the use of military commissions in such circumstances. Article 21 of the [Uniform Code of Military Justice (UCMJ)], the language of which is substantially identical to the old Article 15 and was preserved by Congress after World War II,[22] reads as follows:

> Jurisdiction of courts-martial not exclusive.
> The provisions of this code conferring jurisdiction upon courts-martial shall not be construed as depriving military commissions, provost courts, or other military tribunals of concurrent jurisdiction in respect of offenders or offenses that by statute or by the

---

22. Article 15 was first adopted as part of the Articles of War in 1916. When the Articles of War were codified and reenacted as the UCMJ in 1950, Congress determined to retain Article 15 because it had been "construed by the Supreme Court."

law of war may be tried by such military commissions, provost courts, or other military tribunals.

We have no occasion to revisit *Quirin*'s controversial characterization of Article of War 15 as congressional authorization for military commissions. Contrary to the Government's assertion, however, even *Quirin* did not view the authorization as a sweeping mandate for the President to "invoke military commissions when he deems them necessary." Rather, the *Quirin* Court recognized that Congress had simply preserved what power, under the Constitution and the common law of war, the President had had before 1916 to convene military commissions — with the express condition that the President and those under his command comply with the law of war.[23] That much is evidenced by the Court's inquiry, *following* its conclusion that Congress had authorized military commissions, into whether the law of war had indeed been complied with in that case.

The Government would have us dispense with the inquiry that the *Quirin* Court undertook and find in either the AUMF or the DTA specific, overriding authorization for the very commission that has been convened to try Hamdan. Neither of these congressional Acts, however, expands the President's authority to convene military commissions. First, while we assume that the AUMF activated the President's war powers, see Hamdi v. Rumsfeld, 542 U.S. 507 (2004) (plurality opinion), and that those powers include the authority to convene military commissions in appropriate circumstances, there is nothing in the text or legislative history of the AUMF even hinting that Congress intended to expand or alter the authorization set forth in Article 21 of the UCMJ. . . .

Together, the UCMJ [and] the AUMF . . . at most acknowledge a general Presidential authority to convene military commissions in circumstances where justified under the "Constitution and laws," including the law of war. Absent a more specific congressional authorization, the task of this Court is, as it was in *Quirin*, to decide whether Hamdan's military commission is so justified. It is to that inquiry we now turn. . . .

[In Part V, a plurality of the Court reasons that the government must make a "substantial showing that the crime for which it seeks to try a defendant by military commission is acknowledged to be an offense against the law of war," and it concludes that the government has not met that burden here because "[t]he crime of 'conspiracy' has rarely if ever been tried as such in this country by any law-of-war military commission not exercising some other form of jurisdiction, and does not appear in either the Geneva Conventions or the Hague Conventions — the major treaties on the law of war."]

VI

Whether or not the Government has charged Hamdan with an offense against the law of war cognizable by military commission, the commission lacks power to proceed. The UCMJ conditions the President's use of military commissions on compliance not only with the American common law of war, but also with the rest of the

---

23. Whether or not the President has independent power, absent congressional authorization, to convene military commissions, he may not disregard limitations that Congress has, in proper exercise of its own war powers, placed on his powers. *See* Youngstown Sheet & Tube Co. v. Sawyer, 343 U.S. 579, 637 (1952) (Jackson, J., concurring). The Government does not argue otherwise.

UCMJ itself, insofar as applicable, and with the "rules and precepts of the law of nations," *Quirin*, 317 U.S. at 28 — including, *inter alia,* the four Geneva Conventions signed in 1949. The procedures that the Government has decreed will govern Hamdan's trial by commission violate these laws.

A

[The Court summarizes the commission's procedures. Under these procedures, promulgated by the Department of Defense in Military Commission Order No. 1, the accused was entitled to appointed military counsel and civilian counsel; a presumption of innocence; and certain other rights typically afforded criminal defendants in civilian courts and courts-martial. The accused and his civilian counsel could be precluded, however, from learning what evidence was presented during any part of the proceeding that either the Appointing Authority or the presiding officer decided to "close." Grounds for such closure included "the protection of information classified or classifiable . . .; information protected by law or rule from unauthorized disclosure; the physical safety of participants in Commission proceedings, including prospective witnesses; intelligence and law enforcement sources, methods, or activities; and other national security interests." Appointed military defense counsel would have access to these closed sessions, but could, at the presiding officer's discretion, be forbidden to reveal to his or her client what took place therein. The procedures also permitted the admission of any evidence that, in the opinion of the presiding officer, "would have probative value to a reasonable person," including hearsay, and evidence obtained through coercion. Moreover, the accused and his civilian counsel could be denied access to evidence in the form of "protected information" (i.e., classified information and "information protected by law or rule from unauthorized disclosure" and "information concerning other national security interests"), so long as the presiding officer concluded that the evidence is "probative" and that its admission without the accused's knowledge would not "result in the denial of a full and fair trial." A two-thirds vote of commission members sufficed for both a verdict of guilty and for imposition of any sentence not including death (the imposition of which requires a unanimous vote). Appeals would go to a three-member review panel composed of military officers designated by the Secretary of Defense, which would make a recommendation to the Secretary, who could either remand for further proceedings or forward the record to the President with a recommendation about final disposition. The President then would make the "final decision" or delegate the task to the Secretary. He could change the commission's findings or sentence only in a manner favorable to the accused.] . . .

C

In part because the difference between military commissions and courts-martial originally was a difference of jurisdiction alone, and in part to protect against abuse and ensure evenhandedness under the pressures of war, the procedures governing trials by military commission historically have been the same as those governing courts-martial. . . .

The uniformity principle is not an inflexible one; it does not preclude all departures from the procedures dictated for use by courts-martial. But any departure must be tailored to the exigency that necessitates it. That understanding is reflected in Article 36 of the UCMJ, which provides:

(a) The procedure, including modes of proof, in cases before courts-martial, courts of inquiry, military commissions, and other military tribunals may be prescribed by the President by regulations which shall, so far as he considers practicable, apply the principles of law and the rules of evidence generally recognized in the trial of criminal cases in the United States district courts, but which may not be contrary to or inconsistent with this chapter.

(b) All rules and regulations made under this article shall be uniform insofar as practicable and shall be reported to Congress.

Article 36 places two restrictions on the President's power to promulgate rules of procedure for courts-martial and military commissions alike. First, no procedural rule he adopts may be "contrary to or inconsistent with" the UCMJ — however practical it may seem. Second, the rules adopted must be "uniform insofar as practicable." That is, the rules applied to military commissions must be the same as those applied to courts-martial unless such uniformity proves impracticable. . . .

Without reaching the question whether any provision of Commission Order No. 1 is strictly "contrary to or inconsistent with" other provisions of the UCMJ, we conclude that the "practicability" determination the President has made is insufficient to justify variances from the procedures governing courts-martial. Subsection (b) of Article 36 was added after World War II, and requires a different showing of impracticability from the one required by subsection (a). Subsection (a) requires that the rules the President promulgates for courts-martial, provost courts, and military commissions alike conform to those that govern procedures in *Article III courts,* "so far as *he considers* practicable." 10 U.S.C. §836(a) (emphasis added). Subsection (b), by contrast, demands that the rules applied in courts-martial, provost courts, and military commissions — whether or not they conform with the Federal Rules of Evidence — be "uniform *insofar as practicable.*" §836(b) (emphasis added). Under the latter provision, then, the rules set forth in the Manual for Courts-Martial must apply to military commissions unless impracticable.

The President here has determined, pursuant to subsection (a), that it is impracticable to apply the rules and principles of law that govern "the trial of criminal cases in the United States district courts," §836(a), to Hamdan's commission. We assume that complete deference is owed that determination. The President has not, however, made a similar official determination that it is impracticable to apply the rules for courts-martial. And even if subsection (b)'s requirements may be satisfied without such an official determination, the requirements of that subsection are not satisfied here.

Nothing in the record before us demonstrates that it would be impracticable to apply court-martial rules in this case. There is no suggestion, for example, of any logistical difficulty in securing properly sworn and authenticated evidence or in applying the usual principles of relevance and admissibility. Assuming *arguendo* that the reasons articulated in the President's Article 36(a) determination ought to be considered in evaluating the impracticability of applying court-martial rules, the only reason offered in support of that determination is the danger posed by international terrorism. Without for one moment underestimating that danger, it is not evident to us why it should require, in the case of Hamdan's trial, any variance from the rules that govern courts-martial.

The absence of any showing of impracticability is particularly disturbing when considered in light of the clear and admitted failure to apply one of the most fundamental protections afforded not just by the Manual for Courts-Martial but also by the UCMJ itself: the right to be present. Whether or not that departure technically is "contrary to or inconsistent with" the terms of the UCMJ, the jettisoning of so basic a right cannot lightly be excused as "practicable."

Under the circumstances, then, the rules applicable in courts-martial must apply. Since it is undisputed that Commission Order No. 1 deviates in many significant respects from those rules, it necessarily violates Article 36(b). . . .

D

The procedures adopted to try Hamdan also violate the Geneva Conventions. . . .

[R]egardless of the nature of the rights conferred on Hamdan [by the Conventions] . . . they are, as the Government does not dispute, part of the law of war. And compliance with the law of war is the condition upon which the authority set forth in Article 21 [of the UCMJ] is granted. . . .

ii

[T]he Court of Appeals concluded that the Conventions did not . . . apply to the armed conflict during which Hamdan was captured. The court accepted the Executive's assertions that Hamdan was captured in connection with the United States' war with al Qaeda and that that war is distinct from the war with the Taliban in Afghanistan. It further reasoned that the war with al Qaeda evades the reach of the Geneva Conventions. We . . . disagree with the latter conclusion.

The conflict with al Qaeda is not, according to the Government, a conflict to which the full protections afforded detainees under the 1949 Geneva Conventions apply because Article 2 of those Conventions (which appears in all four Conventions) renders the full protections applicable only to "all cases of declared war or of any other armed conflict which may arise between two or more of the High Contracting Parties." Since Hamdan was captured and detained incident to the conflict with al Qaeda and not the conflict with the Taliban, and since al Qaeda, unlike Afghanistan, is not a "High Contracting Party" — *i.e.,* a signatory of the Conventions, the protections of those Conventions are not, it is argued, applicable to Hamdan.

We need not decide the merits of this argument because there is at least one provision of the Geneva Conventions that applies here even if the relevant conflict is not one between signatories. Article 3, often referred to as Common Article 3 because, like Article 2, it appears in all four Geneva Conventions, provides that in a "conflict not of an international character occurring in the territory of one of the High Contracting Parties, each Party to the conflict shall be bound to apply, as a minimum," certain provisions protecting "persons taking no active part in the hostilities, including members of armed forces who have laid down their arms and those placed *hors de combat* by . . . detention." One such provision prohibits "the passing of sentences and the carrying out of executions without previous judgment pronounced by a regularly constituted court affording all the judicial guarantees which are recognized as indispensable by civilized peoples."

The Court of Appeals thought, and the Government asserts, that Common Article 3 does not apply to Hamdan because the conflict with al Qaeda, being "'international in scope,'" does not qualify as a "'conflict not of an international character.'" That reasoning is erroneous. The term "conflict not of an international character" is used here in contradistinction to a conflict between nations. . . . Common Article 2 provides that "the present Convention shall apply to all cases of declared war or of any other armed conflict which may arise between two or more of the High Contracting Parties." High Contracting Parties (signatories) also must abide by all terms of the Conventions vis-à-vis one another even if one party to the conflict is a nonsignatory "Power," and must so abide vis-à-vis the nonsignatory if "the latter accepts and applies" those terms. Common Article 3, by contrast, affords some minimal protection, falling short of full protection under the Conventions, to individuals associated with neither a signatory nor even a nonsignatory "Power" who are involved in a conflict "in the territory of" a signatory. The latter kind of conflict is distinguishable from the conflict described in Common Article 2 chiefly because it does not involve a clash between nations (whether signatories or not). In context, then, the phrase "not of an international character" bears its literal meaning.

Although the official commentaries accompanying Common Article 3 indicate that an important purpose of the provision was to furnish minimal protection to rebels involved in one kind of "conflict not of an international character," *i.e.*, a civil war, the commentaries also make clear "that the scope of the Article must be as wide as possible." In fact, limiting language that would have rendered Common Article 3 applicable "especially [to] cases of civil war, colonial conflicts, or wars of religion," was omitted from the final version of the Article, which coupled broader scope of application with a narrower range of rights than did earlier proposed iterations.

iii

Common Article 3, then, is applicable here and, as indicated above, requires that Hamdan be tried by a "regularly constituted court affording all the judicial guarantees which are recognized as indispensable by civilized peoples." The Government offers only a cursory defense of Hamdan's military commission in light of Common Article 3. As Justice Kennedy explains, that defense fails because "the regular military courts in our system are the courts-martial established by congressional statutes." At a minimum, a military commission "can be 'regularly constituted' by the standards of our military justice system only if some practical need explains deviations from court-martial practice." As we have explained, no such need has been demonstrated here.

iv

[A plurality of the Court reasons here that the reference in Common Article 3 to "the judicial guarantees which are recognized as indispensable by civilized peoples" incorporates "at least the barest of those trial protections that have been recognized by customary international law," and that many of these protections are described in Article 75 of Protocol I to the Geneva Conventions, which has not been ratified by the United States. The plurality also concludes that provisions in Commission Order No. 1 "dispense with the principles, articulated in Article 75 and indisputably part of the customary international law, that an accused must, absent disruptive conduct or consent, be present for his trial and must be privy to the evidence against him."]

VII

We have assumed, as we must, that the allegations made in the Government's charge against Hamdan are true. We have assumed, moreover, the truth of the message implicit in that charge — *viz.*, that Hamdan is a dangerous individual whose beliefs, if acted upon, would cause great harm and even death to innocent civilians, and who would act upon those beliefs if given the opportunity. It bears emphasizing that Hamdan does not challenge, and we do not today address, the Government's power to detain him for the duration of active hostilities in order to prevent such harm. But in undertaking to try Hamdan and subject him to criminal punishment, the Executive is bound to comply with the Rule of Law that prevails in this jurisdiction. . . .

THE CHIEF JUSTICE took no part in the consideration or decision of this case.

JUSTICE BREYER, with whom JUSTICE KENNEDY, JUSTICE SOUTER, and JUSTICE GINSBURG join, concurring.

The dissenters say that today's decision would "sorely hamper the President's ability to confront and defeat a new and deadly enemy." They suggest that it undermines our Nation's ability to "prevent future attacks" of the grievous sort that we have already suffered. That claim leads me to state briefly what I believe the majority sets forth both explicitly and implicitly at greater length. The Court's conclusion ultimately rests upon a single ground: Congress has not issued the Executive a "blank check." Indeed, Congress has denied the President the legislative authority to create military commissions of the kind at issue here. Nothing prevents the President from returning to Congress to seek the authority he believes necessary.

Where, as here, no emergency prevents consultation with Congress, judicial insistence upon that consultation does not weaken our Nation's ability to deal with danger. To the contrary, that insistence strengthens the Nation's ability to determine — through democratic means — how best to do so. The Constitution places its faith in those democratic means. Our Court today simply does the same.

JUSTICE KENNEDY, with whom JUSTICE SOUTER, JUSTICE GINSBURG, and JUSTICE BREYER join as to Parts I and II, concurring in part.

Military Commission Order No. 1, which governs the military commission established to try petitioner Salim Hamdan for war crimes, exceeds limits that certain statutes, duly enacted by Congress, have placed on the President's authority to convene military courts. This is not a case, then, where the Executive can assert some unilateral authority to fill a void left by congressional inaction. It is a case where Congress, in the proper exercise of its powers as an independent branch of government, and as part of a long tradition of legislative involvement in matters of military justice, has considered the subject of military tribunals and set limits on the President's authority. Where a statute provides the conditions for the exercise of governmental power, its requirements are the result of a deliberative and reflective process engaging both of the political branches. Respect for laws derived from the customary operation of the Executive and Legislative Branches gives some assurance of stability in time of crisis. The Constitution is best preserved by reliance on standards tested over time and insulated from the pressures of the moment.

These principles seem vindicated here, for a case that may be of extraordinary importance is resolved by ordinary rules. The rules of most relevance here are those pertaining to the authority of Congress and the interpretation of its enactments.

It seems appropriate to recite these rather fundamental points because the Court refers, as it should in its exposition of the case, to the requirement of the Geneva Conventions of 1949 that military tribunals be "regularly constituted" — a requirement that controls here, if for no other reason, because Congress requires that military commissions like the ones at issue conform to the "law of war," 10 U.S.C. §821. Whatever the substance and content of the term "regularly constituted" as interpreted in this and any later cases, there seems little doubt that it relies upon the importance of standards deliberated upon and chosen in advance of crisis, under a system where the single power of the Executive is checked by other constitutional mechanisms. All of which returns us to the point of beginning — that domestic statutes control this case. If Congress, after due consideration, deems it appropriate to change the controlling statutes, in conformance with the Constitution and other laws, it has the power and prerogative to do so. . . .

[Parts I and II of Justice Kennedy's concurrence in *Hamdan* express agreement with most aspects of the majority opinion. Justice Kennedy then concludes in Part III by noting the issues he does not reach:

> In light of the conclusion that the military commission here is unauthorized under the UCMJ, I see no need to consider several further issues addressed in the plurality opinion by Justice Stevens and the dissent by Justice Thomas. First, I would not decide whether Common Article 3's standard — a "regularly constituted court affording all the judicial guarantees which are recognized as indispensable by civilized peoples" — necessarily requires that the accused have the right to be present at all stages of a criminal trial. I likewise see no need to address the validity of the conspiracy charge against Hamdan. . . . In light of the conclusion that the military commissions at issue are unauthorized Congress may choose to provide further guidance in this area. Congress, not the Court, is the branch in the better position to undertake the "sensitive task of establishing a principle not inconsistent with the national interest or international justice." Banco Nacional de Cuba v. Sabbatino, 376 U.S. 398, 428 (1964). Finally, for the same reason, I express no view on the merits of other limitations on military commissions described as elements of the common law of war.

548 U.S. at 653-54.]

[Justice Scalia, in an opinion joined by Justices Thomas and Alito, dissented on the ground that the DTA deprived the Supreme Court of jurisdiction.]

[Justice Thomas wrote a dissent joined in most respects by Justices Scalia and Alito. Among many other disagreements with the majority opinion, Justice Thomas disagreed with the conclusion that Hamdan's military commission was unlawful because it violated Common Article 3 of the Geneva Conventions. He reasoned:

> Under this Court's precedents, "the meaning attributed to treaty provisions by the Government agencies charged with their negotiation and enforcement is entitled to great weight." Our duty to defer to the President's understanding of the provision at issue here is only heightened by the fact that he is acting pursuant to his constitutional authority as Commander in Chief and by the fact that the subject matter of Common Article 3 calls for a judgment about the nature and character of an armed conflict.
>
> The President's interpretation of Common Article 3 is reasonable and should be sustained. The conflict with al Qaeda is international in character in the sense that it is occurring in various nations around the globe. Thus, it is also "occurring in the territory of" more than "one of the High Contracting Parties." The Court does not dispute the President's judgments respecting the nature of our conflict with al Qaeda, nor does it suggest that the President's interpretation of Common Article 3 is implausible or foreclosed by the text of the treaty. Indeed, the Court concedes that Common Article 3 is principally concerned with "furnishing minimal protection to rebels involved in . . . a civil war," precisely the type of conflict the President's interpretation envisions to be subject to Common Article 3. Instead, the Court, without acknowledging its duty to defer to the President, adopts its own, admittedly plausible, reading of Common Article 3. But where, as here, an ambiguous treaty provision ("not of an international character") is susceptible of two plausible, and reasonable, interpretations, our precedents require us to defer to the Executive's interpretation.

Id. at 719.]

Notes and Questions

1. President Bush's November 13, 2001, military order authorizing military commissions was crafted to be similar to the language of the Roosevelt military commission orders that were upheld in *Quirin*. The order also cited as authority, among other things, the successor statute to Article 15 of the Articles of War that *Quirin* held authorized the Roosevelt military commission. In 1950, Congress recodified Article 15 as §821 of the Uniform Code of Military Justice without changing the reference to military commissions. Moreover, as footnote 22 of *Hamdan* suggests, the legislative history of §821 indicates that Congress was aware of and accepted the Court's interpretation in *Quirin*. Why, then, didn't the Court uphold the Bush military commissions? What had changed between 1942 and 2006? In what relevant ways was World War II different from the "war on terrorism"? How had the pertinent statutes changed?

2. The Court in *Hamdan* did not hold that military commissions were per se invalid, but rather that the President had violated the statutory prerequisites to and limitations upon military commissions. What does the Court's reasoning imply about the President's concurrent power with Congress to establish military commissions? What does it imply about the President's exclusive power to create military commissions? How is footnote 23 relevant to these issues? Does it say anything more than the truism that the President cannot circumvent congressional restrictions that Congress has the authority to impose on the President? If not, why did the Court say it? Truism or not, does this footnote have relevance to other issues in the war on terrorism?

3. Are you convinced by the *Hamdan* Court's interpretation of Article 36 of the UCMJ? Do you agree that Article 36 requires military commissions to utilize the same procedures as courts-martial? Do you agree with its conclusion that the President erred in determining that it was not "practicable" for military commissions to use court-martial procedures? The Court says that there is "no suggestion of any logistical difficulty in securing properly sworn and authenticated evidence or in applying the usual principles of relevance and admissibility." Is this view consistent with the plurality's determination in *Hamdi*, two years earlier, that "the exigencies of the circumstances" during a military conflict may demand that enemy combatant status proceedings "be tailored to alleviate their uncommon potential to burden the Executive at a time of ongoing military conflict" and can properly result in the introduction of hearsay and a shift in the burden of proof? Won't the potential burden on the Executive Branch and the military be even greater when it comes to securing and presenting evidence needed to prove guilt at trial beyond a reasonable doubt? What about the unusual need in this war to use classified information? Is the Court institutionally competent to second-guess the commander in chief's assessment of these issues? Why didn't the Court give deference, under the principles discussed in Chapter 2, to the President's "practicability" determination?

4. The Court in *Hamdan* also held that the Executive Branch's military commission system violated Common Article 3 of the Geneva Conventions. Why is Common Article 3 relevant to the Court's statutory analysis? And once again, why didn't the Court defer to the President's determination, on February 7, 2002, that Common Article 3 of Geneva does not apply to either Al Qaeda or Taliban detainees, because, among other reasons, the relevant conflicts are international in scope and Common Article 3 applies only to "armed conflict not of an international character"? Is the Court's failure to defer here consistent with its usual deference to the Executive

Branch's interpretation of treaties? Who has the better of the argument on the interpretation of Common Article 3, the majority or Justice Thomas? What are the implications of the Court's Common Article 3 holding beyond the issue of military commissions?

5. The concurring opinions of Justices Kennedy and Breyer emphasize that the Court's opinion leaves it entirely open for Congress to reconfigure military commissions in a way better suited to the current "war on terrorism." In this regard, the Court's decision appears simply to force the President to go to Congress to ensure that both political branches consent to the use and constitution of military commissions. Do you think the Court was self-consciously engaged in this "democracy-forcing" role? Is this a legitimate function for the Court? Why didn't Congress regulate military commissions after the September 11 attacks on its own initiative? What is the relationship between a democracy-forcing role for the Court and Justice Jackson's three categories of analysis in *Youngstown*? Is such a role more or less legitimate when the Court is interpreting presidential authority during military conflict? Does the Court place any limitations on a congressionally approved military commission?

6. Congress accepted the Court's invitation to address the issue of military commissions. About four months after the decision, Congress enacted the Military Commissions Act (MCA) of 2006. The MCA of 2006 established an express statutory foundation for the use of military commissions "to try alien unlawful enemy combatants engaged in hostilities against the United States for violations of the laws of war and other offenses triable by military commissions." It defined "unlawful enemy combatant" as

> (i) a person who has engaged in hostilities or who has purposefully and materially supported hostilities against the United States or its co-belligerents who is not a lawful enemy combatant (including a person who is part of the Taliban, al Qaeda, or associated forces); or
>
> (ii) a person who, before, on, or after the date of the enactment of the Military Commissions Act of 2006, has been determined to be an unlawful enemy combatant by a Combatant Status Review Tribunal or another competent tribunal established under the authority of the President or the Secretary of Defense.

7. The MCA of 2006 outlined the procedures required to be followed in the military commissions and defined the crimes that could be tried before the commissions. It also stated that a military commission established pursuant to its terms "is a regularly constituted court, affording all the necessary 'judicial guarantees which are recognized as indispensable by civilized peoples' for purposes of common Article 3 of the Geneva Conventions." MCA of 2006, §948b(f). Why, in light of *Hamdan*, did Congress think it needed to say this? Is this determination binding on a court trying to determine whether the MCA is consistent with Common Article 3? If it is not binding, how much deference, if any, should courts give it? Do the answers to these questions depend on the force or validity of the next sentence in the MCA, which provides that "No alien unlawful enemy combatant subject to trial by military commission . . . may invoke the Geneva Conventions as a source of rights"? MCA of 2006, §948b(g). Assuming that the Geneva Conventions otherwise would be domestically enforceable (something that remains unsettled), is this provision legally valid?

8. Before the enactment of the MCA of 2006, the War Crimes Act, 18 U.S.C. §2441, provided that "any conduct . . . which constitutes a violation of common Article 3" was a war crime under U.S. law. The MCA of 2006 amends the War Crimes

Act to specify that only "grave breaches" of Common Article 3 constitute war crimes, and it defines these grave breaches.* Neither failure to use "a regularly constituted court" nor "humiliating or degrading treatment" are included as grave breaches, even though they are prohibited by Common Article 3. Why do you think Congress made this amendment? This section of the MCA of 2006 also states, "No foreign or international source of law shall supply a basis for a rule of decision in the courts of the United States in interpreting the prohibitions enumerated in subsection (d) of such section 2441." MCA of 2006, §6(a)(2). Is this provision valid? Can Congress control what courts look at in interpreting statutory provisions? There is also a provision in this section of the MCA stating, "As provided by the Constitution and by this section, the President has the authority for the United States to interpret the meaning and application of the Geneva Convention and to promulgate higher standards and administrative regulations for violations of treaty obligations which are not grave breaches of the Geneva Conventions." MCA of 2006, §6(a)(3). How does this provision relate to the deference courts often give to the Executive Branch on issues of foreign relations law, as discussed in Chapter 2? For a discussion of this and other aspects of the MCA, see Curtis A. Bradley, *The Military Commissions Act, Habeas Corpus, and the Geneva Conventions*, 101 Am. J. Int'l L. 322 (2007); Carlos M. Vazquez, *The Military Commissions Act, the Geneva Conventions, and the Courts: A Critical Guide*, 101 Am. J. Int'l L. 73 (2007).

9. Section 7 of the MCA of 2006 amended the basic federal habeas corpus statute to provide, "No court, justice, or judge shall have jurisdiction to hear or consider an application for a writ of habeas corpus filed by or on behalf of an alien detained by the United States who has been determined by the United States to have been properly detained as an enemy combatant or is awaiting such determination." Instead of habeas review, the MCA of 2006 allowed, like the DTA of 2005, only for review of CSRT determinations and military commission judgments in the D.C. Circuit. Unlike the DTA, however, Congress in the MCA of 2006 made clear that the restriction on habeas "shall apply to all cases, without exception, pending on or after the date of the enactment of this Act, which relate to any aspect of the detention, transfer, treatment, trial or conditions of detention of an alien detained by the United States since September 11, 2001." The legality of this habeas restriction is the subject of the next section.

10. Shortly after taking office, President Obama suspended all military commission proceedings and many commentators believed that he might abolish commissions altogether. By the spring of 2009, however, President Obama had concluded that commissions were "an appropriate venue for trying detainees for violations of the laws of war" because they "allow for the protection of sensitive sources and methods of intelligence-gathering; they allow for the safety and security of participants; and for the presentation of evidence gathered from the battlefield that cannot always be effectively presented in federal courts." Remarks by the President on National Security, May 21, 2009, *at* https://obamawhitehouse.archives.gov/the-press-office/remarks-president-national-security-5-21-09.

In November 2009, President Obama signed into law the Military Commissions Act of 2009. The 2009 Act changes the label of persons eligible for military commission trials from "alien unlawful enemy combatants engaged in hostilities against the United States for violations of the law of war and other offenses triable by military

---

* The current version of the War Crimes Act is excerpted in Section C of Chapter 9.

commission" to "alien unprivileged enemy belligerents for violations of the law of war and other offenses triable by military commission." *See* 2009 Act, §948b. An "alien unprivileged enemy belligerent" is defined as:

> an individual (other than a privileged belligerent) who — (A) has engaged in hostilities against the United States or its coalition partners; (B) has purposefully and materially supported hostilities against the United States or its coalition partners; or (C) is a member of al Qaeda.

The 2009 Act also eliminated §948b(f) of the MCA of 2006, which had provided, "A military commission established under this chapter is a regularly constituted court, affording all the necessary 'judicial guarantees which are recognized as indispensable by civilized peoples' for purposes of common Article 3 of the Geneva Conventions." The 2009 Act thus does not purport to take a position on whether the military commissions satisfy Common Article 3.

In addition, the 2009 Act softened the restriction on the use of the Geneva Conventions by military commission defendants. Whereas the MCA of 2006 disallowed these defendants from invoking the Geneva Conventions "as a source of rights," the 2009 Act disallows them only from invoking the Conventions "as a basis for a private right of action." *See* 2009 Act, §948b(e). The 2009 Act left in place, however, the provision in the MCA of 2006 that disallowed habeas corpus petitioners from invoking the Conventions "as a source of rights."*

Another important change was that, whereas the MCA of 2006 had permitted the use in military commissions of statements obtained by cruel, inhuman, or degrading treatment in certain specified circumstances, the 2009 Act entirely eliminates the use of such statements. *See* 2009 Act, §948r.

11. Military commissions and the D.C. Circuit have struggled with the question whether material support of terrorism and conspiracy can be prosecuted as offenses when they occurred prior to the statutory specification of material support and conspiracy as crimes in the MCA of 2006.

The material support question arose in connection with Salim Hamdan's conviction in a military commission of material support for terrorism. Hamdan appealed his sentence even after he was transferred to his home country of Yemen in 2008. The U.S. Court of Military Commission Review, an appellate body of military judges established by the MCA of 2006, upheld Hamdan's conviction. *See* United States v. Hamdan, CMCR 09-002, June 24, 2011. However, the D.C Circuit reversed, concluding that the material support provision in the MCA of 2006 should not be applied retroactively to Hamdan's conduct. Hamdan v. United States, 696 F.3d 1238 (D.C. Cir. 2012) (*Hamdan II*). The court in *Hamdan II* reasoned that material support was a new crime that was not previously available for prosecution in military commissions before 2006. It further reasoned that material support for terrorism was not included within the violations of the "law of war" recognized by 10 U.S.C. §821. The court reasoned that the term "law of war" referred to "the international law of war" rather than the law of war as developed in U.S. common law precedents, as the Executive Branch had argued. Because the crime of material support was not an international war crime, the Court concluded that any prosecution of Hamdan

---

* In Noriega v. Pastrana, 564 F.3d 1290 (11th Cir. 2009), the court relied on this "source of rights" provision in refusing to consider a Geneva Convention claim raised by General Manuel Noriega, who had finished serving a prison term in the United States and was seeking to block his extradition from the United States to France.

for material support would implicate the constitutional ban on *ex post facto* application of criminal law. In light of this constitutional concern, and based on evidence in the text and legislative history of the MCA of 2006 that Congress did not intend retroactive application of new crimes, the court concluded that Congress had not authorized Hamdan's conviction for material support of terrorism during a period prior to 2006.

The holding in *Hamdan II* raised the question whether courts might also disallow charges of conspiracy in the commissions on similar grounds. The issue arose in connection with the 2008 military commission conviction of Ali Hamza Ahmad Suliman al-Bahlul for conspiring with Osama Bin Laden and others to commit murder of protected persons and attacking civilians. The U.S. government acknowledged that *Hamdan II* required reversal of Bahlul's conviction because his stand-alone conspiracy charges were, like the material support charges in *Hamdan II*, not an "international-law war crime" before 2006. The government later sought rehearing en banc in *Bahlul*, however, arguing that *Hamdan II* was itself wrongly decided because the phrase "law of war" in 10 U.S.C. §821 should be interpreted to include the U.S. common law of war in addition to the international law of war. The D.C. Circuit granted the petition and overruled the statutory holding of *Hamdan II*. *See* United States v. Al Bahlul, 767 F.3d 1 (D.C. Cir. 2014). Writing for the majority of the Court, Judge Henderson reasoned in relevant part that the 2006 MCA "is unambiguous in its intent to authorize retroactive prosecution for the crimes enumerated in the statute — regardless of their pre-existing law-of-war status." The court then turned aside Bahlul's *ex post* facto challenge to his conspiracy conviction, because he had not preserved an objection on that ground and it was not "plain error" for the military commission to try him on that charge. The court thus upheld Bahlul's conviction without resolving the merits of whether the Ex Post Facto Clause applied.

The government in *Bahlul* and other cases has argued that the Constitution was ratified against the background of, and should be presumed not to have called into question, military adjudication during the Revolutionary War of offenses that would not have violated the international laws of war, such as the conduct of certain spies and disloyal civilians. For a detailed treatment of the Revolutionary War precedents that seeks to rebut this argument, see Martin S. Lederman, *Of Spies, Saboteurs, and Enemy Accomplices: History's Lessons for the Constitutionality of Wartime Military Tribunals,* 105 Geo. L.J. 1529 (2017).

12. In a subsequent decision also involving Bahlul that was not limited to the issue of pre-2006 offenses, the D.C. Circuit held that it violates Article III of the Constitution for military commissions to adjudicate the crime of conspiracy. Al Bahlul v. United States, 792 F.3d 1 (D.C. Cir. 2015), vacated, 2015 U.S. App. LEXIS 16967 (D.C. Cir. Sept. 25, 2015). The court noted that federal criminal prosecutions fall within the judicial power of the federal courts, and it reasoned that if a case falls within the federal judicial power, it must normally be tried before an Article III court. While noting that there are "limited exceptions" to this requirement based on historical practice and judicial precedent, and that one such exception is for law-of-war military commissions such as those used at Guantanamo, the court found that the crime of conspiracy does not fall within the scope of that exception. Relying heavily on reasoning in *Ex parte Quirin,* the court concluded that the exception to Article III for law-of-war military commissions extends only to the trial of offenses against the international laws of war, and it noted that the government had conceded that conspiracy does not constitute such an offense. The court also concluded that there was insufficient historical practice to support the use of law-of-war military commissions to try non-international offenses, and that neither the Define and Punish Clause nor the Necessary and Proper Clause gave Congress the authority to allow for such use of the commission.

Even with this decision, the Bahlul saga was not over. The D.C. Circuit subsequently granted rehearing en banc, vacated the panel opinion, and proceeded to uphold Bahlul's conspiracy conviction. The decision was 6-3. Of the six judges in the majority, four concluded that it does not violate the Constitution for Congress to make conspiracy a war crime triable by military commission, one concluded that Bahlul's conviction should be upheld under plain error review, and another concluded that Bahlul was not in fact convicted of an inchoate conspiracy offense. *See* Al Bahlul v. United States, 840 F.3d 757 (D.C. Cir. 2016).

13. A number of individuals associated with Al Qaeda have been subjected to criminal prosecution in federal court. Before the September 11 attacks, individuals implicated in the 1993 bombing of the World Trade Center and the 1998 bombings of the U.S. embassies in Kenya and Tanzania were tried in federal court. *See* United States v. Yousef, 327 F.3d 56 (2d Cir. 2003); United States v. Bin Laden, 91 F. Supp. 2d 600 (2000). After September 11, Richard Reid, a U.S. citizen who attempted to detonate a shoe bomb on a U.S. airliner, was prosecuted in a federal district court in Massachusetts. He pleaded guilty and was subsequently sentenced to life imprisonment. The "American Taliban," John Walker Lindh, also was prosecuted in federal court. He pleaded guilty in return for a 20-year prison sentence. *See* United States v. Lindh, 212 F. Supp. 2d 541 (E.D. Va. 2002). Finally, the alleged "20th hijacker" in the 9/11 attacks, Zacarias Moussaoui, was prosecuted in a federal district court in Virginia, and he eventually pleaded guilty. And as noted in the last section, Yaser Hamdi and Ali Saleh Kahlah al-Marri, both of whom were held for a while in military detention in the United States, were ultimately convicted of crimes.

The Obama Administration came into office with the intention of prosecuting many additional alleged terrorists, including a number of Al Qaeda members detained at the Guantanamo Bay detention center, in federal criminal court. However, when the administration proposed bringing Khalid Sheikh Mohammad, the alleged mastermind of the September 11 attacks, and certain other detainees to the United States for trial, the proposal generated significant controversy and prompted the congressional restrictions on the transfer of detainees to the United States discussed in Section B. The administration subsequently announced that it would try Mohammad before a military commission. Nevertheless, the Obama Administration successfully prosecuted a number of terrorists in federal court, including Al Qaeda members who conspired to kill Americans in the 1998 U.S. embassy bombings. *See* Nicole Hong, *Saudi Arabian Convicted in 1998 U.S. Embassy Bombings Trial*, Wall St. J., Feb. 26, 2015. And, although President Trump announced a preference during the 2016 presidential campaign for military commissions over federal court trials for alleged terrorists, his administration has continued to prosecute terrorists in federal court.

In the absence of congressional restriction, what factors does the Executive Branch consider when deciding whether to try someone in a civilian court versus a military commission? Former Assistant Attorney General for National Security David Kris provided some insight into the government's thinking in a 2010 speech. Kris identified a number of advantages to using military commissions over civilian trials: lower proof requirements, no *Miranda* warning requirement, increased ability to close the courtroom, and admissibility of hearsay. By contrast, Kris noted, civilian trials provide five advantages over military commissions: more certain rules that better promote guilty pleas, more available crimes, better mechanisms for defendant cooperation, tougher sentencing rules, and better international cooperation. The government, Kris argued, should make a "relentlessly pragmatic and empirical" decision between these two trial fora, and military detention, based on which one works "best under the circumstances." *See* David Kris, Speech at the Brookings Institution, June 11, 2010, at http://www.justice.gov/nsd/opa/pr/speeches/2010/nsd-speech-100611.html.

Should the government be free to choose between the use of civilian and military trials? Does the overlap between federal criminal law and the military commission system in the war on terrorism suggest that the latter is unwarranted in this context? Does the government's freedom of choice implicate fairness concerns? If so, do those concerns have constitutional significance?

14. For additional scholarship relating to the use of military commissions, see, for example, Curtis A. Bradley & Jack L. Goldsmith, *The Constitutional Validity of Military Commissions*, 5 Green Bag 2d 249 (2002); David Glazier, *Precedents Lost: The Neglected History of the Military Commission*, 46 Va. J. Int'l L. 5 (2005); David Glazier, *The Misuse of History: Conspiracy and the Guantanamo Military Commissions*, 66 Baylor L. Rev. 295 (2014); Jonathan Hafetz, *Policing the Line: International Law, Article III, and the Constitutional Limits of Military Jurisdiction*, 2014 Wis. L. Rev. 681; Neal K. Katyal & Laurence H. Tribe, *Waging War, Deciding Guilt: Trying the Military Tribunals*, 111 Yale L.J. 12159 (2002); Peter Margulies, *Justice at War: Military Tribunals and Article III*, 49 U.C. Davis L. Rev. 305 (2015); Michael A. Newton, *Some Observations on the Future of U.S. Military Commissions*, 42 Case W. Res. J. Int'l L. 151 (2009); Scott L. Silliman, *On Military Commissions*, 37 Case W. Res. J. Int'l L. 529 (2005); Detlev F. Vagts, *Military Commissions: Constitutional Limits on Their Role in the War on Terror*, 102 Am. J. Int'l L. 573 (2008); and Stephen I. Vladeck, *Military Courts and Article III*, 103 Geo. L.J. 933 (2015).

D. TERRITORIAL SCOPE OF HABEAS JURISDICTION

Since early 2002, the United States has detained hundreds of foreign citizens at the U.S. naval base at Guantanamo Bay, Cuba. The United States occupies the base under a 1903 lease agreement with Cuba, pursuant to which the United States "recognizes the continuance of the ultimate sovereignty of the Republic of Cuba over the [leased areas]," while the Republic of Cuba "consents that during the period of occupation by the United States . . . the United States shall exercise complete jurisdiction and control over and within said areas." A 1934 treaty between Cuba and the United States further provides that the lease will remain in effect "[s]o long as the United States of America shall not abandon the . . . naval station at Guantanamo." Relying on the fact that Guantanamo Bay was not part of U.S. sovereign territory, as well as on the reasoning of Johnson v. Eisentrager (excerpted above in Section A), the Justice Department's Office of Legal Counsel concluded in late 2001 "that the great weight of legal authority indicates that a federal district court could not properly exercise habeas jurisdiction over an alien detained at [Guantanamo Bay]." Memorandum from Patrick F. Philbin and John C. Yoo, Deputy Assistant Attorneys General, Office of Legal Counsel, to William J. Haynes II, General Counsel, Dept. of Defense, "Possible Habeas Jurisdiction Over Aliens Held in Guantanamo Bay" (Dec. 28, 2001).

In a decision issued the same day as Hamdi v. Rumsfeld, the Supreme Court reached a different conclusion. In Rasul v. Bush, 542 U.S. 466 (2004), the Court held that, under the general federal habeas statute, 28 U.S.C. §2241, courts "have jurisdiction to determine the legality of the Executive's potentially indefinite detention of individuals [at Guantanamo] who claim to be wholly innocent of wrongdoing." The Court noted that the petitioners in this case

> differ from the *Eisentrager* detainees in critical respects: They are not nationals of countries at war with the United States, and they deny that they have engaged in or plotted acts of aggression against the United States; they have never been afforded access to any tribunal, much less charged with and convicted of wrongdoing; and for more than two years they have been imprisoned in territory over which the United States exercises exclusive jurisdiction and control.

Justice Kennedy concurred in the judgment to explain why this case was distinguishable from *Eisentrager.* Whereas in *Eisentrager* the detainees "were proven enemy aliens found and detained outside the United States, and . . . the existence of jurisdiction would have had a clear harmful effect on the Nation's military affairs," he reasoned, Guantanamo Bay "is in every practical respect a United States territory, and it is one far removed from any hostilities," and "the detainees at Guantanamo Bay are being held indefinitely, and without benefit of any legal proceeding to determine their status."

The Court in *Rasul* relied only on the statutory right of habeas corpus. Congress responded with the Detainee Treatment Act of 2005 (DTA), which established judicial review of Combatant Status Review Tribunals (CSRTs) and military commissions, but sought to overrule *Rasul's* statutory holding by precluding habeas corpus petitions brought by aliens held by the military at Guantanamo. The Court in Hamdan v. Rumsfeld concluded that this habeas exclusion did not apply to cases that were pending on the date of the DTA's enactment. As described in the previous section, in Section 7 of the Military Commissions Act of 2006, enacted in response to *Hamdan,* Congress once again sought to deny habeas corpus jurisdiction over Guantanamo, and it attempted to make clear that its effort applied to pending cases. The elimination of habeas corpus review by Congress in 2006 raised the question whether Congress had acted consistently with Article I, Section 9 of the U.S. Constitution, also known as the Suspension Clause, which provides that the "privilege of the Writ of Habeas Corpus shall not be suspended, unless when in Cases of Rebellion or Invasion the public Safety may require it." The Supreme Court has construed this clause as conferring a constitutional right of habeas corpus that applies unless Congress provides an adequate substitute for habeas or validly suspends the writ. It was unclear, however, whether and to what extent such a right applied to foreign citizens held at Guantanamo and other places outside the United States.

Boumediene v. Bush

553 U.S. 723 (2008)

[The petitioners in this case were aliens detained at the U.S. naval base at Guantanamo Bay, Cuba, as enemy combatants after being captured abroad. Some were captured on the battlefield in Afghanistan and others were captured in places such as Bosnia and Gambia. They denied that they were members of Al Qaeda or the Taliban forces and sought a writ of habeas corpus in federal court. The court of appeals held that Section 7 of the Military Commissions Act of 2006 precluded habeas corpus jurisdiction, and that the petitioners did not have a constitutional right to habeas review. The court therefore did not reach the issue whether the DTA's system of review of the CSRTs was a constitutionally adequate substitute for habeas review.]

JUSTICE KENNEDY delivered the opinion of the Court. . . .

[The Court first concludes that Section 7 of the MCA of 2006 denies the federal courts jurisdiction to hear habeas corpus challenges brought by detainees at Guantanamo, including challenges pending at the time when the Act was passed. The Court then proceeds to consider whether this restriction violates the Suspension Clause.]

Drawing from its position that at common law the writ ran only to territories over which the Crown was sovereign, the Government says the Suspension Clause affords petitioners no rights because the United States does not claim sovereignty over the place of detention.

Guantanamo Bay is not formally part of the United States. And under the terms of the lease between the United States and Cuba [concluded in 1903], Cuba retains "ultimate sovereignty" over the territory while the United States exercises "complete jurisdiction and control." Under the terms of [a 1934 treaty between the United States and Cuba], however, Cuba effectively has no rights as a sovereign until the parties agree to modification of the 1903 Lease Agreement or the United States abandons the base.

The United States contends, nevertheless, that Guantanamo is not within its sovereign control. This was the Government's position well before the events of September 11, 2001. And in other contexts the Court has held that questions of sovereignty are for the political branches to decide. Even if this were a treaty interpretation case that did not involve a political question, the President's construction of the lease agreement would be entitled to great respect.

We therefore do not question the Government's position that Cuba, not the United States, maintains sovereignty, in the legal and technical sense of the term, over Guantanamo Bay. But this does not end the analysis. . . .

The Government's formal sovereignty-based test [for application of the Constitution] raises troubling separation-of-powers concerns. . . . The political history of Guantanamo illustrates the deficiencies of this approach. The United States has maintained complete and uninterrupted control of the bay for over 100 years. At the close of the Spanish-American War, Spain ceded control over the entire island of Cuba to the United States and specifically "relinquishe[d] all claim[s] of sovereignty . . . and title." See Treaty of Paris, Dec. 10, 1898, U.S.-Spain, Art. I. From the date the treaty with Spain was signed until the Cuban Republic was established on May 20, 1902, the United States governed the territory "in trust" for the benefit of the Cuban people. And although it recognized, by entering into the 1903 Lease Agreement, that Cuba retained "ultimate sovereignty" over Guantanamo, the United States continued to maintain the same plenary control it had enjoyed since 1898. Yet the Government's view is that the Constitution had no effect there, at least as to noncitizens, because the United States disclaimed sovereignty in the formal sense of the term. The necessary implication of the argument is that by surrendering formal sovereignty over any unincorporated territory to a third party, while at the same time entering into a lease that grants total control over the territory back to the United States, it would be possible for the political branches to govern without legal constraint.

Our basic charter cannot be contracted away like this. The Constitution grants Congress and the President the power to acquire, dispose of, and govern territory, not the power to decide when and where its terms apply. Even when the United States acts outside its borders, its powers are not "absolute and unlimited" but are subject "to such restrictions as are expressed in the Constitution." Murphy v. Ramsey, 114 U.S. 15, 44 (1885). Abstaining from questions involving formal sovereignty and territorial governance is one thing. To hold the political branches have the power to switch the Constitution on or off at will is quite another. The former position reflects this Court's recognition that certain matters requiring political judgments are best left to the political branches. The latter would permit a striking anomaly in our tripartite system of government, leading to a regime in which Congress and the President, not this Court, say "what the law is." Marbury v. Madison, 5 U.S. 137, 177 (1803).

These concerns have particular bearing upon the Suspension Clause question in the cases now before us, for the writ of habeas corpus is itself an indispensable mechanism for monitoring the separation of powers. The test for determining the scope of this provision must not be subject to manipulation by those whose power it is designed to restrain.

[T]he outlines of a framework for determining the reach of the Suspension Clause are suggested by the factors the Court relied upon in *Eisentrager*. In addition to the practical concerns discussed above, the *Eisentrager* Court found relevant that each petitioner:

> (a) is an enemy alien; (b) has never been or resided in the United States; (c) was captured outside of our territory and there held in military custody as a prisoner of war; (d) was tried and convicted by a Military Commission sitting outside the United States; (e) for offenses against laws of war committed outside the United States; (f) and is at all times imprisoned outside the United States.

Based on this language from *Eisentrager*, and the reasoning in our other extraterritoriality opinions, we conclude that at least three factors are relevant in determining the reach of the Suspension Clause: (1) the citizenship and status of the detainee and the adequacy of the process through which that status determination was made; (2) the nature of the sites where apprehension and then detention took place; and (3) the practical obstacles inherent in resolving the prisoner's entitlement to the writ.

Applying this framework, we note at the onset that the status of these detainees is a matter of dispute. The petitioners, like those in *Eisentrager*, are not American citizens. But the petitioners in *Eisentrager* did not contest, it seems, the Court's assertion that they were "enemy alien[s]." In the instant cases, by contrast, the detainees deny they are enemy combatants. They have been afforded some process in CSRT proceedings to determine their status; but, unlike in *Eisentrager*, there has been no trial by military commission for violations of the laws of war. The difference is not trivial. The records from the *Eisentrager* trials suggest that, well before the petitioners brought their case to this Court, there had been a rigorous adversarial process to test the legality of their detention. The *Eisentrager* petitioners were charged by a bill of particulars that made detailed factual allegations against them. To rebut the accusations, they were entitled to representation by counsel, allowed to introduce evidence on their own behalf, and permitted to cross-examine the prosecution's witnesses.

In comparison the procedural protections afforded to the detainees in the [status review hearings held by the U.S. military at Guantanamo] are far more limited, and, we conclude, fall well short of the procedures and adversarial mechanisms that would eliminate the need for habeas corpus review. . . .

As to the second factor relevant to this analysis, the detainees here are similarly situated to the *Eisentrager* petitioners in that the sites of their apprehension and detention are technically outside the sovereign territory of the United States. As noted earlier, this is a factor that weighs against finding they have rights under the Suspension Clause. But there are critical differences between Landsberg Prison, circa 1950, and the United States Naval Station at Guantanamo Bay in 2008. Unlike its present control over the naval station, the United States' control over the prison in Germany was neither absolute nor indefinite. Like all parts of occupied Germany, the prison was under the jurisdiction of the combined Allied Forces. The United States was therefore answerable to its Allies for all activities occurring there. The Allies had not planned a long-term occupation of Germany, nor did they intend to displace all German institutions even during the period of occupation. . . . In every practical sense Guantanamo is not abroad; it is within the constant jurisdiction of the United States.

As to the third factor, we recognize, as the Court did in *Eisentrager*, that there are costs to holding the Suspension Clause applicable in a case of military detention abroad. Habeas corpus proceedings may require expenditure of funds by the Government and may divert the attention of military personnel from other pressing tasks. While we are sensitive to these concerns, we do not find them dispositive. Compliance with any judicial process requires some incremental expenditure of resources. Yet civilian courts and the Armed Forces have functioned along side each other at various points in our history. The Government presents no credible arguments that the military mission at Guantanamo would be compromised if habeas corpus courts had jurisdiction to hear the detainees' claims. And in light of the plenary control the United States asserts over the base, none are apparent to us.

The situation in *Eisentrager* was far different, given the historical context and nature of the military's mission in post-War Germany. When hostilities in the European Theater came to an end, the United States became responsible for an occupation zone encompassing over 57,000 square miles with a population of 18 million. In addition to supervising massive reconstruction and aid efforts the American forces stationed in Germany faced potential security threats from a defeated enemy. In retrospect the post-War occupation may seem uneventful. But at the time *Eisentrager* was decided, the Court was right to be concerned about judicial interference with the military's efforts to contain "enemy elements, guerilla fighters, and 'were-wolves.'"

Similar threats are not apparent here; nor does the Government argue that they are. The United States Naval Station at Guantanamo Bay consists of 45 square miles of land and water. The base has been used, at various points, to house migrants and refugees temporarily. At present, however, other than the detainees themselves, the only long-term residents are American military personnel, their families, and a small number of workers. The detainees have been deemed enemies of the United States. At present, dangerous as they may be if released, they are contained in a secure prison facility located on an isolated and heavily fortified military base.

There is no indication, furthermore, that adjudicating a habeas corpus petition would cause friction with the host government. No Cuban court has jurisdiction over American military personnel at Guantanamo or the enemy combatants detained there. While obligated to abide by the terms of the lease, the United States is, for all practical purposes, answerable to no other sovereign for its acts on the base. Were that not the case, or if the detention facility were located in an active theater of war, arguments that issuing the writ would be "impracticable or anomalous" would have more weight. Under the facts presented here, however, there are few practical barriers to the running of the writ. To the extent barriers arise, habeas corpus procedures likely can be modified to address them. . . .

In light of this holding the question becomes whether the statute stripping jurisdiction to issue the writ avoids the Suspension Clause mandate because Congress has provided adequate substitute procedures for habeas corpus. The Government submits there has been compliance with the Suspension Clause because the DTA review process in the Court of Appeals, provides an adequate substitute. Congress has granted that court jurisdiction to consider

(i) whether the status determination of the [CSRT] . . . was consistent with the standards and procedures specified by the Secretary of Defense . . . and (ii) to the extent the Constitution and laws of the United States are applicable, whether the use of such standards and procedures to make the determination is consistent with the Constitution and laws of the United States.

The Court of Appeals, having decided that the writ does not run to the detainees in any event, found it unnecessary to consider whether an adequate substitute has been provided. In the ordinary course we would remand to the Court of Appeals to consider this question in the first instance. It is well settled, however, that the Court's practice of declining to address issues left unresolved in earlier proceedings is not an inflexible rule. Departure from the rule is appropriate in "exceptional" circumstances.

The gravity of the separation-of-powers issues raised by these cases and the fact that these detainees have been denied meaningful access to a judicial forum for a period of years render these cases exceptional. The parties before us have addressed the adequacy issue. . . . Under the circumstances we believe the costs of further delay substantially outweigh any benefits of remanding to the Court of Appeals to consider the issue it did not address in these cases.

. . . [The Court reviews the text and legislative history of the DTA and concludes:] In passing the DTA Congress did not intend to create a process that differs from traditional habeas corpus process in name only. It intended to create a more limited procedure. It is against this background that we must interpret the DTA and assess its adequacy as a substitute for habeas corpus. . . .

We do not endeavor to offer a comprehensive summary of the requisites for an adequate substitute for habeas corpus. We do consider it uncontroversial, however, that the privilege of habeas corpus entitles the prisoner to a meaningful opportunity to demonstrate that he is being held pursuant to "the erroneous application or interpretation" of relevant law. And the habeas court must have the power to order the conditional release of an individual unlawfully detained — though release need not be the exclusive remedy and is not the appropriate one in every case in which the writ is granted. These are the easily identified attributes of any constitutionally adequate habeas corpus proceeding. But, depending on the circumstances, more may be required. . . .

The idea that the necessary scope of habeas review in part depends upon the rigor of any earlier proceedings accords with our test for procedural adequacy in the due process context. . . .

Accordingly, where relief is sought from a sentence that resulted from the judgment of a court of record . . . considerable deference is owed to the court that ordered confinement. Likewise in those cases the prisoner should exhaust adequate alternative remedies before filing for the writ in federal court. Both aspects of federal habeas corpus review are justified because it can be assumed that, in the usual course, a court of record provides defendants with a fair, adversary proceeding. In cases involving state convictions this framework also respects federalism; and in federal cases it has added justification because the prisoner already has had a chance to seek review of his conviction in a federal forum through a direct appeal. The present cases fall outside these categories, however; for here the detention is by executive order.

Where a person is detained by executive order, rather than, say, after being tried and convicted in a court, the need for collateral review is most pressing. A criminal conviction in the usual course occurs after a judicial hearing before a tribunal disinterested in the outcome and committed to procedures designed to ensure its own independence. These dynamics are not inherent in executive detention orders or executive review procedures. In this context the need for habeas corpus is more urgent. The intended duration of the detention and the reasons for it bear upon the precise scope of the inquiry. Habeas corpus proceedings need not resemble a criminal trial, even when the detention is by executive order. But the writ must be effective. The habeas court must have sufficient authority to conduct a meaningful review of both the cause for detention and the Executive's power to detain.

To determine the necessary scope of habeas corpus review, therefore, we must assess the CSRT process, the mechanism through which petitioners' designation as enemy combatants became final. Whether one characterizes the CSRT process as direct review of the Executive's battlefield determination that the detainee is an enemy combatant — as the parties have and as we do — or as the first step in the collateral review of a battlefield determination makes no difference in a proper analysis of whether the procedures Congress put in place are an adequate substitute for habeas corpus. What matters is the sum total of procedural protections afforded to the detainee at all stages, direct and collateral.

Petitioners identify what they see as myriad deficiencies in the CSRTs. The most relevant for our purposes are the constraints upon the detainee's ability to rebut the factual basis for the Government's assertion that he is an enemy combatant. [At] the CSRT stage the detainee has limited means to find or present evidence to challenge the Government's case against him. He does not have the assistance of counsel and may not be aware of the most critical allegations that the Government relied upon to order his detention. The detainee can confront witnesses that testify during the CSRT proceedings. But given that there are in effect no limits on the admission of hearsay evidence — the only requirement is that the tribunal deem the evidence "relevant and helpful" — the detainee's opportunity to question witnesses is likely to be more theoretical than real.

The Government defends the CSRT process, arguing that it was designed to conform to the procedures suggested by the plurality in *Hamdi*. Setting aside the fact that the relevant language in *Hamdi* did not garner a majority of the Court, it does not control the matter at hand. None of the parties in *Hamdi* argued there had been a suspension of the writ. Nor could they. The §2241 habeas corpus process remained in place. Accordingly, the plurality concentrated on whether the Executive had the authority to detain and, if so, what rights the detainee had under the Due Process Clause. True, there are places in the *Hamdi* plurality opinion where it is difficult to tell where its extrapolation of §2241 ends and its analysis of the petitioner's Due Process rights begins. But the Court had no occasion to define the necessary scope of habeas review, for Suspension Clause purposes, in the context of enemy combatant detentions. The closest the plurality came to doing so was in discussing whether, in light of separation-of-powers concerns, §2241 should be construed to forbid the District Court from inquiring beyond the affidavit Hamdi's custodian provided in answer to the detainee's habeas petition. The plurality answered this question with an emphatic "no."

Even if we were to assume that the CSRTs satisfy due process standards, it would not end our inquiry. Habeas corpus is a collateral process that exists, in Justice Holmes' words, to "cu[t] through all forms and g[o] to the very tissue of the structure. It comes in from the outside, not in subordination to the proceedings, and although every form may have been preserved opens the inquiry whether they have been more than an empty shell." Frank v. Mangum, 237 U.S. 309, 346 (1915) (dissenting opinion). Even when the procedures authorizing detention are structurally sound, the Suspension Clause remains applicable and the writ relevant. . . .

Although we make no judgment as to whether the CSRTs, as currently constituted, satisfy due process standards, we agree with petitioners that, even when all the parties involved in this process act with diligence and in good faith, there is considerable risk of error in the tribunal's findings of fact. . . .

For the writ of habeas corpus, or its substitute, to function as an effective and proper remedy in this context, the court that conducts the habeas proceeding must have the means to correct errors that occurred during the CSRT proceedings. This includes some authority to assess the sufficiency of the Government's evidence against the detainee. It also must have the authority to admit and consider relevant exculpatory evidence that was not introduced during the earlier proceeding. Federal habeas petitioners long have had the means to supplement the record on review, even in the postconviction habeas setting. Here that opportunity is constitutionally required.

Consistent with the historic function and province of the writ, habeas corpus review may be more circumscribed if the underlying detention proceedings are more thorough than they were here. In two habeas cases involving enemy aliens tried for war crimes, In re Yamashita, 327 U.S. 1 (1946), and Ex parte Quirin, 317 U.S. 1 (1942), for example, this Court limited its review to determining whether the Executive had legal authority to try the petitioners by military commission. Military courts are not courts of record. . . . [On] their own terms, the proceedings in *Yamashita* and *Quirin*, like those in *Eisentrager*, had an adversarial structure that is lacking here. The extent of the showing required of the Government in these cases is a matter to be determined. We need not explore it further at this stage. We do hold that when the judicial power to issue habeas corpus properly is invoked the judicial officer must have adequate authority to make a determination in light of the relevant law and facts and to formulate and issue appropriate orders for relief, including, if necessary, an order directing the prisoner's release.

We now consider whether the DTA allows the Court of Appeals to conduct a proceeding meeting these standards. "[W]e are obligated to construe the statute to avoid [constitutional] problems" if it is " 'fairly possible' " to do so. There are limits to this principle, however. The canon of constitutional avoidance does not supplant traditional modes of statutory interpretation. We cannot ignore the text and purpose of a statute in order to save it.

The DTA does not explicitly empower the Court of Appeals to order the applicant in a DTA review proceeding released should the court find that the standards and procedures used at his CSRT hearing were insufficient to justify detention. This is troubling. Yet, for present purposes, we can assume congressional silence permits a constitutionally required remedy. In that case it would be possible to hold that a remedy of release is impliedly provided for. The DTA might be read, furthermore, to allow the petitioners to assert most, if not all, of the legal claims they seek to advance, including their most basic claim: that the President has no authority under the AUMF to detain them indefinitely. . . . At oral argument, the Solicitor General urged us to adopt both these constructions, if doing so would allow MCA §7 to remain intact.

The absence of a release remedy and specific language allowing AUMF challenges are not the only constitutional infirmities from which the statute potentially suffers, however. The more difficult question is whether the DTA permits the Court of Appeals to make requisite findings of fact. The DTA enables petitioners to request "review" of their CSRT determination in the Court of Appeals; but the "Scope of Review" provision confines the Court of Appeals' role to reviewing whether the CSRT followed the "standards and procedures" issued by the Department of Defense and assessing whether those "standards and procedures" are lawful. Among these standards is "the requirement that the conclusion of the Tribunal be supported by a preponderance of the evidence . . . allowing a rebuttable presumption in favor of the Government's evidence." Assuming the DTA can be construed to allow the Court of Appeals to review or correct the CSRT's factual determinations, as opposed to merely certifying that the tribunal applied the correct standard of proof, we see no way to construe the statute to allow what is also constitutionally required in this context: an opportunity for the detainee to present relevant exculpatory evidence that was not made part of the record in the earlier proceedings.

On its face the statute allows the Court of Appeals to consider no evidence outside the CSRT record. In the parallel litigation, however, the Court of Appeals determined that the DTA allows it to order the production of all " 'reasonably available information in the possession of the U.S. Government bearing on the issue of whether the detainee meets the criteria to be designated as an enemy combatant,' " regardless of whether this evidence was put before the CSRT. . . . [We] can assume that the Court of Appeals was correct that the DTA allows introduction and consideration of relevant exculpatory evidence that was "reasonably available" to the Government at the time of the CSRT but not made part of the record. Even so, the DTA review proceeding falls short of being a constitutionally adequate substitute, for the detainee still would have no opportunity to present evidence discovered after the CSRT proceedings concluded.

Under the DTA the Court of Appeals has the power to review CSRT determinations by assessing the legality of standards and procedures. This implies the power to inquire into what happened at the CSRT hearing and, perhaps, to remedy certain deficiencies in that proceeding. But should the Court of Appeals determine that the CSRT followed appropriate and lawful standards and procedures, it will have reached the limits of its jurisdiction. There is no language in the DTA that can be construed to allow the Court of Appeals to admit and consider newly discovered evidence that could not have been made part of the CSRT record because it was unavailable to either the Government or the detainee when the CSRT made its findings. This evidence, however, may be critical to the detainee's argument that he is not an enemy combatant and there is no cause to detain him. . . .

By foreclosing consideration of evidence not presented or reasonably available to the detainee at the CSRT proceedings, the DTA disadvantages the detainee by limiting the scope of collateral review to a record that may not be accurate or complete. In other contexts, *e.g.,* in post-trial habeas cases where the prisoner already has had a full and fair opportunity to develop the factual predicate of his claims, similar limitations on the scope of habeas review may be appropriate. In this context, however, where the underlying detention proceedings lack the necessary adversarial character, the detainee cannot be held responsible for all deficiencies in the record. . . .

We do not imply DTA review would be a constitutionally sufficient replacement for habeas corpus but for these limitations on the detainee's ability to present exculpatory evidence. For even if it were possible, as a textual matter, to read into the statute each of the necessary procedures we have identified, we could not overlook the cumulative effect of our doing so. To hold that the detainees at Guantanamo may, under the DTA, challenge the President's legal authority to detain them, contest the CSRT's findings of fact, supplement the record on review with exculpatory evidence, and request an order of release would come close to reinstating the §2241 habeas corpus process Congress sought to deny them. The language of the statute, read in light of Congress' reasons for enacting it, cannot bear this interpretation. Petitioners have met their burden of establishing that the DTA review process is, on its face, an inadequate substitute for habeas corpus.

Although we do not hold that an adequate substitute must duplicate §2241 in all respects, it suffices that the Government has not established that the detainees' access to the statutory review provisions at issue is an adequate substitute for the writ of habeas corpus. MCA §7 thus effects an unconstitutional suspension of the writ. In view of our holding we need not discuss the reach of the writ with respect to claims of unlawful conditions of treatment or confinement. . . .

In cases involving foreign citizens detained abroad by the Executive, it likely would be both an impractical and unprecedented extension of judicial power to assume that habeas corpus would be available at the moment the prisoner is taken into custody. If and when habeas corpus jurisdiction applies, as it does in these cases, then proper deference can be accorded to reasonable procedures for screening and initial detention under lawful and proper conditions of confinement and treatment for a reasonable period of time. Domestic exigencies, furthermore, might also impose such onerous burdens on the Government that here, too, the Judicial Branch would be required to devise sensible rules for staying habeas corpus proceedings until the Government can comply with its requirements in a responsible way. Here, as is true with detainees apprehended abroad, a relevant consideration in determining the courts' role is whether there are suitable alternative processes in place to protect against the arbitrary exercise of governmental power.

The cases before us, however, do not involve detainees who have been held for a short period of time while awaiting their CSRT determinations. . . . In some of these cases six years have elapsed without the judicial oversight that habeas corpus or an adequate substitute demands. And there has been no showing that the Executive faces such onerous burdens that it cannot respond to habeas corpus actions. To require these detainees to complete DTA review before proceeding with their habeas corpus actions would be to require additional months, if not years, of delay. The first DTA review applications were filed over a year ago, but no decisions on the merits have been issued. While some delay in fashioning new procedures is unavoidable, the costs of delay can no longer be borne by those who are held in custody. The detainees in these cases are entitled to a prompt habeas corpus hearing.

Our decision today holds only that the petitioners before us are entitled to seek the writ; that the DTA review procedures are an inadequate substitute for habeas corpus; and that the petitioners in these cases need not exhaust the review procedures in the Court of Appeals before proceeding with their habeas actions in the District Court. The only law we identify as unconstitutional is MCA §7. Accordingly, both the DTA and the CSRT process remain intact. Our holding with regard to exhaustion should not be read to imply that a habeas court should intervene the moment an enemy combatant steps foot in a territory where the writ runs. The Executive is entitled to a reasonable period of time to determine a detainee's status before a court entertains that detainee's habeas corpus petition. . . .

Although we hold that the DTA is not an adequate and effective substitute for habeas corpus, it does not follow that a habeas corpus court may disregard the dangers the detention in these cases was intended to prevent. . . . Certain accommodations can be made to reduce the burden habeas corpus proceedings will place on the military without impermissibly diluting the protections of the writ. . . .

[One] of Congress' reasons for vesting exclusive jurisdiction in the Court of Appeals, perhaps, was to avoid the widespread dissemination of classified information. The Government has raised similar concerns here and elsewhere. We make no attempt to anticipate all of the evidentiary and access-to-counsel issues that will arise during the course of the detainees' habeas corpus proceedings. We recognize, however, that the Government has a legitimate interest in protecting sources and methods of intelligence gathering; and we expect that the District Court will use its discretion to accommodate this interest to the greatest extent possible.

These and the other remaining questions are within the expertise and competence of the District Court to address in the first instance. . . .

In considering both the procedural and substantive standards used to impose detention to prevent acts of terrorism, proper deference must be accorded to the political branches. *See* United States v. Curtiss-Wright Export Corp., 299 U.S. 304, 320 (1936). Unlike the President and some designated Members of Congress, neither the Members of this Court nor most federal judges begin the day with briefings that may describe new and serious threats to our Nation and its people. The law must accord the Executive substantial authority to apprehend and detain those who pose a real danger to our security.

Officials charged with daily operational responsibility for our security may consider a judicial discourse on the history of the Habeas Corpus Act of 1679 and like matters to be far removed from the Nation's present, urgent concerns. Established legal doctrine, however, must be consulted for its teaching. Remote in time it may be; irrelevant to the present it is not. Security depends upon a sophisticated intelligence apparatus and the ability of our Armed Forces to act and to interdict. There are further considerations, however. Security subsists, too, in fidelity to freedom's first principles. Chief among these are freedom from arbitrary and unlawful restraint and the personal liberty that is secured by adherence to the separation of powers. It is from these principles that the judicial authority to consider petitions for habeas corpus relief derives. . . .

Because our Nation's past military conflicts have been of limited duration, it has been possible to leave the outer boundaries of war powers undefined. If, as some fear, terrorism continues to pose dangerous threats to us for years to come, the Court might not have this luxury. This result is not inevitable, however. The political branches, consistent with their independent obligations to interpret and uphold the Constitution, can engage in a genuine debate about how best to preserve constitutional values while protecting the Nation from terrorism. . . .

CHIEF JUSTICE ROBERTS, with whom JUSTICE SCALIA, JUSTICE THOMAS, and JUSTICE ALITO join, dissenting.

Today the Court strikes down as inadequate the most generous set of procedural protections ever afforded aliens detained by this country as enemy combatants. The political branches crafted these procedures amidst an ongoing military conflict, after much careful investigation and thorough debate. The Court rejects them today out of hand, without bothering to say what due process rights the detainees possess, without explaining how the statute fails to vindicate those rights, and before a single petitioner has even attempted to avail himself of the law's operation. And to what effect? The majority merely replaces a review system designed by the people's representatives with a set of shapeless procedures to be defined by federal courts at some future date. One cannot help but think, after surveying the modest practical results of the majority's ambitious opinion, that this decision is not really about the detainees at all, but about control of federal policy regarding enemy combatants.

The majority is adamant that the Guantanamo detainees are entitled to the protections of habeas corpus — its opinion begins by deciding that question. I regard the issue as a difficult one, primarily because of the unique and unusual jurisdictional status of Guantanamo Bay. I nonetheless agree with Justice Scalia's analysis of our precedents and the pertinent history of the writ, and accordingly join his dissent. The important point for me, however, is that the Court should have resolved these cases on other grounds. Habeas is most fundamentally a procedural right, a mechanism for contesting the legality of executive detention. The critical threshold question in these cases, prior to any inquiry about the writ's scope, is whether the system the political branches designed protects whatever rights the detainees may possess. If so, there is no need for any additional process, whether called "habeas" or something else.

Congress entrusted that threshold question in the first instance to the Court of Appeals for the District of Columbia Circuit, as the Constitution surely allows Congress to do. But before the D.C. Circuit has addressed the issue, the Court cashiers the statute, and without answering this critical threshold question itself. The Court does eventually get around to asking whether review under the DTA is, as the Court frames it, an "adequate substitute" for habeas, but even then its opinion fails to determine what rights the detainees possess and whether the DTA system satisfies them. The majority instead compares the undefined DTA process to an equally undefined habeas right — one that is to be given shape only in the future by district courts on a case-by-case basis. This whole approach is misguided.

It is also fruitless. How the detainees' claims will be decided now that the DTA is gone is anybody's guess. But the habeas process the Court mandates will most likely end up looking a lot like the DTA system it replaces, as the district court judges shaping it will have to reconcile review of the prisoners' detention with the undoubted need to protect the American people from the terrorist threat — precisely the challenge Congress undertook in drafting the DTA. All that today's opinion has done is shift responsibility for those sensitive foreign policy and national security decisions from the elected branches to the Federal Judiciary. . . .

The Court acknowledges that "the ordinary course" would be not to decide the constitutionality of the DTA at this stage, but abandons that "ordinary course" in light of the "gravity" of the constitutional issues presented and the prospect of additional delay. It is, however, precisely when the issues presented are grave that adherence to the ordinary course is most important. A principle applied only when unimportant is not much of a principle at all, and charges of judicial activism are most effectively rebutted when courts can fairly argue they are following normal practices.

The Court is also concerned that requiring petitioners to pursue "DTA review before proceeding with their habeas corpus actions" could involve additional delay. The nature of the habeas remedy the Court instructs lower courts to craft on remand, however, is far more unsettled than the process Congress provided in the DTA. There is no reason to suppose that review according to procedures the Federal Judiciary will design, case by case, will proceed any faster than the DTA process petitioners disdained. . . .

The majority's overreaching is particularly egregious given the weakness of its objections to the DTA. Simply put, the Court's opinion fails on its own terms. The majority strikes down the statute because it is not an "adequate substitute" for habeas review, but fails to show what rights the detainees have that cannot be vindicated by the DTA system.

Because the central purpose of habeas corpus is to test the legality of executive detention, the writ requires most fundamentally an Article III court able to hear the prisoner's claims and, when necessary, order release. Beyond that, the process a given prisoner is entitled to receive depends on the circumstances and the rights of the prisoner. After much hemming and hawing, the majority appears to concede that the DTA provides an Article III court competent to order release. The only issue in dispute is the process the Guantanamo prisoners are entitled to use to test the legality of their detention. *Hamdi* concluded that American citizens detained as enemy combatants are entitled to only limited process, and that much of that process could be supplied by a military tribunal, with review to follow in an Article III court. That is precisely the system we have here. It is adequate to vindicate whatever due process rights petitioners may have. . . .

[Chief Justice Roberts reviews the procedures in the CSRTs, and the provisions in the DTA for appeal to the D.C. Circuit, and concludes that "[a]ll told the DTA provides the prisoners held at Guantanamo Bay adequate opportunity to contest the bases of their detentions, which is all habeas corpus need allow."]

Despite these guarantees, the Court finds the DTA system an inadequate habeas substitute, for one central reason: Detainees are unable to introduce at the appeal stage exculpatory evidence discovered after the conclusion of their CSRT proceedings. The Court hints darkly that the DTA may suffer from other infirmities, but it does not bother to name them, making a response a bit difficult. As it stands, I can only assume the Court regards the supposed defect it did identify as the gravest of the lot.

If this is the most the Court can muster, the ice beneath its feet is thin indeed. As noted, the CSRT procedures provide ample opportunity for detainees to introduce exculpatory evidence — whether documentary in nature or from live witnesses — before the military tribunals. And if their ability to introduce such evidence is denied contrary to the Constitution or laws of the United States, the D.C. Circuit has the authority to say so on review.

. . . While the majority is correct that the DTA does not contemplate the introduction of "newly discovered" evidence before the Court of Appeals, petitioners and the Solicitor General agree that the DTA does permit the D.C. Circuit to remand a detainee's case for a new CSRT determination. In the event a detainee alleges that he has obtained new and persuasive exculpatory evidence that would have been considered by the tribunal below had it only been available, the D.C. Circuit could readily remand the case to the tribunal to allow that body to consider the evidence in the first instance. The Court of Appeals could later review any new or reinstated decision in light of the supplemented record. . . .

The Court's hand wringing over the DTA's treatment of later-discovered exculpatory evidence is the most it has to show after a roving search for constitutionally problematic scenarios. But "[t]he delicate power of pronouncing an Act of Congress unconstitutional," we have said, "is not to be exercised with reference to hypothetical cases thus imagined." United States v. Raines, 362 U.S. 17, 22 (1960). . . . The Court's second criterion for an adequate substitute is the "power to order the conditional release of an individual unlawfully detained." As the Court basically admits, the DTA can be read to permit the D.C. Circuit to order release in light of our traditional principles of construing statutes to avoid difficult constitutional issues, when reasonably possible. . . .

The basis for the Court's [conclusion that the DTA does not provide an adequate substitute for habeas] is summed up in the following sentence near the end of its opinion: "To hold that the detainees at Guantanamo may, under the DTA, challenge the President's legal authority to detain them, contest the CSRT's findings of fact, supplement the record on review with newly discovered or previously unavailable evidence, and request an order of release would come close to reinstating the §2241 habeas corpus process Congress sought to deny them." In other words, any interpretation of the statute that would make it an adequate substitute for habeas must be rejected, because Congress could not possibly have intended to enact an adequate substitute for habeas. The Court could have saved itself a lot of trouble if it had simply announced this Catch-22 approach at the beginning rather than the end of its opinion. . . .

JUSTICE SCALIA, with whom THE CHIEF JUSTICE, JUSTICE THOMAS, and JUSTICE ALITO join, dissenting. . . .

The writ of habeas corpus does not, and never has, run in favor of aliens abroad; the Suspension Clause thus has no application, and the Court's intervention in this military matter is entirely *ultra vires*. . . .

The Court purports to derive from our precedents a "functional" test for the extraterritorial reach of the writ, which shows that the Military Commissions Act unconstitutionally restricts the scope of habeas. That is remarkable because the most pertinent of those precedents, Johnson v. Eisentrager, 339 U.S. 763 (1950), conclusively establishes the opposite. . . .

There is simply no support for the Court's assertion that constitutional rights extend to aliens held outside U.S. sovereign territory, and *Eisentrager* could not be clearer that the privilege of habeas corpus does not extend to aliens abroad. By blatantly distorting *Eisentrager*, the Court avoids the difficulty of explaining why it should be overruled. The rule that aliens abroad are not constitutionally entitled to habeas corpus has not proved unworkable in practice; if anything, it is the Court's "functional" test that does not (and never will) provide clear guidance for the future. *Eisentrager* forms a coherent whole with the accepted proposition that aliens abroad have no substantive rights under our Constitution. Since it was announced, no relevant factual premises have changed. It has engendered considerable reliance on the part of our military. And, as the Court acknowledges, text and history do not clearly compel a contrary ruling. It is a sad day for the rule of law when such an important constitutional precedent is discarded without an *apologia,* much less an apology.

What drives today's decision is neither the meaning of the Suspension Clause, nor the principles of our precedents, but rather an inflated notion of judicial supremacy. The Court says that if the extraterritorial applicability of the Suspension Clause turned on formal notions of sovereignty, "it would be possible for the political branches to govern without legal constraint" in areas beyond the sovereign territory of the United States. That cannot be, the Court says, because it is the duty of this Court to say what the law is. It would be difficult to imagine a more question-begging analysis. . . . Our power "to say what the law is" is circumscribed by the limits of our statutorily and constitutionally conferred jurisdiction. And that is precisely the question in these cases: whether the Constitution confers habeas jurisdiction on federal courts to decide petitioners' claims. It is both irrational and arrogant to say that the answer must be yes, because otherwise we would not be supreme.

But so long as there are *some* places to which habeas does not run — so long as the Court's new "functional" test will not be satisfied *in every case* — then there will be circumstances in which "it would be possible for the political branches to govern without legal constraint." Or, to put it more impartially, areas in which the legal determinations of the *other* branches will be (shudder!) *supreme.* In other words, judicial supremacy is not really assured by the constitutional rule that the Court creates. The gap between rationale and rule leads me to conclude that the Court's ultimate, unexpressed goal is to preserve the power to review the confinement of enemy prisoners held by the Executive anywhere in the world. The "functional" test usefully evades the precedential landmine of *Eisentrager* but is so inherently subjective that it clears a wide path for the Court to traverse in the years to come.

Notes and Questions

1. The Court in *Boumediene* holds that §7 of the MCA is unconstitutional as applied to Guantanamo. Should the Court have reached this issue, or should it have remanded to the D.C. Circuit so that it could consider the issue in the first instance? The Court expresses concern that there already has been too much delay, but will its decision eliminate further delay? In considering whether the DTA procedures provided an adequate substitute for habeas review, should the Court have tried harder to interpret them in a way that would have preserved the constitutionality of §7? Is the Court's concern about subsequently discovered exculpatory evidence a sufficient reason to invalidate the statute?

2. The Supreme Court has rarely invalidated a war-related measure supported by both the President and Congress. (In *Ex parte Milligan,* a majority of the Court held that the military commission would have been unconstitutional even if authorized by Congress, but the Court found that the commission was not in fact authorized, and the decision was also issued after the Civil War was over.) Did the Court in *Boumediene* give sufficient deference to the political branches about what counterterrorism steps were necessary in the war on terrorism? Is the decision consistent with Justice Jackson's framework in *Youngstown,* which provides that "[w]hen the President acts pursuant to an express or implied authorization of Congress, his authority is at its maximum," and is "supported by the strongest of presumptions and the widest latitude of judicial interpretation"?

3. As noted in Section C, a number of the Justices in *Hamdan* emphasized that the Court's holding did not prevent the President from going to Congress and seeking the legislation he thought necessary. Does *Boumediene* undermine that message? Or was the invitation to go to Congress directed only at the establishment of military commissions rather than at the restriction on habeas corpus?

4. There is significant debate in *Boumediene* between the majority and Justice Scalia's dissent over the implications of Johnson v. Eisentrager, 339 U.S. 763 (1950), which is excerpted in Section A. In *Eisentrager*, German nationals were captured by the U.S. Army in China, tried and convicted in China by a U.S. military commission for violations of the laws of war, and imprisoned in Germany. In an opinion by Justice Jackson, the Supreme Court held that the detainees were not entitled to petition for habeas corpus relief in a U.S. court. The Court observed early in its opinion that: "We are cited to no instance where a court, in this or any other country where the writ is known, has issued it on behalf of an alien enemy who, at no relevant time and in no stage of his captivity, has been within its territorial jurisdiction. Nothing in the text of the Constitution extends such a right, nor does anything in our statutes." The Court subsequently noted that each petitioner in this case:

> (a) is an enemy alien; (b) has never been or resided in the United States; (c) was captured outside of our territory and there held in military custody as a prisoner of war; (d) was tried and convicted by a Military Commission sitting outside the United States; (e) for offenses against laws of war committed outside the United States; (f) and is at all times imprisoned outside the United States.

339 U.S. at 777. While acknowledging that aliens within the United States are entitled to the "privilege of litigation," the Court explained that this was because "permitting their presence in the country implied protection," whereas "[n]o such basis can be invoked here, for these prisoners at no relevant time were within any territory over which the United States is sovereign, and the scenes of their offense, their capture, their trial and their punishment were all beyond the territorial jurisdiction of any court of the United States." *Id.* at 777-78.

Does the majority in *Boumediene* persuasively distinguish *Eisentrager*? To what extent did the holding in *Eisentrager* turn on formal, as opposed to functional, considerations?

5. In a decision announced on the same day as *Boumediene,* the Supreme Court unanimously held that the habeas corpus *statute* extended to two U.S. citizens being held in Iraq by U.S. forces operating as part of a U.N. multinational force. *See* Munaf v. Geren, 553 U.S. 674 (2008). Building on the government's acknowledgment that the individuals were in the custody of U.S. forces operating under an American chain of command, the Court concluded that the individuals were "in custody under . . . the authority of the United States" for purposes of the habeas statute, 28 U.S.C. §2241(c)(1). The Court distinguished Hirota v. MacArthur, 338 U.S. 197 (1949), a short *per curiam* opinion that had disallowed habeas corpus petitions filed by Japanese citizens detained in Japan after World War II pursuant to the judgments of an international military tribunal. The Court stated in *Munaf* that "we decline to extend our holding in *Hirota* to preclude American citizens held overseas by American soldiers subject to a United States chain of command from filing habeas petitions." On the merits, however, the Court denied the petitioners the relief that they were seeking, which was an injunction to prevent the U.S. military from transferring them to Iraqi authorities for criminal prosecution.

Note that the habeas statute does not distinguish between U.S. citizens and foreign citizens held in U.S. custody. Does *Munaf* therefore mean that non-U.S. citizens held in Iraq by the U.S. military have a right to seek habeas relief in a U.S. court? Of potential relevance to this question, the Court noted in *Munaf* that "[t]hese cases concern American citizens while *Hirota* did not, and the Court has indicated that habeas jurisdiction can depend on citizenship."

6. In September 2017, militia forces in Syria captured a dual U.S.-Saudi national who allegedly had been fighting as part of ISIL. They turned him over to the U.S. military, which subsequently detained him in Iraq. The government did not release his name, so he was referred to as "John Doe." In October 2017, the ACLU filed a habeas corpus petition on Doe's behalf in federal district court. The court concluded that the ACLU had standing to sue, and it entered a preliminary injunction requiring the government to provide 72 hours' notice before transferring Doe to any other country. After the government informed the court of its intent to transfer Doe to a particular third country (which public documents referred to merely as "Country B," but which was thought by most observers to have been Saudi Arabia), the court enjoined the government from doing so. A divided panel of the U.S. Court of Appeals for the D.C. Circuit affirmed. *See* Doe v. Mattis, 889 F.3d 745 (D.C. Cir. 2018).

The appeals court first reasoned that this situation is not covered by the Supreme Court's decision in *Munaf v. Geren*. In this case, unlike in *Munaf*, the government was seeking to transfer Doe to a third country, and the court observed that "[w]e know of no instance — in the history of the United States — in which the government has taken an American citizen found in one foreign country and forcibly transferred her to the custody of another foreign country." The court did agree with the government that, "if Doe is an enemy combatant, the military can transfer him to the custody of Country B, a partner in the campaign against ISIL." But, relying heavily on *Hamdi v. Rumsfeld*, the court said that two conditions must be met for such a transfer: "(i) there must be legal authority for the Executive to wage war against the enemy, and (ii) there must be an opportunity for the citizen to contest the factual determination that he is an enemy combatant fighting on behalf of that enemy." The court noted that "[n]either the legal inquiry nor the factual inquiry has taken place in this case."

The dissent argued, by contrast, that the majority decision represented "a hazardous expansion of the judiciary's role in matters of war and diplomacy." *Hamdi* was not on point, contended the dissent, because it did not purport to "empower a court to enjoin our military from *transferring* a battlefield captive not facing extended detention," much less to "authorize injunctive relief where, as here, the receiving country has a facially strong interest in the captive and the Executive Branch has determined in good faith that he is an enemy combatant." The dissent also thought that the majority decision was inconsistent with the Supreme Court's reasoning in *Munaf*.

It was later learned that Doe's name is Abdulrahman Ahmad Alsheik. In October 2018, the government released Alsheik, transferred him to Bahrain, and canceled his U.S. passport. For discussion, see Robert Chesney, *Doe v. Mattis Ends with a Transfer and a Cancelled Passport: Lessons Learned*, Lawfare (Oct. 29, 2018). In June 2019, the D.C. Circuit released an unredacted version of its opinion in the case, which confirmed that Country B was Saudi Arabia.

7. A central question after *Boumediene* and *Munaf* is whether the *constitutional* right of habeas corpus extends to non-U.S. citizens in places other than Guantanamo, such as in Iraq or Afghanistan. The D.C. Circuit addressed this question in Maqaleh v. Gates, 605 F.3d 84 (D.C. Cir. 2010). The court there considered the constitutionality of §7 of the Military Commissions Act of 2006 as applied to three alien detainees held at Bagram Airfield Military Base in Afghanistan, at least two of whom were captured outside Afghanistan. The court rejected the constitutional challenge to the statute in this context based on a consideration of the three factors articulated by the Supreme Court in *Boumediene.*

The first factor was "the citizenship and status of the detainee and the adequacy of the process through which that status determination was made." The Court noted that while the detainees' alien status made them similarly situated to the detainees in *Boumediene* and *Eisentrager,* the adequacy of the process underlying their detention cut in favor of granting them habeas rights since they received less extensive process than the detainees in either *Eisentrager* or *Boumediene.* The court concluded that "examining only the first of the Supreme Court's three enumerated factors, petitioners have made a strong argument that the right to habeas relief and the Suspension Clause apply in Bagram as in Guantanamo." However, the court went on to reason that the second and third factors cut sharply against habeas relief and controlled the disposition of the case. The second factor is "the nature of the sites where apprehension and then detention took place." This factor, the court reasoned, "weighs heavily in favor" of upholding the preclusion of habeas because, whereas "[t]he United States has maintained its total control of Guantanamo Bay for over a century, even in the face of a hostile government maintaining *de jure* sovereignty over the property," at Bagram "there is no indication of any intent to occupy the base with permanence, nor is there hostility on the part of the 'host' country." The court further held "that the third factor, that is 'the practical obstacles inherent in resolving the prisoner's entitlement to the writ,' particularly when considered along with the second factor, weighs overwhelmingly in favor of the position of the United States." The reason for this conclusion was that Bagram and all of Afghanistan remain a "theater of war," making the government's arguments against habeas relief more powerful than in *Eisentrager* (which concerned detention in a place where active hostilities had ceased but many security threats remained) or *Boumediene* (which involved detention in a place where there were no active hostilities and few security threats from the enemy).

The court took note of the petitioners' concern that the government "chose the place of detention and might be able 'to evade judicial review of Executive detention decisions by transferring detainees into active conflict zones, thereby granting the Executive the power to switch the Constitution on or off at will,'" but insisted that "that is not what happened here" and stated that it did not need to make any "determination on the importance of this possibility, given that it remains only a possibility; its resolution can await a case in which the claim is a reality rather than a speculation." Finally, the court stated that a final factor that heavily supported its decision was "the fact that the detention is within the sovereign territory of another nation, which itself creates practical difficulties" because the court could not "say with certainty what the reaction of the Afghan government would be" if the court tried to assert habeas corpus jurisdiction to a detention in that country. (A year after *Maqaleh* was decided, the federal district court in D.C. reaffirmed that the constitutional right of habeas corpus does not extend to detainees held by the United States in Afghanistan, rejecting arguments that "new evidence" relating to U.S. detention policy in Afghanistan called for a different outcome. *See* Amanatullah v. Obama, 904 F. Supp. 2d 45 (D.D.C. 2012); Maqaleh v. Gates, 899 F. Supp. 2d 10 (D.D.C. 2012).)

Did the court in *Maqaleh* properly reconcile *Eisentrager* and *Boumediene*? Why should the ongoing military conflict in Afghanistan justify the denial of habeas rights to detainees picked up outside of Afghanistan and brought to Bagram? Why is the court so sure that the Executive did not send these detainees to Afghanistan in part to avoid judicial review? Should the Executive's reasons for sending a detainee to Afghanistan as opposed to Cuba matter to the constitutional scope of habeas corpus? Why or why not? If the Obama Administration transferred detainees from Guantanamo to Bagram, would they no longer be entitled to seek habeas corpus review? In answering these questions, keep in mind that in recent years the military has accorded Afghanistan detainees increasingly robust procedural protections, as well as improved detention facilities. *See generally* Jeffrey Bovarnick, *Detainee Review Boards in Afghanistan: From Strategic Liability to Legitimacy*, Army Lawyer (June 2010). Should this fact affect the availability of habeas review?

8. The Court in *Boumediene* merely held that the federal courts were open to hear habeas challenges by the detainees at Guantanamo and did not resolve any of the substantive issues concerning the scope of the government's detention authority. Instead, it indicated that these issues should be resolved in the first instance by the federal courts in D.C. (where the Guantanamo cases have been centralized). As discussed above in the notes to Section B, the district court and court of appeals in D.C. have since developed the law of detention on a case-by-case basis, and as of the fall of 2016, Congress had not provided any concrete additional guidance.

Is such a common law approach to the development of the law of detention in the war on terrorism desirable? Judge Brown on the D.C. Circuit thinks not, arguing:

> [I]t is important to ask whether a court-driven process is best suited to protecting both the rights of petitioners and the safety of our nation. The common law process depends on incrementalism and eventual correction, and it is most effective where there are a significant number of cases brought before a large set of courts, which in turn enjoy the luxury of time to work the doctrine supple. None of those factors exist in the Guantanamo context. The number of Guantanamo detainees is limited and the circumstances of their confinement are unique. The petitions they file, as the *Boumediene* Court counseled, are funneled through one federal district court and one appellate court. And, in the midst of an ongoing war, time to entertain a process of literal trial and error is not a luxury we have.
>
> While the common law process presents these difficulties, it is important to note that the Supreme Court has not foreclosed Congress from establishing new habeas standards in line with its *Boumediene* opinion. Having been repeatedly rebuffed [in its enactment of habeas restrictions in the DTA and MCA], Congress may understandably be reluctant to return to this arena to craft appropriate habeas standards as it has done for other habeas contexts in the past. But the circumstances that frustrate the judicial process are the same ones that make this situation particularly ripe for Congress to intervene pursuant to its policy expertise, democratic legitimacy, and oath to uphold and defend the Constitution. These cases present hard questions and hard choices, ones best faced directly. Judicial review, however, is just that: *re*-view, an indirect and necessarily backward looking process. And looking backward may not be enough in this new war. The saying that generals always fight the last war is familiar, but familiarity does not dull the maxim's sober warning. In identifying the shape of the law in response to the challenge of the current war, it is incumbent on the President, Congress, and the courts to realize that the saying's principle applies to us as well. Both the rule of law and the nation's safety will benefit from an honest assessment of the new challenges we face, one that will produce an appropriately calibrated response.

Al-Bihani v. Obama, 590 F.3d 866, 882 (D.C. Cir. 2010) (Brown, J., concurring). Do you agree with this assessment? Are there ways in which case-by-case development of the standards might actually be better than a legislative rule in this context?

Are some issues (such as the proper length of detention, for example) always best resolved by the political branches?

9. For articles on the significance of *Boumediene*, see, for example, Janet Cooper Alexander, *The Law-Free Zone and Back Again*, 2013 U. Ill. L. Rev. 551 (2013); Bahzer Azmy, *Executive Detention*, Boumediene, *and the New Common Law of Habeas*, 95 Iowa L. Rev. 445 (2010); *Developments in the Law—Extraterritoriality, Extraterritoriality and the War on Terror*, 124 Harv. L. Rev. 1258 (2011); Paul Diller, *Habeas and (Non-Delegation*, 77 U. Chi. L. Rev. 585 (2010); Richard H. Fallon, Jr., *The Supreme Court, Habeas Corpus, and the War on Terror: An Essay on Law and Political Science*, 110 Colum. L. Rev. 352 (2010); Aziz Z. Huq, *What Good Is Habeas?*, 26 Const. Comm. 385 (2010); Jules Lobel, *Separation of Powers, Individual Rights, and the Constitution Abroad*, 98 Iowa L. Rev. 1629 (2013); Daniel J. Meltzer, *Habeas Corpus, Suspension, and Guantanamo: The* Boumediene *Decision*, 2008 Sup. Ct. Rev. 1; and Gerald L. Neuman, *The Extraterritorial Constitution After* Boumediene v. Bush, 82 S. Cal. L. Rev. 259 (2009).

E. INTERROGATION AND TARGETED KILLING

This section considers two controversial issues in the war on terrorism that raise legal issues connected to the themes of this casebook: coercive interrogation (which may or may not amount to torture), and targeted killing of alleged terrorists.

1. Coercive Interrogation

Third Geneva Convention Relative to the Treatment of Prisoners of War

Entered into force Oct. 21, 1950; *Ratified by United States* Feb. 8, 1955

Article 3

In the case of armed conflict not of an international character occurring in the territory of one of the High Contracting Parties, each party to the conflict shall be bound to apply, as a minimum, the following provisions:

1. Persons taking no active part in the hostilities, including members of armed forces who have laid down their arms and those placed hors de combat by sickness, wounds, detention, or any other cause, shall in all circumstances be treated humanely, without any adverse distinction founded on race, colour, religion or faith, sex, birth or wealth, or any other similar criteria.

To this end the following acts are and shall remain prohibited at any time and in any place whatsoever with respect to the above-mentioned persons:

(a) Violence to life and person, in particular murder of all kinds, mutilation, cruel treatment and torture;

(b) Taking of hostages;

(c) Outrages upon personal dignity, in particular, humiliating and degrading treatment;

(d) The passing of sentences and the carrying out of executions without previous judgment pronounced by a regularly constituted court affording all the judicial guarantees which are recognized as indispensable by civilized peoples. . . .

Article 17

. . . No physical or mental torture, nor any other form of coercion, may be inflicted on prisoners of war to secure from them information of any kind whatever. Prisoners of war who refuse to answer may not be threatened, insulted, or exposed to any unpleasant or disadvantageous treatment of any kind.

Convention Against Torture and Other Cruel, Inhuman or Degrading Treatment or Punishment

Entered into force June 26, 1987; *Ratified by United States* Oct. 21, 1994

Article 1

1. For the purposes of this Convention, torture means any act by which severe pain or suffering, whether physical or mental, is intentionally inflicted on a person for such purposes as obtaining from him or a third person information or a confession, punishing him for an act he or a third person has committed or is suspected of having committed, or intimidating or coercing him or a third person, or for any reason based on discrimination of any kind, when such pain or suffering is inflicted by or at the instigation of or with the consent or acquiescence of a public official or other person acting in an official capacity. It does not include pain or suffering arising only from, inherent in or incidental to lawful sanctions. . . .

Article 2

1. Each State Party shall take effective legislative, administrative, judicial or other measures to prevent acts of torture in any territory under its jurisdiction.

2. No exceptional circumstances whatsoever, whether a state of war or a threat or war, internal political instability or any other public emergency, may be invoked as a justification of torture.

3. An order from a superior officer or a public authority may not be invoked as a justification of torture.

Article 3

1. No State Party shall expel, return ("refouler") or extradite a person to another State where there are substantial grounds for believing that he would be in danger of being subjected to torture.

2. For the purpose of determining whether there are such grounds, the competent authorities shall take into account all relevant considerations including, where applicable, the existence in the State concerned of a consistent pattern of gross, flagrant or mass violations of human rights.

Article 4

1. Each State Party shall ensure that all acts of torture are offences under its criminal law. The same shall apply to an attempt to commit torture and to an act by any person which constitutes complicity or participation in torture.

2. Each State Party shall make these offences punishable by appropriate penalties which take into account their grave nature. . . .

Article 16

1. Each State Party shall undertake to prevent in any territory under its jurisdiction other acts of cruel, inhuman or degrading treatment or punishment which do not amount to torture as defined in article 1, when such acts are committed by or at the instigation of or with the consent or acquiescence of a public official or other person acting in an official capacity. . . .

U.S. Reservations, Declarations, and Understandings, Convention Against Torture and Other Cruel, Inhuman or Degrading Treatment or Punishment, Cong. Rec. S17486-01

(Daily ed., Oct. 27, 1990)

I. The Senate's advice and consent is subject to the following reservations:

(1) That the United States considers itself bound by the obligation under article 16 to prevent "cruel, inhuman or degrading treatment or punishment," only insofar as the term "cruel, inhuman or degrading treatment or punishment" means the cruel, unusual and inhumane treatment or punishment prohibited by the Fifth, Eighth, and/or Fourteenth Amendments to the Constitution of the United States. . . .

II. The Senate's advice and consent is subject to the following understandings, which shall apply to the obligations of the United States under this Convention:

(1)(a) That with reference to article 1, the United States understands that, in order to constitute torture, an act must be specifically intended to inflict severe physical or mental pain or suffering and that mental pain or suffering refers to prolonged mental harm caused by or resulting from (1) the intentional infliction or threatened infliction of severe physical pain or suffering; (2) the administration or application, or threatened administration or application, of mind altering substances or other procedures calculated to disrupt profoundly the senses or the personality; (3) the threat of imminent death; or (4) the threat that another person will imminently be subjected to death, severe physical pain or suffering, or the administration or application of mind altering substances or other procedures calculated to disrupt profoundly the senses or personality. . . .

(2) That the United States understands the phrase, "where there are substantial grounds for believing that he would be in danger of being subjected to torture," as used in article 3 of the Convention, to mean "if it is more likely than not that he would be tortured." . . .

III. The Senate's advice and consent is subject to the following declarations:

(1) That the United States declares that the provisions of articles 1 through 16 of the Convention are not self-executing.

18 U.S.C. §2340

As used in this chapter —

(1) "torture" means an act committed by a person acting under the color of law specifically intended to inflict severe physical or mental pain or suffering (other than pain or suffering incidental to lawful sanctions) upon another person within his custody or physical control;

(2) "severe mental pain or suffering" means the prolonged mental harm caused by or resulting from —

(A) the intentional infliction or threatened infliction of severe physical pain or suffering;

(B) the administration or application, or threatened administration or application, of mind-altering substances or other procedures calculated to disrupt profoundly the senses or the personality;

(C) the threat of imminent death; or

(D) the threat that another person will imminently be subjected to death, severe physical pain or suffering, or the administration or application of mind-altering substances or other procedures calculated to disrupt profoundly the senses or personality; and

(3) "United States" means the several States of the United States, the District of Columbia, and the commonwealths, territories, and possessions of the United States.

18 U.S.C. §2340A

(a) Offense. — Whoever outside the United States commits or attempts to commit torture shall be fined under this title or imprisoned not more than 20 years, or both, and if death results to any person from conduct prohibited by this subsection, shall be punished by death or imprisoned for any term of years or for life.

(b) Jurisdiction. — There is jurisdiction over the activity prohibited in subsection (a) if —

(1) the alleged offender is a national of the United States; or

(2) the alleged offender is present in the United States, irrespective of the nationality of the victim or alleged offender.

(c) Conspiracy. — A person who conspires to commit an offense under this section shall be subject to the same penalties (other than the penalty of death) as the penalties prescribed for the offense, the commission of which was the object of the conspiracy.

Memorandum from Jay S. Bybee, Assistant Attorney General, Office of Legal Counsel, to Alberto R. Gonzales, Counsel to the President, "Standards of Conduct for Interrogation Under 18 U.S.C. §§2340-2340A"

At https://www.justice.gov/olc/file/886061/download (Aug. 1, 2002)

You have asked for our Office's views regarding the standards of conduct under the Convention Against Torture and Other Cruel, Inhuman and Degrading Treatment or Punishment as implemented by Sections 2340-2340A of title 18 of the United States Code. As we understand it, this question has arisen in the context of the conduct of interrogations outside of the United States. . . .

[The memorandum proceeds to interpret the meaning of the terms in §§2340 and 2340A. It concludes, among many other things, that the term "severe pain" in §2340 means "excruciating and agonizing" pain, or pain "equivalent in intensity to the pain accompanying serious physical injury, such as organ failure, impairment of bodily function, or even death." The memorandum then considers the constitutionality of the torture statute.]

Even if an interrogation method arguably were to violate Section 2340A, the statute would be unconstitutional if it impermissibly encroached on the President's constitutional power to conduct a military campaign. As Commander-in-Chief, the President has the constitutional authority to order interrogations of enemy combatants to gain intelligence information concerning the military plans of the enemy. The demands of the Commander-in-Chief power are especially pronounced in the middle of a war in which the nation has already suffered a direct attack. In such a case, the information gained from interrogations may prevent future attacks by foreign enemies. Any effort to apply Section 2340A in a manner that interferes with the President's direction of such core war matters as the detention and interrogation of enemy combatants thus would be unconstitutional. . . .

As the Supreme Court has recognized, and as we will explain further below, the President enjoys complete discretion in the exercise of his Commander-in-Chief authority and in conducting operations against hostile forces. Because both "[t]he executive power and the command of the military and naval forces is vested in the President," the Supreme Court has unanimously stated that it is "*the President alone*[]" who is constitutionally invested with the *entire charge of hostile operations.*" Hamilton v. Dillin, 88 U.S. (21 Wall.) 73, 87 (1874) (emphasis added). That authority is at its height in the middle of a war.

In light of the President's complete authority over the conduct of war, without a clear statement otherwise, we will not read a criminal statute as infringing on the President's ultimate authority in these areas. We have long recognized, and the Supreme Court has established a canon of statutory construction that statutes are to be construed in a manner that avoids constitutional difficulties so long as a reasonable alternative construction is available. This canon of construction applies especially where an act of Congress could be read to encroach upon powers constitutionally committed to a coordinate branch of government. . . .

In the area of foreign affairs, and war powers in particular, the avoidance canon has special force. *See, e.g.,* Dep't of Navy v. Egan, 484 U.S. 518, 530 (1988) ("unless Congress specifically has provided otherwise, courts traditionally have been reluctant to intrude upon the authority of the Executive in military and national security affairs."); Japan Whaling Ass'n v. American Cetacean Soc'y, 478 U.S. 221, 232-33 (1986) (construing federal statutes to avoid curtailment of traditional presidential prerogatives in foreign affairs). We do not lightly assume that Congress has acted to interfere with the President's constitutionally superior position as Chief Executive and Commander in Chief in the area of military operations. . . .

In order to respect the President's inherent constitutional authority to manage a military campaign against al Qaeda and its allies, Section 2340A must be construed as not applying to interrogations undertaken pursuant to his Commander-in-Chief authority. As our Office has consistently held during this Administration and previous Administrations, Congress lacks authority under Article I to set the terms and conditions under which the President may exercise his authority as Commander in Chief to control the conduct of operations during a war. . . . As we discuss below, the President's power to detain and interrogate enemy combatants arises out of his constitutional authority as Commander in Chief. A construction of Section 2340A that applied the provision to regulate the President's authority as Commander-in-Chief to determine the interrogation and treatment of enemy combatants would raise serious constitutional questions. Congress may no more regulate the President's ability to detain and interrogate enemy combatants than it may regulate his ability to direct troop movements on the battlefield. Accordingly, we would construe Section 2340A to avoid this constitutional difficulty, and conclude that it does not apply to the President's detention and interrogation of enemy combatants pursuant to his Commander-in-Chief authority. . . .

It could be argued that Congress enacted 18 U.S.C. §2340A with full knowledge and consideration of the President's Commander-in-Chief power, and that Congress intended to restrict his discretion in the interrogation of enemy combatants. Even were we to accept this argument, however, we conclude that the Department of Justice could not enforce Section 2340A against federal officials acting pursuant to the President's constitutional authority to wage a military campaign. . . .

The text, structure and history of the Constitution establish that the Founders entrusted the President with the primary responsibility, and therefore the power, to ensure the security of the United States in situations of grave and unforeseen emergencies. The decision to deploy military force in the defense of United States interests is expressly placed under Presidential authority by the Vesting Clause, U.S. Const. Art. I, §1, cl. 1, and by the Commander-in-Chief Clause, *id.*, §2, cl. 1. This Office has long understood the Commander-in-Chief Clause in particular as an affirmative grant of authority to the President. . . . The Framers understood the Clause as investing the President with the fullest range of power understood at the time of the ratification of the Constitution as belonging to the military commander. In addition, the structure of the Constitution demonstrates that any power traditionally understood as pertaining to the executive — which includes the conduct of warfare and the defense of the nation — unless expressly assigned in the Constitution to Congress, is vested in the President. Article II, Section 1 makes this clear by stating that the "executive Power shall be vested in a President of the United States of America." That sweeping grant vests in the President an unenumerated "executive power" and contrasts with the specific enumeration of the powers — those "herein" — granted to Congress in Article I. The implications of constitutional text and structure are confirmed by the practical consideration that national security decisions require the unity in purpose and energy in action that characterize the Presidency rather than Congress.

As the Supreme Court has recognized, the Commander-in-Chief power and the President's obligation to protect the nation imply the ancillary powers necessary to their successful exercise. "The first of the enumerated powers of the President is that he shall be Commander-in-Chief of the Army and Navy of the United States. And, of course, the grant of war power includes all that is necessary and proper for carrying those powers into execution." Johnson v. Eisentrager, 339 U.S. 763, 788 (1950). In wartime, it is for the President alone to decide what methods to use to best prevail against the enemy. The President's complete discretion in exercising the Commander-in-Chief power has been recognized by the courts. In the Prize Cases, 67 U.S. (2 Black) 635, 670 (1862), for example, the Court explained that whether the President "in fulfilling his duties as Commander in Chief" had appropriately responded to the rebellion of the southern states was a question "to be decided by him" and which the Court could not question, but must leave to "the political department of the Government to which this power was entrusted."

One of the core functions of the Commander in Chief is that of capturing detaining, and interrogating members of the enemy. . . . It is well settled that the President may seize and detain enemy combatants, at least for the duration of the conflict, and the laws of war make clear that prisoners may be interrogated for information concerning the enemy, its strength, and its plans. Numerous Presidents have ordered the capture, detention, and questioning of enemy combatants during virtually every major conflict in the Nation's history, including recent conflicts such as the Gulf, Vietnam, and Korean wars. Recognizing this authority, Congress has never attempted to restrict or interfere with the President's authority on this score.

Any effort by Congress to regulate the interrogation of battlefield combatants would violate the Constitution's sole vesting of the Commander-in-Chief authority in the President. There can be little doubt that intelligence operations, such as the detention and interrogation of enemy combatants and leaders, are both necessary and proper for the effective conduct of a military campaign. Indeed, such operations may be of more importance in a war with an international terrorist organization than one with the conventional armed forces of a nation-state, due to the former's emphasis on secret operations and surprise attacks against civilians. It may be the case that only successful interrogations can provide the information necessary to prevent the success of covert terrorist attacks upon the United States and its citizens. Congress can no more interfere with the President's conduct of the interrogation of enemy combatants than it can dictate strategic or tactical decisions on the battlefield. Just as statutes that order the President to conduct warfare in a certain manner or for specific goals would be unconstitutional, so too are laws that seek to prevent the President from gaining the intelligence he believes necessary to prevent attacks upon the United States. . . .

Memorandum from Daniel Levin, Acting Assistant Attorney General, Office of Legal Counsel, to James B. Comey, Deputy Attorney General, "Legal Standards Applicable Under 18 U.S.C. §§2340-2340A"

At https://www.aclu.org/files/torturefoia/released/082409/ olcremand/2004olc96.pdf (Dec. 30, 2004)

Torture is abhorrent both to American law and values and to international norms. This universal repudiation of torture is reflected in our criminal law, for example, 18 U.S.C. §§2340-2340A; international agreements, exemplified by the United Nations Convention Against Torture (the "CAT"); customary international law; centuries of Anglo-American law; and the longstanding policy of the United States, repeatedly and recently reaffirmed by the President.

This Office interpreted the federal criminal prohibition against torture . . . in *Standards of Conduct for Interrogation under 18 U.S.C. §§2340-2340A* (Aug. 1, 2002) ("August 2002 Memorandum"). The August 2002 Memorandum also addressed a number of issues beyond interpretation of those statutory provisions, including the President's Commander-in-Chief power, and various defenses that might be asserted to avoid potential liability under sections 2340-2340A.

Questions have since been raised, both by this Office and by others, about the appropriateness and relevance of the non-statutory discussion in the August 2002 Memorandum, and also about various aspects of the statutory analysis, in particular the statement that "severe" pain under the statute was limited to pain "equivalent in intensity to the pain accompanying serious physical injury, such as organ failure, impairment of bodily function, or even death." We decided to withdraw the August 2002 Memorandum, a decision you announced in June 2004. At that time, you directed this Office to prepare a replacement memorandum. Because of the importance of — and public interest in — these issues, you asked that this memorandum be prepared in a form that could be released to the public so that interested parties could understand our analysis of the statute.

This memorandum supersedes the August 2002 Memorandum in its entirety. Because the discussion in that memorandum concerning the President's Commander-in-Chief power and the potential defenses to liability was — and remains — unnecessary, it has been eliminated from the analysis that follows. Consideration of the bounds of any such authority would be inconsistent with the President's unequivocal directive that United States personnel not engage in torture....

[Among other things, the new memorandum rejects the 2002 memorandum's interpretation of the term "severe pain" in §2340A, reasoning that "[a]lthough there is some support for [the 'excruciating and agonizing' formulation] in the ratification history of the [Convention Against Torture]," a proposed express understanding to that effect was "criticized for setting too high a threshold of pain, S. Exec. Rep. No. 101-30 at 9, and was not adopted," and "[w]e are not aware of any evidence suggesting that the standard was raised in the statute and we do not believe that it was." The new memorandum also rejected the "organ failure" analogy as misplaced.]

Notes and Questions

1. Recall that on February 7, 2002, President Bush issued a memorandum (discussed in Section B above) that determined for the Executive Branch that Common Article 3 of the Geneva Conventions did not apply to Al Qaeda or Taliban detainees, which meant that the government did not think that Common Article 3's restrictions on interrogation applied to those detainees. One consequence of this decision was that from February 2002 until June 2006, when the Supreme Court in *Hamdan* held that Common Article 3 *did* apply to Al Qaeda detainees, the main legal prohibitions regulating interrogation of enemy combatants, from the U.S. government's perspective, were the Convention Against Torture and its implementing criminal statute, 18 U.S.C. §§2340-2340A.

2. The United States ratified the Torture Convention in 1994. Article 2 provides that each State Party "shall take effective legislative, administrative, judicial or other measures to prevent acts of torture in any territory under its jurisdiction," and Article 16 says that each State Party shall "undertake to prevent in any territory under its jurisdiction other acts of cruel, inhuman or degrading treatment or punishment which do not amount to torture as defined in article 1." What is the difference between torture on the one hand, and cruel, inhuman, or degrading treatment or punishment on the other? The answer, according to the Senate Foreign Relations Committee Report on the Torture Convention, is that torture is an "extreme form" of cruel, inhuman, or degrading treatment. S. Exec. Rep. No.

101-30, at 6 (1990); *see also* J. Herman Burgers & Hans Danelius, The United Nations Convention Against Torture: A Handbook on the Convention Against Torture and Other Cruel, Inhuman or Degrading Treatment or Punishment 80 (1988) (noting that Article 16 implies "that torture is the gravest form of [cruel, inhuman, or degrading] treatment [or] punishment").

Why is the obligation to prevent torture in Article 2 worded differently than the obligation to prevent cruel, inhuman, and degrading treatment in Article 16? Is the obligation under Article 2 stronger? Does the obligation under Article 16 require domestic implementing legislation? When the United States implemented the treaty in Sections 2340-2340A, it criminalized only torture and not cruel, inhuman, and degrading treatment. The Senate Report explains the reason for the different treatment of the two norms as follows: " 'Torture' is . . . distinguished from lesser forms of cruel, inhuman, or degrading treatment or punishment, which are to be deplored and prevented, but are not so universally and categorically condemned as to warrant the severe legal consequences that the Convention provides in the case of torture." S. Exec. Rep. No. 101-30, at 13.

3. Examine Article II(1)(A) of the United States' reservations, declarations, and understandings for the Torture Convention. Does this "understanding" narrow the United States' obligations under the treaty? Why would the United States impose a specific intent requirement not found in the treaty, clarify that "mental pain" refers to "prolonged mental harm," and add other narrowing interpretations to the treaty's prohibitions? Note that the limiting provisions of Article II(1)(A) are reflected in the domestic criminal statute.

4. In late April 2004, photographs of abuses by the U.S. military at the Abu Ghraib prison in Iraq became public, and a few weeks later, the Bybee memorandum excerpted above was leaked to the press. It later became known that in November 2002, the General Counsel of the Department of Defense had issued a memorandum (which had been withdrawn a month later) approving the use of stress positions, 30-day isolation, light deprivation, forced grooming, use of phobias, and "mild, non-injurious physical contact such as grabbing, poking in the chest with the finger, and light pushing," and stating that while other techniques (such as threats to the detainee or his family, the "use of a wet towel and dripping water to induce the misperception of suffocation," and exposure to cold weather) "may be legally available," their use was "not warranted at this time," in part because of the military's "tradition of restraint." In April 2004, a Department of Defense Working Group Report recommended the use of less aggressive interrogation techniques, and in September 2006, the Department of Defense issued a revised Army Field Manual on interrogation that cut back even further on permissible interrogation techniques for the military. It later was revealed, however, that the Central Intelligence Agency had a program of interrogation that used more aggressive techniques, including the use of "waterboarding" on three high-level members of Al Qaeda.

5. The Torture Convention and implementing criminal statute prohibit, among other things, an act under color of law that specifically intends to cause "severe physical pain." What does this latter term mean? What materials should an Executive Branch lawyer look to in interpreting the term "severe pain"? Should doctors be consulted? Is it useful to set forth a general and abstract interpretation of the meaning of "torture" without reference to the legality of particular techniques?

6. The August 1, 2002, memorandum proclaims an extraordinarily broad understanding of the President's exclusive Commander-in-Chief powers. Do the materials in Chapter 9 support this understanding? Why doesn't the memorandum consider the relevance of Congress's Article I military powers, as well as its powers under the Define and Punish Clause? Why doesn't it consider the relevance of *Youngstown*? Are the memorandum's assertions about presidential power consistent with the analysis in Justice Jackson's framework in that case? The memorandum claims that "[a]ny effort by Congress to regulate the interrogation of battlefield combatants would violate the Constitution's sole vesting of the Commander-in-Chief authority in the President." Does the analysis in the memorandum establish this claim? Does the memorandum conflate independent or inherent presidential authority with exclusive presidential authority? If the analysis in the memorandum were correct, what implications would it have for the constitutionality of the War Crimes Act, excerpted in Section C of Chapter 9?

Note that the December 2004 replacement memorandum declines to address the earlier memorandum's analysis of presidential power on the ground that such analysis was "unnecessary" because of the "President's unequivocal directive that United States personnel not engage in torture." If this is true, why did the first memorandum go into such great detail on the Commander-in-Chief override argument?

7. The August 2002 memorandum relies heavily on the canon of constitutional avoidance, pursuant to which courts construe statutes, where fairly possible, to avoid serious constitutional concerns. Does the memorandum properly apply the canon? Should Executive Branch lawyers even be invoking the canon in this context? For an argument counseling caution, see Trevor W. Morrison, *Constitutional Avoidance in the Executive Branch*, 106 Colum. L. Rev. 1189 (2006). Professor Morrison contends that the avoidance canon potentially serves two different values: it facilitates judicial deference to legislative majorities, and it furthers the underlying substantive legal norm in question (here, the Commander-in-Chief power). Morrison argues that the former value has no application to the Executive Branch, and that because executive officials have better access to and knowledge of statutory purpose than do the courts, some facially ambiguous texts may in fact be entirely unambiguous to the executive interpreter, in which case the avoidance canon has no role to play. Is this latter point true of the interpretation of the torture statute?

8. Article 16 of the Torture Convention requires the United States to undertake to prevent cruel, inhuman, or degrading treatment or punishment "in any territory under its jurisdiction." The United States attached a reservation to Article 16 stating that the United States was bound by the Article "only insofar as the term 'cruel, inhuman or degrading treatment or punishment' means the cruel, unusual and inhumane treatment or punishment prohibited by the Fifth, Eighth, and/or Fourteenth Amendments to the Constitution of the United States." Relying on these terms, the government after September 11 apparently concluded that Article 16's obligation did not apply outside U.S. sovereign territory, either because such territory was not under its jurisdiction, or because the Fifth and Fourteenth Amendments, the scope of which are incorporated into the treaty obligation by reference, do not have extraterritorial application.

In 2014, the Obama Administration reversed course, accepting that Article 16 had some extraterritorial application. In a statement to the Committee Against Torture, Acting State Department Legal Adviser Mary McLeod announced:

> In an effort to ensure that we are doing the utmost to prevent torture and cruel treatment, the United States has carefully reviewed the extent to which certain obligations under the Convention apply beyond the sovereign territory of the United States and is prepared to clarify its views on these issues for the Committee today. In brief, we understand that where the text of the Convention provides that obligations apply to

a State Party in "any territory under its jurisdiction," such obligations, including the obligations in Articles 2 and 16 to prevent torture and cruel, inhuman or degrading treatment or punishment, extend to certain areas beyond the sovereign territory of the State Party, and more specifically to "all places that the State Party controls as a governmental authority." We have determined that the United States currently exercises such control at the U.S. Naval Station at Guantanamo Bay, Cuba, and with respect to U.S. registered ships and aircraft.

Opening Statement of Mary E. McLeod, Acting Legal Adviser, U.S. Department of State, Before the Committee Against Torture (Nov. 12-13, 2014), *at* https://geneva.usmission.gov/2014/11/12/acting-legal-adviser-mcleod-u-s-affirms-torture-is-prohibited-at-all-times-in-all-places/. Under the Obama Administration's interpretation of Article 16, what other places might constitute areas that the United States "controls as a governmental authority" outside the United States? What about detention facilities that the United States controls in a foreign territory during an armed conflict?

9. In December 2005, Congress enacted the Detainee Treatment Act, §1003 of which provides: "No individual in the custody or under the physical control of the United States Government, regardless of nationality or physical location, shall be subject to cruel, inhuman, or degrading treatment or punishment." President Bush issued the following statement when he signed the bill containing this provision into law:

> The executive branch shall construe [the provisions in the Act relating to detainees] in a manner consistent with the constitutional authority of the President to supervise the unitary executive branch and as Commander in Chief and consistent with the constitutional limitations on the judicial power, which will assist in achieving the shared objective of the Congress and the President . . . of protecting the American people from further terrorist attacks.

President's Statement on Signing of H.R. 2863 (Dec. 30, 2005), *at* https://georgewbush-whitehouse.archives.gov/news/releases/2005/12/20051230-8.html.

10. As noted above, in June 2006, the Supreme Court held in *Hamdan* that Common Article 3 of the Geneva Conventions governed the conflict between the United States and Al Qaeda and its affiliates. This holding had at least two consequences for interrogation. First, it meant that the interrogation provisions in Common Article 3 applied to the conflict. Second, it meant that the War Crimes Act, 18 U.S.C. §2441, which criminalizes violations of Common Article 3, also applied to the conflict. A few weeks after the *Hamdan* decision, the Department of Defense announced that Common Article 3 of the Geneva Conventions "applies as a matter of law to the conflict with Al Qaeda," and ordered full compliance with its standards. *See* Memorandum from Gordon England, Deputy Secretary of Defense, to Secretaries of the Military Departments et al., "Application of Common Article 3 of the Geneva Conventions to the Treatment of Detainees in the Department of Defense" (July 7, 2006), available at https://fas.org/sgp/othergov/dod/geneva070606.pdf. Three months after the decision in *Hamdan*, Congress enacted the Military Commissions Act (MCA) of 2006, which, among other things, amended the War Crimes Act to define criminal violations of Common Article 3, and to exclude from criminal punishment under the Act violations of Common Article 3's prohibition on "outrages upon personal dignity, in particular humiliating and degrading treatment," as well as violations of Common Article 3's guarantee of a "regularly constituted court." *See* MCA of 2006, §6(b). The MCA of 2006 also allowed evidence obtained by coercion (but not evidence obtained by torture) to be introduced into military commission trials if (among other things) it was reliable. If the evidence was obtained by a method that was cruel, inhuman, or degrading, it was allowed only if it was obtained before the Detainee Treatment Act extended the prohibition on cruel, inhuman, and degrading treatment abroad in December 2005. *See* 10 U.S.C. §948r(c). The subsequent MCA of 2009 completely disallowed the admission of evidence obtained by cruel, inhuman, or degrading treatment. *See* 2009 Act, §948r.

11. Before September 11, 2001, the government began a program of "rendition" that involved the apprehension of alleged terrorists in one country and the transportation of them to another country for questioning, trial, and punishment. *See* Richard Clarke, Against All Enemies 143-44 (2004). According to press reports, this program grew extensively after September 11, and expanded to include renditions for purposes of interrogation alone. The head of the CIA's Bin Laden station and the person who created and ran the original rendition program has said that Clinton-era White House officials "knew that taking detainees to Egypt or elsewhere might yield treatment not consonant with United States legal practice." Michael Scheuer, *A Fine Rendition*, N.Y. Times (Mar. 11, 2005). And, according to press reports, the treatment of rendered detainees was worse after September 11. What is the relevance of the Torture Convention and the torture statute to renditions? Article 3(1) of the Torture Convention states: "No State Party shall expel, return (refouler) or extradite a person to another State where there are substantial grounds for believing that he would be in danger of being subjected to torture." But Article II(2) of the United States' reservations, declarations, and understandings contains an understanding that interprets Article 3(1) to mean "if it is more likely than not that he would be tortured." Does this mean that the United States can, based on its view of the Torture Convention, render someone to another country if it believes that there is a 49 percent chance that he will be tortured? Note that the criminal torture statute does not mention renditions, but it does make it a crime to engage in conspiracy to commit torture. Might this provision be implicated by the practice of renditions?

12. On January 22, 2009, President Obama issued Executive Order 13,491, titled "Ensuring Lawful Interrogations." The executive order prohibited all interrogation techniques for all terrorist detainees, including those in CIA custody, except for the relatively benign ones found in the Army Field Manual. It also ordered the CIA to close its secret "detention facilities," although it defined the term "detention facility" not to refer to facilities "used only to hold people on a short-term, transitory basis." With respect to rendition, the administration maintained the prerogative to engage in the practice, while pledging that it would not render suspects to other countries for purposes of torture. An Obama Administration task force later announced that the administration would "strengthen[] U.S. procedures" for evaluating "assurances from the receiving country" that it would not engage in torture and for monitoring claims about torture. *See* Press Release, Department of Justice, Special Task Force on Interrogations and Transfer Policies Issues its Recommendations to the President (Aug. 24, 2009), *available at* https://www.justice.gov/opa/pr/special-task-force-interrogations-and-transfer-policies-issues-its-recommendations-president. In §1045 of the National Defense Authorization Act of 2016, Congress built on many of these Executive Branch directives. Section 1045 applies the Army Field Manual standard to the interrogation of any person in the custody or control of *any* agency of the federal government. It also mandates that the Army Field Manual be reviewed at least every three years to ensure that its interrogation approaches are lawful, and requires the International Committee of the Red Cross be provided timely notification of and access to detainees taken into U.S. custody.

13. Some detainees have attempted to sue U.S. government officials for alleged torture and other mistreatment. These suits have sometimes been brought under the Alien Tort Statute (ATS), which is discussed in detail in Chapter 7. The ATS provides that, "The district courts shall have original jurisdiction of any civil action by an alien for a tort only, committed in violation of the law of nations or a treaty of the United States." In Rasul v. Bush, 542 U.S. 466 (2004), the Supreme Court indicated that federal courts would have jurisdiction to hear ATS claims brought by detainees at Guantanamo. *See id.* at 484. ATS claims against U.S. officials have generally been unsuccessful, however, because of (among other things) official and governmental immunity doctrines. *See, e.g.,* Ali v. Rumsfeld, 649 F.3d 762 (D.C. Cir. 2011); Rasul v. Myers, 563 F.3d 527 (D.C. Cir. 2009). Some detainees have also sought relief directly under the U.S. Constitution, pursuant to "*Bivens* actions," though, again, with little success. The Supreme Court has said that *Bivens* actions are not appropriate where there are "special factors counseling hesitation" by the judiciary, *see, e.g.,* Correctional Services Corp. v. Malesko, 534 U.S. 61, 68 (2001), and courts have generally declined to recognize *Bivens* claims relating to the war on terrorism. *See* Vance v. Rumsfeld, 701 F.3d 193 (7th Cir. 2012) (en banc) (disallowing civilian U.S. citizens allegedly tortured by U.S. forces in Iraq to bring *Bivens* action); Arar v. Ashcroft, 585 F.3d 559 (2d Cir. 2008) (en banc) (disallowing *Bivens* action by foreign citizen for rendition to a third country that allegedly resulted in torture).

A significant hurdle for detainees suing U.S. government officials for alleged mistreatment is the doctrine of qualified immunity. "Qualified immunity gives government officials breathing room to make reasonable but mistaken judgments about open legal questions." Ashcroft v. al-Kidd, 563 U.S. 731, 743 (2011). It "shields federal and state officials from money damages unless a plaintiff pleads facts showing (1) that the official violated a statutory or constitutional right, and (2) that the right was 'clearly established' at the time of the challenged conduct." *Id.* at 735. Under the second prong of this test, a "Government official's conduct violates clearly established law when, at the time of the challenged conduct, '[t]he contours of [a] right [are] sufficiently clear' that every 'reasonable official would have understood that what he is doing violates that right.'" *Id.* at 741. The Court does "not require a case directly on point, but existing precedent must have placed the statutory or constitutional question beyond debate." *Id.*

An important decision applying these principles in the context of the war on terrorism is Padilla v. Yoo, 678 F.3d 748 (9th Cir. 2012). In that case, Jose Padilla (whose status and fate are discussed in Section B) sued John Yoo, who, as Deputy Assistant Attorney General in the Bush Administration, wrote legal memoranda and helped craft policies that Padilla alleged violated his constitutional rights. The Ninth Circuit dismissed the case on qualified immunity grounds for two reasons. First, because Yoo offered his legal advice before the Supreme Court's decision in *Hamdi*, at a time when *Ex parte Quirin* was the leading precedent, it was not "beyond debate" during Yoo's tenure that Padilla was, as he alleged, "entitled to the same constitutional protections as an ordinary convicted prisoner or accused criminal." Second, Padilla's allegations of detention and interrogation abuses — which included prolonged isolation, light deprivation, extreme variations in temperature, sleep adjustment, threats of severe physical abuse, death threats, administration of psychotropic drugs, and various stress positions — were not clearly unlawful at the relevant time. The court reasoned that "although it has been clearly established for decades that torture of an American citizen violates the Constitution, and we assume without deciding that Padilla's alleged treatment rose to the level of torture, that such treatment was torture was not clearly established in 2001-03." *Id.* at 750.

14. Another barrier to suits challenging the government's actions in the War on Terror is the "state secrets privilege," a common law evidentiary privilege that allows the government to prevent discovery of military and state secrets. In order for the privilege to apply, "the court must be satisfied that under the particular circumstances of the case, 'there is a reasonable danger that compulsion of the evidence will expose military matters which, in the interest of national security, should not be divulged.'" United States v. Reynolds, 345 U.S. 1, 10 (1953). "Where there is a strong showing of necessity, the claim of privilege should not be lightly accepted, but even the most compelling necessity cannot overcome the claim of privilege if the court is ultimately satisfied that military secrets are at stake." *Id.* at 11. Application of the privilege can have three effects:

> First, by invoking the privilege over particular evidence, the evidence is completely removed from the case. The plaintiff's case then goes forward based on evidence not covered by the privilege. . . . If, after further proceedings, the plaintiff cannot prove the *prima facie* elements of her claim with nonprivileged evidence, then the court may dismiss her claim as it would with any plaintiff who cannot prove her case. Alternatively, "if the privilege deprives the *defendant* of information that would otherwise give the defendant a valid defense to the claim, then the court may grant summary judgment to the defendant." . . . Finally, notwithstanding the plaintiff's ability to produce non-privileged evidence, if the "very subject matter of the action" is a state secret, then the court should dismiss the plaintiff's action based solely on the invocation of the state secrets privilege.

Kasza v. Browner, 133 F.3d 1159, 1166-67 (9th Cir. 1997).

In El-Masri v. United States, 479 F.3d 296 (4th Cir. 2007), the court applied the state secrets privilege as a basis for dismissing a civil suit brought by an individual who had allegedly been detained and interrogated by the CIA as part of its "extraordinary rendition" program in the war on terrorism. The court reasoned that even though the CIA's rendition program had been reported in the press, the plaintiff's suit would require evidence showing "how the CIA organizes, staffs, and supervises its most sensitive intelligence operations," evidence that would implicate privileged state secrets.

When running for President, Barack Obama criticized the Bush Administration's reliance on the state secrets privilege. The Obama Administration invoked the privilege, however, in a number of cases concerning surveillance and rendition of terrorist suspects. In September 2009, Obama's Attorney General, Eric Holder, issued a memorandum setting forth "Policies and Procedures Governing Invocation of the State Secrets Privilege." The memorandum states that the Justice Department's policy is to invoke the privilege "only to the extent necessary to protect against the risk of significant harm to national security," and that it will not invoke the privilege "in order to: (i) conceal violations of the law, inefficiency, or administrative error; (ii) prevent embarrassment to a person, organization, or agency of the United States government; (iii) restrain competition; or (iv) prevent or delay the release of information the release of which would not reasonably be expected to cause significant harm to national security." The memorandum also provides that the privilege will be invoked only after recommendation from an Assistant Attorney General, an evaluation by a State Secrets Review Committee (consisting of senior Department of

Justice officials), and approval by the Attorney General. How, if at all, will these policies change the actual practice of state secret assertions by the Executive Branch? For a skeptical perspective, with evidence from Obama Administration practice following the promulgation of this policy, see Glenn Greenwald, *Obama's Latest Use of "Secrecy" to Shield Presidential Lawbreaking*, at https://www.salon.com/2009/11/01/state_secrets_4/. (Nov. 1, 2009). Why was Obama more supportive of the state secrets privilege as President than he was as senator?

In an en banc decision, the Ninth Circuit upheld the Obama Administration's invocation of the state secrets privilege in Mohamed v. Jeppesen Dataplan, Inc., 614 F.3d 1070 (9th Cir. 2010). The case involved a suit against a government contractor, Jeppesen Dataplan, relating to Jeppesen's alleged involvement in the government's program of "extraordinary rendition," whereby terrorist suspects were turned over to other countries for interrogation. The court said that it had "thoroughly and critically reviewed the government's public and classified declarations and [was] convinced that at least some of the matters it [sought] to protect from disclosure in this litigation [were] valid state secrets." It then explained its decision to direct dismissal of the plaintiff's claims:

> We reach this conclusion because all seven of plaintiffs' claims, even if taken as true, describe Jeppesen as providing logistical support in a broad, complex process, certain aspects of which, the government has persuaded us, are absolutely protected by the state secrets privilege. Notwithstanding that some information about that process has become public, Jeppesen's alleged role and its attendant liability cannot be isolated from aspects that are secret and protected. Because the facts underlying plaintiffs' claims are so infused with these secrets, *any* plausible effort by Jeppesen to defend against them would create an unjustifiable risk of revealing state secrets, even if plaintiffs could make a prima facie case on one or more claims with nonprivileged evidence.

Id. at 1088. Five judges dissented, arguing that the court should have "remand[ed] to the district court to determine whether Plaintiffs can establish the prima facie elements of their claims or whether Jeppesen could defend against those claims without resort to state secrets evidence."

For additional discussion of the privilege, see Robert M. Chesney, *State Secrets and the Limits of National Security Litigation*, 75 Geo. Wash. L. Rev. 1249 (2007); Laura K. Donohue, *The Shadow of State Secrets*, 159 U. Pa. L. Rev. 77 (2010); Amanda Frost, *The State Secrets Privilege and Separation of Powers*, 75 Fordham L. Rev. 1931 (2007); and D. A. Jeremy Telman, *Our Very Privileged Executive: Why the Judiciary Can (and Should) Fix the State Secrets Privilege*, 80 Temp. L. Rev. 499 (2007). For discussion of an invocation of the state secrets privilege by the Trump Administration, see James Risen, Sheri Fink, and Charlie Savage, *State Secrets Privilege Invoked to Block Testimony in C.I.A. Torture Case*, N.Y. Times (Mar. 8, 2017).

15. There is an enormous literature on the issues discussed in this subsection. Representative examples include Jack Goldsmith, The Terror Presidency: Law and Judgment Inside the Bush Administration (2007); Karen J. Greenberg, ed., The Torture Debate in America (2005); Sanford Levinson, ed., Torture: A Collection (2006); Benjamin Wittes, Law and the Long War: The Future of Justice in the Age of Terror ch. 7 (2008); Harold Hongju Koh, *Can the President Be Torturer in Chief?*, 81 Ind. L.J. 1145 (2005); David J. Luban, *Liberalism, Torture, and the Ticking Time Bomb*, 91 Va. L. Rev. 1425 (2005); Catherine Powell, *Tinkering with Torture in the Aftermath of* Hamdan: *Testing the Relationship Between Internationalism and Constitutionalism*, 40 N.Y.U. J. Int'l L. & Pol'y 723 (2008); Michael D. Ramsey, *Torturing Executive Power*, 93

Geo. L.J. 1213 (2005); Leila Nadya Sadat, *Ghost Prisoners and Black Sites: Extraordinary Rendition Under International Law,* 37 Case W. Res. J. Int'l L. 309 (2006); Louis Michael Seidman, *Torture's Truth,* 72 U. Chi. L. Rev. 881 (2005); and David Weissbrodt & Amy Bergquist, *Extraordinary Rendition and the Torture Convention,* 46 Va. J. Int'l L. 585 (2006). For a description of U.S. interrogation policy before September 11, showing that "[t]here has been a remarkable continuity between interrogation policies that prevailed after 9/11 and those employed in previous eras of heightened security threats," see William Ranney Levi, Note, *Interrogation's Law,* 118 Yale L.J. 1434, 1439 (2009).

2. Targeted Killing

Al-Aulaqi v. Obama

727 F. Supp. 2d 1 (D.D.C. 2010)

[The plaintiff, a Yemeni citizen, claimed that the U.S. government had unlawfully authorized the targeted killing of his son, Anwar Al-Aulaqi, a dual U.S.-Yemeni citizen who was hiding in Yemen. The United States government alleged that Al-Aulaqi had an operational role in Al Qaeda in the Arabian Peninsula (AQAP), a terrorist organization affiliated with Al Qaeda. Al-Aulaqi allegedly recruited individuals to join AQAP, facilitated terrorist training camps in Yemen, and was the operational leader of planned attacks on the United States, including the failed "underwear bomb" attack by Umar Farouk Abdulmutallab, in December 2009, on a plane traveling to Detroit, Michigan. The plaintiff brought suit against the President, the Secretary of Defense, and the Director of the CIA. He alleged that his son was on a U.S.-government-approved "kill list," and that the use of lethal force against his son without charge, trial, or conviction would violate both the Constitution and international law. As the court noted, the plaintiff sought both declaratory and injunctive relief:

> First, he requests a declaration that, outside of armed conflict, the Constitution prohibits defendants "from carrying out the targeted killing of U.S. citizens," including Anwar Al-Aulaqi, "except in circumstances in which they present a concrete, specific, and imminent threat to life or physical safety, and there are no means other than lethal force that could reasonably be employed to neutralize the threat." Second, plaintiff requests a declaration that, outside of armed conflict, "treaty and customary international law" prohibit the targeted killing of all individuals — regardless of their citizenship — except in those same, limited circumstances. Third, plaintiff requests a preliminary injunction prohibiting defendants from intentionally killing Anwar Al-Aulaqi "unless he presents a concrete, specific, and imminent threat to life or physical safety, and there are no means other than lethal force that could reasonably be employed to neutralize the threat." Finally, plaintiff seeks an injunction ordering defendants to disclose the criteria that the United States uses to determine whether a U.S. citizen will be targeted for killing.]

JOHN D. BATES, DISTRICT JUDGE. . . .

This is a unique and extraordinary case. Both the threshold and merits issues present fundamental questions of separation of powers involving the proper role of the courts in our constitutional structure. Leading Supreme Court decisions from Marbury v. Madison, 5 U.S. (1 Cranch) 137 (1803), through Justice Jackson's celebrated concurrence in Youngstown Sheet & Tube Co. v. Sawyer, 343 U.S. 579 (1952), to the more recent cases dealing with Guantanamo detainees have been invoked to guide this Court's deliberations. Vital considerations of national security and of military and foreign affairs (and hence potentially of state secrets) are at play.

Stark, and perplexing, questions readily come to mind, including the following: How is it that judicial approval is required when the United States decides to target a U.S. citizen overseas for electronic surveillance, but that, according to defendants, judicial scrutiny is prohibited when the United States decides to target a U.S. citizen overseas for death? Can a U.S. citizen — himself or through another — use the U.S. judicial system to vindicate his constitutional rights while simultaneously evading U.S. law enforcement authorities, calling for "jihad against the West," and engaging in operational planning for an organization that has already carried out numerous terrorist attacks against the United States? Can the Executive order the assassination of a U.S. citizen without first affording him any form of judicial process whatsoever, based on the mere assertion that he is a dangerous member of a terrorist organization? How can the courts, as plaintiff proposes, make real-time assessments of the nature and severity of alleged threats to national security, determine the imminence of those threats, weigh the benefits and costs of possible diplomatic and military responses, and ultimately decide whether, and under what circumstances, the use of military force against such threats is justified? When would it ever make sense for the United States to disclose in advance to the "target" of contemplated military action the precise standards under which it will take that military action? And how does the evolving AQAP relate to core Al Qaeda for purposes of assessing the legality of targeting AQAP (or its principals) under the September 18, 2001 Authorization for the Use of Military Force?

These and other legal and policy questions posed by this case are controversial and of great public interest. "Unfortunately, however, no matter how interesting and no matter how important this case may be . . . we cannot address it unless we have jurisdiction." United States v. White, 743 F.2d 488, 492 (7th Cir. 1984). Before reaching the merits of plaintiff's claims, then, this Court must decide whether plaintiff is the proper person to bring the constitutional and statutory challenges he asserts, and whether plaintiff's challenges, as framed, state claims within the ambit of the Judiciary to resolve. These jurisdictional issues pose "distinct and separate limitation[s], so that either the absence of standing or the presence of a political question suffices to prevent the power of the federal judiciary from being invoked by the complaining party." Schlesinger v. Reservists Comm. to Stop the War, 418 U.S. 208, 215 (1974). . . .

[The court first concludes that the plaintiff lacks standing to sue because, among other things, the plaintiff had "failed to provide an adequate explanation for his son's inability to appear on his own behalf." The court then considers the defendants' political question argument for dismissal.]

Defendants argue that even if plaintiff has standing to bring his constitutional claims or states a cognizable claim . . . his claims should still be dismissed because they raise non-justiciable political questions. . . .

Judicial resolution of the "particular questions" posed by plaintiff in this case would require this Court to decide: (1) the precise nature and extent of Anwar Al-Aulaqi's affiliation with AQAP; (2) whether AQAP and al Qaeda are so closely linked that the defendants' targeted killing of Anwar Al-Aulaqi in Yemen would come within the United States's current armed conflict with al Qaeda; (3) whether (assuming plaintiff's proffered legal standard applies) Anwar Al-Aulaqi's alleged terrorist activity renders him a "concrete, specific, and imminent threat to life or physical safety"; and (4) whether there are "means short of lethal force" that the United States could "reasonably" employ to address any threat that Anwar Al-Aulaqi poses to U.S. national security interests. Such determinations, in turn, would require this Court, in defendants' view, to understand and assess "the capabilities of the [alleged] terrorist operative to carry out a threatened attack, what response would be sufficient to address that threat, possible diplomatic considerations that may bear on such responses, the vulnerability of potential targets that the [alleged] terrorist[] may strike, the availability of military and non-military options, and the risks to military and nonmilitary personnel in attempting application of non-lethal force." Viewed through these prisms, it becomes clear that plaintiff's claims pose precisely the types of complex policy questions that the D.C. Circuit has historically held non-justiciable under the political question doctrine. . . .

[T]here are no judicially manageable standards by which courts can endeavor to assess the President's interpretation of military intelligence and his resulting decision — based on that intelligence — whether to use military force against a terrorist target overseas. Nor are there judicially manageable standards by which courts may determine the nature and magnitude of the national security threat posed by a particular individual. . . .

The type of relief that plaintiff seeks only underscores the impropriety of judicial review here. Plaintiff requests both a declaration setting forth the standard under which the United States can select individuals for targeted killing as well as an injunction prohibiting defendants from intentionally killing Anwar Al-Aulaqi unless he meets that standard — i.e., unless he "presents a concrete, specific, and imminent threat to life or physical safety, and there are no means other than lethal force that could reasonably be employed to neutralize the threat." Yet plaintiff concedes that the " 'imminence' requirement" of his proffered legal standard would render any "real-time judicial review" of targeting decisions "infeasible," and he therefore urges this Court to issue his requested preliminary injunction and then enforce the injunction "through an after-the-fact contempt motion or an after-the-fact damages action." But as the D.C. Circuit has explained, "[i]t is not the role of judges to second-guess, with the benefit of hindsight, another branch's determination that the interests of the United States call for military action." El-Shifa Pharm. Indus. Co. v. United States, 607 F.3d 836, 844 (D.C. Cir. 2010) (en banc). Such military determinations are textually committed to the political branches. Moreover, any post hoc judicial assessment as to the propriety of the Executive's decision to employ military force abroad "would be anathema to . . . separation of powers" principles. See El-Shifa, 607 F.3d at 845. The first, fourth, and sixth Baker factors thus all militate against judicial review of plaintiffs' claims, since there is a "textually demonstrable constitutional commitment" of the United States's decision to employ military force to coordinate political departments (Congress and the Executive), and any after-the-fact judicial review of the Executive's decision to employ military force abroad would reveal a "lack of respect due coordinate branches of government" and create "the potentiality of embarrassment of multifarious pronouncements by various departments on one question." Baker v. Carr, 369 U.S. 196, 217 (1962). . . .

[T]here is inadequate reason to conclude that Anwar Al-Aulaqi's U.S. citizenship — standing alone — renders the political question doctrine inapplicable to plaintiff's claims. Plaintiff cites two contexts in which courts have found claims asserting violations of U.S. citizens' constitutional rights to be justiciable despite the fact that those claims implicate grave national security and foreign policy concerns. Courts have been willing to entertain habeas petitions from U.S. citizens detained by the United States as enemy combatants, see, e.g., Hamdi v. Rumsfeld, 542 U.S. 507, 509 (2004), and they have also heard claims from U.S. citizens alleging unconstitutional takings of their property by the U.S. military abroad, see, e.g., Ramirez de Arellano v. Weinberger, 745 F.2d 1500, 1511-12 (D.C. Cir. 1984) (en banc). But habeas petitions and takings claims are both much more amenable to judicial resolution than the claims raised by plaintiff in this case.

Courts have been willing to hear habeas petitions (from both U.S. citizens and aliens) because "the Constitution specifically contemplates a judicial role" for claims by individuals challenging their detention by the Executive. While the Suspension Clause reflects a "textually demonstrable commitment" of habeas corpus claims to the Judiciary, see *Baker*, 369 U.S. at 217, there is no "constitutional commitment to the courts for review of a military decision to launch a missile at a foreign target," *El-Shifa*, 607 F.3d at 849. Indeed, such military decisions are textually committed not to the Judiciary, but to the political branches. Moreover, the resolution of habeas petitions does not require expertise beyond the purview of the Judiciary. Although plaintiff is correct to point out that habeas cases involving Guantanamo detainees often involve judicial scrutiny of highly sensitive military and intelligence information, such information is only used to determine whether "the United States has unjustly deprived an American citizen of liberty through acts it has already taken." Abu Ali v. Ashcroft, 350 F. Supp. 2d 28, 65 (D.D.C. 2004). These post hoc determinations are "precisely what courts are accustomed to assessing." *Abu Ali*, 350 F. Supp. 2d at 65. But courts are certainly not accustomed to assessing claims like those raised by plaintiff here, which seek to prevent future U.S. military action in the name of national security against specifically contemplated targets by the imposition of judicially-prescribed legal standards enforced through "after-the-fact contempt motion[s]" or "after-the-fact damages action[s]." Hence, the *Baker* factors dictate a different outcome for plaintiff's claims than for habeas petitions filed by detainees at Guantanamo Bay.

Plaintiff's claims are also fundamentally distinct from those in which U.S. citizens have been permitted to sue the United States for alleged unconstitutional takings of their property by the U.S. military abroad. In *Ramirez de Arellano*, the D.C. Circuit declined to dismiss as non-justiciable the claims brought by U.S. citizens who asserted that the U.S. military had unlawfully expropriated their cattle ranch in Honduras in violation of the Fifth Amendment. The D.C. Circuit, ruling en banc, explained that the plaintiffs' claims did not constitute a challenge "to the United States military presence in Honduras" but instead were "narrowly focused on the lawfulness of the United States defendants' occupation and use of the plaintiffs' cattle ranch." *Id.* at 1512. Once the court characterized the case as a land dispute between the plaintiffs and the U.S. government, it had little difficulty concluding that "adjudication of the defendants' constitutional authority to occupy and use the plaintiffs' property" did not require "expertise beyond the capacity of the Judiciary" or "unquestioning adherence to a political decision by the Executive." . . .

Unlike *Ramirez*, the questions posed in this case do require both "expertise beyond the capacity of the Judiciary" and the need for "unquestioning adherence to a political decision by the Executive." Here, plaintiff asks the Judiciary to limit the circumstances under which the United States may employ lethal force against an individual abroad whom the Executive has determined "plays an operational role in AQAP planning terrorist attacks against the United States." The injunctive and declaratory relief sought by plaintiff would thus be vastly more intrusive upon the powers of the Executive than the relief sought in *Ramirez*, where the court was only called upon to adjudicate "the defendants' constitutional authority to occupy and use the plaintiffs' property." *Ramirez*, 745 F.2d at 1513. Moreover, although resolution of the plaintiffs' claims in *Ramirez* only required "interpretations of the Constitution and of federal statutes," which are "quintessential tasks of the federal Judiciary," see *id.*, resolution of the claims in this case would require assessment of "strategic choices directing the nation's foreign affairs [that] are constitutionally committed to the political branches," *El-Shifa*, 607 F.3d at 843.

Contrary to plaintiff's assertion, in holding that the political question doctrine bars plaintiff's claims, this Court does not hold that the Executive possesses "unreviewable authority to order the assassination of any American whom he labels an enemy of the state." Rather, the Court only concludes that it lacks the capacity to determine whether a specific individual in hiding overseas, whom the Director of National Intelligence has stated is an "operational" member of AQAP, presents such a threat to national security that the United States may authorize the use of lethal force against him. . . . Because decision-making in the realm of military and foreign affairs is textually committed to the political branches, and because courts are functionally ill-equipped to make the types of complex policy judgments that would be required to adjudicate the merits of plaintiff's claims, the Court finds that the political question doctrine bars judicial resolution of this case.

Speech by Harold Hongju Koh, State Department Legal Adviser, at the Annual Meeting of the American Society of International Law

(Mar. 25, 2010), at http://2009-2017.state.gov/s/l/releases/remarks/139119.htm

. . . [A]s a matter of international law, the United States is in an armed conflict with al-Qaeda, as well as the Taliban and associated forces, in response to the horrific 9/11 attacks, and may use force consistent with its inherent right to self-defense under international law. As a matter of domestic law, Congress authorized the use of all necessary and appropriate force through the 2001 Authorization for Use of Military Force (AUMF). These domestic and international legal authorities continue to this day.

As recent events have shown, al-Qaeda has not abandoned its intent to attack the United States, and indeed continues to attack us. Thus, in this ongoing armed conflict, the United States has the authority under international law, and the responsibility to its citizens, to use force, including lethal force, to defend itself, including by targeting persons such as high-level al-Qaeda leaders who are planning attacks. As you know, this is a conflict with an organized terrorist enemy that does not have conventional forces, but that plans and executes its attacks against us and our allies while hiding among civilian populations. That behavior simultaneously makes the application of international law more difficult and more critical for the protection of innocent civilians. . . .

In U.S. operations against al-Qaeda and its associated forces — including lethal operations conducted with the use of unmanned aerial vehicles — great care is taken to adhere to these principles in both planning and execution, to ensure that only legitimate objectives are targeted and that collateral damage is kept to a minimum.

Recently, a number of legal objections have been raised against U.S. targeting practices. While today is obviously not the occasion for a detailed legal opinion responding to each of these objections, let me briefly address four:

First, some have suggested that the *very act of targeting* a particular leader of an enemy force in an armed conflict must violate the laws of war. But individuals who are part of such an armed group are belligerents and, therefore, lawful targets under international law. During World War II, for example, American aviators tracked and shot down the airplane carrying the architect of the Japanese attack on Pearl Harbor, who was also the leader of enemy forces in the Battle of Midway. This was a lawful operation then, and would be if conducted today. Indeed, targeting particular individuals serves to narrow the focus when force is employed and to avoid broader harm to civilians and civilian objects.

Second, some have challenged *the very use of advanced weapons systems*, such as unmanned aerial vehicles, for lethal operations. But the rules that govern targeting do not turn on the type of weapon system used, and there is no prohibition under the laws of war on the use of technologically advanced weapons systems in armed conflict — such as pilotless aircraft or so-called smart bombs — so long as they are employed in conformity with applicable laws of war. Indeed, using such advanced technologies can ensure both that the best intelligence is available for planning operations, and that civilian casualties are minimized in carrying out such operations.

Third, some have argued that the use of lethal force against specific individuals fails to provide adequate process and thus constitutes *unlawful extrajudicial killing*. But a state that is engaged in an armed conflict or in legitimate self-defense is not required to provide targets with legal process before the state may use lethal force. Our procedures and practices for identifying lawful targets are extremely robust, and advanced technologies have helped to make our targeting even more precise. In my experience, the principles of distinction and proportionality that the United States applies are not just recited at meetings. They are implemented rigorously throughout the planning and execution of lethal operations to ensure that such operations are conducted in accordance with all applicable law.

Fourth and finally, some have argued that our targeting practices violate *domestic law*, in particular, the long-standing *domestic ban on assassinations*. But under domestic law, the use of lawful weapons systems — consistent with the applicable laws of war — for precision targeting of specific high-level belligerent leaders when acting in self-defense or during an armed conflict is not unlawful, and hence does not constitute "assassination."

Speech by Attorney General Eric Holder, at Northwestern University School of Law

(Mar. 5, 2012), at https://www.justice.gov/opa/speech/attorney-general-eric-holder-speaks-northwestern-university-school-law

. . . Now, it is an unfortunate but undeniable fact that some of the threats we face come from a small number of United States citizens who have decided to commit violent attacks against their own country from abroad. Based on generations-old legal principles and Supreme Court decisions handed down during World War II, as well as during this current conflict, it's clear that United States citizenship alone does not make such individuals immune from being targeted. But it does mean that the government must take into account all relevant constitutional considerations with respect to United States citizens — even those who are leading efforts to kill innocent Americans. Of these, the most relevant is the Fifth Amendment's Due Process Clause, which says that the government may not deprive a citizen of his or her life without due process of law.

The Supreme Court has made clear that the Due Process Clause does not impose one-size-fits-all requirements, but instead mandates procedural safeguards that depend on specific circumstances. In cases arising under the Due Process Clause — including in a case involving a U.S. citizen captured in the conflict against al Qaeda — the Court has applied a balancing approach, weighing the private interest that will be affected against the interest the government is trying to protect, and the burdens the government would face in providing additional process. Where national security operations are at stake, due process takes into account the realities of combat.

Here, the interests on both sides of the scale are extraordinarily weighty. An individual's interest in making sure that the government does not target him erroneously could not be more significant. Yet it is imperative for the government to counter threats posed by senior operational leaders of al Qaeda, and to protect the innocent people whose lives could be lost in their attacks.

Any decision to use lethal force against a United States citizen — even one intent on murdering Americans and who has become an operational leader of al-Qaeda in a foreign land — is among the gravest that government leaders can face. The American people can be — and deserve to be — assured that actions taken in their defense are consistent with their values and their laws. So, although I cannot discuss or confirm any particular program or operation, I believe it is important to explain these legal principles publicly.

Let me be clear: an operation using lethal force in a foreign country, targeted against a U.S. citizen who is a senior operational leader of al Qaeda or associated forces, and who is actively engaged in planning to kill Americans, would be lawful at least in the following circumstances: First, the U.S. government has determined, after a thorough and careful review, that the individual poses an imminent threat of violent attack against the United States; second, capture is not feasible; and third, the operation would be conducted in a manner consistent with applicable law of war principles.

The evaluation of whether an individual presents an "imminent threat" incorporates considerations of the relevant window of opportunity to act, the possible harm that missing the window would cause to civilians, and the likelihood of heading off future disastrous attacks against the United States. As we learned on 9/11, al Qaeda has demonstrated the ability to strike with little or no notice — and to cause devastating casualties. Its leaders are continually planning attacks against the United States, and they do not behave like a traditional military — wearing uniforms, carrying arms openly, or massing forces in preparation for an attack. Given these facts, the Constitution does not require the President to delay action until some theoretical end-stage of planning — when the precise time, place, and manner of an attack become clear. Such a requirement would create an unacceptably high risk that our efforts would fail, and that Americans would be killed.

Whether the capture of a U.S. citizen terrorist is feasible is a fact-specific, and potentially time-sensitive, question. It may depend on, among other things, whether capture can be accomplished in the window of time available to prevent an attack and without undue risk to civilians or to U.S. personnel. Given the nature of how terrorists act and where they tend to hide, it may not always be feasible to capture a United States citizen terrorist who presents an imminent threat of violent attack. In that case, our government has the clear authority to defend the United States with lethal force.

Of course, any such use of lethal force by the United States will comply with the four fundamental law of war principles governing the use of force. The principle of necessity requires that the target have definite military value. The principle of distinction requires that only lawful targets — such as combatants, civilians directly participating in hostilities, and military objectives — may be targeted intentionally. Under the principle of proportionality, the anticipated collateral damage must not be excessive in relation to the anticipated military advantage. Finally, the principle of humanity requires us to use weapons that will not inflict unnecessary suffering. . . .

Some have argued that the President is required to get permission from a federal court before taking action against a United States citizen who is a senior operational leader of al Qaeda or associated forces. This is simply not accurate. "Due process" and "judicial process" are not one and the same, particularly when it comes to national security. The Constitution guarantees due process, not judicial process.

The conduct and management of national security operations are core functions of the Executive Branch, as courts have recognized throughout our history. Military and civilian officials must often make real-time decisions that balance the need to act, the existence of alternative options, the possibility of collateral damage, and other judgments — all of which depend on expertise and immediate access to information that only the Executive Branch may possess in real time. The Constitution's guarantee of due process is ironclad, and it is essential — but, as a recent court decision makes clear, it does not require judicial approval before the President may use force abroad against a senior operational leader of a foreign terrorist organization with which the United States is at war — even if that individual happens to be a U.S. citizen.

That is not to say that the Executive Branch has — or should ever have — the ability to target any such individuals without robust oversight. Which is why, in keeping with the law and our constitutional system of checks and balances, the Executive Branch regularly informs the appropriate members of Congress about our counterterrorism activities, including the legal framework, and would of course follow the same practice where lethal force is used against United States citizens. . . .

Notes and Questions

1. A United Nations Special Rapporteur has defined "targeted killing" as the "intentional, premeditated, and deliberate use of lethal force, by States or their agents acting under colour of law, or by an organized armed group in armed conflict, against a specific individual who is not in the physical custody of the perpetrator." Report of the Special Rapporteur on Extrajudicial, Summary, or Arbitrary Executions, U.N. Doc. A/HRC/14/24/Add.6 (May 28, 2010). In general, there is nothing unusual about killing members of enemy forces in an "armed conflict," which is the modern term for war. In an armed conflict, the soldiers of one party to the conflict are permitted to target "military objectives" of the other party to the conflict, including its soldiers. In World War II, for example, U.S. soldiers used guns and tanks and bombs from aircrafts to kill German soldiers and destroy German military installations in Germany and in other countries. The international laws of war (also known as the *jus in bello*) require soldiers in an armed conflict to distinguish themselves from civilians (by, for example, wearing a uniform or some distinguishing mark). They further require those firing weapons in war to distinguish between military and civilian objectives and to target only the former. And they also ban attacks on military targets that produce civilian damage that is excessive in relation to the military advantage gained. Soldiers who target enemy soldiers in compliance with these and related laws of war possess a "combatant's privilege," which means that international law gives them immunity from prosecution for murder or other crimes associated with the attack. *See generally* Gary D. Solis, The Law of Armed Conflict: International Humanitarian Law in War (2d ed. 2016); Yoram Dinstein, The Conduct of Hostilities Under the Law of International Armed Conflict (3d ed. 2016). As the Koh excerpt indicates, targeting particular individuals in an armed conflict is in general deemed lawful so long as *jus in bello* rules are followed. Several elements of the war against Al Qaeda and its affiliates nonetheless raise novel issues for the traditional wartime practice of targeting enemy soldiers.

2. One novelty in the "war on terrorism" is the technology that is sometimes used in targeting, in particular the deployment of unmanned aerial vehicles (UAVs), also known as "drones," for targeted killings. A UAV is an aerial vehicle that can maintain flight for up to 24 hours and that is piloted remotely, often thousands of miles from the battlefield. Traditionally, UAVs were used only for surveillance, but beginning in 2001, the United States began to deploy and fire guided missiles from them, first in Afghanistan, and then in other locations around the world, including Pakistan, Yemen, and Somalia. In 2008, the Bush Administration stepped up the use of UAVs for lethal attacks, and the Obama and Trump Administrations increased their use even further. The fact that the missiles from UAVs are fired remotely by persons far away from the battlefield does not by itself affect the legality of UAV targeting killing operations. The same is true to some degree of cruise missiles fired from submarines or from a far-away military base, and other forms of firing at a distance. But the way that UAVs are deployed in this conflict, the unusual nature of the conflict, the identity of the persons firing the weapons, and the identity and geographical location of the persons targeted raise a number of complex and to some degree novel questions under domestic and international law.

3. To understand the general legal issues before exploring the complexities, consider the use of UAVs to kill Al Qaeda members in Afghanistan, which raises both domestic and international legal issues.

On the domestic law front, the AUMF authorizes the President to use all necessary and appropriate "force" against Al Qaeda. As the plurality noted in *Hamdi*, the authorized force in the AUMF includes the fundamental incidents of waging war. Killing enemy soldiers is a fundamental incident of waging war. The government therefore argues that the AUMF authorizes the President and his subordinates to use military force against Al Qaeda forces, including its leadership, in Afghanistan. Such targeted killings, the government further argues, do not violate the assassination ban discussed in Section D of Chapter 9 because, as explained there, and as reiterated in the Koh excerpt, that ban does not extend to lawful killings of enemy soldiers during wartime. A possible alternative to the AUMF as a basis of authority for targeted killing is Article II of the Constitution. Recall from Chapter 9 that throughout U.S. history, presidents have used force abroad in the absence of congressional authorization pursuant to their Article II powers, and that one basis for doing so has been self-defense. So, for example, President Clinton's cruise missile attack on Al Qaeda training camps in Afghanistan and Somalia in response to the African embassy bombings, and his 1998 covert operation to capture or kill Bin Laden, were justified as an exercise of Article II powers of self-defense.

On the international law front, the first issue is whether the targeted killing complies with the *jus in bello* rules of distinction and proportionality described above in Note 1. When the U.S. military fires a missile from a UAV that targets an Al Qaeda soldier and that does not cause excessive collateral damage, the primary requirements of *jus in bello* are arguably satisfied. The next international law issue concerns the U.N. Charter. Article 2(4) prohibits one nation from using force "against the territorial integrity or political independence of any state," with three general exceptions. The first exception is that a nation can consent to uses of force within its territory. The second exception is that the U.N. Security Council can authorize a use of force, as it did, for example, in Libya in 2011. The third exception is that a nation can, under Article 51 of the Charter, use force in self-defense in response to an "armed attack" and, under some interpretations of the Charter or of related customary international law, in anticipation of imminent attacks. The U.S. invasion of Afghanistan in 2001 was initially justified as an exercise of self-defense under Article 51 of the Charter. The United States' continuing military activities in Afghanistan since the defeat of the Taliban and the creation of a transitional Afghan government in late 2001 have been conducted on the basis of consent.

4. Now consider how these relatively straightforward propositions of law become more complex with respect to the anticipated targeted killing at issue in the *Al-Aulaqi* case.

a. *Geographic Scope of the AUMF.* It is generally agreed that Congress in the AUMF authorized the President to use force in Afghanistan, the country from which Al Qaeda plotted the September 11 attacks. The United States has subsequently used force outside Afghanistan to target alleged terrorists under the AUMF in Pakistan, Iraq, Yemen, Syria, Somalia, and Libya. Does the AUMF authorize the use of force in Yemen and any other country in the world where Al Qaeda members may be found? Recall from Section B that the Bush and Obama Administrations asserted that the detention power under the AUMF is not limited to persons captured on the battlefields of Afghanistan. Does the same interpretation of the AUMF apply to targeted killings? Is there any implied geographic limitation on the "force" authorized by the AUMF? Does the AUMF provide the President with authority to target an Al Qaeda operative in Europe? In the United States? In *Al-Aulaqi*, does it matter to the AUMF analysis that many parts of Yemen are effectively beyond the control of the Yemeni government?

b. *Substantive Scope of the AUMF.* It is generally agreed that Congress in the AUMF intended to authorize the President to target Al Qaeda members. But Anwar Al-Aulaqi was not, technically, a member of Al Qaeda. He was, rather, a leader of Al Qaeda in the Arabian Peninsula (AQAP). AQAP is a terrorist organization created in 2009 out of the remnants of Al Qaeda organizations, but its ongoing ties to Al Qaeda leadership are — at least in the public record — uncertain. One indication of the uncertain relationship between Al Qaeda and AQAP is that the government, in its motion to dismiss in *Al-Aulaqi*, stated that it had "determined that AQAP is an organized armed group that is either part of al-Qaeda, *or* is an associated force, *or* cobelligerent, of al-Qaeda that has directed armed attacks against the United States in the non-international armed conflict between the United States and al-Qaeda that the Supreme Court recognized in Hamdan v. Rumsfeld" (emphasis added). The

Obama Administration also invoked the AUMF in its military strikes against members of the Al Shabaab terrorist organization in Somalia and the Khorasan Group in Syria — entities that are either members of or associated forces of Al Qaeda (the administration was not clear on this). Note also that the controversial extension of the AUMF to ISIL, described in Section B, was done in connection with air strikes against that terrorist organization, first in Iraq and then later in Syria and Libya. Does the AUMF properly authorize the use of targeted force against members of these groups? Recall that Congress, in the National Defense Authorization Act of 2012, expressly recognized *detention* authority under the AUMF, at least for "associated forces" of Al Qaeda that are "engaged in hostilities against the United States." But Congress has not expressly authorized the use of military force against "associated forces," or ISIL, and courts have weighed in on AUMF scope issues only in the context of detention. The extension of the AUMF beyond Al Qaeda and the Taliban thus technically rests entirely on the Executive's Branch's interpretation of the AUMF, albeit informed by what the other two branches have done in the detention context. In response to criticisms that the Obama Administration's legal interpretation of the AUMF conferred on the President overbroad authority to use force, the administration placed a restrictive policy and procedural overlay on these legal conclusions to guide counterterrorism targeting decisions outside areas of active hostilities (defined to be areas other than in Afghanistan, Iraq, and Syria). *See* U.S. Policy Standards and Procedures for the Use of Force in Counterterrorism Operations Outside the United States and Areas of Active Hostilities (May 23, 2013), at https://obamawhitehouse.archives.gov/the-press-office/2013/05/23/fact-sheet-us-policy-standards-and-procedures-use-force-counterterrorism; Procedures for Approving Direct Action Against Terrorist Targets Located Outside the United States and Areas of Active Hostilities (May 22, 2013), at https://www.aclu.org/other/presidential-policy-guidance. The Trump Administration reportedly lifted some of the Obama Administration's restrictions on targeted killings outside of areas of active hostilities. For example, the Trump Administration seems to have designated sections of Somalia and Yemen as areas of active hostilities to which the restrictions do not apply and to have allowed U.S. forces to target not only high-level militants but also foot-soldiers. Charlie Savage & Eric Schmitt, *Trump Poised to Drop Some Limits on Drone Strikes and Commando Raids*, N.Y. Times (Sept. 21, 2017). In March 2019, President Trump issued an executive order that ended a requirement, imposed by President Obama in 2016, of reporting the number of strikes undertaken by the United States against terrorist targets outside areas of active hostilities and assessing the combatant and non-combatant deaths resulting from those strikes. *See* Executive Order on Revocation of Reporting Requirement (Mar. 6, 2019), at https://www.whitehouse.gov/presidential-actions/executive-order-revocation-reporting-requirement/.

   c. *Domestic Legal Bases for Targeted Killing.* The U.S. government argued in its motion to dismiss in *Al-Aulaqi* that, "[i]n addition to the AUMF, there are *other legal bases under U.S.* and international *law* for the President to authorize the use of force against al-Qaeda and AQAP, including the inherent right to national *self-defense*" (emphasis added). The reference to self-defense implies that the government believes that the President has Article II authorities to engage in targeted killings in Yemen. Another possible domestic legal basis for a targeted killing of Al-Aulaqi in Yemen is the covert action statute discussed in Chapter 9, 50 U.S.C. §3093. It has been reported that targeted killings in Yemen were conducted by CIA UAVs, in addition to Defense Department UAVs, as part of a covert action program. As a matter of domestic law authority, is the covert action statute a substitute for the

AUMF? Do you see why it potentially gives the President broader powers to target and kill terrorists than the AUMF? What are the different implications of each statute in terms of the President's reporting obligations to Congress? If the President has three domestic legal bases for targeted killings in the "war on terrorism" — the AUMF, the covert action statute, and Article II — which will the President presumptively prefer and why?

d. *Armed Conflict.* As the Koh excerpt above makes plain, the Obama Administration, like its predecessor, maintained that the United States is in an armed conflict with Al Qaeda and associates under the international laws of war, a position that the Trump Administration has followed. The Koh speech and Obama Administration actions appear to imply that the armed conflict extends beyond Afghanistan and may have been a legal basis for targeting Al-Aulaqi lawfully under international law in Yemen. The plaintiff in *Al-Aulaqi* maintained that any lethal action in Yemen against Al Qaeda affiliates would be "outside of armed conflict" because it takes place outside a traditional battlefield like Afghanistan, and thus the lawful killing permitted by international law in armed conflicts does not extend to Yemen. The question is unsettled in international law, but which rule makes most sense? Should the armed conflict between the United States and Al Qaeda extend to any place where an Al Qaeda member is found? If not, does that mean that top Al Qaeda operators can escape U.S. military force simply by relocating outside Afghanistan?

e. *U.N. Charter.* Circumstantial evidence suggests that the Yemeni government secretly supported U.S. lethal operations against Al Qaeda and affiliate fighters in Yemen. *See, e.g.,* Dana Priest, *U.S. Military Teams, Intelligence Deeply Involved in Aiding Yemen on Strikes,* Wash. Post (Jan. 27, 2010). Some commentators have suggested that this consent must be public to be effective, see *Report of the Special Rapporteur, supra,* at 27, but the U.N. Charter is silent on the issue. Even if Yemen's consent is ineffective or not forthcoming, the United States might argue, and the Koh excerpt might be read to suggest, that U.S. targeting actions in Yemen are consistent with the U.N. Charter because they are acts of self-defense, perhaps in response to AQAP-sponsored attacks and threats directed toward the United States. But if so, self-defense against whom? Against AQAP? Against Yemen? Can the United States continue to use targeted military force in Yemen in self-defense until it defeats AQAP there? In its AUMF-related targeting actions in Pakistan and Syria, and possibly other countries, the United States has employed an expansive conception of self-defense that allows it to target terrorists in a nation that is "unwilling or unable" to suppress the terrorist threat. *See* Charlie Savage, Power Wars: Inside Obama's Post-9/11 Presidency 263-64 (2016); Monica Hakimi, *Defensive Force Against Non-State Actors: The State of Play,* 91 Int'l L. Stud. 1 (2015). For a general discussion of the "unwilling or unable" concept, see Ashley Deeks, *"Unwilling or Unable": Toward a Normative Framework for Extraterritorial Self-Defense,* 52 Va. J. Int'l L. 483 (2012).

f. *International Law Implications of CIA Involvement.* The CIA officers and contractors who conduct UAV targeting operations in Yemen — unlike their Defense Department counterparts — typically do not wear uniforms or otherwise distinguish themselves from civilians. Nor do they typically operate within the military chain of command. Does this make these officials unlawful combatants? Consider this analysis:

> In terms of international armed conflict, those CIA agents are, unlike their military counterparts but like the fighters they target, unlawful combatants. No less than their insurgent targets, they are fighters without uniforms or insignia, directly participating

in hostilities, employing armed force contrary to the laws and customs of war. Even if they are sitting in Langley, the CIA pilots are civilians violating the requirement of distinction, a core concept of armed conflict, as they directly participate in hostilities.

Gary Solis, *CIA Drone Attacks Produce America's Own Unlawful Combatants*, Wash. Post (Mar. 12, 2010). Two consequences appear to follow if this analysis is correct: The CIA officials are legitimate military targets in the armed conflict with Al Qaeda and AQAP, and CIA officers would not receive the combatant's privilege if captured, and could presumably be prosecuted for crimes committed by the UAVs that they operate. Are these troubling implications? Do they have any practical impact if CIA officials are operating UAVs in Yemen from the safe confines of CIA headquarters in Langley, Virginia?

5. The complicated legal issues involved in targeting and killing Al Qaeda and affiliate fighters in the "war on terrorism" outside of traditional battlefields become more complex and controversial when the target is a U.S. citizen. These issues came to a head in connection with the United States's targeted killing of Anwar Al-Aulaqi in Yemen on September 30, 2011, nine months after the District Court in the excerpted case above dismissed the lawsuit brought by Al-Aulaqi's father. The Al-Aulaqi killing raises the same domestic authorization and international law issues discussed in the last note, but also raises additional issues under the U.S. Constitution and U.S. federal criminal law.

a. *Individual Rights.* The plaintiff in *Al-Aulaqi* argued that the Executive Branch's secret unilateral decision to target and kill his son violated his son's Fourth Amendment right to be free from unreasonable seizures and his Fifth Amendment right not to be deprived of life without due process of law. The District Court did not reach these issues, but Attorney General Holder addressed some of them in general terms in his speech, and additional details about the Justice Department's legal position can be found in a Department White Paper leaked to the public in February 2013, *see* Lawfulness of a Lethal Operation Directed Against a U.S. Citizen Who Is a Senior Operational Leader of Al-Qa'ida or An Associated Force (Nov. 8, 2011) ("*White Paper*"), at http://fas.org/irp/eprint/doj-lethal.pdf, and in the underlying 2010 legal opinion by the Office of Legal Counsel, which the Second Circuit ordered the Department of Justice to release in 2014 in partly redacted form as the result of a Freedom of Information Act case brought by The New York Times and the ACLU. *See* Memorandum for the Attorney General, "Applicability of Federal Criminal Laws and the Constitution to Contemplated Lethal Operations Against Shaykh Anwar al-Aulaqi," at https://www.justice.gov/sites/default/files/olc/pages/attachments/2015/04/02/2010-07-16_-_olc_aaga_barron_-_al-aulaqi.pdf.

b. *Due Process.* Attorney General Holder says that the Due Process Clause mandates "procedural safeguards that depend on specific circumstances," and requires the government to engage in "a balancing approach, weighing the private interest that will be affected against the interest the government is trying to protect, and the burdens the government would face in providing additional process." (The OLC opinion makes clear that this test is the same one used for the Due Process analysis in *Hamdi*, discussed above in Section B.) On the private interest side, the Attorney General says that the U.S. citizen has an interest "in making sure that the government does not target him erroneously." But, he adds, the government's interest is very high (because the target, an enemy belligerent, presents an "imminent threat") and the government cannot easily provide additional process (because it was not feasible to capture Al-Aulaqi).

In considering how to balance these factors, note the Attorney General's broad conception of "imminent threat," which the White Paper operationalizes as follows:

> With this understanding [of imminent threat], a high-level official could conclude, for example, that an individual poses an "imminent threat" of violent attack against the United States where he is an operational leader of al-Qa'ida or an associated force and is personally and continually involved in planning terrorist attacks against the United States. Moreover, where the al-Qa'ida member in question has recently been involved in activities posing an imminent threat of violent attack against the United States, and there is no evidence suggesting that he has renounced or abandoned such activities, that member's involvement in al-Qa'ida's continuing terrorist campaign against the United States would support the conclusion that the member poses an imminent threat.

White Paper, supra, at 8. Note further the Attorney General's vague conception of the feasibility of capture, which he acknowledges is "fact-specific." In light of these understandings, do you think the due process balance properly favors the government in depriving Al-Aulaqi of his life? In war, won't the government always have an incentive to tip the scales in favor of its own interests? How would these due process principles apply if Al-Aulaqi were plotting his attacks inside the United States and targeted there? Would they differ because capture is more feasible in this context?

Even assuming that the Due Process Clause allows the government to kill the operational leader of a group covered by the AUMF who presents an imminent threat and cannot feasibly be captured, how much confidence should we have in the government's factual and legal support for these conclusions? How can we be sure, in other words, that the government does not make a factual or legal mistake, and thus erroneously target and kill a U.S. citizen? Holder did not describe the government's processes for making such determinations related to targeted killing. But based on documents submitted by the government in the *Al-Aulaqi* lawsuit, and other sources, it appears that these determinations were based on extensive human, communication, UAV, satellite, and other intelligence sources, and elaborate vetting and scrutiny by lawyers and senior policy officials. Under the Obama Administration, it also appeared that if (like Al-Aulaqi) the target were a particularly sensitive or high-value one, the President or the Secretary of Defense, often preceded by a full-blown National Security Council meeting, had to review the evidence and approve the decision to fire. Does this process provide enough information to minimize the risk of error in targeting?

c. *Fourth Amendment.* Attorney General Holder did not address the Fourth Amendment's prohibition on "unreasonable . . . seizures," but the Office of Legal Counsel's 2010 opinion did, and it concluded that the Amendment would not be violated by a targeted killing of a U.S. citizen in Al-Aulaqi's situation. The Office of Legal Counsel stated that "the constitutionality of a seizure is determined by 'balanc[ing] the nature and quality of the intrusion on the individual's Fourth Amendment interests against the importance of the governmental interests alleged to justify the intrusion. Tennessee v. Garner, 471 U.S. 1, 8 (1985).'" 2010 Opinion, *supra,* at 41. It then stated:

> [A]s we understand the facts, the U.S. citizen in question has gone overseas and become part of the forces of an enemy with which the United States is engaged in an armed conflict; that person is engaged in continual planning and direction of attacks upon U.S. persons from one of the enemy's overseas bases of operations; the U.S. government does not know precisely when such attacks will occur; and a capture operation

would be infeasible. . . . [A]t least where high-level government officials have determined that a capture operation overseas is infeasible and that the targeted person is part of a dangerous enemy force and is engaged in activities that pose a continued and imminent threat to U.S. persons or interests[,] the use of lethal force would not violate the Fourth Amendment" because "any intrusion on any Fourth Amendment interests would be outweighed by the 'importance of the governmental interests [that] justify the intrusion,' *Garner*, 471 U.S. at 8. . . .

Id. How, if at all, does this test differ from the Due Process test?

d. *Federal Criminal Law.* The 2010 OLC opinion also addressed federal criminal law possibly implicated by the targeted killing of a U.S. citizen. Section 1119(b) of Title 18 prohibits a U.S. national from killing another U.S. national outside the United States. The OLC Opinion concluded that this statute did not apply to a targeted killing because Congress implicitly intended §1119(b) to contain a "public authority" exception for lawful killings during warfare. It also concluded that the contemplated lethal operations complied with the War Crimes Act, 18 U.S.C. §2441, because the contemplated operations were against individuals taking active part in hostilities and otherwise complied with the laws of war.

e. *Separation of Powers.* The district court in the *Al-Aulaqi* case concluded that the plaintiff was not the proper person to bring the claim and that the case raised political questions that were for the political branches, and not the judiciary, to decide. Are you convinced by the court's political question doctrine analysis? Is it consistent with the political question doctrine materials in Chapter 2? Are there truly no judicially manageable standards by which courts could ascertain the legality of the targeted killing of the plaintiff's son? Isn't it odd (as the court suggests) to require judicial approval under FISA when the United States targets a U.S. citizen overseas for electronic surveillance, but not require judicial approval when the United States targets a U.S. citizen overseas for killing? Why are the judicial inquiries and judgments in this context any more difficult or sensitive than the judicial inquiries and judgments in the habeas corpus cases concerning the detention of alleged terrorists at Guantanamo, which require courts to assess intelligence, to determine the membership of and relationship between terrorist organizations, and the like? Is there something about a military targeting decision that is especially beyond the ken of courts? What incentives does the combination of extensive judicial review for Guantanamo detentions but no judicial review for targeted killings give the Executive Branch when choosing between the two options?

Attorney General Holder was widely criticized for claiming in the excerpted speech that "[t]he Constitution guarantees due process, not judicial process." What does *Hamdi* say on this issue? The Attorney General also suggests that the Executive Branch's targeting decisions receive "robust oversight" from congressional intelligence committees, to which the Executive Branch "regularly informs" about its counterterrorism activities, including targeting killing. Do you think this oversight is truly robust? Do you think the congressional committees pore over the factual basis for targeting to the same degree that *Hamdi* suggested that courts or military commissions should assess the factual bases for detention? And are the informal means of congressional pushback as powerful as judicial review?

6. Two weeks after killing Anwar Al-Aulaqi, the U.S. military killed Al-Aulaqi's teenage son in another drone strike, although it had not specifically targeted him. Relatives of both the father and son sued various U.S. officials for damages, arguing that the officials had violated the due process rights of the decedents. A federal district court concluded that the suit was not barred by the political question doctrine, and that the plaintiffs had stated a plausible Fifth Amendment due process claim with respect to the killing of the father. But the court reasoned that it would not be appropriate to imply a constitutional damages remedy for the overseas targeting of a U.S. citizen determined to be an active enemy. *See* Al-Aulaqi v. Panetta, 35 F. Supp. 3d 56 (D.D.C. 2014).

7. On May 2, 2011, several dozen U.S. military and CIA officials flew in helicopters to a compound in Abbottabad, Pakistan, where they killed Osama Bin Laden, the leader of Al Qaeda. Based on the principles outlined above, was this operation lawful? State Department Legal Adviser Harold Koh provided this explanation of the legal basis for the attack:

> Given bin Laden's unquestioned leadership position within al Qaeda and his clear continuing operational role, there can be no question that he was the leader of an enemy force and a legitimate target in our armed conflict with al Qaeda. In addition, bin Laden continued to pose an imminent threat to the United States that engaged our right to use force, a threat that materials seized during the raid have only further documented. Under these circumstances, there is no question that he presented a lawful target for the use of lethal force. By enacting the AUMF, Congress expressly authorized the President to use military force "against . . . *persons* [such as bin Laden, whom the President] determines planned, authorized, committed, or aided the terrorist attacks that occurred on September 11, 2001 . . . in order to prevent any future acts of international terrorism against the United States by such . . . persons" (emphasis added). Moreover, the manner in which the U.S. operation was conducted — taking great pains both to distinguish between legitimate military objectives and civilians and to avoid excessive incidental injury to the latter — followed the principles of distinction and proportionality described above, and was designed specifically to preserve those principles, even if it meant putting U.S. forces in harm's way. Finally, consistent with the laws of armed conflict and U.S. military doctrine, the U.S. forces were prepared to capture bin Laden if he had surrendered in a way that they could safely accept. The laws of armed conflict require acceptance of a genuine offer of surrender that is clearly communicated by the surrendering party and received by the opposing force, under circumstances where it is feasible for the opposing force to accept that offer of surrender. But where that is not the case, those laws authorize use of lethal force against an enemy belligerent, under the circumstances presented here.

Harold Hongju Koh, *The Lawfulness of the U.S. Operation Against Osama bin Laden*, at http://opiniojuris.org/2011/05/19/the-lawfulness-of-the-us-operation-against-osama-bin-laden. Is this explanation persuasive? Is it complete? For a more elaborate explanation, see Marty Lederman, *The U.S. Perspective on the Legal Basis for the bin Laden Operation*, Balkinization, May 24, 2011, *at* http://balkin.blogspot.com/2011/05/us-perspective-on-legal-basis-for-bin.html.

8. The joint CIA-Defense Department operation to kill Bin Laden exemplifies an important trend in the post-September 11 era: CIA and Defense authorities and operations increasingly overlap and intersect. The CIA's involvement in paramilitary and other war-like covert actions has become much more commonplace after September 11, especially with the growth in the fleet and deployment of CIA UAVs, but also in other respects. Similarly, the Defense Department's fleet of UAVs has grown enormously since September 11. So too have its Special Operations Forces, which frequently conduct highly secretive counterterrorism operations, some of which, like CIA covert actions, are unacknowledged. Many of these operations take place in Afghanistan, but some of them take place in other countries like Pakistan, Somalia, Yemen, and Libya.

As a result of these trends, the President has significant discretion in deciding which agency of the U.S. government to deploy in a secret counterterrorism
operation or, as in the Bin Laden operation, whether to deploy the forces of the
CIA and the Defense Department together. The President's discretion, however,
is channeled to some degree by domestic law. If the CIA engages in paramilitary
and related war-like actions that otherwise satisfy the covert action definition, the
operation must be conducted in accordance with 50 U.S.C. §3093, which, as we
learned in Chapter 9, has a special regime of reporting and oversight. When the
CIA and Defense Department conduct an operation jointly, the operation is usually
governed by Title 50 covert action authorities. The Bin Laden operation, in fact,
was executed by the U.S. military Joint Special Operations Command, but it was
nonetheless authorized as a Title 50 covert action that was technically commanded
by CIA Director Leon Panetta. *See* Jim Lehrer Interview with Leon Panetta, PBS
NewsHour (May 3, 2011). As a result, the Bin Laden operation was conducted pursuant to a presidential finding that was reported to the congressional intelligence
committees, or some appropriate subset.

Often, however, U.S. military special operations forces conduct secret counterterrorism activities that are not deemed to be covert actions, either because the
predicates to covert action (such as the operation being unacknowledged) are not
satisfied, or because the operation (including unacknowledged military operations)
falls within the covert action statute's exceptions for certain intelligence missions
or "traditional . . . military activities," see 50 U.S.C. §3093(e). The AUMF arguably
authorizes many "traditional military activities," and not surprisingly secret Special
Operations counterterrorism activities, in many corners of the globe, have grown
enormously in the post-September 11 era. Many commentators worry that the
Executive Branch has increasingly relied on secret military operations as a substitute for covert actions because the reporting and oversight requirements for these
secret military operations are much less onerous than the reporting and oversight
requirements for covert action. *See, e.g.,* Alfred Cumming, *Covert Action: Legislative
Background and Possible Policy Questions,* Congressional Research Service, April 6, 2011,
at 5. For various perspectives on this issue, see Robert Chesney, *Military-Intelligence
Convergence and the Law of the Title 10/Title 50 Debate,* 5 J. Nat'l Sec. L. & Pol. 539
(2012); Richard Gross, *Different Worlds, Unacknowledged Special Operations and Covert
Action,* U.S. Army War College, Strategy Research Project (2009), at http://www
.fas.org/man/eprint/gross.pdf; Jennifer D. Kibbe, *Covert Action and the Pentagon,* 22
Intel. & Nat'l Sec. 57 (2007).

9. There is a large literature on the targeted killing issues discussed in this sub-
section, including Philip Alston, *The CIA and Targeted Killings Beyond Borders,* 2 Harv.
Nat'l Sec. J. 283 (2011); Kenneth Anderson, *Targeted Killing in U.S. Counterterrorism
Strategy and Law,* in Legislating the War on Terror: An Agenda for Reform 346
(Benjamin Wittes ed., 2009); Louis René Beres, *After Osama Bin Laden: Assassination,
Terrorism, War, and International Law,* 44 Case W. Res. J. Int'l L. 93 (2011); Gabriela
Blum & Philip Heymann, *Law and Policy of Targeted Killing,* 1 Harv. Nat'l Sec. J. 145
(2010); Robert Chesney, *Who May Be Killed? Anwar al-Aulaqi as a Case Study in the
International Legal Regulation of Lethal Force,* 13 Y.B. Int'l Hum. L. 3 (2011); Jennifer
Daskal, *The Geography of the Battlefield: A Framework for Detention and Targeting Outside
the 'Hot' Conflict Zone,* 161 U. Pa. L. Rev. 1165 (2013); John C. Dehn & Kevin Jon
Heller, *Targeted Killing: The Case of Anwar al-Aulaqi,* 159 U. Pa. L. Rev. PENNumbra
175 (2011); Toren G. Evers-Mushovic & Michael Hughes, *Rules for When There Are No
Rules: Examining the Legality of Putting American Terrorists in the Crosshairs Abroad,* 18

New Eng. J. Int'l & Comp. L. 157 (2012); Mary Ellen O'Connell, *Unlawful Killing with Combat Drones: A Case Study of Pakistan, 2004-2009,* in Shooting to Kill: Socio-Legal Perspectives on the Use of Lethal Force (Simon Bronitt, Miriam Gani, & Saskia Hufnagel eds., 2012); Richard Murphy & Afsheen John Radsan, *Due Process and Targeted Killing of Terrorists,* 31 Cardozo L. Rev. 405 (2009); Jordan J. Paust, *Self-Defense Targetings of Non-State Actors and Permissibility of U.S. Use of Drones in Pakistan,* 19 J. Transnat'l L. & Pol. 237 (2010); Afsheen John Radsan & Richard Murphy, *The Evolution of Law and Policy for CIA Targeted Killing,* 5 J. Nat'l Security L. & Pol'y 439 (2012); John Yoo, *Assassination or Targeted Killings After 9/11,* 56 N.Y. Sch. L. Rev. 57 (2011). For a detailed account of the Obama Administration's decision to kill Al-Aulaqi, see Scott Shane, Objective Troy: A Terrorist, A President, and the Rise of the Drone (2015). For a more general account of the Obama Administration's approach to the war on terrorism, with an emphasis on the role and influence of lawyers, see Charlie Savage, Power Wars, *supra.*

Appendices

A

Articles of Confederation and Perpetual Union

Article I.

The style of this confederacy shall be, "The United States of America."

Article II.

Each State retains its sovereignty, freedom, and independence, and every power, jurisdiction, and right, which is not by this confederation expressly delegated to the United States, in Congress assembled.

Article III.

The said States hereby severally enter into a firm league of friendship with each other, for their common defence, the security of their liberties, and their mutual and general welfare, binding themselves to assist each other, against all force offered to, or attacks made upon them, or any of them, on account of religion, sovereignty, trade, or any other pretence whatever.

Article IV.

§1. The better to secure and perpetuate mutual friendship and intercourse among the people of the different States in this Union, the free inhabitants of each of these States, paupers, vagabonds, and fugitives from justice excepted, shall be entitled to all privileges and immunities of free citizens in the several States; and the people of each State shall have free ingress and regress to and from any other State, and shall enjoy therein all the privileges of trade and commerce, subject to the same duties, impositions, and restrictions, as the inhabitants thereof respectively; provided that such restrictions shall not extend so far as to prevent the removal of property imported into any State, to any other State, of which the owner is an inhabitant; provided also, that no imposition, duties, or restriction, shall be laid by any State on the property of the United States, or either of them.

§2. If any person guilty of, or charged with, treason, felony, or other high misdemeanor in any State, shall flee from justice, and be found in any of the United States, he shall, upon demand of the governor or executive power of the State from which he fled, be delivered up, and removed to the State having jurisdiction of his offense.

§3. Full faith and credit shall be given, in each of these States, to the records, acts, and judicial proceedings of the courts and magistrates of every other State.

Article V.

§1. For the more convenient management of the general interests of the United States, delegates shall be annually appointed in such manner as the legislature of each State shall direct, to meet in Congress on the first Monday in November, in every year, with a power reserved to each State to recall its delegates, or any of them, at any time within the year, and to send others in their stead, for the remainder of the year.

§2. No State shall be represented in Congress by less than two, nor by more than seven members; and no person shall be capable of being a delegate for more than three years, in any term of six years; nor shall any person, being a delegate, be capable of holding any office under the United States, for which he, or another for his benefit, receives any salary, fees, or emolument of any kind.

§3. Each State shall maintain its own delegates in a meeting of the States, and while they act as members of the committee of these States.

§4. In determining questions in the United States in Congress assembled, each State shall have one vote.

§5. Freedom of speech and debate in Congress shall not be impeached or questioned in any court or place out of Congress, and the members of Congress shall be protected in their persons from arrests and imprisonments, during the time of their going to and from, and attendance on, Congress, except for treason, felony or breach of the peace.

Article VI.

§1. No State, without the consent of the United States, in Congress assembled, shall send any embassy to, or receive any embassy from, or enter into any conference, agreement, alliance, or treaty with any king, prince or State; nor shall any person holding any office of profit or trust under the United States, or any of them, accept of any present, emolument, office, or title of any kind whatever, from any king, prince or foreign State; nor shall the United States, in Congress assembled, or any of them, grant any title of nobility.

§2. No two or more States shall enter into any treaty, confederation, or alliance whatever, between them, without the consent of the United States, in Congress assembled, specifying accurately the purposes for which the same is to be entered into, and how long it shall continue.

§3. No State shall lay any imposts or duties which may interfere with any stipulations in treaties, entered into by the United States, in Congress assembled, with any king, prince, or State, in pursuance of any treaties already proposed by Congress to the courts of France and Spain.

§4. No vessels of war shall be kept up in time of peace, by any State, except such number only as shall be deemed necessary by the United States, in Congress assembled, for the defence of such State, or its trade; nor shall any body of forces be kept up, by any State, in time of peace, except such number only as, in the judgement of the United States, in Congress assembled, shall be deemed requisite to garrison the forts necessary for the defense of such State; but every State shall always keep up a well-regulated and disciplined militia, sufficiently armed and accoutered, and shall provide and constantly have ready for use, in public stores, a due number of field-pieces and tents, and a proper quantity of arms, ammunition, and camp equipage.

§5. No State shall engage in any war without the consent of the United States, in Congress assembled, unless such State be actually invaded by enemies, or shall have received certain advice of a resolution being formed by some nation of Indians to invade such State, and the danger is so imminent as not to admit of a delay till the United States, in Congress assembled, can be consulted; nor shall any State grant commissions to any ships or vessels of war, nor letters of marque or reprisal, except it be after a declaration of war by the United States, in Congress assembled, and then only against the kingdom or State, and the subjects thereof, against which war has been so declared, and under such regulations as shall be established by the United States, in Congress assembled, unless such State be infested by pirates, in which case vessels of war may be fitted out for that occasion, and kept so long as the danger shall continue, or until the United States, in Congress assembled, shall determine otherwise.

Article VII.

When land forces are raised by any State, for the common defense, all officers of, or under the rank of colonel, shall be appointed by the legislature of each State respectively by whom such forces shall be raised, or in such manner as such State shall direct, and all vacancies shall be filled up by the State which first made the appointment.

Article VIII.

All charges of war, and all other expenses that shall be incurred for the common defence or general welfare, and allowed by the United States, in Congress assembled, shall be defrayed out of a common treasury, which shall be supplied by the several States, in proportion to the value of all land within each State, granted to, or surveyed for, any person, as such land and the buildings and improvements thereon shall be estimated, according to such mode as the United States, in Congress assembled, shall, from time to time, direct and appoint. The taxes for paying that proportion shall be laid and levied by the authority and direction of the legislatures of the several States, within the time agreed upon by the United States, in Congress assembled.

Article IX.

§1. The United States, in Congress assembled, shall have the sole and exclusive right and power of determining on peace and war, except in the cases mentioned in the sixth Article—of sending and receiving ambassadors; entering into treaties and alliances, provided that no treaty of commerce shall be made, whereby the legislative power of the respective States shall be restrained from imposing such imposts and duties on foreigners, as their own people are subjected to, or from prohibiting the exportation or importation of any species of goods or commodities whatsoever; of establishing rules for deciding, in all cases, what captures on land or water shall be legal, and in what manner prizes taken by land or naval forces in the service of the

United States, shall be divided or appropriated; of granting letters of marque and reprisal in times of peace; appointing courts for the trial of piracies and felonies committed on the high seas; and establishing courts for receiving and determining finally appeals in all cases of captures; provided that no member of Congress shall be appointed a judge of any of the said courts.

§2. The United States, in Congress assembled, shall also be the last resort on appeal, in all disputes and differences now subsisting, or that hereafter may arise between two or more States concerning boundary, jurisdiction, or any other causes whatever; which authority shall always be exercised in the manner following: Whenever the legislative or executive authority, or lawful agent of any State in controversy with another, shall present a petition to Congress, stating the matter in question, and praying for a hearing, notice thereof shall be given, by order of Congress, to the legislative or executive authority of the other State in controversy, and a day assigned for the appearance of the parties by their lawful agents, who shall then be directed to appoint, by joint consent, commissioners or judges to constitute a court for hearing and determining the matter in question: but if they cannot agree, Congress shall name three persons out of each of the United States, and from the list of such persons each party shall alternately strike out one, the petitioners beginning, until the number shall be reduced to thirteen; and from that number not less than seven, nor more than nine names, as Congress shall direct, shall, in the presence of Congress, be drawn out by lot; and the persons whose names shall be so drawn, or any five of them, shall be commissioners or judges, to hear and finally determine the controversy, so always as a major part of the judges, who shall hear the cause, shall agree in the determination; and if either party shall neglect to attend at the day appointed, without showing reasons which Congress shall judge sufficient, or being present, shall refuse to strike, the Congress shall proceed to nominate three persons out of each State, and the secretary of Congress shall strike in behalf of such party absent or refusing; and the judgment and sentence of the court, to be appointed in the manner before prescribed, shall be final and conclusive; and if any of the parties shall refuse to submit to the authority of such court, or to appear or defend their claim or cause, the court shall nevertheless proceed to pronounce sentence, or judgment, which shall in like manner be final and decisive; the judgment or sentence and other proceedings being in either case transmitted to Congress, and lodged among the acts of Congress, for the security of the parties concerned; provided, that every commissioner, before he sits in judgement, shall take an oath, to be administered by one of the judges of the supreme or superior court of the State where the cause shall be tried, "well and truly to hear and determine the matter in question, according to the best of his judgment, without favor, affection or hope of reward." Provided, also, that no State shall be deprived of territory for the benefit of the United States.

§3. All controversies concerning the private right of soil claimed under different grants of two or more States, whose jurisdictions as they may respect such lands, and the States which passed such grants are adjusted, the said grants or either of them being at the same time claimed to have originated antecedent to such settlement of jurisdiction, shall, on the petition of either party to the Congress of the United States, be finally determined, as near as may be, in the same manner as is before prescribed for deciding disputes respecting territorial jurisdiction between different States.

§4. The United States, in Congress assembled, shall also have the sole and exclusive right and power of regulating the alloy and value of coin struck by their own authority, or by that of the respective States; fixing the standards of weights and measures throughout the United States; regulating the trade and managing all affairs with the Indians, not members of any of the States; provided that the legislative right of any State, within its own limits, be not infringed or violated; establishing and regulating post offices from one State to another, throughout all the United States, and exacting such postage on the papers passing through the same, as may be requisite to defray the expenses of the said office; appointing all officers of the land forces in the service of the United States, excepting regimental officers; appointing all the officers of the naval forces, and commissioning all officers whatever in the service of the United States; making rules for the government and regulation of the said land and naval forces, and directing their operations.

§5. The United States, in Congress assembled, shall have authority to appoint a committee, to sit in the recess of Congress, to be denominated, "*A Committee of the States*," and to consist of one delegate from each State; and to appoint such other committees and civil officers as may be necessary for managing the general affairs of the United States under their direction; to appoint one of their number to preside; provided that no person be allowed to serve in the office of president more than one year in any term of three years; to ascertain the necessary sums of money to be raised for the service of the United States, and to appropriate and apply the same for defraying the public expenses; to borrow money or emit bills on the credit of the United States, transmitting every half year to the respective States an account of the sums of money so borrowed or emitted; to build and equip a navy; to agree upon the number of land forces, and to make requisitions from each State for its quota, in proportion to the number of white inhabitants in such State, which requisition shall be binding; and thereupon the Legislature of each State shall appoint the regimental officers, raise the men and cloathe, arm, and equip them, in a soldier-like manner, at the expense of the United States; and the officers and men so cloathed, armed, and equipped, shall march to the place appointed, and within the time agreed on by the United States, in Congress assembled; but if the United States, in Congress assembled, shall, on consideration of circumstances, judge proper that any State should not raise men, or should raise a smaller number than its quota, and that any other State should raise a greater number of men than the quota thereof, such extra number shall be raised, officered, clothed, armed, and equipped in the same manner as the quota of such State, unless the Legislature of such State shall judge that such extra number cannot be safely spared out of the same, in which case they shall raise, officer, clothe, arm, and equip, as many of such extra number as they judge can be safely spared, and the officers and men so clothed, armed, and equipped, shall march to the place appointed, and within the time agreed on by the United States in Congress assembled.

§6. The United States, in Congress assembled, shall never engage in a war, nor grant letters of marque or reprisal in time of peace, nor enter into any treaties or alliances, nor coin money, nor regulate the value thereof, nor ascertain the sums and expenses necessary for the defence and welfare of the United States, or any of them, nor emit bills, nor borrow money on the credit of the United States, nor appropriate money, nor agree upon the number of vessels of war to be built or purchased, or the number of land or sea forces to be raised, nor appoint a commander-in-chief of the army or navy, unless nine States assent to the same, nor shall a question on any other point, except for adjourning from day to day, be determined, unless by the votes of the majority of the United States in Congress assembled.

§7. The Congress of the United States shall have power to adjourn to any time within the year, and to any place within the United States, so that no period of adjournment be for a longer duration than the space of six months, and shall publish the journal of their proceedings monthly, except such parts thereof relating to treaties, alliances, or military operations, as in their judgment require secrecy; and the yeas and nays of the delegates of each State, on any question, shall be entered on the journal, when it is desired by any delegate; and the delegate of a State, or any of them, at his or their request, shall be furnished with a transcript of the said journal, except such parts as are above excepted, to lay before the legislatures of the several States.

Article X.

The committee of the States, or any nine of them, shall be authorized to execute, in the recess of Congress, such of the powers of Congress as the United States, in Congress assembled, by the consent of the nine States, shall, from time to time, think expedient to vest them with; provided that no power be delegated to the said committee, for the exercise of which, by the articles of confederation, the voice of nine States, in the Congress of the United States assembled, is requisite.

Article XI.

Canada acceding to this confederation, and adjoining in the measures of the United States, shall be admitted into, and entitled to all the advantages of this Union: but no other colony shall be admitted into the same, unless such admission be agreed to by nine States.

Article XII.

All bills of credit emitted, moneys borrowed, and debts contracted by or under the authority of Congress, before the assembling of the United States, in pursuance of the present confederation, shall be deemed and considered as a charge against the United States, for payment and satisfaction whereof the said United States, and the public faith are hereby solemnly pledged.

Article XIII.

Every State shall abide by the determinations of the United States, in Congress assembled, on all questions which by this confederation are submitted to them. And the articles of this confederation shall be inviolably observed by every State, and the Union shall be perpetual; nor shall any alteration at any time hereafter be made in any of them, unless such alteration be agreed to in a Congress of the United States, and be afterwards confirmed by the legislatures of every State.

And whereas it hath pleased the great Governor of the world to incline the hearts of the legislatures we respectively represent in Congress, to approve of, and to authorize us to ratify the said articles of confederation and perpetual union, Know ye that we, the undersigned delegates, by virtue of the power and authority to us given for that purpose, do, by these presents, in the name and in behalf of our respective constituents, fully and entirely ratify and confirm each and every of the said articles of confederation and perpetual union, and all and singular the matters and things therein contained. And we do further solemnly plight and engage the faith of our respective constituents, that they shall abide by the determinations of the United States, in Congress assembled, on all questions, which by the said confederation are submitted to them; and that the articles thereof shall be inviolably observed by the States we respectively represent, and that the Union shall be perpetual.

In witness whereof, we have hereunto set our hands in Congress. Done at Philadelphia in the State of Pennsylvania, the 9th day of July, in the year of our Lord 1778 , and in the third year of the Independence of America.

Agreed to by Congress 15 November 1777. In force after ratification by Maryland, 1 March 1781.

B

Constitution of the United States

We the People of the United States, in Order to form a more perfect Union, establish Justice, insure domestic Tranquility, provide for the common defense, promote the general Welfare, and secure the Blessings of Liberty to ourselves and our Posterity, do ordain and establish this Constitution for the United States of America.

Article I.

Section 1. All legislative Powers herein granted shall be vested in a Congress of the United States, which shall consist of a Senate and House of Representatives.

Section 2. The House of Representatives shall be composed of Members chosen every second Year by the People of the several States, and the Electors in each State shall have the Qualifications requisite for Electors of the most numerous Branch of the State Legislature.

No Person shall be a Representative who shall not have attained to the Age of twenty five Years, and been seven Years a Citizen of the United States, and who shall not, when elected, be an Inhabitant of that State in which he shall be chosen.

Representatives and direct Taxes shall be apportioned among the several States which may be included within this Union, according to their respective Numbers, which shall be determined by adding to the whole Number of free Persons, including those bound to Service for a Term of Years, and excluding Indians not taxed, three fifths of all other Persons. The actual Enumeration shall be made within three Years after the first Meeting of the Congress of the United States, and within every subsequent Term of ten Years, in such Manner as they shall by Law direct. The Number of Representatives shall not exceed one for every thirty Thousand, but each State shall have at Least one Representative; and until such enumeration shall be made, the State of New Hampshire shall be entitled to chuse three, Massachusetts eight, Rhode-Island and Providence Plantations one, Connecticut five, New-York six, New Jersey four, Pennsylvania eight, Delaware one, Maryland six, Virginia ten, North Carolina five, South Carolina five, and Georgia three.

When vacancies happen in the Representation from any State, the Executive Authority thereof shall issue Writs of Election to fill such Vacancies.

The House of Representatives shall chuse their Speaker and other Officers; and shall have the sole Power of Impeachment.

Section 3. The Senate of the United States shall be composed of two Senators from each State, chosen by the Legislature thereof for six Years; and each Senator shall have one Vote.

Immediately after they shall be assembled in Consequence of the first Election, they shall be divided as equally as may be into three Classes. The Seats of the Senators of the first Class shall be vacated at the Expiration of the second Year, of the second Class at the Expiration of the fourth Year, and of the third Class at the Expiration of the sixth Year, so that one third may be chosen every second Year; and if Vacancies happen by Resignation, or otherwise, during the Recess of the Legislature of any State, the Executive thereof may make temporary Appointments until the next Meeting of the Legislature, which shall then fill such Vacancies.

No Person shall be a Senator who shall not have attained to the Age of thirty Years, and been nine Years a Citizen of the United States, and who shall not, when elected, be an Inhabitant of that State for which he shall be chosen.

The Vice President of the United States shall be President of the Senate, but shall have no Vote, unless they be equally divided.

The Senate shall chuse their other Officers, and also a President pro tempore, in the Absence of the Vice President, or when he shall exercise the Office of President of the United States.

The Senate shall have the sole Power to try all Impeachments. When sitting for that Purpose, they shall be on Oath or Affirmation. When the President of the United States is tried, the Chief Justice shall preside: And no Person shall be convicted without the Concurrence of two thirds of the Members present.

Judgment in Cases of Impeachment shall not extend further than to removal from Office, and disqualification to hold and enjoy any Office of honor, Trust or Profit under the United States: but the Party convicted shall nevertheless be liable and subject to Indictment, Trial, Judgment and Punishment, according to Law.

Section 4. The Times, Places and Manner of holding Elections for Senators and Representatives, shall be prescribed in each State by the Legislature thereof; but the Congress may at any time by Law make or alter such Regulations, except as to the Places of chusing Senators.

The Congress shall assemble at least once in every Year, and such Meeting shall be on the first Monday in December, unless they shall by Law appoint a different Day.

Section 5. Each House shall be the Judge of the Elections, Returns and Qualifications of its own Members, and a Majority of each shall constitute a Quorum to do Business; but a smaller Number may adjourn from day to day, and may be authorized to compel the Attendance of absent Members, in such Manner, and under such Penalties as each House may provide.

Each House may determine the Rules of its Proceedings, punish its Members for disorderly Behaviour, and, with the Concurrence of two thirds, expel a Member.

Each House shall keep a Journal of its Proceedings, and from time to time publish the same, excepting such Parts as may in their Judgment require Secrecy; and the Yeas and Nays of the Members of either House on any question shall, at the Desire of one fifth of those Present, be entered on the Journal.

Neither House, during the Session of Congress, shall, without the Consent of the other, adjourn for more than three days, nor to any other Place than that in which the two Houses shall be sitting.

Section 6. The Senators and Representatives shall receive a Compensation for their Services, to be ascertained by Law, and paid out of the Treasury of the United States. They shall in all Cases, except Treason, Felony and Breach of the Peace, be privileged from Arrest during their Attendance at the Session of their respective Houses, and in going to and returning from the same; and for any Speech or Debate in either House, they shall not be questioned in any other Place.

No Senator or Representative shall, during the Time for which he was elected, be appointed to any civil Office under the Authority of the United States, which shall have been created, or the Emoluments whereof shall have been encreased during such time; and no Person holding any Office under the United States, shall be a Member of either House during his Continuance in Office.

Section 7. All Bills for raising Revenue shall originate in the House of Representatives; but the Senate may propose or concur with Amendments as on other Bills.

Every Bill which shall have passed the House of Representatives and the Senate, shall, before it become a Law, be presented to the President of the United States: If he approve he shall sign it, but if not he shall return it, with his Objections to that House in which it shall have originated, who shall enter the Objections at large on their Journal, and proceed to reconsider it. If after such Reconsideration two thirds of that House shall agree to pass the Bill, it shall be sent, together with the Objections, to the other House, by which it shall likewise be reconsidered, and if approved by two thirds of that House, it shall become a Law. But in all such Cases the Votes of both Houses shall be determined by yeas and Nays, and the Names of the Persons voting for and against the Bill shall be entered on the Journal of each House respectively. If any Bill shall not be returned by the President within ten Days (Sundays excepted) after it shall have been presented to him, the Same shall be a Law, in like Manner as if he had signed it, unless the Congress by their Adjournment prevent its Return, in which Case it shall not be a Law.

Every Order, Resolution, or Vote to which the Concurrence of the Senate and House of Representatives may be necessary (except on a question of Adjournment) shall be presented to the President of the United States; and before the Same shall take Effect, shall be approved by him, or being disapproved by him, shall be repassed by two thirds of the Senate and House of Representatives, according to the Rules and Limitations prescribed in the Case of a Bill.

Section 8. The Congress shall have Power To lay and collect Taxes, Duties, Imposts and Excises, to pay the Debts and provide for the common Defence and general Welfare of the United States; but all Duties, Imposts and Excises shall be uniform throughout the United States;

To borrow Money on the credit of the United States;

To regulate Commerce with foreign Nations, and among the several States, and with the Indian Tribes;

To establish an uniform Rule of Naturalization, and uniform Laws on the subject of Bankruptcies throughout the United States;

To coin Money, regulate the Value thereof, and of foreign Coin, and fix the Standard of Weights and Measures;

To provide for the Punishment of counterfeiting the Securities and current Coin of the United States;

To establish Post Offices and post Roads;

To promote the Progress of Science and useful Arts, by securing for limited Times to Authors and Inventors the exclusive Right to their respective Writings and Discoveries;

To constitute Tribunals inferior to the supreme Court;

10   To define and punish Piracies and Felonies committed on the high Seas, and Offences against the Law of Nations;

11   To declare War, grant Letters of Marque and Reprisal, and make Rules concerning Captures on Land and Water;

To raise and support Armies, but no Appropriation of Money to that Use shall be for a longer Term than two Years;

To provide and maintain a Navy;

To make Rules for the Government and Regulation of the land and naval Forces;

To provide for calling forth the Militia to execute the Laws of the Union, suppress Insurrections and repel Invasions;

To provide for organizing, arming, and disciplining, the Militia, and for governing such Part of them as may be employed in the Service of the United States, reserving to the States respectively, the Appointment of the Officers, and the Authority of training the Militia according to the discipline prescribed by Congress;

To exercise exclusive Legislation in all Cases whatsoever, over such District (not exceeding ten Miles square) as may, by Cession of particular States, and the Acceptance of Congress, become the Seat of the Government of the United States, and to exercise like Authority over all Places purchased by the Consent of the Legislature of the State in which the Same shall be, for the Erection of Forts, Magazines, Arsenals, dock-Yards, and other needful Buildings;—And

18   To make all Laws which shall be necessary and proper for carrying into Execution the foregoing Powers, and all other Powers vested by this Constitution in the Government of the United States, or in any Department or Officer thereof.

Section 9. The Migration or Importation of such Persons as any of the States now existing shall think proper to admit, shall not be prohibited by the Congress prior to the Year one thousand eight hundred and eight, but a Tax or duty may be imposed on such Importation, not exceeding ten dollars for each Person.

The Privilege of the Writ of Habeas Corpus shall not be suspended, unless when in Cases of Rebellion or Invasion the public Safety may require it.

No Bill of Attainder or ex post facto Law shall be passed.

No Capitation, or other direct, Tax shall be laid, unless in Proportion to the Census or enumeration herein before directed to be taken.

No Tax or Duty shall be laid on Articles exported from any State.

No Preference shall be given by any Regulation of Commerce or Revenue to the Ports of one State over those of another; nor shall Vessels bound to, or from, one State, be obliged to enter, clear, or pay Duties in another.

No Money shall be drawn from the Treasury, but in Consequence of Appropriations made by Law; and a regular Statement and Account of the Receipts and Expenditures of all public Money shall be published from time to time.

No Title of Nobility shall be granted by the United States: And no Person holding any Office of Profit or Trust under them, shall, without the Consent of the Congress, accept of any present, Emolument, Office, or Title, of any kind whatever, from any King, Prince, or foreign State.

Section 10. No State shall enter into any Treaty, Alliance, or Confederation; grant Letters of Marque and Reprisal; coin Money; emit Bills of Credit; make any Thing but gold and silver Coin a Tender in Payment of Debts; pass any Bill of Attainder, ex post facto Law, or Law impairing the Obligation of Contracts, or grant any Title of Nobility.

No State shall, without the Consent of the Congress, lay any Imposts or Duties on Imports or Exports, except what may be absolutely necessary for executing it's inspection Laws: and the net Produce of all Duties and Imposts, laid by any State on Imports or Exports, shall be for the Use of the Treasury of the United States; and all such Laws shall be subject to the Revision and Controul of the Congress.

No State shall, without the Consent of Congress, lay any Duty of Tonnage, keep Troops, or Ships of War in time of Peace, enter into any Agreement or Compact with another State, or with a foreign Power, or engage in War, unless actually invaded, or in such imminent Danger as will not admit of delay.

Article II.

Presidential Powers (orange)

Section 1. The executive Power shall be vested in a President of the United States of America. He shall hold his Office during the Term of four Years, and, together with the Vice President, chosen for the same Term, be elected, as follows:

Each State shall appoint, in such Manner as the Legislature thereof may direct, a Number of Electors, equal to the whole Number of Senators and Representatives to which the State may be entitled in the Congress: but no Senator or Representative, or Person holding an Office of Trust or Profit under the United States, shall be appointed an Elector.

The Electors shall meet in their respective States, and vote by Ballot for two Persons, of whom one at least shall not be an Inhabitant of the same State with themselves. And they shall make a List of all the Persons voted for, and of the Number of Votes for each; which List they shall sign and certify, and transmit sealed to the Seat of the Government of the United States, directed to the President of the Senate. The President of the Senate shall, in the Presence of the Senate and House of Representatives, open all the Certificates, and the Votes shall then be counted. The Person having the greatest Number of Votes shall be the President, if such Number be a Majority of the whole Number of Electors appointed; and if there be more than one who have such Majority, and have an equal Number of Votes, then the House of Representatives shall immediately chuse by Ballot one of them for President; and if no Person have a Majority, then from the five highest on the List the said House shall in like Manner chuse the President. But in chusing the President, the Votes shall be taken by States, the Representation from each State having one Vote; A quorum for this purpose shall consist of a Member or Members from two thirds of the States, and a Majority of all the States shall be necessary to a Choice. In every Case, after the Choice of the President, the Person having the greatest Number of Votes of the Electors shall be the Vice President. But if there should remain two or more who have equal Votes, the Senate shall chuse from them by Ballot the Vice President.

The Congress may determine the Time of chusing the Electors, and the Day on which they shall give their Votes; which Day shall be the same throughout the United States.

No Person except a natural born Citizen, or a Citizen of the United States, at the time of the Adoption of this Constitution, shall be eligible to the Office of President; neither shall any Person be eligible to that Office who shall not have attained to the Age of thirty five Years, and been fourteen Years a Resident within the United States.

In Case of the Removal of the President from Office, or of his Death, Resignation, or Inability to discharge the Powers and Duties of the said Office, the Same shall devolve on the Vice President, and the Congress may by Law provide for the Case of Removal, Death, Resignation or Inability, both of the President and Vice President, declaring what Officer shall then act as President, and such Officer shall act accordingly, until the Disability be removed, or a President shall be elected.

The President shall, at stated Times, receive for his Services, a Compensation, which shall neither be increased nor diminished during the Period for which he shall have been elected, and he shall not receive within that Period any other Emolument from the United States, or any of them.

Before he enter on the Execution of his Office, he shall take the following Oath or Affirmation:—"I do solemnly swear (or affirm) that I will faithfully execute the Office of President of the United States, and will to the best of my Ability, preserve, protect and defend the Constitution of the United States."

Section 2. The President shall be Commander in Chief of the Army and Navy of the United States, and of the Militia of the several States, when called into the actual Service of the United States; he may require the Opinion, in writing, of the principal Officer in each of the executive Departments, upon any Subject relating to the Duties of their respective Offices, and he shall have Power to grant Reprieves and Pardons for Offences against the United States, except in Cases of Impeachment.

He shall have Power, by and with the Advice and Consent of the Senate, to make Treaties, provided two thirds of the Senators present concur; and he shall nominate, and by and with the Advice and Consent of the Senate, shall appoint Ambassadors, other public Ministers and Consuls, Judges of the supreme Court, and all other Officers of the United States, whose Appointments are not herein otherwise provided for, and which shall be established by Law: but the Congress may by Law vest the Appointment of such inferior Officers, as they think proper, in the President alone, in the Courts of Law, or in the Heads of Departments.

The President shall have Power to fill up all Vacancies that may happen during the Recess of the Senate, by granting Commissions which shall expire at the End of their next Session.

Section 3. He shall from time to time give to the Congress Information of the State of the Union, and recommend to their Consideration such Measures as he shall judge necessary and expedient; he may, on extraordinary Occasions, convene both Houses, or either of them, and in Case of Disagreement between them, with Respect to the Time of Adjournment, he may adjourn them to such Time as he shall think proper; he shall receive Ambassadors and other public Ministers; he shall take Care that the Laws be faithfully executed, and shall Commission all the Officers of the United States.

Section 4. The President, Vice President and all civil Officers of the United States, shall be removed from Office on Impeachment for, and Conviction of, Treason, Bribery, or other high Crimes and Misdemeanors.

Article III.

Section 1. The judicial Power of the United States shall be vested in one supreme Court, and in such inferior Courts as the Congress may from time to time ordain and establish. The Judges, both of the supreme and inferior Courts, shall hold their Offices during good Behaviour, and shall, at stated Times, receive for their Services a Compensation, which shall not be diminished during their Continuance in Office.

Section 2. The judicial Power shall extend to all Cases, in Law and Equity, arising under this Constitution, the Laws of the United States, and Treaties made, or which shall be made, under their Authority;—to all Cases affecting Ambassadors, other public Ministers and Consuls;—to all Cases of admiralty and maritime Jurisdiction;—to Controversies to which the United States shall be a Party;—to Controversies between two or more States;—between a State and Citizens of another State;—between Citizens of different States;—between Citizens of the same State claiming Lands under Grants of different States, and between a State, or the Citizens thereof, and foreign States, Citizens or Subjects.

In all Cases affecting Ambassadors, other public Ministers and Consuls, and those in which a State shall be Party, the supreme Court shall have original Jurisdiction. In all the other Cases before mentioned, the supreme Court shall have appellate Jurisdiction, both as to Law and Fact, with such Exceptions, and under such Regulations as the Congress shall make.

The Trial of all Crimes, except in Cases of Impeachment, shall be by Jury; and such Trial shall be held in the State where the said Crimes shall have been committed; but when not committed within any State, the Trial shall be at such Place or Places as the Congress may by Law have directed.

Section 3. Treason against the United States, shall consist only in levying War against them, or in adhering to their Enemies, giving them Aid and Comfort. No Person shall be convicted of Treason unless on the Testimony of two Witnesses to the same overt Act, or on Confession in open Court.

The Congress shall have Power to declare the Punishment of Treason, but no Attainder of Treason shall work Corruption of Blood, or Forfeiture except during the Life of the Person attainted.

Article IV.

Section 1. Full Faith and Credit shall be given in each State to the public Acts, Records, and judicial Proceedings of every other State. And the Congress may by general Laws prescribe the Manner in which such Acts, Records and Proceedings shall be proved, and the Effect thereof.

Section 2. The Citizens of each State shall be entitled to all Privileges and Immunities of Citizens in the several States.

A Person charged in any State with Treason, Felony, or other Crime, who shall flee from Justice, and be found in another State, shall on Demand of the executive Authority of the State from which he fled, be delivered up, to be removed to the State having Jurisdiction of the Crime.

No Person held to Service or Labour in one State, under the Laws thereof, escaping into another, shall, in Consequence of any Law or Regulation therein, be discharged from such Service or Labour, but shall be delivered up on Claim of the Party to whom such Service or Labour may be due.

Section 3. New States may be admitted by the Congress into this Union; but no new State shall be formed or erected within the Jurisdiction of any other State; nor any State be formed by the Junction of two or more States, or Parts of States, without the Consent of the Legislatures of the States concerned as well as of the Congress.

The Congress shall have Power to dispose of and make all needful Rules and Regulations respecting the Territory or other Property belonging to the United States; and nothing in this Constitution shall be so construed as to Prejudice any Claims of the United States, or of any particular State.

Section 4. The United States shall guarantee to every State in this Union a Republican Form of Government, and shall protect each of them against Invasion; and on Application of the Legislature, or of the Executive (when the Legislature cannot be convened), against domestic Violence.

Article V.

The Congress, whenever two thirds of both Houses shall deem it necessary, shall propose Amendments to this Constitution, or, on the Application of the Legislatures of two thirds of the several States, shall call a Convention for proposing Amendments, which, in either Case, shall be valid to all Intents and Purposes, as Part of this Constitution, when ratified by the Legislatures of three fourths of the several States, or by Conventions in three fourths thereof, as the one or the other Mode of Ratification may be proposed by the Congress; Provided that no Amendment which may be made prior to the Year One thousand eight hundred and eight shall in any Manner affect the first and fourth Clauses in the Ninth Section of the first Article; and that no State, without its Consent, shall be deprived of its equal Suffrage in the Senate.

Article VI.

All Debts contracted and Engagements entered into, before the Adoption of this Constitution, shall be as valid against the United States under this Constitution, as under the Confederation.

This Constitution, and the Laws of the United States which shall be made in Pursuance thereof; and all Treaties made, or which shall be made, under the Authority of the United States, shall be the supreme Law of the Land; and the Judges in every State shall be bound thereby, any Thing in the Constitution or Laws of any State to the Contrary notwithstanding.

The Senators and Representatives before mentioned, and the Members of the several State Legislatures, and all executive and judicial Officers, both of the United States and of the several States, shall be bound by Oath or Affirmation, to support this Constitution; but no religious Test shall ever be required as a Qualification to any Office or public Trust under the United States.

Article VII.

The Ratification of the Conventions of nine States, shall be sufficient for the Establishment of this Constitution between the States so ratifying the Same.

ARTICLES IN ADDITION TO, AND AMENDMENT OF, THE CONSTITUTION OF THE UNITED STATES OF AMERICA

Amendment I

Congress shall make no law respecting an establishment of religion, or prohibiting the free exercise thereof; or abridging the freedom of speech, or of the press; or the right of the people peaceably to assemble, and to petition the Government for a redress of grievances.

Amendment II

A well regulated Militia, being necessary to the security of a free State, the right of the people to keep and bear Arms, shall not be infringed.

Amendment III

No Soldier shall, in time of peace be quartered in any house, without the consent of the Owner, nor in time of war, but in a manner to be prescribed by law.

Amendment IV

The right of the people to be secure in their persons, houses, papers, and effects, against unreasonable searches and seizures, shall not be violated, and no Warrants shall issue, but upon probable cause, supported by Oath or affirmation, and particularly describing the place to be searched, and the persons or things to be seized.

Amendment V

No person shall be held to answer for a capital, or otherwise infamous crime, unless on a presentment or indictment of a Grand Jury, except in cases arising in the land or naval forces, or in the Militia, when in actual service in time of War or public danger; nor shall any person be subject for the same offence to be twice put in jeopardy of life or limb; nor shall be compelled in any criminal case to be a witness against himself, nor be deprived of life, liberty, or property, without due process of law; nor shall private property be taken for public use, without just compensation.

Amendment VI

In all criminal prosecutions, the accused shall enjoy the right to a speedy and public trial, by an impartial jury of the State and district wherein the crime shall have been committed, which district shall have been previously ascertained by law, and to be informed of the nature and cause of the accusation; to be confronted with the witnesses against him; to have compulsory process for obtaining witnesses in his favor, and to have the Assistance of Counsel for his defence.

Amendment VII

In suits at common law, where the value in controversy shall exceed twenty dollars, the right of trial by jury shall be preserved, and no fact tried by a jury, shall be otherwise reexamined in any Court of the United States, than according to the rules of the common law.

Amendment VIII

Excessive bail shall not be required, nor excessive fines imposed, nor cruel and unusual punishments inflicted.

Amendment IX

The enumeration in the Constitution, of certain rights, shall not be construed to deny or disparage others retained by the people.

Amendment X

The powers not delegated to the United States by the Constitution, nor prohibited by it to the States, are reserved to the States respectively, or to the people.

Amendment XI

Passed by Congress March 4, 1794. Ratified February 7, 1795.

The Judicial power of the United States shall not be construed to extend to any suit in law or equity, commenced or prosecuted against one of the United States by Citizens of another State, or by Citizens or Subjects of any Foreign State.

Amendment XII

Passed by Congress December 9, 1803. Ratified June 15, 1804.

The Electors shall meet in their respective states and vote by ballot for President and Vice-President, one of whom, at least, shall not be an inhabitant of the same state with themselves; they shall name in their ballots the person voted for as President, and in distinct ballots the person voted for as Vice-President, and they shall make distinct lists of all persons voted for as President, and of all persons voted for as Vice-President, and of the number of votes for each, which lists they shall sign and certify, and transmit sealed to the seat of the government of the United States, directed to the President of the Senate;—the President of the Senate shall, in the presence of the Senate and House of Representatives, open all the certificates and the votes shall then be counted;—The person having the greatest number of votes for President, shall be the President, if such number be a majority of the whole number of Electors appointed; and if no person have such majority, then from the persons having the highest numbers not exceeding three on the list of those voted for as President, the House of Representatives shall choose immediately, by ballot, the President. But in choosing the President, the votes shall be taken by states, the representation from each state having one vote; a quorum for this purpose shall consist of a member or members from two-thirds of the states, and a majority of all the states shall be necessary to a choice. And if the House of Representatives shall not choose a President whenever the right of choice shall devolve upon them, before the fourth day of March next following, then the Vice-President shall act as President, as in case of the death or other constitutional disability of the President. The person having the greatest number of votes as Vice-President, shall be the Vice-President, if such number be a majority of the whole number of Electors appointed, and if no person have a majority, then from the two highest numbers on the list, the Senate shall choose the Vice-President; a quorum for the purpose shall consist of two-thirds of the whole number of Senators, and a majority of the whole number shall be necessary to a choice. But no person constitutionally ineligible to the office of President shall be eligible to that of Vice-President of the United States.

Amendment XIII

Passed by Congress January 31, 1865. Ratified December 6, 1865.

Section 1. Neither slavery nor involuntary servitude, except as a punishment for crime whereof the party shall have been duly convicted, shall exist within the United States, or any place subject to their jurisdiction.

Section 2. Congress shall have power to enforce this article by appropriate legislation.

Amendment XIV

Passed by Congress June 13, 1866. Ratified July 9, 1868.

Section 1. All persons born or naturalized in the United States, and subject to the jurisdiction thereof, are citizens of the United States and of the State wherein they reside. No State shall make or enforce any law which shall abridge the privileges or immunities of citizens of the United States; nor shall any State deprive any person of life, liberty, or property, without due process of law; nor deny to any person within its jurisdiction the equal protection of the laws.

Section 2. Representatives shall be apportioned among the several States according to their respective numbers, counting the whole number of persons in each State, excluding Indians not taxed. But when the right to vote at any election for the choice of electors for President and Vice-President of the United States, Representatives in Congress, the Executive and Judicial officers of a State, or the members of the Legislature thereof, is denied to any of the male inhabitants of such State, being twenty-one years of age, and citizens of the United States, or in any way abridged, except for participation in rebellion, or other crime, the basis of representation therein shall be reduced in the proportion which the number of such male citizens shall bear to the whole number of male citizens twenty-one years of age in such State.

Section 3. No person shall be a Senator or Representative in Congress, or elector of President and Vice-President, or hold any office, civil or military, under the United States, or under any State, who, having previously taken an oath, as a member of Congress, or as an officer of the United States, or as a member of any State legislature, or as an executive or judicial officer of any State, to support the Constitution of the United States, shall have engaged in insurrection or rebellion against the same, or given aid or comfort to the enemies thereof. But Congress may by a vote of two-thirds of each House, remove such disability.

Section 4. The validity of the public debt of the United States, authorized by law, including debts incurred for payment of pensions and bounties for services in suppressing insurrection or rebellion, shall not be questioned. But neither the United States nor any State shall assume or pay any debt or obligation incurred in aid of insurrection or rebellion against the United States, or any claim for the loss or emancipation of any slave; but all such debts, obligations and claims shall be held illegal and void.

Section 5. The Congress shall have the power to enforce, by appropriate legislation, the provisions of this article.

Amendment XV

Passed by Congress February 26, 1869. Ratified February 3, 1870.

Section 1. The right of citizens of the United States to vote shall not be denied or abridged by the United States or by any State on account of race, color, or previous condition of servitude.

Section 2. The Congress shall have the power to enforce this article by appropriate legislation.

Amendment XVI

Passed by Congress July 2, 1909. Ratified February 3, 1913.

The Congress shall have power to lay and collect taxes on incomes, from whatever source derived, without apportionment among the several States, and without regard to any census or enumeration.

Amendment XVII

Passed by Congress May 13, 1912. Ratified April 8, 1913.

The Senate of the United States shall be composed of two Senators from each State, elected by the people thereof, for six years; and each Senator shall have one vote. The electors in each State shall have the qualifications requisite for electors of the most numerous branch of the State legislatures.

When vacancies happen in the representation of any State in the Senate, the executive authority of such State shall issue writs of election to fill such vacancies: *Provided,* That the legislature of any State may empower the executive thereof to make temporary appointments until the people fill the vacancies by election as the legislature may direct.

This amendment shall not be so construed as to affect the election or term of any Senator chosen before it becomes valid as part of the Constitution.

Amendment XVIII

Passed by Congress December 18, 1917. Ratified January 16, 1919. Repealed by amendment 21.

Section 1. After one year from the ratification of this article the manufacture, sale, or transportation of intoxicating liquors within, the importation thereof into, or the exportation thereof from the United States and all territory subject to the jurisdiction thereof for beverage purposes is hereby prohibited.

Section 2. The Congress and the several States shall have concurrent power to enforce this article by appropriate legislation.

Section 3. This article shall be inoperative unless it shall have been ratified as an amendment to the Constitution by the legislatures of the several States, as provided in the Constitution, within seven years from the date of the submission hereof to the States by the Congress.

Amendment XIX

Passed by Congress June 4, 1919. Ratified August 18, 1920.

The right of citizens of the United States to vote shall not be denied or abridged by the United States or by any State on account of sex.

Congress shall have power to enforce this article by appropriate legislation.

Amendment XX

Passed by Congress March 2, 1932. Ratified January 23, 1933.

Section 1. The terms of the President and the Vice President shall end at noon on the 20th day of January, and the terms of Senators and Representatives at noon on the 3d day of January, of the years in which such terms would have ended if this article had not been ratified; and the terms of their successors shall then begin.

Section 2. The Congress shall assemble at least once in every year, and such meeting shall begin at noon on the 3d day of January, unless they shall by law appoint a different day.

Section 3. If, at the time fixed for the beginning of the term of the President, the President elect shall have died, the Vice President elect shall become President. If a President shall not have been chosen before the time fixed for the beginning of his term, or if the President elect shall have failed to qualify, then the Vice President elect shall act as President until a President shall have qualified; and the Congress may by law provide for the case wherein neither a President elect nor a Vice President shall have qualified, declaring who shall then act as President, or the manner in which one who is to act shall be selected, and such person shall act accordingly until a President or Vice President shall have qualified.

Section 4. The Congress may by law provide for the case of the death of any of the persons from whom the House of Representatives may choose a President whenever the right of choice shall have devolved upon them, and for the case of the death of any of the persons from whom the Senate may choose a Vice President whenever the right of choice shall have devolved upon them.

Section 5. Sections 1 and 2 shall take effect on the 15th day of October following the ratification of this article.

Section 6. This article shall be inoperative unless it shall have been ratified as an amendment to the Constitution by the legislatures of three-fourths of the several States within seven years from the date of its submission.

Amendment XXI

Passed by Congress February 20, 1933. Ratified December 5, 1933.

Section 1. The eighteenth article of amendment to the Constitution of the United States is hereby repealed.

Section 2. The transportation or importation into any State, Territory, or Possession of the United States for delivery or use therein of intoxicating liquors, in violation of the laws thereof, is hereby prohibited.

Section 3. This article shall be inoperative unless it shall have been ratified as an amendment to the Constitution by conventions in the several States, as provided in the Constitution, within seven years from the date of the submission hereof to the States by the Congress.

Amendment XXII

Passed by Congress March 21, 1947. Ratified February 27, 1951.

Section 1. No person shall be elected to the office of the President more than twice, and no person who has held the office of President, or acted as President, for more than two years of a term to which some other person was elected President shall be elected to the office of President more than once. But this Article shall not apply to any person holding the office of President when this Article was proposed by Congress, and shall not prevent any person who may be holding the office of President, or acting as President, during the term within which this Article becomes operative from holding the office of President or acting as President during the remainder of such term.

Section 2. This article shall be inoperative unless it shall have been ratified as an amendment to the Constitution by the legislatures of three-fourths of the several States within seven years from the date of its submission to the States by the Congress.

Amendment XXIII

Passed by Congress June 16, 1960. Ratified March 29, 1961.

Section 1. The District constituting the seat of Government of the United States shall appoint in such manner as Congress may direct:

A number of electors of President and Vice President equal to the whole number of Senators and Representatives in Congress to which the District would be entitled if it were a State, but in no event more than the least populous State; they shall be in addition to those appointed by the States, but they shall be considered, for the purposes of the election of President and Vice President, to be electors appointed by a State; and they shall meet in the District and perform such duties as provided by the twelfth article of amendment.

Section 2. The Congress shall have power to enforce this article by appropriate legislation.

Amendment XXIV

Passed by Congress August 27, 1962. Ratified January 23, 1964.

Section 1. The right of citizens of the United States to vote in any primary or other election for President or Vice President, for electors for President or Vice President, or for Senator or Representative in Congress, shall not be denied or abridged by the United States or any State by reason of failure to pay poll tax or other tax.

Section 2. The Congress shall have power to enforce this article by appropriate legislation.

Amendment XXV

Passed by Congress July 6, 1965. Ratified February 10, 1967.

Section 1. In case of the removal of the President from office or of his death or resignation, the Vice President shall become President.

Section 2. Whenever there is a vacancy in the office of the Vice President, the President shall nominate a Vice President who shall take office upon confirmation by a majority vote of both Houses of Congress.

Section 3. Whenever the President transmits to the President pro tempore of the Senate and the Speaker of the House of Representatives his written declaration that he is unable to discharge the powers and duties of his office, and until he transmits to them a written declaration to the contrary, such powers and duties shall be discharged by the Vice President as Acting President.

Section 4. Whenever the Vice President and a majority of either the principal officers of the executive departments or of such other body as Congress may by law provide, transmit to the President pro tempore of the Senate and the Speaker of the House of Representatives their written declaration that the President is unable to discharge the powers and duties of his office, the Vice President shall immediately assume the powers and duties of the office as Acting President.

Thereafter, when the President transmits to the President pro tempore of the Senate and the Speaker of the House of Representatives his written declaration that no inability exists, he shall resume the powers and duties of his office unless the Vice President and a majority of either the principal officers of the executive department or of such other body as Congress may by law provide, transmit within four days to the President pro tempore of the Senate and the Speaker of the House of Representatives their written declaration that the President is unable to discharge the powers and duties of his office. Thereupon Congress shall decide the issue, assembling within forty-eight hours for that purpose if not in session. If the Congress, within twenty-one days after receipt of the latter written declaration, or, if Congress is not in session, within twenty-one days after Congress is required to assemble, determines by two-thirds vote of both Houses that the President is unable to discharge the powers and duties of his office, the Vice President shall continue to discharge the same as Acting President; otherwise, the President shall resume the powers and duties of his office.

Amendment XXVI

Passed by Congress March 23, 1971. Ratified July 1, 1971.

Section 1. The right of citizens of the United States, who are eighteen years of age or older, to vote shall not be denied or abridged by the United States or by any State on account of age.

Section 2. The Congress shall have power to enforce this article by appropriate legislation.

Amendment XXVII

Originally proposed Sept. 25, 1789. Ratified May 7, 1992.

No law, varying the compensation for the services of the Senators and Representatives, shall take effect, until an election of representatives shall have intervened.

C

Select Jurisdictional Provisions

28 U.S.C. §1330: Actions against foreign states

(a) The district courts shall have original jurisdiction without regard to amount in controversy of any nonjury civil action against a foreign state as defined in section 1603(a) of this title as to any claim for relief in personam with respect to which the foreign state is not entitled to immunity either under sections 1605-1607 of this title or under any applicable international agreement.

(b) Personal jurisdiction over a foreign state shall exist as to every claim for relief over which the district courts have jurisdiction under subsection (a) where service has been made under section 1608 of this title.

(c) For purposes of subsection (b), an appearance by a foreign state does not confer personal jurisdiction with respect to any claim for relief not arising out of any transaction or occurrence enumerated in sections 1605-1607 of this title.

28 U.S.C §1331: Federal question

The district courts shall have original jurisdiction of all civil actions arising under the Constitution, laws, or treaties of the United States.

28 U.S.C. §1332: Diversity of citizenship; amount in controversy; costs

(a) The district courts shall have original jurisdiction of all civil actions where the matter in controversy exceeds the sum or value of $75,000, exclusive of interest and costs, and is between —

(1) citizens of different States;

(2) citizens of a State and citizens or subjects of a foreign state, except that the district courts shall not have original jurisdiction under this subsection of an action between citizens of a State and citizens or subjects of a foreign state who are lawfully admitted for permanent residence in the United States and are domiciled in the same State;

(3) citizens of different States and in which citizens or subjects of a foreign state are additional parties; and

(4) a foreign state, defined in section 1603(a) of this title, as plaintiff and citizens of a State or of different States.

(b) Except when express provision therefor is otherwise made in a statute of the United States, where the plaintiff who files the case originally in the Federal courts is finally adjudged to be entitled to recover less than the sum or value of $75,000, computed without regard to any setoff or counterclaim to which the defendant may be adjudged to be entitled, and exclusive of interest and costs, the district court may deny costs to the plaintiff and, in addition, may impose costs on the plaintiff.

(c) For the purposes of this section and section 1441 of this title —

(1) a corporation shall be deemed to be a citizen of every State and foreign state by which it has been incorporated and of the State or foreign state where it has its principal place of business, except that in any direct action against the insurer of a policy or contract of liability insurance, whether incorporated or unincorporated, to which action the insured is not joined as a party-defendant, such insurer shall be deemed a citizen of —

(A) every State and foreign state of which the insured is a citizen;

(B) every State and foreign state by which the insurer has been incorporated; and

(C) the State or foreign state where the insurer has its principal place of business; and

(2) the legal representative of the estate of a decedent shall be deemed to be a citizen only of the same State as the decedent, and the legal representative of an infant or incompetent shall be deemed to be a citizen only of the same State as the infant or incompetent.

(d)(1) In this subsection —

(A) the term "class" means all of the class members in a class action;

(B) the term "class action" means any civil action filed under rule 23 of the Federal Rules of Civil Procedure or similar State statute or rule of judicial procedure authorizing an action to be brought by 1 or more representative persons as a class action;

(C) the term "class certification order" means an order issued by a court approving the treatment of some or all aspects of a civil action as a class action; and

(D) the term "class members" means the persons (named or unnamed) who fall within the definition of the proposed or certified class in a class action.

(2) The district courts shall have original jurisdiction of any civil action in which the matter in controversy exceeds the sum or value of $5,000,000, exclusive of interest and costs, and is a class action in which —

(A) any member of a class of plaintiffs is a citizen of a State different from any defendant;

(B) any member of a class of plaintiffs is a foreign state or a citizen or subject of a foreign state and any defendant is a citizen of a State; or

(C) any member of a class of plaintiffs is a citizen of a State and any defendant is a foreign state or a citizen or subject of a foreign state.

(3) A district court may, in the interests of justice and looking at the totality of the circumstances, decline to exercise jurisdiction under paragraph (2) over a class action in which greater than one-third but less than two-thirds of the members of all proposed plaintiff classes in the aggregate and the primary defendants are citizens of the State in which the action was originally filed based on consideration of —

(A) whether the claims asserted involve matters of national or interstate interest;

(B) whether the claims asserted will be governed by laws of the State in which the action was originally filed or by the laws of other States;

(C) whether the class action has been pleaded in a manner that seeks to avoid Federal jurisdiction;

(D) whether the action was brought in a forum with a distinct nexus with the class members, the alleged harm, or the defendants;

(E) whether the number of citizens of the State in which the action was originally filed in all proposed plaintiff classes in the aggregate is substantially larger than the number of citizens from any other State, and the citizenship of the other members of the proposed class is dispersed among a substantial number of States; and

(F) whether, during the 3-year period preceding the filing of that class action, 1 or more other class actions asserting the same or similar claims on behalf of the same or other persons have been filed.

(4) A district court shall decline to exercise jurisdiction under paragraph (2) —

(A) (i) over a class action in which —

(I) greater than two-thirds of the members of all proposed plaintiff classes in the aggregate are citizens of the State in which the action was originally filed;

(II) at least 1 defendant is a defendant —

(aa) from whom significant relief is sought by members of the plaintiff class;

(bb) whose alleged conduct forms a significant basis for the claims asserted by the proposed plaintiff class; and

(cc) who is a citizen of the State in which the action was originally filed; and

(III) principal injuries resulting from the alleged conduct or any related conduct of each defendant were incurred in the State in which the action was originally filed; and

(ii) during the 3-year period preceding the filing of that class action, no other class action has been filed asserting the same or similar factual allegations against any of the defendants on behalf of the same or other persons; or

(B) two-thirds or more of the members of all proposed plaintiff classes in the aggregate, and the primary defendants, are citizens of the State in which the action was originally filed.

(5) Paragraphs (2) through (4) shall not apply to any class action in which —

(A) the primary defendants are States, State officials, or other governmental entities against whom the district court may be foreclosed from ordering relief; or

(B) the number of members of all proposed plaintiff classes in the aggregate is less than 100.

(6) In any class action, the claims of the individual class members shall be aggregated to determine whether the matter in controversy exceeds the sum or value of $5,000,000, exclusive of interest and costs.

(7) Citizenship of the members of the proposed plaintiff classes shall be determined for purposes of paragraphs (2) through (6) as of the date of filing of

the complaint or amended complaint, or, if the case stated by the initial pleading is not subject to Federal jurisdiction, as of the date of service by plaintiffs of an amended pleading, motion, or other paper, indicating the existence of Federal jurisdiction.

(8) This subsection shall apply to any class action before or after the entry of a class certification order by the court with respect to that action.

(9) Paragraph (2) shall not apply to any class action that solely involves a claim —

(A) concerning a covered security as defined under 16(f)(3) of the Securities Act of 1933 (15 U.S.C. 78p(f)(3)) and section 28(f)(5)(E) of the Securities Exchange Act of 1934 (15 U.S.C. 78bb(f)(5)(E));

(B) that relates to the internal affairs or governance of a corporation or other form of business enterprise and that arises under or by virtue of the laws of the State in which such corporation or business enterprise is incorporated or organized; or

(C) that relates to the rights, duties (including fiduciary duties), and obligations relating to or created by or pursuant to any security (as defined under section 2(a)(1) of the Securities Act of 1933 (15 U.S.C. 77b(a)(1)) and the regulations issued thereunder).

(10) For purposes of this subsection and section 1453, an unincorporated association shall be deemed to be a citizen of the State where it has its principal place of business and the State under whose laws it is organized.

(11)(A) For purposes of this subsection and section 1453, a mass action shall be deemed to be a class action removable under paragraphs (2) through (10) if it otherwise meets the provisions of those paragraphs.

(B)(i) As used in subparagraph (A), the term "mass action" means any civil action (except a civil action within the scope of section 1711(2)) in which monetary relief claims of 100 or more persons are proposed to be tried jointly on the ground that the plaintiffs' claims involve common questions of law or fact, except that jurisdiction shall exist only over those plaintiffs whose claims in a mass action satisfy the jurisdictional amount requirements under subsection (a).

(ii) As used in subparagraph (A), the term "mass action" shall not include any civil action in which —

(I) all of the claims in the action arise from an event or occurrence in the State in which the action was filed, and that allegedly resulted in injuries in that State or in States contiguous to that State;

(II) the claims are joined upon motion of a defendant;

(III) all of the claims in the action are asserted on behalf of the general public (and not on behalf of individual claimants or members of a purported class) pursuant to a State statute specifically authorizing such action; or

(IV) the claims have been consolidated or coordinated solely for pretrial proceedings.

(C)(i) Any action(s) removed to Federal court pursuant to this subsection shall not thereafter be transferred to any other court pursuant to section 1407, or the rules promulgated thereunder, unless a majority of the plaintiffs in the action request transfer pursuant to section 1407.

(ii) This subparagraph will not apply —

          (I) to cases certified pursuant to rule 23 of the Federal Rules of Civil Procedure; or

          (II) if plaintiffs propose that the action proceed as a class action pursuant to rule 23 of the Federal Rules of Civil Procedure.

    (D) The limitations periods on any claims asserted in a mass action that is removed to Federal court pursuant to this subsection shall be deemed tolled during the period that the action is pending in Federal court.

(e) The word "States", as used in this section, includes the Territories, the District of Columbia, and the Commonwealth of Puerto Rico.

28 U.S.C. §1333: Admiralty, maritime and prize case

The district courts shall have original jurisdiction, exclusive of the courts of the States, of:

(1) Any civil case of admiralty or maritime jurisdiction, saving to suitors in all cases all other remedies to which they are otherwise entitled.

(2) Any prize brought into the United States and all proceedings for the condemnation of property taken as prize.

28 U.S.C. §1350: Alien's action for tort

The district courts shall have original jurisdiction of any civil action by an alien for a tort only, committed in violation of the law of nations or a treaty of the United States.

28 U.S.C. §1351: Consuls, vice consuls, and members of a diplomatic mission as defendant

The district courts shall have original jurisdiction, exclusive of the courts of the States, of all civil actions and proceedings against —

    (1) consuls or vice consuls of foreign states; or

    (2) members of a mission or members of their families (as such terms are defined in section 2 of the Diplomatic Relations Act).

28 U.S.C. §1356: Seizures not within admiralty and maritime jurisdiction

The district courts shall have original jurisdiction, exclusive of the courts of the States, of any seizure under any law of the United States on land or upon waters not within admiralty and maritime jurisdiction, except matters within the jurisdiction of the Court of International Trade under section 1582 of this title.

28 U.S.C. §1391: Venue generally

(a) Applicability of Section. — Except as otherwise provided by law —

    (1) this section shall govern the venue of all civil actions brought in district courts of the United States; and

    (2) the proper venue for a civil action shall be determined without regard to whether the action is local or transitory in nature.

(b) Venue in General. — A civil action may be brought in —

(1) a judicial district in which any defendant resides, if all defendants are residents of the State in which the district is located;

(2) a judicial district in which a substantial part of the events or omissions giving rise to the claim occurred, or a substantial part of property that is the subject of the action is situated; or

(3) if there is no district in which an action may otherwise be brought as provided in this section, any judicial district in which any defendant is subject to the court's personal jurisdiction with respect to such action.

(c) Residency. — For all venue purposes —

(1) a natural person, including an alien lawfully admitted for permanent residence in the United States, shall be deemed to reside in the judicial district in which that person is domiciled;

(2) an entity with the capacity to sue and be sued in its common name under applicable law, whether or not incorporated, shall be deemed to reside, if a defendant, in any judicial district in which such defendant is subject to the court's personal jurisdiction with respect to the civil action in question and, if a plaintiff, only in the judicial district in which it maintains its principal place of business; and

(3) a defendant not resident in the United States may be sued in any judicial district, and the joinder of such a defendant shall be disregarded in determining where the action may be brought with respect to other defendants.

(d) Residency of Corporations in States with Multiple Districts. — For purposes of venue under this chapter, in a State which has more than one judicial district and in which a defendant that is a corporation is subject to personal jurisdiction at the time an action is commenced, such corporation shall be deemed to reside in any district in that State within which its contacts would be sufficient to subject it to personal jurisdiction if that district were a separate State, and, if there is no such district, the corporation shall be deemed to reside in the district within which it has the most significant contacts.

(e) Actions Where Defendant Is Officer or Employee of the United States —

(1) In General. — A civil action in which a defendant is an officer or employee of the United States or any agency thereof acting in his official capacity or under color of legal authority, or an agency of the United States, or the United States, may, except as otherwise provided by law, be brought in any judicial district in which (A) a defendant in the action resides, (B) a substantial part of the events or omissions giving rise to the claim occurred, or a substantial part of property that is the subject of the action is situated, or (C) the plaintiff resides if no real property is involved in the action. Additional persons may be joined as parties to any such action in accordance with the Federal Rules of Civil Procedure and with such other venue requirements as would be applicable if the United States or one of its officers, employees, or agencies were not a party.

(2) Service. — The summons and complaint in such an action shall be served as provided by the Federal Rules of Civil Procedure except that the delivery of the summons and complaint to the officer or agency as required by the rules may be made by certified mail beyond the territorial limits of the district in which the action is brought.

(f) Civil Actions Against a Foreign State — A civil action against a foreign state as defined in section 1603(a) of this title may be brought —

(1) in any judicial district in which a substantial part of the events or omissions giving rise to the claim occurred, or a substantial part of property that is the subject of the action is situated;

(2) in any judicial district in which the vessel or cargo of a foreign state is situated, if the claim is asserted under section 1605(b) of this title;

(3) in any judicial district in which the agency or instrumentality is licensed to do business or is doing business, if the action is brought against an agency or instrumentality of a foreign state as defined in section 1603(b) of this title; or

(4) in the United States District Court for the District of Columbia if the action is brought against a foreign state or political subdivision thereof.

(g) Multiparty, Multiforum Litigation — A civil action in which jurisdiction of the district court is based upon section 1369 of this title [relating to certain mass tort cases] may be brought in any district in which any defendant resides or in which a substantial part of the accident giving rise to the action took place.

28 U.S.C. §1441: Removal of civil actions

(a) Generally. — Except as otherwise expressly provided by Act of Congress, any civil action brought in a State court of which the district courts of the United States have original jurisdiction, may be removed by the defendant or the defendants, to the district court of the United States for the district and division embracing the place where such action is pending.

(b) Removal Based on Diversity of Citizenship. — (1) In determining whether a civil action is removable on the basis of the jurisdiction under section 1332(a) of this title, the citizenship of defendants sued under fictitious names shall be disregarded.

(2) A civil action otherwise removable solely on the basis of the jurisdiction under section 1332(a) of this title may not be removed if any of the parties in interest properly joined and served as defendants is a citizen of the State in which such action is brought.

(c) Joinder of Federal Law Claims and State Law Claims. — (1) If a civil action includes —

(A) a claim arising under the Constitution, laws, or treaties of the United States (within the meaning of section 1331 of this title), and

(B) a claim not within the original or supplemental jurisdiction of the district court or a claim that has been made nonremovable by statute,

the entire action may be removed if the action would be removable without the inclusion of the claim described in subparagraph (B).

(2) Upon removal of an action described in paragraph (1), the district court shall sever from the action all claims described in paragraph (1)(B) and shall remand the severed claims to the State court from which the action was removed. Only defendants against whom a claim described in paragraph (1)(A) has been asserted are required to join in or consent to the removal under paragraph (1).

(d) Actions Against Foreign States. — Any civil action brought in a State court against a foreign state as defined in section 1603(a) of this title may be removed by the foreign state to the district court of the United States for the district and division embracing the place where such action is pending. Upon removal the action shall be tried by the court without jury. Where removal is based upon this subsection, the time limitations of section 1446(b) of this chapter may be enlarged at any time for cause shown.

(e) Multiparty, Multiforum Jurisdiction. — (1) Notwithstanding the provisions of subsection (b) of this section, a defendant in a civil action in a State court may remove the action to the district court of the United States for the district and division embracing the place where the action is pending if —

      (A) the action could have been brought in a United States district court under section 1369 of this title; or

      (B) the defendant is a party to an action which is or could have been brought, in whole or in part, under section 1369 in a United States district court and arises from the same accident as the action in State court, even if the action to be removed could not have been brought in a district court as an original matter.

The removal of an action under this subsection shall be made in accordance with section 1446 of this title, except that a notice of removal may also be filed before trial of the action in State court within 30 days after the date on which the defendant first becomes a party to an action under section 1369 in a United States district court that arises from the same accident as the action in State court, or at a later time with leave of the district court.

(2) Whenever an action is removed under this subsection and the district court to which it is removed or transferred under section 1407(j) has made a liability determination requiring further proceedings as to damages, the district court shall remand the action to the State court from which it had been removed for the determination of damages, unless the court finds that, for the convenience of parties and witnesses and in the interest of justice, the action should be retained for the determination of damages.

(3) Any remand under paragraph (2) shall not be effective until 60 days after the district court has issued an order determining liability and has certified its intention to remand the removed action for the determination of damages. An appeal with respect to the liability determination of the district court may be taken during that 60-day period to the court of appeals with appellate jurisdiction over the district court. In the event a party files such an appeal, the remand shall not be effective until the appeal has been finally disposed of. Once the remand has become effective, the liability determination shall not be subject to further review by appeal or otherwise.

(4) Any decision under this subsection concerning remand for the determination of damages shall not be reviewable by appeal or otherwise.

(5) An action removed under this subsection shall be deemed to be an action under section 1369 and an action in which jurisdiction is based on section 1369 of this title for purposes of this section and sections 1407, 1697, and 1785 of this title.

(6) Nothing in this subsection shall restrict the authority of the district court to transfer or dismiss an action on the ground of inconvenient forum.

(f) Derivative Removal Jurisdiction. — The court to which a civil action is removed under this section is not precluded from hearing and determining any claim in such civil action because the State court from which such civil action is removed did not have jurisdiction over that claim.

D

Foreign Sovereign Immunities Act

28 U.S.C. §1602: Findings and declaration of purpose

The Congress finds that the determination by United States courts of the claims of foreign states to immunity from the jurisdiction of such courts would serve the interests of justice and would protect the rights of both foreign states and litigants in United States courts. Under international law, states are not immune from the jurisdiction of foreign courts insofar as their commercial activities are concerned, and their commercial property may be levied upon for the satisfaction of judgments rendered against them in connection with their commercial activities. Claims of foreign states to immunity should henceforth be decided by courts of the United States and of the States in conformity with the principles set forth in this chapter.

28 U.S.C. §1603: Definitions

For purposes of this chapter—

(a) A "foreign state," except as used in section 1608 of this title, includes a political subdivision of a foreign state or an agency or instrumentality of a foreign state as defined in subsection (b).

(b) An "agency or instrumentality of a foreign state" means any entity—

(1) which is a separate legal person, corporate or otherwise, and

(2) which is an organ of a foreign state or political subdivision thereof, or a majority of whose shares or other ownership interest is owned by a foreign state or political subdivision thereof, and

(3) which is neither a citizen of a State of the United States as defined in section 1332(c) and (e) of this title, nor created under the laws of any third country.

(c) The "United States" includes all territory and waters, continental or insular, subject to the jurisdiction of the United States.

(d) A "commercial activity" means either a regular course of commercial conduct or a particular commercial transaction or act. The commercial character of an activity shall be determined by reference to the nature of the course of conduct or particular transaction or act, rather than by reference to its purpose.

(e) A "commercial activity carried on in the United States by a foreign state" means commercial activity carried on by such state and having substantial contact with the United States.

28 U.S.C. §1604: Immunity of a foreign state from jurisdiction

Subject to existing international agreements to which the United States is a party at the time of enactment of this Act [enacted Oct. 21, 1976] a foreign state shall be immune from the jurisdiction of the courts of the United States and of the States except as provided in sections 1605 to 1607 of this chapter.

28 U.S.C. §1605: General exceptions to the jurisdictional immunity of a foreign state

(a) A foreign state shall not be immune from the jurisdiction of courts of the United States or of the States in any case—

(1) in which the foreign state has waived its immunity either explicitly or by implication, notwithstanding any withdrawal of the waiver which the foreign state may purport to effect except in accordance with the terms of the waiver;

(2) in which the action is based upon a commercial activity carried on in the United States by the foreign state; or upon an act performed in the United States in connection with a commercial activity of the foreign state elsewhere; or upon an act outside the territory of the United States in connection with a commercial activity of the foreign state elsewhere and that act causes a direct effect in the United States;

(3) in which rights in property taken in violation of international law are in issue and that property or any property exchanged for such property is present in the United States in connection with a commercial activity carried on in the United States by the foreign state; or that property or any property exchanged for such property is owned or operated by an agency or instrumentality of the foreign state and that agency or instrumentality is engaged in a commercial activity in the United States;

(4) in which rights in property in the United States acquired by succession or gift or rights in immovable property situated in the United States are in issue;

(5) not otherwise encompassed in paragraph (2) above, in which money damages are sought against a foreign state for personal injury or death, or damage to or loss of property, occurring in the United States and caused by the tortious act or omission of that foreign state or of any official or employee of that foreign state while acting within the scope of his office or employment; except this paragraph shall not apply to—

(A) any claim based upon the exercise or performance or the failure to exercise or perform a discretionary function regardless of whether the discretion be abused, or

(B) any claim arising out of malicious prosecution, abuse of process, libel, slander, misrepresentation, deceit, or interference with contract rights; or

(6) in which the action is brought, either to enforce an agreement made by the foreign state with or for the benefit of a private party to submit to arbitration all or any differences which have arisen or which may arise between the parties with respect to a defined legal relationship, whether contractual or not, concerning a subject matter capable of settlement by arbitration under the laws of the United States, or to confirm an award made pursuant to such an agreement to arbitrate, if (A) the arbitration takes place or is intended to take place in the United States, (B) the agreement or award is or may be governed by a

treaty or other international agreement in force for the United States calling for the recognition and enforcement of arbitral awards, (C) the underlying claim, save for the agreement to arbitrate, could have been brought in a United States court under this section or section 1607, or (D) paragraph (1) of this subsection is otherwise applicable.

(b) A foreign state shall not be immune from the jurisdiction of the courts of the United States in any case in which a suit in admiralty is brought to enforce a maritime lien against a vessel or cargo of the foreign state, which maritime lien is based upon a commercial activity of the foreign state: *Provided*, That—

(1) notice of the suit is given by delivery of a copy of the summons and of the complaint to the person, or his agent, having possession of the vessel or cargo against which the maritime lien is asserted; and if the vessel or cargo is arrested pursuant to process obtained on behalf of the party bringing the suit, the service of process of arrest shall be deemed to constitute valid delivery of such notice, but the party bringing the suit shall be liable for any damages sustained by the foreign state as a result of the arrest if the party bringing the suit had actual or constructive knowledge that the vessel or cargo of a foreign state was involved; and

(2) notice to the foreign state of the commencement of suit as provided in section 1608 of this title is initiated within ten days either of the delivery of notice as provided in paragraph (1) of this subsection or, in the case of a party who was unaware that the vessel or cargo of a foreign state was involved, of the date such party determined the existence of the foreign state's interest.

(c) Whenever notice is delivered under subsection (b)(1), the suit to enforce a maritime lien shall thereafter proceed and shall be heard and determined according to the principles of law and rules of practice of suits in rem whenever it appears that, had the vessel been privately owned and possessed, a suit in rem might have been maintained. A decree against the foreign state may include costs of the suit and, if the decree is for a money judgment, interest as ordered by the court, except that the court may not award judgment against the foreign state in an amount greater than the value of the vessel or cargo upon which the maritime lien arose. Such value shall be determined as of the time notice is served under subsection (b)(1). Decrees shall be subject to appeal and revision as provided in other cases of admiralty and maritime jurisdiction. Nothing shall preclude the plaintiff in any proper case from seeking relief in personam in the same action brought to enforce a maritime lien as provided in this section.

(d) A foreign state shall not be immune from the jurisdiction of the courts of the United States in any action brought to foreclose a preferred mortgage, as defined in section 31301 of title 46. Such action shall be brought, heard, and determined in accordance with the provisions of chapter 313 of title 46 and in accordance with the principles of law and rules of practice of suits in rem, whenever it appears that had the vessel been privately owned and possessed a suit in rem might have been maintained.

[Subsections (e) and (f) were repealed in 2008.]

(g) Limitation on Discovery.—

(1) In general.—

(A) Subject to paragraph (2), if an action is filed that would otherwise be barred by section 1604, but for section 1605A or section 1605B, the court, upon request of the Attorney General, shall stay any request, demand, or order for discovery on the United States that the Attorney

General certifies would significantly interfere with a criminal investigation or prosecution, or a national security operation, related to the incident that gave rise to the cause of action, until such time as the Attorney General advises the court that such request, demand, or order will no longer so interfere.

(B) A stay under this paragraph shall be in effect during the 12-month period beginning on the date on which the court issues the order to stay discovery. The court shall renew the order to stay discovery for additional 12-month periods upon motion by the United States if the Attorney General certifies that discovery would significantly interfere with a criminal investigation or prosecution, or a national security operation, related to the incident that gave rise to the cause of action.

(2) Sunset.—

(A) Subject to subparagraph (B), no stay shall be granted or continued in effect under paragraph (1) after the date that is 10 years after the date on which the incident that gave rise to the cause of action occurred.

(B) After the period referred to in subparagraph (A), the court, upon request of the Attorney General, may stay any request, demand, or order for discovery on the United States that the court finds a substantial likelihood would—

(i) create a serious threat of death or serious bodily injury to any person;

(ii) adversely affect the ability of the United States to work in cooperation with foreign and international law enforcement agencies in investigating violations of United States law; or

(iii) obstruct the criminal case related to the incident that gave rise to the cause of action or undermine the potential for a conviction in such case.

(3) Evaluation of Evidence.—The court's evaluation of any request for a stay under this subsection filed by the Attorney General shall be conducted ex parte and in camera.

(4) Bar on Motions to Dismiss.—A stay of discovery under this subsection shall constitute a bar to the granting of a motion to dismiss under rules 12(b)(6) and 56 of the Federal Rules of Civil Procedure.

(5) Construction.—Nothing in this subsection shall prevent the United States from seeking protective orders or asserting privileges ordinarily available to the United States.

(h) Jurisdictional Immunity for Certain Art Exhibition Activities.—

(1) In general.—If—

(A) a work is imported into the United States from any foreign state pursuant to an agreement that provides for the temporary exhibition or display of such work entered into between a foreign state that is the owner or custodian of such work and the United States or one or more cultural or educational institutions within the United States;

(B) the President, or the President's designee, has determined, in accordance with subsection (a) of Public Law 89-259 (22 U.S.C. 2459(a)), that such work is of cultural significance and the temporary exhibition or display of such work is in the national interest; and

(C) the notice thereof has been published in accordance with subsection (a) of Public Law 89-259 (22 U.S.C. 2459(a)),

any activity in the United States of such foreign state, or of any carrier, that is associated with the temporary exhibition or display of such work shall not be considered to be commercial activity by such foreign state for purposes of subsection (a)(3).

(2) Exceptions.—

(A) Nazi-era claims.—Paragraph (1) shall not apply in any case asserting jurisdiction under subsection(a)(3) in which rights in property taken in violation of international law are in issue within the meaning of that subsection and—

> (i) the property at issue is the work described in paragraph (1);
>
> (ii) the action is based upon a claim that such work was taken in connection with the acts of a covered government during the covered period;
>
> (iii) the court determines that the activity associated with the exhibition or display is commercial activity, as that term is defined in section 1603(d); and
>
> (iv) a determination under clause (iii) is necessary for the court to exercise jurisdiction over the foreign state under subsection (a)(3).

(B) Other Culturally Significant Works.—In addition to cases exempted under subparagraph (A), paragraph (1) shall not apply in any case asserting jurisdiction under subsection (a)(3) in which rights in property taken in violation of international law are in issue within the meaning of that subsection and—

> (i) the property at issue is the work described in paragraph (1);
>
> (ii) the action is based upon a claim that such work was taken in connection with the acts of a foreign government as part of a systematic campaign of coercive confiscation or misappropriation of works from members of a targeted and vulnerable group;
>
> (iii) the taking occurred after 1900;
>
> (iv) the court determines that the activity associated with the exhibition or display is commercial activity, as that term is defined in section 1603(d); and
>
> (v) a determination under clause (iv) is necessary for the court to exercise jurisdiction over the foreign state under subsection (a)(3).

(3) Definitions.—For purposes of this subsection—

(A) the term "work" means a work of art or other object of cultural significance;

(B) the term "covered government" means—

> (i) the Government of Germany during the covered period;
>
> (ii) any government in any area in Europe that was occupied by the military forces of the Government of Germany during the covered period;
>
> (iii) any government in Europe that was established with the assistance or cooperation of the Government of Germany during the covered period; and

(iv) any government in Europe that was an ally of the Government of Germany during the covered period; and

(C) the term "covered period" means the period beginning on January 30, 1933, and ending on May 8, 1945.

28 U.S.C. §1605A: Terrorism exception to the jurisdictional immunity of a foreign state

(a) In General.—

(1) No immunity.—A foreign state shall not be immune from the jurisdiction of courts of the United States or of the States in any case not otherwise covered by this chapter in which money damages are sought against a foreign state for personal injury or death that was caused by an act of torture, extrajudicial killing, aircraft sabotage, hostage taking, or the provision of material support or resources for such an act if such act or provision of material support or resources is engaged in by an official, employee, or agent of such foreign state while acting within the scope of his or her office, employment, or agency.

(2) Claim heard.—The court shall hear a claim under this section if—

(A)(i)(I) the foreign state was designated as a state sponsor of terrorism at the time the act described in paragraph (1) occurred, or was so designated as a result of such act, and, subject to subclause (II), either remains so designated when the claim is filed under this section or was so designated within the 6-month period before the claim is filed under this section; or

(II) in the case of an action that is refiled under this section by reason of section 1083(c)(2)(A) of the National Defense Authorization Act for Fiscal Year 2008 or is filed under this section by reason of section 1083(c)(3) of that Act, the foreign state was designated as a state sponsor of terrorism when the original action or the related action under section 1605(a)(7) (as in effect before the enactment of this section) or section 589 of the Foreign Operations, Export Financing, and Related Programs Appropriations Act, 1997 (as contained in section 101(c) of division A of Public Law 104-208) was filed;

(ii) the claimant or the victim was, at the time the act described in paragraph (1) occurred—

(I) a national of the United States;

(II) a member of the armed forces; or

(III) otherwise an employee of the Government of the United States, or of an individual performing a contract awarded by the United States Government, acting within the scope of the employee's employment; and

(iii) in a case in which the act occurred in the foreign state against which the claim has been brought, the claimant has afforded the foreign state a reasonable opportunity to arbitrate the claim in accordance with the accepted international rules of arbitration; or

(B) the act described in paragraph (1) is related to Case Number 1:00CV03110 (EGS) in the United States District Court for the District of Columbia.

(b) Limitations. An action may be brought or maintained under this section if the action is commenced, or a related action was commenced under section 1605(a)(7) (before the date of the enactment of this section [enacted January 28, 2008]) or section 589 of the Foreign Operations, Export Financing, and Related Programs Appropriations Act, 1997 (as contained in section 101(c) of division A of Public Law 104-208) not later than the latter of—

    (1) 10 years after April 24, 1996; or

    (2) 10 years after the date on which the cause of action arose.

(c) Private Right of Action. A foreign state that is or was a state sponsor of terrorism as described in subsection (a)(2)(A)(i), and any official, employee, or agent of that foreign state while acting within the scope of his or her office, employment, or agency, shall be liable to—

    (1) a national of the United States,

    (2) a member of the armed forces,

    (3) an employee of the Government of the United States, or of an individual performing a contract awarded by the United States Government, acting within the scope of the employee's employment, or

    (4) the legal representative of a person described in paragraph (1), (2), or (3),

> for personal injury or death caused by acts described in subsection (a)(1) of that foreign state, or of an official, employee, or agent of that foreign state, for which the courts of the United States may maintain jurisdiction under this section for money damages. In any such action, damages may include economic damages, solatium, pain and suffering, and punitive damages. In any such action, a foreign state shall be vicariously liable for the acts of its officials, employees, or agents.

(d) Additional Damages. — After an action has been brought under subsection (c), actions may also be brought for reasonably foreseeable property loss, whether insured or uninsured, third party liability, and loss claims under life and property insurance policies, by reason of the same acts on which the action under subsection (c) is based.

(e) Special Masters.—

    (1) In general.—The courts of the United States may appoint special masters to hear damage claims brought under this section.

    (2) Transfer of funds. — The Attorney General shall transfer, from funds available for the program under section 1404C of the Victims of Crime Act of 1984 (42 U.S.C. 10603c), to the Administrator of the United States district court in which any case is pending which has been brought or maintained under this section such funds as may be required to cover the costs of special masters appointed under paragraph (1). Any amount paid in compensation to any such special master shall constitute an item of court costs.

(f) Appeal.—In an action brought under this section, appeals from orders not conclusively ending the litigation may only be taken pursuant to section 1292(b) of this title.

(g) Property Disposition.—

    (1) In general.—In every action filed in a United States district court in which jurisdiction is alleged under this section, the filing of a notice of pending action pursuant to this section, to which is attached a copy of the complaint filed in the action, shall have the effect of establishing a lien of lis pendens upon any real property or tangible personal property that is—

(A) subject to attachment in aid of execution, or execution, under section 1610;

(B) located within that judicial district; and

(C) titled in the name of any defendant, or titled in the name of any entity controlled by any defendant if such notice contains a statement listing such controlled entity.

(2) Notice. — A notice of pending action pursuant to this section shall be filed by the clerk of the district court in the same manner as any pending action and shall be indexed by listing as defendants all named defendants and all entities listed as controlled by any defendant.

(3) Enforceability. — Liens established by reason of this subsection shall be enforceable as provided in chapter 111 of this title.

(h) Definitions. — For purposes of this section —

(1) the term "aircraft sabotage" has the meaning given that term in Article 1 of the Convention for the Suppression of Unlawful Acts Against the Safety of Civil Aviation;

(2) the term "hostage taking" has the meaning given that term in Article 1 of the International Convention Against the Taking of Hostages;

(3) the term "material support or resources" has the meaning given that term in section 2339A of title 18;

(4) the term "armed forces" has the meaning given that term in section 101 of title 10;

(5) the term "national of the United States" has the meaning given that term in section 101(a)(22) of the Immigration and Nationality Act (8 U.S.C. 1101(a)(22));

(6) the term "state sponsor of terrorism" means a country the government of which the Secretary of State has determined, for purposes of section 6(j) of the Export Administration Act of 1979 (50 U.S.C. App. 2405(j)), section 620A of the Foreign Assistance Act of 1961 (22 U.S.C. 2371), section 40 of the Arms Export Control Act (22 U.S.C. 2780), or any other provision of law, is a government that has repeatedly provided support for acts of international terrorism; and

(7) the terms "torture" and "extrajudicial killing" have the meaning given those terms in section 3 of the Torture Victim Protection Act of 1991 (28 U.S.C. 1350 note).

28 U.S.C. §1605B: Responsibility of foreign states for international terrorism against the United States

(a) Definition. — In this section, the term 'international terrorism' —

(1) has the meaning given the term in section 2331 of title 18, United States Code; and

(2) does not include any act of war (as defined in that section).

(b) Responsibility of Foreign States. — A foreign state shall not be immune from the jurisdiction of the courts of the United States in any case in which money damages are sought against a foreign state for physical injury to person or property or death occurring in the United States and caused by —

(1) an act of international terrorism in the United States; and

(2) a tortious act or acts of the foreign state, or of any official, employee, or agent of that foreign state while acting within the scope of his or her office,

employment, or agency, regardless where the tortious act or acts of the foreign state occurred.

(c) Claims by Nationals of the United States. — Notwithstanding section 2337(2) of title 18, a national of the United States may bring a claim against a foreign state in accordance with section 2333 of that title if the foreign state would not be immune under subsection (b).

(d) Rule of Construction. — A foreign state shall not be subject to the jurisdiction of the courts of the United States under subsection (b) on the basis of an omission or a tortious act or acts that constitute mere negligence.

28 U.S.C. §1605B (Note) [Pub. L. No. 114-222, §5, 130 Stat. 852, 854 (2016)]: Stay of Actions Pending State Negotiations

(a) Exclusive Jurisdiction. — The courts of the United States shall have exclusive jurisdiction in any action in which a foreign state is subject to the jurisdiction of a court of the United States under section 1605B of title 28, United States Code, as added by section 3(a) of this Act.

(b) Intervention. — The Attorney General may intervene in any action in which a foreign state is subject to the jurisdiction of a court of the United States under section 1605B of title 28, United States Code, as added by section 3(a) of this Act, for the purpose of seeking a stay of the civil action, in whole or in part.

(c) Stay. —

(1) In general. — A court of the United States may stay a proceeding against a foreign state if the Secretary of State certifies that the United States is engaged in good faith discussions with the foreign state defendant concerning the resolution of the claims against the foreign state, or any other parties as to whom a stay of claims is sought.

(2) Duration. —

(A) In general. — A stay under this section may be granted for not more than 180 days.

(B) Extension. —

(i) In general. — The Attorney General may petition the court for an extension of the stay for additional 180-day periods.

(ii) Recertification. — A court shall grant an extension under clause (i) if the Secretary of State recertifies that the United States remains engaged in good faith discussions with the foreign state defendant concerning the resolution of the claims against the foreign state, or any other parties as to whom a stay of claims is sought.

Pub. L. No. 114-222, §7, 130 Stat. 852, 855 (2016) [Note to 18 U.S.C. §2333]: Effective Date

The amendments made by this Act [including 28 U.S.C. §1605B] shall apply to any civil action —

(1) pending on, or commenced on or after, the date of enactment of this Act [enacted September 28, 2016]; and

(2) arising out of an injury to a person, property, or business on or after September 11, 2001.

28 U.S.C. §1606: Extent of liability

As to any claim for relief with respect to which a foreign state is not entitled to immunity under section 1605 or 1607 of this chapter, the foreign state shall be liable in the same manner and to the same extent as a private individual under like circumstances; but a foreign state except for an agency or instrumentality thereof shall not be liable for punitive damages; if, however, in any case wherein death was caused, the law of the place where the action or omission occurred provides, or has been construed to provide, for damages only punitive in nature, the foreign state shall be liable for actual or compensatory damages measured by the pecuniary injuries resulting from such death which were incurred by the persons for whose benefit the action was brought.

28 U.S.C. §1607: Counterclaims

In any action brought by a foreign state, or in which a foreign state intervenes, in a court of the United States or of a State, the foreign state shall not be accorded immunity with respect to any counterclaim —

(a) for which a foreign state would not be entitled to immunity under section 1605 or 1605A of this chapter had such claim been brought in a separate action against the foreign state; or

(b) arising out of the transaction or occurrence that is the subject matter of the claim of the foreign state; or

(c) to the extent that the counterclaim does not seek relief exceeding in amount or differing in kind from that sought by the foreign state.

28 U.S.C. §1608: Service; time to answer; default

(a) Service in the courts of the United States and of the States shall be made upon a foreign state or political subdivision of a foreign state:

(1) by delivery of a copy of the summons and complaint in accordance with any special arrangement for service between the plaintiff and the foreign state or political subdivision; or

(2) if no special arrangement exists, by delivery of a copy of the summons and complaint in accordance with an applicable international convention on service of judicial documents; or

(3) if service cannot be made under paragraphs (1) or (2), by sending a copy of the summons and complaint and a notice of suit, together with a translation of each into the official language of the foreign state, by any form of mail requiring a signed receipt, to be addressed and dispatched by the clerk of the court to the head of the ministry of foreign affairs of the foreign state concerned, or

(4) if service cannot be made within 30 days under paragraph (3), by sending two copies of the summons and complaint and a notice of suit, together with a translation of each into the official language of the foreign state, by any form of mail requiring a signed receipt, to be addressed and dispatched by the clerk of the court to the Secretary of State in Washington, District of Columbia, to the attention of the Director of Special Consular Services—and the Secretary shall transmit one copy of the papers through diplomatic channels to the foreign state

and shall send to the clerk of the court a certified copy of the diplomatic note indicating when the papers were transmitted.

As used in this subsection, a "notice of suit" shall mean a notice addressed to a foreign state and in a form prescribed by the Secretary of State by regulation.

(b) Service in the courts of the United States and of the States shall be made upon an agency or instrumentality of a foreign state:

(1) by delivery of a copy of the summons and complaint in accordance with any special arrangement for service between the plaintiff and the agency or instrumentality; or

(2) if no special arrangement exists, by delivery of a copy of the summons and complaint either to an officer, a managing or general agent, or to any other agent authorized by appointment or by law to receive service of process in the United States; or in accordance with an applicable international convention on service of judicial documents; or

(3) if service cannot be made under paragraphs (1) or (2), and if reasonably calculated to give actual notice, by delivery of a copy of the summons and complaint, together with a translation of each into the official language of the foreign state—

(A) as directed by an authority of the foreign state or political subdivision in response to a letter rogatory or request or

(B) by any form of mail requiring a signed receipt, to be addressed and dispatched by the clerk of the court to the agency or instrumentality to be served, or

(C) as directed by order of the court consistent with the law of the place where service is to be made.

(c) Service shall be deemed to have been made—

(1) in the case of service under subsection (a)(4), as of the date of transmittal indicated in the certified copy of the diplomatic note; and

(2) in any other case under this section, as of the date of receipt indicated in the certification, signed and returned postal receipt, or other proof of service applicable to the method of service employed.

(d) In any action brought in a court of the United States or of a State, a foreign state, a political subdivision thereof, or an agency or instrumentality of a foreign state shall serve an answer or other responsive pleading to the complaint within sixty days after service has been made under this section.

(e) No judgment by default shall be entered by a court of the United States or of a State against a foreign state, a political subdivision thereof, or an agency or instrumentality of a foreign state, unless the claimant establishes his claim or right to relief by evidence satisfactory to the court. A copy of any such default judgment shall be sent to the foreign state or political subdivision in the manner prescribed for service in this section.

28 U.S.C. §1609: Immunity from attachment and execution of property of a foreign state

Subject to existing international agreements to which the United States is a party at the time of enactment of this Act [enacted Oct. 21, 1976] the property in the United

States of a foreign state shall be immune from attachment arrest and execution except as provided in sections 1610 and 1611 of this chapter.

28 U.S.C. §1610: Exceptions to the immunity from attachment or execution

(a) The property in the United States of a foreign state, as defined in section 1603(a) of this chapter, used for a commercial activity in the United States, shall not be immune from attachment in aid of execution, or from execution, upon a judgment entered by a court of the United States or of a State after the effective date of this Act, if—

(1) the foreign state has waived its immunity from attachment in aid of execution or from execution either explicitly or by implication, notwithstanding any withdrawal of the waiver the foreign state may purport to effect except in accordance with the terms of the waiver, or

(2) the property is or was used for the commercial activity upon which the claim is based, or

(3) the execution relates to a judgment establishing rights in property which has been taken in violation of international law or which has been exchanged for property taken in violation of international law, or

(4) the execution relates to a judgment establishing rights in property—

(A) which is acquired by succession or gift, or

(B) which is immovable and situated in the United States: *Provided,* That such property is not used for purposes of maintaining a diplomatic or consular mission or the residence of the Chief of such mission, or

(5) the property consists of any contractual obligation or any proceeds from such a contractual obligation to indemnify or hold harmless the foreign state or its employees under a policy of automobile or other liability or casualty insurance covering the claim which merged into the judgment, or

(6) the judgment is based on an order confirming an arbitral award rendered against the foreign state, provided that attachment in aid of execution, or execution, would not be inconsistent with any provision in the arbitral agreement, or

(7) the judgment relates to a claim for which the foreign state is not immune under section 1605A or section 1605(a)(7) (as such section was in effect on January 27, 2008), regardless of whether the property is or was involved with the act upon which the claim is based.

(b) In addition to subsection (a), any property in the United States of an agency or instrumentality of a foreign state engaged in commercial activity in the United States shall not be immune from attachment in aid of execution, or from execution, upon a judgment entered by a court of the United States or of a State after the effective date of this Act if—

(1) the agency or instrumentality has waived its immunity from attachment in aid of execution or from execution either explicitly or implicitly, notwithstanding any withdrawal of the waiver the agency or instrumentality may purport to effect except in accordance with the terms of the waiver, or

(2) the judgment relates to a claim for which the agency or instrumentality is not immune by virtue of section 1605(a)(2), (3), or (5) or 1605(b) of this chapter, regardless of whether the property is or was involved in the act upon which the claim is based, or

(3) the judgment relates to a claim for which the agency or instrumentality is not immune by virtue of section 1605A of this chapter or section 1605(a)(7) of this chapter (as such section was in effect on January 27, 2008), regardless of whether the property is or was involved in the act upon which the claim is based.

(c) No attachment or execution referred to in subsections (a) and (b) of this section shall be permitted until the court has ordered such attachment and execution after having determined that a reasonable period of time has elapsed following the entry of judgment and the giving of any notice required under section 1608(e) of this chapter.

(d) The property of a foreign state, as defined in section 1603(a) of this chapter, used for a commercial activity in the United States, shall not be immune from attachment prior to the entry of judgment in any action brought in a court of the United States or of a State, or prior to the elapse of the period of time provided in subsection (c) of this section, if—

(1) the foreign state has explicitly waived its immunity from attachment prior to judgment, notwithstanding any withdrawal of the waiver the foreign state may purport to effect except in accordance with the terms of the waiver, and

(2) the purpose of the attachment is to secure satisfaction of a judgment that has been or may ultimately be entered against the foreign state, and not to obtain jurisdiction.

(e) The vessels of a foreign state shall not be immune from arrest in rem, interlocutory sale, and execution in actions brought to foreclose a preferred mortgage as provided in section 1605(d).

(f)(1)(A) Notwithstanding any other provision of law, including but not limited to section 208(f) of the Foreign Missions Act (22 U.S.C. 4308(f)), and except as provided in subparagraph (B), any property with respect to which financial transactions are prohibited or regulated pursuant to section 5(b) of the Trading with the Enemy Act (50 U.S.C. App. 5(b)), section 620(a) of the Foreign Assistance Act of 1961 (22 U.S.C. 2370(a)), sections 202 and 203 of the International Emergency Economic Powers Act (50 U.S.C. 1701–1702), or any other proclamation, order, regulation, or license issued pursuant thereto, shall be subject to execution or attachment in aid of execution of any judgment relating to a claim for which a foreign state (including any agency or instrumentality or such state) claiming such property is not immune under section 1605(a)(7) (as in effect before the enactment of section 1605A) or section 1605A.

(B) Subparagraph (A) shall not apply if, at the time the property is expropriated or seized by the foreign state, the property has been held in title by a natural person or, if held in trust, has been held for the benefit of a natural person or persons.

(2)(A) At the request of any party in whose favor a judgment has been issued with respect to a claim for which the foreign state is not immune under section 1605(a)(7) (as in effect before the enactment of section 1605A) or section 1605A, the Secretary of the Treasury and the Secretary of State should make every effort to fully, promptly, and effectively assist any judgment creditor or any court that has issued any such judgment in identifying, locating, and executing against the property of that foreign state or any agency or instrumentality of such state.

(B) In providing such assistance, the Secretaries—

(i) may provide such information to the court under seal; and

(ii) should make every effort to provide the information in a manner sufficient to allow the court to direct the United States Marshall's office to promptly and effectively execute against that property.

(3) Waiver.—The President may waive any provision of paragraph (1) in the interest of national security.

(g) Property in Certain Actions.—

(1) In general.—Subject to paragraph (3), the property of a foreign state against which a judgment is entered under section 1605A, and the property of an agency or instrumentality of such a state, including property that is a separate juridical entity or is an interest held directly or indirectly in a separate juridical entity, is subject to attachment in aid of execution, and execution, upon that judgment as provided in this section, regardless of—

(A) the level of economic control over the property by the government of the foreign state;

(B) whether the profits of the property go to that government;

(C) the degree to which officials of that government manage the property or otherwise control its daily affairs;

(D) whether that government is the sole beneficiary in interest of the property; or

(E) whether establishing the property as a separate entity would entitle the foreign state to benefits in United States courts while avoiding its obligations.

(2) United States Sovereign Immunity Inapplicable.—Any property of a foreign state, or agency or instrumentality of a foreign state, to which paragraph (1) applies shall not be immune from attachment in aid of execution, or execution, upon a judgment entered under section 1605A because the property is regulated by the United States Government by reason of action taken against that foreign state under the Trading With the Enemy Act or the International Emergency Economic Powers Act.

(3) Third-party Joint Property holders.—Nothing in this subsection shall be construed to supersede the authority of a court to prevent appropriately the impairment of an interest held by a person who is not liable in the action giving rise to a judgment in property subject to attachment in aid of execution, or execution, upon such judgment.

28 U.S.C. §1611: Certain types of property immune from execution

(a) Notwithstanding the provisions of section 1610 of this chapter, the property of those organizations designated by the President as being entitled to enjoy the privileges, exemptions, and immunities provided by the International Organizations Immunities Act shall not be subject to attachment or any other judicial process impeding the disbursement of funds to, or on the order of, a foreign state as the result of an action brought in the courts of the United States or of the States.

(b) Notwithstanding the provisions of section 1610 of this chapter, the property of a foreign state shall be immune from attachment and from execution, if—

(1) the property is that of a foreign central bank or monetary authority held for its own account, unless such bank or authority, or its parent foreign government, has explicitly waived its immunity from attachment in aid of execution,

or from execution, notwithstanding any withdrawal of the waiver which the bank, authority or government may purport to effect except in accordance with the terms of the waiver; or

    (2) the property is, or is intended to be, used in connection with a military activity and

        (A) is of a military character, or

        (B) is under the control of a military authority or defense agency.

(c) Notwithstanding the provisions of section 1610 of this chapter, the property of a foreign state shall be immune from attachment and from execution in an action brought under section 302 of the Cuban Liberty and Democratic Solidarity (LIBERTAD) Act of 1996 to the extent that the property is a facility or installation used by an accredited diplomatic mission for official purposes.

Table of Cases

Principal cases are in italics. Cases cited in excerpted materials are not listed here.

Index